Innovations in Computing Sciences and Software Engineering

Tarek Sobh · Khaled Elleithy
Editors

Innovations in Computing Sciences and Software Engineering

Editors
Dr. Tarek Sobh
University of Bridgeport
School of Engineering
University Avenue 221
06604 Bridgeport Connecticut
USA
sobh@bridgeport.edu

Prof. Khaled Elleithy
University of Bridgeport
School of Engineering
University Avenue 221
06604 Bridgeport Connecticut
USA
elleithy@bridgeport.edu

ISBN 978-94-007-9416-0 ISBN 978-90-481-9112-3 (eBook)
DOI 10.1007/978-90-481-9112-3
Springer Dordrecht Heidelberg London New York

Softcover re-print of the Hardcover 1st edition 2010

Cover design: eStudio Calamar S.L.

Printed on acid-free paper

Springer is part of Springer Science+Business Media (www.springer.com)

To our families
Their continuing support makes all our endeavors possible
And
To the memory of Professor Natalia Romalis
Her spirit will always be with us

Acknowledgements

The 2009 International Conference on Systems, Computing Sciences and Software Engineering (SCSS 09) and the resulting proceedings could not have been organized without the assistance of a large number of individuals. SCSS is part of the International Joint Conferences on Computer, Information, and Systems Sciences, and Engineering (CISSE). CISSE was founded by Professors Tarek Sobh and Khaled Elleithy in 2005, and we set up mechanisms that put it into action. Andrew Rosca wrote the software that allowed conference management and interaction between the authors and reviewers online. Mr. Tudor Rosca managed the online conference presentation system and was instrumental in ensuring that the event met the highest professional standards. We also want to acknowledge the roles played by Sarosh Patel and Ms. Susan Kristie, our technical and administrative support team.

The technical co-sponsorship provided by the Institute of Electrical and Electronics Engineers (IEEE) and the University of Bridgeport is gratefully appreciated. We would like to express our thanks to Prof. Toshio Fukuda, Chair of the International Advisory Committee and the members of the SCSS Technical Program Committee.

The excellent contributions of the authors made this world-class book possible. Each paper received two to four reviews. The reviewers worked tirelessly under a tight schedule and their important work is gratefully appreciated. In particular, we want to acknowledge the contributions of all the reviewers. A complete list of reviewers is provided in the book.

Tarek Sobh and Khaled Elleithy

Bridgeport, Connecticut
January 2010

Contents

Reviewers List

Adam Piorkowski
Adrian Runceanu
Ahmad Sofian Shminan
Ahmed Nada
Alejandro Regalado
Alen Hajnal
Ana Beatriz Alvarez
Andrew Dimmond
Andrew Rosca
Anna Derezinska
Atif Mohammad
Ausif Mahmood
Aymé Perdomo
Barry Stein
Biju Issac
Buket Barkana
Danaysa Macías Hernández
Daniel G. Schwartz
Daniela López De Luise
David Bracewell
David Wyld
David Moore
Denis Berthier
Deniss Kumlander
Dmitry Zub
Erki Eessaar
Ernest Hibbs
fei cheng
Felix Farcas
Gunnar Piho
Hao Wu
Hector Soza
Hector Barbosa Leon
Igor Aguilar Alonso
Igor Petukhov
Ilias Karasavvidis
Ilie Borcosi
Ilona Bluemke
Indrajit Mandal
Ivica Dimitrovski
Jiri Giesl
Joao Ferreira
João Batista Furlan Duarte
Jonathan Lori
Jonathan Sidi
Jyotirmay Gadewadikar
Khaled Elleithy
Krystyna Maria Noga
Kurtulus Kullu
Leonardo Jelenkovic
Lifeng Wang
Madhuri Rao
Maduranga Dassanayake
Manan Joshi
Margareth Stoll
Marius Marcu
Miao Song
miguel vargas
Mircea Popa
Mohamed Abdelfattah
Mohamed Firdhous
Mohammad Hadi Zahedi
Monika Arora
Monika Verma
Muhammad Ali Khan
Nazleeni Samiha Haron
Neeta Verma
Noor Shalasiah Osman
Novac Ovidiu
Oleg Starostenko
Paul Sagayda
Paulo Brito
Petra Marešová
Piotr Gawkowski
Richard Millham
Rick Leopoldi
Rosenberg J Romero
Rünno Sgirka
S. Shervin Ostadzadeh
Sachin Patil
Safwan Shatnawi
Sara McCaslin
Serguei Mokhov
Shafqat Hameed
Shmuel Miller
Sridhar Chandran
Susana María
Sylvia Encheva
Taner Arsan
Temur Jangveladze
Thierry Simonnet
Thubaasini Prabhakaran
Tien D. Nguyen
Timothy Highley
Tzong-An Su
Van Sinh Nguyen
Vikas Deep
Wanessa Amaral
William Westermann
Xiaoqiong Zhen
xiulei qin
Yasir Safeer
Ying Gao
Yoichiro Iwasaki
Zhiqiang Niu
Zunera Jalil

Recursive Projection Profiling for Text-Image Separation

Shivsubramani Krishnamoorthy, R. Loganathan, K P Soman
Centre for Excellence in Computational Engineering,
Amrita University, Coimbatore 641105
{shiv, r_logu}@ettimadai.amrita.edu, kp_soman@amrita.edu

***Abstract:* This paper presents an efficient and very simple method for separating text characters from graphical images in a given document image. This is based on a Recursive Projection Profiling (RPP) of the document image. The algorithm tries to use the projection profiling method [4] [6] to its maximum bent to bring out almost all that is possible with the method. The projection profile reveals the empty space along the horizontal and vertical axes, projecting the gaps between the characters/images. The algorithm turned out to be quite efficient, accurate and least complex in nature. Though some exceptional cases were encountered owing to the drawbacks of projection profiling, they were well handled with some simple heuristics thus resulting in a very efficient method for text-image separation.**

I. Introduction

An Optical Character Recognition (OCR) system zeroes upon recognizing individual characters and images with least error possible, from an optically read document image. The Character Recognition system is trained based on perfectly segmented characters [8] [10] [11] from the binarized document image. Thus character segmentation [11] process critically influences the efficiency of the recognition system as a whole. The character segmentation needs to address the problem of separating the text characters properly from the graphical images in the document so as to make the system training and classification process efficient.

This paper discusses an algorithm which recursively performs projection profiling over the document image to segment the individual characters and graphical images. Projection profiling [5] is a naïve method for segmenting characters based on empty space between them. Projection profiling projects the pixel accumulation along the vertical and horizontal axes. Segmentation is performed based on the peaks and valleys created in the projection.

When the document is digitized by scanning, there is a high possibility that the document gets skewed to a certain angle. With recursive steps involved, by further sub segmenting a segment, the algorithm goes deep into pixel level of the document image. Thus the algorithm is least affected by considerable skew present in the scanned document image.

This paper presents some examples of the algorithm applied on Tamil, Malayalam and English document images. The method turned out to be very efficient and least complex, fetching us promising results in segmenting individual characters and graphical images from a given document image.

II. Projection Profiling

Projection Profile is usually considered as a naïve method of segmenting textual documents into lines. This is performed based on the analysis of regularity of peaks and valleys which represent the occurrence of a line and space between lines respectively [1], [6].

Projection profiling mainly includes two phases, namely

- Horizontal Segmentation phase – as depicted by figure 1.a and 1.b. Here the textual image is separated into lines of characters.
- Vertical Segmentation phase, where a horizontally segmented line of character is vertically projection profiled to spot the space between individual characters in the line.

Figure 1.b shows the horizontal projection profiling of document image as in Figure 1.a.

Figure 1.a: Sample Document Image

T. Sobh, K. Elleithy (eds.), *Innovations in Computing Sciences and Software Engineering*,
DOI 10.1007/978-90-481-9112-3_1, © Springer Science+Business Media B.V. 2010

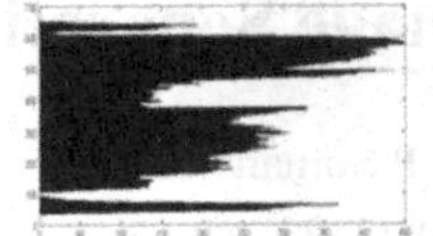

Figure 1.b: Projection Profiling

In this example, the projection profile displays two major valleys corresponding to the document image. It successfully identifies only the lines on the top and the bottom. But the other components in the middle are not recognized separately. This is the drawback of projection profile method. The high density between pixel rows 150 and 600 shows the presence of a graphical image. Our algorithm overcomes the drawback by introducing recursion in the projection profiling process.

III. Recursive Projection Profiling

Recursive Projection Profiling (RPP) follows the phases as in normal projection profiling. As and when a segment is formed, its completeness is verified. An incomplete segment is considered as a new document image and the whole process is repeated on the same, thus bringing in the concept of recursion. Figure 2 is a flowchart depiction of Recursive Projection Profiling.

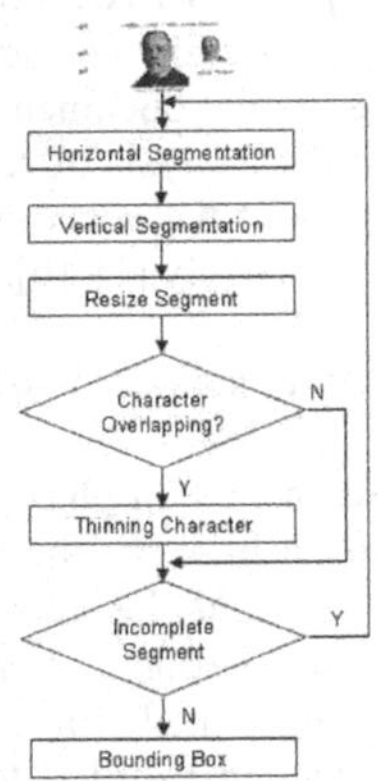

Figure 2: RPP Flow Chart

Horizontal Segmentation: RPP begins with the horizontal segmentation where the image document is segmented into lines of characters based on the peaks and valleys created by the horizontal projection profile of the same.

Vertical Segmentation: Here, the gap between the characters in a particular line, which was obtained by horizontal segmentation, is recognized by means of peaks and valleys created by the vertical projection of the line.

Resize Segment: After vertical segmentation, each character/image is segmented as shown in Figure 3 (top). But, each segment bears the same height as that of the tallest character/image in the line. Each of these segments had to be resized eliminating the empty spaces on the top and the bottom of the characters as depicted in Figure 3

Figure 3: Resizing the Segments

Character Overlapping: Owing to the drawbacks of projection profiling, some exceptions were encountered during the segmentation process. Character overlapping was such an issue to be dealt with. The exception was identified based on some simple heuristics and was handled by the process of Character Thinning. This process helps, to a certain extent, in case of a slanting text encountered as a part of a graphical image

Incomplete Segment: The algorithm reaches a stage where the whole document image is segmented in some manner. All the segments identified may not be purely perfect. Such segments are referred to as incomplete segments. A segment is considered incomplete when a gap/empty space is observed in it after resizing, as shown in Figure 4. Empty space would mean in effect the rows of empty pixels.

பண்புகளை

Figure 4: Incomplete Segment

Recursion: The algorithm works as a simple projection profiling method if all the segments generated are complete, which is most unlikely. Therefore, when an incomplete segment is spotted, the algorithm switches to recursive mode. The incomplete segment is, as such, considered as a document image and is fed back to the initial stage of horizontal segmenting. It has been observed that a recursion level of 3 almost ends up in a perfect segmented document but for some exceptions which are recognized and handled with simple heuristics.

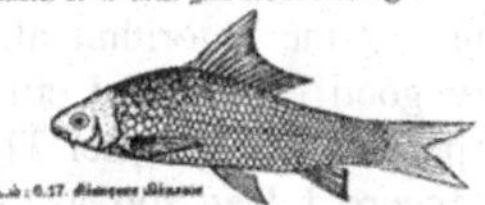

Figure 5: Sample Document Image

Table 1 shows the results produced by RPP Segmentation performed on a sample Tamil document as shown in Figure 5. The result drastically improves as each recursion takes place.

Table 1: Sample Result

Recursion Level	Characters segmented correctly	Characters segmented incorrectly	Pictures Segmented
1	568	884	0
2	984	468	0
3	1446	6	2

It was observed that since each recursion leads deeper into pixel level, too many recursions also led to incorrect segmentation as shown in Figure 6. It was noticed that sometimes due to the poor quality of the document or scanning device, the algorithm even detects the small gaps within a character/images leading to multiple segmentation of the same. Thus, based on experimentations, the magic number of 3 was arrived at as the maximum level of recursion; i.e. the algorithm was found to require a maximum of third level of recursion to obtain a perfect segmentation.

Figure 6: Incorrect Segmentation

IV. Text-Image Separation

Text-Image separation [12] is a very critical issue in Character Segmentation. RPP handles the case based on simple heuristics, avoiding any kind of complexity. Figure 9 displays the perfect segmentation of a sample document with Tamil and English characters and some images. The document was purposely created in this manner so as to verify all the different possibilities in Text-Image Separation.

Figure 7: Perfect String-Image Separation

RPP performs segmentation, as an end result of which are obtained a set of numerous segments. RPP just segments all the characters and images but does not, as such, specify whether a segment formed contains a character or graphical image [11]. Simple heuristics is applied here, based on which the text segment is actually separated from a graphical segment [7].

The heuristics is applied on two levels:

- The height and the width property of the segment are made use of to understand whether a segment obtained contains a character or a graphical image.
    - The average height and average width of all the segments in the document image are calculated.
    - The height and width of each segment is compared with the average value
    - If the segment is large enough than the average, it is considered as an image. Implementation of the same is done based threshold value for height and width.

  - o Character segments [8][10] will more or less be of the same size and in or around the threshold value.

- Every large segment may not be a graphical image as such. There is a possibility that it could be a character of large font size. A second level of heuristics is applied here where the pixel density within the segment is looked upon. A graphical image would, obviously, have high pixel density in comparison with characters.

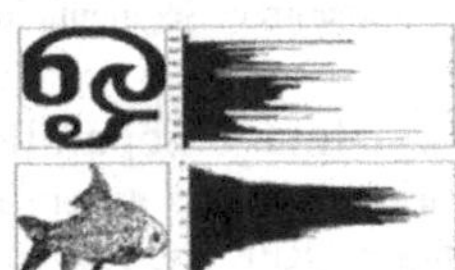

Figure 8: Pixel Density of Text and Image

Figure 8 exhibits the row wise pixel density of a segmented character and a segmented image which pass the first level of heuristics applied, based on the height and width of the segment formed. Thus it isn't yet clear whether the segment actually contains a character or a graphical image. But when the second stage of heuristics is applied, the pixel densities of the two segments are looked into and their difference is quite evident. The segment is understood as an image or character based on the variance observed in the pixel density row wise or column wise. A character segment would produce high variance in the pixel density whereas the variance is comparatively very less in case of an image.

The heuristics applied here may seem to be quite very simple and insignificant. But experimental results reveal that the method actually is very efficient and accurate and Table 1 does prove the same.

There are often cases where a segmented image has some embedded text within its bounds or due to certain disabilities of projection profiling; some text may get clubbed along with an image during segmentation as shown in Figure 9. Based on experimentation it is understood that such cases usually occur only with the possibility of the text being present in or near the corners of the image segment. To handle such cases, the image segments undergo an additional process wherein the corners of the image segments are looked for the presence of some characters.

Figure 9: Exceptional cases

The dimensions of the corner slice will be calculated as:

Horizontal Range = 1/3 * (Width of the Segment).

Vertical Range = 3 * (Average character segment Height in the document)

V. The Skew Problem

A skew [1] [5] [6] that is present in a document image is quite negligible unless two characters/images overlap horizontally. Due to the skew, the characters/image in the first part of a line/paragraph may overlap with characters/images in the last part of the adjacent line/paragraph. Thus not a single row of empty pixels can be identified between the adjacent lines/paragraphs.

Recursive nature of the algorithm alone solved the problem to a very good extent. But still, it had to be coupled with the process of Character Thinning [2], [3] when such a case occurred. Here too, as mentioned in the previous topic, simple heuristics of measuring the height of the segment is used to identify such an exception. Figure 8 exhibits a sample case with a document image with skew. Lines of the paragraph were not segmented properly in a single pass. The figure later displays the perfect segmentation performed with recursive algorithm.

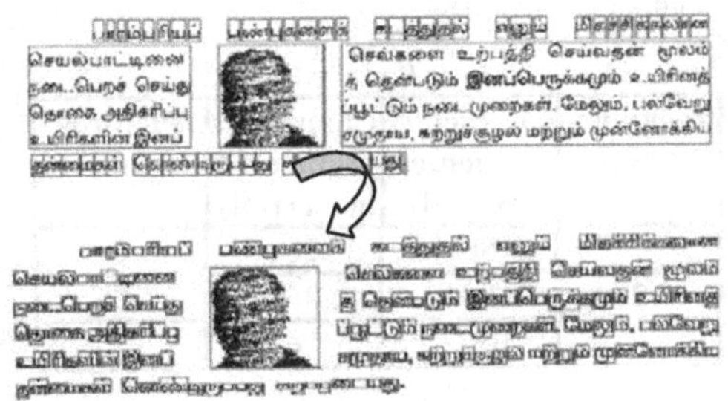

Figure 10: Handling Skew

VI. Enhancements

It is understood that RPP is quite very efficient method of Character Segmentation [11]. It handles almost all the issues regarding character segmentation and separation from graphical images. The algorithm can be still more efficient taking into account the following and our group is already working on it.

- The algorithm can be most reliable and efficient if the document image is totally free from skew. A skew corrected document fed to the algorithm will be segmented perfectly.
- The algorithm was initially designed for a customized requirement and then generalized. The algorithm still needs to address the issue

where a graphical image itself contains slanting text within its bounds.

VII. Conclusion

The paper presented an effective and very simple method of segmenting a document image and separation of text from graphical images. The various aspects regarding RPP were discussed with sample examples. RPP was tested on document images with Tamil, English and Malayalam characters. To a very good extent the algorithm proved to be language independent except for some very typical problems specific to a particular language.

REFERENCES

[1] S.N Srihari and V Govindaraju, Analysis of Textual Images Using the Hough Transform, *Machine Vision and Applications, 2(3):*141-153, 1989.

[2] N. J. Naccache and R Shinghal, Proposed Algorithm for Thinning Binary Patterns, *IEEE Transactions on Systems, Man. and Cybernatics, SMC-14*:409-418, 1984.

[3] P. C. K Kwok, A Thinning Algorithm by Contour Generation, Communications of the *ACM, Vol-31*, No. 11, PP. 1314-1324, 1988.

[4] T. Taxt, P. J. Flynn & A. K. Jain, Segmentation of Document Images, *IEEE Transaction on Pattern Analysis and Machine Intelligence, 11(12):*1322-1329, December 1989.

[5] H. S. Baird, The Skew Angle of Printed Documents, In Proc. of the *Conference Society of Photographic Scientists and Engineers, Volume 40*, Pages 21-24, Rochester, NY, May, 20-21 1987.

[6] R. Cattani, T. Coianiez, S. Messelodi & C. Modena, Geometric Layout Analysis Techniques for Document Image Understanding: A Review, *IRST Technical Report,* Trento, Italy, 1998, 68pp.

[7] D. Wang, S. Srihari *Classification of Newspaper Image Blocks Using Texture Analysis.* Computer Vision, Graphics, and Image Processing, Vol. 47, 1989, pp.327-352.

[8] A. K. Jain and S. Bhattacharjee, *Text Segmentation Using Gabor Filters for Automatic Document Processing,* Machine Vision and Applications, Vol. 5, No. 3, 1992, pp. 169-184.

[9] O. Okun, D. Doermann, Matti P. *Page Segmentation and zone classification.* The State of the Art, Nov 1999.

[10] C.L. Tan, Z. Zhang *Text block segmentation using pyramid structure.* SPIE Document Recognition and Retrieval, Vol. 8, January 24-25, 2001, San Jose, USA, pp. 297-306.

[11] H. Makino. *Representation and segmentation of document images.* Proc. of IEEE Computer Society Conference on Pattern Recognition and Image Processing, 1983, pp. 291-296.

[12] J. Duong, M. Ct, H. Emptoz, C. Suen. *Extraction of Text Areas in Printed Document Images.* ACM Symposium on Document Engineering, DocEng'01, Atlanta (USA), November9-10, 2001, pp. 157-165.

Risk in the Clouds?: Security Issues Facing Government Use of Cloud Computing

David C. Wyld
Southeastern Louisiana University
Department of Management – Box 10350
Hammond, LA 70402-0350 USA

Abstract- **Cloud computing is poised to become one of the most important and fundamental shifts in how computing is consumed and used. Forecasts show that government will play a lead role in adopting cloud computing – for data storage, applications, and processing power, as IT executives seek to maximize their returns on limited procurement budgets in these challenging economic times. After an overview of the cloud computing concept, this article explores the security issues facing public sector use of cloud computing and looks to the risk and benefits of shifting to cloud-based models. It concludes with an analysis of the challenges that lie ahead for government use of cloud resources.**

I. INTRODUCTION

A. *The "Cloud"*

In the world of computing, clouds have always served a metaphorical – almost mystical role. They have been used traditionally to represent the Internet in a networked environment in diagramming and mapping operations [1]. Knorr and Gruman [2] opined that "as a metaphor for the Internet, 'the cloud' is a familiar cliché, but when combined with 'computing,' the meaning gets bigger and fuzzier."

Today, there is a new development - "cloud computing." What is the cloud? The cloud model represents nothing less than a fundamental change to the economics of computing and the location of computing resources [3]. With the growth in Internet usage, the proliferation of mobile devices, and the need for energy and processing efficiency, the stage has been set for a different computing model.

There has been a suggestion to define the concept using the name "cloud" as an acronym, standing for computing that is: "Common, Location-independent, Online, Utility that is available on-Demand" [4]. The term "cloud computing" has at its core a common element – in that with the cloud model, computing services are delivered over the Internet, on demand, from a remote location, rather than residing on one's desktop, laptop, mobile device, or even your own organization's servers. For an organization, this would mean that for a set or variable, usage-based fee – or even possibly for free, it would contract with a provider to deliver applications, computing power and storage via the Web. The cloud can take on various forms, including: SaaS (Software as a Service), PaaS (Platform as a Service), and IaaS (Infrastructure as a Service) [5].

The basic idea behind cloud computing is that *anything* that could be done in computing – whether on an individual PC or in a corporate data center – from storing data to communicating via email to collaborating on documents or crunching numbers on large data sets - can be shifted to the cloud. Certainly, one of the hallmarks of cloud computing is that it enables users to interact with systems, data, and each other in a manner "that minimizes the necessary interaction with the underlying layers of the technology stack" [6]. According to the *Cloud Computing Manifesto*, "The key characteristics of the cloud are the ability to scale and provision computing power dynamically in a cost efficient way and the ability of the consumer (end user, organization or IT staff) to make the most of that power without having to manage the underlying complexity of the technology" [7].

B. *The Growth of the Cloud*

Global IT spending hit $3.4 trillion in 2008, although the aggregate total is expected to decline for the first time since 2001 in the current year – and perhaps for 2010 as well [8]. Indeed, across the private sector, IT spending is under fire. In fact, due to the interrelated impacts of the recession and the credit crisis, capital budgeting and credit availability for large IT projects has declined significantly. Thus, the only areas of IT that are growing in the wake of the economic crisis are outsourced IT and IT services [9]. Additionally, as new entrants, many of them tied to cloud services, enter the marketplace, the prices for outsourced IT are likely to decline over the next few years as competition intensifies between larger, entrenched competitors and these upstart firms [10].

Roughly ten percent of the approximately $64 billion spent on business applications worldwide in 2008 was spent on cloud computing applications [11]. Many analysts, including Gartner, project growth rates for cloud computing in excess of 20% or more for years to come [12]. The growth rate over the next few years could be as high as 30%, with analysts estimating that the global market for cloud computing services could reach $42 billion by 2012 [13]. Gartner sees the cloud computing marketplace as an even larger market, and it predicts that the market for cloud services already surpasses $40 billion today, and that it will grow to over $150 billion annually by 2013 [14].

Why cloud – and why now? According to the results of the 2009 Cloud Computing Survey, surveying over 500 IT decision-makers, the shift to cloud computing can be seen as organizations are increasingly "turning to new technologies to cut costs, rather than cutting back on their technology uptake" [15]. Cloud computing is also by no means an "all or nothing" proposition. Indeed, it has been seen in practice that cloud involvement often starts when organizations

T. Sobh, K. Elleithy (eds.), *Innovations in Computing Sciences and Software Engineering*, DOI 10.1007/978-90-481-9112-3_2, © Springer Science+Business Media B.V. 2010

initially use cloud resources for part of their non-mission-critical applications or as resources for test projects [16].

C. *Cloud Computing and Government IT*

Many analysts [17] believe that the present economic situation – and its resulting financial strain placed on governments – will only serve to accelerate the adoption of cloud computing in the public sector. As Golden [18] discussed, cloud computing offers "undeniable financial payback—higher utilization, lower energy use, and better application availability. The benefits are so large that IT organizations have been willing—eager, even—to tolerate the challenges that accompany the technology." Indeed, a July 2009 *Computerworld* report found that the larger the organization, the greater the likelihood that it would be engaged in using cloud computing [19].

The economy and the resulting tightness of all governmental budgets – on every level – may indeed speed and heighten the rise of cloud computing. Dan Israel, an executive with Google's federal group, recently observed that: "Given that we're in a very tight budget situation, looking to the cloud is a very cost-effective means of bringing new technologies into the government. By moving to cloud computing, we can also help government IT get out of the business of using and managing servers and focusing instead on more mission-critical technology projects in their agencies" [20]. As such, cloud computing gives organizations greater abilities to focus on their core business [15]. Likewise, Ron Ross, the Director of Security for The National Institute of Standards and Technology (NIST), commented that: ""In an era where there's going to be tight resources, there will be compelling ways to do things more effectively on the IT side…(But) we have to be able to do that in an environment that is well protected" [21].

In this budgetary context, the forecast impact of cloud computing on just the U.S. federal government's IT spending is certainly eye-opening. The public sector market analyst firm, INPUT recently projected that over the next five years, overall federal IT spending will grow at a compound annual rate of 3.5%, reaching $90 billion by 2014. INPUT forecasts that federal cloud computing-related spending will grow almost *eight times* as fast, with a growth rate of approximately 30% annually over the same time frame [22]. According to INPUT's projections, federal spending on cloud computing services will triple over the next five years, growing from $277 million in 2008 to $792 million annually by 2013. This would mean that by 2014, over $1 billion of the federal IT budget would be devoted to cloud computing [22]. Projections from Market Research Media [23] are even more optimistic, saying that cloud computing represents "a fundamental re-examination of investments in technology infrastructure." Their market analysis projects a 40% CAGR (compound annual growth rate) for cloud computing spending in the federal sector and predicts that cloud spending will top $7 billion annually by 2015 [23].

While there are many significant positives to be gained by the increasing use of cloud computing, the shift raises a whole host of security concerns as well. This article explores the security issues facing public sector IT leaders as they consider shifting increasing data and computing applications to cloud providers.

II. SECURITY CONCERNS FOR PUBLIC SECTOR IT

Security is indeed a significant issue facing IT executives as they consider shifting data and processing to cloud providers. One of the principal concerns about cloud computing is the reliability question, and this is certainly a case where when a tree falls (i.e. an outage occurs), everyone hears the sound. Unfortunately, worries over cloud reliability and availability – or specifically, the lack thereof when such instances arise - are not just theoretical. There have been well-publicized outages of many of the most popular public cloud services, including Gmail and GoogleApps [24, 25], Apple's MobileMe service [26], and Amazon's S3 cloud service [27]. When service disruptions do occur, these events tend to paint all cloud services with a broad brush. As one observer characterized the September 2009 Gmail outage: "E-mail is a mission-critical application for business users -- period. If customers perceive that Gmail isn't reliable, they won't adopt it. Every Gmail outage makes companies think twice before adopting the free e-mail solution" [25]. Indeed, the security of cloud computing is an issue that will inevitably "blow-up" each time data breaches occur in cloud offerings and hit the media. And, as Schwartz astutely pointed-out, when cloud service outages or inaccessibility occur, "most of the risk and blame if something goes wrong will fall directly on the shoulders of IT -- and not on the cloud computing service providers" (n.p.).

When a cloud provider sees a data breach or service failure occur, this calls into question the efficacy of storing files and information online, causing huge security concerns for all affected users and not just the target cloud provider, but indeed, the whole cloud computing universe, which could be painted with a broad brush in such security matters. Yet, as Condon [21] observed, "Perfect security on the cloud is an illusory goal…and the vulnerabilities of the cloud will have to be weighed against (its) benefits" (n.p.). Indeed, many security experts believe that the notion of putting more data and more applications on the Internet via the cloud model could present vast new opportunities for criminal activity through identity theft and misappropriating intellectual property, hacking, and other forms of malicious activities [29].

The degree to which *any* organization engages in cloud computing – whether outside or inside its own "four-wall" environment - will certainly depend on its need for security [30]. Yet, some will see the risks of moving data outside their own four walls too great to ever consider a cloud-based option. For private sector IT executives, there is a reluctance to shift core, mission-critcal data storage or applications to public cloud environments, even if the cost savings and efficiency arguments are there, over concerns about the reliability and security of cloud offerings. Take for instance the case of the Princeton, New Jersey-based Educational

Testing Service (ETS), which administers the SAT and other standardized tests. While ETS uses SaaS platforms for non-core functions, the firm's CIO, Daniel Wakeman, recently expressed his reluctance to shift data storage and processing for the tests themselves to a cloud environment. This is in spite of the fact that due to the highly cyclical nature of test administrations, scoring, and reporting around specific testing schedules throughout the year, ETS has an average server utilization rate of just around eight percent, making the firm a prime candidate for acquiring computing resources on-demand. Wakeman simply stated that due to security issues which have yet to be worked-out in what he and other perceive to be an "immature market," ETS will monitor developments in the cloud marketplace and "not (be) putting anything up there that we really care about" [31].

The security debate is perhaps even more intense when it comes to public sector IT. Take for instance the stance of Chiu Sai-ming, who serves as the Chief Assessor at Hong Kong's Inland Revenue Department. While Mr. Sai-ming believes it vital to take advantage of new technologies, he believes that the very notion of housing taxpayer data outside of his ministry is "out of the question" [32]. Many in public sector IT will echo the concerns expressed by Ray Roxas-Chua, who serves as the Chairman of the Commission on Information and Communications Technology (CICT) for the Government of the Philippines. Cabinet Minister Roxas-Chua recently stated that: "The 'inherent risks' of cloud computing need to be addressed before government embraces it is a viable way of managing information" [33].

Certainly, how to make cloud computing secure is one of the biggest issues for making it viable for the federal government – or for any government agency. As with prior shifts in information technology with the advent of the Internet and the Web, the introduction of e-mail, and the explosion of social media, their growth and adoption rates have been slowed by initial fears – some justified and some very unjustified – over security concerns and the loss of control over data and operations [15]. Certainly, privacy and security questions will need to be addressed as public data and applications move into a cloud environment. As Adrienne Thomas, who is the Acting Archivist of the United States, plainly stated recently "It's a very big issue for government in terms of someone else to have control of our stuff" [34]. Yet, as Arun Gupta observed, in order to succeed today, "You have to have the confidence to say, 'I don't need to control everything.' That's very much a Web 2.0 mentality." [35]. Linda Cureton, CIO of NASA's Goddard Space Flight Center, urged IT decision-makers in government that it is imperative when considering a cloud-shift: "Don't confuse control and ownership with security and viability" [36].

Kaplan [37] categorized the widely-held perception that cloud computing and SaaS applications were less secure and less reliable than applications housed on an organization's own network was nothing less than a "myth." Indeed, cloud offerings may be significantly more reliable that an organization's internal offerings [24]. The difference is that when a company's email server crashes or a power outage disrupts operations at its data center, these internal failings do not make media headlines, as is the case anytime there is an outage or data breach with a Google, an Apple, or an Amazon cloud offering. As Kash [38] framed the issue, large-scale cloud providers are often-times more secure than a government agency's or private sector company's internal IT operations simply because they have the "talent, resources and focus" that their customers – and their smaller counterparts – do not have. Still, IT executives stridently believe that their own, hosted systems are far more secure than cloud-based resources [39], and public sector IT managers stridently believe that their internal operations are more secure than a private sector vendor could provide [40].

Musico [41] characterized the need to retain control and protection of sensitive, private data, in an age of information sharing the "Catch-22" for government IT in regards to cloud computing. However, Ron Ross, NIST's Director of Security, observed that it is important to consider the sensitivity of the data in question and develop and employ "a range of security controls (that) will be appropriate for differing levels of data sensitivity" [21]. Data security questions then are dependent on the nature and sensitivity of the data involved. Major Larry Dillard, a program manager in the Army's Office of the Chief Marketing Officer, recently commented on overcoming the security concerns of his superior by stating: ""All data is not created equal…(and) all the challenges we've faced have been self-imposed. We're not putting nuclear launch codes on Salesforce.com, we're putting the street addresses of 17-year-olds" [21].

One of the complicating factors in the shift to a cloud computing environment will be federal requirements for agencies to certify the security of their IT contractors' systems - with no cloud-specific security standards in place. From the perspective of NIST's Peter Mell: "Compliance is going to be tricky in the cloud space for several reasons, but one reason is that clouds are likely to use new security technologies that aren't well understood or widely adopted, and that will make it difficult to prove the required level of security to auditors and to authorizing officials" [42]. Some have questioned whether the federal government would be precluded – from a regulatory standpoint – from using cloud-based services for such reasons. In fact, it has been commented that: "For many agency applications, stringent compliance requirements in areas such as privacy, financial controls, and health information will preclude use of public clouds, regardless of the actual security controls of the provider" [43]. Analysts have already voiced concern that cloud providers methods of logging activities and document reads/access are presently insufficient for meeting the needs of government agencies to assure their compliance through audit controls [44].

Analysts have stated that one of the benefits for small companies is that they may, in fact, be able to raise the level of their computing security by moving more data and applications to the cloud. This is simply because cloud providers will have more resources to spend on security for their operations than most individual firms. Plus, their investments in security can be spread over their entire present – and prospective – clients (perhaps hundreds or thousands of firms), producing far greater results in improving computer security than individual firm's investments in such efforts [28]. The same principle will hold true for government clients as well, especially those at the state and local levels. Yet, analysts have said that this may also be true even at the federal level, as large cloud providers – whose business depends on secure operations – may provide better security than internal federal operations [45].

What are the other benefits of cloud computing in the security area? One of the best ways to improve security is to have a single-point of access, controlled by the organization, and mandating users follow their procedures and policies for access privileges. However, while such access controls return power to the client, they may well serve to defeat some of the robust advantages for remote access fundamental to the cloud computing model [46]. A recent study from researchers at the University of Michigan showed that by shifting virus protection from individual PCs to the cloud that connected them by raising the level of protection to the network, significantly improving the ability of antivirus software to detect viruses and malware [47].

Cloud computing is also a relatively quick and easy solution to the significant problem of laptop theft, which poses a very real, intransigent security and financial headache for IT managers [48]. This is because should a user lose his or her laptop, there would be no security threat, simply because the data would reside in the cloud, rather than on the machine itself [49]. In fact, some have said this would actually mean that cloud storage would increase security for the federal government by reducing the security risk inherent with the hundreds of thousands of laptops in employee possession both inside and outside of federal facilities [50].

Cloud providers have been characterized as addressing such security concerns by going "over the top" with their physical and data security measures. For instance, SaaS-provider Salesforce.com's data center employs "five levels of biometric hand geometry scanners and even 'man trap' cages designed to spring on those without the proper clearances" [49]. This is evidence that cloud providers are very much aware of and attune to both their clients' concerns in the security area and the legal and regulatory risks that are being taken on by both the client and their firm by accepting a sizable portion of the client's IT operations [51].

There are signs that there is some backlash against cloud providers to improve their security safeguards and practices. For instance, in response to a data breach that occurred with Google Docs, The Electronic Privacy Information Center (EPIC) asked the Federal Trade Commission (FTC) to investigate Google's privacy and security measures for Gmail and Google Apps [52]. Likewise, the Constitution Project, concerned that a user's personal information has weaker privacy protections in the cloud than when contained on a single device, has called for the cloud computing industry to set privacy standards and for the Congress to examine the privacy issues as well [53].

And for the concerns about security and privacy, centralizing operations in a cloud environment may not just make computing more secure, but make compliance easier – and cheaper - as well. From the viewpoint of Federal CIO Vivek Kundra, "When you look at security, it's easier to secure when you concentrate things than when you distribute them across the government" [54].

Yet, as Golden [51] observed, those who view cloud computing as too risky may be "overly optimistic" in their view on how well there own security and risk management efforts work – both in reality and in comparison to the cloud model. He remarked that: "This attitude reflects a common human condition: underestimating the risks associated with current conditions while overestimating the risks of something new. However, criticizing cloud computing as incapable of supporting risk management while overlooking current risk management shortcomings doesn't really help, and can make the person criticizing look reactive rather than reflective."

As ever-greater amounts of governmental and private sector firms' work is shifted to cloud computing, could this shift in the locus of computation indeed be creating a national security risk? Cohen [55] noted that: "Cyber-threats against the country and the government are growing exponentially, and the desire to connect agencies and make government open, transparent and interoperable makes it easier for hackers to carry out their attacks -- (thus) will openness and interoperability make us as a nation less secure?" He went on to note that government will have significant interest in protecting cloud resources for the private sector and individuals as well, noting the huge economic impact and disruption that can occur if a major cloud resource, such as Gmail, were to go down for an extended period of time or be lost forever [55]. Such risks are not without precedent, as the government of Estonia was hit by a well-coordinated denial-of-service attack – suspected to be Russian in origin – during a period of tension between the two nations in 2007 [56], and just this summer, several agencies in the U.S. government and sites in South Korea were cyberattacked by what was widely believed to be a scheme conducted by the North Korean government [57]. Such a risk has led Carr [3] to label this as the threat of a "Cold War 2.0" – and it is certainly an area where federal policymakers need to be concerned.

III. CONCLUSION

Security is undoubtedly a hard metric to quantify. And, all too often, the IT community has a somewhat damaging tendency to treating all risks – whatever the real nature of them – as the very worst case scenario and not judging the true impact – and likelihood – of their occurrence [51].

Analogies have been drawn between the advent of cloud computing today with the introduction of wireless technologies a decade ago. As Ron Ross, NIST's Director of Security recently observed, "When wireless came along, we didn't really know a lot about how to protect it, but we developed that understanding as we went forward, and now we do a pretty good job of protecting wireless" [58]. However, Kash [59] warned that the shift to cloud computing could be slowed by what he termed as "a darker cloud of Internet security vulnerabilities" (n.p.). John Garing, who serves as the CIO and Director of Strategic Planning for the Defense Information Systems Agency (DISA), characterized the cloud computing security dilemma as the classic case of the "irresistible force versus immovable object," where "the irresistible force is the incredible thirst for collaboration and information-sharing that Web 2.0 tools and many young people have brought on board and the immovable object is security" [60].

It is likely that governments at all levels will be a significant part of the cloud computing market, as the inherent advantages of cloud models, combined with economic pressures, will drive more and more IT procurement to cloud-based resources. As the cloud model advances, it will be incumbent on government IT leaders – and well as vendor executives – to be mindful of the unique security challenges facing the public sector use of cloud computing resources. Certainly, there are a whole host of legal, privacy and workforce issues that will need to be dealt with as well. Thus, the governmental IT marketplace will be an important focus for much activity – and discussion – for the next decade.

REFERENCES

[1] K. Hartig, "What is cloud computing?" *Cloud Computing Journal*, April 15, 2009. [Online]. Available: http://cloudcomputing.sys-con.com/node/579826 [Accessed: April 21, 2009].

[2] E. Knorr and G. Gruman, "What cloud computing really means," *InfoWorld*, April 7, 2008. [Online].Available: http://www.infoworld.com/article/08/04/07/15FE-cloud-computing-reality_1.html [Accessed: February 18, 2009].

[3] N.G. Carr, "The many ways cloud computing will disrupt IT," *InfoWorld*, March 25, 2009. [Online]. Available: http://www.tmcnet.com/usubmit/2009/03/25/4084363.htm [Accessed: April 1, 2009].

[4] T. Chan, "Full interview: AT&T's Joe Weinman. *Green Telecom Live*, March 16, 2009. [Online]. Available: http://www.greentelecomlive.com/2009/03/16/full-interview-att's-joe-weinman/ [Accessed: May 20, 2009].

[5] J.F. Rayport and A. Heyward, *White paper: Envisioning the cloud: The next computing paradigm, a Marketspace point of view*. March 20, 2009. [Online]. Available: http://www.marketspaceadvisory.com/cloud/Envisioning-the-Cloud.pdf [Accessed: March 24, 2009].

[6] K. Langley, "Cloud computing: Get your head in the clouds," *Production Scale*, April 24, 2008. [Online]. Available: http://www.productionscale.com/home/2008/4/24/cloud-computing-get-your-head-in-the-clouds.html [Accessed: June 3, 2009].

[7] *The open cloud manifesto: A call to action for the worldwide cloud community* (Draft 1.0.9). *OpenCloudManifesto.org*, March 30, 2009. [Online]. Available: http://opencloudmanifesto.org/opencloudmanifesto1.htm [Accessed: April 1, 2009].

[8] S. Ferguson, "Gartner says IT spending will decline 4 percent in 2009," *eWeek*, March 31, 2009. [Online]. Available: http://www.eweek.com/index2.php?option=content&task=view&id=52598&pop=1&hide_ads=1&page=0&hide_js=1 [Accessed: April 2, 2009].

[9] J. Davis, "Gartner and Forrester now forecast 2009 decline in IT spending," *Channel Insider*, April 1, 2009. [Online]. Available: http://www.channelinsider.com/c/a/News/Gartner-and-Forrester-Now-Forecast-2009-Decline-in-IT-Spending-204121/ [Accessed: May 2, 2009].

[10] J. Davis, "Gartner: Outsourced IT services prices could fall 20%," *Channel Insider*, March 27, 2009. [Online]. Available: http://www.channelinsider.com/c/a/News/Gartner-Outsourced-IT-Services-Prices-Could-Fall-20-145259/ [Accessed: April 1, 2009].

[11] M.V. Copeland, "The client-server model: Not dead yet," *Fortune*, February 16, 2009. [Online]. Available: http://money.cnn.com/2009/02/16/technology/copeland_oracle.fortune/index.htm [Accessed: March 28, 2009].

[12] M. O'Gara, "Washington itching to take the lead on cloud computing," *SOA Journal*, July 31, 2009. [Online]. Available: http://govit.sys-con.com/node/1055764 [Accessed: August 21, 2009].

[13] IDC, *Press Release: IDC Finds Cloud Computing Entering Period of Accelerating Adoption and Poised to Capture IT Spending Growth Over the Next Five Years*. October 20, 2008. [Online]. Available: http://www.idc.com/getdoc.jsp?containerId=prUS21480708 [Accessed: January 24, 2009].

[14] S. Hamm, "How cloud computing will change business," *Business Week*, June 4, 2009. [Online]. Available: http://www.businessweek.com/print/magazine/content/09_24/b4135042942270.htm [Accessed: July 15, 2009].

[15] Kelton Research, *2009 Cloud Computing Survey*, February 2009. [Online]. Available: http://www.avanade.com/people/thought_detail.aspx?id=70 [Accessed: May 8, 2009].

[16] J. Schwan, "Open source software, cloud computing can save government money," *Government Technology*, June 26, 2009. [Online]. Available: http://www.govtech.com/gt/articles/697935 [Accessed: July 29, 2009].

[17] T. Ferguson, "Cloud could be 'more important than the PC,'" *Silicon.com*, February 23, 2009. [Online]. Available: http://www.silicon.com/publicsector/0,3800010403,39398330,00.htm?s_cid=59 [Accessed: March 8, 2009].

[18] B. Golden, "The case against cloud computing: Conclusion," *CIO*, March 2, 2009. [Online]. Available: http://www.cio.com/article/482691/The_Case_Against_Cloud_Computing_Conclusion [Accessed: March 4, 2009].

[19] J. King, "5 key questions about cloud storage," *Computerworld*, July 13, 2009. [Online]. Available: http://www.computerworld.com/s/article/340471/Cloud_Storage_Illuminated [Accessed: July 23, 2009].

[20] A. Sternstein, "Cloud computing could help agencies track stimulus funds," *NextGov*, April 30, 2009. [Online]. Available: http://www.nextgov.com/nextgov/ng_20090430_4418.php [Accessed: May 5, 2009].

[21] S. Condon, "Is Washington ready for cloud computing?" *CNet News*, February 25, 2009. [Online]. Available: http://news.cnet.com/8301-13578_3-10172259-38.html [Accessed: March 23, 2009].

[22] INPUT, *Press Release: Obama's budget reveals technology spending trends for next five years: Comprehensive INPUT report identifies key developments shaping federal IT investment*, July 9, 2009. [Online]. Available: http://www.prweb.com/releases/Government_Business/Federal_IT_Market/prweb2627004.htm [Accessed: July 15, 2009].

[23] Market Research Media, "U.S. Federal cloud computing market forecast - 2010-2015," *PRWeb*, May 22, 2009. [Online]. Available: http://www.emediawire.com/releases/2009/5/prweb2446074.htm [Accessed: June 1, 2009].

[24] B. Worthen and J.E. Vascellaro, "Gmail glitch shows pitfalls," *The Wall Street Journal*, February 23, 2009. [Online]. Available: http://online.wsj.com/article/SB123561652440078567.html?mod=#printMode [Accessed July 17, 2009].

[25] S. Gaudin and D. Nystedt, "Gmail outages could turn off enterprises," *Computerworld*, September 10, 2009. [Online]. Available: http://www.computerworld.com/s/article/342708/Gmail_Outages_Could_Turn_Off_Enterprises?taxonomyId=16 [Accessed: September 10, 2009].

[26] R. Parr, "Lost in the clouds: MobileMe is facing problems endemic to

cloud computing," *Technology Review*, July 28, 2008. [Online]. Available: http://www.technologyreview.com/computing/21133/ [Accessed: March 13, 2009].

[27] C. Waxer, "Is the cloud reliable enough for your business?" *Computerworld*, June 1, 2009. [Online]. Available: http://www.computerworld.com/action/article.do?command=printArticleBasic&taxonomyName=Servers+and+Data+Center&articleId=339152&taxonomyId=154 [Accessed: June 15, 2009].

[28] E. Schwartz, "The dangers of cloud computing," *InfoWorld*, July 7, 2008. [Online]. Available: http://www.infoworld.com/article/08/07/07/28NF-cloud-computing-security_1.html. [Accessed: August 1, 2009].

[29] B. Bailey, "Cloud computing may create new venues for high-tech criminals," *San Jose Mercury News*, July 10, 2009. [Online]. Available: http://www.mercurynews.com/businessbreakingnews/ci_12812412?nclick_check=1 [Accessed: July 30, 2009].

[30] K. North, "3 steps to managing data in the cloud," *Information Week*, July 20, 2009. No. 1,236, pp. 40-44.

[31] C. Stedman, "Cloud computing not fully enterprise-ready, IT execs say," *Computerworld*, March 2, 2009. [Online]. Available: http://www.computerworld.com/action/article.do?command=viewArticleBasic&articleId=9128840 [Accessed: June 12, 2009].

[32] R. Hicks, "Hong Kong's Tax Office casts doubt over the cloud," *FutureGov*, April 15, 2009. [Online]. Available: http://www.futuregov.net/articles/2009/apr/15/hong-kongs-tax-office-casts-doubt-over-cloud/ [Accessed: May 17, 2009].

[33] R. Hicks, "Philippine CICT Chairman cool on cloud computing," *FutureGov*, March 2, 2009. [Online]. Available: http://www.futuregov.net/articles/2009/mar/02/philippine-cict-chairman-cool-cloud-computing/ [Accessed: May 15, 2009].

[34] J.N. Hoover, "Government wrestles with social media records retention policies," *InformationWeek*, May 28, 2009. [Online]. Available: http://www.informationweek.com/story/showArticle.jhtml?articleID=217700689 [Accessed: June 7, 2009].

[35] K. Hart, "D.C.'s kinetic tech czar," *Washington Post*, January 5, 2009. [Online]. Available: http://www.washingtonpost.com/wp-dyn/content/article/2009/01/04/AR2009010401235.html [Accessed: March 8, 2009].

[36] L. Cureton, "Cloud computing in the federal government," *Goddard CIO Blog*, March 14, 2009. [Online]. Available: http://blogs.nasa.gov/cm/blog/Goddard-CIO-Blog.blog/posts/post_1237089048316.html [Accessed: July 15, 2009].

[37] J. Kaplan, "Five myths about SaaS," *CIO*, March 23, 2009. [Online]. Available: http://www.cio.com/article/print/486091 [Accessed: March 31, 2009].

[38] W. Kash, "The pros and cons of moving to the cloud," *Government Computer News*, July 9, 2009. [Online]. Available: http://gcn.com/articles/2009/07/13/gcn-interview-ron-markezich-microsoft-cloud-computing.aspx [Accessed: July 15, 2009].

[39] J. Foley, "Survey: Fear slows cloud computing adoption," *InformationWeek*, February 25, 2009. [Online]. Available: http://www.informationweek.com/cloud-computing/blog/archives/2009/02/survey_fear_slo.html [Accessed: May 12, 2009].

[40] J. Brodkin, "Cloud computing vendors converge on standard definition, goals," *Network World*, March 31, 2009. [Online]. Available: http://www.networkworld.com/news/2009/033109-cloud-computing-definition.html [Accessed: June 3, 2009].

[41] C. Musico, "Can cloud computing get 'Army Strong?'" *Destination CRM*, April 29, 2009. [Online]. Available: http://www.destinationcrm.com/Articles/PrintArticle.aspx?ArticleID=53589 [Accessed: May 11, 2009].

[42] E. Chabrow, "Slowing the rush to cloud computing," *GovInfoSecurity.com*, April 16, 2009. [Online]. Available: http://blogs.govinfosecurity.com/posts.php?postID=172 [Accessed: May 26, 2009].

[43] J. Foley, "Uncle Sam's cloud computing dilemma, *InformationWeek*, March 24, 2009. [Online]. Available: http://www.informationweek.com/cloud-computing/blog/archives/2009/03/cloud_computing_10.html [Accessed: April 1, 2009].

[44] R. Westervelt, "Researchers say search, seizure protection may not apply to SaaS data," *SearchSecurity.com*, July 31, 2009. [Online]. Available: http://searchsecurity.techtarget.com/news/article/0,289142,sid14_gci1363283,00.html [Accessed: August 4, 2009].

[45] K. Hart, "Tech firms seek to get agencies on board with cloud computing," *The Washington Post*, March 31, 2009. [Online]. Available: http://www.washingtonpost.com/wp-dyn/content/article/2009/03/30/AR2009033002848_pf.html [Accessed: April 21, 2009].

[46] W. Jackson, "Advantages of cloud computing can come with a serious price tag," *Government Computer News*, July 30, 2009. [Online]. Available: http://gcn.com/Articles/2009/07/30/Black-Hat-Briefings-cloud-computing.aspx. [Accessed: August 3, 2009].

[47] K. Greene, "Moving security to the cloud," *Technology Review*, August 26, 2008. [Online]. Available: http://www.technologyreview.com/computing/21303/ [Accessed: June 27, 2009].

[48] Wyld, D.C., "Help! Someone stole my laptop!: How RFID technology can be used to counter the growing threat of lost laptops," *Journal of Applied Security Research*, May 2009, vol. 4, no. 3, pp. 363-373.

[49] B. Gardiner, "The future of cloud computing: A long-term forecast," *Portfolio*, March 9, 2009. [Online]. Available: http://www.portfolio.com/views/columns/dual-perspectives/2009/03/09/A-Long-Term-Forecast [Accessed: May 17, 2009].

[50] K. Hickey, "Feds on board with online apps," *Government Computer News*, April 1, 2008. [Online]. Available: http://gcn.com/articles/2008/04/01/feds-on-board-with-online-apps.aspx [Accessed: January 24, 2009].

[51] B. Golden, "The case against cloud computing, part two," *CIO*, January 29, 2009. [Online]. Available: http://www.cio.com/article/478419/The_Case_Against_Cloud_Computing_Part_Two [Accessed: June 4, 2009].

[52] L. Rao, "The perils of cloud computing," *TechCrunch*, March 17, 2009. [Online]. Available: http://www.techcrunch.com/2009/03/17/the-perils-of-cloud-computing-privacy-group-wants-to-take-your-gmail-away/ [Accessed: March 23, 2009].

[53] A. Lipowicz, "Coalition: Cloud computing raises privacy issues," *Federal Computer Week*, November 19, 2008. [Online]. Available: http://fcw.com/articles/2008/11/19/coalition-cloud-computing-raises-privacy-issues.aspx [Accessed: March 2, 2009].

[54] J.N. Hoover, "Federal CIO scrutinizes spending and eyes cloud computing," *InformationWeek*, March 14, 2009. [Online]. Available: http://www.informationweek.com/news/showArticle.jhtml?articleID=215900079 [Accessed: March 20, 2009].

[55] R. Cohen, "Is cloud computing becoming a national security risk?" *Cloud Security Journal*, March 16, 2009. [Online]. Available: http://cloudsecurity.ulitzer.com/node/879324 [Accessed: May 2, 2009].

[56] J. Kirk, "Estonia recovers from massive DoS attack," *Computerworld*, May 17, 2007. [Online]. Available: http://www.computerworld.com/s/article/9019725/Estonia_recovers_from_massive_DDoS_attack [Accessed: July 20, 2009].

[57] M. Williams, "Was North Korea behind the DOS attack? *PC World*, July 10, 2009. [Online]. Available: http://www.pcworld.com/businesscenter/article/168219/was_north_korea_behind_the_ddos_attack.html [Accessed: July 20, 2009].

[58] D. Beizer, "The other silver linings," *Federal Computer Week*, July 23, 2009. [Online]. Available: http://fcw.com/articles/2009/07/27/tech-early-cloud-adopters-find-perks.aspx?sc_lang=en [Accessed: August 17, 2009].

[59] W. Kash, "Darkness in the cloud," *Government Computer News*, July 28, 2008. [Online]. Available: http://gcn.com/articles/2008/07/28/editors-desk--darkness-in-the-cloud.aspx [Accessed: January 24, 2009].

[60] D. Harris, "DISA CIO: Cloud computing 'something we absolutely have to do.'" *On-Demand Enterprise*, October 20, 2008. [Online]. Available: http://www.on-demandenterprise.com/features/DISA_CIO_Cloud_Computing_Something_We_Absolutely_Have_to_Do_31270309.html [Accessed: February 28, 2009].

Open Source Software (OSS) Adoption Framework for Local Environment and its Comparison

U. Laila and S. F. A. Bukhari
Computer Engineering Department
Sir Syed University of Engineering and Technology, Karachi-75300, Pakistan
Email: ulaila2002@gmail.com, sfaisal_bukhari@yahoo.com

***Abstract-* According to Business Software Alliance (BSA) Pakistan is ranked in the top 10 countries having highest piracy rate [1]. To overcome the problem of piracy local Information Technology (IT) companies are willing to migrate towards Open Source Software (OSS). Due to this reason need for framework/model for OSS adoption has become more pronounced.**

Research on the adoption of IT innovations has commonly drawn on innovation adoption theory. However with time some weaknesses have been identified in the theory and it has been realized that the factors affecting the adoption of OSS varies country to country. The objective of this research is to provide a framework for OSS adoption for local environment and then compare it with the existing framework developed for OSS adoption in other advanced countries. This paper proposes a framework to understand relevant strategic issues and it also highlights problems, restrictions and other factors that are preventing organizations from adopting OSS. A factor based comparison of propose framework with the existing framework is provided in this research.

I. INTRODUCTION

Free and Open Source Software (FOSS) has gradually made its way across the shores of Pakistan. Major organizations can benefit massively from its arrival. Numerous companies have switched from a closed source to an open source development model in an effort to win market share & to expand product growth.

In FOSS the source code is distributed along with the executable program which can be accessible via the Internet without charge. The concept of free software is not new. It has been around since 1960s in universities such as MIT and corporate firms such as Bell Labs, who freely used source code for research. Software was not a source of revenue generation but it was used to attract more and more customers for purchase of new computers. In the early 1980s, Microsoft started writing distributed softwares for the sole purpose of profit. The source code was hidden from users. This move had a great impact and could be consider as the birth of open source. Richard Stallman, researcher at MIT, founded the 'Free Software Foundation' (FSF) to develop and distribute software under the General Public License history (GPL). Bruce Perens defined a set of guidelines to grant software license to the users and he used the term of Open Source Initiative (OSI) for these guidelines ([2], [3]).

II. FRAMEWORK FOR OSS ADOPTION

Innovation adoption theory initially focuses excessively on individual level and not on organizational level [4]. In 1994 Swanson identified shortcomings in this theory, he provided proofs for its failure to take adequate consideration of the business context.

In Fig. 1 each of the factors which inclined toward increase in the degree of adoption are marked with (↑) while other factors which are negative for the adoption of OSS are marked with (↓). These factors and their impact are taken out from the results of the market investigation and their probabilities are then calculated using probability distribution ([7], [8]). On the basis of the factor's probability the framework is proposed. The majority of organizations working in Pakistan with a stable IT department and diverse area of operations are included. In this research a survey to allow an in depth study based on the estimates and the actual number of completed interviews is included. The response rate was calculated to be 85%. The total sample size is 40 out of which 30 were usable responses [7].

TABLE I
SURVEY STRUCTURE

Total Sample Size	40
Accepted Sample	34
Response Rate	85%
Method	Quantitative
	Qualitative

The details regarding OSS adoption factors is given below

A. Intrinsic Factors

Intrinsic factors are identified as the factors that emphasize on the needs of an organization for being adequate for OSS adoption. It includes the organizational internal affairs like top managements support for adoption, availability of OSS literate IT staff and greater savings possible by using OSS.

Organizational adoption of new technologies depends on having the prerequisite skills for effective deployment. The availability of external skills (through integrators or consultants) is essential for adoption by some organizations.

Intrinsic factors are sub divided into two following categories.

T. Sobh, K. Elleithy (eds.), *Innovations in Computing Sciences and Software Engineering*,
DOI 10.1007/978-90-481-9112-3_3, © Springer Science+Business Media B.V. 2010

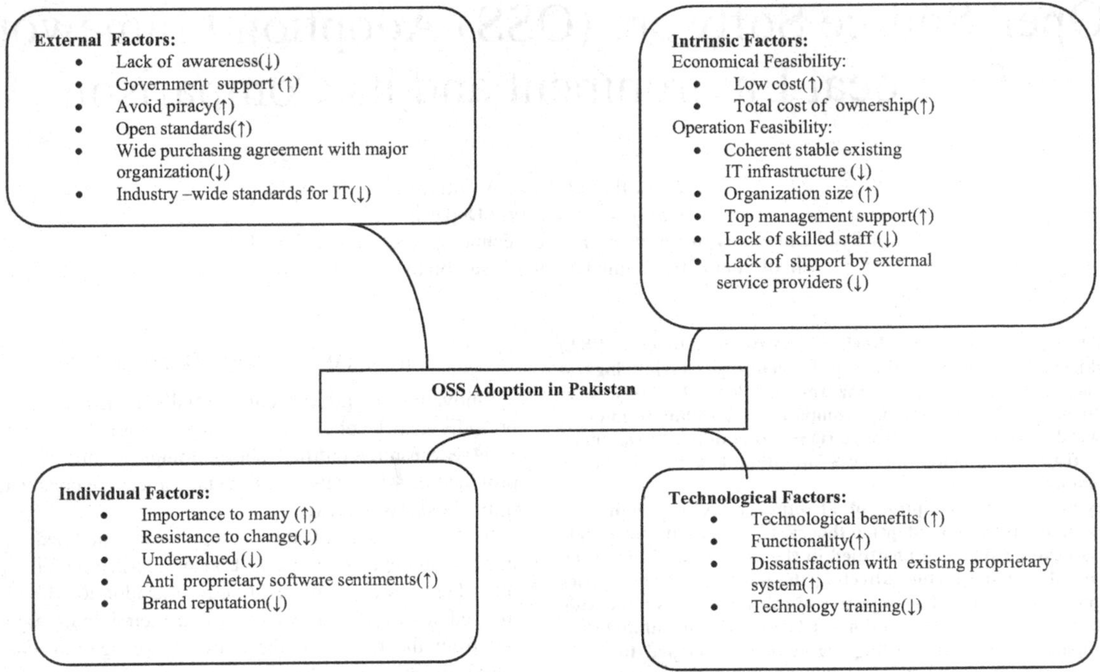

Fig. 1. A Framework for OSS Adoption in Pakistan

Where
(↑). Positive Factors. (↓). Negative Factors.

1) Economical Feasibility

Financial resources are the significant issues in adoption. The budget allocation for IT in Pakistani organizations is limited. Therefore it is insufficient to acquire licensed software. The IT managers of many organizations do not forecast for budget allocation in the near future. They have two choices, i.e. either to reduce their over all level of services or to find some alternative. The open source market-place is open for the organizations to find the alternate solution (low cost) for the required level of services.

The software being free with the low total cost of ownership (TCO) is the main attraction for OSS adoption. In addition, the hidden charges such as hardware cost, administration cost, upgrade cost, technical support, end-user operation cost etc. are not associated with OSS.

2) Operational Feasibility

Some organizations have a stable IT Infrastructure in Pakistan and they are reluctant to change. The source code availability of OSS attracts the organizations because of ease of management of software.

The Organization size appears relevant in the OSS implementation because all desktops software will be converted from proprietary to OSS. This is based on the economic savings in reduction of per-seat license fees being paid for many proprietary applications. Also, large organizations are likely to have access to a pool of specialist IT staff who can assist in solving technical issues that arise in OSS implementation.

Top management support is critical for major, high-risk initiatives because users of proprietary software can turn to the vendor for technical support and there is no vendor of open source software available, only a loose community of developers is there who are not on call when a system crashes. In fact, top managements support is more important for future as OSS adoption moves out of the domain of invisible infrastructure systems to visible, high-profile desktop systems. [4].

One of the principle issues in adoption is the availability of the OSS literate staff. Many developers consider that migrating toward the OSS will deskilled them because most of the companies use proprietary software. It has been observed that the cost of finding appropriately trained personnel for proprietary applications are lower than for OSS. Lack of external service provider is a barrier in the OSS adoption because if an organization lacks support staff then there is no one who will facilitates them.

B. External Factors

Awareness is the critical enabler in the OSS adoption because if people are aware of the technological benefits of OSS then they might think about adoption.

Open source software adoption requires government support and grants for proper execution. Although piracy is the main issue, OSS adoptions evade piracy, which is a sign of honor.

Open source software is typically based on open standards making it easier to share information than with proprietary systems. Unlike CSS applications and platforms, OSS is often portable to a dozen or more different operating systems or platforms.

C. *Individual Factors*

Individual factors are identified as those factors that emphasize on the need to expand the focus of OSS adoption at individual level. Individual factors are also important for OSS acceptance because if people within organization support OSS then they definitely go for OSS adoption.

Users do not want to migrate from CSS to OSS (resistance to change) because of less user friendly OSS products.

Anti proprietary sentiment is also the driving force behind the adoption and it is prevalent, particularly throughout the open source communities. Brand reputation is barrier in OSS adoption, because if people go for brand they won't go for OSS adoption.

D. *Technological Factors*

Technological factors highlight those factors that emphasize on the needs of organizational technological prospective for adopting new technology. The basic issue in adopting a new technology is training. Although most OSS applications, user-interface and functionalities are similar to the Microsoft or other applications that are to be replaced, there are still a lot of differences that hamper the usage of OSS.

Training is needed in order to overcome this obstacle and for new users to become more familiar with the new working environment. Companies need to train their staff to facilitate them to work on OSS product. They try to hire OSS literate people in their companies. Skills to use OSS applications can also be learnt through associating with the OSS communities.

Source code availability enable the user to customize the products according to there need. Companies that develop in-house OSS applications can maintain their software easily. While in proprietary software bug can create a huge problem and it can even stop a project.

III. Order Of Adoption

The order of OSS adoption for an organization is as follows

1. Intrinsic Factors.
2. External Factors.
3. Technological Factors.
4. Individual Factors.

This order is generated with respect to the importance of the factors identified in the survey [7].The most important factor is intrinsic factors because if top management decides to go for OSS then other factors are of no importance i.e. individual, external or technological factors. The reason of giving lesser importance to individual factors is because nobody pays attention to the employees will.

IV. Comparison Of Proposed Framework Factors With Existing Framework Factors

The available framework [4] was developed for the OSS adoption in advanced countries and it is also the motivation for this research. Its factor based comparison with the proposed framework is as follows.

A. *Differences in Intrinsic Factors*

The software with low TCO is the main attraction for OSS adoption because Pakistan is a developing country and money is the main issue. OSS provides lower TCO than CSS.

TABLE II
Organizational Factors

Organizational Factors		
FRAMEWORK	PROPOSED	EXISTING
Financial Resources/Low Cost	√	√
Availability of Skilled Staff	√	√
Organization Size	√	√
Top Management Support	√	√
Total cost of Ownership	√	X
Lack of Support by External Service Provider	√	X
Coherent Stable IT Infrastructure	√	X

Lack of support by external service providers places a negative impact on OSS adoption but in fact it can not be neglected because local environment lacks service providers. Although this is not a big issue in European country but it can be a huge problem in local environment.

Coherent stable IT infrastructure is included because companies that have experience of more than 5 years definitely had a stable IT infrastructure and it is hard for such companies to adopt OSS easily. This factor is included in the technological factors of the existing framework because in developed countries, environmental stability exists which is a major issue locally.

B. *Differences in Technological Factors*

TABLE III
Technological Factors

Technological Factors		
FRAMEWORK	PROPOSED	EXISTING
Technological benefits	√	√
Dissatisfaction with existing system	√	√
Ability of OSS to run on older hardware	X	√
Coherent stable IT infrastructure	X	√
Technological training	√	X
Functionality	√	X

Using open source software on older hardware is an important factor that is included in the existing framework because it targeted a specific case study for migration toward OSS but the proposed framework is general designed. Having a stable IT Infrastructure is a barrier for OSS adoption in local environment.

Technological training is required for proper OSS adoption that's why it is included in proposed framework because without training it is hard to switch to some other technology. Functionality provided by OSS is the main attraction for its adoption.

C. Differences in External Factors

Risk associated with the industry is considered in existing framework because they consider single scenario and they are supposed to check the risk factor for OSS adoption because it was for government sector. The propose framework is general and it considers overall risk of adoption. Organizations will check their overall eligibility/risk for OSS adoption by using this generalize framework.

TABLE IV
EXTERNAL FACTORS

External Factors		
FRAMEWORK	PROPOSED	EXISTING
General attitude to risk in industry	X	√
Successful exemplars	√	√
Government support	√	√
Value for public money	X	√
Industry wide purchase agreement	√	√
Industry wide standard for IT	√	√
Lack Of awareness	√	X
Open standard	√	X

Value for public money factor is included in the existing framework because it focuses on government sectors and saving money for them is a public right. Local environment lacks awareness, which is a barrier for OSS adoption.

Resistance to change factor is in proposed framework because normally people are afraid to switch. Open standard factor is included in the proposed framework because compatibility with the available softwares is required which can easily achievable by using OSS.

D. Differences in Individual Factors

TABLE V
INDIVIDUAL FACTORS

Individual Factors		
FRAMEWORK	PROPOSED	EXISTING
Importance to Many	√	√
Undervalued because Free	√	√
Existence of OSS champions	X	√
Resistance to Change	√	X
Anti Proprietary s/w Sentiments	√	X
Brand Reputation	√	X

Existence of OSS champion's factor is in existing framework because in Europe people are aware of the OSS and there is a possibility of OSS champions. While it is hard to find OSS champions locally because OSS is in preliminary stage.

Anti proprietary software sentiment factor is in proposed framework because there are lot of people who have anti proprietary sentiments. It is because of monopoly of various companies and high licensing cost. Brand reputation factor is in proposed framework because brand reputation plays important role in lowering down the adoption.

V. CONCLUSION

OSS is an emerging technology in Pakistan. The main reason for its popularity is its low cost. This paper has proposed a Framework through which companies can understand the problem they face in proper OSS adoption.

It has been observed that compatibility, skilled staff and maintenance/support are main barriers in proper adoption of OSS at certain times and these problems will get diminished with the passage of time. People are now realizing that the benefits of OSS adoption are more than the problems they can face in adopting OSS.

In future this framework for OSS adoption for local environment will be used to derive a mathematical model [8].

REFERENCES

[1] Business Software Alliance, "Global Software Piracy Study," *http://global.bsa.org/globalpiracy2008/studies/globalpiracy2008.pdf,* 2008.

[2] Open Source Initiative and The Open Source definition, *http://www.opensource.org/osd.html,* 2008.

[3] Peter.B and Sierra Charlie Associates, "Open Source Software Background and Scenarios," 2005.

[4] Glynn. E, Fitzgerald. B and Exton. C, "Commercial Adoption of Open Source Software: An Empirical Study", *International IEEE Symposium Empirical Software Engineering*, 2005, pp 225-234.

[5] Bajaj. A, "A study of senior IS managers' decision models In adopting new computing architecture," *JAIS- Journal of the Association of Information Systems*, Vol. 1, Issue 4. 2000.

[6] Chau. P and Tam. K ,"Factors affecting the adoption of open systems: An exploratory study," *Management Information Systems Quarterly*, Vol. 21, 1997, pp. 1-24.

[7] Laila. U and Khurram. M , "Trends of Open Source Software Adoption in Pakistan," *Interdisciplinary International Conference on Media and Social Change Faculty of Arts, University of Karachi*, 2008.

[8] Laila. U and Abbas. A, "Mathematical Model of Open Source Software Adoption in Pakistan," *International Conference on Open-Source Systems and Technologies (ICOSST) Lahore*, 2007.

Ubiquitous Data Management in a Personal Information Environment

Atif Farid Mohammad
Department of Computer Science, University of North Dakota, Grand Forks, ND USA
atif.mohammad@und.edu

Abstract

This paper presents a novel research work on Personal Information Environment (PIE), which is a relatively new field to get explored. PIE is a self managing pervasive environment. It contains an individual's personal pervasive information associated within user's related or non-related contextual environments. Contexts are vitally important because they control, influence and affect everything within them by dominating its pervasive content(s). This paper shows in depth the achievement of Personal Information Environment, which deals with a user's devices, which are to be spontaneous, readily self-manageable on autonomic basis. This paper shows an actual implementation of pervasive data management of a PIE-user, which contains append and update of PIE's data from the last device used by the user to another PIE devices for further processing and storage needs. Data recharging is utilized to transmit and receive data among PIE devices.

1. Introduction

Computers and computing devices are a ubiquitous part of our lives. We have seen the progress and evolution of these devices over the years from handling one job to juggling many simultaneously. One simple statement mistake by a programmer used to require weeks, sometimes months, to correct. Today, such errors are resolved with astounding speed. As a result of this evolutionary period, computers can now be considered electronic brains, playing an essential part in all of our major activities, including education, business, communication, transportation, and many forms of innovation. Pervasive computing makes devices, as well as applications used by the devices for processing, invisible to the users [01].

Mark Weiser, one of the first visionaries of pervasive computing [02] said in 1991 that we are heading to a "state where computing devices are so pervasive and critical to our activities that they are taken for granted and effectively disappear into the background". This statement describes the notion of "Pervasive/Ubiquitous computing", which is the next generation of computing where individuals have access to their data anywhere and anytime.

This paper provides an examination of such an environment, that being the Personal Information Environment or PIE. The PIE may contain any number of interconnected devices and it provides seamless and transparent access to a PIE user's information using data communication networks at any location. The PIE can have several devices that utilize a wireless connection over the Internet. As per [03], "*Heterogeneity and mobility of devices poses new challenges for information delivery applications in this environment*". This paper presents discussions on data distribution background; it also introduces a novel notion of an individual's Personal Information Environment or PIE and its achievement.

Several possibilities and challenges exist for future work and applications of PIE. The prototype presented in this paper can work for any types of devices attached to the computing environment as pervasive devices.

It is a fact that data management can be achieved efficiently using distributed file system. A Distributed File System is a step by step technique of data storage and availability for any processing need(s) in computing devices. In a Personal Information Environment or PIE, data is saved on one or more devices and can be available for any on demand processing.

2. Background of Data Distribution

This paper provides information about the use of any PIE-device by the user to work on any user related data. Dr. Tanenbaum wrote in his book "Distributed Operating Systems" in 1995 [04] *the design of a world-wide fully transparent distributed file system for simultaneous use by millions of mobile and frequently disconnected users is left as an exercise for the reader.*

The *Coda* file system [05] was the first after *Andrew File System* (AFS) [06] to introduce consistent availability of data in case of intermittent connectivity. In contrast to *Coda* in an *Andrew File System* (AFS) all

T. Sobh, K. Elleithy (eds.), *Innovations in Computing Sciences and Software Engineering*,
DOI 10.1007/978-90-481-9112-3_4, © Springer Science+Business Media B.V. 2010

the data is to be available from one central server for any processing needs on a network. *Frangipani* [07] is another distributed file system that manages a collection of disks on multiple machines as a single shared pool of storage.

3. PIE - Unleashed

The goal of this paper is to achieve by creating and deploying a pervasive Personal Information Environment (PIE) for an individual user. This environment is embedded pervasively and unassumingly in the PIE-user's day to day activities of any kind of stationary or mobile devices and data self-management. A PIE can contain several contexts. An example of a university student can be taken to describe a PIE. Home context of a PIE is described in the Figure 3.1.

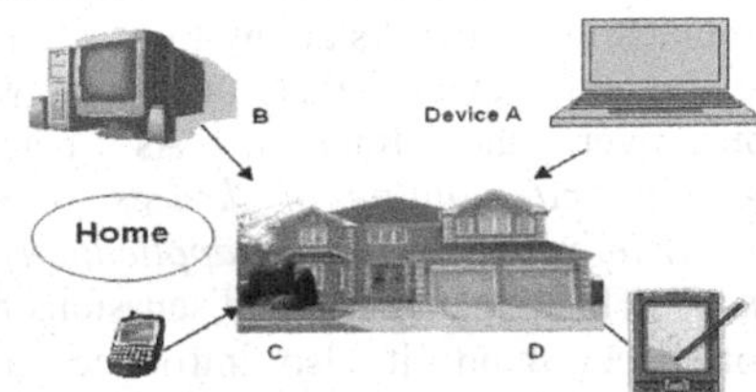

Figure 3.1: A PIE Home Context

Figure 3.1 depicts a device **A,** which is a Personal Laptop of user assumingly having all data from all other PIE-related contexts available for any required data self-management and processing. The cellular devices such as device **C** is a Cell Phone or device **D** is a PDA can access user related data needs to be altered or created for an urgent or immediately required data processing need to be available in PIE for further processing if needed at any other PIE-device(s). Device **B** is Home desktop can be configured with a profile to access school's data as well as any personal work processing needs.

In the School context the student utilizes few devices, such as a computer lab's desktop computer, user's personal laptop, a mobile phone and a PDA for data management at any given time in either at computer lab or in a class session or in library. Two ubiquitous data management scenarios of a PIE are presented in next section. These scenarios are extracted from master-slave [08] model. This replication model is given in sub-section 3.1 as the base theoretical example on which a PIE is designed using data recharging. These scenarios contain hypothetical examples of data objects creation and transmission among PIE devices. These scenarios are the detailed description of a PIE and how the data objects are either pushed or pulled among PIE devices.

3.1 Master-Slave Data Distribution. Master-slave model of data replication as shown in Figure 3.2 is a prime model [09] employed to design the PIE prototype using data recharging. In this replication model, all PIE devices hold the master data with a logical time stamp. We call this logical timestamp an Index Key.

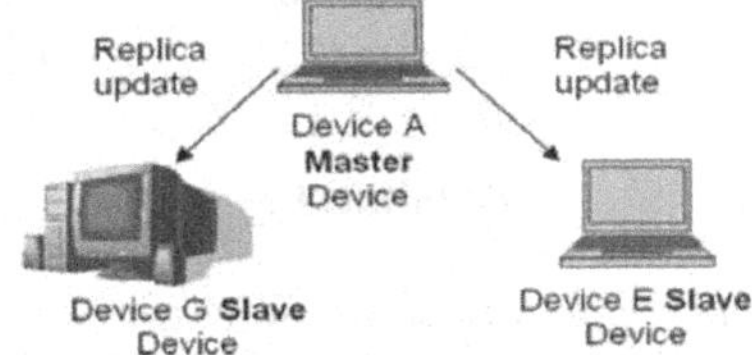

Figure 3.2: Master-Slave Data Replication Scheme

3.2 Design of PIE Prototype. This section contains two scenarios describing the use a PIE on the basis of master-slave model given in previous section. These scenarios display the data management of an individual users PIE. First data management scenario of a PIE where all devices have equal data management options might also contain a PDA, where data needs to be available for one-time processing only and transported to all other devices after the alteration is completed. These data updates can be removed by the user from the PDA to make memory available for any other processing needs. PIE data recharging has a data push as depicted in Figure 3.3 to recharge all PIE–associated devices with profiles configured to get the transaction with the latest updates for future processing needs.

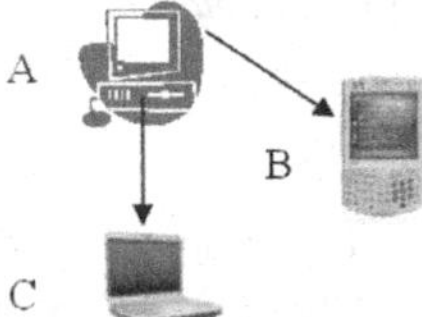

Figure 3.3: Master data dissemination from A to B & C

Figure 3.3 depicts that master data on device A or we can call it *Home-PC* will be available to be pulled by both devices B or *PDA* and C as *Laptop*. Only one data push transaction at a time occurs on individual devices. At the time the master data is updated, the key index value is also changed and is committed at the time the data is saved at both local device's central data recharging folder as well as central node's data recharging repository. An index value is digital proof of a data's creation logical time at any computing device.

Second data management scenario of a PIE is where several devices *A, B, C* and *D* as shown in Figure 3.4, provide efficient data management using the profile property of "Device Denied".

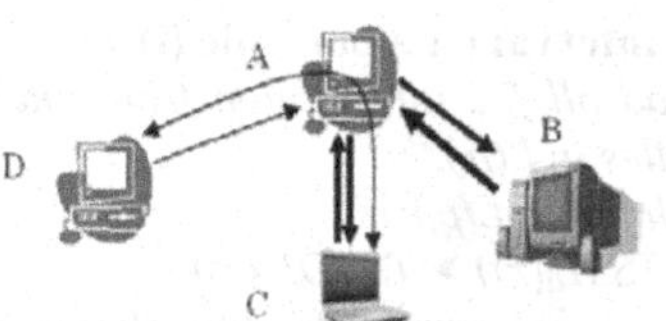

Figure 3.4: Data management using a device profile

Assume that device *A* is a central node as well as a local Home PC as well, and can get data from all devices within a PIE. Device *B*, on the other hand, has a profile restriction not to send and/or receive data from device *D*.

This scenario can be applied on professionals, who join an educational/training institution for any upgrade requirements. Due to the privacy and security issues, these users are often bound not to access official data, while they are on an unofficial site. In this case a PIE user can have a device provided by his organization to use for such data processing. A UML diagram is given in Figure 3.6 to explain these scenarios.

3.3 Data Recharging and Available Solutions. The notion of data recharging was established in the year 2000 by Cherniack, Franklin and Zdonik [10] on the basis of Dissemination-Based Information System (DBIS). The most recent work done in data recharging is *Project 54* [11, 12]. It is pervasive system designed to create an organizational pervasive computing environment within the police cruiser. There is a class of commercial products available for data transmission like data recharging for an official and/or personal use. *Availl Wide Area File Services* (WAFS) [13], *PowerSync 5.0 WS* [14], *Avvneu Access and Share* [15] and rsync [16] is an open source utility that provides fast incremental file transfer over Unix. It is freely available under the GNU General Public License [17] are few examples.

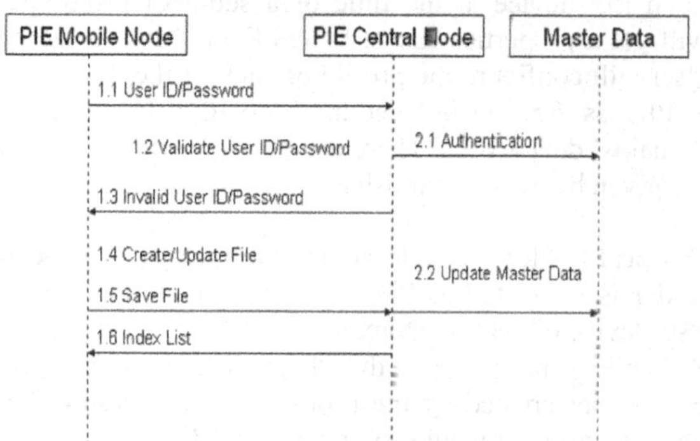

Figure 3.5: Data Recharging Sequence Diagram

3.4 PIE Prototype Processing for Limited Devices. PIE prototype and related actions for both PIE stationary and limited devices; such as PDA, iPaq or Black Berry as mobile devices, are given in the sequence diagram given in the following Figure 3.6 shows the data flow among PIE-Devices. A mobile node does not have the capacity to be a central node.

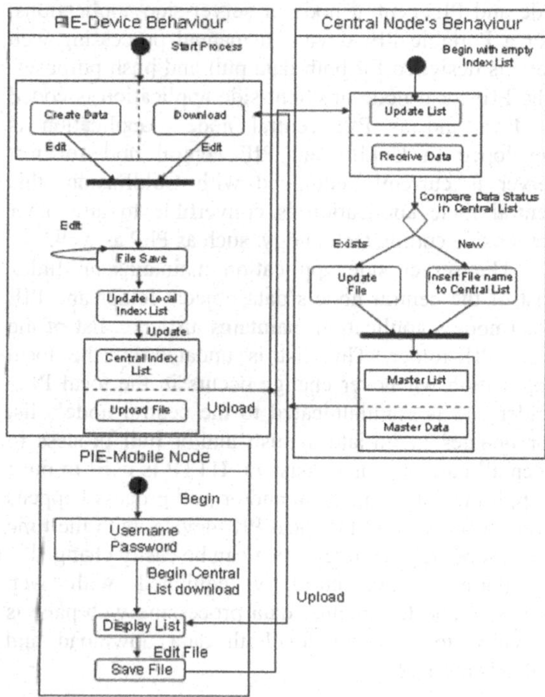

Figure 3.6: Data Recharging within PIE-Devices

4. Design of a Self-Manageable PIE

The PIE prototype uses a set of *n* devices, where devices can be numbered from *0* to *n*. Each device stores profile information for its data processing, management and propagation/recharging purposes. We use an example of a student's PIE. The student is assumed to be a working professional as well.

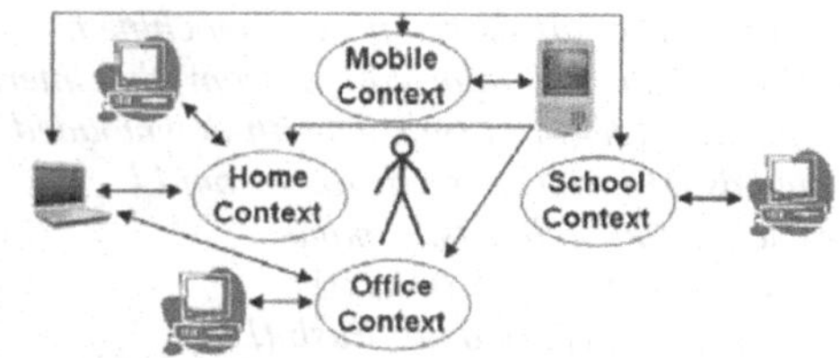

Figure 4.1: A PIE of a student's several contexts

We take a student's different contexts and the devices used within each as in a Home; Home PC, Laptop, PDA, at School Lab PC, Laptop, PDA, at Office Office PC, Laptop, PDA and at Mobile a PDA is utilized. We provide a functional example of data recharging using data replication for a PIE using our solution QUIT. Our PIE solution facilitates automated data propagation in all PIE-devices without the need for human intervention.

QUIT is a combination of PIE local node or client-side and PIE central node or server-side applications. For a Portable PIE device, a manual processing web page is designed for both data pull and push purposes. The PIE local node or client-side application is coded in Java and as PIE central node's application is developed in Coldfusion. PIE central node or test server is currently equipped with ColdFusion; this central node application is convertible to any other server side coding technology, such as PhP as well.

The server side application maintains an Index List of the central node's data objects folder and PIE local node's application maintains an index list of the local PIE-folder. This list is updated by the local application whenever change occurs in the local PIE-folder and is communicated to the central node's list for updates to initiate a push and/or pull process to keep all data objects consistent. HTTP is used to push or pull the data. This push and/or pull process happens every 5 seconds on the local PIE-device, with the time interval being a parameter that can be easily changed.

Portables are currently equipped with web browsers and the manual data processing web page is provided to the user for both data download and uploads purposes.

4.1 Data Recharging Algorithm. Replication is used to develop data recharging for a PIE user to access the PIE-data. If a PIE-device is switched off for any reason, [18] as soon as it restarts the PIE prototype solution will restart and will bring in all the changed files (if any) from the master server so as to be equivalent with all related peers. The pseudocode for the data recharging solution is as follows for a standard device as well as PIE-related portables:

1. At every interval on a machine (i)

1) Take a census of all shared files on machine ***i****.*

2) Download all file information from the internet server for the folders in $\mathbf{L(m_i)}$. *The* ***ith*** *downloaded list is denoted as* ***DLi*** *so as to be distinct from* ***Li****.*

3) For each file in both lists, compare

If $TS(L_i(x)) > TS(DL_i(x))$

Secure data: Push $(L_i(x))$

If $TS(L_i(x)) < TS(DL_i(x))$

Pull $(DL_i(x))$*: Decrypt data*

For each file in DL_i*, not in* L_i

Pull $(DL_i(x))$*:Decrypt data*

For each file in L_i*, not in* DL_i

Secure data:Push $(L_i(x))$

2. Every interval on a portable (i)

1) Download all file information from internet server for the files in $L(p_i)$*.*

2) For each file in $L(p_i)$*:*

If $TS(L_i(x)) > TS(DL_i(x))$

Secure data:Push $(L_i(x))$

If user initiates the handheld device capable of handling all data:

If $TS(L_i(x)) < TS(DL_i(x))$

Pull $(DL_i(x))$*:Decrypt data*

The last step mentioned above will only occur on the user's initiative, and is dependent on the availability of both enough memory and storage in the user's handheld device. It is a fact that smaller devices, such as PDAs, Blackberries etc., are clearly a resource–constrained in memory and storage when compared to Laptop or desktop computers. This suggests a PIE prototype solution which minimizes the use of communication bandwidth and memory usage. Data recharging produces PIE-data duplicates and distributes copies to the other same PIE-devices as soon as a change happens in any of the data. This recharging is done on-demand as well as per a device's profile provided by the user. This profile is to be defined by the user to add a computing device into user related PIE. Table 4.1 contains an actual profile of Home Desktop computer of a student's PIE.

Profile Property	Values
Local Folder	C:\\Home_Desktop\\Docs
User of the PIE	Maf
Deleted	1
File Types	doc;xls;ppt;txt
Device	Home-Desktop
Devices Denied	OfficePC

Table 4.1: PIE-Device Profile Properties file

Each PIE-device at the time of a setup of prototype will get a properties file to be configured by the user. User will configure the profile of each of the device in a PIE as per his/her required devices for various domains' data access. There are two scenarios of a PIE are given below to establish a device's profile:

❖ Local Folder = C:\\Home_Desktop\\Docs -- A local folder is dedicated as "Data Recharging Folder" at a PIE-device of "Home Domain".

❖ Name = maf (User of the PIE) -- This is an identity of the user created by the prototype to make sure the data recharging remains in one user's PIE.

❖ Deleted = 1 -- The "deleted" property of profile can be either "0" or "1". In case of its parameter is "0", upon deletion of the files from PIE-dedicated folder, the deleted files will not be recharged from the master node. If the property is set to be "1", none of the files in PIE dedicated folder can be allowed to be deleted. This profile property makes sure that data is safe and available all the time.

❖ File Types = doc; xls; ppt; txt -- A PIE-user can setup preferences as per the device's context, such as school's or home's and/or office's device of the data files to be appended to the master data repository at the central node defined by the PIE-user. As well as these types of the files will only be downloaded on this typical device for it's recharging. Every PIE-device contains a data index list of the user for the data traceability needs containing last update location, file name, extension and the timestamp.

❖ Device = Home-Desktop -- This typical device is given name as Home-Desktop. This device name's uniqueness is the key to inform the user of the last updated status of the data file, in case PIE-user needs this information for any traceability requirement.

❖ Device Denied = OfficePC -- This device will not get any files created at OfficePC. All other PIE devices data will be transmitted to and from this device.

The results of our prototype implementation shows accurate data recharging as described earlier in the algorithm.

4.2 Resultant Data Sets. The step by step processes of given algorithm yield resultant data. These data sets of few PIE-devices are given below in tables 4.2, 4.3 and 4.4 for a better understanding of the index list. The index key is generated by the PIE prototype and is stored in the index list at all PIE-devices. The central node contains all files uploaded from all PIE devices.

No.	File Name	Index Key	Recharging Device
1	abc.txt	58302180000	Home-PC
2	xyz.xls	60831084000	Home-PC
3	ph.doc	62904152000	School-PC
4	ghi.txt	66063406000	Laptop

Table 4.2: Central Node's Data Index List

No.	File Name	Index Key	Recharging Device
1	abc.txt	58302180000	Home-PC
2	xyz.xls	60831084000	Home-PC
3	ghi.txt	66063406000	Laptop

Table 4.3: Home-PC Index List display

No.	File Name	Index Key	Recharging Device
1	abc.txt	58302180000	Home-PC
2	xyz.xls	60831084000	Home-PC
3	ph.doc	62904152000	School-PC
4	ghi.txt	66063406000	Laptop

Table 4.4: School-PC Index List display

5. Contributions and Future Work

Personal Information Environment is an element of Pervasive Computing. We have seen and are experiencing the technology evolution and growth of Pervasive Computing use over last several decades as in current times. Devices are getting thinner and more efficient. This thesis examines the concept of Personal Information Environment based upon the idea of having information available, as it is needed. To make sure that this data is available in a PIE, we use data recharging, which, in turn, uses data replication to ensure that relevant information is available on all PIE-devices.

5.1 Contributions. The pervasive data of a PIE user can amass and become so widespread that its updates, editions, and transportation can pose difficulties with archiving and publication. This paper contributes the study of an individual user's Personal Information Environment. The use of standard requirements engineering [19, 20] in this research work has lead to an algorithm design for data availability in a PIE to make a PIE achievable. The study of data recharging has provided a valid solution. There can be *n* number of devices attached to a user's PIE. The PIE data-recharging structure facilitates efficient, snapshot-consistent data availability for any processing needs on these devices. The PIE prototype has been designed specifically for individual users only.

5.2 Future Work. This study can further be evaluated for the PIE's relevance to the health care industry for monitoring data associated with patients in care facilities or at their homes. For example, a patient in acute or palliative care needs several pervasive devices to reduce or remove pain to facilitate recovery. Data associated with these devices must be transmitted via a certain computing device from a patient's care facility on an as-soon-as-possible (ASAP) basis to the medical authorities. Hospice staff needs to expedite decisions about patient care to advise attending staff regarding procedures to provide relief for patients. This data transmission is possible with our research work on pervasive data management and recharging. A PIE prototype can also be used to maintain *n* versions of any desired file or folder by the PIE user. A PIE can be extended in the collaborative environment for read-only or write-only basis permission-granting by the PIE user to family, friends or co-workers.

It is also a possibility that a user uses a device, which has been disconnected for a period of time. There will be two files with the same name and different index keys available in the PIE as the connectivity resumes between these two nodes. Two of the following solutions can be adapted to resolve this conflict. An e-mail can be generated by the prototype for the user to inform that there are two files with the same name and different index key values available. The available file at central node can be accessed by using the web-portal used for hand held device. This file can be downloaded in any other folder on the device in use by the user for comparison either to merge data or discard one of the files. A second solution that could be adapted is to have multiple versions available of a file with an information display that can be designed for the user to be available on the web-portal for the user to make a choice, which file he/she wishes to process.

6. Conclusion

This paper introduced the novel notion of data recharging in a pervasive Personal Information Environment. Data recharging makes a PIE much simpler for the user requiring data processing at anytime, anywhere availability. The PIE prototype is a way to process one's data and transmit it over the physical network backbone. There are no third-party servers involved that could generate data security breach issues, due to the fact that a user can use one of his/her own device as a central node. Our prototype implementation of QUIT, maintains a synchronized index list of files recharged among all PIE devices. This index list contains the data file name, its transmission/recharging time, and a device's profile information, where the data has been processed, and its last processing time at the data recharging phase.

References

[01] E. Loureiro, L. Oliveira and H. Almeida: "Improving flexibility on host discovery for pervasive computing middlewares", in Proceedings of the 3rd International Workshop on Middleware for Pervasive and Ad-Hoc Computing, pp. 1- 8, November 2005

[02] M. J. Franklin, "Challenges in Ubiquitous Data Management", Lecture Notes In Computer Science. Informatics - 10 Years Back. 10 Years Ahead. Volume 2000, pp. 24-33, January 2001

[03] G. Berhe, L. Brunie and J. Pierson: "Modeling service-based multimedia content adaptation in pervasive computing", in Proceedings of the 1st Conference on Computing Frontiers, pp. 60-69, April 2004

[04] Tanenbaum, A.S.: Distributed Operating Systems, Prentice Hall, Upper Saddle River, NJ U.S.: Prentice Hall, 614 pages, 1995.

[05] James J. Kistler and M. Styanarayanan, "Disconnected Operation in the CODA File System," ACM Transactions on Computer Systems, Volume 10, Issue 1, pages: 3 - 25, February 1992

[06] Morris, J., Satyanarayanan, M., Conner, M. H., Howard, J. H., Rosenthal, D. S., Smith, F. D.; Andrew: a distributed personal computing environment. Comms. ACM, vol. 29, no. 3, pp. 184-201.

[07] Chandramohan A. Thekkath, TimothyMann, Edward K. Lee: Frangipani: A Scalable Distributed File System. ACM SIGOPS Operating Systems Review Volume 31 , Issue 5 Pages: 224 – 237. Dec, 1997

[08] D. Ratner, P. Reiher, G. J. Popek and G. H. Kuenning, "Replication requirements in mobile environments", in Dial M for Mobility: Discrete Algorithms and Methods for Mobile Computing and Communication, Vol 6 , Issue 6, pp. 525-533, November 2001

[09] E. Pacitti, P. Minet and E. Simon, "Replica Consistency in Lazy Replicated Databases", in Proceeding of Distributed and Parallel Databases, Volume 9, Issue 3, pp. 237-267, May 2001

[10] M. J. Franklin, S. Zdonik. "A Framework for Scalable Dissemination-Based Systems", in Proceedings of the 12th ACM SIGPLAN Conference on Object-Oriented Programming, Systems, Languages, and Applications, pp. 94 – 105, October 1997

[11] Jacob LeBlanc, Thomas E. Hurton, W. Thomas Miller III and Andrew L. Kun : "Design and evaluation of a vehicle data distribution and collection system," Fifth International Conference on Pervasive Computing (Adjunct Proceedings), Toronto, Canada, 2007

[12] W. Thomas Miller, III, Andrew L. Kun and William H. Lenharth, "Consolidated Advanced Technologies for Law Enforcement Program," IEEE Intelligent Transportation Systems Conference, October, 2004

[13] http://www.availl.com/wafs/ accessed on Jun 18, 2009

[14] http://www.linkpro.com/ accessed on Jun 18, 2009

[15] http://www.avvenu.com accessed on Jul 04, 2009

[16] http://rsync.samba.org; Accessed on Jul 10, 2009

[17] http://rsync.samba.org/GPL.html; Accessed on Jul 12, 2009

[18] Atif Farid Mohammad; Use of Data Recharging for Personal Information Environment. In proceedings of International Conference on Software Engineering Research and Practice, Las Vegas, NV pp. 718-724 July 2008

[19] Atif Farid Mohammad, Dustin E. R. Freeman; Supply Chain Requirements Engineering: A Simulated Reality Check. in IEEE Conference on Systems, Computing Sciences and Software Engineering. Bridgeport, CT. December 2008

[20] Atif Farid Mohammad; A New Perspective in Scientific Software Development. in IEEE Conference on Systems, Computing Sciences and Software Engineering. Bridgeport, CT. December 2008

Semantics for the Asynchronous Communication in LIPS, a Language for Implementing Parallel/distributed Systems

Amala VijayaSelvi Rajan*
Dubai Women's College - Higher Colleges of Technology, Dubai, UAE

Arumugam Siri Bavan[†] and Geetha Abeysinghe[‡]
Middlesex University, London, UK

Abstract

This paper presents the operational semantics for the message passing system for a distributed language called LIPS. The message passing system is based on a virtual machine called AMPS(Asynchronous Message Passing System) designed around a data structure that is portable and can go with any distributed language. The operational semantics that specifies the behaviour of this system uses structured operational semantics to reveal the intermediate steps that helps with analysis of its behaviour. We are able combine this with the big-step semantics that specifies the computational part of the language to produce a cohesive semantics for the language as a whole.

I. INTRODUCTION

Operational Semantics defines the meaning of programs in terms of their behaviour. For example, it describes the executional behaviour of a programming language for implementation purposes and gives a computational model for the programmers to refer to. This paper presents the operational semantics that models the asynchronous message passing behaviour of LIPS, a Language for Implementing Parallel/distributed Systems [1].

LIPS is an asynchronous point-to-point message passing language which can handle its communication and computational components independently. A LIPS program consists of a network of nodes described by a network definition and node definitions which describe the nodes in the network. Each node consists of a set of guarded processes. Each guarded process has a statement block which forms the computational part of LIPS. In order to adequately provide implementation information for both computational and communication parts when describing the semantics for of LIPS, we follow a mixed two step strategy where

- computations are defined using big-step semantics and
- communication part of LIPS is defined using Structured Operational Semantics (SOS).

SOS has been chosen to describe the communication as it tells us how the intermediate steps of the execution are performed which are crucial in message passing. The combined semantics describes the operational behaviour of LIPS programs by modelling how different statements are executed while capturing both the result of computation and how the result is produced. This can help to implement the language and its debugging tools. Many languages which include parallelism and concurrency or any other special features have adopted similar type of mixed approaches. Following are few examples:

- operational semantics for functional logic languages is defined in[2] by using the big-step semantics in natural style to relate expressions and their evaluated results and extended it with small-step semantics to cover the features of modern functional logic languages;
- The semantics for SML has been generated by integrating the concurrency primitives with process algebra [3];
- Big-step semantics has been extended with a relational approach to handle concurrent languages [4].

The asynchronous communication in LIPS has been implemented using Asynchronous Message Passing System (AMPS) conceptualised by Bavan [5]. AMPS is based on a simple architecture comprising of a Data Structure (DS), a Driver Matrix (DM), and interface codes. In a LIPS program, a message is sent and received using simple assignment statements and the program is not concerned with how the data is sent or received. With the network topology and the guarded process definitions, it is easy to identify the variables participating in the message passing. The DS and the DM for the AMPS are defined using these variables. A detailed explanation of AMPS can be found in [5] and its initial version of the Operational Semantics can be found in [6]. The work presented here on the operational semantics for the communication part of LIPS is a refinement of the work

---

*Electronic address: amala.rajan@hct.ac.ae
†Electronic address: s.bavan@mdx.ac.uk
‡Electronic address: g.abeysinghe@mdx.ac.uk

T. Sobh, K. Elleithy (eds.), *Innovations in Computing Sciences and Software Engineering*,
DOI 10.1007/978-90-481-9112-3_5,

published in [6].

The operational semantics for the communication part of LIPS is implemented using the following:

- connect statements which express the topology of the network.
- Node which contains the set of guarded processes.
- Asynchronous Message Passing System (AMPS).

As a first step to describing the SOS for the communication part of LIPS, the primitives of AMPS and the communication schema are described in the following section (Section II).

II. PRIMITIVES AND COMMUNICATION SCHEMA FOR THE ASYNCHRONOUS MESSAGE PASSING IN THE LIPS

The AMPS of LIPS makes three main function calls and the data involved in the message passing is always sent to the Data Structure (DS) or received from the DS thereby the sender or receiver never waits for the recipient or the sender respectively. The basic types of data have been extended with the additional data types and functions to handle the asynchronous communication. The extended data types and their associated syntactic categories are described in subsection II A.

The following are the functions used in the AMPS of LIPS:

1. **IS_ok_to_send (Src_node_number, Vnum)**: Sender checks whether it can send data to the AMPS.
2. **Is_input_available(node_number, Vnum)**: Receiver checks the availability of the data in the AMPS.
3. **Send(data_packet)**: Sender sends the data packet.

When one of these functions is called, the statement block is executed. The set of statements belong to the computational part of LIPS is defined using the big-step semantics.

A. Syntactic Categories for Asynchronous Communication

The existing data types have to be extended and the extended data types will be used implicitly by the LIPS compiler. The extended data types are given as below:

σ `::= int | real | bool | string | char | channel | flag | node_number | node_name | counter | vnum | vname | type_number | data_packet | inlist | outlist | data_structure | cmd`

According to the extended data types, the syntactic categories of LIPS have been extended and are listed below:

i. **Set of Channel Numbers - positive integer values:**

$$\texttt{CHANNEL} \stackrel{def}{=\!=} \{ch_1, ch_2, ..., ch_n\}$$

ii. **Set of flags which can take Boolean values:**

$$\texttt{FLAG} \stackrel{def}{=\!=} \{fch_1, fch_2, ..., fch_n\}$$

iii. **Set of node numbers**

$$\texttt{NODE\_NUMBER} \stackrel{def}{=\!=} \text{k } \{\text{finite set of integers}\}$$

iv. **Set of node names**

$$\texttt{NODE\_NAME} \stackrel{def}{=\!=} \{\text{finite set of integers}\}$$

v. **Set of Channel Variable Numbers**

$$\texttt{VNUM} \stackrel{def}{=\!=} \{\text{finite set of integers}\}$$

vi. **Data Type Numbers**

$$\texttt{TYPE\_NUMBER} \stackrel{def}{=\!=} \{1, 2, 3, 4, 5, 6, 7, 8, 9\}$$

vii. **The original data in string form**

$$\texttt{DATA} \stackrel{def}{=\!=} \{\text{data — data} \in \textbf{STR}\}$$

viii. **Data Packet**

$$\texttt{DATA\_PACKET} \stackrel{def}{=\!=} \text{¡node\_number, vnum, type\_number, data¿}$$

ix. **List of Input channels**

$\texttt{InList} \stackrel{def}{=\!=}$

```
Struct inlist {
        vnum, vname, flag, data,
        Struct inlist *next}
```

x. **List of Output channels**

$\texttt{OutList} \stackrel{def}{=\!=}$

```
Struct outlist {
     vnum, vname, counter, data,
     Struct outlist *next}
```

xi. **Data Structure**

$\texttt{DS} \stackrel{def}{=\!=}$

```
Struct data_struct {
       nnum, nname, inlist, outlist,
       Struct data_struct *next}
```

xii. **Data Matrix**

$$\texttt{Data\_Matrix} \stackrel{def}{=\!=} \text{DM}\,[m][n]$$

where m is the number of rows which is equal to the number of variables and n is the number of columns which is equal to the number of nodes in the network plus three. The various columns in the network are Vnum, node_number, type_number, node_number of the nodes in the network.

xiii. **Checking the availability of data**

$\texttt{IsInputAvail} \stackrel{def}{=\!=}$ Is_input_available(node_number, vnum)

When this function is called, a set of actions take place which are represented by the following code segment:

```
int availstatus = 0
while (DS != null){
  if(DS.node_number = node_number) then{
     while(inlist != null) do {
        if (inlist.vnum = vnum) then{
            if (inlist.flag = 1) then{
                availstatus = 1
                break whileloop
                } }
         inlist = inlist.next
        } if (availstatus = 1) then
                   break whileloop
    } DS = DS.next
   }
return availstatus
```

xiv. **Checking the readiness for of sending the data**

$\texttt{ISOKTOSEND} \stackrel{def}{=\!=}$ Is_ok_to_send(Src_node_number, vnum)

When this function is called, a set of actions take place which are represented by the following code segment:

```
int status = 0
while (DS != null) do {
 if(DS.node_number = Src_node_number) then{
    while(outlist != null){
        if (outlist.vnum = vnum) then{
          if (outlist.counter = 0) then{
              status = 1
              break whileloop
          }} outlist = outlist.next
        } if (status = 1) then
                 break whileloop
        } DS = DS.next
        } return status
```

xv. **Sending data**

$$\texttt{SEND} \stackrel{def}{=\!=} \text{Send(data\_packet)}$$

where the data_packet consists of the node number, variable number, `vnum`, type of data, `type_number`, and the actual data, `data`, in string form. On the receipt of this packet, the AMPS checks the data structure, `DS`, to see whether the variable number, and type are correct and stores the data in the appropriate field. The counter is set to the number of nodes that are to receive the data by consulting the data matrix, DM, which consists of `m` number of rows and `n` number of columns where `m` is the number of variables where `n` is 3 (to store the variable number, its source node number and type number) + number of nodes. The Send function returns a 1 to indicate a success. The code segment to find counter value for a given node number, variable number and its type by using the data matrix is given below:

```
int i, j
int counter = 0
for (i = 0 to m -1){
  if (DM[i][0] = vnum) then{
    if ((DM[i][1] = node_number) ^
           (DM[i][2] = type_number)) then{
         for (j = 3 to n - 1){
            if (DM[i][j] = 1) then
              counter = counter + 1
}}}}
return counter
```

The code segment to place the data in the data structure and set the counter value is give below:

```
int status = 0
while (DS != null) do {
   if(DS.node_number = Src_node_number){
      while(outlist != null){
         if (outlist.vnum = vnum) then{
             outlist.data = data
             outlist.counter = counter
             status = 1
}}}}
return status
```

After storing the data, the AMPS consults the DM, distributes the data to other DS nodes, and decrements the copy counter accordingly. Here the data is written to the input channel variable of a receiving DS node, provided the status counter of that input channel variable is 0 (that is, the channel is free to receive new data). Once the data is received, the status is set to 1. If any of the DS destination nodes are unable to receive the new data, the AMPS periodically checks whether they are free to accept the data.

```
while (DS != null){
  if(DS.node_number = node_number){
     while(inlist != null){
       if ((inlist.vnum = vnum)
             ^ (inlist.flag = 0)) then{
          inlist.data = data
          inlist.flag = 1
          counter = counter - 1
        }
       inlist = inlist.next
   }}}
return counter;
```

xvi. **Guard**

$$G_i \stackrel{def}{=\!=} fch_{i1} \wedge fch_{i2} \wedge fch_{i3} \wedge ..., \wedge fch_{im}$$

xvii. **Guarded Process**

$$\left\{ \begin{array}{l} gp_i \stackrel{def}{=\!=} \\ \quad if\ (fch_{i1} \wedge fch_{i2} \wedge fch_{i3} \wedge ... \wedge fch_{im}) \\ \quad\quad then\ P_{i1}; P_{i2}; P_{i3}; ...; P_{ik} \end{array} \right.$$

xviii. **Node**

$$\left\{ \begin{array}{l} R_j \stackrel{def}{=\!=} \\ while\ (true)\ do \\ \quad if\ \ (fch_{i1} \wedge fch_{i2} \wedge fch_{i3} \wedge ... \wedge fch_{im}) \\ \quad then\ \ P_{i1}; P_{i2}; P_{i3}; ..., P_{ik} \\ od \end{array} \right.$$

for all $1 \le i \le n$ where n is the number of guarded processes for a node $R_j \in R$.

xix. **Connect Statement**

$$\left\{ \begin{array}{l} \texttt{CONNECT} \stackrel{def}{=\!=} \\ \quad R_i(ich_{i1} \wedge ich_{i2} \wedge ... \wedge ich_{im}) \\ \quad \rightarrow (och_{i1} \wedge och_{i2} \wedge ... \wedge och_{is}) \end{array} \right.$$

where $R_i \in R$
$ich_{i1}, ich_{i2}, ..., ich_{im} \in ch$
$och_{i1}, och_{i2}, ..., och_{is} \in ch$

In this section, we define the type assignments used in the computational part of LIPS. In the next section, the operational semantics using its evaluation relation is defined.

III. STRUCTURAL OPERATIONAL SEMANTICS (SOS) FOR THE ASYNCHRONOUS COMMUNICATION

In SOS, the behaviour of the processes is modelled using the Labelled Transition System (LTS). These transitions are caused by the inference rules that follow the syntactic structure of the processes.

Definition 1. Labelled Transition System
A Labelled Transition System (LTS) is a triplet {S, K, T} where S is a set of states, K is a set of labels where $\overline{K}$= {$\overline{k}$— k ∈ K}, and T = {$\xrightarrow{k}$, k ∈ K } is a transition relation where $\xrightarrow{k}$ is a binary transition relation on S.

The translation can be written as $s \xrightarrow{k} s'$ instead of (s,s')∈$\xrightarrow{k}$.

LTS is a set of inference rules used to specify the operational semantics of the calculus. It is defined using the syntactical structure of the term defining the processes and it describes the observational semantics. The general form of SOS for a function can be defined as follows:

Let f be the name of the function.
Let $x = \{x_1, x_2, ... xn\}$ be the set of argument parameters associated with the function.
Let $x_i : 1 \le i \le n$ where

type of x_i ∈ `CHANNEL` ∨ `FLAG` ∨ `NODE_NUMBER` ∨ `VNUM` ∨ `VNAME` ∨ `TYPE_NUMBER` ∨ `DATA` ∨ `DATA_PACKET` ∨ `COUNTER` ∨ `DATA_STRUCTURE` ∨ `INLIST` ∨ `OUTLIST`.

Let y be the value returned by the function where y is either a 0 or a 1. Let s_1 and s_2 be the initial and final state of the caller respectively. The SOS is

$$\frac{}{(f(x_1, x_2, ... x_n), s_1) \xrightarrow{x_1, x_2, ..., x_n} (y, s_2)} :: f$$

Following are the inference rules used to specify the SOS for the asynchronous message passing in LIPS:

Guard and Guarded Process

The SOS for a guarded process GP_i is given below:
Let $FCH_i = \{fch_{i1}, fch_{i2}, ..., fch_{im}\}$ be the set of flags associated with the input channels $CH_i = \{ch_{i1}, ch_{i2}, ..., ch_{im}\}$ respectively for some positive integer $m \ge 0$. Let $G_i = (fch_{i1}, \wedge fch_{i2}, \wedge ... \wedge fch_{im})$ be a guard or condition to be satisfied for the associated process body to be executed.
Let GN_i is guard number and VNUM is variable number. For a fch_{ij} to be true, $Is\_input\_available(GN_i, VNUM\ of\ ch_i)$ should return 1. When a 1 is returned, the `Send` function will be initiated which sends the data to the Data Structure (DS) of the AMPS. The SOS for a guard G_i is defined

as below:

$$\frac{\dfrac{}{(fch_{i1}{:=}\underline{T}, s_1) \xrightarrow{\underline{T}} (ch_{i1}, s)} \quad \cdots \quad \dfrac{}{(fch_{im}{:=}\underline{T}, s_1) \xrightarrow{\underline{T}} (ch_{im}, s)}}{(fch_{i1} \wedge fch_{i2} \wedge \ldots \wedge fch_{im}, s_1) \xrightarrow{\underline{T}} (\underline{T}\{ch_{i1}, ch_{i2}, \ldots, ch_{im}\}, s_2)} :: G_i$$

Let $P_i = P_{i1}; P_{i2}; \ldots ; P_{ik}$ be the set of statements in the process body for some $k \geq 0$. These statements may contain assignment statements to assign values for the output channels. When such a statement is encountered, the function, *Is_ok_to_send* will be called. If this call returns a 1 then the **Send** function will be called to send the data to the DS of the AMPS.

Let $OCH_i = \{val_{i1}, val_{i2}, \ldots, val_{is}\}$ be the set of values associated with the output channels for the guard G_i where $s \geq 0$.
The SOS for the guarded process GP_i is specified as follows:

$$\frac{\dfrac{}{(G_i, s_1) \xrightarrow{\underline{T}} (\underline{T}, s_1\{G_i{=}\underline{T}\})} \quad \dfrac{}{(P_i, s_1) \xrightarrow{CH_i} (OCH_i, s_2\{G_i{=}\underline{F}\})}}{(if\ G_i\ then\ P_i, s_1) \xrightarrow{CH_i} (OCH_i, s_2\{G_i = \underline{F}\})} :: GP_i$$

Node

The node $R_i \in R$, which is a collection of guarded processes, is illustrated using an infinite while loop. The SOS for a node using `while statement` is given below:

Let $GP = \{GP_1, GP_2, \ldots, GP_n\}$ be the set of guarded processes where $n \geq 0$.

Let $FCH_i = \{fch_{i1}, fch_{i2}, \ldots, fch_{im}\}$ be the set of flags associated with the input channels $CH_i = \{ch_{i1}, ch_{i2}, \ldots, ch_{im}\}$ respectively for some positive integer $m \geq 0$.

Let $OCH_i = \{val_{i1}, val_{i2}, \ldots, val_{is}\}$ be the set of output channels associated with the guarded process GP_i where $s \geq 0$.

$$\frac{A \quad B}{(while\ (\underline{T})\ do\ (GP_1\ else\ GP_2\ else\ \ldots\ GP_n), s_1) \xrightarrow{\underline{T}} (if\ (\underline{T}\ then\ (GP_i;\ while\ \underline{T}\ do\ (GP_1\ else\ GP_2\ else\ \ldots\ GP_n))), s_k)} :: R_i$$

$$A \stackrel{def}{=\!=} \frac{}{(\underline{T}, s_j) \xrightarrow{\underline{T}} (\underline{T}, s_j)} \quad \frac{\dfrac{}{(G_i, s_j) \xrightarrow{CH_i} (\underline{T}, s_j)} \quad \dfrac{}{(P_i, s_j) \xrightarrow{CH_i} (OCH_i, s_j)}}{(if\ G_i\ then\ P_i, s_j) \xrightarrow{CH_i} (OCH_i, s_{j+1})} :: GP_i$$

where $1 \leq j \leq k$ and k is some positive integer.

$$B \stackrel{def}{=\!=} \frac{A \quad B}{(while\ (\underline{T})\ do\ (GP_1\ else\ GP_2\ else\ \ldots\ GP_n), s_j) \xrightarrow{\underline{T}} (if\ (\underline{T}\ then\ (GP_i;\ while\ \underline{T}\ do\ (GP_1\ else\ GP_2\ else\ \ldots\ GP_n))), s_k)} :: R_i$$

Network definition

Let n be the number of nodes in a network and m and s are the number of input channels and output channels respectively whose value changes for every node in the network. A `connect` statement is closely associated with the node's definition and it specifies the set of input and output channels associated with a node.
Let R_i be a node in a system under consideration.
Let $ICH_i = \{ich_{i1}, ich_{i2}, \ldots, ich_{im}\}$ be the set of input channels associated with R_i where $m \geq 0$.

Let $OCH_i = \{och_{i1}, och_{i2}, \ldots, och_{is}\}$ be the set of output channels associated with R_i where $s \geq 0$.
The SOS for one connect statement is given below:

$$\frac{}{(R_i(ich_{i1} \wedge ich_{i2} \wedge \ldots \wedge ich_{im}), s_1) \longrightarrow ((och_{i1}, och_{i2}, \ldots, och_{is}), s_2)} :: Connect$$

The SOS for the network defined using these n number of connect statements where is given below:

$$\frac{}{\forall i : 1 \leq i \leq n((R_i(ich_{i1} \wedge ich_{i2} \wedge \ldots \wedge ich_{im}), s_1) \longrightarrow ((och_{i1}, och_{i2}, \ldots, och_{is}), s_2))} :: Connect$$

Is_input_available, Is_ok_to_send, and Send

The labelled transitions for the function,

IS_INPUT_AVAIABLE, returning a 1 is given as:

$$\frac{\dfrac{(while\ (\underline{T})\ do\ (A), s_1) \xrightarrow{\underline{T}} (if\ (\underline{T}\ then\ (A;\ while\ (DS\,!{=}\,null)\ do\ \ (A))), s_2)}{(while(DS\,!{=}\,null)\ do\ A, s_1) \xrightarrow{\underline{T}} (1, s_2)}}{(Is\_input\_available(node\_number,\ vnum),\ s_1) \xrightarrow{node\_number,\ vnum} (1,\ s_2)} \; :: IS\_INPUT\_AVAILABLE$$

$$A \stackrel{def}{=\!=} \frac{\overline{(DS.node\_number{=}node\_number\ , s_1) \xrightarrow{\underline{T}} (\underline{T}, s_1\{DS.node\_number{=}node\_number\})} \quad \overline{(B, s_1) \xrightarrow{\underline{T}} (B, s_2)}}{(if\ (DS.node\_number = node\_number)\ then\ B,\ s_1) \xrightarrow{node\_number} (\underline{T}, s_1)}$$

$$B \stackrel{def}{=\!=} \frac{(while\ (\underline{T})\ do\ (C),\ s_1) \xrightarrow{\underline{T}} (if\ (\underline{T}\ then\ (C;\ while\ (inlist! = null)\ do\ \ (C))),\ s_1)}{(while(inlist! = null)\ do\, C, s_1) \xrightarrow{\underline{T}} (1,\ s_1)}$$

$$C \stackrel{def}{=\!=} \frac{\overline{(inlist.vnum{=}vnum\ , s_1) \xrightarrow{\underline{T}} (\underline{T}, s_1\{inlist.vnum{=}vnum\})} \quad \overline{(D, s_1) \xrightarrow{\underline{T}} (D, s_1)}}{(if\ (inlist.vnum = vnum)\ then\ D,\ s_1) \xrightarrow{vnum} (\underline{T}, s_1)}$$

$$D \stackrel{def}{=\!=} \frac{\overline{(inlist.flag{=}1\ , s_1) \xrightarrow{\underline{T}} (\underline{T}, s_1\{inlist.flag{=}1\})} \quad \overline{(availstatus{=}1, s_1) \xrightarrow{availstatus} (availstatus{=}1, s_2\{availstatus{=}1\})}}{(if\ (inlist.flag = 1)\ then\ availstatus = 1,\ s_1) \xrightarrow{vnum} (\underline{T}, s_2\{availstatus = 1\})}$$

In the above sequence, if the `inlist.flag` stores 0 then the function *Is_input_available* will return a 0. Similar transitions have been derived for the functions: *Is_ok_to_send* and *Send.*

IV. CONCLUSION

The research presented here involves the defining the operational semantics which can be used to refine the LIPS compiler. The defined semantics can also be used for the specification and verification of LIPS programs. This paper explains the operational semantics for only the communication part of LIPS. But, we have not only defined the operational semantics for the computational part of LIPS but also an abstract machine called LIPS Abstract Machine (LAM) for LIPS which works on the basis of single-step rewrite rules. This abstract machine has been verified for its correctness against the operational semantics [7].

[1] A. S. Bavan and E. Illingworth, *A Language for Implementing Parallel and distributed Systems using asynchronous point-to-point communication* (Nova Science Publishers, Inc., Commack, NY, USA, 2001), ISBN 1-59033-116-8.

[2] E. Albert, M. Hanus, F. Huch, J. Olvier, and G. Vidal, in *Proc. of the Int'l Workshop on Reduction Strategies in Rewriting and Programming (WRS 2002)* (Elsevier Science Publishers, 2002), vol. 70 of *Electronic Notes in Theoretical Computer Science.*

[3] D. Berry, R. Milner, and D. N. Turner, in *Annual Symposium on Principles of Programming Languages, Proceedings of the 19th ACM SIGPLAN-SIGACT* (1992), pp. 119–129.

[4] K. Mitchell, Tech. Rep., LFCS report ECS-LFCS-94-311 (1994).

[5] A. S. Bavan, A. V. S. Rajan, and G. Abeysinghe, in *Proceedings of IADIS International Conference Applied Computing 2007, Salamanca, Spain (18th–20th February 2007)* (IADIS, 2007), URL `http://www.pms.ifi.lmu.de/publikationen/#REWERSE-RP-2007-012`.

[6] A. V. S. Rajan, A. S. Bavan, and G. Abeysinghe, *Semantics for an Asynchronous Message Passing System* (Springer, 2007), vol. XVIII of *Advances and Innovations in Systems, Computing Sciences and Software Engineering*, ISBN 978-1-4020-6263-6.

[7] A. V. S. Rajan, A. S. Bavan, and G. Abeysinghe, *An equivalence theorem for the specification of asynchronous communication systems(SACS) and Asynchronous Message Passing Systems(AMPS)* (Springer, Due in 2010), Advanced Techniques in Computing Sciences and Software Engineering, ISBN 978-90-481-3659-9.

Separation of Concerns in Teaching Software Engineering

Izzat M. Alsmadi, and Mahmoud Dieri

Abstract – Software Engineering is one of the recently evolving subjects in research and education. Instructors and books that are talking about this field of study lack a common ground of what subjects should be covered in teaching introductory or advance courses in this area. In this paper, a proposed ontology for software engineering education is formulated. This ontology divides the software engineering projects and study into different perspectives: projects, products, people, process and tools. Further or deeper levels of abstractions of those fields can be described on levels that depend on the type or level of the course to teach.

The goal of this separation of concerns is to organize the software engineering project into smaller manageable parts that can be easy to understand and identify. It should reduce complexity and improve clarity. This concept is at the core of software engineering. The 4Ps concerns overlap and distinct. The research will try to point to the two sides. Concepts such as; ontology, abstraction, modeling and views or separation of concerns (which we are trying to do here) always include some sort of abstraction or focus. The goal is to draw a better image or understanding of the problem. In abstraction or modeling for example, when we model students in a university in a class, we list only relevant properties, meaning that there are many student properties that are ignored and not listed due to the fact that they are irrelevant to the domain. The weight, height, and color of the student are examples of such properties that will not be included in the class. In the same manner, the goal of the separation of the concerns in software engineering projects is to improve the understandability and consider only relevant properties. In another goal, we hope that the separation of concerns will help software engineering students better understand the large number of modeling and terminology concepts.

Keywords: Software engineering, ontology, separation of concerns, project, product, process and people.

1 Introduction

In teaching software engineering courses to students, it is noticed that some students complain from the lots of models that they need to know without having to know the overall picture first.

This is similar to the problem we have also in formal methods. There are tons of formal method tools and sectors to learn without having an overall ontology that illustrates the big picture.

Ontological studies simplify the structure of some domain knowledge. It includes abstraction, representations, and assumptions, but it is useful to make better understanding of that domain. Ontology or conceptual models facilitate communication or knowledge sharing on common grounds. In any ontology, we agree to "focus" on some objects or entities and specify the relation between those entities. Software engineering is lacking a comprehensive ontology that covers the overall knowledge body.

Izzat M Alsmadi is an assistant professor in the CIS department at Yarmouk university in Jordan. www.faculty.yu.edu.jo\izzat, Email: ialsmadi@yu.edu.jo

Students should be able to manage the different views and move easily between them. However, a major problem in Software Engineering education is to avoid transmitting a rigid methodology involving one dominant separation of concerns. There are some other alternative views for software engineering modules and separation of concerns. We can separate them into the dimensions; data; that focuses on entities, functional; which is concerned with functions or services, user view, reusing, and distribution dimensions. This separation is usually considered in software projects. For example in design, we talk about class diagrams, activity or sequence diagram and user interface design. This means that we are considering many dimensions of those considered in the earlier reference.

Out of the four views listed above, the software process and project views are the two that have the highest percent of documentation and models in literature. Nevertheless, they are tightly coupled that makes it hard to distinguish whether this is a process or project model. Part of this confusion is understood since the software project management can be seen as a software process or activity. However, we should differentiate between software processes that are product oriented such as requirements, design and coding of the product, and the processes that are people oriented such as the project management.

There are numerous software process models existed in the software engineering field. We will try to classify those models according to the aspects and properties that distinguish each view. The software process is the set of activities and methods employed in the production of a software. The software project is how we manage and

T. Sobh, K. Elleithy (eds.), *Innovations in Computing Sciences and Software Engineering*,
DOI 10.1007/978-90-481-9112-3_6, © Springer Science+Business Media B.V. 2010

organize the process, the people and the product. This view makes the software project the main view that includes the three other views. The software product is the ultimate goal for the project, process and product. We measure the software project success through the product success. A successful project, people and process should result in a successful product. The people are the real and main resources in software projects. Without talented and dedicated people, we can't have a successful project and product. This shows that the four views are highly depending on each other and that we have to guarantee each ones success to guarantee the overall success.

On the other side of the picture, there are many trials for integrating the different views in one large view. An overall picture draws a plan for where the project and organization should go. I think that the two paths do not contradict with each other. We decompose a project design to facilitate communication, tracking and planning of the project and its components. We eventually combine those sub components to test their integrity and cooperation.

In the following sections, we will consider the four dimensions; process, product, people and project. Each one will be considered in a chapter. The project dimension is intentionally left to the end as it combines the three and includes them.

2 Software Processes; Activities and Models

As mentioned earlier, out of the 4P dimensions, the process is the one that has most of the existed literature or documentation. Software processes are the activities involved in producing and evolving the software. Examples of some of those major activities include; requirements gathering and specifications, software architectural and design, software implementation, testing and maintenance or evolution. We have to differentiate between software processes and software process models. Software process models are abstract representations for the models and their interaction. Similar to abstractions, models involve focus on particular concerns or perspectives. As a result, each model has certain scenarios that can be best used in. For example, the water fall process model is used when we have fixed and stable requirements.

The difference between the different models is largely depending on how the processes interact with each other (that's why they are process models). There are two possibilities on how processes can interact with other.

A. Straight forward processes. In those models, each major software activity is completed first before moving to the next process. Once a process is completed, we can't go back and modify it. The largely known and used model in this type is the Waterfall model. Waterfall is used when we have stable and fixed requirements as it can hardly deal with changes or accommodations.

B. Iterative or evolutionary processes. In those models, major activities are completed partially in cycles and evolve to reach the final product. The goal is to deal with the instability of requirements and the need to accept and accommodate changes. With the exception of the waterfall model, all other software process models, such as the incremental model, spiral model, prototyping, and agile models, are examples of the Iterative models. Some models iterate through all process activities, others gather all requirements, then iterate through the rest of the activities. Spiral models make explicit risk assessments in every cycle, agile models combine iteration with project and people techniques to include a larger model that simply being a process model.

There are some software engineering books who consider some other software process models such as formal specification or Commercial Off-The shelf Software (COTS) as process models. The usage of formal specification or off-shelf software does not have to be in a special process models. Any of those methods can be used in the process models described earlier and hence do not need to be a process model by itself. It implies using certain technology or technique. For example, formal specification methods are used to verify requirements formally before start the construction process. This is a specific extra activity that is added to the requirement stage.

3 People, the software project resources

A software process model is an explicit description of the process through which software artifacts (or products) are implemented. Most of those process models focus on the products, time or goals as the factors that control the tasks for each stage of the model. In real environment the employees are the main resource and in each stage each employee, should have a specific task. Many of those current software process models do not consider some scenarios where a company may start a new project and each team or team member, whether from the business analysis's team, from the development, testers or from the document writers, is expected to do some work at any development stage.

Humans play an important role in the success of software projects. Communication is very important to ensure all team collaborations and contributions. Some methods, such as agile development models are customer oriented where the customer suggestions and concerns are always considered.

Software process models are abstract representations of software development activities. They guide and instrument the development process and indicate the main tasks and goals to be done in each stage or time of the software life cycle. In most of the traditional software development models, the focus is in achieving the goals or the requirements that the application is expected to fulfill. In agile methodologies, the time is more sensitive giving the fact that requirements and/or many other factors may change with a relatively short time.

Although those models target most of business scenarios in developing projects, in some cases we may have all company employees required to work simultaneously. Following for example a traditional approach in that case, requires developers to wait or take a vacation if they don't have other projects to work on till business analysis's team finish colleting the requirements. Testers and documents' writers are expected to wait longer time waiting for developers to design or implement the project or part of it.

In small business environment, this is expected to happen specially when there are no earlier versions of the application that those testers or document writers can work on through early stages. We have to have a model that take into consideration such scenarios and implement the stages depending on the humans and not the applications (i.e. people models rather than process models). Developers, testers, and document writers for example, have to have certain tasks to do from the beginning of the project (although the main focus at this stage will be on the requirement gathering people, or the business analysts).

Agile community defines agile methodologies as people oriented development processes. In general there are 4 critical groups that contribute to the software development; developers, testers, customers, and managers. For a project to be successful, all those groups should be fully involved and supportive all throughout the project. In traditional processes, the development stage is the main factor where we define the current stage (i.e. design for example), and then we assign time and resources for such stage.

In Agile development, achievements or deliverables are the key. We define time and resources that will achieve those tasks. A people oriented model is a model that considers the people or the resources first, and rather than defining a deliverable or a stage, we define the people or the role of those people and then we define deliverables and expected time for them.

In this context, there are three related words: concepts, individuals, and roles. Concepts, areas of knowledge, or subjects are general knowledge in life or life science (such as software engineering, programming, testing, physics, and religion) which have some common characteristics. Roles are classes of people (classified based on their professional) belong to those concepts or areas of knowledge (i.e. software engineer, programmer, and tester. Physician and religious people may have different meanings or more details). Concepts are classes while roles are the human subjects of those classes. Individuals are instances, actors, or players of the roles. For example, Brian is a software engineer who works in the software engineering field.

A role can be for an individual (served or played by individuals such as programmers), or for a group (served or played by a group such as stakeholders which is served by several classes of people: owners, managers, users, etc.). A good software project manager should have teams that are replaceable in their roles. This means that a manager should not depend on particular individuals to do certain tasks. All individuals in a role should be able to do all tasks assigned for that role (in theory).

4 TOOLS, THE PEOPLE HELPERS

Tools play a major role in software engineering processes and development. In several cost estimation models such as COCOMO, the amount of assistance tools gave to developers is important information needed to estimate the development time. They can noticeably improve the overall productivity of the team members.

Software engineering is a field rich of a large amount of tools exists to help software project team in the different development stages. Without such tools, tasks will be far more complicated, slower to achieve, and evaluate. Software tools that assist in the software engineering activities are usually called Computer Aided Software Engineering (CASE) tools. They are divided into upper and lower cases depending on the early or late developed stages they are assisting in. Those tools try to automate the specific process that if usually done manually will take more time and resources. For example a software test automation tool can save large amount of testing (especially regression testing). They can work day and night, in time or over time, in the week start or the week end. This can ultimately reduce the amount of time required to complete a specific task or the overall project. There are several classifications for case tools. They can be classified into upper and lower case tools depending on the development stage. Similarly, they can be classified into front end and back end tools. They can be also categorized into: tools, workbenches and environment to support a single task, stage of several tasks (e.g. the requirement or testing stage) or more than one stage of the development lifecycle.

The general goals for developing a CASE tool can be summarized in the following reasons:

- Decrease the time required to perform a specific task or the overall project. As described earlier, through automating an activity using a tool, time can be saved in regular working hours. Tools can also work continuously and in parallel. If developed with a high speed or good performance, it can finish tasks faster than humans. Usually, tools are more reliable or consistent especially for structured tasks that do not need reasoning.
- Perform some tasks that are considered uninteresting and time consuming for humans to do. This is true for example for regression testing where same tests need to be executed over and over again.
- Efficient transfer of information between tools. This is true if tools agree on the same data format. As such, it is important when acquiring a commercial or

open source CASE tool to look for the type of inputs or outputs this tool generates or requires.

• Decreasing the time required to develop a task or a project can contribute to reduce the overall cost of the software. This is true in all manufacturing areas where products produced using large manufacturing automated tools are usually cheaper than those crafted by hand.

Following are general classification of CASE tools according to the development stage or process.

1. Tools for software project management. Software management includes several activities such as project management, cost estimation, risk assessment and management, metrics, configuration management, scheduling and tasks distribution. There are different tools for those tasks. Some of the general management tools for software projects are? Microsoft project, ProjectTrack, SPR (Software Productivity Research), KickStart, Xpdproject, MinuteMan, PlanBee, ProjeX, Mission Manager, KIDASA software, Chronicle Graphics, DescisionEdge, Intellisys Project Desktop. Open Workbench, Sure Track, Milestones Professional, etc. Those tools help creating and modifying, and publish project schedule and tasks distribution to be available for all project team members. They should effectively allocate resources and financial planning. They can also locate critical items or paths in the project.

2. Tools for the requirement stage. The requirement stage includes several tasks such as the feasibility study, requirement elicitation, analysis, management and verification. In general, all tools in this stage in particular and in all development stages in general should facilitate and foster communication among project team members. Those tools should have a central database in the backend where a modification by one team member can be seen by all others. Database central control and management is also vital to ensure that changes for requirement are traced and allowed only through the right people (i.e. requirement traceability). Traceability is very important to make sure that we didn't skip any requirement, that the sources and relations among requirements are known and clear. The ability to work and integrate with other tools in design, implementation, etc is an important factor in selecting requirement management tools. Requirement tool can also address change management and control. A Requirement Verification Tool should be able to verify Completion and Correctness of Requirements so that broken links can be addressed. Requirement tools classify requirement into different types, levels or priorities depending on the user preferences. Requirement tools keep tracking of requirement modifications or history. This is important to know who edit a particular requirement, why and when? Requirement tools may also have some metrics capabilities regarding metrics, classifications, etc.

Besides features, requirement tools can be selected based on their learning curve or the ease of use and learning.

There are several products designed specifically for requirement management, such as IBM Rational Requisite Pro, Rational Rose, MS Visio, MS Office, RDD, DOORs, CORE, RTM Workshop and Caliber-RM, UML diagrams, Vital Link, Cradle REQ, RDT, etc.

There are also several Software Configuration Management (SCM) tools such as MS Visual Source Safe (VSS/ Source safe), Subversion, PVCS, ClearCase, Perforce, ClearCase, AcuuRev, PlasticSCM, SCCS, RVS, Aegis, CVS, etc. Those tools are also called version controls tool. Those software tools are responsible for tracking software code updates and modifications. For example, developers need to be all working on the exact same copy of code to make sure that there are no conflicts. Before a developer can update the server central code (i.e. check in code), he or she should have the up to date current copy of the code from the server (i.e. check out). This is particularly important for companies developing using agile or iterative methods where software code integration is continuous (continuous integration). In case of any conflict, developers should be able to see the locations of the conflict and should be able to resume to earlier versions of the code. Those software can be usually accessed from the web as they have web interfaces. They save the code from all developers to a code centric database or repository. Central code should also have a locking mechanism to control modifications. Other features include merging and branching of the code, tools or algorithms for version labeling, integration with other tools specially development and testing tools.

3. Tools for the design stage. Software design stage is a stage that relies heavily on graphics to visualize or model the artifacts. Examples of tools, notations, or applications include UML, IBM Rational Rose, MS Visio, Together, Describe, Rhapsody, Poseidon, Borland, Jdeveloper, Netweaver, DIA, Violet, Kennedy-Carter, XDE, Ensemble systems, MagicDraw, Popkin's System Architect , MasterCraft, UMLGraph, UMLet, JUDE, OmniGraffle, Argo/UML, Action Semantics, ARTiSAN software, BoldSoft, BridgePoint, GDPro, Ideogramic, Objecteering, Softera, . Several other graphics and editor or word processor tools such as MS Word, Power Point, Excel, etc. can be used in design as well. Those tools can be found under Modeling, design or UML tools. There are some other design details who are specific for database design or schema such as Erwin and ER studio. The link to UML and the ability to cover some or all UML diagrams such as use case, class, package, sequence, activity, collaboration, state, component, deployment, etc. diagram, is a major feature or requirement for design tools. Another important feature that is growing recently is the round trip engineering between design and requirement from one side and design and code from another side. Some tools can auto generate the code from the design.

4. Tools for the development stage. As mentioned earlier, the development (also called coding or implementation) stage is a major stage in the software development lifecycle where the design is translated into a working model.

Software code tools can be as simple as editors such as Notepad, to the Graphical User Interface Integrated Development Environment (IDE) tools with rich tools and components such as MS .NET, Java Eclipse, Java Netpeans, etc. The first category of the development tools are IDEs such as Eclipse and Netbeans for Java and Microsoft studio and .NET for MS programming languages such as C# and VB. Other example are: Adobe/Macromedia Studio 8, Borland Delphi, Borland JBuilder, IBM Rational App Developer, IBM WebSphere Studio, Oracle JDeveloper, Sun Java Studio, Sybase PowerBuilder, ActiveState Komodo, WinDev, Visual Web developer, phpDesigner, PHPEdit, Expression Web, PhpEd, Coda, CSSEdit, BlueFish, Dreamweaver CS4, Aptana Studio, Nvu, Spket IDE, BlueJ, XWP, RHide, KDevelop, C-Forge, IntlliJ Idea, Komodo IDE, Zend Studio, etc. IDE major features includes the following components: Compiler/Interpreter, Debugger, Editor, Make/Build Functions, Documentation, Application Modeling Tools, Web Design Tools, Profiler, Compiler Performance, Sample Applications, Performance of Resulting Applications, An easy to use interface, Ability to Integrate 3rd Party Tools, Availability of 3rd Party Tools, Quality of Technical Support Options, Size and Quality of Developer Community.

Other types of development tools include editors (e.g. Notepad, Emacs, jEdit, THE, MED), make tools (e.g. NMAKE, GNU Make), source and binary code generators, code interpreters, debugging tools, code libraries, installers and versioning tools. There are also automatic code generation tools that generate the initial parts of the code (that can be extracted from the design and requirements). Examples of those tools are: MathWorks Real Time Workshop, Rhapsody UML code generator, Flex, and Yacc, Rational Rose, Class diagrammer, and Artisan.

- Tools for the testing stage. Software testing may be performed in all stages to test and verify the different activities or artifacts. Compilers are testing tools done by the programming languages to verify that the written code is consistent with the programming language rules. Testing the developed code in particular is performed in 3 stages: testing individual units. This is usually done by developers. Examples of CASE tools here are unit testing tools such as JUnit and NUnit, and debugger tools which usually come as part of the IDE. Test automation is an important feature in this stage to reduce the amount required for testing. The second stage of testing is the black box or functional testing of the code to make sure it fulfills all its requirements. This is usually accomplished in integration and system testing. Test automation is also an important feature in this stage where we want to automatic the generation, execution and verification of the test cases. Examples of tools in this area include: IBM Rational Robot, XDE/Functional, Manual, and Performance testers, HP Mercury WinRunner, QuickTest, Segue SilkTest, Compuware TestPartner, AccordSQA SmarteScript. Other testing tools are: Abbot, AberroTest, AutoIt, AutoPilot, Axe, CAPBAK, Certify, CitraTest, CrashFinder, Eggplant for Mac OS X, EMOS Framework, eValid, Eventcorder suite, expecco, GUIdancer, imbus GUI Test Case Library, incisif.net, Jacareto, Jemmy, QARun, jfcUnit, JStudio SiteWalker, KD Executor, LISA Functional Testing, Marathon, MITS.GUI, Oracle Application Testing Suite, Perl GUITest, PesterCat, Phantom, Pounder, PureTest, pywinauto, Q1, QC/Replay, QF-Test, Ruby GuiTest, SAFS (Software Automation Framework Support), SilkTest, Smalltalk Test Mentor, Squish, Tasker, TestComplete, TestAgent, TestArchitect, TestBench for iSeries, Tester, TestGUI, TestQuest Pro Test Automation System, TestSmith, TRecorder, Unified TestPro (UTP), Vermont HighTest Plus, VistaTask Pro, Visual Test, VNCRobot, vTest , web2test , WebCorder, WebKing, X-Unity, xrc - X Remote Control, and XRunner.

The third stage of testing which is the acceptance or user testing. This stage can't be automated as it is usually hard and complex to teach tools or program to evaluate user interfaces in the same way humans do. The major sub tasks of the software testing process include: test case generation, execution, verification, regression testing, test oracle or database. A complete test automation tool (which may not be practical) should be able to automate all those activities. However, regression testing where earlier or all test cases are re-executed in case of codes change.

Although most debugging tools come as part of the IDE (i.e. VS .NET, Eclipse, Netbeans), however, there are some standalone debugging tools such as: DTrace, mdb, Sherlock, CodeView, gdb, JProbe, Wireshark, Jdb, Firebug lite.

5. Tools for the deployment stage. By deployment we mean the stage of preparing the software for packaging and shipment to the users and then test them on the user environment. This is why it is referred to in some literature or books as the implementation stage. Here largely we will talk about packaging, translating or installer tools. Examples of software installers are InstallShield, Microsoft MSI and Wise.

6. Tools for the evolution and maintenance stage. Evolution and maintenance activities occur after the first deployment of the application to the user. All activities after this step (even if its design, implementation or testing) should be called maintenance or evolution. Both activities including modifications in the original software or code. Evolution is more generic that includes changing the code for any reason (adding new features, updating or removing current features, responding to problems from the customer, etc). However, maintainability focuses on modifying the code to fix errors.

All tools listed in previous stages can be used in the maintenance and evolution phases as they include all activities. Other maintenance and evolution tools include: source code static analyzers or metrics such as: Compilers, Analyzers, Auditors, Complexity Measurers or Metrics, Cross Referencing Tools, Size Measurers, Structure Checkers and analyzers, Syntax and Semantics Analyzers, Test Preparation Tools, Data Extractors, Requirements-Based Test Case Generators, Test Data Generators, Test Planners, Test Execution Tools (Dynamic Analyzers), Reverse engineering tools (such as de-compilers, Rigi, SHriMP, Klocwork Insight, Imagix 4D, SPOOL, REGoLive, Columbus/CAN, Understand), Reengineering tools, Assertion Analyzers, Capture-Replay Tools, and many other types.

5 THE SOFTWARE PRODUCT, THE GOAL OF THE SOFTWARE PROJECT

The software product is the ultimate deliverable or goal of software projects. Having a successful process, people and project will not help us much if we are not having eventually a successful product. It makes sense to have a successful product if we have the right people and process. However, that may not always be true.

Software products can be the product or the goal such as MS Office, they can be a tool for a goal such as the programming languages. They can host other programs such as operating systems. They can also be embedded within hardware components. Software can be installed on a local drive, network drive, removable drive, or embedded on integrated circuits. It can be also used as a service through the network or the internet without local installation.

Software can be also generic such as MS Windows built for general market and not specific customers. It can also be specific built for a particular client, domain or market. It can Commercial Off The Shelf (COTS) bought and used as is. Software can also be free available to download through the internet. It can be shareware available for usage temporarily. Finally software can be open source available for download executable and source code so that users can customize and redistribute it for their own usage or to others without required license.

Other classification of software includes applications and systems software. Computer software consists of system software that control computer hardware and application software that typically helps users solves problems. System software consists of operating systems (e.g., Windows, Linux), device drivers, utilities, and programming languages. Application software consists of a variety of programs that help individuals carry out tasks effectively. Application software can be divided into different categories based on how it is used. These categories include word processing, spreadsheets, data management, entertainments, games, education, etc. Application software can also be classified into: productivity software, graphics and multimedia software, software for home, personal and educational uses, communication software, etc. System software is the combination of operating systems, utility programs and driver programs. Utility programs are system software that allow users to manage a computer. Examples are file viewer, file compression utility, diagnostic utility, disk scanner, uninstaller, file defragmenter, backup utility, screen saver, anti-virus software, etc. System software can be also divided into: system control, support and development software. System software can be also classified into: operating systems, DBMSs, network systems, developing tools and programming languages.

Software can be also classified according to the environment or the operating system that may work under such as Windows, Unix, Mac, etc. On the distance between the machine and the users, software can be classified into six categories: The first and closest category to the machine is the machine language that consists of binary values: zero and one. The next level is the operating system that manages the relation between applications and the hardware. The 4 next levels are respectively: High level programming languages, programming environment, programming tools (e.g. Excel, DBMS, etc), and finally applications. In this chapter we will describe product models based on earlier product classifications. One more classification of software divide software productions into 2 categories: commercial and academic software.

Based on the target of the software, the software can be classified into 3 categories: Software products for hardware components (e.g. embedded software, drivers, bios, etc), software products for other software (e.g. APIs, Dlls, interfaces, etc), and software for humans or end users.

Separation of concerns in the product section means that we should consider the type of the product we are developing in consideration when we are deciding the software process or project management. A software process that may work well for certain types of products may not for other types.

Software product models are less popular relative to software process models. In process models such as waterfall and iterative models, process activities are distributed over time and deliverables. Activities are the sub parts of the process and the two variables that may define or distinguish an activity from another is time, size, and deliverables or outputs. Drawing a similar comparison with the product, software products are composed of components, entities, classes, modules, etc. All those names refer to a product sub components (with different levels of abstraction). What can distinguish a component from others is its size, inputs, outputs and its level of abstraction. In software process models, the software product is the deliverable. Hence we want to make the activities as our deliverables in the software product models.

In literature, COTS product model is usually mixed with software process models which cause a serious clash between process and product models. There is no contradiction to say that we will follow the agile process model in developing COTS as those models belong to different concerns. In related subject, Component Based Software Engineering (CBSE) focuses on trying to build software products as manufacturing assembly lines where software components can be built to be easily reusable, replaceable and updatable. In reality, however, this may not be practically true as software products are not similar to manufacturing product lines such as cars, toys, etc where a company can deliver millions of exact same original model. In software, each business and domain may have certain characteristics to distinguish from business in the same domain. Perhaps software companies can learn from sales and marketing concepts of "mass customization". A concept adapted by Dell for example where they allow each customer to build their own "version" of their desktop or laptop.

In some literatures, product models refer to software activities (i.e. requirements, design, code, etc). Those are the software project deliverables or products. Examples of such models are: formalizing informal requirements for the requirement stage (http://csse.usc.edu/csse/research/requirement.html), and in Design: Alfa (http://sunset.usc.edu/~softarch/Alfa/index.html), DRADEL (http://sunset.usc.edu/~softarch/dradel2/index.html), Focus (http://sunset.usc.edu/~neno/Focus/index.html), Mae (http://sunset.usc.edu/~softarch/mae.html), Prism (http://sunset.usc.edu/~softarch/Prism).

However, the code itself is the final product or the product of all products and as such, it should be the focus of product models.

1. Waterfall software product model (Bottom up integration). A waterfall-like software product model is a model in which we start building software product modules bottom up where we don't leave a lower level of components until we complete it. We also don't start a higher level component until finish all lower level components. In this case we don't need to build any stubs (lower level virtual components needed for testing). As we learned earlier, waterfall structure is more stable and easier to manage. However, sometimes it is convenient when we are not sure how finally a certain component should look like and we need to eventually go back and evolve such component.

2. Top down product models. In these models, components integration start from the top (such as building the GUI shell first). All uncompleted lower components are replaced by stubs. The convenient part of this approach is that we can see the end of the project first and then we start filling up the empty pieces. This is very similar in concept to prototyping in software or engineering products. Users need to see the overall program and approve it before going further in the project. Users need to understand that this is just a prototype of shells and largely of no working features. Developers may need extra time developing number of stubs , that they will through away eventually, to make such early prototype suitable for demonstration. This approach is suitable for certain parts of the project such as the user interface and not for all project parts.

This approach is already used in software product integration. However, software process models do not include such top-down style of development where project team may go counter clock wise in the software activities. This will be very similar to reverse engineering processes where we start from a working product to end up of generating the design and requirements. Can we fake (i.e. stubs) some software activities such as requirements and design and start coding and find out eventually which design or requirements can fulfill this code ?! This model can be called code driven development where code guides the development process.

3. Agile software product models. In agile process models, all software activities (i.e. requirements, design, coding, testing) are visited in every cycle. Similarly, we want software product subcomponents to evolve through the iterations or cycles. All software modules or components should be visited in every cycle. Of course in agile models, earlier cycles will have large percent of the cycle dedicated to requirements. Eventually focus is shifted to design, then coding and testing. Similarly, some components will eventually go out of the cycles as they reach a stable stage. This flexibility allows us to have the chance to improve some components as times goes and more components are integrated or added to the system.

Based on the access level for the software, we can classify software into: private, commercial, COTS, Open Source, Free, and software as a service.

Private software products are those build and used (by large) locally in one company. In some large software companies such as Microsoft and IBM, there are large numbers of small proprietary applications that are built and used in house. On the other hand, most software companies build software products for commercial use to target specific or large domain of users or companies. Commercial software can be classified into several categories depending on the access right level. In some cases licenses are sold to individuals for temporary time or for good. In other cases, software can be sold for companies to be used by all individuals in this company within the premises of the company. Software can be also sold as a service to be used through the network or the internet without having a local copy of the software. Software can be sold on CDs or removable storages or it can be downloaded from the internet.

COTS: COTS are software product models based on building software products from ready components. The website (http://www.componentsource.com/index.html) include examples of different COTS for all types of applications.

Open source software products are low cost alternative for commercial or proprietary software. The low total cost of ownership is a major advantage for open source software. Other advantages include reducing the dependency on software vendors through having control over the source code. They can be relatively easier to customize in comparison to commercial software where they can't be customized locally due to the fact that the company does not have control on the source code. Security can be another advantage due to the local control of the source code. Open source software is not absolutely free as it requires maintenance and support expenses. In many surveys and literatures reviewed, independent factors of the open source outweigh the lower costs advantages. People love to have freedom on their business decisions away from environment or other companies' risks or pressure.

Also called Application Service Provider (ASP), Software as a Service (SaaS) is an alternative type of acquiring or selling software products. The vendor licenses the users or customers to use the software as a service on demand. Despite the fact that in this type of services, the vendor usually hosts the application through web servers, however, in some cases users can download the software on their local machines. Vendor has the control on the software and can switch the service on and off depending on their contract with their clients. This is very similar in principles to internet services where Internet Service Providers (ISPs) sell the internet services to the public.

6 THE SOFTWARE PROJECT; THE UMBRELLA THAT COVERS ALL VIEWS

Project is the container for the process, people and product models. Project management activities and decisions affect directly the people, process and the product. In software engineering, project models are usually mixed with process models. For example, agile process models do not take processes only into consideration. They can also be considered as product or project models as they consider those 2 elements in their activities.

In the software process model, the activities: requirements, design, coding, testing, etc are the major blocks that distinguish a model from another. For example, in the waterfall process model, all those activities are implemented in a straightforward fashion without forwarding until completing the current activity. However, in iterative models, activities are in a loop with time and in each cycle all those activities are visited. In the people models, we mentioned that the project members and roles (i.e. designers, managers, testers, developers, etc) are the major elements that distinguish a model from another. In product models components are the elements that distinguish a model from another. Here in the project models, project activities such as: tasks distributions, cost estimation, requirements managements, projects' planning, resources' allocation, deciding the software process model, risk assessment and management, etc. Projects may follow a waterfall project model having to complete all what can be completed from these activities earlier in the project. However, some activities such as cost estimation, risk assessment, resource allocation can be iterative and update over time.

Software project management activities can be divided based on the time line into 3 stages: The feasibility phase, the requirements phase, and the detailed or implementation phase. Software projects can be classified to: new, reengineering and maintenance projects. Other classification of software projects according to their complexity divided them into: simple or organic, semi detached or medium and embedded or complex. Software projects can be built totally in house, totally outsourced, or something in between. Project management activities will be different in those different scenarios. Software projects can be also divided into single projects (one time or one-off project) or a product line. Software projects can be also divided in size into small (typically less than 20,000 lines of code), medium (20,000 to 250,000 lines of code), and large projects (more than 250,000 lines of code). Projects can also be divided into deterministic where we largely know the amount of time and resources required or un-deterministic projects. This is necessary as known stable projects should be handled different than Research and Development (R &D) projects where the whole final outcome is unknown. Success factors or metrics in those two types of projects may not be the same. Projects could start deterministic and end up otherwise.

The main challenge of software project management is dealing with viewpoints of 4 major players: managers, stakeholders, developers and customers. Project management tasks should have a win-win solution for all those 4 groups. Problems that projects' managers may have is the lack of experience and knowledge in certain areas, the conflict of interests among all project stakeholders, lack or incorrect of estimation or team members' experience, deadline pressure, lack of information and documentation, and the challenge of facing project triple constraints; i.e. budget, time and resources.

Software projects main productivity attributes are: time, milestones and deliverables. Project managers assign milestones as dates for revision and evaluation. Those are usually marked as end of stages such as requirements, coding, testing, etc. Deliverables are product metric to measure how many requirements, tasks, goals, etc are completed in a certain cycle or period of time. Examples of some of the projects' milestones and deliverables are: Identifying major key project decision-maker, creating proposals and business case for the software, establishing preliminary effort and schedule targets, creating change control plan, etc.

Examples of software project models listed in software engineering literature: agile development methodologies. Rapid Application Development (RAD), Joint Application Development (JAD), Capability Maturity Models (CMM), Rational Unified Process (RUP), etc.

Software project management have certain characteristics that distinguish it from other projects' management. First, people are the main and most critical resource in software projects. As such, it is usually hard to assess people abilities in the way we can do it for machines or equipments. Humans can call for sick or have personal problems which may limit their productivities. Software projects are always unique and it is very hard to copy a successful story from one project to another in the exact same approach. What works good in some case, may not work as well in another. Software project managers need to be creative in dealing with such changing and volatile environment. Communication skills are a must for software project managers. They need to be able to deal with different opinions and interest and reach to an optimal solution that can be accepted by all different project partners. They need also to be able to handle conflicts and problems among team members. Without proper coordination between all team members projects can reach a dead lock. This is true for many software projects where personal conflicts lead to projects' failures. Errors and mistakes are normal for humans. Managers need to review and test tasks frequently to minimize the amount of errors or mistakes. A complete exhausting testing is not a choice. We test to improve the confidence in the product and reduce, not eliminate the amount of errors. Managers need to be flexible to change a wrong route, need to be open to team members to listen and accept different opinions. They also need to continuously assess and monitor risks.

Increasing the number of team members can make work faster. However, it may cause higher communication overheads and complexity. For large groups managers may need to divide project team into several teams with a team leader for each group. This may make communication easier and faster. Project managers must monitor costs, efficiency and quality without being excessively ceremonial.

There are several attributes that distinguish a software project from others. Many management decisions require thorough knowledge of those attributes. Examples of those attributes are: Cost, duration, effort, budget, resources, size, etc.

1. Cost, budget, and benefits. Those terms are related to expenses. Cost calculated the total cost of the project. There are several techniques used for cost estimations. Examples of those techniques are : calculating cost through models such as the COCOMO, calculating cost through analogy, and calculating cost through experts. Cost estimation is not expected to be precise as it is just estimation. However, far unrealistic estimation may put software projects in serious risks. Project managers need also to know how much budget is allocated or available to the project in order to make early decisions whether this project is feasible or not. Overall, money is a critical factor in the success or the failure of software projects. Project managers need to be transparent and open with all stakeholders in concern with budget, cost and benefits.

2. Time and duration. Time and duration attributes make estimates for required time of all project or individual tasks. Cost estimation techniques usually give cost, time and resource estimations. Besides cost estimation techniques, project managers need to understand also project team members' abilities to be able to distribute tasks realistically. In iterative development, projects' velocity is calculated from early cycles to adjust all tasks allocations and duration.

3. Resources. Project resources include humans, software, hardware, and network requirements. There are some challenges facing resources' allocation. Software managers need to find the right people for the right tasks. This means that we may have 4 alternatives:

a. Right people for the right tasks. This is the perfect situation (if it can exist). This requires managers to be able to know where each person can best fit in the project. In software projects, managers have two choices: Either they can select the team that they will work with or the company allocates certain employee from the company to this particular project. In the first scenario, the project manager has the choice of selecting the "right" people. However, it will be challenging and needs deep knowledge of all company employee and their skills. It also requires knowledge of the project to be able to know who can best fit in a specific task. Project managers need to study project tasks, skills and level of experience needed each task (if possible).

You may have more than one person fits for a specific task and you may not have any person who can fit in another task. Finally, managers need to best allocate or optimize their resources, of humans and money. This may include training some team members or outsourcing some tasks. You may also need to hire new employees, contract them, or buy some of the COTS components.

However, in some choices, project managers may not have the freedom to choose their project team members. The project will be assigned to selected company employees (for a specific amount of time). In some cases, the only full time employee in this project is the project manager. All other team members could be working on some other tasks at the same time. In those cases, the project manager needs to best allocate available team members to the tasks he or she has. An example of this situation is to typically assign a senior good developer a development task.

Employees' interests may not always match their experience. Should project managers assign people based on what they know or what they like to know? Typically, he or she should assign them tasks according to what they best know. However, a negotiation or a win-win solution may be needed in some scenarios.

b. Right people for the wrong tasks. Companies are not always very successful in selecting the right people for the right tasks. In some cases, highly qualified people are working in several projects. In some other cases, risk is very high that those members may find a better opportunity and leave the company. Putting the right people in the wrong tasks may courage them to leave the project and the company. However, companies may do this due to different reasons. This could be the worst situation of the 4 as we not only lost a qualified team member to perform tasks that they excel in, but we also had them perform tasks that they are not good at. This is a loose-loose solution for this person and for the company. A typical example of this situation is to assign a senior expert software developer routine tasks such as document writing or test case execution.

c. Wrong people for the right tasks. Politics may play roles in projects' decision making and some people may be assigned a higher tasks to give them new chances or opportunities. Those people may proof that they are up to these challenging tasks or they could fail miserably. If risks are highly already, managers need to do their best to avoid such situations. A typical example of this scenario is to assign a new fresh CS graduate student as an architect or a team leader of the software project.

d. Wrong people for the wrong tasks. It may not make a difference if we have wrong people whether they will be assigned the right or wrong tasks. Tasks are not "wrong" by themselves. They become wrong if they are assigned to the wrong people. However, the different here is that tasks can be wrong in their estimated time or cost for example assuming that this task is going to be finished in a day or two while it may take much more time.

7 Conclusion

This paper suggests a methodology to teach software engineering on the basis of the different perspectives or views. Such views are expected to develop and overall conceptual understanding that seems to be missing for many students who learn software engineering basics. We described those different views in brief to proof the concept. As this is a suggestion for a book or a course, later on, it will include more details and elaborations. We will introduce all software engineering terms, and concepts in terms of this view.

Ontology definitions are expected to improve the overall understanding for any beginners in any knowledge or science. We hope this can be incorporated into the software engineering tools to be always part of the software development process.

8 References

[1] Ian Sommerville. *Software Engineering* (Seventh Edition). Addison-Wesley, 2004

[2] Roger S. Pressman. *Software Engineering: A Practioner's Approach* (Sixth Edition, International Edition). McGraw-Hill, 2005.

[3] Habra, Naji. Separation of concerns in software engineering education. ICSE 2001.

[4] Jessica Keyes. *Software Engineering Handbook.* Auerbach Publications (CRC Press), 2003.

[5] Hans van Vliet. *Software Engineering: Principles and Practice* (Second Edition). Wiley, 1999.

[6] Timothy C. Lethbridge & Robert Laganière. *Object-Oriented Software Engineering: Practical Software Development using UML and Java* (Second Edition). McGraw-Hill, 2005.

[7] Andrew Hunt, David Thomas. *The Pragmatic Programmer: From Journeyman to Master*. Addison-Wesley Pub Co, 1999.

[8] Barry Boehm. *Software Engineering Economics*. Prentice Hall, 1982.

[9] J. Fairclough (Ed.). *Software Engineering Guides*. Prentice Hall, 1996.

[10] C. Mazza. *Software Engineering Standard.* Prentice Hall, January 1995.

[11] Alan M. Davis. *201 Principles of Software Development.* McGraw-Hill, 1995.

[12] I. Jacobson, G. Booch, and J. Rumbaugh, The Unified Software Development Process, Addison-Wesley, Reading, MA, 1998.

[13] J. Scott Hawker. Integrating Process, Product, and People Models to Improve Software Engineering Capability. < http://cs.ua.edu/research/TechnicalReports/TR-2002-05.pdf>. 2002.2008.

[14] C. Wille, A. Abran, J-M Desharnais, R. Dumke, The Quality concepts and sub concepts in SWEBOK: An ontology challenge, in International Workshop on Software Measurement (IWSM) , Montreal , 2003 , pp. 18,

[15] C. Wille, R. Dumke, A. Abran, J-M, Desharnais, E-learning Infrastructure for Software Engineering Education: Steps in Ontology Modeling for SWEBOK, in Ontology Modeling for SWEBOK , in Software Measurement European Forum , Rome, Italy , 2004

[16] Software Engineering Research Laboratory. Institute of Electrical and Electronics Engineers, Inc. <www.swebok.org>. 2008.

[17] Framework and Tool for Modelling and Assessing Software Development Processes. J. G. Doheny and I. M. Filby AIAI-TR-204. August 1996.

[18] Ed Yourdons software journal, Vol 3 No. 7-8.

Authors' information

[1] **Izzat Alsmadi.** Dr Izzat Alsmadi is a Jordanian native born in 1972. He earned B.sc in telecommunication engineering from Mutah University in Jordan, MS in CIS from University of Phoenix, USA, Master in Software engineering from NDSU, USA, and PhD in Software engineering from NDSU, USA.

Dr Alsmadi research interests include: software engineering, testing, test automation, and software metrics.

Dr Alsmadi is an assistant professor teaching currently in the CIS department at Yarmouk University, Irbid, Jordan

Student Model Based On Flexible Fuzzy Inference

Dawod Kseibat, Ali Mansour, Osei Adjei, Paul Phillips
Dawod.kseibat@beds.ac.uk, Ali.Mansour@beds.ac.uk, Osei.Adjei@beds.ac.uk, Paul.Phillips@beds.ac.uk
Department of Computer Science and Technology
University of Bedfordshire, UK

Abstract-In this paper we present a design of a student model based on generic fuzzy inference design. The membership functions and the rules of the fuzzy inference can be fine-tuned by the teacher during the learning process (run time) to suit the pedagogical needs, creating a more flexible environment. The design is used to represent the learner's performance. In order to test the human computer interaction of the system, a prototype of the system was developed with limited teaching materials. The interaction with the first prototype of the system demonstrated the effectiveness of the decision making using fuzzy inference.

I. INTRODUCTION

An intelligent tutoring system (ITS) can be defined as educational software containing some artificial intelligence components. An ITS should be capable of emulating a teacher's behaviour in all aspects relating to supporting learners as they acquire knowledge [1]. While existing ITSs vary in their structures, they typically consist of at least three basic components or subsystems. Hartley and Sleeman [2] described the requirements of ITS for the first time in 1973. ITSs rely on: 1) the Domain model, or Domain knowledge, that contains the expertise of the human teacher in certain knowledge domain, 2) the Learner model that contains the student knowledge and behaviour, and 3) the Pedagogical model that controls the learning process and provides teaching and learning aims, curriculum content and the approach to delivery [3][4]. The interactions between the learners and ITS provided via user interface. Fig 1 provides presentation of the subsystems of ITS.

Fuzzy logic has been used in diverse ITSs because it makes decisions in a similar way to the human teacher. Without complex formulae it utilises a set of rules similar to those a teacher would apply in judging a student's performance or activities. Moreover, Fuzzy logic provides flexibility when used to implement mathematical formalisations based on natural language or working with imprecise information [5].

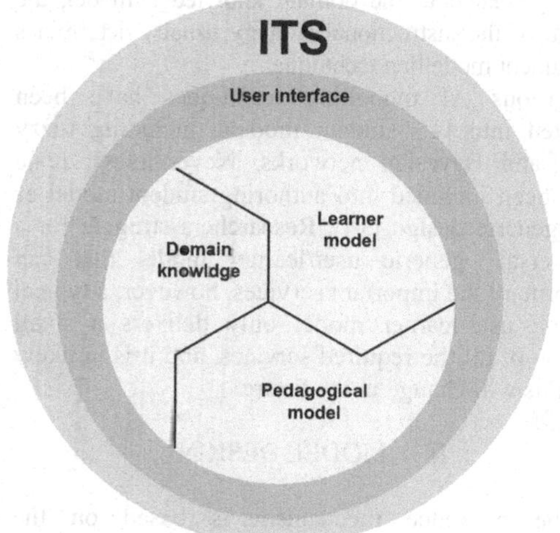

Fig. 1. Subsystems of ITS

Nedic [6] designed a fuzzy rule-based decision making system aimed at adaptively adjusting the teaching of a first year engineering course on electrical circuit theory, based on students' performance. Each student's performance was based on the membership functions for a particular topic, difficulty and importance levels. A "virtual student" model which simulated human learning behaviour was developed by Negoita and Pritchard [7] based on fuzzy logic technologies. Stathacopoulou *et al.* [8] proposed a neuro-fuzzy model to encode teachers' knowledge. This was applied to diagnose students' learning characteristics. The experimental results from testing the model in a learning environment were encouraging, showing good capability of handling uncertainty as confirmed by the advice of five experienced teachers. Chen *et al.* [9] presented a learning performance assessment scheme by combining a neuro-fuzzy classifier and a fuzzy inference. The inferred learning performance results can be used as a reference for teachers, and provide feedback for learners. Fuzzy logic was used as it handles uncertainty and provides a mode of qualitative reasoning closer to human decision making [9][10][11].

T. Sobh, K. Elleithy (eds.), *Innovations in Computing Sciences and Software Engineering*,
DOI 10.1007/978-90-481-9112-3_7, © Springer Science+Business Media B.V. 2010

The Learner model represents the system beliefs about a student's knowledge and skills, and guides pedagogical decision-making. The model is updated regularly by data collected from several sources implicitly by observing student activities or explicitly by requesting information directly from the student [12]. Adaptive tutoring systems can modify the learning process to best fit student's needs, characteristics and preferences by discovering the strengths and weaknesses of each student. The effectiveness of adaptive tutoring system depends on how accurate the Learner model is [13]. Although the learner model is directly related to the domain knowledge model, the design of the instructional strategy usually determines the student modelling technique.

Various AI modelling techniques have been adapted into ITS student models, including fuzzy logic and Bayesian networks. Nevertheless, none have been included into authoring student model or in a generic design [14]. Researchers struggle for a "universal" generic user/learner model that can perform all the important services, however, a typical generic user/learner model only delivers a small portion of all the required services, and it is unlikely that this will change in the future.

II MODEL DESIGN

The inference mechanism is based on the Mamdani fuzzy inference method since this is the most commonly used. Two fuzzy functions types were used: the triangular and the trapezoidal membership functions. This is because it is preferable to use these functions to handle fuzzy Linguistic terms and variables, and these functions have the advantage of simplicity which makes them easy to be modified by the teachers or non-experts. Additionally, these functions have been used successfully in many different ITSs applications [6][9][10]. A flexible fuzzy membership function $f_i(x)$ was developed in this research where $f_i(x): f_i(x) \rightarrow [0,1]$ is represented by four points P1, P2, P3, and P4. P1 and P2 represent the starting and the ending point of the increasing section (IS) of the function $f_i(x)$ respectively. P3 and P4 represent the starting and the ending point of the decreasing section (DS) of the function $f_i(x)$ respectively (see Figs 2 and 3). The equal section (ES) of the function are represented by the set {P1,P2} or {P3,P4} depends weather it is a right shoulder or left shoulder function as presented in Figs 2 and 3. The increasing section, the decreasing section, and the equal section (ES) of the function $f(x)$ are represented mathematically by equation 1 where H is the membership value for the equal section. The values of the points: P1, P2, P3, P4, and H can be modified at the learning process (run time) and replaced with new values: N1, N2, N3, N4 and H1 as represented in Figs 2 and 3.

If-then rule constructs are used to formulate the conditional statements that comprise the fuzzy inference. The structure of these rules takes the following general form:

Rule I: IF first Fuzzy input$_f$ AND second Fuzzy input$_j$ THEN Fuzzy output$_k$

$$f(x) = \begin{cases} \dfrac{x - P1}{P2 - P1} & \text{for IS} \\ \dfrac{P4 - x}{P4 - P3} & \text{for DS} \\ H & \text{for ES} \end{cases} \qquad (1)$$

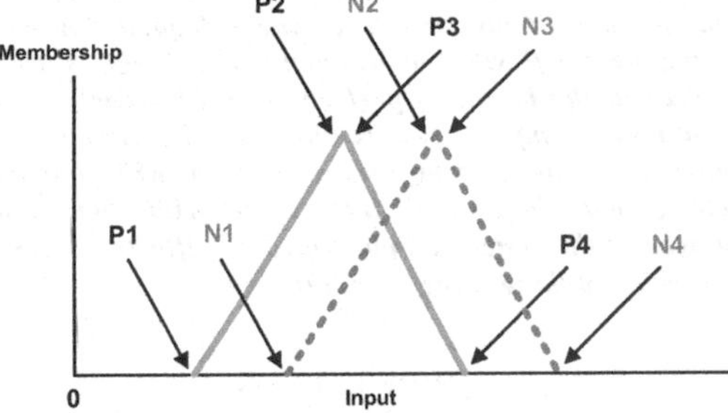

Fig. 2. The triangular fuzzy membership function

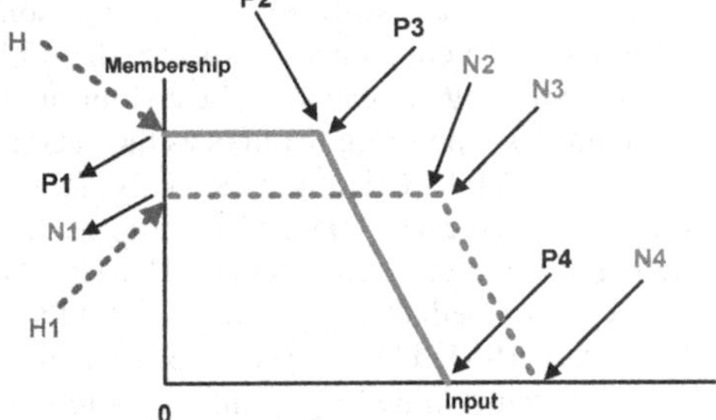

Fig. 3.a. The trapezoidal fuzzy membership function (left shoulder)

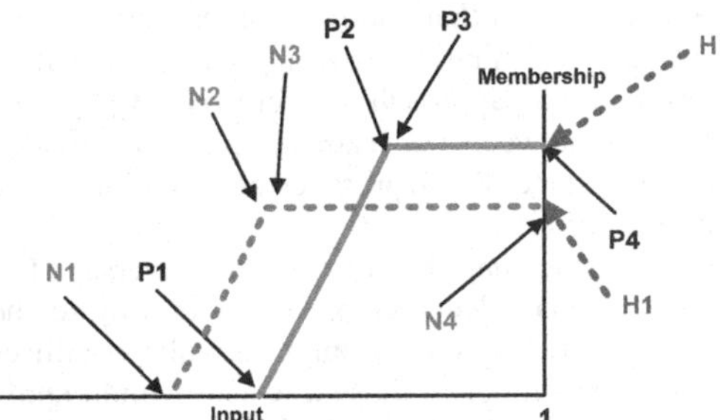

Fig. 3.b. The trapezoidal fuzzy membership function (right shoulder)

The input to each rule is the current values for the input variables, and the output is the entire fuzzy set assigning one value to the output variable (O_k). The set O where O_k (*k*=1, 2, 3, 4) is a linguistic term (word) that describes the kth response that represents the learner's observable behaviour. As a result of two fuzzy variables, each of them having four classes, 16 different rules and its conditions are formulated. The design of these rules is based on a flexible design so as to allow for the modification of these rules during the learning process by the teacher. The information on these rules are coded and saved in the file 'FuzzyRules' while the information of the fuzzy membership functions are coded and saved in the file 'FuzzyInfo'. This information can be accessed and modified by the teacher through the teacher's interface as presented in Figs 8 and 9. The structure of the files FuzzyInfo and FuzzyRules is represented by Tables I and II respectively.

TABLE I
THE STRUCTURE PF FUZZYINFO FILE

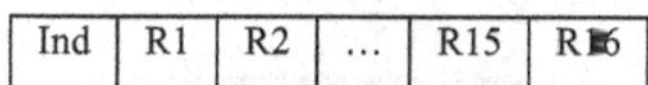

Ind	R1	R2	…	R15	R16

TABLE II
THE STRUCTURE OF FUZZYRULEFILE

Ind	Title	Type	P1	P2	P3	P4

Where **Ind** is the index of the file, **Title** is the title (name) of each membership function (input or output), **Type** is the type of each function (e.g. triangular or trapezoidal), and **R*i*** is the output of the *i*th rule. The initial values for the file 'FuzzyRules' and 'FuzzyInfo' are represented in Table III and Table IV respectively.

III FUZZY INFERENCE

The fuzzy inference design was used to represent the learner's performance (see Fig 4). The system uses four sets of stereotypes (classes) to represents the learner's performance (Pr) since it is an important factors in indicating the online learner's attitudes toward the learning process [15][16]. The system collects information from the learner activities during the learning process and tests it against the membership functions of each measurement.

In order to design the membership functions for input/output, sub ranges of the continuous (numeric) input/output variables (IOVs) were defined since IOVs$\in$[0,1]. The measurement for all IOVs has four separate membership functions defining different ranges. Therefore, any IOV has four "truth values" — one for each of the four functions (see Fig 5, 6 and 7).

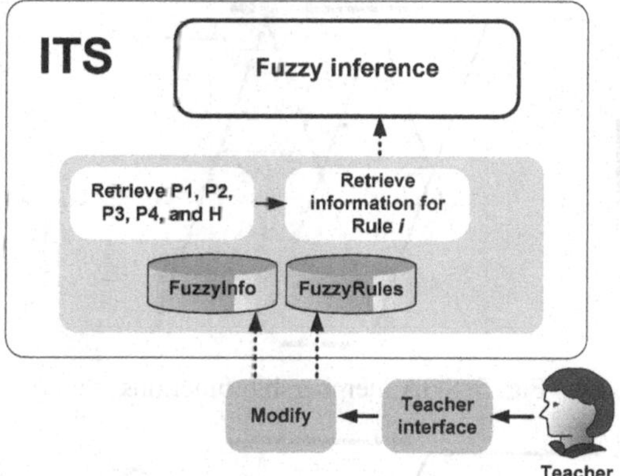

Fig. 4. Fuzzy flexible design

IV MEMBERSHIP FUNCTIONS

The learner's Performance is defined as the learner's involvement in his/her developmental courses, which results in an improvement of the presented course and a positive change in his/her attitude towards learning [15][16]. Average grades of both exams and questions taken by the learner during the learning process were used as inputs to the fuzzy inference to calculate the Performance since questions and exams are well proven measurements of a learner's knowledge, skills and performance in a certain topic. The first input is the learner's exam average grade (SGA). SGA represents the average grade value of all exams taken by the learner plus the placement test result (SPG). SGA can be calculated by equation 2.

$$SGA = \frac{\left(\sum_{i=1}^{3} \text{Exam Grade}_i\right)}{Xn} + SPG \quad (2)$$

$$SQAG = \frac{\left(\sum_{i=1}^{3}\sum_{j=1}^{n} \text{Question Grade}_i^j\right)}{Qn} \quad (3)$$

Where *Xn* is the number of exams taken by the learner and *i* is the learning level. The second input is the learner's question average grade (SQAG). SQAG represents the average grade of all the questions answered by the learner in all the learning levels and all the learning level classes. SQAG can be calculated by equation 3 where *Qn* is the number of questions taken by the learner, *i* is the learning level and *j* is the number of questions taken by the learner in each learning level class. The inputs and the output membership functions are represented by the following graphs.

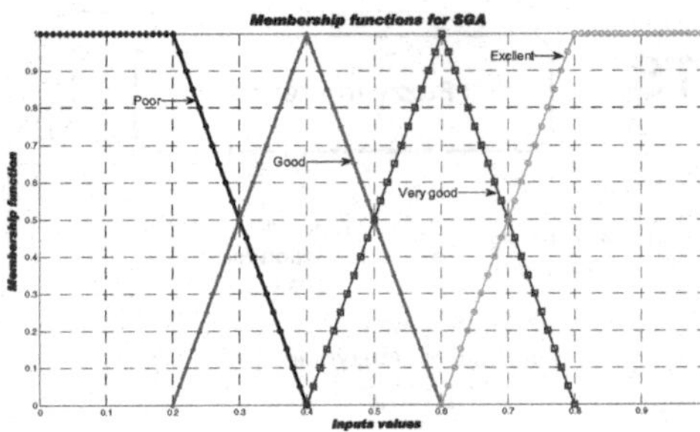

Fig. 5. SGA membership functions

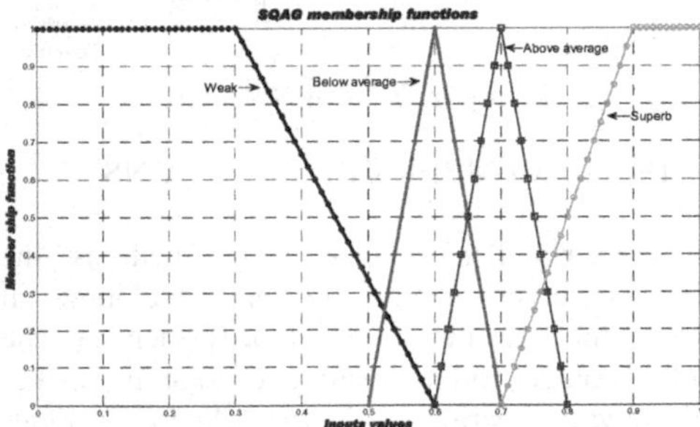

Fig. 6. SQAG membership functions

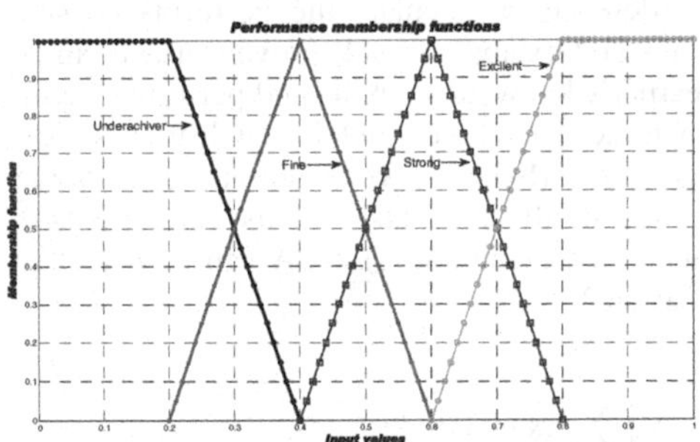

Fig. 7. Performance membership functions

TABLE III
INITIAL VALUES FOR FUZZYINFO FILE

Ind	Title	Type	P1	P2	P3	P4
1	Poor	0	0	0.2	0.2	0.4
2	Good	1	0.2	0.4	0.4	0.6
3	Very good	1	0.4	0.6	0.6	0.8
4	Excellent	0	0.6	0.8	0.8	1
5	Weak	0	0	0.3	0.3	0.6
6	Below average	1	0.5	0.6	0.6	0.7
7	Above average	1	0.6	0.7	0.7	0.8
8	Superb	0	0.7	0.9	0.9	1
9	Underachiever	0	0	0.2	0.2	0.4
10	Fine	1	0.2	0.4	0.4	0.6
11	Strong	1	0.4	0.6	0.6	0.8
12	Excellent	0	0.6	0.8	0.8	1

TABLE IV
INITIAL VALUES OF FUZZYRULES FILE

Ind	R1	R2	R3	R4	R5	R6	R7	R8
1	0	1	1	2	3	2	3	3
	R9	R10	R11	R12	R13	R14	R15	R16
	2	0	0	0	0	0	0	0

V IMPLEMENTATION

The proposed system is developed using PHP and MySql. A graphic interface is used to create effective system-user interface. Using this interface, a user can control subsystems and review the results. The fuzzy membership functions and their rules can be modified by the teacher via the teacher's interface (Figs 8 and 9).

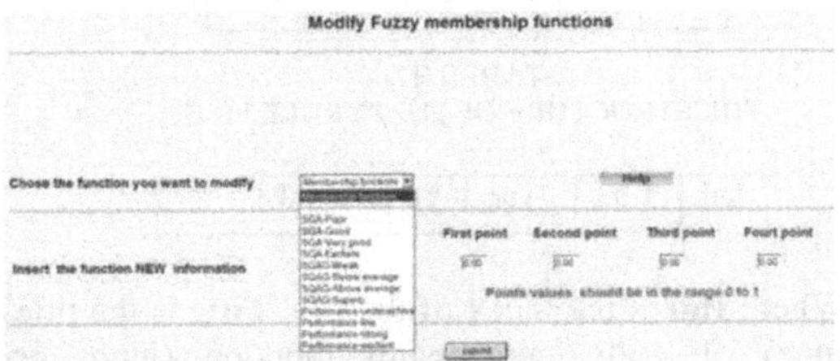

Fig. 8. Teacher interface for modifying membership functions

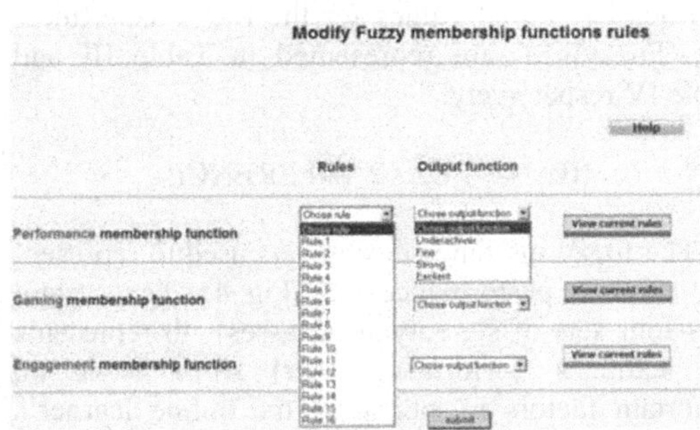

Fig. 9. Teacher interface for modifying inference fuzzy rules

VI ADVANTAGES OF FLEXIBLE FUZZY INFERENCE

The design of the flexible fuzzy inference offers many advantages that can be described as follows:

- The design of the fuzzy system provides a way to capture the student's characteristics with fuzzy descriptions. It introduced a system of fuzzy linguistic constructors, to model the structure of fuzzy linguistic expressions in rule and query.
- An ability to tune the parameters of the Fuzzy Inference (fuzzy rules and membership functions), i.e. produce a system with improved performance.

- The possibility for teachers to customise the inference mechanism during the learning process.
- The elimination of the need for the teacher to use a programming language to customise the system.

VII SYSTEM EVALUATION

The first prototype of the system was developed and populated with limited teaching materials. In order to test the human computer interaction of the system a log file that captures the student actions, and the system output, was produced for each student. Sample results from two log files of two students' learning sessions are presented in Table V. By comparing the two log files we can see that the system was adapting to the student activities during the learning process, and this prevented the system from giving the same teaching materials repeatedly. The interaction with the first prototype of the system showed the effectiveness of the decision making using fuzzy inference and demonstrated that the system is adapting to the students needs during the learning process.

TABLE V SAMPLE RESULTS FROM TWO LOG FILES

	First student	Second student
1	Log file opened in : 12-04-2008 User : DAWOD System : your placement test results is 100% System : your stereotype is >>>> Performance = underachiever -	Log file opened in : 12-04-2008 User : Ahmed System : your placement test results is 0% System : your stereotype is >>>> Performance = underachiever
2	System : your stereotype is >>>> Performance = strong	System : your stereotype is >>>> Performance = underachiever
3	System : LOADING LESSON ... Lesson : 2 ---------------------------- SORRY, No EXTRA TUTORING set up for you by the instructional strategy	System : LOADING EXTRA TUTORING MATERIALS ... FOR LESSON : 2

VIII CONCLUSION

In this work the design of an Intelligent Tutoring System for teaching Modern Standard Arabic language was introduced. Based on learner's performance a fuzzy inference was designed to handle the uncertainty and the inference mechanism in the system during the learning process since it imitates "human" reasoning style.

The design of the membership functions and their rules were based on flexible designs which allow the adjustment of these functions by the teacher during the learning process. The interaction with the first prototype of the system showed the effectiveness of the decision making using fuzzy inference. The design of the learner's performance can be extended to measure different learner characteristics.

REFERENCES

[1] Hatzilygeroudis, I., Prentzas, J., (2004), "Using a hybrid rule-based approach in developing an intelligent tutoring system with knowledge acquisition and update capabilities", Expert Systems with Applications, Vol. 26, pp. 477–492.

[2] Hartley, J., Sleeman, D., (1973), "Toward more intelligent teaching systems", International Journal of Man-Machine studies, pp. 215-236.

[3] Karlstrom, P., Pargman, T., Ramberg, R., (2005), "Designing for Collaboration in Intelligent Computer Assisted Language Learning", 5th IEEE International Conference on Advanced Learning Technologies (ICALT'05), pp. 321-322.

[4] Kseibat, D., Mansour, A., Adjei, O., Onley, P., (2007), "A Prototype for the Design of Intelligent Tutoring Systems for Teaching Modern Standard Arabic Language", IASK, E-Activity and Leading Technologies, 2-6 DEC, Porto, Portugal.

[5] Sanchez–Torrubia, M., Torres–Blanc, C., Krishnankutty, S., (2008), "Mamdani's Fuzzy Inference eMathTeacher: A Tutorial for Active Learning", WSEAS transactions on computers, Vol. 7.

[6] Nedic, Z., Nedic, V., Machotka, J., (2002), "Intelligent Tutoring System for teaching 1st year engineering", World Transactions on Engineering and Technology Education, Vol. 1, No.2.

[7] Negoita, M., Pritchard, D., (2004), "Using a virtual student model for testing intelligent tutoring systems", Interactive Technology and Smart Education, Vol. 1, 195–203, Troubador Publishing Ltd.

[8] Stathacopoulou, R., Magoulas, G., Grigoriadou, M., Samarakou, M., (2005), "Neuro-fuzzy knowledge processing in intelligent learning environments for improved student diagnosis", Information Sciences, pp. 273-307.

[9] Chen, C., Hong, C., Chen, S., Liu, C., (2006), "Mining Formative Evaluation Rules Using Web-based Learning Portfolios for Web-based Learning Systems", Educational Technology & Society, Vol. 9, No. 3, pp. 69-87.

[10] Nykanen, O., (2006), "Inducing Fuzzy Models for Student Classification", Educational Technology and Society, Vol. 9, No. 2, pp. 223-234.

[11] Stathacopoulou, R., Grigoriadou, M., Samarakou, M., Mitropoulos, D., (2007), "Monitoring students' actions and using teachers' expertise in implementing and evaluating the neural network-based fuzzy diagnostic model", Expert Syst. Appl. Vol. 32, No. 4.

[12] Esposito, F., Licchelli, O., Semeraro, G., (2004), "Discovering Student Models in e-learning Systems", Journal of Universal Computer Science, vol. 10, no. 1, p. 47-57.

[13] Carmona, C., Castillo, G., Millan, E., (2007), "Discovering Student Preferences in E-Learning", Proceedings of the International Workshop on Applying Data Mining in e-Learning, ADML-07, pp. 33-43.

[14] Murray, T., Ainsworth, S., and Blessing, S., (2003), "Authoring Tools for Adv. Tech. Learning Env", Kluwer Academic Publishers. pp. 493–546.

[15] Anderson, T., (2008), "The theory and practice of learning", Second Edition, AU press, Canada.

[16] Luppicini, R., (2007), "Learning Communities in Online Education", Information Age Publishing.

PlanGraph: An Agent-Based Computational Model for Handling Vagueness in Human-GIS Communication of Spatial Concepts

Hongmei Wang
Department of Computer Science
Northern Kentucky University
Highland Heights, KY, U. S. A.
wangh1@nku.edu

***Abstract*—A fundamental challenge in developing a usable conversational interface for Geographic Information Systems (GIS) is effective communication of spatial concepts in natural language, which are commonly vague in meaning. This paper presents a design of an agent-based computational model, *PlanGraph*. This model is able to help the GIS to keep track of the dynamic human-GIS communication context and enable the GIS to understand the meaning of a vague spatial concept under constrains of the dynamic context.**

I. INTRODUCTION

A Geographic Information System (GIS) is a computer-based information system for capturing, storing, querying, analyzing and displaying geospatial data (geographically referenced data) [1]. One stream of attempts to improve the usability of GIS and enable wider adoption of GIS is to develop natural communication modalities (e. g. speech, gesture, gaze, etc.) based interfaces for GIS [2-6]. Most existing natural interface-based GIS are conversational (speech enabled). A fundamental challenge in developing a usable conversational interface for GIS is how to handle the vagueness problem in human-GIS communication through natural language. The meaning of a spatial concept communicated through natural language can be context-dependent and fuzzy [7]. For example, the spatial concept *near* represents the spatial distance relationship between spatial entities. The meaning of *near* is different in different contexts, and does not have a clear boundary in a given context. Existing studies (see summary in [7]) have addressed the fuzziness aspect of the vagueness problem to a great extent, but little work [7-9] has been done to handle the context-dependency sub-problem.

The goal of this study is to facilitate handling the vagueness problem in human-GIS communication of spatial concepts through natural language, in particular, the context-dependency sub-problem. In human-human natural language communication, human communicators usually can successfully handle the vagueness problem through making use of the communication context. Driven by the success of human-human communication, an agent-based computational model, *PlanGraph,* is developed in this study for the GIS to keep track of the dynamic human-GIS communication context, and further helps to constrain the system's understanding of the meaning of a vague spatial concept. This model is implemented in a conversational GIS, *Dave_G* [2, 4]. Our previous papers [2, 8, 10] related to *PlanGraph* focus on application of this model for managing collaborative dialogues. This paper will focus on design and implementation of this model for handling the vagueness problem in human-GIS communication of spatial concepts.

The rest of this paper is organized as follows. Section II details the design of the agent-based model, *PlanGraph*, and its implementation details in a conversational GIS, *Dave_G*. Section III gives a sample dialogue between the human user and the conversational GIS, which illustrates how this model helps the GIS to handle the vagueness problem. The conclusion and future work is summarized at Section IV.

II. THE PLANGRAPH MODEL

Following human-human communication principles[8] and the Human Emulation approach [11] in the human-computer collaboration field, the design principle in this study is to enable the computer, a conversational GIS, to emulate a human GIS operator's role in natural language communication between a GIS user and a GIS operator. By emulating the GIS operator's role, the system needs to be able to keep track of the dynamic communication context, and use the context to constrain its understanding of the vague spatial concept.

The *PlanGraph* model is designed by following the *SharedPlan* theory [12, 13], and the computational collaborative discourse theory [14]. The human-GIS communication (mainly task-oriented collaborative dialogues) is modeled as a human-GIS collaboration process. During the collaboration process, the two agents, including the user agent and the system agent, both contribute to the collaboration plan, represented as a *SharedPlan*, which represents the dynamic human-GIS communication context. The *PlanGraph* model is designed to keep track of the *SharedPlan*.

To illustrate how the *PlanGraph* model helps to handle the vagueness problem, we have implemented this model in the prototype conversational GIS, *Dave_G* [2, 4, 10]. The GIS command-related functions used in *Dave_G* are provided by

T. Sobh, K. Elleithy (eds.), *Innovations in Computing Sciences and Software Engineering*,
DOI 10.1007/978-90-481-9112-3_8, © Springer Science+Business Media B.V. 2010

ArcIMS, which is a commercial web-based map server product by ESRI, Inc. [15]. The *PlanGraph* helps *Dave_G:* 1) to keep track of the human-GIS dialogue process and 2) to reason about how to interpret the user request, how to evolve the dialogue toward its success and how to respond to the user in terms of the current human-GIS dialogue status. For more details, see our previous papers [2, 4, 10].

This section describes the structure of *PlanGraph* and implementation details of this model in *Dave_G*, in particular, those related to handling the vagueness problem.

A. *Structure*

The *PlanGraph* model enables the GIS agent to keep track of the *SharedPlan* between the system and the user through use of the *PlanGraph* (see its structure from our previous paper [2]). The *PlanGraph* represents the dynamic knowledge that the GIS agent holds on the *SharedPlan* at a given time point during the human-GIS communication process. This model also provides a set of reasoning algorithms associated with the *PlanGraph.*

By following [14], the *PlanGraph* records three interrelated structures of the collaborative human-GIS dialogue, including the linguistic structure, the intentional structure, and the attentional state. The *PlanGraph* consists of the root plan representing the common goal of the system agent and the user, and all its sub-plans for sub-goals, which represents the intentional structure of the human-GIS dialogue. Each plan node in the *PlanGraph* is a complex data structure which records an action (and associated parameters if possible) together with a set of mental states that the system agent holds on that action at the given time point. The *PlanGraph* also records the attention focus that the system agent holds on the *SharedPlan* at that given time point. The discourse segments (phrases and sentences) are recorded as properties of plans in the *PlanGraph.* Thus, the linguistic structure of the collaborative human-GIS dialogue is also recorded in the *PlanGraph.*

B. *Actions and Recipes Knowledge*

The system needs to have general knowledge of actions and their recipes involved in construction of *PlanGraph* before being able to construct the *PlanGraph.* We designed the GIS agent's general knowledge by following the human GIS operator's knowledge involved in human-human communication involving spatial information requests. For example, such knowledge can include: (1) how to understand the meaning of a vague spatial concept based on major contextual information; (2) how to infer the context event behind the user's map requests; (3) how to handle the context-dependency problem through collaborative dialogues.

To illustrate the capabilities of the *PlanGraph* model in *Dave_G*, we have implemented a set of actions and recipes by following human communication principles. For example, the recipe *Infer Near* for the action *Instantiate Distance* (Figure 1(a)) represents one way for the agent G to instantiate the *Distance* parameter value by inferring the *near* distance value based on several major contextual factors. Due to space limitations, the recipe *Infer Near* in Figure 1(a) shows only three parameters representing three major contextual factors among many. Another example is the recipe *Travel1* (see Figure 1(b)). This is implemented for the system to understand the context that involves the user's spatial information requests. The last example recipe in Figure 1(c) is implemented for the system and the user to clarify one parameter's information, such as the goal of the user's map request or the transportation mode in the user's context event. For more actions and recipes implemented in *Dave_G*, please see the example in Section IV and our previous papers [2, 8, 10].

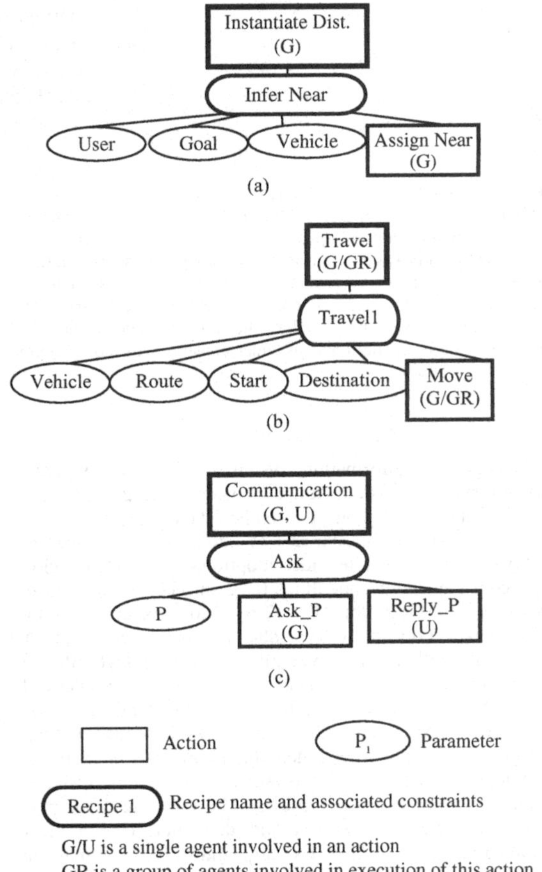

Figure 1. Sample Actions and Reciples in *Dave_G*

C. *Mental States*

The GIS agent's mental states on action/parameter nodes in the *PlanGraph* are designed by following the *SharedPlan* theory [12, 13]. According to the plan evolution process described in the *SharedPlan* theory [12, 13], a plan towards the goal/action α in collaboration usually evolves from partial to complete through several major steps. At each of these steps, the agent responsible for the plan needs to hold a set of mental states (intention, commitment, mental belief etc.) in order to evolve the partial plan toward the more complete plan. We design the system agent's mental states by following these mental states required at each major step of a plan evolution process.

A set of numerical labels, Mental State Numbers (MSNs) (Table 1), are designed to represent mental states that the GIS agent holds on an action node or a parameter node in the *PlanGraph* at each step of the *SharedPlan* evolution process. We use the numbers 4.1 and 4.2 to represent uncertain mental states that the GIS holds on action/parameter nodes which involves vagueness in two situations, respectively, including: 1) not enough context information is shared; 2) enough context information is shared between the system and the user. Only these two mental states are newly designed for handling the vagueness problem. However, the entire table including all MSNs is listed here for convenience of this paper's readers.

TABLE I. MSNS AND THEIR MEANINGS

MSN	Meaning of an MSN on an action α	Meaning of an MSN on a parameter *p*
0	The goal of α is proposed for α.	*p* is proposed in an action involved in the collaboration.
1	The goal of α is agreed by all agents in collaboration.	*p* is necessary for the collaboration and is waiting for instantiation.
2	α is a basic action ready to be executed.	*p* under the instantiation process is optional.
3	α is a complex action, and one plan is selected for this action.	*p* under the instantiation process is required.
4	The plan selected for α is executed, and the plan execution result contains uncertainties.	*p* is instantiated with a parameter value involving uncertainties.
	MSN=4.0 in case no vagueness is involved; MSN=4.1 in case that not enough context information is shared; MSN=4.2 in case that enough context information is shared.	
5	The plan selected for α fails.	Instantiation of *p* fails.
6	The plan selected for α is successfully executed, and the plan execution result does not involve any uncertainties.	*p* is successfully instantiated with a parameter value without any uncertainties.

D. *Reasoning Algorithms*

During the human-GIS communication process, the system needs to know: 1) how to understand the user's requests, in particular, the spatial concepts expressed in natural language, 2) how to evolve the *SharedPlan* toward its success, and 3) when and what to send out as responses. These three steps are called *Interpretation*, *Elaboration*, and *Response Control*, respectively, in this study. The *PlanGraph* model also provides reasoning algorithms for these three steps, including *Interpretation Algorithms* (**IAs**), *Elaboration Algorithms* (**EAs**), and *Response Algorithms* (**RAs**). For details of these reasoning algorithms, please see our previous papers [2, 10]. This section focuses on those reasoning algorithms related to handling the vagueness problem.

The **EAs** are designed and implemented as a depth-first recursive process. Detailed **EAs** related to how to handle the vagueness problem at different situations are designed by following the human-human communication principles. For example, a human communicator usually tries to understand the meaning of a vague spatial concept based on context information available from the existing communication context and/or inferred context information if the required context information is not available from communication; if the other communicator does not agree with the existing inference on the vague spatial concept, the two communicators can use collaborative dialogues to further clarify some context information which is not clear and/or negotiate the meaning of a vague spatial concept based on the existing inference. Therefore, *Dave_G* is implemented as always selecting a recipe like the one in Figure 1(a) to understand the meaning of a vague spatial concept based on context information at first; trying to share context information with the user or to ask for context information from the user if its MSN on the vague spatial concept is 4.1; trying to negotiate the meaning of the vague spatial concept with the user if its MSN on it is 4.2.

III. HANDLING VAGUENESS IN HUMAN-GIS DIALOGUE

This section explains a sample collaborative dialogue (Figure 2) between a human user and the conversational GIS, *Dave_G*. This dialogue example is used to illustrate how the *PlanGraph* model can help the GIS agent to handle the vagueness problem, in particular, the context-dependency sub-problem.

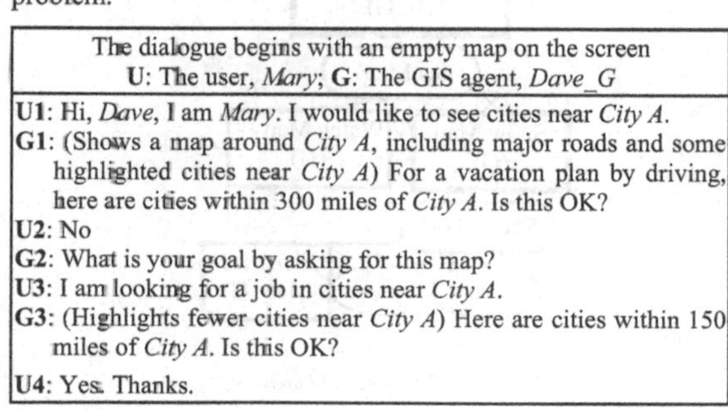
The dialogue begins with an empty map on the screen
U: The user, *Mary*; **G**: The GIS agent, *Dave_G*

U1: Hi, *Dave*, I am *Mary*. I would like to see cities near *City A*.
G1: (Shows a map around *City A*, including major roads and some highlighted cities near *City A*) For a vacation plan by driving, here are cities within 300 miles of *City A*. Is this OK?
U2: No
G2: What is your goal by asking for this map?
U3: I am looking for a job in cities near *City A*.
G3: (Highlights fewer cities near *City A*) Here are cities within 150 miles of *City A*. Is this OK?
U4: Yes. Thanks.

Figure 2. Sample Collaborative Human-GIS Dialogue

After receiving the first user input, U1, from the GIS interface, the GIS agent analyzes the semantic meaning of the input, and knows that the user's intention underlying U1 is to see a map, and the intention is represented by the action, *See Map*. Then, it starts to interpret the input U1 by calling the **IAs** from *Reasoning Engine*. The system initiates the *PlanGraph* with the user's intention, *See Map*, with MSN 0 (see Figure 3) because it believes that it can help the user to see a map.

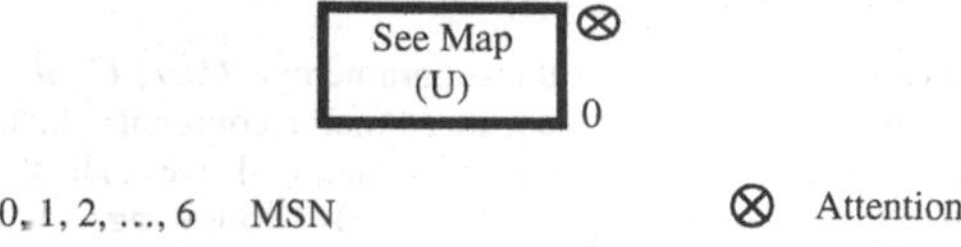

Figure 3. Initial *PlanGraph*

By calling the **EAs** from *Reasoning Engine*, the system tries to advance the focus action, *See Map*, in *PlanGraph* toward its success. In this study, we assume that the system and the user always agree with each other's requests related to GIS use and take them as part of their collaboration. Under this assumption, the system updates its MSN on *See Map* from 0 to 1. Then, the system finds the recipe *SeeMap1* (see this recipe in Figure 4) from its *Knowledge Base* for *See Map* and extends it with the recipe *SeeMap1*. At the same time, and updates its MSN on the focus action *See Map* from 1 to 3, and initiates its MSN on each sub-action node as 0 (see Figure 4). By following the recursive depth-first **EAs**, the system agent moves its attention to the first child node, *Show Map*, of *See Map* and elaborates the new focus node with its recipe *ShowMap1* (Figure 5)).

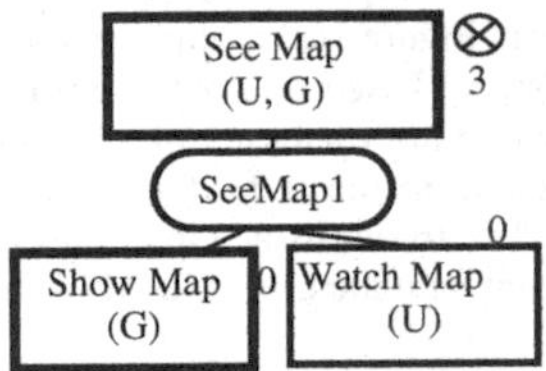

Figure 4. Temporary *PlanGraph*

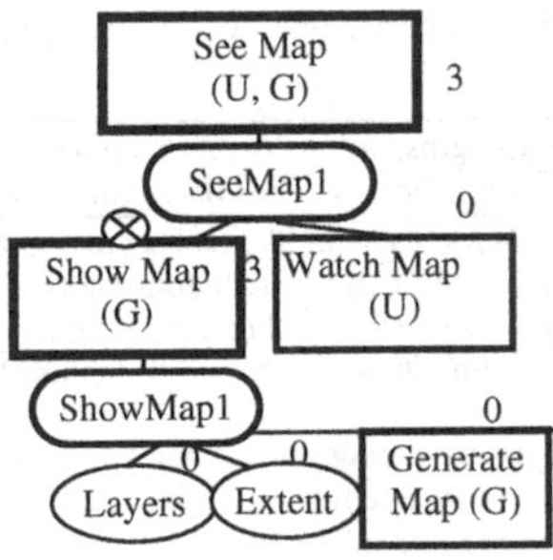

Figure 5. Temporary *PlanGraph*

Similarly, by following the recursive depth-first **EAs**, the system moves its attention to the first child node, *Layers*, of *Show Map1* and tries to instantiate this parameter by using the action *Instantiate Layer*. It uses the recipe *Select by Distance* (which corresponds to a GIS query command) of *Instantiate Layer* to generate a layer value for *Layers*. The system successfully identifies the target layer (that is, *cities*) and the reference location (*City A*) from U1 for the two parameters, *Target* and *Refer*, in this recipe, but needs to infer the *Distance* parameter value from the vague spatial concept *near* with the recipe *Infer Near* (see Figure 6).

As explained before, the three parameters, *User*, *Goal* and *Vehicle* in *Infer Near* represent three major contextual factors which influence the meaning of *near*, and we call these parameters as context parameters. By following human communication principles, to instantiate these context parameters, the system needs to retrieve corresponding context information from the existing *PlanGraph* (which represents the system knowledge kept on the human-GIS communication context) or infers the context behind the user's spatial information request, *See Map*. In this example, the current *PlanGraph* contains the *User* information (from U1), but does not have *Vehicle* and *Goal* information. Therefore, the system has to infer the context event, *Travel*, behind of the user's map request and its *Goal* event behind *Travel* and integrate them with the existing *PlanGraph*. In the *Travel* context event (see Figure 7), the system infers the *Vehicle* as *car* (because most people living around *City A* travel by car), the *Routes* as *major roads* (whose information is then added to the map to be shared with the user), the *Start* location as *City A*, and the *Target* is the spatial information that the user is asking for in *See Map*. In addition, the system also infers the *Goal* of the user's traveling plan is to have a vacation (because the goal of most users who ask for spatial information about cities is to plan for a vacation). See the top part in Figure 7 for the context event that the system has inferred.

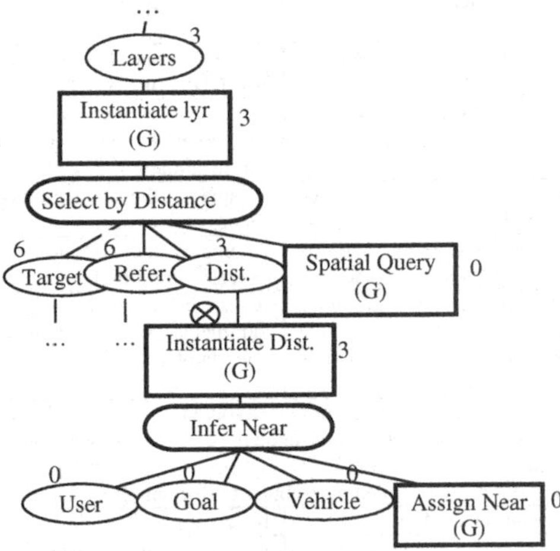

Figure 6. Temporary *PlanGraph*

After inferring the context event behind the user's spatial information request, the system comes back to execute the plan *Infer Near*. It instantiates the context parameters by retrieving context information from the updated *PlanGraph*, and assigns *near* as 300 miles through executing the action *Assign Near*. By executing *Spatial Query*, the system calls the GIS component to generate a GIS layer showing all cities within 300 miles of *City A*. At this time, the two context parameters, *Goal* and *Vehicle*, are estimated by the system. Therefore, the system's MSN on the action *Assign Near*, *Instantiate Distance* and the parameter *Distance* are updated as 4.1.

By following the recursive depth-first **EAs**, the system moves its attention to the second parameter, *Extent*, in the plan *ShowMap1*, and estimates its value as the extent of the new layer generated by the GIS component. Then, it moves its attention to the action *Generate Map*. By calling the GIS component to generate a map response based on the *Layers* parameter values instantiated so far and an estimated map *Extent*, the system generates a map response and a text response in G1 through executing *Generate Map*.

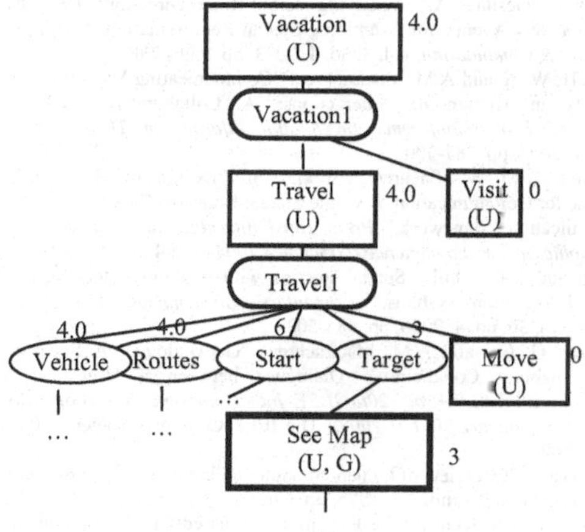

Figure 7. Temporary *PlanGraph*

Show Map is a communicative action assigned to be performed by the system. So, the system calls the **RAs** from *Reasoning Engine*, and decides to send out all responses in G1. By assuming that the user usually can successfully execute the action *Watch Map*, the system moves its attention on the common goal between the system and the user, *See Map,* and looks forward to the user's comment on the collaboration result—the map. At this moment, because the parameter value of *Distance* contains vagueness, this node's parent nodes and the other nodes that use the vague distance value all contain certain vagueness. Therefore, the MSNs on these codes are all updated as 4.1. See the current *PlanGraph* at this moment in Figure 8.

From the user's negative reply in U2 on the map response in G1, the system knows that it needs to improve its plan toward their common goal, *See Map*. So, it updates the MSN on this plan as 3 and traces all its sub-plans with vagueness (that is, those with MSN 4.1). When the system traces back to the node *Instantiate Distance* action and its children nodes, it knows that it needs to get a better idea on the *Goal* information to better infer the *near* distance because the MSN on *Goal* is 4.0. Therefore, by following human communication principles, the system uses collaborative dialogues to ask the user for such context information in G2. The user's reply in U3, *I am looking for jobs in City A*, helps the system to update not only the *Goal* parameter value, but also the background event behind the spatial information request *See Map*. U3 is interpreted as the context event action, *Work with Job*. Therefore, the system replaces the previous root action, *Vacation*, in the *PlanGraph* with the new context event action, *Work with Job*. Then, the system retrieves the updated context information from the updated *PlanGraph* to re-fill parameter values for the context parameters with MSN 4.0. In this case, they are *Goal* and *Vehicle* in the plan *Infer Near* (see Figure 8). The MSN on *Goal* is updated as 6 and that on *Vehicle* is still 4.0 because there is no update on the vehicle information. By re-executing the action, *Assign Near*, with updated parameter values in the plan *Infer Near*, the system re-assigns 150 miles as the *near* distance. Consequently, it regenerates another map response showing cities within 150 miles of *City A* in G3. Finally, the system receives the user's confirmation in U4 on the new *near* distance shown in G3.

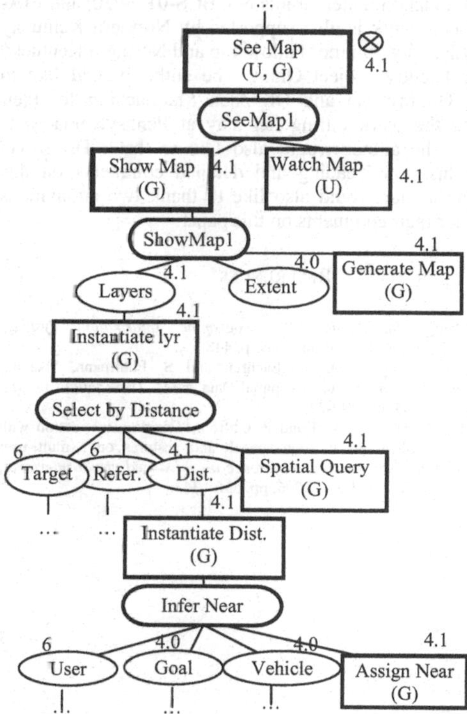

Figure 8. Partial *PlanGraph* after G1

IV. CONCLUSION AND FUTURE WORK

In this paper, we present the agent-based computational model, *PlanGraph*. It helps the conversational GIS to handle the vagueness problem in human-GIS communication, in particular, the context-dependency sub-problem. The capabilities of this model are demonstrated by the performance of a conversational GIS, *Dave_G*, which incorporates this model. This model can help the GIS to keep track of the dynamic human-GIS communication context, which can further help to constrain the system's understanding of a vague spatial concept involved in communication.

The performance of a natural language enabled GIS in handling the vagueness problem depends highly on the knowledge of actions and their recipes stored in the system's knowledge base. Such knowledge in *Dave_G* is pre-built as static knowledge, which does not get updated along with communication with the user. In the future, we will consider to improve the system so that it can dynamically accumulate and update its knowledge of actions and recipes in the *Knowledge Base*. The system with dynamically accumulated and updated knowledge would be able to handle the vagueness problem more intelligently.

ACKNOWLEDGMENT

This material is based upon work supported by the National Science Foundation under Grants No. BCS-0113030, and EIA-0306845. This work is also supported by Northern Kentucky University Faculty Summer Fellowship and Northern Kentucky University Faculty Project Grant. The author would like to thank Dr. Guoray Cai and Dr. Alan MacEachren for their advising to the work during her stay at Pennsylvania State University. The author would also like to thank Dr. Kevin Kirby for his proof-reading and detailed comments on this paper. The author would also like to thank two anonymous reviewers for their comments on this paper.

REFERENCES

[1] K.-t. Chang, *Introduction to Geographic Information Systems*, McGrawHIll Higher Education, 2009, p. 448.

[2] G. Cai, H. Wang, A.M. MacEachren and S. Fuhrmann, "Natural Conversational Interfaces to Geospatial Databases," *Transactions in GIS*, vol. 9, no. 2, 2005, pp. 199-221.

[3] T. Edward, S. Chia, G. Saul and F. Clifton, "Enabling interaction with single user applications through speech and gestures on a multi-user tabletop," *Proc. The working conference on Advanced visual interfaces*, ACM New York, NY, USA, 2006, pp. 336 - 343.

[4] A.M. MacEachren, G. Cai, R. Sharma, I. Rauschert, I. Brewer, L. Bolelli, B. Shaparenko, S. Fuhrmann and H. Wang, "Enabling Collaborative GeoInformation Access and Decision-Making Through a Natural, Multimodal Interface," *International Journal of Geographical Information Science*, vol. 19, no. 3, 2005, pp. 293-317.

[5] D. Wilson, J. Doyle, J. Weakliam, M. Bertolotto and D. Lynch, "Personalised maps in multimodal mobile GIS," *International Journal of Web Engineering and Technology*, vol. 3, no. 2, 2007, pp. 196-216.

[6] G.L. Allen, "Gestures Accompanying Verbal Route Directions: Do They Point to a New Avenue for Examining Spatial Representations?," *Spatial Cognition & Computation*, vol. 3, no. 4, 2003, pp. 259 - 268.

[7] G. Cai, H. Wang and A.M. MacEachren, "Communicating Vague Spatial Concepts in Human-GIS Interactions: A Collaborative Dialogue Approach," *Proc. Conference on Spatial Information Theory 2003*, Springer, 2003, pp. 287-300.

[8] H. Wang, A.M. MacEachren and G. Cai, "Design of Human-GIS Dialogue for Communication of Vague Spatial Concepts Based on Human Communication Framework," *Proc. Third International Conference on Geographic Information Science (GIScience 2004)*, 2004, pp. 220-223.

[9] X. Yao and J.-C. Thill, "Spatial queries with qualitative locations in spatial information systems," *Computers, Environment and Urban Systems*, vol. 30, no. 4, 2006, pp. 485-502.

[10]H. Wang, G. Cai and A.M. MacEachren, "GeoDialogue: A Software Agent Enabling Collaborative Dialogues between a User and a Conversational GIS," *Proc. 20th IEEE Int'l Conference on Tools with Artificial Intelligence (ICTAI 2008)*, The IEEE Computer Society, 2008, pp. 357-360.

[11]L.G. Terveen, "Overview of human-computer collaboration," *Knowledge-based Systems*, vol. 8, no. 2-3, 1995, pp. 67-81.

[12]B.J. Grosz and S. Kraus, "The Evolution of SharedPlans," *Foundations and Theories of Rational Agency*, A. Rao and M. Wooldridge, ed., 1999, pp. 227-262.

[13]B.J. Grosz and S. Kraus, "Collaborative plans for complex group action," *Artificial Intelligence*, vol. 86, no. 2, 1996, pp. 269-357.

[14]B.J. Grosz and C.L. Sidner, "Attention, intentions, and the structure of discourse," *Computational Linguistics*, vol. 12, no. 3, 1986, pp. 175--204.

[15]I. ESRI, "ArcIMS," 2009; http://support.esri.com/index.cfm?fa=software.filteredGateway&PID=16.

Risk-Based Neuro-Grid Architecture for Multimodal Biometrics

Sitalakshmi Venkataraman[1], Siddhivinayak Kulkarni[2]
Academic Research Members of Internet Commerce and Security Laboratory,
Graduate School of Information Technology and Mathematical Sciences,
University of Ballarat, PO Box 663, Ballarat, VIC 3353, Australia
[1] s.venkatraman@ballarat.edu.au
[2] s.kulkarni@ballarat.edu.au

Abstract—Recent research indicates that multimodal biometrics is the way forward for a highly reliable adoption of biometric identification systems in various applications, such as banks, businesses, government and even home environments. However, such systems would require large distributed datasets with multiple computational realms spanning organisational boundaries and individual privacies.

In this paper, we propose a novel approach and architecture for multimodal biometrics that leverages the emerging grid information services and harnesses the capabilities of neural network as well. We describe how such a neuro-grid architecture is modelled with the prime objective of overcoming the barriers of biometric risks and privacy issues through flexible and adaptable multimodal biometric fusion schemes. On one hand, the model uses grid services to promote and simplify the shared and distributed resource management of multimodal biometrics, and on the other hand, it adopts a feed-forward neural network to provide reliability and risk-based flexibility in feature extraction and multimodal fusion, that are warranted for different real-life applications. With individual autonomy, scalability, risk-based deployment and interoperability serving the backbone of the neuro-grid information service, our novel architecture would deliver seamless and robust access to geographically distributed biometric data centres that cater to the current and future diverse multimodal requirements of various day-to-day biometric transactions.

Keywords: Biometric Technologies, Transaction Risks, Multimodal Biometrics, Grid Services, Data Grids, Neural Networks

I. Introduction

With the escalating increase in digital impersonation being witnessed today, biometric identification becomes a highly secure personal verification solution to the problem of identity theft [1]. Since a biometric trait of a person (e.g. fingerprint, hand geometry, signature, retina, voice, gait, etc.) has a strong relationship to his or her identity, it confirms the person making a transaction leading to satisfying the authentication, authorisation and non-repudiation objectives of information security. Hence, biometric verification is being increasingly considered in a wide variety of everyday applications in business, service and even home and schools [2]. However, in order for biometrics to be successful, such advanced systems should also be able to deal with privacy concerns, performance problems and multiple trait issues [3].
Biometric technology needs to address the following critical problems:

i) Permanence – Biometric data may be required to be revoked and reissued due to security breach or changes in the person's features due to factors such as aging or deformity [4].
ii) Multiple Traits - Different biometric technologies are at different stages of maturity [5] and there is no single trait that could become the standard for all applications. Multiple biometric enrolments for different situations pose a major inconvenience to the users [6].
iii) Individual Privacy – User confidence in biometrics is based on whether the system allows exchange of biometric data with other databases that could lead to function creep [7].

To solve the above said problems, multimodal biometric systems, which consolidate information from a person's multiple biometric samples (e.g. fingerprints of the same finger), multiple instances (e.g. fingerprints of different fingers) and multiple traits (e.g. fingerprint and iris scan), are becoming popular While there is a strong motivation for multimodal biometrics, such systems would require advanced biometric technology interfaces and policy framework that caters to performance, security and privacy issues for a successful adoption in everyday life [8]. Generally, the main limitations of the present systems that use multimodal biometrics are: a) fixed calibration that does not adapt to different user / application / service requirements, b) lack of interoperability among multiple distributed heterogeneous environments, c) shared resources issues, and d) poor data optimisation leading to low quality of service (QoS).

Grid information services, which provide scalability, security and high-performance features to the distributed and heterogeneous resources [9], offer promise to overcome the aforesaid limitations of the current unimodal and multimodal biometric systems. Hence, this paper aims to present a biometric grid architecture that could launch an adaptive multimodal biometrics effectively through the use of neural networks for addressing security and privacy risks in real-life applications. Such a neuro-grid architecture could compensate the weakness of any biometric classifier by other stronger biometric classifiers through the distributed grid service to achieve accuracy and reliability of multimodalities in a collaborative and flexible manner. In this way, biometric systems could be tuned to meet the changing business and user requirements. In other words, this paper explores the

T. Sobh, K. Elleithy (eds.), *Innovations in Computing Sciences and Software Engineering*,
DOI 10.1007/978-90-481-9112-3_9, © Springer Science+Business Media B.V. 2010

integration of two concepts, namely neural networks and grid computing for an improved multimodal biometric system of the future.

The rest of the paper is organized as follows. Section 2 presents a brief overview of the essential features of Grid Information Services required for biometric transaction processing. Section 3 describes how the complex fusion scheme of multimodal biometrics could be enabled through neural network fusion technique that uses a risk-based classification of biometric transactions. In Section 4, we propose risk-based neuro-grid architecture for multimodal biometrics using a feed-forward neural network. Finally, in Section 5, we provide conclusions and directions of future work.

II. Grid Information Services in Biometrics

A grid is a collection of distributed services launched in a portal through which users or business applications interact for their information processing services [9]. In this section, we provide an overview of typical grid information services (Fig. 1) that could cater to the needs of various biometric users or applications. As depicted in Fig. 1, we describe below, the main basic and advanced functions of grid information services that are highly useful for processing biometric transactions:

i) Basic functions – The basic features of discovery and brokering, data sharing, monitoring and policy controlling are essential for processing multiple biometric classifiers in a distributed grid environment.

ii) Advanced functions – The advanced features associated with security and resource management capabilities of grid information services play a crucial role in achieving accuracy and reliability of biometric transactions in a distributed grid environment.

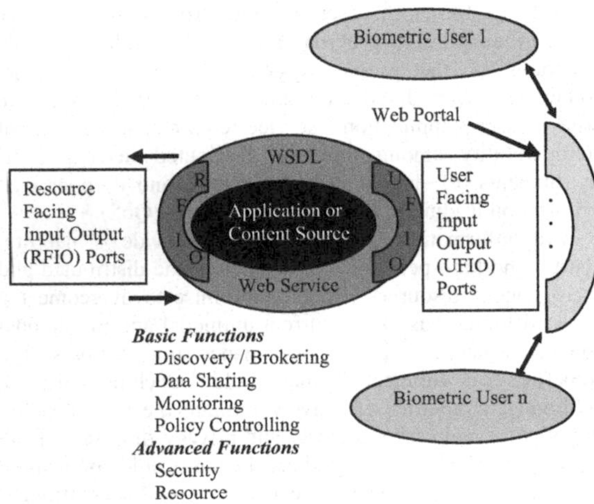

Fig. 1. Typical grid information services for biometric users

Discovery and Brokering: This functionality helps in the discovery of biometric resources and brokering of different biometric traits in the discovered resources.

Data Sharing: This feature allows access to very large databases of biometric data and other personal identification data in a distributed and shared fashion. Other data services such as metadata cataloguing, data caching, data replication, backup and storage services are also essential aspects for biometric transactions.

Monitoring: The multimodal biometric processing is to be monitored closely so that the matching measures are computed successfully over large databases. A good matching should avoid false positives and false negatives and at the same time inter-operate on different types of biometric traits with inherent noise.

Policy controlling: This feature controls the access mechanisms for the biometric databases and the rules for notification processes as well.

Security: Grid information services are capable of providing the security controls for multiple distributed infrastructures and the authentication, authorisation and accounting mechanisms required for processing biometric data. The capability of grid information services with dynamic instantiation of new security features and services becomes an advanced feature for biometric applications.

Resource Management: This feature involves dynamic scheduling, load balancing, workflow management, fault tolerance and error recovery of biometric systems transacting in distributed grid environments.

III. Multimodal Biometric Fusion using Neural Networks

Recent research studies indicate that privacy and security risks are the prime factors for society to be slow in embracing biometrics [7]. Hence, in order to reap the benefits of this emerging technology as a highly secure personal verification solution against information security threats, we need to identify and address the possible privacy and security risks that biometric transactions could pose within commercial as well as non-commercial scenarios. More importantly, a classification of these transactions based on the risk levels, such as , 'Basic', 'Intermediate' and 'Advanced' [10], would aid in providing the necessary flexibility and adaptability that Grid information services could leverage upon while matching with each user's multimodal biometric preferences.

A. Complexities of Multimodal Biometric Fusion

In multimodal biometrics of a multiple classifier system, the fusion module chosen by the grid information service is required to be based on a few associated criteria so that the grid-based architecture could match the user-centric preferences of the biometric traits with the business transaction requirements towards addressing the privacy and security risk issues. We identify the following criteria with which the grid information service could be modeled to adopt the most appropriate fusion algorithm:

i) Level of system balance – The level of accuracy of multiple biometric classifiers could vary among different traits [11]. If all the classifiers to be included in the fusion module are of high level of accuracy, then the level of system balance is set to be high. Hence, the level of system balance could be determined based on the classifier accuracy levels and their differences.
ii) Degree of complexity – This is determined based on the computational complexity of the fusion algorithm in the matching process of multiple biometrics. There are simple techniques such as the sum rule, decision tree, plain averaging formula, etc. [12]. Some of the highly complex techniques adopt trained rule base classifiers that make use of Support Vector Machines (SVM), neural networks, Bayes / radial basis network, etc [13].
iii) Level of privacy / security risk – Biometric transactions could be classified based on the risk levels associated, such as, basic, medium or advanced. This gives an indication to the grid information service the type of biometric classifiers to be used for processing the transaction. A holistic analysis of risk levels for biometric authentication would be based on technology, privacy, safety, performance and security issues that surround biometrics in an integrated manner [14].

Many research studies have demonstrated that fusion is more effective in the identification of an individual than single classifiers [15]. However, if unbalanced classifiers are combined, a highly complex fusion technique may take more time to optimise and would eventually degrade the system performance. Hence, for many simple transactions that fall under basic risk level, the grid information system could make use of unimodal biometrics. On the other hand, certain financial transactions, even though assigned basic privacy risk level, may require classifiers with high system balance as preferred by the user and may involve complex fusion techniques. In open-population applications such as airports, simple sum fusion could be more effective, whereas in closed-population applications such as office, user weighting fusion methods could be more effective. Hence, the above three inter-related criteria could be incorporated as privacy policy rules for the grid information system to be flexible in adopting the appropriate fusion technique for biometric authentication based on the transaction scenario. To achieve this, we propose the use of neural networks for the feature extraction step and fusion technique adoption step that are required for processing a biometric identification transaction. These steps are briefly summarized next.

B. Neural Network-Based Feature Extraction

Overall, privacy and security risks could be identified with biometrics during the very first interaction with the user, namely, the enrolment process, when biometric data is collected and stored as signatures or normalised as templates. Neural network models that have been successfully adopted in image analysis and pattern recognition [16] [17], could be considered for biometric applications. We propose a Multi Layer Perceptron (MLP) neural network that learns the same biometric trait at the input and output neurons and provides a characteristic through its hidden layer as a feature vector. The main advantages of using a MLP neural network are adaptability, noise tolerance and collective computability [18], which are the main features required for multimodal biometrics. The number of hidden layers may vary depending upon the characteristics of the feature vectors and the synaptic weights are determined to minimize error [19].

We provide an example MLP as a fingerprint feature extractor in Fig. 2. Here, the features are extracted from fingerprint images which are usually texture patterns. The output obtained from the hidden layer of MLP will be taken as fingerprint feature vectors. In general, the feature vector obtained (hidden layer output) can be considered as a two dimensional block of hidden node outputs, each hidden node having N_i outputs so that the total dimension of a feature is N_h by N_i, where N_h is the number of hidden nodes in the hidden layer and N_i is the number of inputs applied to the MLP. As shown in Fig. 2, the example MLP given here learns the same patterns with a single hidden layer in the feed-forward neural network that provides the biometric feature vector. The MLP with the same texture patterns at input and output could be trained using a supervised learning algorithm. A compelling advantage of this technique is that the training is quite fast and provides consistency between the extracted features of the same class [20]. This will help in the classification of extracted features accurately and to adopt appropriate fusion algorithm in the verification and application stages based on the risks associated with the biometric transaction.

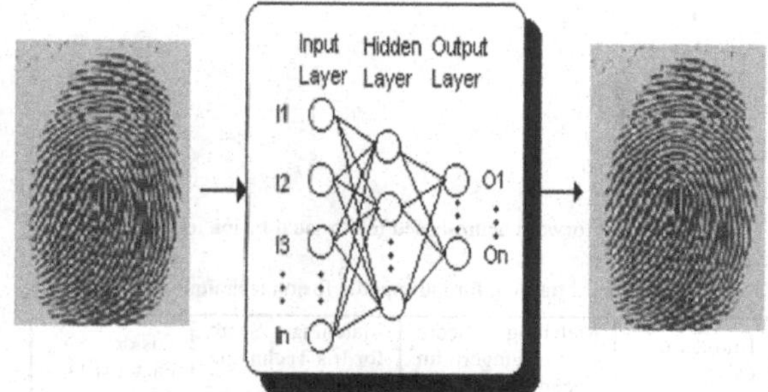

Fig. 2. Multi Layer Perceptron (MLP) as feature extractor

C. Neural Network-Based Multimodal Fusion Scheme

We propose a fusion scheme that is based on N-layer feed-forward neural network. The number of inputs to the neural network is equivalent to the number of biometric techniques used and the output of the neural network is called the Fusion Factor. The neural network decides the final fusion factor for the combination of the N different biometric classifiers, where MS_i denotes the matching score of classifier i. Fig. 3 depicts a typical N-layer feed-forward neuro-based multimodal fusion approach.

We illustrate a 2-layer feed-forward neural network with two traits, namely fingerprint and iris for training bimodal biometric fusion technique in Table 1. If the matching score (MS) for the first classifier is MS_1 and the matching score for the second classifier is MS_2, these two scores could be applied to neural network as input and the resulting fusion factor is indicated by F_1 in the first iteration. As illustrated in Table 1, let the matching scores be 0.7 and 0.9 for two different biometric traits (Case-I), and 0.8 and 0.7 (Case-II) for another instance of these traits. The neural network determines the fusion factor for Case-I and Case-II as A and B respectively, which are compared. For the illustrated dataset, we would expect the fusion factor B to be less than A and the neural network could discard B and consider another bimodal dataset for the next training iteration. This way, the feed-forward neural network gets trained with the prime objective of minimising False Acceptance Rate (FAR) and False Rejection Rate (FRR). Through the generation of fusion factors, the expected threshold values of the three criteria, namely, level of system balance, degree of complexity and risk levels are determined for risk-based biometric transaction processing.

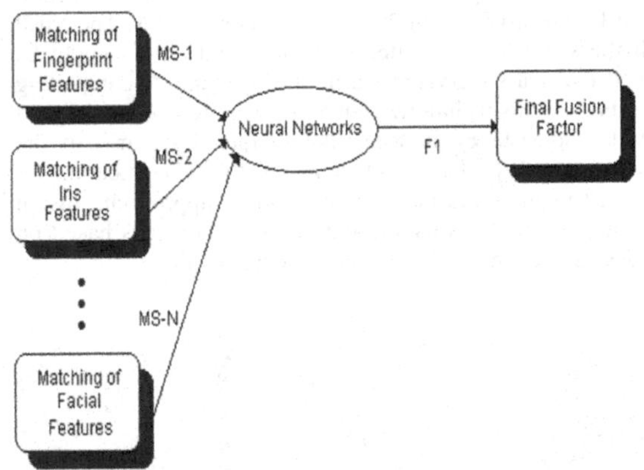

Fig. 3. Feed-forward neuro-based multimodal fusion technique

Table 1: Neuro-based training for multimodal fusion technique

Biometric Cases	Matching Score for Fingerprint Technique (MS1)	Matching Score for Iris Technique (MS2)	Fusion Factor (F1)
Case-I	0.7	0.9	A
Case-II	0.8	0.7	B (A>B)

IV. Risk-Based Biometric Neuro-Grid Architecture

We propose a grid architecture that uses a feed-forward neural network for incorporating risk-based multimodal biometric fusion schemes. It provides the flexibility at the client services layer for both users and business transactions to choose the suitable biometric modalities that are compatible with the user-preferred and transaction-specific risk levels that are assigned for different business applications. We present an overview of the biometric neuro-grid architecture in Fig. 4, which shows the major components involved. We describe briefly the components that constitute our risk-based biometric neuro-grid architecture from the top layer to the bottom layer, with inputs of risk parameters and biometric fusion parameters that would get processed from one layer to the other using a feed-forward neural network.

A. Biometric Client Application Layer

This layer consists of a Web portal, which provides a user-friendly and browser-based interface for the users and businesses to make use of the Discovery and Brokering features of grid services for finding the suitable biometric resources for their biometric authentication transactions. It allows different businesses, government and home applications, such as, bank applications, e-passport services, driver licence applications, e-shopping, and public services (e.g., community, library and transport), to setup their biometric requirements and neural network parameters, that serve as inputs to the next level of grid service. This layer also includes neuro-grid client for the users to determine their biometric trait preferences for different applications based on the risk levels associated with those biometric-enabled transactions. The portal uses such parameters to associate biometric metadata with datasets that are utilized in the next layer to determine their resource location for data retrieval and publication.

B. High-level and Multimodal Biometric Services

In this second layer of the grid architecture, the high-level grid service provides the capabilities of reliable data movement, cataloguing, metadata access, data subsetting and aggregation. Such high-level data features form the sub-components that are based on the Open Grid Services Architecture Data Access and Integration (OGSA-DAI) service, which uses the Replica Location Service (RLS) to retrieve the location information from the distributed RLS databases [21]. This layer provides the neuro-grid paradigm and simulation services for mapping the inputs with metadata that is required for processing the multimodal biometrics. The neuro-grid paradigm and simulation services determine the archive data rules and adaptive fusion rules that are required for training and processing the feed-forward MLP in the next layer.

C. Neuro-Grid (Globus) Infrastructure

This layer provides remote, authenticated access to shared data resources such as biometric data, risk-based and neuro-based metadata through Meta Directory Services (MDS), and other services such as RLS and transaction management services. This is accomplished by the Grid Security Infrastructure (GSI) for secure authentication. A shared data access could be incorporated for integrating shared authorisation service for both group-based and individual access to datasets through GridFT [22]. Apart from enforcing data encryption through GSI, reliability could also be enhanced through the monitoring infrastructure through the use of Globus Toolkit's grid information services [23]. The Grid Resource Allocation and Management (GRAM) sub-component provides the necessary service to communicate between the multimodal biometric recognition module provided by the feed-forward MLP and the grid services modules to access and process biometric data.

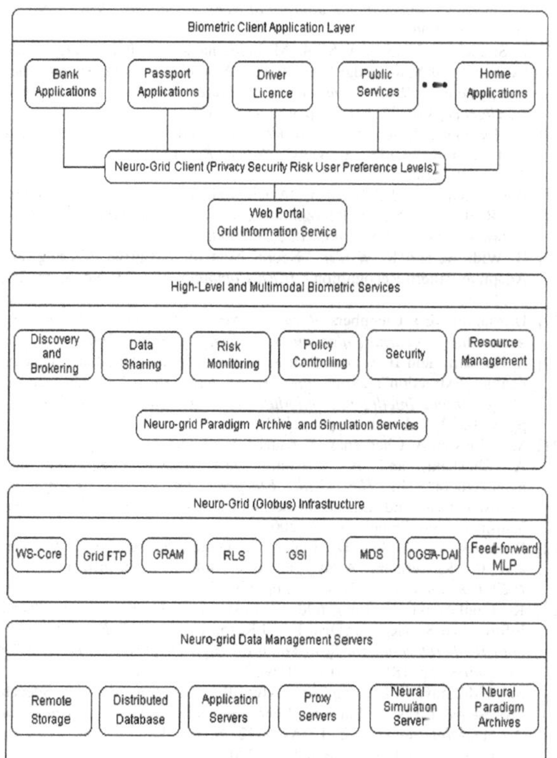

Fig. 4. Neuro-grid architecture for multimodal biometrics

D. *Neuro-Grid Data Management Servers*

This is the lower-most layer of the grid architecture consisting of all the computational resources such as Web servers, application servers, database servers, neural simulation servers, neural paradigm archives and mass storage systems including CPU, cache, buffers, etc. This lowest layer provides scalable, dependable and secure access to the distributed resources that is required for biometric applications as grid computing maintains administrative autonomy and allows system heterogeneity. The database servers are used to store metadata, biometric features, privacy policy rules, etc. The application servers are for running the Open Grid Services Architecture (OGSA) applications or legacy applications (non-OGSA) such as servlets running in Java application server containers, neural network servers running the training simulators, and the Web servers for hosting the Internet portal services for the different biometric applications. The neural simulation servers consist of the MLP as biometric feature extractor and the feed-forward neurons for the multimodal fusion adoption scheme. The fusion adoption scheme determines the best of available algorithms that are configured through machine learning and training to suit each particular biometric-enabled business transaction. Such training mechanisms have been successfully adopted, especially in speech processing [24]. The training paradigms in this context are preserved as archives of the machine learning process for future references. In summary, this layer provides all the necessary resources for executing biometric transactions and to provide computational power to users who make use of the Web grid services at the client-end of the various biometric applications.

V. Conclusions and Future Work

In this paper, we have presented a novel risk-based grid architecture that uses feed-forward neural network for multimodal biometric fusion. The motivation of the proposed architecture is to address the risk-based adoption issues surrounding biometrics. While multimodal biometrics are capable of overcoming the limitations posed by unimodal biometrics, such as, permanence, multiple traits and individual privacy, its success in adoption require information sharing among large, heterogeneous and distributed multimodal data centres. This warrants features such as, advanced biometric data access, sophisticated multimodal fusion algorithms and more importantly, an adaptive privacy policy framework, and these form the main backbone of our proposed risk-based neuro-grid architecture for multimodal biometrics.

Our proposed neuro-grid architecture takes advantage of the recent evolution of OGSA's GSI3 that provides an improved security model, network services and other information services through a Web portal. It provides the optimal setting for the discovery, data sharing, monitoring and managing multimodal biometric resources that are diverse, large, dynamic and distributed among organisations. Further, by combining with neural network capabilities, the proposed architecture caters to three parameters such as multimodal biometric system balance, degree of complexity of fusion schemes and privacy / security risk levels that feed into the training and adaptive rules of the policy framework. Since such a feed-forward neural network combines the information from different biometric modalities as preferred by the individual user for specific biometric transactions and checks the compatibility within the policy framework of each application environment, it is aimed at providing the necessary risk-based decisions for an improved diffusion of multimodal biometrics.

Looking forward, there is much to be gained from neural network and grid computing researchers, and this paper provides motivation for such inter-disciplinary research with applications in multimodal biometrics. With the increased interest in neural network based multimodal biometric fusion, an interesting topic for future research entails investigation of different number of hidden layers in the feed-forward neural network that could impact on the performance and accuracy of fusion schemes. Another topic of future research is to explore collaborative data sharing of multimodal biometrics among different organisations to take advantage of the proposed neuro-grid information service.

system and CASE systems. We discuss some queries that one can use to check artifacts. Finally, we draw conclusions and point to the future work with the current topic.

II. Related Work

Bernstein and Dayal [8] define repository as "[a]a shared database of information about engineered artifacts". It is possible to use a DBMS as the basis of repository manager that "provides services for modeling, retrieving, and managing the objects in a repository" [8]. CASE and meta-CASE systems record artifacts in a repository. Are there any systems, the part of which is a repository and which use a $RDBMS_{SQL}$ or an $ORDBMS_{SQL}$ as their basis? Do these systems allow users to construct and execute queries?

Rasmussen [9] describes different constraint checking mechanisms in CASE tools. A possibility is to "[a]allow everything initially, but let the model go through a validation process, that will flush out any errors in the model" [9]. In this case one can use queries to find problems in artifacts. Dittrich et al. [10] acknowledge that database technology can help the designers of software engineering systems in case of querying and retrieval of artifacts and enforcement of integrity and consistency of artifacts. Bernstein [11] writes about the implementation of a software engineering system and concludes: "Given technology trends, an object-relational system is likely to be the best choice, but an XML database system might also be suitable".

In his previous work [12], one of the authors of this paper proposes a web-based and database-based CASE system for creating models according to the methodological framework for the Enterprise Information System strategic analysis. The system records data in an OR_{SQL} database. He proposes to use 22 queries to find consistency or completeness problems.

Gray and Ryan [13] present a CASE system that fulfils the requirements of PARallel Software Engineering (PARSE) project. The system uses the help of Oracle $RDBMS_{SQL}$. The authors [13] stress that advanced query mechanism of the DBMS makes it easier to implement the CASE system. The PARSE design rules are implemented as integrity constraints, which are enforced by the DBMS.

Lutteroth [14] proposes AP1 platform for the development of model-based CASE tools. Firebird $RDBMS_{SQL}$ forms the core of the system. Many constraints, like referential integrity are implemented as integrity constraints, which are enforced by the DBMS. Lutteroth [14] notes that SQL makes it easy to integrate AP1 with other platforms.

General Modeling Environment (GME) [15] stores data in the Microsoft Repository [16] or in the files with a proprietary binary file format. Microsoft Repository is an object-oriented layer that encapsulates $RDBMS_{SQL}$s MS SQL Server or MS Access. GME has a Constraint Manager subsystem, the task of which is to enforce model constraints.

Lavazza and Agostini [17] propose UML Model Measurement Tool that can be used to measure UML class models and state models. The system uses the help of MySQL $RDBMS_{SQL}$. It reads data from XML Metadata Interchange files and populates a database. Therefore, it is possible to use SQL queries to calculate the values of software measures.

Sneed and Dombovari [18] present a system for recording models that specify requirements and object-oriented implementation of a stock broker trading system GEOS. The system also records associations between the requirements and implementation elements. It allows users to execute Ad Hoc queries and to see the results of predefined queries.

There exist attempts to use Object Constraint Language (OCL) to express queries about UML models. Some authors like Akehurst and Bordbar [19] propose to use only OCL and extend OCL, if necessary. On the other hand, Ritter and Steiert [20] present an $ORDBMS_{SQL}$ based repository of UML models. The system allows users to express design guidelines and goals as OCL expressions. The system is able to translate these constraints to integrity constraints or queries that can be used to check design goals on demand. Mahnke et al. [21] present a system that is called SERUM (Software Engineering Repositories using UML). This $ORDBMS_{SQL}$-based system allows developers to build customized repository managers for the different types of artifacts. The authors acknowledge that it is reasonable to exploit benefits of DBMSs like the use of queries. However, they do not discuss thoroughly the use of queries in their proposed system.

In conclusion, the presented reviews of systems do not discuss thoroughly query facilities or describe systems that allow users to manage and use relatively small amount of different types of artifacts or queries. Some of the authors (like [17]) propose to use generic database administration / management software to perform SQL queries about artifacts.

On the other hand, we have developed a system that can be used to create systems for managing many different types of artifacts. Its query subsystem allows developers to perform various queries about artifacts. For instance, queries can be used for finding completeness and consistency problems of artifacts. We do not use an intermediate language (like OCL) to express queries and generate SQL statements. We do not use OCL due to its complexity and limitations. For instance, OCL is not as expressive as relational calculus and cannot compute all the recursive functions [22].

Current commercial file-based CASE systems provide also limited support to model checking. For instance, CASE system StarUML™ 5.0 [23] allows developers to use a set of rules to verify models. CASE system Rational Rose™ 2003 [24] allows developers to check consistency of models. In these systems one can extend the model checking by creating *procedural* programs that read and check the models.

III. A Web-Based and Database-Based Meta-CASE System

In this section, we shortly introduce a web-based and database-based meta-CASE system. Both the meta-CASE system and the CASE systems that are created by using the meta-CASE system use an $ORDBMS_{SQL}$ as their basis. We have created a prototype of the system by using PostgreSQL™ 8.0 $ORDBMS_{SQL}$ and PHP 5.0 language.

Fig. 1 presents the general architecture of the system. The database allows us to integrate different parts of the system. At the logical level the database consists of exactly one *metamodel base*, exactly one *query base*, and zero or more *artifact bases*. We implement the metamodel base and the query base in a database as a single SQL schema, which is "a persistent, named collection of descriptors" [6]. In addition, each artifact base is implemented as a separate SQL schema. We use different schemas to prevent possible name conflicts.

The meta-CASE system allows administrators to create web-based CASE systems by using a web-based user interface. Developers (end-users) use the CASE systems to manage (create, read, update, and delete) artifacts. The administrators and developers do not have to use Java Applets or to install additional plug-ins to their computer to use the system. Specifications of CASE systems (metamodels) as well as artifacts, which have been created by using these systems, are recorded in one OR_{SQL} database. The meta-CASE and CASE systems provide currently form-based user interface.

Each CASE system, which is created by using our meta-CASE system, allows developers to create artifacts by using exactly one software language. The administrators of each new CASE system have to specify the abstract syntax of its underlying language by creating a metamodel. In addition, administrators have to register settings of the user interface and user identification of the CASE system as well as manage queries. The system records the queries in the query base. Developers can execute these queries based on artifacts.

Meta Object Facility (MOF) Specification [25] describes four-layer metadata architecture. Fig. 2 characterizes the proposed system in terms of MOF. A meta-metamodel specifies the abstract syntax of a language for specifying new metamodels. We implement the meta-metamodel layer as a set of base tables (tables) that together form the metamodel base. All these tables are in exactly one SQL schema.

The proposed system allows administrators to use exactly one meta-metamodeling language to create metamodels. We have tried to keep the language as simple as possible. In our system administrators have to specify metamodels in terms of objects and sub-objects. Therefore, the metamodel base contains tables *Object* and *Sub_object* among others.

Our system records metamodels in the tables of the metamodel base. In addition, each metamodel that is recorded in the metamodel base has exactly one corresponding artifact base, which is implemented as a separate SQL schema. If an administrator defines a metamodel *m*, then the system creates exactly one corresponding schema *s* in the database. If an administrator defines a new object *o* that belongs to *m*, then the system creates corresponding table *t* in *s*. If an administrator defines a new sub-object *so* of *o*, then the system creates corresponding column *c* in *t*. The type of *so* determines the type of *c*. If the sub-object is used to specify a relationship between *o* and *o'* (objects that both belong to *m*), then the system also creates a foreign key constraint to *c*.

The use of an $ORDBMS_{SQL}$ as the basis of the repository means that other software systems can also use the data that corresponds to M1–M3 layers. These systems can access the repository directly through the interface of the $ORDBMS_{SQL}$.

In this paper, we use SimpleM modeling language [26] as an example. The elements of this language are *State*, *StartState*, and *Event*. Fig. 3 illustrates possible data in the database, based on a CASE system for managing SimpleM models. Part a) is a metamodel that is presented as a UML class diagram. Part b) presents some true propositions about the metamodel that are recorded in the metamodel base. Part c) presents a fragment of a SimpleM model. Part d) illustrates how this fragment is recorded in the artifact base that is created based on the metamodel of SimpleM.

The proposed system has some similarities to the AP1 platform [14] and the SERUM system [21]. What are its main differences and advantages? Our system is completely web-based and does not require the installation of plug-ins to the computers of their users. AP1 provides a generic editor, which is an integrated development environment that a user must install to his/her computer. The SERUM system is used to generate repository managers, but not the systems that end-users can use to access the repositories.

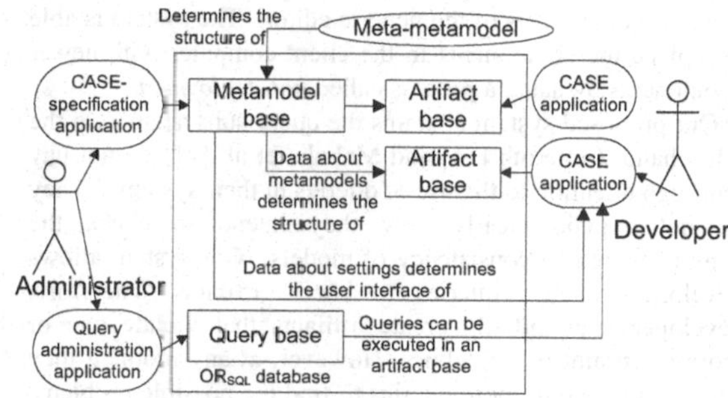

Fig. 1. Architecture of the meta-CASE system.

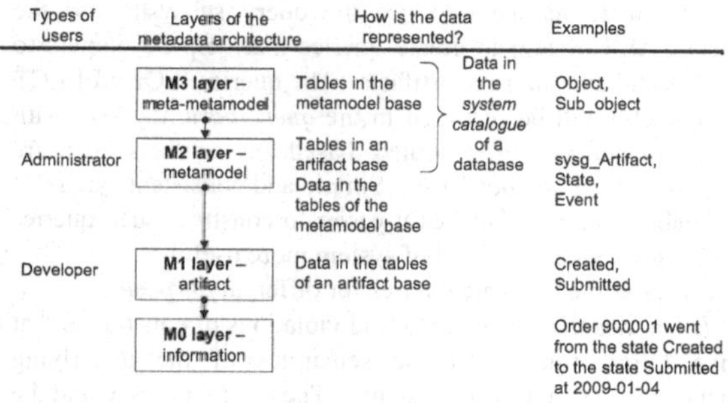

Fig. 2. Layers of the meta-CASE system.

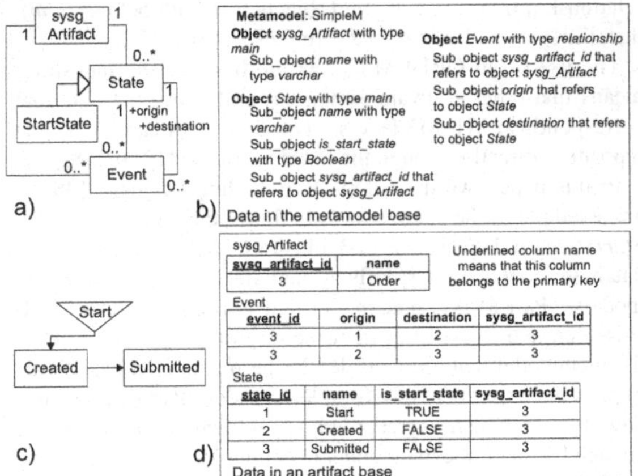

Fig. 3. An example of data in the metamodel base and in the artifact base of SimpleM models.

Our system records specifications of the user interface of the CASE systems in the metamodel base. If an administrator *ad* makes changes in the specification, then the result will be visible to developers after *ad* commits the changes. It simplifies the propagation of changes to the potential users (developers). AP1 records configuration information of the generic editor in its repository. In addition, the repository contains components of the generic editor. The system is able to replace the components in the client computer with newer components by using a process called *hot-deployment*.

Our proposed system contains the query subsystem. On the other hand, Lutteroth [14] and Mahnke et al. [21] do not pay thorough attention to the use of queries in their systems. They do not explain clearly how they intend to check the completeness and consistency of models. Our system allows developers to use queries to check artifacts. Therefore, developers can initially create artifacts that violate one or more constraint or guideline. However, at any moment they can execute one or more queries to find the possible problems and start to make gradual improvements in the artifacts.

IV. QUERY SUBSYSTEM

Administrators have to use the query subsystem of the meta-CASE system to create queries that help developers to understand and improve artifacts. The queries (SQL SELECT statements) will be recorded in the *query base*, together with their metadata, and executed based on artifacts that are recorded in an *artifact base*. Simple and consistent syntax of a database language makes it easier to construct such queries and hence makes this kind of system more useful.

It is possible to create queries for different *purposes*.

1) Queries that allow us to find violations of constraints that give information about the semantics of the underlying metamodel of a CASE system. These violations could be related to consistency or completeness of artifacts.

2) Queries for searching violations of design guidelines. Ritter and Steiert [20] distinguish global design guidelines, temporary design guidelines, and process-related design rules.

3) Queries for calculating values of software measures.

4) General queries that we cannot classify to any of the previous category.

In case of *1)* and *2)*, we can differentiate between queries that return a Boolean value (whether or not an artifact satisfies a constraint/guideline) and queries that allow us to find artifact elements that are incorrect in terms of a constraint/guideline.

Queries can have different *scope*.

1) Queries, the results of which will be found based on exactly one artifact.

2) Queries, the results of which will be found based on all the artifacts that are in one artifact base.

The *expected results* of queries have different *types*.

1) Queries, the results of which are scalar values (for instance, with type Boolean). More precisely, the results are tables with one column and zero or one row.

2) Queries, the results of which are tables where there are one or more columns and zero or more rows.

All the queries that can be used in our system have to be written by using the SQL dialect of the underlying DBMS (PostgreSQL™ in this case). If an administrator wants to check the syntax of a query, then the system tries to execute the query and reports whether it was successful or not. The system allows administrators to save and check only SELECT statements. The statements cannot contain reserved words like INSERT, UPDATE or DELETE that are not delimited (not between ""). It is needed to prevent *SQL injection* attacks.

In Table I, we present examples of queries, the purpose of which is a completeness check, the scope of which is one artifact, and the expected result of which is a scalar value. *#A#* is a placeholder. If a developer selects an artifact *af* and executes the query, then the system replaces the placeholder with the identifier of *af* before executing the query.

All the queries in Table I are Boolean queries. For each Boolean query that is recorded in the system, an administrator has to specify the expected result (value TRUE or FALSE).

TABLE I

QUERIES THAT ALLOW DEVELOPERS TO DETECT PROBLEMS OF SIMPLEM MODELS

ID	Query	Expected value
1	SELECT public.is_empty ('SELECT S.state_id FROM State S, Event E WHERE S.state_id = E.destination AND S.sysg_artifact_id = #A# AND S.is_start_state = TRUE') AS result;	TRUE
2	SELECT (SELECT Count(*) FROM State WHERE sysg_artifact_id = #A# AND is_start_state = TRUE) = 1 AS result;	TRUE
3	SELECT public.is_empty ('SELECT * FROM Event WHERE sysg_artifact_id = #A# AND origin = destination') AS result;	TRUE
4	SELECT public.is_empty ('SELECT S.state_id FROM State S, Event E WHERE S.state_id = E.origin AND S.sysg_artifact_id = #A# AND S.is_start_state = TRUE') AS result;	FALSE

If the query result is equal to the expected value, then *af* conforms to the constraint/guideline that is expressed in terms of this query, otherwise it does not conform.

Serrano [26] presents a set of constraints that give information about the semantics of SimpleM. "The StartState can only be connected to States by outgoing Events" [26]. The query is in Table I (ID=1). *is_empty* is a user-defined function that has one parameter, the expected value of which is a SELECT statement *s*. The function is in schema *public*. The function was created to simplify the creation of queries. It returns TRUE if the result of *s* contains zero rows. It returns FALSE if the result of *s* contains more than zero rows.

As you can see, the table names in the query statements are *unqualified* names. If a user executes a query that is associated with a metamodel *m*, then the system modifies the *schema search path* to ensure that the result will be found based on tables that are in the schema that corresponds to *m*.

"In a diagram there must be one and only one StartState" [26]. The query is in Table I (ID=2). In our case the diagram corresponds to the object *sysg_artifact*. In case of each metamodel in the metamodel base, the system automatically creates object *sysg_artifact* with sub-object *name* ("sysg_" like *system generated*). This object is necessary because it allows developers to create different artifacts, which are all recorded in the same artifact base and have the same metamodel. The system also automatically ensures that the tables in each artifact base (except classifier tables) contain identifiers of artifacts. It simplifies the creation of queries about a single artifact – the queries must perform the restriction operation based on column *sysg_artifact_id* (see Table I).

"Loop Events, i.e. Events that connect a State to itself, are not allowed" [26]. The query is in Table I (ID=3). "The minimum diagram is composed by a StartState connected to a State by an outgoing Event" [26]. Query 4 in Table I allows us to find whether a SimpleM model contains a StartState connected to a State by an outgoing Event.

Developers can also use queries to find elements of artifacts that have problems. For each possible problem, an administrator can create one or more queries, the scope of which is one artifact and the expected value of which is a table. For instance, the following query finds the names of the states that have associated loop events.

```
SELECT DISTINCT O.name AS result FROM Event E,
State O WHERE E.origin = O.state_id AND
E.sysg_artifact_id = #A# AND E.origin = E.destination;
```

Choinzon and Ueda [27] present a set of software design measures together with their thresholds of undesirable value. Our system supports the use of *measure defect queries* that allow developers to determine design defects based on the values of measures. For each such query *q* there are one or more non-overlapping ranges of scalar values that have the same type as the expected results of *q*. Let us assume that one of the ranges that are associated with *q* is *v1–vn*. Let us also assume that if *q* is executed in case of an artifact *af*, then the result is a scalar value *v*. If the expression (v≥v1 AND v≤vn) evaluates to TRUE, then *af* can be characterized by using the assessment that is associated with *v1–vn*. For instance, one could specify that each SimpleM model must ideally contain between 4 and 15 States. One could define the measure defect query *amount of states* that has associated ranges <4 "too few", 4–15 "reasonable amount", and >15 "too many".

```
SELECT Count(*) AS result FROM State WHERE
sysg_artifact_id = #A#;
```

Administrators can construct *tests* based on Boolean queries and measure defect queries. The scope of the queries that belong to a test must be one artifact. Developers can execute these tests in order to evaluate artifacts. Let us assume that a test *t* contains queries *q1,..., qn*. Each query in a test is a subtest of this test. For each query that belongs to *t*, administrators have to define a set of acceptable values. If a developer executes *t* in case of an artifact, then *t* fails if at least one query that belongs to *t* returns a value that does not belong to the set of acceptable values of this query.

The following query is an example of a query, the answer of which will be found based on all the artifacts that are recorded in an artifact base. It allows developers to find the average amount of states in different artifacts that are recorded in the artifact base of SimpleM models.

```
SELECT Avg(amt) AS result FROM (SELECT Count(*) AS
amt FROM State GROUP BY sysg_artifact_id) AS foo;
```

The following *general query*, the scope of which is one artifact, is used to find states that do not have outgoing events.

```
SELECT name FROM State S WHERE sysg_artifact_id=#A#
AND state_id NOT IN (SELECT origin FROM Event
WHERE sysg_artifact_id=#A# AND origin IS NOT NULL);
```

Part 1 of Fig. 4 presents SimpleM model *Order2* that violates some constraints. This model contains a loop event and the start state is the destination of one of the events.

A developer has to select queries based on their purpose. In addition, he/she has to select an artifact. Part 2 of Fig. 4 presents the result of executing the queries 1–4 from Table I based on *Order2*. A developer can execute all these queries together because their expected results are scalar (Boolean) values. For each selected query the system presents the name of the query and its result. If the result is the same as the expected result of the query, then the system displays message "correct". Otherwise it shows message "incorrect". Part 3 of Fig. 4 presents the result of executing a test based on *Order2*. The test contains queries that are presented in Table I. It also contains measure defect query *amount of states*. We defined that in the context of this test the acceptable amount of states in an artifact is between 3 and 15 (endpoints included). Hence, the model is correct in terms of this subtest. The test in general failed because its two subtests failed.

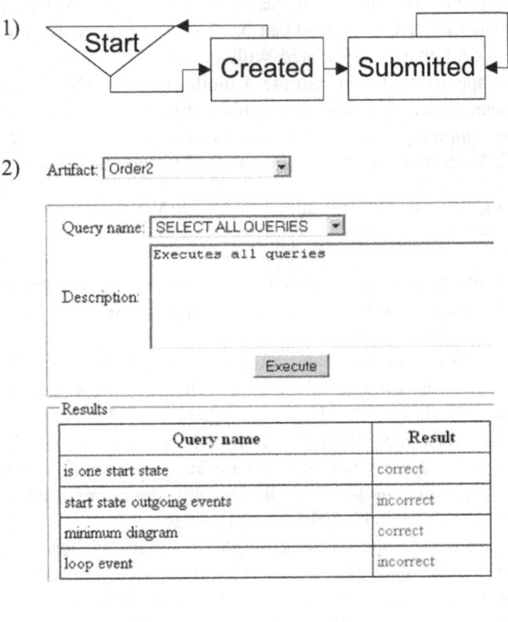

Fig. 4. Execution of queries and tests in a CASE system that is created by using the proposed meta-CASE system.

V. CONCLUSIONS

In this paper, we presented a database-based and web-based meta-CASE system that can be used to create database-based and web-based CASE systems. If someone specifies a new CASE system, then the system generates a database schema and tables based on the specification. The query subsystem allows administrators to continuously define SQL queries about artifacts and create tests based on the queries. The system allows developers to execute the queries and tests and hence to gradually improve the quality of artifacts. It is a functionality that is not well supported in current CASE systems, but is needed to produce high quality artifacts.

Future work should include formal and empirical evaluation of the system. We must extend the functionality of the CASE systems to support the versioning of artifacts and the generation of new artifacts based on existing artifacts.

This research was supported by the Estonian Doctoral School in Information and Communication Technology.

REFERENCES

[1] M. Roost, R. Kuusik, K. Rava, and T. Veskioja, "Enterprise Information System Strategic Analysis and Development: Forming Information System Development Space in an Enterprise," in *Proc. ICCI 2004*, 2004, pp. 215-219.

[2] E. Giaccardi and G. Fischer, "Creativity and evolution: a metadesign perspective," *Digital Creativity*. vol. 19, no. 1, pp. 19-32, 2008.

[3] D. Delen, N.P. Dalal, and P.C. Benjamin, "Integrated modeling: the key to holistic understanding of the enterprise," *Communications of the ACM*, vol. 48, issue 4, pp.107-112, April 2005.

[4] T. Kyte, *Expert Oracle Database Architecture: 9i and 10g Programming Techniques and Solutions*. Apress, 2005.

[5] E. Eessaar and R. Sgirka, "A Database-Based and Web-Based Meta-CASE System," in *Proc. SCSS 08*, 2009, in press.

[6] J. Melton (Ed.), ISO/IEC 9075-1:2003 (E) Information technology — Database languages — SQL — Part 1: Framework (SQL/Framework), August, 2003.

[7] "PostgreSQL 8.3.8 Documentation," [Online document] [2009 Nov 23], Available at http://www.postgresql.org/docs/8.3/interactive/index.html

[8] P.A. Bernstein and U. Dayal, "An Overview of Repository Technology," in *Proc. VLDB 1994*, 1994, pp. 705-713.

[9] R.W. Rasmussen, "A framework for the UML meta model," University of Bergen Institute for informatics, 2000.

[10] K. Dittrich, D. Tombros, and A. Geppert, "Databases in Software Engineering: A Roadmap. The Future of Software Engineering," in *Proc. ICSE'00*, 2000, pp. 293-302.

[11] P.A. Bernstein, "Applying Model Management to Classical Meta Data Problems," in *Proc. CIDR 2003*, 2003, pp. 209-220.

[12] E. Eessaar, "Integrated System Analysis Environment for the Continuous Consistency and Completeness Checking," in *Proc. JCKBSE'06*, 2006, pp. 96 -105.

[13] J.P. Gray and B. Ryan, "Integrating Approaches to the Construction of Software Engineering Environments," in *Proc. SEE 1997*, 1997, pp. 53-65.

[14] C. Lutteroth, "AP1: A Platform for Model-Based Software Engineering," in *Proc. TEAA 2006*, LNCS 4473, 2007, pp. 270-284.

[15] A. Lédeczi, M. Maroti, A. Bakay, and G. Karsai, "The Generic Modeling Environment," in *Proc. WISP'2001*, 2001.

[16] P.A. Bernstein, T. Bergstraesser, J. Carlson, S. Pal, P. Sanders, and D. Shutt, "Microsoft repository version 2 and the open information model," *Information Systems*, vol. 24, issue 2, pp. 71-98, April 1999.

[17] L. Lavazza and A. Agostini, "Automated Measurement of UML Models: an open toolset approach," *Journal of Object Technology*, vol. 4, pp. 115-134, May-June 2005.

[18] H. Sneed and T. Dombovari, "Comprehending a complex, distributed, object-oriented software System - a Report from the Field," in *Proc. Seventh International Workshop on Program Comprehension*, 1999, pp. 218-225.

[19] D.H. Akehurst and B. Bordbar, "On Querying UML Data Models with OCL," in *Proc.UML 2001*, LNCS 2185, 2001, pp. 91-103.

[20] N. Ritter and H.P Steiert, "Enforcing Modeling Guidelines in an ORDBMS-based UML-Repository," in *Proc. 2000 IRMA International Conference*, 2000, pp. 269-273.

[21] W. Mahnke, N. Ritter, and H.P. Steiert, "Towards Generating Object-Relational Software Engineering Repositories," *Tagungsband der GI-Fachtagung 'Datenbanksysteme in Büro, Technik und Wissenschaft'. Informatik aktuell, Freiburg*, pp. 251-270, März 1999.

[22] L. Mandel and M.V. Cengarle, "On the Expressive Power of OCL," in *Proc. FM'99*, LNCS 1708, 1999, pp. 854-874.

[23] "StarUML 5.0 User Guide (Verifying Model)," [Online document] [2009 Oct 03], Available at http://staruml.sourceforge.net/docs/user-guide(en)/ch09.html

[24] "Rational Rose," [Online] [2009 Oct 03], Available at http://www-01.ibm.com/software/awdtools/developer/rose/

[25] MetaObjectFacility(MOF) Specification. Version 1.4.1. formal/05-05-05

[26] J.A. Serrano, "Formal Specifications of Software Design Methods," in *Proc. 3rd Irish Workshop on Formal Methods*, 1999.

[27] M. Choinzon and Y. Ueda, "Design Defects in Object Oriented Designs Using Design Metrics," in *Proc. JCKBSE'06*, 2006, pp. 61-72.

An Intelligent Control System Based on Non-Invasive Man Machine Interaction

Darius Drungilas[1], Antanas Andrius Bielskis[1], Vitalij Denisov[1],
[1]Department of Computer Science, University of Klaipeda, 84 Manto str., 92294, Klaipeda, Lithuania
dorition@gmail.com, andrius.bielskis@ik.ku.lt, vitalij.denisov@ik.ku.lt

Abstract- **This paper presents further development of intelligent multi-agent based e-health care system for people with movement disabilities. The research results present further development of multi-layered model of this system with integration of fuzzy neural control of speed of two wheelchair type robots working in real time by providing movement support for disabled individuals. An approach of filtering of skin conductance (SC) signals using Nadaraya-Watson kernel regression smoothing for emotion recognition of disabled individuals is described and implemented in the system by R software tool. The unsupervised clustering by self organizing maps (SOM) of data sample of physiological parameters extracted from SC signals was proposed in order to reduce teacher noise as well as to increase of speed and accuracy of learning process of multi-layer perceptron (MLP) training.**

Keywords- multiple agent system control, bio-robots, distributed information systems, knowledge representation techniques, fuzzy logic, neural networks

I. Introduction

The developing process of intelligent systems with adaptive e-services is very complex and important problem, especially if the systems are aimed to provide user-friendly e-health and e-social care for people with movement disabilities. Such systems usually include different intellectual components for control and monitoring of sensors by supporting multi-agent activities and, in accordance to the recognition of certain situations, integrate the possibilities to affect and control the devices of disable persons [2, 5]. Being able both to provide an intelligent accident preventive robot-based support for people with movement disabilities and to include affect sensing in Human Computer Interaction (*HCI*), such system should depend upon the possibility of extracting emotions without interrupting the user during *HCI* [1, 3, 4, and 10]. Emotion is a mind-body phenomenon accessible at different levels of observation (social, psychological, cerebral and physiological). The model of an intelligent multi-agent based e-health care system for people with movement disabilities is recently proposed by [2]. The continuous physiological activity of disabled person is being made accessible by use of intelligent agent-based bio-sensors coupled with computers. The aim of this research is to integrate different knowledge representation techniques for further development of the reinforcement framework of interaction of intelligent remote bio robots. This framework incorporates multiple cooperative agents' whose activities are aimed at recognition and prediction of emotional situation of disabled persons (see Fig.1 and 2). The research results present further development of the concept model of physiological parameters recognition to transform exploratory analogue signal into parameters to be used by embedded intelligent control system. This system is based on intelligent fuzzy neural control of two wheelchair type robots working in real time and providing movement support for disabled individuals. The method of clustering emotional states using self organizing maps (SOM) for skin conductance (SC) parameters was proposed to reduce noise to classify data by SOM for training of multi-layer perceptron (MLP). The selected SC parameters include: a) latency, b) rise time, c) amplitude, and d) half recovery time (see Fig.5 a).

It includes two adaptive moving wheelchair-type robots which are remotely communicating with two wearable human's affect sensing bio-robots. To capture towards e-social and e-health care context relevant episodes based on humans affect stages [13], the context aware sensors are incorporated into the design of the Human's Affect Sensing Bio Robot-x (*HASBR-x*) for every disabled individual, and information based on these episodes is used by local Intelligent Decision Making Agent-x (*IDMA-x*) for control of every intelligent support providing robot. Those values are used by proposed in [5] *NN Learning Agent* on Fig.2b for learning of *Artificial NN* on Fig.2a. The output of the *Artificial NN* generates percentage value of pulse width change $\Delta PW\ (k)$ to describing how much pulse width value $PW(k)$ of the real motor speed control value should be changed at the moment k and generated in real time by the *ATmega32* microcontroller to perform online calculating of

$$PW\left(k\right)=PW\left(k-1\right)+\Delta PW\left(k\right). \quad (1)$$

The amplified signals are digitized and recorded to *Firebird* database by *ATmega Oscilloscope* [4] to be used for emotion recognition.

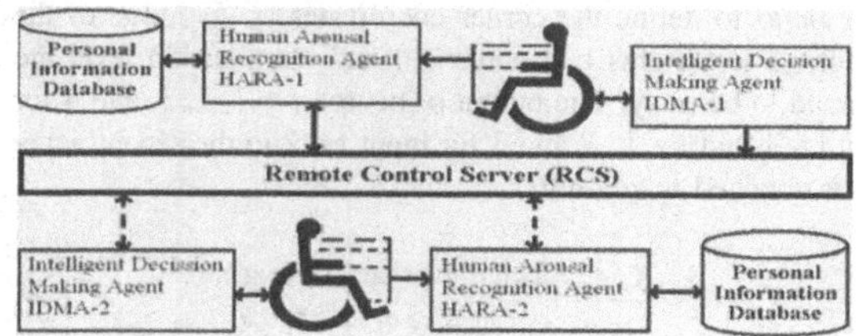

Fig.1. The reinforcement framework of an intelligent remote bio robots interaction based on distributed information systems by [2].

T. Sobh, K. Elleithy (eds.), *Innovations in Computing Sciences and Software Engineering*,
DOI 10.1007/978-90-481-9112-3_11, © Springer Science+Business Media B.V. 2010

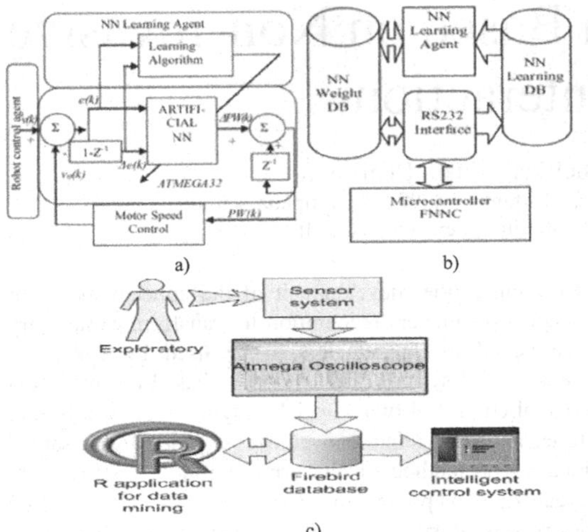

Fig.2. Multi-agent based adaptive robot motor speed control system: a) Modified agent based adaptive FNNC-type DC motor speed controller by [6], b) Agent-based NN learning system [5], and c) Intelligent instrumentation of physiological parameters recognition system.

The *R* software tool is connected to *Firebird* database, and it was used in order to extract specified information from collected data. *R* tool is used for data filtering and physiological parameters mining. The extracted information as a result is recorded to *Firebird* database to be used by Human arousal recognition agents *HARA-1* and *HARA-2* of Fig.1. The connection between *R* tool and *Firebird* database is implemented by Open Database Connectivity (*ODBC*) interface by using *sql** commands to read, save, copy and manipulate data between data frames and *sql* tables [8].

II. An Intelligent Robot Motion Control Subsystem

A simplified architecture of the neural-fuzzy controller [6] is presented on Fig.3. The layer 1 in Fig.3 represents inputs $X=e\ (k)$ and $Y=\Delta e\ (k)$ to the fuzzy neural controller, the speed error $e\ (k)$ and the change in speed error $\Delta e\ (k)\ =e\ (k)–e\ (k\text{-}1)$, respectively. The layer 2 consists of 7 input membership nodes with four membership functions, *A1, A2, A3,* and *A4,* for input *X* and three membership functions, *B1, B2,* and *B3,* for input *Y* [6], the membership value specifying the degree to which an input value belongs to a fuzzy set is determined in this layer. The triangular membership function is chosen for the change in motor speed error $\Delta e(k)$ to define the corner coordinates aj, b_j and c_j of the triangle. The weights between input and membership level are assumed to be unity. The output of neuron j = 1, 2, 3, and 4 for input i = 1 and j = 1, 2, and 3 for input i = 2 in the second layer can be obtained as follows:

$$\begin{cases} O_j^2 = \dfrac{X_i - a_j}{b_j - a_j}, & \text{for positive slope of triangle, when } X_i \geq a_j \text{ and } X_i \leq b_j \\ O_j^2 = \dfrac{X_i - c_j}{b_j - c_j}, & \text{for negative slope of triangle, when } X_i \geq b_j \text{ and } X_i \leq c_j \end{cases}, \quad (2)$$

where a_j , b_j , and c_j are the corners of the jth triangle type membership function in layer 2 and X_i is the ith input variable to the node of layer 2, which could be either the value of the error or the change in error. The layer 1 in Fig.3 represents inputs $X = e(k)$ and $Y=\Delta e(k)$ to the fuzzy neural controller, the speed error $e(k)$ and the change in speed error $\Delta e(k)=e(k)–e(k–1)$, respectively. The layer 2 consists of 7 input membership nodes with four membership functions, *A1, A2, A3,* and *A4,* for input *X* and three membership functions, *B1, B2,* and *B3,* for input *Y,* as shown in Fig.3. The weights between input and membership level are assumed to be unity. Each node in Rule layer 3 of Fig.3 multiplies the incoming signal and outputs the result of the product representing one fuzzy control rule. It takes two inputs, one from nodes *A1–A4* and the other from nodes *B1–B3* of layer 2. Nodes *A1–A4* defines the membership values for the motor speed error and nodes *B1–B3* define the membership values for the change in speed error. Accordingly, there are 12 nodes in layer 3 to form a fuzzy rule base for two input variables, with four linguistic variables for the input motor speed error $e(k)$ and three linguistic variables for the input change in motor speed change error $\Delta e(k)$. The input/output links of layer 3 define the preconditions and the outcome of the rule nodes, respectively. The outcome is the strength applied to the evaluation of the effect defined for each particular rule. The output of neuron k in layer 3 is obtained as $O_k^3 = \prod_l w_{jk}^3 y_j^3$, where y_j^3 represents the jth input to the node of layer 3 and w_{jk}^3 is assumed to be unity. Neurons in the output membership layer 4 represent fuzzy sets used in the consequent fuzzy rules. An output membership neuron receives inputs from corresponding fuzzy rule neurons and combines them by using the fuzzy operation union. This was implemented by the maximum function. The layer 4 acts upon the output of layer 3 multiplied by the connecting weights. These link weights represent the output action of the rule nodes evaluated by layer 3, and the output is given $O_m^4 = \max(O_k^3 w_{km})$, where the count of k depends on the links from layer 3 to the particular m^{th} output in layer 4 and the link weight w_{km} is the output action of the mth output associated with the kth rule. This level is essential in ensuring the system's stability and allowing a smooth control action. Layer 5 is the output layer and acts as a defuzzifier. The single node in this layer takes the output fuzzy sets clipped by the respective integrated firing strengths and combines them into a single fuzzy set. The output of the neuro-fuzzy system is crisp, and thus a combined output fuzzy set must be defuzzified. The sum-product composition method was used. It calculates the crisp output as the weighted average of the cancroids of all output membership functions as

$$O_o^5 = \left(\sum_m \left(O_m^4 ac_m \cdot bc_m \right) \right) \Big/ \left(\sum_m O_m^4 bc_m \right), \quad (3)$$

where ac_m and bc_m for m = 1, 2, .., and 5 are the centres and widths of the output fuzzy sets, respectively. The values for the bc_m's were chosen to be unity. This scaled output corresponds to the control signal (percent duty cycle) to be applied to maintain the motor speed at a constant value. The only weights that are trained are those between layers 3 and layer 4 of Fig.3. The back-propagation network is used to train the weights of this layer. The weights of the neural network were trained offline by using an open source type *R* programming environment before they were used in the online real time experimental by applying the modified learning algorithm from [6]: Step (1): Calculate the error for the change in the control signal (duty cycle) for ATmega32-based microcontroller as $E_o = T_o - O_o^5$, where E_o, T_o, and O_o^5 are the output error, the target control signal, and the actual control signal; Step (2): Calculate the error gradient

$$\delta_m = E_o \cdot \left(\left(\sum_{\substack{j=1 \\ j \neq m}}^{m-1} O_j^4 (ac_m - ac_j) \right) \middle/ \left(\sum_{j=1}^{m} O_j^4 \right)^2 \right), \tag{4}$$

where ac_i *for* $i = 1 \ldots 5$ are the centres of the output fuzzy sets and O_j^4 is the firing strength from node *j* in layer 4; Step (3): Calculate the weight correction $\Delta w_{km} = \eta \delta_m O_j^3$ to increasing the learning rate. Here Sejnowski-Rosenberg updating mechanism was used, which takes into account the effect of past weight, changes on the current direction of the movement in the weight space. This is given by

$$\Delta w_{km}(t) = \eta(1-\alpha)\delta_m O_m^3 + \alpha \Delta w_{km}(t-1), \tag{5}$$

where α is a smoothing coefficient in the range of 0…1,0, and η is the learning rate. Step (4): Update the weights

$$w_{km}(t+1) = w_{km}(t) + \Delta w_{km}(t), \tag{6}$$

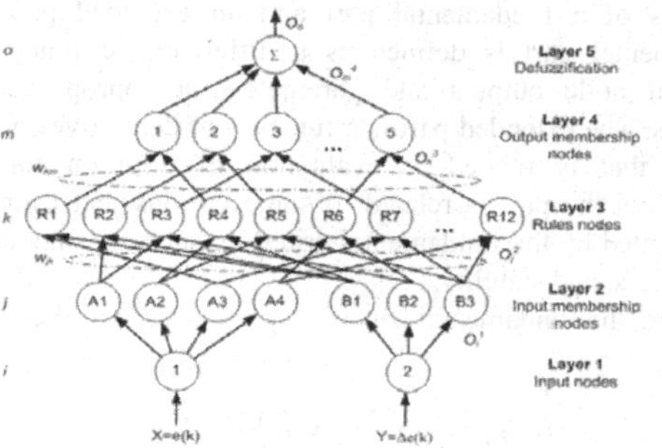

Fig.3. Architecture of the neural-fuzzy controller by [6] for DC motor speed control of wheelchair type robot

where *t* is the iteration number. The weights linking the rule layer (layer 3) and the output membership layer (layer 4) are trained to capture the system dynamics and therefore minimize the ripples around the operating point.

III. Human Computer Interactions In The System

A. Emotion Recognition and Data Mining Subsystem

The concept model of the main processes in the system of physiological parameters recognition is shown in Fig.4. The main purpose of physiological parameters recognition subsystem is to transform exploratory analog signal into physiological parameters so that they could be used by any intelligent control system, to take patient monitoring and caring.

B. Smoothing Method

Kernel regression smoothing was used to remove noise from recorded signals [7] by applying the Nadaraya–Watson estimator

$$\hat{m}(x) = \left(\sum_{i=1}^{n} K_h(x - x_i) y_i \right) \middle/ \left(\sum_{i=1}^{n} K_h(x - x_i) \right), \tag{7}$$

where $K(\cdot)$ is a function satisfying $\int K(u)du = 1$, which we call the kernel, and *h* is a positive number, which is usually called the bandwidth or window width [7]. We see the larger the bandwidth – the smoother the result. By [8], the kernels are scaled so that their quartiles (viewed as probability densities) are at +/- (0.25*bandwidth).

C. Data Analysis

From stimulus point (when emotional change occurs), four characteristics can be extracted from *SC* data: latency, rise time, amplitude and half recovery time (see Fig.5a.).

The purpose is to transform these four parameters into particular emotional state. In this case, we used eight discrete emotional states by [10] shown in Fig.5b. The clustering was done in order to make sure that the parameters classes of different states differs enough that could be used in prediction. As the errors could come from labeling the data points (teacher noise) classifying data into somewhat similar clusters can lead to noise reduction, and therefore, higher accuracy [11]. For clustering, *SOM*, unsupervised self-learning algorithm, was used, that discovers the natural association found in the data. *SOM* combines an input layer with a competitive layer where

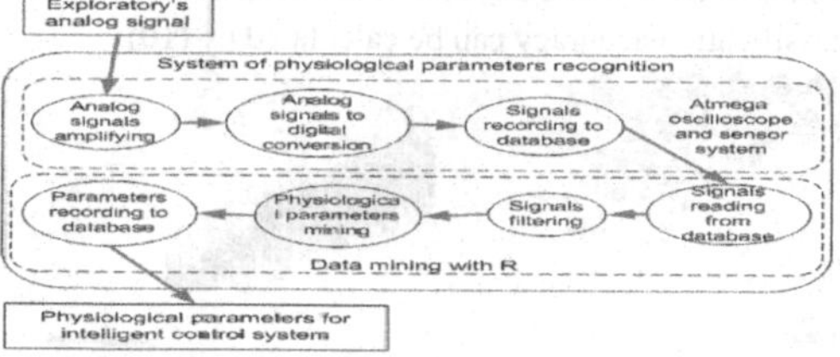

Fig.4. Concept model of physiological parameters recognition subsystem.

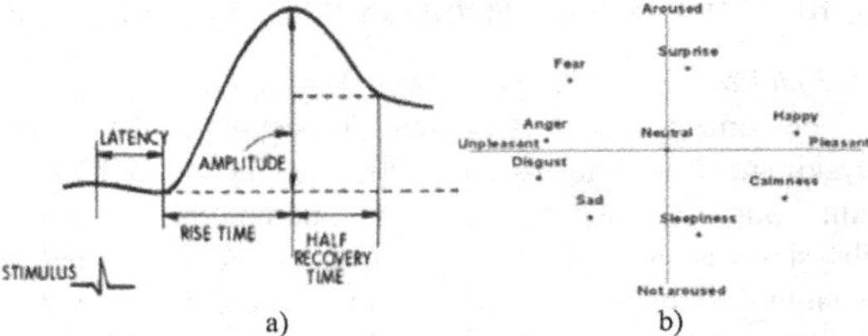

Fig.5. a) SC characteristics by [9], and b) Emotional states by [10].

the units compete with one another for the opportunity to respond to the input data. The winner unit represents the category for the input pattern. Similarities among the data are mapped into closeness of relationship on the competitive layer [12]. The *SOM* here defines a mapping from the input data space R^4 onto a two-dimensional array of units. Each unit in the array is associated with a parametric reference vector weight of dimension four. Each input vector is compared with the reference vector weight w_j of each unit. The best match, with the smallest Euclidean distance,

$$d_j = \|x - w_j\| \tag{8}$$

is defined as response, and the input is mapped onto this location. Initially, all reference vector weights are assigned to small random values and they are updated as

$$\Delta w_j = \alpha_n(t) h_j(g,t)(x_i - w_j(t)), \tag{9}$$

where $\alpha(t)$ is the learning rate at time t and $h_n(g, t)$ is the neighborhood function from winner unit neuron g to neuron n at time t. The *kohonen R* package was used to provide simple-to-use functions such as *som*, *xyf*, *bdk*, and *supersom* to define the mapping of the objects in the training set to the units of the map [13].

In Fig.6a, we can see 10x10 *SOM* grids, where each unit contains R^4 weight vector that groups *SC* parameters by similarities. The numbers represent training data classes, and colors – different clusters after training. The *SOM*'s training progress is shown in Fig.6b. The *SOM*'s units on competitive layer are arranged by similarities i.e. by distance, so the training is measured as mean distance to the closest unit.

The classification accuracy can be calculated by (10):

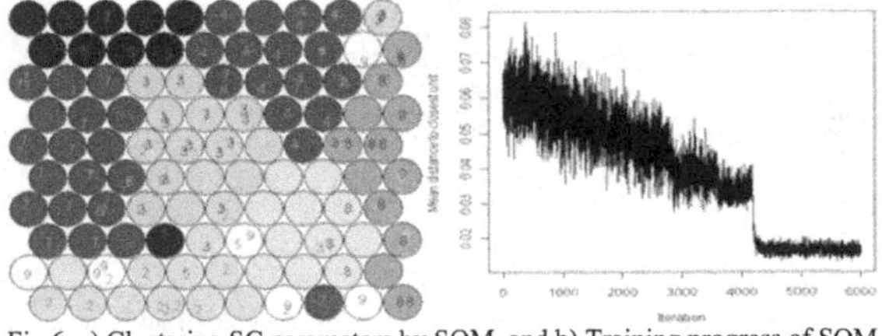

Fig.6. a) Clustering SC parameters by SOM, and b) Training progress of SOM.

$$A(h \mid X) = \frac{\sum_{i=1}^{N} h(x^i) = r^i}{N} \cdot 100\ \%, \tag{10}$$

where $h(x)$ is hypothesis of assigning x to appropriate class, r^i – experts indicated class, N – classification sample. $h(x^i) = r^i$ is equal to 1, when x^i is classified as r^i, and is equal to 0 otherwise.

D. Prediction of SC Parameters Using MLP

Prediction of discrete emotional states can be done by using multi-layer perceptron (*MLP*). As clustering data reduces noise, we will use classified data by *SOM* for *MLP* training. *MLP* was constructed by topology shown in Fig.7. It is feed forward neural network containing two hidden layers. There are four neurons in input layer for *SC* parameters and 8 neurons in output layer representing predictable states. Adaptive gradient descend with momentum algorithm was used to train *MLP*. The weights are updated as:

$$w_{ij}^l(t) = w_{ij}^l(t-1) + \Delta w_{ij}^l(t), \tag{11}$$

$$\Delta w_{ij}^l(t) = -\gamma(t)\frac{\partial E_s(t)}{\partial w_{ij}^l(t-1)} + \lambda \Delta w_{ij}^l(t-1), \tag{12}$$

where $w_{ij}^l(t)$ is the weight from node i of lth layer to node j of $(l+1)^{th}$ layer at time t, $\Delta w_{ij}^l(k)$ is the amount of change made to the connection, $\gamma(t)$ is the self-adjustable learning rate, λ is the momentum factor, $0 < \lambda < 1$, and E_S is the criterion function.

Minimizing the E_S by adjusting the weights is the object of training neural network. The criterion function E_S usually consists of a fundamental part and an extended part. The fundamental part is defined as a differentiable function of relevant node outputs and parameters at appropriate time instants. The extended part is a function of derivatives of node output that is related to evaluation of criterion function. Therefore, the part is related to some notions that cannot be represented by the fundamental criterion, such as, smoothness, robustness, and stability.

Here, the fundamental part is only considered as the

$$E_S(t) = \frac{1}{2}\sum_{i=1}^{S}\sum_{j=1}^{2}\left(y_j(t) - \hat{y}_j(t)\right)^2, \tag{13}$$

where S is the total number of training samples. The learning rate $\gamma(t)$ is usually initialized as a small positive value and it is able to be adjusted according to the following information presented to the network:

$$\gamma(t) = \begin{cases} \gamma(t-1)\cdot a_1, 0 < a_1 < 1, E_S(t) \geq E_S(t-1) \\ \gamma(t-1)\cdot a_2, a_2 > 1, E_S(t) < E_S(t-1) \end{cases}. \tag{14}$$

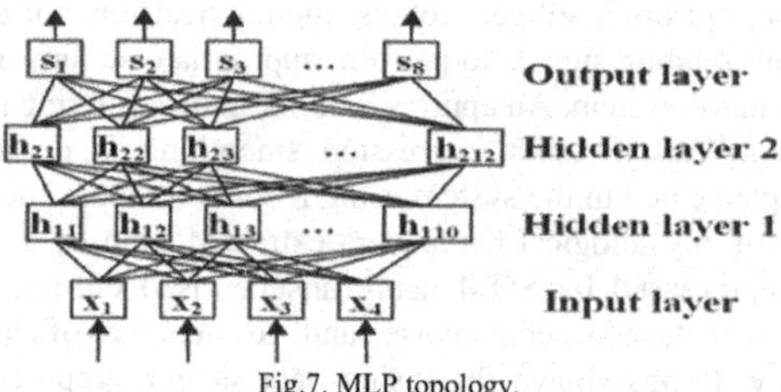

Fig.7. MLP topology.

It has to be noted that the weights only are substituted by the new weights when E_S decreases. This measure can assure the convergence of the neural network model. Repeat the training process until E_S is either sufficiently low or zero [14].

IV. Results And Discussion

A. *Smoothing of SC Signals*

For the *SC* data filtering, *R* tool's function *ksmooth()* was used which implements the Nadaraya-Watson kernel regression estimation [8]. As can be seen in Fig.8, this data smoothing, with bandwidth=9, properly removes data noises and allows to do further data analysis.

B. *Clustering of SC Parameters Using SOM*

The clustering accuracy calculated by (10) is 75.00%. It means that classes of parameters of different states differ enough to make emotional state recognition. In order to know which factor is most important for emotional state classification, the clustering with *SOM* by each factor was made and clustering accuracy was calculated. The clustering accuracies by latency, rise time, amplitude, and half recovery time were 44.70%, 52.27%, 52.27%, and 48.48% respectively. So the rise time and amplitude correlates with emotional states the most, and latency is least significant parameter for emotional state recognition. However all four *SC* parameters combined together give 22.73% higher accuracy (75.00%), than the best clustering accuracy (52.27%) by separate *SC* parameters. Fig.9 illustrates the influence of *SC* parameters on each neuron, and it proves that the clustering of emotional states by *SOM*, as shown in Fig.6a, could be made.

C. *Prediction of Emotional States from SC Parameters Using MLP*

Several packages are provided in *R* software tool to implement feed forward neural networks: *AMORE*, *nnet*, *neural* and other. In this case, the *AMORE* package was used as it provides the user with an unusual neural network simulator.

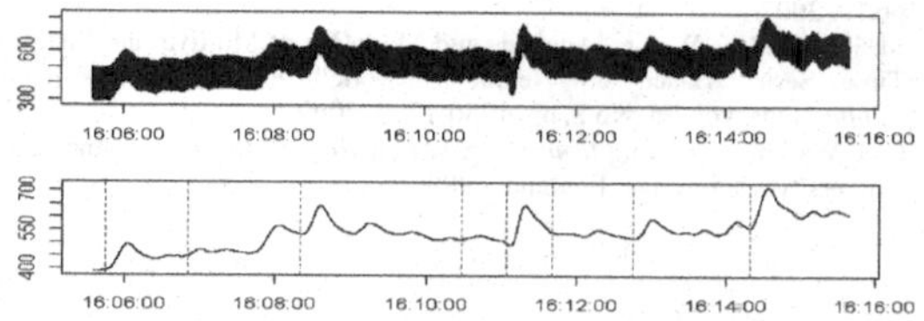

Fig.8. SC signal filtering using Nadaraya-Watson kernel regression smoothing.

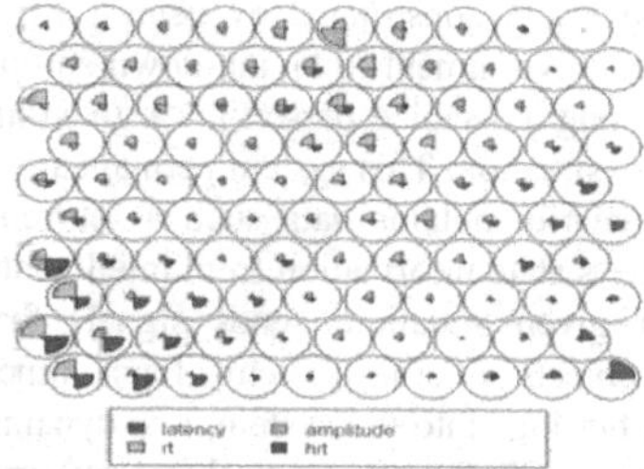

Fig.9. Influence of SC parameters on each neuron of the SOM

It is a highly flexible environment that should allow the user to get direct access to the network parameters, providing more control over the learning details and allowing the user to customize the available functions in order to suit their needs. The package is capable of training a multilayer feed forward network according to both the adaptive and the batch versions of the gradient descent with momentum back propagation algorithm.

Thanks to the structure adopted, expanding the number of available error criteria is as difficult as programming the corresponding *R* costs functions [13]. For experiment, two samples were used each containing training and testing data – 60% and 40% of all data sample respectively. First training sample was made from *SOM*'s predicted data, second – from data not processed by *SOM*. *MLP* training progress using *AMORE* package is shown in Fig.10 for the first and the second training samples – bold and thin lines respectively. As we see, training is much faster for the first training sample. So it was useful to preprocess training samples of *MLP* with *SOM*, as *MLP* easier finds the pattern. Another good point of training sample preprocessing with *SOM* is that *MLP* classification accuracy increases by 2.27% from 47.73% to 50.00%.

D. *Reasoning Algorithms Used by Human Arousal Recognition Agents*

Human Computer Interaction (*HCI*) in the system was realized in providing of necessary e-health care support actions for *user1* and *user2* discovered in the *Personal Information Databases* of Fig.1. To proposing of precisely controllable social care aware movement actions by robot 1 and 2 for given user with movement disabilities, a real-time *Off-Policy Agent Q-learning algorithm* [15] was used:

$$Q(s,a) \leftarrow Q(s,a)+\alpha[r+\gamma max_{a'} Q(s',a')-Q(s,a)]. \quad (15)$$

It was implemented by using multi-agent based human computer interaction system, proposed in [2].

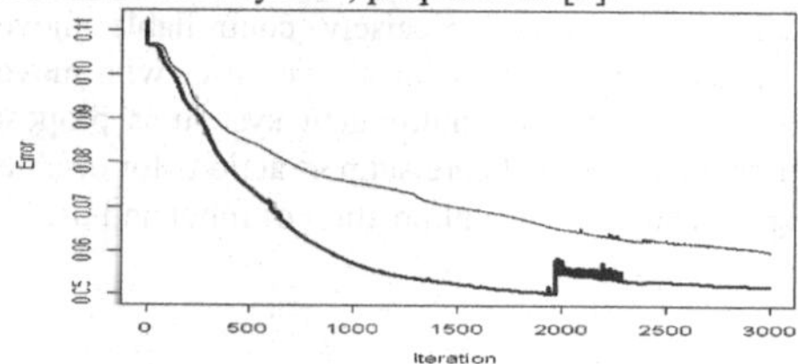

Fig.10. MLP training errors for different training samples

The system was constructed by using *Java*–based *JACK* agent oriented environment to laying-down an optimal path of robot in assisting a disabled person for a given his/her arousal context aware situation. This system permanently performs the following scenario: obtains data such as current position of robot and user's state information from intelligent robots; finds decision for given situation; sends signals for appropriate actions to objects of the system. Each time when new intelligent robot logs into the system, two dynamic agents, the *Dispatcher* and *RCS* (Remote Control System) are created. The *Dispatcher* is responsible for TCP/IP–based communications between logged robot and system. When *Dispatcher* gets new message it creates an event *NewMessage*. The *NewMessage* has capability *IdentifyMessage* to recognizing what data obtained and where it was delivered. Then an event *NewCondition* is created for an agent *RCS* that controls an intelligent robot and sends data to the object which is found necessary to be updated in a given context aware situation. By using new data as well as saved person's e-health history data obtained, one of 4 plans is performed. If plans *BadCondition* or *CriticalCondition* are being selected each plan creates 3 new events: *GoToBed, AskHelp,* and *InformDoctor.* If situation of any individual in the system becomes critical a help message is sent to both of intelligent robots of the system. By given scenario, if such message is obtained a plan *InformationMessage* of the agent *Dispatcher* is performed. It then creates an event *HelpFriend.* If a necessity of providing such a help is discovered the plan *FinDirection* obtains coordinates where the disabled individual was being delivered, and another robot is directed to this place for providing social care aware help.

Conclusion

An approach is proposed in creating of an intelligent e-health care environment by modelling of an adaptive multi-agent-based e-health and e-social care system for people with movement disabilities. Human's Arousal Recognition Module is described based on online recognition of human's skin conductance (SC parameters) by using embedded Atmega32 type microcontrollers. Multi-agent based online motion control of two wheelchair-type robots is realized by real-time adaptive Fuzzy Neural Network Control algorithm, integrated into *ATmega32* microcontroller. Human Computer Interaction in the system is implemented within *Java*–based *JACK* agent oriented environment and was used to provide necessary e-health care support actions for users with some movement disabilities. A real-time Off-Policy Agent Q-learning algorithm was used to provide of precisely controllable movement actions by social care robots for a given user with movement disabilities. The dynamic multi-agent system is proposed to realize permanent e-social care support actions for disabled by: gathering data such as current position of robot and user's state information from intelligent robots; finding decisions for given situation; sending signals to perform appropriate actions of the objects in the system. An approach of *SC* signals filtering using Nadaraya-Watson kernel regression smoothing is described and implemented in the system using *R* software tool. The data sample of physiological parameters extracted from *SC* signals was preprocessed by SOM using unsupervised clustering in order to reduce teacher noise and to achieve of higher accuracy. It was shown that using data sample preprocessed with *SOM*, the learning process in *MLP* training is much faster than using not preprocessed data sample. The proposed approach of data preprocessing also increases accuracy of *MLP* based classification of human emotional states by 2.27%.

References

[1] A. Bielskis, V. Denisov, G. Kučinskas, O. Ramašauskas, and N. Romas. "Modeling of Human Physiological Parameters in an E-Laboratory by SOM Neural Networks", *Elektronika ir elektrotechnika* , vol. 3 , No 75, pp.77-82 ,2007.

[2] A. Bielskis, V. Denisovas, D. Drungilas, G. Gricius, and O. Ramašauskas. "Modeling of Intelligent Multi-Agent based E-health Care System for People with Movement Disabilities", *Elektronika ir elektrotechnika*, vol.6, No 86, pp.37-42, 2008.

[3] A.A. Bielskis, D. Dzemydiene, V. Denisov, A. Andziulis, and D. Drungilas. "An Approach of Multy-Agent Control of Bio-Robots Using Intelligent Recognition Diagnosis of Persons with Moving Disabilities". *Technological and Economic Development of Economy*, vol. 15, No 3, pp. 377-394, 2009.

[4] G. Gricius, and A.A. Bielskis. "Development of "ATmega Oscilografas" as a Device for Autonomous Emotion Recognition System". *Journal of Management,* vol.1, No 14, pp. 89-106, 2009.

[5] G. Gricius, D. Drungilas, A. Šliamin, K. Lotužis, and A.A. Bielskis. "Multi-Agent-Based E-Social Care System for People with Movement Disabilities". *Technological Research Works in Western Lithuania*, vol.6, pp. 67-77, 2008.

[6] A. Rubaai, A.R. Ofoli, L.Burge, and M. Garuba. "Hardware Implementation of an Adaptive Network-Based Fuzzy Controller for DC–DC Converters", *IEEE Trans. on Ind. Appl.*, vol. 41, No 6, pp. 1557-1565, 2005.

[7] S. Zhang, and X.F. Huang. "An Improved Kernel Regression Method Based on Taylor Expansion", *Applied Mathematics and Computation,* vol. 193, No 2, pp. 419-429, 2007.

[8] R Development Core Team. "R: A Language and Environment for Statistical Computing", *R Foundation for Statistical,* URL http://www.R-project.org, 2008.

[9] P. Wang, and H. McCreary. "EDA sensor". URL http://courses.cit.cornell.edu/ee476/FinalProjects/s2006/hmm32_pjw32/index.html, 2006.

[10] J. A. Russell. "A Circumplex Model of Affect", *Journal of Personality and Social Psychology* , vol. 39, No 6, pp. 1161–1178, 1980

[11] M.R Amin-Naseri, and A. Soroush. "R Combined Use of Unsupervised and Supervised Learning for Daily Peak Load Forecasting", *Energy Conversion and Management,* vol. 49, No 6, pp. 1302-1308, 2008.

[12] M.L. Talbi, and A. Charef. "PVC Discrimination Using the QRS Power Spectrum and Self-Organizing Maps", *Computer Methods and Programs in Biomedicine*, vol. 94, No 3, pp. 223-231, 2009.

[13] R. Wehrens, and L.M.C. Buydens. "Self- and Super-Organizing Maps in R: the Kohonen Package", *Journal of Statistical Software*, vol. 21 No 5, pp.19, 2007.

[14] M. Han, and Y. Wang. "Analysis and Modeling of Multivariate Chaotic Time Series Based on Neural Network", *Expert Systems with Applications*, vol. 36, No 2, pp. 1280-1290, 2009.

[15] C. J. Watkins. *Learning from Delayed Rewards: PhD thesis*. Cambridge University, Cambridge, England, 1989.

A UML Profile for Developing Databases that Conform to the Third Manifesto

Erki Eessaar
Department of Informatics, Tallinn University of Technology,
Raja 15, 12618 Tallinn, Estonia
eessaar@staff.ttu.ee

***Abstract*- The Third Manifesto (TTM) presents the principles of a relational database language that is free of deficiencies and ambiguities of SQL. There are database management systems that are created according to TTM. Developers need tools that support the development of databases by using these database management systems. UML is a widely used visual modeling language. It provides built-in extension mechanism that makes it possible to extend UML by creating profiles. In this paper, we introduce a UML profile for designing databases that correspond to the rules of TTM. We created the first version of the profile by translating existing profiles of SQL database design. After that, we extended and improved the profile. We implemented the profile by using UML CASE system StarUML™. We present an example of using the new profile. In addition, we describe problems that occurred during the profile development.**

I. Introduction

The concept "data model" is semantically overloaded. One of its meanings is that it is an abstract programming language that describes data structures, constraints, and operators that can be used in many different databases. In this paper, we denote the data model that is specified in The Third Manifesto (TTM) [1] as OR_{TTM}. TTM uses generic concepts *variable*, *value*, *type*, and *operator* to define the relational data model. According to TTM each database is a set of relational variables (relvars). Users of a database perform operations to assign new values (relations) to these variables and to derive new values based on the values of relvars. Tutorial D is a database language that has been created based on OR_{TTM}.

SQL is a well-known implementation of the relational data model. The SQL-standard specifies both the data model and its corresponding database language. In this paper, we denote the underlying data model of SQL [2] as OR_{SQL}.

UML is a widely used visual language for describing requirements and design of systems [3]. It is possible to extend UML in a lightweight manner by creating *profiles* (by specializing the semantics of standard UML metamodel elements) that consist of stereotypes (specific metaclasses), tag definitions (standard metaattributes), and constraints [3]. UML is used in the context of Model Driven Architecture [4], according to which it is possible to generate program code based on UML models by using a sequence of transformations. There exist extensions of UML that allow developers to describe the design of OR_{SQL} databases [5, 6, 7]. It is possible to generate SQL code based on these models. There exist database management systems that are based on the principles of OR_{TTM} [8, 9]. However, currently there are no specific modeling methods and tools for the development of OR_{TTM} databases. If developers can use UML for designing OR_{TTM} databases, then they can use existing UML CASE systems and their existing knowledge of UML.

The *first goal* of the paper is to present a *UML profile* that allows developers to design OR_{TTM} databases by using a visual modeling language. The *second goal* of the paper is to discuss problems that occurred during the development of the profile. The *third goal* is to present a metamodel of the metamodel-based translation method [10], which was used to create the first version of a UML OR_{TTM} profile.

Each metamodel describes abstract syntax of a language. In [10], we introduced a method for creating first versions of UML profiles by using metamodel-based translation. We also presented a *partial* UML OR_{TTM} profile as an example of the use of the method. In this paper, we present a *more complete* profile and discuss the problems that occurred during its development. We also present a metamodel of the translation method. This metamodel can be used as a basis to create a system that assists the translation process.

The paper is organized as follows. *Firstly*, we present a UML OR_{TTM} profile. *Secondly*, we present a metamodel of the method that was used to create the first version of the profile. *Thirdly*, we explain the problems that occurred during the development of the profile. *Fourthly*, we present an example of using the profile. *Finally*, we conclude and point to the future work with the current topic.

II. A UML OR_{TTM} Profile

We use a format, which is similar to the one used by Mora et al. [11], to present the new profile. For each *stereotype*, we present its name, base class (UML metamodel element, based on which the stereotype is defined), a short informal description, a list of constraints (in a natural language), and a list of tag definitions that are associated with the stereotype. We plan to use textual stereotype display and hence we do not present special icons for the stereotypes.

For each *tag definition*, we present its name, the type of its possible values, and a short informal description. One also has to specify the maximum number of values that can be associated with a tag definition in case of a model element [11]. The maximum number is 1 in case of all the tag definitions in the profile.

T. Sobh, K. Elleithy (eds.), *Innovations in Computing Sciences and Software Engineering*,
DOI 10.1007/978-90-481-9112-3_12,

A. Stereotypes of Class

Name: User-defined scalar type

Base class: Class

Description: Classes of this stereotype represent scalar types that have been created by users. A scalar type is a type with no user-visible components. However, it has one or more possible representations and these possible representations *do have* user-visible components [13].

Constraints:

All attributes of a User-defined scalar type must be Component.

A User-defined scalar type must have at least one Component.

All operations of a User-defined scalar type must be Type constraint.

Name: Tuple type

Base class: Class

Description: Classes of this stereotype represent tuple types, which are nonscalar types that have user-visible, directly accessible components [13]. Each tuple type has the form TUPLE {H} where {H} is a heading.

Constraints: Tuple types cannot have operations.

All attributes of a Tuple type must have multiplicity 1.

Attributes of a Tuple type cannot have initial values.

Name: Relation type

Base class: Class

Description: Classes of this stereotype represent relation types, which are nonscalar types that have user-visible, directly accessible components [13]. Each relation type has the form RELATION {H} where {H} is a heading.

Constraints: Relation types cannot have operations.

All attributes of a Relation type must have multiplicity 1.

Attributes of a Relation type cannot have initial values.

Name: Base relvar

Base class: Class

Description: Classes of this stereotype represent relational variables that are not defined in terms of other relational variables [14].

Constraints:

All attributes of a Base relvar must have multiplicity 1.

All operations of a Base relvar must be Candidate key or Foreign key.

A Base relvar must have at least one Candidate key.

Tag definitions. Name: init_relational_expression

Type: UML::Datatypes::String

Description: "An expression denoting a relation" [14, p80]. It specifies the initial value of the base relvar and must have the same type as the relvar.

Name: Snapshot

Base class: Class

Description: Classes of this stereotype represent relational variables that are defined in terms of other relational variables and have their own separately materialized copy of data [14].

Constraints:

All attributes of a Snapshot must have multiplicity 1.

All operations of a Snapshot must be Candidate key or Foreign key.

A Snapshot must have at least one Candidate key.

Tag definitions. Name: relational_expression

Type: UML::Datatypes::String

Description: "An expression denoting a relation" [14, p80]. A relation with heading {H} is a value that has the relation type RELATION {H}.

Name: now_and_then

Type: UML::Datatypes::String

Description: Specifies when the snapshot is refreshed – its current value is disregarded and the relational expression is reevaluated to find the new current value of the snapshot [13].

Name: Virtual relvar

Base class: Class

Description: Classes of this stereotype represent relational variables (relvars) that are defined in terms of other relvars but have not their own separately materialized copy of data [13].

Constraints:

All attributes of a Virtual relvar must have multiplicity 1.

All operations of a Virtual relvar must be Candidate key or Foreign key.

A Virtual relvar must have at least one Candidate key.

Tag definitions. Name: relational_expression

Type: UML::Datatypes::String

Description: "An expression denoting a relation" [14, p80].

Name: Set of constraints

Base class: Class

Description: Classes of this stereotype represent collections of integrity constraints in a database.

Constraints: A Set of constraints cannot have attributes.

All operations of a Set of constraints must be Relvar constraint or Database constraint.

Name: Set of operators

Base class: Class

Description: Classes of this stereotype represent collections of user-defined read-only and update operators in a database.

Constraints: A Set of operators cannot have attributes.

All operations of a Set of operators must be User-defined read-only operator or User-defined update operator.

B. Stereotypes of Attribute

Name: Component

Base class: Attribute

Description: These attributes represent user-visible components of a possible representation of a scalar type [13].

Constraints: The multiplicity of a Component must be 1.

Components of a User-defined scalar type cannot have initial values.

Components can only be associated with User-defined scalar types.

Tag definitions. Name: name_of_possrep

Type: UML::Datatypes::String

Description: The name of a possible representation, the part of which is the current component. Each scalar type has one or more possible representations.

C. Stereotypes of Operation

Name: User-defined read-only operator

Base class: Operation

Description: Operations of this stereotype represent user-defined operators that update no variables (except maybe local to the implementation) but return a value [14].

Constraints: A User-defined read-only operator must have exactly one parameter with ParameterDirectionKind = return. All other parameters must have ParameterDirectionKind = in. An operator must not have two or more parameters with the same name.

Name: User-defined update operator

Base class: Operation

Description: Operations of this stereotype represent user-defined operators that update at least one variable, which is not local to the implementation, but return no value [14].

Constraints: All the parameters of a User-defined update operator must have ParameterDirectionKind = in. An operator must not have two or more parameters with the same name.

Tag definitions. Name: subject_to_update

Type: UML::Datatypes::String

Description: A comma-separated list of names of parameters that are subject to update – the expected values of each such parameter is the name of a variable that must get a new value due to the invocation of the operator. The order of the names in the list is unimportant.

Name: Candidate key

Base class: Operation

Description: Operations of this stereotype represent integrity constraints that specify unique identifiers [14].

Constraints: A Candidate key must have zero parameters.

Tag definitions. Name: attributes_in_key

Type: UML::Datatypes::String

Description: A comma-separated list of names of attributes of the relvar that form the key. The order of the names in the list is unimportant.

Name: Foreign key

Base class: Operation

Description: Operations of this stereotype represent referential constraints (foreign key constraints) [14].

Constraints: A Foreign key must have zero parameters.

Tag definitions. Name: attributes_in_key

Type: UML::Datatypes::String

Description: A comma-separated list of names of attributes of the relvar that form the foreign key. The order of the names in the list is unimportant.

Name: referenced_relvar

Type: UML::Datatypes::String

Description: The name of a relvar that is the referenced (parent) relvar in the context of the foreign key constraint.

Name: referenced_relvar_key

Type: UML::Datatypes::String

Description: A comma-separated list of names of attributes of the referenced relvar R that form a candidate key of R. The order of the names in the list is unimportant.

Name: on_delete

Type: UML::Datatypes:Enumeration {no action, cascade, set default}

Description: The compensating action that a database management system (DBMS) must perform to keep referential integrity if the value of the referenced relvar is changed in a way that the new value does not contain one or more tuples.

Name: on_update

Type: UML::Datatypes::Enumeration {no action, cascade, set default}

Description: The compensating action that a DBMS must perform to keep referential integrity if the value of the referenced relvar is changed in a way that in the new value, one or more tuples have new candidate key values.

Name: Type constraint

Base class: Operation

Description: These operations represent specifications that define the set of values that make up a given type [14].

Constraints: A Type constraint must have zero parameters.

Tag definitions. Name: boolean_expression

Type: UML::Datatypes::String

Description: An expression that denotes a truth value [14].

Name: name_of_possrep

Type: UML::Datatypes::String

Description: The name of a possible representation, the part of which is the current constraint.

Name: Relvar constraint

Base class: Operation

Description: Operations of this stereotype represent integrity constraints that refer to exactly one relvar [14].

Constraints: A Relvar constraint must have zero parameters.

Tag definitions. Name: boolean_expression

Type: UML::Datatypes::String

Description: An expression that denotes a truth value [14].

Name: Database constraint

Base class: Operation

Description: These operations represent integrity constraints that refer to two or more distinct relvars [14].

Constraints:

A Database constraint must have zero parameters.

Tag definitions. Name: boolean_expression
Type: UML::Datatypes::String
Description: An expression that denotes a truth value [14].

In addition, there is a constraint that the components of a possible representation of a scalar type (components in short) as well as the attributes of a tuple type, a relation type, or a relational variable must have unique names within a class that is used to represent it. All components, attributes, and parameters must have a type. One cannot use Base relvars, Virtual relvars, Snapshots, Sets of constraints, and Sets of operators as types of components, attributes or parameters. Recursively defined scalar types and headings are not permitted [1]. A scalar type or a heading is recursively defined, if it is defined, directly or indirectly, in terms of itself.

D. Other Extensions

We implemented the profile in StarUML™ (ver. 5.0) CASE system as a module [15]. The system allows us to define new diagram types and to determine model elements that can be used on a diagram. One can create a program by using JScript to check models based on the constraints.

We defined two types of diagrams.

Type Design Diagram (TDD). It is created based on a class diagram. It is possible to describe User-defined scalar types, Tuple types, and Relation types on this kind of diagram.

Relvar Design Diagram (RDD). This diagram is created based on a class diagram. It is possible to describe Base relvars, Virtual relvars, Snapshots, Sets of constraints, and Sets of operators on this diagram.

We can also use Notes and NoteLinks on both diagrams.

TTM states that the only scalar type that is required by the relational model is BOOLEAN. In addition, each database management system can provide more system-defined scalar types. Definition of a new profile in StarUML™ can contain specification of data types (these are system-defined scalar types). Based on [1], we defined the following types in the profile: BOOLEAN, CHAR, INTEGER, and REAL.

If one wants to use a type that is not a system-defined scalar type, then he/she must specify it on a TDD. Each type can be used as the type of a component of a scalar type, the type of an attribute of a relvar, relation type or a tuple type, or the type of a parameter of an operator. On the other hand, if one wants to define a new relvar, then he/she must not specify the relation type of the relvar on a TDD. In case of a base relvar one has to specify the attributes of the relvar and possibly its initial value (as a tagged value). In case of a virtual relvar or a snapshot one has to specify attributes as well as the relational expression and register the latter as a tagged value.

III. Development of a New Profile

We used a metamodel-based translation method [10] to create the first version of a UML OR_{TTM} profile. Firstly, we introduce the notation that we use in the next sections.

P – a non-empty set of source profiles, based on which we want to create a new profile. We use SQL profiles [5, 6, 7] as the source profiles. p' – the *candidate* profile that will be created by translating profiles that belong to P.

In this paper, we present a UML OR_{TTM} profile, the first version of which was created by using the metamodel-based translation. L – the language that is represented by all the profiles that belong to P. L is OR_{SQL} in case of this paper. L' – the language that is represented by p'. L' is OR_{TTM} in case of this paper. The profiles in P and the metamodel of L must use the same natural language (in this case English). S and S' denote the set of stereotypes in P and p', respectively. s and s' denote a stereotype that belongs to S and S', respectively.

L and L' may have more than one metamodel that are created for different purposes (teaching, code generation etc.). One has to select one of the metamodels of L and one of the metamodels of L' to create a new profile by using the metamodel-based translation [10]. The idea of the metamodel-based translation method of profiles [10] is that each stereotype and tag definition in profiles in P should *ideally* have a corresponding element in the selected metamodel of L. Let M denote the set of elements of the metamodel of L that have one or more corresponding elements in profiles in P. During the translation one has to find elements in the selected metamodel of L', which are semantically equivalent or similar to the elements in M. After that one has to describe p' based on these elements of the metamodel of L' (see Fig. 1). We used metamodels of OR_{SQL} and OR_{TTM} and a mapping between the metamodels that is specified in [12].

For instance, Marcos et al. [5] present stereotype <<ROW type>>. It has the corresponding metaclass *Row type* in a metamodel of OR_{SQL} [12]. The corresponding metaclass in a metamodel of OR_{TTM} [12], which represents semantically similar concept, is *Tuple type*. Therefore, the resulting profile of OR_{TTM} has stereotype <<Tuple type>>.

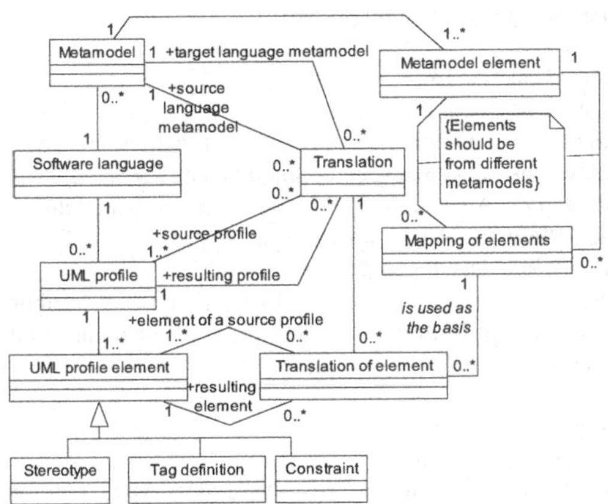

Fig. 1. A metamodel of a metamodel-based translation method of UML profiles.

IV. Problems During the Profile Development

It is possible that one cannot create some stereotypes by using translation. What could be the reasons of that?

It is possible that the source language L does not use a concept, based on which to find a corresponding element in the metamodel of L' and hence to create s'. For instance, reference [1] does not mention *snapshots* but Date [13] foresees the possibility to use them in the context of OR_{TTM}. Therefore, we included them to the profile. Some OR_{SQL} DBMSs allow developers to create *materialized views*. This concept is semantically similar to the concept *snapshot*. However, OR_{SQL} does not specify materialized views [2]. SQL standard contains a specification of a language opportunity according to which "[t]the next edition of the SQL standard should standardize the syntax and semantics of materialized views" [2, Notes–22]. Hence, we did not find stereotype <<Snapshot>> as a result of translation.

It is possible that the source language L uses a concept, based on which it is possible to find a corresponding element in the metamodel of L' and hence to create s'. However, the profiles in P do not contain a corresponding stereotype s, based on which to create s'. For instance, OR_{TTM} prescribes the use of relation types (a kind of data type) that have the general form RELATION {H} where {H} is a heading. Each such type is created by invoking the relation type generator operator. The concept *relation type* is semantically similar to *table type* in OR_{SQL} [12]. The profiles [5, 6, 7] do not specify stereotype <<Table type>>. Hence, we did not find stereotype <<Relation type>> as a result of translation.

SQL [2] specifies *assertions* that are used to constrain values in one or more tables. The corresponding concept in OR_{TTM} is *database constraint* that constrains values of two or more relational variables [12]. The profiles [5, 6, 7] do not specify stereotype <<Assertion>>. Hence, we did not find stereotype <<Database constraint>> as a result of translation.

It is also possible that one cannot create a profile element in p' based on elements of profiles in P. For instance, Gornik [7] proposes to use tagged values that are associated with columns to indicate whether the column is mandatory (prohibits NULLs) or optional (allows NULLs). In contrast, TTM prohibits the use of NULLs to represent missing data. Hence, one does not need similar tag definition in a UML OR_{TTM} profile. Another example is stereotype <<Index>> [7]. An index is a physical data structure that supports faster data access [7]. The relational data model does not prescribe how to implement a database at the physical level. Hence, there is no need for stereotype <<Index>> in a UML OR_{TTM} profile.

UML forces us to represent some OR_{TTM} constructs in a way that is not consistent with the principles of OR_{TTM}. The OR_{TTM} profile contains stereotypes <<Relation type>> and <<Tuple type>>. The following description is based on <<Relation type>>, but the same is true in case of the <<Tuple type>> as well. <<Relation type>> as well as <<User-defined scalar type>> are created based on the metamodel class (metaclass) *Class*. TTM proposes a statement for creating scalar types. On the other hand, there is nwo separate statement for creating relation types. A relation type is created automatically if the *relation type generator* operator is invoked. This invocation occurs if one defines a variable, expression, component, attribute, or parameter with a relation type. However, representing <<Relation type>> based on *Class* may give a wrong impression that there is also a possibility for creating a relation type for the later usage (just like a scalar type). We had to define <<Relation type>> based on *Class* because otherwise it will not be possible to show in a consistent manner that a component, an attribute or a parameter has a relation type.

The profile specifies stereotypes <<Set of constraints>> and <<Set of operators>> to allow us to *group* integrity constraints (relvar and database constraints) and operators, respectively. On the other hand, TTM does not specify this kind of constructs.

The name of a relation type is RELATION {H} where {H} is the heading. Heading is "[a]a set of attributes, in which (by definition) each attribute is of the form <*A*, *T*>, where *A* is an attribute name and *T* is the type name for attribute *A*" [14, p47]. Therefore, users of the OR_{TTM} profile cannot give an artificial name to a relation type. For instance, if the heading is {person_code CHAR, last_name CHAR}, then the name of the relation type is RELATION {person_code CHAR, last_name CHAR}. As you can see, one has to specify attributes in the name of the relation type. The same is true in case of tuple types. The name of a tuple type is TUPLE {H} where {H} is the heading.

One has to make decisions during the development of a profile. For instance, an existing SQL profile [7] defines stereotypes for primary key <<PK>> and foreign key <<FK>>. TTM suggests that each relvar must have one or more candidate key and that it is not necessary to mark one of the keys as the most important (primary) key. Therefore, we did not create a stereotype or a tag definition for specifying *primary keys* in case of the OR_{TTM} profile. Each relvar has one or more candidate keys. We decided to define <<Candidate key>> as a stereotype that can be associated with an operation. According to TTM each relvar must have at least one candidate key. Therefore, one must be allowed to specify keys in case of base relvars as well as virtual relvars and snapshots. This is different from UML SQL profiles where one can define keys only in case of base tables.

The profile contains stereotypes <<Relvar constraint>> and <<Database constraint>> that allow developers to define constraints. On the other hand, candidate key and foreign key constraints are special kind of relvar constraints or database constraints. Hence, there is a question whether it is necessary to create separate profile elements (stereotypes or tag definitions) for certain types of constraints. We decided to do so due the importance of these particular constraints. Any given relvar has at least one candidate key [1]. TTM strongly suggests that a database language must provide some declarative shorthand to represent foreign key constraints [1].

The profile requires some *redundancy* in the specification of a database. If one defines a virtual relvar or a snapshot, then he/she must a) describe the attributes of the relvar and b) describe the relational expression that is associated with the relvar. The attributes of the relvar can also be found by evaluating the expression. The profile has this redundancy because a SQL profile [7] uses the same approach – one has to define the columns of a view as well as specify the underlying SELECT statement of the view. It means that there can be inconsistencies between different parts of a specification of the same database. Therefore, the users of the profile must be extra careful. Another redundancy is in case of relation types and tuple types. If one defines this kind of type, then a) he/she must specify the heading as a part of the name of the type and b) describe the attributes that belong to the heading as attributes of the class. We decided to use this kind of approach in order to minimize the amount of exceptions in the profile. If one can define attributes in case of a virtual relvar, then it must also possible in case of a relation type.

V. An Example of Using the Profile

We created the example based on an example that is presented by Marcos et al. [5]. On Fig. 2, we define user-defined scalar type *AddressType* and relation type *RELATION {id_c_room INTEGER, building CHAR, campus CHAR}*. *AddressType* has one possible representation named *address* with four components. The possible representation has a type constraint, according to which *number* must be a positive integer. The Boolean expression of the constraint is *number>0*. On Fig. 3, we use the types to define base relvar *Teacher* that has one candidate key. Attribute *address* has type *AddressType*. Attribute *reserves* has a relation type.

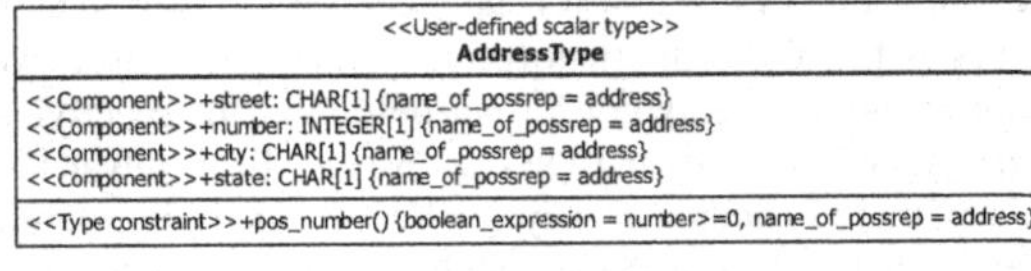

<<Relation type>>
RELATION {id_c_room INTEGER, building CHAR, campus CHAR}
+id_c_room: INTEGER[1]
+building: CHAR[1]
+campus: CHAR[1]

Fig. 2. An example of Type Design Diagram.

<<Base relvar>>
Teacher
+id_teacher: INTEGER[1]
+name: CHAR[1]
+e_mail: CHAR[1]
+address: AddressType[1]
+reserves: RELATION {id_c_room INTEGER, building CHAR, campus CHAR}[1]
<<Candidate key>>+key_teacher() {attributes_in_key = id_teacher}

Fig. 3. An example of Relvar Design Diagram.

VI. Conclusions

Developers are familiar with UML and there exists many UML CASE systems. Therefore, if there are new approaches to database development, then it would be useful to still use UML for specifying the design of databases. UML provides a lightweight, built-in extension mechanism that allows developers to extend UML by creating profiles.

The Third Manifesto (TTM) describes the relational data model and tries to avoid problems that are associated with SQL. In this paper, we presented a UML profile for developing databases that correspond to the rules of TTM. It is a candidate profile that must be accepted by interested parties. We created the first version of the profile by using a metamodel-based translation method. In this paper, we presented a metamodel of this method. We also discussed some problems and questions that rose during the development of the new profile. In conclusion, it is possible to design OR_{TTM} databases by using UML. However, UML forces us to represent some OR_{TTM} constructs in a way that is not consistent with the principles of OR_{TTM}.

The future work must include empirical studies of the use of the profile. One has to create a code generator for generating database language statements based on OR_{TTM} database design models. If the underlying data model of the profile evolves, then the profile must also be changed accordingly. We also have to extend the profile to support the subtyping and inheritance that one can use to define new types.

References

[1] C.J. Date and H. Darwen, *Databases, Types and the Relational Model*, 3rd ed.. Addison Wesley, 2006.

[2] J. Melton (Ed.), IWD 9075-2:200x (E) Information technology — Database languages — SQL — Part 2: Foundation (SQL/Foundation). April, 2006.

[3] Object Management Group, Unified Modeling Language: Superstructure, version 2.1.1, formal/2007-02-03. February 2007.

[4] MDA Guide Version 1.0.1, OMG document omg/03-06-01, 2003.

[5] E. Marcos, B. Vela, and J.M. Cavero, "A Methodological Approach for Object-Relational Database Design using UML," *Journal on Software and Systems w*, vol. 2, pp. 59-72, 2003.

[6] S.W. Ambler and P.J. Sadalage, *Refactoring Databases: Evolutionary Database Design*. Addison Wesley, 2006.

[7] D. Gornik, "UML Data Modeling Profile," Rational Software White Paper TP162, 05/2002.

[8] D. Voorhis, "An Implementation of Date and Darwen's Tutorial D database language," [Online document] [2009 June 29], Available at http://dbappbuilder.sourceforge.net/Rel.php

[9] "Dataphor," [Online document] [2009 June 29], Available at http://dataphor.org

[10] E. Eessaar, "On Translation-Based Design of UML Profiles," in *Proc. SCSS 07*, 2008, pp. 144-149.

[11] S.L. Mora, J. Trujillo, and I.Y. Song, "Extending the UML for Multidimensional Modeling," in *Proc. UML 2002*, 2002, LNCS 2460, pp. 290-304.

[12] E. Eessaar, *Relational and Object-Relational Database Management Systems as Platforms for Managing Software Engineering Artifacts*, Ph.D. thesis, Tallinn University of Technology, 2006. Available at http://digi.lib.ttu.ee/i/?85

[13] C.J. Date, *An Introduction to Database Systems*, 8th ed.. Boston: Pearson/Addison Wesley, 2003.

[14] C.J. Date, *The Relational Database Dictionary*. O'Reilly, 2006.

[15] "StarUML – The Open Source UML/MDA Platform," [Online document] [2009 June 29], Available at http://staruml.sourceforge.net

Investigation and Implementation of T-DMB Protocol in NCTUns Simulator

Tatiana Zuyeva
Saint-Petersburg State University of Aerospace Instrumentation
Saint-Petersburg, Russia
tatiana.zuyeva@gmail.com

Adnane Cabani, Joseph Mouzna
ESIGELEC/IRSEEM
Saint-Etienne du Rouvray, France
cabani@esigelec.fr
mouzna@esigelec.fr

***Abstract*- Investigation of T-DMB protocol forced us to create simulation model. NCTUns simulator which is open source software and allows addition of new protocols was chosen for implementation. This is one of the first steps of research process. Here we would like to give small overview of T-DMB (DAB) system, describe proposed simulation model and problems which we have met during the work.**

Keywords: T-DMB; Digital Radio; NCTUns.

I. Introduction

T-DMB (Terrestrial Digital Multimedia Broadcasting) [1][2] is a mobile television service that targets mobile devices such as mobile phones, handheld and portable devices. Nowadays one of the most popular topics in investigation of transmission system is a transmission of data on high speed. In our work we are analyzing transmission of data using T-DMB protocol on high speed. The first step which was defined in this research is implementation of T-DMB in NCTUns simulator. This system uses DAB transmission system (Digital Audio Broadcasting), therefore here we are talking about implementation of DAB system.

II. Overview of DAB Transmission System

DAB transmission system is designed to carry several digital audio signals together with data signals. From the view point of 7-layers OSI model DAB system as well as T-DMB can be represented in 3 layers: Presentation layer, Data link layer, Physical layer. In such hierarchy presentation layer is charged with work of audio codecs, data link layer is responsible for forming of DAB transmission frame and on physical layer coding and decoding schemes defined by the protocol are working. Step by step work of DAB transmission system is shown on Figure 1.

In this overview we will point only most important parts for our implementation of this process.

Data coming from presentation layer is multiplexed according to DAB frame format (which is exactly the same for

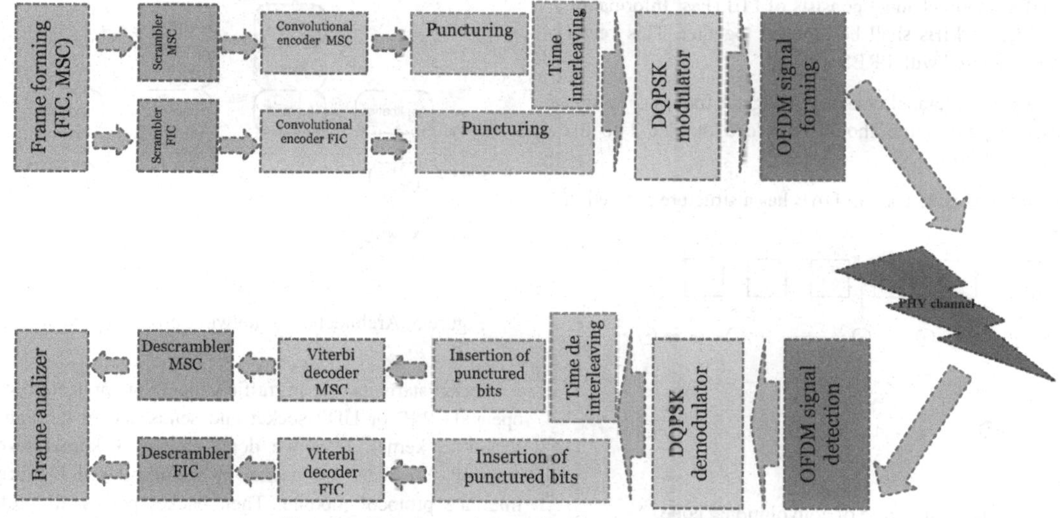

Figure 1. Forming and detecting process of DAB system.

T. Sobh, K. Elleithy (eds.), *Innovations in Computing Sciences and Software Engineering*,
DOI 10.1007/978-90-481-9112-3_13, © Springer Science+Business Media B.V. 2010

T-DMB system) on Data link layer. Then Energy Dispersal scrambler, Convolutional encoder with puncturing procedure and Time-interleaver work on Physical layer. The DAB transmission frame consist of three channels (Figure 2): synchronization channel, fast information channel used for rapid access of information by a receiver and main service channel used to carry audio and data service components.

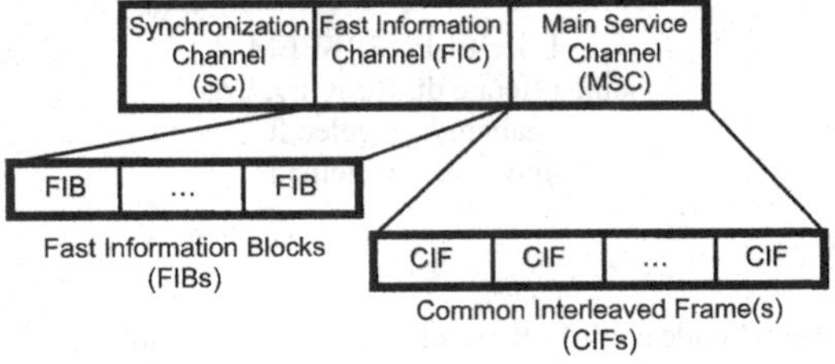

Figure 2. DAB (T-DMB) transmission frame structure.

In order to ensure appropriate energy dispersal in the transmitted signal, the individual inputs of energy dispersal scramblers shown in Figure 3 shall be scrambled by a modulo-2 addition with a Pseudo-Random Binary Sequence (PRBS).

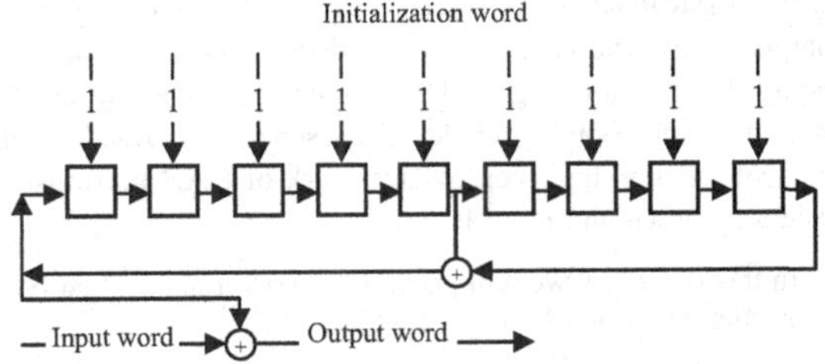

Figure 3. Energy dispersal scrambler structure.

Fast information channel consists of FIB (Fast Information Blocks). Every 3 FIBs shall be grouped together. This vector should be scrambled with PRBS.

Main Service Channel consists of logical frames. The first bit of each logical frame should be added modulo-2 to the PRBS bit of index 0.

Convolutional code used in DAB has a structure showed in Figure 4.

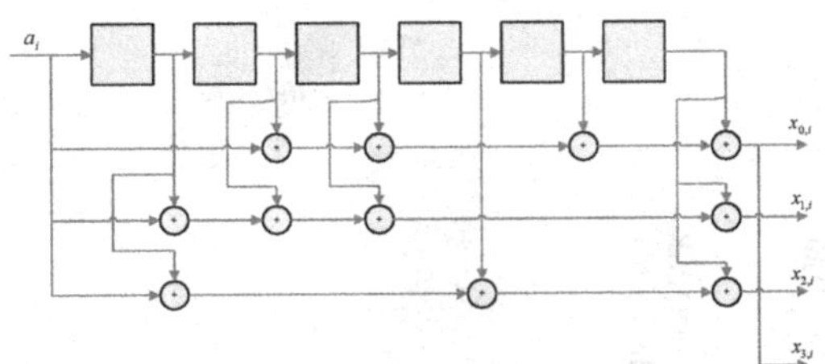

Figure 4. Structure of convolutional code.

DAB system uses the same code in FIC and MSC. Puncturing procedure is applied for both of channels: MSC and FIC.

Scheme shown in Figure 1 was implemented in NCTUns simulator. We used schemes mentioned above to form appropriate message. We would like to point in decoding process Viterbi algorithm was used.

III. OVERVIEW OF NCTUNS SIMULATOR

NCTUns simulator [3][4] is open source network simulator and emulator. This simulator works under Linux platform. Through a set of API functions provided by its simulation engine, we can develop a new protocol module and add the module into the simulation engine. The simulation engine could be described as a small operating system kernel. It performs basic tasks such as event processing, timer management, packet manipulation, etc. Its API plays the same role as the system call interface provided by an UNIX operating system kernel. By executing API functions, a protocol module can request service from the simulation engine without knowing the details of the implementation of the simulation engine.

NCTUns provides a module-based platform. A module corresponds to layer in a protocol stack. Modules can be linked together to form protocol stack to be used by a network device. We can insert a new module into existing protocol stack, delete an existing module from a protocol stack, or replace an existing module in a protocol stack with own module. So, we can control and change the behavior of a network device. Architecture of network protocol simulation is shown on Figure 5.

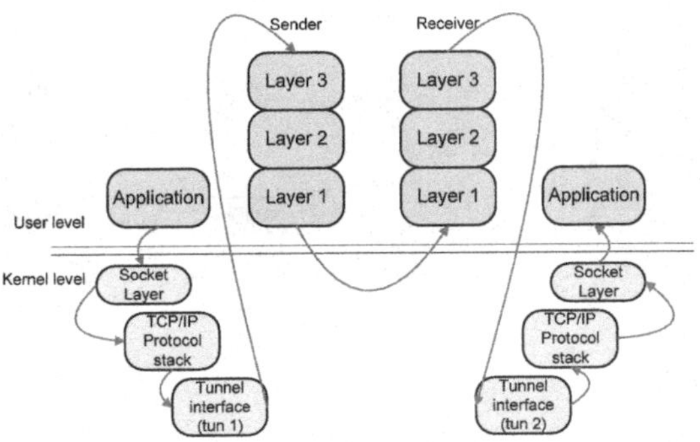

Figure 5. Architecture of network protocol simulation.

Packet starts its way in traffic generating application which opens TCP/IP or UDP socket and sends packet through this socket to kernel. Here we don't care how kernel level is working. We meet our packet in Module-Based Platform in Interface protocol module. Then packet passes all protocol modules from one node to second. After that Interface protocol module of second node puts packet to kernel level. Application on receiving side (here it is also called a traffic generator) waits for incoming packet on its TCP/IP or UDP socket. Combination of API function send() and recv() in module moves packet through all simulated modules from sender to receiver.

Packet-object is used to encapsulate sending packing to well-known format in NCTUns. Figure 6 illustrates example of encapsulating data into Packet-Object. PT_INFO, PT_DATA and PT_SDATA are memory buffers that are called "Packet Buffer" or "pbuf". The "pbuf" is most basic unit in a Packet-Object. Default length for each "pbuf" is 128 bytes. But PT_DATA and PT_SDATA pbuf allows using cluster buffer. For PT_DATA pbuf the size of cluster is 1024 bytes. The size of cluster for PT_SDATA is unlimited. In DAB transmission system we have to work with packet which has big size. Therefore the best way for us to use PT_SDATA type pbuf and keep frame in the cluster that has unlimited size.

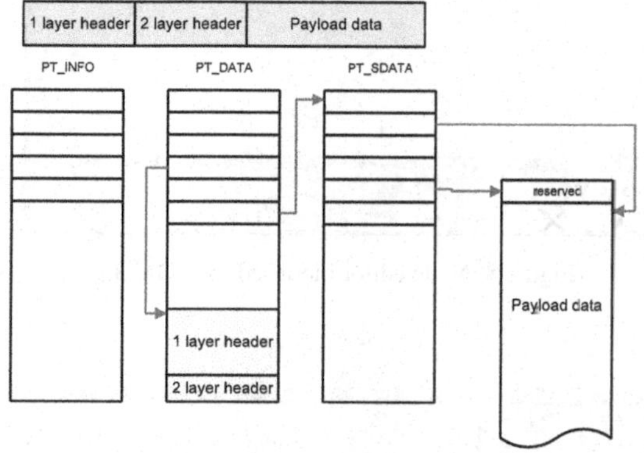

Figure 6. Encapsulating data into Packet-Object.

One of the benefits of NCTUns simulator is friendly GUI which allows user create different network topologies and observe simulation process.

IV. IMPLEMENTATION MODEL

Implementation process can be divided on two parts. First part is creation of new module in NCTUns and embedding it into simulator, second part is adjusting of GUI according to new module.

Because NCTUns provides module based platform, first we should represent DAB transmission system in terms of module. The topology of network using T-DMB assumes that we have two types of nodes: Base Station (BS) that only transmit information broadcast and Subscriber Station (SS) that receives information and tries to make decision if packet is correct or not. One module called OFDM_TDMB will perform both of these functions. Keeping in mind structure (Figure 5) of NCTUns we propose following approach of node's protocol stack based on 3-Layers model defined in previous close (Figure 7):

Application stg generates packet and send it to tunnel interface. Packet goes through Interface module. We receive packet from Interface module and create packet according to DAB frame structure.

Function send() of TDMB module generates Packet-Object with such data inside, performs scrambling, encoding (according to code from Figure 4) and puncturing procedures, attaches it to ePacket object and then sends to next layer. All procedures are implemented according to standard. Some points were given in previous close.

On receiving side, recv() function, whenever it receives a packet, starts a timer rvTimer to simulate transmission time. When rvTimer expires recvHandler() function is called. This function performs insertion of punctured bits with 0 value. After that it calculates BER (Bit Error Rate) for used modulation and adds error bit in received sequence. Finally decoding and descrambling procedures are applied. This function also is responsible for logging of not collided packets. Log file contains following information: current time, packet id, BER applied for this packet, number of errors occurred in the channel, number of error bits (which were not corrected during decoding).

We have made changes in GUI. TDMB topology is based on graphical objects for 802.11(p) network nodes: one is the

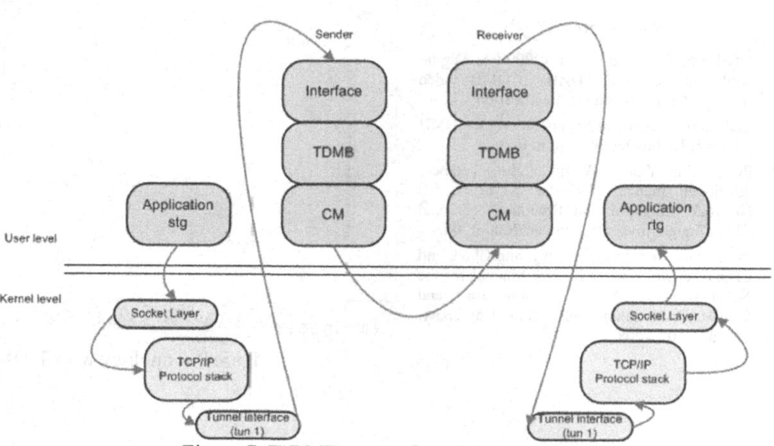

Figure 7. T-DMB protocol module approach.

802.11 (p) on-board unit (OBU) which represents a vehicle equipped with radio receiver; the second is the 802.11(p) road-size unit (RSU) which represents a fixed device with radio transmitter. To change these nodes to TDMB receiver and transmitter we have to change protocol stack in this nodes, using Node Editor. Therefore new units have been added to Node Editor. Node Editor allows us to delete existing blocks and insert new blocks for every type of Nodes. Figure 8 illustrates TDMB protocol stack in Node Editor. Here we can see all the layers which have been mentioned above: interface, TDMB (called OFDM_T_DMB) and CM layer which simulates physical transmission layer and responsible for calculating SNR (Signal to Noise Ratio). CM and Interface layers are reused from Simulator and don't have any changes.

Investigated topology consist of one T-DMB Base station (RSU) and car with T-DMB receiver. We set up moving path for car. When simulation is started car starts to move with speed 10 m/sec defined by default settings. stg application sends packet every 1 sec. Figure 9 illustrates the topology. Car keeps moving till end of path and then stays on the same position. If Base station continues to transmit data car will receive it but without moving.

When simulation process is over NCTUns generates tdmblog file and put it in appropriate directory. Format of file is following: Time, Packet ID, Bit Error Ratio, Number of occurred Errors and Number of Errors after decoding.

V. Conclusion and Future Work.

Possibilities of created model are very limited nowadays. However it has some benefits. Implementation in NCTUns simulator allows user to work with very friendly GUI. Also this work increases NCTUns simulator functionality and can make it interesting for more researchers. Future work assumes to compare results of practical experiments with simulation results.

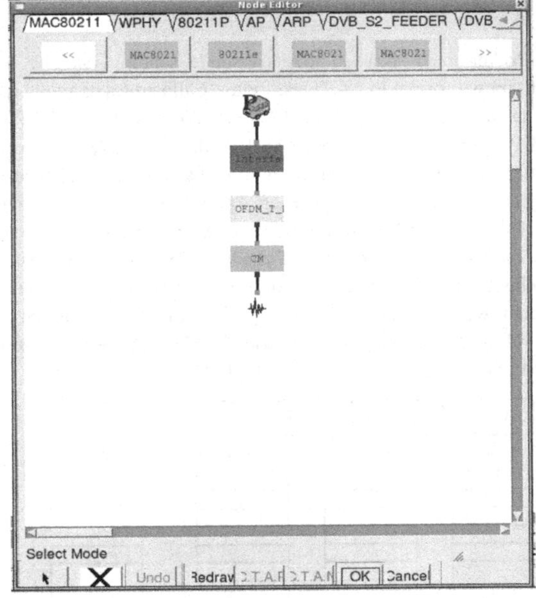

Figure 8. Node editor modified for TDMB.

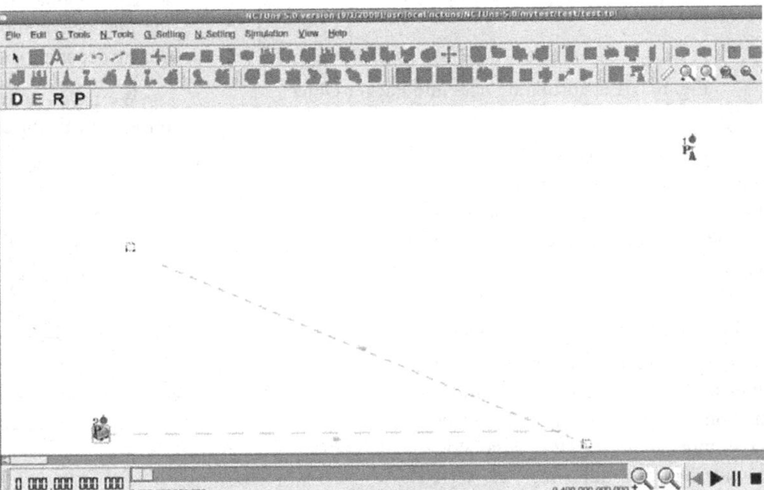

Figure 9. Topology with T-DMB nodes and moving path.

References

[1] ETSI EN 102 428 v1.2.1 (2009-04) Digital Audio Broadcasting (DAB) ; DMB video service ; User application specification.

[2] TDF 2008, Technical Specifications for DMB – Digital Radio Deployment in France.

[3] Prof. Shie-Yuan Wang "The protocol developer manual for the NCTUns 5.0 Network Simulator and Emulator" National Chiao Tung University, Taiwan 2000-2008.

[4] Prof. Shie-Yuan Wang, Chih-Liang Chou, and Chih-Che Lin "The GUI User Manual for the NCTUns 5.0 Network Simulator and Emulator", National Chiao Tung University, Taiwan 2000-2008.

Empirical Analysis of Case-Editing Approaches for Numeric Prediction

Michael A. Redmond[1], Timothy Highley[1]

Abstract– **One important aspect of Case-Based Reasoning (CBR) is Case Selection or Editing – selection for inclusion (or removal) of cases from a case base. This can be motivated either by space considerations or quality considerations. One of the advantages of CBR is that it is equally useful for boolean, nominal, ordinal, and numeric prediction tasks. However, many case selection research efforts have focused on domains with nominal or boolean predictions. Most case selection methods have relied on such problem structure. In this paper, we present details of a systematic sequence of experiments with variations on CBR case selection. In this project, the emphasis has been on case quality – an attempt to filter out cases that may be noisy or idiosyncratic – that are not good for future prediction. Our results indicate that Case Selection can significantly increase the percentage of correct predictions at the expense of an increased risk of poor predictions in less common cases.**

Index Terms: case-based reasoning, case editing, numeric prediction, case selection.

I. Introduction

Case-Based Reasoning (CBR) has been an active research area and has been used successfully in many practical applications. In CBR, previous examples or cases are used to solve future similar problems. Generalizations of the CBR process include the CBR Cycle [1]. In the CBR Cycle, stages include: Retrieve – identify previous similar case(s), Reuse – identify the answer or solution that can be transferred from the previous case to the current situation, Revise – adapt the previous solution to differences between the previous situation and the current situation, and Retain – store the current situation and solution as a new case. A more detailed discussion of basic CBR methodology is not included here. Interested readers desiring extended introduction can review basic CBR methodology in [2], [3], and [4]. In CBR, it has been widely acknowledged that not all cases should be retained. Depending on perspective, the choice of which cases to retain could be part of the Retain stage (in incremental learning approaches, not all new cases need necessarily be retained), or as part of an additional Review stage (if the approach is a batch / retrospective approach). Perhaps due to interest in cognitive modeling, early research (e.g. [5]) focused on incremental approaches. With more recent interest in Data Mining, more efforts have used retrospective review of an existing "full" collection of cases. While not receiving nearly as much attention as feature selection/weighting, case selection has received a significant amount of research. Much of that research has been motivated by space considerations – how can a CBR system obtain as good performance while retaining only a fraction of the available cases. An alternative perspective is an emphasis on quality – can prediction accuracy be improved via removing some cases, presumably via removal of anomalous or noisy cases? This latter perspective puts the focus not on removing large numbers of cases, but rather on removing the proper set of cases.

CBR presents several advantages over other learning / data mining approaches in prediction tasks. One of these is that CBR easily uses all types of variables (versus some other models which are limited to binary, nominal, ordinal, or interval variables). Most importantly, CBR can accommodate prediction of all types of variables. However, most research efforts in case selection have been carried out in domains in which predictions are of a given class (nominal or binary). The algorithms generally reflect that in their search bias. In this research, a fairly simple CBR approach has been used to make numeric predictions[1], and research has focused on case selection. In this work, the focus is on non-incremental approaches from the case-base quality perspective, all for a numeric prediction domain: community crime rate prediction.

A. Background

Case selection/editing is a problem that has received considerable attention. However, most of the existing work in this area differs from what is presented in this paper because the previous work either focuses on reducing the size of the case base rather than finding anomalies, or it uses an approach that is inherently tied to nominal predictions instead of numeric predictions.

Case selection research pre-dates CBR. Wilson [6] presents an approach to case-editing where a case is assumed to be noisy if it disagrees with a majority of its *k*-nearest neighbors (*k*=3 typically), and is removed. This work has influenced many succeeding efforts and is a common standard for comparison.([7], [8]; [9]; [10]).

More recent case selection algorithms include Aha's [2] IB3; Wilson and Martinez's [8],[9] RT3 / DROP-3; Smyth and McKenna's [11] case-base competence model; Brighton and Mellish's [10] Iterative Case Filtering (ICF); Morring and Martinez 's [12] Weighted Instance Typicality Search; Massie,

Manuscript received October 12, 2009.

Both authors are with La Salle University, Philadelphia, PA 19141 USA (corresponding author M.A. Redmond phone: 215-951-1096; e-mail: redmond@ lasalle.edu).

[1] Numeric prediction is called "regression" by some researchers, after the statistical technique long used for it

T. Sobh, K. Elleithy (eds.), *Innovations in Computing Sciences and Software Engineering*, DOI 10.1007/978-90-481-9112-3_14, © Springer Science+Business Media B.V. 2010

Craw and Wiratunga's [13] Threshold Error Reduction algorithm; and Pasquier, Delany, and Cunningham's [14] Blame-Based Noise Reduction. All of these algorithms or approaches include the assumption that predictions are classifications. In some cases, the inclusion is of a nature of "if the prediction is correct" as part of the algorithm. In others, it is more fundamental, for instance with pseudocode including "loop through possible classes." The latter obviously are more difficult to adjust to use in numeric prediction.

The research presented in this paper attempts to pursue case selection / filtering with the goal of noise reduction in a knowledge-poor, non-incremental numeric prediction task. As Wilson's [6] algorithm is mostly consistent with the goals of this research, and is still competitive with the most successful approaches, and is used as part of some of the most successful approaches, it made sense to investigate converting that approach to be used with numeric prediction. A series of variations was tried, along with a new algorithm.

II. EXPERIMENTAL METHODOLOGY

The researchers utilized data about communities within the United States gathered by the first author and first used for [15]. The data combines socio-economic data from the 1990 United States Census [16], law enforcement data from the 1990 Law Enforcement Management and Administrative Statistics survey [17], and crime data from the 1995 FBI Uniform Crime Report [18]. The datasets needed to be combined via programming; details of this process are discussed in [16]. The researchers chose any potentially relevant variables for inclusion as independent variables (features) (N=122), plus the attribute to be predicted (Per Capita Violent Crimes). The per capita violent crimes variable was calculated using population and the sum of crime variables considered violent crimes in the United States: murder, rape, robbery, and assault. In order to avoid using incorrect/missing "answer" attribute values, 221 cases were removed, leaving 1994.

Prior to the current work, all features were normalized to be in the range from 0 to 1. This removes any issues with the scale of the variables. The resulting dataset has been made available at the UCI machine learning dataset repository: http://archive.ics.uci.edu/ml/datasets/Communities+and+Crime [19].

All experiments followed a 10-fold cross validation methodology. Thus, in each experiment, for each fold being tested, there are approximately 1795 training cases and 199 test cases. During testing, in addition to calculating the mean absolute error for each prediction, a threshold was established to judge "correct" or "incorrect." Any prediction within 5% of the actual value was judged to be "correct"[2]. The results are averaged across the results from each of the 10 folds to get a mean of mean absolute error and mean percent correct. All tests were done on the same randomly generated folds, so paired sample statistics can be used.

[2] As will be seen, during training one of the aspects varied was the threshold for cases "agreeing". During testing a threshold for a "very good" prediction was desired for judging "correctness" percentage.

III. CBR EXPERIMENTS

In order to predict crime rates, the researchers first pilot tested a small variety of simple nearest neighbor methods. In terms of the common CBR terminology, none of the experiments involved use of "Adaptation," ("Revise") or complex "Retrieval," such as using "Indexing." The k-nearest neighbor approach to CBR retrieval ([20], [21]), sometimes referred to as instance-based learning, was used for all CBR experiments. Based on the best results from pilot testing, the baseline ("no editing") approach was to use k-nearest neighbor with similarity for attributes combined via "Euclidean" (or "Crow Flies") metric in which difference for a case is the sum of the squared differences. Prediction is done using a weighted average; nearer neighbors have more impact on the prediction than do more distant neighbors. This no editing approach will be compared to the editing approaches.

A. Initial Experiments

The initial experiments are attempts to convert Wilson's [6] Edited Nearest Neighbor algorithm to handle numeric prediction. In Wilson's method, instances are removed that do not agree with the majority of their k-nearest neighbors. With numeric prediction (especially without adaptation), some metric for "agree" is needed. In the experiments to follow, two thresholds were established and experimented with. First is the "agreeThreshold" that sets how close the numeric dependent variable values have to be in order to consider the cases to "agree" with each other. The second is the "acceptThreshold" that sets what percentage of neighbors have to "agree" with the case in order for it to be kept[3].

The first numeric conversion of Wilson's algorithm (henceforth NWF1) is shown in Figure 1. This process is carried out for each fold in the 10-fold cross validation experiments. Each training case is compared to its k nearest neighbors. Based on the threshold for agreement, the percentage of neighbors who "agree" with the training case is calculated. If the percentage agreeing with the training case is below the acceptance threshold, then the case is dropped from the case base.

```
For each case in training data
  NumAgree = 0
  Find k nearest neighbors among training data
  For each neighbor
    Calculate difference on dependent variable
    If difference <= agreeThreshold then
      numAgree incremented
  End inner loop
  If (numAgree / k) < acceptThreshold then
    Drop training case
End outer loop
```

Figure 1: Numeric Wilson Filter 1 Algorithm

As with the original Wilson filter approach, this tends to remove noisy *and* border cases and keep "internal" points in the case space. A pilot test was carried out using initial thresholds of (agreeThreshold = .2; acceptThreshold = 0.5) and k=3, 5, and 7, and results were not satisfactory. Around

[3] Wilson's algorithm set this permanently as 0.50 (50%), but with typically using k=3, not a lot of precision was necessary for this value.

2/3 of cases were removed each time, leaving mainly cities with low crime. The majority of cities have relatively low crime, so the approach was treating most cities with significant crime as noisy. See Figure 2 for a distribution of the normalized violent crime rates. To obtain an idea of the difficulty of the prediction task, consider that the average case has a normalized crime rate 0.17 away from the mean. So a mean absolute error (MAE) for the straw man of always predicting the mean would be around 0.17. Around 20% of pair-wise differences among normalized crime rates among all cases are within the somewhat arbitrary "correctness" threshold of 0.05, so a straw man of predicting using a random case might be expected get around 20% "correct".

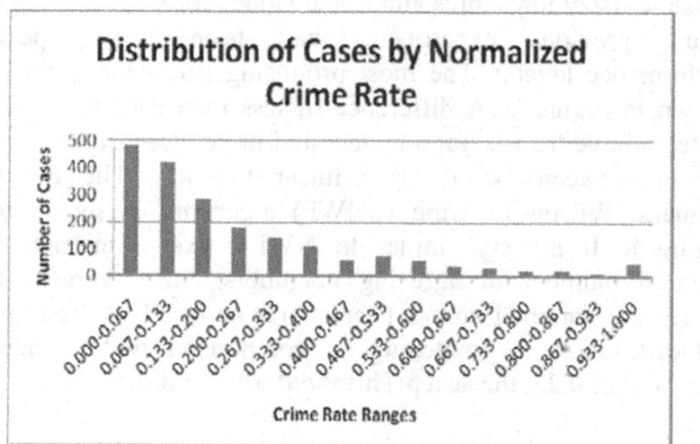

Figure 2: Distribution of Normalized Per Capita Violent Crime Rates

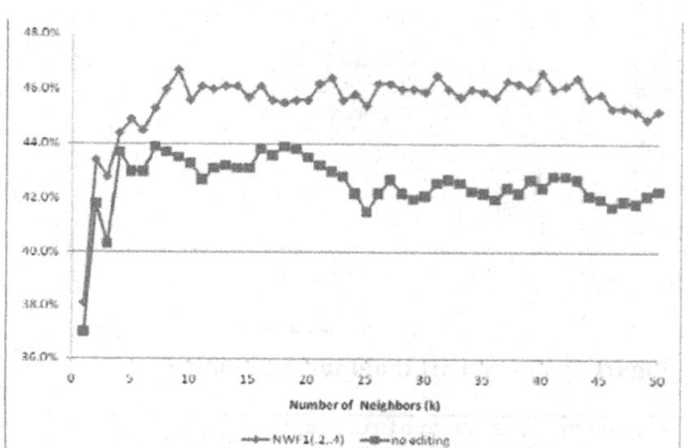

Figure 3: Percent "Correct" NWF1 vs. No Edit

For the first full experiment, the acceptThreshold was adjusted down to 0.4. Results for these initial thresholds, along with the baseline (no editing) are shown in Figure 3 and Figure 4. Better performance is obtained, to a point, by using more neighbors. One similar neighbor could be unusual and could lead to an incorrect prediction. Adding more neighbors (increasing k) essentially brings more information to bear on the prediction. However, as more neighbors are added, the neighbors being used are getting less similar to the case being predicted. At some point it is expected that increasing k will lead to worse performance instead of better, and this indeed happens.

In this case, with the somewhat arbitrary threshold for "correct", peak percent correct occurs a little bit later and is a little bit higher with NWF1 than with no editing (for all k's above 7, except for 17, 18, and 19, the difference is significant). However, for mean absolute error, NWF1 peaks earlier, does not get as low, and retreats faster than with no editing (for all k's above 6, except for 10, the differences are significant).

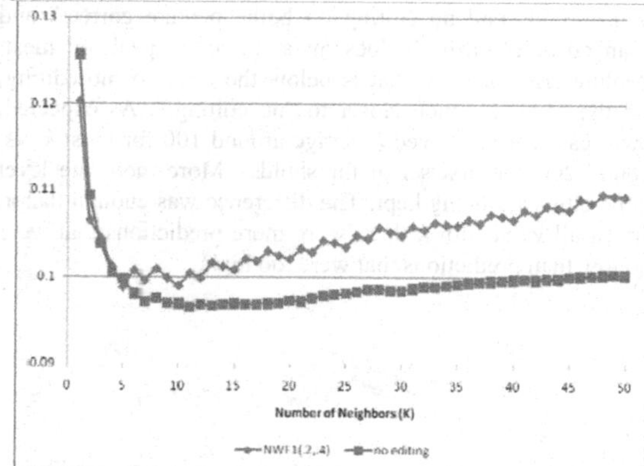

Figure 4: Mean Absolute Error NWF1 vs. No Editing

Analysis

Note that each case is a training case in 9 folds, and a test case in one fold. So a case can potentially be removed 0-9 times during a 10-fold cross validation experiment. A detailed analysis was done for a few values of k, to see whether the same cases were being consistently removed in the different folds. The results are shown in Table 1. By far, most cases were never removed across all 9 training folds. The second most common times removed is 9 times. Thus it appears that the algorithm is identifying something consistently, be it noisy or border cases. Further analysis reveals that for k=7, the average normalized crime rate for cases removed is .6543, while the average normalized crime rate for retained cases is .1983. Thus, the algorithm appears to be biased toward removing cases from high crime cities. This helps get more of the many low crime cities to be "correctly" predicted (close to actual) but tends toward worse predictions for high crime cities, leading to higher average error. In general, higher k increases the effect.

Table 1: How often cases are removed

	Number of Cases for each k		
Times Removed	3NN	5NN	7NN
9	203	107	141
8	65	20	19
7	84	15	15
6	0	13	13
5	0	7	5
4	0	0	2
3	0	0	11
2	60	39	33
1	81	62	49
0	1501	1731	1706

If too many normal cases are being removed, then one adjustment that can be tried is to adjust the thresholds to make it harder to remove a case. In the next experiment, the agreeThreshold was increased to 0.25, and the acceptThreshold was reduced to 0.30. Results showing the comparison among the two sets of thresholds and no editing are shown in Figure 5 and Figure 6. The less rigorous thresholds are in general the middle path, between the first set of thresholds and no editing on both "percent correct" and mean absolute error. It does hit a minimum peak on mean absolute error at k=10 that is below the error for no editing, and the MAE is much closer to "no editing"[4]. As expected, fewer cases are removed (average around 100 for most k, vs. around 200 for first set of thresholds). More moderate level crime cities are being kept. The difference was enough that at almost all values for k there were more predictions that were too low than predictions that were too high.

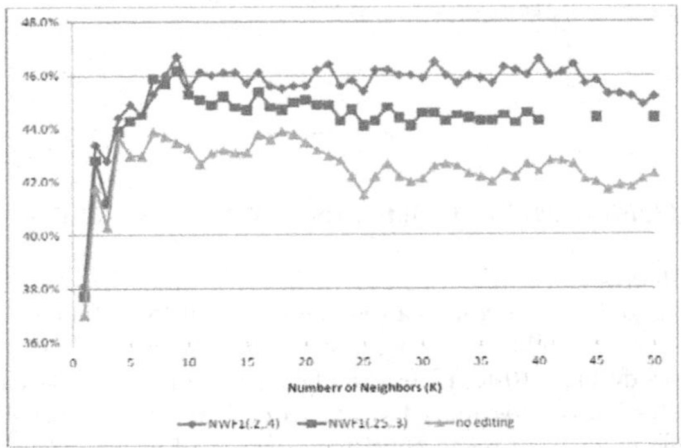

Figure 5: NWF1 Comparison Percent Correct

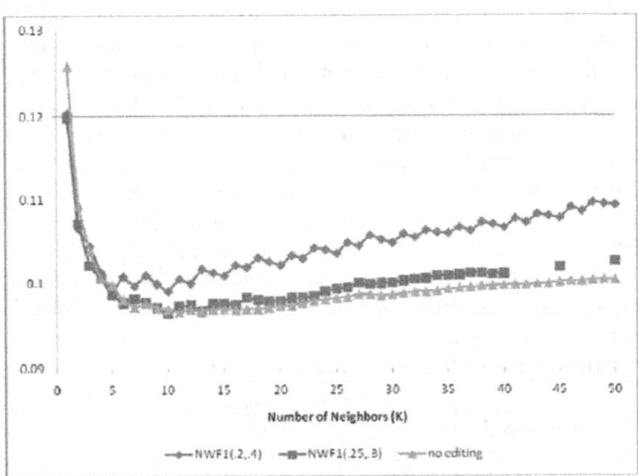

Figure 6: NWF1 Comparison Ave Error

B. Fuzzy Agreement Experiments

The initial approach to Numeric Wilson Filtering showed some promise. However, it seemed doubtful that continued easing of thresholds would be promising. A 0.25 difference in normalized crime rate is a pretty loose definition of "agreement" when over 65% of the pairwise differences across the case-base are 0.25 or lower. Setting the agreeThreshold as high as 0.30 would push that to over 70% of cases "agreeing" with each other on the "answer." Of course, any such threshold is arbitrary and suffers from its discreteness.

An alternative is to use a "fuzzy" threshold in the sense of fuzzy logic. The idea would be that above a certain level of agreement, the agreement would be considered total (fuzzy membership in "agreement" = 1.0), below a certain level of agreement, there is no agreement (fuzzy membership in "agreement" = 0), and in between there is some in between level of agreement (frequently in fuzzy logic a linear function is used). Some pilot testing was done working with a few possible fuzzy thresholds and a few values for k (in the range where previous experiments had been hitting peak performance levels). The most promising fuzzy threshold is shown in Figure 7. A difference of less than 0.15 is a total match; above 0.25 is not a match, and in-between differences are in between, based on a linear function. The Fuzzy Numeric Wilson Filtering (FNWF) algorithm is shown in Figure 8. It is very similar to NWF1, except instead of counting number of agreeing neighbors, fuzzy agreement values are summed across nearest neighbors[5] To adjust for reduced credit for matching in comparison with a hard threshold of 0.25, the acceptThreshold was set down to 0.2.

Figure 7: Fuzzy Threshold for Agreement

```
For each case in training data
  AgreementSum = 0
  Find k nearest neighbors among training data
  For each neighbor
    Calculate difference on dependent variable
    Convert difference into fuzzy agreement
      membership
    AgreementSum += current fuzzy agreement
  End inner loop
  If (AgreementSum / k) < acceptThreshold then
    Drop training case
End outer loop
```

Figure 8: Fuzzy Numeric Wilson Filtering Algorithm

[4] The gaps for high values of K for the second set of parameters represent tests that were skipped because the pattern of results was established.

[5] i.e. This is NOT a full Fuzzy Logic approach with rules, inference, composition, and defuzzification. There is merely a fuzzy membership function for "agrees with neighbor"

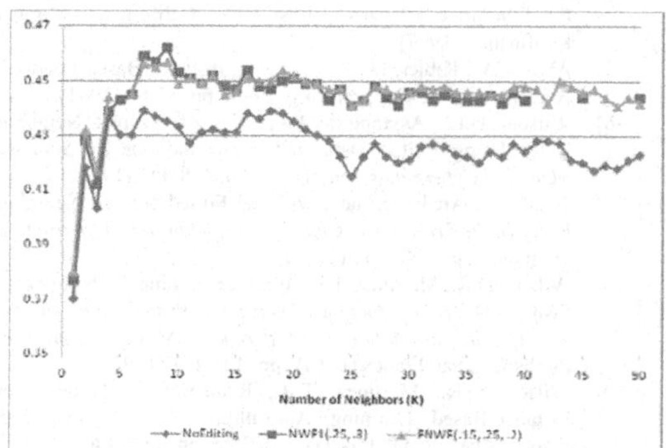

Figure 9: Fuzzy vs. NonFuzzy Pct Correct

The results for the second experiment, with FNWF are shown in Figure 9 and Figure 10. The percent correct results are very similar to the NWF1, and the mean absolute error is also very similar, with perhaps some slight advantage for the fuzzy approach in the lowest peaks. The differences are probably not meaningful, but further experiment results are compared to the fuzzy approach

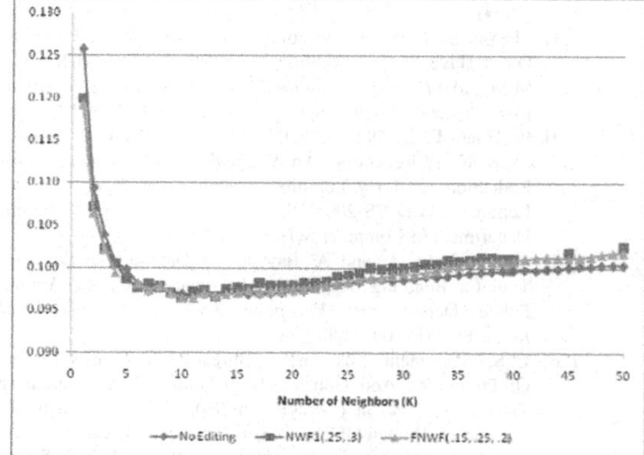

Figure 10: Fuzzy vs. NonFuzzy Ave Error

C. Greedy Hill Climbing Experiments

The next step was to try an algorithm built from scratch for editing case bases used in numeric prediction. It shares a lot in common with previous approaches developed for classification. In fact, it shares the basic assumption dating at least to [6]: that a training case whose neighbors disagree with it might be noisy (as opposed to the neighbors). It also follows a common machine learning pattern of being a greedy hill climbing wrapper approach. It meets with our assumptions in that it is not incremental, it is based on numeric prediction, and it is biased (at least slightly) toward keeping cases rather than removing them. The algorithm is shown in Figure 11.

```
Repeat until no improvement on avg error
  For each case in validation data
    Predict using normal method
    Calculate prediction error for validation case
  End inner loop
  Remove case with greatest error
  Calculate average error for validation cases
End outer loop
```

Figure 11: Greedy Hill Climbing Algorithm

The algorithm separates a portion of training data to serve as "validation data" [22, p146], which is used as sort of a "pre-test" during training. Using separate validation data during training is an attempt to avoid overfitting. The algorithm shown is run for each fold during the 10-fold cross validation. The algorithm is conservative towards deleting cases since it stops when improvement is not found rather than when performance worsens – ties mean stop. It looks not at which cases disagree with their neighbors, but rather at which cases drastically disagree with their neighbors. In other words, instead of adjusting non-numeric algorithms to determine if cases "agree" in their predictions, it makes use of the actual numeric differences. This might allow greater sensitivity than a mere difference in classification.

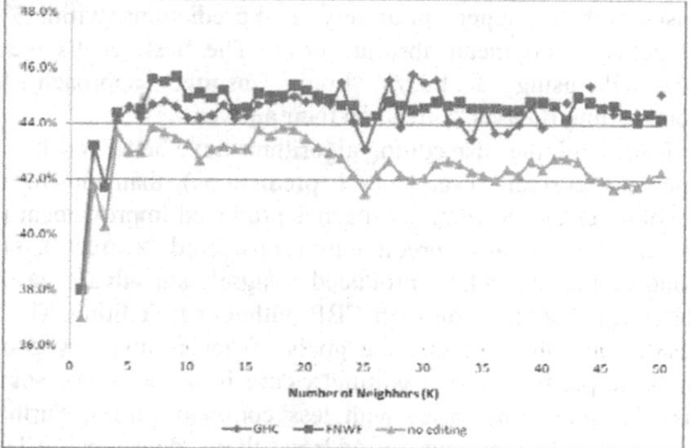

Figure 12: GHC vs FNWF vs No edit

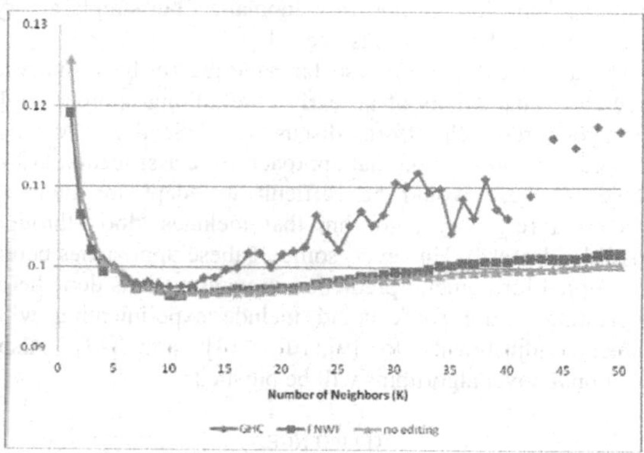

Figure 13: Ave Error GHC vs. FNWF vs. No Editing

The results for the third experiment, with greedy hill climbing method are shown in Figure 12 and Figure 13. The percent correct results are more variable than the FNWF approach, and peak at higher *k*. The results for mean absolute error are not as low as the other approaches, and they get significantly worse quickly with greater *k*. It is possible that this approach is more heavily sacrificing high crime cities as *k* goes up, aiding prediction of low crime cities but producing large errors for high crime cities. This will be investigated further. Ideas for improving on this method have been developed; based on further analysis of detailed results some of these directions will be pursued.

IV. Discussion and Conclusions

We have presented a study of several algorithms for numeric prediction using CBR. One of the important benefits of CBR is that it can be used to provide any kind of answer – binary, nominal, ordinal, numeric, and even structural (e.g. meal plans, designs, etc). Full-fledged knowledge-rich CBR efforts have focused attention on case evaluation as part of Retain or Review stages. However, research on case selection / editing within knowledge-poor domains has focused almost entirely on classification tasks. In this research, several experiments have been carried out exploring variations of case editing algorithms for numeric prediction, including both adjustments of previous algorithms developed for classification domains and new algorithms. Evaluation was based both on the percent of very good predictions (within 5% of actual), and mean absolute error. The best results were obtained using a Fuzzy Logic inspired approach to determining if cases "agree" on their answer.

In general, the case editing algorithms have better results on "percent correct" (very good predictions) than on mean absolute error. Several approaches produced improvement in the number of close predictions (considered "correct"), but none of the algorithms produced a significant advantage on the mean absolute error over CBR without case editing. These results may indicate that the goals of generating very good numeric predictions via editing a case base may have some risk for predicting cases with less common values. Further research will continue to address these dual goals. The detrimental effect on predicting less common cases may actually make sense if the anomalous values that are removed via Case Selection are not truly anomalies, but simply a very rare case. Further analysis is needed.

The approaches pursued so far have mostly been numeric prediction adaptations of an early case editing approach [6]. Numerous research efforts discussed in Section I.A have worked at improving on that approach for classification tasks. Some of these would be difficult to adapt for numeric prediction (e.g. any algorithm that includes "loop through possible classes"). However, some of these approaches could be adapted for numeric prediction in ways such as done here. Interesting future work could include experimenting with numeric adjustments to [9],[10], [13], and [14]. Also, additional novel algorithms will be pursued.

References

[1] Aamodt, A., Plaza, E., Case-Based Reasoning : Foundational Issues, Methodological Variations, and System Approaches; In *Artificial Intelligence Communications*. IOS Press. 7:1, pp. 39-59. (1994).

[2] Kolodner, J. Case-Based Reasoning. Los Altos, CA: Morgan Kaufmann. (1993)

[3] Leake, D. Case Based Reasoning: Experiences, Lessons, and Future Directions. Menlo Park, California: AAAI Press/MIT Press. (1996)

[4] Watson, I.D. Applying Case-Based Reasoning: Techniques for Enterprise Systems. Los Altos, California: Morgan Kaufmann,. (1997)

[5] Aha, D.W., Kibler, D., Albert, M.K. Instance Based Learning Algorithms. *Machine Learning.* Vol 6, pp. 37-66 (1991).

[6] Wilson, D.L., Asymptotic Properties of Nearest Neighbor Rules Using Edited Data. *IEEE Transactions on Systems, Man, and Cybernetics*, vol 2, no 3, pp. 408-421 (1972)

[7] Tomek, I., An Experiment with the Edited Nearest-Neighbor Rule. *IEEE Transactions on Systems, Man, and Cybernetics,* vol 6, no 6, pp. 448-452 (1976)

[8] Wilson, D.R., Martinez, T.R., Instance Pruning Techniques. In Fisher, D. (ed) *Machine Learning: Proceedings of the Fourteenth International Conference*, Mogan Kaufmann Publishers, San Francisco, CA, pp. 404-411 (1997)

[9] Wilson, D.R., Martinez, T.R., Reduction Techniques for Instance-Based Learning Algorithms. *Machine Learning.* Kluwer Academic Publishers. Vol 38:3, pp. 257-286 (2000).

[10] Brighton, H., Mellish, C. Advances in Instance Selection for Instance-Based Learning Algorithms. *Data Mining and Knowledge Discovery*, Kluwer Academic Publishers, vol 6, pp. 153-172 (2002)

[11] Smyth, B., McKenna, E., Building Compact Competent Case-Bases. In *Proceedings of the Third International Conference on Case-Based Reasoning.* Springer, pp. 329-342 (1999)

[12] Morring, B.D., Martinez, T.R., Weighted Instance Typicality Search (WITS): A Nearest Neighbor Data Reduction Algorithm. In *Intelligent Data Analysis*, vol 8, no 1, pp. 61-78. (2004)

[13] Massie, S., Craw, S., Wiratunga, N. When Similar Problems Don't Have Similar Solutions. In Weber, R.O. and Richter, M.M. (eds) *Proceedings of the 7th International Conference on Case-Based Reasoning*, Springer-Verlag, pp 92-106 (2007)

[14] Pasquier, F.X., Delany, S.J., and Cunningham, P. Blame-Based Noise Reduction: An Alternative Perspective on Noise Reduction for Lazy Learning. Computer Science Technical Report, TCD-CS-2005-29, Trinity College Dublin, Department of Computer Science (2005)

[15] Redmond, M. A. and A. Baveja: A Data-Driven Software Tool for Enabling Cooperative Information Sharing Among Police Departments. *European Journal of Operational Research* 141 (2002) 660-678.

[16] U. S. Department of Commerce, Bureau of the Census, Census Of Population And Housing 1990 United States: Summary Tape File 1a & 3a (Computer Files), U.S. Department Of Commerce, Bureau Of The Census Producer, Washington, DC and Inter-university Consortium for Political and Social Research Ann Arbor, Michigan. (1992)

[17] U.S. Department of Justice, Bureau of Justice Statistics, Law Enforcement Management And Administrative Statistics (Computer File) U.S. Department Of Commerce, Bureau Of The Census Producer, Washington, DC and Inter-university Consortium for Political and Social Research Ann Arbor, Michigan. (1992)

[18] U.S. Department of Justice, Federal Bureau of Investigation, Crime in the United States (Computer File) (1995)

[19] Asuncion, A. & Newman, D.J. UCI Machine Learning Repository [http://www.ics.uci.edu/~mlearn/MLRepository.html]. Irvine, CA: University of California, School of Information and Computer Science. (2007).

[20] Cost S., and S. Salzberg: A weighted nearest neighbor algorithm for learning with symbolic features. *Machine Learning* 10 (1993) 57-58.

[21] Aha, D.W. Lazy Learning. Artificial Intelligence Review, vol 1, pp. 1-5 (1997)

[22] Witten, I.H. and Frank, E. *Data mining: practical machine learning tools and techniques*, Morgan Kaufmann. (2005)

Towards a Transcription System of Sign Language for 3D Virtual Agents

Wanessa Machado do Amaral, José Mario De Martino
Department of Computer Engineering and Industrial Automation,
FEEC, University of Campinas,
13083-970 Campinas, SP, Brazil

Abstract-**Accessibility is a growing concern in computer science. Since virtual information is mostly presented visually, it may seem that access for deaf people is not an issue. However, for prelingually deaf individuals, those who were deaf since before acquiring and formally learn a language, written information is often of limited accessibility than if presented in signing. Further, for this community, signing is their language of choice, and reading text in a spoken language is akin to using a foreign language. Sign language uses gestures and facial expressions and is widely used by deaf communities. To enabling efficient production of signed content on virtual environment, it is necessary to make written records of signs. Transcription systems have been developed to describe sign languages in written form, but these systems have limitations. Since they were not originally designed with computer animation in mind, in general, the recognition and reproduction of signs in these systems is an easy task only to those who deeply know the system. The aim of this work is to develop a transcription system to provide signed content in virtual environment. To animate a virtual avatar, a transcription system requires explicit enough information, such as movement speed, signs concatenation, sequence of each hold-and-movement and facial expressions, trying to articulate close to reality. Although many important studies in sign languages have been published, the transcription problem remains a challenge. Thus, a notation to describe, store and play signed content in virtual environments offers a multidisciplinary study and research tool, which may help linguistic studies to understand the sign languages structure and grammar.**

KEYWORDS: computer graphics, sign language, XML, accessibility, virtual reality.

I. INTRODUCTION

There are estimated to be 5,7 million people with hearing disabilities in Brazil [3], 20 million in U.S [5] and 278 million people worldwide [16]. Kennaway [6] shows that the reading performance of deaf children is poor compared to that of their hearing peers. Thus, situations in which information is presented primarily in written form place them at a substantial disadvantage.

The access that deaf people have to virtual content could be greatly improved by the provision of sign language information. Sign language is being displayed on computer environment using video content. However, there are disadvantages to this means of providing information, since it is necessary to use specific equipments and trained people who deeply know the sign language. The maintenance of video content is another problem. There are continuity issues, like use the same signer, in the same clothing and with the same background. Thus, create pieces of signing that can be joined together to make signed phrases is nontrivial. Each time any content detail changes, new videos must be made, increasing the costs. Storing and downloading videos can also be problematic as they are large files. For displayed content on Web sites using Internet connection, the time and cost involved in downloading video sequences may be prohibitive.

A virtual avatar driven by animation software provides an attractive alternative to video. Virtual signing has some advantages. Signed content can be created by one person on a desktop computer. No video capture equipment is required. A virtual avatar can generate real time content, so continuity is not a problem since details of the content can be edited at any time, without having to rerecord whole sequences. Storing the content is further advantage. Disk space demands to store sign description are negligible. Data transmission is improved, since transcription content can be stored in text files, which are smaller than video files and can be downloaded faster. Another advantage is the extra control by user, which is not possible with video. The view angle can be continuously adjusted during playback.

To animate a virtual avatar, the first need is to develop an accurate transcription system, to explicitly specify how sign is articulated. The challenge is to ensure the realistic animation of virtual agents.

II. RELATED WORK

A. *Stokoe*

Stokoe, the founder of the sign language linguistics, proposed the first notation system for a sign language [14]. The original Stokoe notation is consisted of 55 symbols, divided in three groups, called *chemeres*, representing aspects of sign:

- Tabula: hand location;
- Designator: hand shape;
- Signation: movement.

Hand shape symbols are based on Latin letters and numerals. Location and movement symbols are iconic. Stokoe shows how these three parts, meaningless alone, fit together to form a linguistic structure, identical to the phonemes of spoken language [11].

T. Sobh, K. Elleithy (eds.), *Innovations in Computing Sciences and Software Engineering*,
DOI 10.1007/978-90-481-9112-3_15, © Springer Science+Business Media B.V. 2010

Despite the simultaneity of aspects of sign, Stokoe notation sequentially writes the symbols that represent each aspect. This sequential structure can be read by humans who know the notation and the sign language. However, it is nontrivial to understand by someone not familiar with Stokoe notation, and even more by a computer program.

On the other hand, there is sequentiality in the internal structure of signs. For example, the sign "deaf" in ASL is articulated with two face touches with the index finger, the first one in the region below the ear and the second in the region next to the mouth, with an arc trajectory between them. Change the order of these movements results in a meaningless articulation in ASL.

It is important to note that simultaneity and sequentiality are unresolved issues in existing notations, and they are treated in the transcription system proposed here. Typically, traditional notations sequentially write the sign aspects, which are simultaneous during articulation. In the other side, there is a sequence in *holds* and *movements* of a single sign, and this order must be respected and explicitly stored.

There are defined hand shapes in Stokoe notation. To write a sign with a new hand shape, it is necessary to look at the whole hand shape set and matches the new shape with an existing one that resembles most. This can also be problematic, since sign language is not static and new signs may arises requiring new hand shapes.

Stokoe notation does not provide non-manual aspects, such as facial expressions. However, signs showing emotions such as joy or anger need to be accompanied by the appropriate facial expression. Liddell [9] shows that to reproduce a story with characters that has no name, the signers can use facial expressions to refer different characters. Thus, facial expressions play a very important role, and are necessary to effectively convey meaning.

B. *SignWriting*

SignWriting [13] was created in 1974 and is defined by a combination of iconic symbols to represent hand shapes, body locations, facial expressions, contacts and movement. Hand shapes can have variations of three basic form of the fist: closed, open or flat. The symbols in SignWriting are all shown from the expressive, not the receptive, viewpoint. That is, signs are written with the signer perspective, looking at their own hands. There are also symbols to represent palm, back and hand side. The articulation space is represented in SignWriting using arrows.

C. *HamNoSys*

A later system, HamNoSys [12], was first made publicly available in 1989 and consists of about 200 symbols covering the parameters of hand shape, location and movement, like Stokoe Notation. HamNoSys is still being improved and extended, and it is possible to note down facial expressions, but their development is not finished yet.

The eSign [7] project uses an XML-based scripting notation, SiGML, based in HamNoSys. The project presents a web browser plug-in to animate signs using an avatar-independent scripting notation. Nevertheless, SiGML has some limitations. There are some omitted information, such as default locations of sign articulation and the duration of each movement, specified on SiGML merely as fast, slow, or ordinary speed [6]. In real situations, speed may vary during the signing, for example, to assign intonation. In this case, a sign can start running at normal speed and have fast speed at the end of articulation. This issue will be treated on this work.

III. TRANSCRIPTION

A. *Xml and diagrams*

Digital information provided in sign language is not common. Sign language can be displayed using video. However, this is not an appropriate alternative for computational environment. Kennaway [6] shows that the traditional transcription systems were not created to virtual animation purposes.

This work addresses a transcription system for sign languages for virtual 3D agents implementation. The main challenge is to develop a model that represents the signs without having to store all existing gestures combinations, which would certainly result in a combinatorial explosion and make the work impossible.

The transcription system proposed in this paper considers the following main limitations of previous approaches: movement speed, sign concatenation, sequentiality and non-manual expressions. Moreover, the information was grouped hierarchically using XML (eXtensible Markup Language) files, which have the advantages below:

- Are text files, editable in any simple text editor.
- Are hierarchical files, validated and consolidated.
- Low cost. Existence of free editors and validators.
- Are files easy to share and store.

To facilitate comprehension, the XML description is illustrated by UML diagrams. Each XML element is represented in diagram as a class. The cardinality between classes means how many times the element may appear in the document. Each attribute is illustrated as a class attribute. The possible values that attributes can assume will be written immediately in front of the attribute name and may refer to a set of values, for example, 0,..,10, and preceded by the equal sign (=), or a value type, string or integer, preceded by a colon sign (:).

B. *Notation*

As mentioned above, Stokoe identified three aspects: hand shape, location and movement. Later, Battison [1] and Friedman [4] identified the palm orientation, which already existed in Stokoe original notation system, but with secondary importance. Klima and Bellugi [8] identified the hands arrangement, which hand holds the sign and if in active or passive form. Liddell and Johnson [11] grouped the movements in local and global. The work of Battison [2] has two restrictions that significantly limit the number of possible combinations of signs articulated with two hands: symmetry and dominance conditions. Symmetry condition states that when both hands move independently, they will have the same hand shape, place, orientation and movement. Dominance condition states that if the two hands have different hand shapes, then the weak hand will be passive. Liddell [10] argued that any sign is composed of movements and/or holds. Hold is the moment when hand shape, location and palm orientation are the same, that is, when the hands are stooped. Holds can be joined by movements, with the displacement of the hands in space.

Based on Liddell studies, the notation presented here first grouped information in two parts: *hold* and *globalMovement* (Fig.1). The hold element has three children: *rightHand*, *leftHand* and *face*. The *number* attribute is used to store sequentiality information, and order the *holds* and *movements* that compose the sign.

Each hand has four children: *handConfiguration*, *location*, *orientation* and *localMovement* (Fig.2). The *leftHand* has additional symmetry attribute, which is set to yes when the sign has the symmetry condition.

The *handConfiguration* element describes hand shapes and has only one attribute, *preDefined*. There are most commonly used hand configurations in sign languages, so a set of pre-defined hand shape was created, but this set can increase if necessary.

Element *location* (Fig.3) describes the region where signs are articulated, and can be set as a point in space (Fig.4), or as a contact point, which can be with other hand (Fig.5), body (Fig.6) or face (Fig.7). When *location* is omitted, the sign will be articulated in front of body.

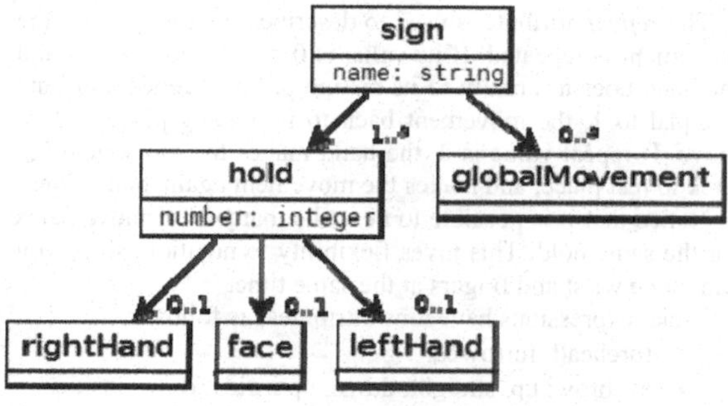

Fig.1. Hierarchical description of signs.

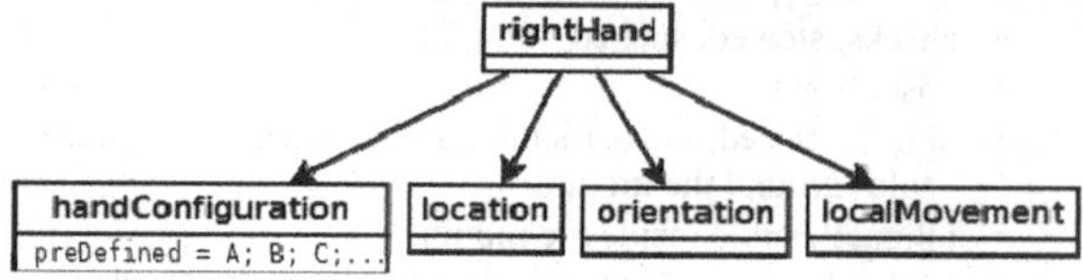

Fig.2. Hand description.

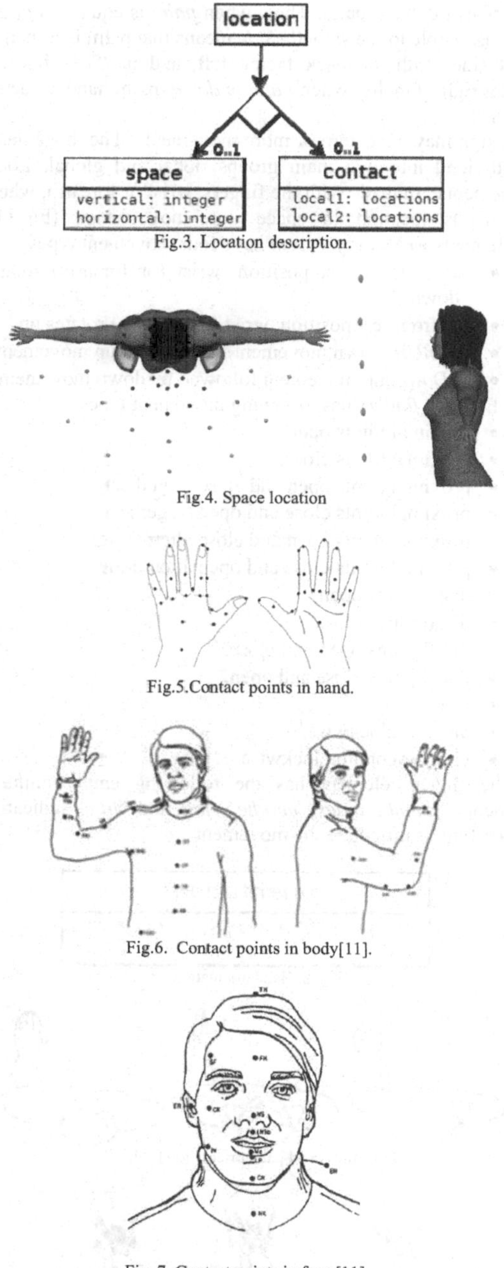

Fig.3. Location description.

Fig.4. Space location

Fig.5. Contact points in hand.

Fig.6. Contact points in body[11].

Fig. 7. Contact points in face [11].

Palm orientation is an important aspect, that in some cases distinguishes two signs. Like in SignWriting, the *orientation* element considers the signer is looking at her own hands, from her perspective (Fig.8). Orientation *forearm* attribute can be *horizontal* (Fig.9) or *vertical* (Fig.10). The *palm* attribute describes the hand palm. Thus, when *palm* is equal to *up*, the palm is visible to the signer. *rSide* means that palm is turned to right side, with the back facing left, and in *lSide*, back is facing right. Finally, when *palm* is *down*, palm hand is facing down.

A sign may have zero or more movements. The movements are divided into two main groups: local and global. Local movements are made with the fingers, wrist or forearm, where the hands location in space does not change (Fig.11).

Elements *wrist* and *forearm* have four movement types:

- *down*: from rest position, wrist (or forearm) rotates down
- *up*: from rest position, wrist (or forearm) rotates up.
- *downUP*: down movement followed by up movement.
- *upDown*: up movement followed by down movement.

Element *fingers* has following movement types:

- proximal joints open.
- proximal joints close.
- proximal joints open and close (together).
- proximal joints close and open (together).
- proximal joints open and close alternating.
- proximal joints close and open alternating.
- distal joints open.
- distal joints close.
- distal joints open and close.
- distal joints close and open.
- rub.
- circular clockwise.
- circular counterclockwise.

The fingers element has the following empty children elements: *thumb*, *index*, *middle*, *ring* and *little*, indicating which fingers articulate the movement.

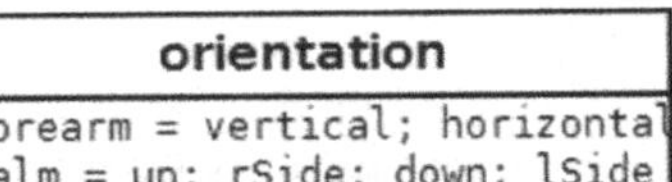

Fig. 8. Hand orientation.

Fig. 9. Horizontal palm orientation [15].

Fig. 10. Vertical palm orientation [15].

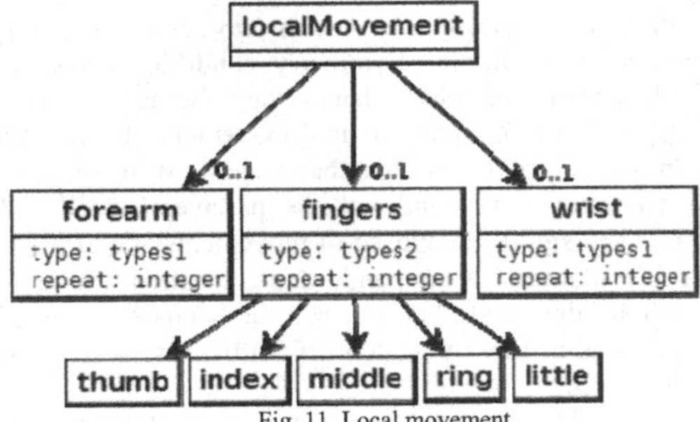

Fig. 11. Local movement.

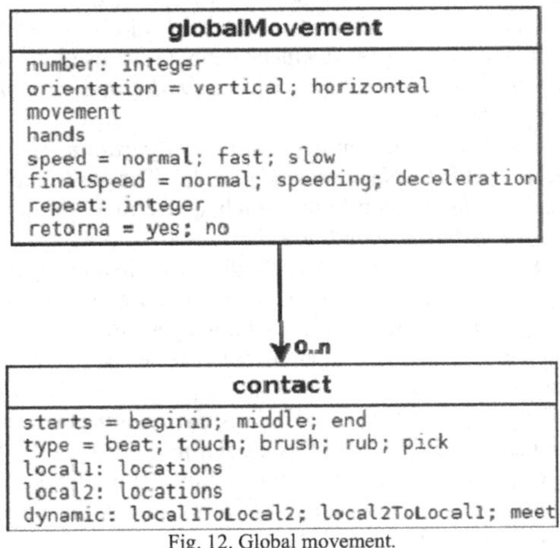

Fig. 12. Global movement.

The *repeat* attribute is used to describe how many times the movement is repeated. If its value is 0, the motion occurs and the hand does not return to its resting place. If repeat attribute is equal to 1, the movement back to its resting place, before move. If repeat value is 2, the hand makes the movement, go back to rest place, and makes the movement again, and so on.

Notice that it is possible to describe many local movements for the same hold. This gives flexibility to notation, since you can move wrist and fingers at the same time.

Facial expressions have nine attributes, as follows:

- forehead: furrowed.
- eyebrow: up, straight, down, up inside, down inside.
- eyes: open, squeezed, closed, half open, wide open.
- look: up, up and side, sideways, down, down and side.
- cheeks: stewed, sucked, tight, blow.
- nose: frown.
- mouth: closed, closed smile, smile, yawn, kiss, tense, folds around the mouth.
- tongue: visible inside the mouth.
- teeth: above touching the lower lip, lower lip touching.

The *face predefined* attribute was created to carry values like happy, sad or angry. This attribute can be used when high accuracy is not necessary, that is, describe facial expression just as happy or unhappy is enough for a good articulation.

Global movement (Fig.12) is trajectory between two holds, in the same sign. The movement direction can be vertical or horizontal, described by *orientation* attribute. The *move* attribute can be *circular* (clockwise or counterclockwise), *halfCircle* (clockwise or counterclockwise), straight (right, left, back, front) or *zigzag* (from right and front, from right and back, from left and front, from left and back.).

The *hands* attribute describes the dynamics of movement, how the movement is performed, with one or two hands, alternate, consecutive, simultaneous or mirrored.

Possible values for *hands* attribute are:

- *right*: only right hand moves.
- *left*: only left hand moves.
- *simultaneous*: both hands move together.
- *alternate*: both hands move alternately, for example, right hand moves in the opposite direction to the left hand.
- *consecutiveR*: hand A moves while hand B is stopped. Then hand B moves while hand A is stopped. Right hand moves first.
- *consecutiveL*: same as *consecutiveR*, left hand moves first.
- *mirror*: both hands move in mirrored movements.
- *mirroredConsecutiveR*: both hands move in mirrored movements, one at a time. Right hand moves first.
- *mirroredConsecutiveL*: same as *mirroredConsecutiveR*, but left hand moves first.

GlobalMovement speed attribute can be *fast*, *slow* or *normal*. When not filled, the attribute value is considered *normal*. The movement may have its speed changed during sign articulation, setting *final* attribute.

It is possible to add contact during global movement, described with child element *contact* of element *globalMovement*. The *time* attribute is the moment which contact is made. Contact *type* attribute can have the following values: *beat*, *touch*, *brush*, *rub* (move, and remains on the surface) and *pick*. The attributes *local1* and *local2* refer to contact points with the hand (Fig.5), body (Fig.6) or face (Fig.7), identical to those used in the description of the location element. Contact can occurs from one location to another or between two places. The *dynamic* attribute defines how the contact occurs, and its values can be *local1ToLocal2*, *local2ToLocal1* or *meet*.

The *repeat* attribute, as well as in the local movement, is used to describe how many times the movement is repeated. If 0, the movement occurs and the hand does not return to their resting place. If 1, the hands came back to their resting place, before the movement. If repeat value is 2, the hands make the movement, go back to rest place, and make the movement again, and so on.

The notation system presented above describes isolated signs. However it is also necessary to describe

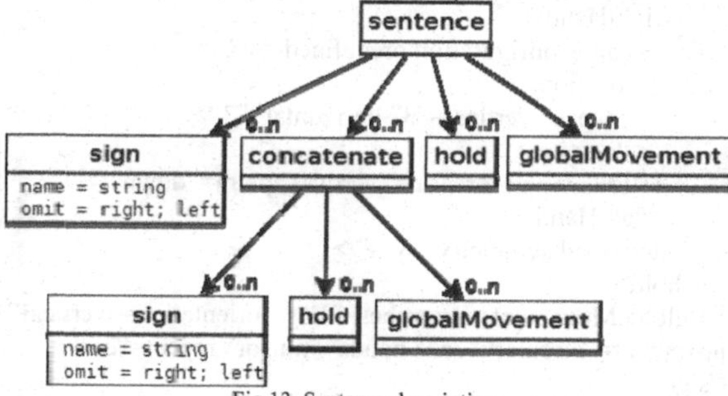

Fig.13. Sentence description.

whole sentences. Thus, some further problems arises, as signs concatenation (omission of parts of signs), and articulations that have no corresponding sign. The diagram in Fig.13 illustrates a sentence description.

The *sentence* element has four children elements:

- *sign*: to cite a signal has been described
- *concatenate*: allows the concatenation of a sign with another sign or suspension. Everything that is inside this element will be played at the same time.
- *hold*: when the suspension does not correspond to any known, it can be described in one sentence as an isolated suspension.
- *globalMovement*: when the movement does not correspond to any known, it can be described in one sentence as an isolated move.

Important information for virtual avatar animation, which does not appear in the existing notations, is sign concatenation. Instead, traditional transcription systems usually represent signs separately. But for a computational articulation, the way sign is placed in the sentence context must also be interpreted. The sign concatenation occurs when parts of a sign is omitted with the overlap of another sign. For example, it may occurs the A sign starts before the end of B sign, occurring overlap of these signals.

The *concatenate* element has three children elements:

- *sign*: reference to a sign.
- *hold*: description of an isolated.
- *globalMovement*: description of a movement.

IV. Transcription Examples

To illustrate the system transcription, the sign "computer" of Libras (Brazilian Sign Language) will be described. The sign computer is articulated with both hands, mirrored, and C hand shape. Circular clockwise global movement with right hand is articulated, and left hand movement is mirrored. The XML below describes sign "computer":

```
<sign name="computer">
   <hold number="1">
      <rightHand>
         <handConfiguration predefined="c"/>
         <location>
            <space vertical="3" horizontal="3">
         </location>
         <orientation forearm="vertical" palm="down"/>
      </rightHand>
      <leftHand symmetry="yes"/>
   </hold>
   <globalMovement number="1" orientation="vertical"
movement="circularClock" hands="mirror" repeat="2"/>
</sign>
```

The sign "computer" in ASL is quiet similar, but with a slightly different hand shape.

Two sentences are described to illustrate the transcription of content. The first sentence is "*He's crying because the ball is gone away*", with the following XML:

```
<sentence>
   <sign name="he"/>
   <sign name ="cry"/>
   <sign name ="because"/>
   <sign name ="ball"/>
   <sign name ="away"/>
</sentence >
```

This sentence is just a sequence of signs. Another example show sign concatenation. An example of concatenation in sentences is the description of situations that occur simultaneously. For example, the bike sign is articulated with both hands closed and circular mirrored movement, as if holding the handlebars of the bicycle, but making the movement of the pedals. To articulate the sentence: "*While riding his bicycle, his hat felt off.*", the bike sign can the concatenated with the movement of hat falling from head. The two hands of bike sign is mirrored, so one of them can be omitted and articulate the sign corresponding of dropping hat from head, indicating that his hat felt off his head while he was riding his bicycle. The XML that describes this sentence is:

```
< sentence >
   <sign name="bike">
   <concatenate>
      <sign name="bike" omit="right"/>
      <hold> (describe articulation of hat falling from head)
      </hold>
   </concatenate >
</sentence >
```

With two signs the whole sentence is articulated. However, the articulation of this two signs separately, in sequential order, does not achieve the same meaning.

V. Conclusion

This work presented an XML transcription system for sign languages. Describe signs in written form is nontrivial task. Existing transcription systems were not designed to computer animation purposes. The work presented here aims to record most relevant information for sign language computer playback. Thus, it is possible to increase the computational accessibility to deaf people, improving human-computer interaction for these users. It is important to highlight the multidisciplinary nature of this work, since the detailed study of sign aspects may help in linguistic studies of sign languages.

The examples mentioned above describe Libras signs. Next work is to extend the descriptions for ASL signs, in an attempt to prove that the transcription system is suitable for any sign language.

References

[1] Battison, R.. Phonological deletion in American Sign Language. *Sign Language Studies 5* (1974), 1-19.

[2] Battison, R. *Linguistics of American Sign Language: An introduction.* Washington, DC: Clerc Books: Gallaudet University Press, 2000.

[3] IBGE:http://www.ibge.gov.br/home/estatistica/populacao/censo2000/tabulacao_avancada/tabela_brasil_1.1.3.shtm, accessed 15/09/2009.

[4] Friedman, L.. Phonological deletion in American Sign Language. *Sign Language Studies* 51 (1975), 940-961.

[5] Gallaudet Research Institute. http://gri.gallaudet.edu/Demographics/factsheet.htm, accessed 05/10/2009.

[6] Kennaway, R.J. Experience with and requirements for a gesture description language for synthetic animation. *Lecture Notes in Computer Science 2915* (2004), 300-311.

[7] Kennaway, R.J.., Glauert, J.R.W. e Zwitserlood, I. Providing Signed Content in the Internet by Synthesized Animation. *ACM Trans Comput Hum Interact (TOCHI) 14,* 3 (2007).

[8] Klima, E e Belluigi, U. *The signs of language.* Cambridge, Mass: Harvard University Press.,1997.

[9] Liddell, S.K.. Nonmanual signals and relative clauses in American Sign Language. *In: P. Siple, P. (Ed.). Understanding language through sign language research.* (1978), 59-90.

[10] Liddell, S.K.. THINK and BELIEVE: Sequentiality. *In American Sign Language 60*(1984), 372-99.

[11] Liddell, S.K. e Johnson, R.E. American Sign Language: the phonological base. *Sign Language Studies. 64* (1989), 195-278.

[12] Prillwitz, S., Leven, R., Zienert, H., Hanke, T., Henning, J and Colleagues. HamNoSys Version 2.0: Hamburg Notation System for Sign Languages:An Introductory Guide. *International Studies on Sign Language and the Communication of the Deaf 5* (1989), 195-278.

[13] http://www.signwriting.org, accessed 15/09/2009.

[14] Stokoe, W.C. Sign Language Structure: An Outline of the Visual Communication System of the American Deaf. *Studies in Linguistics: Occasional Papers 8* (1960).

[15] Stumpf, M. R. Lições sobre o SignWriting. Tradução Parcial e Adaptação do Inglês/ASL para Português LIBRAS do livro 'Lessons in SignWriting', de Valerie Sutton, publicado originalmente pelo DAC, Deaf Action Committe for SignWriting. accessed 15/09/2009. http://sign-net.ucpel.tche.br/licoes-sw/licoes-sw.pdf

[16] World Health Organization, http://www.who.int/mediacentre/factsheets/fs300/en/, acessed 05/10/2009.

Unbiased Statistics of a Constraint Satisfaction Problem – a Controlled-Bias Generator

Denis Berthier
Institut Telecom ; Telecom & Management SudParis
9 rue Charles Fourier, 91011 Evry Cedex, France

Abstract: We show that estimating the complexity (mean and distribution) of the instances of a fixed size Constraint Satisfaction Problem (CSP) can be very hard. We deal with the main two aspects of the problem: defining a measure of complexity and generating random unbiased instances. For the first problem, we rely on a general framework and a measure of complexity we presented at CISSE08. For the generation problem, we restrict our analysis to the Sudoku example and we provide a solution that also explains why it is so difficult.
Keywords: constraint satisfaction problem, modelling and simulation, unbiased statistics, Sudoku puzzle generation, Sudoku rating.

I. Introduction

Constraint Satisfaction Problems (CSP) constitute a very general class of problems. A finite CSP is defined by a finite number of variables with values in fixed finite domains and a finite set of constraints (i.e. of relations they must satisfy); it consists of finding a value for each of these variables, such that they globally satisfy all the constraints. General solving methods are known [1, 2]. Most of these methods combine a blind search algorithm (also called depth-first or breadth-first structured search, Trial and Error with Guessing, …) with some form of pattern-based pruning of the search graph.

In [3, 4, 5], we introduced a new general framework, based on the idea of a constructive, fully pattern-based solution and on the concepts of a candidate (a value not yet known to be impossible) and a resolution rule (which allows to progressively eliminate candidates). In [6], we introduced several additional notions, also valid for any CSP, such as those of a chain and a whip, and we showed how these patterns lead to general and powerful kinds of resolution rules.

The present paper relies on these general concepts (that are briefly recalled in order to make it as self-contained as possible) to analyse another question: *how can we define a measure of complexity for the instances of a given "fixed size" CSP and how can we estimate the statistical distribution of this complexity measure?* As yet, this question has received little interest and it could hardly have, because any method allowing blind search will rely on chance and hide the complexity of the various instances. With our constructive resolution approach, we can define a realistic mesure of complexity.

It should be clear that the above question is independent of a widely investigated problem, the NP-completeness of some types of CSPs. NP-completeness [7] supposes the CSP has a parameter (such as the size of a Sudoku grid: 9x9, 16x16; or the number of resources and tasks in a resource allocation problem) and one concentrates on worst case analysis as a function of this parameter. Here, on the contrary, we fix this parameter (if any), we consider the various instances of this fixed size CSP (e.g. all the 9x9 Sudoku puzzles) and we are more interested in mean case than in worst case analysis.

II. Minimal instances

Instances of a fixed size CSP are defined by their givens (or clues): a *given* is a value pre-assigned to a variable of the CSP.

Instances of a CSP with several solutions cannot be solved in a purely constructive way: at some point, some choice must be made. Such under-constrained instances can be considered as ill-posed problems. We therefore concentrate on instances with a single solution.

It should also be obvious that, given an instance of a CSP, the more givens are added to it, the easier the resulting instances should become – the limit being when all the non given variables have only one possible value. This leads to the following definition: an instance of a CSP is called *minimal* if it has one and only one solution and it would have several solutions if any of its givens was deleted.

In statistical analyses, only samples of minimal instances are meaningful because adding extra givens would multiply the number of easy instances. We shall show that *building random unbiased samples of minimal instances may be very hard.*

III. zt-whips and the associated measure of complexity

The following definitions were introduced in [3], in the Sudoku context, and generalised to the general CSP in [6].

Definition: two different candidates of a CSP are *linked* by a direct contradiction (or simply linked) if one of the constraints of the CSP directly prevents them from being true at the same time *in any state* in which they are present (the

T. Sobh, K. Elleithy (eds.), *Innovations in Computing Sciences and Software Engineering*,
DOI 10.1007/978-90-481-9112-3_16, © Springer Science+Business Media B.V. 2010

fact that this notion does not depend on the state is fundamental). If two candidates are not linked, they are said *compatible*.

For any CSP, two different candidates for the same variable are always linked; but there may be additional direct contradictions; as expliciting them is part of modelling the CSP, we consider them as given with the CSP.

In Sudoku, two different candidates $n_1r_1c_1$ and $n_2r_2c_2$ are linked if: ($n_1 \neq n_2$ & $r_1c_1 = r_2c_2$) or ($n_1 = n_2$ & share-a-unit(r_1c_1, r_2c_2)), where "share-a-unit" means "in the same row or in the same column or in the same block".

A. zt-whips in a general CSP

Definition: given a candidate Z (which will be called the target), a *zt-whip* of length n built on Z is a sequence L_1, R_1, L_2, R_2, … L_n, of 2n-1 (notice that there is no R_n) *different* candidates (alternatively called left-linking and right-linking candidates) for possibly different variables, such that, additionally:

for any $1 \leq k \leq n$, L_k is linked to R_{k-1} (setting $R_0 = Z$),

for any $1 \leq k < n$, L_k and R_k are candidates for the same variable (and they are therefore linked),

R_k is the only candidate for this variable compatible with Z and with the previous right-linking candidates (i.e. with all the R_j, for $j < k$),

for the same variable as L_n, there is no candidate compatible with the target and the previous right-linking candidates.

zt-whip theorem for a general CSP: in any knowledge state of any CSP, if Z is a target of a zt- whip of any length, then it can be eliminated (formally, this rule concludes ¬Z). The proof was given in [6].

B. The ZT measure of complexity

For any CSP, we are now in a position to define an increasing sequence of theories (i.e. sets of resolution rules) based on zt-whips, an increasing sequence of sets of minimal puzzles solved by these theories and a rating for these instances:

L_0 is the set of resolution rules expressing the propagation of constraints (elimination of candidates due to the presence of a value for a variable) and of resolution rules asserting values for variables that have a unique candidate left;

for any n>0, L_n is the union of L_0 with set of resolution rules for whips of length $\leq$ n.

as there can be no confusion between sets of rules and sets of instances, L_n is also used to name the set of minimal instances of the CSP that can be solved with rules in L_n;

given an instance of a CSP, its *ZT rating* is defined as the smallest n such that this instance is in L_n.

In Sudoku, the zt-rating has a nice structural property: it is invariant under the (n, r, c) natural super-symmetries of the game, i.e two puzzles that are isomorphic under any of these symmetries have the same zt-rating. For this reason, we named zt-whips nrczt-whips [4, 5] and the zt-rating NRCZT.

There was an anterior measure of complexity, the SER, based on a very different approach and compatible with the players intuition of complexity, but not invariant under symmetries. It appears that the correlation coefficient (computed on several collections of a million puzzles each) between the NRCZT and the SER is always high: 0.895.

Finally, there is also a very good correlation between the NRCZT and the logarithm of the number of partial whips used in the resolution process: 0.946. This number is an intuitive measure of complexity, because it indicates among how many useless whips the useful ones must be found.

These two properties show that the NRCZT rating is a good (logarithmic) measure of complexity, from both theoretical and pragmatic points of view. We can therefore conclude that the first task we had set forth is accomplished.

C. First statistical results for the Sudoku nrczt-whips

In the Sudoku case, we have programmed all the rules for nrczt-whips in our SudoRules solver, a knowledge based system, running indifferently on the CLIPS [8] or the JESS [9] inference engine.

The following statistics are relative to a sample of one million puzzles obtained with the suexg [10] top-down random generator. This was our first, naive approach to the generation problem: using a generator of random minimal puzzles widely available and used by the Sudoku community.

Row 2 of Table 1 below gives the number of puzzles with NRCZT rating n. Row 3 gives the total number of puzzles solved when whips of length $\leq$ n (corresponding to resolution theory L_n) are allowed. This shows that more than 99% of the puzzles can be solved with whips of length $\leq$ 5 and more than 99.9% with whips of length $\leq$ 7. But there remain a few exceptional cases with much larger complexity.

0	1	2	3	4	5	6	7	8	9	10	11	12	13
417,624	120,618	138,371	168,562	122,946	24,187	5,511	1,514	473	130	38	15	9	2
417,624	538,242	676,613	845,175	968,121	992,308	997,819	999,333	999,806	999,936	999,974	999,989	999,998	1,000,000

Table 1: Number of puzzles in 1,000,000 with NRCZT rating n (row2) and solved with nrczt-whips of length $\leq$ n (row 3).

IV. STANDARD TOP-DOWN AND BOTTOM-UP GENERATORS

A little after the above results were obtained, additional statistics led to suspect that the top-down suexg generator may have some bias. There is a very simple procedure for generating an unbiased Sudoku puzzle:

```
1) generate a random complete grid P;
2) for each cell in P, delete its value with probability ½, thus obtaining a puzzle Q;
3)if Q is minimal, return it, otherwise goto 1.
```

Unfortunately, the probability of getting a valid puzzle this way is infinitesimal and one has to rely on other generators. Before going further, we introduce the two classical algorithms for generating minimal puzzles: bottom-up and top-down.

A. The classical bottom-up and top-down generators [12]

A standard bottom-up generator works as follows to produce ***one*** minimal puzzle (it has to be iterated n times to produce n minimal puzzles):

```
1) start from an empty grid P
2a) in P, randomly choose an undecided cell and a value for it, thus getting a puzzle Q;
2b) if Q is minimal, return it and exit;
2b) if Q has several solutions, set P = Q and GOTO 2a;
2c) if Q has no solutions, then goto 2a (i.e. backtrack, forget Q and try another cell).
```

A standard top-down generator works as follows to produce ***one*** minimal puzzle (it has to be iterated n times to produce n minimal puzzles):

```
1) choose randomly a complete grid P;
2a) choose one clue randomly from P and delete it, thus obtaining a puzzle P2;
2b) if P2 has several solutions, GOTO 2a (i.e. reinsert the clue just deleted and try deleting another);
2c) if P2 is minimal, printout P2 and exit the whole procedure;
2d) otherwise (the puzzle has more than one solution), set P=P2 and GOTO 2a.
```

Clause 2c in the bottom-up case and clause 2b in the top-down case make any analysis very difficlut. Moroever, it seems that they also cause the generator to look for puzzles with fewer clues. It may thus be suspected of introducing a strong, uncontrolled bias with respect to the number of clues.

C. Existence of a bias and a (weak) correlation

The existence of a (as yet non measurable) bias in the number-of-clues distribution may in itself introduce a bias in the distribution of complexities (measured by the NRCZT or SER ratings). This bias may not be very large, as the correlation coefficient between the number of clues and the NRCZT or the SER was estimated (on our 1,000,000-puzzle sample) to be only 0.12. But it cannot be completely neglected either because it is an indication that other kinds of bias, with a potentially larger impact, may be present in these generators.

V. A CONTROLLED-BIAS GENERATOR

No generator of minimal puzzles is currently guaranteed to have no bias and building such a generator with reasonable computation times seems out of reach.

We therefore decided to proceed differently: taking the generators (more or less) as they are and applying corrections for the bias, if we can estimate it.

The method was inspired by what is done in cameras: instead of complex optimisations of the lenses to reduce typical anomalies (such as chromatic aberration, purple fringing, barrel or pincushion distortion…) – optimisations that lead to large and expensive lenses –, some camera makers now accept a small amount of these in the lenses and they correct the result in real time with dedicated software before recording the photo.

The main question was then: can we determine the bias of the classical top-down or bottom-up generators? Once again, the answer was negative. But there appears to be a medium way between "improving the lens" and "correcting its small defects by software": we devised a modification of the top-down generators such that it allows a precise mathematical computation of the bias.

A. Definition of the controlled-bias generator

Consider the following, modified top-down generator, the ***controlled-bias generator***; the procedure described below produces ***one*** minimal puzzle (it has to be iterated n times to produce n minimal puzzles):

```
1) choose randomly a complete grid P;
2a) choose one clue randomly from P and delete it, set P2 = the resulting puzzle;
2b) if P2 has several solutions, GOTO 1 (i.e. restart with another complete grid);
2c) if P2 is minimal, printout P2 and exit the whole procedure;
2d) otherwise (the puzzle has more than one solution), set P=P2 and GOTO 2a
```

The only difference with the top-down algorithm is in clause 2b: if a multi-solution puzzle is encountered, instead of backtracking to the previous state, the current complete grid is merely discarded and the search for a minimal puzzle is restarted with another complete grid.

Notice that, contrary to the standard bottom-up or top-down generators, which produce one minimal puzzle per complete grid, the controlled-bias generator will generally use several complete grids before it outputs a minimal puzzle. The efficiency question is: how many? Experimentations show that many complete grids (approximately 250,000 in the mean) are necessary before a minimal puzzle is reached. But this question is about the efficiency of the generator, it is not a conceptual problem.

The controlled-bias generator has the same output and will therefore produce minimal puzzles according to the same probability distribution as its following "virtual" counterpart:

```
Repeat until a minimal puzzle has been printed:
1) choose randomly a complete grid P;
2) repeat while P has at least one clue:
   2a) choose one clue randomly from P and delete it,
   thus obtaining a puzzle P2;
   2b) if P2 is minimal, print P2 (but do not exit the
   procedure);
   2c) set P=P2.
```

The only difference with the controlled-bias generator is that, once it has found a minimal or a multi-solution puzzle, instead of exiting, this virtual generator continues along a useless path until it reaches the empty grid.

But this virtual generator is interesting theoretically because it works similarly to the random uniform search defined in the next section and according to the same transition probabilities and it outputs minimal puzzles according to the probability Pr on the set B of minimal puzzles defined below.

B. Analysis of the controlled-bias generator

We now build our formal model of this generator.

Let us introduce the notion of a *doubly indexed puzzle.* We consider only (single or multi solution) consistent puzzles P. The double index of a doubly indexed puzzle P has a clear intuitive meaning: the first index is one of its solution grids and the second index is a sequence (notice: not a set, but a sequence, i.e. an ordered set) of clue deletions leading from this solution to P. In a sense, the double index keeps track of the full generation process.

Given a doubly indexed puzzle Q, there is an underlying singly-indexed puzzle: the ordinary puzzle obtained by forgetting the second index of Q, i.e. by remembering the solution grid from which it came and by forgetting the order of the deletions leading from this solution to Q.

Given a doubly indexed puzzle Q, there is also a non indexed puzzle, obtained by forgetting the two indices.

Notice that, for a single solution doubly indexed puzzle, the first index is useless as it can be computed from the puzzle; in this case singly indexed and non indexed are equivalent. In terms of the generator, it could equivalently output minimal puzzles or couples (minimal-puzzle, solution).

Consider now the following layered structure (a forest, in the graph-theoretic sense, i.e. a set of disjoint trees, with branches pointing downwards), the nodes being (single or multi solution) doubly indexed puzzles:

- floor 81 : the N different complete solution grids (considered as puzzles), each indexed by itself and by the empty sequence; notice that all the puzzles at floor 81 have 81 clues;

- recursive step: given floor n+1 (each doubly indexed puzzle of which has n+1 clues and is indexed by a complete grid that solves it and by a sequence of length 81-(n+1)), build floor n as follows:

each doubly indexed puzzle Q at floor n+1 sprouts n+1 branches; for each clue C in Q, there is a branch leading to a doubly indexed puzzle R at floor n: R is obtained from Q by removing clue C; its first index is identical to that of Q and its second index is the (81-n)-element sequence obtained by appending C to the end of the second index of Q; notice that all the doubly indexed puzzles at floor n have n clues and the length of their second index is equal to 1 + (81-(n+1)) = 81-n.

It is easy to see that, at floor n, each doubly indexed puzzle has an underlying singly indexed puzzle identical to that of (81 - n)! doubly indexed puzzles with the same first index at the same floor (including itself).

This is equivalent to saying that, at any floor n < 81, any singly indexed puzzle Q can be reached by exactly (81 - n)! different paths from the top (all of which start necessarily from the complete grid defined as the first index of Q). These paths are the (81 - n)! different ways of deleting one by one its missing 81-n clues from its solution grid.

Notice that this would not be true for non indexed puzzles that have multiple solutions. This is where the first index is useful.

Let N be the number of complete grids (N is known to be close to 6.67×10^{21}, but this is pointless here). At each floor n, there are N . 81! / n! doubly indexed puzzles and N . 81! / (81-n)! / n! singly indexed puzzles. For each n, there is therefore a uniform probability P(n) = 1/N . 1/81! . (81-n)! . n! that a singly indexed puzzle Q at floor n is reached by a random (uniform) search starting from one of the complete grids. What is important here is the ratio:

P(n+1) / P(n) = (n + 1) / (81 - n).

This formula is valid globally if we start from all the complete grids, as above, but it is also valid for all the single solution puzzles if we start from a single complete grid (just forget N in the proof above). (Notice however that it is not valid if we start from a subgrid instead of a complete grid.)

Now, call B the set of (non indexed) minimal puzzles. On B, all the puzzles are minimal. Any puzzle strictly above B has redundant clues and a single solution. Notice that, for all the puzzles on B and above B, singly indexed and non indexed puzzles are in one-to-one correspondence.

On the set B of minimal puzzles there is a probabily Pr naturally induced by the different Pn's and it is the probability that a minimal puzzle Q is output by our controlled-bias generator. It depends only on the number of clues and it is defined, up to a multiplicative constant k, by Pr(Q) = k P(n), if Q has n clues. k must be chosen so that the probabilities of all the minimal puzzles sum up to 1.

But we need not know k. What is important here is that, by construction of Pr on B (a construction which models the workings of the virtual controlled bias generator), the fundamental relation ***Pr(n+1) / Pr(n) = (n + 1) / (81 - n)*** holds for any two minimal puzzles, with respectively n+1 and n clues.

For n < 41, this relation means that a minimal puzzle with n clues is more likely to be reached from the top than a minimal puzzle with n+1 clues. More precisely, we have:

Pr(40) = Pr(41),

Pr(39) = 42/40 . Pr(40),

Pr(38) = 43/39 . Pr(39).

Repeated application of the formula gives Pr(24) = 61.11 Pr(30) : a puzzle with 24 clues has ~ 61 more chances of being output than a puzzle with 30 clues. This is indeed a strong bias.

A non-biased generator would give the same probability to all the minimal puzzles. The above relation shows that ***the controlled bias generator:***

- is unbiased when restricted (by filtering its output) to n-clue puzzles, for any fixed n,

- is biased towards puzzles with fewer clues,

- this bias is well known.

As we know precisely the bias with respect to uniformity, we can correct it easily by applying correction factors cf(n) to the probabilities on B. Only the relative values of the cf(n) is important: they satisfy cf(n+1) / cf(n) = (81 - n) / (n + 1). Mathematically, after normalisation, cf is just the relative density of the uniform distribution on B with respect to the probability distribution Pr.

This analysis also shows that a classical top-down generator is still more strongly biased towards puzzles with fewer clues because, instead of discarding the current path when it meets a multi-solution puzzle, it backtracks to the previous floor and tries again to go deeper.

C. Computing unbiased means and standard deviations using a controlled-bias generator

In practice, how can one compute unbiased statistics of minimal puzzles based on a (large) sample produced by a controlled-bias generator? Consider any random variable X defined (at least) on minimal puzzles. Define: on(n) = the number of n-clue puzzles in the sample, E(X, n) = the mean value of X for n-clue puzzles in the sample and sd(X, n) = the standard deviation of X for n-clue puzzles in the sample.

The (raw) mean of X is classically estimated as: sum[E(X, n) . on(n)] / sum[on(n)].

The corrected, unbiased mean of X must be estimated as (this is a mere weighted average):

unbiased-mean(X) =

sum[E(X, n).on(n).cf(n)] / sum[on(n).cf(n)].

Similarly, the raw standard deviation of X is classically estimated as: sqrt{sum[sd(X, n)^2 . on(n)] / sum[on(n)]}.

And the unbiased standard deviation of X must be estimated as (this is merely the standard deviation for a weighted average):

unbiased-sd(X) =

sqrt{sum[sd(X, n)^2.on(n).cf(n)] / sum[on(n).cf(n)]}.

These formulæ show that the cf(n) sequence needs to be defined only modulo a multiplicative factor.

It is convenient to choose cf(26) = 1. This gives the following sequence of correction factors (in the range n = 19-31, which includes all the puzzles of all the samples we have obtained with all the random generators considered here):

[0.00134 0.00415 0.0120 0.0329 0.0843 0.204 0.464 1 2.037 3.929 7.180 12.445 20.474]

It may be shocking to consider that 30-clue puzzles in a sample must be given a weight 61 times greater than a 24-clue puzzle, but it is a fact. As a result of this strong bias of the controlled-bias generator (strong but known and smaller than the other generators), unbiased statistics for the mean number of clues of minimal puzzles (and any variable correlated with this number) must rely on extremely large samples with sufficiently many 29-clue and 30-clue puzzles.

D. Implementation, experimentations and optimisations of the controlled-bias generator

Once this algorithm was defined, it was easily implemented by a simple modification of the top-down suexg – call it ***suexg-cb***. The modified generator, even after some optimisations, is much slower than the original one, but the purpose here is not speed, it is controlled bias.

V. Comparison of Results for Different Generators

All the results below rely on very large samples. Real values are estimated according to the controlled-bias theory.

A. Complexity as a function of the generator

Generator sample size	bottom-up 1,000,000	top-down 1,000,000	ctr-bias 5,926,343	real
SER mean	3.50	3.77	4.29	4.73
std dev	2.33	2.42	2.48	2.49
NRCZT mean	**1.80**	**1.94**	**2.22**	**2.45**
std dev	1.24	1.29	1.35	1.39

Table 2: SER and NRCZT means and standard deviations for bottom-up, top-down, controlled-bias generators and real estimated values.

	0	1	2	3	4	5	6	7	8	9	10	11	12-16
bottom-up	46.27	13.32	12.36	15.17	10.18	1.98	0.49	0.19	0.020	0.010	0 *	0.01 *	0 *
top-down	41.76	12.06	13.84	16.86	12.29	2.42	0.55	0.15	0.047	0.013	3.8e-3	1.5e-3	1.1e-3
ctr-bias	35.08	9.82	13.05	20.03	17.37	3.56	0.79	0.21	0.055	0.015	4.4e-3	1.2e-3	4.3e-4
real	**29.17**	**8.44**	**12.61**	**22.26**	**21.39**	**4.67**	**1.07**	**0.29**	**0.072**	**0.020**	**5.5e-3**	**1.5e-3**	**5.4e-4**

Table 3: The NRCZT-rating distribution (in %) for different kinds of generators, compared to the real distribution.

Table 2 shows that the mean (NRCZT or SER) complexity of minimal puzzles depends strongly on the type of generator used to produce them and that all the generators give rise to mean complexity below the real values.

Table 3 expresses the NRCZT complexity bias of the three kinds of generators. All these distributions have the same two modes, at levels 0 and 3, as the real distribution. But, when one moves from bottom-up to top-down to controlled-bias to real, the mass of the distribution moves progressively to the right. This displacement towards higher complexity occurs mainly at the first nrczt-levels, after which it is only very slight.

B. Number-of-clues distribution as a function of the generator

Table 4 partially explains Tables 2 and 3. More precisely, it explains why there is a strong complexity bias in the samples produced by the bottom-up and top-down generators, in spite of the weak correlation coefficient between the number of clues and the (SER or NRCZT) complexity of a puzzle: the bias with respect to the number of clues is very strong in these generators; *controlled-bias, top-down and bottom-up are increasingly biased towards easier puzzles with fewer clues.*

#clues	bottom-up %	top-down %	ctr-bias %	real %
20	0.028	0.0044	0.0	0.0
21	0.856	0.24	0.0030	0.000034
22	8.24	3.45	0.11	0.0034
23	27.67	17.25	1.87	0.149
24	36.38	34.23	11.85	2.28
25	20.59	29.78	30.59	13.42
26	5.45	12.21	33.82	31.94
27	0.72	2.53	17.01	32.74
28	0.054	0.27	4.17	15.48
29	0.0024	0.017	0.52	3.56
30	0	0.001	0.035	0.41
31	0	0	0.0012	0.022
mean	**23.87**	**24.38**	**25.667**	**26.577**
std-dev	1.08	1.12	1.116	1.116

Table 4: Number-of-clues distribution (%) for the bottom-up, top-down and controlled-bias generators and real estimated values.

VI. STABILITY OF THE CLASSIFICATION RESULTS

A. Insensivity of the controlled-bias generator to the source of complete grids

There remains a final question: do the above results depend on the source of complete grids. Until now, we have done as if this was not a problem. But producing unbiased collections of complete grids, necessary in the first step of all the puzzle generators, is all but obvious. It is known that there are 6.67 x 10^{21} complete grids; it is therefore impossible to have a generator scan them all. Up to isomorphisms, there are "only" 5.47 x 10^{9} complete grids, but this remains a very large number and storing them would require about 500 Gigabytes.

Very recently, a collection of all the (equivalence classes of) complete grids became available in a compressed format (6 Gb); at the same time, a real time decompressor became available. Both were provided by Glenn Fowler. All the results reported above for the controlled bias generator were obtained with this *a priori* unbiased source of complete grids.

Before this, all the generators we tried had a first phase consisting of creating a complete grid and this is where some type of bias could slip in. Nevertheless, several sources of complete grids based on very different generation principles were tested and the classification results remained very stable.

The insensitivity of the controlled-bias generator to the source of complete grids can be understood intuitively: it deletes in the mean two thirds of the initial grid data and any structure that might be present in the complete grids and cause a bias is washed away by the deletion phase.

B. Insensivity of the classification results to the choice of whips or braids

In [6], in addition to the notion of a zt-whip, we introduced the apparently much more general notion of a zt-braid, to which a B-NRCZT rating can be associated in the same way as the NRCZT rating was associated to zt-whips. The above statistical results are unchanged when NRCZT is replaced by B-NRCZT. Indeed, in 10,000 puzzles tested, only 20 have different NRCZT and B-NRCZT ratings. The NRCZT rating is thus a good approximation of the (harder to compute) B-NRCZT rating.

VII. COLLATERAL RESULTS

The number of minimal Sudoku puzzles has been a longstanding open question. We can now provide precise estimates for the mean number of n-clue minimal puzzles per complete grid and for the total number (Table 5).

number of clues	number of n-clue minimal puzzles per complete grid: mean	number of n-clue minimal puzzles per complete grid: relative error (= 1 std dev)
20	6.152e+6	70.7%
21	1.4654e+9	7.81%
22	1.6208e+12	1.23%
23	6.8827e+12	0.30%
24	1.0637e+14	0.12%
24	6.2495e+14	0.074%
26	1.4855e+15	0.071%
27	1.5228e+15	0.10%
28	7.2063e+14	0.20%
29	1.6751e+14	0.56%
30	1.9277e+13	2.2%
31	1.1240e+12	11.6%
32	4.7465e+10	70.7%
Total	**4.6655e+15**	**0.065%**

Table 5: Mean number of n-clue minimal puzzles per complete grid

Another number of interest is the mean proportion of n-clue minimal puzzles among the n-clue subgrids of a complete grids. Its inverse is the mean number of tries one should do to find an n-clue minimal by randomly deleting 81-n clues from a complete grid. It is given by Table 6.

number of clues	mean number of tries
20	7.6306e+11
21	9.3056e+9
22	2.2946e+8
23	1.3861e+7
24	2.1675e+6
24	8.4111e+5
26	7.6216e+5
27	1.5145e+6
28	6.1721e+6
29	4.8527e+7
30	7.3090e+8
31	2.0623e+10
32	7.6306e+11

Table 6: Inverse of the proportion of n-clue minimals among n-clue subgrids

One can also get, still ***with 0.065% relative error***: after multiplying by the number of complete grids (known to be 6,670,903,752,021,072,936,960 [13]), ***the total number of minimal Sudoku puzzles: 3.1055e+37***; after multiplying by the number of non isomorphic complete grids (known to be 5,472,730,538 [14]), ***the total number of non isomorphic minimal Sudoku puzzles: 2.5477e+25***.

VIII. CONCLUSION

The results reported in this paper rely on several months of (3 GHz) CPU time. They show that building unbiased samples of a CSP and obtaining unbiased statistics can be very hard.

Although we presented them, for definiteness, in the specific context of the Sudoku CSP, the sample generation methods described here (bottom-up, top-down and controlled-bias) could be extended to many CSPs. The specific P(n+1)/P(n) formula proven for the controlled-bias generator will not hold in general, but the general approach can in many cases help understand the existence of a very strong bias in the samples. Even in the very structured and apparently simple Sudoku domain, none of this was clear before the present analysis.

REFERENCES

[1] E.P.K. Tsang, *Foundations of Constraint Satisfaction*, Academic Press, 1993.

[2] H.W. Guesgen & J. Herztberg, *A Perspective of Constraint-Based Reasoning*, Lecture Notes in Artificial Intelligence, Springer, 1992.

[3] D. Berthier: *The Hidden Logic of Sudoku*, Lulu.com, May 2007.

[4] D. Berthier: *The Hidden Logic of Sudoku (Second Edition)*, Lulu.com Publishers, December 2007.

[5] D. Berthier: From Constraints to Resolution Rules; Part I: conceptual framework, *CISSE08/SCSS, International Joint Conferences on Computer, Information, and System Sciences, and Engineering*, December 4-12, 2009.

[6] D. Berthier: From Constraints to Resolution Rules; Part II: chains, braids, confluence and T&E, *CISSE08/SCSS, International Joint Conferences on Computer, Information, and System Sciences, and Engineering*, December 4-12, 2009.

[7] M. Gary & D. Johnson, *Computers and Intractability: A Guide to the Theory of NP-Completeness*, Freeman, 1979.

[8] G. Riley, *CLIPS online documentation*, http://clipsrules.sourceforge.net/OnlineDocs.html, 2008.

[9] E.J. Friedmann-Hill, *JESS Manual*, http://www.jessrules.com/jess/docs/71, 2008.

[10]G. Stertenbrink, *suexg*, http://www.setbb.com/phpb/viewtopic.php?t=206&mforum=sudoku, 2005.

[11]B. Felgenhauer & F. Jarvis, Sudoku enumeration problems, http://www.afjarvis.staff.shef.ac.uk/sudoku/, 2006.

[12]E. Russell & F. Jarvis, There are 5472730538 essentially different Sudoku grids, http://www.afjarvis.staff.shef.ac.uk/sudoku/sudgroup.html, 2006.

Factors that Influence the Productivity of Software Developers in a Developer View

Edgy Paiva
UNIFOR, IVIA
Fortaleza, Brazil
Email: edgy.paiva@ivia.com.br

Danielly Barbosa
UNIFOR
Fortaleza, Brazil
Email: daniellybg@gmail.com

Roberto Lima Jr
UNIFOR, E-NOVAR
Fortaleza, Brazil
Email: roberto@enovar.com.br

Adriano Albuquerque
UNIFOR
Fortaleza, Brazil
Email: adrianoba@unifor.br

Abstract- **To measure and improve the productivity of software developers is one of the greatest challenges faced by software development companies. Therefore, aiming to help these companies to identify possible causes that interfere in the productivity of their teams, we present in this paper a list of 32 factors, extracted from the literature, that influence the productivity of developers. To obtain the ranking of these factors, we have applied a questionnaire with developers. In this work, we present the results: the factors that have the greatest positive and negative influence on productivity, the factors with no influence and the most important factors and what influences them. To finish, we present a comparison of the results obtained from the literature.**

I. INTRODUCTION

One of the fundamental issues facing the software engineering industry is programmer productivity. Over the past several years, many studies have demonstrated a wide disparity in the productivity of similarly experienced programmers [1].

According to [1], if a company is able to identify the most productive programmers and eliminate or further train the least productive, the resulting productivity increases would be a competitive advantage.

With software development viewed more as an art than a science, it has been difficult to study the productivity factors, which affect software projects, and to accurately predict software development costs. The lack of understanding of software productivity and productivity measurement methods has caused confusion in software cost estimation. In order to improve the quality of a software product, and the productivity of the development process, accurate measurements of development costs and productivity factors are required [2].

In the software industry, productivity and quality are primordial and must be considered simultaneously because the fact that a professional is able to perform his/her task fast, but without quality, does not mean that he/she is productive. The most important, for the issue of productivity, is to perform a task with quality in the shortest time possible.

For a matter of competitiveness, companies need to increasingly improve the productivity of their development teams and, for that, acknowledge the factors that influence such productivity. However, it is observed that companies usually do not know these factors and, furthermore, cannot measure the influence of such factors.

According to [3], basically there are three major stages in the process of software productivity improvement: measuring, analyzing, and improving software productivity.

There are several articles that aim to identify the factors that have influence on the productivity of developers, but no article was found that lists a ranking of these factors. Our work aims to identify the factors that influence the productivity of developers and to define a ranking.

This article is organized as follows: The second section presents studies about productivity in the software industry. The third section presents the survey performed. In the fourth section, we present the result obtained from applying the questionnaires. The fifth section presents a comparison of the result of our survey with existing works. Finally, we finish by presenting the conclusion.

II. RELATED WORKS ON PRODUCTIVITY IN THE SOFTWARE INDUSTRY

A. *Systematic Review*

Since a systematic review aims to reach a higher level of scientific rigor, we have decided not to do a conventional literature review, but to do a systematic review [4]. Unlike conventional literature reviews, in which the researcher does not follow a defined process, a systematic review is done in a formal manner, following a pre-defined protocol. This way, the result tends to be more reliable since it uses a methodology that is rigorous and capable of being audited and repeated.

According to [4], a systematic literature review is defined as a way to identify, evaluate and interpret the available research that is relevant to an issue or discipline, or phenomenon of interest of a specific research domain.

The activities of a systematic review should include: formulate a research question; identify the need to conduct a systematic review; exhaustive and thorough search, including primary studies; evaluate the quality of the selected studies; extract data; summarize the results of the study; interpret the results to determine its applicability; and write the report [5].

This systematic review aims to identify relevant publications that comment on factors that influence the productivity of developers. The search for articles was done in the ACM (Association for Computing Machinery) and the IEEE (Institute of Electrical and Electronics Engineers) digital libraries, using the term "software productivity" and "factors".

We have not limited the date to search on the libraries and the articles have been selected from inclusion and exclusion criteria.

We have excluded articles that do not present factors that influence the productivity and included articles that presented factors that influence the productivity.

T. Sobh, K. Elleithy (eds.), *Innovations in Computing Sciences and Software Engineering*,
DOI 10.1007/978-90-481-9112-3_17,

In the first search, we have found 28 articles in the IEEE digital library and 5 articles in the ACM digital library. From these articles, we have selected 10 articles from IEEE and one article from ACM. Therefore, a total of 33 articles were analyzed, but only 11 articles were selected for this review.

There are several factors that influence the productivity of developers; however, each author lists distinct factors. Therefore, aiming to include the factors in a questionnaire, it was necessary to unify some of them, since it is one of the goals of this work to define a ranking of the factors.

B. *Main Identified Factors*

In the researched studies, we have identified several factors that influence the productivity in the software development because according to [6], productivity is impacted by a great number of factors.

In this systematic review, the most frequently mentioned factors were: experience of the team, programming language used, code reuse, size of the project and consistent requirements.

In the next section, we will detail the factors used in our survey.

Peck and Callahan [1] affirm that the difference in the productivity in certain situations is higher, with a ratio of 28:1 from the most productive to the least productive. Even though this is an extreme scenario, many studies show a ratio of 10:1. Besides, other researchers have also showed that the most productive programmers also produce the best code.

III. Survey

The survey of the factors that influence the productivity of software developers was composed of several steps.

In the first survey step, for the systematic review, we have selected articles that are relevant to the topic of productivity in software development, and from these articles, we have listed the previously mentioned factors and grouped the ones with the same meaning, resulting in 32 factors, as presented in Table 1.

TABLE 1
FINAL LIST OF FACTORS

Factor	Description
Agile Methodology	Adoption of a methodology that uses agile processes and/or practices (XP, SCRUM).
Architecture	A software architecture that is clear and adequate.
Benefits	The company offers additional benefits, such as health insurance, food stamps and participation in profits.
Code Reuse	Existence of a code library for reuse and policies for code reuse.
Commitment	Professional is devoted and committed with his/her work.
Communication	Appropriate communication in projects, frequent meetings to review the status, etc.
Consistent Requirements	The requirements given by the analyst are clear, complete and stable.
Development Tool	Use adequate tools for software development. Example: Visual Studio, Eclipse, etc.
Documentation	Updated documentation for all phases of the software development lifecycle.
Domain of the Application	Knowledge on the domain of the application that is being developed. Example: Medical Systems.
Experience	Knowledge and experience on processes, methodology, technology and tools used in the work.
Home Office	Work in the "home-office" format.
Internet Access	Free access to the Internet, including chats, YouTube, social networks, etc.
Interpersonal Relationship	Have a good relationship with colleagues and customers.
Knowledge Management	Have an environment and policies for knowledge management.
Maturity Level	The company has a specific level of process maturity (e.g. MPSBR, ISO or CMMI).
Methodology	The company has a formal software development methodology.
Modernity	Always use the new technologies available in the market.
Motivation	Be motivated with the work.
Physical Location	Easy access to the workspace (e.g. no traffic, availability of public transportation).
Programming Language	Programming language is part of the latest generation.
Project Management	Have an adequate project management.
Project Size	The size of the project (effort) is very high.
Prototyping	Project has used software prototyping
Salary	Have a salary according to the market.
Team Size	The project has a large number of people in the team (more than 20).
Technological Gap	Use of obsolete tools / software versions. Example: Fortran.
Test	The project has policies for tests (the test is done before the code is sent to the customer).
Training	Adequate training prior to performing specific activities.
Type of Project	The project is for development or maintenance.
Work Environment	A pleasant work environment, with a nice, silent and comfortable space.
Workstation	Use of an appropriate workstation (physical infra-structure) to perform activities.

After selecting the factors, a questionnaire was created for developers to assess the type and level of influence that each factor has in the productivity during software development. The questionnaire was administered as a pilot-study with five developers and one university professor, who could give their opinions and criticisms, aiming to assemble the final version of the questionnaire.

After the application in the pilot-study, the necessary adjustments were made and the final questionnaire to be applied was created, containing three sections: contextualization of the company, profile of the respondent and evaluation of the factors.

The section for the contextualization of the company collected data related to the companies, such as: sector in which the company is active (public or private), quantity of employees, for how long it has been in operation and if it applies evaluation methods (e.g. CMMI [7], MPS.BR [8] or ISO 9001[9]).

The section for the profile of the respondent identified some characteristics of the respondents, such as: time of experience in this job, if they have any certification (PMI, Microsoft, IBM, Sun or others) and the level of education.

These two sections were useful to group the collected data, to identify patterns related to the level of maturity of the companies and of the respondents and to identify whether this data influences the way they see the productivity in software development.

For the section about the evaluation of the factors, each factor was explained with a brief description to facilitate understanding. Each factor was classified according to the following options: High positive influence (HPI), Low positive influence (LPI), No influence (NI), Low negative influence (LNI), High negative influence (HNI) and No comment (NC).

At the end of the questionnaire, we requested the respondents to list five factors that have more positive influence on the productivity in software development and the factors that influenced these five factors the most.

We have applied the questionnaire in 11 (eleven) companies in Ceará, a state in the Northeast of Brazil. The sample size was 77 (seventy seven) respondents.

IV. Results

In this section, we will present the results obtained from the data analysis of the questionnaires. Since we have used different scales to measure the influence of productivity (HPI, LPI, NI, LNI, HNI, NC), for this study, in which we aim to identify the factors that have a greater influence on the productivity of developers, it is relevant only to present the results that have High positive influence (HPI), No influence (NI) and High negative influence (HNI), excluding the results from

Low positive influence (LPI) and Low negative influence (LNI).

The factors Home Office, Knowledge Management and Agile Methodology were the ones that had the highest response rates of NO. We concluded that the respondents, possibly, do not have experience in working in the home-office format and in using knowledge management and agile methodologies.

A. *Profile of Surveyed Companies*

The questionnaire was applied in 11 (eleven) companies, being 1 (one) public and 10 (ten) private companies.

The greatest part of the companies (72,73%) has more than 9 (nine) years of existence and only one company has less than 3 years of existence, which we concluded that the surveyed companies have a certain level of maturity. From the surveyed companies, only 27,27% was evaluated by CMMI [7] or MPS.BR [8], and 36,36% have ISO 9001 certificate [9], therefore most of the surveyed companies do not have a formal process that is well defined and evaluated.

B. *Profile of Surveyed Professionals*

Only 6,49% of the respondents has more than 9 (nine) years of experience and 11,69% of the respondents has up to 6 years of experience in the job. It is apparent then, that in the profile of developers, there are many people who do not have much experience.

From the surveyed professionals, 38,96% has an official certificate of a manufacturer and 54,55% has not yet finished college. Therefore, besides not having experience in the job, most of the developers are still attending the university.

C. *Factors that have High Positive Influence (HPI)*

According to our survey, as depicted in Table 2, the factors that have highest positive influence on productivity are: Commitment and Motivation. We understand that this result is related with the fact that these factors are the basis for any professional who wants to productively perform their activities.

For the developers, the fact that requirements are consistent increases the productivity because not understanding requirements leads to doubts and, consequently, reduces productivity.

TABLE 2
Factors that have High Positive Influence (HPI) on Productivity

POSITION	FACTOR	QTY	%
1	Commitment	67	87,0%
2	Motivation	67	87,0%
3	Consistent requirements	65	84,4%
4	Work Environment	64	83,1%
5	Salary	63	81,8%
6	Workstation	61	79,2%
7	Development Tool	60	77,9%
8	Project Management	58	75,3%
9	Experience	56	72,7%
10	Interpersonal Relationship	56	72,7%

The work environment and a good workstation have also been considered as important. Simple actions, such as replacing the equipment of the developer or adding extra memory and maybe even changing to a more comfortable chair can positively influence the productivity.

Development tools have also been considered as important and, indeed, tools that facilitate editing the code, debugging and other aspects, provide better productivity.

The salary is also among the ones with highest influence on productivity. Developers are the lowest paid professionals involved in the project, therefore, they end up having financial problems that influence the productivity.

Interpersonal relationship has also been considered as an important factor, mainly because, in software projects, there is a great need to interact with the team members of a project.

Considered by most of the articles as a very important factor, the Experience factor was 15% below the factor that was considered the most important. Possibly, the majority of the respondents consider that they have a level of experience appropriate to perform their activities and do not consider that they would produce more if they were more experienced.

Project management, which is a key success factor for any software project, was also considered as important by the respondents.

D. Factors with No Influence on Productivity (NI)

For factors that do not influence the productivity (Table 3), the main factor is the "Home Office" factor, possibly the majority of the respondents is not used to work in this format, therefore, they believe that this factor has no influence on productivity.

TABLE 3
FACTORS THAT HAVE NO INFLUENCE ON PRODUCTIVITY (NI)

POSITION	FACTOR	QTY	%
1	Home Office	12	15,6%
2	Knowledge Management	12	15,6%
3	Agile Methodology	10	13,0%
4	Type of Project	7	9,1%
5	Architecture	5	6,5%
6	Maturity Level	5	6,5%
7	Team Size	5	6,5%
8	Project Size	5	6,5%
9	Prototyping	5	6,5%
10	Technological Gap	4	5,2%

The knowledge management, the type of project (development or maintenance) and the project size (when the effort is very high) were evaluated as not having influence on productivity. This makes sense since the survey was conducted directly with developers, who, possibly, receive an artifact to be developed and it makes no difference if the artifact is for development or maintenance. Usually, they also not use knowledge management tool and it does not make any difference whether the team is large or not because each developer will perform the activities assigned to him/her.

The "Agile Methodology" factor was considered to have no influence, which is justifiable because most respondents do not work with agile methods. The fact that maturity level was also considered with no influence may have been for the same reason.

E. Factors that have High Negative Influence (HNI) on Productivity

According to Table 4, the Technological Gap (Use of obsolete tools / software versions. Example: Fortran) was considered to have the Highest Negative Influence on Productivity. Because of that, it is important for the development team to work with recent technologies (not obsolete).

TABLE 4
FACTORS THAT HAVE HIGH NEGATIVE INFLUENCE (HNI) ON PRODUCTIVITY

POSITION	FACTOR	QTY	%
1	Technological Gap	46	59,7%
2	Methodology	38	49,4%
3	Home Office	11	14,3%
4	Team Size	10	13,0%
5	Internet Access	6	7,8%
6	Project Size	3	3,9%
7	Maturity Level	2	2,6%
8	Modernity	1	1,3%
9	Documentation	1	1,3%
10	Workstation	1	1,3%

The fact that the company does not have a formal software development methodology ("Methodology" factor) was also considered as a high negative influence on productivity. We have, therefore, considered as highly important for companies to have a formal software development methodology.

Some of the respondents considered negative the fact of working at home, which is a tendency in some corporations. We believe that this result is related to the greater difficulty to interact with the other participants of the project.

The fact that the team is large ("Team Size" factor) has also been considered as a negative influence on productivity. This makes perfect sense especially because in a project with a large team, the management effort is much higher and it becomes necessary to interact with more people.

Even though it has been mentioned as a factor that has no influence on productivity (NI), Internet Access has also been considered negative, since some people disperse with free Internet access, they browse for long hours and, consequently, their productivity decreases.

The other factors did not have great quantitative relevance and, therefore, they will not be mentioned.

F. Most Important Factors and What Influences Them

At the end of the survey, we asked what were the 5 (five) most important factors from the list of High Positive Influence. We have also asked which factors influenced these items. The result is depicted in Table 5.

The factors considered as most important were: Motivation, Salary, Work environment, Commitment and Experience.

Among the factors that were considered as MORE IMPORTANT (Table 5) and the factors that were selected as HIGH POSITIVE INFLUENCE ON PRODUCTIVITY (Table 2), we have concluded that, from 10 (ten) factors most voted as HPI, 9 (nine) were considered as the most important ones and there are only changes in order of position from Table 2 and Table 5.

TABLE 5
FACTORS WITH HIGHEST DEGREE OF IMPORTANCE AMONG THE FACTORS WITH HIGH POSITIVE INFLUENCE

POS.	FACTOR	QTY.	INFLUENCE 1	INFLUENCE 2	INFLUENCE 3
1	Motivation	47	Salary	Work Environment	Benefits
2	Salary	37	Benefits	Experience	Commitment
3	Work Environment	32	Workstation	Interpersonal Relationship	Physical Location
4	Commitment	25	Motivation	Work Environment	Salary
5	Experience	25	Training	Commitment	Motivation
6	Interpersonal Relationship	18	Communication	Team Size	Work Environment
7	Consistent Requirements	18	Documentation	Communication	Domain of the Application
8	Project Management	17	Experience	Methodology	Communication
9	Workstation	15	Work Environment	Development Tool	Architecture
10	Domain of the Application	14	Training	Experience	Communication

F. Most Important Factors and What Influences Them

At the end of the survey, we asked what were the 5 (five) most important factors from the list of High Positive Influence. We have also asked which factors influenced these items. The result is depicted in Table 5.

The factors considered as most important were: Motivation, Salary, Work environment, Commitment and Experience.

Among the factors that were considered as MORE IMPORTANT (Table 5) and the factors that were selected as HIGH POSITIVE INFLUENCE ON PRODUCTIVITY (Table 2), we have concluded that, from 10 (ten) factors most voted as HPI, 7 (seven) were considered as the most important ones.

V. COMPARISON OF THE SURVEY WITH THE LITERATURE

In Table 6, we compare our ranking with the most important factors that were indicated in the literature.

The "Experience" and "Consistent Requirements" factors were the only ones that were considered as very important in both studies.

In the literature, it is also presented as important factors the following: Programming Language, Code Reuse and Project Size. In our survey, these factors appear in the last positions.

According to [6], the "Project Size" factor is the most basic factor in the analysis of productivity. There is a tendency to increase the productivity as the project size increases. In the survey, this factor was not considered as important since, for developers, the productivity of developers is the same whether the project is large or small.

According to [10], the "Communication" factor has a great influence on productivity. In large projects, many of the problems, if not most of them, are the result of the lack of communication. In the survey, communication is also considered important (14th position).

Enthusiasm can be contagious and people tend to produce more in an optimistic environment than in an environment that is "negative towards work" [11]. The "Work Environment" factor proves this, besides having influence on the motivation of the developer.

Reuse of previously tested code improves productivity and, consequently, decreases the development time because it reduces the need to create new code [12]. Code reuse was not considered important in our survey, possibly because the interviewed developers do not practice reuse in their companies.

TABLE 6
COMPARISON OF THE SURVEY AND THE LITERATURE

POS.	MOST IMPORTANT FACTOR	QTY.	FACTORS FROM THE LITERATURE
1	Motivation	47	**Experience**
2	Salary	37	Programming Language
3	Work Environment	32	**Consistent Requirements**
4	Commitment	25	Code Reuse
5	**Experience**	25	Project Size
6	Interpersonal Relationship	18	
7	**Consistent Requirements**	18	
8	Project Management	17	
9	Workstation	15	
10	Domain of Application	14	
24	**Programming Language**	3	
26	Code Reuse	3	
32	Project Size	0	

The time spent learning what the customer wants or needs at the beginning of the project should reduce the frequency of future changes in the specification [12]. Indeed, the "Consistent Requirements" factor is very important for the productivity of developers since re-work is discouraging for any professional.

Finally, contracting the best people and supporting them with training increases productivity and speed [12]. There is no doubt that the "Experience" factor is primordial to increase productivity.

VI. Conclusion and Future Works

Several factors influence the productivity of software developers. For a company to become more competitive, it is necessary to measure, analyze and improve the main factors that influence the productivity of developers.

For instance, in a company where it is identified that a workstation has a high influence on the productivity of the developer, the investment in new workstations (low cost in comparison to the developer salary) could bring a high gain in productivity for the company.

We have had some divergences between the survey and the literature. This is due to the fact that the survey is subjective and expresses the opinion of developers, while some articles in the literature make a real measurement of projects and come to more objective conclusions. However, in this work, it is extremely relevant to understand the factors that influence the productivity of developers from their own opinion.

According to the item *C.Factors that have High Positive Influence (HPI)*, the "Motivation" and "Commitment" factors are the basis for any professional to productively perform their activities. Since they are in the literature, these factors were included in our survey, however for future surveys in other regions, it would be important not to consider them since they will always be mentioned as HPI.

We consider important for future works to perform a survey in other regions in Brazil because we understand that some factors can be relevant in one region and not so relevant in another one.

After identifying the factors that have highest influence on the productivity, we will also seek to define a model capable of measuring each factor individually (developer) and organizationally. This model could be used as a basis for developer productivity improvement programs in companies.

Another future work is to perform a bibliographical study to identify what can be done to minimize the effect of factors that have HPI on the developer. For instance: how to improve communication in projects? What must be done to improve the developer work environment?

Last, but not least, since software development is done by people and it is considered more an "art" than a "science", it is necessary to have continuous investment on what is more important so companies have more productivity and quality: the People.

References

[1] Peck, C., Callahan, D.W.. "A proposal for measuring software productivity in a working environment", 2002. [Online]. Website: http://ieeexplore.ieee.org/search/freesrchabstract.jsp?arnumber=1027063&isnumber=22050&punumber=7971&k2dockey=1027063@ieeecnfs

[2] Yu, W. D. "A Modeling Approach to Software Cost Estimation", 1990. [Online]. Website: http://ieeexplore.ieee.org/search/freesrchabstract.jsp?arnumber=46886&isnumber=1775&punumber=49&k2dockey=46886@ieeejrns

[3] Yu, W. D., Smith, D. P., Huang, S. T. "Software productivity measurements", 1990. [Online]. Website: http://ieeexplore.ieee.org/search/freesrchabstract.jsp?arnumber=170239&isnumber=4410&punumber=342&k2dockey=170239@ieeecnfs

[4] Kitchenham, B. (2004), "Procedures for Performing Systematic Reviews", Keele technical report SE0401 and NICTA technical report 0400011T.1.

[5] Pai, M., McCulloch, M., Gorman, J., Pai, N., Enanoria, W., Kennedy, G., Tharyan, P., Colford Jr., J. (2004), "Systematic reviews and meta-analyses: An illustrated step-by-step guide". The National Medical Journal of India, 17(2), pp: 86-95.

[6] Wang, Hao, Wang, Haiqing, Zhang,H. "Software Productivity Analysis with CSBSG Data Set", 2008. [Online]. Website: http://ieeexplore.ieee.org/search/freesrchabstract.jsp?arnumber=4722120&isnumber=4721981&punumber=4721667&k2dockey=4722120@ieeecnfs

[7] CMMI – Capability Maturity Model Integration. Website: http://www.cmmi.de/cmmi_v1.2/browser.html

[8] MPS.BR – Melhoria no Processo de Desenvolvimento de Software. Website: http://www.softex.br/mpsbr/_home/default.asp

[9] NBR ISO 9001 - ASSOCIAÇÃO BRASILEIRA DE NORMAS TÉCNICAS.– Sistema de Gestão da Qualidade – Requisitos. Rio de Janeiro, 2008. Website: http://www.abnt.org.br

[10] Simmons, D. B. "Communications : a software group productivity dominator", 1991. [Online]. Website: http://ieeexplore.ieee.org/xpl/freeabs_all.jsp?isnumber=3440&arnumber=120430

[11] Sherdil, K., Madhavji, N. H. "Personal 'Progress Functions' in the Software Process", 1994. [Online]. Website: http://ieeexplore.ieee.org/search/freesrchabstract.jsp?arnumber=512780&isnumber=11304&punumber=3880&k2dockey=512780@ieeecnfs

[12] Blackburn, J. D., Scudder, G. D., Wassenhove, N. V. "Improving Speed and Productivity of Software Development: A Global Survey of Software Developers", 1996. [Online]. Website: http://ieeexplore.ieee.org/search/freesrchabstract.jsp?arnumber=553636&isnumber=11972&punumber=32&k2dockey=553636@ieeejrns

Algorithms for Maintaining a Consistent Knowledge Base in Distributed Multiagent Environments

Stanislav Ustymenko
Meritus University, NB, Canada
sustymenko@meritusu.ca

Daniel G. Schwartz
Florida State University, Tallahassee, FL, USA, schwartz@cs.fsu.edu

Abstract

In this paper, we design algorithms for a system that allows Semantic Web agents to reason within what has come to be known as the Web of Trust. We integrate reasoning about belief and trust, so agents can reason about information from different sources and deal with contradictions. Software agents interact to support users who publish, share and search for documents in a distributed repository. Each agent maintains an individualized topic taxonomy for the user it represents, updating it with information obtained from other agents. Additionally, an agent maintains and updates trust relationships with other agents.

When new information leads to a contradiction, the agent performs a belief revision process informed by a degree of belief in a statement and the degree of trust an agent has for the information source.

The system described has several key characteristics. First, we define a formal language with well-defined semantics within which an agent can express the relevant conditions of belief and trust, and a set of inference rules. The language uses symbolic labels for belief and trust intervals to facilitate expressing inexact statements about subjective epistemic states. Second, an agent's belief set at a given point in time is modeled using a Dynamic Reasoning System (DRS). This allows the agent's knowledge acquisition and belief revision processes to be expressed as activities that take place in time. Third, we explicitly describe reasoning processes, creating algorithms for acquiring new information and for belief revision.

1. Introduction

The Semantic Web (SW) [2] is a vision of knowledge management on a global scale. The SW retains the massively decentralized nature of the current World Wide Web, with an unlimited number of knowledge sources identifiable by unique URIs. It supports rich metadata annotation, including expressive ontology languages. The SW addresses two distinct but mutually influencing trends.

The first trend is towards integrating heterogeneous knowledge artifacts into common virtual repositories. Digital artifacts (textual documents, databases, images, and other media files) and expertise sources (individuals, groups, and organizations) are catalogued, searched, and accessed through common interfaces and techniques.

To support such integration, elaborate metadata technologies are utilized. The more diverse are the resources that are being managed, the more the users' efficiency relies on common classification schemata. At the same time, metadata complexity increases. This makes managing the metadata increasingly difficult. In this context, there is demand for flexible formal approaches and representation formats.

The second trend involves the desire to engage the users in knowledge producing activities. The recent explosion in social software popularity demonstrates that large groups of users, operating in an essentially autonomous fashion and motivated by self-interest, can successfully create and maintain large knowledge repositories. Social dynamics can be unleashed to effect information filtering, collaborative knowledge creation, classification, and quality management. Tools and practices referred to as Web 2.0 and Enterprise 2.0 are in the mainstream of the knowledge management field.

Consider an archive of publicly available resources updated by a community of knowledge workers (e.g., a preprint archive of scientific papers). Indexing information in a digital archive requires extensive metadata schemas, enabling accurate categorization for navigation and search. Such a metadata system would include concepts organized in a taxonomic hierarchy, thesaurus, or more complex knowledge structure utilizing ontology semantics.

One obstacle for utilizing ontology-based techniques for large and/or evolving archives, such as digital repositories of research papers, is defining an ontology of concepts so as to satisfy the needs of the majority of users, who might have conflicting perspectives on overlapping areas of inquiry. Ideally, metadata created should reflect perspectives of different groups while spanning all the content and recognizing links between alternative conceptualizations. At the same time the system should maximize the quality of the ontology.

Our position is that the task of constructing a comprehensive ontology is best left to the evolving community of users to carry out. We describe a Web-based system which allows users, individually and through collaboration, to define ontologies to classify

T. Sobh, K. Elleithy (eds.), *Innovations in Computing Sciences and Software Engineering*,
DOI 10.1007/978-90-481-9112-3_18,

documents in a collection. Users will form online communities around domains of interest, contributing to ontology engineering through discussions and collaborative editing. A software system that would support such collaboration has to have ability to handle inconsistencies, by performing belief revision.

Schwartz's Dynamic Reasoning System (DRS) [4, 5] framework allows one to portray belief revision as a form of back tracking along the lines of the "truth maintenance," or "reason maintenance," systems devised by Doyle [3]. A DRS contains a "derivation path" consisting of propositions that are either instances of logical axiom schemas, expressions of information obtained from outside sources (human users, sensors, etc.), or derived from propositions appearing earlier in the path by means of logical rules of inference. In this manner the derivation path represents the current belief set, or knowledge base, of the reasoning agent. Whenever a proposition is entered into the path it is attached with a "label" containing information about how it was obtained (in particular, if it was derived by applying an inference rule, what premises were involved), its current "status" (believed or disbelieved), Moreover, if the proposition is derived from some premises by means of a rule, then the labels of the premises are updated to show that this new proposition depended on them.

If, at some point in time, a contradictory proposition is entered into the path, then this triggers a process (typically human assisted) of working backwards through the path, following the information stored in the labels, looking for "culprit" propositions that may be held responsible for having led to the contradiction. Some of these propositions are then removed from the set of currently held beliefs, so as to eliminate the contradiction, and one uses the proposition labels once again to forward chain through all deductions that originated from these propositions and remove them from the current belief set as well. This process can obviously give rise to complexity issues, but it is nonetheless both theoretically feasible and finitary.

Elsewhere [6] we present a formal logic system that can support multiagent communication, by explicitly representing agents, agents' beliefs, and trust relationships between agents. Here, we present reasoning procedures that can support consistency of a bibliographic knowledge base, developed as part of doctoral dissertation [6]. The same algorithms can be extended to work with other limited domains.

2. Logic and knowledge base

The agent's knowledge base includes the following:

- A Dynamic Reasoning System containing taxonomic knowledge of the agent in the form of a derivation path at a given point in time.
- A taxonomy tree, containing a topic hierarchy calculated using the DRS. This can serve as an index, helping to guide the inference process.
- A list of documents. A document record will link to all the topics to which the document belongs.
- Trust information. A list of all currently held trust relationships of a particular agent.

For a formal representation system, we require a logic that enables us to speak about individual documents. To this end we now extend the propositional calculus for belief and trust presented in [6] to a first-order predicate calculus. This somewhat follows the line of development in [5], but, whereas that work concerns only belief conditions, the present treatment additionally incorporates the notion of trust.

First, following [6], let us adopt the following notations:

$\mathcal{B}_4$ *unequivocally believes*
$\mathcal{B}_3$ *strongly believes*
$\mathcal{B}_2$ *fairly confidently believes*
$\mathcal{B}_1$ *somewhat believes*
$\mathcal{B}_0$ *neither believes nor disbelieves*
$\mathcal{B}_{-1}$ *somewhat disbelieves*
$\mathcal{B}_{-2}$ *fairly |confidently disbelieves*
$\mathcal{B}_{-3}$ *strongly disbelieves*
$\mathcal{B}_{-4}$ *unequivocally disbelieves*

These are taken to express various grades of strength in the agent's disposition towards believing in a given proposition. In particular, $\mathcal{B}_0$ expresses uncertainty, either in the sense that the agent has information to both support and refute the proposition in question, or in the sense that the agent suffers from a complete lack of information regarding the truth or falsehood of the proposition.

Similarly, let us define the following notation for trust:

$\mathcal{T}_4$ for *total trust*
$\mathcal{T}_3$ for *strong trust*
$\mathcal{T}_2$ for *medium trust*
$\mathcal{T}_1$ for *low trust*
$\mathcal{T}_0$ for *no trust*

Here, trust is treated as a positive value. "No trust" can mean either justified distrust or lack of information.

Proposition are here expressed as formulas and may have any of the following forms (cf. [6] for further details):

$F_1 = \{p(t_1, \ldots, t_n) \mid p \text{ is an n-ary predicate symbol, } n \geq 1, \text{ and the } t_i \text{ are terms}\}$

$F_2 = F_1 \cup \{\neg P, (P \vee Q), (P \wedge Q), (P \rightarrow Q) \mid P, Q \in F_1 \cup F_2\}$

$F_3 = \{\mathcal{B}_i(a, P) \mid P \in F_2, i = -4, \ldots, 4 \text{ and } a \in \{a_1, a_2, \ldots\}\}$

$F_4 = F_3 \cup \{(\dot{\neg} P), (P \dot{\vee} Q), (P \dot{\wedge} Q), (P \dot{\rightarrow} Q) \mid P, Q \in F_4\}$

$F_5 = \{\mathcal{T}_i(a, b) \mid i = -4, \ldots, 4 \text{ and } a, b \in \{a_1, a_2, \ldots\}\}$

$F_6 = F_5 \cup \{(\dot{\neg} P), (P \dot{\vee} Q), (P \dot{\wedge} Q), (P \dot{\rightarrow} Q) \mid P, Q \in F_6\}$

where a, a_1, etc are names of individual objects, e.g., documents. The following statement forms will constitute axiom schemas for our system.

(S1) $\mathcal{A} \dot{\rightarrow} (\mathcal{B} \dot{\rightarrow} \mathcal{A})$

(S2) $(\mathcal{A} \dot{\rightarrow} (\mathcal{B} \dot{\rightarrow} \mathcal{C})) \dot{\rightarrow} ((\mathcal{A} \dot{\rightarrow} \mathcal{B}) \dot{\rightarrow} (\mathcal{A} \dot{\rightarrow} \mathcal{C}))$

(S3) $(\dot{\neg}\mathcal{A} \dot{\rightarrow} \dot{\neg}\mathcal{B}) \dot{\rightarrow} (\mathcal{B} \dot{\rightarrow} \mathcal{A}))$

(S4) $\mathcal{B}_1(a, \mathcal{A} \rightarrow (\mathcal{B} \rightarrow \mathcal{A}))$

(S5) $\mathcal{B}_1(a, (\mathcal{A} \rightarrow (\mathcal{B} \rightarrow \mathcal{C})) \rightarrow ((\mathcal{A} \rightarrow \mathcal{B}) \rightarrow (\mathcal{A} \rightarrow \mathcal{C}))$

(S6) $\mathcal{B}_1(a, \neg\mathcal{A} \rightarrow \neg\mathcal{B}) \rightarrow (\mathcal{B} \rightarrow \mathcal{A}))$

(S7) $\mathcal{A} \dot{\rightarrow} \mathcal{A}(y/x)$, if y does not occur in $\mathcal{A}$

(S8) $\mathcal{A} \dot{\rightarrow} \mathcal{A}(c/x)$, where c is a constant symbol

(S9) $\mathcal{B}_i(a, P) \dot{\wedge} \mathcal{B}_j(a, Q) \dot{\rightarrow} \mathcal{B}_{min[i,j]}(a, P \wedge Q)$

(S10) $\mathcal{B}_i(a, P) \dot{\wedge} \mathcal{B}_j(a, Q) \dot{\rightarrow} \mathcal{B}_{max[i,j]}(a, P \vee Q)$

(S11) $\mathcal{T}_i(a, b) \dot{\wedge} \mathcal{T}_j(b, c) \dot{\rightarrow} \mathcal{T}_{min[i,j]}(a, c)$

In addition, the following rules of inference are defined:

(R1) *Instantiation*: From schema S infer $S(P_1,...,P_n/A_1,...,A_n)$, i.e., replacement of the schema variables A_i with the formulas P_i, assuming the substitution results in a formula of the language.

(R2) *Modus ponens*: From $\mathcal{A}$ and $\mathcal{A} \dot{\rightarrow} \mathcal{B}$, infer $\mathcal{B}$.

(R3) *Modified modus ponens*: From $\mathcal{B}_i P$ and $\mathcal{B}_j P \rightarrow Q$, infer $\mathcal{B}_{min[i,j]} Q$.

(R4) *Trust Application*: From $\mathcal{T}_i(a, b)$ and $\mathcal{B}_j(b, P)$, infer $\mathcal{B}_k(a, P)$, where k is determined as in [6].

(R5) *Belief Combination*: From $\mathcal{B}_i(a, P)$ and $\mathcal{B}_j(a, P)$, infer $\mathcal{B}_k(a, P)$ where k is determined as in [6].

To simplify our notation, we will use $\mathcal{B}_j P$ as an abbreviation for $\mathcal{B}_i(a, P)$, where a is the name of the agent doing the reasoning. To represent the contents of an agent's knowledge base, we choose the following types of statements:

1. *Subtypes*: $\mathcal{B}_i(p_1(x) \rightarrow p_2(x))$
2. *Disjointness*: $\mathcal{B}_i(p_1(x) \rightarrow \neg p_2(x))$
3. *Or-Definition*: $\mathcal{B}_i(p_1(x) \rightarrow p_2(x) \vee p_3(x))$
4. *And-Definition*: $\mathcal{B}_i(p_1(x) \leftrightarrow (p_2(x) \wedge p_3(x))$
5. *Document Classification*: $\mathcal{B}_i p_1(doc_1)$, $\mathcal{B}_i \neg p_1(doc_1)$
6. *Trust relationship*: $\mathcal{T}_i(a1, a2)$

In the following, we will refer to statements of forms 1–4 as *taxonomy statements*. Statements having forms 5 are positive or negative *document classification statements*. We will refer to statements of form 6 as trust statements.

The goal of the system is to provide accurate classification of documents. An additional desire is for the system to automatically detect and, preferably, remove sources of any contradictory classifications. There is no direct need to infer new taxonomy statements. Thus, we can concentrate on inferences that result in new document classifications. In Table 1, we summarize inference forms that lead to new classification.

Premise 1	Premise(s) 2	Conclusion
$\mathcal{B}_i(p_1(x) \rightarrow p_2(x))$	$\mathcal{B}_j p_1(doc1)$	$\mathcal{B}_{min[i,j]} p_2(doc1)$
$\mathcal{B}_i(p_2(x) \rightarrow p_1(x)))$	$\mathcal{B}_j \neg p_1(doc1)$	$\mathcal{B}_{min[i,j]} \neg p_2(doc1)$
$\mathcal{B}_i(p_1(x) \rightarrow \neg p_2(x))$	$\mathcal{B}_j p_1(doc1)$	$\mathcal{B}_{min[i,j]} \neg p_2(doc1)$
$\mathcal{B}_i(p_1(x) \rightarrow \neg p_2(x))$	$\mathcal{B}_j p_2(doc1)$	$\mathcal{B}_{min[i,j]} \neg p_1(doc1)$
$\mathcal{B}_i(p_1(x) \rightarrow p_2(x) \vee p_3(x))$	$\mathcal{B}_j p_1(doc1)$, $\mathcal{B}_k \neg p_3(doc1)$	$\mathcal{B}_{min[i,j,k]} P2(doc1)$
$\mathcal{B}_i(p_1(x) \leftrightarrow p_2(x)) \wedge p_3(x))$	$\mathcal{B}_j p_1(doc1)$	$\mathcal{B}_{min[i,j]} p_2(doc1)$, $\mathcal{B}_{min[i,j]} p_3(doc1)$
$\mathcal{B}_i(p_1(x) \leftrightarrow p_2(x) \wedge p_3(x))$	$\mathcal{B}_j p_2(doc1)$, $\mathcal{B}_k p_3(doc1)$	$\mathcal{B}_{min[i,j,k]} p_1(doc1)$
$\mathcal{B}_i(p_1(x) \leftrightarrow p_2(x) \wedge p_3(x))$	$\mathcal{B}_j \neg p_2(doc1)$	$\mathcal{B}_{min[i,j]} \neg p_1(doc1)$

Table 1. Inferring new document classifications

3. Inference Process

An agent's knowledge base, represented as the derivation path in a DRS, is an ordered labeled sequence of statements, where the labels are as described above.

3.1 Operations on the knowledge base

To support the purpose of an agent, we define several procedures aimed at maintaining the knowledge base. In this section we present several subroutines, which are then used by the main routines presented in later sections.

- **Adding a statement**: *addStatement.* This enters a new formula into the derivation path.
- **Determining a statement's ancestors**: *getAncestors*.
- **Determining a statement's descendants**: *getDescendants*.
- **Deleting a statement**: *deleteStatement.* When a statement is deleted (its status changed to "disbelieve"}, all statements that are logically dependent on it (traced via the formula labels) are deleted as well.
- **Combining beliefs**: *beliefCombination.* This procedure is called whenever an agent encounters two statements expressing the same document classification but with different belief levels. Two statements are passed to the procedure as arguments. To reach the new belief level for the statement, the agent applies a belief combination rule (R5)

- **Contradiction Removal**: *removeContradiction.* When a reasoning procedure discovers a contradiction, another belief revision process is triggered. We have set up the reasoning in such a way that a discovered contradiction will always take the form $\mathcal{B}_4(Topic1(doc1)) \wedge \mathcal{B}_{-4}(Topic1(doc1))$. The system will respond by removing (using deleteStatement) one taxonomic statement from the ancestors of the contradiction deemed least believed. In case there is more than one culprit with same belief level, the system will choose the statement whose ancestors have the least cumulative belief level, as determined by the following procedure *leastValuable*.
- **Least valuable statement**: *leastValuable.* A subroutine for belief revision process, this procedure chooses the least valuable statement from the set passed to it. Statement *P* is more valuable than statement *Q* if the sum of belief levels of the ancestors of P is greater than the sum of belief levels of the ancestors of *Q*. The use of *leastValuable* helps the belief revision process achieve a form of *informational economy* [1].

3.2 Purposeful reasoning

The principal inference process is triggered when there is a new statement for an agent to assimilate. This new statement comes either from the authorized user or from a trusted agent. In each case, an agent takes appropriate action, depending on the type of statement being processed. Procedure *triggerReasoning* (Fig. 1) represents the main entrance point of the process. When reacting to new input, the system will:

```
Data: knowledge base KB
Input: input statement Input , source
Result: updated KB
St = (P, λ) := new statement;
P := Input;
λ.from = es;
if source = trusted agent then
    trust := Agents[source].TrustLevel;
    belief := P.BeliefLevel;
    P.BeliefLevel := TrustBelief(belief, trust);
switch P do
    case taxonomic statement
        newTaxonomyStatement(St, λ.from);
    case document classification
        newDocumentClassification(St, λ.from);
    case trust statement
        newTrustStatement(St, λ.from);
```

Fig. 1 Procedure triggerInference

- Turn the input statement into a labeled formula.
- If the input statement comes from another agent, combine that agent's belief level and the present agent's trust level in that other agent, to obtain the present agent's belief value for the formula.
- Add the new formula to the path of the Dynamic Reasoning System, invoking appropriate reasoning to compute consequences.

Procedure *newDocumentClassification* is invoked when an agent is given new document classification, identifying a specific document doc_1 with a specific predicate symbol P_1. Two auxiliary procedures, *addPositiveConsequences* and *addNegativeConsequences*, are used to deal with specific inference cases (see Table 1). The computational process can best be described as a recursive walk through the taxonomy. The steps are as follows:

- Check if the system already contains an identical statement. If it does, end procedure.
- Append the statement to the derivatinop path, using *addNewStatement* routine.
- If a conflicting belief level for the same classification exists, invoke *beliefCombination* .
- If a contradiction is identified, call *removeContradiction*.
- Call *addPositiveConsequences* or *addNegativeConsequences* to infer further document classifications.

```
Data: knowledge base KB
Input: input statement, St B_i p1(doc1) , Set from
Result: updated KB
begin
    if St already in the KB then
        return ;
    addNewStatement(St, from);
    if this classification exists with different belief level, St1 ∈ KB then
        newSt := beliefCombination(St, St1);
        if newSt = St OR newSt = St1 then
            return ;
        else
            St := newSt;
    if contradicting statement St1 ∈ KB then
        beliefRevision(St, St1);
        if St1 ∈ KB then
            Note: new statement just got rejected;
            return ;
    if St = B_i p1(doc1) then
        addPositiveConsequences(St, from);
    else
        addNegativeConsequences(St, from);
end
```

Fig. 2 Procedure newDocumentClassification

Procedures *addPositiveConsequences* and *addNegativeConsequences* encapsulate logical inference. Given an argument statement of the form $\mathcal{B}_i p_1(doc1)$ or

$\mathcal{B}_i \neg p_1(doc1)$, these procedures iterate through the list of taxonomic statements that contain the predicate symbol P_1. If a taxonomic statement, combined with the argument, yields a new inferred statement, the procedures call *newDocumentClassification* with the inferred statement as an argument. Since *newDocumentClassification* calls these two fuctions, we have an indirect recursive process traversing the taxonomy tree searching for possible inferences.

```
Data: knowledge base KB
Input: input statement, B_i p1(doc1)
Result: updated KB
begin
  foreach St ∈ p1.Statements do
    fro := { St, B_i p1(doc1) } switch St do
      case B_j(p1(x) → p2(x))
        newDocumentClassification(B_min(i,j) p2(doc1), fro)
      case B_j(p1(x) → ¬p2(x)) OR B_j(p2(x) → ¬p1(x)))
        newDocumentClassification(B_min(i,j) ¬p2(docI), fro)
      case B_j(∀x(p1(x) → p2(x) ∨ p3(x)), fro)
        if B_k ¬p3(doc1) then
          fro := fro ∨ B_k ¬p3(doc1)
          newDocumentClassification(B_min(i,j,k) p2(doc1), fro)
        if B_k ¬p2(doc1) then
          fro := fro ∨ B_k ¬p2(doc1)
          newDocumentClassification(B_min(i,j,k) p3(doc1), for)
      case B_j(p1(x) ↔ (p2(x) ∧ p3(x)))
        newDocumentClassification(B_min(i,j) p2(doc1), fro)
        newDocumentClassification(B_min(i,j) p3(doc1), fro)
      case B_j(p2(x) ↔ (p1(x) ∧ p3(x))
        if B_k p3(doc1) then
          fro := fro ∨ B_k p3(doc1)
          newDocumentClassification(B_min(i,j,k) p2(doc1), fro)
end
```

Fig.3 Procedure *addPositiveConsequences*

The taxonomy tree that will guide the reasoning process is not explicitly represented in the knowledge base. In that tree, the nodes of the tree are all predicate and document literals in the system, while statements form the links. For the described inference procedure to be effective, we rely on an assumption that sets like *Pred.Statements* are derived efficiently.

In an implemented system, for example, an agent can store information on all predicates and document constants in a statement object, and each predicate symbol object can be associated with the list of all statements containing that symbol.

Adding new taxonomic statements also leads to computing new document classifications. Procedure*newTaxonomyStatement* shows the appropriate process. The basic algorithm involves the following:

- Add the new statement to the DRS.
- Based on the type of statement, identify document classifications that can lead to new inferences (see Table 1).
- For each such classification statement, apply an appropriate rule.
- Invoke *newDocumentClassification* for newly inferred statements.

```
Data: knowledge base KB
Input: input statement St, Set from
Result: updated KB
begin
  addNewStatement(St, from)
  switch St do
    case B_j(p1(x) → p2(x))
      foreach doc1 where B_j p1(doc1) do
        fro := { St, B_j p1(doc1) }
        newDocumentClassification(B_min(i,j) p2(doc1), fro)
      foreach doc1 where B_j ¬p2(doc1) do
        fro := { St, B_j ¬p2(doc1) }
        newDocumentClassification(B_min(i,j) ¬p1(doc1), fro)
    case B_j(p1(x) → ¬p2(x))
      foreach doc1 where B_j p1(doc1) do
        fro := { St, B_j p1(doc1)
      newDocumentClassification(B_min(i,j) ¬p2(doc1), fro)
    foreach doc1 where B_j p2(doc1) do
      fro := { St, B_j p2(doc1) }
      newDocumentClassification(B_min(i,j) ¬p1(doc1), fro)
  case B_j(p2(x) → p1(x) ∨ p3(x))
    foreach doc1 where B_j p1(doc1) and B_k ¬p3(doc1) do
      fro := { St, B_j p1(doc1), B_k ¬p2(doc1) }
      newDocumentClassification(B_min(i,j,k) p3(doc1), fro)
  case B_j(p2(x) ↔ p1(x) ∧ p3(x))
    foreach doc1 where B_j ¬p3(doc1) or B_j ¬p1(doc1) do
      fro := { St, B_j ¬p1(doc1) (or B_j ¬p3(doc1)) }
      newDocumentClassification(B_min(i,j,k) ¬p2(doc1), fro)
    foreach doc1 where B_j p1(doc1) do
      fro := { St, B_j ¬p1(doc1) }
      newDocumentClassification(B_min(i,j) ¬p2(doc1), fro)
      newDocumentClassification(B_min(i,j) ¬p3(doc1), fro)
end
```

Fig. 4. Procedure *newTaxonomyStatement*

As before, we rely on an assumption that the set of documents associated with a given predicate can be derived efficiently. This can be achieved by the use of appropriate data structures.

Along with taxonomic information, an agent also maintains trust relations with other agents. We adopt a simplifying assumption that an agent only receives new statements from trusted agents. We also assume that change in trust in a particular agent does not automatically lead to a belief revision process involving all previously adopted knowledge. If such trust revision is desired by users, then one can invoke an algorithm similar to belief revision procedures defined above.

Procedure *newTrustStatement* takes an acquired trust statement as input. We assume that a denotes the agent doing reasoning. Given a previously unknown statement $T_i(a_1, a_2)$ and assuming that the statement of the form $T_j(a, a_1)$ is already in the KB, the procedure arrives at the new statement $T_{min[i,j]}(a, a_2)$. This conclusion follows from (S11) and Modus Ponens.

```
Data: knowledge base KB
Input: input statement St = T_i(a_1, a_2), Set from
Result: updated KB
begin
    addNewStatement(St, {ec});
    trust_level = min(i, TrustLevel(a, a_1);
    addNewStatement(T_trust_level(a, a_2), {St}));
end
```

Fig. 5. Procedure *newTrustStatement.*

4. Conclusion

Modern information systems promise easy access to vast amounts of information. The Semantic Web and Web 2.0 provide a rich information environment, allowing people and machines to collaborate and exchange information. Judging the reliability of distributed information therefore becomes a necessity. The goal of this research has been to extend existing approaches to reasoning and reason maintenance to support explicit handling of belief and trust, suitable for supporting the semantic Web of Trust.

Our starting point was the logic for agent-oriented epistemic reasoning proposed by Schwartz [4]. We extended this logical framework with a support for multiple agents and the notion of trust. The result was a formal logic language based on intuitive linguistic categories, complete with a clear semantics and plausible rules for belief and trust combination.

We used the previously described notion of Dynamic Reasoning System [4] to provide means of modeling an agent's inference process, allowing it to address conflicting and contradictory information. Two situations of belief revision are identified: one requiring simple belief combination to arrive at a new belief level and one that requires removing a formula that leads to a contradiction. The description of these formalisms is found in Section 2.

We have described a potential application for our formalisms: a collaborative, multi-user bibliographic database. The defining feature of the proposed system is that the users define their own classification taxonomies and contribute their own document classifications. Human users interact with software agents that represent them. In turn, agents can get information from each other, extending users' taxonomies and enhancing search capabilities. Agents can use trust relations to establish their individual belief levels assigned to taxonomy links and to perform necessary belief revision.

Armed with logical formalism and problem understanding, we proceeded to introduce, in Section 3, a formal reasoning system capable of dealing with bibliographic taxonomies. We described an agent with a knowledge base of taxonomic data stored in a DRS. We limited our logic language to five types of statements sufficient to express rich taxonomic structures.

We then defined procedures an agent may use to achieve its goal: to adopt new information while maintaining the quality of the knowledge base. When given new data, the agent will derive all document classifications this new information entails. It will also identify and address all evident contradictions. Procedures for belief revision are defined, implementing a discrete version of the principle of informational economy.

5. References

[1] Alchourrón, C.E., Gärdenfors, P., Makinson, D., On the logic of theory change: partial meet contraction and revision functions, *Journal of Symbolic Logic*, **50**, 2 (1985) 510–530.

[2] Berners-Lee, Sir T., Hendler, J., Lassila, O., "The Semantic Web". Scientific American, May 2001

[3] Doyle, J., A truth maintenance system, *Artificial Intelligence*, **12** (1979), 231–272.

[4] Schwartz ,D. G., A Logic of Qualified Syllogisms, in *Proceedings of 2008 International Conference on Systems, Computing Sciences and Software Engineering (CISSE08), University of Bridgeport, CT, December 5--13, 2008.*

[5] Schwartz, D.G., Dynamic reasoning with qualified syllogisms, *Artificial Intelligence*, **93** (1997) 103–167.

[6] Ustymenko, S., Schwartz, D.G., An Agent-Oriented Logic for Reasoning about Belief and Trust, in *Proceedings of 30th IEEE Annual International Computer Software and Applications Conference*, September 17-21, 2006, Chicago, IL.

[7] Ustymenko, S., *Multiagent Dynamic Reasoning about Belief and Trust*, Doctoral Dissertation, Florida State University, Tallahassee, Florida, USA, 2008.

Formal Specifications for a Document Management Assistant

Daniel G. Schwartz
Department of Computer Science
Florida State University
Tallahassee, FL, 32306-4530
schwartz@cs.fsu.edu

***Abstract*— The concept of a *dynamic reasoning system* (DRS) provides a general framework for modeling the reasoning processes of a mechanical agent, to the extent that those processes follow the rules of some well-defined logic. It amounts to an adaptation of the classical notion of a formal logical system that explicitly portrays reasoning as an activity that takes place in *time*. Inference rule applications occur in discrete time steps, and, at any given point in time, the *derivation path* comprises the agent's *belief set* as of that time. Such systems may harbor inconsistencies, but these do not become known to the agent until a contradictory assertion appears in the derivation path. When this occurs one invokes a Doyle-like reason maintenance process to remove the inconsistency, in effect, disbelieving some assertions that were formerly believed. The notion of a DRS also includes an extralogical control mechanism that guides the reasoning process. This reflects the agent's *goal* or *purpose* and is context dependent. This paper lays out the formal definition of a DRS and illustrates it with the case of ordinary first-order predicate calculus, together with a control mechanism suitable for reasoning about taxonomic classifications for documents in a library. As such, this particular DRS comprises formal specifications for an agent that serves as a document management assistant.**

I. Introduction

The notion of a Dynamic Reasoning System was introduced in [8] for purposes of formulating reasoning involving a logic of "qualified syllogisms". This notion has been applied more recently for reasoning about belief and trust relationships in the emerging Semantic Web [9]. The present paper represents a rethinking and partial reorganization of those treatments, aimed at making the underlying concepts more explicit and precise. This is undertaken as a necessary prerequisite for any eventual implementation.

The DRS framework is here viewed as a general framework for nonmonotonic belief revision and is thought to be applicable to a wide variety of reasoning activities. Due to space limitations an in-depth comparison of the relation between this and other approaches must be remanded to a future publication. Here it will only be noted that this work has been inspired by the truth/reason maintenance methods of Doyle [2] and the belief revision systems developed by Gärdenfors and others [1], [3], [4] (the so-called AGM systems), and in part represents a synthesis of the two approaches. It differs significantly from the AGM approach, however, by dispensing with two of their "rationality postulates", these being the requirements that the underlying belief set be at all times (i) consistent, and (ii) closed with respect to logical entailment. The latter is sometimes called the "omniscience" postulate, inasmuch as the modeled agent is thus characterized as knowing all possible logical consequences of its beliefs.

These postulates are dropped here primarily in order to accommodate implementation. Consistency is known to be undecidable for any system at least as strong as first-order logic, and, even for decidable systems that are nontrivial, it typically is computationally intractable. Omniscience is problematic since, for any nontrivial system, it is infinitary—no computer can determine all logical consequences of the belief set in finite time.

Dropping these postulates has anthropomorphic rationale, moreover. Humans obviously cannot be omniscient in the sense described, and, because of this, they often harbor inconsistent beliefs without being aware of it, and without it threatening their survival or in any way interfering with their daily activities. Thus it is not unreasonable that our artificial agents should exhibit the same characteristics. Consistency nonetheless clearly is desirable and should be strived for to whatever extent this is feasible.

II. Dynamic Reasoning Systems

A *dynamic reasoning system* (DRS) is comprised of a "path logic", which provides all the elements necessary for reasoning, and a "controller", which guides the reasoning process. A *path logic* consists of a language, axiom schemas, inference rules, and a derivation path, as follows.

Language: Here denoted $\mathcal{L}$, this consists of all *expressions* (or *formulas*) that can be generated from a given set σ of *symbols* in accordance with a collection of production rules (or an inductive definition, or some similar manner of definition). As symbols typically are of different types (e.g., individual variables, constants, predicate symbols, etc.) it is assumed that there is an unlimited supply (uncountably many if necessary) of each type. Moreover, as is customary, some symbols will be *logical symbols* (e.g., logical connectives, quantifiers, and individual variables), and some will be *extralogical symbols* (e.g., individual constants and predicate symbols). It is assumed that $\mathcal{L}$ contains at least the logical connectives for expressing *negation* and *conjunction*, herein denoted $\neg$ and $\wedge$, or a means for defining these connectives in terms of the given connectives. For example, in the following we take $\neg$ and $\rightarrow$ as given and use the standard definition of $\wedge$ in terms of these.

Axiom Schemas: Expressed in some meta notation, these describe the expressions of $\mathcal{L}$ that are to serve as *logical axioms*.

T. Sobh, K. Elleithy (eds.), *Innovations in Computing Sciences and Software Engineering*,
DOI 10.1007/978-90-481-9112-3_19, © Springer Science+Business Media B.V. 2010

Inference Rules: These must include one or more rules that enable instantiation of the axiom schemas. All other inference rules will be of the usual kind, i.e., stating that, from expressions having certain forms (premise expressions), one may infer an expression of some other form (a conclusion expression). Of the latter, two kinds are allowed: *logical rules*, which are considered to be part of the underlying logic, and *extralogical rules*, which are associated with the intended application. Note that logical axioms are expressions that are derived by applying the axiom schema instantiation rules.

Derivation Path: This consists of a sequence of triples $(L_0, R_0, B_0), (L_1, R_1, B_1), \ldots$, where L_t is the sublanguage of $\mathcal{L}$ that is in use at time t, R_t is the set of inference rules in use at time t, and B_t is *belief set* in effect at time t. This sequence may be defined as follows. Since languages are determined by the symbols they employ, it is useful to speak more directly in terms of the set σ_t comprising the symbols that are in use at time t and then let L_t be the sublanguage of $\mathcal{L}$ that is generated by the symbols in σ_t. With this in mind, let σ_0 be the logical symbols of $\mathcal{L}$, so that L_0 is the minimal language employing only logical symbols, let R_0 be the schema instantiation rules together with the logical rules, and let $B_0 = \emptyset$. Then, given (L_t, R_t, B_t), the pair $(L_{t+1}, R_{t+1}, B_{t+1})$ is formed in one of the following ways:

1) $\sigma_{t+1} = \sigma_t$ (so that $L_{t+1} = L_t$) and B_{t+1} is obtained from B_t by adding an expression that is derived by application of an inference rule that instantiates an axiom schema,
2) $\sigma_{t+1} = \sigma_t$ and B_{t+1} is obtained from B_t by adding an expression that is derived from expressions appearing earlier in the path by application of an inference rule of the kind that infers a conclusion from some premises,
3) $\sigma_{t+1} = \sigma_t$ and an expression employing these symbols is added to B_t to form B_{t+1},
4) some new extralogical symbols are added to σ_t to form σ_{t+1}, and an expression employing the new symbols is added to B_t to form B_{t+1},

Whenever one of the above actions are performed, either $R_{t+1} = R_t$ or one or more new rules are added to R_t to form R_{t+1}. Such new rules may be extralogical, motivated by the application domain, or derived rules intended to simplify deductions. Derived rules encapsulate frequently used argument patterns.

The act of adding an expression to the current belief set in any of these manners may be expressed more simply as that of "entering" the expression "into the (derivation) path". Expressions entered into the path in accordance with either (3) or (4) will be *extralogical axioms*. Whenever an expression is entered into the path it is assigned a *label* λ comprised of:

1) A *time stamp*, this being the value of the subscript $t+1$ on the set B_{t+1} formed by entering the expression into the path in accordance with any of the above items (1) through (4). The time stamp effectively serves as an *index* indicating the expression's position in the path.
2) A *from-list*, indicating how the expression came to be entered into the path. In case the expression is entered in accordance with the above item (1), i.e., using a schema instantiation rule, this list consists of the name (or other identifier) of the schema and the name (or other identifier) of the inference rule if the system has more than one such rule. In case the expression is entered in accordance with above item (2), the list consists of the indexes (time stamps) of the premise expressions and the name (or other identifier) of the inference rule. In case the expression is entered in accordance with either of items (3) or (4), i.e., is a extralogical axiom, the list will consist of some code indicating this (e.g., *es* standing for "external source") possibly together with some identifier or other information regarding the source.
3) A *to-list*, being a list of indexes of all expressions that have been entered into the path as a result of rule applications involving the given expression as a premise. Thus to-lists may be updated at any future time.
4) A *status indicator* having the value *bel* or *disbel* according as the proposition asserted by the expression currently is believed or disbelieved. The primary significance of this status is that only expressions that are believed can serve as premises in inference rule applications. Whenever an expression is first entered into the path, it is assigned status *bel*. This value may then be changed during belief revision at a later time. When an expression's status is changed from *bel* to *disbel* it is said to have been *retracted*.
5) An *epistemic entrenchment factor*, this being a numerical value indicating the strength with which the proposition asserted by the expression is held. This terminology is adopted in recognition of the the work by Gärdenfors, who initiated this concept [3], [4], and is used here for essentially the same purpose, namely, to assist when making decisions regarding belief retractions. Depending on the application, however, this value might alternatively be interpreted as a degree of belief, as a certainty factor, as a degree of importance, or some other type of value to be used for this purpose. In the present treatment, epistemic entrenchment values are assigned only to axioms. No provision for propagating these factors to expressions derived via rule inferences is provided, although this would be a natural extension of the present treatment. It is agreed that logical axioms always receive the highest possible epistemic entrenchment value, whatever scale or range may be employed.
6) A *knowledge category specification*, having one of the values *a priori*, *a posteriori*, *analytic*, and *synthetic*. These terms are employed in recognition of the philosophical tradition initiated by Kant [7]. Logical axioms are designated as a priori; extralogical axioms are designated as a posteriori; expressions whose deriva-

tions employ only logical axioms are designated as analytic; and expressions whose derivations employ any extralogical axioms are designated as synthetic. The latter is motivated by the intuition that an ability to apply inference rules and thereby carry out logical derivations is itself a priori knowledge, so that, even if the premises in a rule application are all a posteriori, the rule application entails a combination of a priori and a posteriori knowledge, and the conclusion of the application thus qualifies as synthetic under most philosophical interpretations of this term.

Thus when an expression P is entered into the path, it is more exactly entered as an expression-label pair, here denoted (P, λ). A DRS's language, axiom schemas, and inference rules comprise a *logic* in the usual sense. It will be assumed that this logic is *consistent*, i.e., for no expression P is it possible to derive both P and $\neg P$. The belief set may become inconsistent, nonetheless, through the introduction of contradictory extralogical axioms.

In what follows, only expressions representing a posteriori and synthetic knowledge may be retracted; expressions of a prior knowledge are taken as being held unequivocally. Thus the term "a priori knowledge" is taken as synonymous with "belief held unequivocally", and "a posteriori knowledge" is interpreted as "belief possibly held only tentatively" (some a posteriori beliefs may be held unequivocally). Thus the distinction between knowledge and belief is herein blurred somewhat, and what is referred to as a "belief set" might alternatively be called a "knowledge base", as is often the practice in AI systems.

A *controller* manages the DRS's interaction with its environment and guides the reasoning process. This amounts to performing the following operations.

1) Receiving input from its environment, e.g., human users, sensors, or other artificial agents, expressing this input as formulas in the given language $\mathcal{L}$, and entering these formulas into the derivation path in the manner described above (derivation path items (3) and (4)). During this operation, new symbols are appropriated as needed to express concepts not already represented in the current L_t.
2) Applying inference rules in accordance with some extralogical objective (some plan, purpose, or goal) and entering the derived conclusions into the derivation path in the manner described above (derivation path items (1) and (2)).
3) Performing any actions as may be prescribed as a result of the above reasoning process, e.g., moving a robotic arm, returning a response to a human user, or sending a message to another artificial agent.
4) Carrying out belief revision in the manner described below.

A *contradiction* is an expression of the form $P \wedge \neg P$. Sometimes it is convenient to represent the general notion of contradiction by a special symbol $\perp$ representing falsehood. Belief revision is triggered whenever a contradition or a designated equivalent expression is entered into the path. We may assume that this only occurs as the result of an inference rule application, since it obviously would make no sense to enter a contradiction directly as an extralogical axiom. The process of belief revision involves three steps:

1) Starting with the from-list in the label on the contradictory expression, backtrack through the derivation path following from-lists until one identifies all extralogical axioms that were involved in the contradiction's derivation. Note that such extralogical axioms must exist, since, by the consistency of the logic, the contradiction cannot constitute analytical knowledge, and hence must be synthetic.
2) Change the belief status of one or more of these extralogical axioms, as many as necessary to invalidate the derivation of the given contradiction. The decision as to which axioms to retract may be dictated, or at least guided by, the epistemic entrenchment values. In effect, those expressions with the lower values would be preferred for retraction. In some systems, this retraction process may be automated, and in others it may be human assisted.
3) Forward chain through to-lists starting with the extralogical axiom(s) just retracted, and retract all expressions whose derivations were dependent on those axioms. These retracted expressions should include the contradiction that triggered this round of belief revision (otherwise the correct extralogical axioms were not retracted).

Thus defined a DRS may be viewed as representing the "mind" of an intelligent agent, where this includes both the agent's reasoning processes and its memory. At any time t, the belief set B_t represents the agent's conscious awareness as of that time. Since the extralogical axioms can entail inconsistencies, this captures the fact that an agent can "harbor" inconsistencies without being aware of this. The presence of inconsistencies only becomes evident to the agent when they lead to a contradictory expression being explicitly entered into the belief set, in effect, making the agent consciously aware of an implicit contradiction in its beliefs. This then triggers a belief revision process aimed at removing the inconsistency that gave rise to the contradiction.

This belief revision process is reminiscent of Hegel's "dialectic", described as a process of "negation of the negation" [6]. In that treatment, the latter (first occurring) negation is a perceived internal conflict (here a contradiction), and the former (second occurring) one is an act of transcendence aimed at resolving the conflict (here removing the contradiction). In recognition of Hegel, the belief revision/retraction process formalized above will be called *dialectical belief revision*.

Note that the use of axiom schemas together with schema instantiation rules here replaces the customary approach of defining logical axioms as all formulas having the "forms" described by the schemas and then including these axioms among the set of "theorems". The reason for adopting this alternative approach is to ensure that the DRS formalism is finitary, and hence, machine implementable—it is not possible to represent an infinite set of axioms (or theorems) on a computer. That the two approaches are equivalent should be obvious.

Depending on the application, the controller may be programmed to carry out schema instantiations and perform derivations based on logical axioms. Such might be the case, for example, if the logical rules were to include a "resolution rule" and the controller incorporated a Prolog-like theorem prover. In many applications, however, it likely will be more appropriate to base the controller on a few suitably chosen derived rules. The objective in this would be to simplify the controller's design by encapsulating frequently used argument patterns. In such cases, the use of axiom schemas and logical inference rules is implicit, but no logical axioms per se need be entered into the derivation path. Accordingly, all members of the belief set will be either a posteriori or synthetic and thus subject to belief revision. This is illustrated in the example that follows.

III. First-Order Logic

This section presents classical first-order logic in a form suitable for incorporation into a DRS. The treatment follows [5]. As symbols for the language $\mathcal{L}$ we shall have: individual variables, $\mathbf{x}_1, \mathbf{x}_2, \ldots$, denoted generically by x, y, z, etc.; individual constants, $\mathbf{a}_1, \mathbf{a}_2, \ldots$, denoted generically by a, b, c, etc.; predicate letters, infinitely many for each arity, $\mathbf{A}_1^1, \mathbf{A}_2^1, \ldots; \mathbf{A}_1^2, \mathbf{A}_2^2, \ldots; \ldots$, denoted generically by α, β, γ, etc.; punctuation marks, namely, the comma and left and right parentheses; the logical connectives $\neg$ and $\rightarrow$; the quantifier symbol, $\forall$; and the absurdity symbol, $\bot$.[1] The *atomic formulas* will be the absurdity symbol and all expressions of the form $\alpha(x_1, \ldots, x_n)$ where α is an n-ary predicate letter and $x_1, \ldots, x_n$ are individual variables. The *formulas* will be the atomic formulas together with all expressions having the forms $(\neg P)$, $(P \rightarrow Q)$, and $(\forall x)P$, where P and Q are formulas and x is an individual variable.

Further connectives can be introduced as means for abbreviating other formulas:

$(P \wedge Q)$ for $(\neg(P \rightarrow (\neg Q))$
$(P \vee Q)$ for $((\neg P) \rightarrow Q))$
$(P \leftrightarrow Q)$ for $((P \rightarrow Q) \wedge (Q \rightarrow P))$

In a formula of the form $(\forall x_i)P$, the expression $(\forall x_i)$ is a *quantifier* and P is the *scope* of the quantifier. Moreover, any occurrence of x_i in P is said to be *bound* by this quantifier. Individual variable occurrences not bound by quantifiers are *free*. Where P is a formula, let $P(a_1, \ldots, a_n/x_1, \ldots, x_n)$ be the formula obtained from P by replacing all occurrences of $x_1, \ldots, x_n$, respectively, with occurrences of $a_1, \ldots, a_n$, where it is understood that no substitution takes place for any x_i not actually occurring in P.

The axiom schemas will be the meta-level expressions:

[1] This omits the customary *function letters* and associated set of *terms*, as they are not needed for the examples discussed here.

1) $(\mathcal{A} \rightarrow (\mathcal{B} \rightarrow \mathcal{A}))$
2) $((\mathcal{A} \rightarrow (\mathcal{B} \rightarrow \mathcal{C}) \rightarrow ((\mathcal{A} \rightarrow \mathcal{B}) \rightarrow (\mathcal{A} \rightarrow \mathcal{C})))$
3) $((\neg\mathcal{A} \rightarrow \neg\mathcal{B}) \rightarrow (\mathcal{B} \rightarrow \mathcal{A}))$
4) $(\bot \leftrightarrow (\mathcal{A} \wedge \neg\mathcal{A}))$
5) $((\forall \mathbf{x})\mathcal{A} \rightarrow \mathcal{A})$
6) $((\forall \mathbf{x})(\mathcal{A} \rightarrow \mathcal{B}) \rightarrow (\mathcal{A} \rightarrow (\forall \mathbf{x})\mathcal{B}))$

Let the *formula meta symbols* $\mathcal{A}, \mathcal{B}, \mathcal{C}$ be denoted generically by $\mathcal{A}_1, \mathcal{A}_2, \ldots$. Where $\mathbf{S}$ is a schema, let $\mathbf{S}(P_1, \ldots, P_n/\mathcal{A}_1, \ldots, \mathcal{A}_n)$ be the formula obtained from $\mathbf{S}$ by replacing all occurrences of $\mathcal{A}_1, \ldots, \mathcal{A}_n$, respectively, with occurrences of $P_1, \ldots, P_n$. The inference rules will be:

- *Schema Instantiation 1*: Where S is one of axiom schemas (1) through (4), infer $\mathbf{S}(P_1, \ldots, P_n/\mathcal{A}_1, \ldots, \mathcal{A}_n)$, where $\mathcal{A}_1, \ldots, \mathcal{A}_n$ are all the distinct formula meta symbols occurring in $\mathbf{S}$, and $P_1, \ldots, P_n$ are formulas.
- *Schema Instantiation 2*: Where S is axiom schema (5), infer $((\forall x)P \rightarrow P)$, where P is any formula, and x is any individual variable that does not occur free in P.
- *Schema Instantiation 3*: Where S is axiom schema (5), infer $((\forall x)P \rightarrow P(a/x))$, where P is any formula, a is any individual constant, and x is an individual variable that occurs free in P.
- *Schema Instantiation 4*: Where S is axiom schema (6), infer $((\forall x)(P \rightarrow Q) \rightarrow (P \rightarrow (\forall x)Q))$, where P, Q are any formulas, and x is any individual variable that does not occur free in P.
- *Modus Ponens*: From P and $(P \rightarrow Q)$ infer Q, where P, Q are any formulas.
- *Generalization*: From P infer $(\forall x)P$, where P is any formula, and x is any individual variable.

The "soundness" and "adequacy" proofs presented in [5] can be adapted to establish similar results for this logic. Soundness amounts to consistency in the sense defined above.

An example of a derived rule that might be entered into the rule set for a DRS employing this logic is

- *Hypothetical Syllogism*: From $(P \rightarrow Q)$ and $(Q \rightarrow R)$ infer $(P \rightarrow R)$, where P, Q, R are any formulas.

The validity of this rule as a consequence of Schema Instantiation 1 and Modus Ponens can be established by adapting the corresponding argument in [5]. Two other rules that can be derived using standard techniques are

- *Aristotelean Syllogism*: From $(\forall x)(P \rightarrow Q)$ and $P(a/x)$, infer $Q(a/x)$, where P, Q are any formulas, x is any individual variable, and a is any individual constant.
- *Subsumption*: From $(\forall x)(P \rightarrow Q)$ and $(\forall y)(Q \rightarrow R)$, infer $(\forall z)(P \rightarrow R)$, where P, Q, R are any formulas, and x, y, z are any individual variables (not necessarily distinct).

The former captures the reasoning embodied in the famous argument "All men are mortal; Socrates is a man; therefore Socrates is mortal", by taking P for "is a man", Q for "is mortal", and a for "Socrates". A concept A "subsumes" concept B if the set of objects represented by A contains the set represented by B as a subset. Thus the latter rule captures the transitivity of this subsumption relationship. Either of these rules may be derived using formal proof techniques, or their derivability may be established by appeal to the logic's soundness, mentioned above, and verifying that the indicated inferences are semantically valid.

IV. Application To Document Classification

In general, a DRS would be used to represent the reasoning processes of an artificial agent interacting with its environment. For this purpose the belief set should include a model of the agent's environment, with this model evolving over time as the agent acquires more information about the environment. This section illustrates this idea with a simple DRS based on first-order logic representing an agent that assists its human users in creating and managing a taxonomic document classification system. Thus the environment in this case consists of the document collection together with its human users. The objective in employing such an agent would be to build concept taxonomies suitable for browsing.

In the associated DRS, documents are represented by individual constants, and document classes are represented by unary predicate letters. Then membership of document a in class α is expressed by the atomic formula $\alpha(a)$; the property of class α being a subclass of class β can be expressed by $(\forall x)(\alpha(x) \rightarrow \beta(x))$, where x is any individual variable; and the property of two classes α and β being disjoint can be expressed by $(\forall x)(\neg(\alpha(x) \wedge \beta(x)))$, where x is any individual variable. A taxonomic classification hierarchy may thus be constructed by entering formulas of these forms into the derivation path as extralogical axioms. It will be assumed that these axioms are input by the users.

It is desired to organize the classification taxonomy with respect to its subclass-superclass relationship as a directed acyclic graph. To this end the controller will maintain a data structure that represents the current state of this graph. Whenever an axiom expressing a document-class membership is entered into the path, a corresponding is-an-element-of link with be entered into the graph; whenever an axiom expressing a subclass-superclass relationship is entered into the path, a is-a-subclass-of link will be entered into the graph, unless this would create either a cycle or a redundant path (i.e., creating more than one path between two nodes); and whenever an axiom expressing class disjointedness is entered in the path, a corresponding link expressing this will be entered into the graph. To accommodate this activity, the derivation path as a sequence of triples is augmented to become a sequence of quadruples (L_t, B_t, R_t, G_t), where G_t is the state of the graph at time t.

This is illustrated in Figure 1, showing a graph that would be defined by entering the following formulas into the path, where TheLibrary, Science, Engineering, Humanities, ComputerScience, Philosophy, and ArtificialIntelligence are taken as alternative labels for the predicate letters $A^1_1, \ldots, A^1_7$, Doc1, Doc2, Doc3 are alternative labels for the individual constants $\mathbf{a}_1, \mathbf{a}_2, \mathbf{a}_3$, and x is the individual variable $\mathbf{x}_1$:

$(\forall x)(\mathrm{Science}(x) \rightarrow \mathrm{TheLibrary}(x))$
$(\forall x)(\mathrm{Engineering}(x) \rightarrow \mathrm{TheLibrary}(x))$
$(\forall x)(\mathrm{Humanities}(x) \rightarrow \mathrm{TheLibrary}(x))$
$(\forall x)(\mathrm{ComputerScience}(x) \rightarrow \mathrm{Science}(x))$
$(\forall x)(\mathrm{ComputerScience}(x) \rightarrow \mathrm{Engineering}(x))$
$(\forall x)(\mathrm{Philosophy}(x) \rightarrow \mathrm{Humanities}(x))$
$(\forall x)(\mathrm{ArtificialIntelligence}(x) \rightarrow \mathrm{ComputerScience}(x))$
$(\forall x)(\neg(\mathrm{Engineering}(x) \wedge \mathrm{Humanities}(x)))$
$\mathrm{Science}(\mathrm{Doc1})$
$\mathrm{Engineering}(\mathrm{Doc1})$
$\mathrm{ArtificialIntelligence}(\mathrm{Doc2})$
$\mathrm{Philosophy}(\mathrm{Doc3})$

As described in the foregoing, entering each such formula into the derivation path also entails expanding the current language by adding the needed new symbols and assigning the new formula an appropriate label. For the above formulas, the to-list will consist of an indication that the source of the formula was a human user; let us use the code *hu* for this (as an alternative to the aforementioned *es*). As an epistemic entrenchment value, let us arbitrarily assign each formula the value 0.5 on the scale $[0, 1]$. Thus each label will have the form

$$\{t, \{hu\}, \emptyset, bel, 0.5, a\ posteriori\}$$

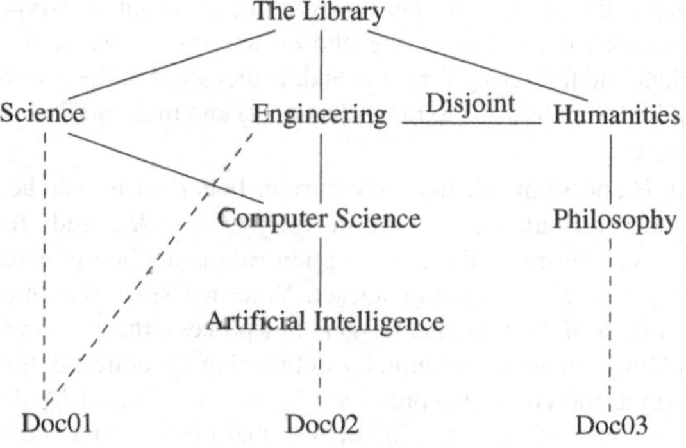

Fig. 1. A taxonomy fragment.

For the intended document management assistant, whenever a new extralogical formula is entered into the path, a reasoning process it triggered, depending on the type of formula and/or its source. To facilitate these processes, let the rule set R_1 be formed from R_0 by adding the Hypothetical Syllogism, Aristotelean Syllogism, and Subsumption rules described above. In addition, we shall have

- *Conflict Detection*: From $(\forall x)(\neg(P \wedge Q))$, $P(a/x)$, and $Q(a/x)$ infer $\perp$, where P, Q are any formulas, x is any individual variable, and a is any individual constant.

The reasoning processes are as follows. Here P, Q, R are atomic formulas involving unary predicate letters.

Event Type 1: A formula of the form $(\forall x)(P \rightarrow Q)$ is entered into the path by a human user. First it is checked whether P and Q are identical, and, if so, the formula is rejected (is immediately removed from the belief set) and the user is informed that the formula is not allowed. The reason for this provision is that formulas of this form are tautologous with respect to the subsumption relationship and contribute nothing to the taxonomy.

If P and Q are distinct, then (i) some corresponding nodes and is-a-subset-of link are entered into the graph (nodes for P and Q are entered only if they do not already exist), and (ii) the current belief set is searched for any formulas of the form $(\forall x)(Q \rightarrow R)$, and, for each such formula, the Subsumption rule is applied to enter $(\forall x)(P \rightarrow R)$ into the belief set.

Event Type 2: A formula of the form $(\forall x)(P \rightarrow Q)$ is entered into the path as a result of a rule application. In this case the to-lists of any formulas that served as premises in the rule application are updated to contain the time stamp (index) of this formula. First it is checked whether P and Q are identical, indicating the discovery of a loop in the subsumption hierarchy represented by the graph. If they are, then a backtracking process is carried out utilizing from-lists to obtain a list of all extralogical axioms involved in deriving this formula, and some view of the list is returned to the user for inspection. The user is then required to change the status of one or more such axioms from *bel* to *disbel*, after which the controller then starts with these chosen axioms and, using to-lists, forward chains through the indicated derivations and changes the status from *bel* to *disbel* for all formulas whose derivations depended on the chosen axioms. These should include the triggering formula, and, if they do not, the user is required to review his axiom selection(s) and make additional changes.

If P and Q are distinct, the current belief set is searched for any formulas of the form $(\forall x)(Q \rightarrow R)$, and, for each such formula, the Subsumption rule is applied to enter $(\forall x)(P \rightarrow R)$ into the belief set. Note that since the latter formula is of the type that triggers this process, the process is implicitly recursive, eventually delineating all concepts that subsume the concept represented by P, as indicated by the current state of the graph. Note also, that links are not added to the graph as a result of entering such derived formulas into the path, as such would constitute redundant paths in the graph.

Event Type 3: A formula of the form $P(a/x)$ is entered into the path by a human user. First it is checked whether the formula P is already in the current belief set, and, if not, the formula is rejected (immediately removed from the belief set) and the user is informed of this action. The reason for this is that, for the purposes of building a classification taxonomy, it makes no sense to assign a document to a category that does not exist.

If the formula P is found in the current belief set, then (i) a node representing document a and an is-an-element-of link connecting this node to the node representing P is added to the graph (it will be a consequence of these reasoning processes that all atomic P appearing in formulas entered into the path will have graph representations), (ii) the current belief set is searched for any formulas having the form $(\forall x)(P \rightarrow Q)$, and, for each such formula, Aristotelian Syllogism is applied to enter $Q(a/x)$ into the path.

Event Type 4: A formula of the form $P(a/x)$ is entered into the path as a result of a rule application. Then the current belief set is searched for any formulas having the form $(\forall x)(P \rightarrow Q)$, and, for each such formula, Aristotelian Syllogism is applied to enter $Q(a/x)$ into the path. Note that since the latter formula is of the type that triggers this process, the process is implicitly recursive, eventually delineating all concepts that apply to (include as a member) document a as indicated by the current state of the graph. Note also, that links are not added to the graph as a result of entering such derived formulas into the path, as such would constitute redundant paths in the graph.

Event Type 5: The above recursive process initiated by an event of type 4 terminates. The current belief set is searched for formulas of the forms $(\forall x)(\neg(P \wedge Q))$ and $Q(a/x)$, where P is the formula involved in the type 4 event, and, if found, the Conflict Detection rule is applied to enter the formula $\perp$ into the path.

Event Type 6: A formula of the form $(\forall x)(\neg(P \wedge Q))$ is entered into the path by a user. The current belief set is searched for formulas of the forms $P(a/x)$ and $Q(a/x)$, and, if found, the Conflict Detection rule is applied to enter the formula $\perp$ into the path.

Event Type 7: The formula $\perp$ is entered into the path (as a result of applying the Conflict Detection rule). A dialectical belief revision process is applied to remove the detected conflict. This should result in changing the status of this occurrence of $\perp$ to *disbel*, and, if not, the user is required to make further changes. Note that removing the conflict may entail reclassifying some documents, or it may entail removing the associated disjointedness constraint and thereby allowing that the concepts overlap. When a formula's status is changed from *bel* to *disbel*, any entry that may have been made in the associated graph when that formula was entered into the path must be removed.

Applying these procedures whenever a formula is entered into the path will ensure that the belief set remains consistent.

REFERENCES

[1] C.E. Alchourrón, P. Gärdenfors, and D. Makinson, On the logic of theory change: partial meet contraction and revision functions, *Journal of Symbolic Logic*, **50**, 2 (1985) 510–530.

[2] J. Doyle, A truth maintenance system, *Artificial Intelligence*, **12** (1979) 231–272.

[3] P. Gärdenfors, *Knowledge in Flux: Modeling the Dynamics of Epistemic States* (MIT Press/Bradford Books, Cambridge, MA, 1988).

[4] P. Gärdenfors, ed., *Belief Revision* (Cambridge University Press, New York, 1992).

[5] A.G. Hamilton, *Logic for Mathematicians, Revised Edition* (Cambridge University Press, 1988).

[6] G.W.F. Hegel, *Phenomenology of Mind*, tr. J. B. Baillie, Clarendon Press, Oxford, 1910; 2nd ed. 1931.

[7] I. Kant, *Critique of Pure Reason*, trans. N.K. Smith, Macmillan, London, England, 1929.

[8] D.G. Schwartz, Dynamic reasoning with qualified syllogisms, *Artificial Intelligence*, **93** (1997) 103–167.

[9] S. Ustymenko, *Multiagent Dynamic Reasoning about Belif and Trust*, Doctoral Dissertation, Florida State University, Tallahassee, Florida, USA, 2008.

Towards a Spatial-Temporal Processing Model

Jonathan B. Lori

Abstract—**This paper discusses architecture for creating systems that need to express complex models of real world entities, especially those that exist in hierarchical and composite structures. These models need to be persisted, typically in a database system. The models also have a strong orthogonal requirement to support representation and reasoning over time.**

***Index Terms*—Spatial-temporal processing, object-relational mapping, entity-relationship modeling, design patterns, dynamic composites**

I. Introduction

SINCE using relational databases and object oriented programming (OOP) languages have become commonplace for developers, it is only natural that systems have evolved to facilitate using relational databases as data persistence mechanisms for programs developed in object oriented languages. For example, the Java Database Connectivity (JDBC) API [1] provides database-independent connectivity between the Java programming language and a wide range of databases.

Object-based systems are founded on a set of fundamental concepts [2]. Objects have state, so they can model memory. They have behavior, so that they can model dynamic processes. And they are encapsulated, so that they can hide complexity. There are only two kinds of relationships in an object model [3], a static relationship: inheritance ('is-a") and a dynamic relationship: composition ('has-a").

As OOP has advanced, other structuring facilities have emerged in designs and code based on idioms and best practices that have evolved in OOP-based systems. Some of these practices have been codified as "Design Patterns" [4]. One such object oriented design pattern is **Composite**. This pattern composes objects into tree structures to represent part-whole hierarchies. Composite lets clients treat individual objects and compositions of objects uniformly.

Evolution was also occurring in the database world. Although initially discounted by the relational community at large, the ER model [5] is based on strong mathematical foundations, including: Set Theory, Mathematical Relations, Algebra, Logic and Lattice Theory.

Manuscript received October 10, 2009.

J. Lori is a PhD candidate at the University of Bridgeport, Bridgeport, CT, 06066 USA (email: jlori@bridgeport.edu).

This work was partially funded by the Pratt and Whitney Corporation, 400 Main Street, East Hartford, CT 06453 USA.

At the beginning of this decade, Dr. Ralph Kimball, one of the leading visionaries in the architecture of Data Warehouse systems described his goals for the marriage of database technology, ER models, and object oriented programming systems. In his newsletter [6], Kimball proposes four kinds of data warehouse business rules: "These rules included simple data formats, relationships between the keys of connected tables, declarations of entity relationships, and 'complex business logic'…" Kimball wanted direct support in the programming system for the third rule, particularly in the situation where many-to-many relationships were used.

Describing the fourth rule, Kimball states: "Complex business logic will always remain a combination of static data relationships and adherence to procedural sequences…"

Dr. Kimball sought an approach that uses OOP to manage entity-relationship data models and implements the associated processing logic to form an effective basis for data warehouses. While both OOP and Data Warehouse design had matured, a major stumbling block remained to be overcome. The problem is known as "object-relational impedance mismatch". Ambler [7] supplies this definition, which focuses on the orthogonal approaches to search and navigation in the two models: "The object/relational impedance mismatch is the difference resulting from the fact that relational theory is based on relationships between tuples that are queried, whereas the object paradigm is based on relationships between objects that are traversed."

As software technology moved forward through the first decade of the twenty-first century, a new technology emerged for integrating OOP and database systems. This technology is known as Object-Relational Mapping (ORM). ORM is defined as follows [8]: "Object-relational mapping (ORM, O/RM, and O/R mapping) in computer software is a programming technique for converting data between incompatible type systems in relational databases and object-oriented programming languages. This creates, in effect, a 'virtual object database' that can be used from within the programming language."

By the middle of the decade, ORM systems became highly sophisticated and had achieved significant results. Some of the best ORM implementations are open source Java-based systems [9]. These systems brought back a lightweight, object-oriented persistence model based on the concept of POJOs (Plain Old Java Objects) [9].

II. Problem Space

The architecture discussed here is realized in a system called Phoenix [10]. The system is designed to implement a management suite for jet engines. The heart of the suite is an

T. Sobh, K. Elleithy (eds.), *Innovations in Computing Sciences and Software Engineering*,
DOI 10.1007/978-90-481-9112-3_20, © Springer Science+Business Media B.V. 2010

application known as On Wing Tracker (OWT). The purpose of OWT is to track the configuration and utilization of engines, engine components and parts. Essentially, this is a classic Bill of Materials (BOM) problem. However, there are a few other critical elements to the problem. Engines are complex and expensive assemblies that last for decades. Engines evolve. Components wear out. Modules and parts are moved from one engine to another. Information on the state of the engine may be "late arriving" and sometimes missing.

Utilization may be expressed in multiple ways, from simply accumulating run time hours to more sophisticated event-based modes such as throttle operations per flight. What is required to solve such a set of problems is not simply a system structured around a spatial dimension i.e. a BOM model, but one which can also reason over temporal dimensions as well.

III. DESIGN PATTERNS

As stated earlier, object models contain two types of relationships: composition and inheritance. As Wirfs-Brock [3] points out: "Both (models) have analogs in a family tree. A composite relationship is like a marriage between objects. It is dynamic, it happens during the participating objects' lifetimes, and it can change. Objects can discard partners and get new partners to collaborate with. Inheritance relations are more like births into the family. Once it happens, it is forever… We can extend an object's capabilities by composing it from others. When it lacks the features that it needs to fulfill one of its responsibilities, we simply delegate the responsibility for the required information or action to one of the objects that the object holds onto. This is a very flexible scenario for extension."

When first considering a BOM model, which is essentially a tree structure, an architect may be tempted to begin modeling based on inheritance. However, an architecture organized around composition is a dynamic and flexible approach, and more extensible. There is a long-recognized design axiom [11] that states: "Prefer composition to inheritance."

The interesting point in the Phoenix architecture is that if there is one major organizing principle it is this: the system is organized around the notion of Dynamic Composites [10]. By this it is meant that BOM hierarchies are built as Composites, where a Composite, while already a dynamic OO relationship, is also assembled from a dynamic search. The search is through information stored in a generic ER model that is in turn stored in a relational database.

Phoenix is logically composed as a generic Entity-Relationship model that is persisted in a relational DBMS system. (Fig. 1) The generic ER model is then mirrored by a generic object model. (Fig. 2) The two models are mapped together through an object-relational mapping system. In the Phoenix architecture, Hibernate is the ORM [9]. The ER model is decimated enough to produce the desired flexibility, including the capability of "decorating" entities with any required attributes. Thus, the ER model provides a unified data model for the system. The object model is closely matched to the ER model. Therefore it is easy to fulfill all of Kimball's goals for using OOP to drive an ER model-based data warehouse.

Note also that there are no entities or classes called "Composite". This is because the dynamic composites exist only as sets of instances in memory. Finally, note that the entities (tables) and their mirrored classes contain strategically embedded timestamp fields. The object model contains both Java code (procedural logic) and embedded queries and parameters (SQL/HQL). (SQL is the Structured Query Language. HQL is the Hibernate Query Language [9]).

IV. TEMPORAL PROCESSING

Temporal reasoning [12] is handled as follows. A Bitemporal Database is implemented using the foundation provided by the Phoenix Architecture. Facts are stored in a database at a point in time. After the fact is stored, it can be retrieved. The time when a fact is stored in a database is the transaction time of the fact. Transaction times are consistent with the serial order of the transactions. The past cannot be changed; therefore transaction times cannot be changed. A transaction time also cannot be later than the current time. Typically, the commit time of a database transaction is used as the transaction time.

Conversely, the valid time of a fact is the time when such a fact is true in the modeled reality. A fact can be associated with any number of events and intervals. The system uses transactional storage mechanisms to persist data. Such a storage event corresponds to a transaction time for that event. Meanwhile, the data being stored also contains representations of a valid time event: "Something was done to an entity or a characteristic of an entity at some (valid) time". A transaction-time database supports transaction time and such a transaction can be rolled back to a previous state. A valid-time database contains the entire history of the entities it contains. Phoenix maintains and uses both the transaction time and the valid time information to provide temporal reasoning in Domain Models built using the Phoenix Architecture. Hence, the Bitemporal Database is a built from the combination of the Domain Model, the structuring of entities within the Dynamic Composites that comprise the model and the ability to track the history of each entity and its characteristics in an arbitrary fashion.

V. SYSTEM ARCHITECTURE

The Phoenix Architecture has implemented a novel approach for processing, tracking and calculating information when the representative structure, characteristics of the structure, and the temporal history of both the structure and the characteristics of its components may be easily tracked and modified over time. This includes the capability to re-materialize the representative state at some arbitrary point in time. The innovations are in three primary areas:

1. A mirrored generic data model coupled with a mirrored generic object model.
2. The mirrored models can impose an overarching relationship on arbitrary subsets of information termed a Dynamic Composite.
3. The mirrored models organize temporal information and processing into a Bitemporal Database.

Therefore, the object model (behavior) drives the ER model (date) through the ORM to dynamically create composites (state). By adding to or altering these queries with additional parameters based on the timestamps in the object and ER models, bi-temporal reasoning is fully subsumed within the standard operations of the system. Ergo, the problems of fully integrating ER and OO systems, resolving the O-R impedance mismatch, and providing temporal processing support are resolved in Phoenix. A spatial-temporal processing system has been fully realized.

This approach enables the creation of flexible and dynamic software models of real world entities, while allowing for lossless processing and reversible changes in the entities, characteristics and their tracked time attributes (history). Full support for "slowly changing data" and the ability to support "late arriving edits" are natural consequences of the approach, including the ability of the system to maintain processing history.

The system is organized as follows:

1. Strongly-typed generic types as used as foundational elements:
a. Attribute
b. Characteristic
c. Entity
d. Tracked Characteristic
2. Key dynamic relations are maintained as data:
a. Hierarchy Type – Attribute Type
b. Entity Type – Attribute Type
c. Hierarchy Type – Characteristic Type
d. Entity Type – Characteristic Type
3. Attribute semantics are treated as decorator and bridge tables:
a. Attribute Type
b. Attribute Reference
c. Attribute Type Descriptor
d. Hierarchy Type Attribute
4. Independent metadata for generic types:
a. Attribute Type
b. Characteristic Type
c. Entity Type
d. Hierarchy Type
5. Independent metadata for Bill of Material (BOM) structures:
a. BOM Structure
b. BOM Rule

Metadata, Semantics and Relations are found dynamically via search, and therefore they do not coerce the compositional structure, characteristics of the components, or their temporal information.

The Dynamic Composite structuring mechanism in Phoenix provides for bi-directional and recursive relationships. Any component in the composite can find its children or parent entity. Any Composite can contain other composites. Therefore, the Composite can represent notions of inheritance "is-a", ownership "owns", containment "has a", as well as composition "part of". Any member in the Composite Structure (i.e. an actual entity) can also have Characteristics. This includes the Structures themselves. Characteristics can also have attributes (Tracked Characteristics). Such an attribute can be used to associate historical information with a Characteristic, and thus by relationship, these Characteristics can be associated with an Entity or Structure of Entities. This Characteristic/Tracked Characteristic mechanism can be used to "decorate" any specific entity or entity structure any number of times. Thus, Tracked Characteristics can be used to hold "time varying" streams for Characteristics. Characteristics may or may not be applied to an Entity. Such Characteristics may or may not change over time. Time Series can be represented, as well as slowly changing data that carries its own temporal information as opposed to relying on a fixed index/constant time delta relationship.

Entities may stand alone, or they may be combined into Composites. These structures are completely arbitrary in size and shape. There can be many levels, or no levels. Levels can be missing altogether. Components at any given level can be missing. Conversely, as many structural levels or as many Entities at a given Structural level can be represented as desired.

Phoenix also records errors and provides an Audit Trail using its System Framework logic. The Business Logic within applications built on the Phoenix Architecture may not allow certain classes of errors, such as an erroneous edit, to persist. However, because of the issues related to erroneous, missing or out of sequence data, the system might consider data as being valid (the valid time is accepted as being true at the time of a transaction), but later the system can consider new inputs that may augment or even invalidate previous data. Therefore, the complete history of these changes and the original values being replaced may all be kept so that they are available for reprocessing.

The mirrored data and object models allow information to be stored in a relational database but to be realized as Object Oriented structures in memory. The object structures are built as POJOs (Plain Old Java Objects). This architecture allows full use of the power of the underlying Relational Database technology to provide relational operations (project, intersect, etc.) upon the data sets. The POJO-based object model allows the full use of the powerful capabilities of a modern Object Oriented language (Java) to implement algorithms and Business Logic.

An ORM (Object Relational Mapping) layer maintains a consistent mapping between the object and data models. The combination of the two, mirrored models, along with the embedded timestamp fields and embedded queries in the OOP code, provides the foundation necessary to implement the Bitemporal Database functionality. Attributes such as

"Recorded Date", "To Date" and "From Date" as evidenced in the Tracked Characteristics table are used to track temporal information. The Entity Structure Table contains "Begin Date" and "End Date" attributes, as well as keyed attributes for Parent and Child Entity Ids and Hierarchy Type Ids. This is how elements of Dynamic Composites are related spatially while maintaining the time interval endpoints that allow the materialization of Dynamic Composites as they existed during that time interval (valid time temporal relationship).

VI. Conclusion

This paper describes a system architecture built using a combination of a generic ER model mirrored by a generic object model, mapped together by an ORM system. This approach implements Kimball's requirements for the marriage of an ER Data Warehouse along with full OOP support. Building on these capabilities, and by adding the appropriate temporal attributes to the co-models and queries in the OOP code, a fully realized spatial-temporal processing system has been created.

Note also that the instances in memory are lightweight POJO's, that the entire software stack is built with Open Source packages, that an industry standard OOP (Java) is used and that a industry standard relational DBMS (Oracle) is used. This in turn implies that standard tools and development environments can be used. Furthermore, no special extensions to the OOP or the database system are required to implement the temporal processing features.

References

[1] *JDBC Overview*. Sun Microsystems, Inc., Santa Clara, CA, 2006.

[2] T. Reeskaug, P. Wold, O.A. Lehne. *Working with Objects: The OOram Software Engineering Method*. Greenwich, CT: Manning Publications, 1996.

[3] R. Wirfs-Brock, A. McKean. *Object Design: Roles, Responsibilities and Collaborations*. Reading, MA: Addison-Wesley, 2003, p. 16.

[4] E. Gamma, R. Helm, R. Johnson, and J. Vlissides. *Design Patterns: Elements of Reusable Object-Oriented Software*. Reading, MA: Addison-Wesley, 1995.

[5] P. Chen, "The Entity-Relationship Model: Toward a Unified View of Data," *ACM transactions on Database Systems*, vol. 1, no. 1, pp. 1-36, March 1976.

[6] R. Kimball. (2000, Aug. 18). *The Intelligent Enterprise Data Web House*. vol. 3, no. 13. Available: http://intelligent-enterprise.informationweek.com/000801/webhouse.jhtml

[7] S. Ambler. *Building Object Applications That Work*. Cambridge, UK: University Press, 1998, p. 311.

[8] *Object-Relational Mapping*. Wikipedia, 2009. Available: http://en.wikipedia.org/wiki/Object-Relational_Mapping

[9] C. Bauer, G. King, *Java Persistence with Hibernate*. Greenwich, CT: Manning Publications, 2006.

[10] J. Lori, "*ADEM Phoenix Enterprise Architecture*", East Hartford, CT: Pratt and Whitney Aircraft Corp, 2006.

[11] H. Sutter, A. Alexandrescu. *C++ Coding Standards: 101 Rules, Guidelines and Best Practices*. Reading, MA: Addison-Wesley, 2004.

[12] A.U. Tansel, J. Clifford. S. Gadia, S. Jajodia, A. Segev, R. Snodgrass. *Temporal Databases: Theory, Design and Implementation*. Menlo Park, California: Benjamin/Cummings, 1993.

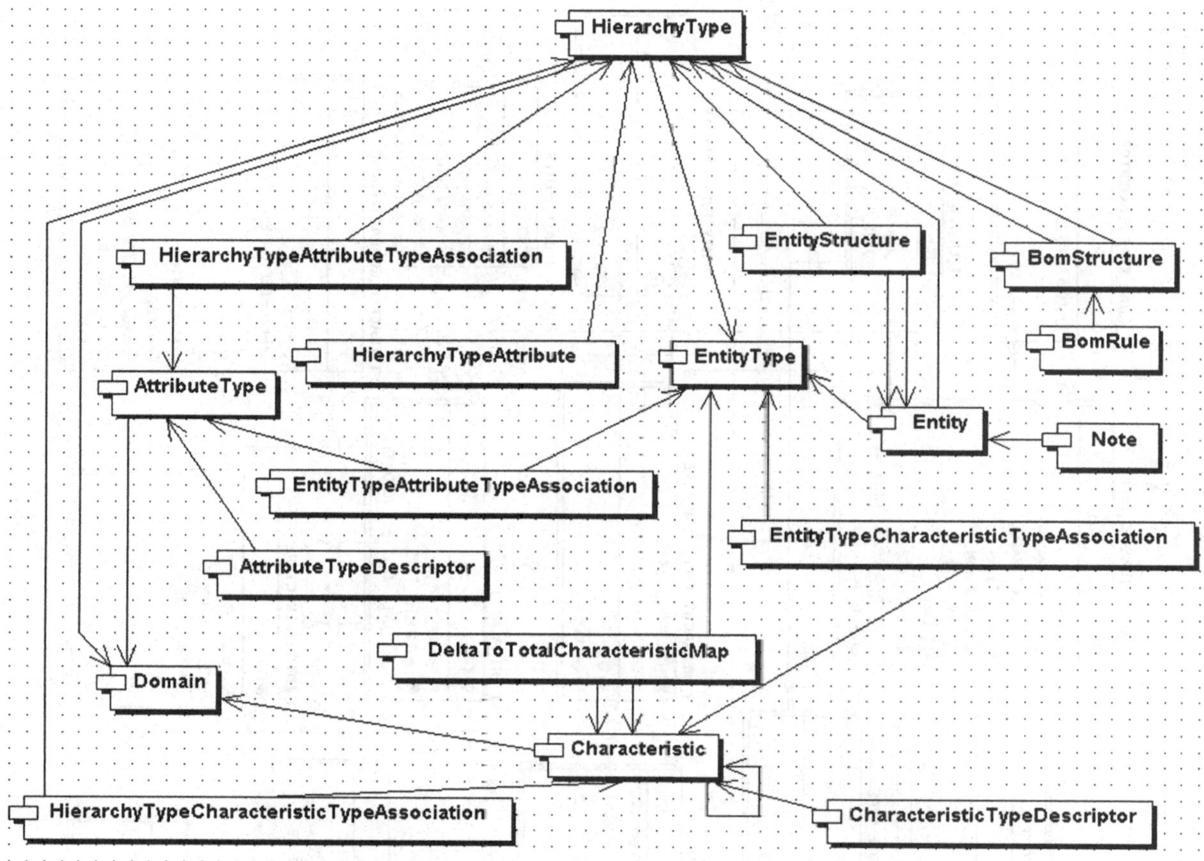

Figure 1: Phoenix Mirrored Object Model

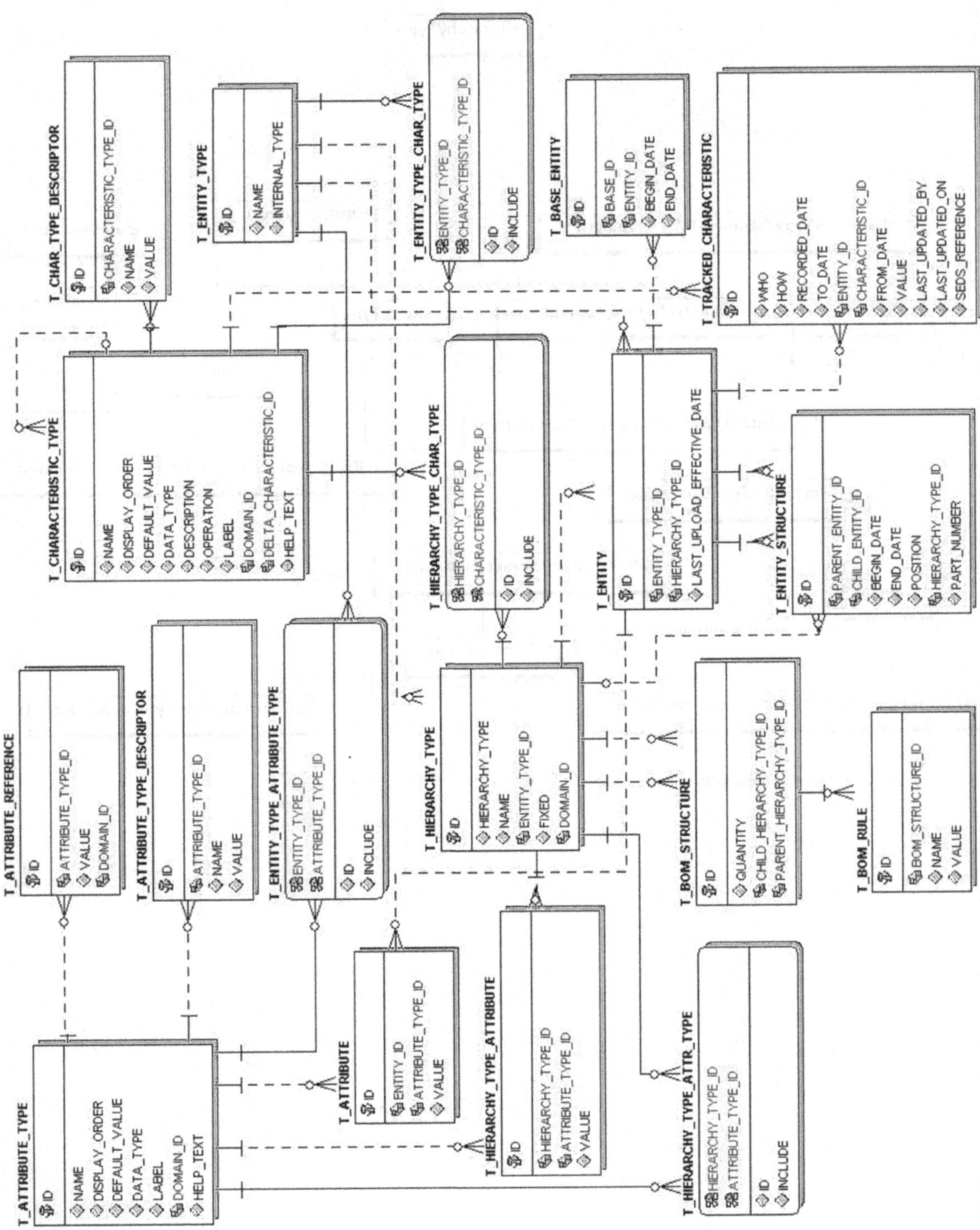

Figure 2: Phoenix Generic Entity-Relationship Model

Structure, Context and Replication in a Spatial-Temporal Architecture

Jonathan Lori

Abstract—**This paper examines some general aspects of partitioning software architecture and the structuring of complex computing systems. It relates these topics in terms of the continued development of a generalized processing model for spatial-temporal processing. Data partitioning across several copies of a generic processing stack is used to implement horizontal scaling by reducing search space and enabling parallel processing. Temporal partitioning is used to provide fast response to certain types of queries and in quickly establishing initial context when using the system.**

Index Terms—**Spatial-temporal processing, horizontal scaling, partitioning, MVCC, dynamic composites, anti-corruption layer.**

I. Introduction

PHOENIX [1] is a system that provides spatial-temporal processing capabilities for the management of configuration and utilization of aircraft engines and components.

The core spatial-temporal capability of Phoenix is completely generic. The first implementation of the system was used to create a suite of applications to manage aircraft engines. In this embodiment, a complex dynamic composite in Phoenix represents a real world jet engine with approximately one thousand components that are being tracked. These components are at varying levels of the particular bill of materials (BOM) hierarchy, ranging from the entire engine itself to various modules and assemblies. Ultimately, the composite structure goes all of the way down to the level of actual parts. Queries are driven both parametrically and by navigating against a model of the particular bill of materials of the physical assembly. Parameters represent qualification both in the spatial aspect of the composite and in the temporal aspect. For example, a serial number of a component would be chosen, as well as an "as-of" date.

Since the system manages the entire history of all of the components, performance demands turned to considering horizontal scaling [2] or "scaling out". There are natural groupings within the data that help make this possible. For example, there is a strong locality of data that represents parts on the same engine. Engines tend to last for decades, and the same parts tend to remain on the same engine until they wear out. There is also a natural grouping of engines and parts within the same engine family. And there is another large bifurcation, for security reasons, of military versus commercial engines. So an easy horizontal partitioning approach is to simply deploy multiple identical copies of the application on the application server and to deploy multiple copies of the database schema and partition the system data accordingly among the different installations. An interesting facet of Phoenix is that even though there could be replicated copies of the software that are ultimately managing the same overall set of data, the system will tend to run faster on the same exact hardware for the exact same workload when decimated into multiple instances, with each instance containing only a subset of data. This is due to decreased memory footprint per instance, better use of inline caches, reduced virtual memory paging, and in particular better database performance. A set of SQL queries for full engine materialization might require thirty full table scans in the database. One approach to improving performance would be to carefully control the generation and allocation of database ids to the system, and then use table partitioning to improve table scan performance. However, it is easy to take advantage of the natural partitioning in the datasets, and simply deploy multiple copies of the system using data that is decimated to the natural data alignment. It is also straightforward to host these deployments on multiple servers for even more performance. Thus there is a simple avenue to horizontal scaling. The tradeoff is that a user needs to access a specific installation of the system. As long as the system partitioning follows the natural data partitioning, this is not really an issue. There are also mechanisms, such as reporting, that allow for a "rolled-up" view of the information captured by multiple installations of the system.

Ultimately, an arbitrary partitioning scheme could be adapted. This approach would be based on using grid-based software to provide the additional functionality to support the arbitrary horizontal scaling. Examples of such technology include software grid systems such as Coherence [3] or GigaSpaces [4]. (Fig. 1) Maintaining spatial-temporal data locality in any given partition of the system (data) would still be a desirable quality in order to ensure maximal performance. Such a system would require facilities for directing searches to a specific partition. To maintain performance, some replication of data might be required. For example, suppose an assembly were moved from one engine to another. If these engines were to exist in two different partitions of the system, the grid implementation would need to account for this in the totality of the history of the components in any given partition. However, the goal of partitioning is to improve performance. Ideally, any given search should be limited to involving the smallest

Manuscript received October 10, 2009.

J. Lori is a PhD candidate at the University of Bridgeport, Bridgeport, CT, 06066 USA (email: jlori@bridgeport.edu).

T. Sobh, K. Elleithy (eds.), *Innovations in Computing Sciences and Software Engineering*,
DOI 10.1007/978-90-481-9112-3_21, © Springer Science+Business Media B.V. 2010

number of stacks, preferably one. The better approach is to move the data for the containing aggregate and the component such that they are collocated with the moved component's target aggregate. The move event would trigger an ETL (Extract-Transform-Load) process managed by the system software. In either case, such an approach becomes a sophisticated "anti-corruption" layer [5].

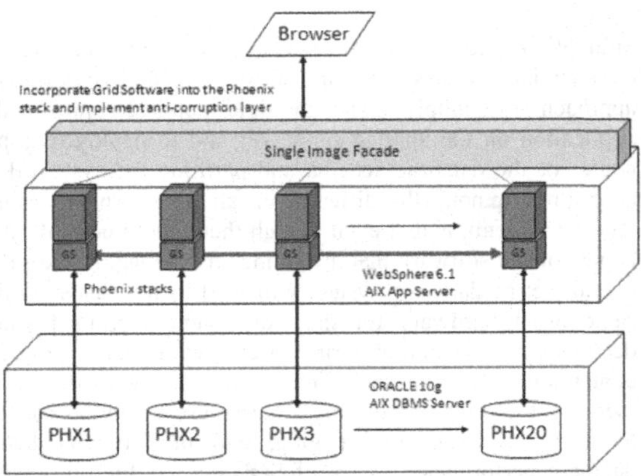

Fig. 1 Phoenix Scale-out using a Grid Architecture

Grid systems such as Coherence and GigaSpaces are built around a distributed architecture model. This means that by incorporating such technology into the system implicitly provides a foundation such that each partition could run on its own dedicated server. The combination of partitioning, distribution, anti-corruption, and genericity with the core spatial-temporal abilities of Phoenix makes for a unique and powerful system that is widely useful in many applications. Prototypes of certain parts of Phoenix using both GigaSpaces and Coherence have been implemented to drive further refinement of the architecture.

II. Caching

It is important to note that both Coherence and GigaSpaces can act as second-level caches for the Hibernate [6] object-relational mapping system used in Phoenix. Additionally, these packages can act as caching mechanisms in their own right. This means global metadata such as BOM models could be cached. Certain operations in Phoenix could benefit from a generic global scratchpad in memory as well. Materialized dynamic composites could be cached. A key question is what exactly should be cached.

III. COG Model

Another partitioning approach has been implemented to provide the next level of scaling in the Phoenix architecture beyond implementing a data grid. It is described in this section. It is postulated in this paper that there are almost always multiple models in any large system. Or, perhaps, there should be. Structuring paradigms such as layers and tiers contribute to this. Different database models for transaction processing versus analysis or reporting are another example of this effect. Useful software is used software, and software which is used inevitably undergoes change. So maintenance and augmentation tends to drive large, long lived systems in this direction as well. In a discussion on Domain Driven Design, Evans [7] provides an excellent rationale for the multiple model approach. Evans discusses decimating a system into corresponding domains such as a core domain, generic domains, and sub-domains. He postulates that while architects are taught to eschew duplication and that there should be a single, unified model within any one such context; he then states that duplication should be embraced between contexts.

Phoenix [1] uses a very generic Entity Relationship data model. This model is represented inside the database, and it is mirrored by an object model. Instances of dynamic composites are instantiated in memory using this object model. The co-models were designed to support the storage, searching and materialization of any type of dynamic composite. Despite this genericity, the need for performance and functionality has driven the architecture to multiple copies of the same model, as well as multiple copies of the same data in different models.

Some criticisms of the system were directed at the lack of a more specific (strongly-typed in the domain of discourse) set of entities and classes. In the application domain such as that which is served by Phoenix, this would include tables and classes such as "Engine". However, the Phoenix core domain is really "composites in time". State is viewed as the "value of an identity at a time" [8]. It just so happens that the applications currently built on Phoenix deal with composites of engine components. They could be composites of anything.

Besides the persistent Phoenix ER data model and its mirrored object model, the data in the system is also represented in a Dimensional Data Mart (DDM) [9]. The DDM provides a system-wide data rollup in a format amenable to relational tools, especially reporting tools.

The new model that will be discussed in this section is called Composite Object Graph (COG). Here, a COG is defined as object graph that is built in such a way that it is capable of representing the information and structure of a dynamic composite and is compatible with the requirements of the persistence mechanism that will be used to store the COG. The COG might use an Object Database (OODBMS) as its persistence mechanism. Or, it might exist in the distributed cache on a grid system such as Coherence or GigaSpaces. Typical compatibility requirements might include constraints such as the need for the persistent classes to implement a no-argument constructor. The classes might be required to implement language specific elements. The system is currently implemented in Java, so there may be a need to implement the Java Serializable or Externalizable interfaces. Another requirement might be that native Java collection classes could not be used, so the COG would have to forego the use of native Java collections, create its own simple collections, or use collection classes supplied by the persistence mechanism. In order to keep as many options open as possible, while leveraging identical or very similar constraints, the COG is designed to work on as many of the potential storage, distribution and caching systems as possible. Currently, the COG is implemented using the DB4O open source OODBMS [10].

In an earlier system, NextGen [11], an important distinction was made between having a current time model as well as the full (historical) model. The spatial-temporal model is vastly simplified by reducing the time dimension to "now" in the current time model. Many common operations are performed in the "current time". For example, typical current-time queries in Phoenix include "What is the current configuration of engine X? What modifications has the engine incorporated to this point? What modifications are available?" The important distinction here is that if the system can be partitioned in yet another dimension, along the time axis, then the performance for these operations can be radically improved over searching through all historical data. A COG also has the benefit of being able to be stored in an object-oriented representation. Using object-based persistence can be a big win in performance for complex object systems versus using relational storage. In general, if a point in time can be established, the spatial-temporal graph can readily be built and stored as a COG.

One choice for the current time model is to simply keep the same exact system application, but achieve improved performance by replicating out the current time information into a separate data store that uses the same data model as well. The replicated store would be used to handle only the current time processing. As discussed earlier [1], it has already been demonstrated that simply reducing the amount of data in the spatial-temporal model has a strong, positive effect on Phoenix performance.

Another approach is to implement an entirely different storage model for the current time structures, and then use both structures in the system. This is the approach currently being taken, and it utilizes the COG model. Thus, the COG model acts as a persistent object cache of current-time data. There is a facade that acts as the entry point to the system. The application starts off with the current-time context, and then optionally if there is a need to drill down or perform an edit, it deals with processing against the entire historical data set. This can be done either synchronously or asynchronously. The synchronous approach can use read-through/write-through access to the underlying data store when everything must be kept in synch. Write-behind approaches update the cache and then asynchronously update the underlying data store.

The façade makes the system appear as a "single image" to an end user and also acts as a router to channel interaction to the appropriate copy of the stack containing the required data.

Brewer's Law [12] states: "You can have any two of the following three qualities in your system: consistent, available, or partitioned". Since partitioning is a deliberate first choice to allow the system to scale out, this leaves only a single axis of freedom. Since the operational context of these designs is that of a Web-based system, the second choice is availability. Therefore, some modicum of consistency may be sacrificed (temporarily) in order to produce a large (partitioned) and performant (available) system.

The COG model for Phoenix (Fig. 2) is BOM-based, as this matches the approach of engine management applications in Phoenix that use BOM structures as metadata. The NextGen system used a process of "double writes" to update both the current time model and the historical model. The historical model update process in NextGen used a queued, write-behind approach. In an earlier version of the Phoenix system, certain edits to the data store could use an asynchronous write-behind approach to update the system. A "headless" version of the Phoenix stack was developed in parallel with the full stack. The headless version was used to perform background processing tasks against the same data store. These tasks are the same operations normally done by the full stack, but the headless stack is distributed to another server and communicates via messaging.

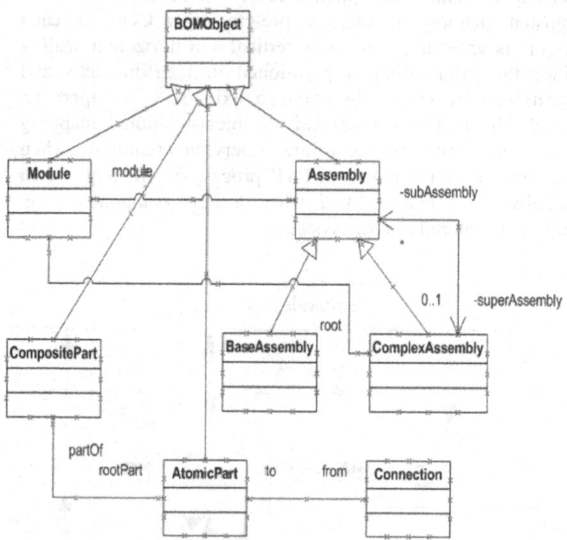

Fig. 2 Generalized BOM-based Composite Object Graph

All system edits are transactional, but in the asynchronous mode, the edit carries both the current state and the new state, and the system first checks to see that the current state matches that which is contained in the edit message. The edit occurs as an "all or nothing" transaction and it will not occur if there is a mismatch between the current system state and the current state contained within the message. The edit is then reflected in the COG store, and eventually in the DDM store as well. The DDM is rebuilt each night. Both the COG and DDM models are considered "read only" outside this update process. Updates are always made first to "back end" i.e. the Phoenix stack, and then propagated back to the other models. As stated previously, edits that must be done in real time can always go directly through the full Phoenix stack in a synchronous fashion. Ultimately, this approach might change as the Grid vendors continue to expand their feature set in these areas. For example, the COG could be cached and updated first, while an asynchronous process updates the underlying data store.

In 2007, a Business Process Engine [13] was added to Phoenix. The thinking at that time was to use the process engine to manage COG images and updates and the message flow between the front end (façade) and back end store. It is also notable that systems such as Coherence and GigaSpaces both evolved their facilities in a direction that better supports the COG implementation. Since these mechanisms are built in as part of the distribution, replication and control architecture of the Grid packages, the need for the Process Engine in this area has been superseded.

The current COG implementation (Fig. 3) is based on DB4O, an open source OODBMS that supports both Java and C#. The benefit of using an object database is that a COG can be persisted directly and rematerialized quickly. Having another persistence engine and model that supports a COG directly means that a COG can be pre-created, stored persistently and then quickly recreated in a cache or in transient memory. In essence, pre-creating a COG for each engine is an example of both vertical and horizontal scaling since the information is partitioned in the time axis and partitioned by engine in the data axis. A COG approach avoids the real-time overhead of object-relational mapping and much of the real-time querying required when materializing an engine. An ETL process is still required to initially instantiate a COG when a new component (e.g. engine) is entered into the system.

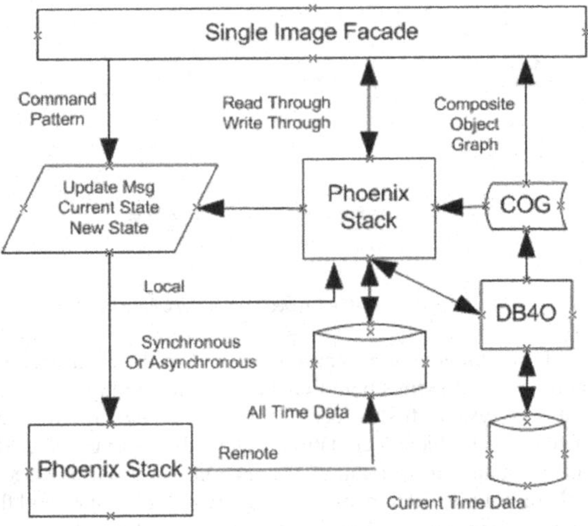

Fig. 3 Incorporating COG's into the Architecture

An earlier approach [14] used database rows to store blobs of serialized object graphs of COG structures. Future approaches may involve persistent concurrent data structures such as bit-partitioned hash tries [8]. These structures support efficient, immutable copies that implement Software Transactional Memory (STM) [15]. Again, the architecture is driven by the notion of having the same data, but storing it in a different representation (model). The bifurcation with STM is mutability versus immutability when dealing with concurrency and state.

IV. Summary

The fundamental capability of the Phoenix system to flexibly represent and reason over spatial-temporal information in a very generic form makes it applicable to solve a large and important range of problems. As the system progressed, the biggest requirement became the ability to scale it to handle larger data sets. This paper describes the evolution of the Phoenix system to provide increased performance and scalability.

The main techniques used in scaling the Phoenix architecture include:

Achieve parallelism and reduce search footprint with a scale-out design
Horizontal partitioning with multiple generic stacks and data stores
Grid computing
Domain-driven design
Caching
Foreground/background processing
Multiple models of representation
Unified model within a context
Duplication between contexts
Optional read-through/write-through edits to the underlying data store
Optional asynchronous updates to the underlying data store
Anti-corruption layer and mechanisms
Carrying current and new state during asynchronous updates (example of anti-corruption)
Data re-collocation after splitting historical data (example of anti-corruption)
Maintaining context with the front-end façade (single image system / software router)
Continuous ETL to update multiple models
Composite Object Graphs
Temporal partitioning of the current time representation independently of all historical data
Domain-driven design

The work has been successful. In general, good solutions have been reached and other performance enhancements are being investigated. The scale-out approach over natural data partitioning provides proportional performance increases. Partitioning over an arbitrary division of data can extend these gains by leveraging Grid computing software in a straightforward manner. The Grid software facilities then become part of the anti-corruption layer.

Future work will involve partitioning the system in yet another way. Identity is forever, and Structure typically changes slowly. Some data captured in the system, while temporal in nature, has frequent updates. There needs to be more isolation and flexibility between representing a Slowly Changing Dimension (SCD) [16] and a Fast Changing Dimension (FCD) in the system.

REFERENCES

[1] J. Lori, "Towards a Spatial-Temporal Processing Model", Dept. of Eng., University of Bridgeport, Bridgeport, CT, 2009.

[2] M. Fowler, *Patterns of Enterprise Architecture,* Reading, MA: Addison-Wesley, 2002, p. 9.

[3] *Oracle Coherence Suite*. Oracle Corporation, Redwood City, CA, 2008.

[4] *GigaSpaces Extreme Application Platform*. GigaSpaces Technologies Inc., New York, NY, 2009.

[5] *Anti-corruption Layer*. Domain Driven Design Community. 2009. Available: http://www.domaindrivendesign.com.

[6] C. Bauer, G. King, *Java Persistence with Hibernate*. Greenwich, CT: Manning Publications, 2006.

[7] E. Evans, *Domain Driven Design*, Reading, MA: Addison-Wesley, 2003, p. 335.

[8] R. Hickey, "Persistent Data Structures and Managed References", presented at 2009 InfoQ QCon, San Francisco, CA.

[9] C. Ballard, D. Farrell, A. Gupta, C. Mazuela, S. Vohnik. *Dimensional Modeling: In a Business Intelligence Environment*. Armonk, NY: IBM Redbooks, 2006.

[10] *DB4Objects Database System*. Versant Corporation, Redwood City, CA, 2009.

[11] J. Lori, "*The NextGen System Architecture*", Stamford, CT: Pitney-Bowes Corp, 1994.

[12] E. Brewer, "*Towards Robust Distributed Systems*", ACM PODC Keynote Paper, July 2000.

[13] *Oracle Business Process Management Suite*. Oracle Corporation, Redwood City, CA, 2008.

[14] J. Lori, "*ADEM Phoenix Enterprise Architecture*", East Hartford, CT: Pratt and Whitney Aircraft Corp, 2006.

[15] *Software Transactional Memory*. Wikipedia. 2009. Available: http://en.wikipedia.org/wiki/Software_transactional_memory

[16] R. Kimball, J. Caserta. *The Data Warehouse ETL Toolkit*, Indianapolis, IN: John Wiley & Sons, 2004, pp. 183 - 194.

Service Oriented E-Government

Dr. PhD Margareth Stoll Margareth.stoll@eurac.edu
Dr. Dietmar Laner dlaner@eurac.edu
EURAC Research, Drususallee, 1
39100 Bozen, South Tyrol, Italy

Abstract- **Due to different directives, the growing request for citizen-orientation, improved service quality, effectiveness, efficiency, transparency and reduction of costs, as well as administrative burden public administrations apply increasingly management tools and IT for continual service development and sustainable citizens' satisfaction. Therefore public administrations implement always more standard based management systems, such as quality ISO9001, environmental ISO 14001 or others. Due to this situation we used in different case studies as basis for e-government a the administration adapted, holistic administration management model to analyze stakeholder requirements and to integrate, harmonize and optimize services, processes, data, directives, concepts and forms. In these case studies the developed and consequently implemented holistic administration management model promotes constantly over more years service effectiveness, citizen satisfaction, efficiency, cost reduction, shorter initial training periods for new collaborators, employee involvement for sustainable citizen-oriented service improvement and organizational development.**

Keywords: e-government, administration management, process management, service management, organizational development, management system

I. Introduction

A Starting Situation

Due to globalization and ever shorter change cycles organizations and also public administrations must improve increasingly faster their services, organization and technologies inclusive IT in accordance to citizens and legal requirements. Thus the largest potential is continual improvement by organizational learning based on individual learning and the management of information, data, knowledge [1] and directives. In this respect an effective holistic interdisciplinary systemic administration management and an optimal exploitation of data, information, directives and knowledge within the public administrations are central for new public management. However, existing systems have not kept pace with the evolving complexity and diversity of challenges facing knowledge workers to support their daily work [2]. Therefore integrating job relevant data, information, directives and knowledge into the business processes of public administrations has become a topic of general interest [3], [4], [6].

Management tools, successfully applied in great sized private organizations, can not be transferred without changes into public administrations. The prevalent influence of laws and directives, the differences between single proceedings caused by to the individual citizen situation, the fragmentation of services and processes over different departments or administrations, the undefined client as all citizens for some services, the important influences and role of politicians, the considerable amount of data including sensitive data, the increasing data protection demands require adapted management models. Therefore existing models must be adapted regarding their specially conditions for the use in public administrations.

More than one million organizations of different sizes and scopes are implementing already since several years management systems, such as quality ISO9001, environmental ISO14001, information security ISO27001, hygienic ISO22000 or others [7]. They are based on international standards with common principles: organizational objectives and strategies, business processes, resource management and the continuously optimization of the organization [8]. These systems are implemented more frequently in a holistic way. Thereby are integrated according to organizational purpose and objectives different aspects, like quality, environment, hygiene, data security, occupational health and safety, personnel development, resource management, IT - management, communication management, controlling, and/or knowledge management.

The established standard based management system must be documented, communicated, implemented and continual improved. Thus the system documentation contains the entire actual explicit knowledge and supports individual and organizational learning. Thereby the management system pushes constantly the knowledge and learning spiral, change organizational knowledge and promote sustainable organizational development.

B Purpose of the Article

In the public administration processes and services are often fragmented over different departments or administrations. If projects and actions are taken independently of each other to promote efficiency, effectiveness and cost reduction for single sub organizations, the holistic service and business process of the administration is neglected. Consequently different departments use for the same administration service different procedures, directives, regulations, forms, concepts, methods and/or IT solutions. Just at the end of the 20th century new public management required process redesign.

T. Sobh, K. Elleithy (eds.), *Innovations in Computing Sciences and Software Engineering*,
DOI 10.1007/978-90-481-9112-3_22,

Nevertheless it was applied frequently in a fragmented way [9].

Organizations commit a radical error and analyze their organization by the lens of their lived processes. They ask themselves "how can we use new technology to optimize our processes" instead of, "how we can do something new with the technology: automation instead innovation" [10]. The prior IT objective must be to promote in the best way possible the objectives of the organization.

Thus we need a holistic, systematic administration management approach, which regards the special requirements of public administrations, to respond to ambient changes, to increase efficiency, citizen satisfaction, effectiveness and cost reduction and to promote continually organizational development for fulfilling sustainable citizens and stakeholder requirements.

C Research Approach

The always stronger request for citizen orientation, citizen satisfaction, efficiency, effectiveness, cost reduction, shorter improvement cycles in the public administration, the increasing implementation of standard based management systems, the growing informatization, and the great importance of citizen-oriented organizational development leaded us to introduce a the administration adapted, holistic administration management model, which is based on standard management systems. Thereby we analyze stakeholder requirements, integrate, harmonize and improve services, processes, directives, law interpretations, concepts and documents to promote the fulfillment of the objectives of the administration and citizen-oriented organizational development.

D Structure of the Article

Firstly we describe based on the starting situation the project objectives [II]. Afterwards we explain our holistic management model for the public administration [III]. After that we present our approach [IV]. Finally we document the project experiences and results [V] including the achievement of the project principles [V A] and a reflection about success factors and social aspects [V B]. At the end we express an outlook [VI] and our conclusion [VII].

II. Project Objectives

How can we establish the objectives and strategies of a public administration regarding stakeholder and citizen requirements? Howe we analyze, integrate, improve, harmonize and communicate processes, services, data, directives, law interpretations, concepts and documents in a holistic and systemic way in accordance with the established requirements in order to be considered, used and continual improved as an organizational knowledge base for sustainable citizen-oriented organizational development?

With our holistic administration management approach we expect to foster:

- effectiveness and citizen satisfaction,
- efficiency and cost reduction,
- shorter initial training periods for new collaborators,
- organizational development by employee involvement and service improvement.

This holistic administration management model includes all relevant processes, services, data, directives and information and should improve knowledge representation, knowledge communication, learning, service implementation and knowledge use, employee involvement, knowledge generation, process and service improvement and organizational development.

III. Holistic Administration Management Model

For the holistic administration management model we use the ISO9001 model [8]. The distinct standard based management systems have different specialized focuses, but are all based on common principles [8], [fig.1.]:

- Organizational objectives and strategies must be established regarding stakeholder requirements.
- All administration processes including management process, support processes, resource processes and optimization processes must be defined and promote optimized fulfillment of organizational objectives under the focus of respective standard.
- Process oriented resource management must be promoted including human resource development, IT – management and other infrastructures, tools and instruments.
- The administrations, their objectives and strategies, services, products and processes must be continually optimized according to established processes in the sense of a PDCA cycle (plan, do, check / study, act).

The established administration management system must be structured and systematically documented, as well as communicated within the administration. The collaborators must be continually motivated for implementing the established processes and for recommending improvements.

These standard based management systems are implemented more frequently in a holistic way. In accordance to organizational purposes and objectives different aspects like quality, environment, data security, occupational health and safety, as well as human resource development, IT, data, communication, knowledge and infrastructure management, controlling are integrated.

Fig. 1. Main requirements of standard based management systems

IV. APPROACH

Due to the large relevance and range of a project for implementing a holistic administration management model we use a holistic project management method for planning and implementing it in accordance with stakeholder project requirements. The achievement of the project objectives is controlled constantly by concrete measurement methods.

A Stakeholder Oriented Organizational Objectives

For establishing the vision, mission statement, administrations' objectives and strategies we use Quality Function Deployment [11]. We define and prioritize the stakeholder (politicians, citizens, customer, collaborators, supplier, environment and society) with the collaborators and managers involved. Due to the experiences from intensive contacts between stakeholders and collaborators and, or due to interviews, literature research or citizen surveys the stakeholder requirements and expectations are identified. Subsequently they are prioritized. The vision, mission statement, longer-term strategic objectives and concrete full year objectives for the administration are deduced from the prioritized requirements. To achieve these objectives we elaborate appropriate programs and projects, define responsible organizational units, measurement methods, metrics, deadlines and necessary resources. Thereby we regard all relevant aspects (e.g. quality, environment, hygiene, data security, occupational health and safety, human resource development, resource management, IT - management, communication, controlling, knowledge management). Thus the entire administration is focused on stakeholder requirements.

B Process Analysis and Process / Service Improvement

Afterwards the services and applied processes are analyzed bottom up by interviewing the collaborators involved [10]. For process modeling we apply simple structured flowcharts [Fig.2] with three or four columns (4th for annotations, conditions, terms), which are limited to one page. Therefore they are deeply structured. For time critical descriptions we use Gantt charts. All processes receive also a short textual summary.

Thereby we consider all processes of the administration beginning from the management process, all service processes inclusive the development of new services, as well as all supporting processes, resources processes and improvement processes. In accordance to the objectives of the administration we consider and integrate thereby all relevant aspects (e.g. quality, information security, data protection, environment, human resource development, resource management, IT - management, communication management, controlling, knowledge management or others).

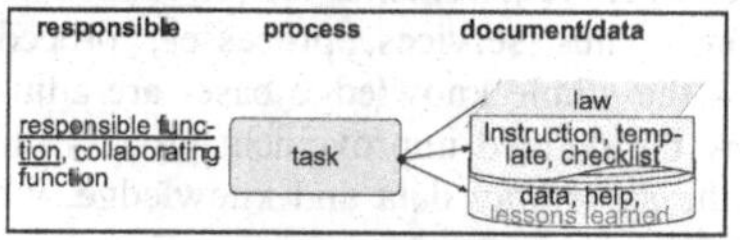

Fig. 2. Process modeling method

All processes are analyzed and improved regarding the established administrations' objectives, legal and directive requirements, efficiency, effectiveness and cost reduction. They are harmonized and integrated inclusive the procedures, directives, regulations, legal interpretations, concepts, checklist, forms as well as the information and data flow and all databases and IT systems [3].

To harmonize the services, processes and data we define in the first step the main services with their corresponding processes and analyze these in the single departments. Afterwards we harmonize common process segments, legal interpretations, directives, concepts and forms (apart from some specific data and calculations) and integrate them. Thus we establish a reduced number of common, harmonized, integrated main services and processes (ca. one until five) with related data, documents, instructions, information, relevant laws, directives and legal interpretations. Afterwards parameterization resolves specific differences. Thereby we define and apply also a common organizational glossary.

For all activities the responsible function, the applied documents, checklists, procedures, forms, IT applications, the relevant laws and directives are studied. Also the necessary data, information and knowledge for all tasks and their exchange and storage are analyzed. In that way the whole document and data logistic is identified (creation, control, approval, signature, release, distribution, retrieval, modification, archive and destruction). Thereby also the data interfaces are defined. All treated data are examined for necessity and lawfulness. This is also an optimal basis for establishing signature regulations including signature rights and signature procedures. In accordance to the administration purpose and objectives, as well as the data protection code, the required data encryptions and necessary encryption procedures are identified. Further the procedures for current, intermediate and historical archiving with archive duration and the requirements for data and service confidentiality, availability and integrity are elaborated. Thereby we regard the data protection law. This is also an important part of a holistic information security management system in accordance to ISO/IEC 27001.

Templates are developed for all necessary documents and forms (e.g. application forms). Thus they are examined only once by specialized experts and jurisprudents. Afterwards every collaborator can fill them easily with the personal data of the single applicant. The specialized knowledge of experts is integrated also into all checklists. Thereby implicit knowledge is externalized. Further the checklists are continually extended or changed according to experiences taken during the application in the administrations' everyday life. Also changes in the law, modified directives or regulations or altered stakeholder requirements or circumstances causes modifications. Thus services, processes, procedures and documents - the whole knowledge base- are adjusted flexible. Thereby the defined improvement process must be observed. In the same way data and knowledge, which is no more needed, is removed in time.

During process analysis we recognize these process steps, in which experiences and interpretations of laws or directives (lessons learned) are developed. That should be documented for later use. Thus data collection and information processing are planed and implemented systematically and structured accordingly to the relevant data protection codes and all other legal requirements. We integrated into the process models, directly at the single process steps, a context sensitive interface to the relevant laws and directives. Further users can integrate into the process models individual or common accessible personal notes and thereby represent their knowledge.

Function profiles, necessary requirement profiles, knowledge and competences are deduced from the single process steps. Thus knowledge carriers are specified and knowledge maps - yellow pages- are constructed [12], [13], [14].

C Resource Management

The administration must determine and provide due to standard requirements necessary resources, tools and instruments to achieve the established objectives and to continual improve the administration.

The increasing strengthened informatization effects job modifications, redistribution of responsibilities and job enlargements. Therefore the personnel regulations (such as career profiles, requirement profiles, selection procedures) must be adapted. This, the growing service and citizen orientation and increased service quality requirements demands self and social competencies, communication skills, IT – competences, interest in new knowledge, change and learning willingness, team ability, openness and tolerance, empathy, entrepreneurial spirit, as well as self-driven, objective and system oriented acting in accordance to the established objectives and regulations. The standards require the planning and implementation of trainings and competence objectives accordingly to defined processes. The effectiveness of the processes must be evaluated.

D Continually Improvement

Due to standard requirements we deduce from established administrations' objectives service and process objectives. Therefore we define corresponding measurement methods to demonstrate the service and process ability to achieve planned results. This is the basis for the continually improvement of the administration. Based on the required systemic approach of the standards, the interrelations between single services, processes and objectives must be identified, understand and managed [8]. The ability of the organization to achieve planned service, process and administration objectives, inclusive citizen/customer satisfaction, is evaluated periodically by data and information in accordance to established measurement methods. If planned results are not achieved appropriate corrective and eventually preventive actions must be determined, implemented and their effectiveness evaluated. All corrective actions, improvements or changes must be checked by the involved collaborators, approved, documented, communicated, implemented and their effectiveness evaluated. Therefore appropriate systematically and structured processes must be established. Optimizations and preventive actions are introduced also by means of collaborators' ideas and suggestions. Periodically internal and external audits, feedbacks from stakeholders, the collaboration with supplier and praxis experiences promote improvements, which are handled systematically in accordance to established processes.

Thereby holistic administration management, knowledge use, systematically and continually knowledge generation, organizational learning, process and service improvement for continual organizations' development, as well as service and/or process innovations in accordance to established objectives and stakeholder requirements are promoted. Theoretical considerations are tested in practice. In that way we integrate optimally process modeling, service and process standardization, service and process improvement with need and objective oriented flexible process implementation. Changing organizational knowledge new individual learning becomes possible. Thereby the knowledge and learning spiral is pushed constantly again and the organizational knowledge base is extended.

E System Documentation

The established management system with vision, mission, objectives, strategies, service and process models including directives, legal interpretations, concepts, documents, the data management, the relevant laws, directives, necessary law interpretations, function profiles, templates, checklists and others must be documented. All collaborators and every new collaborator at his/her entrance receive the documentation traceable. Also all changes must be distributed traceable. The collaborators and particularly the directors must constantly implement the established processes, regulations and directives. To promote need-oriented, workplace integrated access to system documentation we prepare it regarding media-pedagogical, motivation-psychological and didactical principles [15] and distribute it electronically through web-based intranets or pdf. The way for accessing the single modules must be as short as possible, optimal structured and practice oriented. The requirements of all collaborators must be analyzed and considered as early as possible (e.g. an efficient and effective search function). We used a constructivist method. Need-oriented workplace integrated learning, knowledge communication and knowledge sharing can be promoted further by an organizational learning and knowledge system [16].

F IT Implementation

A consequently implemented and improved, the administration optimally adapted, holistic administration management system offers due to its strong stakeholder and objective orientation, the systematically, structured and holistic approach, the collaborators' involvement, the harmonized, burden reduced services, the in the practice "tested" and optimized processes and forms an optimal basis for e-government. Due to a strong and early user involvement and this holistic, systematically approach the IT will be best adapted to all stakeholder and user requirements' and promotes a sustainable citizen-oriented organizational development.

V. Project Experiences and Results

This holistic administration management model is implemented successfully since more years in several public administrations with distinct management systems. Thereby implementing customer and service orientation, process thinking, harmonizing and simplifying processes, directives, concepts, procedures and forms, as well as controlling and maintaining service and process improvement were great challenges.

A Achieving the Project Objectives

This holistic administration management leads to the following case study results collected by established service, process and system measurement methods and interviewing directors and collaborators:

- Effectiveness and citizen satisfaction: the fulfillment of established objectives is periodically controlled by defined measurement methods, studied and if necessary, appropriate corrective or prevention actions are elaborated, implemented and their effectiveness is controlled. Therefore in an administration e.g. could be improved the citizen satisfaction constantly from 85% at the end of 2002 to 92% at the end of 2006. The administrations can achieve their established objectives in average at more than 95%. By an optimal IT support the measurements can be continually evaluated with no or little additional expenditure. Many collaborators and specially directors felt the clear definition of objectives and aligned measurement methods as a great help and assistance. This improved achieving of administrations' objectives secures sustainable citizen orientation.
- Efficiency and cost reduction: Due to constantly optimized processes and services in accordance to established stakeholder oriented objectives the adherence to delivery dates could be increased in an administration from 77% in 2002 to 95% in 2006.
- Shorter initial training periods for new collaborators: new collaborators are quickly introduced into the structure of the system documentation at their first working day. Afterwards they learn all relevant contents for their specific administration job in a self-driven, need oriented, work integrated way. Thus the documentation is always accessible a new collaborator can focus at the start only on the principle information and after she/he access need-oriented to all necessary directives, regulations, laws, law interpretations, procedures and process models to fulfil her/his job. Thereby the lead time could be abbreviated around a half. New collaborators feel themselves substantially earlier integrated into the administration and can execute their job faster well, whereby the productivity increase and possible errors are avoided.
- Organizational development by employee involvement and process / service improvement: Due to the standard requirements all ideas, optimizations and suggestions of the collaborators are evaluated, eventually implemented systematically and structured and their effectiveness is controlled. Thereby we received averaged monthly 0.1 until 0.6 ideas from each collaborator. Thus service and process improvement is promoted, the system documentation (organizational knowledge base) continually improved and the achievement of the administrations' objectives sustainable optimized.

The optimized information and communication flows, the improved service and process thinking, which promotes organizational relationships, the implemented human resource development, knowledge exchange and knowledge generation, and the enhanced collaborators' involvement increase the collaborators' satisfaction.

In periodically internal and external audits the compliance between the lived processes/services and the process models (organizational knowledge base) is examined. This supports a constantly updating and changing of the process models and services. Thereby we integrate optimal process/service modeling, process/service standardization and transparency with need and objective oriented flexible process/servcie implementation.

B Success Factors and Social Aspects

Corporate culture, processes and IT technology must be integrated optimally according to administration objectives, collaborators needs and stakeholder requirements. Thereby didactical principles should be considered also in order to support the continual improvement of processes, services, organization, technology and the administration itself. Technology, models and methods are thereby only tools, which support the optimization of the administration including its services and processes so far as this is admitted by the culture. Therefore we need an open, confident based, participative, esteeming, fault-tolerant, objective oriented corporate and learning culture with criticism and change readiness.

The collaborators should be interested in new knowledge, able for self-driven learning, have personal employment, team ability and change willingness. All managers must elaborate constantly and actively new ideas and motivate their collaborators in following these principles. A strengthening point for achieving this is the maintenance of an optimal internally communication as well with external partners.

The system documentation must be analyzed and improved bottom up by involving the concerned collaborators. Thereby the collaborators support the project, develop practice oriented services and process models with daily used terms. In that way the documentation contains most of the explicit organizational knowledge. A great challenge is also the right process depth: to promote an efficiently and effectively application of the documentation there should be regulated as much as needed and as less as possible.

Using holistic administration management as basis for organizational learning and organizational development requires the administration best adapted process and service models. This certainly can not be achieved by using purchased general manuals, which do not correspond with lived processes, services and objectives. Further the system must be consequently and effectively implemented and can not be only an alibi - action.

This holistic administration management model requires from the system manager or e-government specialist a part from system and administration management skills the expertise about all relevant laws and directives and necessary competences in change management, organizational learning, knowledge management, information and data management, information security management, data protection, controlling, technology and infrastructure management, and others.

Sufficient IT-infrastructure and IT-support are also very important for the project success. A need and objective oriented workflow based holistic database supported e-government system promotes continual organization development in accordance to administrations' objectives, as well as effectiveness, efficiency and cost reduction.

VI. OUTLOOK

Due to these excellent project experiences in different administrations with distinct management systems holistic administration management systems should be introduced enhanced by regarding all success factors [V B].

Administration management should be considered more in a holistic way. Thereby different aspects, like quality, environment, hygiene, data security, occupational health and safety, personnel development, resource management, IT - management, information management, knowledge management, controlling and others should be integrated accordingly to administration purpose and objectives.

Administration management should underline and promote the importance of an open, confident based, fault tolerant corporate and learning culture with criticism and change readiness.

Trainings for system manager, e-government specialists or IT analyst should consider more this holistic administration management approach and teach all aspects of this model and the importance of corporate and learning culture.

VII. CONCLUSION

Due to our holistic administration management model we analyze stakeholder requirements, integrate, improve and harmonize services, processes, data, directives, legal interpretations, concepts and documents bottom up by interviewing the collaborators involved and prepare the system documentation in accordance to didactical principles. In the various case studies this holistic administration management model promotes effectiveness and citizen satisfaction, efficiency and cost reduction, shorter initial training periods for new collaborators, employee involvement and process/service improvement for sustainable citizen-oriented organizational development,

REFERENCES

[1] H. Takeuchi and I. Nonaka, *Hitotsubashi on Knowledge Management*, John Wiley & Sons, Singapore, 2004.

[2] R. Maier, *Knowledge management systems*, Springer, Berlin, 2002.

[3] T. Davenport and L. Prusak, *Working Knowledge*, Harvard Business School Press, Boston, 1998.

[4] G. Probst, S. Raub and K. Romhardt, *Wissen managen*, Gabler, Wiesbaden, 1999.

[5] M. Stoll, *Managementsysteme und Prozessorientiertes Wissensmanagement*, in N. Gronau Eds. Proc. 4th Conference professional knowledge management – experiences and visions, Gito, Berlin, volume 1, pp. 433-434, 2007.

[6] K. Lenk and R. Traunmüller: *Electronic Government*, Computer kommunikativ, 4, pp. 15—18, 2001.

[7] ISO, *ISO Survey of Certifications – 2006*, www.iso.org/iso/pressrelease.htm?refid=Ref1089, ISO, 2007.

[8] ISO, *ISO 9001:2008*, Quality Managemnt Systems – requirements, ISO, 1.12.2008.

[9] H. Metzen, *Schlankheitskur für den Staat*, Lean Management in der öffentlichen Verwaltung, Campus, Frankfurt, 1994.

[10] M. Hammer, *Beyond reengineering*, HarperCollins Business, London, 1996.

[11] Y. Akao, *Quality Function Deployment*, integrating customer requirements into product design, Productivity Press, Portland, 1990.

[12] G. Riempp, *Integrierte Wissensmanagementsysteme*: Architektur und praktische Anwendung, Springer, Berlin, 2004.

[13] F. Lehner, *Wissensmanagement*: Grundlagen Methoden und technische Unterstützung, Hanser, München, 2006.

[14] S. Güldenberg, *Wissensmanagement und Wissenscontrolling in lernenden Organisationen*. Deutscher Universitäts-Verlag, Wiesbaden, 1997.

[15] G. Reinmann-Rothmeier, *Mediendidaktik und Wissensmanagement*, in MedienPädagogik 10, www.medienpaed.com/02-2/reinmann1.pdf, 2002.

[16] M. Stoll, *Workplace Process Integrated Learning and Knowledge Organization*, in H. Maurer and K. Tochtermann Eds. Proc. I-Know 07, 7th International Conference on Knowledge Management, J.UCS Journal of Universal Computer Science, Graz, 2007.

Fuzzy-rule-based Adaptive Resource Control for Information Sharing in P2P Networks

Zhengping Wu
Department of Computer Science and Engineering
University of Bridgeport
221 University Avenue, CT 06604, USA
zhengpiw@bridgeport.edu

Hao Wu
Department of Computer Science and Engineering
University of Bridgeport
221 University Avenue, CT 06604, USA
wuhao@bridgeport.edu

***Abstract*—With more and more peer-to-peer (P2P) technologies available for online collaboration and information sharing, people can launch more and more collaborative work in online social networks with friends, colleagues, and even strangers. Without face-to-face interactions, the question of who can be trusted and then share information with becomes a big concern of a user in these online social networks. This paper introduces an adaptive control service using fuzzy logic in preference definition for P2P information sharing control, and designs a novel decision-making mechanism using formal fuzzy rules and reasoning mechanisms adjusting P2P information sharing status following individual users' preferences. Applications of this adaptive control service into different information sharing environments show that this service can provide a convenient and accurate P2P information sharing control for individual users in P2P networks.**

Keywords – adaptive resource control; fuzzy logic; P2P technology; information sharing; collaborative social network

I. Introduction

P2P technology has been proven to be a good solution for maximizing the cost-benefit ratio over information sharing [1]. With the use of storage space and other resources in a large scale supported by P2P systems, information retrieval also becomes convenient and efficient. As the rapid expansion of online social networks, people start to share information and collaborate with each other over the Internet. P2P technology is also a good solution for sharing information such as large data sets with separate pieces in distributed locations and/or generated by real-time sources, which cannot be easily shared over online social networks. Although people can benefit from a more flexible and convenient information-sharing environment augmented by P2P technologies in online social networks, the actual sharing capability between peer users may be impacted by the communication channel's capacity, the communication channel's reliability, and access point control, in which channel capacity determines the transfer speed of information, channel reliability determines integrity and safety of transferred information; access point control determines the trustworthiness of peer users and their access activities. As described in [2], the relationships between users in online social networks are more complex than a simple indication of two people's mutual acquaintance. The complex relationships between people in online social networks may raise confusion when users have to determine the trust degrees between each other. Thus it is difficult for users to control the safety and privacy of the information being shared through P2P technologies between peers within online social networks because of these uncertain factors.

To manage a collection of uncertain factors in the decision-making process for control of information sharing, we provide an adaptive control service to help users manage these factors according to users' own preferences represented in decision-making policies. We introduce "fuzziness" into policy representation and enforcement in this service. Applying fuzzy logic into a policy-based access control service for P2P information sharing in online social networks can help users handle multiple factors in decision-making activities with a certain level of uncertainty. We propose and implement a P2P information sharing service over online social networks using policy-based access control and combining various types of control information following users' own preferences based on fuzzy enforcement of policies containing uncertain factors.

II. Related Work

Peer-to-peer (P2P) technologies have received great attention for information sharing in recent years [3]. A P2P network can be described as a self-organizing decentralized network where participating nodes can elect to consume as well as provide services and/or resources at the same time [4]. One node in a P2P network may act as a service/resource consumer and service/resource provider at the same time. In P2P networks, all resources are stored and provided in a decentralized fashion. P2P technologies have been proven as a good solution for designing and implementing successful information-sharing applications such as instant message (MSN & ICQ), file sharing (BT & eMule), VoIP (Skype), and streaming media (YouTube). Although using large scale storage space and resources provided by P2P systems, information retrieving and sharing become more and more convenient and efficient, how can people trust other peers becomes a big issue. We believe that introduction of an adaptive control service into online social networks is a good way to solve these problems. In next section, we will illustrate an adaptive

T. Sobh, K. Elleithy (eds.), *Innovations in Computing Sciences and Software Engineering*,
DOI 10.1007/978-90-481-9112-3_23,

control service using fuzzy logic to control information sharing, using this service to manage trustworthiness between peer users in information sharing, and how to manage uncertainty in multi-factor decision-making for information access control involving trustworthiness factors.

III. System Architecure

Our system is a build in service which for online social networks. In online social networks, when a user uses P2P technologies for information sharing, he or she needs to coordinate trustworthiness of other peer users, the capacity of the communication channel, and the reliability of the communication channel. The trustworthiness between peers is hard to define because it is from an indirect source; uncertainty in this factor is unavoidable. The capacity and the reliability of one communication channel are also hard to define, because these are subjective judgments. So it is hard for a user to evaluate peer users who are currently accessing shared information and control the information sharing between these peer users dynamically. Thus we introduce a P2P information sharing mechanism using users' preferences to provide a solution for this kind of evaluation and control problems.

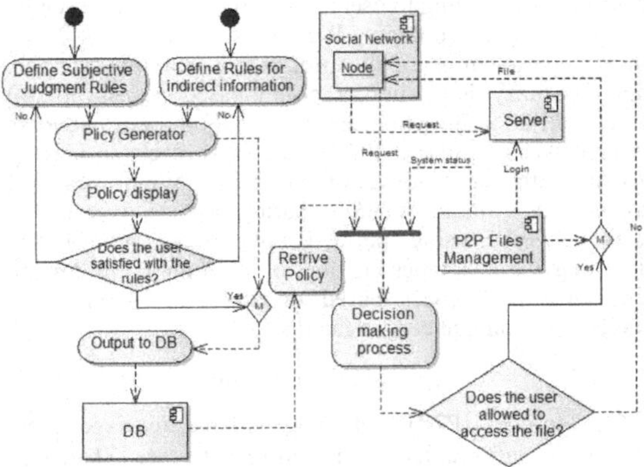

Figure 1. System Architecture

Figure 1 illustrates the system architecture of our framework. After users defining their fuzzy policies, the system stores these policies in a database. Then, when a peer user from online social network tries to access the shared information within the system, the system retrieves policies from the policy database and applies these policies onto the decision-making process based on the information gathered from peer users and system itself, such as the level of trustworthiness of the user and the state of the communication channel. Finally the system will decide whether the user is allowed or rejected to access the shared information and the upper limit speed of the allowed access channel, and then adjust the states of all connected peers dynamically.

IV. Fuzzy Model

A. *Fuzzy Model of Uncertainty*

The trust relationships in P2P information sharing are hard to assess due to the uncertainties involved. If a trust relationship relies upon a subjective judgment based on indirect information, it will be very uncertain and any access operations related to that trust relationship may cause unexpected results.

Fuzzy logic is a suitable way to represent uncertainties, especially when they need to be handled quantitatively. Two advantages of using fuzzy logic to quantify uncertainty in trust management are: (1) Fuzzy inference is capable of quantifying imprecise data or uncertainty in measuring different levels of trust. (2) Different membership functions and inference rules could be developed for different trust relationships independently, without changing the fuzzy inference engines and enforcement mechanisms.

L. Zadeh first introduced fuzzy logic in the development of the theory of fuzzy sets. The theory of fuzzy logic extends the ontology of mathematical research to be a composite that leverages quality and quantity and contains certain fuzziness. Introducing fuzzy logic into the research of trust management, we try to solve the issues associated with uncertainty in trust management for information-sharing activities. First, we need to identify the subjects of these issues. These subjects are either the sources of trust-related information needed in trust management or the entities with which trust relationships are built. This subject set can be defined as follows.

Definition 4.1 Set of subjects in trust management

The set of subjects in trust management is all the subjects that are either the sources of trust-related information or are the entities with which trust relationships are built. This set is represented as X in this paper.

Then we need to define a general fuzzy set in trust management.

Definition 4.2 Fuzzy set for trust management

For every element x in the set of subjects X, there is a mapping $x \rightarrow \delta(x)$, in which $\delta(x) \in [0,1]$. The set $\Delta = \{(x, \delta(x))\}$ for $\forall x \in X$ is defined as a fuzzy set for trust management. $\delta(x)$ is defined as the membership function for every x in Δ.

All the fuzzy sets on X are represented as $Z(X)$. Then we can use a group of fuzzy sets from $Z(X)$ to group all the elements of X into several sets with different levels of uncertainty. For example, we can use a group of three sets $Z_i \in Z(X)$ to categorize of uncertainty in trust management.

Z_1 represents not recommended;
Z_2 represents normally recommended;
Z_3 represents highly recommended.

In real life, the level of uncertainty cannot be limited to only one set, and the degrees to these sets are not simply 'total' or 'none'; additionally, it is sometimes difficult to determine which set or sets should be used for certain kinds of uncertainty. In other words, these sets are not exclusive to each other. So when we deal with certain kinds of uncertainty, a vector consisting of the degrees of belongingness to each set $D = \{d_1, d_2, d_3\}$ is more appropriate for describing the actual trustworthiness-based judgment from daily life, in which d_i (i = 1, 2, 3) is the degree of belongingness to set Z_i (i = 1, 2, 3). Meanwhile, there are several ways to determine or calculate the degrees d_i. One way is direct judgment that determines the degree from direct experience or evaluation. Another one is indirect inference that determines the degree via an analysis of an indirect source such as reputation or recommendation. The first one is relatively subjective while the evaluation method may be very objective; and the second one is relatively objective while the source of information may be subjective. Other ways to determine the degrees also exist, which will not be discussed in this paper.

B. Fuzzy Representation of Uncertainty

To reason among the degrees of uncertainty in trust management for further inference or decision-making-making, we need to represent uncertainty formally. Direct trust is formally described as $a \overset{D}{\rightarrow} b[Z]$, which means entity a is willing to rely upon entity b to degree D for the categorized uncertainty Z. D is a vector with corresponding degrees of belongingness for each set in categorization Z. Direct trust is from direct experience of the trustworthiness of the other entity or from a judgment with subjective/objective evaluation. Indirect trust is described as $a \underset{P}{\overset{D}{\rightarrow}} b[Z]$, which means entity a is willing to rely upon b to degree D following P's recommendation for the categorized uncertainty Z. P is one or more entities constructing a path that gives a recommendation to entity a for entity b. D is a vector with corresponding degrees of belongingness for each set in categorization Z. Indirect trust is derived from the recommendation passed through one or more intermediate entities. There are also two types of recommendations. One type is that the recommender had direct experience with the recommended entity so that the P has only one entity; the other is that the final recommender formed the recommendation from further recommendations of other recommenders so that the P has more than one entity constructing a chained recommending path or a compound recommending graph. But from the recommendee's (entity a's) point of view, there is no big significance related to with the number of entities forming the recommending path; the recommendee (entity b) only cares about the final recommender's capability to make accurate recommendation based on its own experience and trustworthiness.

The use of fuzzy rules to describe uncertain rules in trust management can involve rules in which we have antecedent terms of the form:

"If the probability of (some event) is high, then a certain action is performed."

We apply this general form to describe fuzzy rules in a trustworthiness-based decision-making system for information sharing in online social networks to express real life uncertainty in trust management and decision-making making with human linguistics. Here different formats of the probability function W introduce different types of rules. If W is a threshold function, the rule becomes a threshold decision-making rule; if W has a fuzzy definition, the rule is a fuzzy rule; if W uses a granular probability distribution, the rule becomes most suitable for uncertainty description in human linguistics.

C. Fuzzy Enforcement

Currently, most people use Zadeh operators $\wedge$ and $\vee$ to perform calculation and analysis with fuzzy logic. But these operators are too imprecise in that too much information will be lost if these are the only operators used. Thus several general class fuzzy operators are proposed [8]. To adapt to different sources of uncertainties in trust management, a parameterized general intersection operator and union operator are needed. They are also called T-norm and S-norm. With different values of the parameters, these operators can maximize the expressiveness and flexibility of the system to capture people's intentions toward these uncertainties. Here we choose a general class of parameterized fuzzy operators proposed by Dubois and Prade [9] to perform further calculation and analysis. Because these operators are suitable for policy analysis and have clear semantic meanings [9], the intention embedded in fuzzy sets can be easily enforced. So we define T-norm and S-norm as follows.

Definition 4.3 T-norm

For fuzzy set $A, B \in Z(X)$ *and* $\alpha \in [0,1]$,

$(A \cap B)(x) = T(A(x), B(x), \alpha) = \dfrac{A(x)B(x)}{\max\{A(x), B(x), \alpha\}}$, *in which* $A(x)$ *and* $B(x)$ *represent x's degrees of member function to fuzzy sets A and B.*

Definition 4.4 S-norm

For fuzzy set $A, B \in Z(X)$ *and* $\alpha \in [0,1]$,

$(A \cup B)(x) = S(A(x), B(x), \alpha) = \dfrac{A(x) + B(x) - A(x)B(x) - \min\{A(x), B(x), (1-\alpha)\}}{\max\{1 - A(x), 1 - B(x), \alpha\}}$, *in which* $A(x)$ *and* $B(x)$ *represent x's degrees of member function to fuzzy sets A and B.*

Then we define two calculators on vectors of fuzzy values. Suppose we have two fuzzy value vectors $D_1 = \{d_{11}, d_{12}, \ldots, d_{1P}\}$ and $D_2 = \{d_{21}, d_{22}, \ldots, d_{2P}\}$.

Definition 4.5 Connection calculator

$D_1 \otimes D_2 = \{T(d_{11}, d_{21}, \alpha), T(d_{12}, d_{22}, \alpha), \ldots, T(d_{1P}, d_{2P}, \alpha)\}$

Definition 5.4 Union calculator

$D_1 \oplus D_2 = \{S(d_{11}, d_{21}, \alpha), S(d_{12}, d_{22}, \alpha), \ldots, S(d_{1P}, d_{2P}, \alpha)\}$

After we define the above calculators, we can perform formal analysis on fuzzy sets and fuzzy rules used for uncertainty expressions. Here we define two sets of derivation rules (deduction rules and consensus rules) to handle different types of uncertainty. Below are the formal descriptions of deduction rules.

Definition 4.6 Deduction rules

$$a \xrightarrow{D} b[Z] \wedge b \xrightarrow{D'} c[Z] \Rightarrow a \xrightarrow[P'']{D''} c[Z] \wedge (P'' = \{b\}) \wedge (D'' = D \otimes D')$$

$$a \xrightarrow{D} b[Z] \wedge b \xrightarrow[P']{D'} c[Z] \Rightarrow a \xrightarrow[P'']{D''} c[Z] \wedge (P'' = \{b, P'\}) \wedge (D'' = D \otimes D')$$

$$a \xrightarrow[P]{D} b[Z] \wedge b \xrightarrow[P']{D'} c[Z] \Rightarrow a \xrightarrow[P'']{D''} c[Z] \wedge (P'' = \{P, P'\}) \wedge (D'' = D \otimes D')$$

Deduction rules are used for a recommendation's connection to construct a whole recommendation chain that allows the trustworthiness to be transferred from one end to the other end. For the trust relationships from the same categorization, deduction rules can form a new connection using the trust relationship between the recommender and the recommendee and embed the content of that recommendation into the new connection. Below are the formal descriptions of consensus rules.

Definition 4.7 Consensus rules

$$a \xrightarrow{D_1} b[Z] \wedge a \xrightarrow{D_2} b[Z] \wedge \ldots \wedge a \xrightarrow{D_n} b[Z] \Rightarrow a \xrightarrow{D''} b[Z] \wedge (D'' = D_1 \oplus D_2 \oplus \ldots \oplus D_n)$$

$$a \xrightarrow[P_1]{D_1} b[Z] \wedge a \xrightarrow[P_2]{D_2} b[Z] \wedge \ldots \wedge a \xrightarrow[P_n]{D_n} b[Z] \Rightarrow a \xrightarrow[P'']{D''} b[Z] \wedge (P'' = \{P_m \mid |P_m| = \min\{|P_i| (i = 1 \ldots n)\}\}) \wedge (D'' = D_1 \oplus D_2 \oplus \ldots \oplus D_n)$$

Consensus rules are used for combining of multiple recommendations for the same kind of categorization. When two or more recommendation paths appear simultaneously, consensus rules can synthesize the opinions to form a comprehensive recommendation. The shortest recommending path is the easiest path to verify that indirect information, even if the value of the trust degree vector is not as high as others. We use this path as the recommending path for verification of that recommendation. But more likely we will only use the unified trust degree vector alone after the composition.

With the help of the fuzzy operations and rules defined above, we can form a formal decision-making process to handle uncertainty in the management of trustworthiness. The diagram of the process is illustrated in figure 2. Users need to define the categorization of uncertainty. Then the decision-making process uses fuzzy operations to combine uncertain information from different sources. After defuzzification of the trustworthiness degrees, users need to judge whether the final decision is consistent with their own rules. If not, the parameters of the fuzzy operations need to be adjusted.

V. TRUSTWORTHINESS BWTWEEN PEOPLE

To manage a collection of trust-related activities across P2P information sharing in online social networks, we need to understand trust itself. From different points of views, trust can be categorized into different classes. Following the categorization described by Beth et al. [5], we categorize trust into two classes - direct trust and indirect trust. A trust relationship formed from direct experience or negotiations can be characterized as direct trust; a trust relationship or a potential trust relationship built from recommendations by a trusted third party or a chain of trusted parties, which create a trust path, is called indirect trust.

In [2], authors stated that trust has three main properties, which are transitivity, asymmetry, and personalization. The primary property is transitivity, which means trust can be passed between people. For the example, Alice asks Bob for the trustworthiness of Cindy, and Bob's trust on Cindy will be passed to Alice. However, trust between people is not always transitive. For example, Alice trusts Bob, and Bob trusts Cindy, but Alice does not necessarily trust Cindy. So asymmetry of trust is also an important property. That means trust between people do not have to be bi-directional. For instance, Alice is highly trusted by Bob, but Alice does not have to trust Bob. The personalization property of trust means different people have different opinions on trust. From Alice's point of view, Cindy is highly trustable; however, from Bob's point of view, Cindy may not be trustable at all.

Although some of the online social networks allow users assigning trust levels for friends and all other users [6], trust between users in most online social networks are based on FOAF relationships. Although Golbeck and Hendler propose a binary method to calculate the trust between users in online social networks [2], and other methods such as the ones described in [7] also give some algorithms to calculate the trust between users, in most online social networks, trusts between users are simply calculated from the levels of FOAF relationships. As discussed before, personalization of trust reduces the adaptability of those algorithms. They cannot always satisfy any particular users on online social networks, because everyone has his or her own opinion on trust, and he or she may remain uncertain when defining trust between users in online social networks. We introduce fuzzy logic into the definition of trustworthiness in our framework for information sharing. For peer users, the trustworthiness to the target peer user can be calculated by the degree of the trust path and the fuzzy rules and membership function defined by users.

VI. PROTOTYPE SYSTEM

Following the system architecture described above, we describe some practical fuzzy policies, the user interface to input fuzzy policies, and the enforcement mechanism to enforce these policies for P2P information sharing in an online social network. Here, we try to provide a tool to help users dynamically control the P2P information sharing in an online social network environment.

A. *User Interface*

The prototype system is implemented an "application" in Facebook. We provide an interface for users to share information with their Facebook friends and other peer users who are using the system. Users can view what files their friends are sharing, and they can download the file they have interests. Users are also allowed to search files from their friends, and chat with their friends by using the integrated instant message function.

Since the control of information sharing involves both indirect information and subjective judgment, we have two sets of policies to describe corresponding fuzzy rules. All the policies follow the general rule (policy) format discussed in section 4.2. The fuzzy policy for indirect information is illustrated below.

- *If the trustworthiness of a peer user is high/normal/low and(or) the number of connected users is many/ medium /few and(or) the total download speed is high/normal/low and(or) the accumulated downloaded volume is large /medium /small then the user will be limited/allowed/blocked to access the files.*

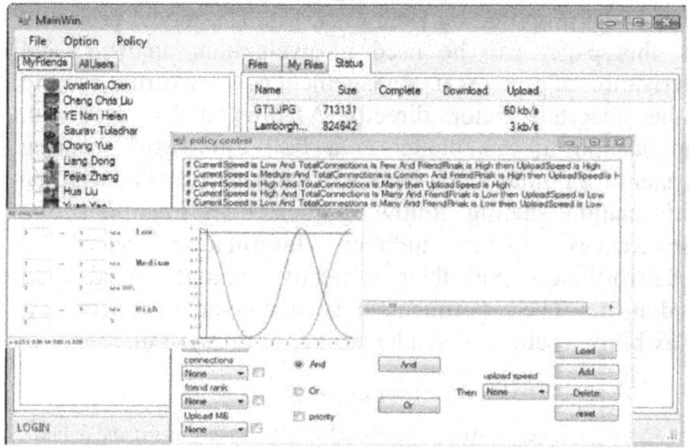

Figure 2. Fuzzy Policy Input Interface and sharing states

After we have defined the policy format, we design and implement a user interface to assist users to input these policies consistent with the accurate rules or intentions in their minds. As illustrated in figure 2, the policy input interface allows users to change the flexible parts in fuzzy policies according to their information sharing control needs. Furthermore users can select different types of membership functions they need rather than use the default membership functions provided by the system and combine the membership functions between any two of the involved factors. The prototype system provides default membership functions for all the fuzzy terms and allows users to modify all the membership functions if the default membership functions do not accurately capture users' intentions. Once the definitions of fuzzy polices are finally determined, the system uses a policy generator to translate the fuzzy policies into XACML format, and store them in a policy database. When the system is in use, once an access request together with a connection request arrives the system, the system will decide whether to grant this access request, determine an upload speed limit, and dynamically adjust the information sharing (file sharing) states, which is illustrated in figure 2. Users can also train the system by adjusting the parameters in the decision-making process to refine the system's accuracy.

VII. A Case Study and Experiments

To examine the performance and usability of the system, we set up an experiment environment including 30 users and implement the P2P information sharing framework in a file sharing system. First, we tested our system on two different policy sets. Then we tested the system performance on different users downloading one particular file at the same time from a particular user. Then we compared our system with some other popular P2P file sharing systems.

A. Experiments on Different Policy Sets

We define two different policy sets in the system. One policy set is following the common sense that the file upload speed varies as the level of trustworthiness changes. The other policy set prefers the most trustable peer users.

First, we estabish a peer user, and allow this user sharing files with others. Then three other peer users which with different trust levels with the established peer user are connected to that user. And all these three peer users download the same file from the. The system-wide download speed limit is 200 KB/s. Once a new peer connects to the established peer user and tries to download files, the system will recalculate all the connected peer and allocate a new bandwidth for each of them following the formular illustrated below:

$$B_i = B \cdot \frac{F(i) \cdot P_i}{\sum_{i=0}^{Connection} (F(i) \cdot P_i)}$$

in which, B represents the system-wide download speed limit, $F(i)$ is the fuzzy function to calculate the trust level of ith peer according to the policies and membership functions defined by the established peer user and P_i represents its priority which calculated by the connection order and fraction of the remain downloading amont.

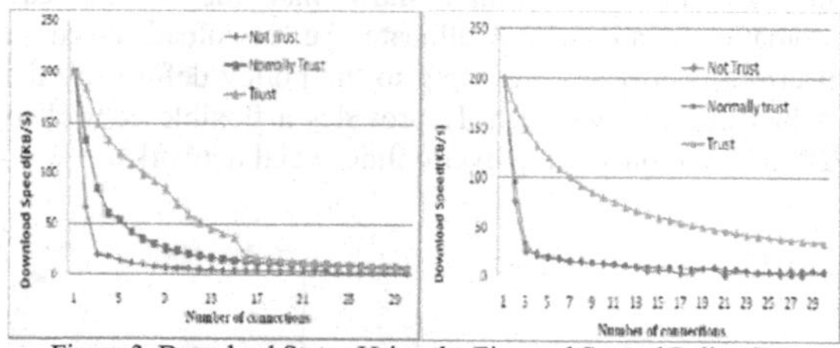

Figure 3. Download Status Using the First and Second Policy Sets

When the system adopts the first policy set, the upload speeds of three peer users change as illustrated in figure 3. When the number of connections increases, the download speed for the not trusted peer user drops off dramatically. The normally trusted peer user also drops rapidly and has the same trend as the not trusted peer user, but the drop speed is not as dramatic as the trusted peer user. The download speed of the trusted peer user decreases very slowly as the number of connections increases and it always gets a higher download speed than other peer users. So figure 3 clearly shows us that the system always allocates higher download speed for the trusted peer user of the established peer user.

As illustrated in figure 3, when the system adopts the second policy set, the situation is different. We can tell from the figure that only the trusted peer user gets a good download speed. The speeds of other two peer users drop to almost the same level. Compared with the result based on the first policy set, the speed of the trusted peer users always has the top priority in the system. The result shows the system's flexibility, which reflects users' preferences represnted in different policy sets, and the system's accuracy to capture users' preferences and enforce them.

B. *Experiment on Dynamic User Behaviors*

Following the first experiment on the different policy sets, we perform the second experiment on downloads of the same file from different peer users with different trust levels to examine the flexibility and adaptability of the system. This experiment is based on the first policy set. At the very beginning, three peer users with different trust levels download the same file simultaneously. Then these three peer users try to download the same file at different time. The untrusted peer user starts downloading first; then the trusted peer starts downloading after 1 minute; 1 more minute later, the third normally trusted peer user starts downloading. The dynamic downloading behaviors are illustrated in figure 4. When these three peer users start downloading at the same time, the trusted peer user can get the highest priority, and the normally trusted peer user gets higher priority than the untrusted peer user. So the trusted peer user can finish downloading first with the highest allocated speed following the rules in the first policy set. After the trusted peer user's downloading is completed and releases the bandwidth occupied, the other two are allocated more bandwidth, and download speeds increase with the same amount. The results show that the system can automatically adjust and allocate the download speed to differrent peer users according to the policy defined by the established user, which truly provides a flexible control of P2P information sharing over online social networks.

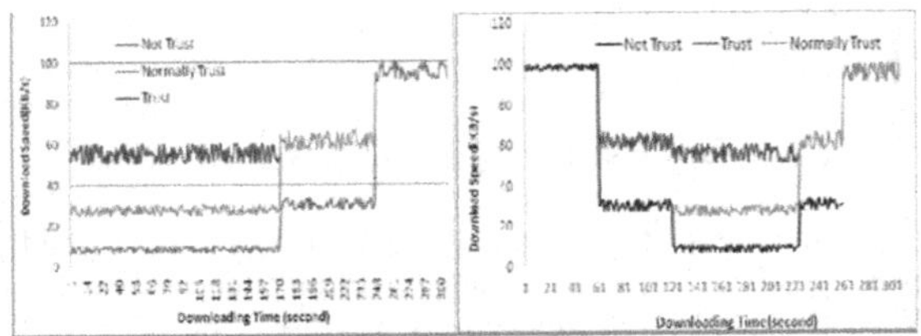

Figure 4. Download at Same Times and Different Times

VIII. CONCLUSION

In this paper a framework of adaptive control service based on fuzzy logic is proposed to handle uncertainty and fuzziness in decision-making process for P2P information sharing activities in online social networks based on trustworthiness. This paper addresses the issues that how can people trust their peer friends in social networks for information sharing. This paper introduces membership functions from fuzzy logic into policy definition to describe uncertainty and fuzziness in trustworthiness, and defines a trust degree vector to evaluate different levels of trustworthiness. This paper also introduces a general categorization of fuzziness to describe various types of trustworthiness in daily life and in P2P information sharing environments. In addition, the derivation rules proposed in this paper incorporate a parameter to allow users to adjust membership functions through a feedback mechanism in order to make the decision-making process adaptable to users' changing intentions and preferences, which addresses the inadequacies in the model proposed by Josang[10] and the model proposed by Beth et al. [5]. The model proposed in this paper can be used in evaluation, analysis, and derivation of policies in management of trustworthiness and other uncertain factors directly. As illustrated in section 4, application of this model in a P2P information sharing system for online social networks can help users control the information sharing following their own intentions and preferences using indirect information such as trustworthiness and their subjective upload speed limit judgments. The experiments in section 6 show the accuracy, flexibility, usability and adaptability of the system.

REFERENCES

[1] J.M. Gallaugher, P. Auger, Anat BarNir, "Revenue streams and digital content providers: an empirical investigation," *Information & Management*, vol. 38 (7), 2001, pp. 473-485.

[2] J. Golbeck, J. Hendler, "Inferring Binary Trust Relationships in Web-Based Social Networks," *ACM Transactions on Internet Technology*, Vol. 6 (4), 2006, pp. 497-529.

[3] R. Steinmetz, K. Wehrle, *Peer-to-Peer Systems and Applications*, LNCS 3485, Springer, 2005.

[4] P. Golle, K. Leyton-Brown, I. Mironov, M. Lillibridge, "Incentives for Sharing in Peer-to-Peer Networks," *Proc. of the Second International Workshop on Electronic Commerce*, 2001, pp. 75-87.

[5] T. Beth, M. Borcherding, B. Klein, "Valuation of Trust in Open Networks," *Proc. of the 1994 European Symposium on Research in Security*, 1994, pp. 3-18.

[6] J. Sabater-Mir, "Towards the next generation of computational trust and reputation models," *Modeling Decision-makings for Artificial Intelligence*, LNCS 3885, Springer-Verlag, 2006, pp. 19–21.

[7] Josiane Xavier Parreira, Debora Donato, Carlos Castillo, Gerhard Weikum, "Computing trusted authority scores in peer-to-peer web search networks," *Proc. of the 3rd International Workshop on Adversarial Information Retrieval on the Web*, 2007, pp. 73-80.

[8] S. Weber, "A general concept of fuzzy connectives, negations, and implications based on t-norms," *Fuzzy Sets System*, 1983(11), pp. 115-134.

[9] D. Dubois and H. Prade, "New results about properties and semantics of fuzzy set theoretic operators," *Fuzzy sets: theory and applications to policy analysis and information systems*, 1980, pp. 59-75.

[10] A.Josang, Ross Hayward, Simon Pope "Trust network analysis with subjective logic" *Proc. of the 29th Australasian Computer Science Conference*, Volume 48, 2006, pp. 85 - 94.

Challenges in Web Information Retrieval

Monika Arora[1], and Uma Kanjilal[2], Dinesh Varshney[3,4],
[1]Department of IT, Apeejay School of Management, Dwarka Institutional Area, New Delhi, India
[2]Department of Library and Information Science, Indira Gandhi Open University Maidan Garhi, New Delhi-110 068,India
[3]School of Physics, Devi Ahilya University, Khandwa road Campus, Indore, M. P. India
[4]Multimedia regional Centre, Madhya Pradesh Bhoj (open) University, Khandwa road Campus, Indore- 452001, M. P. India

Abstract— **The major challenge in information access is the rich data available for information retrieval, evolved to provide principle approaches or strategies for searching. The search has become the leading paradigm to find the information on World Wide Web. For building the successful web retrieval search engine model, there are a number of challenges that arise at the different levels where techniques, such as Usenet, support vector machine are employed to have a significant impact. The present investigations explore the number of problems identified its level and related to finding information on web. This paper attempts to examine the issues by applying different methods such as web graph analysis, the retrieval and analysis of newsgroup postings and statistical methods for inferring meaning in text. We also discuss how one can have control over the vast amounts of data on web, by providing the proper address to the problems in innovative ways that can extremely improve on standard. The proposed model thus assists the users in finding the existing formation of data they need. The developed information retrieval model deals with providing access to information available in various modes and media formats and to provide the content is with facilitating users to retrieve relevant and comprehensive information efficiently and effectively as per their requirements. This paper attempts to discuss the parameters factors that are responsible for the efficient searching. These parameters can be distinguished in terms of important and less important based on the inputs that we have. The important parameters can be taken care of for the future extension or development of search engines**

Key words: Information Retrieval, Web Information Retrieval, Search Engine, Usenet, Support Vector machine

I. Introduction

Search engines are extensively important to help users to find relevant retrieval of information on the World Wide Web. In order to give the best according to the needs of users, a search engine must find and filter the most relevant information matching a user's query, and then present that information in a manner that makes the information most readily presentable to the user. Moreover, the task of information retrieval and presentation must be done in a scalable fashion to serve the hundreds of millions of user queries that are issued every day to a popular web search engines [1]. In addressing the problem of Information Retrieval (IR) on the web, there are a number of challenges researchers are involve, some of these challenges in this paper and identify additional problems that may motivate future work in the IR research community. It also describes some work in these areas that has been conducted at various search engines. It begins by briefly outlining some of the issues or factors that arise in web information retrieval. The people/User relates to the system directly for the Information retrieval as shown in Figure 1. They are easy to compare fields with well-defined semantics to queries in order to find matches. For example the Records are easy to find for example bank database query. The semantics of the keywords also plays and important role which is send through the interface. System includes the interface of search engine servers, the databases and the indexing mechanism, which includes the stemming techniques. The User defines the search strategy and also gives the requirement for searching .The documents available in www apply subject indexing, ranking and clustering [2] .The relevant matches easily found

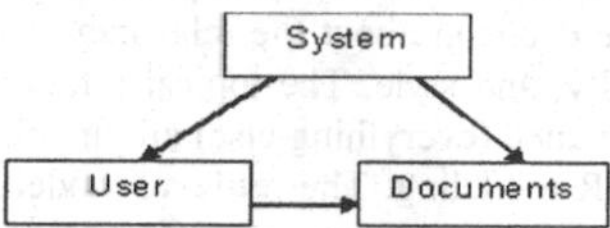

Figure1: IR System Components

by comparison with field values of records. It will be simple for the database it terms of maintenance and retrieval of records but for the unstructured documents it is difficult where we use text.

II. Information Retrieval on the Web Searches

The some criteria for searching will give the better matches and also the better results. The different dimensions of IR have become vast because of different media, different types of search applications, and different tasks, which is not only a text, but also a web search as a central. The IR approaches to search and evaluation are appropriate in all media is an emerging issues of IR. The information retrieval involved in

T. Sobh, K. Elleithy (eds.), *Innovations in Computing Sciences and Software Engineering*,
DOI 10.1007/978-90-481-9112-3_24, © Springer Science+Business Media B.V. 2010

the following tasks and sub tasks: 1) Ad-hoc search involve with the process where it generalizes the criteria and searches for all the records, which finds all the relevant documents for an arbitrary text query; 2) Filtering is an important process where the users identify the relevant user profiles for a new document. The user profile is maintained where the user can be identified with a profile and accordingly the relevant documents are categorized and displayed; 3) Classification involve with respect to the identification and lies in the relevant list of the classification, this works in identifying the relevant labels for documents; 4) Question answering Technique involves for the better judgment of the classification with the relevant questions automatically frames to generate the focus of the individuals. The tasks are described in the Figure 2.The Field of IR deals with the

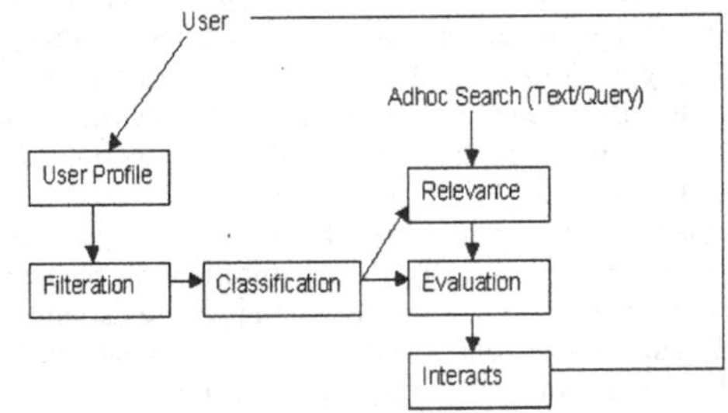

Figure 2: Proposed Model of Search

relevance, evaluation and interacts with the user to provide them according to their needs/query. IR involves in the effective ranking and testing. Also it measures of the data available for the retrieval. The relevant document contains the information that a person was looking for when they submitted a query to the search engine. There is many factors influence a person's to take the decision about the relevancy that may be task, context, novelty, and style. The topical relevance (same topic) and user relevance (everything else) are the dimensions, which help in the IR modeling. The retrieval models define a view of relevance. The user provides information that the system can use to modify its next search or next display. The relevance feedback is the how much system understand user in terms of what the need, and also to know about the concept and terms related to the information needs.

The phases uses the different techniques such as the web pages contain links to other pages and by analyzing this web graph structure it is possible to determine a more global notion of page quality. The remarkable successes in this area include the Page Rank algorithm [1], which globally analyzes the entire web graph and provided the original basis for ranking in the various search engines, and Kleinberg's hyperlink algorithm [2,3], which analyzes a local neighborhood of the web graph containing an initial set of web pages matching the user's query. Since that time, several other linked-based methods for ranking web pages have been proposed including variants of both PageRank and HITS [3, 4], and this remains an active research area in which there is still much fertile research ground to be explored.

This may refer to the recent work on Hub and researchers from where, it identifies in the form of equilibrium for WWW sources on a common theme/topic in which we explicitly build into the model by taking care of the diversity of roles between the different types of pages [2]. Some pages, are the prominent sources of primary data/content, are considered to be the authorities on the topic; other pages, equally essential to the structure, accumulate high-quality guides and resource lists that act as focused hubs, directing users to suggested authorities. The nature of the linkage in this framework is highly asymmetric. Hubs link heavily to authorities, and they may have very few incoming links linked to themselves, and the authorities are not link to other authorities. This, is completely a suggested model [2], is completely natural; relatively anonymous individuals are creating many good hubs on the Web. A formal type of equilibrium consistent model can be defined only by assigning the weights to the two numbers called as a hub weight and an authority weight .The weights to each page in such a way that a page's authority weight is proportional to the sum of the hub weights of pages that link to it to maintain the balance and a page's hub weight is proportional to the sum of the authority weights of pages that it links to.

The adversarial Classification [5] may be dealing with Spam on the Web. One particularly interesting problem in web IR arises from the attempt by some commercial interests to excessively heighten the ranking of their web pages by engaging in various forms of spamming [4]. The SPAM methods can be effective against traditional IR ranking schemes that do not make use of link structure, but have more limited utility in the context of global link analysis. Realizing this, spammers now also utilize link spam where they will create large numbers of web pages that contain links to other pages whose rankings they wish to rise. The interesting technique applied will continually to the automatic filters. The spam filtering in email [7] is very popular. This technique with concurrently involved the applying the indexes the documents

III. An Approach of Retrieval in UseNet Archive

The UseNet archive is considered to be less visible document collections in the context of general-purpose search engines, which is conservatively estimated to be at least 800 million documents. The UseNet archive, have 20 newsgroups data set used in text classification tasks—is extremely interesting. UseNet started as a loosely structured collection of groups that people could post to. Over the years, it evolved into a large hierarchy of over 50,000 groups with topics ranging in different dimensions. IR in the context of UseNet articles raises some very interesting issues. One previously explored possibility is to address retrieval in UseNet as a two-stage IR problem: (1) find the most relevant newsgroup, and (2) find the most relevant document within that newsgroup. This 20-years of archive of

Usenet is the largest to serve as a powerful reference tool. This repository can be used as the insight to the history and culture of the Internet. The Google Groups was very popular with more than 700 million postings in more than 35,000 topical categories

Along these lines, previous research has examined building models of newsgroups, communication patterns within message threads, and language models that are indicative of content [11 - 13]. Still, questions remain of how to go about using such factors to build an effective ranking function [8] and how to display these results to the users. This can also attempt to compute the quality or reliability of an author independent of the query, much as PageRank [1] does for the Web. Such a computation would operate on a graph of relatively modest size since, for example, if we were to filter authors to only those that had posted at least twice in a year to the same newsgroup, we would be left with only on the order of 100,000 authors. This is a much more manageable size than the web graph which has several billion nodes. Computing community structures rather than pure linear structures as in posting threads can also generate interesting insights as to how various authors and groups participate in and influence discussions. More recently, work on filtering technologies in the context of information retrieval [8] has also focused attention on building better models of the likely content in messages and routing them to appropriate people, bringing together work on user modeling, IR, and text analysis.

An advantage of working with the UseNet archive is the fact that it improves many of the infrastructural problems that might otherwise slow research in the web domain, such as building HTML parsers, properly handling different languages and character sets, and managing the exceptional volume of available data (even small potions of the Web would require several hundred gigabytes to store). For the smaller scale problems, making the archive relatively easy to store, index and process on a single machine. It is a challenging task to use the rich structure of the bulletin board domain (i.e., author information, posting content, thread history, etc.) to predict both the label and score for new postings. More generally, improving ranking methods for UseNet or bulletin board postings is an open area of research with many interesting similarities to the web, but also with very many significant differences that make it a fascinating subject of further.

There is another classification technique named, as Support Vector Machines (SVM) is a Kernel-based technique. Other techniques such as Bayes point machines, Gaussian processes and kernel principal component analysis represents a major development in machine learning algorithms. The Support vector machines (SVM) is based on the group of supervised learning methods which can applied to the principles of classification or regression. Support vector machines represent the extension to nonlinear models. However, because there is no theoretical tool to predict which kernel will give the best results for a given dataset, experimenting with different kernels is the only way to identify the best function [7]. This can be implemented where the huge dataset can be divided based on the criteria. The actions can be defined based on the roles separated.

The latest filtering tool can be applied and course of action can be seen further. The latest search engine 'INDRI' which is focused on the research articles and tried to be efficient and effective one i.e. the Indri search engine is designed to address the following goals: a) The query language should support complex queries involving evidence combination and the ability to specify a wide variety of constraints involving proximity, syntax, extracted entities, and document structure, b) The retrieval model should provide superior effectiveness across a range of query and document types (e.g. Web, cross-lingual, ad-hoc2), c) The query language and retrieval model should support retrieval at different levels of granularity (e.g. sentence, passage, XML field, document, multi-document), and d) The system architecture should support very large databases, multiple databases, optimized query execution, fast indexing, concurrent indexing and querying, and portability.

IV. Architecture of Search Engine

The retrieval system should be fast at indexing and retrieval, and still be able to handle the complex data and information needs. In addition, this system was required to handle concurrent indexing and querying. Indri Search engine is based on the original interference network retrieval frame work [10]. The cast retrieval as inference in simple graphical model. It is en extension to the original model [9]. This also incorporates of probabilities and also supports multi languages in network environment. At the time of indexing the belief nodes are created dynamically based on the query. This are derived from the link matrices. Firstly it combines the evidence from the parents in various ways and secondly it allows fast inference by making marginalization computationally tractable. Information need node is simply a belief node that combines all the network evidence into a single value. The documents are ranked according to $P(I|\alpha,\beta,D)$.It is an extension of INQUERY. The structured query language follows the term weighting, ordered and unordered windows and the synonyms. It gives the additional features as language modeling construct, add flexibility to deal the fields via context and also generalization of passage retrieval. Finally, as this system is meant to be usable in an academic setting, we wanted the code to be clear and easy to modify. During the development of the system, we constantly made decisions that supported one goal at the expense of another. However, we believe that the Indri system has achieved a functional balance between its design goals: 1) Parsing: Indri parsers the variety of the document formats like TREC formatted text, XML, HTML, and plain text documents. These parsers translate the documents into an intermediate representation, called a Parsed Document that also have the indexer can store directly. These parsers can be configured to pass tag information from documents on to the indexer so that this can be used for querying document structure. Indri provides a small library of Transformation objects for parsing

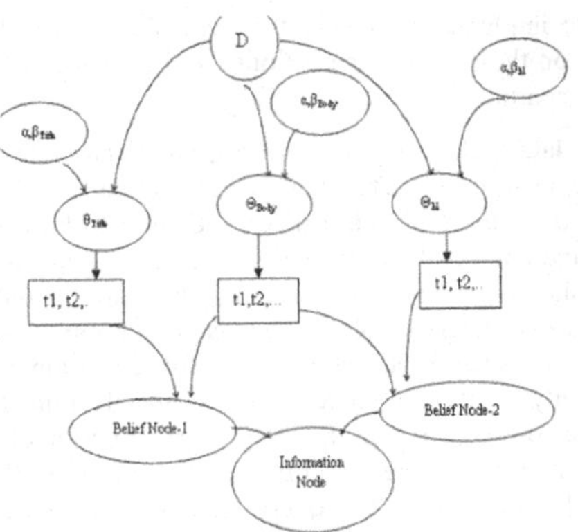

Figure 3: Indri working Model.

as well. Transformation objects transform a Parsed Document into another Parsed Document; therefore, they can be easily chained together. 2) Indexing: The indexing system builds compressed inverted lists for each term and field in memory. It contains all information necessary to perform queries on that data. In a sense, an Indri index can be considered a set of smaller indexes. The indexer also stores a copy of the incoming document text in compressed form. This text is commonly used to produce document snippets at retrieval time. The index subsystem is capable of storing any text that can be represented in Unicode. 3) Retrieval: When a query is submitted to the Indri system, it is parsed into an intermediate query representation. This intermediate representation is then passed through a variety of query transformations. In the event that the indexes are not on the same machine as the query director process, the query director connects to an Indri daemon on the remote machine which performs some of the query processing.

Query evaluation proceeds in two phases. In the first phase, statistics about the number of times terms and phrases appear in the collection are gathered. In the second phase, the statistics from the first phase are used to evaluate the query against the collection. The query evaluation code in Indri incorporates the max-score optimization in order to speed query evaluation [10]. 4) Concurrency: Indri supports multithreaded operation, where document insertions, deletions and queries can be processed simultaneously. In the implementation, we have been careful to arrange data such that locks are held as briefly as possible. Indri stores indexed documents in a repository, which is composed of an ordered set of indexes. At any one time, only one of these indexes can receive new documents; all other indexes are read-only. The index that receives new documents resides in main memory, and contains only a small fraction of the total indexed documents. This means that the majority of indexed documents are in read-only indexes, which simplifies concurrent execution significantly. When the active in-memory index fills, it is marked read-only and written to disk asynchronously. While the write is taking place, a new in-memory index is created to receive any incoming documents. When the write completes, the old in-memory index is deleted, and the copy on disk takes its place.

V. WORLD'S LARGEST COLLECTION OF WEB DOCUMENTS

The Google is considered to be a world's largest and most comprehensive collection of web documents. It immediately finds the information what we need by using the following services:

Google Web Search is the search service offers more than 2 billion documents - 25 percent of which are other than English language web pages. Google Web Search offers users to search the numerous non-HTML files such as PDF, Microsoft Office, and Corel documents. Google's uses the powerful and scalable technology for searches, which is the comprehensive set of information and it delivers a list of relevant results with in less than half-a-second. Google Groups is a 20-year archive of Usenet conversations as is the largest powerful reference tool, offers the insight into the history and culture of the Internet. Google Groups have more than 700 million postings in more than 35,000 topical categories. Google Image Search Comprises of more than 330 million images, Google Image Search enables users to quickly and easily find electronic images relevant based on the variety of topics, including pictures (celebrities, popular travel destinations). The advanced features also include image size, format (JPEG and/or GIF), and coloration. It also restricts the searches to specific sites or domains.

The Google Groups Usenet archive uses for the different contexts at Google: Spelling Correction and Query Classification. Spelling correction. The Google [6] uses the spelling corrector that takes a Machine Learning approach that builds a very fine-grained probabilistic context sensitive model for the spelling correction.. The fine-grained context sensitivity can be achieved by analyzing very large quantities of text.

It uses a Query Classification into the Open Directory Project. The Open Directory Project (ODP) (http://dmoz.org/) is a large open source topic hierarchy into which web pages have been manually classified. The hierarchy contains roughly 500,000 classes/topics. Since this is a useful source of hand-classified information, we sought to build a query classifier that would identify and suggest categories in the ODP that would be relevant to a user query. At first blush, this would appear to be a standard text classification task. It becomes more challenging when we consider that the "documents" to be classified are user queries, which have an average length of just over two words. Moreover, the set of classes from the ODP is much larger than any previously studied classification task, and the classes are non-mutually exclusive despite these challenges, we have available roughly four million pre-classified documents, giving us quite a substantial training set. The system architecture in Figure 4 shows that there are five modules: (1) the module of Focused Crawler, which is responsible for collecting data; (2) Data cargo module; (3) the module of Data hub; (4) Query Processor and (5) Graphics UI module.

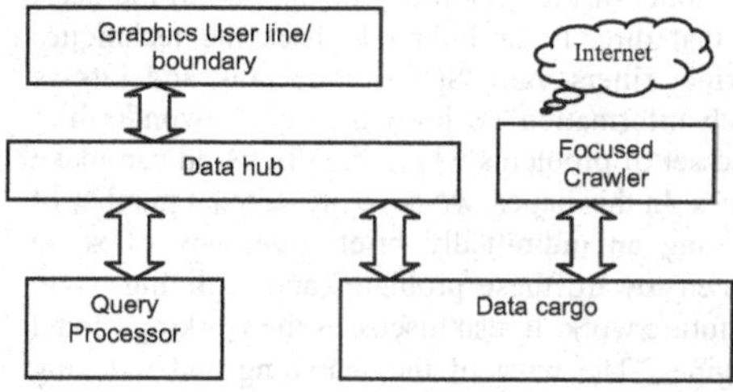

Figure 4: Working Model of Search Engines

Focused Crawler is highly depends on the topic related data, hence focused crawler is to collect data. A novel score function is presented to evaluate the URLs' correlation about the specific topic. Three factors contribute to the score. The first one is the content of given web pages, including title, keyword, text and description as defined in INDRI. The second one is the anchor text of the URL and the third one is the link structure of the connected URLs and pages. For those satisfied Web pages, we access them, analyze the content inside, organize them with XML format, and store them into data storage. The hierarchical structure [12] of the data collecting module and the procedure for data parsing. The Data Cargo/Storage Module used the different file formats of xml files: Paper Document, Book Document, Thesis Document, WWW Document, Organization Document, People Document, and Project Document etc. The Module of data center receives the users' queries and then parses them to get related documents from the storage component. We use Vector Space Model [8] to represent a document. Each word (except for the stop words) in the abstract of document will be an attribute of the vector, and the vector space is stored in the index file.

After analyzing all the related documents, data center returns a document list, a hierarchical tree of the documents, and some statistical information according to the application template. In order to reduce the influence of noisy data, WordNet can be used to find the wrongly spelled words and the different words which have the same meaning. On the other hand, we get the stop words adaptively according to the statistics on the appearance of the words. The main task of query processor is to execute query and provide hierarchical clustering results. We partly borrow the thinking from a global frequent item set hierarchical clustering strategy (FIHCP [8]) to build clusters. This algorithm can be summarized in three phases: First, initial clusters are constructed. Second, a cluster (topic) tree is built. Finally, the cluster trees are pruned in case there are too many clusters. Furthermore, we refine the FIHC algorithm in the labeling aspect to give user a better understanding of the clustering result. A friendly browser-based user interface is presented to the end users finally. The users can get some analysis for each sub-topic respectively, the topics are clustered hierarchically [12]. We tried a variety of different approaches that explored many different aspects of the classifier model space: independence assumptions between words, modeling word order and dependencies for two and three word queries, generative and discriminative models, boosting, and others. The complete list of methods compared is not included since some portions of the study were conducted in an iterative piecemeal fashion, so a direct comparison of all methods applied to all the data is not possible to provide.

Nevertheless, we found that the various algorithms performed as expected relative to previously published results in text classification when training data set sizes were small. Interestingly, as we steadily grew the amount of data available for training, however, we reached a critical point at which most of the algorithms were generally indistinguishable in performance. Even more interesting was the fact that as we moved substantially beyond this critical point by adding even more training data, The classification and the use of a separate model for single word queries), outperformed—by several percentage points in accuracy—every other algorithm employed, even after substantial effort was placed into making them better. Furthermore, most probability smoothing techniques, which generally seem to help in limited data situations, either showed no appreciably improvements or actually decreased performance in the data rich. While the set of alternative algorithms used was by no means exhaustive, and the results here are still somewhat anecdotal, we hypothesize that, as in the case of the abundance of data often can, and usually does, make up for weaker modeling techniques. This can

VI. Survey Interpretations

The above discussion can be finalized and be formulated in the criteria or factors required for the search engines. The survey discusses the interesting parameters for the search engine – the Internet users want quality information, and also want it fast. This survey describes the different parameters and based on the frequency as shown in table 1. The table indicates certain important trends as well as some unimportant areas. Further we also obtained certain alarming area to be considered at the first priority. Positive features of search engine practices for Indian users want the comfortably in usage and also the download time. They are also little inclined towards the regularly updates information and also the quality of the data available at the World Wide Web.

The less significant areas are organization of the content. They are not aware of that. The less important areas for the search engine users are access of the customer service, quantity of contents, displaying search engine at their website and front page layout. They are least important for them is the look and feel of the website. These users don't bother about the animation uses. As a search Engine, the least important areas can be ignored or be given the low priority for the assessment of the usage of the search in the development areas of the search engines. The Alarming trends evident from the table.

Table 1: Search Engine users

Factors for online users	Frequencies				
	Strongly Disagree	Dis-agree	Neutral	Agree	Strongly Agree
Ease Of Use/Navigation of search engine	0%	0%	4%	24%	72%
Fast Download Time	0%	0%	12%	72%	16%
Regularly Updated Information	0%	0%	64%	24%	4%
Quality Of Content	0%	16%	60%	20%	4%
Organization Of Content	0%	52%	28%	16%	4%
Access To Customer Service	0%	48%	36%	16%	0%
comfortable with Quantity Of Content	0%	44%	40%	12%	4%
Search Engine At their webSite	0%	44%	40%	16%	0%
Front Page Layout of the site	0%	44%	24%	28%	4%
time for Fun on internet	60%	20%	20%	0%	0%
the Look And Feel Of The Site	68%	24%	4%	0%	4%
Animated Graphics at the site	64%	24%	8%	0%	4%

include important areas towards consensus building and impact assessment of search engines. The frequency graph representation will give you a clear impact of the above discussions.

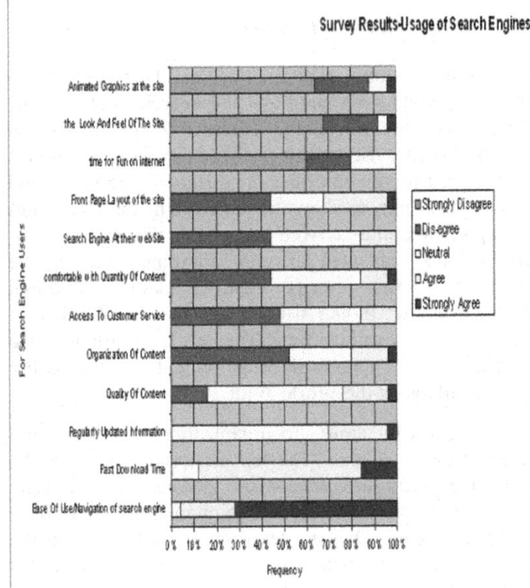

Figure: 4 Frequency graph: Factors influenced to search users.

VII. Conclusions

The proposed model of the search engine applied to the tasks and subtasks that directly or indirectly uses the techniques such as indexing, filters, hub, Spam, page rank and hits as discussed. Web information retrieval presents a wonderfully rich and varied set of problems where the discussed can make critical advances. In this paper, we have presented a number of challenges, giving an (admittedly brief) overview of some approaches taken toward these problems and outlining many directions for future work. It also discusses the working Model of Search Engines. The most of the searching and indexing methods for underlying XML data are exploited. As a result, we hope to stimulate still more research in this area that will make use of the vast amount of information on the web in order to better achieve the goal of organizing the world's information and making it universally accessible. The survey, which was conducted online, gives the significant and non-significant parameters according to the web users. The significant are where the search engines have to improve is the ease of use, latest updated and quality of content and the fast download speed. The others parameters discussed that are least important for the Internet users.

REFERENCES

[1] Brin, S., Page, L.: The Anatomy of a Large-Scale Hypertextual Web Search Engine. In: Proc. of the 7th International World Wide Web Conference (1998) 107-117

[2] Kleinberg, J.M.: Authoritative Sources in a Hyperlinked Environment. Journal of the ACM 46(5) (1999) 604-632

[3] Herbach, J. (2001). Improving Authoritative Searches in a Hyperlinked Environment Via Similarity Weighting. Retrieved September 04, 2009 from http:// www.cs.princeton.edu/~jherbach/hits-sw.pdf

[4] Tomlin, J.A.: A New Paradigm for Ranking Pages on the World Wide Web. In: Proc. of the 12th International World Wide Web Conference (2003) 350-355

[5] Agosti, M., and Melucci, M. (eds.): Workshop on Evaluation of Web Document Retrieval at SIGIR-1999 (1999)

[6] T. Joachims, Evaluating Retrieval Performance Using Clickthrough Data, in J. Franke and G. Nakhaeizadeh and I. Renz, "Text Mining", Physica/Springer Verlag, pp. 79-96, 2003.

[7] Sahami, M., Dumais, S., Heckerman, D., and Horvitz, E.: A Bayesian Approach to Filtering Junk E-Mail. In: Learning for Text Categorization: Papers from the 1998 Workshop. AAAI Technical Report WS-98-05 (1998)

[8] Diez J,del Coz J.J Luaces O. ,Bahamonde A. Clustering for preference criteria, Centro de Inteligencia Artificial. Universidad de Oviedo at Gijón (2004)

[9] J. Ponte and W. B. Croft, A language modeling approach to information retrieval. In SIGIR 1998, pp. 275-281.

[10] H. Turtle and W. B. Croft, Evaluation of an inference network based retrieval model. Trans. Inf. Syst., 9(3):187-222, 1991.

[11] Indri: A language-model based search engine for complex queries. (extended version). Trevor Strohman, Donald Metzler, Howard Turtle and W. Bruce Croft, Center for Intelligence Information Retrieval (2004)

[12] Fung, B., Wang, K., & Ester, M. (2003, May). Hierarchical document clustering using frequent items. SDM'03, San Francisco, CA

An Invisible Text Watermarking Algorithm using Image Watermark

Zunera Jalil and Anwar M. Mirza
FAST National University of Computer and Emerging Sciences, Islamabad, Pakistan
E-mail: {zunera.jalil, anwar.m.mirza}@nu.edu.pk

Abstract- **Copyright protection of digital contents is very necessary in today's digital world with efficient communication mediums as internet. Text is the dominant part of the internet contents and there are very limited techniques available for text protection. This paper presents a novel algorithm for protection of plain text, which embeds the logo image of the copyright owner in the text and this logo can be extracted from the text later to prove ownership. The algorithm is robust against content-preserving modifications and at the same time, is capable of detecting malicious tampering. Experimental results demonstrate the effectiveness of the algorithm against tampering attacks by calculating normalized hamming distances. The results are also compared with a recent work in this domain.**

I. Introduction

Copyright protection and privacy issues have gained importance with the increasing use of internet, digital libraries, e-commerce and other communication and digital technologies. Besides, making it easier to access information within a very short span of time, it has become difficult to protect copyright of digital contents. Digital contents comprises of text, image, audio and videos. Copyright protection of images, audio and video has been given due consideration by researchers in past but the amount of work done to protect text is very scare. Although, text is the most dominant part of internet, e-books, newspapers, articles, legal documents, and journals; but its protection has been seriously ignored in past.

The threats of electronic publishing like illegal copying and re-distribution of copyrighted material, plagiarism and other forms of copyright violations should be seriously and specifically addressed. Copyright protection of digital contents and specifically the text, is such a need of time which cannot be condoned. Digital watermarking is one of the solutions which can watermark the digital contents and can be used to claim ownership later. Digital watermarking methods are used to identify the original copyright owner (s) of the contents which can be an image, a plain text, an audio, a video or a combination of all.

A digital watermark can be described as a visible or an invisible, preferably the latter, identification code that permanently is embedded in the data. It means that unlike conventional cryptographic techniques, it remains present within the data even after the decryption process [1].

The process of embedding a digital watermark (image or text) into a digital text document that carries information unique to the copyright owner or the creator of the document is called Digital Text Watermarking. An illicit re-distribution and reproduction of information content (s) and copyright violations can be avoided by applying text watermarking methods.

A text, being the simplest mode of communication and information exchange, brings various challenges when it comes to copyright protection. Any transformation on text should preserve the meaning, fluency, grammaticality, writing style and value of the text. Short documents have low capacity for watermark embedding and are relatively difficult to protect.

The binary nature, block/line/word patterning, semantics, structure, style, syntax, and language rules are some of the important properties of text documents which are needed to be addressed in any text watermarking algorithm. Also, the inherent properties of a generic watermarking scheme like imperceptibility, robustness, and security need to be satisfied. In this paper, we propose a novel text watermarking algorithm which embeds the logo or signatures of the original copyright owner in text to protect it.

The paper is organized as follows: Section 2 provides an overview of the previous work done on text watermarking. The proposed embedding and extraction algorithm are described in detail in section 3. Section 4 presents the experimental results for the tampering (insertion, deletion and re-ordering) attacks. Performance of the proposed algorithm is evaluated by comparing it with the most recent relevant work. The last section concludes the paper along with directions for future work.

II. Previous Work

Text watermarking is an important area of research; however, the previous work on digital text watermarking is quite inadequate. In past, various text watermarking techniques have been proposed. These include text watermarking using text images, synonym based, pre-supposition based, syntactic tree based, noun-verb based, word and sentence based, acronym based, typo error based methods etc.

The previous work on digital text watermarking can be classified in the following categories; an image based approach, a syntactic approach, a semantic approach and the structural approach. Description of each category and the work done accordingly is as follows:

T. Sobh, K. Elleithy (eds.), *Innovations in Computing Sciences and Software Engineering*,
DOI 10.1007/978-90-481-9112-3_25, © Springer Science+Business Media B.V. 2010

A. An Image-Based Approach

Text document image is used to embed watermark in this approach. Brassil, et al. were the first to propose a few text watermarking methods utilizing text image[2]-[3]. Later Maxemchuk, et al. [4]-[6] analyzed the performance of these methods. Low, et al. [7]-[8] further analyzed the efficiency of these methods. The first method was the line-shift algorithm which moves a line upward or downward (left or right) based on watermark bit values. The second method was the word-shift algorithm which modifies the inter-word spaces to embed the watermark. Sine wave was adjusted to watermark the text. The signals were encoded in the phase, amplitude, and frequency of the sine waves. The third method was the feature coding algorithm in which certain text features are altered to encode watermark bits in the text.

Huang and Yan [9] proposed an algorithm based on an average inter-word distance in each line. The distances are adjusted according to the sine-wave of a specific phase and frequency. The feature and the pixel level algorithms were also developed which mark the documents by modifying the stroke features such as width or serif [10].

Text watermarking algorithms using binary text image are not robust against reproduction attacks and have limited applicability. In some algorithms, watermark can be destroyed by OCR (Optical Character Recognitions).The use of OCR obliterate the changes made to the spaces, margins and fonts of a text to embed watermark.

B. A Syntactic Approach

In this approach towards text watermarking, researchers have used the syntactic structure of text to embed watermark. Mikhail J. Atallah, et al. first proposed the natural language watermarking scheme by using syntactic structure of text [11]-[12] where the syntactic tree is built and transformations are applied to it in order to embed the watermark keeping all the properties of text intact. The NLP techniques are used to analyze the syntactic and the semantic structure of text while performing any transformations to embed the watermark bits [25].

Hassan et al. performed morpho-syntactic alterations to the text to watermark it [13]. The text is first transformed into a syntactic tree diagram where hierarchies and functional dependencies are made explicit and then watermark is embedded. The author states that agglomerative languages like Turkish are easier to watermark than the English language. Hassan et al. provided an overview of available syntactic tools for text watermarking [14].

Text watermarking by using syntactic structure of text and natural language processing algorithms, is an efficient approach but progress is slower than the requirement. NLP is an immature area of research till now and by using in-efficient algorithms, efficient results in text watermarking cannot be obtained.

C. A Semantic Approach

The semantic watermarking schemes focus on using the semantic structure of text to embed the watermark[25]. Atallah et al. were the first to propose the semantic watermarking schemes in the year 2000 [15]-[17]. Later, the synonym substitution method was proposed, in which watermark is embedded by replacing certain words with their synonyms [18]. Xingming, et al. proposed noun-verb based technique for text watermarking [19] which exploits nouns and verbs in a sentence parsed with a grammar parser using semantic networks. Later Mercan, et al. proposed an algorithm of the text watermarking by using typos, acronyms and abbreviation to embed the watermark [20]. Algorithms were developed to watermark the text using the linguistic semantic phenomena of presuppositions [21] by observing the discourse structure, meanings and representations. The text pruning and the grafting algorithms were also developed in the past. The algorithm based on text meaning representation (TMR) strings has also been proposed [22].

The text watermarking, based on semantics, is language dependent. The synonym based techniques are not resilient to the random synonym substitution attacks. Sensitive nature of some documents e.g. legal documents, poetry and quotes do not allow us to make semantic transformations randomly because in these forms of text a simple transformation sometimes destroys both the semantic connotation and the value of text[25].

D. A Structural Approach

This is the most recent approach used for copyright protection of text documents. A text watermarking algorithm for copyright protection of text using occurrences of double letters (aa-zz) in text to embed the watermark has recently been proposed[25]. The algorithm is a blend of encryption, steganography and watermarking, and gives a robust solution for the text watermarking problem. In that algorithm, groups are formed by using full stop period. Text like poetry, quotes, web contents, legal document may not essentially contain full stops; which makes this algorithm inapplicable. To overcome the shortcomings of this algorithm, another algorithm which use preposition besides double letters to watermark text is proposed[29].

The structural algorithms are not applicable to all types of text documents and the algorithm use an alphabetical watermark; hence we propose an algorithm which uses an image watermark that can be a logo, fingerprint or signature of the original author.

III. PROPOSED ALGORITHM

The proposed algorithm exploits occurrences of double letters and prepositions existing in text to embed the watermark as in [29]. The original copyright owner of text logically embeds the watermark in a text and generates a watermark key. Double letters and prepositions are inherent part of English language text which cannot be neglected.

In the proposed approach, text partitions are made based on preposition input. Afterwards these partitions are combined to make groups, where each group contains gs partitions if gs is the group size. Then, the frequency of occurrence of each double letter in each group is analyzed. Afterwards a watermark key is generated by using the AOL list that contains the double letters occurring average number of time. Median average method is used to find averages.

This watermark key is registered with the trusted third party which is called Certifying Authority (CA) with the original watermark and the entry is time stamped. Whenever any conflict of claim about copyright arises, this watermark key can be applied on the text using extraction algorithm to obtain the watermark. That watermark will identify the de- facto owner. The proposed algorithm is a blind watermarking algorithm since the original watermark is not required at the time of watermark extraction. The trusted third party is responsible for performing detection on behalf of the content owner and the detector has to answer who the registered user is/may be[25]. The proposed algorithm caters for combined insertion, deletion and re-ordering attack on the text.

A watermark is a unique logo or signature of an individual or an organization who owns the copyright of a digital content, in this case text. Text can be attacked in a number of ways, but generally an attack is the deliberate insertion, deletion and re-ordering of words and sentences to and from the text [25].

The watermarking process involves two stages, watermark embedding and watermark extraction. Watermark embedding is done by the original author and extraction done later by the Certifying Authority on author behalf.

A. *Embedding Algorithm*

The algorithm which embeds the watermark in the text is called embedding algorithm. The embedding algorithm embeds the watermark in the text logically and generates a watermark key. The watermark embedding process is shown in fig. 1.

The watermark embedding algorithm is as follows:

1. Input WI, GS, Pr and T.
2. Convert W_I to W_T
3. Make partitions of T based on Pr
4. Make groups of text based on GS i.e. Number of groups= Number of partitions/GS
5. Count occurrence of double letters in each group and populate AOL (Average occuring letter) in each group.
6. $\forall w_j \subset AOL \begin{cases} key[i] = 0; \ where\ j = 1,2,3,\ldots n \\ key[i+1] = Group\ Number(AOL \end{cases}$

   $\forall w_j \not\subset AOL \begin{cases} key[i] = 1; \\ key[i+1] = (w_j + k) MOD\ 26 \\ where\ k\ is\ in\ Z_{26} \end{cases}$

   where Z_{26} represents 26 alphabets (a-z)
7. Output WK

W_I: image watermark, GS: Group size, Pr: Preposition, T: text file, W_T: text watermark, WK: Watermark key

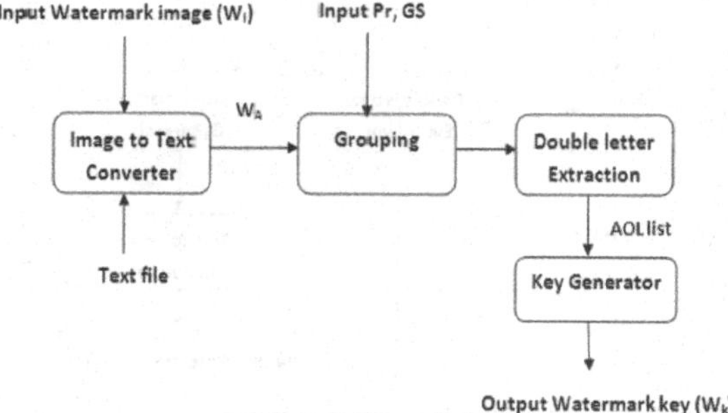

Fig. 1. Watermark embedding process

The watermark image (WI) is first converted to alphabet and we obtain an alphabetical watermark (WA). Then, depending on preposition (Pr) and group size (GS) input by user (partial key), partitions and groups are formed. In the next step, the occurrence of each double letter is counted in each group and the double letter occurring average number of time is identified (AOL). The key generator generates the watermark key by using watermark and AOL list as shown in the algorithm and generates the watermark key. This key is then registered with the CA along with the watermark image, original text, and current date and time.

B. *Extraction Algorithm*

The algorithm used to extract the watermark from the watermarked text is known extraction algorithm. It takes the author key as input and extracts the watermark image from the text. The algorithm is kept with the CA that uses it to resolve copyright issues, if any at a later stage. The watermark extraction process is shown in fig. 2. The detailed algorithm is as follows:

```
1. Input WK and T.
2. Read Pr from Wk and set counter=1.
3. Make partitions of T based on Pr
4. Make groups of text based on GS i.e.
5. Number of groups=
   Number of partitions/GS
6. Count occurrence of double letters in
   each group and populate AOL (Average
   occuring letter) in each group.
7. L=length(WK), Keyindex=L+1
8. While(Keyindex<L)repeat 9 to 10
9.   If(WK(i)equals 0)
       W(I)= AOL(groupnumber)
     else
       W(I)=Cipher letter
10.    I=I+1
11.    Output W
```

In the extraction algorithm, text is partitioned using preposition (Pr) from watermark key (WK). Then partitions are combined to make text groups as done previously in the

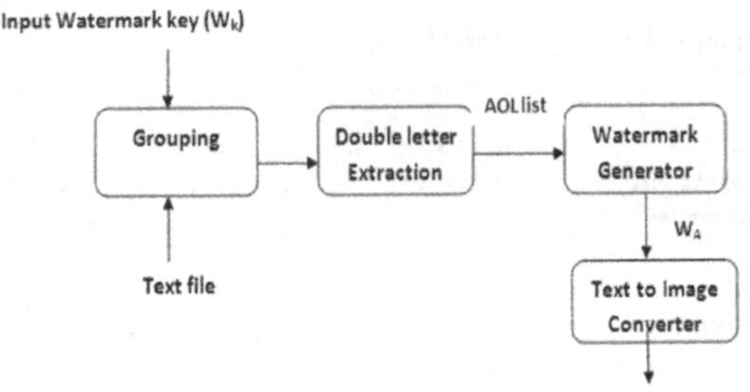

Fig. 2. Watermark extraction process

embedding algorithm. Afterwards, occurrence of double letters in each group is analyzed and average occurring letter in each group is identified. The contents of watermark (WK) are then used to obtain watermark from the text as shown in step 8 to 10 of the algorithm.

IV. Experimental Results

We used 20 samples of variable size text as in [25] and [29]. Group size was kept 2, 3 5 and 10 for Small Size Text (SST), Medium Size Text (MST), Large Size Text (LST) and very Large Size Text (VLST) respectively. The logo of FAST National University of Computer and Emerging Sciences, Islamabad, Pakistan as shown in fig. 3 was used as the watermark image.

In order to evaluate the degree of closeness between original watermark and the extracted watermark image, we selected the normalized hamming distance (NHD) as the similarity measure:

$$NHD(w, w') = \frac{1}{N_w}\sum_{i=1}^{N_w} w(i) \oplus w'(i) \qquad (1)$$

where w and w' are the original and extracted reference watermarks respectively, N_w is the length of the watermark, and $\oplus$ is the exclusive-OR operator. The distance ranges between (0, 1). Ideally, two perceptually similar images should have a distance of close to 0. The possible attacks on text can be random insertion, deletion, and re-ordering of words; to and from the text. The tampering volume was kept same as in [29].

The normalized hamming distances between original and extracted image on all text samples (average of each category) are shown in table I.

TABLE I
NORMALIZED HAMMING DISTANCES BETWEEN ORIGINAL WATERMARK IMAGE (W) AND EXTRACTED WATERMARK IMAGE (W')

Samples	Normalized Hamming Distances			
	'in'	'on'	'to'	'of'
SST	0.0267	0.0098	0.0035	0.0417
MST	0.0577	0.0139	0.0585	0.0591
LST	0.0315	0.0133	0.0429	0.0662
VLST	0.0165	0.0090	0.0263	0.0326

Fig. 3. Watermark image (118 x 118 pixels)

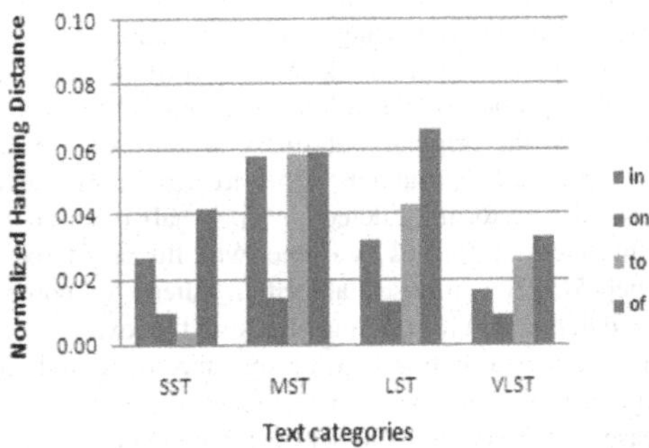

Fig. 4. Normalized hamming distance between original and retrieved watermark (after tampering) on all text sample

Fig. 4 shows the hamming distances between original and extracted watermark image after tampering. It can be clearly observed that the hamming distances are close to zero for every preposition. And the result are more optimal for the preposition 'in' and 'on' on all text samples.

For comparison, we compare the performance of proposed algorithm with a text watermarking algorithm proposed by Peng et al. [22] which is named here as OTMR. To facilitate comparison, we used the same 9 TMR samples from MIKRKOSMOS as input in our experiments used in OTMR. Twenty experiments were conducted on each sample. All text samples fall under the category of Small Size Text (SST).

The ratios of successfully detected watermark as compared with OTMR are shown in table II and graphically represented in fig. 5.

TABLE II
COMPARISON OF PROPOSED ALGORITHM WITH OPTIMIZED TMR ALGORITHM (OTMR) [22]

Sample No.	Ratio of successfully detected watermark			
	OTMR-10	OTMR 20b	OTMR 30b	Proposed Algorithm
TMR0011	38%	92%	62%	99%
TMR0020	42%	90%	56%	100%
TMR0046	24%	86%	48%	99%
TMR0070	24%	84%	50%	99%
TMR0589	36%	86%	44%	98%
TMR0592	22%	78%	42%	100%
TMR2099	40%	90%	58%	99%
TMR2103	26%	84%	44%	98%
TMR2301	22%	88%	46%	100%

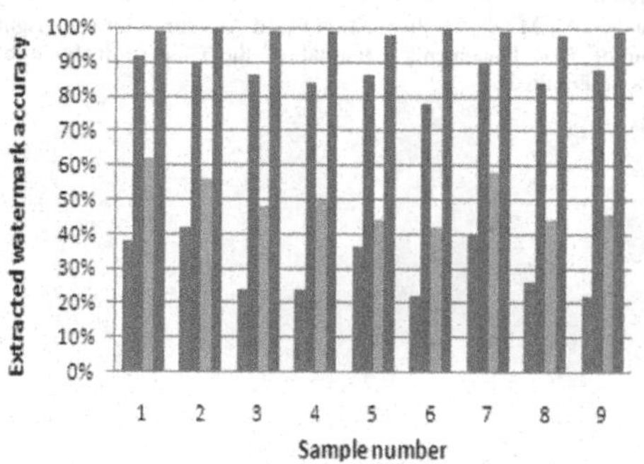

Fig. 5. Comparative accuracy of proposed algorithm as compared with OTMR algorithm.

Fig. 5 shows the comparative results of both algorithms where results of all three versions of Peng algorithm 10 bit, 20 bit and 30 bit are inferior to results of proposed algorithm. The proposed algorithm is effective and has better robustness as compared with OTMR on all 9 samples. The watermark survived even after insertion, deletion and re-ordering attacks.

V. Conclusion

The existing text watermarking algorithms are not robust against random tampering attacks. With the increasing volume of attack, it becomes impossible to detect watermark accurately. We have developed a text watermarking algorithm, which embeds the logo or signature of the copyright owner logically in text and can be later used to prove ownership. We evaluated the performance of the algorithm for random tampering attack in dispersed form on 20 texts. We also compared the performance of the algorithm with a recently proposed algorithm. Results show that our algorithm is more robust, secure and efficient against random tampering attacks.

Acknowledgment

One of the authors, Ms. Zunera Jalil, 041-101673-Cu-014 would like to acknowledge the Higher Education Commission of Pakistan for providing the funding and resources to complete this work under Indigenous Fellowship Program.

References

[1]. Asifullah Khan, Anwar M. Mirza and Abdul Majid, "Optimizing Perceptual Shaping of a Digital Watermark Using Genetic Programming", Iranian Journal of Electrical and Computer Engineering, vol. 3, pp. 144-150, 2004.

[2]. J. T. Brassil, S. Low, N. F. Maxemchuk, and L. O'Gorman, "Electronic Marking and Identification Techniques to Discourage Document Copying," *IEEE Journal on Selected Areas in Communications*, vol. 13, no. 8, October 1995, pp. 1495-1504.

[3]. J. T. Brassil, S. Low, and N. F. Maxemchuk, "Copyright Protection for the Electronic Distribution of Text Documents," *Proceedings of the IEEE*, vol. 87, no. 7, July 1999, pp.1181-1196.

[4]. N. F. Maxemchuk, S. H. Low, "Performance Comparison of Two Text Marking Methods," *IEEE Journal of Selected Areas in Communications (JSAC)*, May 1998. vol. 16 no. 4 1998. pp. 561-572.

[5]. N. F. Maxemchuk, "Electronic Document Distribution," *AT&T Technical Journal, September 1994*, pp. 73-80. 6.

[6]. N. F. Maxemchuk and S. Low, "Marking Text Documents," *Proceedings of the IEEE International Conference on Image Processing*, Washington, DC, Oct. 26-29, 1997, pp. 13-16.

[7]. S. H. Low, N. F. Maxemchuk, and A. M. Lapone, "Document Identification for Copyright Protection Using Centroid Detection," *IEEE Transactions on Communications*, Mar. 1998, vol. 46, no.3, pp 372-381.

[8]. S. H. Low and N. F. Maxemchuk, "Capacity of Text Marking Channel," *IEEE Signal Processing Letters*, vol. 7, no. 12 , Dec. 2000, pp. 345 -347.

[9]. D. Huang and H. Yan, "Interword distance changes represented by sine waves for watermarking text images," *IEEE Trans. Circuits and Systems for Video Technology*, Vol.11, No.12, pp.1237-1245, Dec 2001.

[10]. T. Amano and D. Misaki, "A feature calibration method for watermarking of document images," *Proceedings of ICDAR*, pp.91-94, 1999.

[11]. M. J. Atallah, C. McDonough, S. Nirenburg, and V. Raskin, "Natural Language Processing for Information Assurance and Security: An Overview and Implementations", Proceedings 9th ACM/SIGSAC New Security Paradigms Workshop, September, 2000, Cork, Ireland, pp. 51–65.

[12]. M. J. Atallah, V. Raskin, M. C. Crogan, C. F. Hempelmann, F. Kerschbaum, D. Mohamed, and S.Naik, "Natural language watermarking: Design,analysis, and a proof-of-concept implementation", Proceedings of the Fourth Information HidingWorkshop, vol. LNCS 2137, 25-27 April 2001, Pittsburgh, PA.

[13]. Hassan M. Meral et al., "Natural language watermarking via morphosyntactic alterations", Computer Speech and Language, 23, 107-125, 2009.

[14]. Hasan M. Meral, Emre Sevinç, Ersin Ünkar, Bülent Sankur, A. Sumru Özsoy, Tunga Güngör, Syntactic tools for text watermarking, 19th SPIE Electronic Imaging Conf. 6505: Security, Steganography, and Watermarking of Multimedia Contents, Jan. 2007, San Jose.

[15]. M. Atallah, C. McDonough, S. Nirenburg, and V. Raskin, "Natural Language Processing for Information Assurance and Security: An Overview and Implementations," Proceedings 9th ACM/SIGSAC New Security Paradigms Workshop, September, 2000, Cork, Ireland, pp. 51–65.

[16]. M. Atallah, V. Raskin, C. F. Hempelmann, M. Karahan, R. Sion, U. Topkara, and K. E. Triezenberg, "Natural Language Watermarking and Tamperproofing", Fifth Information Hiding Workshop, vol. LNCS, 2578, October, 2002, Noordwijkerhout, The Netherlands, Springer-Verlag.

[17]. M. Topkara, C. M. Taskiran, and E. Delp, "Natural language watermarking," Proceedings of the SPIE International Conference on Security, Steganography, and Watermarking of Multimedia Contents VII, 2005.

[18]. U. Topkara, M. Topkara, M. J. Atallah, "The Hiding Virtues of Ambiguity: Quantifiably Resilient Watermarking of Natural Language Text through Synonym Substitutions". In Proceedings of ACM Multimedia and Security Conference, Geneva, 2006.

[19]. Xingming Sun, Alex Jessey Asiimwe. Noun-Verb Based Technique of Text Watermarking Using Recursive Decent Semantic Net Parsers. Lecture Notes in Computer Science (LNCS) 3612: 958-961, Springer Press, August 2005.

[20]. Topkara, M., Topraka, U., Atallah, M.J., 2007. Information hiding through errors: a confusing approach. In: Delp III, E.J., Wong, P.W. (Eds.), Security, Steganography, and watermarking of Multimedia Contents IX. Proceedings of SPIE-IS&T Electronic Imaging SPIE 6505. pp. 65050V-1–65050V-12.

[21]. B. Macq and O. Vybornova, "A method of text watermarking using presuppositions," in Proceedings of the SPIE International Conference on Security, Steganography, and Watermarking of Multimedia Contents, January 2007.

[22]. Peng Lu et al., "An optimized natural language watermarking algorithm based on TMR", on proceedings of 9th International Conference for Young Computer Scientists, 2009.

[23]. Carlos Lopez, "Watermarking of digital geospatial datasets: a review of technical, legal and copyright issues", International Journal of Geographical Information Science, 2002. Vol.16, No. 6, 589-607.

[24]. "Reuters corpus," http://about.reuters.com/researchandstandards/corpus/index.asp.

[25]. Z. Jalil and A.M. Mirza, "A Novel Text Watermarking Algorithm Based on Double Letters", International Journal of Computer Mathematics. (Submitted)

[26]. "Preposition" The Columbia Encyclopedia, Sixth Edition. 2008. *Encyclopedia.com.* Aug. 2009

[27]. "English Preposition List", http://www.englishclub.com/grammar/prepositions-list.htm

[28]. Sinclair, J. 1991. Corpus, Concordance, Collocation Oxford: Oxford University Press

[29]. Z. Jalil and A. M. Mirza, "A Preposition based Algorithm for Copyright Protection of Text Documents", Journal of the Chinese Institute of Engineers. (Submitted)

A Framework for RFID Survivability Requirement Analysis and Specification

Yanjun Zuo, Malvika Pimple, Suhas Lande
{yanjun.zuo, malvika.pimple, suhas.lande}@und.edu
University of North Dakota,
Grand Forks, ND, USA 58201

Abstract[1]- **Many industries are becoming dependent on Radio Frequency Identification (RFID) technology for inventory management and asset tracking. The data collected about tagged objects though RFID is used in various high level business operations. The RFID system should hence be highly available, reliable, and dependable and secure. In addition, this system should be able to resist attacks and perform recovery in case of security incidents. Together these requirements give rise to the notion of a survivable RFID system. The main goal of this paper is to analyze and specify the requirements for an RFID system to become survivable. These requirements, if utilized, can assist the system in resisting against devastating attacks and recovering quickly from damages. This paper proposes the techniques and approaches for RFID survivability requirements analysis and specification. From the perspective of system acquisition and engineering, survivability requirement is the important first step in survivability specification, compliance formulation, and proof verification.**

Keywords: Radio Frequency Identification, Survivability, Threat model, Survivability requirements mapping graph

I. Introduction

In today's world competition is a major part of every domain. To be successful, it is important for every individual or organization to hone their skills to gain a competitive advantage over their contenders. For industries, one way of gaining a competitive advantage is by providing high quality services which are highly available, reliable, and secure.

This paper focuses on the survivability requirements and issues in a RFID system. RFID is a wireless technology for automatic item identification and data capture. It uses radio signals to identify a product, animal or person. Many industries are relying on Radio Frequency Identification (RFID) as a technology to automate their routine business processes and thus simplify and enhance the quality and accuracy of services. RFID has been used in various applications including, manufacturing, business automation application, supply chain management and citizen identification by customs and border protection through RFID enabled passports. Major retail chains such as Wal-Mart and Target have mandated that all suppliers introduce RFID. One of the major advantages of RFID is its capability to offer automatic, large scale, and contactless data collection. Although RFID brings various benefits to organizations, it also raises several security and privacy issues. Various security mechanisms and protocols have been developed for secure RFID applications ([1-2], for instance). Among the security issues related to RFID systems, one should distinguish those which cause minor damages to the system from those which could significantly affect the system's survivability. Survivability is defined as the ability of a system to provide essential and dependable services in presence of attacks and failures, and to recover full services in a timely manner [3]. Survivability is considered to be a key inherent property of a reliable system [4]. Survivability is different from security, as security deals with protecting the system components from attack by strengthening the system while survivability encompasses the functioning of the entire system and not individual components [5].

We study survivability issues for RFID systems because RFID is rapidly becoming an important part of enterprises; and because of the high distribution and vulnerability of its components, RFID technology is subject to various threats which can affect system survivability. There are three major components of a RFID system: tags, readers, and a backend RFID server. A tag is a small and cheap device which is combined in an IC chip and an antenna for radio communication which is physically attached to an item with a unique identifier. A reader is a device which can identify the presence of RFID tags and read information supplied by them [3]. Due to the limited computational power and limited memory for a RFID tag, standard security algorithms and protocols (e.g. public key cryptography and full scale access control) cannot be applied to low cost devices such as passive RFID tags.

In this paper, we perform analysis of survivability requirements from a system engineering perspective. We use threat modeling as a basis of specifying survivability requirements. We then categorize the requirements from which system experts can benefit in order to make a system survivable. In this paper, we mainly focus on the threats evolving from the RF subsystem of RFID system since this part represents the most vulnerable component of the entire system.

The rest of the paper is organized as follows. Section 2 discusses related work. Section 3 specifies the structure, functionality and critical services of an example RFID System. Section 4 describes a step by step method of threat modeling of the system and risk management. We also describe the concept of risk management and its importance in achieving system survivability. Section 5 specifies a novel method of specifying system survivability requirements based on the indentified threats to the system in order to achieve survivability goals. Finally, section 6 concludes this paper.

[1] This work was supported in part by US AFOSR under grant FA 9550-09-1-0215.

T. Sobh, K. Elleithy (eds.), *Innovations in Computing Sciences and Software Engineering*,
DOI 10.1007/978-90-481-9112-3_26,

II. Related Work

There are several existing works on threat modeling and requirements engineering. Threat modeling as a basis of security requirements is discussed in [6]. That paper describes a systematic approach towards threat modeling for complex systems. The concept of risk management is briefly explained in [6]. The authors of [7] propose a goal oriented approach to security threat modeling and analysis by using visual model elements. They introduce the notions of negative softgoals for representing threats and inverse contributions for evaluating design alternatives. An analysis procedure is also provided in [7] as a guide to context sensitive selection of countermeasures. Major focus of [6-7] is on system security.

There are intensive studies and definitions of system survivability proposed in the literature. Most survivability studies are based on different abilities a system should have ([8-14], to cite a few). In [8] the authors discuss strategies for achieving survivability and techniques and processes for analyzing survivability in an unbounded network such as the Internet. In [13], the process is described about constructing systems to be dependably reconfigurable without forcing the system to sacrifice desired capabilities.

Work has also been done in the area of requirements engineering for survivable systems. In [15], the author describes the current state of requirements engineering for survivable systems. The requirements engineering definition for survivability strategies are enumerated as resistance, recognition and recovery. The major emphasis of the paper is on the importance of survivability requirements. Various other survivability models proposed which are, usually application or domain specific. However, the survivability models described are very application or domain specific.

Currently, there is a lack of research on systematic reasoning and specification of the requirements for pervasive computing systems such as a RFID system. The proposed framework assists system engineers to enumerate categorized requirements in a systematic approach. Although we relate the survivability requirement model to RFID systems, the proposed methodology can be extended to a wide range of applications and domains (e.g. wireless sensor networks).

III. An Example RFID System

RFID systems are important to many different kinds of applications. The structure of the system may differ with domain. The main mission of RFID systems differ with different applications. A tagged item can have different type of data associated with it which should be readable and revisable whenever/ wherever needed. Thus, we can summarize the system mission as providing trustworthy and accurate data associated with the tagged item in a timely and secure manner to the higher applications.

The structure of a typical RFID system is shown in Figure1. Typically, a multi-enterprise RFID based system is composed of multiple sites. The major components of each site include:

1) A Radio Frequency Subsystem: It consists of components which perform identification and related wireless communications and transactions. Readers and Tags are a part of the RF subsystem.

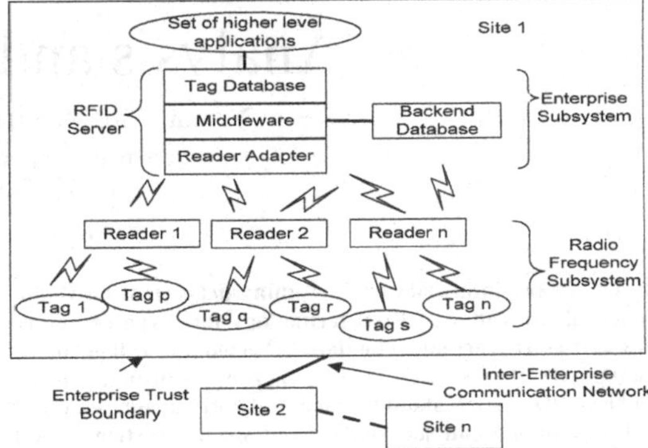

Figure 1: RFID system components

2) An Enterprise Subsystem: It consists of a backend database and a RFID server.
   a) Backend Database: The backend database at least the following information: the tag identification number, the secret key shared between the database and the tag, and optional item descriptions of the tagged item.
   b) RFID Server: This consists of systems and applications which communicate with the readers and process data acquired from the RF subsystem. Three components constitute an RFID server:
      i. Reader adapter: an interface to connect the readers.
      ii. Middleware: An intermediate layer between the lower level RF subsystem and the higher level database which pre-processes data collected from the RF subsystem and provide cleaned data to the higher components. Middleware also contains some security mechanisms to ensure data security.
      iii. Tag Database: Cleaned tag data is stored in this database to be used by the high level applications. This database may also contain high level events.
3) An Inter-Enterprise Subsystem: It connects enterprise subsystems across organizational boundaries. For example, a manufacturing enterprise may communicate with its suppliers, wholesalers and brokers.

The communications between RFID tags and readers are through wireless channels. The RFID server is connected to the higher level user processes within the trusted internal network of the organization. Users should be aware that the RFID server described above only represents a logical RFID server which may encompass a set of distributed RFID servers present in an enterprise.

A. *RFID Critical Services*

Critical services refer to a set of essential services that are critical to the functionality of a system. Failures to provide these services will result in violations of system mission and objectives. Next, we identify critical services that a RFID system should provide. It is essential for survivable systems to maintain the critical services with full or even degrading functionality in case of faults/attacks and recover when the situation improves. In our example system, we assume that the

RFID system is sensitive to error or malicious data injected by adversaries in the RF subsystem. We also assume that the system is data intensive. Under these assumptions, we conclude that the major critical service in this enterprise application is the continuous availability of truthful, consistent and accurate data to the users of the system. We now proceed to the threat modeling, which helps in enumerating the list of possible threats to the system, which can result in the systems inability to provide the set of critical services described above.

IV. Threat Modeling and Risk Management

Threat modeling is an important step towards security/survivability specification of a system. Threat modeling involves understanding the complexity of the system and identifying the possible threats to the system. Based on the identified threats, the system/security developers and administrators can specify realistic and meaningful security/survivability requirements for the system. Proper identification of threats and appropriate selection of countermeasures reduce the likelihood for the attackers to compromise the system.

Threat modeling involves three steps: characterizing the system, identifying assets and access points, and identifying threats [6]. These steps will be discussed in following sections. Although our approach for threat modeling is similar to the approach specified in [6], our main focus is on RFID system. We identify RFID specific threats and the corresponding requirements to thwart attacks to ensure system survivability. Furthermore, we study RFID system characteristics and risk management from a survivability perspective.

A. Characterizing the system

Characterizing a system involves a system model that reveals essential characteristics of the system. Modeling can be done using a number of approaches. In this paper, we use an UML class diagram for a more formal specification of the structure of the example RFID system as shown in Figure 1. From Figure 2, we can see that the major classes of the UML class diagram include enterprise, tag, reader, RFID server, backend database, higher-level applications, reader adapter, tag database and RFID middleware. We specify the attributes and operations of each class. For instance, the class tag has the attributes tag ID and secret key and operations SendMessage(), ReceiveMessage() and UpdateKey().

B. Identifying Assets and Access Points

An asset is a resource of a system which is essential to the system's mission and must be protected. The main assets of the RFID system include: (a) tags; (b) reader; (c) the backend database which contains authentication information; (d) the tag database; and (e) the inter-enterprise networks connecting partner organizations.

Access Points are where the adversary can penetrate the system. The main access points that we identified for the example RFID system include: (a) wireless connections between different components within the RF subsystem, (b) the wireless connection of the reader with the backend database or the RFID server, and (c) the inter-enterprise networks.

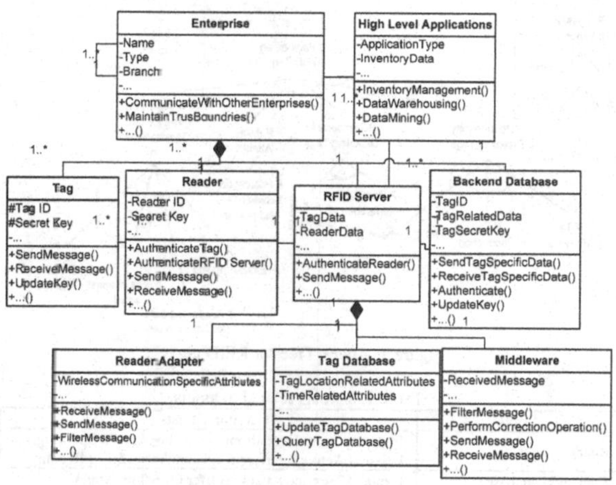

Figure 2: UML Class Diagram for Example RFID System

In general, due to security solution restrictions and RFID systems' characteristics, designing survivability mechanisms for RFID systems are both crucial and challenging.

In this paper, we assume that the main goal for an attacker is to compromise the survivability of a system by attacking the system from various access points described. An important step for the threat analysis is to step through the system's assets, reviewing a list of possible attacks for each asset [6].

C. Identifying Threats

The process of correlating threats to an asset involves creating an adversary hypothesis [6]. In this section, we use attack trees [6, 16] to identify the critical threats related to an asset. An attack tree provides a formal, methodical way of describing the security of the system based on varying attacks. In such tree structure, the root represents the threat corresponding to an asset (the attacker goal) and each node represents the attacker decision process. For each threat, the key P and I are used to describe whether it is possible or impossible for the threat to occur given other restrictions under consideration. Figure 3 shows an attack tree for an RFID tag. Figure 3 shows how an adversary can attack a RFID tag. For a more complete list of threats on a tag, interested readers may refer to [17].

Permanently Disabling Tags: This can be achieved by tag removal, tag destruction or using the KILL command. Although a KILL command is a valid operation performed by the enterprise, an adversary can exploit this method to sabotage RFID communication (17). However, achieving this can be very difficult (if not impossible).

Temporarily Disabling Tags: Aluminum foil can be used to shield a tag from electromagnetic waves to disable it. RFID tags also run the risk of unintentional temporary disablement caused by environmental conditions (example: ice/snow)

Relay Attacks: In a relay attack, an adversary acts as a man-in-the-middle and intercepts/modifies communication between legitimate components.

Similarly, threats can be identified for other important assets and entry points. Due to page limitation, we will not show

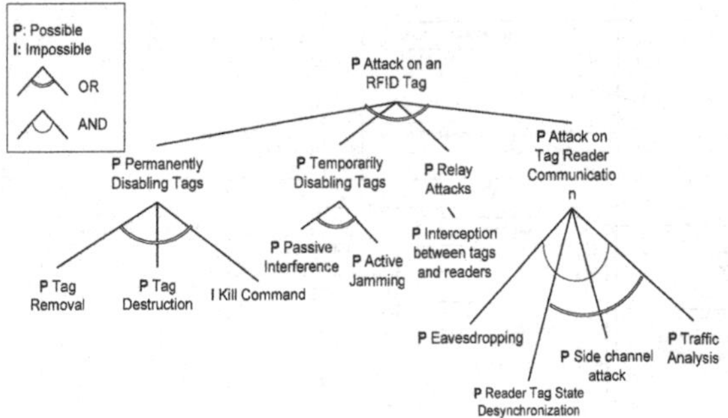

Figure 3: Attack Tree for RFID tag

Table 1: Threats related to assets

Assets	Major Threats
Reader	Impersonation, Eavesdropping, Relay Attack, Spoofing, Passive/ Active Interference, Unauthorized Tag Reading
Backend Database	Denial of Service Attack, Buffer Overflow Attack
RFID Server	Malicious Code Injection
Inter-enterprise Communications	Trust Relationship Misuse, Loss of Network Connection, Competitor Espionage

the detailed attack tree for each component. The major threats for each of those assets are listed in Table 1.

D. *Risk Management*

It is very difficult (if not impossible) to make the system perfectly secure from threats. Well organized attacks are just beyond what security experts can really expect. What we can do is identify the risk specific requirements that enable a system to survive attacks and recover from damages as soon as possible. Risk management is an essential step in survivability specification of the system. The objective of risk management is to systematically address the risks and decide how to cope with each of the threats. After the threats have been identified, it is necessary to prioritize them. Two simple ways of prioritizing the threats are to assess their likelihood and the consequent damage that can be caused by the threat. There are four ways of managing the risk [6]:

- *Accept the risk:* If the possibility of occurrence of a threat is low or it is too costly to mitigate, it can be accepted.
- *Transfer the risk:* Transfer the risk to someone else via insurance, warnings etc.
- *Remove the risk:* Remove the system component or feature associated with the risk if the feature is not worth the risk.
- *Mitigate the risk:* Reduce the risk with countermeasures.

In our example, some risks for the RFID system that can be accepted. For instance, the risk of malware can be accepted because the possibility of its occurrence is very low. The RFID system has various installed defense-in-depth mechanisms to prevent, detect, and remove malware. An example of risk that can be removed is the restriction of physical access to any important assets. Instead of allowing any access to the system remotely, it is more secure to restrict the access to the system from its current physical location. This removes all the corresponding threats related to remote access of important assets and the sensitive data they store. Finally several risks must be mitigated.

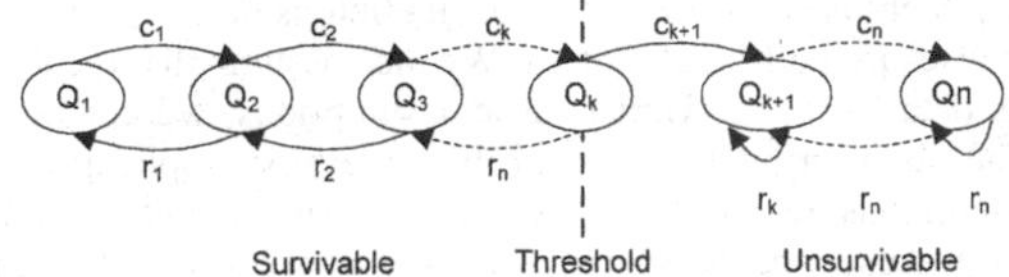

Figure 4: System survivability FSM

One example is a relay attack. By utilizing distance bounding authentication protocols, this risk can be mitigated.

The key for risk management is to identify those threats which could bring a system to an unsurvivable state. We have developed a finite state machine model (FSM) as shown in Figure 4 to show the effect of a particular threat on system survivability. To evaluate the risk level of a threat, a security expert may refer to this FSM to determine if a threat (or a combination of threats) could lead the system to an unsurvivable state. If so, the threat must be mitigated, transferred, or removed.

Figure 4 shows the system states under varying levels of compromise. For instance, state Q_0 represents the state where an RFID system is damage free. When an attack occurs, some degree of the system is damaged. Hence, the system transits to state Q_1. Each of the transition rates $c_1..c_n$ represent the probability that a threat can bring the system from one state to another. When such attacks continue, the system has a probability to transit from state Q_1 to Q_2. In the mean time, the system has a chance to recover as long as some recovery mechanisms are available. The transitions $r_1..r_n$ represent the probability of recovering the compromised components. For instance, while at system state Q_2, the system may have a chance to be recovered to a previous state. If the recovery r_2 is successful and the damage caused by the compromise attempt c_2 is reversed, the system transits back to the state Q_1. Similarly, when the damage caused by compromise c_1 is reversed the system comes back to the initial state Q_0 which again represents the state of fully recovered or the damage free state. All the recovery attempts are assumed to be successful for the attacks that bring the system to the state Q_k or any prior state. State Q_k is the threshold representing survivability break point. After the system reaches Q_k, it transitions into unsurvivable condition. At that point, the critical services cannot be provided and the system must be shut down for manual recovery. By using this model, security experts can identify which sets of risks must be mitigated (i.e., threats that bring the system to a state beyond the threshold Q_k) and which can be accepted (i.e. threats that cannot bring the system to a state beyond Q_k).

V. Mapping Threats to Survivability Requirements

Initial threat modeling reveals all the possible attacks. Risk analysis eliminated those attacks which only cause insignificant threats to system's survivability either because they are less likely to occur or the consequences of those attacks are not very severe. Next, survivability mapping identifies the requirements in terms of system survivability based on those severe attacks which could cause serious damages to affect the system's mission and critical services.

Various severe threats can bring the system to an unsurvivable state thereby hampering the system survivability. These threats must be removed or mitigated by specifying a set of survivability requirements. The set of survivability requirements, when enforced by implementing and deploying the appropriate techniques, can guarantee that the corresponding threat be eliminated. A survivability requirement mapping graph illustrates how we determine the survivability requirements given the severe threats in order to ensure system survivability.

A survivability requirement mapping graph is a directed graph $G = \{V, E\}$ where V represents a set of vertices and E represents a set of directed edges. Each vertex $v \in V$ represents one of these three types of nodes.

1. Survivability Goal Node: Such a node represents a target which is to be achieved in terms of system survivability.
2. Threat Node: Each threat node represents a threat to the survivability objective node.
3. Survivability requirements node: Each survivability requirement node represents a requirement that should be fulfilled in order to overcome the threat and achieve the corresponding survivability goal.

These three types of vertices appear in alternating pattern in a survivability requirement mapping graph G from the root to the leaves; i.e. goal nodes are followed by threat nodes which are followed by the corresponding requirement nodes.

Each weighted edge $e \in E$ in G represents a relationship between the two connected nodes. The relationship can be a contribution represented by the '+' signs or an inverse contribution represented by the '–'signs. By contribution we mean the relationship between two nodes. Positive contribution increases the chance of meeting the goal and inverse contribution decreases it. The severity of the contribution or inverse contribution is denoted by the number of '+' or '-'signs on the corresponding directed edge, respectively. For instance, the survivable goals of the RF subsystem positively contribute to survivability requirements of the entire RFID system as shown in Figure 5. On the other hand, the physical corruption of a tag negatively contributes to the survivability of an RF subsystem since any corruption of RFID tags can inversely affect the critical services of the RF subsystem. In Figure 5, we specify five requirements that, if satisfied, can ensure the tag's ability to resist malicious attacks. However, not all of the five requirements must be satisfied in the same time in order to make the tag attack resilient. We specify the mandatory/optional relationships among those 5 requirements. Those relationships are denoted by and symbols, respectively. As the figure shows, if physical access control function is applied to a tag, it negatively contributes to physical corruption of tags and thus positively contributes to survivability of the RF subsystem. In general, the following steps are applied to build a survivability requirements mapping graph.

1. Identify the major survivability goals of the system under consideration.
2. Refine the major goal to a set of sub goals necessary.
3. Enumerate possible threats that can affect each sub goal. The threats are identified by stepping through the critical components as discussed earlier. The set of threats can be refined at different levels of details.
4. For each threat listed in step 3, identify a set of the corresponding survivability requirements. Those requirements are necessary for the system to mitigate the threat. The implementation security survivability mechanisms based on those requirements effectively help a system survive in event of occurrence of the threat.
5. Categorize the survivability requirements in a set of categories.

In our example, we categorized the survivability requirements in the following categories: physical security, intrusion detection/response, robustness/fault tolerance, and completeness/soundness. Categorizing can help the system expert to perform analysis while focusing on the aspect of system that the requirement contributes to. Table 2 summarizes each survivability requirement category and its quantitative assessment for the assistance of system engineers.

Thus after performing the above five steps on our example RFID system, a survivability requirements mapping graph is developed as shown in Figure 5. The major goal identified for our example RFID system is to ensure the RFID system survivability. Refining this goal in a group of sub goals, we have survivability of RF subsystem, survivability of enterprise subsystem and survivability of inter-enterprise subsystem. Then a set of possible threats are specified which might hinder the sub goal listed in the previous step. From the figure, we can see that the possible threats that can affect the survivability of the RF subsystem include corruptions of readers, introduction of rogue or cloned readers, corruption of tags and compromise of tag-reader communication[2].Next, for each threat a set of survivability requirements are specified which, if satisfied, can help the system thwart the attacks. For example, in term of the threat "corruptions of reader", two survivability requirements are specified: prompt damage assessment/recovery and reader tamper resilience. Those two requirements should be satisfied at the same time (as shown by the in Figure 5) in order to ensure that the reader is tamper free. Finally we categorize the identified requirements based on their common features. For example, both reader tamper resilience and tag physical access control can be categorized into the "physical security" category. Detailed explanation of the requirement and its respective category can be found in Table 3.

We should point out that the survivability mapping graph as show in Figure 5 only represents the detailed threats, survivability requirements (and their categories) for the survivability goal of the RF subsystem. The survivability requirements for other subsystems are only briefly mentioned in the figure. We assume that the RFID enterprise sub-system can use standard security mechanisms such as digital signature and strong authentication to ensure RFID data confidentiality, integrity, and availability.

[2] The threats mentioned in the figure or in the content of this paper may not be a complete list of all the threats that could affect the security or survivability of an RFID system. The threats mentioned are identified based on our threat analysis. An advantage of survivability mapping graph is that more threats and the corresponding requirements can be added if the need arises.

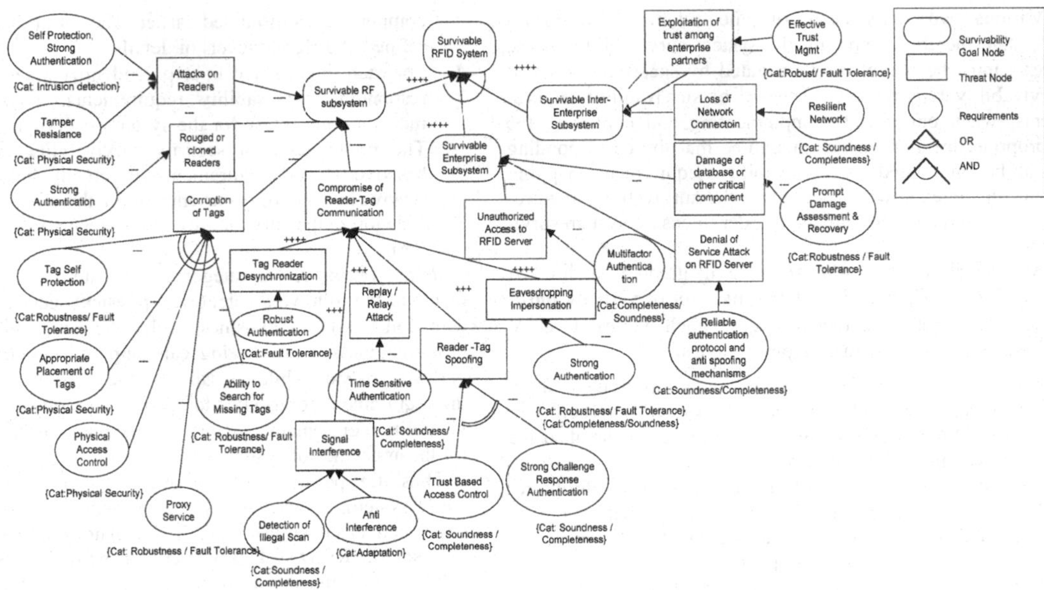

Figure 5: Survivability Requirement Mapping Graph

Table 2: Survivability Requirement Category Quantitative Assessment

Survivability Req. Category	Measurement	Category and Symbol Explanation
Physical Security	$\forall C \in Components(SY$ $Pr(Corruption(C)) \le$	The ability of the RFID system to resist physical attacks. It can be measured as follows: For every component C in the component set of system SYS. the possibility of physically corrupting the component is lower than a pre-defined value α ($0 \le \alpha \le 1$)
Robust-ness/Fault Tolerance	$\frac{N - N_C}{N} > \beta$	The ability of an RFID system to with-stand devastating attacks. It can be measured as a ratio of the difference between the total number of components N and the number of compromised components N_C divided by N at a given moment. The system is resistant to deadly attack if and only if this ratio is larger than a threshold β (the required minimum number of components to support the critical services is maintained).
Intrusion Detection	$Max(DetectionTime($ $Avg(AssessmentTime$ $Max(ResponseTime($	The ability of an RFID system to detect attack *A* promptly (measured by the time for the system to recognize A), evaluate the extent of damage (measured by the time for system to perform survivability analysis and damage assessment) and adjust its behavior (measured by the time for system to respond). System meets the survivability requirements if those parameters are below certain levels.
Sound-ness/Complete ness	$Pr(Accept(c)) \| c \notin Co$ $Pr(Reject(c)) \| c \in Com$	The possibility of acceptance of a component not belonging to the system is negligible (δ is a threshold) –soundness. The possibility of rejecting a legitimate component *c* is negligible (δ' is a threshold) –completeness.

Table 2 provides a summary of categories of the identified survivability requirements as shown in Figure 5 and the quantitative assessments for each category. We use the first order predicate to represent symbols in the measurements. The table lists each survivability requirement, a measurement and the explanation of the notation used in measurement.

Table 3: Survivability Requirements Summery

Survivability Requirements	**Category**	**Explanation**
Tamper Resilience Tag Self Protection	Physical Security	The requirement for an RFID component to be physically resilient to damage and attacks (mechanisms which satisfy this requirements include physical unclonable functions, tag password protection, tag disable in case of emergency situations).
Appropriate Placement of Tags	Physical Security	The requirement for the RFID system to appropriately deploy RFID tags such that physical access or close contact of the tags by the adversary is almost impossible. Placement of tags should also consider such factors as fault tolerance since high correlation of RFID tags make it possible for tag data inference to effectively recover or mask damage of individual tags.
Physical Access Control	Physical Security	The requirement to control and monitor physical premier of RFID infrastructure. For instance, illegal scans of tags by unknown readers should be detected and prevented.
Proxy Service	Robustness / Fault Tolerance	The requirement for the RFID system to strategically deploy relatively more powerful proxy servers (e.g. special readers) to shield and protect low-cost tags. For instance, an RFID system may use proxy servers to respond to tag scans from unknown readers on behalf of the tags to be protected. Each proxy server simulates tags by continuously relabeling their IDs
Ability to Search for Missing Tags	Robustness / Fault Tolerance	The requirement for the RFID system to automatically assess the current status of current tags in the system and detection of any missing tags, tag fraud or tag theft.
Robust Authentication	Robustness / Fault Toler-	The requirement for the mutual authentication protocols between RFID system components to be

	ance	robust against various anomalies such as tag-reader desynchronization and side channel attacks.
Network Reliability and Resilience	Robustness / Fault Tolerance	The requirement for the enterprise or inter-enterprise networks (wired / wireless) to be reliable and resilient to common attacks.
Prompt Damage Recovery	Robustness / Fault Tolerance	The requirement for the RFID system and its component to quickly recover from damage and restore to a health state.
Anti spoofing and anti impersonation	Intrusion Detection/ Response	The requirement for the RFID system to detect rouged and cloned readers by the mechanisms such as behavior observation, data reading analysis and non-self detection.
Strong Authentication, Trust based access control	Soundness/ Completeness	The requirement for strong and reliable authentication protocol tag, reader, RFID server and backend database
Time Sensitive Authentication	Soundness/ Completeness	The requirement for the RFID system to perform time sensitive or distance bounding mechanisms to detect and /or prevent relay attacks.
Protocol and anti-spoofing mechanisms	Intrusion Detection/ Response	The requirement for the RFID system to secure hosts, disallow IP spoofing, disallow ICMP broadcast/multicast addresses from outsiders, tighten firewalls, be vigilant/observant and communicate with peers.
Trust Management	Soundness/ Completeness	The requirement for the RFID inter-enterprise systems to conduct effective trust initiation, trust update and trust management among enterprise partners.
Anti-Interference	Robustness/ Fault tolerance	The requirement for the RFID system to provide adaptive and robust communication protocols by using different frequency bands, spread spectrums and collision arbitration process, multiple channels and different modulation techniques in different environments.

Table 3 summarizes the survivability requirements identified in the survivability requirements mapping graph shown in Figure 5. The table enumerates each survivability requirement, its category and a brief explanation. These tables can assist system experts to incorporate the requirements in their development cycle.

Survivability mapping graph thus provides an effective method of mapping survivability goals to a set of survivability requirements based on the identified threats. Categories of the survivability requirements can be expanded to include different aspects of a desirable system from the survivability point view. This method allows the system engineers to assess system survivability and ensure that the system can provide critical services in face of malicious attacks.

VI. Conclusion

Enumerating survivability requirements through the threat modeling is crucial in empowering a system's ability to withstand devastating attacks. RFID has been applied in various high security and high integrity settings. Given various attacks to an RFID system, it is crucial to develop a formal model to specify survivability requirements in order to make such a system more robust and resilient. In the proposed framework, threat modeling using attack trees provides preliminary insights into all the possible threats to an RFID system. Risk analysis identifies those devastating attacks which could render an RFID system unsurvivable. Then, system survivability requirements are specified based on those identified attacks. These survivability requirements, if implemented, can significantly improve the RFID system's survivability. From system engineering perspective, RFID application vendors and system designers can incorporate those survivability requirements into their software and hardware development cycles. Categorizing the requirements into major categories not only provides a systematic way to organize survivability requirements from users' perspective but also provides the guidelines for the system vendors to develop the most effective security/survivability mechanisms to satisfy the survivability requirements as specified by the users in each category.

Acknowledgement

The authors are thankful to Dr. Robert Herklotz for his support, which made this work possible.

References

[1] Y. Zuo, "Secure and private search protocols for RFID systems", *Information System Frontiers: A Journal for Innovation and Research*, Springer Netherlands, 2009.

[2] M. Hoque, F. Rahman, and S. Ahamed, "Supporting Recovery, Privacy and Security in RFID Systems using a Robust Authentication Protocol", *The 2009 ACM Symposium on Applied Computing*, 2009.

[3] B. Glover, and H. Bhatt, "RFID Essentials", O'Reilly Publisher, 2006.

[4] V. Westmark, "A Definition for Information System Survivability", *The 37th Hawaii International Conference on System Sciences*, 2004.

[5] W. Yurcik, D. Doss, and H. Kruse. "Survivability- Over-Security: Providing Whole System Assurance", *IEEE/SEI/CERT Information Survivability Workshop*, 2004, pp. 201-204.

[6] S. Myagmar, A. Lee, and W. Yurcik, "Threat Modelling as a Basis for Security Requirements", *Symposium on Requirements Engineering for Inforamtion Security (SREIS)*, 2006.

[7] E. Oladimeji, S. Supakkul, and L. Chung, "Security Threat Modeling and Analysis: A Goal Oriented Approach", *The 10th IASTED International Conference on Software*, 2006.

[8] R. Ellison, D. Fisher, R. Linger, and H. Lipson, "Survivable Network Systems: An Emerging Discipline", Technical Report, Carnegie Mellon University , 1997. CMU/SEI-97-TR-013.

[9] J. Knight, E. Strunk and K Sullivan, "Towards a Rigorous Definition of Information System Survivability", *DARPA Information Survivability Conference and Exposition*, 2003, Washington D.C., USA.

[10] M. Hiltunen, R. Schlichting, C. Ugarte and G. Wong, "Survivability Through Customization and Adaptability: The Cactus Approach", *DARPA Information Survivability Conference and Exposition*, 2000, pp. 243-307.

[11] M. Deutsch and R. Willis, "Software Quality Engineering: A Total Technical and Management Approach", NJ : Prentice Hall, 1988.

[12] B. Thiraisingham and J. Maurer, "Information Survivability for Evolvable and Adaptable Real-time Command Control Systems", *IEEE Transactions on Knowledge and Data Engineering*, Jan./Feb. 1999, 11(1), pp. 228-238.

[13] E. Strunk and J. Knight, "Dependability Through Assured Reconfiguration in Embedded Systems Software", *IEEE Transactions Dependable and Secure Computing*, 3(3), July 2006, pp. 172-187.

[14] A. Snow, U. Varshney and A. Malloy, "Reliablility and Survivability of Wireless and Mobile Networks", *IEEE Computer*, 33(7), July 2000, pp. 49-55.

[15] N. Mead, "Requirements Engineering for Survivable Systems", Carnegie Melon University, 2003.

[16] B. Schneier, "Attack Trees", *Dr. Dobb's Journal of Software Tools* 24, December 1999, pp. 12-29.

[17] A. Mitrokotsa, M. Rieback and A. Tanenbaum, "Classification of RFID Attacks", *Information System Frontiers: A Journal for Innovation and Research*, Springer Netherlands, 2009.

[18] C. Williams, R. Bhaumik, R. Burke, and B. Mobasher, "The Impact of Attack Profile Classification on the Robustness of Collaborative Recommendation", *WEBKDD '06*, 2006, Philadelphia, PA, USA.

[19] B. Schneier, "Secrets and lies : Digital Security in a Networked World", New York, NJ : John Wiley & Sons, 2009.

[20] F. Swiderski and W. Snyder, "Threat Modeling", Microsoft Press, 2004.

[21] M. Rieback, B. Crispo, and A. Tanenbaum, "Is Your Cat Infected with a Computer Virus?" *4th IEEE International Conference on Pervasive Computing and Communications*, 2006. pp. 169–179

The State of Knowledge Management in Czech Companies

P. Maresova, M. Hedvicakova
Department of Economics
Faculty of Informatics and Management, University of Hradec Kralove
Rokitanskeho 62, 500 03 Hradec Kralove, Czech Republic

Abstract - In the globalised world, Czech economy faces many challenges brought by the processes of integration. The crucial factors for companies that want to succeed in the global competition are knowledge and abilities to use the knowledge in the best possible way. The purpose of the work is a familiarization with the results of a questionnaire survey with the topic of "Research of the state of knowledge management in companies in the Czech Republic" realized in the spring 2009 in the cooperation of the University of Hradec Králové and the consulting company *Per Partes Consulting, Ltd* under the patronage of the European Union.

I. INTRODUCTION

It is characteristic of the enterprising environment in the Czech Republic that competition has been growing, one of the causes of this being globalization and the related expansion of the free market. One of the basic preconditions for the competitive ability are innovations and speed of companies in innovation processes. Knowledge has been becoming the most important form of capital of a company, traditional capital resources (money, land, technologies) depend on knowledge capital and this dependency has been increasingly deepening. Knowledge needs of organizations have been growing, they have become a strategic resource indispensable for achievement of an enterprising success. The more the need of knowledge grows, the more grows the significance of knowledge management as a tool to manage knowledge in organisations. Knowledge management is the tool which can, to a great extent, determine the near future of Czech companies. Also information and communication technologies play important roles in effective work in the area of knowledge management. The purpose of this paper thus is to make the reader more familiar with the state of knowledge management in Czech companies, with their interest in this issue and with potential barriers of introduction of knowledge management. Further also with the possibilities of use of modern technologies - often already existing in companies - in the area of knowledge management.

II. KNOWLEDGE MANAGEMENT AND THE PRESENT TIME

Knowledge management has become a current topic in the beginning of the 21st century. The attention paid to knowledge and its management has been dramatically growing all over the world. In the area of knowledge management, many researchers have been taking place with various focus ([8], [6], [3], [11], [7], [4], [2], [10], [5]) for example research of suitability of tools for support of knowledge management, application of knowledge management in enterprising environment, development of knowledge management at the academic field etc. There is also a research work called „Directions and trends in research of knowledge“ realised by Georg M. Giaglis from Aegean University in Greece, which explored more than two hundred projects from the are of knowledge management realised within the European Union. Conclusions of the research showed that although it concerns a very prospective area, there are still substantial gaps. These include the fact that the technical infrastructure is not prepared for work with knowledge, saturation with unnecessary knowledge, unwillingness of co-workers to share knowledge or disagreement about benefits of knowledge management in organisations. A no less important problem is how to ascertain efficiency of introduction of knowledge management. In the past, many initiatives in the area of knowledge management consisted in making a great amount of knowledge accessible to a great number of people. However, efficiency of similar widely based initiatives is uncertain and difficult to be measured.

The development of interest in this issue is evidenced by many publications with this focus. As it is shown by the research mentioned in [9], knowledge management is still the forefront issue especially at the academic field. Publications with this topic coming from the corporate sector are still very scarce. This is confirmed by the fact that the pace of introduction of knowledge management as a subject in corresponding study programs has been higher in the past few years than its introduction as a managerial approach in the corporate sphere.

Interest in the knowledge management from the part of the private sector is evidenced by various researches (e.g. [10]) dealing with the fact how companies direct their focus on human capital and the related innovations, knowledge, its creation, storage and sharing. There are more and more companies offering remuneration for innovation and team management, evaluating changes in skills, in knowledge, in procedures etc. In the private sector, the number of consulting companies offering professional consulting for projects of knowledge management has been growing. Not even the newly emerging departments with focus on knowledge management in leading software companies, such as Lotus, Oracle, Microsoft, have been falling behind. A great amount of pages dealing with this issue can be found on the internet. Software companies create new modules for their solutions, focused specifically on projects of knowledge management.

T. Sobh, K. Elleithy (eds.), *Innovations in Computing Sciences and Software Engineering*,
DOI 10.1007/978-90-481-9112-3_27,

It is obvious from the above mentioned statistics that although knowledge management is a young and still developing discipline, its introduction is meaningful and beneficial. This was the reason for realisation of the research titled „ Research of the state of knowledge management in companies in the Czech Republic", the purpose of which was a familiarisation with the state of knowledge management in Czech companies, with the interest in this issue and with potential barriers of introduction of knowledge management.

III. RESEARCH OF THE STATE OF KNOWLEDGE MANAGEMENT IN CZECH COMPANIES

In 2009, a questionnaire survey was realised dealing with the topic of „Research of the state of knowledge management in companies in the Czech". This survey aimed to chart the current attitudes of companies to knowledge management. The survey was conducted in cooperation with the University of Hradec Králové, consulting company Per Partes Constulting, s.r.o and under the patronage of the European Union. 1000 organisations active in the Czech Republic were addressed in total, across all industries with the focus on medium and big companies. 132 filled-out questionnaires were acquired. The aim was to find out what makes companies to be interested in knowledge management, what phase of its use they find themselves in, and also how knowledge is acquired, shared and managed in companies. A no less important area concerned barriers preventing full application of the principles of knowledge management.

With each of the questions, respondents were able to choose from several answers, or they could answer in their own words. They could mark more possibilities both from the point of view of the current situation and from the point of view of what they are planning for future in the horizon of three years. For these reasons, the sum of the percentages mentioned in individual answers may surpass a hundred percent. The purpose of the questions formulated in such way was to find out whether companies would like to deal with the given issue even in the future and if so, whether with greater or lesser intensity.

IV. ANALYSIS OF ANSWERS OF RESPONDENTS

Reasons for introduction of knowledge management

The main motive for the focus on knowledge management in most Czech companies is reduction of costs (44%) and response to the growing abilities of competition in the area of work with knowledge (42%) (see Figure 1). These two factors show that companies are considering the significance of work with knowledge both from the perspective of possibility of more savings and greater efficiency and also from the perspective of the fact that in case of omitting work with knowledge, there is a threat of falling behind the competition.

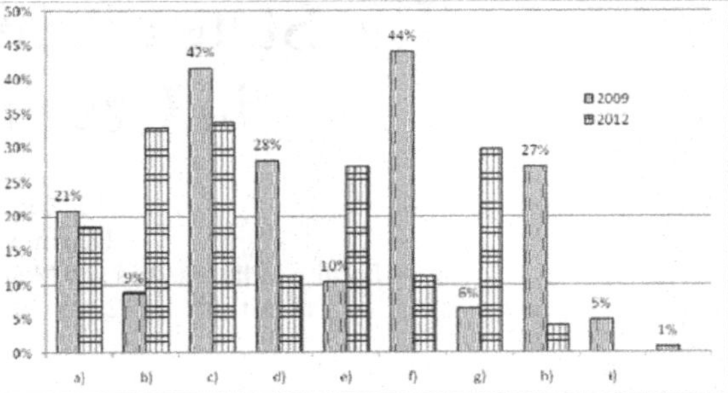

a) increasing the role of intangible intellectual assets in the efficiency of enterprising
b) expected arrival of knowledge of economy in countries with expensive workforce (such as CZR)
c) responses to growing abilities of the competition in this area
d) a growing need of development of individualised and customised products and services
e) need to integrate knowledge into products/services and to achieve their artificial intelligence in the sense of the ability to carry out a dialogue with a human being
f) reduction of internal costs due to an enhanced flow of knowledge about corporate processes
g) elicitation of a need to share knowledge in the network of alliance partners
h) taking advantage of possibilities offered by information technologies
i) pointing out the significance of intellectual capital of EU and determining the year 2009 as the year of creativity and activeness

Fig. 1. Reasons for introduction of knowledge management

Other significant impulses motivating companies to focus their attention in this direction are:

- the growing need of development of individualised and customised products and services,
- taking advantage of the possibilities offered by information technologies,
- need to integrate knowledge into products/services and to achieve their artificial intelligence in the sense of the ability to carry out a dialogue with a human being.

In future, knowledge management will be interesting for companies due to its possibility to create customised products according to wishes of customers and it will also be attractive as a means, in which companies will be able to compete its products against countries with inexpensive workforce.

Crucial knowledge in organisations

Research confirmed that nowadays crucial types of knowledge, viewed as priorities by companies, in three large areas are the following (see Figure 2):

- knowledge of customers and their needs,
- knowledge of the market and of market possibilities and
- knowledge of the competition and its strategy.

Companies are interested in their employees' knowledge to a lesser extent (25%). This is an unfavourable phenomenon from the perspective of knowledge management, as the very employees and their know-how can be a source of a big competitive advantage.

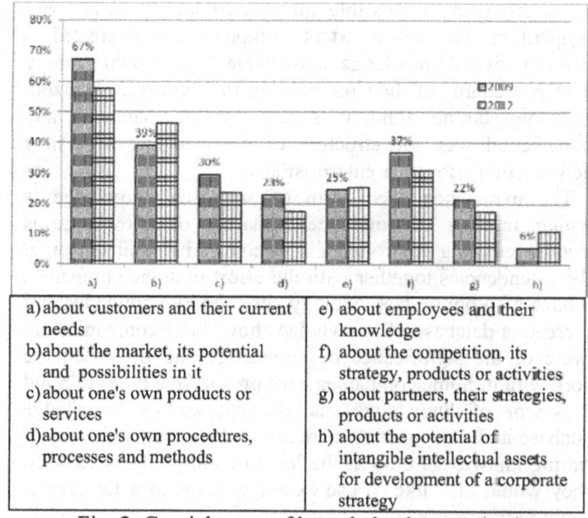

a) about customers and their current needs	e) about employees and their knowledge
b) about the market, its potential and possibilities in it	f) about the competition, its strategy, products or activities
c) about one's own products or services	g) about partners, their strategies, products or activities
d) about one's own procedures, processes and methods	h) about the potential of intangible intellectual assets for development of a corporate strategy

Fig. 2. Crucial types of knowledge in organisations

Companies mention knowledge about the potential of intangible intellectual assets for development of a corporate strategy (6%) as an insignificant area of interest. This again corresponds to the lesser interest in employees' knowledge and thus to the low activity in the area of work with one's own knowledge assets. Companies deal almost to the same extent with strategies and activities of their partner organisations (25%) and with their own established processes and strategies (23%).

In the three-year horizon, companies do not view it as necessary to change in a fundamental manner the infrastructure of the knowledge, which they consider crucial for their enterprising. They expect that a greater accent will be put on knowledge about market possibilities as opposed to the currently preferred knowledge about customer needs.

Acquiring and sharing knowledge

The main mentioned manner of acquiring knowledge is regular training of employees (61%). Sharing of knowledge is supported by a controlled discussion or by brainstorming (33%) and by sharing documents in the information system (30%)(see Figure 3). These tendencies together with the effort of some companies to enrich the corporate methodology by means of knowledge (20%) and to create a database of knowledge (11%) show those companies are not aware of the significance of knowledge and of systematic work with knowledge. On the other hand there is that considerable percentage of answers from the survey, which do not evidence this fact. This concerns respondents who wrote that knowledge are shared above all by an informal discussion in teams (61%). Further the fact that new knowledge is acquired by purchase from the outside (15%) indicates an opposite tendency in relation with knowledge management. In general, this phenomenon is unfavorable, as in the very knowledge of one's own employees one can find a big corporate potential, by means of which one can gain a competitive advantage.

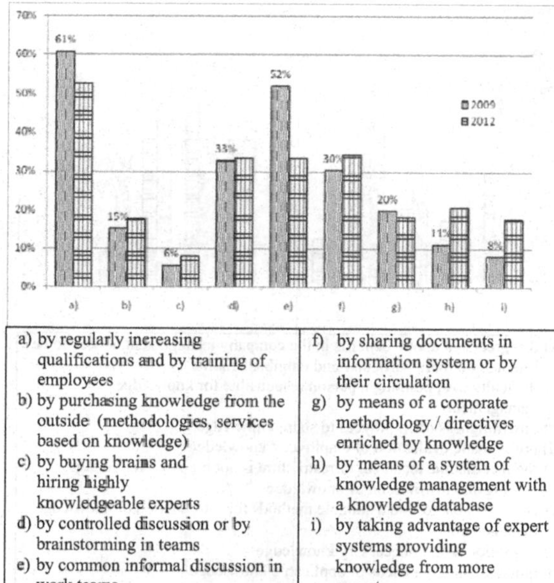

a) by regularly increasing qualifications and by training of employees	f) by sharing documents in information system or by their circulation
b) by purchasing knowledge from the outside (methodologies, services based on knowledge)	g) by means of a corporate methodology / directives enriched by knowledge
c) by buying brains and hiring highly knowledgeable experts	h) by means of a system of knowledge management with a knowledge database
d) by controlled discussion or by brainstorming in teams	i) by taking advantage of expert systems providing knowledge from more experts
e) by common informal discussion in work teams	

Fig. 3. Acquiring and sharing knowledge

Prospective plans of the companies include building of a system of knowledge management and of a knowledge database (21%) and companies would like to markedly reduce their practices of sharing knowledge only at the level of informal discussions (now already 34% as opposed to the current state of 52%). They would also like to use expert systems to a greater extent in their work (18%). Overall, those facts can be summarised thus: companies plan to dedicate more attention to knowledge management and to a systematic work with knowledge.

Barriers of knowledge management

Respondents stated that the greatest barrier is a problematic evaluation of employees' knowledge (30%), further the problem that the company's management has to discern benefits of knowledge management and their tangibility (29%). This category may also include the answer about the uncertainty of the return on investments into knowledge management (25%)(see Figure 4). All these factors indicate that the issue of „measurement"of knowledge management and its benefits should be solved. As it was already said, there are often benefits of a qualitative character. This does not mean that they are less important than quantitative benefits, but it is far more difficult to find a specific definition for them. This particular obstacle has a very unfavorable impact on focus of companies on knowledge management.

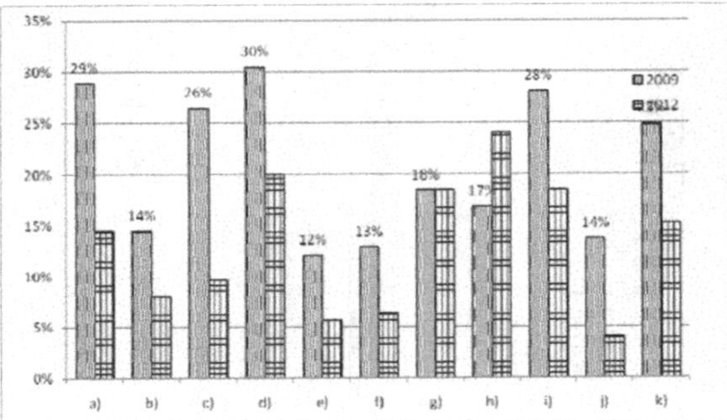

a) disagreement about benefits in the company management, a need to be oriented on more particular and tangible benefits
b) difficulty in appointing a person responsible for knowledge management
c) unwillingness of employees to share knowledge
d) problematic evaluation of employees' knowledge
e) the fact that the technical infrastructure is not prepared for storage, sharing and distribution of knowledge
f) not to be able to find a suitable methods for introduction of knowledge management
g) saturation with unnecessary knowledge
h) quickly changing needs of applicable knowledge
i) insufficient time for activities with a longer period of return
j) expensiveness of introducing knowledge management
k) uncertain return of investments

Fig. 4. Barriers of knowledge management

Another significant barrier is on the part of the employee, for example unwillingness of employees to share knowledge (26%).

Other barriers are, from the perspective of their significance, approximately at the same level. They also include:

- quickly changing needs of applicable knowledge,
- saturation with unnecessary knowledge and thus the necessity to sort them out,
- expensiveness of introduction of knowledge management, etc.

Another barrier is also the fact that the technical infrastructure is not prepared. This factor does not rank among the first places, nonetheless it deserves a special attention in the current times of modern information and communication technologies existing in most Czech companies.

From the point of view of the near future, the worry about potential barriers against introduction of knowledge management has been generally decreasing. There is only a worry about the ability to cope with quickly changing needs of applicable knowledge.

V. SUMMARY OF THE QUESTIONNAIRE SURVEY

The questionnaire survey realised on the sample of 132 companies residing in the Czech Republic aimed to chart the situation of knowledge management. Respondents were medium and big companies across all industries.

It was ascertained from the answers that nowadays companies consider it their priority and crucial knowledge to know as much as possible about customers, market and competition. To a lesser extent, companies are interested in their employees' knowledge, knowledge of their own strategy or of procedures of their partners. In the three-year horizon, companies do not think it is necessary to change in any fundamental way the structure of knowledge, which they view as crucial for their enterprising.

The main mentioned form of acquiring knowledge is regular training of employees. Sharing of knowledge is encouraged by a controlled discussion or by brainstorming. These tendencies together with the effort of some companies to have a corporate methodology enriched by knowledge and to create a database of knowledge show those companies are aware of the significance of knowledge and of systematic work with it. Some companies have prospective plans to build a system of knowledge management and a knowledge database and they want to markedly reduce their practices of sharing knowledge only at the level of informal discussions. They would also like to use expert systems to a far greater extent in their work.

Further, it was apparent from the answer of the respondents that in most cases, knowledge management is not introduced as a whole in companies and the top management leaves this area in the competence of company divisions. Acquiring of knowledge is mostly the task of an employee as an individual. However, in future, companies plan relatively extensive changes from the point of view of use of knowledge. First of all, acquiring of knowledge will be increasingly less dependent only on initiatives of each employee and knowledge will not be administered only within individual company divisions. Companies will focus more on possible benefits of knowledge management and almost 30% respondents stated that they plan to create an overall company strategy for knowledge management.

Respondents stated that the greatest barrier for knowledge management is a problematic evaluation of employees' knowledge. Another barrier was also an inefficient use of available modern technologies in the area of knowledge management and of investments into knowledge management. In the framework of answers concerning this issue in the near future (answers for the year 2012), the worry about potential barriers against introduction of knowledge management has been generally decreasing. Only the worry about the ability to cope with quickly changing needs of applicable knowledge has remained the same.

It can be concluded from the text above that companies are interested in knowledge management, they see its possible use even in future and they are interested to deal with it more than they have done so far. One of the problems they see in this area is especially connected with the ability to use modern information and communication technologies in the are of knowledge management. Technologies suitable for this issue and individual phases of introduction of knowledge management are mentioned in the following overview.

VI. THE SELECTED INFORMATION AND COMMUNICATION TECHNOLOGIES FOR KNOWLEDGE MANAGEMENT

A significant tool in the area of knowledge management is modern information and communication technologies complemented by a suitable software. The software can be helpful in each phase of introduction of knowledge management, it is a fundamental component of an already established knowledge management. The task of individual information, communication and knowledge technologies is for example to secure mutual interconnection of people, interconnection of people with knowledge and a conversion of data into knowledge. The following lines include technologies that could be used in the given phase of introduction of knowledge management. Many technologies can be used in more phases. Introduction of knowledge management can be for example - according to [1] - divided into four basic steps: set-up of an implementation team, analysis of the initial state, creation of a knowledge strategy and implementation of activities of knowledge management. According to activities in each step, corresponding technologies can be recommended.

Set-up of an implementation team

- systems for support of decision-making – Expert Choice, Criterion/ Standard Decision Plus, etc.
- brainstorming applications,
- discussion systems – these systems support sharing of information and knowledge mostly by members of a particular community. These systems make it possible to acquire answers to questions, tips, lesson learned etc.
- CMS (Capability Management Systems) – these systems are sometimes known as Yellow Pages. The systems enable members of an organisation to find out „who knows what", for they can provide information about skills, abilities, experience, achieved education etc.

Analysis of the initial state

- Systems for document administration,
- intelligent agents – this concerns specialised software systems, which are mostly a part of larger systems. The main task of intelligent agents is to provide assistance to people (or to other agents) in various activities.
- Lessons Learned Systems – these systems provide access to a database, where you can find experience related to solving of common problems,
- analytic OLAP applications (MIS, EIS),

Creation of a knowledge strategy

- EDMS (Electronic Document Management Systems) – these systems enable employees to access existing documents more easily,
- expert systems – these systems simulate decision-making of a human expert. Their usefulness was proven for example in situations, in which a great deal of knowledge is necessary to decide about a solution of a problem.
- Knowledge Discovery Systems – these systems explore large databases for the purpose of finding potentially useful information or knowledge,
- products used for project management.

Implementation of activities of knowledge management

The technologies with respect to particular activities of knowledge management will be used in this phase. However, it should generally hold true that all technologies must be integrated into the overall infrastructure of knowledge management. This will secure a more efficient approach of working with data and knowledge and this will bring subsequent benefits for the organisation.

It is obvious from the text above that modern technologies can be used in any phase of introduction of knowledge management, in which a company finds itself in. This will facilitate many activities accelerate communication and access to data and subsequently save costs and increase efficiency of work.

VII. CONCLUSION

Today, high-quality and suitably managed knowledge in an organisation is necessary for the organisation's effective functioning, it has been becoming a significant competitive advantage and it is therefore an efficient tool of competitive fight. Knowledge management provides a certain set of instructions how to work with knowledge.

The purpose of this paper was a familiarisation with the state of knowledge management in Czech companies and with their interest in this issue. As it followed from the survey, Czech companies are interested in the issue, but they come across many obstacles, which finally discourage them from its consistent implementation. One of the problems they see in this area is mainly connected with the ability to take advantage of modern information and communication technologies in the are of knowledge management. Within the horizon of three years, companies plan to deal with knowledge management far more intensively and also to remove potential barriers of its introduction.

REFERENCES

[1] V. Bures, Knowledge management and process of its implementation (Znalostní management a proces jeho zavádění – Průvodce pro praxi), Grada Publishing, 2007, s.216, ISBN 8024719788

[2] J.CH.Chena, J.W. Huang, "How organisational climate and structure affect knowledge management - The social interaction perspective", in International Journal of Information Management, 2007, doi:10.1016/j.ijinfomgt.2006.11.001

[3] G. Dhillon, " Organizational competence for harnessing IT: A case study", in *Information & Management*, vol. 45, 2008,pp. 297–303.

[4] I. M.Faniel, A. Majchrzak, " Innovating by accessing knowledge across departments", in *Decision Support Systems*, vol. 43, 2007, pp.1684–1691.

[5] G. Heijst, R. Spek, E. Kruizinga, " Corporate Memories as a Tool for Knowledge Management", vol. 13, 1997, pp.41-54.

[6] C.W. Holsapple, K.D. Joshi, "Organizational knowledge resources", in *Decision Support Systems*, vol.3, 2001, pp.39–54.

[7] I. Ch Hsu, "Knowledge sharing practices as a facilitating factor for improving organisational performance through human capital: A preliminary test",in *Expert Systems with Applications*, vol. 35, 2008, pp.1316–1326.

[8] R. Maier, Knowledge Management Systems, Berlin-Heidelberg, 2007, s. 720, ISBN 978-3-540-71407-1.

[9] A. Perrin, *Knowledge Management: Publications in Knowledge Management*, 2006, [on-line]. Available from http://km.typepad.com/index/2006/10/publications_in.html.

[10] K. Y. Wonga, E. Aspinwallb, "Development of a knowledge management initiative and system: A case study", in *Expert Systems with Applications,* vol. 30, 2006,pp. 633–641.

[11] J.H. Wu, Y. M. Wang, " Measuring KMS success: A respecification of the DeLone and McLean's model", in *Information & Management,* vol. 43, 2006, pp. 728–739.

A Suitable Software Process Improvement Model for the UK Healthcare Industry

Tien D. Nguyen, Hong Guo, Raouf N.G. Naguib
Biomedical Computing and Engineering Technologies (BIOCORE) Applied Research Group,
Faculty of Engineering and Computing and Health Design & Technology Institute (HDTI),
Coventry University, CV1 5FB, UK

***Abstract* - Over the recent years, the UK Healthcare sector has been the prime focus of many reports and industrial surveys, particularly in the field of software development and management issues. This signals the importance of growing concerns regarding quality issues in the Healthcare domain. In response to this, a new tailored Healthcare Process Improvement (SPI) model is proposed, which takes into consideration both signals from the industry and insights from literature.**

This paper discusses and outlines the development of a new software process assessment and improvement model based on ISO/IEC 15504-5 model. The proposed model will provide the Healthcare sector with newly specific process practices that focus on addressing current development concerns, standard compliances and quality dimension requirements for this domain.

I. Introduction

Software has become an important part of almost every product being developed today. It is embedded in the environment we live in and provides vital functions for our welfare and safety. In an area such as Healthcare, software plays a critical role in delivering safer care for patients and improving job satisfaction for the frontline professionals.

In the past, the Healthcare industry has been put under the microscope with some well-known software disasters caused by poor design and implementation, for example: the Therac-25 (a machine used in radiation therapy for cancer patients) case which cost six people's lives [1]. The high-profile London Ambulance Service failure is merely the best-documented among many other unsuccessful Healthcare IT projects the designers of which failed to pay enough attention to the impacts that the new software systems could bring to working practices [2]. Today, the ongoing UK National Programme for IT (NPfIT) project, branded as the World's largest computer project [3], has already faced many issues and challenges in keeping up with the budget, timescale and technical requirements, which are well documented in many recent reports and studies [4-6].

A recent survey undertaken by the author suggests that Healthcare development issues are not only attributable to the size or the technical challenges, but more frequently down to the management of software users, mainly in the areas which require collaboration between supplier and customer, such as requirement, change and implementation management processes [7]. In addition, there are other issues ranging from specific technical concerns such as security and interoperability to wider organizational and people challenges [8]. These elements in combination suggest that developing and implementing Healthcare applications are extremely daunting and in serious trouble [9].

Software quality can be enhanced or improved in a number of ways. For example, it can be improved by carrying out testing procedures or quality reviews which allow errors to be eliminated at an early stage. Quality improvement is also achievable by improving processes such that the generation of errors can be avoided. This is where the Software Process Improvement (SPI) approach comes into play, acknowledging that the quality of a software system is greatly influenced by the quality of the processes that produced it. There have been over 1,000 studies on software process improvement in the IEEE database to date. A search for "*ISO/IEC 15504*" resulted in 4960 hits in June 2003 but increased to nearly 50,000 hits in October 2005 [10]. The Software Engineering Institute also reported 3,113 formal Capability Maturity Model (CMM) appraisals carried out by 2,674 organizations world-wide for the period April 2002 – December 2007 [11]. This substantial increase in SPI awareness confirms the growth in interest and adoption of these standards. As more organizations are initiating SPI efforts for internal process improvement, SPI is becoming a driving force in the global software industry [12].

With the complexity of patient care delivery, which involves the coordination and management of a large number of highly specialized, distributed personnel and information from various sources, software practitioners must be careful about oversimplifying the parallels between Healthcare and manufacturing and other services industries [13]. Meeting the challenges of ensuring high quality software product delivery in the Healthcare environment will require innovative uses, tailoring and customizations of existing SPI tools. A new SPI model that can work seamlessly with improvements on current management issues and at the same time incorporate industry best practices to support Healthcare development requirements is urgently needed.

The following sections explain the development processes of the proposed Healthcare SPI model.

II. Current SPI Models

Although SPI has become very popular amongst software practitioners nowadays, it is a relatively new concept which was only developed since the early 90s. Most ideas in SPI were adopted from theories and methodologies for improving quality in manufacturing systems by Demin, Crosby and Juran [14-16].

T. Sobh, K. Elleithy (eds.), *Innovations in Computing Sciences and Software Engineering*,
DOI 10.1007/978-90-481-9112-3_28, © Springer Science+Business Media B.V. 2010

This approach identifies best practices for the management of software engineering and provides methods for assessing an organization's capability and maturity level. Currently, there are two most commonly used models in the software industry: the CMMI and the ISO/IEC 15504.

The Capability Maturity Model (CMM) was originally developed for assessing the capability of the US Department of Defence contractors, but it soon became a reference guide for software process development improvement. The further enhancement of the initial CMM were stopped and development efforts were directed from 1998 onwards to the Capability Maturity Model – Integrated [17]. Capability Maturity Model Integration for Development (CMMI-DEV), Version 1.2 is a continuation and update of CMMI [18]. The Software Engineering Institute is now planning Version 1.3 of the CMMI Product Suite which will likely be released in 2010.

ISO/IEC 15504, also called SPICE (Software Process Improvement and Capability dEtermination), is a project granted by the International Committee on Software Engineering Standards ISO/IEC JTC 1/SC7. Its initial version, Version 1.0, was released in 1995 as a Technical Report (draft standard), which became the basis for the development of the ISO/IEC TR 15504 released in 1998. The current version is renamed to ISO/IEC 15504 which comprises of eight parts. The next generation of SPICE will be replaced with the 31k series of standards which is currently under development [19]. The acronym 'SPICE' is also extended to include 'System, Software and Service Process Improvement and Capability dEtermination'.

Developing a new reference and assessment model from scratch was not a viable option due to the substantial efforts and resources that would be required. Looking at the ISO/IEC 15504 model elements as an example; it contains 48 process dimensions with 9 associated process attributes together with process outcomes, process definitions and work-product characteristics – a total of around 1800 elements in the entire model. The historic average development efforts for each process are around 15-20 hours for two experienced developers [20]. Therefore, selecting one of the existing process model as a foundation that can be tailored, adapted and adopted quickly would be a more practical approach. The table below explains the similarities and differences between CMMI-DEV Ver1.2 and ISO/IEC 15504-5 which will be used as the basis for base model selection.

III. Based Model Selection

As stated above, the new Healthcare SPI model would have to be based upon existing process areas, base practices and assessment components from either the CMMI or the ISO/IEC 15504-5 model. Selecting one model over another is very challenging as they both offer similar results for process improvement and process capability determination as shown in Table 1. The authors used Halvorsen & Conradi's taxonomy combining with some additional related works [21, 22, 26-34] to determine the differences and similarities dedicated to CMMI and ISO/IEC 15504 from an array of different characteristics. Furthermore, this analysis provides a structured comparison approach in selecting a model with regard to its practicality (i.e. possibility to adapt within an appropriate timeframe and resources) and its usability (i.e. can be adopted easily understood easily by the users). It can also be used for eliminating any personal preferences and subjective opinions when selecting between SPI models.

The CMMI is no doubt the better known and most widely used model world-wide for software process improvement and process assessment. ISO/IEC 15504 is, however, gaining popularity in the market place, which can be expected to affect the continuing evolution of the CMMI. They are now both influencing each other as they continue to evolve. For instance: ISO/IEC 15504 Part 10 is currently under development to cover Safety issues which will be equivalent to the +Safety Extension of CMMI-Dev Ver1.2; CMMI introduced its Continuous Constellation to offer the same flexibility that ISO/IEC 15504 has; CMMI states in its own specifications that "3.1.6 The CMMI Product Suite shall be consistent and compatible with ISO/IEC 15504" [35]. Therefore, it is of critical importance to recognise that both models should not be seen as rivals, but rather as companions that will contribute to the ongoing success of process improvement and assessment. The following key criteria were the deciding factors for the base model selection:

A. *Primary focus*

The ISO/IEC 15504 model describes the terrain of software process maturity from the perspective of the individual process with its two-dimensional framework structure, hence "process capability" is the main focus, whereas the CMMI provides a roadmap for organizational improvement by arranging a set of Key Process Areas for improvement for each maturity level, and thus focuses more on organization maturity improvement. As one of the main goals of the new model is to introduce tailored best practices to overcome deficiencies in specific Healthcare development and management process areas (e.g. requirement management and implementation management), "process" improvement focus is therefore more beneficial. This difference in primary focus (organization vs. process) makes the ISO 15504 model more favourable.

B. *Adaptability and extendibility*

The current latest ISO/IEC 15504 standard allows organizations to create or extend a new Process Reference/Assessment Model as long as they meet the conformance requirements from Part 2. This enables organizations to select and tailor processes that are unique to their way of conducting business from the exemplar model, the ISO/IEC 15504-5, or even add a new process dimension from other external process standard models such as the ISO/IEC 12207 in a relatively simple way. This idea has enabled a number of industry-specific models to be generated at a large-scale level (International Standards), for instance the Automotive sector (Automotive SPICE) [24], the Aerospace domain (SPICE for SPACE) [23]. Also at a smaller scale (research project at PhD level), there was also a successful attempt to adapt this model for the Tele-working development environment [36]. This flexibility of ISO/IEC 15504 both in

TABLE I
CMMI-DEV VERSION 1.2 VERSUS ISO/IEC 15504-5

Characteristic	CMMI-Dev Version 1.2	ISO/IEC 15504-5
Scientific Origin	Total Quality Management and US Department of Defence (DoD) appraisal standards.	CMM model, Bootstrap model, Trillium model and the UK Ministry of Defence (MoD) standards.
Development	Since 1986	Since early 1990s
Support	The CMMI is actively sponsored by the US DoD with annual Software Engineering Process Group and CMMI conferences.	Supported by the international community with a dedicated user forum (SPICE User Group) to assist, share and discuss technical issues and all the latest developments and annual SPICE conferences.
Motivation	To evaluate contractors/bidders (Software Capability Evaluation) and to guide and support a process improvement initiative.	To perform process improvement and capability determination.
Popularity	Highest (especially in US and India) - The CMM was created first and reached critical 'market' share before ISO 15504 and other models became available.	Growing.
Assessment	Organization maturity.	Process maturity.
Improvement Initiation	Top-down and Process instance.	Process instance.
Improvement Focus	Organization maturity. Suitable for large and process-centric organizations.	Process capability. Suitable to all type and size of organizations and can be adopted in a wide variety of domains [10].
Analysis Techniques	Assessment questionnaires.	Manual and automated.
Documentation Size	Large - CMMI was invented to help military officers quickly assess and describe contractors' abilities to deliver correct software on time, and in this regard, it has been a great success. However CMMI is not the answer for every organization. The CMMI model document is over 700 pages and the SCAMPI is just under 300 pages. It not only contains a vast amount of information but it is also more complicated to understand compared to other models. It is suitable for larger process-centric organizations, the Staged Representation in particular. Its rigid requirements for documentation and step-by-step progress make it better suited to large organizations than to small [21].	ISO/IEC 15504 is almost a third of the CMMI documentation. It is much shorter and simpler to understand.
Progression	Staged and Continuous.	Continuous (staged at process instance level).
Casual Relation	Key Process Areas (KPA) --> Maturity level.	Process attributes --> Capability level.
Comparative	Yes, maturity level.	Yes, maturity profile.
Process Artefacts	Process documentation, assessment result.	Process profile, assessment record.
Public Availability	Free from SEI website.	Must be purchased from ISO store.
Process Evolution	In Staged representation: KPAs are a snapshot of the evolving process. In Continuous representation: KPAs are described similarly to ISO/IEC 15504.	The evolution of processes from ad hoc to continuous improvement is fully described.
Capability Level	1-5 (Initial - Managed - Defined - Quantitatively Managed - Optimizing)	0-5 (Incomplete - Performed - Managed - Established - Predictable - Optimizing)
	With the exception of Level 1, each Maturity Level is composed of several KPAs, 22 in total. Each KPA is organized into five sections called Common Features. The Common Features specify the key practices that accomplish the goals of the KPA.	ISO/IEC 15504 is two-dimensional. One dimension consists of Process Dimension - 48 processes in total that are grouped into three categories and nine process groups. The second dimension consists of the capability scale that is used to evaluate the process capability (the Capability Level).
Process Rating	Each Specific Goal and / or Generic Goal is assessed using Not Rated, Satisfied or Unsatisfied scale.	Each Process Attribute is assessed on a four-point (N-P-L-F) rating scale: Not achieved (0 - 15%) - Partially achieved (>15% - 50%) - Largely achieved (>50%- 85%) - Fully achieved (>85% - 100%).
	ISO/IEC 15504 and CMMI have the ability to perform assessments rating ranging from one process in one project (Continuous Representation for CMMI) to a complete organization-wide assessment (Staged Representation for CMMI). This means it is possible to perform very fast and focus on very comprehensive assessment. In addition, they also have the ability to use the capability scale independently of the process dimension to design higher capability business processes and provide a powerful business advantage.	
Process Implementation	CMMI provides a much greater level of details of the processes. It describes sub-practices (i.e. defines typical work products), which are implementation guidance under the specific practices.	SPICE specifies work products in a generic manner. For this reason, they are consistently defined, but they are too generic to be used without further professional knowledge or assistance.
	CMMI gives more guidance and best practices for implementation. Extensive guidance in the key practices and subpractices provides significant help in understanding what a key practice or goal means, although it is typically oriented towards the practices of large organizations and projects in a contracting environment.	SPICE is equipped with Process Reference Model (PRM) which are primarily designed (with clear purpose and outcomes) to guide users in what processes to implement. The models often divide processes into groups, such as Supporting, Management, and Engineering as a guide to users on the potentially related processes. The PRM does not, however, describe HOW to implement the processes but only WHAT to implement which specifies by work product characteristic.

	Process areas of CMMI are closely related to the PRM described in ISO/IEC 15504-5. Generic goals and practices of CMMI are also closely related to the Process Attributes described in ISO/IEC 15504-2. For this reason, any practitioner adequately implementing, for example, the MAN 5. Risk Management Process in ISO/IEC 15504 could reasonably expect to have satisfied the [RSKM] Risk Management key process area in the Software CMM.	
Maturity Level Mapping	The mapping from each Specific and generic Practices for each Process Area of the CMMI can be compared to the outcomes and process attributes of the ISO 15504 processes. This mapping can provide evidence that the results of a CMMI Staged model assessment can cover the ISO 15504 process capability [22]. CMMI Maturity Level (ML) 2 = ISO 15504 Process Attributes (PA) 1.1, 2.1, 2.2. ML3 = PA 1.1, 2.1, 2.2, 3.1, 3.2. ML4 = PA 1.1, 2.1, 2.2, 3.1, 3.2, 4.1, 4.2. ML5 = All 9 PAs.	
Organization Capability	Established based upon the Staged Representation and measured by Maturity Level. It is more explicit than that described in ISO/IEC 15504.	Established based upon assessed profiles of Process Capability (ISO/IEC 15504 Part 7). It can be intuitively understood by looking at the organizational processes, the process attributes, and their dependencies. There is not presently a clear distinction between Organization Maturity and process capability [10].
Adaptability / Extendibility	Limited - Hard to adapt, little flexibility [22]. It may be difficult for the non-expert to extend the CMMI principles to new disciplines or focus areas. This is one of the major criticisms of the existing SW-CMM, which stems from the fact that it was targeted at large organizations such as defence contractors and had very little means for adaptation to the environments and goals of smaller companies or organizations. The CMMI is not an easy standard [21].	Adding processes and integrating with other models is a relatively straightforward definition, with the application of the capability dimension for rating the processes. A fundamental idea behind this standard is that reference/assessment models may be generated according to certain criteria and may thus be used instead of the example Process Assessment Model (PAM) exemplar model contained in Part 5. In another words, it allows model developers to design different PAM using the same PRM, as long as they meet the conformance requirements from Part 2. This idea enables industry-specific models to be generated without starting from scratch, hence, it offers flexibility for tailoring to suit particular industry and business. E.g. SPICE for SPACE previously used ISO/IEC TR 15504-2:1998 PRM and added Space industry specific extensions [23]. Other major sectors such as Automotive [24] and Medical Device industries are also leading the way with industry relevant variant standards.

terms of process coverage and assessment scope, plus its adaptability to specific industries, is a strong advantage over other standards [21].

Once again, both models are conceptually compatible and have the same fundamental philosophy in process improvement and process assessment, thus deciding which one is better was not the main purpose of this study. However, when putting them into the context of our research work, i.e. to select a model that "best serves Healthcare industry's current development and management concerns" and "best support model developer's goal", the ISO/IEC 15504-5 was the most suitable one.

IV. DEVELOPMENT REQUIREMENTS FOR HEALTHCARE SPI MODEL

As in previous studies [7,8], the authors have highlighted the development and management challenges facing the Healthcare sector, which consequently influenced the decision to develop a new SPI model by adopting ISO/IEC 15504-5 as the based model. In line with this, detailed requirements for the new model were defined, covering both functional and non-functional aspects. A new tailored process improvement model should:

a. accommodate specific UK Healthcare quality dimension requirements, i.e. patient-centred design, safety and confidentiality;
b. adhere to minimum UK Healthcare standard requirements, i.e. clinical standards (Common User Interface, Clinical Safety Management standard), risk & security standards (Evaluation Assurance Level, CRAMM);
c. provide coverage of additional software development practices for critical areas such as: *requirement management, risk/change control process* and *customer-supplier implementation management processes*;
d. be generic enough to be widely applicable (e.g. for all organization sizes) but specific enough to be useful (e.g. introduction of new tailored best practices to comply with UK Healthcare standards);
e. be timely in its development.

These requirements should, therefore, be the main focus for the development of the Healthcare SPI model. Fig. 1 elaborates on the specific Healthcare software quality dimension in combination with particular Healthcare standards and guidelines to provide inputs for the new model development. For example: Usability features of all UK National Health Service (NHS) clinical applications should be designed to adhere to the Common User Interface guideline, requiring software suppliers to comply in the early requirement elicitation process; or strict Training guidelines for training and coaching software users. Current models, ISO/IEC 15504-5 and CMMI, do not cover such specific areas; hence, the success of the projects can be hindered as a consequence. Process improvement and assessment methods must now be extended to incorporate customers' preferences, sector standards requirement and sector best practices to be more effective.

The inputs in Fig. 1 indicate minimum quality expectations for new applications from the UK Healthcare software acquirers. The new Healthcare SPI model will need to incorporate such requirements into its new tailored key process areas and best practices to enhance software development processes. Quality software is defined as software that meets its functional as well as non-functional requirements (e.g. usability, interoperability, etc.) within budget and timescale, but in the Healthcare setting, it must also conform to specific standards.

Apart from integrating Healthcare quality requirements and existing standards conformance, the new SPI model will need to extend and/or adapt existing practices to address current Healthcare development concerns. For this reason, the outputs from Fig. 1 identify requirements for the new Healthcare SPI model which assist the authors to set priorities and to limit the development scope. *Customer-supplier management; Requirement management; Security requirement; Safety management; Risk & change management and implementation management* will be the main areas for development, illustrated in Fig. 1.

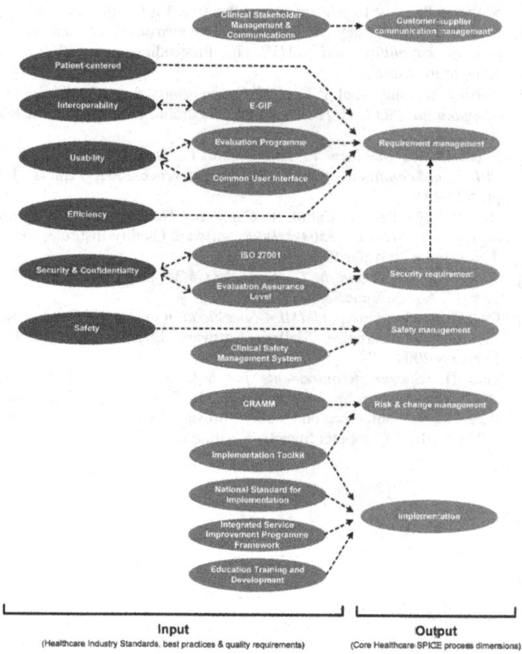

Fig. 1. Development requirements for the Healthcare SPI model

zPRIMARY Life Cycle Processes	SUPPORTING Life Cycle Processes	ORGANIZATIONAL Life Cycle Processes
ACQ.1	SUP.1	MAN.1
ACQ.2	SUP.2	MAN.2
ACQ.3	SUP.3	MAN.3
ACQ.4	SUP.4	MAN.4
ACQ.5	SUP.5	MAN.5
SPL.1	SUP.6	MAN.6
SPL.2	SUP.7	PIM.1
SPL.3	SUP.8	PIM.2
ENG.1	SUP.9	PIM.3
ENG.2	SUP.10	RIN.1
ENG.3		RIN.2
ENG.4		RIN.3
ENG.5		RIN.4
ENG.6		REU.1
ENG.7		REU.2
ENG.8		REU.3
ENG.9		
ENG.10		
ENG.11		
ENG.12		
OPE.1		
OPE.2		Tailored Healthcare PA

Fig. 2. Proposed Healthcare SPI model structure based on ISO/IEC 15504-5

V. CONCLUSIONS AND FUTURE WORK

As UK is leading the world in Healthcare IT investment, everyone is watching its Healthcare system being transformed and supported by a range of new ICT systems. Failure to provide high quality software systems despite vast spending will have negative impacts on the UK's reputation, but more seriously, losing taxpayers' confidence means there will be less support for similar future IT investment projects. At the same time, increasing software's functionalities and dependencies can also increases the significance of software quality enormously. As a result, having the right tool to ensure high quality products is imperative as poorly designed or implemented software in this environment can lead to financial losses and, more importantly place people's lives at risk.

Whilst current SPI models cover the whole software production process, the new Healthcare SPI model heavily concentrates on those sub-processes that directly impact the success of Healthcare software such as requirements management, risk management and change control. This new model will also incorporate Healthcare standards and its critical quality dimension requirement, with a prime focus on the UK, into ISO/IEC 15504-5 model to improve software houses's internal processes. It will further provide assessment mechanisms that enable software acquirers to measure and evaluate their software suppliers to ensure the final product meets its agreed expectations and standards compliances.

Our plan is to develop and tailor the first 12 processes by end of 2009 (see Fig. 2). The remaining two processes, Safety management and Safety engineering, will follow after the official release of ISO/IEC 15504 Part 10 Safety extension.

REFERENCES

[1] Leverson N., and Turner C., *An Investigation of the Therac-25 Accidents*. Computer, pp. 18-41, July 1993.

[2] Field M., and Keller L., *Project Management*. ISBN 1-86152-274-6, Thomson, pp. 75-86, 2002.

[3] Brennan S., *The NHS IT Project: The Biggest Computer Program in the World ... Ever!*. Radcliffe Publishing Ltd., Oxford, 2005, ISBN: 1857757327.

[4] MORI, *A Baseline Study on the National Program for IT*. Mori Social Research Institute, July 2005.

[5] Medix, *Survey of doctors' views about the National Programme for IT (NPfIT)*. Medix Plc UK, 2005.

[6] Medix, *Survey of doctors' views about the National Programme for IT (NPfIT)*. Medix Plc UK, 2006.

[7] Nguyen T.D., Guo H., Naguib N.G., *A survey of industrial experiences for the UK healthcare software development sector. Int.* J. Biomedical Engineering and Technology, Vol. 1, No. 3, p329-341, 2008.

[8] Nguyen T.D., Guo H., Naguib N.G., *Twenty-First Century Healthcare Software Application: the Good, the Bad and the Ugly*. In Proceedings of the 9th International Conference of Software Process Improvement and Capability Determination (SPICE 2009), Turku, Finland, pp. 42-49, May 2009, ISBN 978-952-12-2287-0.

[9] Anderson R., *The NHS's National Program for IT: Dossier of Concerns*. May 2007. Available online: http://nhs-it.info/. Last accessed date: 20 September 2007.

[10] Rout P.T., Khaled El Emam, Mario Fusani, Dennis Goldenson, Ho-Won Jung, *SPICE in retrospect: Developing a standard for process assessment*. Journal of Systems and Software, Volume 80, Issue 9, Evaluation and Assessment in Software Engineering - EASE06, September 2007, pp. 1483-1493.

[11] SEI (Software Engineering Institute), *Process Maturity Profile: CMMI SCAMPI Class A Appraisal Results*. Carnegie Mellon University, Mar 2008.

[12] Card N. D., *Research direction in software process improvement*. In Proceedings of the 28th Annual International Computer Software and Applications Conference (COMPSAC'04), 2004.

[13] Reid P.P., W. Dale Compton, Jerome H. Grossman, and Gary Fanjiang, *Building a Better Delivery System: A New Engineering/Health Care Partnership*. Institute of Medicine and National Academy of Engineering, Washington D.C, 2005.

[14] Demin E., *Out of the Crisis*. MIT Press, 1986.

[15] Crosby P.B., *Quality is Free: The Art of Making Quality Certain*. McGraw-Hill, New York, 1979.

[16] Juran J., *Juran on Planning for Quality*. MacMillan, 1988.

[17] CMMI Product Team, *CMMI for systems engineering/software engineering*, V1.02. CMU/SEI-2000-TR-028. Carnegie Mellon, Software Engineering Institute, 2000.

[18] CMMI Product Team, *CMMI for Development*, Version 1.2 (CMU/SEI-2006-TR-008, ADA455858). Software Engineering Institute, Carnegie Mellon University, 2006. Available online: http://www.sei.cmu.edu/publications/documents/06.reports/06tr008.html . Last accessed date: 25th June 2009

[19] SPICE User Group, *Next Generation* 15504 - *the 31001 series of Standards*. The SPICE User Group News Feed. Available online: http://www.spiceusergroup.org/forum2/topics/next-generation-15504-the. Last accessed date: 7th June 2009.

[20] Ibrahim L., and Menezes W., *Enterprises* SPICE *Update - Status and Lessons Learned*. In Proceedings of the 9th International Conference of Software Process Improvement and Capability Determination (SPICE 2009), Turku, Finland, pp. 113-116, May 2009, ISBN 978-952-12-2287-0.

[21] Loon H., *Process Assessment and ISO/IEC 15504 – A Reference Book*. Springer, 2004, ISBN 0-387-23172-2.

[22] Paulk M.C., *Analyzing the Conceptual Relationship between ISO/IEC 15504 (Software Process Assessment) and the Capability Maturity Model for Software*. In Proceedings of the Ninth International Conference on Software Quality, Cambridge, MA, USA, 1999, pp. 293-303.

[23] Cass A., *et al., SPiCE for SPACE: A Process Assessment and Improvement Method for Space Software Development*. ESA Bulletin 107, European Space Agency, 2001, pp. 112-119.

[24] Automotive SIG, *Automotive SPICE process reference model, V 4.2*. SPICE Users Group 2005. Available online: http://www.automotivespice.com. Last accessed date 15 May 2009.

[25] McCaffery F., and Dorling A., *Medi SPICE: An Overview*. In Proceedings of the 9th International Conference of Software Process Improvement and Capability Determination (SPICE 2009), Turku, Finland, pp. 34-41, May 2009, ISBN 978-952-12-2287-0

[26] Pino F., Baldassarre M., Piattini M., Visaggio G., *Relationship between maturity levels of ISO/IEC 15504-7 and CMMI-Dev V1.2*. In Proceedings of the 9th International Conference of Software Process Improvement and Capability Determination (SPICE 2009), Turku, Finland, pp. 69-76, May 2009, ISBN 978-952-12-2287-0.

[27] Pino F., *Study on the relationship between process reference models and organizational maturity models of the SEI and ISO*. Available online: http://alarcos.inf-cr.uclm.es/competisoft/Comparison.pdf. Last accessed date: 7 July 2009.

[28] Zarour M., Desharnais J.M., Abran B., *A Framework to Compare Software Process Assessment Methods Dedicated to Small and Very Small Organizations*. International Conference on Software Quality - ICSQ 07. In Proceedings of the International Conference on the Software Quality - ICSQ'07, October 16-17, 2007, Lakewood (Denver) Co. USA.

[29] Rout P.T., and Tuffley A., *Harmonizing ISO/IEC 15504 and CMMI*. Software Process: Improvement and Practice, 12(4), 2007, pp. 361-371.

[30] Rout P.T., and Tuffley A., *The ISO 15504 measurement framework for process capability and CMMI*. In Proceedings of SPICE 2005, Klagenfurt, Austria.

[31] Tuffley A., and Rout P.T., *CMMI conformance to ISO/IEC 15504: Mapping to ISO/IEC 12207*. SEPG Australia Conference, Adelaide, Australia, 2004.

[32] Lepasaar M., Makinen T., and Varkoi T., *Structural comparison of SPICE and continuous CMMI*. SPICE conference 2002, Venicia , Italy, pp. 223-234.

[33] Rout P.T., Tuffley, A., Cahill, B., *Capability Maturity Model Integration Mapping to ISO/IEC 15504-2:1998*. Software Quality Institute, Ver 1.0, 7 November 2001, Griffith University.

[34] Rout P.T., *SPICE and the CMM, is the CMM compatible with ISO/IEC 15504?*. AquIS, Venecia, Italy, 1998.

[35] CMMI Steering Group, *CMMI A-Specification for CMMI Product Suite, Version 1.6*. Carnegie Mellon, Software Engineering Institute, 6 February 2004.

[36] Guo H., *Special Requirements for Software Process Improvement Applied in Teleworking Environments*. In Proceedings of the Second Asia-Pacific Conference on Quality Software (December 10 - 11, 2001). APAQS. IEEE Computer Society, Washington, DC, p. 331.

Exploring User Acceptance of FOSS: The Role of the Age of the Users

M. Dolores Gallego
University of Pablo de Olavide
Ctra. Utrera, km.1
Seville, 41013 Spain

Salvador Bueno
University of Pablo de Olavide
Ctra. Utrera, km.1
Seville, 41013 Spain

***Abstract* - Free and open source software (FOSS) movement essentially arises like answer to the evolution occurred in the market from the software, characterized by the closing of the source code. Furthermore, some FOSS characteristics, such as (1) the advance of this movement and (2) the attractiveness that contributes the voluntary and cooperative work, have increased the interest of the users towards free software. Traditionally, research in FOSS has focused on identifying individual personal motives for participating in the development of a FOSS project, analyzing specific FOSS solutions, or the FOSS movement itself. Nevertheless, the advantages of the FOSS for users and the effect of the demographic dimensions on user acceptance for FOSS have been two research topics with little attention. Specifically, this paper's aim is to focus on the influence of the users´ age with FOSS the FOSS acceptance. Based on the literature, users´ age is an essential demographic dimension for explaining the Information Systems acceptance. With this purpose, the authors have developed a research model based on the Technological Acceptance Model (TAM).**

I. Introduction

From a professional, academic, business and political standpoint, few topics are as current as the development and implementation of free and open source software (FOSS). The changes introduced by FOSS in the software industry have been surprising, and represent a radical change of perspective in developmental business models and software distribution. This change has turned FOSS into one of the most debated topics among software users and analysts [1].

In recent years, FOSS use has rapidly grown among organizations and users, thanks to the advantages that it offers when compared to proprietary software [2]. As a consequence of its evolution, a great amount of research has been done on FOSS. Traditionally, this research has focused on, either the identification of the personal motives of the people who participate in the development of an FOSS project [3] [4] [5] [6] [7], the analysis of specific solutions that are developed by the FOSS movement [8] [9] [10] [11] [12], or on the FOSS movement, itself [13] [14] [15] [16] [1] [17] [18] [19] [20] [21].

However, the profile of the FOSS user or the influence of the demographic dimensions the acceptance towards this software solution has received very little attention. For this reason, our purpose is to analyze the effect of the user´ age on the acceptance for FOSS. User´ age is one of the essential demographic dimensions for explaining the Information Systems acceptance. For this development, we have considered the Technology Acceptance Model (TAM) [22] which provides the theoretical and methodological framework capable of explaining the acceptance for FOSS. With this objective in mind, we have carried out a study on users of the Linux operating system. We consider that the TAM application for users of the Linux Operative System serves as a representative sample of potential FOSS users. Thus, we understand that the conclusions reached from our specific study will allow to uncover the factors that influence user acceptance of any technology based on FOSS.

II. TAM Methodology and Hypothesis.

The TAM model developed by [22] has been widely applied with the purpose of understanding the conduct and motivational factors that influence Information Systems and Technologies (IS/IT) adoption and use. Just as [23] indicate, only ten years after the model publication, the Social Science Citation Index listed more than four-hundred articles that had cited both articles which introduced TAM methodology, [22] and [24]. Since then, the model has become well established as a powerful and efficient tool for predicting user acceptance.

The TAM model is an adaptation of the Theory of Reasoned Action (TRA) proposed by [25] to explain and predict the behavior of organizational members in specific situations. TAM adapts the TRA model to provide evidence for the general factors that influence IS/IT acceptance in order to help determine user behavior towards a specific IS/IT. This powerful model allows for a contrast in behavior on the part of the user and is based on four fundamental variables or constructs which are: perceived usefulness (PU), perceived ease of use (PEU), intention to use (IU) and usage behavior (UB).

Independent of the internal constructs of the TAM model, FOSS users consider that the acceptance for FOSS is influenced by some external variables. Therefore, our goal is to identify the external constructs that influence the intention of use a FOSS solution. With this objective in mind, we have taken as a reference the study elaborated previously by the authors [26]. Based on this work, we consider suitable to include four external constructs to the TAM model. These variables are: system capability (SC), software flexibility (SF), software quality (SQ) and social influence (SI).

T. Sobh, K. Elleithy (eds.), *Innovations in Computing Sciences and Software Engineering*,
DOI 10.1007/978-90-481-9112-3_29,

In a same way, based on the TAM model proposed by [26] about FOSS usage behavior, we formulate an acceptance model that was validated in the cited work with a sample with 347 Linux users. This model explains the user behavior for FOSS solutions in a 39.1% (Fig. 1). We asked to the users of the sample how old are they for completing our study.

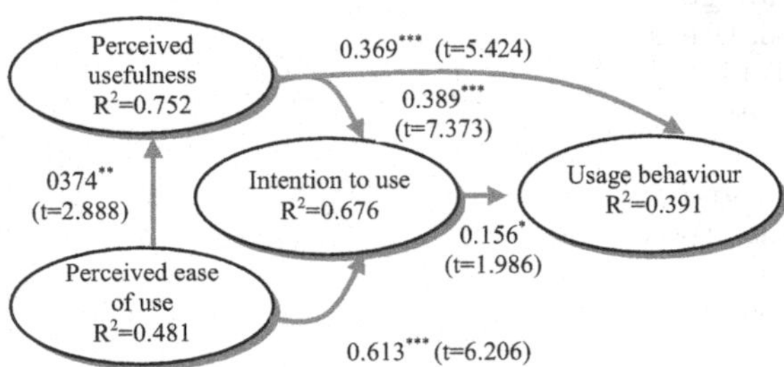

Fig. 1. Reduced research model. Source: [26]

Age has been considered as one of the demographic variables that influences the acceptation of a technology. Its influence is connected with beliefs about the use of the system and attitudes towards its use [27]. Hence, studies such as [28] found that there was a negative connection between the users· age and their technological acceptation. Meanwhile, the study carried out by [29] clearly showed the negative influence of age in the ease of use. In this same line, [30] made it plain that the first to adopt a new technology tend to be the Young. With the aim of determining the influence of age in the adopting a FOSS solution, we put forward the following hypotheses:

Hypothesis 1 (H1): The user's age has a negative effect on Perceived Usefulness of an FOSS solution

Hypothesis 2 (H2): the user's age has a negative effect on Perceived Ease of Use of an FOSS solution

Hypothesis 3 (H3): the user's age has a negative effect on Intention to Use of an FOSS solution

Hypothesis 4 (H4): the user's age has a negative effect on User Behavior of an FOSS solution

III. Sample Information and Preliminary Analysis

We have selected Linux FOSS users for the sample of our study. We understand that these users are a representation of all FOSS users, and the results obtained could extrapolate any solution based on FOSS. In this sense, we turned to The Linux Counter website, where we were able to access the contact information of the users that were registered in the website. The information provided to us happened to be organized by geographic areas. We selected the European countries which tended to have a higher number of registered users. Within each area, the selection made was completely at random. A total of 1,736 study invitations were sent out by electronic mail to registered Linux users in eleven different European countries. In the end, we received 363 survey responses. Of those, 347 were complete and valid for our study. This number represents a response rate of twenty percent.

In order to measure each one the variables included in the TAM model developed for our study, we carried out a review of the literature that allowed to identify items for each one of the constructs. The survey and the selection of the sample used for the study already were validated [26].

In order to cover the main objective of this study, the users of the sample indicated their age. The feedback obtained allows realizing a descriptive analysis about the age of the FOSS users' and classifying the sample in seven categories of users (see Table I). Besides, we have could can observe that the average age of FOSS user is 34 years old. This data shows the maturity of FOSS users towards this type of technology.

TABLE I
DESCRIPTIVE ANALYSIS

Mean	S.D.	Categories	Number of participants
		Less than 20 years	15
		Between 21 and 25	49
		Between 26 and 30	72
34	10.84	Between 31 and 35	64
		Between 36 and 40	48
		Between 41 and 45	28
		More than 45	61

IV. Analysis and Findings

In order to agree upon all the hypotheses collected in the research model, a causal analysis have been developed. The research models were tested by structural equation modeling (SEM) using Lisrel 8.51 with maximum-likelihood estimation. The parameters that represent the regression coefficients among the constructs are indicated with the symbol γ if the relationship it represents is between an independent construct and a dependent one. If the relationship established is between two dependent constructs, it is indicated with the symbol β.

$$PEU = \gamma_1\ SC + \gamma_2\ SI + SF\ \gamma_3 + \varepsilon_1$$

$$PU = \gamma_4\ SQ + SC\ \gamma_5 + SI\ \gamma_6 + \beta_1\ PEU + \varepsilon_2$$

$$IU = \beta_2\ PEU + \beta_3\ PU + \varepsilon_3$$

$$UB = \beta_4\ IU + \beta_5\ PU + \varepsilon_4$$

For the Lisrel, we were able to prove how the model very adequately explains the variance in the perceived ease of use (R^2=0,481), perceived usefulness (R^2=0,752), intention to use (R^2=0,676) and usage behavior (R^2=0,391) [26]. Based on these findings, we have developed a causal analysis to each group of user. After, we will compare the findings. The comparison analysis will allow to obtain significant discussions about the influence of the age of the users with respect FOSS acceptance. We also use Lisrel 8.51 with maximum-likelihood estimation.

V. Research Model Test

The user's demographics dimensions have generally a positive or negative effect on the perceptions and attitudes towards the use of a certain type of technology. In our particular research, we want to test the negative influence of the user's age on FOSS on perceived ease of use (H1), perceived usefulness (H2), intention to use (H3) and usage behavior (H4).

In order to test satisfactorily all the hypotheses, we have divided the sample in two sub-samples (see Table II), users who are 30 years old or less (A-1) and those who are over 30 years old (A-2). This decision is adopted to obtain sufficiently wide sub-samples for reaching estimations of the regression equations with the software Lisrel [30].

TABLE II
MODEL HYPOTHESES CONTRAST

Interval of year	Relationship	γ or β	t-student	R2	R2
Users who are 30 years old or less	SC→ PEU	0.305	4.084		
	SI→ PEU	0.0774	1.070	0.506	0.481
	SF→ PEU	0.123	3.047		
	PEU→ PU	0.194	0.931		
	SQ→ PU	0.506	3.623	0.657	0.752
	SC→ PU	0.305	1.681		
	SI→ PU	0.167	1.362		
	PEU → UB	0.606	3.912	0.624	0.676
	PU → UB	0.364	4.831		
	PU → IU	0.481	4.723	0.469	0.391
	UB→ IU	0.0939	0.749		
User over 30 years old	SC→ PEU	0.628	4.385		
	SI→ PEU	0.0324	0. 742	0.467	0.481
	SF→ PEU	0.108	2.447		
	PEU→ PU	0.447	2.797		
	SQ→ PU	0.910	4.462	0.859	0.752
	SC→ PU	0.135	0.486		
	SI→ PU	0.0376	0.636		
	PEU → UB	0.598	4.467	0.686	0.676
	PU → UB	0.460	5.565		
	PU → IU	0.243	2.603	0.320	0.391
	AU→ IU	0.221	2.148		

With respect to the users· age, the sub-group formed by younger users (A-1), perceived more ease of use (0.506) and usage behavior (0.469) than the older users (A-2: 0.467 and 0.320 respectively). According to these findings (Table III), hypotheses H1 y H4 are significantly tested. Regarding perceived usefulness, older users (A-2) perceive more usefulness (0.859) than younger users (0.657). In this respect, hypothesis H2 has not been tested significantly.

Finally, with respect to hypothesis H3, which defines the negative effect of the users' ages on the intention to use an FOSS solution, we can't accept it. In this respect, the hypothesis H3 has not been tested significantly. Nevertheless, based on these findings, we can't state that the user's age has a positive effect on the intention to use an FOSS solution. We can only confirm that these relationships aren't positive or a significant difference doesn't exist.

VI. DISCUSSIONS

Even though research on FOSS has proliferated in recent years, the acceptance of this type of technological solution on behalf of the users had not been tackled. Thus, the main objective that we pose with this research is to analyze the influence of the age of the user with the acceptance towards FOSS. With this aim, we have formulated a Technology Acceptance Model based on a previous study of the authors. Besides, we have identified relevant discussions about the influence of the age of the user with the FOSS acceptance.

First, we have observed the particularity of FOSS. Specifically, the positive relationship between the age of the user and perceived ease of use for FOSS (H1) and user behavior (H4) has been tested significantly. Nevertheless, there aren't significant differences about the perception of usefulness and the age of the user (hypotheses H2).

Second, with these findings we cannot affirm that exist negative relationships with respect the intention to use of a FOSS solution with the age of the user. For that, these findings show the particularity of the FOSS movement.

Thirds, based on the findings, we can affirm that the FOSS governmental organizations and developers must favorer the flow of FOSS information for fomenting the use of these solutions. With this in mind, we think that the efforts of organizations for increasing the number of FOSS users must be orientated to young people.

REFERENCES

[1] A. Fuggetta, "Open source software—an evaluation". Journal of Systems and Software Vol. 66 (1), pp. 77–90, 2003

[2] C. Ruffin, and C. Ebert, "Using open source software in product development: a primer", IEEE Software Vol. 21 (1), pp. 82-86, 2004.

[3] A. Bonaccorsi and C. Rossi, "Comparing motivations of individual programmers and firms to take part in the Open Source movement. From community to business", http://opensource.mit.edu/papers/bnaccorsirossimotivationlong.pdf, 2003 [25-03-2006].

[4] G. Hertel, S. Niedner, and S. Herrmann, "Motivation of software developers in Open Source projects: an Internet-based survey of contributors to the Linux kernel", Research Policy Vol. 32 (7), pp. 1159-1177, 2003.

[5] Y. Ye and K. Kishida, "Toward an Understanding of the Motivation of Open Source Software Developers", International Conference on Software Engineering (ICSE2003). Portland - Oregon (EE.UU.), 2003.

[6] A. Hars and S. Ou, "Working for Free? Motivations for Participating in Open-Source Projects" International Journal of Electronic Commerce Vol. 6 (3), pp. 25-40, 2002.

[7] R. Ryan, and E. Deci, "Intrinsic and Extrinsic Motivations: Classic Definitions and New Directions", Contemporary Educational Psychology Vol. 25 (1), pp. 54-67, 2000.

[8] M. Federman, "The Penguinist Discourse: A critical application of open source software project management to organization development", Organization Development Journal Vol. 24 (2), pp. 89-100, 2006.

[9] M. Fink, "The business and economics of Linux and Open Source". Ed. Prentience Hall PTR, Upper Saddle River - New Jersey (EE.UU.), 2003.
[10] N. Franke and E. Von Hippel, "Satisfying heterogeneous user needs via innovation toolkits: the case of Apache security software", Research Policy Vol. 32 (7), pp. 1199-1215, 2003.
[11] M. Mustonen, "Copyleft–the economics of Linux and other open source software", Information Economics and Policy Vol. 15 (1), pp. 99-121, 2003.
[12] G. Carbone and D. Stoddard, "Open source enterprise solutions", Ed. Wiley, Nueva York (EE.UU.), 2001.
[13] X. Shen, "Developing Country Perspectives on Software: Intellectual Property and Open Source - A Case Study of Microsoft and Linux in China", International Journal of IT Standards & Standardization Research Vol. 3 (1), pp. 21-43, 2005.
[14] R. Van Wendel and T. Egyedi, "Handling variety: the tension between adaptability and interoperability of open source software". Computer Standards & Interfaces Vol. 28 (1), pp. 109-121, 2005.
[15] B. Dwan, "Open source vs closed", Network Security Vol. 5, pp. 11-13, 2004.
[16] A. Bonaccorsi and C. Rossi, "Why Open Source software can succeed". Research Policy Vol. 32 (7), pp. 1243-1258, 2003.
[17] S. Krishnamurthy, "A managerial overview of open source software", Business Horizons, Vol. 46 (5), pp. 47-56. 2003
[18] K. Lakhani and E. Von Hippel, "How open source software works: "free" user-to-user assistance", Research Policy Vol. 32 (6), pp.923-943, 2003.
[19] J. West, "How open is open enough?: Melding proprietary and open source platform strategies", Research Policy Vol. 32 (7), pp. 1259-1285, 2003.
[20] J.P. Johnson, "Open Source Software: Private Provision of a Public Good", Journal of Economics & Management Strategy Vol. 11 (4), pp. 637-662, 2002.
[21] W. Scacchi, "Understanding the Requirements for Developing Open Source Software Systems", IEE Proceedings--Software Vol. 149 (1), pp. 24-39, 2002.
[22] F.D. Davis, "Perceived usefulness, perceived ease of use, and user acceptance of Information Technology". MIS Quarterly Vol. 13 (3), pp. 319-340, 1989.
[23] V. Venkatesh and F.D. Davis, "A theoretical extension of the technology acceptance model: four longitudinal field studies". Management Science Vol. 46 (2), pp. 186-204, 2000.
[24] F.D. Davis, R.P. Bagozzi and P.R. Warshaw, "User acceptance of computer technology: a comparison of two theoretical models", Management Science Vol. 35 (8), pp. 982–1003, 1989.
[25] M. Fishbein and I. Ajzen, "Belief, Attitude, Intention, and Behavior: An Introduction to Theory and Research". Addison-Wesley. New York, 1985.
[26] M.D. Gallego, P. Luna, and S. Bueno, "Designing a forecasting analysis to understand the diffusion of open source software in the year 2010", Technological Forecasting and Social Change Vol. 75 (5), pp. 672-686, 2008.
[27] M. G. Morris and V. Venkatesh, "Age differences in technology adoption decisions: Implications for a changing work force", Personnel Psychology Vol. 53 (2), pp. 375-403, 2000.
[28] M. Igbaria, "User acceptance of microcomputer technology: An empirical test", Omega, Vol. 21 (1), pp. 73-90, 1993.
[29] G. S. Hubona and E. Kennick, "The impact of external variables on information technology usage behavior", 29th Annual Hawaii International Conference on System Science, Hawaii (EE.UU.), 1996.
[30] J. C. Brancheau and J.C. Wetherbe, "The adoption of spreadsheet software: testing innovation diffusion theory in the context of end-user computing", Information Systems Research, Vol. 1(2), pp. 115-143, 1990.

GFS Tuning Algorithm Using Fuzzimetric Arcs

Issam Kouatli,
Lebanese American University, LAU PO Box 13-5053 Chouran Beirut, Lebanon
Email: Issam.kouatli@lau.edu.lb

Abstract: **Evolutionary learning and tuning mechanism to fuzzy systems is the main concern to researchers in the filed. The optimized final performance on the fuzzy system is dependent on the ability of the system to find the best optimized rule-set(s) as well as the optimized fuzzy variable definition. This paper proposes a mechanism of selection and optimization of fuzzy variables termed as "Fuzzimetric Arcs" and then discusses how this mechanism can become a standard of selection and optimization of fuzzy set shapes to tune the performance of GFS. Genetic algorithm is the technique that can be utilized to alter/modify the initial shape of fuzzy sets using two main operators (Crossover and Mutation). Optimization of rule-set(s) is mainly dependent on the measurement of fitness factor and the level of deviation from fitness factor.**

Keywords: **Fuzzy systems, GFS, Genetic algorithm, Fuzzimetric Arcs, learning and tuning.**

I. INTRODUCTION

Hybridization of Fuzzy logic and genetic algorithm are becoming popular among researchers in the field. The main objective is to achieve means for decision making in the same manner that human brain employ in the process of decision making. As such it can provide a translation of the qualitative abilities of the human brain into quantitative functions. Fuzzy system is the main mechanism allowing the achievement of this objective. However, such mechanism would require an optimization/tuning technique to achieve the adaptability to the environmental changes to the system. Evolutionary systems is usually a term that has resulted from such hybridization where fuzzy systems deal with the uncertainty part and Genetic algorithm deals with the optimization and tuning part. Herrera [1] reviewed the research trends in such systems in more details, where a clear differentiation between the approach areas of learning and tuning mechanisms has been explained. Yun et al [2] proposed some genetic algorithms with adaptive abilities. Crossover and mutation operators of genetic algorithms were used for constructing the adaptive abilities. These algorithms can regulate the rates of crossover and mutation operators during their search process. A good introduction to the applicability of genetic algorithms to fuzzy systems was also written by Herrera et al [3, 4].

This paper introduces the notation of "Fuzzimetric Arcs" mainly as selection and tuning mechanism of fuzzy set shape (Fuzzy variable definition) where crossover and mutation operators used to adapt/tune the fuzzy set shape to achieve optimality of the system. Fuzzimetric Arcs was introduced as a concept by Kouatli et al [5, 6]. However, this paper explains how this concept can be utilized as part of Evolutionary mechanism of GFS. A good illustrative decision making example of how to use Fuzzimetric Arcs can be found in Kouatli [7] where a financial example of whether or not to buy bonds using interest rates as input and bond price as the output of the system. Proposal of implementing such concept in a form of generic inference tool is currently under consideration and termed as FIE "Fuzzy Inference Engine" [8] where the objective is to build a generic fuzzy inference engine with built-in ability of Fuzzimetric Arcs utilization.

II. *FUZZIMETRIC ARCS AND GFS*

Fuzzimetric Arcs is a methodology/tool for a simple universe partitioning technique as well as a methodology for the selection of the optimum shape of the fuzzy sets for the fuzzy variables to be developed. Each arc is mainly composed of three quarters of a trigonometric circle, which has a radius of absolute value of unity. Then the main fuzzy variables zero, Small, Medium and Big of any system may be represented on this arc, which may encompass positive and/or negative values forming the process of partitioning. Hence, for positive values, the members of the universe that belong to the fuzzy variable Positive Zero (PO) for example, would carry a membership value of unity ($\cos 0 = \sin (\pi/2 - 0) = 1$) for the member zero which decreases gradually for the rest of the members until the start of the second quarter of the arc is reached (Fig. 1).

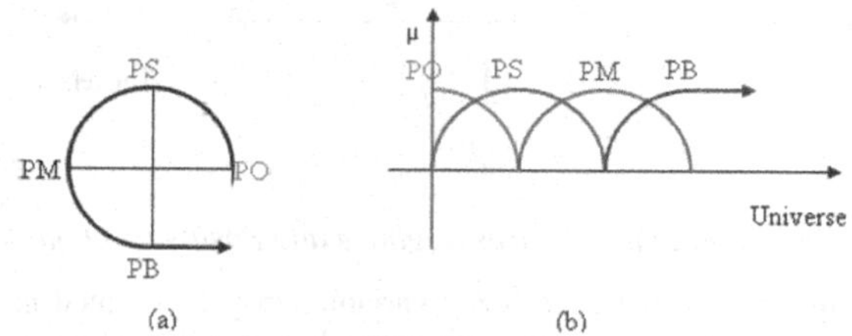

Figure 1: (a) Positive Fuzzimetric Arc
(b) Spread of Fuzzy Variables on the membership-Universe axes.

Similarly, the Positive Small (PS) fuzzy variable should carry a non-zero membership value for any member that lies in the range of 0° to 180° on the arc where a membership value of unity ($\sin \pi/2$) should be at the start

T. Sobh, K. Elleithy (eds.), *Innovations in Computing Sciences and Software Engineering*,
DOI 10.1007/978-90-481-9112-3_30,

of the second quarter of the arc. The members that belong to the fuzzy variable Positive Medium (PM) have a non-zero membership value in the range of 90° to 270° on the arc. The final fuzzy variable Positive Big (PB) would covers all the members that lie in the range of 180° to 270° where the largest member in the universe should have a unity membership value, i.e. $|\sin(3\pi/2)|$. Hence, the fuzzy variables will be defined as:

PO	$= \|\sin(\pi/2 - x)\|$	for $0 < x < \pi/2$
	$= 0$	otherwise
PS	$= \|\sin(x)\|$	for $0 < x < \pi$
	$= 0$	otherwise
PM	$= \|\sin(\pi/2 - x)\|$	for $\pi/2 < x < 3\pi/2$
	$= 0$	otherwise
PB	$= \|\sin(x)\|$	for $\pi < x < 3\pi/2$
	$= 0$	otherwise

Infinity is assumed at any value greater than the maximum value of Positive Big.

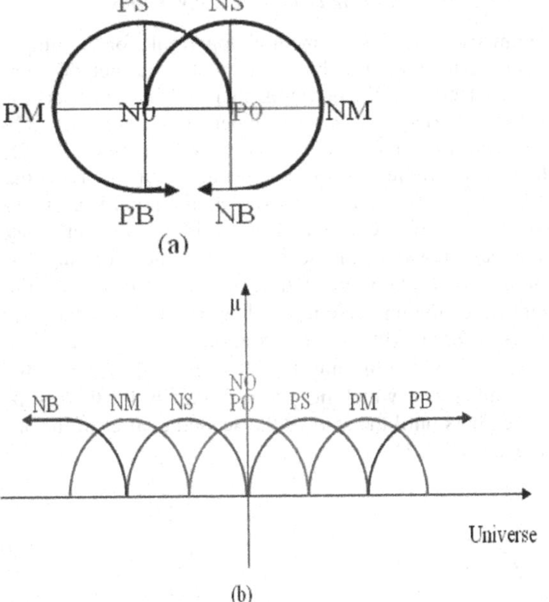

Figure 2: Fuzzimetric Arcs Negative and Positive sections.

Similarly the negative fuzzy variables may be defined in the same manner but in a different direction, i.e. counter-clockwise for the positive direction and clockwise for the negative direction. The zero level may then be shared between the two arcs (Fig. 2). Discretization of the universe in this way will assign a certain number of degrees of the arcs for each member. As an example, assuming a universe of real numbers in the range of –9 to +9, the universe should be assigned segments of 30° per member (+270/9 and –270/9), where infinity is assumed to be the values beyond the extremes. Table 1 shows the partitioned fuzzy variables with their corresponding assigned membership value for each member of the universe.

Some of the characteristics of the fuzzimetric arc are that some of the trigonometric formulae may be used to define fuzzy variables that lie between two adjacent sets, for example:

$+\text{BZS} = \text{PO}^2 + \text{PS}^2$ where $\text{PO}^2 + \text{PS}^2 = 1$, $0° < x < 90°$

$+\text{BSM} = \text{PS}^2 + \text{PM}^2$ where $\text{PS}^2 + \text{PM}^2 = 1$, $90° < x < 180°$

$+\text{BMB} = \text{PM}^2 + \text{PB}^2$ where $\text{PM}^2 + \text{PB}^2 = 1$, $180° < x < 270°$

Similarly:

$-\text{BZS} = \text{NO}^2 + \text{NS}^2$ where $\text{NO}^2 + \text{NS}^2 = 1$, $0° < x < -90°$

$-\text{BSM} = \text{NS}^2 + \text{NM}^2$ where $\text{NS}^2 + \text{NM}^2 = 1$, $-90° < x < -180°$

$-\text{BMB} = \text{NM}^2 + \text{NB}^2$ where $\text{NM}^2 + \text{NB}^2 = 1$, $-180° < x < -270°$

Where:

+BZS = Between zero and Positive Small.

+BSM = Between Positive Small and Positive Medium

+BMB = Between Positive Medium and Positive Big

–BZS = Between Zero and Negative Small.

–BSM = Between Negative Small and Negative Medium.

–BMB = Between Negative Medium and Negative Big.

Thus, with the help of Fuzzimetric Arcs, it is possible to assemble another type of linguistic hedge from two adjacent sets.

If a trapezoidal shape was considered appropriate for the process, then the following relationship should be applied to the fuzzy variables:

$$\mu = \frac{\arcsin(\text{fuzzy vaiable})}{t}$$

$$= 1 \text{ for } \mu > 1$$

Where the fuzzy variable is any of PO, PS… etc. The t parameter is the shape alternation factor (Mutation factor) in the range of $0 < t \leq 90$.

TABLE 1
FUZZY VARIABLE DEFINITIONS

	-9	-8	-7	-6	-5	-4	-3	-2	-1	0	1	2	3	4	5	6	7	8	9
NB	1	0.86	0.5	0	0	0	0	0	0	0	0	0	0	0	0	0	0	0	0
NM	0	0.5	0.86	1	0.86	0.5	0	0	0	0	0	0	0	0	0	0	0	0	0
NS	0	0	0	0	0.5	0.86	1	0.86	0.5	0	0	0	0	0	0	0	0	0	0
NO	0	0	0	0	0	0	0	0.5	0.86	1	0	0	0	0	0	0	0	0	0
PO	0	0	0	0	0	0	0	0	0	1	0.86	0.5	0	0	0	0	0	0	0
PS	0	0	0	0	0	0	0	0	0	0	0.5	0.86	1	0.86	0.5	0	0	0	0
PM	0	0	0	0	0	0	0	0	0	0	0	0	0	0.5	0.86	1	0.86	0.5	0
PB	0	0	0	0	0	0	0	0	0	0	0	0	0	0	0	0	0.5	0.86	1

A special case is when $t = 90$ which produces a triangular shape. If the value is greater than 90, a triangular shape of the fuzzy set would result in which the maximum value of membership is less than unity (Fig. 3). Thus altering the value of parameter t in Equation (1) would result in a different representation of fuzzy sets. This is useful when automatic search for the optimum shape of the fuzzy set is required.

As described so far, "Fuzzimetric Arcs" provides a systematic selection mechanism where the selection "fitness" factor may determine the final shape of the fuzzy set. Moreover, Fuzzimetric Arcs allow a mutation of the fuzzy sets by altering the range where the fuzzy set can be defined. For example assuming 50% mutation would result in an original initial selection of sin wave for the 1st half of the fuzzy set and a "mutated" 2nd half of the fuzzy set which might be half triangular, trapezoidal…etc. Figure 4(a) shows samples of possible 50% mutation combination between different forms of fuzzy set shapes using equation (1). Figure 4 (b) shows an UML notation example of fuzzy variable(shape definition) where the attributes are t, mutation, and angle with two methods select() (selecting sine, trapezoidal, triangular) and mutate(), providing the definition of mutated fuzzy set shape.

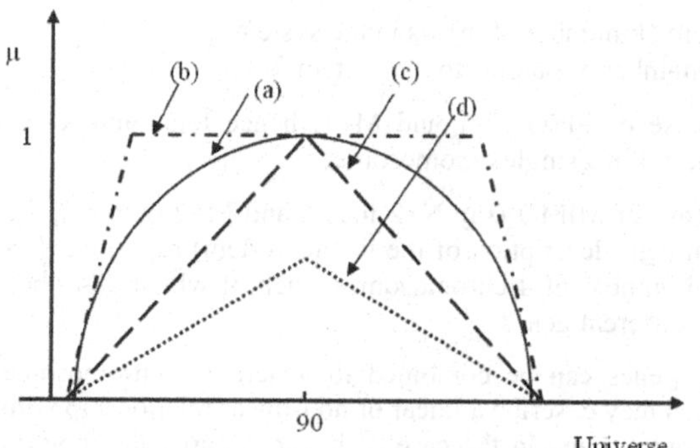

***Fig.** 3 Fuzzy shape of the fuzzy sets; (a) sin wave, (b) trapezoidal (μ arcsine (sin x)/t where t<90), (c) Special case when t = 90, (d) t>90.*

III. FUZZY INFERENCE ENGINE (FIE) USING FUZZIMETRIC ARCS AS THE DESIGN STRUCTURE

As this paper proposes to build a specialized type of generic inference engine using Fuzzimetric Arcs principle, such system will be termed as FIE (Fuzzy inference Engine) where it is composed of 3 main components. These components are: The fuzzification component, the knowledge component and the Inference/De-fuzzification component.

The first component uses Fuzzimetric Arcs as a genetic modification mechanism to find the optimum fuzzy set shape where crossover and mutation operators may be utilized. The second component will use a Knowledge search mechanism to find the trend in the rule-set(s) structure where crossover operator and fitness factor value will play the main role of defining rules suitability. The third component will measure the final performance of the system (after inference) and then decide upon the suitability of rule-set(s) using Cross-over/Fitness factor deviation from desired values and/or Fuzzy set shapes tuning using Crossover and mutation operators. This component will also be responsible for de-fuzzification procedure of the final output(s). Figure 5 below shows the schematic FIE structure in a form of three main components.

III.1. FUZZIFICATION COMPONENT

As mentioned in earlier section fuzzification process is dependent on Fuzzimetric Arcs principle as described above. This can be explained in the following steps:

Step1: Initial selection of Fuzzy variables using the above reviewed Fuzzimetric Arcs principle

a) Find out the range the system would work under (descretization Range). This can be achieved by subtracting the highest possible value form the minimum one

b) Calculate the scaling factors for each of the inputs and outputs.

c) Selection of good initialized "genes" of fuzzy variables (fuzzy set shapes) using Fuzzimetric Arcs standard as explained earlier without any mutation/crossover with a default angle value of 30^0 (for example) which discretize the universe to 10 different levels. This has to be accomplished for each of the input(s) and output(s).

Step 2: Crossover and mutation operations of fuzzy sets (variables) are dependent on the third component after inferring the results and measuring the fitness factor deviation.

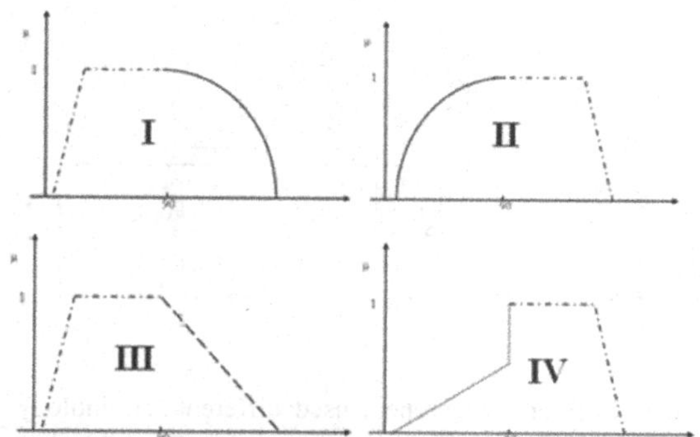

Figure 4(a) Samples of possible mutations using fuzzimetric arcs and equation (1) with 50% mutation (exact half of fuzzy set).

I) Mutation of Trapezoidal (left section) and Sin wave
II) Mutation of Trapezoidal (Right section) and sin wave
III) Mutation of Triangular (t=90) and Trapezoidal (left section)
IV) Mutation of Triangular (t>90) and Trapezoidal (right section)

Fuzzy Variable
Value= Angle= T= Mutation= Chromosome=
Fitness (); Select(); Mutate(); Crossover();

Figure 4(b) Fuzzy Variable can now be represented in a form of an object with attributes and operations as shown.

III.2. KNOWLEDGE/RULE-SETS DEFINITION COMPONENT

This component describes the behavior (collection of if-Then statements) of the system representing the knowledge of the system. Unfortunately there is no standard manual procedure for developing algorithms and therefore the rules must be developed from *a priori* knowledge of the system. Extraction of the knowledge and representing it in algorithmic form is mainly regarded as knowledge engineering, which is gained through communication with human experts. However, by using the concept of Fuzzimetric Arcs together with the concept of multivariable structure proposed by Kouatli [9] can be utilized as a methodology to standardize on rule-set/knowledge extraction where the effect of each of the input(s) to the output(s) of the multi-variable system is treated as separate rule-set modules. Collection of those rule-set modules into one coherent structure of rule-set can be accomplished using weighting factor (a factor to measure the importance level of a specific input). More details can be found in Kouatli [9] which is beyond the scope of this paper.

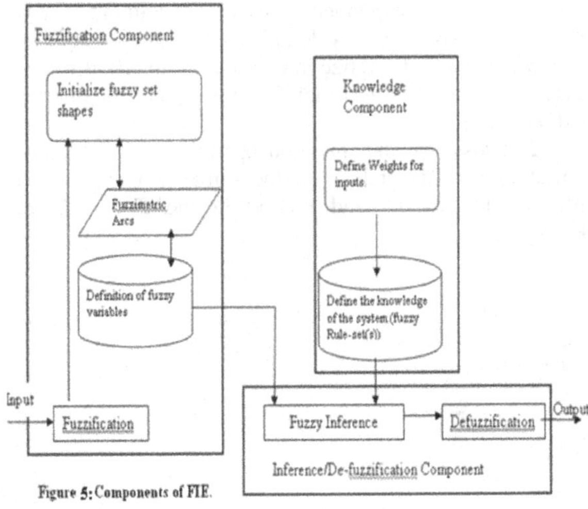

Figure 5: Components of FIE.

In GFS, different researchers used different terminology when describing chromosomes to resembles the GFS. For example, Shi et al [10] assumed that a chromosome represent the whole rule-set (Pittsburgh approach), while Kovacs [11] assumed that a chromosome is a behavior description of single rule (Michigan approach). A full study of using the different terminology can be found in [1]. In this paper and in resemblance to biological context, the following definitions will be adopted:

Definition 1: A Gene: is a specific rule composed of one of the inputs (IF part of the rule) and one of the outputs (THEN part of the rule). The arrangement method of multiple genes resembles the fuzzy-DNA.

Definition 2: A Chromosome: is a collection of the genes in a specific manner. It is composed of rule-set that describe the behavior of a specific input with a specific output.

Definition 3: A Cell: is a collection of multiple chromosomes (Rule-sets in case of MIMO) that describes the behavior of the whole system. In this case, coherent combinations of individual chromosomes (rule-sets) of each of inputs and outputs can be achieved using the multivariable technique described in [9] by using input importance weighting factor. In case of Single-input-single-output system (SISO), then a cell (behavior of the whole system) is composed of only one chromosome.

Completeness and consistency of the chromosomes (Rule-set(s) is important to achieve an efficient system, i.e. it is important that the rule-set covers all possible combinations of the input and output variables. It is also vital to eliminate and replace any contradiction in some of the rules in that rule-set. For example, in case of Single-input-Single-Output system **(SISO)** in conjunction with Fuzzimetric Arcs (four basic variables), the total number of rules required is four rules covering all possible input values to the system. This can be calculated using the general formula:

Number of genes (Rules)= 4*N*M

where N=number of inputs in the system.
M=number of outputs to the system

In case of SISO N=1 and M=1, hence total number of genes=4 in a single chromosome.

In case of MIMO (say N=2 inputs and M=2 outputs), the final cell (description of the whole system) represented in total number of 4 chromosomes, each of which described in 4 different genes.

The genes can be combined to generate a chromosome which may describe a linear or non-linear relationship with the output, and in the case of linear relation, the input(s) could be either directly proportional or inversely proportional with the output(s). Fig 6 shows examples of different possibilities of rule-set definitions.

(a)	(b)
If input 1=PO Then output 1=PO	If input 1=PO Then output 1=PL
If input 1=PS Then output 1=PS	If input 1=PS Then output 1=PM
If input 1=PM Then output 1=PM	If input 1=PM Then output 1=PS
If input 1=PL Then output 1=PL	If input 1=PL Then output 1=PO

(a) Linear directly proportional rule-set, (b) Linear inversly proportional rule-set

If input 1=PO Then output 1=PM
If input 1=PS Then output 1=PM
If input 1=PM Then output 1=PS
If input 1=PL Then output 1=PS

(c) Non-linear rule-set

Fig 6 Examples of Linear and non-linear rule-sets

III.3. FUZZY INFERENCE AND DE-FUZZIFICATION COMPONENT

Using the Multivariable structure described above, the final inference value (optimum) is dependent on the fitness factor value. In brief, the following steps (as described in figure 7)

Step1- starts with the default initializations of fuzzy sets and rule-set.

Step 2- Fuzzify fuzzy variables

Step 3- Infer decision (Output)

Step 4- Measure fitness factor (if actual values equal to the output values then stop) otherwise,

Step5- Check if fuzzy set selection is appropriate (Mutate or crossover when necessary)

Step 6- Check if rule-set chosen is appropriate.

Step 7- modify as applicable and repeat from step 4.

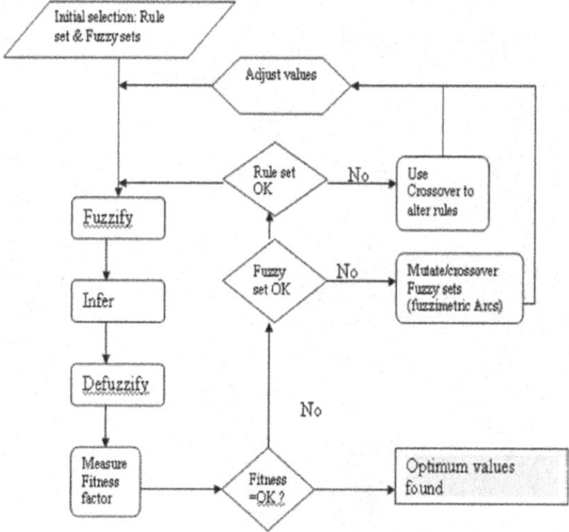

Figure 7 Mechanism of GFA

IV. CONCLUSION

This paper provides a guidance of using genetic algorithm by using a technique termed as "Fuzzimetric Arcs" as a process to tune GFS by altering and optimizing the fuzzy set shape (Fuzzy variable definition) by using two main operators Crossover and Mutation. The effect of this optimization reflected on the GFS performance level. Moreover, tuning of the rule set(s) that describes the behavior of the system can be accomplished by measuring the deviation from the Fitness factor level. The proposed technique/mechanism can be easily incorporated into GFS and provide a possible standardization of selection and tuning of fuzzy set shapes.

References

[1] Herrera, F., "Genetic Fuzzy Systems: Taxonomy, Current Research Trends and Prospects". Evolutionary Intelligence 1 (2008) 27-46

[2] YOUNGSU YUN, MITSUO GEN "Performance Analysis of Adaptive Genetic Algorithms with Fuzzy Logic and Heuristics" in "Fuzzy Optimization and Decision Making", 2, 161– 175, 2003 # 2003 Kluwer Academic Publishers. Printed in The Netherlands.

[3] O.Cordon, F. Herrera, E. Herrera-viedima, M. Lozano « Genetic algorithms and fuzzy logic in control processes » Tech report #DECSAI-95109, 1995

[4] F. Herrera, Leuis Magdalena, "Genetic Fuzzy systems: A tutorial".

[5] Kouatli, I. And Jones, B. (1990) An improved design procedure for fuzzy control systems. International Journal of Machine Tool and Manufacure,

[6] Kouatli I., Jones, B. "A guide to the design of fuzzy control systems for manufacturing processes", Journal of Intelligent Manufacturing, 1-1990, pp 231-244

[7] Kouatli, I. "Definition and selection of fuzzy sets in genetic-fuzzy systems using the concept of Fuzzimetric Arcs" Kybernetes, VOL: 37 NO. 1, 2008 pp 166-181

[8] Kouatli, I., Khayat,H. "FIE: A generic Fuzzy decision making tool with An Example of CRM Analysis" -in Press

[9] Kouatli, I., "A simplified fuzzy multi-variable structure in a manufacturing environment" Journal of Intelligent Manufacturing, 1994 VOL: 5, pp:365-387

[10] Shi, YH, Eberhart R, Chen YB. "Implementation of Evolutionary Fuzzy systems" IEEE Trans Fuzzy systems 1999 7(2): pp 109-119

[11] Kovacs T "Strength or accuracy: Credit assignment in learning classifier systems. 2004- Springler, Berlin.

Multi-Step EMG Classification Algorithm for Human-Computer Interaction

Peng Ren, Armando Barreto and Malek Adjouadi

Biomedical Engineering / Electrical & Computer Engineering Department
Florida International University
Miami, FL 33174 USA

Abstract- **A three-electrode human-computer interaction system, based on digital processing of the Electromyogram (EMG) signal, is presented. This system can effectively help disabled individuals paralyzed from the neck down to interact with computers or communicate with people through computers using point-and-click graphic interfaces. The three electrodes are placed on the right frontalis, the left temporalis and the right temporalis muscles in the head, respectively. The signal processing algorithm used translates the EMG signals during five kinds of facial movements (left jaw clenching, right jaw clenching, eyebrows up, eyebrows down, simultaneous left & right jaw clenching) into five corresponding types of cursor movements (left, right, up, down and left-click), to provide basic mouse control. The classification strategy is based on three principles: the EMG energy of one channel is typically larger than the others during one specific muscle contraction; the spectral characteristics of the EMG signals produced by the frontalis and temporalis muscles during different movements are different; the EMG signals from adjacent channels typically have correlated energy profiles. The algorithm is evaluated on 20 pre-recorded EMG signal sets, using Matlab simulations. The results show that this method provides improvements and is more robust than other previous approaches.**

Keywords-Human-Computer Interaction (HCI), Electromyography (EMG), Mean Power Frequency (MPF), Signal Energy.

I. INTRODUCTION

In modern society, the ability to interact with information technology devices, such as computers, is very important for the social integration of all individuals. Unfortunately, there are still many people suffering from spinal cord injury or spinal dysfunction, who may have their mobility severely restricted. It is estimated that currently there are 250,000-400,000 individuals having these disabilities in the US and these numbers grow by about 7800 cases each year [1].

Human-computer Interaction (HCI) is a sub-discipline that focuses on the interaction between users and computers, and it involves in its research aspects of computer science, electrical engineering, physiology, clinical science etc. Some researchers in this filed seek to provide individuals with motor disabilities, who are unable to use the mouse, touchpad or keyboard, new alternatives to access the computers. For example, "brain-computer interfaces" have been developed, which use electroencephalogram (EEG) signals from the user to send commands to the computer. Wolpaw et al. [2] have utilized the 8-12 Hz Mu rhythm recording from the scalp over the central sulcus of one hemisphere to move a cursor. Leuthardt et al. [3] have used electrocorticographic (ECoG) activity recordings from the surface of the brain to control a one-dimensional computer cursor. However, a substantial disadvantage of these approaches is that an extensive training is required before the users can control the computer efficiently.

Eye-gaze tracking (EGT) is another common approach to address the problem of hands-free cursor control. Video capturing the eye of the user is processed to determine, in real-time, the line of gaze, i.e., the direction in which the user is looking, and, therefore, the location on the screen where the user is looking [16, 17, 18]. Nowadays, modern eye-tracking systems use contrast to locate the bright eye (pupil) center and apply infrared light to obtain a strong corneal reflection. Then the locations of the pupil reflection and the corneal reflection in the video image are used to determine the line of gaze.

Electromyography (EMG) signals, which reflect the electrical potentials generated by muscle cells when these cells are active and at rest, can also be used for cursor control [4,5,6,7,8,9,10]. In [6], two electrodes were placed on both sides of the mouth to implement a continuous decoder, which interpreted the input signal stream in order to achieve cursor control. Barreto et al., [4,5] used two electrodes respectively placed on both sides of the subject's head, to monitor the activity of the left temporalis muscle and right temporalis muscle, and one electrode placed on the forehead of the subject, to monitor the electrical activity of the right frontalis muscle. This approach is suitable for individuals who suffer from severe motor disabilities or are paralyzed from the neck down. In [9,10], one electrode placed on the procerus was added to the original three-electrode system to achieve better performance in implementing UP and DOWN cursor control.

In [5], it is also mentioned that the EMG signal generated by the contraction of one particular muscle tends to have different frequency distribution from EMG reflecting contractions of other muscles. Fig.1. shows the spectrum distribution during a frontalis contraction and a temporalis contraction separately. According to [11], the reasons for these spectral differences may be found in aspects such as muscle fatigue, motor unit recruitment patterns and conduction velocity.

T. Sobh, K. Elleithy (eds.), *Innovations in Computing Sciences and Software Engineering*,
DOI 10.1007/978-90-481-9112-3_31,

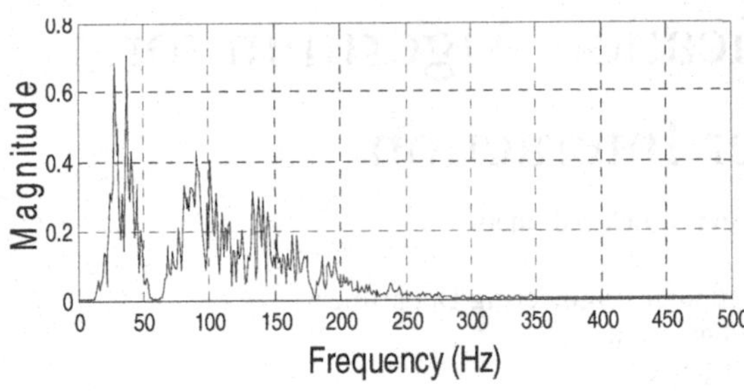

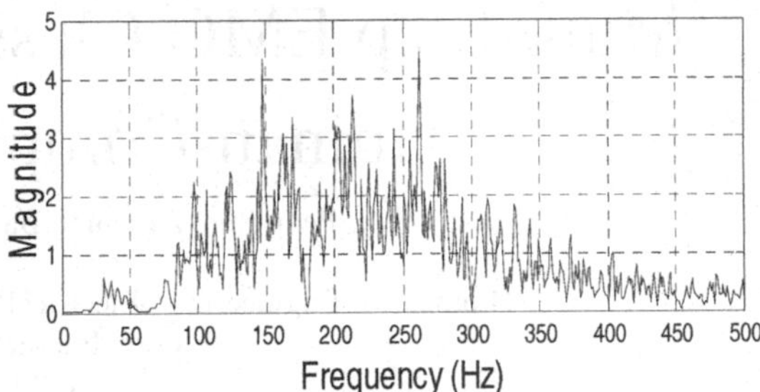

Fig. 1. Spectra observed during a right frontalis contraction (left plot) and left temporalis contraction (right plot)

In [9], Chin et al. successfully used the comparison of the sum of the power spectral density (PSD) of the EMG signals sensed by different electrodes (monitoring different muscles), to perform the classification necessary for cursor control. Similarly, calculation of the Mean Square Value (MSV) of EMG signals extracted from different muscles has been used to identify which muscle performed a specific contraction [12]. In one way or another, all these previous researchers used the assessment of EMG signal energy for classification purposes.

The EMG signal is the composite sum of electrical activity from all the motor unit action potentials occuring in the muscle underlying the skin. A motor unit contains one motor neuron and all the muscle fibers it innervates. When a motor unit fires, the action potential will spread over all of the innervated muscle fibers of that particular motor unit. When the muscle is not contracting, it does not yield action potentials, which means that no EMG signal will be detected [14].

II. METHODS AND MATERIALS

A. Electrode placement for the HCI system

The HCI system provides the basic cursor control commands required for computer interaction (UP, DOWN, LEFT, RIGHT, Left-Click), deriving them from analysis of the activity of serveral cranial muscles. Fig.2 displays the placement of Ag/AgCl electrodes on the head of the subject.

Electrode 1 is placed on the forehead of the subject, displaced about two centimeters to the right, to monitor the activity of the right frontalis muscle. Electrodes 2 and 3 are placed on both sides of the head, at locations assigned for monitoring the left and right temporalis muscles, respectively. A reference electrode is needed to collect three referential EMG signals. The reference electrode is placed on the right mastoid.

B. Hardware Components of the EMG system

The three EMG signals are amplified using Grass® P5 Series AC biopotential preamplifiers (Grass Technologies Product Group, Astro-Med Inc; West Warwick, Rhode Island). These amplifiers preprocess the signals with analog anti-aliasing filters and amplify the signals with a gain of 10,000 V/V.

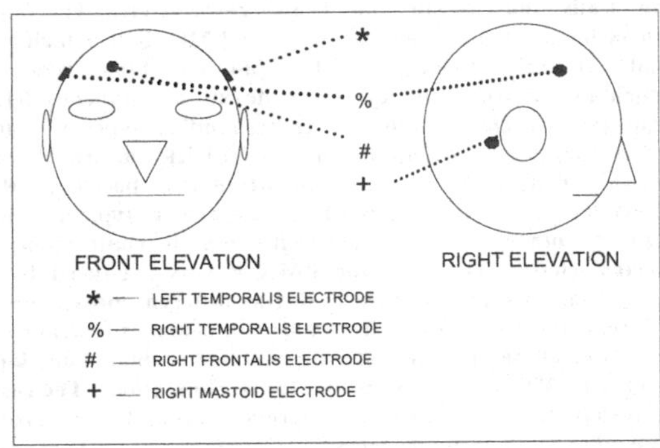

Fig. 2. Electrode placement diagram for the EMG system

A 60 Hz notch-filter is also implemented by each of the thee preamplifiers used to process the 3 EMG signals. The outputs of these preamplifiers have amplitudes in the range of -5 V and +5 V and are sent to the NI DAQPad-6020E analog-to-digital conversion module, to digitize each signal channel at a sampling rate of 1 KHz. The "Traditional" NI-DAQ driver, from National Instruments, was used to store the digital data on a PC. The digital data files gathered from this setup are employed as the inputs to the classification algorithm written in Matlab.

C. The Classification Algorithm

Our approach is aimed at associating a facial movement with a corresponding cursor movement command. In [4,5,9,13], it has been proposed that the left and right temporalis muscles can produce unilateral contractions, meaning that the dominant contraction produced by the left temporalis can lead to a significant increase of EMG amplitude at electrode 3 during the clenching of the left side of the jaw, and the dominant contraction produced by the right temporalis can cause a significant increase of EMG amplitude at electrode 2 during the clenching of the right side of the jaw.

In addition, the clenching of the full jaw (both sides) results in significant EMG amplitude increases at electrodes 2 and 3. In [9], the right frontalis and procerus contractions were used to command the UP and DOWN cursor movements, respectively. It is known that moving the eyebrows up or down, will produce different contraction levels of the fibers of the right frontalis muscle. So our aim is to differentiate these two facial movements from analysis of the signal from just one electrode, placed on the right frontalis. The desired relationships between voluntary facial movements and associated cursor commands are shown in Table I.

TABLE I
Relations between cursor movement, facial movement and muscle contractions

Cursor Action	Facial Movement	Muscle Contracting	Sensing Electrode
Left	Left Jaw Clench	Left Temporalis	3
Right	Right Jaw Clench	Right Temporalis	2
Up	Eyebrows Up	Right Frontalis	1
Down	Eyebrows Down	Right Frontalis	1
Left-Click	Left & Right Jaw Clench	Left & Right Temporalis	2 & 3

The classification algorithm makes use of signal energy estimation of each of the three EMG signals. In discrete signal processing, the signal energy is commonly assessed as the sum of the squared magnitude of the samples. This calculation is performed on windows of 250 consecutive samples (every 0.25 second) of each of the three EMG channels. Mathematically,

$$E_d = \sum_{i=1}^{250} X_i^2 \qquad (1)$$

The Mean Power Frequency (MPF) is also used in our classification algorithm. It is derived from the Power Spectral Density (PSD) estimates. The PSD describes how the energy of a signal is distributed over different frequencies. The MPF is defined as a weighted average frequency where each frequency component (f_i) is weighted by its corresponding power (P_i). The formula for the MPF is given by:

$$MPF = \frac{f_1 \times P_1 + f_2 \times P_2 + \ldots + f_i \times P_i}{P_1 + P_2 + \ldots + P_i} \quad i=1,2,..,250 \qquad (2)$$

In previous publications [4,5,9], it has been noticed that the main spectrum range distribution of the frontalis muscle is below 200 Hz, with the MPF in the range 40 Hz- 170 Hz, while raising the eyebrows. The EMG spectrum of a temporalis contraction has most of its components above 200 Hz, with the MPF in the range 120 Hz-295 Hz. It has also been observed that the spectra of EMG signals from the muscles monitored in this study do not contain significant components below 50 Hz. In contrast, noise signals seem to usually have important components in this frequency range.

The classification algorithm includes three main steps. The first step is to determine whether a block of data (250 samples) reflects "movement" or "no-movement". Movement indicates that the subject performed any of the five facial actions as mentioned above (left jaw clench, right jaw clench, eyebrows up, eyebrows down simultaneous left & right jaw clench). No-movement indicates that during this period, the subject did not perform any voluntary facial movement, which implies that the EMG signal is not generated and the collected signal is mostly noise. If the segment under analysis is found to contain a movement, the second step is to determine which channel has the maximum energy value. Then, the third step is to use specific criteria, described below, to determine which of the five facial movements took place. If the maximum energy value is in channel 1, this situation has two possibilities: eyebrows up or eyebrows down, corresponding to up or down cursor commands, respectively. If the maximum energy value is found in channel 2 or in channel 3, the criteria explained below will be used to determine whether a left jaw clench and/or a right jaw clench took place. If the signals indicate that a simultaneous clench of both sides of the jaw took place, then the system will command a Left-Click cursor action. Otherwise the channel with the highest energy value will determine the corresponding lateral cursor movement.

Several criteria must be met before the HCI will issue a cursor command or a "Left-Click". The identification of the signal as movement or no-movement requires the MPF calculation of the original signal data for channel 1(MPF_{ori1}), because, as mentioned above, typical noise components have lower MPF values compared with any of the five facial movements, which is one of the significant characteristics for distinguishing no-movement periods from movement periods. Then, in order to remove the noise and keep the components of the actual EMG signals, a high-pass filter with a cutoff frequency at 50 Hz is applied to all the EMG channels and each filtered EMG signal is compared against a threshold Th_0. The values of the filtered signals which do not surpass this threshold are zeroed, yielding the 3 new signals X_1, X_2 and X_3. In addition, the signal energy values from X_1, X_2 and X_3 are calculated according to (1) obtaining a value for each 250 samples denoted as E_1, E_2, E_3, respectively. Finally, to account for the common interference energy present in each pair of the channels E_1, E_2 and E_3, the corresponding energy differences ($S_{12}=E_1-E_2$; $S_{13}=E_1-E_3$; $S_{23}=E_2-E_3$) are calculated.

With these preliminary results, the conditions that classify the EMG signals can be summarized as follows:

STEP I

Conditions for classifying MOVEMENT/NO MOVEMENT

(1) $E_1>Th_1$ (Th_1:The threshold for signal energy value of channel 1)

(2) $MPF_{ori1}>40$

(3) ($|S_{12}|<Th_2$) || ($|S_{13}|<Th_2$) || ($|S_{23}|<Th_2$) (Th_2: The threshold for E_1, E_2, E_3 subtraction)

If all three conditions are satisfied
Then: Go Step II.
Else: NO-MOVEMENT

STEP II

Find the channel with the maximum signal energy value of E_1, E_2 and E_3.
If it is in channel 1, go to STEP III-A
If it is in channel 2 or channel 3, go to STEP III-B:

STEP III-A

Conditions for classifying UP/ DOWN CURSOR MOVEMENT

(1) $E_1>Th_3$ (Th_3: The threshold for signal energy value of channel 1)
(2) ($E_2>Th_4$)&&($E_3>Th_4$) (Th_4: The threshold for signal energy value of channel 2 and 3)
(3) $MPF_{fil1}<=170$ (MPF_{fil1}: The mean power frequency of X_1)
(4) $|S_{12}|> 1$

If two or more conditions are satisfied
Then: UP Cursor Movement
Else: DOWN Cursor Movement

STEP III-B

Conditions for classifying CURSOR LEFT/CURSOR RIGHT/LEFT-CLICK MOVEMENT

(1) ($E_2>0.3*(E_3+E_2)$)&& ($E_3>0.3*(E_3+E_2)$)
(2) ($|E_2-E_3|/max(E_2,E_3)$)< 0.8
(3) ($E_2>Th_5$)&& ($E_3>Th_5$) (Th_5: The threshold for signal energy value of channel 2 and 3)
(4) ($S_{12}<-1$)&&($S_{13}<-1$)

If three or more conditions are satisfied
Then: LEFT-CLICK Movement
Else: If the maximum energy is in channel 3
Then: LEFT Cursor Movement
If the maximum energy is in channel 2
Then: RIGHT Cursor Movement

III. TESTING

Twenty pre-recorded multi-channel EMG files were involved in the testing of the classification algorithm. Each file contained the three EMG signals measured from the frontalis (channel 1), the right temporalis (channel 2) and the left temporalis (channel 3). Each file lasted approximately 190 seconds and contained the EMG signals obtained while the subject executed a series of movements and pauses, following the schedule shown in Table II. An experimenter kept track of the timing during the recording and provided verbal cues to the subject, indicating what kind of movement or pause needed to be executed next. Adherence to this schedule during the recording provided us with knowledge of the actual type of movement (or pause) contained in each 250-sample data window analyzed.

TABLE II
Schedule of facial movements and pauses executed by each subject

Time	Sequence of Facial Movement
0-20s	No Movement
20-40s	Left Clench
40-50s	No Movement
50-70s	Eyebrows Up
70-80s	No Movement
80-100s	Left/Right Clench
100-110s	No Movement
110-130s	Eyebrows Down
130-140s	No Movement
140-160s	Right Clench
160-190s	No Movement

IV. RESULTS

In order to directly view the results of the algorithm, the outputs of the algorithm were assigned to be one of six integer values (0-5). Each integer corresponds to a specific classification result and can be used to command a specific cursor action. Table III shows the mapping between classification output values and cursor movement. Following this coding scheme, the classification result for each 250-sample window of EMG data analyzed is expressed as a value from 0 to 5. This allows to present all the classification results for a given data file (representing an experimental session) as a stem plot, such as the example provided in Fig. 3. The example in this figure shows how the majority of the stems appear grouped in segments that reflect the schedule of actions performed by the subject (correct classifications), with only a few stems departing from the value that corresponds to the action in each segment of the file (incorrect classifications). The percentage of correct classifications (with respect to the total number of classifications) in a file determines the accuracy of the method for that test file. The accuracy of classification process for all the 20 files is shown in Table IV.

Table III
Mapping between classification output and cursor movement

Classification Algorithm Output	Cursor Movement
0	No Movement
1	Up
2	Right
3	Left
4	Down
5	Left-click

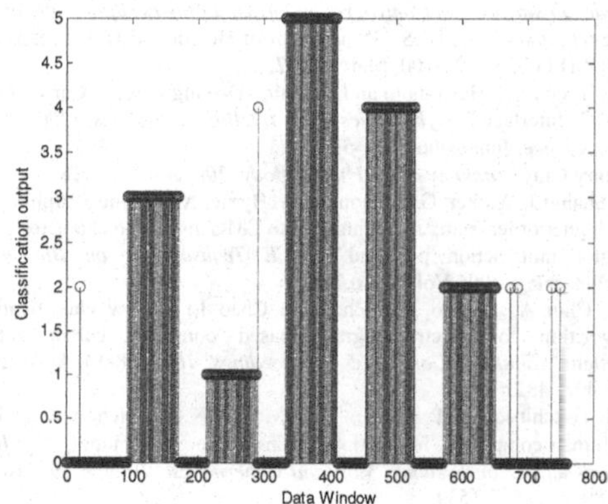

Fig . 3. Example of a classification sequence produced

TABLE IV
Accuracy of the classification algorithm for each test file

File #	Accuracy (%)	File #	Accuracy (%)
1	96.97	11	94.74
2	93.94	12	97.50
3	98.94	13	95.13
4	93.29	14	97.37
5	96.45	15	99.08
6	98.68	16	97.90
7	95.53	17	94.87
8	98.42	18	93.82
9	94.45	19	96.58
10	93.16	20	97.76

V. DISCUSSION

The results show that the three-electrode HCI system has an average accuracy of 96.23% with the maximum correct classification percentage of 99.08% and the minimum correct classification percentage of 93.16%, in the twenty test files used for its evaluation. The standard deviation for the accuracy is 3.85%. These figures represent encouraging results. A previous algorithm that attempted the same classification of 5 muscular contraction conditions from the same three EMG signals had an average classification accuracy of 78.43% with a standard deviation of 22.90% [15]. Therefore the new multi-step classification process presented in this paper has achieved a greater average accuracy, accompanied by a much smaller standard deviation, which is believed to represent a higher level of consistency and robustness.

Previous algorithms for EMG cursor control proposed by our group [15] had demonstrated high levels of accuracy and robustness, but at the cost of placing one more electrode on the forehead of the subject, over the procerus muscle. While the addition of a fourth electrode is not a great burden from the point of view of instrumentation or computational complexity, there is a marked preference on the part of individuals with motor disabilities (the targeted end-users of these developments), for systems that do not add awkward or cumbersome elements to their physical appearance. Therefore, being able to achieve higher accuracy and robustness with only 3 electrodes, conveniently placed under a sports headband, is an important step forward towards achieving a higher level of user comfort with the system.

VI. CONCLUSION

The EMG-based Human-Computer Interaction system presented can, potentially, provide individuals suffering severe motor disabilities with an approach to interact with their environment and with others through a point-and-click computer interface. Its operation is simple, requiring only five kinds of voluntary contraction of cranial muscles, and the placement of only three electrodes on the head of the user, to collect the EMG signals from designated positions. The use of only three electrodes reduces the instrumental requirements and the computational load associated with the operation of the system. Most importantly, eliminating the need for the placement of a fourth electrode in between the eyes of the subject can effectively reduce his/her discomfort when using the system.

The operation of this HCI system is possible due to the following three reasons. First, the EMG signal collected in the neighborhood of the cranial muscle performing a contraction tends to have the largest amplitude or energy of all the EMG signals collected during that contraction. Second, the contractions of different cranial muscles display different spectral compositions in the corresponding EMG signal. Third, the noise components present in the signals collected during the "no-movement" intervals tend to have similar levels of energy and, therefore, are cancelled when pair-wise differences of the energy measures are considered. This facilitates the process of discarding the signal segments collected while no movements are executed.

In comparison with other unassisted interfaces for users with motor disabilities such as the previous four-electrode based EMG HCI system, the EMG HCI interface presented here has advantages of enhanced simplicity, accuracy and robustness. As such it may represent an important contribution to the possibilities available for hands-free computer cursor control.

ACKNOWLEDGEMENTS

This work was sponsored by NSF grants CNS-0520811, CNS-0426125, and HRD-0833093.

REFERENCES

[1] http://www.makoa.org/nscia/fact02.html
[2] Jonathan R. Wolpaw, Niels Birbaumer, Dennis J. McFarland, Gert Pfurtscheller and Theresa M. Vaughan, "Brain-computer interfaces for communication and control," *Clinical Neurophysiology*, vol. 113, Issue 6, pp. 767-791, June 2002.
[3] Eric C. Leuthardt, Gerwin Schalk, Jonathan R. Wolpaw, Jeffrey G. Ojemann and Daniel W. Moran, "A brain-computer interface using

electrocorticographic signals in humans," *J. Neural Eng.*, vol.1, issue 2, June 2004, pp. 63-71 .

[4] A. B Barreto, S. D Scargle, and M. Adjouadi, "A Real-Time Assistive Computer Interface for Users with Motor Disabilities," *SIGCAPH Newsletter*, Issue 64, 1999, pp. 6-16.

[5] A. B Barreto, S. D Scargle, and M. Adjouadi, " A Practical EMG-based Human-Computer Interface for Users with Motor Disabilities," *Journal Of Rehabilitation Research And Development,* vol. 37, Issue 1, January - February 2000, pp.53-63.

[6] http://www.hotamateurprograms.com/

[7] T. Itou, M. Terao, J. Nagata and M. Yoshida, "Mouse cursor control system using EMG," *2001 Conference Proceedings of the 23rd Annual International Conference of the IEEE Engineering in Medicine and Biology Society*, vol. 2, 2001, pp. 1368-1369.

[8] M. Yoshida, T. Itou and J. Nagata, "Development of EMG controlled mouse cursor," *Conference Proceedings, Second Joint EMBS-BMES Conference 2002.24th Annual International Conference of the Engineering in Medicine and Biology Society*, Annual Fall Meeting of the Biomedical Engineering Society, vol. 3, 2002, pp. 2436.

[9] Craig A. Chin, Armando Barreto, Gualberto Cremades and Malek Adjouadi, "Integrated electromyogram and eye-gaze tracking cursor control system for computer users with motor disabilities," *Journal of Rehabilitation Research & Development,* vol. 45, Number 1, 2008, pp.161-174.

[10] G.C. Chang, W.J. Kang, J.J. Luh, C.K. Cheng, J.S. Lai, J.J. Chen and T.S. Kuo, "Real-time implementation of electromyogram pattern recognition as a control command of man-machine interface," *Med Eng Phys.*, vol. 45,1996,18(7),PP.529–37.

[11] B. LeVeau and G. Andersson, "Output forms: data analysis and applications," *Interpretation of the electromyographic signal, selected topics in surface electromyography for use in the occupational setting: expert perspective*, U .S . Department of Health and Human Services, NIOSH Pub. No. 91-100, March 1992.

[12] A. Sasaki, H. Hashimoto and C. Ishii, "Driving Electric Car by Using EMG Interface," *Cybernetics and Intelligent Systems, 2006 IEEE Conference*, June 2006, PP.1-5.

[13] Henry Gray, *Anatomy of the Human Body. 20th edition,* 1918.

[14] S. Shahid,J. Walker, G.M Lyons, C.A. Byrne, A.V. Nene , "Application of higher order statistics techniques to EMG signals to characterize the motor unit action potential," *IEEE Transactions on Biomedical Engineering*, 2005 Vol.52(No.7) .

[15] C. Chin, A. Barreto, Jing Zhai and Chao Li , "New classification algorithm for electromyography-based computer cursor control system," *SoutheastCon, 2005. Proceedings. IEEE*, 8-10 April 2005, PP.428- 432.

[16] T.E Hutchinson, K.P. White, W.N Martin, K.C. Reichert, L.A. Frey "Human-computer interaction using eye-gaze input, " *IEEE Transactions on Systems, Man and Cybernetics*, Volume 19, Issue 6, 1989, pp. 1527-1534.

[17] R.J.K. Jacob, "The use of eye movements in human-computer interaction techniques: what you look at is what you get," *ACM Transactions on Information Systems*, Volume 9, Issue 2, 1991, pp. 152-169.

[18] Lankford Chris; "Effective eye-gaze input into Windows," *Proceedings of the symposium on Eye tracking research & applications*, 2000, pp. 23-27.

Affective Assessment of a Computer User through the Processing of the Pupil Diameter Signal

Ying Gao, Armando Barreto and Malek Adjouadi

Electrical and Computer Engineering Department
Florida International University
Miami, FL 33174 USA

Abstract- **This study proposes to achieve the affective assessment of a computer user through the processing of the pupil diameter (PD) signal. An adaptive interference canceller (AIC) system using the H$^\infty$ time-varying (HITV) adaptive algorithm was developed to minimize the impact of the PLR (pupil size changes caused by light intensity variations) on the measured pupil diameter signal. The modified pupil diameter (MPD) signal, obtained from the AIC, was expected to reflect primarily the pupillary affective responses (PAR) of the subject. Additional manipulations of the AIC output resulted in a Processed MPD (PMPD) signal, from which a classification feature, "PMPDmean", was extracted. This feature was used to train and test a support vector machine (SVM), for the identification of "stress" states in the subject, achieving an accuracy rate of 77.78%. The advantages of affective recognition through the PD signal were verified by comparatively investigating the classification of "stress" and "relaxation" states through features derived from the simultaneously recorded galvanic skin response (GSR) and blood volume pulse (BVP) signals, with and without the PD feature. Encouraging results in affective assessment based on pupil diameter monitoring were obtained in spite of intermittent illumination increases purposely introduced during the experiments. Therefore, these results confirmed the possibility of using PD monitoring to evaluate the evolving affective states of a computer user.**

*Keywords-*Pupil Diameter (PD) Signal, Adaptive Interference Canceller (AIC), H$^\infty$ time-varying (HITV) adaptive algorithm, Support Vector Machine (SVM).

I. Introduction

In order to improve the interaction between humans and computers, research is currently underway to create a computer system that could tailor its responses differently according to the user's emotional state [1]. To achieve this goal, the assessment of the computer user's affective state (e.g., stress), has been considered as one of the key challenges [1].

Over the last decade, many researchers have carried out studies to address the affective assessment challenge. The monitoring and analysis of physiological signals is considered as a particularly promising method, since these signals are inherently controlled by the subject's Autonomic Nervous System (ANS), and they are, therefore, less susceptible to environmental interference or voluntary masking [1]. There are several physiological signals that can be chosen for affective state monitoring. Along with the traditional physiological parameters such as the Galvanic Skin Response (GSR), Blood Volume Pulse (BVP), etc., the Pupil Diameter (PD) has been found to be a variable that changes with the subject's emotional state. However, the affective sensing potential of PD has not been fully investigated. This may be due to the well-known confounding effect of the "Pupillary Light Reflex" or "PLR" (i.e., the pupil diameter changes in response to light intensity variations of the environment).

In this research we propose to minimize the impact of the PLR in the measured PD signal by means of an Adaptive Interference Canceller (AIC) using the H$^\infty$ time-varying (HITV) adaptive algorithm, with the hope that the resulting "Modified Pupil Diameter" (MPD), further enhanced by additional post-processing (PMPD), can be used as an indicator of the PD changes derived solely from the affective response of the subject, which has been termed the Pupillary Affective Response (PAR). We gauge the success of this approach by the classification performance of features extracted from the PMPD signal, using a Support Vector Machine (SVM) classifier. On the other hand, the stress detection results obtained through features derived from the GSR and BVP with and without the PMPD signal are also investigated. This comparative study provides an opportunity to determine the advantage of affective assessment through PD vs. other physiological signals (GSR & BVP).

II. Signal Monitoring

In this work we measured and analyzed PD, GSR and BVP signals to determine the affective state of a computer user. PD records the size of a subject's pupil, which will be increased if the subject experiences stress or if the Illumination Intensity (IL) in the environment decreases. At the same time, it is well known that when a person is experiencing stress, the palms of his/her hands tend to become moist. This emotional sweating can be measured by changes in the GSR signal. The BVP signal reflects the cardiovascular activity of the subject, which is expected to be different in "stress" and "relaxation" states.

A. Software Development

In order to observe the changes in the PD, BVP and GSR signals and their correlation to the affective states of "stress" and "relaxation", we use the "Stroop Color-Word Interference Test" [9] to elicit mild mental stress in the experimental subjects during controlled intervals.

T. Sobh, K. Elleithy (eds.), *Innovations in Computing Sciences and Software Engineering*,
DOI 10.1007/978-90-481-9112-3_32, © Springer Science+Business Media B.V. 2010

In the test, a word presented to the subject designates a color that may ("Congruent") or not ("Incongruent") match its meaning. The subjects were instructed automatically by the program to click one of the five screen buttons to indicate the font color of the word presented. A typical (Incongruent) example of this test interface is shown in Fig. 1. The complete experiment protocol (Fig. 2) comprised three consecutive sections.

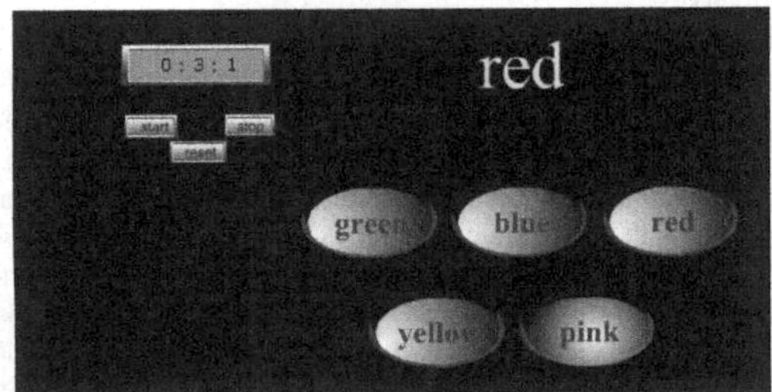

Fig. 1. Sample of the Stroop test interface.

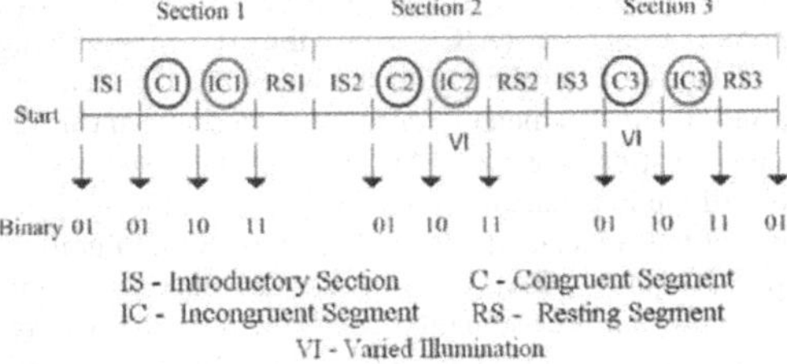

Fig. 2. Stimuli schedule of the experimental protocol.

In each section, there were four segments, including:

- 'IS' – the Introductory Segment to let the subject get used to the task environment, in order to establish an appropriate initial level for his/her psychological state, according to the Law of Initial Values (LIV) [3];
- 'C' – the Congruent segment, comprising 45 Stroop congruent word presentations (font color matches the meaning of the word), which are not expected to elicit significant stress in the subject;
- 'IC' – the Incongruent segment, in which the font color and the meaning of the 30 words presented are different. This is expected to induce stress in the subject, according to previous research reported in the psychophysiological literature [4];
- 'RS' – a Resting Segment to let the subject relax for some time.

At the beginning of each C, IC or RS segments, the binary codes (01, 10 or 11, respectively) shown in Fig. 2, were output as bursts of sinusoidal tones through the two audio output channels of the computer, serving as time-stamps for the recorded physiological signals. Since the aim of this study was to investigate the use of the pupil diameter signal for affective assessment, even in the presence of varied light intensity of the environment surrounding the subject, the illumination intensity (IL) was temporarily increased during the IC2 and C3 segments ("VI" marks in Fig. 2).

B. Hardware Setup

The complete instrumental setup developed for the study is illustrated in Fig. 3. This figure shows that the visual stimuli for the subject (Stroop test) were displayed on the TOBII T60 eye tracker monitor. The program developed for the eye tracking system allows the extraction of selected variables (in this case the PD of both eyes and their validity code) to a file at a frequency of 60 Hz, which, in turn, can be read into MATLAB.

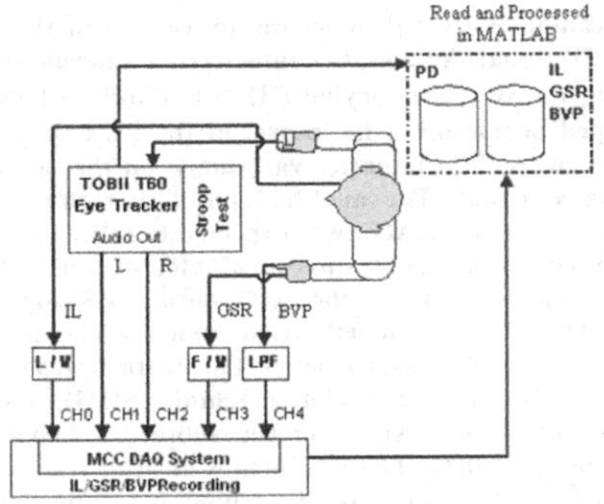

Fig. 3. Complete instrumental setup

While performing the Stroop test, the subject has the GSR and BVP sensors attached to his/her left hand and the IL sensor on his/her forehead, above the eyes. All these three signals, together with the left and right audio output (to provide the corresponding time stamping in the experiment) are recorded and converted to a MATLAB® -readable data file directly at rate 360 samples/second, using a multi-channel MCC DAQ system (PCI-DAS6023 board). Later, IL, GSR, BVP and both audio output channels were down-sampled to 60 Hz, to match the PD sampling rate.

C. Experimental Procedure

In total, 30 individuals (16 female, and 14 male) volunteered to participate in the experiment. Their age ranged from 24 to 34 years. They were from diverse professional and ethnic backgrounds.

In each experiment, the participant was asked to remain seated in front of the TOBII screen, interacting with the "Stroop Test" program for about 30 minutes, while wearing a head band with the IL sensor, the GSR sensor on the middle and ring fingers and the BVP sensor on the index finger. During that time, all the normal lights in the room were kept ON, but an additional level of illumination provided by a desk lamp placed above the eye level of the subject was switched ON intermittently to introduce intervals of higher illumination in the experiment, which would trigger the pupillary light reflex.

III. Signal Processing

A. Physiological Signal Processing

In this research, the signal processing method applied to the PD is an AIC system with the HITV adaptive algorithm. However, prior to the application of the adaptive interference canceller, the interruptions in the PD data, due to blinking (identified as a value of "4" in the validity code provided by the TOBII system), were compensated by linear interpolation. The resulting signal was processed by a low pass, 512th order FIR filter with a cutoff frequency of 0.13Hz, to complete the elimination of the blink responses, and shifted forward 256 sampling intervals to maintain the original time alignment.

The PD signal obtained after blink-removal was applied to the AIC system as the primary input signal *d(k)*, and the reference input *r(k)* was the simultaneously measured IL signal (already downsampled to 60 Hz). The block diagram of the AIC is shown in Fig. 4.

As described above, the equations governing the AIC are:

Primary Input: $$d(k) = s(k) + z(k) \quad (1)$$

Reference Input: $$r(k) = n(k) + u(k) \quad (2)$$

Output: $$e(k) = d(k) - y(k) = d(k) - \hat{z}(k) = \hat{s}(k) \quad (3)$$

where,

- *s(k)*: signal of interest (PD changes driven by PAR), uncorrelated to the reference ($\mathrm{cov}(s(k), r(k)) = 0$);
- *z(k)*: interference in the primary sensor (PD changes driven by PLR);
- *n(k)*: actual source of the interference (IL changes), correlated to *z(k)*, i.e. ($\mathrm{cov}(z(k), r(k)) \neq 0$);
- *u(k)*: measurement noise (assumed negligible).

The core element of the AIC system is an Adaptive Transversal Filter (ATF), where the reference signal *r(k)* is processed to produce an output $y(k) = \hat{z}(k)$ that is an approximation of *z(k)*. The state space model of the ATF is given by [6]:

$$w(k+1) = w(k) + \Delta w(k) \quad (4)$$

$$d(k) = r(k)^T w(k) + v(k) \quad (5)$$

$$z(k) = r(k)^T w(k) + \upsilon(k) \quad (6)$$

$$v(k) = s(k) + \upsilon(k) \quad (7)$$

In these equations,

- *w(k)* = system state vector; which is the ATF coefficient vector of size $m \times 1$ (m is the order of the ATF);
- *d(k)* = measurement sequence, which is the observed pupil diameter (PD) signal;
- *z(k)* = sequence to be estimated;
- $\Delta w(k)$ = process noise vector, which represents the time variation of the ATF weights *w(k)*;
- *v(k)* = measurement noise vector, which includes *s(k)* (PD- driven by PAR) and model uncertainties $\upsilon(k)$;
- $r(k) = [r_k, r_{(k-1)}, \ldots\ldots, r_{(k-m+1)}]^T$, which is the interference vector of size $m \times 1$.

The H^∞ Time-Varying (HITV) adaptive algorithm attempts to remove the interference from the recorded signal by adaptively adjusting the impulse response of the ATF [6].

The robustness of this HITV algorithm is achieved by minimizing the maximum energy gain from the disturbances to the estimation errors with the following solutions [7]:

$$\tilde{P}^{-1}(k) = P^{-1}(k) - \varepsilon_g^{-2} r(k) r^T(k) \quad (8)$$

$$g(k) = \frac{\tilde{P}(k) r(k)}{1 + r^T(k) \tilde{P}(k) r(k)} \quad (9)$$

$$\hat{w}(k+1) = \hat{w}(k) + g(k)(y(k) - r^T(k)\hat{w}(k)) \quad (10)$$

$$P(k+1) = [P^{-1}(k) + (1 - \varepsilon_g^{-2}) r(k) r^T(k)]^{-1} + \gamma_0 \quad (11)$$

$$P(0) = \eta I = \Pi_0, \; \Upsilon_0 = \rho I \quad (12)$$

Here, $g(k)$ is the gain factor; ε_g, η and ρ are positive constants. Note that ρ reflects a priori knowledge of how rapidly the state vector *w(k)* varies with time, and η reflects the a priori knowledge of how reliable the initial estimate available for the state vector *w(0)* is.

In the PD signal processing of this study, we treated the recorded pupil diameter signal as the primary input of the AIC, which is composed by the signal of interest *s(k)* (PD- driven by PAR) and the interference *z(k)* (PD- driven by PLR).

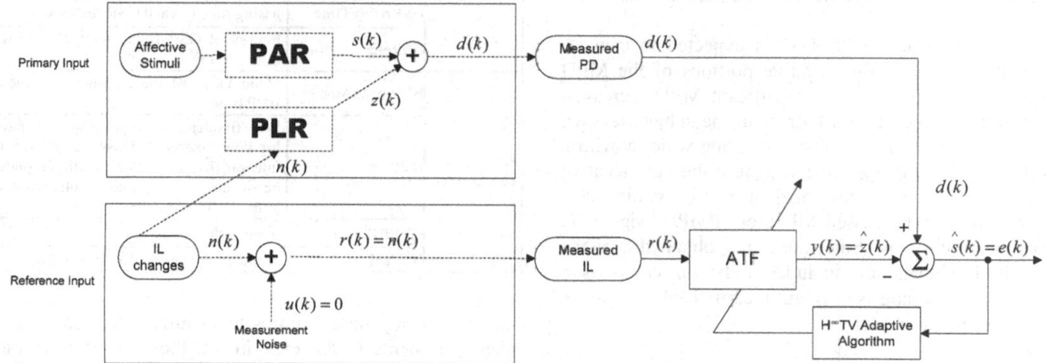

Fig. 4. Adaptive interference canceller (AIC) block diagram.

However, with the assumption that the measurement noise is negligible in our experimental setup, an independent measurement of illumination in the neighborhood of the eye of the subject (IL) is used as the reference input. The ATF is set with 120 weights and adapted by the HITV algorithm ($\eta = 0.001$, $\varepsilon_g = 2.0$ and a time-varying parameter ρ , changed according to the IL value to enable the AIC system to have a quicker response when there is a sudden increase in IL.). It is expected that the ATF will emulate the transformation of the illumination variations to pupil diameter changes, so that the noise *n(k)* will be converted into a close-enough replication of the PLR-driven components of PD (the output *y(k)*). In that case, the error, *e(k)*, designated as the Modified Pupil Diameter (MPD), would be the estimation of the desired signal *s(k)*, containing only the PD variations due to affective changes (PAR).

An example of the processing of this PD signal (after blink removal) together with the IL signal through the AIC system and HITV adaptive algorithm is shown in Fig. 5. The bottom panel represents the AIC output, i.e., the MPD signal.

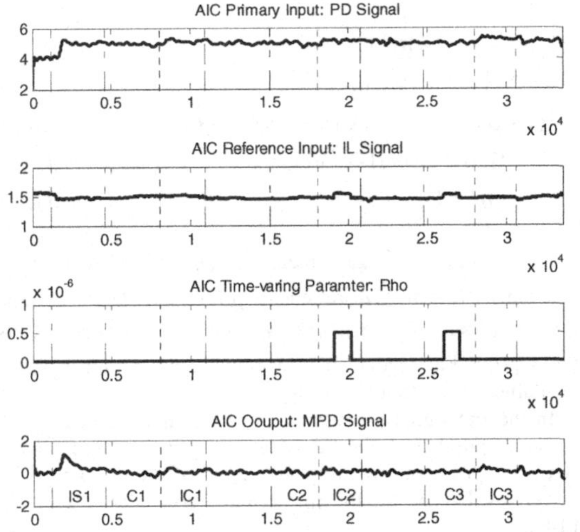

Fig. 5: Example of the processing of the PD signal (after blink removal) together with IL signal through AIC system and HITV algorithm.

As the affective state of "Stress" is expected to cause a dilation of the pupil [7], the negative portions of the MPD signal were zeroed out to isolate significant MPD increases, which indicate the emergence of stress in the subject (shown in the middle panel of Fig. 6). Then, a sliding window with a width of 900 samples is applied throughout the non-negative MPD signal to calculate the median value within each window, yielding the Processed MPD, or "PMPD" signal (in the bottom panel of Fig. 6). Since the results obtained from the GSR and BVP signals are included only for comparison purposes, their processing is only outlined in Table I (Further details could be found in [8]).

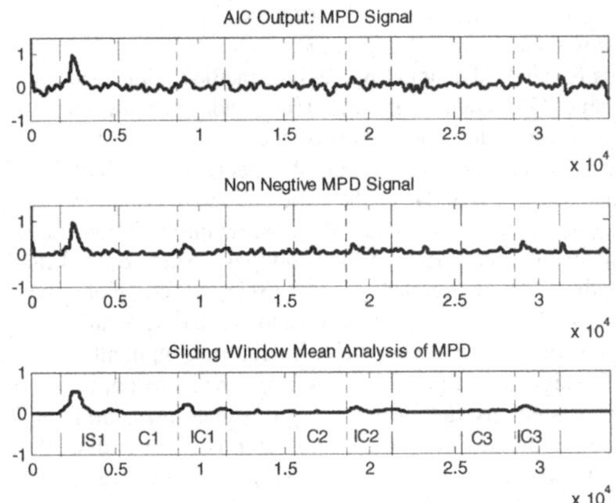

Fig. 6: Example of the further processing of the MPD signal.

B. Feature Extraction and Data Normalization

In this study, the specific aim was to evaluate the affective assessment performance of a single-feature stress detector, derived from PMPD. The efficiency of this single-feature detector is compared to two other detectors that also included features derived from measured GSR and BVP signals. These detectors were assessed in terms of their discriminating power to differentiate between the "relaxed" affective states in the Congruent Stroop segments and the "stressed" states in the Incongruent Stroop segments of the computer user.

Table I shows the features obtained from each of the signals recorded in the experiments, resulting in a single feature value for each "C" or "IC" segment in the test.

TABLE I
FEATURES EXTRACTED FROM THE PD, GSR AND BVP SIGNALS

Signal	Features	Definition
PD (1 feature)	PMPDmean	Average value of the non-negative MPD signal after median processing
GSR (5 features)	GSRmean.	Average value of the GSR samples
	GSRnum	Number of the GSR responses
	GSRmeanAmp	Mean value of the amplitude of each GSR response
	GSRrisingTime	Rising time of each GSR response
	GSReng	Energy of GSR (total under the rising time curve)
BVP (4 features)	BVPmeanAmp	Mean value of the amplitude of each BVP beat
	BVPl2h	Low frequency to high frequency rate for Power spectral density of interbeat interval(IBI) (the time in milliseconds between two normal, consecutive peaks in the BVP) sequence
	BVPIBImean	Mean value of the IBI
	BVPstd	Standard deviation of IBI sequence

Before using these features to identify "stressed" and "relaxed" segments in the experiment, the 9 features extracted from the BVP and GSR signals were normalized according to the following 1), 2) and 3) steps. [The "PMPDmean" feature was only normalized through steps 2) and 3), since the illumination levels used during the preliminary introductory period, prior to the actual experiment, were variable and did not provide a suitable baseline for PD].

1) Reference the features to their baseline level.

$$Y_s = \frac{X_s}{X_r} \qquad (13)$$

Here *Xs* is the raw feature value during "C" and "IC" segments, and *Xr* is the corresponding feature value during the relaxation period, prior to the first congruent segment. (This was done only for GSR and BVP features)

2) Minimize the impact of individual subject responses dividing each feature by the sum of all six segment values.

$$Y_s' = \frac{Y_{si}}{\sum_{i=1}^{6} Y_{si}} \qquad (14)$$

3) Normalize all data to the range of [0, 1] with max-min normalization.

$$Y_{norm} = \frac{Y_s' - Y_s'_{\min}}{Y_s'_{\max} - Y_s'_{\min}} \qquad (15)$$

IV. Affective Assessment With SVM

This study proposes to assess the affective states (stress vs. relaxation) of a computer user through the feature "PMPDmean" derived from the PD signal, using a machine learning algorithm, i.e., a Support Vector Machine (SVM), as a classifier. Subsequently, multi-feature classifiers, also implemented through Support Vector Machines (SVMs), were used to process the features from the GSR and BVP signals, with and without the PMPD feature

SVM is a supervised machine learning method used for classification and regression. Viewing input data as two sets of vectors in an n-dimensional space, an SVM will construct a separating hyperplane in that space which optimally separates the data into two categories. The aim of SVM is to construct a discriminant function for the data points in feature space in such a way that the feature vectors of the training samples are separated into classes, while simultaneously maximizing the distance of the discriminant function from the nearest training set feature vector. Therefore, an important part of SVM classification is the identification of a suitable discriminant function (kernel function) that cannot only capture the essential properties of the data distribution, but also prevent the over-fitting problem.

In this paper, the kernels used for the SVMs are:

Linear: $K(X,Y) = X \bullet Y$ (16)

Polynomial: $K(X,Y) = (X \bullet Y + 1)^p$ (17)

Radial basis function (RBF):

$$K(X,Y) = \exp(-\gamma \|X - Y\|^2),\ \gamma > 0 \qquad (18)$$

Gaussian: $$K(X,Y) = \exp\left(\frac{-\|X - Y\|^2}{2\gamma^2}\right) \qquad (19)$$

Here, γ and p are kernel parameters. The "•" used in these equations represents the dot product of two vectors.

To obtain a more realistic assessment of the performance of the SVM, a k-fold cross validation [9] method is also used in this study, which separates given data sets into two parts: the training sets and a test set, where the labels of test set are considered unknown in the classifier training. Then the accuracy on these sets can more precisely reflect the performance that can be expected in classifying unknown data.

Specifically, in this work, the SVM classification is applied through the "SPIDER" software package for MATLAB, which can be freely downloaded from http://www.kyb.mpg.de/bs/people/spider/. According to the cross validation strategy, the original data is first divided into 20 equal subsets. One subset is tested using the classifier trained on the remaining 19 subsets. This process is repeated until every instance has been used exactly once for testing. The overall success rate for a classifier was evaluated as the number of correct classifications divided by the total number of feature sets tested:

To assess the overall usefulness of the pupil diameter signal, the classification phase of this study was repeated under 3 different conditions:

- P1: Only using the feature extracted from PD (only 1 feature, "PMPDmean", was used for classification);
- P2: Using all features extracted from the monitored PD, GSR and BVP signals (all 10 features were used for classification);
- P3: Excluding the feature extracted from PD signal; (1 feature "PMPDmean" was excluded, 9 features from GSR and BVP were used for classification).

The experimental data of the 180 segments collected from the 30 volunteers (3 "C" and 3 "IC" for each subject) were processed through SVMs with the 4 kernel functions described above, to train and verify the performance of the affective assessment. The accuracy rates from the experiments performed to evaluate the proposed affect recognition system by SVM using the "SPIDER" software are shown in Table II.

TABLE II
Results of Stress Classification by SVM

Phase of Classification	SVM Kernel			
	Linear	**Poly-nomial**	**RBF**	**Gaussian**
		d =3.0	γ =1.0	γ = 1.0
P1: 1 feature from PD	77.78%	77.78%	77.78%	77.78%
P2:10 features from PD, GSR and BVP	76.11%	76.67%	73.33%	37.78%
P3: 9 features from GSR and BVP (no PD)	50.00%	54.44%	48.89%	37.78%

V. DISSCUSSION

The outcomes of the SVM classification show that, under controlled conditions, the monitoring and processing of the PD signal (Phase 1), yields acceptable levels (up to 77.78%) of differentiation between "Non-stressed" and "Stressed" user states, as evoked by congruent and incongruent Stroop stimulation, respectively. Regardless of which kernel was utilized, the SVM classifier is able to deal with the complex pattern distribution, achieving encouraging results for affective assessment.

When the features from GSR and BVP are added to "PMPDmean" into the affective classification process (Phase 2), the observed system accuracy decreases slightly (to 76.67%). This seems to hint that the discrimination performance of the GSR and BVP features is not as good as that of the PMPD feature.

In the third phase of the stress classification, it is also observed that, with the PD signal excluded, the recognition rate dramatically dropped to 54.44% (for the best classifier), which is significantly lower than the accuracy rate in the previous two phases (both of which include "PMPDmean"). This result seems to indicate that the pupil diameter signal may be one of the most important physiological signals to involve in the development of an automated affective recognition system.

An additional important aspect to note in these results is that the encouraging level of affective classification observed from the "PMPDmean" feature was achieved even in spite of the temporary illumination increases introduced during the IC2 and C3 segments of experimentation. This seems to confirm that the AIC system used to process the PD signal may have been successful in minimizing the impact of the PLR effect in these segments. This, in turn, would imply that affective sensing based on the PD signal might be practical even in environments with unconstrained illumination changes.

VI. CONCLUSION

This paper outlined the development of an affective assessment approach to differentiate "stress" vs. "relaxation" states of computer users through the non-invasive monitoring of the Pupil Diameter (PD) signal. An H^{∞} Time-Varying (HITV) adaptive algorithm has been implemented in an Adaptive Interference Canceller (AIC) to discount the dominant influence of PD variation, the pupillary light reflex (PLR), from a measured PD signal. The output of the AIC, the MPD signal, was post-processed with the application of a non-negative constraint followed by median calculation performed on a sliding window, to generate a PMPD signal, as an indicator of user stress. Specifically, the average value of PMPD in each Stroop segment of the experiment ("PMPDmean" feature) was extracted as an indicator of Pupillary Affective Responses (PAR) due to, for example, subject stress, during the corresponding experimental segment.

In the experiment designed for this study, the two affective states to be differentiated were elicited by exposing the subjects to congruent (relaxation) and incongruent (stress) Stroop color naming trials. Digital signal processing techniques were used to extract a total of 10 features from the 3 monitored physiological signals (PD, GSR and BVP) in each congruent and incongruent Stroop segment of the protocol. These features were processed by Support Vector Machine (SVM) classification systems. Using the single feature derived from the processed pupil diameter ("PMPDmean") for the training and testing of the classifier system, an encouraging classification level of 77.78% was achieved by the SVM. The classification achieved using simultaneously all the 10 features derived from the PD, GSR and BVP signals for the SVM classifier yielded a similar accuracy rate of 76.67%. The last phase of classification evaluation was performed excluding the PD feature from consideration (i.e., using only the 9 features extracted from the GSR and BVP signals). The accuracy rate of the classification system trained under this new condition decreased significantly (54.44%). These observations suggest that the PD is an important physiological signal for affective assessment.

ACKNOWLEDGMENTS

This work was sponsored by NSF grants CNS-0520811, CNS-0426125, and HRD-0833093.

REFERENCES

[1] R.W. Picard, *Affective Computing*, MIT Press, Cambridge, Mass, 1997.

[2] J. R. Stroop; 1935. "Studies of interference in serial verbal reactions", *Journal of Experimental Psychology*, vol. 18, pp. 643-662, 1935.

[3] R. M. Stern, W. J. Ray, *Psychophysiological Recording*. Oxford University Press, Quigley, K.S., 2001.

[4] P. Renaud and J. P. Blondin, "The Stress of Stroop Performance: Physiological and Emotional Responses to Color-word Interference, Task Pacing, and Pacing Speed", *International Journal of Psychophysiology*, vol. 27, pp. 87-97, 1997.

[5] A. Todoroki, N. Hana, "Luminance change method for cure monitoring of GFRP", *Key Engineering Materials*, vol. 321-323, pp. 1316-1321. 2006.

[6] B. Hassibj, T. Kailath, "H^{∞} adaptive filtering", *Proc. Int. Conf. Acoustics, Speech, Signal Processing*, pp. 945-952, 1995.

[7] S. Puthusserypady, "H^{∞} adaptive filters for eye blink artifact minimization from electroencephalogram". *IEEE Signal Processing Letters*, vol. 12, pp. 816-819.

[8] A. Barreto, J. Zhai,; M. Adjouadi, "Non-intrusive physiological monitoring for automated stress detection in human-computer interaction", *Lecture Notes in Computer Science*, Springer-Verlag, vol. 4796, pp. 29–38, 2007.

[9] B. Efron and R. Tibshirani, "An Introduction to the Bootstrap." New York, London: Chapman and Hall, 1993.

MAC, A System for Automatically IPR Identification, Collection and Distribution

[1]Carlos Serrão

[1]ISCTE-IUL/DCTI/ADETTI, Ed. ISCTE, Av. Das Forças Armadas, 1649-026 Lisboa, Portugal
[1]carlos.serrao@iscte.pt

***Abstract*— Controlling Intellectual Property Rights (IPR) in the Digital World is a very hard challenge. The facility to create multiple bit-by-bit identical copies from original IPR works creates the opportunities for digital piracy. One of the most affected industries by this fact is the Music Industry. The Music Industry has supported huge losses during the last few years due to this fact. Moreover, this fact is also affecting the way that music rights collecting and distributing societies are operating to assure a correct music IPR identification, collection and distribution. In this article a system for automating this IPR identification, collection and distribution is presented and described. This system makes usage of advanced automatic audio identification system based on audio fingerprinting technology. This paper will present the details of the system and present a use-case scenario where this system is being used.**

***Index Terms*— digital music, audio fingerprinting, intellectual property rights, piracy, music rights distribution**

I. Introduction

In the digital Era, managing properly and efficiently digital Intellectual Property is an enormous challenge. This is particularly important in a rights distribution scenario that ensures that the appropriate rights are distributed as real as possible to the creators. Such perfect system does not exist at the moment.

Technology plays an important role in the establishment of this distribution scenario and a mechanism has to be established to enable an automated music identification system. This automated system must rely on audio fingerprint technology to automatically identify music tracks from its psycho-acoustic intrinsic characteristics.

This paper presents a method for audio identification on audio streams based on the division of the latter ones in smaller audio elements. Those small parts of audio identified kept in order permit to obtain a more reliable audio identification. The proposed paper will further describe this audio-fingerprinting process, analyze the results obtained in automatic audio identification and introduce an integrated system where it is being tested and used.

The system that was developed to help the correct identification, collection and distribution of the music IPR, covered the different aspects a derived rights collective society has to deal, in order to become more efficient and business centric.

This paper starts by providing an overview of the music rights collecting society processes and describe how these processes are manually handled. From this, a system for automating these processes is presented – the Music Active Control system. A specific technology of the system is presented and described as the technology that enables the system to be fully automated – the audio fingerprinting system. Finally, some details about how the system operates are also provided.

II. Music Related Rights Management Societies

Related Rights (RR) or Neighboring Rights (NR) are terms in copyright law that represent the rights which are similar to the author rights but which are not connected with the actual author of the work. Both the author rights and the related rights are copyrights. The RR/NR is independent of any authors' rights, which may also exist in the work. The rights of performers, phonogram producers and broadcasting organizations are certainly covered, and are internationally protected by the RR/NR legislation. In the specific case of the music industry, and as an example, four different copyright-types rights will concurrently protect a CD recording of a song:

- The authors' rights of the composer of the music;
- The authors' rights of the lyricist;
- The performers' rights of a singer and the musicians;
- The producers' rights of the person or corporation, which made the recording.

Therefore one the most important activities of these Music Related/Neighboring Rights Management Societies (MRNRMS) is the collection of neighboring rights on behalf of producers and performers related to public performance of recorded music.

Therefore the mission of a MRNRMS can be resumed in the following four major objectives:

- Raise public awareness to the reality of related/neighboring rights - which are the rights of artists and producers - and the need for its protection (a fact still relatively new and little known);

T. Sobh, K. Elleithy (eds.), *Innovations in Computing Sciences and Software Engineering*,
DOI 10.1007/978-90-481-9112-3_33, © Springer Science+Business Media B.V. 2010

- Boosting the delivery of remuneration for distribution to the holders, be they producers or artists;
- Realize the collection of related/neighboring rights to all places of public performance using recorded music for commercial purposes, as well as all the inspectors to use of recorded music, by any means. The spaces where it is used recorded music for public performance can be clubs, transport systems, hotels, amusement parks and parking, banks, call centers, stadiums, street music, local music and recorded, among others;
- The community awareness in relation to associated rights will, in large part, be accomplished with the collaboration of public authorities with powers of supervision on Copyright and Related/Neighboring Rights, as well as the users of recorded music in various areas and industries that in compliance with the law, should ask for their license.

These MRNRMS are responsible for issuing licenses to businesses that use represented recording music as a mean to conduct their own business models. Moreover, they are also responsible for the effective collection and distribution of the associated fees to the music producers, performers and authors.

Most of this work is accomplished using manual procedures. The verification process is conducted manually as well as the distribution. Moreover the MRNRMS often uses a flat rate fee to charge from their clients. This flat rate fee is calculated based on the type of business and the business space. It is also difficult to know exactly what type of recorded music does the licensee uses – most of the times this evaluation is conducted using a direct sample of music listened during some discrete periods of time. In terms of rights distribution, most of the producers, performers and authors will receive the same amount of money independently if their music was or not used by the client.

This situation creates issues both in terms of rights charging (charging the right price for the music that was effectively used by the client) and in terms of distribution (distributing the right amount of money to the producers, performers and authors whose music was used by the clients). The MRNRMS should pursue the means to be as efficient as possible on the accomplishment of its mission.

In order to solve these problems in terms of collection of fees from the clients, management of the represented repertory and distribution of the producers, performers and author rights, the MRNRMS has to employ the necessary automatic means to become more efficient on its mission.

In the following sections a system that was developed to deal with these issues is presented. The Music Active Control system is a networked based system that empowers the MRNRMS to perform better in the different aspects of their activity.

III. The Music Active Control System

In order to accomplish its mission in an effective way, the MRNRMS developed a distributed system, based on set of open components and on audio-fingerprinting technology, called Music Active Control (MAC). The MAC system is a web-based system that enables the integration into the MRNRMS value-chain, the different elements that are part of the Related/Neighboring Rights ecosystem. MAC allows the upstream integration of the music producers, and the downstream integration of the music using business clients and the RR/NR proprietary's (Figure 1).

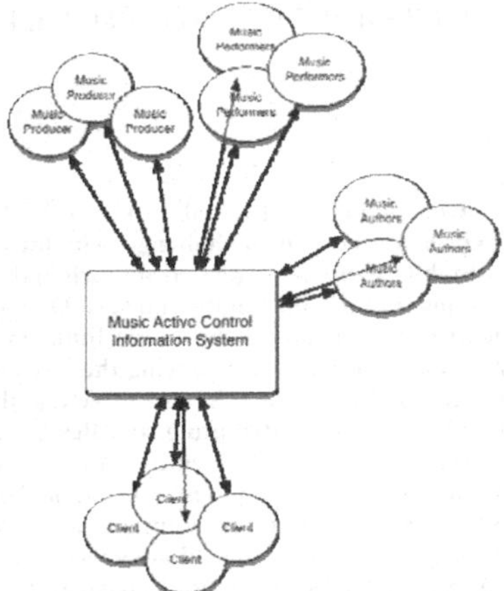

Figure 1. The Music Active Control actor's ecosystem

The MAC system aggregates the information from the music releases from the different music producers, the information of the representative of the music in the specific country (a specific label may be representing this music or artist in the country), information about the performers and information about the music authors.

A. *MAC Audio and Metadata Grabber*

It is an objective of the MAC system that the different actors themselves should update the data on the system – this way it will be possible for the system to grow with little central coordination and control effort. In order for this objective to be achieved, the MAC system uses a web-based portal as well as a client-side application (Figure 2) to feed the MAC system database with the necessary data.

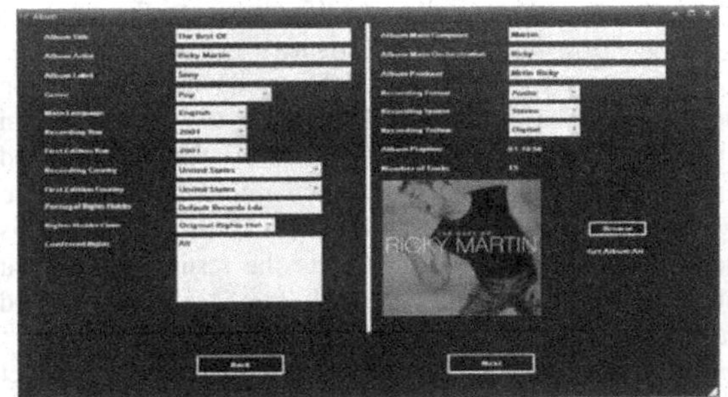

Figure 2. Client application that allows the data entry on the MAC system

The client side application, the MAC Audio and Matadata Grabber that is distributed to the music producers, allows an easy and seamless way to capture the MAC system required data. This application, not only captures the information from the new music releases, but also crucial information about the audio music itself. The audio data is analyzed and extracted from the audio CD, high-quality MP3 files are created and an audio-fingerprint is generated from the original audio CD content. The full process can be described on the following steps:

- The producer starts the application;
- The producer inserts an newly released audio CD on an optical computer drive;
- The application analyses the audio CD data, and tries to extract metadata both from the audio CD and from several Internet databases. This makes the data filling task less complex and faster;
- The producer verifies the metadata that was automatically from the audio CD or the Internet, corrects it and or completes it – there are some information that is impossible to extract directly from the Internet and must be manually input;
- The application analyses the audio CD data, and generates a unique fingerprint for each of the music tracks that are part of the CD;
- The application extracts the audio from the CD and converts it to an high-quality MP3 file;
- Finally, the application sends all the metadata, MP3 files and the audio fingerprints to the MAC system.

The MAC system stores all the information on a centralized database and indexes the MP3 music files. Also, the audio fingerprints are associated to the music track metadata, for later matching processes. When this process completes, the MAC system contains the information about all the different music tracks that the MRNRMS represents, and that require licensing from businesses using that music for commercial purposes.

B. MAC.box

The other important process of the MAC system is the automatically identification system that will be used at the client business side, to collect the exact information of the music that was used by the client, in order for the MRNRMS to charge the appropriated fee and to correctly distribute the RR/NR rights associate to the music that was used.

In order to accomplish this, the Mac system makes available on the client side, a small hardware/software appliance, called MAC.box. This appliance is responsible for recording the audio data, from the used audio source, and to perform the generation of audio fingerprints. From time to time, the MAC.box connects to the MAC system and sends the captured information. This information is matched on the MAC system side, and the represented music that has been used by the client is automatically identified.

The identification and matching process can be described in the following steps:

- The MAC.box is connected directly to the output of the audio device that will be playing music on the client business;
- The MAC.box captures ("listens") the audio being played by the audio device, on specific time intervals and for short periods of time, recording the captured data;
- MAC.box computes the audio fingerprints of the different samples captured;
- The MAC.box sends a report containing the list of computed fingerprints, and the date and hour of capture to the central MAC system;
- The MAC system, compares the received captured fingerprints against the original fingerprints that are stored on the system;
- If both fingerprints are a match the music is identified;
- The final result of this process is a series of reports that list the music tracks that were used by a certain client, during a certain period of time.

With this information, the MRNRMS can charge the customer better and perform a fairer distribution of rights to producers, performers and authors.

All of the processes described related to the identification of the music tracks are only possible because of a key-enabling technology: the audio-fingerprinting system. In the following sections, a more detailed description of the audio-fingerprinting system used on the MAC system for music matching, is described.

IV. THE MAC SYSTEM AND AUDIO-FINGERPRINTING

As it was previously referred on this paper, the system is based on the automatic identification of the different music tracks that are used by the clients. For this automatic music identification to work, two different processes are necessary in the system (Figure 3):

1. The creation of the original audio-fingerprint from the original CD music tracks and their storage associated with music metadata;
2. The comparison between an audio-fingerprint candidate (or multiple audio-fingerprint candidates) and the original audio-fingerprint stored on the system. If a match is found than the music is identified and the corresponding metadata is pulled from the system.

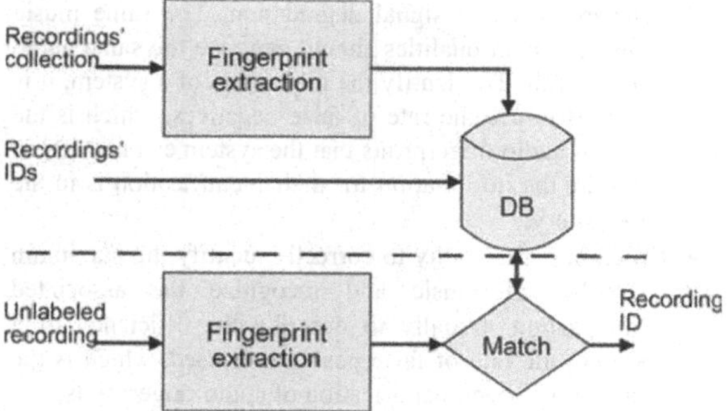

Figure 3. Processes involved in the generation and matching of audio-fingerprints

Both these processes rely on the capability of the audio-fingerprinting algorithm for correct audio identification. The audio-fingerprint or acoustic fingerprint is a condensed digital summary, deterministically generated from an audio signal that can be used to identify an audio sample or quickly locate similar items in an audio database.

V. AUDIO FINGERPRINTING BASED ON SVD

Any complete audio identification system based on audio fingerprinting technology is normally divided in two distinct parts. First, an audio fingerprint extraction process that is responsible for extracting an unique identifier (fingerprint) from the music track and second, the matching process that tries to find a match between the generated fingerprint and the different fingerprint identifiers stored on a database and the corresponding meta-information.

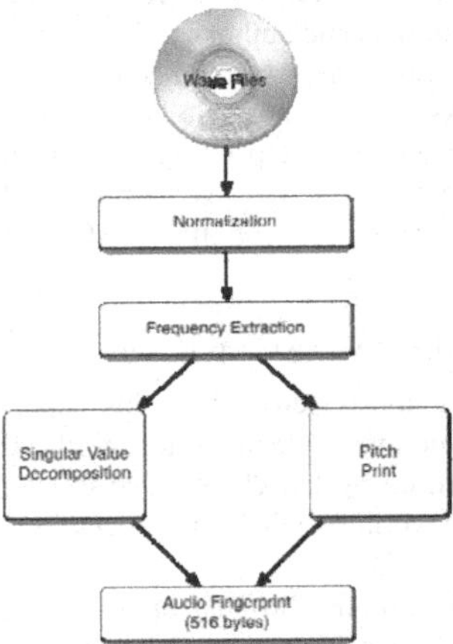

Figure 4. Description of the process for the creation of audio-fingerprints

Considering the specific requirements of the system to be developed, there is a set of requirements that the audio-fingerprint generation process [1] [2] should be able to comply to:

- **Robustness**: precise identification of the audio, despite the existence of signal degradation. The same music with different qualities should generate the same audio fingerprint. To identify the robustness of a system, it is normal to use the rate of false negatives, which is the rate of audio fingerprints that the system can not detect, despite the information for their identification is in the repository;
- **Efficiency**: the ability to correctly identify the maximum possible of music and recognize the associated information. Usually to describe the efficiency of a system the rate of false positives is used, which is the rate of incorrect identification of audio fingerprints;
- **Granularity**: the ability to identify audio samples with just a few seconds duration. This implies working with synchronization between audio fingerprints taken and those that are stored in the repository. As this parameter depends on the objectives of the system in some situations it may be necessary to use the entire song instead of just an excerpt;
- **Dimension**: for quick searches, it is necessary to store the audio fingerprint in RAM. Consequently, the memory resources to the server database will have to be determined taking into account this parameter;
- **Scalability**: the ability to find an audio fingerprint in a reasonable time, taking into account the number of existing audio fingerprint in the repository. The larger the database, the greater the physical capacity of storage required. It should be possible to resize the system with ease, due to the high growth potential of these systems.

The production of an audio-fingerprint with the about requirements is not an easy task. It involves a different set of tasks from the audio source, until the final fingerprint is computed [3].

The pre-processing of the audio signal is performed in order to prepare it for the following analysis, carried out by other components.

As a first step the audio is passed to mono format (in the case of a stereo signal), the silence is removed, followed by removal of DC offset, given that its existence does not allow to maximize the volume during the normalization process.

The pre-processing finishes by converting the signal to 44.100Hz. Finally, the 10 initial seconds of music are removed in order to avoid the silence that could have been introduced in the audio. The remaining audio signal after the initial 120 seconds is ignored, allowing larger music coverage and preventing a file manipulation attack [4].

After the normalization of the signal the frequency is extracted using the Fast Fourier Transform (FFT).

Upon receiving the data returned by the FFT, the spectrum series are examined, each one representing a small audio frame (185 milliseconds). In turn, each frame is composed by a set of frequencies (frequencies matrix).

The system proposed on this paper will use the Singular Value Decomposition (SVD) applied to the matrix of audio frequencies for the extraction of audio fingerprints, which produces a smaller size matrix result resuming the audio features [5]. In order to represent an audio element X as a matrix, it will have to be divided in M audio segments, each of them containing N frequency bins, originating therefore a matrix $M*N$, where $M>N$. With the aim of obtaining a more reduced matrix is applied to the matrix X the SVD, decomposing it as

$$X = USV^T$$

where U with size $M*M$ and V with dimension $N*N$ are orthogonal matrices and their columns are called respectively left and right singular vectors. S is a diagonal matrix of singular values. These singular values are sorted in a decreasing order and represent the importance of the correspondent singular vectors in the matrix structure. In general the first singular values contain most part of the information relative to the matrix, thus in order to reduce redundant information it is advised to only keep primary singular values. In the proposed system, it was decided to keep four singular values, after the analysis of experimental results. Those singular values together with the correspondent right singular vectors, which contain spectral principle components, can be used to represent the main features of the audio element. In the system presented on this paper they are used as part of the audio fingerprint that has been called CorePrint. The other part is composed by four numbers that correspond to the most prominent frequencies of the audio pitch and is called PitchPrint. PitchPrint is useful for the lookup and matching procedures [6] [7].

At the end of the fingerprint extraction process, a 408 bytes fingerprint (8 bytes from the Pitch, 320 bytes from the right singular vectors and 80 bytes correspondent to the singular values) resuming the audio element analysed, is obtained.

The matching process is based on a first part possible results reduction, using a pitch match procedure. The obtained results are produced by a more complex and time consuming matching process in order to obtain the identification to each audio fingerprint. After this, the outcomes are analyzed as a whole, and the decision about which music is being played is made. The foremost part of the matching procedure (pitch match) is a very simple one, consisting in the direct comparison of the audio element pitch numbers analyzed with the ones stored on a database. This way all the fingerprints that do not have equal PitchPrint will be discarded as possible match. With the possibilities reduced, the system will aim at the CorePrint match. For that it is necessary to compute the similarity value between each print, as defined here

$$S = \sum_{i=1}^{m} \sum_{j=1}^{m} w_{i,j} s_{i,j}$$

where ***Wi,j***

$$w_{i,j} = \frac{\lambda_{c1,i} \lambda_{c2,j}}{\sqrt{\sum_{i=1}^{m} \lambda_{c1,i}^{2} \sum_{j=1}^{m} \lambda_{c2,j}^{2}}}$$

is the variable weight.

This specifies how each ***Si,j*** will contribute to the similarity calculation, and ***Si,j*** is the dot product between two groups of ***S*** vectors (right singular vectors). The higher similarity will correspond to a match and the corresponding audio identification. This is only valid if its value is superior to a pre-defined threshold, therefore reducing the false positives probability. When an audio stream is divided in audio elements and those are analysed, a set of audio elements identifications will be produced. Setting the size of the audio elements to a relative small size comparing with the normal size of a music, and maintaining the output results ordered will probably originate consecutive equal identifications [8]. The system presented on this paper will consider that music has been correctly identified when a defined number of equal consecutive audio elements identifications are found.

VI. Tests and Results

In order to assess the quality of the system and in particular the robustness of the audio-fingerprint some tests were conducted. In this assessment a set of different music tracks (from different artists and different albums') were selected (20 audio music tracks), and three different tests were conducted to evaluate this robustness.

The first test aimed to confirm the ability of the audio-fingerprint to work with different sampling patterns. Each file was converted to a lossy MP3 format, and for different sampling frequencies (32, 44 and 48 kHz) and sampling speeds (32, 48, 64, 96, 128, 160, 192 kbps). The following table (Table 1) summarizes the results for the different sampling rates, taking into account that this factor did not alter the results.

Table 1. Testing the Different Rhythms and Sampling Frequencies (P: Passed; F: Fail; NT: Not Tested)

Artist	Music	32kbs	48kbs	64kbs	96kbs	128kbs	160kbs	192kbs
Green Day	Nice Guys Finish Last	P	P	P	P	P	P	P
Green Day	Hitchin'A Ride	P	P	P	P	P	P	P
Green Day	The Grouch	P	P	P	P	P	P	P
Green Day	Redundant	P	P	P	P	P	P	P
Green Day	Scattered	P	P	P	P	P	P	P
Smashing Pumpkins	I am one	P	P	P	P	P	P	P
Smashing Pumpkins	Siva	P	P	P	P	P	P	P
Smashing Pumpkins	Rhinoceros	P	P	P	P	P	P	P
Smashing Pumpkins	Bury me	P	P	P	P	P	P	P
Smashing Pumpkins	Crush	P	P	P	P	P	P	P
Queen	Keep yourself Alive	P	P	P	P	P	P	P
Queen	Doing All Right	P	P	P	P	P	P	P
Queen	Great King Rat	P	P	P	P	P	P	P
Queen	My Fairy King	P	P	P	P	P	P	P
Queen	Liar	P	P	P	P	P	P	P
Silence 4	Goodbye Tomorrow	P	P	P	P	P	P	P
Silence 4	Borrow	P	P	P	P	P	P	P
Silence 4	Dying Young	P	P	P	P	P	P	P
Silence 4	Old Letters	P	P	P	P	P	P	P
Silence 4	Angel Song	P	P	P	P	P	P	P

As shown by the results obtained, the audio fingerprint system worked with all the rhythms and frequencies of sampling with which it was tested.The aim of this second test was to test the ability of the audio fingerprinting to deal with the introduction of silence at the beginning of the audio files. The following table (Table 2) summarizes the results obtained.For this second test has been included at the beginning of each of the audio files, 5, 10, 15 and 20 seconds of silence. The audio music files used on the test were in MP3 format with sampling frequency of 44kHz and 128kbs sampling rate (typical values for audio files). After this, the fingerprints were generated for the music audio files containing the silence and analyzed the results by comparing with the fingerprints of the original unmodified audio files. As shown by the results table (Table 2) obtained from the test the ability to fight the introduction of silence at the beginning of the audio is yet not ideal.

Table 2. Testing the introduction of silence at the beginning of the audio music files (P: Passed; F: Fail; NT: Not Tested)

Artist	Music	5s	10s	15s	20s
Green Day	Nice Guys Finish Last	P	F	F	F
Green Day	Hitchin'A Ride	P	P	F	F
Green Day	The Grouch	P	P	F	F
Green Day	Redundant	F	P	P	F
Green Day	Scattered	P	F	F	F
Smashing Pumpkins	I am one	F	P	P	F
Smashing Pumpkins	Siva	F	F	F	F
Smashing Pumpkins	Rhinoceros	NT	NT	NT	NT
Smashing Pumpkins	Bury me	P	F	F	F
Smashing Pumpkins	Crush	P	P	F	F
Queen	Keep yourself Alive	P	F	F	F
Queen	Doing All Right	F	F	F	F
Queen	Great King Rat	F	F	F	F
Queen	My Fairy King	F	F	F	F
Queen	Liar	F	F	F	F
Silence 4	Goodbye Tomorrow	NT	NT	NT	NT
Silence 4	Borrow	NT	NT	NT	NT
Silence 4	Dying Young	P	F	F	F
Silence 4	Old Letters	F	F	F	F
Silence 4	Angel Song	F	F	F	F
	Passaram	8	5	2	0
	Falharam	9	12	15	17

In this third test, as before, were used MP3 files with a sampling frequency of 44kHz and 128kbs rhythm sampling.

Table 3. Simulation of AM reception and introduction of distortion (P: Passed; F: Fail; NT: Not Tested)

Artist	Music	AM Effect	2x AM Effect	0,5 Distortion	1,0 Distortion
Green Day	Nice Guys Finish Last	F	F	P	P
Green Day	Hitchin'A Ride	P	P	P	F
Green Day	The Grouch	P	F	P	F
Green Day	Redundant	F	F	P	F
Green Day	Scattered	P	F	P	F
Smashing Pumpkins	I am one	F	F	P	F
Smashing Pumpkins	Siva	P	F	P	F
Smashing Pumpkins	Rhinoceros	NT	NT	NT	NT
Smashing Pumpkins	Bury me	P	F	P	F
Smashing Pumpkins	Crush	P	F	P	F
Queen	Keep yourself Alive	P	F	P	F
Queen	Doing All Right	P	F	P	P
Queen	Great King Rat	F	F	P	F
Queen	My Fairy King	F	F	P	F
Queen	Liar	F	F	P	F
Silence 4	Goodbye Tomorrow	NT	NT	NT	NT
Silence 4	Borrow	NT	NT	NT	NT
Silence 4	Dying Young	F	P	P	F
Silence 4	Old Letters	F	F	P	F
Silence 4	Angel Song	F	F	F	F
	Passaram	8	2	16	2
	Falharam	9	15	1	15

In this final test errors were introduced in the audio signal such as distortion or effect caused by bad signal reception (different levels of signal distortion). The results (Table 3) shown that the audio fingerprinting can correctly identify the music if the distortion rate is low. When the distortion rate increases the identification capability diminishes considerably. However this was not one of the biggest requirements of the system, because we will have direct access to the audio device output with low distortion.

VII. Conclusions

This paper presented a system that empowers the Music Related/Neighboring Rights Management Societies (MRNRMS) to perform much better. This reflects in the way the clients are charged and on the way the different related or neighboring rights are distributed to the producers, performers and authors. The systems uses the new information and communication technologies, in a distributed system, over the Internet, to create and collect information about the managed music portfolio, and for the collection of information about the music consumption on the business clients. The music portfolio is updated by the music producers through the automatic introduction of metadata, and by the generation of unique audio identifiers – the audio/acoustic fingerprint – that will enable the automatic identification of the different audio tracks. At the business client side, the MRNRMS relies on a set of small appliances (MAC box) that is connected to the audio output of the audio device, and that captures small samples of the audio in discrete periods of time, generating a set of candidate fingerprints. These candidate fingerprints, as well as some additional capture data is sent over the Internet, to the MAC system, for the matching process. On the MAC system, the different audio-fingerprint candidates will be searched on the database against a similarity threshold that will allow the identification of the audio music track that was played. As such, the music identification processes that were previously perform using a manual procedure can now be completely automated and the system brings important performance gains for the operation of MRNRMS.

References

[1] Burges, C. J., Platt, J. C., & Goldstein, J. (8 de Novembro de 2003). Identifying Audio Clips with RARE. Berkeley, California, U.S.A.

[2] Burges, C. J., Platt, J. C., & Jana, S. (2002). EXTRACTING NOISE-ROBUST FEATURES FROM AUDIO DATA. International Conference on Acoustics, Speech, and Signal Processing, (pp. 1021-1024). Redmond.

[3] Cano, P., Batlle, E., KALKER, T., & HAITSMA, J. (2005). A Review of Audio Fingerprinting. Journal of VLSI Signal Processing , 41, 271–284.

[4] Doets, P., & Lagendijk, R. Stochastic Model Of A Robust Audio Fingerprinting System. Delft.

[5] Haitsma, J., & Kalker, T. (2002). A Highly Robust Audio Fingerprinting System. IRCAM.

[6] KLEMA, V. C., & LAUB, A. J. (2 de Abril de 1980). The Singular Value Decomposition: Its Computation and Some Applications. IEEE TRANSACTIONS ON AUTOMATIC CONTROL, , pp. 164-176.

[7] Lu, L., & Hanjalic, A. (27 de Outubro de 2006). Towards Optimal Audio "Keywords" Detection for Audio Content Analysis and Discovery. Santa Barbara, California, USA.

[8] MusicIP. (2006, Março 12). Open Fingerprin Architecture WhitePaper v1. Monrovia, California, U.S.A.

Testing Distributed ABS System with Fault Injection

Dawid Trawczyński, and Janusz Sosnowski and Piotr Gawkowski
Institute of Computer Science, Warsaw University of Technology, Warsaw, Poland
{D.Trawczynski, P.Gawkowski, J.Sosnowski}@ii.pw.edu.pl

***Abstract*- The paper deals with the problem of adapting software implemented fault injection technique (SWIFI) to evaluate dependability of reactive microcontroller systems. We present an original methodology of disturbing controller operation and analyzing fault effects taking into account reactions of the controlled object and the impact of the system environment. Faults can be injected randomly (in space and time) or targeted at the most sensitive elements of the controller to check it at high stresses. This approach allows identifying rarely encountered problems, usually missed in classical approaches. The developed methodology has been used successfully to verify dependability of ABS system. Experimental results are commented in the paper.**

I. Introduction

In many applications an important issue is to evaluate their behaviour in the case of appearing faults. In embedded control systems (e.g. used in automotive controllers) transient faults resulting from various disturbances are especially critical [5,7,11,18]. In the literature various fault injection techniques have been described to evaluate fault effects [3,12,14,15]. The most universal approach bases on software implemented fault injection (SWIFI) [3,8,17,18]. Its usefulness was verified analysing many calculation oriented applications. In embedded real time systems we have to take into account their reactive nature. Only a few papers deal with this problem for simple examples e.g. [5,18,21]. We have also some experience in this area with chemical controllers [9]. This paper is targeted at more complex system combined with several interconnected and co-operating controllers in automotive antilock braking system (ABS). Here we have faced new problems related to combining the tested controller with the environment model (involving the control object), developing efficient fault injection strategies targeted at the controller and qualification of results from the application perspective.

To resolve the presented problems we have adapted and extended the capabilities of our previously developed fault injector (FITS) [8]. In particular we added an interface to external environment models (e.g. based on TrueTime and Simulink simulators [2,16]) and result qualification procedures which check the output signal trajectories in relevance to specified behavioural properties. The environment covers not only complex models interacting with the controllers (wheel and road properties) but also such elements as interconnection network and real time kernel (not covered in the literature). All this results in an original heterogeneous simulation test bed.

In section 2 we present the developed test bed, model of the controller and environment. Section 3 presents fault injection experiments and results. Two strategies have been performed: classical random distribution of faults and a new strategy allowing to drill down the most critical points. The gained experience is summarised in section 4.

II. Specification of the Test Bed

A. System Structure

The analyzed anti-lock braking system is a composition of 4 distributed microcontrollers interconnected via CAN or TTCAN bus. We have developed its model on the x86 architecture and Visual Studio 2005 integrated programming platform. This model has been developed in C++ and consists of over 20,000 lines of source code: about 12,000 lines of real-time simulator TrueTime [2] and 8,000 lines of the distributed ABS application model.

Each microcontroller corresponds to single car wheel. The idea of controlling a single wheel to avoid wheel locking or slippage was described in [16] and its fault robustness was analyzed in [20]. Extending this analysis to the complete 4-wheel system was a big challenge, due to the need of introducing communication network between the controllers and adaptation of the control algorithms, so as to take into account messages exchanged between controllers and serving them tasks. This added also the need of modeling operating system kernels in each controller (node).

The distributed ABS model instantiated four main modules (the first three modules are replicated for all four wheels):

- *Wheel and Tire Dynamics Module ($WTDM_i$)*: responsible for simulation of the wheel dynamics based on suspension and associated quarter of the vehicle mass,
- *Brake Torque Modulator Module (BTM_i):* responsible for simulation of the brake fluid pressure modulator,
- *Control Node (n_i):* responsible for the simulation of an ABS microcontroller that contains the ABS controller object (CLB_i), the signal filter object (SPB_i) and the real-time operating system kernel ($KERNEL_i$),
- *Network Node (N):* responsible for the simulation of a network protocol and interface.

Each control node n_i (big circles in fig. 1) executes specific control tasks. In our ABS simulation model, each node executes four periodic and one aperiodic task. The periodic tasks are control dedicated while the aperiodic task is

T. Sobh, K. Elleithy (eds.), *Innovations in Computing Sciences and Software Engineering*,
DOI 10.1007/978-90-481-9112-3_34,

responsible for processing incoming network interrupts (generated by the received messages). These tasks execute according to the selected scheduling algorithm. A scheduler is a part of the TrueTime operating system kernel model implementation, and generates the task execution scheduling policy (i.e., sharing of a single processor among tasks). The scheduler supports standard real-time scheduling algorithms (e.g., round-robin, rate monotonic and earliest-deadline-first discussed in [11]) but in our simulations we only used the priority with preemption due to its wide use in many industrial, real-time embedded applications.

While developing the four-wheel ABS model, we needed to assure separate code regions for all four nodes as injecting faults, we only disturb one specified controller. This assumption requires that the code as well as the data of all simulation objects should be disjoint, so while disturbing one object, the remaining are not affected by the disturbance. To avoid object interactions via common code or variables we disable the optimization features of the compiler and implement each controller via a separate dynamic-link-library (DLL - available in Windows). This technique assures high test controllability and observability in relevance to analyzed system objects.

In the sequel we describe in more detail the model of task executions, give the outline of the main control algorithm and the model of the environment interacting with the considered system.

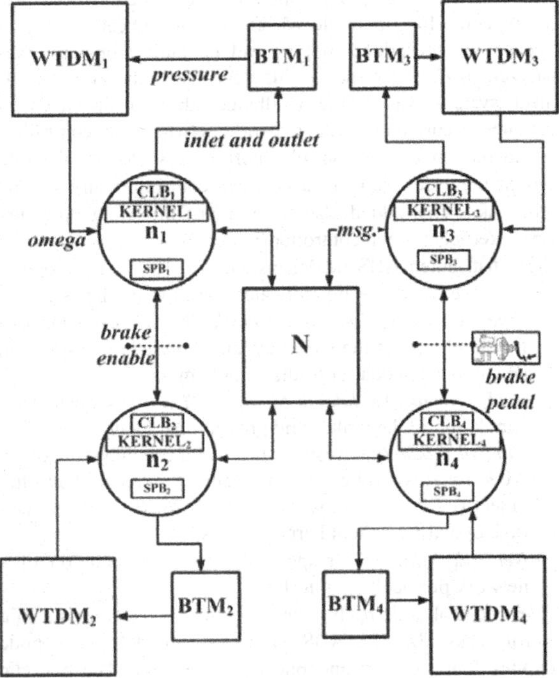

Fig. 1 Distributed ABS model with four control nodes

B. Distributed Task Model

In Fig. 2 we present five tasks ($T_{i,1}$...,$T_{i,5}$) of the distributed ABS model that run on four different processors P_1,...,P_4, where i is the processor index. Note that each processor is mapped to only one node (circle in Fig. 1). Task $T_{i,1}$ is responsible for reading sensor data from the wheel and tire (in Fig. 1 labeled as $WTDM_i$) environment. Task $T_{i,2}$ is responsible for computation of the ABS controller signals. Task $T_{i,3}$ is responsible for the simulation of the environment - the wheel, suspension and tire models. Task $T_{i,4}$ is responsible for sending periodic broadcast messages via the shared CAN or TTCAN bus (network N) to all processors [1]. These messages contain the value of the local wheel slip coefficient. All four control tasks $T_{i,2}$ take into account four slip values when deciding how much brake pressure to apply to each wheel brake disk. Task $T_{i,5}$ is a network interrupt handler that is called by the operating system kernel whenever a slip message arrives from the network. This task is responsible for updating slip values used by the controller task $T_{i,2}$.

For all tasks presented in Fig. 2, a period $p_{i,j}$ or deadline $d_{i,j}$ is specified by the designer, where i is the processor and j is the task index. The period $p_{i,j}$ determines the time interval between task activations. The deadline $d_{i,j}$ specifies the maximum amount of time a task can utilize a processor (i.e., its worst-case-execution-time, WCE). In real-time systems, the WCE is a critical parameter because it assures predictable system behavior. In our simulation approach, all tasks can be preempted and have equal priority.

In addition to the presented task model, in Fig. 2 we also illustrate the task execution schedule for all five tasks that run on distributed processors. This task execution schedule is projected onto the vertical (time) axis, in which the circle indicates a task $T_{i,j}$ that is executing at some simulation time t. Each task's execution start time is marked via a black dot at the top of the circle, and the completion time is marked via a black dot at the bottom of the circle. In Fig. 2, both of these dots are projected onto the time axis to indicate the associated events. Note that the time scale in Fig. 2 is not always linear because our intention is to illustrate only the sequence of periodic activation of tasks and not the entire task schedule. As such, in Fig. 2, the time-line starts at $t = 0$ (i.e., initial simulation time value) and shows task initialization and termination times. The task execution time is defined by these two points.

In Fig. 2, the first time interval [0, 102] (in microseconds) relates to the sequence of three tasks ($T_{i,1}$, $T_{i,2}$, $T_{i,3}$). The activation time for all tasks is specified by the developer via the offset parameter $o_{i,j}$. The offset (not show explicitly in Fig. 2) equals $o_{i,1} = 0$, $o_{i,2} = 50$, $o_{i,3} = 100$, $o_{i,4} = 224$ (μsec.) for tasks $T_{i,1}$, $T_{i,2}$, $T_{i,3}$, and $T_{i,4}$ respectively; the offset for task $T_{i,5}$ is not deterministic (i.e., dynamic) due to variable communication delay introduced by the network N shown in Fig. 2.

The first time interval is followed by the second interval [102, 220] (μsec.) in which three horizontal line segments indicate the second activation of task $T_{i,1}$, $T_{i,2}$, and $T_{i,3}$; this is a consequence of the periodic execution of these tasks. After this

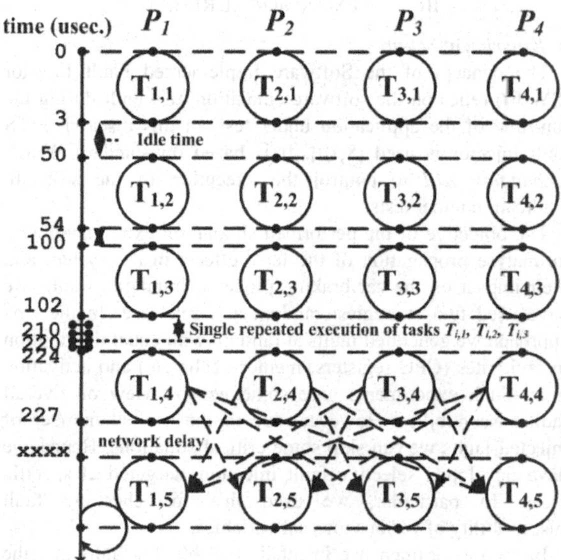

Fig. 2 Distributed ABS tasks model in the context of execution schedule

time interval passes, at time t = 224 microseconds, task $T_{i,4}$ is initiated on each processor P_i; this task sends wheel slip messages to other network nodes via the CAN or TTCAN network interface function *ttSendMsg()*[2]. Sending messages is denoted with dashed arrows.

Finally, some time later, (depending on the transmission and queuing delays) slip messages are received by network nodes, and this is indicated in Fig. 2 by the execution of network interrupt handler task $T_{i,5}$. Note, that the start time of this task is not specified (in Fig.2 this time is shown as *xxxx*) because it is non-deterministic (see discussion above). After the execution of task $T_{i,5}$ is terminated, the same task execution schedule repeats in a loop for the predefined simulation time (in the discussed experiment the logical simulation time is t = 2 seconds). In Fig. 2, the task repetitions are denoted with a looping arrow at the end of the time axis. While simulating the distributed ABS operation, we assumed the simulation time resolution equal to 0.5 microseconds (to capture all system dynamics). In the discussed experiment 4 million loop iterations were performed in each two second simulation time interval. Moreover, within this simulation time interval, a maximum of 18,181 task $T_{i,1}$, $T_{i,2}$, $T_{i,3}$ executions were performed, and 250 tasks $T_{i,4}$, $T_{i,5}$ were executed by each processor P_i. Tasks $T_{i,4}$, $T_{i,5}$ were activated less frequently because their periods were 8 milliseconds, while tasks $T_{i,1}$, $T_{i,2}$, $T_{i,3}$ had periods equal to 0.11 milliseconds.

An important issue is the network (CAN or TTCAN) communication delay. The CAN delay affects the communication schedule because it introduces some indeterminism when activating the network interrupt handler task $T_{i,5}$. TTCAN delay on the other hand, is a function of the slot size, the number of source-destination communication slots in a round, and the cycle length. Due to the time-triggered bus access scheme, in fault-free conditions, the TTCAN delay is constant because the message has guaranteed channel bandwidth within the allocated time slot. Finally, we note that when faults do occur within the network, this delay can significantly differ from the fault-free conditions. We have analyzed this effect in experiments discussed in [19]. Having explained the distributed system and the task model, we outline the distributed ABS control algorithm.

C. ABS Controller Model

An important part of the embedded and distributed ABS is the control algorithm. Authors in [6] and [13] suggest that current algorithms are strongly empirical in nature, and for this reason, we developed our own algorithm called ***DSlip***.

Algorithm: DSlip

```
BEGIN
1. FOR all nodes n_i
2.     IF(free_running_time < FRT)
3.             reff_om = omega * r_eff
4.             local_slip = 1.0 - (reff_om / x2_dot)
5.     ENDIF
6.     ELSE
7.             reff_om = omega * r_eff
8.             local_slip = 1.0 - (reff_om / x2_dot)
9.             Asynchronously receive slip coefficients
               from remaining network nodes N - {n_i}
               through the ttGetMsg() API
10.            FOR all nodes N - {n_i}
11.                  IF slip[wh_nbr] > local_slip
12.                        local_slip = slip[wh_nbr]
13.                  ENDIF
14.            ENDFOR
15.    ENDELSE

16. Update outputs of CLB_i (i.e., inlet and outlet valve
    control signals), BTM_i (i.e., brake pressure applied
    to brake pads),WTDM_i (i.e., wheel angular velocity
    and car's traveled distance)
17. Compute new local_slip and send the slip message
    to remaining nodes N - {n_i} via the ttSendMsg() API
18. ENDFOR
END
```

Fig. 3 DSlip algorithm pseudocode

The ***DSlip*** algorithm (Fig. 3) is based on the message pre-emption concept in which a brake pressure increase or decrease decision is computed from slip messages received from all nodes $n_1,\ldots,n_4$. The message pre-emption is indicated in steps *11* and *12* of the algorithm. In the algorithm we use some specific variables: *reff_om*: wheel peripherial velocity, *omega*:

wheel angular velocity, *local_slip*: wheel slip in current node, *wh_nbr*: is the wheel index, *x2_dot*: car velocity and an array *slip[wh_nbr]:* local wheel slip array that contains slip coefficients of all wheels. Moreover, we use two functions:

ttGetMsg(): API function used to receive network messages in TrueTime,

ttSendMsg(): API function used to send network messages in TrueTime,.

The *free_running_time*: is the time during which the distributed ABS algorithm only uses local wheel slip values to avoid transient and false positive wheel state conditions. FRT is the maximum time during which only local slip computation is used by the ABS controller.

In steps 11 and 12, we see that if at least one node experiences slip, the algorithm will cause a controller to decrease the brake pressure regardless of the local state of the wheel (slip or non-slip); this is indicated in step *12* by assigning the value of distributed *slip[wh_nbr]* received (via network) from other control nodes to a *local_slip* variable.

D. Environment Model

The ABS environment relates to two modules: brake modulator (*BTM*), and tire and wheel dynamics module (*TWDM*) (see Fig.1). The brake modulator module (*BTM*) generates a real value of the simulated brake torque applied at the wheel rotor (disc brake). This module models a physical device and is represented as a hydraulic pressure modulator. *BTM's* input is unaltered brake fluid pressure, while its output is the modulated brake fluid pressure applied to car's brake pads. Note that the pressure can be controlled by opening or closing the associated input and output vales.

The tire and wheel dynamics module (*TWDM*) is responsible for simulation of the wheel angular velocity *omega*. This value is generated based on two inputs – the *slip* (delivered by *CLB*) and applied *brake torque* (delivered by *BTM*). Additionally, the wheel angular velocity is computed based on an initial wheel velocity, moment of inertia of the wheel and tire, unloaded tire radius, vertical tire stiffness, effective tire radius, and normal force due to vehicle mass; these parameters are defined in [16]. Generally, as the slip value increases and brake torque increases, the wheel lock condition can be reached (the angular velocity of the wheel is zero). The controller therefore must adjust the brake torque to avoid the "wheel lock" state.

The *WTDM* also calculates vehicle horizontal acceleration (*hac*) and velocity (*hvel*), and the *vehicle stopping distance* based on only two inputs: the wheel angular velocity *omega* and *brake status* signal. *WTDM* calculates these signals and simulates the motion of the vehicle in the x direction by taking into account the following parameters: vehicle mass, axle and rim mass, initial body translational velocity, initial axle translational velocity, tire belt translational stiffness, tire belt translational damping, vehicle translation dumping suspension, vehicle translation stiffness suspension, stop velocity, damping of translation, and normal force at the tire contact point. These parameters are defined in [16].

III. Experimental Results

A. Experiment Set-up

The concept of the Software Implemented Fault Injector (SWIFI) relies on the software emulation of a fault during the run-time of the application under test. In this research FITS fault injector is used [8,10]. It is based on standard Win32 *Debugging API* to control the execution of the software application under tests.

The objective of the performed simulation experiments was to analyse propagation of the fault effects in the system and their impact on the car braking process. Simulating faults we have used two strategies: random and selective. In the first approach we generated faults at random with equal distribution in fault sites (CPU registers, memory cells etc) and activation time. Such experiments give some general view on overall fault susceptibility. However, due to the limited number of injected faults we can skip some critical situations. Hence, we have developed selective fault injections targeted at specific areas. In particular, we used this for checking fault susceptibility of various internal variables.

In each experiment we injected 1000 bit-flip faults into the program's data memory (MEM), processor registers (REG), program's code memory (CODE), the next (dynamic) instruction (INST), and the processor's floating pointing unit (FPU), or a set of ABS controller parameters. For each fault injection test we then collected data on car trajectory and controller responses and compared that with the reference ones via a special result qualification (RQ) module.

In case of the ABS, the result qualification enabled us to collect braking performance statistics from our SWIFI experiments and classify them as correct (*C*), incorrect (*I*), system exception (*S*) and timeouts (*T*). The correct (C) means that a program executing the ABS controller produced an expected (acceptable) trajectory. The incorrect (*I*) test means that the program provided unexpected (unacceptable) trajectory. The system exception (*S*) test means that some unhandled system/hardware exception was generated (e.g., illegal memory access). The timeout (*T*) means that a program run-time exceeded the maximum expected execution time (e.g., due to the ABS controller lock-down).

To qualify simulation results for the four-wheel ABS, we used measurements of individual wheel trajectories that had to fit within result qualification window, and be within a certain tolerance value ε. In case of the qualification window, each individual wheel stopping distance had to be between $d_{min} = 14.0$ and $d_{max} = 16.5\ m$, the car final velocity between $cwv_{min} = 0$ and $cwv_{max} = 1.5\ m/sec.$, and wheel slip between $ws_{min} = -0.9$ and $ws_{max} = -0.0005$ (no units) within the simulation time range $t_{min} < t < t_{max}$. In our experiments, t_{min} and t_{max} window variables were set to *1.49* and *1.99* seconds respectively. We selected the trajectory tolerance value ε = 10%, which means all four stopping distance and final velocity trajectories for all four wheels can not be different by more than 10% relative to each other. This tolerance value along with window size parameters were derived from our reference (golden-run) ABS simulation experiments, in which the car's initial velocity was set equal *60 km/hr*, the vehicle mass was *1200 kg*, and axle and rim mass was *35 kg* and tire parameters are given in [16].

B. Results for Random Fault Injections

Results for random (in time and space) fault injections are given in Tab. 1. Only single ABS node (out of four) was disturbed. The objective of this experiment was to check if random faults that affect ABS controller's registers (*REG*), data memory (*MEM*), static (*CODE* – disturbed bits in the memory code area), dynamic code (*INST* – disturbed executed instructions) and the floating point unit (*FPU*) lead do dangerous system behavior. To disturb uniquely the ABS controller (not other elements in the test bed) the controller code was explicitly separated via the dynamic link library (DLL). The results of the experiments in Tab. 1 relate to two controller versions: ABS1 uses the event-triggered CAN data bus to connect the four controller nodes, while the second (ABS2) uses the time-triggered TTCAN data bus. We used two different data buses to assess the influence of network medium access control (MAC) protocol on the ABS dependability.

Results in Tab. 1, show that random fault injection into selected processor resources (*REG, MEM, CODE, INST, FPU*) generated 0.8-15% (depending on the fault's location) of undetected errors (I - incorrect results) that could violate the ABS safety. Fault injection covers the whole braking process (period [0, 2] s). Uniform random distribution (in time and space) of faults may not cover some critical situations (low probability of activation). We deal with this problem in selective test scenario.

C. Selective Fault Injections

In this fault injection scenario we selected a set of controller parameters and observed the system behavior in the presence of parameter faults. We analyzed the ABS system with no fault hardening mechanisms (version 1) and an enhanced version with built-in simple software assertions (version 2). These assertions were targeted at critical parameters and their effectiveness was checked experimentally. In this approach an important issue is the selection of critical parameters.

TABLE 1
RESULTS OF RANDOM FAULT INJECTION

ABS1	REG	MEM	CODE	INST	FPU
C	64.84%	97.83%	41.24%	29.68%	90.52%
I	0.80%	1.09%	10.21%	15.14%	4.49%
S	33.76%	0.54%	44.84%	54.58%	1.50%
T	0.6%	0.54%	3.70%	0.60%	3.49%
ABS2	REG	MEM	CODE	INST	FPU
C	64.71%	91.50%	43.82%	28.88%	87.52%
I	0.70%	1.00%	10.46%	15.04%	3.69%
S	33.80%	0.50%	44.92%	54.48%	1.50%
T	0.80%	7.00%	0.80%	1.59%	7.29%

Main parameters selected for experiments were wheel slip threshold (*SL*), low-pass filter time constant (*FT*), low-pass filter amplification gain (*FG*), integrator sample time (*ST*), and effective tire radius (*TR*). The significance and typical values of these ABS controller parameters are discussed in [16].

In Fig.4 we show parameter oriented fault injection results for a controller with CAN network without and with fault hardening mechanisms (application specific assertions). In each experiment we computed the total number of correct (*C*), incorrect (*INC*), system exceptions (*S*) and program timeouts (*T*) to determine the performance of the system in the presence of faults. Each odd column (bar) shows results (i.e., distribution of result categories in percents) for a specific parameter (denoted with acronym as given above), they relate to the non-hardened ABS controller (version 1). Each even column (bar) shows results for the assertion hardened ABS controller (version 2) that protects a specific parameter labeled in the figure. This label is additionally marked with character ', to distinguish it from the non hardened version (e.g. SL stands for non hardened and SL' for fault hardened version, respectively). Errors detected by assertions recover appropriate parameter values.

For the five selected parameters we injected a total of 5000 bit-flip faults that disturbed the controller during the initial (90-900) control iterations (testing region). We disturbed ABS parameters during the initial stages of controller activity because in this time interval ([9.9ms, 99ms], one iteration is equivalent to 0.11 ms) most of the braking force must be generated to stop the vehicle safely.

The results of Fig. 4 show that using simple assertions (10 static machine instructions required for each parameter), one can significantly improve controller's ability to tolerate faults affecting its critical parameters. Only 1-10% of injected faults produce incorrect results and the remaining faults are either detected or tolerated. For some parameters (e.g., SL) the dependability enhancement is very high with low static and dynamic code size overheads (less than 5% when compared to the primary version 1).

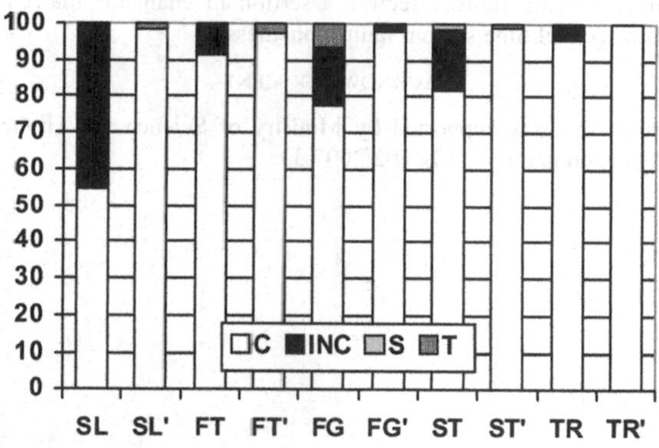

Fig. 4 Fault injections into specific variables

Another interesting issue was the controller fault susceptibility to different bit locations affecting the eight-byte parameters (FPU double precision). Our experiments have shown that disturbing the least significant four bytes (related to the analyzed parameter stored in the memory) did not affect the ABS controller performance significantly. The deviation from the reference value (of the braking performance) was negligibly small. However, injection of bit-flip faults into the most significant four bytes negatively affected the controller. Some results we give for the slip threshold parameter (SL). The reference value of this parameter was equal to 0.2, and in our experiments, we disturbed each bit position (0 to 31) of this parameter in different time moments. The most significant two bytes of the slip threshold parameter (SL) showed high fault sensitivity. Converting the resulting faulty hexadecimal values into decimal representations we found that faults begin to affect the controller at bit position 17, which corresponds to a value of about 0.215. If a wheel slip parameter value is greater than 0.215 (due to a fault), it generates non-negligible lower braking performance. Similar analysis has been performed for other critical parameters.

IV. Conclusions

The paper proved the possibility of integrating different simulation models (based on various software platforms) in a common test bed to check and analyze fault effects. This test bed has been combined with software implemented fault injector. It provides interactions with external environment and assures high fault controllability (within specified test objects). To check fault robustness of the analyzed systems we have developed two complementary test scenarios (random and selective). This approach has been verified for a complex distributed ABS system (several versions were considered including fault hardened one). It is worth noting that the ABS model was much more complex than other systems reported in fault injection experiments by other authors. In particular, it included many complex interacting objects. The gained experience with the ABS system can be used in analyzing other reactive systems. Further research will be focused on finding and accessing more effective assertion mechanisms that can improve real time system fault robustness.

Acknowledgment

This work was supported by Ministry of Science and Higher Education grant 4297/B/T02/2007/33.

References

1. Albert, A., Gerth, W.: Evaluation and Comparison of the Real-Time Performance of CANand TTCAN. Proc. of 9th CAN Conference, Munich (2003)
2. M. Anderson, D. Henriksson, A. Cervin: *TrueTime 1.3 Manual*. Lund Institute of Technology, Sweden, 2005.
3. Aralat et al., "Comparison pf physical and software-implemented fault injection techniques" IEEE Trans. on Computers, vol.52, no.9, pp.1115-1133, 2003.
4. A. Cervin, D. Henriksson, D. Lincoln, K. J. Eker-Årzén *"How does control timing affect performance?"* Proc. IEEE Control Systems Magazine, vol.23, no.3, pp. 16-30, June 2003.
5. J. C. Cunha et. al. *"A study of failure models in feedback control systems"* Proc. International Conference on Dependable Systems and Networks DSN 2001, pp.314-326, Goteborg, Sweden, 2001.
6. T. Frahsure: *Distributed Anti-Lock Braking System*; US Patent Nbr: 20060119174 A1, 2006.
7. P. Gawkowski, J. Sosnowski, "Dependability evaluation with fault injection experiments," *IEICE Transactions on Information & System*, vol. E86-D, pp. 2642-2649, 2003.
8. P. Gawkowski, J. Sosnowski, "Experiences with software implemented fault injection," Proceeding of the International Conference on Architecture of Computing Systems, VDE Verlag GMBH, pp. 73-80, 2007.
9. P. Gawkowski et al.,"Software implementation of explicit DMC algorithm with improved dependability" Novel Algorithms and Techniques in Telecommunications Automation and Industrial Electronics, Springer, pp.214-219, 2008.
10. P. Gawkowski, J. Sosnowski, Developing Fault Injection Environment for Complex Experiments, Proc. of IEEE On-Line Test Symposium, 2008, pp. 179-181.
11. H. Kopetz: *Real-Time Systems - Design Principles for Distributed Embedded Applications*; Kluwer Academic, Netherlands 1998.
12. J. Muranho et. al. *"Failure boundness in discrete applications"* Proc. 3rd Latin-American Symposium on Dependable Computing, pp.160-169, Morella, Mexico, 2007.
13. J. B. Pheonix: Electronic Braking Control System; US Patent Nbr: 5575543, 1996.
14. K. Pattabiraman et al.*"SymPLFIED: Symbolic program level fault injection and error detection framework"* Proc. International Conference on Dependable Systems and Networks DSN 2008, pp.472-481, Anchorage, Alaska, USA, 2008.
15. Portela-Garcia, M. et al., Portela-Garcia, M. et al., "Rapid fault injection approach for measuring SEU sensitivity in complex processors", *Proc. of IEEE IOLTS, 2007*, pp.100-106.
16. K. Rangelov: *Simulink Model of a Quarter-Vehicle with an Anti-Lock Braking System*; Research Report, Eindhoven University of Technology, 2004.
17. M. Rebaudengo, M. S. Reorda, M. Villante, A new software based technique for low cost fault tolerant appliaction, Proc. of IEEE Annula Reliability and Maintanability Symposium, 2003, pp.23-28
18. D. Skarin, J. Karlsson, Software imlemented detection and recovery of soft errors in a break by wire system, Proc. of 7th European Dependable Computing Conference, 2IEEE Comp. Soc., 008, pp.145-154.
19. D. Trawczynski, J. Sosnowski, J. Zalewski: *A Tool for Databus Safety Analysis Using Fault Injection*; Proc. International Conference on Computer Safety, Reliability, and Security, SAFECOMP'06, pp. 261-275, Gdansk, Poland, 2006.
20. D. Trawczynski, J. Sosnowski, P. Gawkowski, *"Analyzing fault susceptibility of ABS microcontroller"* Proc. International Conference on Computer Safety, Reliability, and Security SAFECOMP'08, pp. 320-372, Newcastle, U.K, 2008.
21. J. Vinter et al. *"Experimental dependability evaluation of a fail-bounded jet engine control system for unmanned aerial vehicles"* Proc. International Conference on Dependable Systems and Networks DSN 2005, pp. 666-671, Yokohama, Japan, 2005.

Learning Based Approach for Optimal Clustering of Distributed Program's Call Flow Graph

Yousef Abofathi
Faculty of Computer Engineering,
Islamic Azad University,
Shabestar Branch, Iran
Y.Abofathy@IAUshab.ac.ir

Bager Zarei
Faculty of Computer Engineering,
Islamic Azad University,
Shabestar Branch, Iran
Zarei_Bager@IAUshab.ac.ir

Saeed Parsa
Faculty of Computer Engineering,
Science & Technology University,
Tehran, Iran
Parsa@iust.ac.ir

***Abstract*—Optimal clustering of call flow graph for reaching maximum concurrency in execution of distributable components is one of the NP-Complete problems. Learning automatas (LAs) are search tools which are used for solving many NP-Complete problems. In this paper a learning based algorithm is proposed to optimal clustering of call flow graph and appropriate distributing of programs in network level. The algorithm uses learning feature of LAs to search in state space. It has been shown that the speed of reaching to solution increases remarkably using LA in search process, and it also prevents algorithm from being trapped in local minimums. Experimental results show the superiority of proposed algorithm over others.**

Keywords-Call Flow Graph; Clustering; Learning Automata; Concurrency; Distributed Code

I. INTRODUCTION

Optimization of distributed code with goal of achieving maximum concurrency in execution of distributable components in network level is considered as a new aspect in optimization discussions. Concurrency in execution of distributed code is obtained from remote asynchronous calls. The problem is specifying appropriate calls, with considering amount of yielding concurrency from remote asynchronous calls. In this way, dependency graph between objects are clustered with the base of amount of calls between objects, and each cluster is considered as a component in distributed architecture. Since clustering is a NP-Complete problem, in this paper a learning based non-deterministic algorithm is proposed for optimal clustering of call flow graph.

The proposed algorithm uses learning feature of LAs to search in state space. Resisting against the superficial changes of solutions is the most important characteristic of proposed algorithm. Penalty and reward are characteristics of proposed algorithm.

II. LEARNING AUTOMATA

Learning in LAs is choosing an optimal action from a set of automata's allowable actions. This action is applied on a random environment and the environment gives a random answer to this action from a set of allowable answers. The environment's answer depends statistically on the automata's action. The environment term includes a collection of all outside conditions and their effects on the automata's operation. The interaction between environment and LA is shown in Fig. 1.

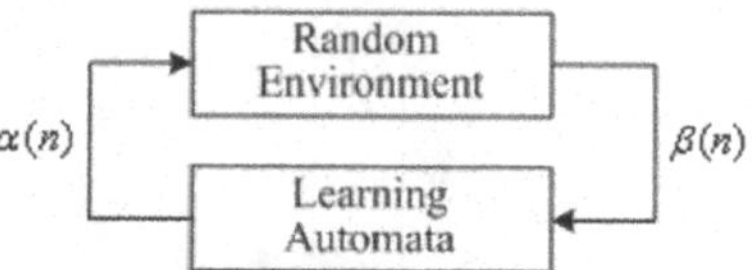

Figure 1. Interaction between environment and LA

III. PROPOSED SEARCHING ALGORITHM FOR OPTIMAL CLUSTERING OF CALL FLOW GRAPH

In fact, this algorithm determines appropriate clustering in a finite search space. Finally each cluster is considered as a component in distributed architecture. In section 3-3 an algorithm is represented for determining amount of yielding concurrency from a given clustering.

A. Showing clustering by learning automata

In proposed algorithm each clustering is shown by a LA of the object migrating type. In this automata $\alpha = \{\alpha_1, \dots, \alpha_k\}$ is the set of allowable actions for the LA. This automata has k actions (actions number of this automata is equal to the number of distributable components or clusters. Determining of appropriate number of clusters is an optimization problem which has not discussed in this paper). Each action shows a cluster.

$\Phi = \{\phi_1, \phi_2, \dots, \phi_{kN}\}$ is the set of states and N is the depth of memory for automata. The states set of this automata is partitioned into the k subset $\{\phi_1, \phi_2, \dots, \phi_N\}$, $\{\phi_{N+1}, \phi_{N+2}, \dots, \phi_{2N}\}$, …, and $\{\phi_{(k-1)N+1}, \phi_{(k-1)N+2}, \dots, \phi_{kN}\}$. Call flow graph nodes are classified on the basis of their states. If node n_i from call flow graph is in the states set $\{\phi_{(j-1)N+1}, \phi_{(j-1)N+2}, \dots, \phi_{jN}\}$, then node n_i will be j^{th} cluster.

T. Sobh, K. Elleithy (eds.), *Innovations in Computing Sciences and Software Engineering*,
DOI 10.1007/978-90-481-9112-3_35,

In the states set of action j, state $\varphi_{(j-1)N+1}$ is called inner (stable) state and state φ_{jN} is called outer (unstable) state. For example, consider call flow graph of fig. 2.

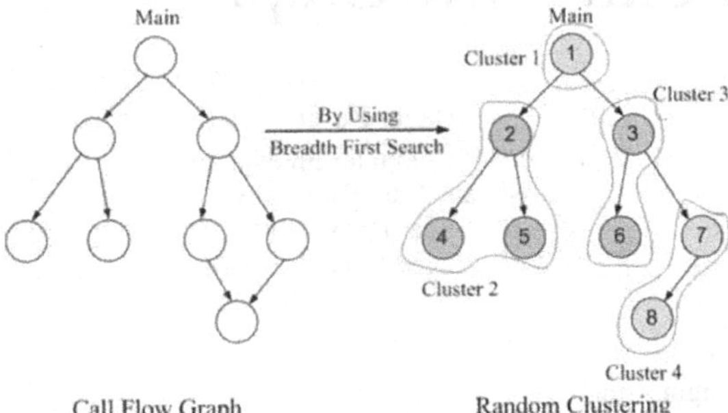

Figure 2. An instance of call flow graph

Clustering of fig. 2 is shown in fig. 3 by a LA with similar connections to Tsetline automata. This automata has 4 (equal to the number of clusters) actions a_1, a_2, a_3, and a_4 and its depth is 5. States set {1,6,11,16} are inner states and states set {5,10,15,20} are outer states of the automata. At the beginning each cluster is placed at the outer state of relative action. For instance since in fig. 3 $C_2=\{n_2, n_4, n_5\}$, so nodes n2, n4, n5 are placed in same cluster (cluster 2).

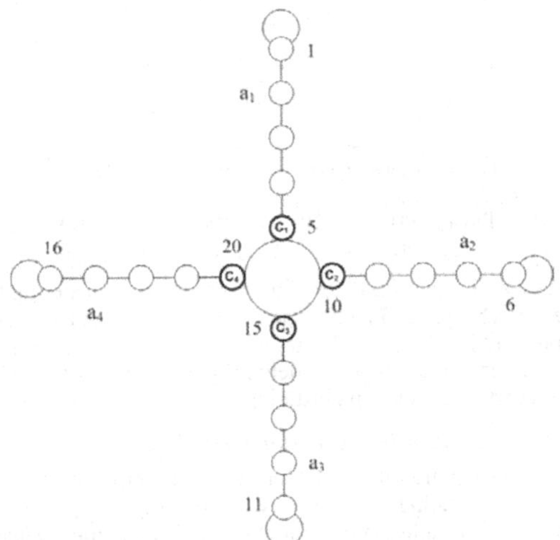

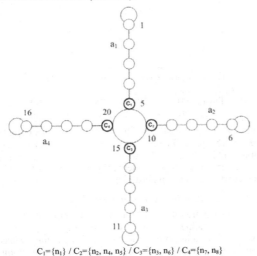

$C_1=\{n_1\}$ / $C_2=\{n_2, n_4, n_5\}$ / $C_3=\{n_3, n_6\}$ / $C_4=\{n_7, n_8\}$

Figure 3. Showing clustering of fig. 2 by a LA with similar connections to Tsetline automata

B. Penalty and reward operators

Since in proposed algorithm, every clustering is shown in the form of LA, in each automata after examining fitness of a cluster (action) which is selected randomly, that cluster will be rewarded or penalized. State of a cluster in the relative action states set will be changed as the result of rewarding or penalizing it. If a cluster is placed at the outer state of an action, penalizing it leads to action of one of its nodes is changed and so a new clustering will created. Reward and penalty operator vary according to the LA types.

For example, in an automata with similar connections to Tsetline automata if cluster C_3 is in the states set {11, 12, 13, 14, 15}, and its execution time without considering remote calls is less than threshold, this cluster is rewarded and it moves to the inner states of its action. If cluster C_3 is in the innermost state (state number 11) and rewarded, it will remain in that state. The movement of such cluster is shown in fig. 4.

If execution time of a cluster without considering remote calls is greater than threshold, this cluster is not appropriate and it is penalized. The movement of such cluster for two different cases is as follows:

- The cluster is at a state other than outer state: Panelizing this cluster reduces its importance and it moves to the outer states. The movement of such cluster is shown in fig. 5.
- The cluster is in outer state: In this case, we find a cluster of automata in which, if one of the cluster nodes is moved to the founded cluster, maximum increase in fitness outcome. In this case, if the founded cluster is not in outer state, first it is moved to outer state of its action and then node is moved to it. The movement of such cluster is shown in fig. 6.

Important subject is determining of threshold value. For this consider concurrent execution time in following three different cases:

- Best Case (100% Concurrency): $T_c = \frac{T_s}{NoClusters}$
- Average Case (50% Concurrency): $T_c = \frac{T_s}{\frac{1}{2}NoClusters}$
- Worst Case (0% Concurrency): $T_c = T_s$

In above criteria, T_c is concurrent execution time, T_s is sequent execution time, and NoClusters is number of clusters. In this paper we considered threshold value be concurrent execution time in average case.

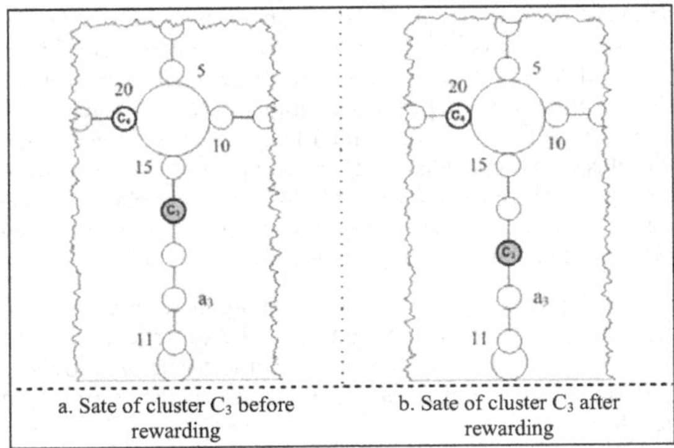

a. Sate of cluster C_3 before rewarding

b. Sate of cluster C_3 after rewarding

Figure 4. The manner of rewarding a cluster

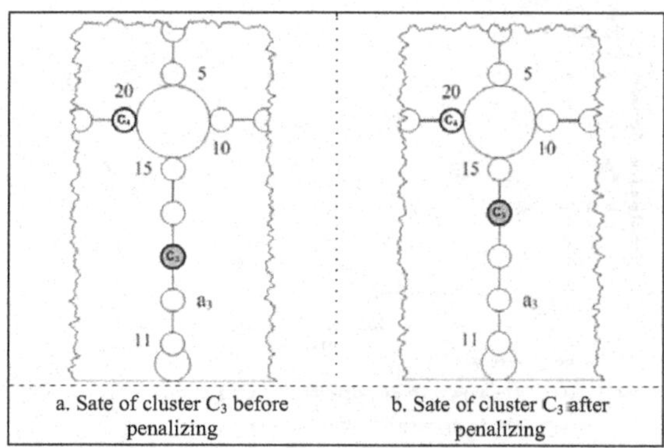

a. Sate of cluster C_3 before penalizing   b. Sate of cluster C_3 after penalizing

Figure 5. The manner of penalizing a cluster palced in a state other than outer state

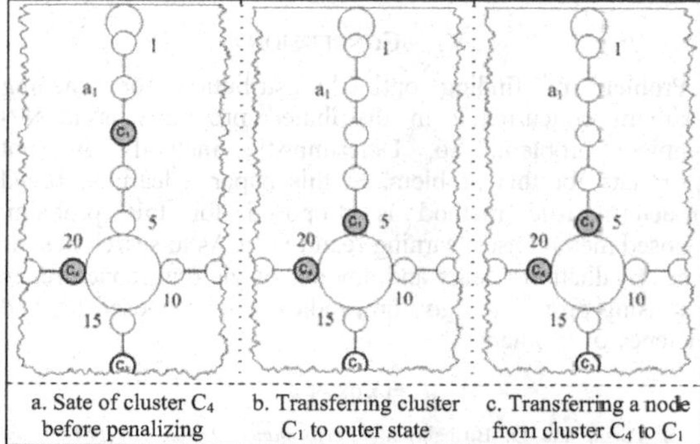

a. Sate of cluster C_4 before penalizing   b. Transferring cluster C_1 to outer state   c. Transferring a node from cluster C_4 to C_1

Figure 6. The manner of penalizing a cluster palced in outer state

C. Determining amount of yielding concurrency from a given clustering

Goal of optimal clustering is reaching maximum concurrency in execution of distributed code; so, for a given clustering amount of yielding concurrency must be calculated. In this section an algorithm is represented for determining amount of yielding concurrency from a given clustering for call flow graph of a distributed code. As you known concurrency is obtained from asynchronous remote calls. When a function such as r is called via function m in a way i=a.r(), caller function m can run synchronous with function r until it does not need to the return value of r. For example consider the fig. 7. In this figure interval between call of function r to the using point of this call's outcome is denoted by T_d, and execution time of function r is denoted by EET_r. Indisputable in the best case $2T_c+EET_r \leq T_d$, which T_c is required time for getting or sending of parameters. In general, waiting time of function m for getting return value from function r is calculated from the following criteria.

$$T_{wait} = (T_d > 2T_c + EET_r)\ ?\ 0 : (2T_c + EET_r) - T_d$$

The problem is calculating T_d and EET_r. Because, for instance, in the time of between call point and using point of this call's outcome or in context of called function may be exist other calls, and since it is unknown these functions will be executed local or remote, the execution time of them are unpredictable. For solving this problem, calculation of execution time must be started from a method in call flow graph in which it has not any call to other methods in call flow graph. In fig. 8 a pseudo code is represented for determining amount of yielding concurrency from a given clustering for call flow graph of a distributed code.

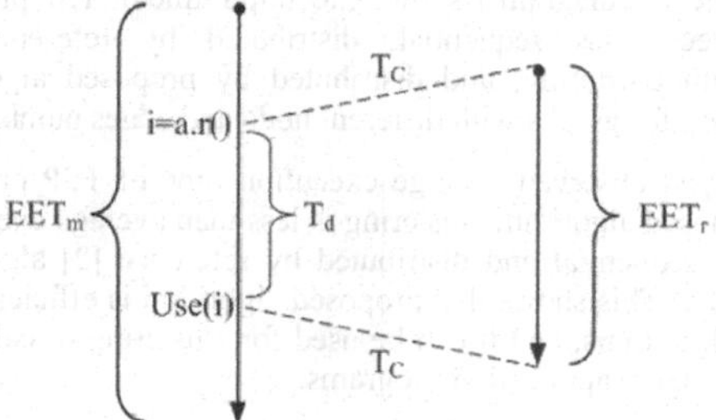

Figure 7. Calculation of exection time in remote calls

```
Function Speedup(CallFlowGraph, LearningAutomata):Speedup
Begin
    Call TopologicalSort(CallFlowGraph);
    for each method m in call flow graph
        if NoCalls_m = 0 then
            EET_m = 0;
            for each not call statement, i, within m
                EET_m = EET_m + ExecutionTime(i);
            for each local call statement, c, within m
                EET_m = EET_m + EET_c;
            for each remote asynchronous call statement, r,
            within m
                EET_m = EET_m + Max(T_d, 2T_c + EET_r);
            for each parent, p, of m within the call flow
            graph
                NoCalls_p = NoCalls_p - 1;
        End if
    End for
End function
```

Figure 8. Pseudo code of determining amount of yielding concurrency from a given clustering

Proposed algorithm pseudo code is shown in fig. 9.

```
Function CFG_Clustering(CallFlowGraph):Clusters or LA
Begin
    LA = Random Clustering of Call Flow Graph;
    while(Speedup(LA) < ConstantValue) do
        C_j = Random * NoClusters;
        if (ExecutionTime(LA_i.C_j) < Threshold) then
            Reward(LA_i , C_j);
        else
            Penalize(LA_i , C_j);
    end while
End function
```

Figure 9. Proposed algorithm pseudo code

IV. PROPOSED METHOD EVALUATION

In order to evaluating proposed algorithm, distributed code of implementation of TSP was used. This distributed code solves TSP by using dynamic methods and finding optimal spanning tree.

Table and diagram 1 shows execution time of TSP program for three cases sequential, distributed by reference [2] algorithm clustering, and distributed by proposed algorithm clustering for graphs with different node and edges number.

As you observed average execution time of TSP program by proposed algorithm clustering is less than average execution time of sequential and distributed by reference [2] algorithm clustering. This shows that proposed algorithm is efficient than other algorithms, and it can be used for clustering of call flow graph of large application programs.

TABLE I. EXECUTION TIME OF TSP PROGRAM FOR THREE CASES SEQUENTIAL, DISTRIBUTED BY REFERENCE [2] ALGORITHM CLUSTERING, AND DISTRIBUTED BY PROPOSED ALGORITHM CLUSTERING FOR GRAPHS WITH DIFFERENT NODE AND EDGES NUMBER

Number of Graph Nodes	Number of Graph Edges	Sequential Execution Time	Distributed Execution Time with Reference [2] Algorithm Clustering	Distributed Execution Time with Proposed Algorithm Clustering
20	40	0.573	7.357	4.859
40	81	1.383	7.81	5.652
60	122	3.246	8.163	6.888
80	163	11.214	11.109	9.738
100	204	19.773	14.741	11.933
120	245	43.517	30.722	24.836
140	286	85.362	60.871	52.022
160	327	145.721	105.227	82.012
180	368	234.871	168.28	125.748
200	409	360.143	261.412	219.746
220	450	576.655	440.343	354.005
240	491	997.653	774.142	606.350
Average Execution Time (ms)		**206.6759**	**157.5148**	**125.316**

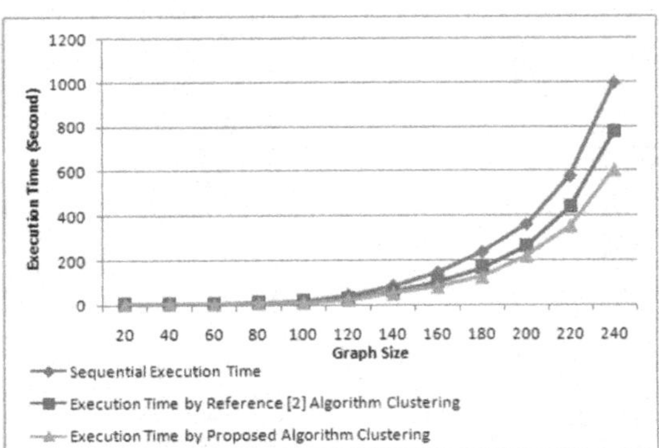

Diagram 1. Execution time of TSP program for three cases sequential, distributed by reference [2] algorithm clustering, and distributed by proposed algorithm clustering for graphs with different node and edges number

V. CONCLUSION

Problem of finding optimal distribution for reaching maximum concurrency in distributed programs is a NP-Complete problem. So, Deterministic methods are not appropriate for this problem. In this paper a learning based non-deterministic method is proposed for this problem. Proposed method uses learning feature of LAs to search in state space. Evaluation results and amount of yielding concurrency from using proposed algorithm, indicator of proposed method efficiency over others.

REFERENCES

[1] S. Parsa, and O. Bushehrian, "*Performance-Driven Object-Oriented Program Remodularization*", ISSN: 1751-8806, INSPEC Accession Number: 10118318, Digital Object Identifier: 10.1049/iet-sen:20070065, Aug, 2008.

[2] S. Parsa, and V. Khalilpoor, "*Automatic Distribution of Sequential Code Using JavaSymphony Middleware*", 32th International Conference On Current Trends in Theory and Practice of Computer Science, 2006.

[3] Roxana Diaconescu, Lei Wang, Zachary Mouri, and Matt Chu, "*A Compiler and Runtime Infrastructure for Automatic Program Distribution*", 19th International Parallel and Distributed Processing Symposium (IPDPS 2005), IEEE, 2005.

[4] S. Parsa, O. Bushehrian, "*The Design and Implementation of a Tool for Automatic Software Modularization*", Journal of Supercomputing, Volume 32, Issue 1, April 2005.

[5] Mohammad M. Fuad, and Michael J. Oudshoorn, "*AdJava-Automatic Distribution of Java Applications*", 25th Australasian Computer Science Conference (ACSC2002), Monash University, Melbourne, 2002.

[6] S. Mitchell Brian, "*A Heuristic Search Approach to Solving the Software Clustering Problem*", Thesis, Drexel University, March 2002.

[7] Thomas Fahringer, and Alexandru Jugravu, "*JavaSymphony: New Directives to Control and Synchronize Locality, Parallelism, and Load Balancing for Cluster and GRID-Computing*", Proceedings of Joint ACM Java Grande ISCOPE 2002 Conference, Seattle, Washington, Nov 2002.

[8] Michiaki Tatsubori, Toshiyuki Sasaki, Shigeru Chiba1, and Kozo Itano, "*A Bytecode Translator for Distributed Execution of Legacy Java Software*", LNCS 2072, pp. 236-255, 2001.

[9] Markus Dahm, "*Doorastha—A Step Towards Distribution Transparency*", JIT, 2000.

[10] Michael Philippsen, and Bernhard Haumacher, "*Locality Optimization in JavaParty by Means of Static Type Analysis*", Concurrency: Practice & Experience, pp. 613-628, July 2000.

[11] Andre Spiegel, "*Pangaea: An Automatic Distribution Front-End for Java*", 4th IEEE Workshop on High-Level Parallel Programming Models and Supportive Environments (HIPS '99), San Juan, Puerto Rico, April 1999.

[12] Saeed Parsa, and Omid Bushehrian, "*Genetic Clustering with Constraints*", Journal of Research and Practice in Information Technology, 2007.

[13] Leng Mingwei, Tang Haitao, and Chen Xiaoyun, "*An Efficient K-means Clustering Algorithm Based on Influence Factors*", Eighth ACIS Int. Conference on Software Engineering, Artificial Intelligence, Networking, and Parallel/Distributed Computing, pp. 815-820, July 2007.

[14] Tapas Kanungo, David M. Mount, Nathan S. Netanyahu, Christine D. Piatko, Ruth Silverman, and Angela Y. Wu, "*An Efficient K-Means Clustering Algorithm: Analysis and Implementation*", IEEE Transaction on Pattern Analysis and Machine Intelligence, Vol. 24, No. 7, July 2002.

[15] Tapas Kanungo, David M. Mount, Nathan S. Netanyahu, Christine D. Piatko, Ruth Silverman, and Angela Y. Wu, "*The Analysis of a Simple K-Means Clustering Algorithm*", Proc. of the Sixteenth Annual Symposium on Computational Geometry, pp. 162, June 2000.

[16] B. Hendrickson, and R. Leland, "*A Multilevel Algorithm for Partitioning Graphs*", Proceedings of the 1995 ACM/IEEE Conference on Supercomputing (CDROM), pp. 28, ACM Press, 1995.

[17] K. A. Dejong , and W. M. Spears, "*Using Genetic Algorithms to Solve NP-Complete Problems*", Proceedings of the Third International Conference on Genetic Algorithms, 1989.

[18] K. S. Narendra, and M. A. L. Thathachar, "*Learning Automata: An Introduction*", Prentice-hall, Englewood cliffs, 1989.

[19] M. R. Meybodi, and H. Beigy, "*Solving Graph Isomorphism Problem by Learning Automata*", Thesis, Computer Engineering Faculty, Amirkabir Technology University, Tehran, Iran, 2000.

[20] H. Beigy, and M. R. Meybodi, "*Optimization of Topology of Neural Networks Using Learning Automata*", Proceedings of 3th Annual International Computer Society of Iran Computer Conference (CSICC-98), Tehran, Iran, pp. 417-428, 1999.

[21] B. J. Oommen, R. S. Valiveti, and J. R. Zgierski, "*An Adaptive Learning Solution to the Keyboard Optimization Problem*", IEEE Transaction On Systems. Man. And Cybernetics, Vol. 21, No. 6, pp. 1608-1618, 1991.

[22] B. J. Oommen, and D. C. Y. Ma, "*Deterministic Learning Automata Solution to the Keyboard Optimization Problem*", IEEE Transaction on Computers, Vol. 37, No. 1, pp. 2-3, 1988.

[23] A. A. Hashim, S. Amir, and P. Mars, "*Application of Learning Automata to Data Compression*", in Adaptive and Learning Systems, K. S. Narendra, Editor, New York, Plenum Press, pp. 229-234, 1986.

[24] M. R. Meybodi, and S. Lakshmivarhan, "*A Learning Approach to Priority Assignment in a Two Class M/M/1 Queuing System with Unknown Parameters*", Proceedings of Third Yale Workshop on Applications of Adaptive System Theory, Yale University, pp. 106-109, 1983.

[25] Bager Zarei, M. R. Meybodi, and Mortaza Abbaszadeh, "*A Hybrid Method for Solving Traveling Salesman Problem*", Proceedings of the 6th IEEE/ACIS International Conference on Computer and Information Science (ICIS 2007), IEEE Computer Society, Melbourne, Australia, pp. 394-399, 11-13 July 2007.

Fuzzy Adaptive Swarm Optimization Algorithm for Discrete Environments

M. Hadi Zahedi[1], M. Mehdi S.Haghighi[2]

zahedi@ieee.org,haghighi@ieee.org

[1]Computer Department, Faculty of Engineering, Ferdowsi University of Mashhad, Iran

[2]Computer Department, Faculty of Engineering, Sadjad Institute of Higher Education, Mashhad, Iran

Abstract: *The heuristic methods have been widely developed for solution of complicated optimization methods. Recently hybrid methods that are based on combination of different approaches have shown more potential in this regard. Fuzzy simulation and Particle Swarm Optimization algorithm are integrated to design a hybrid intelligent algorithm to solve the np-hard problem such as travelling salesman problem in efficient and faster way of solutions. The results obtained with the proposed method show its potential in achieving both accuracy and speed in small and medium size problems, compared to many advanced methods.*

Key Words: *Particle Swarm Optimization, Fuzzy set and systems, Traveling Salesman Problem*

1- INTRODUCTION

The Particle swarm optimization (PSO) algorithm, originally developed by Kennedy and Eberhart [1], is a method for optimization on metaphor of social behavior of flocks of birds and/or schools of fish. Similar to genetic algorithms (GAs), the PSO is also an optimizer based on population. The system is initialized firstly in a set of randomly generated potential solutions, and then is performed to search for the optimum one iteratively. It finds the optimum solution by swarms following the best particle. Compared to GAs, the PSO has much better intelligent background and could be performed more easily. According to its advantages, the PSO is not only suitable for scientific research, but also engineering applications. Presently the PSO has attracted broad attention in the fields of evolutionary computing, optimization and many others [2–5]. Although the PSO is developed for continuous optimization problems initially, there have been some reported works focused on discrete problems recently [6-7].

The Traveling Salesman Problem (TSP) is the problem of a salesman who starts from his hometown and wants to visit a specified set of cities, returning to his hometown at the end. Each city has to be visited exactly once and we are interested in finding the shortest possible tour. TSP is one of the top ten NP-hard problems. It has been used as one of the most important test-beds for new combinatorial optimization methods. Its importance stems from the fact there is a plethora of fields in which it finds applications e.g., shop floor control (scheduling), distribution of goods and services (vehicle routing), product design (VLSI layout), micro-array gene ordering and DNA fragment assembly. Since the TSP as proved to belong to the class of NP-hard problems, heuristics and meta-heuristics occupy an important space in the methods so far developed to provide practical solutions for large instances of TSP [8-18]. It is a well-known and extensively studied benchmark for many new developments in combinatorial optimization. Over decades, besides the well-known variants of simulated annealing (SA) [16], researchers have suggested a multitude of heuristic algorithms, such as genetic algorithms (GAs) [10-13], neural networks [13-15], tabu search [17-18], particle swarm optimization [19-21], and ant colonies [22-25] to solve TSP.

Among recently developed non-derivative-based heuristic methods, the particle swarm optimization (PSO), which is a population-based algorithm for optimization, has shown a very high potential in solving complicated problems. Despite of its noticeable success in solving many continuous space problems, it has difficulties in discrete spaces like TSP. Clerc proposed a brief outline of the PSO method for solving TSP problems [26-27]. By adding a memory capacity to each particle in the PSO algorithm, Hendtlass [28] applied the PSO algorithm to solve smallsize TSP problems, and improved its performance. Wang et al. [29] redefined the PSO operators by introducing the concepts of "Swap operator" and "Swap sequence", therefore the TSP problems could be solved by the PSO in another way. The sizes of cities in [27] and [29] are both 14 (both of them selected Burma14, a benchmark problem in TSPLIB with 14 cities), and that of [19] is 17 (it selected br17, a benchmark problem in TSPLIB with 17 cities). That is to say, the sizes of cities are rather limited in their algorithms. In this paper, we applied the idea of swarm intelligence to discrete space of the TSP and

T. Sobh, K. Elleithy (eds.), *Innovations in Computing Sciences and Software Engineering*,
DOI 10.1007/978-90-481-9112-3_36,

proposed a new simulated annealing process taking the advantage of particle swarm optimization. Although the method is at the beginning of its road towards completion, besides small cities, it has shown its capability to solve medium size problems up to 200 cities.

This paper is organized as follows. First section is devoted to definition of the traveling salesman problem. Section 1-2 and 1.3 presents an overview of PSO algorithms and fuzzy set and systems as well as defining the traveling salesman problem. Section 2 shows our proposed hybrid algorithm that integrated PSO and fuzzy concepts, analyzing how the new method utilizes PSO to solve discrete problem like TSP. The effectiveness of the proposed algorithm and results of implementation are illustrated in Section 3. Further, the comparison between the new PSO algorithm for solving TSP and other methods is discussed through simulation results. We use TSP canonical library, TSPLIB, for comparison of the results with several other methods.

1.1 The Traveling Salesman Problem

A salesman has to visit n nodes, usually named “cities” or “sale points”, c1, c2, …, cn , given an n by (n – 1) matrix of D including the distances between the nodes, where dij is the distance from city ci to city cj; i, j = 1, 2, …, n. The aim is to go through all and each one of them exactly once, and the problem is to know in what sequence the salesman can make it so that the total traveled distance or the total energy consumed, namely E, is minimum. If a sequence of the nodes is defined by s = {s1, s2, …, sn}, then the problem is like equation 1[23]:

$$\min E(s) = d_{s_n s_1} + \sum_{i=1}^{n-1} d_{s_i s_{i+1}} \qquad (1)$$

The previous problem has turned out to have a bigger practical and theoretical importance than the one of facilitating the professional life of salesmen. This problem is a reference point forced in the Combinatorial Optimization and is known internationally by the initials TSP (Travelling Salesman Problem). The problem of the TSP can be formulated as the one of finding a Hamiltonian cycle of minimum distance in the graph of the cities to visit and of the highways that join them. In this context, the Hamiltonian cycles are usually called tours. It is said that a TSP is symmetrical if for any couple of cities, *ci* and *cj*, it is verified that *dij* = *dji*; that is to say, if the square matrix of distances (*n* × *n*), namely ***DT***, is symmetrical. It is called asymmetrical TSP if it is not symmetrical. If the location of the cities is given in terms of their coordinates in a 2 dimensional plane, then distance is measured by equation 2:

$$d_{i,j} = \sqrt{(x_i - x_j)^2 + (y_i - y_j)^2} \quad i,j = 1..n \qquad (2)$$

where *xi, yi, xj* and *yj* are the *i*th and *j*th elements in coordinate vectors, namely ***x*** and ***y***, respectively.

1-2 overview of PSO Algorithm

The particle swarm optimization (PSO) algorithm, proposed by Kennedy and Eberhart [24-25], is a new optimization technique originated from artificial life and evolutionary computation [26-27]. The algorithm completes the optimization through following the personal best solution of each particle and the global best value of the whole swarm. PSO can be implemented with ease and few parameters need to be tuned. Relying on the favor of its inherent intelligence, it has been successfully applied to many areas and proved to be a very effective approach in the global optimization for continuous problems [28-29].

However, as a newly developed optimal method, the PSO algorithm is still in its developmental infancy and further studies are necessary. For example, the original PSO had problems in controlling the balance between exploration and exploitation, because it tends to favor the intensification search around the ‘better’ solutions previously found. In such a context, the PSO appears to be lacking global search ability. Also, its computational efficiency for a refined local search to pinpoint the exact optimal solution is not satisfactory [25]. Many researchers have proposed various kinds of approaches to improve the PSO algorithm [12-14].

An important difficulty that PSO has faced is implementing its discrete version. To enhance the performance of PSO, we first propose a new method for solving discrete problems-such as TSP- with particle swarm optimization algorithms, and then we optimized this proposed algorithm. Like genetic algorithm, the PSO algorithm first randomly initializes a swarm of particles. Each particle is represented by an n-vector pi = (pi,1, pi,2, …, pi,n); i = 1, 2, ..., P, where pij is the position of the ith particle in the jth coordinate, n is the dimension of the space and P is the swarm size. Thus, each particle is randomly placed in the n-dimensional space as a candidate solution. Each particle adjusts its trajectory toward its own previous best position and the previous best position attained by any particle of the swarm, namely p_bi and p_g respectively. At the kth iteration, the swarm positions are updated by the equations (3) and (4):

where vij is the velocity on the jth dimension of the ith particle, α and β are acceleration constants, $u1$ and $u2$ are real numbers drawn from two uniform random sequences of $U(0, 1)$.

1-3 Fuzzy set and systems

In ultra industrial world of today, fuzzy logic has got important and different functions at various scientific courses like controlling engineering systems and artificial intelligence. Dr.Lotfi Zadeh officially presented an article "Fuzzy sets "at 1965 A.C [31]. Fuzzy logic reached to an inclination point in 1974. Fuzzy was applied to "controlling" by Ebrahim Mamdanie for the first time. The international society of fuzzy systems as the first scientific organization was established for fuzzy logic theorists and executors in 1984 [32-34].

The first and the most successful function of fuzzy system are "controlling". Fuzzy systems are based on rules or knowledge. Computing the rules is the first step to design a fuzzy system. The next step is combination of these rules. Definition a fuzzy set "A" might be shown by regular couples (x, MA(x)).If fuzzy set "A" is continuous, it might be shown as $\int \mu_A(x)/_x$ And if it is discrete might be shown as $\sum \mu_A(x)/_x$.

Some of the processes of fuzzy sets are: complementary, intersection (minimum), union (maximum). There are various methods to evaluate rules; one of the most applicable one is Mamdanie inference as shown by equations 5 and 6 [35, 37].

$$\mu_{QMM}(X,Y) = \min\left[\mu f_{p1}(x), \mu f_{p2}(y)\right] \quad (5)$$

$$\mu_{QMp}(X,Y) = \left[\mu f_{p1}(x) \times \mu f_{p2}(y)\right] \quad (6)$$

Generalized Modes ponnes deduction might be used as following: assume the fuzzy set " A' " and fuzzy relation "A ⟶ B" At U*V, A fuzzy set B' at V is like equation 7.

$$\mu_{B}(Y) = \sup t\left[\mu A(X, \mu A \rightarrow B(X,Y))\right] \quad (7)$$

Fuzzy rules bases: fuzzy rules set will be "if ⟶ then"

$$v_{i,j}^{(k+1)} = v_{i,j}^{(k)} + \alpha \times u_1 \times \left[pb_{i,j}^{(k)} - p_{i,j}^{(k)}\right] + \beta \times u_2 \times \left[p_{g_j}^{(k)} - p_{i,j}^{(k)}\right] \quad (3)$$

$$p_{i,j}^{(k+1)} = p_{i,j}^{(k)} + v_{i,j}^{(k+1)} \quad (4)$$

When the rule "I" is presented as follow:

RI: If X1 is Ai1 and X2 is Ai2 ....and Xr is Air then y is Bi

Fuzzy inference engine; principles of fuzzy logic are applied for rules' combinations. There are 2 different methods for Inference:

1) Inference based on rules' combinations

2) Inference based on singular rules.

At second method, each rule has got a fuzzy result and the final result is combination of those fuzzy results. Combination is done by union or intersection. Inference engine has got various kinds. One of them is multiplication inference engine which is computed by equation 8:

$$\mu_B(Y) = \max\left\{\prod_{k=1}^{r} \mu_{Aik}(XK), \mu_{Bi}(y)\right\} \quad \textbf{(8)}$$

2. Adaptive fuzzy discrete PSO optimization

As described previously, PSO algorithm basically has the capability to solve problems in continuous environments where position of each particle is a real number. On the other hand, there are many problems that are basically discrete so there are some constraints on movement of each particle. Population size plays a very important role in evolutionary methods, robustness and computation cost of algorithm are also affected by it. Small population size may result in local convergence; large size will increase computational efforts and may make slow convergence. So an effective population size besides keeping appropriate diversity can reduce computational cost. To achieve these goals, we adopt fuzzy rule base to control population size based on the value of diversity.

2.1 algorithm overview

In the proposed method we consider some important parameters. First, population size has an important role in evolutionary methods and computations. Small population size causes convergence to local minimum. Large population size increases the computation and cost while the convergence is reduced.

As a result a proper population size should optimize computation while keeping the effective diversity. The propose algorithm uses an adaptive method to control the population size by defining cycles where at the end of each cycle diversity is computed. Increasing and decreasing the population size is applied by using fuzzy if-then rules based on diversity value. These if-then rules are defined in a fuzzy knowledge base. Moreover, in discrete environments we have to change basic PSO definitions and equations to adopt with discrete environments.

2.3 Adaptive fuzzy discrete PSO optimization algorithm

In our proposed algorithm, it is assumed that the number of cycles is C and each cycle is repeated P times (P is number of periods). As a result, there is G generations where $G = C \times P$.

The proposed algorithm partitioned to the following sections: (1) randomly initialize population; (2) updating velocity and position of each particle (3) fitness evaluation and ranking particles according to their fitness (4) calculating distance, hamming distance and entropy parameters. Finally evaluating diversity of population according to the three mentioned parameters at the end of each cycle; (5) fuzzification of all the previously computed parameters; (6) executing fuzzy inference engine[1] Specifying the fired rules in FIS in order to determine population of the next cycle; (7) defuzzifying FIS output in order to make decision about Increasing or decreasing population.

The pseudo code of the algorithm is showed in figure 1. Some main parts are designed in the next parts of the paper:

```
FPSO ( )
begin
    Initialize_parameters (np , num_cycle , period);
    initialize_population(InitPop);
    for iter_cycle=1:num_cycle
      num_period=1;
      for num_period=1:period
        for i = 1:np
          if f(x_i) < f(x_pbesti)
            x_pbesti=x_i
          endif
          P_gbest = min(P_neighbors)
          For d=1:dimensions
                v_id(t+1)=wv_id(t)+c1r1(x_pbestid(t)-x_id(t))
                          +c2r2(.)x_gbestid(t)-x_id(t)) );
              x_id(t+1)=x_id(t)v_id(t+1)
              if v_id(t+1)>v_max
                   v_id(t+1)=v_max
              elseif v_id(t+1)<-v_max
                   v_id(t+1)=-v_max
              end
              if x_id(t+1)>x_max
                  x_id(t+1)=x_max
              elseif x_id(t+1)<x_min
                   x_id(t+1)=x_min
              end
          end
        end
      end
    end
end
```

Figure. 1: Pseudo code of FPSO

2.3.1 Initialize population

In the algorithm, by assuming np as the number of particles, positions and velocities of the particles are generated randomly by normal distribution function.

2.3.2 Updating velocity and position

Since PSO is a population based search technique, each particle represents a potential solution within the search space. Each particle has a position vector and a velocity vector, which should be updated in the general algorithm based on equations (3) and (4). On the other hand, the general velocity definition is no longer valid for our problem and should be adapted on our special problem. In our method, velocity is defined by the number of changes in the order of nodes in each particle. The more the velocity is, the more the number of swaps in the order of nodes in each particle. Therefore, the formula for updating velocity is changed to the formula in equation 9:

$$v_{id}(t+1) = wv_{id}(t) + c_1r_1\left(x_{pbestid}(t) - x_{id}(t)\right) + c_2r_2\left(x_{gbestid}(t) - x_{id}(t)\right) \quad (9)$$

[1] FIS

Where, in equation (9) the value of $(x_{pbestid}(t) - x_{id}(t))$ shows the swap sequence based on local status while $(x_{gbestid}(t) - x_{id}(t))$ is the swap sequence based on global status. The coefficients can determine effectiveness of each part in the final status of particle, each between 0 and 1. For updating position same equation (4) are used.

2.3.3 Particles ranking

At the end of each cycle, fitness of each particle is computed. Next, according to one of the selection methods, like q-tournament, the particles are ranked based on their fitness. When ranks of all particles are derived, the population can be arranged from high to low according to the ranks which they achieved. Particle ranking is necessary for making decision about population of next generation. For increasing the population, some new particles should be added to the population; these new particles are chosen among the particles with high rank. On the other hand, for decreasing the population, the particles with lowest rank are chosen for elimination.

2.3.4 Diversity computing

Distribution of particles in search space has an important role in finding optimum position such that proper distribution may result to find better solutions. On the other hand, improper distribution causes undesirable solution. A suitable method lead the population distribution in problem space, is to define special parameters like hamming distance and entropy. Based on these parameters, it is possible to define a new parameter called diversity. By controlling the diversity in every cycle, population distribution will be under control. Definition of the parameters is as follow:

Definition1: Hamming distance between two particles Pi and Pj is calculated by equation 10 while, average Hamming distance at each end of cycle is calculated by equation 11:

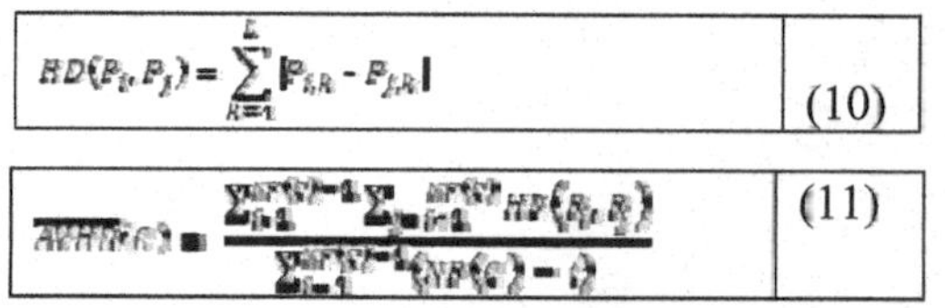

Definition 2: Entropy is defined as equation 12.entropy shows degree of similarity between particles of a population. The lower the similarity, the higher entropy is and vice versa.

$$E_c = -\sum_{j=1}^{Q} P_j \log(P_j) \quad \text{where} \quad P_j = \frac{|S_{c,j}|}{N} \qquad (12)$$

Definition 3: based on equations 2 and 3, diversity is defined by equation 13. The more types in population, the more monotonically distributed population.

$$div(C) = \left[\frac{1}{\pi}\left(atan(AVHD) + \frac{\pi}{2}\right)\right]\frac{E_c}{\log(N)} \qquad (13)$$

Note: there is an interesting relation between diversity and density. Diversity is talking about the kinds of particles whereas the density concentrates on particle distribution in problem space. The lower the diversity of population, the higher the density of population is and vice versa.

2.3.5 Problem Fuzzification

As equation 4 shows, the value of diversity is a real value limited in the range [0, 1]. Diversity is used to make decision about increasing or decreasing population. This decision can be adopted according to the crisp value of diversity. But, this way of using diversity alleviates accuracy and efficiency of the algorithm because there is a strong relation between diversity value and population such that a little variation in the value of diversity may change the decision. To improve efficiency and accuracy of the algorithm, we propose to use fuzzy set theory. For this purpose, the algorithm is changed to make decisions according to the fuzzified value of diversity. Gaussian membership functions were used to fuzzify input variables as shown in figure 2.

2.3.6 Fuzzy inference engine

After fuzzification of inputs, fuzzy rule base or if-then rules should be extracted based on some predefined knowledge. Nevertheless, range of Input variable which is the diversity obtained by equation 4, is divided in 9 different partitions labeled from very low to extra high. Next, output of the inference engine which is the value of increasing or decreasing population is divided to 5 different partitions. Therefore, $9 \times 5 = 45$ if-then rules are generated to be used in the fuzzy inference engine. On the other hand, mamdani min-max fuzzy inference system with centroid defuzzifier is used for reasoning.

Benchmark / Method	burma 14	eil51	eil76	kroA100	berlin52	att48
Optimal Solution In TSPLIB	3323	426	538	21282	7542	10628
CONN (Average δ)	0	2.58	5.02	2.57	8.18	2.17
SA1 (Average δ)	0.42	4.1908	6.8464	5.3199	5.2826	2.2970
SA2 (Average δ)	0	3.3455	2.4713	1.3283	0.8456	1.0147
(COA) (Average δ)	0.1489	3.7558	-------	-------	-------	3.0845
Novel discrete PSO without c (Average δ)	0.5982	11.112	16.5315	30.2762	15.7541	-----
C3DPSO (Average δ)	0.03129	1.7934	2.5501	1.9138	0.7525	-------
PSO_TS (Average δ)	9.12	35.47	9.98	--------	7.37	------
FPSO(Average δ)	0.0125	2.361	3.7659	4.2485	3.1175	2.1758

2.3.7 Increasing or decreasing population

According to the results obtained from inference engine, it is time to apply the results on the current population to produce the next generation. In general if diversity of current population is inside an interval, we should add or delete some particles to improve the diversity of population in next cycle. In order to make the added particles inherit features from their parents, some particles with high fitness are selected to be added. In contrast, in order to decrease population size, some particles with lowest fitness are selected for omission. It should be noted that rate of increasing or decreasing population depends on the position of the interval.

Benchmark / Method	Berlin52	Eil76	Eil51	Kroa100	Burma14
Optimal Solution In TSPLIB	7542	538	426	21282	3323
PSO without C3 Average	8730.18	626.94	473.34	27725.4	3342.88
C3DPSO	7598.76	551.72	433.64	21689.3	3324.04
PSO-TS Average	8100.105	588.712	582.501	-----	3369
PSO-TS-2opt	7938.041	564.523	459.273	-----	3323
PSO-TS-CO	8323.432	604.126	500.231	-----	3654
PSO-TS-CO-2opt	7704.242	560.712	440.9	-----	3323
ACO	7694.92	560.72	434.14	21821.16	3329
FPSO	7604	553	438.5	21693	3332

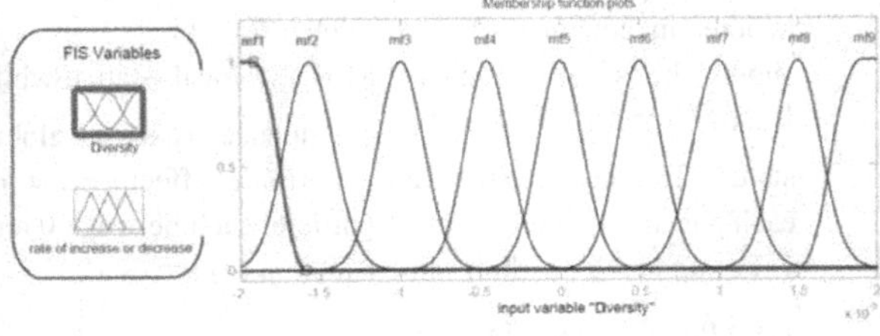

Figure.2Input membership function

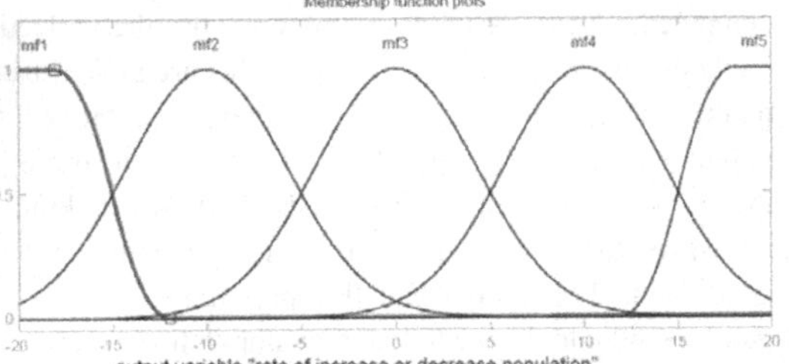

Figure.3 output membership function

3. Applications: Travelling Salesman Problem (TSP)

The results found with the technique proposed in this work for the TSPLIB's cases are compared with other PSOs algorithm. Several methods were used to compare with the technique presented in this work. Results are shown in tables 1 and 2.

Table 1
Results of the experiments for the TSP

Table 2
Results of the experiments for the TSP

Figures 4 thru 7 execution of the proposed algorithm for some known standard TSP benchmarks are shown. The figures show that the algorithm successfully found optimum tour.

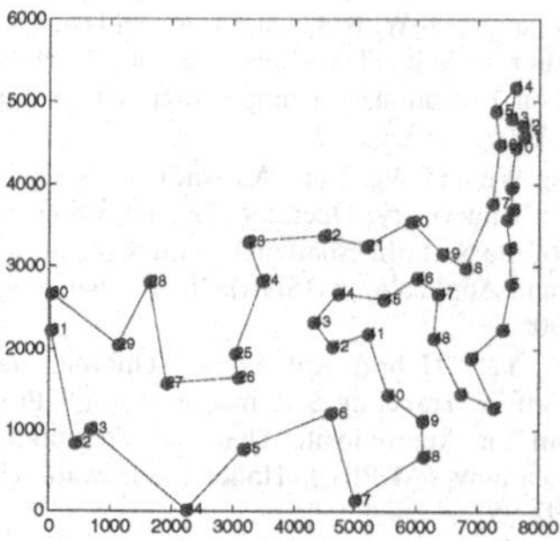

Figure.4: Att48 Benchmark

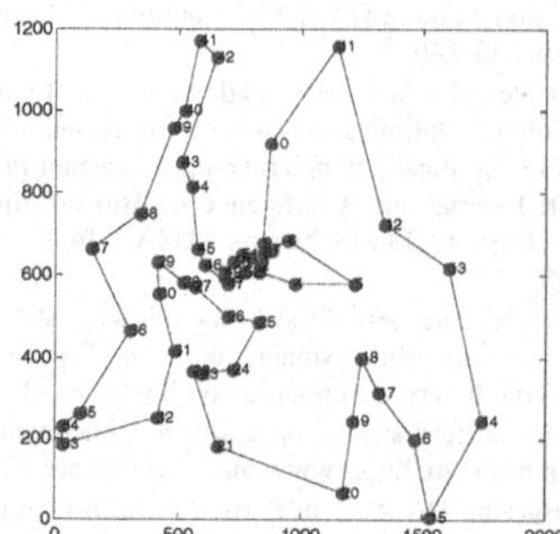

Figure.5:berlin52 Benchmark

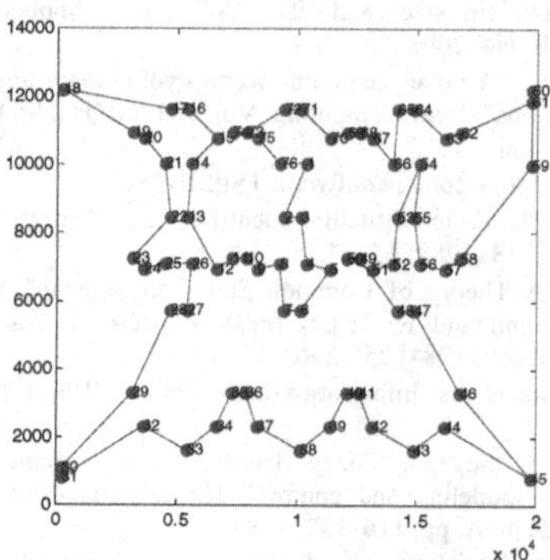

Figure.6:pr76 Benchmark

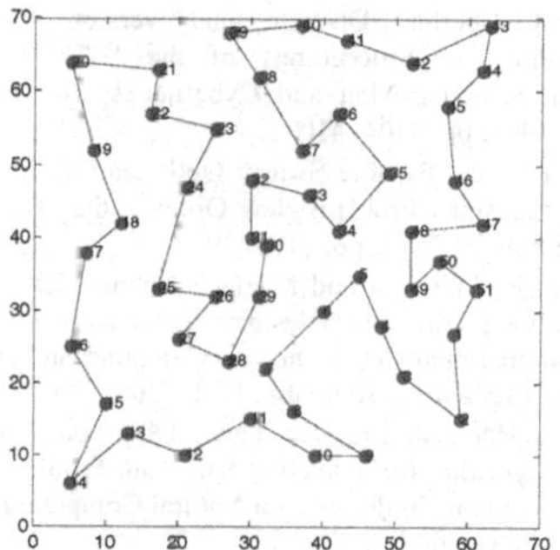

Figure.7: Eili5 Benchmark

Conclusion

In this paper, we have proposed a Fuzzy PSO algorithm; the hybrid algorithm combining the adaptive PSO algorithm with Fuzzy sets concepts, which is to combine the particle swarm optimization algorithm's strong ability in global and local search. We can get better search result using this hybrid algorithm. In this hybrid algorithm, the initial particles are distributed randomly in the problem space; a global searching is assured around the global optimum. But due to some parameters such diversity, fitness and population size, we adopt a new decision about population size. In adaptive particle swarm optimization (PSO) algorithm, we introduced a Ranking selection strategy. In the FPSO–BP algorithm, to know when the searching process is transited from the current state to next state (because of this we call ladder) a fuzzy rule base way was introduced. That is when the best fitness value in the history of all particles has not changed for some generations (i.e., ten generations), the search process would be transferred to next state.

References

[1] J. Kennedy, R.C. Eberhart, Particle swarm optimization, in: Proceedings of the IEEE International Conference on Neural Networks,Perth, Australia, vol. 4, IEEE Service Center, Piscataway, NJ, 1995, pp. 1942–1948.

[2] P.J. Angeline, Evolutionary optimization versus particle swarm optimization: philosophy and performance differences, Evolutionary Programming 7 (1998) 601–610.

[3] M. Clerc, J. Kennedy, The particle swarm-explosion, stability, and convergence in a multidimensional complex space, IEEE Transactions on Evolutionary Computation 6 (2002) 58–73.

[4] I.C. Trelea, The particle swarm optimization algorithm: convergence analysis and parameter selection, Information Processing Letters 85 (2003) 317–325.

[5] J.F. Chang, S.C. Chu, J.F. Roddick, J.S. Pan, A parallel particle swarm optimization algorithm with communication strategies, Journal of Information Science and Engineering 4 (21) (2005) 809–818.

[6] J. Kennedy, R.C. Eberhart, Discrete binary version of the particle swarm algorithm, in: Proceedings of the IEEE International Conference on Systems, Man and Cybernetics, vol. 5, Orlando, Florida, USA, 1997, pp. 4104–4108.

[7] M. Clerc, in: Discrete Particle Swarm Optimization, illustrated by the Traveling Salesman Problem New Optimization Techniques in Engineering, Springer, 2004, pp. 219–239.

[8] Bager Zarei, M.R. Meybodi and Mortaza Abbaszadeh, “A Hybrid Method for Solving Traveling Salesman Problem”, Proc. of the 6th IEEE/ACIS International Conference on Computer and Information Science (ICIS), Melbourne, Australia, 11-13, July, 2007.

[9] Xue-song Yan, Han-min Liu, Jia Yanl, Qing-hua Wu, “A Fast Evolutionary Algorithm for Traveling Salesman Problem”, Proc. of the Third International Conference on Natural Computation (ICNC), China, 24-27 August 2007.

[10] K. Ghoseiri and H. Sarhadi, “A 2opt-DPX Genetic Local Search for Solving Symmetric Traveling Salesman Problem”, Proc. of the Industrial Engineering and Engineering Management (IEEM) Singapore, 2-5, December, 2007 pp. 903-906.

[11] Ioannis Mavroidis, Ioannis Papaefstathiou, Dionisios Pnevmatikatos, “Hardware Implementation of 2-Opt Local Search Algorithm for the Traveling Salesman Problem” 18th IEEE International Workshop on Rapid System Prototyping (RSP), Poeto Alegre, Brazil, 28-30 May, 2007.

[12] Manuel I. Capel Tunon, Mario Rossainz Lopez, "Design and use of the CPAN Branch & Bound for the solution of the Traveling Salesman Problem (TSP)", Proc. of the 15th International Conference on Electronics, Communications and Computers (CONIELECOMP), Puebla, Mexico, 28 February- 2 March, 2005.

[13] Hannes Schabauer, Erich Schikuta, Thomas Weish¨aupl, “Solving Very Large Traveling Salesman Problems by SOM Parallelization on Cluster Architectures”, Proc. of the Sixth International Conference on Parallel and Distributed Computing, Applications and Technologies (PDCAT), Dalian, China, 5-8 December, 2005.

[14] Rodrigo Pasti and Leandro Nunes de Castro, "A Neuro-Immune Network for Solving the Traveling Salesman Problem", Proc. of the International Joint Conference on Neural Networks, Vancouver, BC, Canada, July 16-21, 2006, pp. 3760-3766.

[15] Jiu-Sheng Chen, Xiao-Yu Zhang and Jing-Jie Chen “An Elastic Net Method for Solving The Travelling Salesman Problem”, Proc. of the International Conference on Wavelet Analysis and Pattern Recognition, Beijing, China, 2-4 Nov. 2007, pp. 608-612.

[16] J. Jang, C. Sun, E. Mizutani, “Neuro-Fuzzy and Soft Computing”, Proc. of the Prentice Hall 1997.

[17] Yi HE, Yuhui QIU, Guangyuan LIU, Kaiyou LEI, "A Parallel Adaptive Tabu Search Approach for Traveling Salesman Problems" Proc. of IEEE International Conference on Natural Language Processing and Knowledge Engineering (NLP-KE), Island, Korea, 11-13 October, 2005, pp. 796-801.

[18] NingYang, PingLi and Baisha Mei, “An Angle-based Crossover Tabu Search for the Traveling Salesman Problem” Proc. of the Third International Conference on Natural Computation (ICNC), China, 24-27 August 2007.

[19] Zhenglei Yuan, Liliang Yang, Yaohua Wu, Li Liao, Guoqiang Li, “Chaotic Particle Swarm Optimization Algorithm for Traveling Salesman Problem”, Proc. of the IEEE International Conference on Automation and Logistics August 2007, Jinan, China, 1121 -1124.

[20] W. L. Zhong, J. Zhang, and W. N. Chen, “A Novel Discrete Particle Swarm Optimization to Solve Traveling Salesman Problem”, Proc. of the Congress on Evolutionary Computation (CEC), Singapore, 25-28 September 2007, pp. 3283-3287.

[21] Jinglei Guo, Yong Wu and Wei Liu, "An Ant Colony Optimization Algorithm with Evolutionary Operator for Traveling Salesman Problem", Proc. of the Sixth International Conference on Intelligent Systems Design and Applications (ISDA), Jinan, Shandong, China, 16-18 October 2006.

[22] H. Duan and X. Yu, "Hybrid Ant Colony Optimization Using Memetic Algorithm for Traveling Salesman Problem ", Proc. of the IEEE Symposium on Approximate Dynamic Programming and Reinforcement Learning (ADPRL), Honolulu, Hawaii, USA, 1-5 April 2007, pp. 92-95.

[23] Daniel Angus, “Crowding Population-based Ant Colony Optimization for the Multi-objective Traveling Salesman Problem”, Proc. of the IEEE Symposium on Computational Intelligence in Multicriteria Decision Making (MCDM), Honolulu, Hawaii, USA, 1-5 April 2007, pp. 333-340.

[24] Yi Zhang, Zhi-li Pei, Jin-hui Yang and Yan-chun Liang, “An Improved Ant Colony Optimization Algorithm Based on Route Optimization and Its Applications in Traveling Salesman Problem”, Proc. of the IEEE International Conference on Bio-Informatics & Bio-Engineering, Boston, Massachusetts, USA, 14-17 October 2007, pp. 693-698.

[25] M. Clerc, J. Kennedy, The particle swarm-explosion, stability,and convergence in a multidimensional complex space, IEEE Transactions on Evolutionary Computation 6 (2002) 58–73.

[26] M. Clerc, Discrete particle swarm optimization illustrated by the traveling salesman problem, http://www.mauriceclerc.net, (2000).

[27] T. Hendtlass, Preserving Diversity in Particle Swarm Optimization, in: Lecture Notes in Computer Science, vol. 2718, Springer (2003) 4104–4108.

[28] Chen DeBao,Zhao ChunXi, Particle swarm optimization with adaptive population size and its application, Applied Soft Computing , Elsevier,2008

[29] Yan Wang et al, “A novel quantum swarm evolutionary algorithm and its applications”, Neurocomputing, Vol. 70 (2007) 633-640.

[30] http://www.iwr.uni-heidelberg.de/groups/comopt/software/TSPLIB95

[31] M. Sugeno, G.T. Kang, Structure identification of fuzzy model, Fuzzy Sets Syst. 28 (1988) 15–33.

[32] L.A. Zadeh, "A Theory of Common Sense Knowledge", in H.J. Skala, S. Termini, and E. Trillas (eds), Aspects of Vagueness, Dodrecht: D.Riedel, (1984) 257-296.

[33] Zadeh, L. A,Fuzzy sets. Information and Control,. (1965). 8, 338–353.

[34] T. Takagi and M. Sugeno, “Fuzzy identification of systems and its applications to modeling and control,” IEEE Trans. Syst., Man, Cybern.,vol. 15, pt. A, pp. 116–132, 1985.

[35] E.H. Mamdani, "Applications of Fuzzy Logic to Approximate Reasoning Using Linguistic Systems", IEEE Trans. Comput., 26 (1977) 1182-1191.

[36] D. Dubois and H. Prade, "Fuzzy Sets and Systems: Theory and Applications, Academic Press, New York, (1980).

[37] E.H. Mamdani, "Advances in the Linguistic Synthesis of Fuzzy Controllers", J. Man-Mach. Studies, 8 (1976) 669-678.

Project Management Software for Distributed Industrial Companies

M. Dobrojević[1], B. Medjo[2], M. Rakin[3], A. Sedmak[4]

[1] Innovation Center of Faculty of Mechanical Engineering, University of Belgrade, Kraljice Marije 16, 11120 Belgrade, Serbia

[2] Faculty of Technology and Metallurgy, University of Belgrade, Karnegijeva 4, 11120 Belgrade, Serbia, bmedjo@tmf.bg.ac.rs

[3] Faculty of Technology and Metallurgy, University of Belgrade, Karnegijeva 4, 11120 Belgrade, Serbia

[4] Faculty of Mechanical Engineering, University of Belgrade, Kraljice Marije 16, 11120 Belgrade, Serbia

Key words: Project management software, Web based software, Resources planning, Task accomplishment tracking, Project team communication improvement

Abstract - **This paper gives an overview of the development of a new software solution for project management, intended mainly to use in industrial environment. The main concern of the proposed solution is application in everyday engineering practice in various, mainly distributed industrial companies. Having this in mind, special care has been devoted to development of appropriate tools for tracking, storing and analysis of the information about the project, and in-time delivering to the right team members or other responsible persons. The proposed solution is Internet-based and uses LAMP/WAMP (Linux or Windows - Apache - MySQL - PHP) platform, because of its stability, versatility, open source technology and simple maintenance. Modular structure of the software makes it easy for customization according to client specific needs, with a very short implementation period. Its main advantages are simple usage, quick implementation, easy system maintenance, short training and only basic computer skills needed for operators.**

INTRODUCTION

Distributed industrial companies, which include outsourcing of activities like planning, management and fabrication, are very challenging for business management, because the project members and teams have to be able to communicate the status of on-going project or projects. Efficient way to collect, analyze and transfer the project information, as well as tracking and coordination of information exchange are crucial for successful project finalization. A proper software solution can greatly improve the management of information among the project members and between the project team and other parties involved in the project.

In order to cover these functional aspects, this software solution will be able to collect accurate information between organization units in real time. The final goal of such system is to provide the right information at the right time to the right person or group of persons (project member, group of members, project manager, etc). Also, documents concerning the project activities are a very important issue in this context.

Monitoring and tracking of the project team activities is very important, in order to carry out corrective actions when needed, thus avoiding additional work, duplication of data and other related costs (some reasons that lead to project failures, cost and time overruns are explained in [1]). By developing easy-to-use tool which enables an end user to efficiently access relevant data, the above issues can be solved, reducing delays and costs and increasing project efficiency.

The subject of this paper is development of flexible, but easy to use project management engine, designed to help end users to track processes and solve problems related to project management in industry. Software will be set as a highly secured web application (or communication interface), accessible through any standard web browser working on any platform (PC, PDA or mobile). Access to project data will be controlled through multiple layers of user levels, each corresponding to real-life access rights of project team members. All this will enable access to relevant data in real time, when and where needed. In situation when project members are scattered on different locations (and often in different cities, countries and/or continents), such software tool based on modern Internet technologies will be able, in many cases, to solve communication and coordination problems. In addition, close cooperation between management, field engineers, supervisors and other team members can significantly improve the process of problem solving and help to minimize delays and off-time.

Research that led to development of this software was conducted through interviews, discussions and experience exchange with managers, engineers and technicians working in several large or medium companies and their branches in Serbia. Software itself is being developed under Eureka

T. Sobh, K. Elleithy (eds.), *Innovations in Computing Sciences and Software Engineering*,
DOI 10.1007/978-90-481-9112-3_37,

E!4573 project. Development of this system is based on experience concerning many real-life engineering problems in several industry areas.

PROPOSED SOFTWARE SOLUTION

Having in mind that this software is intended for use mainly in medium and large companies, very important goal is to improve possibilities for company management to simultaneously track, coordinate and manage multiple projects within the company (Fig. 1). From the point of view of the end user (i.e. engineers or other staff members working on site), this application should help them to track their task list within the project (or multiple projects) and to coordinate activities of team members in the most efficient way and in accordance with planned budget and timeframe. Regarding benefits for the project manager, he or she will get precise overview of the current state of the project, financial balance (income, expenses, etc), degree of completion of planned goals, activities and tasks assigned to project members, results etc.

Basic information about the project, i.e. the project initiation data, including the planned and actual income/expenses, are summed on the General data screen - Project overview, as shown in Fig. 2.

Project teams are defined in a flexible and easy way, allowing users to participate at different levels with different roles, depending on the project type and characteristics. Access rights are granted in accordance with access rights which specific person has in real life. Projects are defined with resources of different kind and they can be split into different tasks (Fig. 3), each with defined time schedules. The resources and time schedules can be viewed as tables, Gantt charts or other appropriate according to client specification (Fig. 4).

As in real life, it is not mandatory for each team member to have access rights to project data or even a user account (i.e. technicians, operators, etc.). Depending on role in the team and degree of involvement, project manager with assistance of system administrator will be able to specify which project members will have user accounts (either active or inactive). For team members with user account, project manager will be able to specify their access/moderator rights to the project.

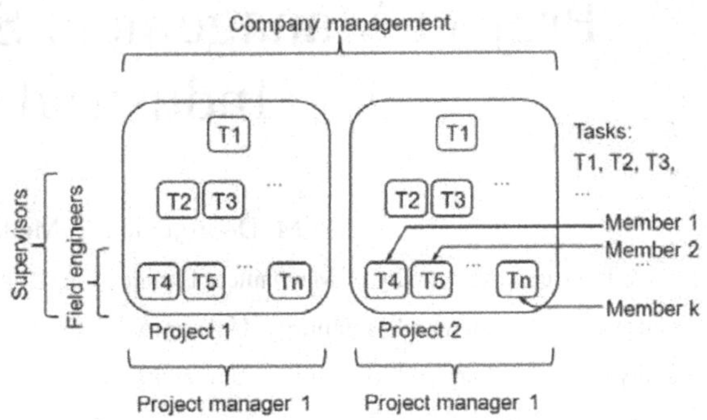

Fig. 1. Organization scheme

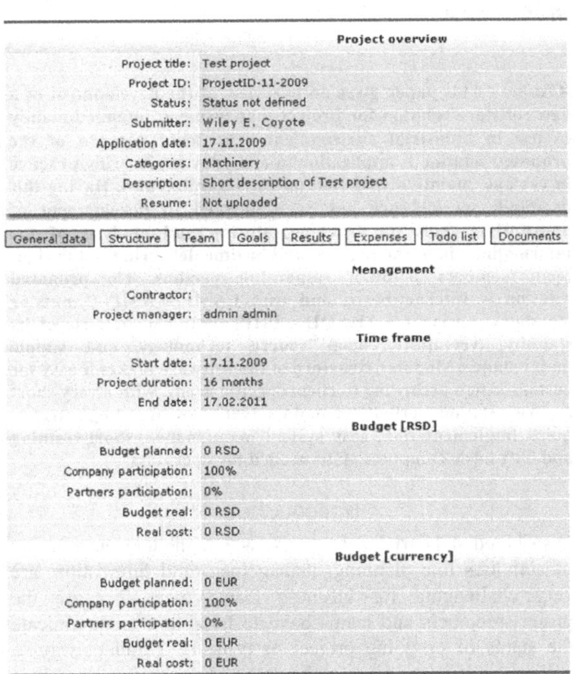

Fig. 2. Project overview

Also, in case that project member has active user account but no access rights to project data, he or she will still be able to track his/hers task list and granted access rights through "My profile" module. This module tracks information on tasks and accomplishments of that project member, while his/hers supervisor confirms in the project administration panel which task/activity/etc. is successfully finished.

The main channel of communication among the project members is Internet; hence it does not matter on how the user approaches to relevant information. In addition to standard access with PC, laptop or webbook, it is also necessary to enable access through mobile devices, like web enabled cell phones or PDAs (i.e. for repair and maintenance staff on site, to fetch needed information from the database). Also, one of the main features of the software is an easy access, tracking and control of the relevant documentation.

Development of this software will be conducted throughout the following stages:

- Software design, which will accommodate common needs of companies from various industrial branches in the field of project management.
- Development of software engine as web application.
- Development of the user interface for different platforms:
  - PC/laptop/webbook,
  - Mobile devices (PDA, cell phone).

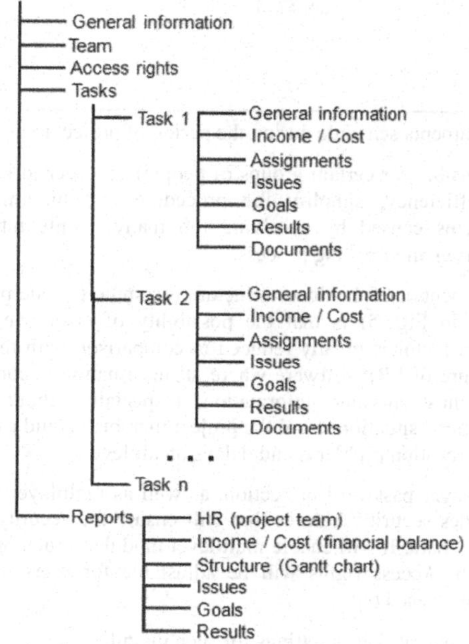

Fig. 3. Project subdivision

In this paper, only basic application modules will be discussed, which are currently being developed. User interface is very easy for use. Each module will have a user front-end and administrative back-end, including the distribution of the options in accordance with the assigned user level and access rights defined for each user.

MAIN FEATURES OF THE APPLICATION

Software automation of project management process enables the following: remarkable saving of time, application of planned execution procedure, quick response to unpredicted situations and problems, visualization of data, exceptionally fast and easy comparison of the planned and actual (on-site) state of the project and its phases or activities. Besides, considering that it is a Web based software, the results of each database updating or updating of the software code itself are immediately visible for the end users and available without delay on their computers (no additional installations, local updates etc).

The proposed software solution is flexible and open, and is not rigidly connected to the company structure, i.e. it can be adjusted in accordance with the requirements of a project and especially with the real on-site situation. It is intended for use mainly by engineers and management, without a strict dependence on book-keeping, accounting or enterprise resource planning (ERP) software used in the company (challenges of ERP software implementation are discussed in [2,3]). In fact, the proposed solution can be used in parallel with other software, enabling the management better insight into the real state of the project (mainly from the engineering point of view).

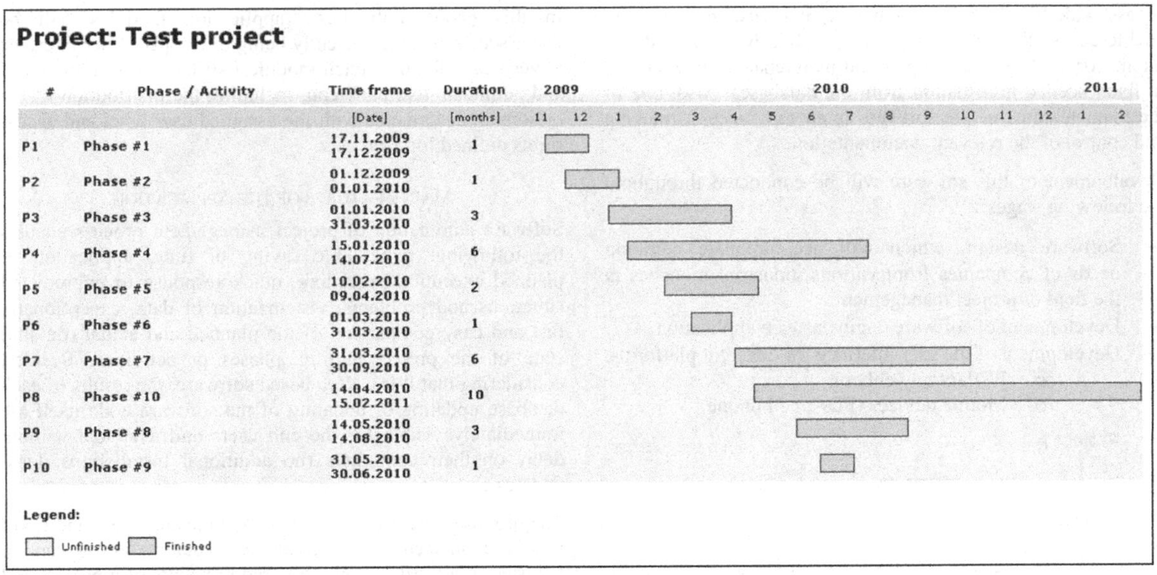

Project: Test project

#	Phase / Activity	Time frame [Date]	Duration [months]
P1	Phase #1	17.11.2009 17.12.2009	1
P2	Phase #2	01.12.2009 01.01.2010	1
P3	Phase #3	01.01.2010 31.03.2010	3
P4	Phase #4	15.01.2010 14.07.2010	6
P5	Phase #5	10.02.2010 09.04.2010	2
P6	Phase #6	01.03.2010 31.03.2010	1
P7	Phase #7	31.03.2010 30.09.2010	6
P8	Phase #10	14.04.2010 15.02.2011	10
P9	Phase #8	14.05.2010 14.08.2010	3
P10	Phase #9	31.05.2010 30.06.2010	1

2009: 11 12 — 2010: 1 2 3 4 5 6 7 8 9 10 11 12 — 2011: 1 2

Legend: Unfinished, Finished

Fig. 4. An example of the report: Gantt chart of the activities and assignments schedule during the period of project realization

The state-of-the-art technology is implemented, in order to insure efficient, robust and safe functioning of the application. Standard SQL database system is used as a core database, but all relevant data will be encrypted using advanced 128-bit encryption algorithms, to obtain maximum security. The platform for main application engine development is LAMP (Linux - Apache - MySQL - PHP) or WAMP (Windows - Apache - MySQL - PHP). All the components of these platforms are very reliable, often-used and robust systems already installed on many commercial servers [4]. Company staff required to maintain the system is reduced to minimum, resulting in a moderate cost of software exploitation. Due to its user-friendly environment, administration doctrine and access rights distribution, training course for system administrators and operators will be reduced from several months to only 2-5 work days. Dynamic user interface with various visualization tools shall enable the management of distributed industrial company to have real-time insight into work progress on projects.

Concerning the representation and accuracy of the project data in this software, it is created in the simplest possible manner, in order to emulate typical project structure and provide all the necessary information for users. Such approach can be applied in most companies, without the need for significant changes. Further, only limited number of responsible team members will have access rights (typically engineers and managers responsible for certain groups of people), in order to increase the efficiency, simplify the procedure and minimize the problems caused by involving too many people into data acquiring and tracking process.

Great benefit of this loose structure (example for one phase is given in Fig. 5) is that the possibility of error caused by human factor is greatly reduced in comparison with the rigid structure of ERP software where all information is correlated and thus missing information (especially about some unplanned situation) from the project members could cause by chain reaction problems and delays on all levels.

Multilayer password protection, as well as multilayer access, provides security features that will ensure the security of all project data. It will enable multilevel modular structure of the system. Access rights will be adjustable for users on each module, based on:

- General access settings for each module,
- Each team member working on specific project can be given special access rights (or access denial for some submodules),
- List of users with full and/or partial access rights to the project can be specified (e.g. project manager(s) vs. company manager(s)). In that way, real-time management would be achieved, enabling quick response on each project task.

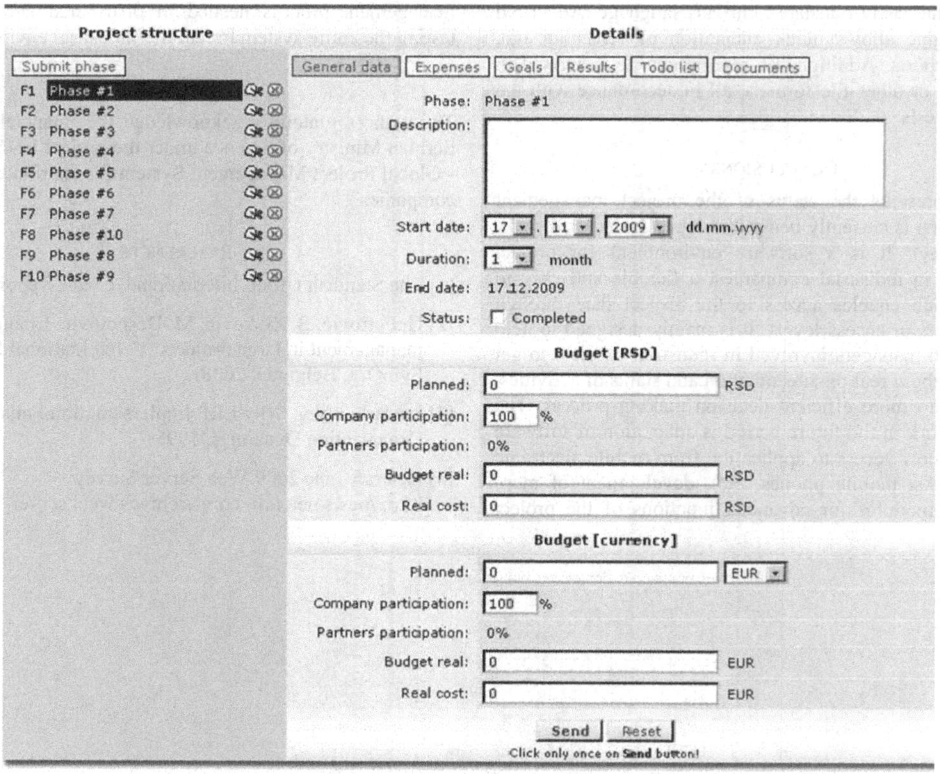

Fig. 5. The structure of the project

Relevant industrial standards concerning information security are taken into account, through verification of the access rights, access location and format/content of submitted data. Concerning the access locations, access could be granted only for machines working in virtual private network (VPN), Intranet and/or local network, or from any location by HTTPS protocol, depending on the company size, business type, management preferences, security policy and network configuration. Verification of format and content of data entering the system is another important feature of this application - all the data submitted by users will be checked by format, length and content.

The platform for the application consists of a database and web server, as shown by the schematic representation given in Fig. 6. Basic module list and accompanying features embedded in application are:

- General access rights control
- Administration panels for each module / submodule
- User accounts management
- Project management
- Template engine

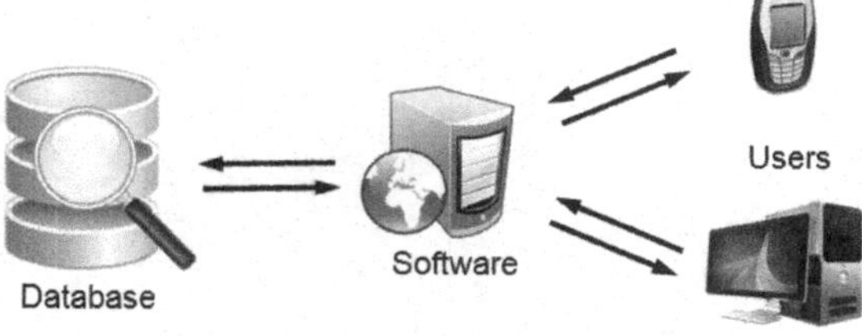

Fig. 6. Application structure

The project management module is split into several basic submodules:

- General information
- Income / expenses
- Goals
- Results
- Team
- Diagrams and reports

Due to the concept of the application, it is important to emphasize that the user interface and all generated reports can be quickly and easily translated into any language. Advanced template engine allows quick adaptation of screen design, forms and reports. Additionally, reports can be generated in HTML, PDF or other file formats, all in accordance with the end user requests.

CONCLUSIONS

The paper presents the status of the project management software which is currently being developed under the Eureka E!4573 project. It is a software environment for project management in industrial companies, a flexible and easy to use tool which enables access to the project data through multiple layers of access levels. It is mainly designed to help engineers and managers involved in industrial projects to get information about real on-site situation and status of activities, which leads to more efficient decision making process. The aim of the work in the future period is adaptation of software in order to allow access to application from mobile electronic devices (PDAs, mobile phones, etc), development of more options and modules for advanced functions of the project management process needed in distributed companies and testing the entire system in real life industrial environment.

ACKNOWLEDGMENTS

The authors gratefully acknowledge the financial support of Serbian Ministry of Science under the project E!4573 "GPMS - Global Project Management System for distributed industrial companies"

REFERENCES

[1] The Standish Group International, Chaos Report, 1995

[2] G. Petrović, B. Živković, M. Despotović, Change management in large projects, 1st International Symposium SymOrg, Belgrade, 2008.

[3] J. Markowsky, Why ERP Implementation Fails, Organization Dynamics, 1995

[4] Netcraft June 2009 Web Server Survey: http://news.netcraft. com/archives/web_server_survey.html

How to Construct an Automated Warehouse Based on Colored Timed Petri Nets

Fei Cheng, Shanjun He
Management School, Zhejiang University
Management College, HangZhou Dianzi University
Hangzhou 310008, China

***Abstract-* The automated warehouse considered here consists of a number of rack locations with three cranes, a narrow aisle shuttle, and several buffer stations with the roller. Based on analyzing of the behaviors of the active resources in the system, a modular and computerized model is presented via a colored timed Petri net approach, in which places are multicolored to simplify model and characterize control flow of the resources, and token colors are defined as the routes of storage/retrieval operations. In addition, an approach for realization of model via visual c++ is briefly given. These facts allow us to render an emulate system to simulate a discrete control application for online monitoring, dynamic dispatching control and off-line revising scheduler policies.**

***Keywords*-colored timed Petri net(CTPN); automated warehouse; automated storage and retrieval system; modeling; multicolor**

I INTRODUCTION

Automated warehouse are computer-directed storage and transport facilities for large capacity and high volumes of handled materials. In a typical automated warehouse, it can be composed of three subsystems. The first one is called crane subsystem which consists of storage racks erected along aisles with the automated stacker cranes which travel within an aisle performing storage from buffer station and retrieval operations from racks; The next is shuttle subsystem, in which the shuttle machine transfers pallets from main input stations to the buffer stations with the roller; the third is buffer stations to the buffer station subsystems which consisting of several buffer stations with the roller which provide transporting between crane subsystem and shuttle subsystem. The case addressed in this paper is more general than others presented in the literatures[1,2,3,4,5,6], since the presence of the buffer station subsystem is considered.

A two-hierarchical control structure is proposed ad the system operational level [4]; the first is called the scheduler, which decides a control strategy on the basis of current subsystems' state in order to maximize the system through put; it receives from a higher scheduler system loading/unloading orders with a set of possible destinations in different aisle and produces the route for a pallet, crane or shuttle. The other is the resource controller, which receives and fulfils the route from the scheduler. The model in the paper aims to the resource controller. In the resource controller level, the main and almost operations are resource-oriented; therefore, it is necessary for modeling the resource controller system to study the behavior of resources, especially for active resources consisting of the pallets, the cranes and the shuttle. The behaviors of resources are divided seven types in the paper, and the control flow of automated warehouse is unified of all these types of the behaviors.

Colored Timed Petri Nets (CTPN) have resulted to be effective tool for automated warehouse modeling [4,6,8,9]. The literature [4] proposed a CTPN model to describe in concise and efficient way the dynamics of an AS/RS (automated storage and retrieval system) serviced by rail guided vehicles in control perspective; The literature [6] obtained model modularity of AS/RS by CPN, which was decomposed in six modules which communicates via fusion places. However, in these literatures [4,6,8,9], the behaviors of resources are not clearly clarified in modeling, so that not only the model intends to complex, but also the information of the system easily loses. This paper aims to model automated warehouse in fig 1 based on the behaviors of resources via CTPN in modular way, and the model is to be more concise and more conveniently computerized; in addition, the approach of CTPN here is to multicolor places in order to simplify the model and characterize control flow of the resources.

The paper is organized as follows: in section2 an automated warehouse under study is described, including its control structure and analyzing of its active resources' behaviors, in section 3, following a brief approach of CTPNs, a modular model of behaviors of active resources is explained; in section 4, the approach of realization for model in section 3 via visual c++ is briefly given; finally, several concluding remarks are reported.

T. Sobh, K. Elleithy (eds.), *Innovations in Computing Sciences and Software Engineering*,
DOI 10.1007/978-90-481-9112-3_38, © Springer Science+Business Media B.V. 2010

II. SYSTEM DESCRIPTION AND BEHAVIOR ANALYSISE

An automated warehouse considered here is decomposed into three subsystems (see fig1): crane subsystem, buffer station subsystem and shuttle subsystem. In crane subsystem, each narrow aisle stacker crane serves two storage racks, the marks 101,111,134 in fig 1 represent crane input stations from which crane carries a pallet and transfers to the rack location; the marks 106,117,127 represent crane output stations to which crane transfers a pallet from rack locations. In buffer station subsystem, each buffer station is equipped with the roller, a pallet van be transferred between consecutive buffer stations. In shuttle subsystem, there are three main input stations and one shuttle.

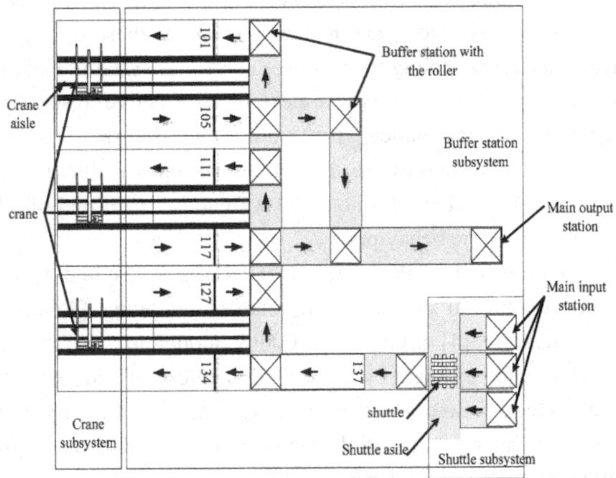

Fig. 1. Automated warehouse layout

In order to identify all resources, the automated warehouse layout in fig 1 is marked in fig 4, where v denotes the shuttle, its aisles are divided into three positions: pv1,pv2 and pv3; rs1,rs2 and rs3 represent three cranes; p29,p30, p31 are three cranes' home positions; p01, p02 and p03 are main input stations, p3 is main output station, others are buffer stations, there into, p15,p16, p19 and p25 is shared buffer stations which can transfer storage/retrieval pallets. On the other hand, for sake of simplicity, it is supposed that every crane serves two racks, each with four locations; Fig 2 shows the rack locations and crane positions where crane rs3 can shift.

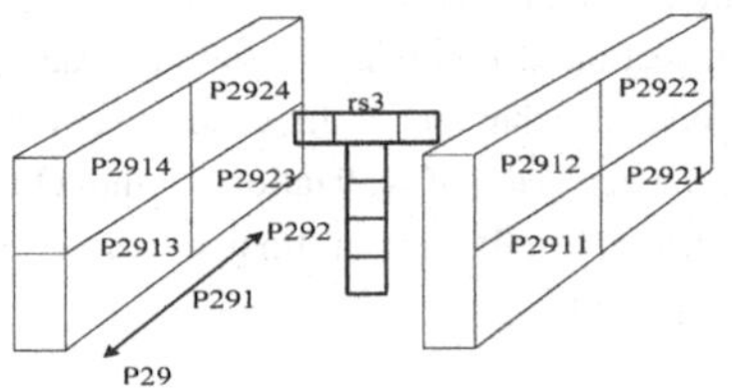

Fig. 2. Example of a servicing two opposite racks.

A. Hierarchical Control Structure

In control system of automated warehouse, A two-hierarchical control structure (Fig 3) is proposed at the system operational level [4], the first is called the scheduler, which decides a control strategy on the basis of current subsystems' state (in fig 3, the arrow to the scheduler from the resource controller is omitted) in order to maximize the system throughput; it receives from a higher scheduler system loading/unloading orders with a set of possible destinations in different aisle; it produces the route for a crane, a shuttle or a pallet, and assigns shared buffer stations to carry a pallet in their consecutive stations; the other is the resource controller, which receives and fulfils the route from the scheduler. The model in the paper aims to resource controller.

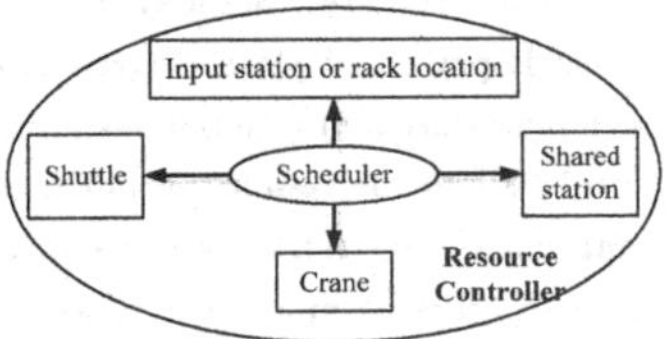

Fig. 3. Hierarchical Control Structure

B. The Workflow of Resource Controller

1)The storage operation: When a new pallet arrives at one of main input station, the scheduler assigns a storage route to the pallet which starting from main input station, following a certain number of shuttle aisle locations to several buffer stations and a certain number of crane aisle locations to the corresponding rack location. i.e. when a pallet in p_{01} is to be stored in storage location p_{2924}, the scheduler will assign such route to the pallet as $p_{01}\rightarrow p_{v1}\rightarrow p_{v2}\rightarrow p_{12}\rightarrow p_{13}\rightarrow p_{14}\rightarrow p_{15}\rightarrow p_{16}\rightarrow p_{17}\rightarrow p_{18}\rightarrow p_{19}\rightarrow p_{20}\rightarrow p_{21}\rightarrow p_{9}\rightarrow p_{29}\rightarrow p_{291}\rightarrow p_{292}\rightarrow p_{2924}$; then the shuttle v is booked, loads the pallet from p_{01} and transfers to p_{12}; the buffer stations then transmit it to p_9, finally, the crane is booked and carries it from p_4 and sends to rack location p_{2924}.

2)The retrieval operation: If a pallet is to be retrieved, a crane will be booked b scheduler to travel to the rack location and loads it to buffer station (i.e.p_5, p_6 and p_8), then the pallet will be transferred to main output station p_3. A route of the pallet assigned by the scheduler is like: $p_{2924}\rightarrow p_{292}\rightarrow p_{291}\rightarrow p_{29}\rightarrow p_{8}\rightarrow p_{19}\rightarrow p_{22}\rightarrow p_{23}\rightarrow p_{24}\rightarrow p_{25}\rightarrow p_{28}\rightarrow p_{3}$.

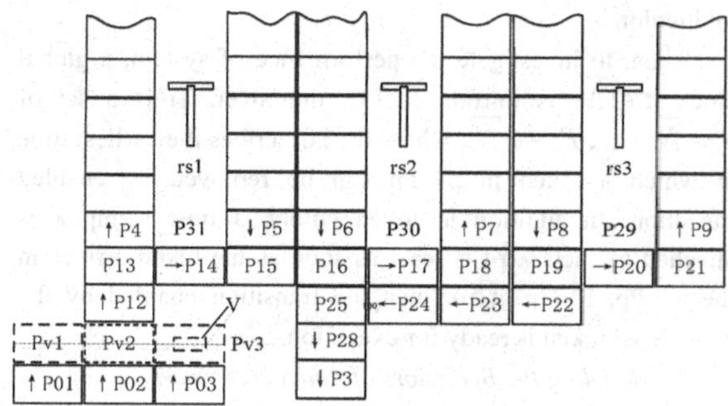

Fig. 4. Automated warehouse marked layout

C. The Behavior of Active Resources

In resource controller level, the main and almost operations are resource-oriented, therefore, it is necessary for modeling the resource controller system to study the behavior of resources, especially for active resources consisting of pallets, especially for active resources consisting of pallets, cranes and the shuttle. It is the behaviors of these resources that can change the control system'state. A route of an active resource represents a set of places along which an active resource can be transited. In following sections, the main study aims to analyze the behaviors of active resources and classify them, in section 3, and then a CTPN is applied to model the events of these behaviors.

Firstly, the behaviors of a pallet in clued getting the route, loaded, transferred and unloaded by the shuttle or a crane, transmitted by buffer stations. Secondly, the behaviors of the shuttle or a crane is composed of getting route from the scheduler, loading and unloading one pallet, and moving between shuttle or crane aisles with a pallet or not.

Being considered enabling conditions of these behaviors and their results fired, seven types of behaviors are identified as follows:

1-type behavior: called entering. When a pallet enters the system or is to be retrieved, the scheduler will assign a route to this pallet, the result is that the pallet will get the route.

2-typr behavior: called loading. A pallet is to be loaded by a booked shuttle/crane. Including that the booked shuttle loading a pallet from main input station, and a booked crane loading a pallet from buffer stations/rack locations. The result is that the pallet will enter the shuttle or crane; its route will be changed with cutting current place, which represents that a shuttle or crane has carried a pallet, then, the information of the pallet's current place will be cleared.

3-type behavior: called transferring. A booked or loaded shuttle/crane shifts, or a pallet is transferred between consecutive buffer stations. The result is that the pallet, the shuttle or the crane enters next place; its route will be changed with cutting current place, and the information of current place will be cleared.

4-type behavior: called unloading. The shuttle or a crane unloads a pallet into the buffer station or rack location. The result is that the pallet enters a buffer station or rack location and its route will be changed with cutting current place, and the shuttle or a crane becomes idle in current place.

5-type behavior: called booking. The shuttle or a crane is booked by the scheduler to carry a pallet. A route from current place to place of the pallet will be assigned by the scheduler. The result is that the shuttle or a crane gets this route.

6-type behavior: called sharing. When one more pallets is enabled to transfer to shared buffer stations such as p15, p16, p19 and p25, the scheduler will give an instruction to shared buffer stations to tell which pallet can be loaded.

7-type behavior: called leaving. A pallet is to leave from main output station. The result is that the information of main output station will be cleared.

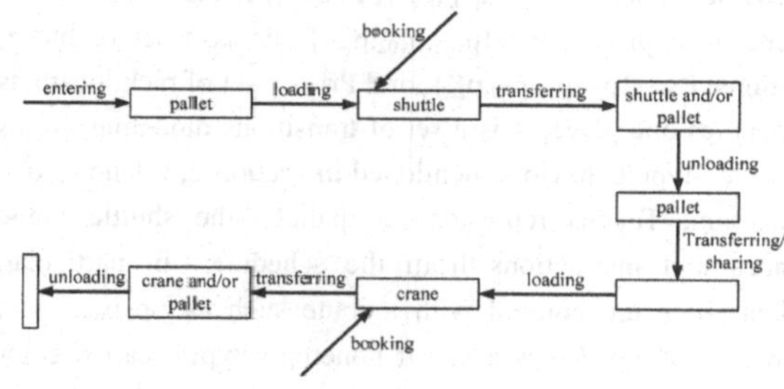

Fig. 5. The process of storage operation

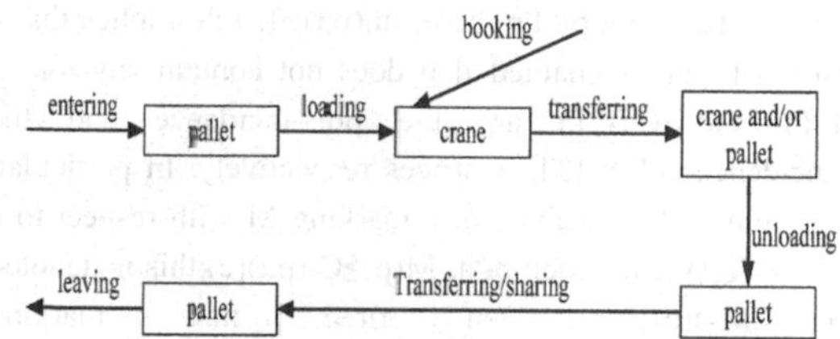

Fig. 6. The process of retrieval operation

Based on seven types of behaviors mentioned above, the process of storage/retrieval operation in automated warehouse can be described as fig5 and fig6.

III MODELING OF THE SYSTEM VIA CTPN

This section describes the CTPN modeling seven type behaviors mentioned above. A modular and resource-oriented CTPNs model is proposed. In particular, places are such stations as main input/output stations, buffer stations, rack locations, and crane/shuttle aisle places; tokens are the pallets, the shuttle and the cranes, while token colors represent the storage/retrieval routes. In addition, transitions model events of seven-type behaviors of the active resources. In the following section we briefly review such modeling approach.

A. The approach of CTPN modeling the system

The CTPN setting extends the framework of PN by adding color, time and modular attributes to the net [7]. The color attribute is developed to deal with systems that have similar or redundant logical structures [6]. The time attribute allows various time-based performance measures to be added in the system model. A time delay can be assigned to places to model the time properties of a system. We assume that the reader already knows concepts and terminology of Colored Petri Nets(CPN). Nevertheless, [4,7,8] can be consulted about the overview of CTPN. Let us briefly describe the approach of CTPN modeling the system shown in fig 1.

A colored timed Petri net is a 9-tuple CTPN= (P, T, Co, Inh, C_+, C_-, Ω, Ti, Mo)where P is a set of places, P=Pp∪P', P' is a set of virtual places which are introduced to accommodate instructions from the scheduler, Pp=Pv∪Pin∪Pc∪Prs∪Prl∪Pout∪Psc, Pin={p_{01},p_{02},p_{03}}, Pout={p_3},Prs is a set of the crane aisle places, Pv={p_{v01},p_{v02},p_{v03}}, Pc is a set of buffer stations, Psc={p_{15},p_{16},p_{19},p_{25}}, and Prl is a set of rack locations; p denotes one place; T is a set of transitions modeling events of seven-type behaviors mentioned in section 2, t denotes one transition; Tokens represent the pallets, the shuttle, three cranes and instructions from the scheduler; in particular, tokens here are colored with a route such as <p_i,p_m,...,p_n>, p_i,p_m,...,p_n ∈ Pp; Co is a set of nonempty types, called color sets, Co(P) is a set of p∈P, Co(p) is the token color in p∈P, Co(T) is a set of t∈T and Co(t) represents two consecutive p∈Pp. Inh is a weight function for an inhibitor arc which connects a t∈T to a p∈Pp, here Inh(p,t)=1, Inh implies that a transition t can be enabled if p does not contain any token. C_+(P,T) and C_-(P,T) are the post-incidence and the pre-incidence |P| × |T| matrices respectively. In particular, a transition t T is enabled at a marking M with respect to a color c∈Co(t) if for each p∈t, M(p)≥C-(p,t)(c):this is denoted with M{t(c)}. When fired, new marking M'(p)=M(p)-C-(p,t)(c)+C_+(p,t)(c).

The set Ω is defined as follows: $\Omega = \cup_{x\in P\cup T}\{C(x)\}$. Mo is the initial marking of the net.

Definition 1: a transition $t_{i,m}$ represents a token in p_i∈Pp is to be transferred from p_i∈Pp to p_m∈Pp (i,m∈N), and:

Co (token) =< p_i,p_m,... >;

Co (p_i) = Co (token); Co(p_m)=0;

C_-(p_i, $t_{i,m}$)(c) =< p_i,p_m >;

C_+(p_m,$t_{i,m}$)(c) = Co(p_i)-< p_i >;

M(p_i) = Co(p_i), M(p_m) = Co (p_m).

Definition 2: M(p_i)=<p_i> describes that a pallet is in p_i and with no route if p_i ∈Prc, a shuttle is in p_i and idle if p_i ∈Pv, or a crane is in p_i and idle if ∈Prs.

Definition3: If P_1⊂P, P_1={p_1,p_2,...,p_n}, n∈N and colored token in p_i ∈P_1, then the color Co(P_1) of P_1 is <p_1,p_2,...,p_n>, and the color Co(p_i) of p_i is token color. Such is called places multicolor.

Then, to investigate the performance of system, a global clock $\tau \in \overline{N}$ is introduced [4]; moreover, Ti is a set of $t_i \in \overline{N}$, $t_i : P_p \rightarrow \overline{N}$, where ti(p) describes the earliest time at which a token in p∈Pp can be removed by enabled transition. In addition to token colors, a time stamp λ is attached to each. λ(p) is reset as soon as the token arrives in the p∈Pp. If λ(p)>t_i(p), then the transition enabled by the considered token is ready for execution.

B. Modeling the Behaviors of Active Resources

In following subsections, The CTPN is applied to model the behaviors of active resources, and a rectangle shows a virtual place p'; if following transition fired, the information in virtual place p' will be cleared.

1) The CTPN modeling entering behavior

The dynamics of entering behavior is modeled by the CTPN in fig 7. P' is a set of virtual places, Pi=Pin∪Prl, $T_{p',pi}$ describes events that the scheduler assigns a route to the pallet in Pi, for storage or retrieval.

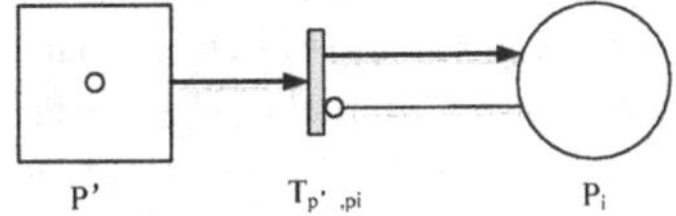

Fig. 7. The CTPN modeling entering behavior.

For each t∈$T_{p'pi}$, its enabling conditions are:

A1) M(p_i) =0, p_i∈Pin; M(p_i) =<p_i>, p_i∈Prl.

A2) M(p')=<p_1,...>.

If t∈$T_{p'pi}$ is ready and fires, then the new marking M' is the following:

$$M'(p_i)=\langle p_i,\ldots\rangle \quad (1)$$

$$M'(p')=0 \quad (2)$$

Then λ(pi) is reset and begins to count.

2) The CTPN modeling loading behavior

Fig 8 shows loading behavior including the shuttle loading a pallet from p_{01},p_{02} and p_{03}, or the crane loading a pallet from buffer stations or rack locations.

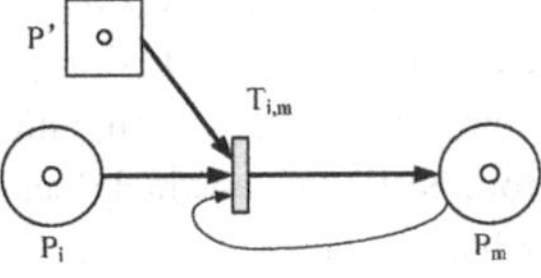

Fig. 8. The CTPN modeling loading behavior.

In fig 8, p_i =Pin∪P_{rl}∪{p_4, p_7,p_9}; P_m=P_v∪P_{rs}. Here, if p_i is one of elements in Pin, then pm∈Pv; else pm∈Prs. $T_{i,m}$ describes that a pallet with the route will be loaded into a shuttle or a crane from p_i to p_m. P' is a set of virtual places containing the instructions that which pallet the shuttle or a crane is to carry.

For each $t_{i,m} \in T_{i\ m}$, if $p_m \in P_m$, $p_i \in Pi$ and $p' \in P'$, its enabling conditions are:

B1) $M(p_m)=<p_m>$ B2) $\lambda(p_i) \geq t_i(p_i)$.

B3) $M(p_i) \geq C\text{-}(p_i, t_{i,m})(c) =< p_i, p_m>$

B4) $M(p') = C\text{-}(p', t_{i,m})(c) =< p_i, p_m >$

If $t_{i,m} \in T_{i\ m}$, is ready and fires, then the new marking M' is the following:

$$M'(p_m)=C+(P_m, t_{i,m})(c) + M(p_m) =< p_m, \ldots > \quad (3)$$

$$M'(p_i) = 0 \quad (4)$$

$$M'(p')= 0 \quad (5)$$

Then $\lambda(p_m)$ is reset and begins to count.

3) The CTPN modeling unloading behavior

Unloading behavior includes that the shuttle unloading the pallet into buffer station and crane unloading the pallet intorack location or buffer station, shown fig 9.

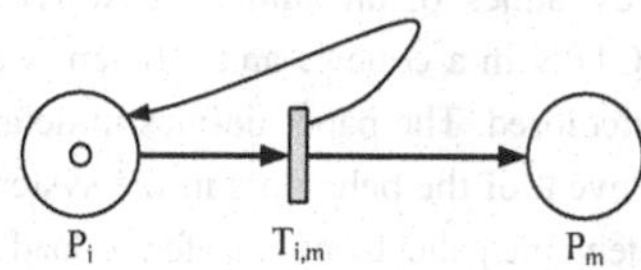

Fig. 9. The CTPN modeling unloading behavior.

$Pi=Pv \cup Prs$, $P_m=\{p_{12}, p_5, p_6, p_8\} \cup Prl$. Here, if $Pi=Pv$, then p_m is p_{12}; else $p_m \in (Pr \cup \{p_5, p_6, p_8\})$; Ti,m describes that a pallet in the shuttle/crane will be unloaded from Pi to Pm.

For each $t_{i,m} \in T_{i\ m}$, if $p_m \in Pm$ and $p_i \in Pi$, its enabling conditions are:

C1) $M(p_m) = 0$. C2) $\lambda(p_i) \geq t_i(p_i)$.

C3) $M(p_i) \geq C\text{-}(p_i, t_{i,m})(c) =<p_i, p_m>$.

If $t_{i,m} \in T_{i\ m}$ is ready and fires, then the new marking M' is the following:

$$M'(p_m)=C_+(p_m,t_{i,m})(c)+M(p_m)=<p_m,\ldots> \quad (6)$$

$$M'(p_i)=<p_i> \quad (7)$$

Then $\lambda(p_m)$ is reset and begins to count.

4) The CTPN modeling transferring behavior

Fig 10 shows the CTPN model of transferring behavior.

$P_i,P_m=P_v \cup Prs \cup Pc$; Here, either $P_i,P_m=Pv$, or $P_i,P_m=Prs$, or $P_i,P_m=Pc$; $T_{i,m}$ describes events of all transferring behavior.

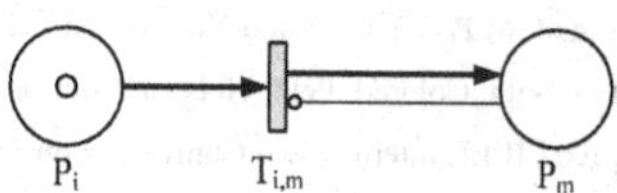

Fig. 10. The CTPN modeling transferring behavior.

For each $t_{i,m} \in T_{i\ m}$, if $p_m \in P_m$ and $p_i \in P_i$, its enabling conditions are:

DI) $M(p_m)=0$. D2) $\lambda(p_i) \geq t_i(p_i)$.

D3) $M(p_i) \geq C\text{-}(p_i, t_{i,m})(c) =<p_i, p_m>$

If $t_{i,m} \in T_{i\ m}$ is ready and fires, then the new marking M' is the following:

$$M'(p_m)=C_+(p_m, t_{i,m})(c) + M(p_m) =<p_m,\ldots> \quad (8)$$

$$M'(pi)=0 \quad (9)$$

Then $\lambda(p_m)$ is reset and begins to count.

5) The CTPN modeling leaving behavior

In fig 11, p_3 is main output station, $T_{3,0}$ describes a pallet is to leave the system.

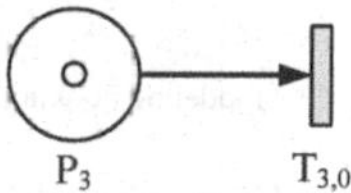

Fig. 11. The CTPN modeling leaving behavior.

For each $t_{3,0} \in T_{3,0}$, its enabling conditions are:

El) $M(p_3) =<p_3,0>$ E2) $\lambda(p_3) \geq t_i(p_3)$

If $t_{3,0}$ is ready and fires, then the new marking M' is the following:

$$M'(p_3)=0 \quad (10)$$

6) The CTPN modeling sharing behavior

In fig 2, when a storage pallet, i.e. in p_{14} and a retrieval pallet in p_5 arrives at the same time, the conflict will occur in p_{15}. In such condition, the scheduler will intervene; here p_{15} is called a sharing station ($Psc=\{p_{16}, p_{15}, p_{19}\ p_{25}\}$). Fig 12 shows the CTPN model of such sharing operation.

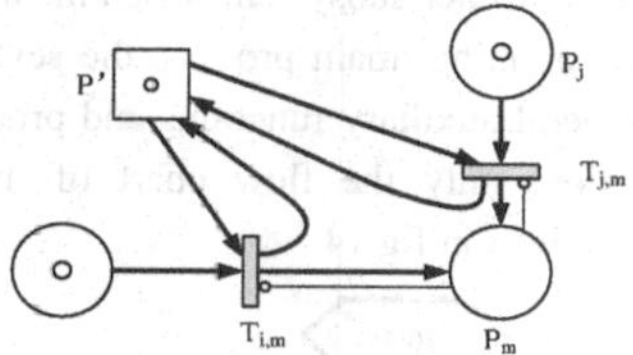

Fig. 12. The CTPN modeling sharing behavior.

In fig 12, P' is a set of virtual places containing the instructions that decide either $T_{i,m}$ or $T_{j,m}$ is to occur. Here, (P_i,P_j,P_m) is $\{(p_{14},p_5,p_{15}); (p_{15},p_6,p_{16}); (p_{18},p_8,p_{19}); (p_{24},p_{16},p_{25})\}$; $T_{i,m}(T_{j,m})$ describe a pallet in $P_i(P_j)$ is to be transferred to P_m.

For each $t_{i,m} \in T_{i\ m}$, if $p_m \in P_m$ and $p_i \in P_i$, its enabling conditions are:

Fl) $M(p_m)=0$. F2) $\lambda(p_i) \geq ti(p_i)$.

F3) $M(p_i) \geq C_-(p_i,t_{i,m})(c) =<P_i,P_m>$

F4) $M(p') =<p_i,p_m>$

If $t_{i,m} \in T_{i\ m}$ is ready and fires, then the new marking M' is the following:

$$M'(p_m)=C_+(p_m, t_{i,m})(c) + M(p_m) =<P_m,\ldots> \quad (11)$$

$$M(p_i)=0 \quad (12)$$

$$M'(p_i)=<p_j, p_m> \quad (13)$$

Then $\lambda(p_m)$ is reset and begins to count.

M' $(p')=<p_j, p_m>$ denotes that a pallet in p_i has been transferred into p_m, the next operation is $T_{j,m}$. For each $t_{j,m} \in T_{j\ m}$, the operation is similar to $t_{i,m} \in T_{i\ m}$.

7) The CTPN modeling booking behavior

In fig 13, $P_i = P_v \cup P_{rs}$. For each $t \in T_{p',pi}$, its enabling conditions are:

G1) $M(p_i) = <p_i>$. G2) $M(p') = <p_j, \ldots>$

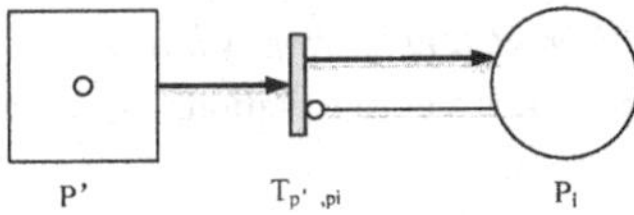

Fig. 13. The CTPN modeling booking behavior.

If $t \in T_{p',pi}$ is ready and fires, then the new marking M' is the following:

$$M'(P_i) = <P_i, \ldots> \quad (14)$$

$$M'(p') = 0 \quad (15)$$

M'(pi) =<P,... > denotes a shuttle or a crane is booked with a route from current location to destination for loading.

IV. IMPLEMENTING MODEL OF CTPN WITH VC++

Based on the approach of the CTPN modeling seven-type behaviors of the active resources in automated warehouse described above, the simulations of the whole system can be performed in the Visual C++ environment, where seven transition functions emulate the seven-type behaviors. The whole system is mainly composed of the scheduler subsystem and the resource controller subsystem which includes such the modules as class defining, main process, the seven transition functions and several auxiliary functions and procedures; due to space limitation, only the flow chart of main process module is briefly given in fig 14.

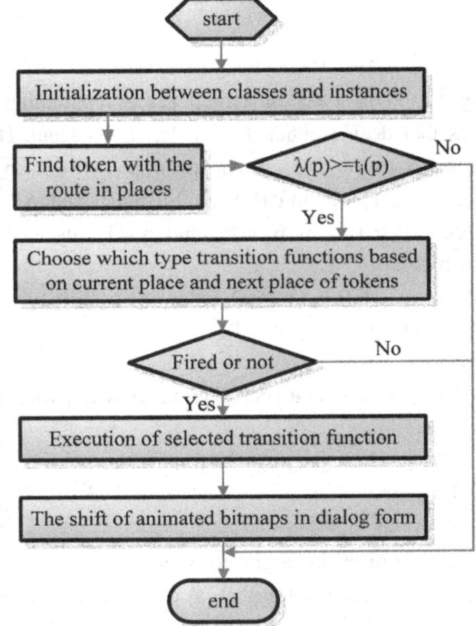

Fig. 14. The flow chart ofmain process of the resource controller module.

In main process module, a dialog form simulates the work flow of all resources in fig 1,and many animated bitmaps describe the shift of the active resources. When one of transition functions has been chosen, it's enabling conditions base on either A1-A2, or B1-B4, or C1-C3, or D1-D3, or El-E2, or F1-F4, or G1-G2;then fired, new marking M' is updated either according to equations (1)-(2), or (3)-(5), or (6)-(7), or (8)-(9), or (10), or (11)-(13), or (14)-(15).

V. CONCLUDING REMARKS

CTPN results to be effective for modeling the resource-oriented systems such as the automated warehouse. It is necessary for modeling resource-oriented systems to analyze the behaviors of the resources, especially for active resources. Based on study of the behaviors of the active resources, the dynamics of an automated warehouse can be modeled with CTPN in a concise and efficient way, in which places are multicolored. The paper defines in detail the CTPN modeling each event of the behaviors in the system: the pallet entering the system, the pallet being transferred/loaded /unloaded, a pallet leaving from system, a crane or a shuttle being booked or shifting, and a buffer station being shared. To do so, the implement of the model becomes easier via Visual C++. The approach allows us to obtain a resource-oriented model suitable for real-time control applications. Further study on developing the scheduler model and designing favorable dispatch policies to improve the whole system performances is now in progress.

REFERENCES

[1] B.R.Sarker and P.S. Babu. "Travel time models in automated storage/retrieval systems: a critical review," International Journal of Production Economics, 40, pp. 173-184, 1995.

[2] van den J.P. Berg and A.J.R.M. (NOUD) Gademann, "Simulation study of an automated storage/retrieval system," International Journal of Production Research, 38(6), pp. 1339-1356, 2000.

[3] M.J. Rosenblatt, Y. Roll and V. Zyser, "A combined optimization and simulation approach for designing automated storage/retrieval systems," IIE, Transactions, 25(1), pp. 40-50, 1993.

[4] M. Dotoli and M.P. Fanti, "Modeling of an AS/RSServiced by Rail-Guided Vehicles with Colored Petri Nets: a Control Perspective," in Proceedings of the 2002 IEEE International Conference on Systems, Man and Cybernetics, Hammamet, Tunisia, pp. 162-167.

[5] F. Amato and F. Basile, "Optimal Control of Warehousing Systems with Simultaneous Crane and Shuttle Optimization," in Proceedings of the 2001 IEEE international Conference on Emerging Technologies and Factory Automation, Antibes,France, pp. 95- 104.

[6] F. Basile, C. Carbone, P. Chiacchio, "Modeling of AS/RS via Coloured Petri Nets," in Proceedings of the 2001 IEEEIASME International Conference on Advanced intelligent Mechatronics, Como, Italy, pp. 1029-1034

[7] K.Jensen, Colored Petri nets,Basic concepts,analysis methods and practical use, vol.1, Monographs on Theoretical Computer Sciences. New York: Springer Verlag, 1995.

[8] S.Hsieh, J. S. Hwang, and H.C. Chou, "A Petri net based structure for AS/RS operation modeling," Int. Journal ofProduction Research, vol.36, n. 12, pp. 3323-3346, 1998.

[9] S.C. Lin and H.P.B. Wang, "Modeling an automated storage and retrieval system using Petri nets," Int. Journal of Production Research, vol.33, n1, pp. 237-260, 1995.

[10] ShanJun HE, Fei CHENG and Jian LUO, "Modeling and Implementing of an Automated Warehouse via Colored Timed Petri Nets: A Behavior Perspective", in Proceeding of the IEEE ICCA 2007, pp:2823-2828.

Telecare and Social Link Solution for Ambient Assisted Living Using a Robot Companion with Visiophony

Thibaut Varène, Paul Hillereau, Thierry Simonnet
ESIEE-Paris,
Noisy le Grand – FRANCE
Email: {t.varene, hillerep, t.simonnet}@esiee.fr

***Abstract*- An increasing number of people are in need of help at home (elderly, isolated and/or disabled persons; people with mild cognitive impairment). Several solutions can be considered to maintain a social link while providing tele-care to these people. Many proposals suggest the use of a robot acting as a companion. In this paper we will look at an environment constrained solution, its drawbacks (such as latency) and its advantages (flexibility, integration...). A key design choice is to control the robot using a unified Voice over Internet Protocol (VoIP) solution, while addressing bandwidth limitations, providing good communication quality and reducing transmission latency**

I. INTRODUCTION

As part of ongoing projects, research has been conducted towards efficient solutions for audio/video communication between people and robot remote control, using an unified channel.

In Europe, there is an increasing demand [1] for maintaining dependent people at home, to reduce hospital load, improve their quality of life and strengthen their social link. To this extent, a need for communication systems and telecare technologies arose. Maintaining such people at home often requires medical assistance, excellent and reliable communication tools, used by their relatives and the caregivers, as well as means for physical interaction between the remote operator and the person at home. Thus, the use of a "robot companion" was suggested [2, 3, 4].

Nonetheless, several constraints have to be taken into account: these systems make use of an internet connection and as such rely on bandwidth availability. Most European personal internet accesses use Asymmetric Digital Subscriber Line (ADSL) technology, offering a limited upload bandwidth.

Still, in order to offer accurate and exploitable communication, image and sound quality must be maintained. Video quality is usually highly dependent on available bandwidth, and how different compression algorithms perform with limited bandwidth.

As the robot companion will also act as a visiophony relay, it seemed natural to integrate remote control into that channel. Yet, in order to remote control the robot, low latency must be achieved. It has been observed that an operator can be disturbed by delays larger than 250 ms [5, 6, 7].

This article is organized as follows. We present a platform overview and an explanation of our choices in Section II. A detail of its technical drivers is given in Section III. Then the identified remaining issues are discussed in Section IV before concluding in Section V.

II. PROJECT OVERVIEW

A. Existing Platform

As presented in Figure 1, the current platform is composed of three parts: a master server, a smart home and a remote client.

- A master server, handling:
- Lightweight Directory Access Protocol (LDAP) server (registry and authentication).
- Mail server.
- Collaborative environment based on Horde Groupware.
- Asterisk Internet Protocol Private Branch eX change (IP-PBX, or IPBX) for voice/video communications routing.

A Smart Home, equipped with:
- A robot companion featuring a camera, a display and a VoIP client.
- Various sensors for person monitoring.
- Internet gateway (local IPBX).
- A remote client system, basically a Personal Computer with:
- A web browser.
- A VoIP Client

Our main concern is the VoIP communication channel between the VoIP users and its use to control the robot.

T. Sobh, K. Elleithy (eds.), *Innovations in Computing Sciences and Software Engineering*,
DOI 10.1007/978-90-481-9112-3_39, © Springer Science+Business Media B.V. 2010

B. *Initial Choices*

Several options have been considered to answer the implementation constraints. One of the most interesting implementation previously studied was based on the open source videoconferencing tool OpenMeetings [8].

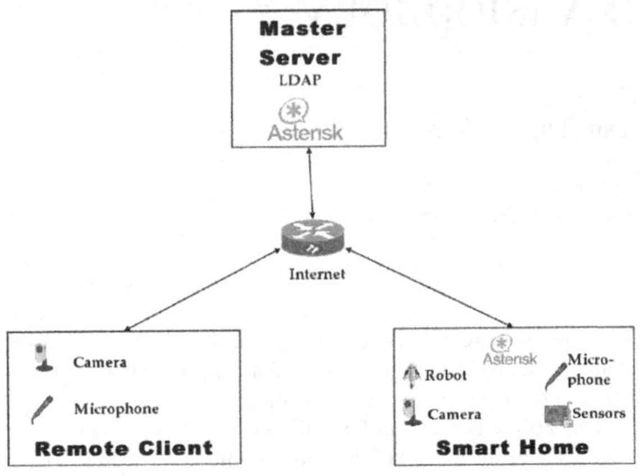

Fig. 1. Existing Platform

It was a web-based solution, requiring only a web browser and a Flash R plugin to operate. It was thus very unintrusive on the client system and very easy to install (contrary to a dedicated client).

Nevertheless, this approach was eventually discarded because of several drawbacks: low image quality, no possibility to control bandwidth usage. The source code was also sufficiently complicated to abandon the idea of making major changes to resolve these issues.

C. *Current Solution*

The current approach uses a dedicated software client, Ekiga[9] and an Asterisk IPBX[10], both being opensource.

This new architecture enabled us to choose the video and audio codec independently. Both Asterisk and Ekiga are also easily modifiable, with a strong opensource community, open to changes and feedback.

Asterisk has the major advantage of being compatible with dedicated VoIP hardware (such as IP phones). It also permits to segment and establish a clear dialplan for various user categories, thus making it easier to manage the platform. Due to the fact that Asterisk is very modular, and supports many protocols, adding a new channel to control the robot does not present a major difficulty.

Ekiga is opensource, it has been developped for Linux and Windows, and it offers among other opensource VoIP clients the largest set of features. In particular, Ekiga already implements a text channel for chat purpose. Moreover, Ekiga's user interface is well abstracted from the actual VoIP client, making it easy to adapt.

Obviously, such an approach is more intrusive on the client system (need to install a dedicated software). Setup at the server level is also more complex.

A particular problem quickly appeared with this new setup: Network Address Translation (NAT - A system used to accomodate several computers sharing a single public IP address. Often enabled by default on ADSL set top boxes -) issues. Specifically, Ekiga uses a lower level protocol than OpenMeetings (which is working over HyperText Transfer Protocol - HTTP), introducing additional complexity when dealing with NATed clients. This problem has been resolved by introducing a gateway, embedding a local Asterisk server which routes incoming and outgoing calls.

Overall, the resulting architecture complexifies: handling NAT problems, having to install software on remote ends and managing point of failures (the NAT gateway being one) makes the whole system harder to administrate.

III. TECHNICAL DRIVERS

The current solution has been designed to meet several criteria. It is driven by the need to satisfy exploitation constraints: it must be easy to use, it must tolerate limited available bandwidth and it must have reduced processing power requirements.

A. *User Interface*

As we have previously mentioned, Ekiga offers a highly configurable Graphical User Interface (GUI) framework. This is especially useful to us as we have different requirements depending on the current user of the software.

Telecare operators might want a detailed interface, to be able to call any recipient, integrated with robot control interface. Family relatives would use the standard GUI, while some users could use a very simplified interface, with e.g. four pictures representing four recipients, clicking on any of which would initiate the call. We have developed such a simplified interface.

B. *Video Codec*

The key issue is the choice of video codec. Bandwidth and processing power requirements for video compression far exceed that of audio or text channels. For instance, voice audio can be encoded with Speex [11] with bit rates comprised between 0.3 and 2 kilobytes/s [12]. The remaining free bandwidth will thus be used for video. As we can see on Figure 2, for a typical upload bandwidth of 100 kilobytes/s, video uses the most of it.

We have three primary constraints to deal with, which are interdependent:

- Bandwidth
- Processing power
- Latency

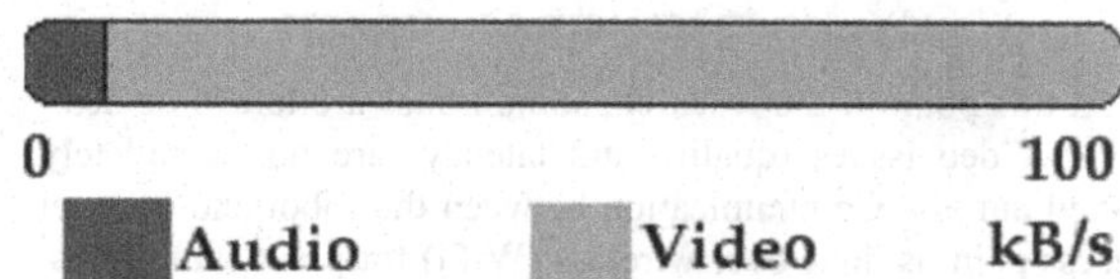

Fig 2. Illustrated bandwidth assignment between audio and video

The last two items make it mostly impossible to consider doing video codec translation on the IPBX, as it would require too much processing power on the server platform and introduce unacceptable latency between the source and the viewer. As such, the chosen codec must be suitable for all elements in the chain.

1. Networking

Target audience will be equipped with standard ADSL Internet access, which has the main drawback of providing an asymmetrical upload vs. download bandwidth. Specifically, upload bandwidth (data sent by the user) is typically apped in e.g. France at about 100 kilobytes/s, which is an order of magnitude slower than download bandwidth.

This implies a major restriction on the video codec: indeed, video will be the primary consumer of bandwidth. Image quality in compressed video formats is usually a balance of three parameters:

- Bitrate (i.e. target bandwidth).
- Frame size and frame rate.
- Buffer size (how many frames will be buffered for the compression to happen. Directly impacts latency from live feed).

2. Processing Power

Another constraint that we have to keep in mind is limited available processing power. In particular the robot has hardware limitation: it runs on battery, with hardware aimed at low power consumption. Thus it has limited processing power.

Another option that we want to keep open is for users to be able to communicate using portable devices (such as smart phones). These devices also have limited processing power by design.

3. Options

The targeted audience includes elderly people, whose visual acuity often requires a good picture (large, well defined image). Moreover, in order to remotely operate the robot, we also need a good picture quality, with reasonable dimensions, good frame rate (the industry standard 24 frames/s has been retained due to its proven results[3]), and as little delay as possible (to be close to realtime control). These demands usually imply a very high bandwidth. Several codecs offer trade-offs for a given low bitrate such as:

Motion JPEG Very low latency, very low picture quality, low processing power requirements.

H.261 Medium latency, low picture quality, low processing power requirements.

H.263 An evolution of H.261, with improved video quality and slightly higher processing requirements.

H.264 Baseline Profile Medium latency, good picture quality, high processing power requirements.

Motion JPEG (MJPEG) is not really a video codec: it simply takes each individual frame of a video stream and compress them using the JPEG format. The compression rate of this format is also very low compared to video oriented codecs which use motion compensation. Still, it's commonly found on entry-level IP cameras.

H.261 and H.263 have been directly developed for video conferencing applications over limited network bandwidth. They are our prime candidate for video compression and are currently being evaluated for implementation. H.261 has the drawback of offering only two pre-defined image sizes (176x144 and 352x288 [13]), whilst H.263 offers five (from 128x96 to 1408x1152 [14]).

H.264 Baseline Profile (H.264-BP) is a proposed successor to H.263. H.264 [15] is very flexible on image size, offers the highest video quality for low bit rates (half the bit rate necessary for a given level of fidelity compared to predecessor video coding standards [16]) at the expense of very high processing power required for both encoding and decoding. Also, H.264 patent situation has yet to be resolved [17]. Until these issues can be addressed, we cannot consider using it.

Considering our needs and the processing power on the robot, we chose H261 as our main video codec. We worked to integrate H261, H263 and H264 in Ekiga. Using H261 codec, we were able to reduce delay from 10 to 1: average delay is now in the range 30 ms to 80 ms.

C. Robot Control

For some applications, such as telecare, it is necessary to pilot the robot based on the video feed it provides. Several options were evaluated based on the following environmental constraints:

- Commands sent to the robot must be synchronized with the video feed to account for latency.
- Driving the robot must be a straightforward operation.

The first constraint quickly prompted toward sending robot commands over the same carrier as the voice and video were. Two primary options were studied, as presented in following 1 and 2 paragraphs.

1. Sending commands over the voice channel

This could be achieved with e.g. inband Dual-Tone Multi-Frequency (DTMF).

Synchronisation would be guaranteed (the VoIP client handles synchronisation between voice/video feeds and between each end's feeds).

This would have had the drawback of introducing a new complexity as the audio channel would have had to be processed in order to filter out DTMF command signals and translate them to the robot controls. Also, this approach would rely on good audio quality, and introduced some latency (duration of the DTMF code and processing).

Also, a loss of audio signal (in case of "lag" for instance) would also mean a loss of control over the robot, which might be a security risk.

2. *Sending commands over a third channel*

A simpler approach was then devised: instead of encapsulating commands into the voice channel, we thought about using a dedicated text channel. The reasons for this are numerous:

- No more signal processing required.
- Does not rely on audio channel (more resilient).
- Groundwork for the text channel already exist in Ekiga, and simple to implement in Asterisk.
- No latency: complexity of commands virtually unlimited (any amount of text is sent almost instantaneously).
- Assigning "missions" to the robot, or even completely reprogramming it, could be done this way.

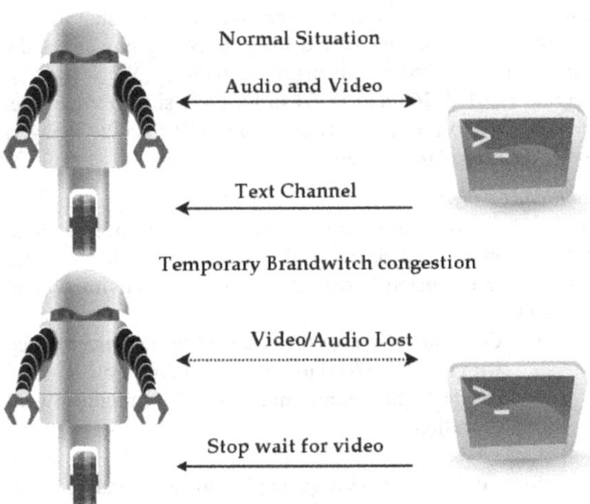

Fig 3. Use of the text channel in bandwitdh congestion situation

Using a separate channel limits the risk of loosing control over the robot, see Figure 3. Text data requiring very little bandwidth, it is most likely to be the last channel to go in case of bandwidth congestion.

IV. Issues remaining to address

At this point of the research, some issues are left to be dealt with. Video issues (quality and latency) are not completely sorted out yet. Communication between the robot and Internet access point is done over wireless (WiFi) for practical reasons. This introduces new problems.

A. *Video*

As we have seen, the key problem in the current setup is video quality. Video is central to maintaining a decent social link: it conveys more information than voice only, to either family members and telecare operators.

We want to provide the robot with good picture quality so that people with reduced visual acuity can enjoy decent experience and we need to provide remote operators with good video and lowest possible latency.

At the moment, we have retained H.261 and H.263 codecs as best candidates, but they do not deliver the expected video quality given our bandwidth limitations.

H.264-BP could be a promising replacement, but its processing power requirements (let aside patent issues) make it unfit for our current platform. This problem could be mitigated by using dedicated hardware encoding/decoding devices.

We also lack the possibilty to directely interact with IP cameras. It is still not possible to connect from the VoIP client to an IP camera to have a real time video stream. We have planned to develop a Real Time Streaming Protocol (RTSP) module on Asterisk IPBX. Such module would offer the ability of calling a remote IP camera as any other VoIP client, by its SIP number, and get its video stream.

B. *Robot connection : WiFi*

The robot connects to the Internet (and the rest of the system) wirelessly for obvious practical reasons. The current architecture implements a WiFi connexion, which is an industry standard (802.11[18]).

Unfortunately, WiFi introduces new problems[19], which may degrade the video quality:

- Interferences: WiFi operates in the 2.4 GHz band, subject to interferences from other devices such as BlueTooth devices, microwave ovens, and concurrent (neighbouring) WiFi "pollution".
- Latency and packet loss: they are usually caused by network congestion, i.e. when the available bandwidth is saturated. They can also be a result of interferences.
- Bandwidth: degrades as the radio signal gets weaker or polluted. In-house environments with reinforced concrete walls can significantly reduce WiFi signal range [20].

All these problems introduce more latency and reduce useable bandwidth. Some solutions have already been proposed to address these issues, though [21, 22, 23].

V. Conclusion and Outlook

The current platform presented here is a prototype for a pilot project, but the technologies used can be further expanded to other fields. In particular, the only source and display for the Audio/Video feed is the robot.

Thus, we plan to add IP cameras to the platform to offer more inputs for telecare operators. Live switching between video sources would also be implemented using the third text channel. In a broader view, considering a Smart Home Environment (SHE) equipped with automation devices, we plan to perform remote operations of those devices (lights control, window shades, water system, etc) using the text channel.

Moreover, reprogramming the robot and/or the SHE would be a matter of defining a simple protocol (lead-in, payload, lead-out, checksum) that the equipments could collect from the text channel and execute on a scheduled basis.

Also, we have presented the text channel as a one-way communication channel in the current setup. But we plan to use it to receive feedback from the remote systems, e.g. real-time monitoring of life signs, status reports of the smarthome equipments, battery alert for the robot, etc.

Finally, it is technically possible to port a compatible VoIP client to mobile devices (e.g. smart phones), making it possible for users to communicate and/or control the platform (robot, SHE...) from mobile devices.

Acknowledgment

ESIEE-Paris team works in close cooperation for platform validation, especially for Alzheimer disease people with:

- Broca Hospital (Assistance Publique Hpitaux de Paris leader of Tandem project)) for content generation for cognitive stimulation and day-time management as well as ethics,
- INT for monitoring and sensors,
- IBISC, Université d'Evry, leader of QuoVadis project,
- Private companies like Legrand, Verklizan and SmartHomes for smart homes and services,
- University of Reading, leader of CompanionAble project.

Some research leading to these results has received funding from the European Community's seventh Framework Programme (FP7/2007-2013) under grant agreement n°216487.

References

[1] World Health Organization, 2002, *The European Health Report*, European Series, N° 97.

[2] B. Burger, I. Ferran, and F. Lerasle, Multimodal Interaction Abilities for a Robot Companion, *Conference on Computer Vision Systems (ICVS'08)*, Santorini, Greeee, 2008.

[3] J.L. Baldinger *et al.*, Tele-surveillance System for Patient at Home: the MEDIVILLE system, *9th International Conference, ICCHP 2004, Paris France, Series : Lecture Notes in Computer Science, Ed. Springer, 2006.*

[4] J. Boudy et al., Telemedecine for elderly patient at home : the TelePat project, *International Conference on Smart Homes and Health Telematics*,Belfast UK, 2006.

[5] K. Barron *et al.*, "Graphical User Interfaces for Engineering Design: Impact of Response Delay and Training on User Performance", *ASME Design Engineering Technical Conferences - Design Theory & Methodology Conference, 2004.*

[6] G.Armitage, "An Experimental Estimation of Latency Sensitivity in Multiplayer Quake3", *11th IEEE International Conference on Networks*, 2003.

[7] T. Henderson, "Latency and user behaviour on a multiplayer game server", *3rd International Workshop on Networked Group Communications*, 2001.

[8] OpenMeetings, "Open-Source Webconferencing", *http://code.google.com/p/openmeetings/.*

[9] D. Sandras, Ekiga, *http://ekiga.org.*

[10] Digium, The Open Source PBX & Telephony Platform, *http://www.asterisk.org/.*

[11] Xiph.Org Foundation, "Speex: A Free Codec For Free Speech", *http://speex.org/.*

[12] G. Herlein *et al.*, RTP Payload Format for the Speex Codec, *draft-ietf-avt-rtp-speex-07, http://tools.ietf.org/html/draft-ietf-avt-rtp-speex-07*, 2009.

[13] International Telecommunication Union, "H.261: Video codec for audiovisual services at p x 64 kbit/s", *Line Transmission of Non-Telephone Signals,* 1993.

[14] International Telecommunication Union, "H263: Video coding for low bit rate communication", *SERIES H: Audiovisual and Multimedia Systems Infrastructure of audiovisual services, Coding of moving Video, 2005.*

[15] International Telecommunication Union, "H264: Advanced video coding for generic audiovisual services", *SERIES H: Audiovisual and Multimedia Systems Infrastructure of audiovisual services, Coding of moving Video,* 2003.

[16] T. Wiegand, G. J. Sullivan, G. Bjontegaard and A. Luthra, Overview of the H.264/AVC Video Coding Standard, *IEEE TRANSACTIONS ON CIRCUITS AND SYSTEMS FOR VIDEO TECHNOLOGY,* 2003.

[17] MpegLA, List of patents (Attachment 1) covered by the AVC Patent Portfolio License as of May 1, 2009, *http://www.mpegla.com/avc/avc-patentlist.cfm*, 2009,

[18] IEEE Standards Association, "IEEE Standard for Information technology— Telecommunications and information exchange between systems— Local and metropolitan area networks— Specific requirements", *Part 11: Wireless LAN Medium Access Control (MAC) and Physical Layer (PHY) Specifications,* 2007.

[19] S. G. Nelwamondo, *Adaptive video streaming over IEEE 802.11,* F'SATIE, 2005.

[20] 3COM, 3COM Wireless Antennas, *http://www.3com.com/other/pdfs/products/en_US/101900.pdf.*

[21] J. Apostolopoulos, "Reliable Video Communication over Lossy Packet Networks using Multiple State Encoding and Path Diversity", *Visual Communications and Image Processing (VCIP),* 392,409, 2001.

[22] S. Chen et al., "An adaptative rate control streaming mechanism with optimal buffer utilization", *Journal of System and Software, 75:271,281,* 2005

[23] M. Armstrong, D. Flynn, M. Hammond, S. Jolly and R. Salmon, High Frame-Rate Television, *BBC Research White Paper WHP 169,* 2008.

Contextual Semantic: A Context-aware Approach for Semantic Web Based Data Extraction from Scientific Articles

Deniss Kumlander
Department of Informatics, TTU
Raja 15, 12618
Tallinn, Estonia
e-mail: kumlander@gmail.com

Abstract—**The paper explores whether the semantic context is good enough to cope with ever increasing number of available resources in different repositories including the web. Here a problem of identifying authors of scientific papers is used as an example. A set of problem still do arise in case we apply exclusively the semantic context. Fortunately contextual semantic can be used to derive more information required to separate ambiguous cases. Semantic tags, well-structured documents and available databases of articles do provide a possibility to be more context-aware. Under the context we use co-authors names, references and headers to extract key-words and identify the subject. The real complexity of the considering problem comes from the dynamical behaviour of authors as they can change the topic of the research in the next paper. As the final judge the paper proposes applying words usage patterns analysis. Final the contextual intelligence engine is described.**

Keywords-Semantic net, library analysis, context-aware.

I. Introduction

The quick evolution of technologies, globalisation of the world and quick growth of the educational level in countries that are just now merging the world scientific society generated the huge number of information and articles. The growth of those papers models the growth of published document in the web and certainly exceeds expectations of researchers. In this situation analysis of those works and consequently the search of key papers by keywords become more and more complicated and nowadays nearly impossible.

The first task that librarians, including online libraries and search engines, have to solve is the correct linking of articles to authors. This task is trivial on small amount of articles in limited training amount of those become fairly complex on real examples. The paper do stop on this in more details in the forth chapter. In order to solve this problem the semantic web, described in the chapter two, was mainly used so far. Unfortunately this important technology is not good enough to cope with all kind of complexities, but still do provide an excellent basis for further processing of papers. Here, we do propose to strength the semantic net approach with context-aware systems approaches. Saying that we do warn the reader that the semantic context and semantic and context should be distinguished as those do represent completely different approaches as we will demonstrate in more details in the third chapter.

The firth chapter does specify the proposed approaches including problems and solutions and the final chapter concludes the paper.

II. Semantic Web

The Semantic web [1] idea is the further evolution of the web proposed in 1990th where the global network doesn't only stores the data, but also contains semantic information and relates different documents on this basis. Documents in the web are published using HTML, which does provide certain information in some extend, but is first of all limited and secondly is a mixture of design, styling, types and other kind of tags requiring to present the document correctly to web browsers, but not really good enough to process any document efficiently. The semantic web, basing on technologies like RDL, OWL and XML allow giving additional information to data (text of the document) described in the published document and understand at least key information like for example the name of the author, the main topic of the document and so forth

The semantic net can be seen as a further generalisation of the semantic web, as documents can be stored in any kind of repository, which is not always the Web.

The semantic net shifts abilities to process information stored in documents to the new level. If the old data representation was primary used for machines to process and display information for humans, then in the semantic net the information can be processed, displayed and understood by the machine. Basing on this understanding the computer can do additional activities, for example fetching additional links which are similar and are likely to be interested for the human requested the current document.

III. Context Aware Systems

A context aware software development principal defines the computer reaction can be organized using more than just direct data input. It could and probably should consider circumstances under which the input is defined, sense the environment in

T. Sobh, K. Elleithy (eds.), *Innovations in Computing Sciences and Software Engineering*,
DOI 10.1007/978-90-481-9112-3_40, © Springer Science+Business Media B.V. 2010

which the request is formulated and so forth. In the result the system response will be different for the same request depending on those extra (request context) parameters.

Some authors [5, 6] say that this behaviour can be described by the system ability to adapt to specific contexts under which the system operates or reacts on the request and ability to collect and recognize the context information.

Consider for example web applications, which do normally react on the request, but could collect and modify behaviour depending on the following extra parameters:

- Previous requests that are not considered as direct input to the current one. For example so far collected preferences of a user without asking him to define those directly like previously made searches in case of search engines etc.
- Internet browser type. A request made using IE browser should be responded differently in compare to Firefox as those browsers standards (JavaScript, HTML) etc. are different so the response will be rendered differently;
- Accessing device – obviously the page should look different in case the user accesses the page using mobile version of the device due space, keyboard etc restrictions;
- Vary the response depending on geo location of the requester (country, time-zone, language);
- Connection speed – in order to provide either a short and restricted answer or expanded and large one;

... and so forth.

The example above deals with hardware context used in most cases, but obviously it is not the only context that can be acquired. Following the same principals, it is possible to use history of communication or different other messages as a context of the current communication.

The context-aware approach is used to increase relevancy of the response (service) provided by the system and target to bridge the gap between formal and [7] human-human type interaction. Generally context-aware application contain 3 types of sub-activity elements: they should detect context, interpret it and react on it, although the first activity is sometimes delegated to other systems (alternatively it can be said that the system relies on other one to collect context and provide it and so depends on the front-system in terms of how well it can adapt as the smaller context is the less flexibility the system could provide).

IV. Sample Case

The modern society provides much more opportunities for researches and consequently for publishing novel approaches in forms of articles. The overall speed of knowledge transfer is permanently increasing allowing collaborating and picking up the current knowledge quickly and efficiently. It does provide much better starting position for any research to be done than ever before. Fifty years ago the post looked like an incredible invention in compare to what scientists had in the 19th century been isolated into local country communities. Only major invention was floating more or less freely having still a sufficient shift in time between been acquired and transferred to any other community. The same shift has been done once again with invention of Internet system 25 years ago allowing much faster access information and what is much more important much easier publish information. Nowadays search engines do simplify the process of searching information even more grouping it, tagging by key words, so the user doesn't have to know the exact address to obtain information from, but could use keywords or paper names in the search process.

The growth of population and involvement into active science other countries used to be called the „third world" sufficiently increased the number of contributions made each year.

Imagine that our task is to structure articles by authors. At the first glance the process is obvious. Current articles' format requirements contain semantic tag to be used to identify authors of the paper. Therefore in most cases authors can be easily extracted as well as other information like references, keywords, topics of the papers orienting on headers of different level.

The real problem comes with the overall world involvement and the size of available papers that makes exactly similar names of totally different persons to be quite common nowadays. In the next chapter we will try to resolve this problem applying context-aware systems techniques. We will call such persons below in the paper – "co-persons".

V. Semantic Contextual Web

Is semantic enough to derive the correct result? The first answer on this question has been got already in early days of artificial intelligence algorithms implementation when automatic translation assistants were developed. Clearly semantic of any statement can be interpreted differently and so the meaning is very ambiguous. The context is what defines the meaning of most concrete statements. Following the best practises from this (translation) area the first level of deriving context will be exploring the neighbourhood of the statement by examining other statements. During this process the algorithm searches for interdependencies and attempts to narrow down the topic. This process can be called a semantic context.

Unfortunately the semantic context is not enough to derive required information in many cases. For example if we do analyse messages transferred during communication between two persons then backgrounds of communicating parties are required parts of the puzzle, which is missing as in not directly send (and so written down) during the communication messages exchange. Therefore we need to consider other context of the information, which is not directly linked to the semantic of language or parsed tags. In other words we propose also using contextual semantic.

Returning to our task defined earlier, we would like to reformulate it slightly by providing the background. The problem is not about processing one and only one article. On the contrary it is first of all an analysis a set of unparsed data for example in search engines. Consider for example Google Scholar producing a list of articles by an author name. Clearly it is a mix. If the author has co-person then currently there is no possibility to group this list by „real" persons. This makes impossible to do certain analytical activities like understanding an impact of the scientist calculating for example the Hirsch index [8]. Clearly in this task we have to split all articles by real authors instead of merging separate scientists into one person within the index. Unfortunately there are many countries whether certain names are very common including first names making such analysis nearly impossible without extra data mining logic described next.

Having a database of already collected resources we can extra different kinds contextual information form an article and track the same information in the history of this author in order to uniquely identify him. This process of identification can be divided into several levels of required sophistication. First of all the author is identified by the name. If there is no such author then it will be added and analysis is completed. Otherwise we need to analyse further. At the first glance the problem will exist only if there are n authors and n is more than 1. Then we need to decide among candidates. Actually the problem still exists even when n equals to 1. The algorithm always should assume that this person is a new researcher with exactly the same name as an existing one. The goal here is to recognise his work and do not associate it to the existing candidate. In other words the number of persons with a name always equals to the count of already recognised individuals and a virtual, new one. Therefore we can carry on the analysis on all levels until we collected enough evidence that the person is uniquely recognised.

The first and simplest information we could obtain is co-authors. It is quite unlikely that the same co-authors appear in articles of co-persons.

Secondly the algorithm should pick up and analyse used references on other articles. Analyses of references will first of all clearly identify the area of the paper research. Thereafter continuous research is likely to use the same references or even self-citations.

If results on previous stages are still ambiguous then much more complex analysis should be carried on. The words usage patters and typical mistakes (linguistic, grammatical and so forth) should support the author recognition process as it is well-known that different authors do use different words and phrases. This kind of analysis has already been used to recognised authors of some unsigned, but important paper written several decades or hundreds years ago.

Finally we would like to do a step back and discuss possible scenarios of reasons the article appears in order to understand better strategies we need to implement in the algorithm identifying the paper. Those scenarios will be aligned to the goal of the algorithm work.

The "working" goal is to associate the article author with an existing author or introduce a new one choosing between alternatives as it was described above.

The "evolving" goal is about tracking down the evolution of the author topics, thought and consequently of his/her research. For example there is always a possibility that the well-known, from the system point of view, person has picked a new topic of changed the institution s/he works for. Obviously the change of topic cannot be dramatic and is likely to stay within the same subject like for example "software engineering".

VI. Context Intelligence Engine

Implementation of the so far described intelligence identifying the author of the paper requires building and synchronizing activities that form on the general level a context intelligence engine to be described in this chapter.

A. *Knowledge Base*

First of all the algorithm will produce new data and consume intensively historical data. Therefore the algorithm does require either an access via some sort of interface to a global repository of scientific works or should contain a local data-base of such works. The acquired knowledge should also be stored locally or in the cloud of other software components working together. This is motivated by the fact that the extracted author information is the basis for other kinds of analysis like mentioned earlier Hirsch or g-index, evaluating and tracking efficiency of authors, services to see trends by subjects and most respectful scientists. All these services will consume results of our algorithm work and as articles indexes are mostly public then there is no privacy reasons to protect results.

B. *Semantic Context Acquisition Engine*

Secondly the semantic based extractor should be implemented basing on modern approaches. It should be able to process the paper and extract certain information requested by the context intelligence algorithm. This component should be able to return:

- Data basing on requests by tags, like an author, a co-author, institution and references;
- Headers and sub-headers;
- Text in the free form (in order to process it in the word usage pattern identification step);
- Meaning of words basing on semantic context, i.e. include sub-components to analyze neighborhood of key-words and uniquely identify them among synonyms.

C. *Clustering and Patterns Identifier*

This component is designed to combine two similar solvers. The first one is responsible for process the text and extracting the patterns of words and phrases usage. There are two alternatives to process results of this module work. First of all the module can return a pattern by the work and then another components will compare it to patterns extracted from candidate authors works and identify the match using a predefined matching factor, which will identify how close patterns should be to consider those as equivalent and should be tuned during the system work. The system would function very mach similar to the soft biometrical students' identification systems [9]. Alternatively the word usage pattern identifying engine could take so far identified patterns by possible authors as an input parameter and return the probability of matching by those persons. The selection of one or another method of implementation greatly depends on the required flexibility and availability of third parts components that can be consumed as such engines.

The second part of this component should be responsible for data mining algorithm basing of available parameters in order to traverse the data and cluster authors by those parameters. This raw information will be consumed further by the context intelligence module described next.

D. *Context Intelligence Module*

The context intelligence module will model rules described in the fifth chapter of this paper. Reading authors' information from the knowledge base, requesting smart tags information via the semantic context acquisition engine will allow moving by the authors name identifying decision tree identifying the precise author.

The module contains a set of declarative rules to follow, reasoning module and policies of communication to all other components unifying the data extraction process and synchronising different steps.

VII. Conclusion

In this paper a problem of identifying author of scientific papers is revised as an example of applying semantic net approaches. During this process a set of problems is demonstrated as the number of papers has increased dramatically in the last years and semantic context is not enough any longer to acquire the correct and unique author name among co-persons having exactly the same name, working in the same universities and so forth. Basically the same conclusion was made in the artificial intelligence algorithms of the automatic translation area much earlier. Fortunately semantic tags, well-structured documents and available databases of previous articles do provide us with a possibility to be more context-aware than in the auto-translation case as this paper does propose. Under the context we do mean using co-authors names, references and headers to extract key-words and identify the subject. The real complexity comes from the dynamical behaviour of authors. They can change the topic of the research at any moment or go to another university changing the place s/he belongs to and research directions been included into the other group of scientists. Alternatively the paper can be written by a new author, unknown to the system and therefore it will be incorrect to associate him/her to any existing. As the final judge the paper proposes applying words usage patterns analysis that should identify clearly having narrowed down possible authors list and so eliminating sufficiently this approach complexity. A brief, but clear description of the context extracting intelligence is given in the paper. It provides guidelines for building an engine for processing scientific papers basing on the proposed method.

References

[1] T. Berners-Lee, J., Hendler, and O. Lassila, "The semantic web", *Scientific American*, 2001.

[2] M. H. Coen, "Design principles for intelligent environments", *Proceedings of AAAI/IAAI*, 1998, pp. 547–554.

[3] A. Roy, S. K. D. Bhaumik, A. Bhattacharya, K. Basu, D.J. Cook, and S.K. Das, "Location aware resource management in smart homes", *Proceedings of First IEEE International Conference on Pervasive Computing and Communications* (PerCom'03), 2003, pp. 481-488.

[4] H. Chen, T. Finin, and A. Joshi, "Semantic Web in the context broker architecture", *Proceedings of the 2nd IEEE Annual Conference on Pervasive Computing and Communications (PerCom '04)*, 2004, pp. 277–286.

[5] P. Chang, A. Gul, "Towards Context-Aware Web Applications", *7th IFIP International Conference on Distributed Applications and Interoperable Systems (DAIS)*, Springer, vol. 4531, 2007, pp. 239–252.

[6] W.Y. Lum, and F.C.M. Lau, "A context-aware decision engine for content adaptation", *IEEE Pervasive Computing*, vol. 1 (3), 2002, pp. 41–49.

[7] J. Pascoe, "Adding Generic Contextual Capabilities to Wearable Computers", *Proc. 2nd Int'l Symp. Wearable Computers*, IEEE CS Press, Los Alamitos, Calif., 1998, pp. 92–99.

[8] J.E. Hirsch, "An index to quantify an individual's scientific research output", *Proceedings of the National Academy of Science*, vol. 102 (46), 2005, pp. 16569-16572.

[9] D. Kumlander, "Soft Biometrical Students Identification Method for e-Learning", *Proceedings of Advances in Computer and Information Sciences and Engineering*, Springer, Netherlands, 2008, pp. 114 – 118.

Motivating Company Personnel by Applying the Semi-self-organized Teams Principle

Deniss Kumlander
Department of Informatics, TTU
Raja 15, 12618
Tallinn, Estonia
e-mail: kumlander@gmail.com

***Abstract*—The only way nowadays to improve stability of software development process in the global rapidly evolving world is to be innovative and involve professionals into projects motivating them using both material and non material factors. In this paper self-organized teams are discussed. Unfortunately not all kind of organizations can benefit directly from agile method including applying self-organized teams. The paper proposes semi-self-organized teams presenting it as a new and promising motivating factor allowing deriving many positive sides of been self-organized and partly agile and been compliant to less strict conditions for following this innovating process. The semi-self organized teams are reliable at least in the short-term perspective and are simple to organize and support.**

Keywords-Personnel motivating, software engineering, key success factors.

I. Introduction

Invention of agile methodology of software development has sufficiently decreased the gap between software engineering process results and customers expectations, but wasn't able to eliminate software projects failures completely. Those failures costs and risks are still sufficiently increasing the overall cost of software development process and are ultimately carried by customers. It is important to examine reasons of failures and try to avoid them in order to make products' investments much more competitive considering modern software business society and involved risks.

Recent researches [2] have shown that nearly one third of all software projects fail directly since customers are not satisfied with the delivered packaging. A lot of others failures were also indirectly connected to this factor as software vendors were not able to meet time of budget expectations mostly trying to bridge gaps between vision of the project and/or customers and scopes that were defined either in the beginning or during the project. The more interesting fact is that a situation with so called "successful" projects is far from been ideal: just one fifth of the developed functionality was reported to be used "often" or "always" and extra 16% was marked as been used "sometimes". Clearly, there is a lot of functionality, which is not correct, not working or not usable and all this took considerable time to develop and deliver [1].

Rapidly increasing competition between software vendors on the global market, much more demanding customers and quick change of business rules force software companies to stabilize their productivity and improve their development process in all possible ways [2] considering risks stated above very seriously. The key factor of this process is personnel strategy as personnel is recognized as a very important aspect of any company success [3]. Unfortunately the software industry is a highly technological sector [4] with a shortness of resources in many areas. Therefore the process of motivating employees become crucial to keep the current team stable and involved into projects. Unfortunately the motivation task is elementary and companies are still loosing skilled professionals despite all modern motivating approaches [5, 6, 7], like good salaries, friendly working environment etc. Therefore, it is important to address all kinds of needs and motivate personnel using innovating approaches recognizing their abilities and providing them with possibilities to use all their skills increasing this way their attachments to the organization.

Moreover it should be mentioned that the software development process quality also depends on the team performance and willingness to develop the product. The communication between all involved team that are not necessary bounded to the strict hierarchical way of pushing things is one of the key issues improving the quality [8]. Many modern software development methodologies do rely on the advanced team-work, which is stimulated by certain level of freedom in making decisions as long as those serve company targets.

II. Material and Non Material Motivating Techniques: Why Do We Care?

Highly professional and motivated personnel are a key factor of the company success and unmotivated personnel can be seen as a major risk factor [5, 7] since workers either decrease their productivity or leaving the company. In the last case the company loses a professional and had to educate a new person losing a huge slice of experience with the gone person.

There are a lot of motivation techniques as we have already mentioned in the introduction, but the majority of those are materialistic and could not be always available for the organization. Moreover, reasons of losing one or another

T. Sobh, K. Elleithy (eds.), *Innovations in Computing Sciences and Software Engineering*,
DOI 10.1007/978-90-481-9112-3_41, © Springer Science+Business Media B.V. 2010

person could also be different and some could be just tired from doing the same, routine things using the same set of tools, others could like a rotation of environment and persons s/he communicates with or just fill that the knowledge in terms of using technologies become outdated and it is important to find a new place that will guarantee updating skills.

All stated previously clearly demonstrates that there are also non material reasons for losing experts and obviously there should be non material approaches to address stated risks. Besides, a consequence of been under motivated could be less dramatic than migrating to another work-place. It can be decrease of involvement into projects, drop of quality etc. All those risks need permanent attention primary using special personnel management techniques like for example recognizing the person inside the organization as an outstanding professional.

The technological needs can be addressed by recently proposed technique of organizing motivational software projects using novel technologies. This provides an opportunity for both involved parties. It is a perfect possibility for workers to upgrade their skills, learn something new and see novel technologies and approaches. At the same time the organization benefits from exploring new ways of building products that can ensure better quality, performance or usability than in current products. This clearly allows bridging the gap to highly technological products of competitors or coming up with a novel product to the market. Obviously such projects does require investments in term of resources and time, but those will be comparable to the re-education investments in case the company needs to find a new worker and having high chances to produce something novel and highly useful for the company future. Therefore, software engineering projects using novel approaches can be seen as an important motivation tool. At the same time motivating software projects have certain restrictions. First of all those do not fully address persons' efforts recognizing needs. Secondly it has a short-term effect from the time perspective depending on the result of these pilot projects. Finally, and this is the most crucial, piloting using modern software techniques requires certain organization of the team, which is not very traditional at the moment and therefore requires changing management attitude to the teams hierarchies. Ideally those motivating projects should be executed within self-organized teams that are discussed in the next chapter.

III. SEMI-SELF-ORGANIZED TEAMS

Semi-self organized teams are a kind of teams that locates between traditional teams and self-organized teams identified as a vital component of agility practices. Therefore the presentation of semi-self-organized teams requires a clear description of self-organized teams in the first place.

The self-organized teams can be described using the major property of those – ability to act fully autonomously during unrestricted period of time and can be recognized within the organization as a kind of "black" box receiving targets and tasks and producing required results within predefined constraints. Those teams do not require external management efforts and use several kinds of autonomy in order to ensure positive experience dealing with those.

There are different types of autonomy. First of all it is an external autonomy which was already mentioned as an ability to act without management efforts constantly pushing the team in required direction and focusing it on targets. Obviously it doesn't mean that the team is expected to act independently since it is just a part of the organization. The autonomy here mean that the team is granted rights to decide by themselves and the influence of any teams, persons that do not belong to the team is minimized and is defined just in forms of targets or constraints defining the scope of the requirement arriving to the input of the team "box".

Secondly there is an internal autonomy that defines the team internal procedure of arriving to decisions and on what degree each member of the team is involved into this process. In most cases decisions are made jointly and in some rare cases this right is delegated to a restricted set of internal experts.

Finally there is an individuals' autonomy showing in which respect each member of the team has rights to pick up tasks and influence the tasks-to-persons assignment process. It also defines in what degree the person can set the sequence in which s/he does those tasks obviously following tasks interdependencies. A level of agreement shows how many tasks per person were not picked by team members by themselves and had to be assigned. For many successful teams this indicator will equal to zero as individuals will rather volunteer than bargain distributing tasks.

Although proposing the idea of semi-self-organized teams was motivated by certain factors, it will be much clearer if the semi-self-organized team concept is defined first and only then framed by factors, conditions and other concepts creating a framework where those can be applied.

Semi-self-organized teams can be described both as an individual concept and by outlining the difference from fully self-organized teams. As an individual concept it is a kind of teams that can act independently during certain restricted period of time obtaining a certain level of autonomy of any kind, but doesn't necessarily and rather rarely all of them. As you can see from this definition the difference from self-organized teams is both sufficient and relatively small depending on predefined goals. Semi-self-organized teams do not act independently during the long or undefined period of time, so their mobility and encapsulation is rather weak. At the same there are a lot of companies that would actually like this kind of teams. We will compare these two kinds of teams on more detailed level in the following chapter.

IV. SELF ORGANIZED VS. SEMI-SELF-ORGANIZED TEAMS

Although agility methods have clear advantages in most business software projects, those do require in many cases presence of conditions that are not acquirable for some organizations. Self organized teams should be built using, at least as a core, highly skilled professionals with very good analytical thinking abilities. Unfortunately not all organizations have such personnel and there are a lot of persons that either are not able or do not want to be fully committed during the work time. Secondly there are a lot of organizations having strict hierarchy rules. In some cases applying agility approaches there is either impossible or could produce too high stress for both workers and the entire organization and negatively impact the overall performance for the very long time.

Fortunately it is possible to apply the proposed semi-self-organized teams in many cases described earlier either as a temporary approach moving toward true agility methods or as a hybrid approach employing some positive sides of autonomous teams and avoiding negative impacts of doing too radical changes.

V. SEMI-SELF-ORGANIZED TEAMS FRAMEWORK

The idea of applying semi-self-organized teams serves first of all motivational goals. It is important to recognize individuals efforts, their ability to act autonomy for some time still producing high quality and been dedicated into their work looking for better ways to do it. Even better is to recognize their collective efforts of been efficient and innovating. The synergy is the factor sufficiently increasing the productivity and if it already presented it is worth to care about it and motivate. If it is not presented, then creating semi-self-motivated teams can produce such effects since individuals are recognized as experts and the formed team is composed of such persons. In the result we have a group of people having similar interests, close level of knowledge so they help each other rather than been distracted by a need to communicate to younger developers on the permanent basis.

It is worth to mention that although been semi-self-organized is discussed so far as a motivation technique, as teams are granted the right to be self-organized, it is not always the case. There are in practice cases when the team acquired the right to be semi-self-organized by themselves. Even in this case it is still possible to use this fact in order to motivate personnel. Moreover the team will be probable expecting that. In most cases the team has either broken some kind rule in order to be efficient or nobody noticed or carried about that.

Finally we would like to merge the idea of motivating via been semi-self-organized with the idea of motivational software projects. As it was demonstrated already fully self-organized teams are not available in many kinds of organizations. At the same time motivational projects do require he certain autonomy level. Therefore applying those two motivation techniques simultaneously we can ensure success of both as those do support each other. It is hard to be semi-self-organized without a clear goal and it is impossible to develop innovating projects been always distracted by side tasks, need to develop much more important standard features. The last is especially destructive as shows to the team that management doesn't value their innovating efforts.

VI. GUIDELINES ON EXECUTING SEMI-SELF-ORGANIZED TEAMS

Although semi-self-organized teams are sufficiently easier to build than fully self-organized teams there still certain problems that should be overcome in order to ensure positive output doing that. In order to analyze arising difficulties we need to identify reasons why we do want to apply semi-self-organized teams and what prevents us from choosing the fully self-organized teams' route. The following reasons were most noticeable in our practice:

- Available personnel is not able to be fully self-organized;
- Management does not want them to be fully self-organized;
- Semi-self organization is granted as a certain freedom and so autonomy is motivating rather than the general managing technique;
- Distance between locations is forcing gaining certain autonomy to a team;
- Lack of interest to the team projects allows a team to acquire the self-organized title been enough autonomous in decisions.

The hardest autonomy to execute properly granting the team a right to be autonomous is the internal one. There is always a possibility that in absence of an "external" manager somebody will grab his role and in many cases this persons will be the loudest one, not the most knowledgeable. If it will be the case the team will be exploded and there will be no force team members accept orders from. At the same time conservative members are not used to discuss and make join decisions and therefore are very slow to obtain group/internal autonomy. It is also possible that the group is composed of people having different level of productivity and knowledge. It is very dangerous combination and happens purely because we normally do lack highly skilled professionals. It is dangerous since formally all members of the team are having a right to vote and those votes are equal. In practice it is not so and therefore there is normally a manger that is supposed to support the most valuable opinions. As you can see, the problem arises only if less knowledgeable team members have high ego. That is basically why semi-self organized teams are designed for. A certain person can be appointed to the "temporary" manager position suppressing the internal autonomy, but keeping other types of autonomies and so still deriving certain positive sides of self-organized teams. If there is no conflicts and less experience persons do respect more experience persons opinions then the team self-balance and the internal autonomy is not very high (as there is no joined decisions), but it is still presented as decisions are made by each area experts internally.

Rotating the internal conductor role is an interesting technique we used in practice recently. Obviously there is no manager as the team should have the internal autonomy and is preferably making decisions using joined efforts. At the same time, there is one person appointed to the role of synchronizing efforts and communicating to other teams. The person in this role has an ability to understand internal and external processes, see the full picture and learn to respect others seeing the amount of work they are doing. It also clearly demonstrates all processes involved in making different kinds of decisions, which is essential for the team to stay stably autonomous as each team member is fully aware of different decisions consequences.

Considering the individual autonomy, it is important to give certain right to select tasks for each team member as shows that s/he is valued by the team and managers. At the same time it is important to stimulate co-work. The last should serve several goals. First of all it should spread the knowledge inside the team and to provide to each involved individual new, sometimes completely unexpected, point of view on things, development techniques etc. In many cases, persons will very much like it as they avoid been isolated and can discuss, communicate and in the result progress faster and more efficiently. Secondly it sufficiently improves the communication between team members, which is well-known vital element of been self-organized.

VII. CONCLUSION

In this paper semi-self-organized teams were explored as a motivating approach for company personnel. The semi-self-organized teams are teams that are able to act autonomously during relatively short-time using different kind of autonomy. Those teams still do require mangers attentions, but on sufficiently lower level than in case of standard hierarchical structure of the organization. Building semi-self-organized teams can be used as an excellent motivation techniques since allow recognizing outstanding members of organization granting them autonomy rights having still management control over the team.

Besides, the motivational effort of organizing such teams can be merged with other kinds of non material motivation approaches like for example starting motivation software projects involving novel techniques and languages. Each of these techniques relies on another and together they produce a synergy ensuring success of the motivational project. As the result the performance and emotional attachment to the organization is sufficiently increased among involved personnel, which is crucial for stabilizing good productivity of any software vendors engineering process.

REFERENCES

[1] A.A. Khan, "Tale of two methodologies for web development: heavyweight vs agile", *Postgraduate Minor Research Project*, 2004, pp. 619-690.

[2] D. Kumlander, "Software design by uncertain requirements", *Proceedings of the IASTED International Conference on Software Engineering*, 2006, pp. 224-2296.

[3] M. A. Armstrong, "*Handbook of Personnel Management Practice*", Kogan Page, London, UK, 1991.

[4] M. Rauterberg, O. Strohm, "Work organization and software Development", *Annual Review of Automatic Programming*, vol. 16, 1992, pp. 121-128.

[5] D. Daly, and B. H. Kleiner, "How to motivate problem employees", *Work Study*,vol. 44 (2), 1995, pp. 5-7.

[6] B. Gerhart, "How important are dispositional factors as determinants of job satisfaction? Implications for job design and other personnel programs", *Journal of Applied Psychology*, vol. 72 (3), 1987, pp. 366-373.

[7] F. Herzberg, "One more time: How do you motivate employees?" *Harvard Bus. Rev.*, vol. 65 (5), 1987, pp. 109-120.

[8] R.E. Miles, C.C. Snow, and G. Miles, "TheFuture.org", *Long range planning*, vol. 33 (3), 2000, pp. 300-321.

[9] R. A. Guzzo, and M.W. Dickson, "Teams in organizations: Recent research on performance and effectiveness", *Annual Review of Psychology*, vol. 47, 1997, pp. 307-338.

[10] N.B. Moe, T. Dingsoyr, and T. Dyba, "Understanding Self-Organizing Teams in Agile Software Development", *Australian Software Engineering Conference*, 2008, pp. 76-85.

[11] D. Kumlander, "On using software engineering projects as an additional personnel motivating factor", *WSEAS Transactions on Business and Economics*, vol. 3 (4), 2006, pp. 261-267.

[12] M. Fenton-O'Creevy, "Employee involvement and the middle manager: evidence from a survey of organizations", *J. of Organizational Behavior*, vol. 19 (1), 1998, pp. 67-84.

[13] M. Hoegl, and K.P. Parboteeah, "Autonomy and teamwork in innovative projects", *Human Resource Management*, vol. 45 (1), 2006, pp. 67-79.

[14] C.W. Langfred, "The paradox of self-management: Individual and group autonomy in work groups", *J. of Organizational Behavior*, 2000, vol. 21 (5), 2000, pp. 563-585.

Route Advising in a Dynamic Environment – A High-Tech Approach

M F M Firdhous[1], D L Basnayake[2], K H L Kodithuwakku[3], N K Hatthalla[4], N W Charlin[5], P M R I K Bandara[6]

Faculty of Information Technology
University of Moratuwa
Sri Lanka

[1]firdhous@uom.lk, {[2]dlbs.lk, [3]harshanikhl, [4]nimali.devi, [5]nwcharlin, [6]isuri86}@gmail.com

Abstract* - *Finding the optimal path between two locations in the Colombo city is not a straight forward task, because of the complex road system and the huge traffic jams etc. This paper presents a system to find the optimal driving direction between two locations within the Colombo city, considering road rules (one way, two ways or fully closed in both directions). The system contains three main modules – core module, web module and mobile module, additionally there are two user interfaces one for normal users and the other for administrative users. Both these interfaces can be accessed using a web browser or a GPRS enabled mobile phone. The system is developed based on the Geographic Information System (GIS) technology. GIS is considered as the best option to integrate hardware, software, and data for capturing, managing, analyzing, and displaying all forms of geographically referenced information. The core of the system is MapServer (MS4W) used along with the other supporting technologies such as PostGIS, PostgreSQL, pgRouting, ASP.NET and C#.

Keywords: **Dijkstra's Algorithm, GIS, Route Advising, Shortest Path**

I. INTRODUCTION

The city of Colombo in Sri Lanka has a large floating population. This population enters the city for various purposes like getting their official work done in a government department, visiting relatives and friends, for business purposes, etc., The main reason for this is almost all the government offices like ministries, head offices of all the government departments and private companies are located in Colombo. Also Colombo is the main commercial city in the country. In addition to this floating population, Colombo has a large permanent population too. The people who come to Colombo or travelling inside Colombo like to get to their destination fast. But for most of them, find it very difficult to reach their intended destination on time due to various reasons like the large number of roads within the city, traffic jams, regular closure of roads, accidents, unannounced road closures etc., [1]. Therefore a route advising system will help these travellers immensely by advising them with the shortest distance path from the origin location to the destination. This paper proposes such a system as a solution to the Colombo city's travelling problems.

The proposed system has two interfaces thorough which users can access the system. They are namely the web interface and the mobile interface. The web interface can be used to access the system through any standard web browser running on computer while the mobile interface helps to access the system through a GPRS enabled mobile phone.

This paper is organized into different sections, and each section discusses the different aspect of the project. Section I is the introduction that discusses the problem at hand, Section II discusses the currently available approaches to solve this problem, Section III discusses the technologies adopted in this project, Section IV discusses the Route Advising System design and implementation in brief, Section V presents the evaluation of the system and Section VI is the conclusion and recommendations for future work.

II. ROUTE ADVISING – CURRENT APPROACHES

A numbers of web sites are available that provide detailed Sri Lankan maps with directions to famous places like the ruined cities with historical value, hot sunny beaches, the upcountry etc., for the travellers [2],[3],[4],[5],[6]. The target audience of these web sites is tourists who would like visit these places. The downside of these web sites is that none of these websites contain any information to help a person who likes to get to one place from another place inside a city like Colombo. Also these sites lack information on the status of the road network

T. Sobh, K. Elleithy (eds.), *Innovations in Computing Sciences and Software Engineering*,
DOI 10.1007/978-90-481-9112-3_42, © Springer Science+Business Media B.V. 2010

like if the road is a one-way or two-way road, the road is closed for vehicular traffic, or changes to the status of the road depending on the time of the day etc.,

There are systems like Yahoo Maps, Google Maps or London Map like web based applications that help travellers find driving directions from one location to another in other countries like the USA or UK [7],[8],[9]. The objective of this project is to build a system that can be used find the best or the most appropriate path or driving direction between any two locations in Colombo even under the dynamic conditions like road closures. Also, the system must help the travellers plan their journeys advance depending on the conditions on the intended day and time of travelling. The mobile interface provided with the system makes the system available anywhere anytime as the system can be accessed even with a mobile phone provided that phone has GPRS capability.

III. TECHNOLOGIES USED

Route Advising System is mainly based on GIS – MapServer and the ASP.NET mobile web application projects with GPRS connectivity. In addition to these technologies, postgreSQL with postGIS, pgRouting, C# based on the ASP.NET framework was also used.

Geographic Information System (GIS), captures, stores, analyzes, manages and presents data that is linked to location [10]. Basically a GIS handles geographical information in such a manner, as it integrates hardware, software, and data for capturing, managing, analyzing, and displaying all forms of geographically referenced information [11]. In this project the Open Source GIS software MapServer 5.4 or MS4W is used. MS4W is used to display dynamic spatial maps over the Internet. It allows users to create "geographic image maps", that is, maps that can direct users to content [1]. C# mapscripts were used to extend the capabilities of MS4W to suit the requirements of the project. The back end database is hosted on the Open Source Objcet Relational Database System, PostgreSQL. PostgreSQL runs on almost all known major operating systems and supports advanced features like foreign keys, joins, views, triggers, and stored procedures. PostgreSQL can also store binary large objects, including pictures, sounds or video. The routing capability to PostGIS/PostgreSQL is provided by pgRouting. pgRouting is part of PostLBS that provides core tools for Location Based Services [12]. pgRouting contains three methods to compute the shortest path between the two given points. They are namely, Dijkstra, A* and Shooting Star. In this project Dijkstra was selected as the routing algorithm, due to its advantages over the other two methods including the performance factor of having lower response time [13][14][15]. ASP.NET, the next version of ASP (Active Server Pages), is a programming framework is used to create enterprise-class Web Applications. The .NET framework consists of many class libraries and it can be used with different languages and has the capability of execution in different platforms. It is a very flexible framework and a developing Internet application with the .NET framework is very easy [16]. ASP.NET 3.5 was used in this project.

IV. THE ROUTE ADVISING SYSTEM

The Route Advising System was developed with two types of users, namely admin users and general users.
Admin users have administrative rights to change the system such as selecting a road segment from the road network and updating the schedule information or the direction information such as one-way, both ways or change direction of one-way. The admin users also can insert new records, update records or delete records depending on the requirement.

Any person interested in getting direction information from location to another can log into the system as a general or common user. Anybody can become a general user by registering with the system by providing certain personal information such as username, password, full name, email address, phone number, residential address, closest city etc., The closest city information is used to select the start location automatically, when the user logs in. This start location information can be changed, if the start location is different. A logged in user can access advanced features of the system such as checking the shortest path for a future date, driving directions in text format etc., The data provided by registered users are stored in the system. This information will be used for informing users with improvements to the system, changes in their routine driving directions via email.

It is also possible to get restricted access to information from the system without logging in. These anonymous users can check driving directions between any two locations like registered users. But the result will be restricted to the current time of the day. They will not be able to check the condition of the road network or the driving directions on a future date or time.

The system consists of three main modules and two user sections. The modules are namely the Web Module, the Mobile Module and the Core Module. The main two user sections are Application User Section and the Admin User Section. Figure 1 shows the architecture of the system.

The front end modules, namely the Web Module and the Mobile Module handles the user data and the final presentation of the results, while the Core Module handles the processing the of the data presented and computes the shortest path between the given locations.

In addition to the main module the road status data, user data are stored in a back end relational database. The map information is stored in a map server.

The Core Module is the most important module of the system as this carries out the central management of the entire system. This module contains functionality for connecting to the map server and the database server, and producing the shortest path marked map by using the Dijkstra's algorithm. When a mobile or a web user sends their request with the source and the destination point details in text format, the text points are converted to map coordinates to identify the locations in the map. Then these map coordinates along with the time information are supplied as inputs to this module for further processing.

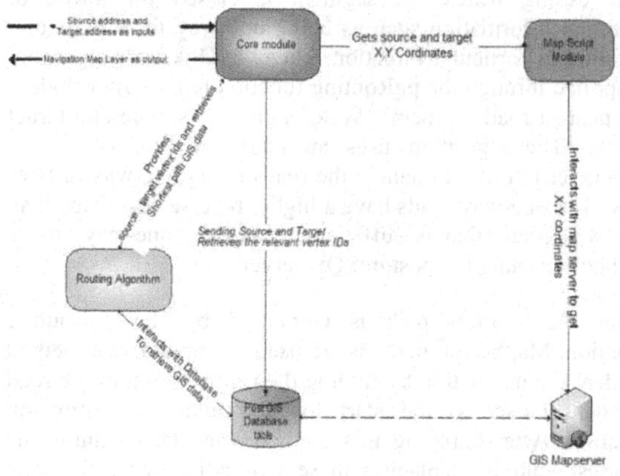

Figure 1: Architecture of the System

The Web Module serves the desktop users. The IIS server is used to host the Web Module. This module collects user input though web forms and forwards it to the Core Module. Also the Web Module is used to forward the final output to the user. Hence, the Web Module works as the input collector as well as the output displayer for the Core Module.

The Mobile Module serves the users who access the system via their GPRS enabled mobile devices. The user who accesses the system via the Mobile Module will be presented with a map on which he can enter the source and destination locations. The input collected from the user using this module will be presented to the Core Module after initial processing for the computation of the shortest path. Finally again the Mobile Module will be used to transfer the resulting map with the shortest path marked back to the user. Figure 2 shows how a interaction takes place with the system depending on if he is logged in or not.

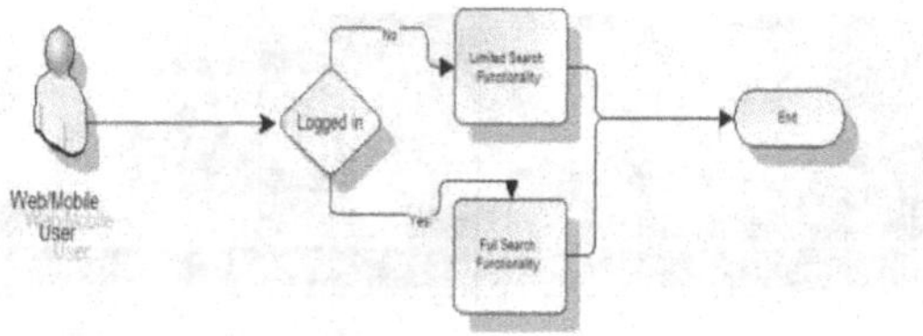

Figure 2: User Interaction with the System

Figure 3 shows the user interface in which a general web based user can access the system. Here the user has not logged onto the system, so he is presented with the advanced search facilities. Figure 4 is the interface presented to the advanced user (logged in user), where the user can supply additional search parameters such as the date and time of intended travel.

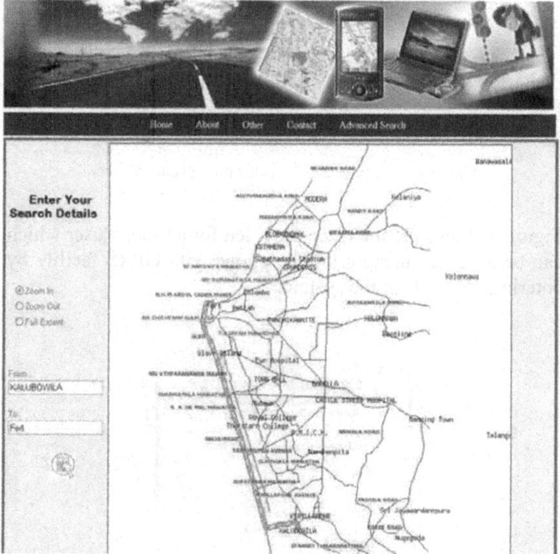

Figure 3: User Interface Provided for Web Users

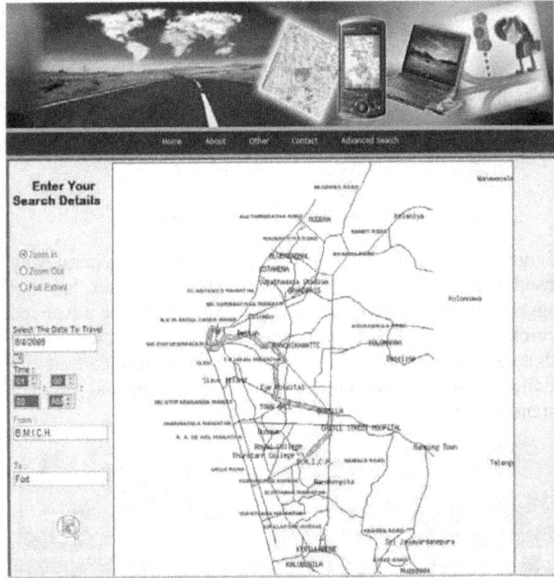

Figure 4: User Interface Provided for Advanced Users

Figure 5 shows the interface provided for a mobile user which can be accessed using a mobile phone with GPRS facility by entering the URL of the system.

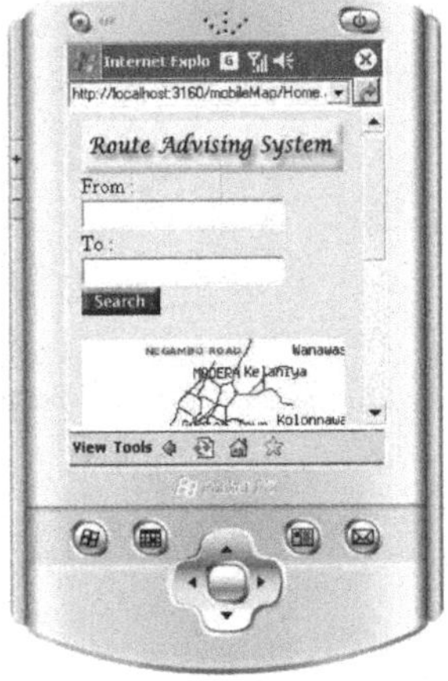

Figure 5: User Interface Provided for Mobile User.

Users input their start and destination location information to the system through the text boxes provided in the web interface and the mobile interface. These inputs are originally in text format and get converted in to point coordinates that is compatible with the map server through the methods implemented using C# map script. The registered users can also perform a future search by giving a future date and time to travel and get the system to predict the best available shortest route for travelling on the particular date and time. If the search is performed without logging in, then the route will be as per the current time. When a search query is entered by a user, the available road network information in the system gets filtered either by the user-entered time or by the system time by connecting to the Schedule Information Table in the postgreSQL database. In the Schedule Information Table, each road segment is associated with information such as the time during which the segment is closed for traffic or direction information such as being one way for a particular duration in particular direction. Then the Dijkstra's algorithm is applied through the pgRouting function library after finding the nearest road segment's vertex points as source and target points. The algorithm uses an added reverse cost as a parameter in order to handle the roads being one-way or two-way. The one-way roads have a higher reverse cost value than two-way roads that is sufficient to support one-way streets without crashing the postgreSQL server.

After the shortest path is computed by the pgRouting function, MapScript methods are used to implement a method to clear the navigation by finding the nearest point of the road segment closer to the start location and the destination location. After applying this method, the query returns the shortest path by replacing these two points with the start vertex and the end vertex of the shortest path that was calculated using the Dijkstra's algorithm. This increases the accuracy of the returned path result. Then the complete path from the start location to the destination location is returned in a raster map image. This image is then delivered to the user via the web module as a web page or via the mobile module to the user's GPRS enabled mobile phone.

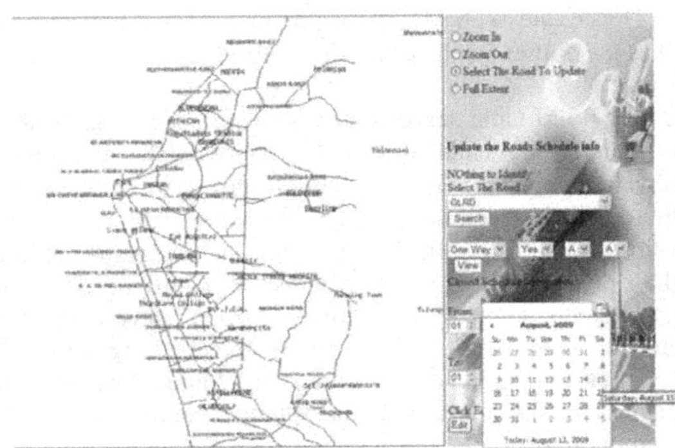

Figure 6: Interface for Administrators

Figure 6 is the Administrator's interface. The administrator can select a road segment and change the parameters of the segment such as the type of road (one-way, two-way or closed). These parameters can be set for a specific period from a given date and time to another date and time. Also the administrator can add or delete a road segment to the system. All the changes made by the administrator are stored in the backend database and available to other users immediately.

V. EVALUATION

This section provides the evaluation of the final system. Figure 7 shows the driving directions from one location (A) in the Colombo city to another location (B). Figure 8 shows the driving directions from (B) to (A), That is the directions are reversed while keeping all the other information same.

From these figures, it can be seen when the driving directions are reversed, it gives two different results. That is due to the reason that the road segment indicated in Figure 7 is one-way in the direction from (B) to (A). So, that segment is not taken into consideration for the computation of the shortest path even though that segment is part of the shortest pat. Other than this segment all the other parts of the road are same in both direction. This is due to the reason that those portions of the road are two-way and available for vehicular traffic in both directions.

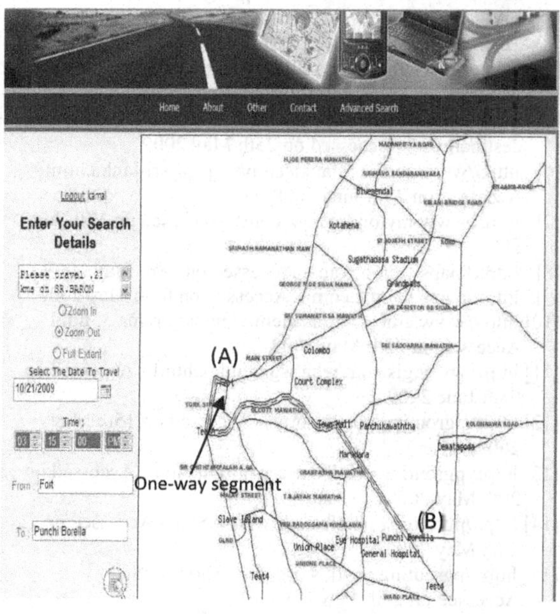

Figure 7: Driving Directions from (A) to (B)

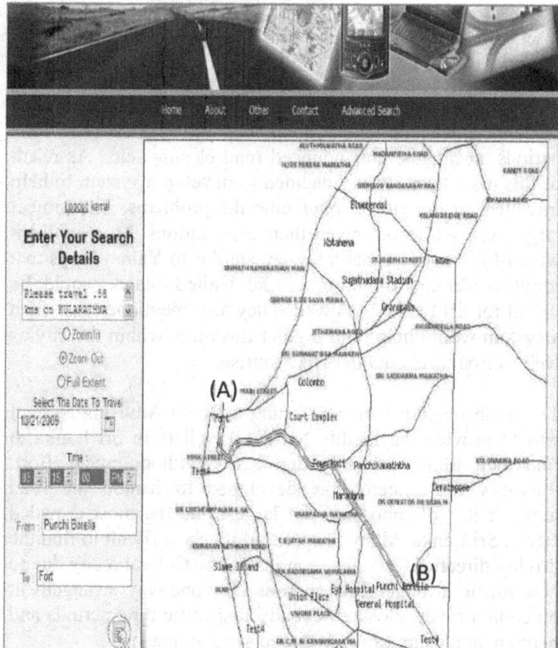

Figure 8: Driving Directions from (B) to (A)

Figure 9 shows the results on a mobile device. The result on the mobile device is restricted compared to the results displayed on a web browser.

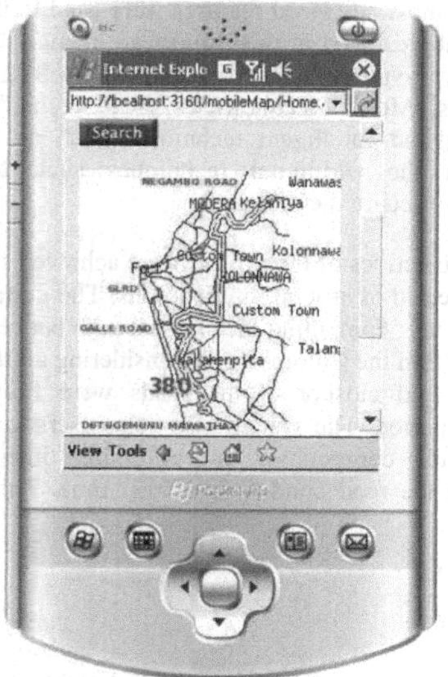

Figure 9: Driving Directions on a Mobile Device

VI. CONCLUSIONS AND FUTURE WORK

Several people were consulted and discussed about the problem they faced when travelling in Sri Lankan cities. Most of them mentioned about the large number of roads within the city, traffic jams, closure roads during a specific time periods, accidents, unannounced road closures etc., As result of this discussion, it was decided to develop a system to help travellers in the city to overcome the problems. The project target was set according to their expectations. Most of them were of the opinion that a system similar to Yahoo Maps that provides driving direction in the United States would be useful for Sri Lankans as well. They also mentioned that such a system would help both regular travellers within the city as well as first time travellers like tourists.

The main objective of developing a Route Advising System was to provide the facility for the travellers in Sri Lanka to find their routes correctly and easily without much effort. Presently the system was developed to handle the road network in Colombo city, the largest and the most crowded city in Sri Lanka. Many people find it very difficult to find the driving directions to a location inside the Colombo city due to new traffic arrangements such as new one-way arrangement on certain roads, closure of roads at specific time periods and permanent closure of roads due to security reasons.

The web and the mobile were selected the platforms to implement this project as the penetration of these technologies is very high within the Sri Lankan population especially within main cities.

In order to make the system user friendly while keeping cost of development at the lowest, open source technologies that provide the most advanced features were used in this project. The technologies used in this project are namely Geographic Information System technologies, PostgreSQL database technologies, Mobile technologies, Web technologies, and Networking and Intelligent techniques such as Algorithms along with the additional techniques such as security techniques to secure the system.

The main objectives of the project were achieved successfully in a short period of around three months. The initial objective of the project of computing the shortest path between any two locations within the Colombo city considering all the one-way restrictions and closure of the roads were fully achieved during this period. The system also helps users to carry out a shortest path computation at a future time and date considering the road conditions at that time. This helps the users to plan their travel well in advance. This feature is missing in systems like Yahoo Maps where the search can only be carried out at present conditions as date and time of travels cannot be entered as a travel parameter.

As future work, it is proposed to extend the system to other major cities in Sri Lanka, finally covering the entire island. It is also proposed to enhance the system by including additional information like the public places like hospitals, schools, restaurants, cinemas etc.,

It is also proposed to include the time to travel between two locations as a parameter to enhance the system as what is more useful for the user would be the shortest time to travel between two locations rather than the physically shortest path between the locations. This would be very useful in cities like Colombo where traffic congestion is very high.

REFERENCES

[1] http://www.dailynews.lk/2006/02/18/fea02.asp - Accessed on 07th June 2009

[2] http://beijing.asiaxpat.com/travel/destinations/ sri-lanka/ - Accessed on 08th May 2009

[3] http://ocw.mit.edu/NR/rdonlyres/Electrical-Engineering-and-Computer-Science/6-871Spring-2005/468C8A59-EAC8-4E7D-9DB9-AA4C43FC8096/0/watugala _fin_rep.pdf - Accessed on 15th May 2009

[4] http://www.world66.com/asia/southasia/ srilanka - Accessed on 20th June 2009

[5] http://travel.mapsofworld.com/sri-lanka/sri-lanka-tourist-destinations/ - Accessed on 25th May 2009

[6] http://www.scenicsrilanka.com/map-of-sri-lanka.html - Accessed on 20th June 2009

[7] http://www.mylondonmap.com - Accessed on 12th June 2009

[8] http://maps.yahoo.com – Accessed on 08th May 2009.

[9] http://maps.google.com – Accessed on 08th May 2009

[10] http://www.cmb.ac.lk/academic/medicine/ma 3. html - Accessed on 25th May 2009

[11] http://www.gis.com/whatisgis/index.html - Accessed on 08th June 2009

[12] http://pgrouting.postlbs.org/ - Accessed on 15th May 2009

[13] http://pgrouting.postlbs.org/wiki/Dijkstra - Accessed on 20th May 2009

[14] http://pgrouting.postlbs.org/wiki/AStar - Accessed on 20th May 2009

[15] http://pgrouting.postlbs.org/wiki/ShootingStar - Accessed on 20th May 2009

[16] http://www.startvbdotnet.com/aspsite/asp/ -Accessed on 20th June 2009

Building Security System Based on Grid Computing To Convert and Store Media Files

Hieu Nguyen Trung, Duy Nguyen, Tan Dang Cao

Department of Network and Telecom
Faculty of Information Technology, University of Sciences HCMC
{nthieu@fit.hcmus.edu.vn, nguyenduy0606@yahoo.com, cdtan@fit.hcmus.edu.vn}

Abstract-In the recent years, Grid Computing (GC) has made big steps in development, contributing to solve practical problems which need large store capacity and computing performance. This paper introduces an approach to integrate the security mechanisms, Grid Security Infrastructure (GSI) of the open source Globus Toolkit 4.0.6 (GT4) into an application for storing, format converting and playing online media files, based on the GC.

Keywords: Grid Computing, Grid Security, Video/Media Format Conversion, Grids Video System.

I. INTRODUCTION

The trend to use large media file with multiple format is increasing. In fact, the business organizations and individuals using format converting to reduce storage size or to a format most used. Some applications of Government, Security, and Defense ... may need high security media files and only people with special permission could access, change the formats and play them. Currently there are many systems for the converting media file formats. They run on a single machine but take quite a long time. To solve the problem we have set up a system which takes advantage of idle computers allowing individuals and organizations to upload, convert media file formats and play them online via web interface if they have permissions.

To build a strong service, capable of hosting large media files, with high performance and security, the Grid Computing (GC) was selected. The GC based system will gain the benefits which are inheriting from GC technology.

High security mechanisms to ensure authentication, permission (for different groups and users) and security communications.

Grid distributed storage for large files.

The high performance processing based on distributed and parallel processing of GC.

This article offers a solution to integrate the security mechanisms of GSI to a specific application to store, convert media file formats and play online. The system (named as GridMediaSystem) was implemented in Grid Lab, Department of Network and Telecom, Faculty of Information Technology, University of Sciences, HCM City.

II. SECURITY IN GRID APPLICATIONS

A. Security issues with an Grid application

There are two ways to execute an Grid application. In the first way the request to execute a Grid application comes from a Grid node (called local host) and in the second one, the request comes from a non-Grid node (called remote host). Although the request could come from local or remote host, it must be requested by certain user and the Grid application must start at a Grid node (called Start Node). The Start Node splits the media file into small blocks and then distributed them to other nodes in the Grid, including it. Each node will perform data processing and send result back to the Start Node to form the final result and returned it to the user. Related security issues are following.

Start Node must be authenticated to the Grid environment and will be issued a Certificate (called the Host Certificate - signed by the CA) to verify it as a node in the Grid.

User who submits jobs must be authenticated before participating in the Grid and issued a Certificate (called the User Certificate - signed by the CA). On the other hand the user must have a certificate (Proxy Credential) which delegates himself to work in all Grid nodes without need to submit user certificate every time when his job enters to a new Grid node.

The job and result transfer between Grid nodes is safety and accuracy by GridFTP protocol.

General security solution of the Grid application:

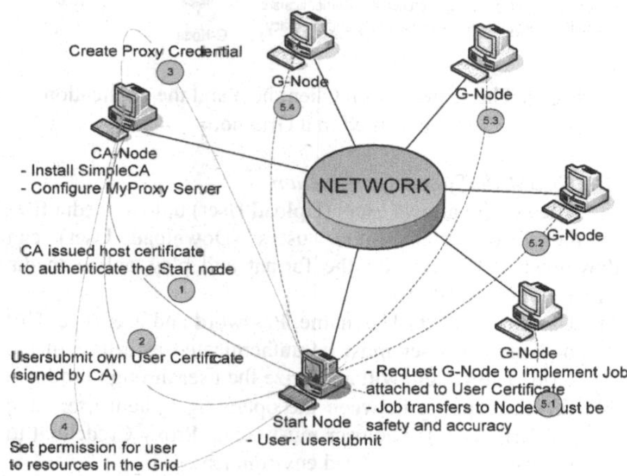

Fig. 1: The request and application execution in Local host (Start Node)

T. Sobh, K. Elleithy (eds.), *Innovations in Computing Sciences and Software Engineering*,
DOI 10.1007/978-90-481-9112-3_43, © Springer Science+Business Media B.V. 2010

The application execution in Local host:

1) Grid administrator must create a new account for a user, called submit-user
2) To work on Start Node as a Grid user the submit-user need to validate as a user of Grid.
3) Submit-user can execute the application at the local or send request and jobs to the remote nodes, then gets results back to form final result

Application execution in Remote host:

1) The web application GridMediaSystem is installed in a Grid node.
2) Remote user through web browser to register himself and executes functions of GridMediaSystem: submit jobs and get results returned back.
3) Grid Admin will make permission policy for registered users.

The application execution at remote host:

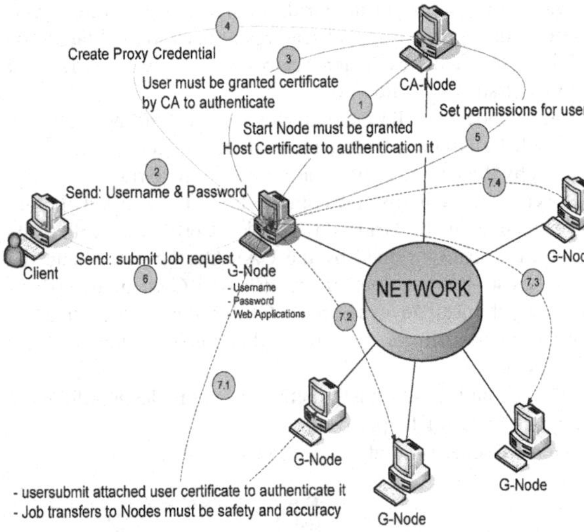

Fig. 2. The request from Client host and the application executed in a Grid node

B. *GridMediaSystem Introduction*

The system allows users (Upload User) upload media files to the Grid system, other users (Download User) can download and/or convert the format and play online media file. Detail is as followed:

1) Users register for Username, Password and user type: VIP or Normal). User must be authenticated as a user of the Grid. The system will authorize the user through Gridmap file (a mapping between the operating system users and the Grid users). The user must create Proxy Credential to represent him on the Grid environment.
2) After successful registration, the users through the web interface to log into the system and use the services of the application.
3) The Upload/Download User via the web interface stores converts or downloads to play media files remotely to/from the Grid system if he has related right.

Application is built and deployed on the GT4, using API library of COG Kit 4.1.2 to provide interaction with GSI.

Application covers three major areas of the GC: Grid Security, Compute Grid and Data Grid.

To implement above functions, the following components are used:

1) MyProxy: to store the user's proxy (called Proxy Credential). When in need, a Node contact with MyProxy to receive user's Proxy Credential to authenticate, authorize the user to work in the Grid. The advantage of MyProxy is:
   - ✓ The user can stay anywhere and log into the GridMediaSystem.
   - ✓ Reduce the number of certificate transmission between nodes.
   - ✓ Myproxy supports both Single-Sign-On and Delegation.
2) Gridmap file: to manage the user rights on grid resources.
3) Gsiftp: to secure transmission of some blocks of media files to a Grid node.

C. *Detail functions*

Register:

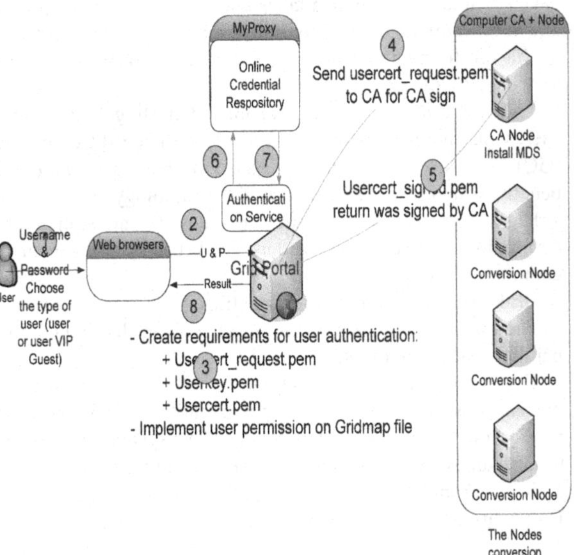

Fig. 3. Function register

Upload:

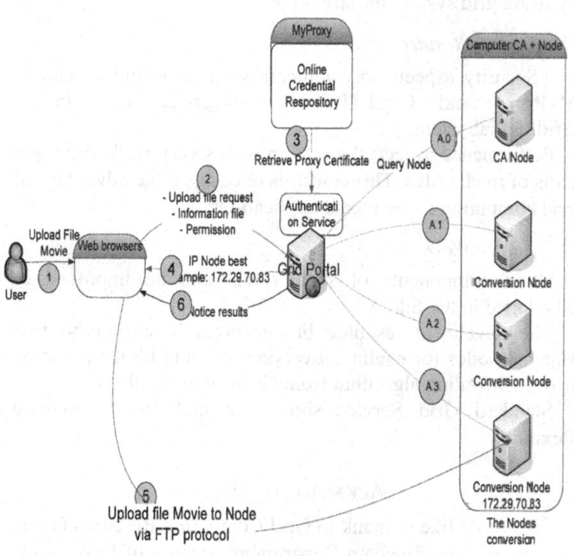

Fig. 4. Function upload

Media files will be uploaded to the best node, through best node selection algorithm based on parameters such as free CPU, RAM, HDD..., If upload process was successful, the system will return a logic link to user and then user can convert, download and play media files online.

Download:

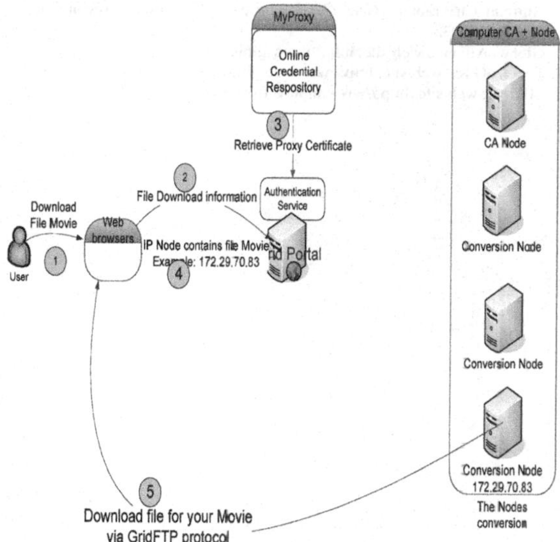

Fig. 5. Function download

When user sends request to download a media file or play online from above logical link, the system checks the validity of this link, and check permission for this user. If user has permission, user can convert, download and play media file online.

Convert:

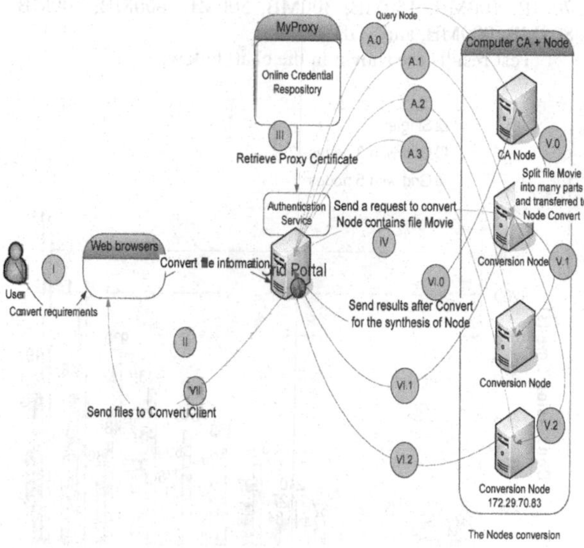

Fig. 6. Function Convert

Users will select the file movie and output format which he wants to convert, then sends the request to the system. The system will check user's rights to convert movie files or not. If user has rights, the system will split media files into a number of parts according to available nodes.

By Network Weather Service (NWS), the client can gather useful information like computational capabilities, CPU loading, number of available nodes, etc. Then, GridMediaSystem submits jobs (divided parts of media files) to conversion nodes by using GridFTP.

After that, each conversion node will convert and return its part to Start Node to be merged. Converted file will be returned to the user via the logic link on the web interface

III. EXPERIMENT ENVIRONTMENT

A. Experiment Grid Environment

Test system was built in Grid Lab of Network and Telecom Department, Faculty of Information Technology, University of Sciences The system has 6 Linux PCs (CPU Intel Core 2 dual 2.66GB, 2GB RAM, 60GB HDD) installed middleware GT4 as follows:

- 1 PC as CA Node: for Authenticating hosts and users on the Grid.
- 5 PCs as Computing Nodes: for converting and storing.

B. Performance Results

We have tested convert function on three different systems:

1) A single system
2) Grid system consists of three conversion nodes.
3) Grid system consists of five conversion nodes

Media file sizes are following: 5MB, 10MB, 50MB, 70MB, 100MB, 150MB, 300MB, 500MB, 600MB, 700MB, 800MB, 900MB, and 1GB.

Test results are shown in the chart below:

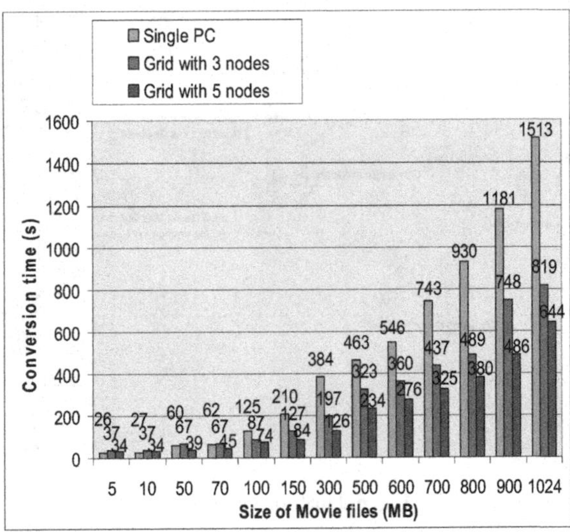

Fig. 7. Comparison of conversion time from AVI to WMV of single PC and grid systems

Conversion time of Media files on grid system with small size is longer than on single PC, because media files must be split, converted and merged. In addition, system must authenticate, transfer the media parts to conversion nodes, receive and merge results after converting. Other hand, the conversion time will be significantly reduced by using grid system for larger parts

C. Testing Results

Security aspect: host authentication, user authentication, MyProxy and GridFTP were integrated well in to GridMediaSystem.

Performance aspect: the system works very well with large parts of media files. This confirms once again the advantage of grid computing in the media applications

D. Future Work

Many components of system that can be improved or developed in the future:

The developed resource broker takes long time to find suitable nodes for media conversion. It could be improved by using scheduling algorithm from Gridway or Gridbus.

Standard Grid Service should be included to increase flexibility

ACKNOWLEDGMENT

We would like to thank to Grid Computing Research Group at Network and Telecom Department, Faculty of Information Technology, University of Sciences, HCM City for their good advices and technical support.

REFERENCES

[1] Bart Jacob, Michael Brown, Kentaro Fukui, Nihar Trivedi, "*Introduction to Grid Computing*", Redbooks, IBM Corp, 12/2005.
[2] Jim Basney, *Using the MyProxy Online Credential Repository",* National Center for Supercomputing Applications University of Illinois.
[3] Bart Jacob, Luis Ferreira, Norbert Bieberstein, Candice Gilzean, JeanYves Girard, Roman Strachowski, Seong (Steve) Yu, *Enabling Applications for Grid Computing with Globus*, Redbooks, IBM Corp, 06/2003.
[4] Anirban Chakrabarti, *Grid Computing Security*, Infosys Technologies Limited, 2007.
[5] Globus Alliance web site, http://www.globus.org.
[6] Java CoG Kit web site, http://www.Cogkit.org/release/4_1_2.
[7] MPlayer web site, http://www.mplayerhq.hu.

A Tool Supporting C code Parallelization

Ilona Bluemke, Joanna Fugas
Institute of Computer Science, Warsaw University of Technology
Nowowiejska 15/19, 00-665 Warsaw, Poland
I.Bluemke@ii.pw.edu.pl

Abstract - **In this paper a tool, called ParaGraph, supporting C code parallelization is presented. ParaGraph is a plug-in in Eclipse IDE and enables manual and automatic parallelization. A parallelizing compiler inserts automatically OpenMP directives into the outputted source code. OpenMP directives can be also manually inserted by a programmer. ParaGraph shows C code after parallelization. Visualization of parallelized code can be used to understand the rules and constraints of parallelization and to tune the parallelized code as well.**

I. INTRODUCTION

Parallel programming has been attracting programmers and researchers attention for many years. At the beginning parallel code was simultaneously executed on processors of a supercomputer. Currently many cores are present even in modern PC so they can be used to run parallel code as well. Sequential program code can be parallelized and simultaneously executed on multiple cores. Parallelization is a very difficult task and may cause many runtime errors so some methods and tools facilitating this process are necessary. Parallel code can be prepared by a programmer or automatically by some compilers. As both approaches have advantages and disadvantages, some of them are mentioned in section II, it seems that a tool enabling for manual and automatic parallelization can be very useful in the production of fast programs. Many tools have been built to support automatic or/and manual code parallelization. SUIF Explorer [1] combines static and dynamic compiler analysis with indications given by programmer. In compiler of Fortran 77 Polaris [2] directives introduced by user are used in the process of translating code into parallel dialect of Fortran. ParaWise [3] is able to generate parallel code for distributed or for multiprocessor system. HTGviz [4] also enables manual and compiler parallelization. The result is a program in the same source language with inserted OpenMP directives. Additionally visualization tool shows the static control flow graph of the program, with data dependences.

At the Institute of Computer Science Warsaw University of Technology a tool, called ParaGraph, was designed and implemented. In ParaGraph code in C programming language can be manually, as well as automatically, parallelized and presented in a graphical form. To our best knowledge there are no similar tools dedicated to C programming language. Usually programmers have difficulties writing code which can be highly parallelizable so code visualization may be very useful in teaching how to built easily parallelizable program. ParaGraph was designed as a tool which can be used in compiler construction course. The presence of back-end information was identified by Binkley et al. in Feedback compiler [5] as very important in teaching compiler construction. ParaGraph is platform independent, it is a plug-in in Eclipse IDE.

The organization of this paper is as follows. The main approaches to parallelization are briefly presented in section II. Section III contains the description of ParaGraph. In section IV examples showing the usage of our tool and its advantages are given. Section V contains some conclusions.

II. CODE PARALLELIZATION

Code of a program can be parallelized automatically by a parallelizing compiler or a programmer can identify all parallelizable fragments and implement the parallel code. OpenMP [6] is an environment in which programmer is able to decide where to insert parallelizing directives indicating the parallel code. The compiler then uses platform specific mechanisms to make the program executable in parallel on multiple processors. Programmer, knowing the implemented algorithm, can precisely indicate code suitable for parallelization and accelerate the execution of the algorithm. On the other hand an inexperienced programmer can slow down the execution of a program, make it unstable or even introduce some races.

A parallelizing compiler works automatically, is not driven by user, so the parallelization is very limited. Compilers, which are independent of the platform, usually perform only static analysis and are able to efficiently parallelize loops. If in a loop there are no data dependences between loop iterations, it can be easily parallelized. Otherwise a synchronization of data is needed thus decreasing the efficiency of generated program. Furthermore, loops which are parallelized automatically usually contain only few instructions, so the parallelization granularity is fine and the speedup in execution time is not very convincing.

Finding data dependence constraints is the basic step in detecting loop level parallelism in a program [7]. Briefly, the data dependence determines whether two references to the same array within a nest of loops may reference to the

T. Sobh, K. Elleithy (eds.), *Innovations in Computing Sciences and Software Engineering*,
DOI 10.1007/978-90-481-9112-3_44,

same element of that array. Many algorithms have been proposed to solve the problem by analyzing the linear equations formed by a pair of array references. Data dependence test, which is very important in automatic parallelization, is applied to array accesses in a loop. Compiler can only determine dependences between a pair of affine (linear) accesses. Examples of affine and non affine accesses are given in listing 1.

```
for( i = 0; i<N; ++i)
{
for( j = 0; j<N; ++j)
{
Z[i];       //affine: outer loop index
Z[i+j+10]; //affine: outer index +
                    inner + constant
Z[0];       //affine: constant
Z[3*j]; //affine: index multiplied
                    by a constant
Z[i*j]; //non-affine: multiplication
}
}
```

Listing 1 Examples of affine and non-affine subscripts

Type of access affine/not affine in a program depends on the code style and data structures. If programmer chooses a structure to which an access has to be affine, the compiler will not be able to compute the dependences and will have to assume that the synchronization exists. Viitanen and Hamalainen in [8] show that data dependence tests may fail to find all dependences in a program. Finding all data dependences in affine accesses is NP-complete problem. Despite some limitations, auto parallelization can speed up many programs but some effort is necessary to be able to write programs suitable for parallelization.

Giordano and Funari proposed in [4] a tool called HTGviz which combines two methods of parallelization. The sequential code is parallelized automatically by a compiler. The result of compilation is a program in the same source language with inserted OpenMP directives. A visualization tool shows the static control flow graph of the program, with data dependences that were found by the compiler. This graph can help the programmer to tune the code with his own parallelizing directives. The advantages of manual and automatic parallelization are combined so the code can be made more efficient.

We propose a tool – ParaGraph – taking advantages of both parallelization approaches and useful in studying how to prepare a highly parallelizable program. ParaGraph, presented in section III, is dedicated to code in C programming language and works in Eclipse environment. ParaGraph was designed for didactic purposes so more emphasis was put on back-end information than the efficiency of the parallelized code.

ParaGraph works as an Eclipse plug-in, precisely it is an additional element of the well-known plug-in CDT (C/C++ Development Tool) [9]. The idea of ParaGraph operation is presented in figure 1. An external compiler is used to generate parallelized code and a file containing the control flow graph of compiled program. The graph is shown in a graphical editor, with textual information accessible in "properties view" (Fig. 4). A direct link from blocks on the graph, to the source code after parallelization, is kept to help the programmer access the fragment of code, which seems interesting to her/him.

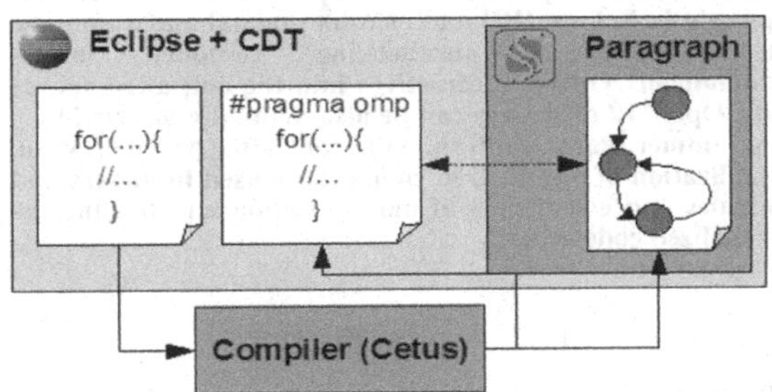

Fig.1 ParaGraph an Eclipse plug-in

The reasons to implement ParaGraph as an Eclipse/CDT plug-in are following:

1. Eclipse is very popular.
2. There was no need to implement editor or other tools.
3. If a programmer has program already in CDT he has only to create another project for the source files generated by the parallelizing compiler, and point the original code as an input to ParaGraph.
4. ParaGraph uses API called GEF (Graphic Editing Framework, part of Eclipse project). This meant less effort to create visualization because GEF library is dedicated to create graphical editors and views.
5. The implementation of association between graph and source code was very simple to implement with the use of CDT parser.

Programmer may use other Eclipse plug-ins to improve parallelization, for example Parallel Tools Platform (PTP) [10]. This plug-in contains tools for parallel environments like OpenMP, MPI, a parallel debugger and performance analyzing tools. A dynamic analyzer, which is also included in PTP, can also decrease the execution time of the program. As was proved by Blume et al. in [2] after static parallelization it is possible to add some improvements at runtime.

A. Compiler

ParaGraph is able to work with any compiler, which can generate code with OpenMP and a control-flow graph. Currently, it uses an open-source compiler (fig.1) named Cetus [11]. Cetus was created for research purposes at Purdue University School of Electrical and Computer Engineering. It is intended to *source-to-source* processing. It currently supports ANSI C and is under development to support C++. Cetus is written in Java in a very intuitive way, so it is easy to understand and easy to modify. Current release of Cetus is able to parallelize certain types of loops and insert "*omp parallel for*" directives. We had to implement generation of control flow and data dependence on the same graph (in *dot* format) to use Cetus in ParaGraph.

Following features of Cetus are used in ParaGraph:

1. privatization (which variable in a loop is private for each iteration) and reduction (which variable in a loop is a result of the same computation that all iterations perform)
2. data dependence testing with Banerjee-Wolfe inequalities [12] and data dependence graph construction,
3. generation of OpenMP directives (`#pragma omp parallel for`),
4. control flow graph drawing.

A source-to-source compiler enables manual and automatic parallelization. The visualization is used to show the result and to learn how to write a suitable, parallelizable code. Additionally, some information about the loops is displayed to point out the reasons why a loop could not be parallelized. ParaGraph may be used as a tool for increasing efficiency of parallelization. The main components of ParaGraph and the activities executed by a user and compiler are shown in figure 2.

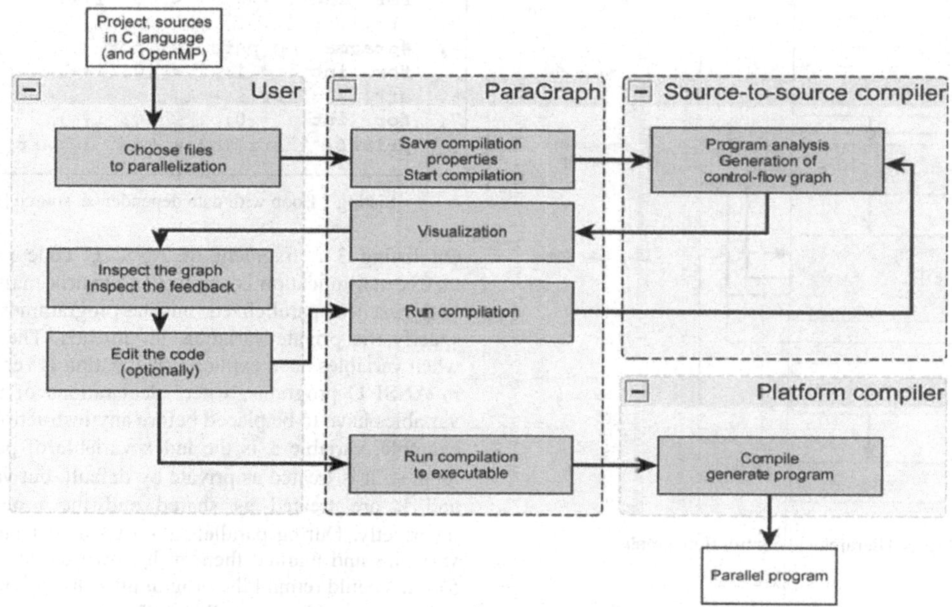

Fig. 2. ParaGraph – main components and parallelizing process

B. *User interface*

The process of building an Eclipse plug-in consists of creating new functionalities in extension points defined in the IDE. In ParaGraph, the extensions were used to create the following elements:

- `Graphical Editor` which display the control flow graph,
- `Outline view` which enables searching for a certain function on the graph,
- `Properties view`, which shows back-end information about loops and data dependences.

The editor is written in the model-view-controller (MVC) pattern, required by GEF. MVC enables creating multiple views for one model, in our software the view is a graph. The editor allows a user to change visual properties of the graph's element. User is not able to edit the graph because changes in the graph structure should impose changes in the source code.

The `Properties View` (lower right part of Fig.4) provides auxiliary information about program parallelization. When user selects non parallelizable loop on the graph the reason why it could not be parallelized is displayed. For data dependency some additional information are also available. Such information will help to understand why the code was or was not parallelized. thrown exception can be seen.

C. *Control Flow graph*

One of the key functionalities in ParaGraph is the visualization of control flow graph of the program (described in [7]), with data dependence edges. Only when these two relations appear on one graph, a programmer may notice the necessity of data synchronization or the possibility of a hazard. The control flow graph, presented on figure 3, consists of following elements:

- a simple node (basic block), contains a sequence of simple instructions,
- a compound node which visualizes a loop, an enclosing directive or a function call,
- a control flow edge, represents the precedence relation between nodes in a program,
- a data dependence edge, which connects two simple nodes which contain two dependent array accesses.

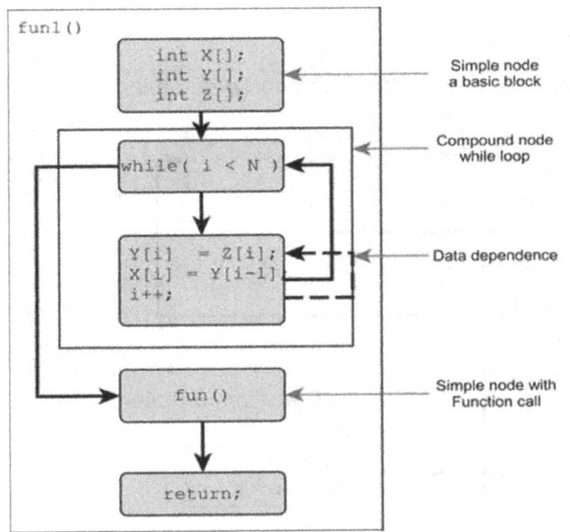

Fig. 3. Hierarchical control flow graph

III. EXAMPLES

Several experiments were conducted to find out if ParaGraph is really a support for manual and automatic parallelization and helps revealing errors in parallelization. We assumed that the code which was given to ParaGraph was written by an inexperienced programmer, who wanted to parallelize his/her program. We used the code from OpenMP traps for C++ developers and converted it into ANSI C (listing 2). Programmer wanted to accelerate the loop operations. Unfortunately, he/she did not notice, that the subscript at line 6 contains a data dependence which forbids parallelization with `#pragma omp for` directive. After compilation in ParaGraph, the programmer can see a graph, on which the dependence is marked with a dashed arrow (figure 4). Additionally, the feedback from Cetus indicates a ">" direction of the dependence and marks the loop as not applicable for parallelization. Such information can help the programmer in realizing that he/she made a mistake and that program will not produce a correct result. It can be seen that the loop cannot be parallelized in the way the programmer suggested. Additionally, ParaGraph parallelized the first loop, which was not indicated for parallelization by the programmer.

```
1. int arr[10];
2. for (int i = 0; i < 10; i++)
3. arr[i] = i;
4. #pragma omp parallel for
5. for (int i = 1; i < 10; i++)
6. arr[i] = arr[i - 1];
7. for (int i = 0; i < 10; i++)
8. printf("\narr[%d] = %d", i, arr[i])
```

Listing 2 Loop with data dependence, source [13]

On listing 3 a fragment of ANSI C code performing matrix multiplication is shown. The matrix multiplication loop nest was parallelized, but the programmer forgot to specify the private variables for threads. The situation, when variables need explicit privatization is very frequent in ANSI C programs, where declarations of temporary variables have to be placed before any instructions. In this example, variable `i` is the index variable of parallelized loop, so it is treated as private by default, but variables `j` and `k` are treated as shared and the program runs incorrectly. During parallelization Cetus detected private variables and marked them in his own directives (figure 5). This could remind the programmer that privatization is necessary for these variables. The directive "`#pragma cetus private(i, j, k)`" – fig 5. was inserted by Cetus compiler.

The above simple examples show, that ParaGraph can be very helpful in code parallelization. We also conducted several experiments measuring the effectiveness of code manually and automatically parallelized, some results are presented in [14]. The best results were obtained when parallelization combined both methods.

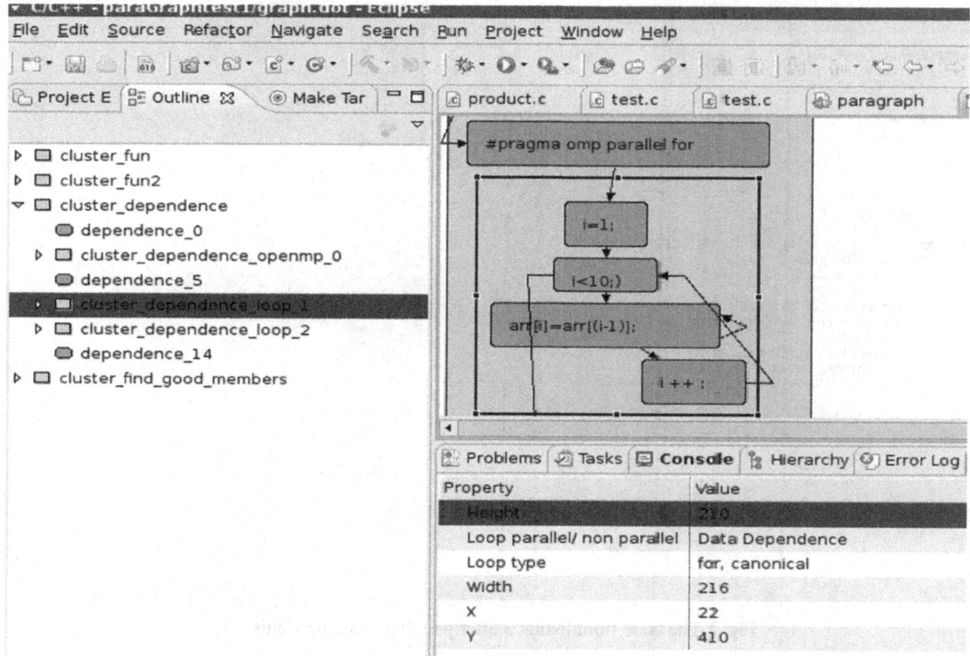

Fig.4 Control flow graph for code from listing 2

```
int matrix_mult (const matrix * A, const matrix * B, matrix * C)
{
        if (A->columns != B->rows || A->rows != C->rows ||
                B->columns != C->columns)
        {
                return ERROR; //error
        }
        else
        {
        double a, b;
        double temp=0;
        int i, j, k;
        #pragma omp parallel for firstprivate(temp)
                for (i = 1; i <= C->rows; i++)
                {
                        for (j = 1; j <= C->columns; j++)
                        {
                                for (k = 1; k <= A->columns; k++)
                                {
                                temp += MATRIX_GET (A, i, k)*MATRIX_GET (B, k, j);
                                }
                        MATRIX_SET (C, i, j, temp);
                        temp=0;
                        }
                }
        return SUCCESS;
        }
}
```

Listing 3 Code for matrix multiplication

```
product.c | test.c | *test.c | paragraph | graph.dot

int matrix_mult(const matrix * A, const matrix * B, matrix * C) {
    if ((((A->columns != B->rows) || (A->rows != C->rows)) || (B->columns
            != C->columns)))
    {
        return 1;
        //error
    }
    else
    {
        double a, b;
        double temp = 0;
        int i, j, k;
        #pragma omp parallel for firstprivate(temp)
        #pragma cetus private(i, j, k)
        for (i = 1; i <= C->rows; i++)
        {
            #pragma cetus private(j, k)
            for (j = 1; j <= C->columns; j++)
            {
                #pragma cetus private(k)
                #pragma cetus reduction(+: temp)
                for (k = 1; k <= A->columns; k++)
                {
                    temp += (A->data[(i - 1)][(k - 1)] * B->data[(k - 1)][(j
                            - 1)]);
                }
                C->data[(i - 1)][(j - 1)] = temp;
                temp = 0;
            }
        }
        return 0;
    }
}
```

Fig. 5 The code from listing 3 after parallelization by Cetus

IV. CONCLUSIONS

In this paper we presented ParaGraph, an Eclipse plug-in, designed and implemented at the Institute of Computer Science Warsaw University of Technology, supporting automatic and manual parallelization of C code. To our best knowledge there are no similar tools dedicated to C programming language. By supporting visualization of code after parallelization, we provide opportunities to understand the use of OpenMP directives and change the program so that it can be easily parallelized. Simple examples given in section III show, that our tool is helpful in C code parallelization, reveals errors. Although ParaGraph was designed for didactic purpose, some experiments conducted by us and presented in [14] show, that the execution of a program after parallelization is visibly faster. An interesting and important study would be to apply ParaGraph in an industry project, to evaluate the benefits of parallel code. We intend also to improve the data dependency analysis and add intra-procedural analysis. The architecture of ParaGraph (fig.1) enables for very simple adaptation to other programming languages. Replacing Cetus C compiler with other source to source parallelizing compiler we can obtain a tool supporting parallelization of other languages.

REFERENCES

[1] S. Moon, B. So, M. W. Hall, "Evaluating Automatic Parallelization in SUIF", *IEEE Transactions on Parallel and Distributed Systems*, vol. 11, no 1 January 2000, pp 36-49

[2] B. Blume et al. "Restructuring Programs for High-speed Computers with Polaris", *International Conference on Parallel Processing Workshop*, 1996, pp.149-161

[3] ParaWise http://www.parallelsp.com/parawise.htm

[4] M. Giordano, M. Funari, "HTGviz, A Graphic Tool for the Synthesis of Automatic and User–Driven Program Parallelization in the Compilation Proce", *LNCS*; vol. 1615, 1999, pp.312 – 319

[5] D. Binkley et. al. "The FeedBack Compile", in: 6th International Workshop on Program Comprehension, *IEEE Computer Society*, USA, 1998, pp.198 – 206

[6] OpenMP specification, http://www.openmp.org/mp-documents/spec30.pdf

[7] A. V. Aho, M. Lam, R Sethi, J. Ullman, *Compilers: Principles, Techniques, Methods And Tools*, Second Edition, Addison Wesley, 2007, chapters 10-12

[8] M. Viitanen, T. D. Hämäläine, "Comparison of Data Dependence Analysis Tests", in *Third International Workshop on Systems, Architectures, Modeling, and Simulation*, 2003, pp. 114-119

[9] CDT - Eclipse C/C++ Development Tool: http://www.eclipse.org/cdt/

[10] Parallel Tools Platform, http://www.eclipse.org/ptp/

[11] Cetus Project, http://arden.ecn.purdue.edu/cetus/public/index.html

[12] U. Banerejee, et. all., "Automatic program parallelization", *Proceedings of the IEEE*, vol. 81, no 2, February 1993, pp. 211-243

[13] OpenMP traps for C++ developers, http://www.codeproject.com/KB/cpp/32_OpenMP_traps

[14] I. Bluemke, J. Chojecka: "Visualization of C code after parallelization" in: *Advances in Web-Age Information Systems*", part 3, chapter 17, Oficyna Wydawnicza Politechniki Wrocławskiej, ISBN 978-83-7493-479-4, 2009, pp. 191-200

Extending OpenMP for Agent Based DSM on GRID

Mahdi S. Haghighi, M. Hadi Zahedi, Mustafa Ghazizadeh A and Farnad Ahangary
Computer Department, Faculty of Engineering
Ferdowsi University of Mashhad, Mashhad, Iran
Haghighi@ieee.org, Zahedi@ieee.org, Mo_gh@stu-mail.um.ac.ir and ahangary@um.ac.ir

Abstract—This paper discusses some of the salient issues involved in implementing the illusion of a shared-memory programming model across a group of distributed memory processors from a cluster through to an entire GRID. This illusion can be provided by a distributed shared memory (DSM) system implemented by using autonomous agents.
Mechanisms that have the potential to increase the performance by omitting consistency latency intra site messages and data transfers are highlighted.
In this paper we describe the overall design/architecture of a prototype system, AOMPG which integrates DSM and Agent paradigms and may be the target of an OpenMP compiler. Our goal is to apply this to GRID Applications.

Keywords— Distributed shared memory; AOMPG; Agent; GRID.

I. Introduction

Development of a standard programming methodology to write efficient programs for all classes of parallel machines is one of the main purpose of parallel software research. In this way training programmers, porting of programs would be easy, and, in general, it would reduce the burden of adopting parallel computing.

So far the most popular way of programming parallel machines, especially clusters and distributed memory machines in general, is to write SPMD (Single Program Multiple Data) programs and use Message-Passing Interface (MPI) library routines [4] for communication and synchronization. The second approach, which dominates when the target machine is a Symmetric Multiprocessor (SMP) with a few processors, is to use thread libraries or OpenMP [3] to write parallel programs assuming a shared memory model. OpenMP resembles HPF because of its reliance on directives. However, the OpenMP standard differs from HPF in that it deals almost exclusively with control flow and synchronization and has practically no mechanism to control data placement and alignment.

Of the two approaches, the former is seen as a low level programming model to the point that MPI has been called the assembly language of parallel programming. Clearly, message-passing programming has the advantage that it gives the programmer direct and explicit control of the communication between threads and provides simple mechanisms to transfer data structures between distributed memory machines to enable the construction of high performance and highly scalable parallel applications. However, the complexity of subscripts that arise when arrays are distributed manually and the difficulty of changing distributions and, in general, modifying message-passing parallel program makes the message-passing programming model inconvenient and costly. So there is considerable burden placed on the programmer whereby send/receive message pairs must be explicitly declared and used, and this is often the source of errors. Implementations of message passing paradigms exist for GRID too [19].

Shared memory is a simpler paradigm for constructing parallel applications, as it offers uniform access methods to memory for all user threads of execution. Therefore it offers an easier way to construct applications when compared to a corresponding message passing implementation.

The disadvantage is limited scalability. But nonetheless, vast quantities of parallel codes have been written in this manner. OpenMP, promoted by multiple vendors in the high performance computing sector, has emerged as a standard for developing these shared memory applications.

Through the use of compiler directives, serial code can be easily parallelized by explicitly identifying the areas of code that can be executed concurrently. This parallelization of an existing serial application can be done in an incremental fashion. This has been an important feature in promoting the adoption of this standard among parallel application developers.

Both OpenMP and thread libraries bring the programming advantages of the shared memory model, but OpenMP has the additional advantage of enforcing a nested structure in the parallel program. This last consideration gives OpenMP an advantage over thread libraries.

We believe it is possible to use OpenMP to generate efficient programs for distributed memory clusters and computer GRIDs. Clearly, to achieve this goal the appropriate runtime systems, OpenMP extensions, and compiler techniques must be developed.

A possible approach to implement OpenMP is to use a Software Distributed Shared Memory (SDSM) system such a TreadMarks [1] to create a shared memory view on top of the target system. By following this approach the implementation of OpenMP on distributed memory systems becomes equivalent in difficulty to implementing OpenMP on an SMP machine. The drawback is that the overhead typical of SDSMs can affect speedup significantly.

A way to reduce the overhead is to translate OpenMP programs so that the SDSM system is implemented by agents. This can be achieved by applying compiler techniques similar to those developed by NavP [7]. This approach does not suffer from the same overhead problems as the SDSM approach in

T. Sobh, K. Elleithy (eds.), *Innovations in Computing Sciences and Software Engineering*,
DOI 10.1007/978-90-481-9112-3_45, © Springer Science+Business Media B.V. 2010

the case of faulting pages and moving pages from one node to another.

To this end, we propose to extend OpenMP to allow users indirect use of agents. This is important because the compiler, especially the earlier versions of it, is not expected to adequately handle all conceivable situations. Providing use of agents through extensions to OpenMP will make it possible for the programmers to take advantage of the compiler in order to optimize OpenMP and also avoid the complexities of message-passing programming. The main goal in this work is gaining good performance while we provide easy programming environment without changes in programming syntax .So we can execute any program written with OpenMP directives on GRID environment without changes in program. Our main goal in this paper is introducing our system and OpenMP directive implementations.

The rest of this paper is organized as follows. Section II provides related works and section III introduces some of optimization techniques implemented by using agents. Section IV details the proposed idea in using agents with combination of GRID. Section V discusses our implementation of some OpenMP directives. Performance evaluation for directives has shown in section VI and section VII is our conclusion.

II. Related Works

Many commercial compilers for modern hardware architectures can compile OpenMP programs. There are also various open-source implementations of the OpenMP standard for SMPs. OdinMP/CCp [8], OmniOpenMP[16], and OpenUH[14]are source-to-source compilers that preprocess source code with OpenMP directives and create a source program that uses a threading library (OdinMP uses pthreads; Omni OpenMP can use different thread packages ;OpenUH can also compile to native Itanium code) . The upcoming GCC version4.2 is expected to also compile OpenMP (C/C++ and Fortran) code to native.

We are aware of no OpenMP specification in Java for GRID. The JOMP [9] source-to-source compiler transforms a subset of the OpenMP standard to regular Java and uses the Java Threading API for parallelism. In contrast to JOMP, JaMP [10] compiler benefits from translating rather than rewriting the OpenMP directives, because the Jackal [11] compiler is aware of the parallelization applied. This enables various compiler optimizations, e.g., data race analysis, use of explicit send/receive operations instead of the DSM protocol, and the like.

There is little OpenMP-related work on clusters like JaMP. Intel Cluster OMP [12] extends the OpenMP specification by a special clause to share data between different cluster nodes. It is based on an extended version of the TreadMarks DSM [1]. Omni/SCASH [13] transparently executes OpenMP-enriched programs in the SCASH-DSM [15].

III. Agent based optimizations

Some of optimizations previously used for SDSM are as follows:

A. *Privatization optimization*

In this kind of optimization, the focus is on read-only access to data. The data that have read-only accesses is privatized. In general, two kinds of shared data can be treated as private data [5, 6]. The shared data with read-only accesses in certain program sections can be made “private with copy-in” during these sections. Similarly, the shared data that are exclusively accessed by the same thread can be privatized during such a program phase.

Our system provides this kind of optimization by using agents. Firstly private data are agent’s variable which is private to that agent. Secondly agents go toward data and locally access data they need. So shared data is also accessed locally and do not need any privatization.

B. *Page Placement and data Distribution on the nodes*

In this optimization all shared variables of a program are allocated after all the threads are created and before all the slaves are suspended for the first time.

The first step makes all the pages of an allocation unit distribute across all the execution threads averagely because the allocation is done at the beginning of the execution. Here “threads” are used instead of “nodes”, which means if several threads are running on one node, the pages associated with these threads are all located in this node.

The second step is to implement the first-touch placement based on home migration provided by JIAJIA [2]. If the page never migrated is referenced only by one thread in a parallel region, it will be migrated into the node on which the thread is running.

We implemented autonomous agents that migrate toward data, so we do not need to use this technique. By using agents communication cost is almost reduced to migrating agents.

We also try to distribute computation at a coarse granularity level and uniformly at the start of execution so that agents do not need to migrate very soon. Fortunately, many algorithms exhibit some degree of locality of access and are coarse grained.

C. *Overlapping data communication with computation*

One of the other optimizations done in OpenMP is to overlap communication and computation. This optimization is used to reduce all spent time (communication time + computation time) for that process.

For doing this, inspectors at compile time and runtime are needed to do the work of restructuring code and reordering the accesses to arrays. Then with respect to reordered access to arrays, program accesses data. At runtime when an access does not have its data available on the same node (locally), the runtime optimizer tries to bring its data before finishing the computation. Here computation and communication overlapping is done.

Since in the agent based system, agents migrate toward data, it is not possible to overlap communication with computation unless we break the agent into two agents. Breaking the agent into two agents should be done at the point of the agent where it needs a data not available on the same node. But here we should consider other circumstances such as dependencies of data.

As proposed in NavP agents can be a good alternative for page faults and migrating data towards code. That is agents (code) migrate to the nodes having data and locally execute there.

NavP says that programmer should distribute data him/herself; Then programmer with respect to the distribution of data write a program. One thing that programmer uses is Hop statement which is used by programmer to verify where the destination of migration is and when should an agent migrate.

So the first disadvantage of their system is that programmer should think exactly with respect to distribution of data.

The other and also important disadvantage is caused by this kind of programming; the structure of the program should be changed if the distribution of data is changed.

In this system no remote data accessing is allowed and all accesses to data is done locally and so is synchronization.

IV. An Agent based OpenMP Programming for Grid Computing

As we discussed in the previous session, agent has advantages to reduce communication cost and result in good performance and also has the affect of some optimizations. Here we show how we use agents for our purpose.

A. *Agents as the main concept*

Scaling OpenMP from distributed machines to GRID is our final goal. Some other models have developed so far, but their performance is low in comparison with MPICH-G2 [19] (which have the best performance until now). MPICH-G2 is based on MPI and message passing. The biggest problem here is the programming complexity especially on GRID.

To Scale OpenMP from distributed shared memory to GRID computing environment we need some changes in recent OpenMP. With respect to this, we decided to use agents to increase performance and scalability.

One debate that remains is how to apply this to GRID. At first we need a suitable distribution of data over clusters and then migrating agents between nodes of clusters.

To achieve this purpose, we used the three-layered architecture proposed in [21] which is shown in Fig.1.

In first layer (transmission layer) message transmission (sending and receiving messages) between nodes in GRID has been implemented.

Communication layer, propose methods that agents can communicate with each other. The method we used in our system is a hierarchical communication architecture shown in Fig.2.

Agent Directors (ADs) are the points of communication between agents with each other and with Agent Directors. Each cluster in GRID only has one AD that can communicate with other ADs in other clusters. Agent Management System (AMS), which has the responsibility of providing information about where agents and other ADs exist, are associated with ADs. Each AMS also registers all data location information in a computation. This information is used by agents to access the data they need. In a collection of clusters a Master AD manages all ADs.

When an agent wants to access a remote data (by migration) it should have known the location of the data. So at first step after creating agents, they ask AMS where the data they need are placed. Here to reduce the number of communications, each agent gets its required data placement information from AMS only at the time it is created and carries that information with itself everywhere it navigates. In this way, agents move autonomously.

In this way shared data on all nodes are global for all agents and they can locate data required. So DSM system is provided here.

Top layer is the application layer and has the code that agents want to execute. An OpenMP program creates agents and gives each a block of code to execute.

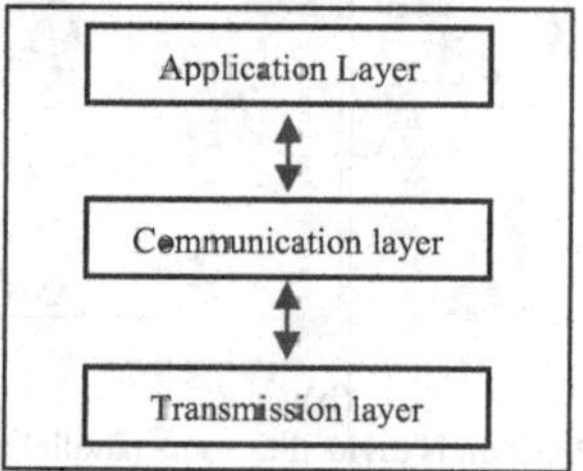

Fig.1 Three-layered architecture for agent communication

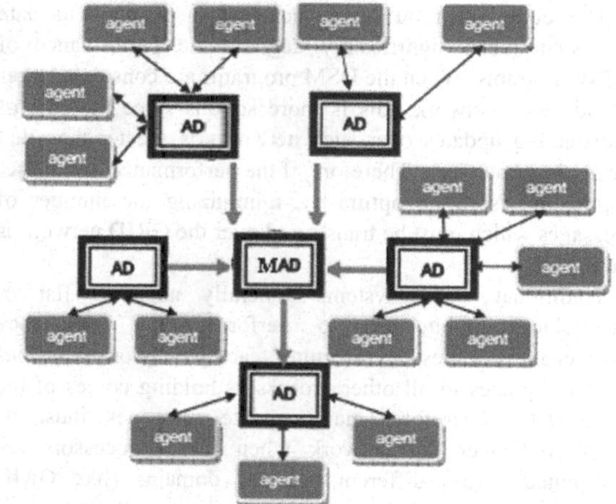

Fig.2 Communication between agents using hierarchical communication architecture

B. *Transparency of data access*

We have provided transparency of data access as follows. As we said in previous session each

Master AMS registers all data location information in a computation. This information is used by agents to access the data they need. As Fig.3 (a) depicts, at first program is divided to some parallel agents. Then they ask AMS where the data they need, are placed. This is done locally at the master node. So information about data locations is also given to that agent at the time of creating agents. Now if an agent wants to access a data, it looks up data location in its local information and with those information moves to where the data is placed.

Migrated agents can be seen in Fig.3 (b).If data is located at the node where agent is currently executing, no migration is done.

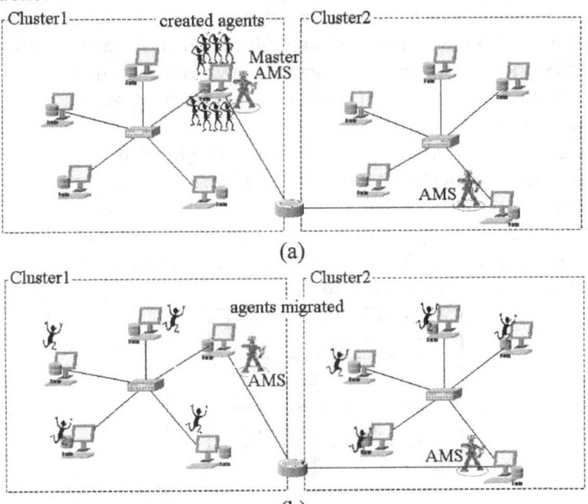

Fig.3 (a) Program is divided to some parallel agents
(b) Agents migrating to where data is placed, using local information

C. Cost of data-consistency maintenance

The communication costs incurred in maintaining data consistency can significantly degrade the performance of DSM programs. When the DSM programs are considered over a wide area network, this is more serious since the cost of propagating updates over such networks is greater than that over a local network. Therefore, if the performance of the user application is to be optimized, minimizing the number of messages which must be transferred over the GRID network is essential.

Traditional DSM systems generally adopt a flat or hierarchical architecture to perform data consistency maintenance. In these architectures, each processor propagates its data updates to all other processors holding copies of the same data. Therefore, many update messages must be transferred over the network when these processors are distributed across different network domains (like GRID environment), and hence the application performance is seriously degraded. To address this problem, we can say that our system has eliminated this data-consistency cost and its alternative cost is migrating agents. To degrade this cost as we said previously, distribution of data and computation should be done at a coarse granularity level and uniformly at the start of execution so that agents do not need to migrate very soon. Fortunately, many algorithms exhibit some degree of locality of access and are coarse grained.

V. AOMPG DIRECTIVES

Since AOMPG directives follow the OpenMP standard, its programming model is as expressive as the OpenMP programming model. An OpenMP programmer can use AOMPG without learning a new syntax for directives.

Since they are missing in the Java specification, AOMPG provides its own implementation of pragmas. Moreover, we have provided a preprocessor to translate directives and add agents.

The parallel directive marks a section of a program as parallel. When an agent reaches a parallel region (we call this agent, Master Agent), it conceptually creates a team of agents that execute the region's code in parallel. At the end of each parallel region, there is an implicit barrier. Only when all agents executing the region reach the barrier, the Master Agent continues. We will describe implementation of barrier later.

AOMPG supports data-access types defined by OpenMP. For variables marked as shared, the same memory location in the DSM is used by all agents that are put to work on the parallel region. This means that if an agent wants to access a shared variable, it should migrate to the node where data is placed, so we do not have any false sharing and we are not worry about inconsistency. As we said before agent migration destination can be found by asking AMSs in each cluster. Private variables are really agent's variables which are local to that agent and other agents can not access them.

The iteration space of a loop can be distributed among a set of created agents by means of the Do directive. In a "*for*" statement, *init* value is the initialization expression of the loop, *cond* is a loop-invariant termination condition, and the *increment* value specifies how to increment the loop variable by some loop-invariant value. According to the OpenMP standard, the loop variable is privatized to each agent:

for (<init >; <cond>; <increment>) {
// some code
}

AOMPG supports multiplication and summation types of arithmetic reduction operations defined by the OpenMP standard. This is done hierarchically by some communication between agents in a cluster and the AD of that cluster and at the end a communication between ADs can gather all the reduction information. This means that firstly a reduction is done in each cluster, and finally a reduction among cluster ADs.

With the single directive it is also possible to have code that is executed by only one agent. Single directive has also an implicit barrier at the end of the construct. User-defined barriers can be created by means of the barrier directive to create program locations at which all agents wait for each other. When an agent arrives at a barrier point, it will send a barrier message to AMS of that cluster. AMS of each cluster collects these messages and increases a counter by 1 for each message. When all agents in a cluster arrive at the barrier point, AMS will aware Master AMS which is the AMS associated with Master AD, and when MAD found that all agents has reached the barrier point, it will send a message to AMSs in each cluster and then those AMSs will aware agents to continue their computation. The critical directive can be used to mark critical sections that may be executed by only one agent at a time. To ensure the implementation of DSM as we said before, we were forced to implement this directive such that if agents are to execute a critical section, all of them should migrate to one node, the node which has the critical data (data that agents want to access in critical section). Critical directive has also an implicit barrier at the end of the critical section.

VI. PERFORMANCE EVALUATION

To simulate our work we used gridsim [20] toolkit as [21] has used and has been described in section IV.*A*. To evaluate performance we used a two-cluster GRID which nodes are distributed uniformly between them.

We have evaluated the AOMPG directives and simulated a set of algorithms to show the performance. The simulation results are depicted in section VI.*B*.

A. Gridsim toolkit

GRID introduces a number of resource management and application scheduling challenges in the domain of security, resource and policy heterogeneity, fault tolerance, continuously changing resource conditions, and politics. The resource management and scheduling systems for GRID computing need to manage resources and application execution depending on either resource consumers' or owners' requirements, and continuously adapt to changes in resource availability.

In a GRID environment, it is hard and even impossible to perform a performance evaluation in a repeatable and controllable manner as resources and users are distributed across multiple organizations with their own policies. To overcome these limitations, GridSim have been developed which is a Java-based discrete-event GRID simulation toolkit [20] and can be programmed to simulate a GRID system, thus it offers support, in terms of classes, for simulating computing elements, storage elements, Virtual Organizations, etc. The toolkit supports modeling and simulation of heterogeneous GRID resources (both time- and space-shared), users and application models. In a GridSim GRID environment there can be multiple users executing applications concurrently in the simulated GRID so that contention for resources can be modeled. The network speed between resources can be specified so that transfer of data is realistic. Static and Dynamic schedulers can be modeled and here is support for statistical analysis of any operations performed in the system. It can be used to simulate application schedulers for single or multiple administrative domains distributed computing systems such as clusters and GRIDs. It provides primitives for creation of application tasks, mapping of tasks to resources, and their management.

The GridSim toolkit provides a comprehensive facility for simulation of different classes of heterogeneous resources, users, applications, resource brokers, and schedulers. These facilities of GridSim with our packages added to it, made it suitable for our goal of using agents to simulate our SDSM model in GRID simulation environment.

Building an ideal GRID-enabled software DSM system is hugely challenging since many problems must first be overcome, including those of heterogeneity, dynamicity, resource allocation and data-consistency costs, etc. Since the problems of heterogeneity and dynamicity, this study focuses specifically on the issue of communication costs incurred in accessing data, without consistency problem over the network.

B. Simulation results

We have evaluated the performance of the AOMPG with a set of benchmarks.

To determine the speed of the basic AOMPG operations, we use the same set of microbenchmarks that has been used to assess the JOMP implementation [17]. As suggested in [18], the microbenchmarks compute the overhead of a particular directive by measuring the runtime of the execution of an empty loop and the runtime of the same loop with the directive added. Fig.4 shows the execution times of the individual AOMPG directives.

The overhead of the *barrier* statement (see Fig.4 (a)) is due to barrier implementation, for which the Master AMS maintains the barrier's counter. Whenever an agent reaches the barrier, it communicates with the cluster AMS and waits until a reply is received. When all agents in a cluster arrive at the barrier point the AMS of that cluster sends its counter to Master AMS, and waits for reply. Master AMS reply messages only after all agents of the team have reached the barrier. Since this is a hierarchical communication model its cost is decreased.

The time needed for a barrier consists of the time required to send 2 communication messages per node in each cluster and 2 communication messages per AMS between each AMS and Master AMS intra cluster. Although in this hierarchical system number of communications between each agent and cluster AMS is high, but the expensive communications which is intra cluster is low and it is cost effective.

The *single* directive takes roughly the same time, as it is currently implemented as a check of the thread ID plus a barrier at the end of the construct (which is required by the OpenMP specification).

Critical directive has a high overhead, and this is because all agents migrate to where the critical data exists. So we have a high overhead in executing a critical section. Whenever a agent encounters a critical region, first it migrates, and after arriving it sends a request to the AMS. If the region is currently not owned by any agent, the AMS immediately replies. Otherwise, the grant message is deferred until the current owner leaves the critical region.

The overhead caused by a *parallel* region is as shown in Fig.4 (b). The overhead consists of (1) creation and initialization of the shared and private objects and also the agents, (2) a sequence of communications between each agent and AMS to get location addresses of the data they require, (3) migrating agents toward data, and (4) the final barrier.

The overhead of a *Do(for)* directive, mainly consists of a barrier at the start of for loop to wait for the initialization of the chunks. The second barrier at the end of the for region which is required to synchronize agents.

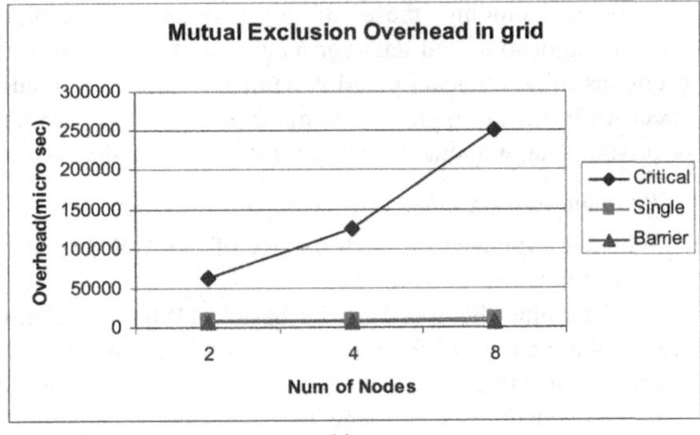

(a)

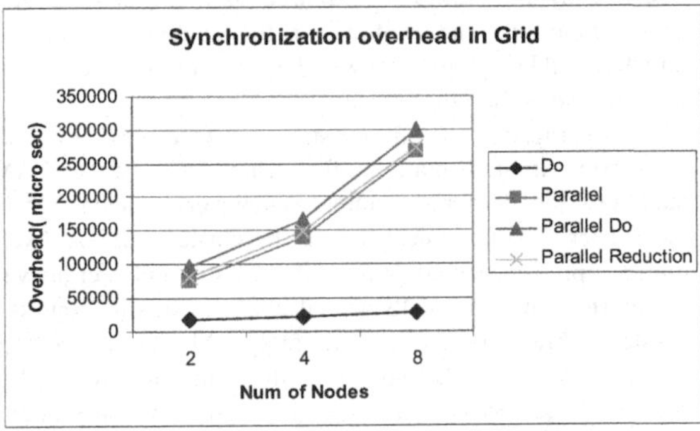

(b)

Fig .4 Overhead of AOMPG directives
(a) Mutual exclusion overheads
(b) Synchronization overheads

The overhead of a *parallel (Do) for* region approximately consist of the overhead needed to execute both *parallel* and *for* region.

For the *parallel reduction*, the overhead consists of the time needed for the parallel region and the time needed to combine the partial results of the worker agents. In Fig.4 (b) reduction overhead is + reduction for a variable of type long.

One of the most important overhead-reduction that we gain in this system is the overhead caused by consistency model that we have omitted it with our DSM model.

We also used the parallel Java Grande Forum (JGF) benchmarks [22] section 2 to show speed-up gained.

Sparse Matrix Multiply computes (200 times) the product of two sparse N × N matrixes in compressed-row format. The main loop is simply divided between agents. The speed-up in Fig.5 (a) is the result. As the number of nodes increases, the relative data size per node decreases and so does the speed-up.

Series computes the first Fourier coefficients of the function $f(x) = (x+1)^x$. The most important component of the program is the loop over the Fourier coefficients. Each iteration of the loop is independent of other loops and the work can be distributed simply between processors. It mainly uses transcendental and trigonometric functions to compute the coefficients. The main loop is divided between agents by means of the parallel for directive. The computation of Series

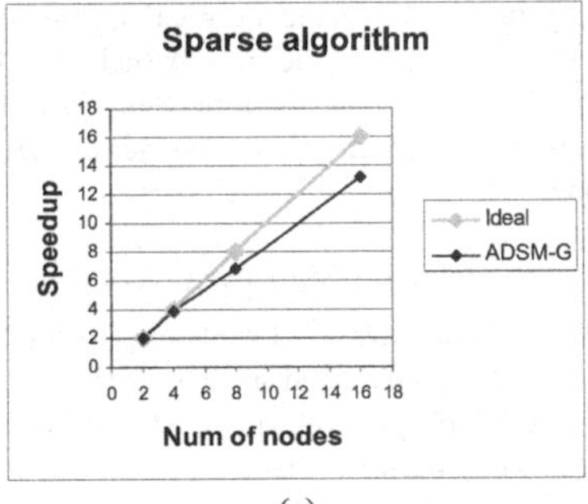

(a)

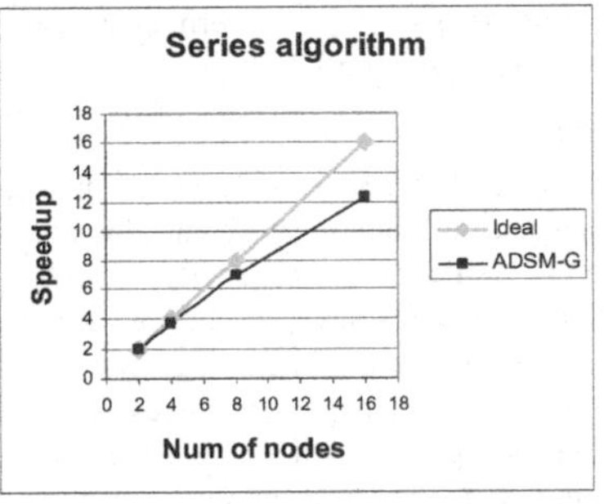

(b)

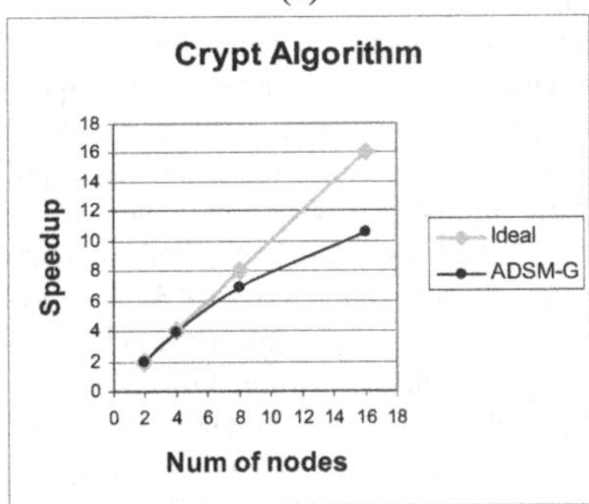

(c)

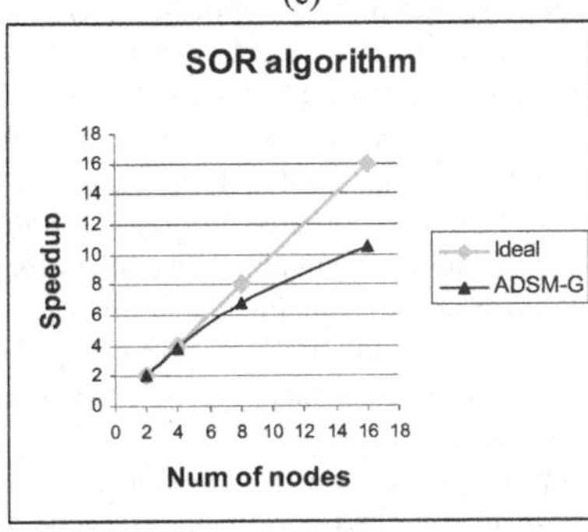

(d)

Fig5. (a) Speedup for Sparse matrixes multiply
(b) Speedup for Series
(c)Speedup for Crypt
(d)Speedup for SOR

is inherently parallel. After the chunks of computations have been divided between agents, only a migration would happen and no remote memory accesses are necessary. Approximately half of agents need to migrate between two clusters. Fig.5 (b) shows the Series benchmark speed-up on the nodes.

Crypt performs IDEA (International Data Encryption Algorithm) encryption and decryption an array with the length of N bytes. Crypt strongly depends on bit and byte operations. The main loop is divided among agents simply, because iterations are independent of each other and each agent receives only parts of the array which is independent of the others. The result has shown in Fig.5 (c).

SOR is a simple over-relaxation with 100 iterations on an N×N grid. As Fig.5 (d) shows, SOR has a reasonable performance, because the amount of shared data is rather small compared to the amount of computations. Since only two rows of the matrix are shared between neighboring agents, the overhead of migration to access remote data is not small compared to the other algorithms. But this is caused without the consistency maintenance cost.

Take this note into consideration: when agents located on different nodes want to access the same data variables, data consistency is maintained automatically by migrating code toward data using agents. Also, in this way consistency is preserved automatically.

VII. Conclusions

In this paper we introduce a new environment for programming in GRID. We have used OpenMP directives in Java and added agent capabilities to it. In this way we integrates DSM simulated with agents to provide a personal shared memory multiprocessor on computational GRIDs and migrating computations toward data. In this system, programmers use the concept of shared memory rather than message passing or even function calls to develop parallel applications on a computational GRID. This allows all OpenMP programs to be applied in a GRID environment.

A programmer can write a sequential Java program and enrich it with parallelization directives to make it a parallel AOMPG program. The directives are expressed as OpenMP standard. We have also omitted consistency overheads exist in previous DSM models. We also show the overheads of the individual AOMPG directives and the speedup of some JGF benchmark algorithms.

The simulations have shown that the proposed consistency maintenance method is effective in minimizing the number of data movement over the network. However, there are many other problems must also be considered, including data distribution, load balancing, and so on.

References

[1] P. Keleher, A.L. Cox, S. Dwarkadas, and W. Zwaenepoel. TreadMarks: Distributed Shared Memory on Standard Workstations and Operating Systems. In Proc. of the Winter 1994 Usenix Conf., pages 115–131,San Francisco, CA, January 1994.

[2] W. Hu, W. Shi, and Z. Tang. JIAJIA: An SVM System Based on A New Cache Coherence Protocol, in Proc. of the High Performance Computing and Networking (HPCN'99), LNCS 1593, pp. 463-472, Springer, Apr. 1999.

[3] OpenMP Application Program Interface, 2008. http://www.openmp.org/.

[4] Message Passing Interface Forum. MPI-2: Extensions to the Message-Passing Interface, July 1997.

[5] A. Basumallik, S.-J. Min, and R. Eigenmann. Towards OpenMP execution on software distributed shared memory systems, Int'l Workshop on OpenMP: Experiences and Implementations (WOMPEI'02), Lecture Notes in Computer Science 2327, Springer Verlag, May, 2002.

[6] R. Eigenmann, J. Hoeflinger, R. Kuhn, D. Padua, A. Basumallik, S.-J. Min and J. Zhu, Is OpenMP for GRIDs? Workshop on Next-Generation Systems, Int'l Parallel and Distributed Processing Symposium (IPDPS'02), May, 2002.

[7] LeiPan, Ming Kin Lai, KojiNoguchi, Javid J.Huseynov, Lubomir Bic, and Michael B. Dillencourt. Distributed parallel computing using navigational programming. International Journal of Parallel Programming, 32(1):1–37, February 2004.

[8] C. Brunschen and M. Brorsson. OdinMP/CCp - a Portable Implementation of OpenMP for Concurrency and Computation: Practice and Experience, 12(12):1193–1203, 2000.

[9] J.M. Bull and M.E. Kambites , JOMP — an OpenMP-like Interface for Java. In Proc. of the ACM 2000 Java Grande Conf., pages 44–53, San Francisco, CA, USA, June 2000.

[10] M. Klemm, M. Bezold, R. Veldema, and M. Philippsen. JaMP: An Implementation of OpenMP for a Java DSM. In M. Arenaz, R. Doallo, B.Fraguela, and J. Tourino, editors, Proceedings of the 12th Workshop on Compilers for Parallel Computers, pages 242–255, A Coruna, Spain, January 2006.

[11] R. Veldema, R. Bhoedjang, and H. Bal. Jackal, A Compiler Based Implementation of Java for Clusters of Workstations. Technical report, Dept. of Mathematics and Computer Science, Vrije Universiteit, Amsterdam, Netherlands.

[12] J.P. Hoeflinger. Extending OpenMP to Clusters. http://www.intel.com /cd/software/products/ asmona/eng/compilers/285865.htm, 2006.

[13] Y. Ojima and M. Sato. Performance of Cluster-enabled OpenMP for the SCASH Software Distributed Shared Memory System. In Proc. of the 3rd Intl. Symp. on Cluster Computing and the Grid, pages 450–456, Tokyo, Japan, May 2003.

[14] C. Liao, O. Hernandez, B. Chapman, W. Chen, and W. Zheng. OpenUH: An Optimizing, Portable OpenMP Compiler. Concurrency and Computation: Practice and Experience.

[15] H. Harada, Y. Ishikawa, A. Hori, H. Tezuka, S. Sumimoto, and T. Takahashi. Dynamic Home Node Reallocation on Software Distributed Shared Memory. In Proc. of the 4th Intl. Conf. on High-Performance Computing in the Asia-Pacific Region, pages 158–163, Bejing, China, May 2000.

[16] M. Sato, S. Satoh, K. Kusano, and Y. Tanaka. Design of OpenMP Compiler for an SMP Cluster. In Proc. of the 1st European Workshop on OpenMP, pages 32–39, Lund, Sweden, September 1999.

[17] J.M. Bull, M.D. Westbed, M.E Kambites, and J. Obdrzealek. Towards OpenMP for Java. In Proc. Of the 2nd European Workshop on OpenMP, pages 98–105, Edinburgh, Scotland, U.K., September 2000.

[18] J.M. Bull. Measuring Synchronization and Scheduling Overheads in OpenMP. In Proc. of 1st European Workshop on OpenMP, pages 99–105, Lund, Sweden, October 1999.

[19] Nicholas T. Karonis , Brian Toonen , Ian Foster, MPICH-G2: a Grid-enabled implementation of the Message Passing Interface, Journal of Parallel and Distributed Computing, v.63 n.5, p.551-563, May 2003

[20] Buyya R, Murshed M. A deadline and budget constrained cost–time optimize algorithm for scheduling parameter sweep applications on the Grid. GridSim Toolkit Release Document, December 2001. http://www.buyya.com/gridsim.

[21] Khatibzadeh M.,A Java Agent-Based Parallel Programming Model for Grid, MSC thesis, Ferdowsi university of Mashhad, Summer 2007

[22] L.A. Smith, J.M. Bull, and J. Obdrzealek. A Parallel Java Grande Benchmark Suite. In Proc. of the 2001 ACM/IEEE Conf. on Supercomputing, pages 97–105, Denver, CO, USA, November 2001.

Mashup – Based End User Interface for Fleet Monitoring

[1]M. Popa, [2]A.S. Popa, [3]T. Slavici, [4]D. Darvasi
[1,2,3]"Politehnica" University from Timisoara, Romania
[4]"Ioan Slavici" University from Timisoara, Romania

Abstract—**Fleet monitoring of commercial vehicles has received a major attention in the last period. A good monitoring solution increases the fleet efficiency by reducing the transportation durations, by optimizing the planned routes and by providing determinism at the intermediate and final destinations. This paper presents a fleet monitoring system for commercial vehicles using the Internet as data infrastructure. The mashup concept was implemented for creating a user interface.**

I. Introduction

Fleet monitoring of commercial vehicles has received a major attention in the last period. It significantly influences correlated fields, such as information exchange between dispatchers and drivers, tracing and tracking, fleet management and planning of handling activities. A good monitoring solution increases the fleet efficiency by reducing the transportation durations, by optimizing the planned routes and by providing determinism at the intermediate and final destinations.

Classical solutions use specific data infrastructures, leading to high installation and maintenance costs. A modern approach tends to use existing data infrastructures, e.g. the Internet.

This paper presents a fleet monitoring system for commercial vehicles using the Internet as data infrastructure. The mashup concept was implemented for creating a user interface. The rest of the paper consists of: the second section presents related work, the third section presents the mashup module, the fourth section describes the proposed solution, the fifth section outlines the conclusions and the last section presents the references.

II. Related Work

The fleet monitoring problem and the mashup concept are consistently discussed in the specific literature.

In reference [1], the authors describe a multiple vehicles tracking system using GSM network and satellite communication. The tracking system is based on the synchronization between the vehicle client unit and the base station. Reference [2] presents an abstract multiagent architecture useful for Decision Support Systems and implements it on the Bus Fleet Management domain. Reference [3] describes a fleet monitoring system for advanced tracking of commercial vehicles. It can identify discrepancies between actual and planned data and automatically updates this database of the logistics system.

In reference [4], a review of six mashup makers from an end user development perspective is presented. Their features are summarized and compared across six different themes. Reference [5] describes fleet management application based on new type of information utilities called mobile location – based services. These services are obtained by converging multiple technologies, including the Internet, wireless communications, geographic information system, location technologies and mobile devices. Reference [6] explores how to realize operational carrier – class mobile mashup services.

III. General Presentation of the Mashup Module

Mashup is an Internet technology that combines data and services from more than one source into a single web application. The information used in such systems is assumed from other sources through a public interface (API).

A mashup application is composed from three parts:

- The content provider: represents the information source; the information is available either through an API or different web protocols, such as RSS or web services;

- The mashup site: it is a web application which provides a new service using different data sources;

- The client browser: it is the interface of the final use of the mashup; in such an application, the information can be aggregated by the client browser using a scripting language, e.g. JavaScript.

The mashup module was used in an application for fleet monitoring of commercial vehicles. According to the specifications, the mashup component takes over information about the fleets of commercial vehicles belonging to different clients form the company data base and together with the system of maps Google Maps offers a visual representation of the information. Other services (e.g. meteorological information from weather.com) can also be offered.

The mechanism for storing the vehicles' localization information is transparent for this application, all the information being in a company data base. Each client can visualize the travels achieved by the own vehicles according to rules established in the specifications document.

The mashup module has the following components:

- XHTML documents, JavaScript scripts and CSS formatting files; these are used by the client's browser;

- Java Servlets running in order to provide information to the client and

- Other public web services.

In order to achieve the mashup, the Google Web Toolkit was used. It is a tool allowing writing code in Java language

T. Sobh, K. Elleithy (eds.), *Innovations in Computing Sciences and Software Engineering*,
DOI 10.1007/978-90-481-9112-3_46,

and the compiler transforms the Java code in JavaScript and HTML documents. GWT allows using Java at the client side, instead of JavaScript. This offers the possibility to use the high number of Java development tools. Another advantage comes from the fact that the Internet applications are more and more complex and with continuously increasing dimensions and Java is more appropriate than JavaScript for this type of applications. More than that, JavaScript is not standardized for all the browsers and using GWT all the differences due to the lack of standardization are masked. Although GWT brings towards Internet all the benefits of Java, it also allows interacting with the existing JavaScript code.

The GWT core contains a Java to JavaScript compiler which produces code able to run in different browsers, such as Internet Explorer, Firefox, Mozilla, Safari and Opera. There are certain library limits.

GWT offers support for Java Servlets from the server. The Servlets can be achieved using extensions of the HttpServlet class which offers facilities for serializing and deserializing the transmitted objects. Objects can be transmitted between the client part of the GWT application and the server part and whole the serializing and deserializing mechanism is transparent for the user. This mechanism is called GWT – RPC (Remote Procedure Call).

The remote call implemented in GWT is asynchronous, meaning that after a remote call for a method, the application on the client side does not stop. This is an advantage over the synchronous solution in which a remote call would produce a blocking of the application until the whole result from the server would become available.

The limits of the libraries imposed by GWT are not found on the server part too. These libraries are specific for compiling the Java code in JavaScript which is necessary only in the client part of the application. On the server part, any Java libraries can be used.

The technologies used for achieving the mashup are:

- on the client side: XHTML, JavaScript, CSS2, AJAX and GWT;

- on the server side: JavaServlets and SQL.

IV. The Proposed Solution

The proposed system monitors fleets of commercial vehicles. The mashup concept was used for creating an end user interface. The application provides good response times for the users, due to the fact that much processing is done at the client level and the requests which cannot be fulfilled only at the client level can be obtained from the server without the need of reloading the web page. The application runs in a browser.

The system is made of the following parts:

- Terminals with GPS receivers,

- The database for localizing information,

- Server for web services and

- The client's browser.

Fig. 1. presents the general diagram of the system. The terminals with GPS receivers are devices installed in each vehicle to be monitored. During the use of the vehicle, these devices receive localizing information from the GPS satellites. The devices store this information and, at certain moments, send them to a server through the GSM network using the GPRS protocol. At the server, this information is processed and stored in databases. Further, the information is available to a client which wants to know the positions of different vehicles. If needed, reports about the vehicles' activity can be obtained. The position of the vehicle can be visualized using the system of maps Google Maps. Together with the Google Maps API, other services can be used also, such as meteorological information (weather.com).

In order to provide the localizing information to the clients, a web server must exist. Through this server, the clients can access the data in different formats. The browsers can receive information as HTML pages, hand – held devices can receive it as XML files and specific applications can obtain other formats.

The Mashup application consists of the following modules:

- QuickSearch: it is the "home" module; when the end user accesses the application he will enter this module; the end user will receive localizing information concerning a vehicle; localizing information mean current position, speed, orientation etc.

- Journeys: is a module through which the user can visualize the list of the rides each vehicle has accomplished;

- Statistics: represents the module for creating reports; the statistics will be created at the server level and will be sent to the client when this one will request such a report;

- Vehicles: contains information about vehicles.

Fig. 2. presents the UML Class Diagram of the QuickSearch module. QuickSearch is a container type class. It implements the EntryPoint interface. The container will aggregate the GMap2 class which represents a Google Maps widget derived from an external library specially created for managing the Google Maps maps. Other objects will be aggregated in the object QuickSearch. These Label type objects will work as text containers regarding localizing information (speed, azimuth etc.) and statically information about the vehicle (model, matriculation number etc.).

An important module is SuggestBox. SuggestBox is a class which will be used for creating the instance of an object will display a special input field for the user. The major difference from a classical input field is the suggestion this one will try to do when the user types a character.

The Callback class defines a type used like an inverse call after running certain routines. A Callback type object will generate the SuggestBox and Label type objects.

InformationSevice is an interface of the services offered by the server. The QuickSearch class depends on this interface because it will call remotely a method which is declared through this interface.

Journeys displays the route diagrams of each vehicle from the fleet. This supposes the use of methods for selecting a time intervals, a vehicle and the display of the rides as tables.

Fig. 3. presents the class diagram of this module. It is used as an EntryPoint class. It will be instantiated and run when its use is required. Several types of classes, belonging especially to the graphical user interface, will be aggregated inside the Journey class.

The ListBox class is the pattern for creating a list with multiple options. These options will be the vehicles from the client's own fleet and the user will be able to select the desired vehicle. The GMap2 class was aggregated in the Journeys module for handling a Google maps map.

The GWTCIntervalSelector class derives from an external library (GWTChismes) and represents an interval selector. In order to select the borders of the interval, two calendars will be displayed in the popup model.

Callback is a class dependent by Grid and GMap2. This fact means that objects Grid and GMap2 are instantiated when the service information becomes available.

Statistics is an EntryPoint type class. As in the precedent cases, all the text containers were modelated as series of Label type aggregated classes.

Fig. 4. presents the class diagram of this module. Collection is a container class for several same type objects. In case of this application it is referred to the Statistic interface. This interface is implemented by several classes which define specific types of reports, such as GeneralReport, SpeedReport etc. The responsibility of instantiating the Statistic type objects was delegated to a class StatisticBuilder. This is a Factory class, having only the role of instantiating a class and returning the Statistic type object.

Each class which implements the Statistic interface must implement several methods, through which also GenerateReport(). GeneralReport will use a StatisticService interface which represents is an abstract remote call. When the remote routine finishes the Callback object will be automatically called for achieving routines for finishing the transaction.

The main tool for developing the mashup application was the Google Web Toolkit (GWT). The four modules of the Mashup application are GWT modules. Each of them contains an interface for obtaining, if necessary, information for a remote service.

The QuickSearch module calls the LocalisationServive.getVehicles remote service. This remote call specifies as parameters the ID of a client and an AsyncCallback type object. This object is used for asynchronous remote calls. Synchronous remote calls could also be used but this functionality is undesirable because the application must not "freeze" when the user achieves a remote call until the information is obtained from the server. The AsyncCallback interface requires that the class which will implement it must also implement two methods:

- public void onSucces (Object result);

- public void onFailure (Throwable caught).

OnFailure() is a method implicitly called when the remote service generates a not treated serial type exception. This occurs when the remote service cannot be called. OnSucces() is a method implicitly called when the remote service returns some results to the caller. The remote call was successfully achieved and the information is available only after the call to the OnSucces() method.

The first widget which is instantiated is the Google Maps map. Several controls are attached to it and the implicit type of map is set, using an API from GWT from a special library for Google Maps. The next widget is a SuggestBox. It is a field in which the user can introduce a text and the field will try to suggest to the user the complete text. In this step, a list of points with the current coordinates of each vehicle is generated. When a user searches a vehicle, it will select one of the suggestions offered by SuggestBox and for that, a method will be called.

Each vehicle is memorized in a GLatLng type list of objects with its current position. This type of object was defined in the special library for handling Google Maps and represents a point on the map, defined by its latitude and longitude. In this way the current position of all the vehicles from the fleet can be displayed on the same image. The GBounds type was designed for taking over a list of objects GLatLng and calculating a virtual border on the map containing all the vehicles. In order to handle the Google map so that the map included in that virtual border can be displayed, a GLatLngBounds type object must be instantiated. It represents a virtual border, centred in a point with certain coordinates. It will receive an object GBounds. The Zoom level of the map is also calculated with the help of the GLatLngBounds object.

The interface LocalisationService extends the RemoteService interface. This extension is necessary in order to specify to the compiler that it has to deal with a remote interface. The service offered by the new interface is called getVehicles(clientId) and returns a list of the client's vehicles to the caller. The interface defines also a static and public attribute representing the name of the remote service and a method getInstance() which returns a LocalisationServiceAsync type object used by the client for calling remotely the service. The name of the remote service will be used for configuring the application and will represent the name used for implementing the interface. The object LocalisationServiceAsync is the one which will be used for calling the remote service.

On the server side, a Servlet must run to implement the LocationSevice interface. The class must also extend the RemoteServiceServlet class. The RemoteServiceServlet class has HttpServlet as a super class.

The way to remotely transmit the objects, through the GWT-RPC service, is transparent for the user. The serializing and services for the objects to be transmitted and deserializing services are under the responsibility of JavaScript, through the interface RemoteService, on the client side, and through the super class RemoteServiceServlet, on the server side.

V. Conclusions

Compared to other similar solutions, the described application has the advantage of severely reducing the traffic at the server level. Most of the processing is done at the client level. If necessary, only specific data are transferred from the server at the client without reloading the whole web page, thus the user waiting times are minimized.

Future development directions can be:

- At the server level: inclusion of more information, such as statistics referring the pollution, frequently used routes etc.

- At the client level: the use of markup languages for hand – held devices, the increase of the number of the services for the mashup operation.

References

[1] M. Ahmad, J. Iqbal, Q. Ul-Ain, Q. Ul-Ain, and S. Ghazal, "Real time fleet monitoring and security system using GSM nerwork", in *Proc. of*

the 6th WSEAS International Conference on Simulation, Modelling and Optimization, September, 2006, Lisbon, Portugal, pp. 498-503

[2] M. V. Belmonte, J. L. Perez-de-la-Cruz, F. Triquero and A. Fernandez, "Agent coordination for bus fleet management", in *Proc. of the 2005 ACM symposium on Applied computing*, March 2005, Santa Fe, New Mexico, pp. 462-466

[3] A. Goel and V. Gruhn, "A Fleet Monitoring System for Advanced Tracking of Commercial Vehicles", in *Proc. of SMC'06, The IEEE International Conference on Systems, Man and Cybernetics*, October, 2006, Taipei, Taiwan, pp. 2517-2522

[4] L. Grammel and M. A. Storey "An End User Perspective on Mashup Makers", *Technical report DCS-324-IR,* September 2008

[5] A. P. Silva and G. R. Mateus, "A mobile location-based vehicle fleet management service application", in *Proc. of IEEE IV2003 Intelligent Vehicles Symposium*, June 2003, Columbus, USA, pp. 25-30

[6] H-y. Xu, M-n. Song, H. Chen and J-d. Song, J-d, "Research on SOA based mobile mashup platform for telecom networks", in *Proc. of the 3rd International Conference on Intelligent Environments*, September 2007, Ulm, Germany

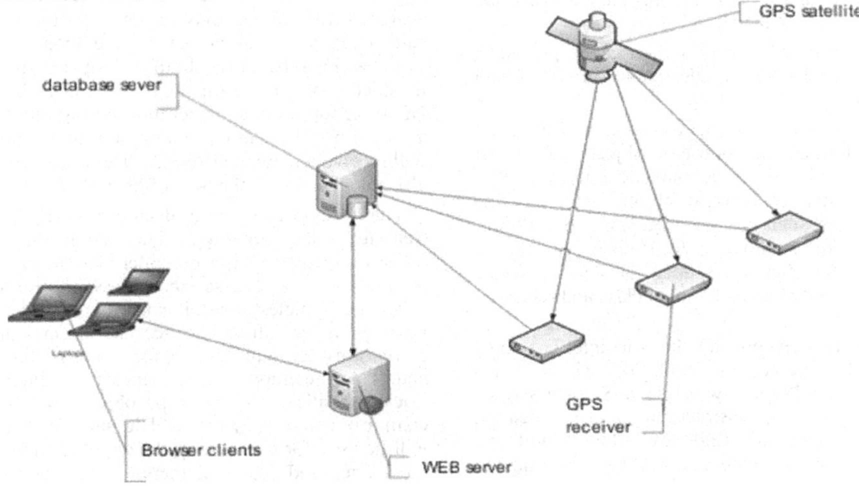

Fig. 1. General structure of the fleet monitoring system

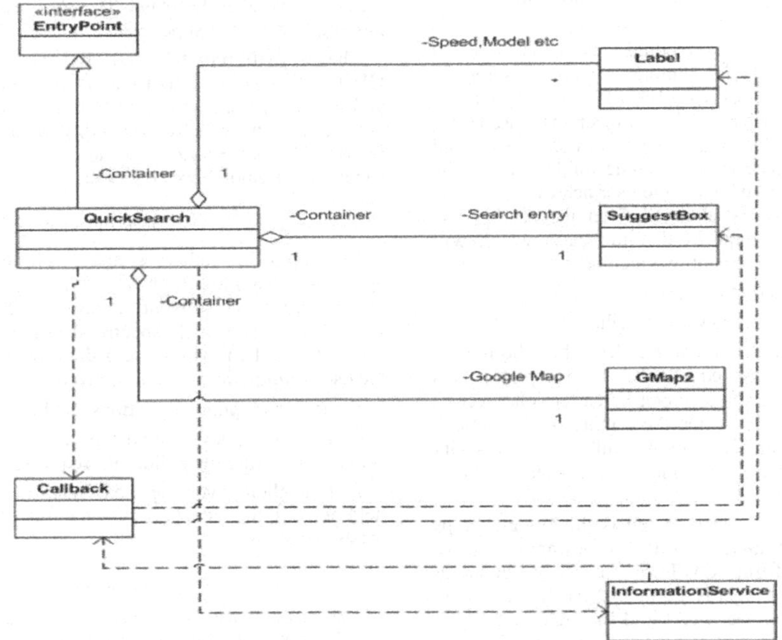

Fig. 2. The components of the QuickSearch module

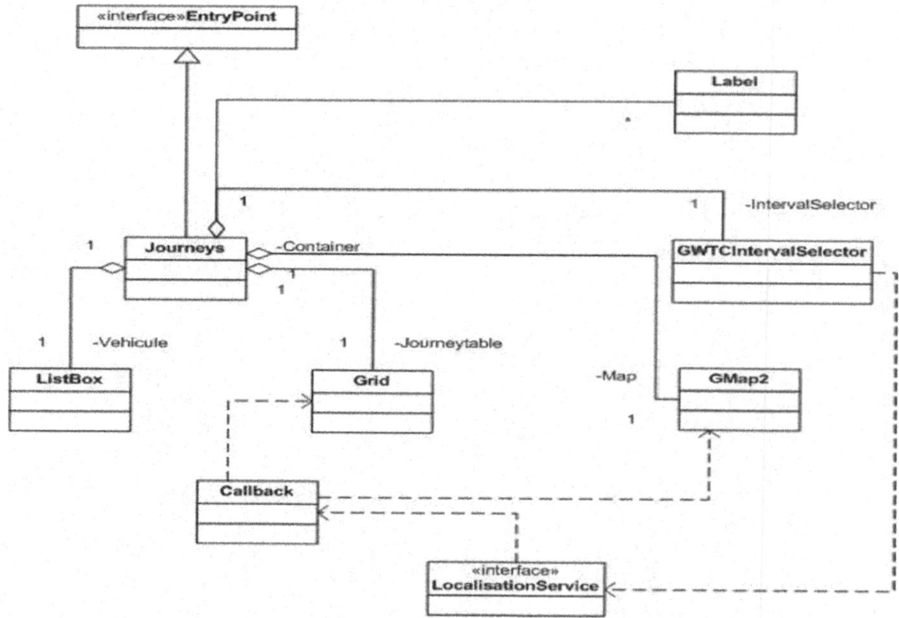

Fig. 3. The components of the Journeys module

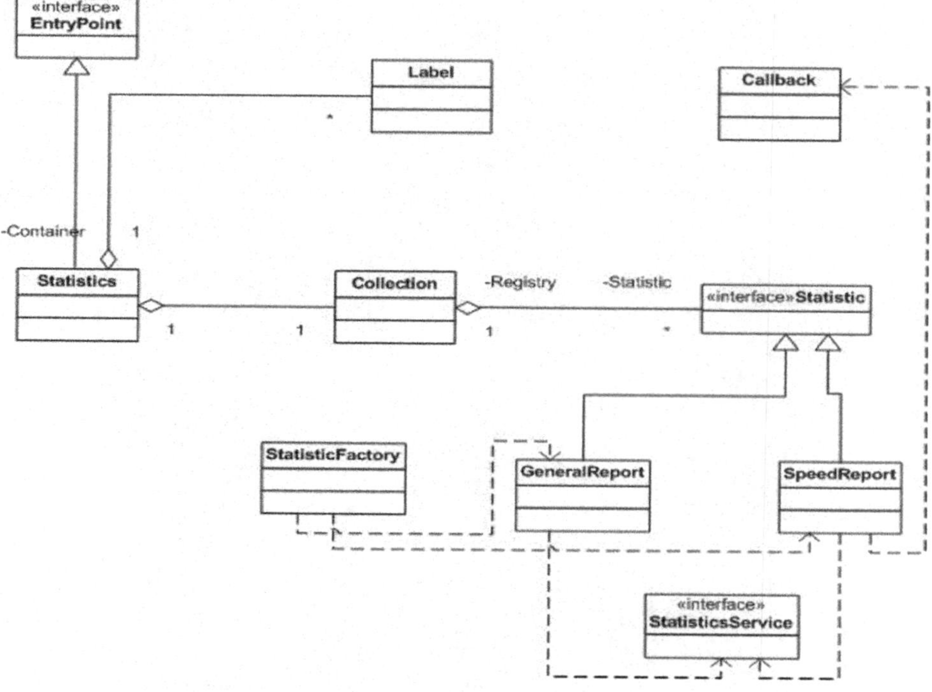

Fig. 4. The components of the Statistics module

The Performance of Geothermal Field Modeling in Distributed Component Environment

A. Piórkowski, A. Pięta, A. Kowal, T. Danek
Department of Geoinfomatics and Applied Computer Science,
AGH University of Science and Technology, Cracow, Poland.
{pioro, tdanek} @agh.edu.pl, apieta@geol.agh.edu.pl

***Abstract*—An implementation and performance analysis of heat transfer modeling using most popular component environments is a scope of this article. The computational problem is described, and the proposed solution of decomposition for parallelization is shown. The implementation is prepared for MS .NET, Sun Java and Mono. Tests are done for various operating systems and hardware platform combinations. The performance of calculations is experimentally indicated and analyzed. The most interesting issue is the communication tuning in distributed component software – proposed method can speed up computational time, but the final time depends also on the network connections performance in component environments. These results are presented and discussed.**

***Index Terms*—heat transfer modeling, component platforms**

I. Introduction

Heat transfer phenomenon plays an important role in such physical problems in Earth science as volcanoes, intrusions, earthquakes, mountain building or metamorphism. Analytically exact solution of heat transfer equation exists only for geological models with simple geometry. In many geologically realistic situations it is necessary to use numerical approaches to obtain valid models of these important processes. Heat-conduction equation and its finite difference solution is a problem which is easy to parallelize. This fact is a great advantage because modeling in huge complex media carry on for a long period of time and in presence of thermal anisotropy can be a very time consuming process [1], [2].

The main disadvantages of created program codes is introduction of newer and newer software and hardware solutions that caused in very short life cycle of created codes. One of the methods used to overcome the problem of short life cycle is use of the component technologies.

II. Component Technologies

Portability, security and independence of hardware are the main advantages of component-based software. A possibility of component code reuse enables coders cooperation. The most popular component platforms are Sun Java [3] and MS .NET [4]. These platforms are developed by commercial providers. There is a free and open alternative for one of them (MS .NET) – a platform Mono [5]. The .NET applications can be run under control of Mono.

The component platforms use a managed code technique to enable hardware independency and portability. This technique is a *bytecode* in Sun Java and *CLI* in MS .NET. The translation to native code by Just-In-Time method is a bottle-neck in terms of performance. There are numerous algorithms for optimization to speed up calculations.

The subsystem of communication is one of the most important parts of component environment in terms of performance in case of parallelization. Sun Java offers a RMI mechanism [6] that enables remote procedure calling, the same function is domain of .NET Remoting for MS .NET and Mono.

III. Test Environment and Applications

A. Hardware specification

The experimental tests of heat transfer modeling computations were performed in two different environments.

The first environment was a notebook:

- 1 processor (Intel Pentium M 1,86 GHz),
- 1 GB RAM.

The second environment was a cluster of 30 PC computers:

- 1 processor with 2 cores (Hyper-Threading Technology Intel Pentium 4 2,8 GHz),
- 1 GB RAM,
- Gigabit Ethernet network adapter.

All nodes of cluster were joined by Gigabit Ethernet switch.

B. Used Operating Systems and Component Environments

The performance of component seismic computing was measured in following operating systems: Linux (Fedora Core 3, kernel: 2.6.12-1.1381 [smp]), MS Windows 2000 (SP4), MS Windows XP (SP2) and MS Windows Vista.

There are two applications for heat transfer modeling written in Java and C# language. To run Java code we use Sun

T. Sobh, K. Elleithy (eds.), *Innovations in Computing Sciences and Software Engineering*,
DOI 10.1007/978-90-481-9112-3_47, © Springer Science+Business Media B.V. 2010

Java SE virtual machine, version 1.6.0. The C# code was tested under control of MS .NET Framework 2.0 and Mono 1.2.6.

IV. HEAT TRANSFER MODELING

A. Basics of heat transfer modeling

Component solutions were tested using heat-conductive equation. In two-dimensional isotropic medium this equation can be written as:

$$\frac{\partial T}{\partial t} = \frac{\lambda}{\rho \cdot c}\left(\frac{\partial^2 T}{\partial x^2} + \frac{\partial^2 T}{\partial z^2}\right) + \frac{Q_w}{\rho \cdot c} \tag{1}$$

where $T(x, z)$ is temperature, $\lambda(x, z)$ is thermal conductivity, $c(x,z)$ is specific heat capacity, $\rho(x, z)$ is density, t is time and Q_w denotes the heat generated in the volume element of the medium during unit time (heat production rate).

Adopting the finite difference to approximate the above equation and using the Simple Explicit Method [7] one can obtain:

$$t_{i,j}^{k+1} = t_{i,j}^{k} + \alpha\Delta t\left[\frac{t_{i+1,j}^{k} - 2t_{i,j}^{k} + t_{i-1,j}^{k}}{(\Delta x)^2} + \frac{t_{i,j+1}^{k} - 2t_{i,j}^{k} + t_{i,j-1}^{k}}{(\Delta z)^2}\right] \tag{2}$$

$$i = 1, \ldots, n_x; \quad j = 1, \ldots, n_z$$

where α is thermal diffusivity, Δt is the time sampling interval, Δx and Δy are distances between grid points in the x and z directions respectively, n_x and n_y are grid points amount in the x and z directions respectively.

To achieve numerical stability the following relationship must be fulfilled [7].

$$\alpha\Delta t\left[\frac{1}{(\Delta x)^2} + \frac{1}{(\Delta z)^2}\right] \leq \frac{1}{2} \tag{3}$$

We used two types of boundary conditions: convective boundary conditions (4) at the top and bottom of the model and Neumann boundary conditions (5) elsewhere.

$$\lambda \left.\frac{\partial T}{\partial n_i}\right|_{r_i} + h_i T(r_i, t) = f_i(r_i, t) \tag{4}$$

$$\lambda \left.\frac{\partial T}{\partial n_i}\right|_{r_i} = f_i(r_i, t) \tag{5}$$

where:
r_i - coordinate at the boundary, i - one of the boundaries,
n_i - the outward-facing normal vector on the body surface,
h_i - the heat transfer coefficient,
f_i - the specified function,
λ - thermal conductivity.

B. An experimental model

There is a simple model prepared for simulation. The parameters of this model are presented in Table I and this model is presented on fig. 1. The model contains of a part of rock at the left and water at the right. The solutions of heat transfer simulation for 10 and 100 years are presented in the fig. 2 and fig. 3.

TABLE I.
PARAMETERS OF SIMPLE MODEL

Parameters of the experimental model	
model dimensions [m x m]	250 x 250
spatial grid steps [m]	1
depth to heat layer [m]	250
temperature of heat layer [°C]	100
thermal conductivity of land [W/m*K]	0,000001201
thermal conductivity of water [W/m*K]	0,000000128
end time [years]	100
time step [days]	1
initial temp. of land (250m) / water	100°C / 0°C

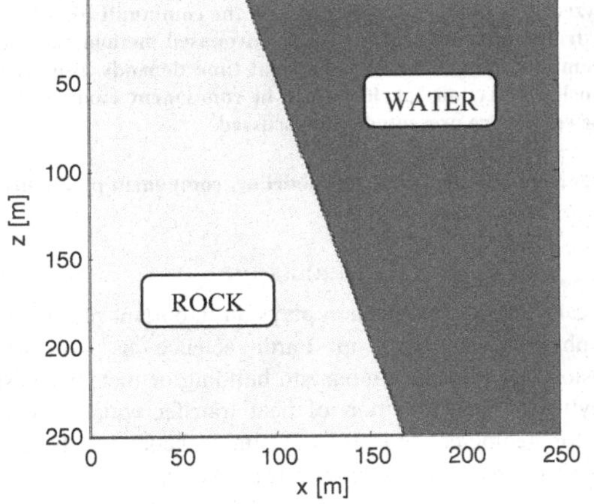

Fig 1. The simple model for simulation.

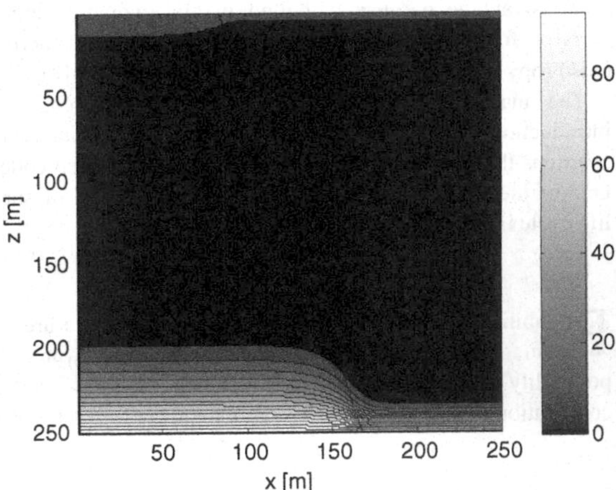

Fig 2. The solution of heat transfer simulation for 10 years.

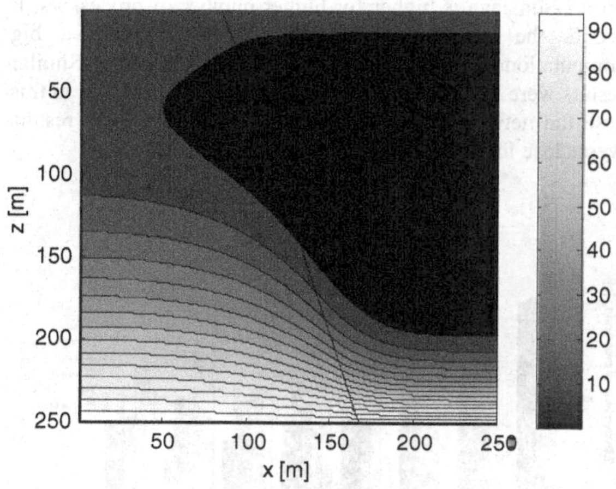

Fig 3. The solution of heat transfer simulation for 100 years.

C. Serial case

At the start we have measured the times of heat transfer modeling computations for the serial case. The experiment took a place in two hardware environments. The reached times are collected in Table II and presented in fig. 4.

TABLE II.
AVERAGE TIMES OF COMPUTATIONS FOR SINGLE MACHINE

	Avg. times in E1 [s]			Avg. times in E2 [s]	
	MS Vista	MS XP	FC 3	MS 2000	FC 3
.NET	99,22	95,73	-	142,43	-
Mono	110,86	107,04	107,93	231,93	181,84
Java	112,64	103,88	113,03	200,22	136,49

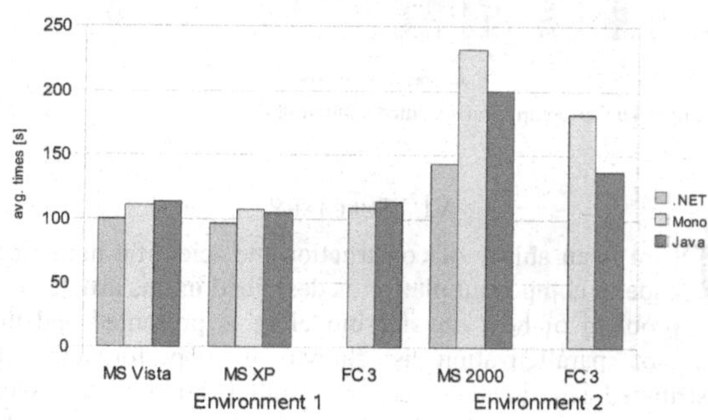

Fig. 4. Graphical comparison of times of computations for various operating systems, programming platforms and hardware.

The fastest computations have been reached in environment 1, under control of MS Windows XP, using .NET Framework. In second environment the fastest code was run under control of Linux using Sun Java platform.

D. Parallel case

Geological model described in the previous chapter and the same set of parameters were used for the parallel modeling of the heat transfer equation. Parallelizm was introduced by domain decomposition of the computational domain (Fig. 5) and master slave paradigm (Fig. 6).

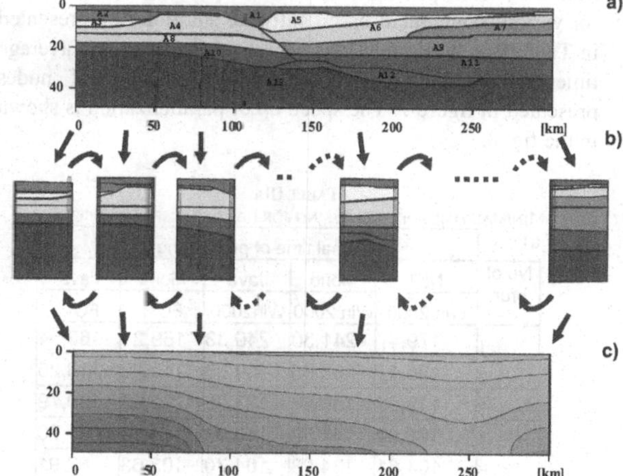

Fig 5. The domain decomposition schema. Global computational domain (a) is divided into smaller subdomains. Results of computation performed by slave nodes (b) are collected by master node (c)

Global computational domain was divided into as much subdomains as independent processors got involved in concurrent heat transfer equation solving. Assignment of computational subdomains to independent processors made computational process much faster and limited the risk of local

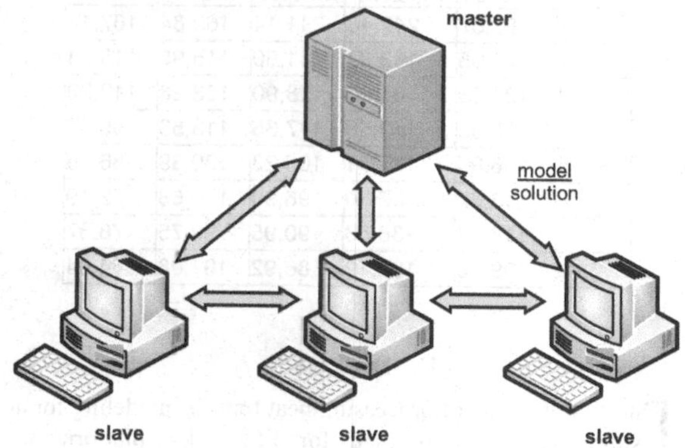

Fig 6. The environment for distributed heat transfer modeling.

RAM exceeding. One of the machines hosted master process, other hosted only slave processes. Master was responsible for creation of numerical model representation, division of the global computational domain, assigning and sending data to slave nodes and finally collecting heat flow modeling results. Slave processes performed computation and were exchanging subdomain border nodes after every step of calculation.

The intra slave communications was the most time consuming part of parallel algorithm. For a test model described above slaves exchanged 80MB of data for about two thousand times. Parallel algorithm with such dense communication pattern strongly limits number of slave nodes especially for small computational models. The entire tests were performed in computational hardware environment described in the previous section. Computation times received for various component-based software solutions are presented in Table IIIA and Table IIIB. There are minimal and average times of computing for consecutive numbers of nodes presented in figure 7. The speed up of parallelization is shown in the fig. 8.

TABLE IIIA
MINIMAL TIMES OF PROCESSING FOR HEAT TRANSFER MODELING

a)

No of proc	Minimal time of processing [s]				
	.NET Win 2000	Mono Win 2000	Java Win2000	Mono FC 3	Java FC 3
1	179,47	241,30	240,33	169,21	166,54
2	126,17	162,86	140,58	115,22	113,26
3	119,92	160,42	127,95	132,05	109,79
4	108,92	141,52	116,02	111,13	91,70
5	104,61	134,28	104,70	103,63	82,91
6	107,77	135,00	95,94	109,62	70,67
7	107,27	137,20	89,79	98,72	74,13
8	104,13	134,59	85,49	98,86	81,32

TABLE IIIB
AVERAGE TIMES OF PROCESSING FOR HEAT TRANSFER MODELING

b)

No of proc.	Average time of processing [s]				
	.NET Win 2000	Mono Win 2000	Java Win2000	Mono FC 3	Java FC 3
1	182,87	242,48	241,14	169,84	167,17
2	128,35	163,07	141,50	115,95	116,34
3	125,38	161,06	128,90	133,28	112,90
4	113,55	142,58	117,35	113,53	95,47
5	106,90	137,31	105,23	130,39	86,76
6	113,72	137,30	96,90	115,68	72,19
7	117,23	138,53	90,95	99,75	76,37
8	109,18	137,19	86,92	101,08	84,04

V. DISCUSSION

The shortest time of processing heat transfer modeling for a single case war reached for MS .NET platform in environment 1. In environment 2 (cluster of PC-s) the fastest combination was Sun Java and Linux (there was no Windows XP installation). For the same environment in distributed case the leader was also Sun Java as platform and Linux as operating system (similar scores are for synthetic tests [9]). The interesting point is the speed ups for these technologies - the network usage by communication was a bottle-neck for .NET and Mono - the speed up is not especially growing for four processors and more. The speed up for Sun Java is higher for higher number of processors. It proofs the necessary of parallelization for such a big computational problem like heat transfer modeling. Similar results were reached for seismic field modeling [8], but in this case the network transfer was smaller and speed ups results were close for all platforms.

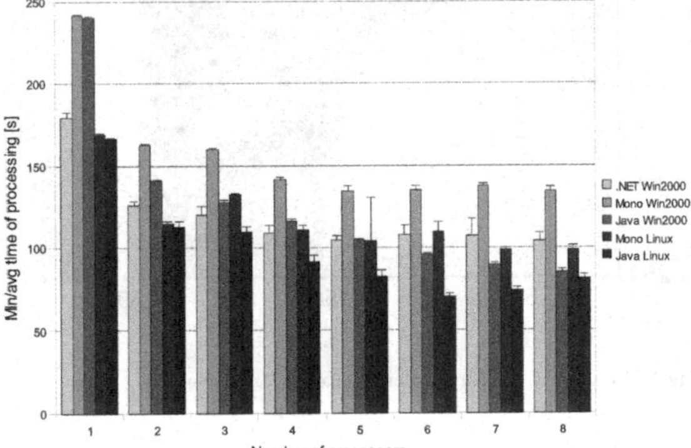

Fig 7. The minimal and average times for distributed simulation.

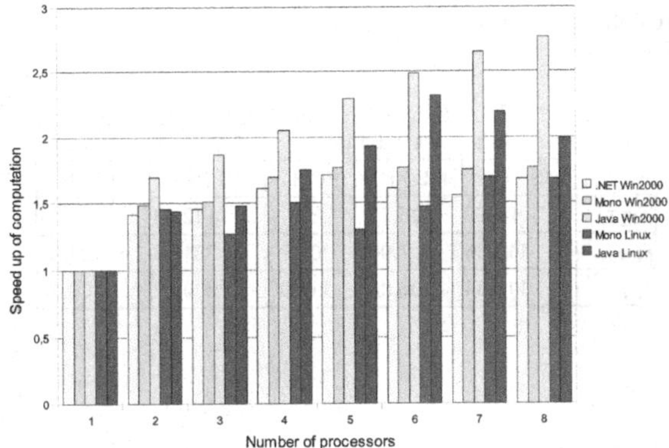

Fig 8. The speed up for distributed simulation.

VI. SUMMARY

There is an ability of construction the scientific numerical code in component platforms described in this article. The problem of heat transfer modeling is presented and the way of parallelization is shown. The performance of distributed solutions in case of parallelization is the main scope of experimental tests. Obtained speed up results proofs, that parallelization is a good way to solve a problem of computations efficiency.

ACKNOWLEDGMENT

This work was financed by the AGH - University of Science and Technology, Faculty of Geology, Geophysics and Environmental Protection as a part of statutory project number 11.11.140.561.

REFERENCES

[1] A. Pięta, “Heat transfer modeling in deep geothermal application,” in Science and supercomputing in Europe - report 2006, Cineca, HPC-Europa, Pan-European Research Infrastructure on High Performance Computing. Bologna 2006, Italy, p. 338–341.

[2] M. Wróblewska, A. Pięta, “Deep lithosphere thermal modeling against surface temperature condition,” in Near Surface 2008 - 14th European meeting of Environmental and engineering geophysics, 15–17 September 2008, Cracow, Poland.

[3] D. Reilly., M. Reilly: Java Network Programming and Distributed Computing. Addison Wesley, 2002.

[4] M. MacDonald: Microsoft .NET Distributed Applications: Integrating XML Web Services and .NET Remoting. Microsoft Press, 2003

[5] H.J. Schonig, E. Geschwinde: Mono Kick Start. Sams, 2003.

[6] E. Pitt, K. McNiff: java.rmi: The Remote Method Invocation Guide. Addison Wesley, 2001.

[7] J. C. Tannehill, D.A. Anderson, R.H. Pletcher: Computational Fluid Mechanics and Heat Transfer, Second Edition, Taylor & Francis, Washington, 1997.

[8] A. Kowal, A. Piórkowski, T. Danek, A. Pięta, “Analysis of selected component technologies efficiency for parallel and distributed seismic wave field modeling,” in Innovations and Advances in Computer Sciences and Engineering, Springer, 2010.

[9] A. Piorkowski, and D. Plodzien, "Efficiency analysis of the server-side numerical computations," in Computer Networks, 16th Conference, CN 2009, Wisla, Poland, June 16-20, 2009, Communications in Computer and Information Science, Springer Berlin Heidelberg, 2009.

An Extension of Least Squares Methods for Smoothing Oscillation of Motion Predicting Function

O. Starostenko, J.T. Tello-Martínez, V. Alarcon-Aquino, J. Rodriguez-Asomoza, and R. Rosas-Romero
Research Center CENTIA, CEM Department, Universidad de las Américas-Puebla, 72820, Mexico
e-mails: {oleg.starostenko, joset.tellomz, vicente.alarcon, jorge.rodriguez, roberto.rosas}@udlap.mx

***Abstract*- A novel hybrid technique for detection and predicting the motion of objects in video stream is presented in this paper. The novelty consists in extension of Savitzky-Golay smoothing filter applying difference approach for tracing object mass center with or without acceleration in noised images. The proposed adaptation of least squares methods for smoothing the fast varying values of motion predicting function permits to avoid the oscillation of that function with the same degree of used polynomial. The better results are obtained when the time of motion interpolation is divided into subintervals, and the function is represented by different polynomials over each subinterval. Therefore, in proposed hybrid technique the spatial clusters with objects in motion are detected by the image difference operator and behavior of those clusters is analyzed using their mass centers in consecutive frames. Then the predicted location of object is computed using modified algorithm of weighted least squares model. That provides the tracing possible routes which now are invariant to oscillation of predicting polynomials and noise presented in images. For irregular motion frequently occurred in dynamic scenes, the compensation and stabilization technique is also proposed in this paper. On base of several simulated kinematics experiments the efficiency of proposed technique is analyzed and evaluated.**

Index Terms—Image processing, motion prediction, least squares model, interpolating polynomial oscillation and stabilization.

I. Introduction

A motion prediction is not a trivial task due to different types of motion and variations that occur in sequence of images where some objects in motion have complex routes with occlusions and with constantly changed illumination. In general, three key problems arise in image segmentation applied to motion analysis:

a) how to extract motion features of an object within image in order to build the appropriate feature space;

b) how to estimate the clusters from a feature space used for segmentation;

c) given the estimated clusters, how to perform spatial grouping to decide which pixels belong to which cluster and to which corresponding object [1], [2].

The complexity of motion analysis consists in a huge quantity of processed data due to necessity of bit by bit image inspection. Usually, the motion detection and prediction can be obtained in short period of time by processing object edges or principal corners instead of analysis of intensity variations or complete object correlation in consecutive frames [2], [3].

Therefore, the principal objectives of the proposed hybrid technique is to provide efficient and fast description of object routes, to apply the clustering to image that permits to trace objects even they are in rotation, to implement the motion compensation or stabilization technique in case of irregular motion frequently occurred in dynamic scenes, and finally, to predict the location of objects in motion within noised images.

The obtained information about motion can be used as input of different subsequent processes including motion detection and compensation, motion-based data compression, 3-D scene reconstruction, autonomous navigation, analysis of dynamic processes in robotics, etc. [4], [5].

II. Analysis of Motion Prediction Techniques

A sequence of images contains all necessary information about dynamic scene and usually it is described by optical flow or motion field, which can be estimated by well-known methods [2], [5]. This is a fact that these methods are too complex and slow to use them in real–time applications.

Another approach for quantitative estimation of motion characteristics is based on the block correspondence technique when the similarity of block features within consecutive frames at the high level (definition of configuration, filtering, distribution) or low level (processing boundaries, corners, textures, color regions) is computed. In this technique the same pattern is used within consecutive frames as reference [4]. It allows overcoming the problem of progressive increment of compared patterns but aggregates accumulative error proportional to time function.

The block correspondence approach has been selected for proposed technique because it is faster than others based on computing the motion field or the optical flow analysis. The accumulative error will be reduced by processing the motion predicting function in subintervals [2], [6].

The proposed technique has been developed on base of previous efforts to generate a model that measures a slowly varying motion usually corrupted by random noise [4]. That research is also referred to Savitzky-Golay filter [7].

In this paper, we expand this model implementing the interpolation and the least squares methods for motion function description as well as the developing motion prediction algorithm.

A. Difference approach and mass center tracing

The most obvious method for detecting changes between two frames $F_j(x, y)$ and $F_k(x, y,)$ consists in comparison of the corresponding pixels applying a binary difference operator $DP_{jk}(x, y)$ according to the equation with threshold τ:

T. Sobh, K. Elleithy (eds.), *Innovations in Computing Sciences and Software Engineering*,
DOI 10.1007/978-90-481-9112-3_48, © Springer Science+Business Media B.V. 2010

$$DP_{jk}(x,y)=\begin{cases}1, if \ |F_j(x,y)-F_k(x,y)|>\tau \\ 0, otherwise\end{cases} \quad (1)$$

The pixels equal to binary "*1*" are interpreted with certain approximation (depended on threshold τ) as an object in motion. In this way the computing accumulative difference in limited sequence of frames gives a set of object locations in a scene. This method is very sensitive and permits to detect small object displacement that may be used for precise motion characteristic estimation.

In previous author's works the spatial features of an object in motion are estimated by computing the position of its mass center representing that object in consecutive images of a video stream [2], [4]. In order to improve the known technique the following procedure is proposed:

a) analyzing two consecutive frames, detect the directions of atomic variation (the smallest displacement taken as a single step) for mass center in one of four possible directions: left-right or up-down;

b) if the difference is positive then an object moves to the right (up) with respect to a reference frame, otherwise the direction of motion of object is to the left (down);

c) if an object moves to the right (up) then the computed position is obtained from the following equations:

$$X_p = x_{max} - \frac{dim}{2}; \quad Y_p = y_{max} - \frac{dim}{2} \quad (2)$$

d) if an object moves to the left (down) then its position is obtained as:

$$X_p = x_{min} + \frac{dim}{2}; \quad Y_p = y_{min} + \frac{dim}{2}, \quad (3)$$

where x_{max} (x_{min}) ; y_{max} (y_{min}) are the maximum (minimum) displacement values on axis x and y of the mass center for object with the dimension *dim*;

In Fig. 1 the procedure for computing x and y coordinates of object location in a sequence of images using the atomic variation is shown.

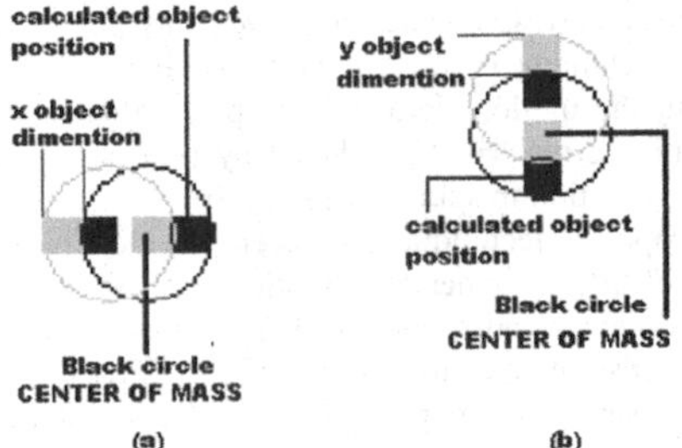

Fig. 1. Detection of object displacement in two consecutive frames

In Fig.1a) an object moves to the right because the difference between mass centers of the black (present state of object) and gray (previous state) circles representing object dimensions is positive for two consecutive positions. Whereas the difference in Fig. 1b) is negative the object moves toward down.

B. *Least squares method*

The principal disadvantage of well-known methods for motion prediction which use interpolation is the oscillating nature of high grade polynomials that introduce significant deviations during approximation. Moreover, if the proper kinematics of an object generates inflexions, the polynomial will oscillate much more. In a practice each object in a scene has its associated transformation matrix, which transfers object from model space to screen space in frame [8].

Frequently for motion prediction the least squares method is used where the following solution is obtained: [9].

$$min \ p\|Ap - s\|^2 , \quad (4)$$

where A is a given model matrix, s is a vector of noisy observations, and p is the sought parameter vector. If s has uniform Gaussian noise the solution is given by: $p = A^+ s$,

where A^+ denotes the pseudo-inverse transform. In general case of operation with a rank deficient model matrix, the minimum solution will be computed from the infinite number of partial solutions. However, in our proposal we will concentrate on the case where A has full column rank. Then the pseudo-inverse transform becomes:

$$A^+ = (A^T A)^{-1} A^T \quad (5)$$

In any case we obtain the parameter vector by multiplying the pseudo-inverse by the data vector.

During the image processing some points representing the object have more importance than others because their distances to the reference point are more important [9]. Therefore, we will denote the measured data by f_i $i=1,2,...,n$ and the smoothed (filtered) data by g_i, $i=1,2,...,n$. So, the polynomial $p(x)$ of degree M fitted to the data f_i is computed as

$$pi(x) = \sum_{k=0}^{M} b_k \left(\frac{x - xi}{\Delta x}\right)^k \quad (6)$$

In order to determine the coefficients b_k, the expression below must be minimum as it is mentioned in eq. 4:

$$\sum_{k=0}^{M} (p(x) - f)^2 = min \quad (7)$$

According to Gander [7] using the equations:

$$A = \begin{bmatrix} (-n_L)^M \cdots - n_L \cdots 1 \\ \vdots \\ 0 \\ \vdots \\ n_R^M \cdots\cdots\cdots - n_R \cdots 1 \end{bmatrix} \in R^{(n_L+n_R+1)x(M+1)}$$

$$b = \begin{bmatrix} b_M \\ \vdots \\ b_1 \\ b_0 \end{bmatrix} \in R^{(M+1)}, \text{ and } f = \begin{bmatrix} f_{i-n_L} \\ \vdots \\ f_{i1} \\ \vdots \\ f_{i+n_R} \end{bmatrix} \in R^{(n_L+n_R+1)}$$

the least squares problem may be solved taking

$$\|Ab - f\|^2 = min \ . \quad (8)$$

It is a fact, that in practice the least squares problem is solved by means of QR-decomposition, thus $A = QR$, where Q is an orthogonal $(n_L+n_R+1)\times(M+1)$ matrix and R is upper triangular $(M+1)\times(M+1)$ matrix. Then the solution c of system is obtained as.

$$c = \left[\frac{1}{r_{M+1,}r_{M+1}}\right] Qe_{M+1}, \quad (9)$$

where e_{M+1} denotes a $(M+1)$ unit vector [10].

A major complexity consists in selection of filter parameters n_L, n_R, and M. So, intuitively we propose the idea that the smoothed value g_i at the point x_i may be calculated by modified average of a nearest weighted vales of data presenting a motion.

In this paper we fit a polynomial through representative points according to the type of motion (constant or with acceleration) as it is shown in Fig. 2. Here n_L and n_R denotes the number of representative points on the left and right with respect to the reference point x_i. The $p_i(x)$ denotes a polynomial of degree M which is fitted to the observed n_L+n_R+1 points in the least squares sense.

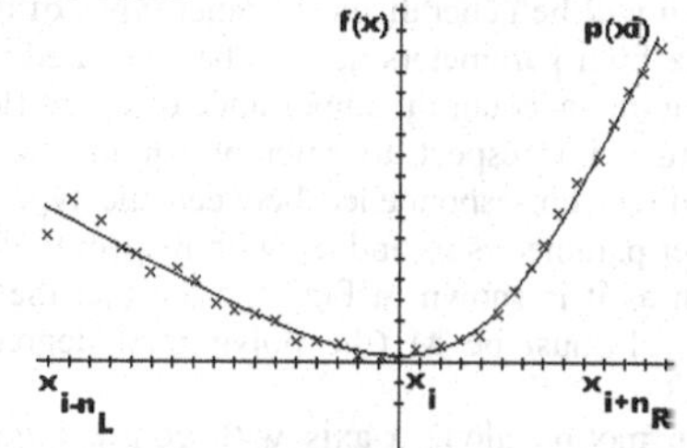

Fig. 2. A fitting the polynomial through representative points

For better illustration of motion type the representative points may be shown as it is presented in Fig. 3 where the cases of positive a) and negative b) acceleration are depicted.

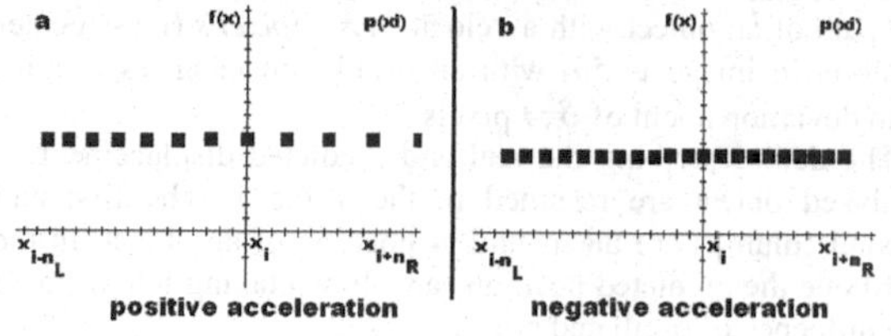

Fig. 3 Representation of the representation points in motion

In these cases, the number of points with respect to reference one x_i (as it has been shown in Fig.1) is taken according to the grade of importance in the construction of polynomial $p(x_i)$. For example, in the case of positive acceleration n_L is less than n_R, therefore, the distance between successive points is increased distorting more and more the polynomial $p(x_i)$. For negative acceleration according to Fig. 3b) $n_L > n_R$ and space between successive point is decreased.

There are some other approaches for motion description. One of them is a statistical approach where Bayesian filters are used for the tracking an object with easy prediction by Brownian motion model. Brownian model is extremely conservative and does not satisfy the dynamics of irregular motion [11]. Kalman's filter is the standard technique for motion prediction by improving state estimation over the time. However, this filter needs data preprocessing to determine which measurements in an image should be used to update the motion model [4], [7].

The multi-hypothesis motion compensated method predicts a block from a weighted sum of multiple reference blocks in the frame buffer. It can provide less prediction errors by efficient combining these reference blocks [5].

After analysis of well-known methods the hybrid approach for motion prediction is introduced, particularly the proposed algorithm is developed taking into account advantages of the interpolation method, least squares approach, block correspondence approach for tracing mass centers of objects in motion [2], and the technique for irregular motion compensation and stabilization.

III. PROPOSED TECHNIQUE FOR MOTION PREDICTION

The proposed technique for motion prediction consists in two procedures: the first one has been developed for fast motion detection and prediction of object presented by its mass center combining partial interpolations with adjustment of approximation function by least squares method. The second one implies adjustment of coefficients for Savitzky-Golay smoothing filter providing the reduction of oscillation of the predicting polynomial describing the object behavior without and with acceleration.

The first procedure is implemented by the following algorithm:

a) the input normalized images are the frames of video stream to be converted to gray scale images;

b) the detection of objects in motion is obtained by analysis of changes $DPjk(x,y)$ between consecutive images $F(x,y,j)$ and $F(x,y,k)$ according to eq.1 where threshold τ is selected with respect to necessary quantity of edges representing an object;

c) the objects in motion detected by step b) are wrapped by circular envelope (with the radius, for example, of 100 pixels). It is used for description of object in the following frame without taking into account small variations of object form. Using the envelope instead of complete borders simplifies manipulation of objects with rotation or occlusions;

d) the center of envelope is computed. It represents the object gravity center;

e) taking previously known envelope center coordinates (x_0, y_0) and (x_1, y_1) the linear interpolation is obtained by

$$y_{pre} = y_1 + \left[\frac{y_1 - y_0}{x_1 - x_0}\right](x_{pre} - x_1), \quad (10)$$

where x_{pre} is the predicted coordinate of envelope center on x axis. The predicted coordinates are found on the same line that connects two known positions. It is obvious that error may be significant, but it is enough for computing the approximate location.

f) In order to fit better the result, three object positions (x_0, y_0), (x_1, y_1), and (x_{pre}, y_{pre}) are used applying the least squares method for the system of 3 equations:

$$y_0 = a + b(x - x_0) + c(x - x_0)^2$$
$$y_1 = a + b(x - x_1) + c(x - x_1)^2$$
$$y_{pre} = a + b(x - x_{pre}) + c(x - x_{pre})^2 \qquad (11)$$

The advantage of this approach is the fast processing which does not accumulate a lot of initial positions as in Lagrange or Newton approaches and polynomial has only second grade.

The second procedure of the proposed technique is used for adjustment of coefficients for Savitzky-Golay smoothing filter which consists in extension of weighted least squares method.

Suppose we have two random variables x and y which have a linear relation: $y = a + bx$. In order to predict the closest next point we seek for sums:

$$\sum_{k=0}^{n} y = an + b\sum_{k=0}^{n} x, \quad \sum_{k=0}^{n} xy = a\sum_{k=0}^{n} x + b\sum_{k=0}^{n} x^2 \qquad (12)$$

Using the experimental readings and minimizing the functional variance, the constants a and b are computed as:

$$a = \frac{(\sum_{k=0}^{n} y)(\sum_{k=0}^{n} x^2) - (\sum_{k=0}^{n} x)(\sum_{k=0}^{n} xy)}{n\sum_{k=0}^{n} x^2 - (\sum_{k=0}^{n} x)^2}$$

$$b = \frac{n(\sum_{k=0}^{n} xy) - (\sum_{k=0}^{n} x)(\sum_{k=0}^{n} y)}{n\sum_{k=0}^{n} x^2 - (\sum_{k=0}^{n} x)^2} \qquad (13)$$

In the same manner for a parabolic function the approximation by the least squares method is presented by $y = a + bx^2$ where the coefficients are:

$$\sum_{k=0}^{n} y = an + b\sum_{k=0}^{n} x + c\sum_{k=0}^{n} x^2$$
$$\sum_{k=0}^{n} xy = a\sum_{k=0}^{n} x + b\sum_{k=0}^{n} x^2 + c\sum_{k=0}^{n} x^3$$
$$\sum_{k=0}^{n} x^2 y = a\sum_{k=0}^{n} x^2 + b\sum_{k=0}^{n} x^3 + c\sum_{k=0}^{n} x^4 \qquad (14)$$

Very good results are provided by spline approach when approximating function is computed by a set of functions which have enough flexibility to adapt to the given data and which can be easily evaluated. Traditionally, polynomials have been used for this purpose. However, for fast varying values the degree of polynomial increases that causes the oscillation of exhibiting function.

The situation changes when the basic interval is divided into subintervals and the function is represented by different polynomials over each subinterval. The polynomials are joined together at the interval endpoints in such a way that a certain degree of smoothness of the resulting function called a polynomial spline function is guaranteed [12].

For the case of linear interpolation the piecewise polynomial is constructed for each of subintervals $[x_{i+1}, x_i]$ as

$$S_i(x) = f(x_i) + \frac{f(x_{i+1}) - f(x_i)}{x_{i+1} - x_i}(x - x_i) =$$
$$= f(x_i) + f[x_{i+1}, x_i](x - x_i) \qquad (15)$$

For quadratic interpolation the next equation is used

$$q_i(x) = f(x_i) + d_i(x - x_i) + \frac{d_{i+1} - d_i}{2(x_{i+1} - x_i)}(x - x_i)^2 \qquad (16)$$

where $d_{i+1} = -d_i + 2\left[\frac{f(x_{i+1}) - f(x_i)}{x_{i+1} - x_i}\right]$

Splines are highly recommended for data fitting whenever there is no particular reason for using a single polynomial or other elementary functions such as sine, cosine, or exponential ones [13].

IV. Experiments and Discussion

We start with the simplest motion type when the object moves along oscillated trajectory without acceleration and then the approach will be generalized for other types of motions. In this case the filter parameters need to be evaluated in different ways, taking into account the importance of the n_L (left) and n_R (right) terms with respect to reference point. Additionally, there is a direct correspondence between the type of motion and the filter parameters n_L and n_R, with respect to the value of acceleration as it is shown in Fig. 4. Note that the sum of n_L and n_R plus 1 must be M (the polynomial degree of fitted points).

Since the motion along x-axis with constant velocity and slight oscillation is symmetric at any time with respect to intermediate points in the path of object, it is evident that distance between neighboring representative points is similar. For demonstration of the experimental results, the initial choice of coefficients is, for example, $n_L=2$ and $n_R=2$. Fig. 5 shows the path of an object with a velocity $v_x=15pixel/s$ (mass center position in image $y=50$) with an oscillation taken as a noise with deviation about of $\delta=4$ pixels.

The data describing the real and predicted displacement of analyzed object are resumed in the Table 1. The first and second columns are the x- and y- position of an object. In the third one the predicted positions are shown taking into account the influence of oscillated noise.

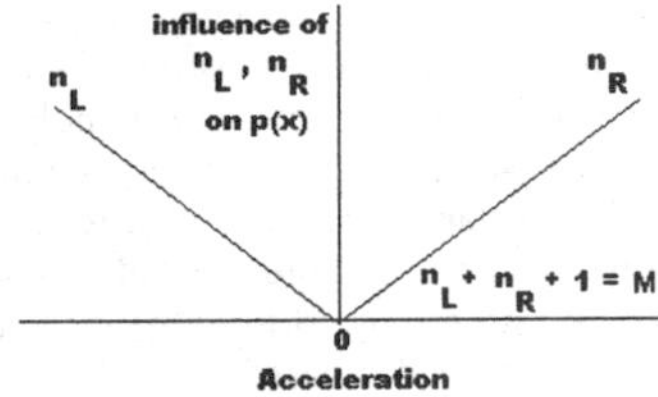

Fig. 4. Weighted least squares coefficients with respect to reference point.

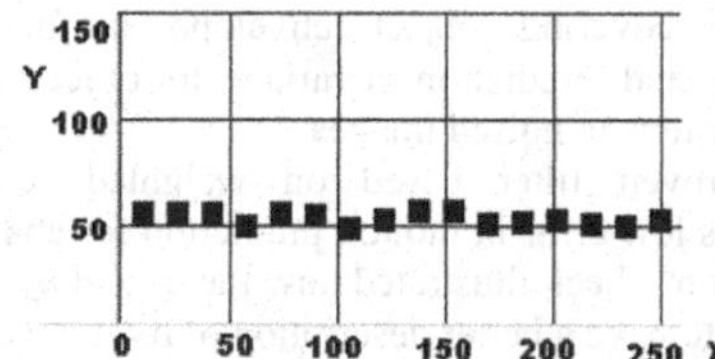

Fig. 5. An object displacement along x-axis with constant velocity and slowly varying y-position.

In the fourth column the average value of relative errors of prediction is presented after applying the equation:

$$\delta = \frac{\sum_{i=1}^{n}\left(\frac{\left|real(y_i)-predicted\,(y_i)\right|}{real(y_i)}\right)}{n} * 100\%, \quad (17)$$

where $\left|real(y_i)-predicted\,(y_i)\right|$ is the absolute value of deviation of predicted positions with respect to real ones and n is the number of computed positions.

TABLE 1
THE REAL AND PREDICTED DISPLACEMENT OF OBJECT

x-axis position	real displacement	predicted displacement	relative error
18.5	55	55	0
34.5	55	55	0
50.5	52	52	0
66.5	52	53.0952	-0.02063
82.5	54.5	52.8651	0.030926
98.5	51	51.127	-0.00248
114.5	50	51.246	-0.02431
130.5	54	53.8571	0.002653
146.5	56	54.9286	0.019505
162.5	53	53.0079	-0.00015
178.5	50.5	51.4683	-0.01881
194.5	51.5	51.1429	0.006982
210.5	51	50.4921	0.010059
226.5	49.5	49.9603	-0.00921
242.5	50.5	50.5	0
258.5	50	52.5	-0.05

Fig.6 shows kinematics of the analyzed motion. The gray line is the real path whereas the black one is the result of computing the interpolated fitting polynomial. The black bold line is the predicted position of the object in the last step.

In a similar way we can obtain polynomials for more complex motion with positive or negative acceleration and with presence of nose. In Fig. 7 $2pixels/s^2$ acceleration is applied to an object at $x=10$ and $y=50$ initial position.

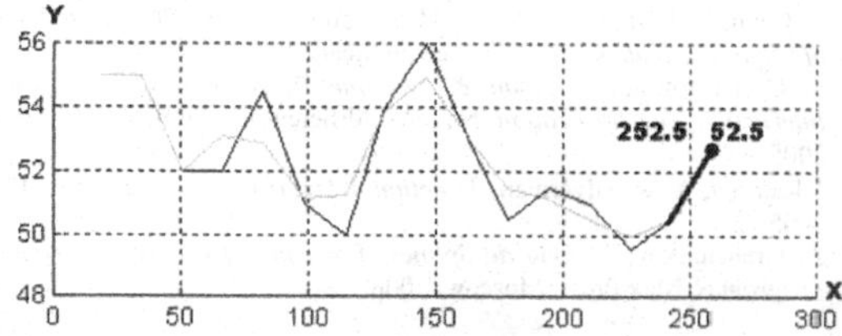

Fig. 6. The kinematics of the analyzed motion

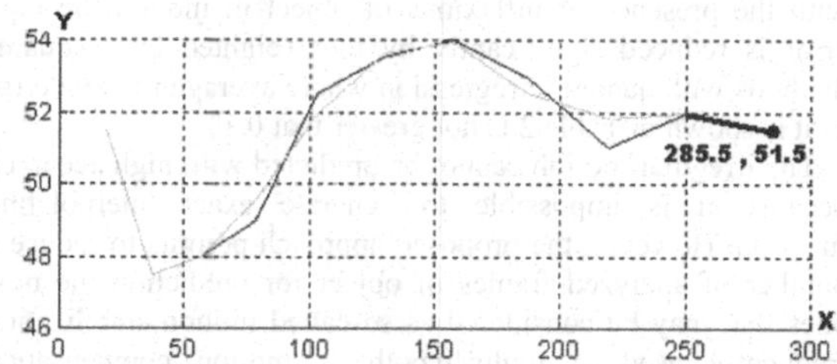

Fig.7. The kinematics of the analyzed motion with acceleration

Note that with a non-uniform motion, the spacing between two successive positions varies with a time.

The most interesting case is the parabolic motion. The arbitrary parameters are: v_{ox} = $20pixels/s$, v_{oy}=$70pixels/s$, acceleration is $-g$=$-9.8pixels/s^2$. The measured data are corrupted by a noise of δ=2 $pixels$. Due to presence of noise the parabolic path, will be distorted. Fig. 8 and the Table 2 describe the experiment for parabolic motion prediction in noised images.

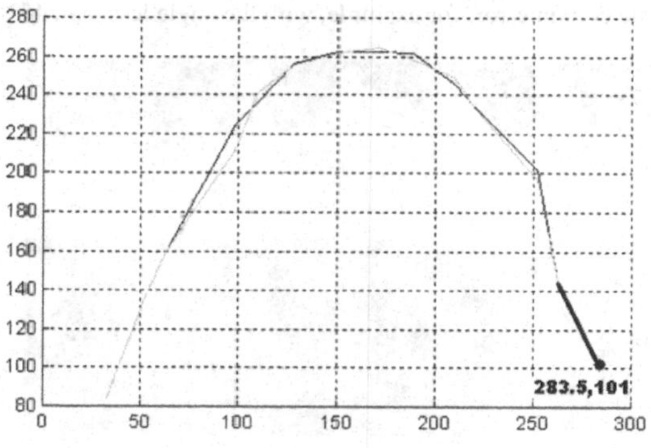

Fig.8. Parabolic motion prediction

TABLE 2.
REAL AND PREDICTED DISPLACEMENT FOR PARABOLIC MOTION

x-axis position	real displacement	predicted displacement	relative error
32.5	84	84	0
52.5	137	137	0
63	159.5	159.5	0
98.5	225	212.4841	0.058903
109.5	236	240.6508	-0.01933
128.5	256.5	255.6825	0.003197
150.5	262.5	261.8571	0.002455
171.5	262.5	264.7222	-0.00839
189	261.5	258.381	0.012071
210	245.5	249.381	-0.01556
220.5	234	233.1349	0.003711
252.5	202	196.627	0.027326
262.5	145	145	0
283.5	91.9	101	-0.09

Due to the high grades of polynomial which oscillates more with the presence of inflexions of object in motion the high error is reduced significantly by the weighted least squares methods with quadratic regression where average relative error as it is shown in Table 2 is not greater that 0.1%.

The irregular motion cannot be predicted with high accuracy because it is impossible to generate exact interpolating function. However, the proposed approach permits to reduce a number of analyzed frames of object for prediction the next ones that may be considered as so-called motion stabilization frequently used in multi-hypothesis motion compensation prediction approach.

The stabilization heuristic function is obtained as a set of possible routes of an object in motion when the error between the predicted and described by interpolating function displacement vector goes to zero. Taking into account interpolating function the probability of each route is computed and more probable one is selected.

In Fig. 9 the stabilization of the interpolation process is shown. The white line presents the direction of real displacement, the black straight one shows the direction of predicted motion. The stabilization is obtained when the real and computed displacement vectors have the similar direction with the certain error, for example, with the angle less than 45°.

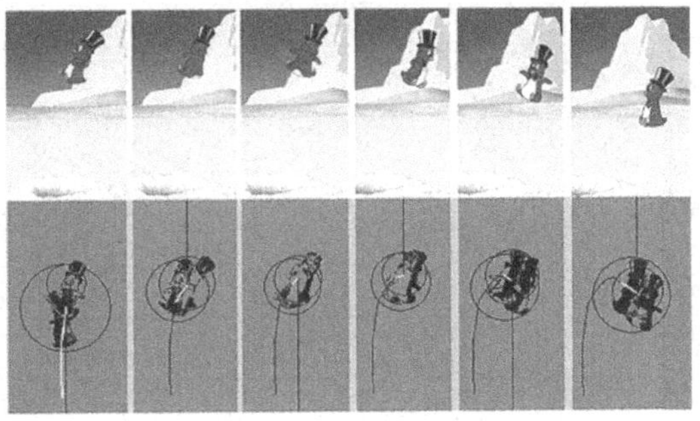

Fig. 9. Oscillation of the interpolating polynomial reaching the stabilization when the real and computed displacement vectors have the similar direction

The proposed technique is one of the possible contributions to still open problem of motion prediction and may be used in applications where reduction of oscillation of predicting polynomial that describes the object behavior in motion in noised images without or with acceleration is required.

V. CONCLUSION

This paper presents early results in development of efficient techniques for motion analysis and prediction. The well-known approaches for motion prediction are not always so useful and fast for real-time applications. The proposed technique is one of possible solution for designing fast facilities for estimating and predicting position of objects in motion based on interpolation of their routes.

For reduction of the processed data the mass center representing the object in motion is used. Its tracing is done by analysis of covering object envelope useful for route construction and prediction invariant to object rotation or partial occlusions in noised images.

The improved filter based on weighted least squares approach has low error in motion prediction for analyzed types of motion. It has been illustrated how the n_L and n_R coefficients can be used to have a better description of motion type.

The principal restriction of proposed technique consists in that the processed video streams captured by a single fixed camera and characteristics of relative motion of objects are not taken into account.

Preliminary experiments with the proposed hybrid technique show fast and accurate motion prediction taking into account irregular motion, possible objects rotation, and illumination changes. One possible extension to this work includes combining the results of multiple interpolation models into efficient one and extension of the technique to other types of motion.

ACKNOWLEDGMENT

This research is sponsored by Mexican National Council of Science and Technology, CONACyT, Projects: #48259, #109115 and #109417.

REFERENCES

[1] G. Farneback. Very high accuracy velocity estimation using orientation tensors, parametric motion, and simultaneous segmentation of the motion field. *In ICCV*, Vancouver, July 2001, pp. 171–177.

[2] O. Starostenko, A. Ramírez, A. Zehe, G. Burlak. Novel algorithms for estimating motion characteristics within a limited sequence of images, in Book *Recent Advances in Interdisciplinary Applied Physics*, Elsevier , UK , 2005, pp. 277-281.

[3] K. Bendjilali, F. Berkhuche and T. Jin, Characterizing the exact collision course in the plane for mobile robotics application, in Book *Novel Algorithms and Techniques in telecommunications, Automation and Industrial Electronics*, Ed. Tarek Sobh, Khaled Elleithy, Springer, 2008 (CISSE 2007 proceedings)

[4] J. T. Tello, O. Starostenko, G.Burlak, "New Motion Prediction Algorithm Invairant to Rotation and Occlusion", *J. Advances in Computer Science in México*, Vol. 13. 2005. pp.23-33

[5] B. Jahne, *Digital image processing*, 5ed., Springer, 2002

[6] G. Papadopoulos, R. Bryant, W. Pitts, "Flow Characterization of Flickering Methane/Air Diffusion Flames Using Particle Image Velocimetry", *J. Experiments in Fluids*, Vol. 33, No. 3, 2002, pp. 472-481.

[7] W. Gander, J.Hrebícek U von Matt. *Smoothing Filters. Solving Problems in Scientific Computing Using Maple and MATLAB*, Springer, Paperback, Jul 27, 2004.

[8] J. Wolberg, *Data Analysis Using the Method of Linear Squares*, Kindle Ed., 2006.

[9] C. Radhakrishna Rao, H.Toutenburg, Heumann, *Linear Models and Generalization: Least Squares and Alternatives*, Springer, 2007.

[10] R. Chan, C.Greif, *Milestones in Matrix Computation: The selected works of Gene H. Golub*, Oxford Science publications, 2007.

[11] S. C. Di Pittinuri, *Human & Machine Perception: Communication, Interaction, and Integration*, NY, World Scientific Publishing Company, 2005.

[12] J Ramsay, B W Silverman, *Functional Data Analysis*, Springer, USA, 2005.

[13] A. Grebennikov, *Método de Splines: Elementos teóricos, Algorítmos y Programas*, Max Press, Moscow, 2008.

Security of Virtualized Applications: Microsoft App-V and VMware ThinApp

Michael Hoppe
Fakultät für Informatik
Otto-von-Guericke University Magdeburg
39106 Magdeburg, Germany
Email: michael.hoppe@st.uvgu.de

Patrick Seeling
Department of Computing and New Media Technologies
University of Wisconsin-Stevens Point
Stevens Point, WI 54481, USA
Email: pseeling@ieee.org

Abstract—**Virtualization has gained great popularity in recent years with application virtualization being the latest trend. Application virtualization offers several benefits for application management, especially for larger and dynamic deployment scenarios. In this paper, we initially introduce the common application virtualization principles before we evaluate the security of Microsoft App-V and VMware ThinApp application virtualization environments with respect to external security threats. We compare different user account privileges and levels of sandboxing for virtualized applications. Furtherwmore, we identify the major security risks as well as trade-offs with ease of use that result from the virtualization of applications.**

I. Introduction and Related Works

Different virtualization technologies have attracted great popularity in recent years, mainly driven by increases in computing power and typically unused system resources. A more recent development in the domain of virtualization is the virtualization of individual applications. Application virtualization can be defined as a technology that decouples applications from desktop operating systems to dynamically deliver applications, see, e.g., [1].

In the application virtualization domain, a virtualization layer sits between the operating system and the virtualized application, which is typically described as being executed in a 'bubble' or sandbox, making the application partially independent from the hosting operating system environment. Current examples for application virtualization environments are, e.g., Microsoft App-V [2], VMware ThinApp [3] or the Feather-weight Virtual Machine [4].

It is initially noteworthy to identify the main differences between different virtualization technologies, which we illustrate in Figure 1. In a typical non-virtualized environment, applications directly consume the resources offered through the operating system. All dependencies for required system resources for a specific application, e.g., complete frameworks or individual dynamically linked libraries (DLL), must be resolved directly. The utilization of these shared system resources can be problematic when different applications are requiring different versions of a shared system resource and upward or downward compatibility is not or only partially given.

In a virtualization environment that relies on a hypervisor to emulate a complete computer system (virtual machine), a complete operating system and all dependencies for a specific application need to be installed. For more than one specific target application, the considerations for the non-virtualized environment are applicable as well.

In a virtualized application environment, resources provided by the hosting operating system are required for the virtual environment to function properly. In a virtual application context, each application is executed inside its own (partially virtualized) environment, which includes the application-specific system resource requirements and dependencies to other applications that are not provided by a standardized version of the operating system. A standardized version of the hosting operating system is required to ensure that the virtualized application can be executed on different configurations of the underlying operating system. (The standardized version of the hosting operating system can be thought of as a baseline of different system resources that will always be available with an installation of the hosting operating system.) Examples for system resources that are provided to the virtualized application through the virtualization layer are access to the registry, file systems or other programs. The overall concept of independent virtualized applications, which themselves include all necessary dependencies, is targeted at system stability and easier manageability of applications. In turn, virtualized applications can be seen to be closer to, e.g., the JAVA virtual machine environment.

While security for computer system virtualization has attracted research interests in the past, see, e.g., [6]–[9], the security of the underlying operating system and related resources through the use of virtualized applications has attracted very little research efforts so far. Most security considerations for virtualized applications to date are focusing on the practical aspects of secure provisioning in virtual application environments, see, e.g., [10]–[12] for the App-V and ThinApp environments we evaluate throughout this paper.

The remainder of this paper is organized as follows. In Section II, we provide a more detailed description of the App-V and ThinApp environments for virtualized applications. In the following Section III, we briefly outline the potential for security breaches in virtualized applications and the hosting operating system. In Section IV, we describe an exemplary evaluation of different security breaches and how they impact

T. Sobh, K. Elleithy (eds.), *Innovations in Computing Sciences and Software Engineering*,
DOI 10.1007/978-90-481-9112-3_49,

the security of the hosting operating system and virtualized applications. We provide an initial investigation of a higher level of isolation between virtualized applications and the hosting operating system in Section V before we conclude in Section VI.

II. VIRTUALIZED APPLICATIONS

Microsoft provides an application virtualization with its App-V solution, which is part of the Microsoft Desktop Optimization Pack. We illustrate the general functionality of the application virtualization environment of App-V (provided through the installation of the App-V client) in Figure 2. We note that the approach followed in the ThinApp environment developed by VMware is similar.

The virtual operating system surrounds the application and provides the required system environment. The virtualized operating components typically provide access to the registry, file system operations, other system resources as well as additionally application-specific requirements. This virtual operating system does not include all functionalities a real operating system offers, but provides only the required infrastructure the virtualized application requires and that is different from the standardized version of the hosting operating system. All higher functions, access to periphery elements like print services, processor access, access to the memory and all processes necessary after the application has been executed, are forwarded to the hosting operating system. This approach allows for a small size of the virtualized application, but creates a dependency to the operating system architecture and assumed standard system resources.

The environmental elements provided by the virtual operating system are stored in the application virtualization container. The application virtualization container appears to the real file system as single file (which could in turn be an executable file or any other file type), that includes the whole application and the virtualized operating system infrastructure around it. The container stores the necessary changes on the file system to encapsulate the application from the real file system. In addition, the container stores the virtual system registry, which contains the required entries for the application. The container does not include the complete registry, but only the entries which are necessary to launch the application and all required additional components. The virtual registry operates together with the system registry, whereby the hosting operating system's registry and the virtual registry are presented to the virtualized application by the virtual operation system. One security measure provided in the ThinApp virtualization environment is the possibility to encapsulate the application access to files completely from its environment. In this particular case, the virtual operating system would present only the virtual file system to the application. Otherwise, the application can be allowed to obtain access to the real file system, which is necessary if the virtualized application should be able to operate on objects outside of the virtualization container, such as typically the case for general office applications. The level of isolation or sandboxing of the virtualized application can hence be adjusted based on the usage scenario.

The permission context of the virtualization container and all interactions between the virtualization environment and hosting operating system are those for the current user. In App-V they are handled through the locally installed App-V client and hosting operating system, while no client installation is required for the ThinApp environment. The App-V client creates a special hard-drive (the 'Q:' drive) on the client workstation as part of the installation process. This drive is not accessible; only the App-V client has access and privileges for this isolated drive. This approach helps to maintain a virtualized application's integrity against common actions of the system or user. In the ThinApp environment,

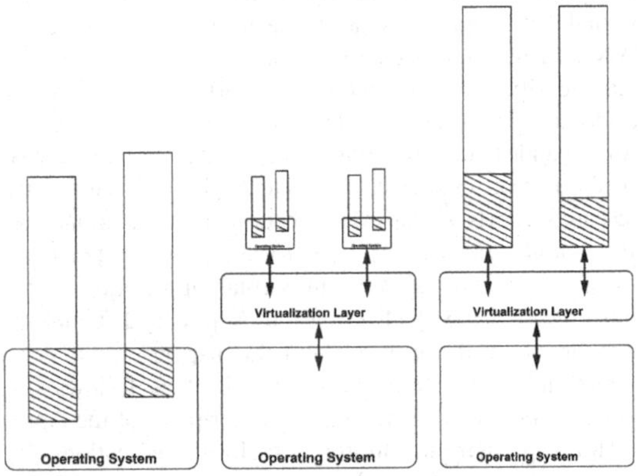

Fig. 1. Traditional applications versus virtualized applications. The virtualized applications have non-standard operating system components in their individual virtualized environment and any access to the underlying operating system is performed through the virtualization layer, see [5].

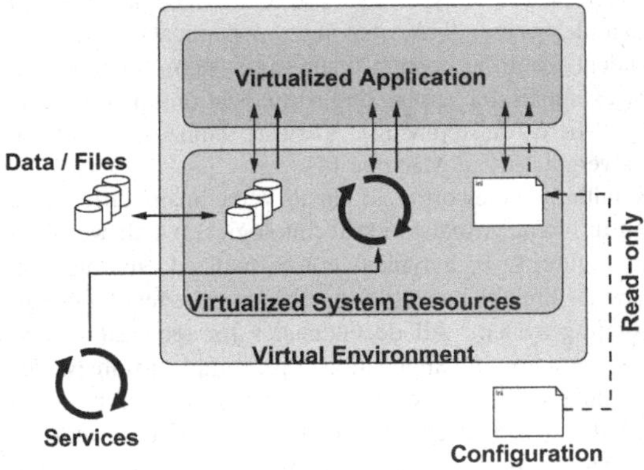

Fig. 2. Default configuration for virtualized applications in Microsoft App-V, see [13]. The virtualized application has full access to application-specific items in the virtualization container (configuration, system services and file system), while access to the hosting operating system is limited the virtualization environment, which can be configured to allow for different levels of isolation.

typically an executable file is created that can be directly executed and provides the virtualization environment directly. The second approach App-V uses to keep the application integrity protected is how changes by the user or the system are handled. Changes on configurations of an application are not always harmful, but also often mandatory to provide correct functioning of one and same application in different scenarios.

Changes on virtualized applications within the App-V environment are differentiated by who made them, the user or the system. User changes are stored individually for the virtual application and for each user in the respective user profile, while system changes are stored centrally on the workstation. This approach offers each user the possibility to make changes for the virtualized application without affecting the base application package. In ThinApp environments, all changes (the sandbox environment) are stored by default in folders created in the user profile, the directory the executed application resides in or a custom directory.

Both evaluated virtualization environments result in a behavior that is similar to a locally installed application, but with one major advantage for integrity: the local (base) application package will never (and should never) be affected. An additional benefit in a multi-user environment is that global customizations for a locally installed application influence all users, while virtualized applications in application virtualization environments can be customized by any user individually without influencing the virtualized applications of other users.

III. Attack Surfaces in Virtualization Environments

Possibilities for exploitable vulnerabilities vary with respect to the employed virtualization environment. In the complete virtualization of computer systems, the hypervisor that simulates the computing environment (virtual machine), the operating system in the virtual machine itself and processes in the virtual machine are typical targets for potential attacks. Typically, the only means of gaining access to the underlying hosting operating system through this type of virtualization is the successful attack of the hypervisor, as it is typically the only component that interacts directly with the hosting operating system[1].

In virtualized application environments, the tight integration between the hosting operating system and the virtualization environment allows for the exploitation of additional potential vulnerabilities. We illustrate these potential attack surfaces in Figure 3.

The attack surfaces for virtualized applications in particular are the application itself, the virtualized system components required by the virtualized application and the virtualization environment. One major difference from the approach of hypervisors and virtual machines is that the tight integration of the virtualized application with the underlying operating system results in the process management for the virtualized

[1]We note that in several virtualization environments additional interaction between the hosting and virtual operating system exist, e.g., through usage of shared folders or clipboards.

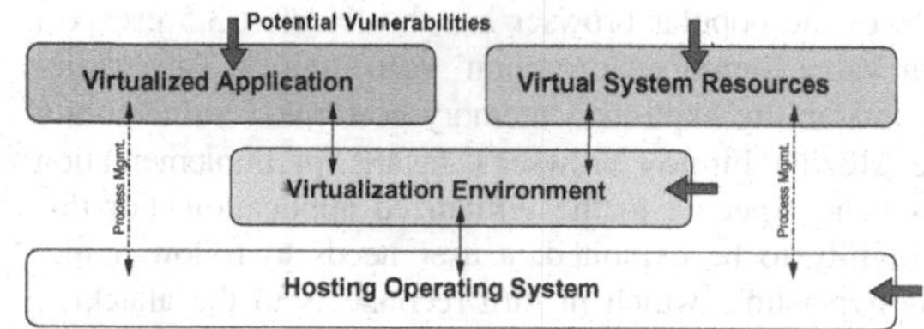

Fig. 3. Attack surfaces for an executing virtualized application are (i) the application itself, (ii) dependent components that are included in the virtual system resources, (iii) the virtualization environment itself and (iv) the hosting operating system.

application being handled through the hosting operating system. Through initial investigations, we observed that the process control for the virtualized application is handled directly by the scheduler of the hosting operating system. In turn, we conclude that the investigated virtualization environments, e.g., the App-V client, do not provide a strict separation between the hosting operating system and the virtualized application, but rather only provides interception of accesses to system resources provided within the virtualized application's context.

This interaction can be fine-tuned to allow for different levels of isolation (or sandboxing), as required by the usage scenario. For a virtualized office application, for example, the user typically will need to save modified documents to a local or remote location. The virtualization environment in turn needs to allow for interaction with the file system through the hosting operating system, in turn increasing the potential attack surface. Other applications, such as web browsers, on the other hand, do not require access to the file system of the hosting operating system.

IV. Virtualized Application Security in Partially Sandboxed Environments

In this section, we present an exemplary evaluation of the potential security breaches that are possible by exploiting existing vulnerabilities in virtualized applications. To simplify the testing of the extends to which a remote attacker would be able to obtain access to the virtualized application and its packaged resources as well as the underlying hosting operating system, we chose to employ the popular Metasploit framework (development version 3.3), which greatly simplifies the associated tasks of evaluating vulnerabilities, see, e.g., [14], [15].

The client operating system utilized was Microsoft Windows XP Professional with Service Pack 3 and all subsequent updates installed until October 1st, 2009, with the Microsoft App-V client installed (version 4.5.1.15580). In addition, we utilized VMware ThinApp (version 4.0.3) with the 'Write-Copy' isolation mode to generate an executable file. We note that in both cases, we assume that the application to be executed within the virtualization environment requires access to the hosting operating system's file system.

The virtualized application with security vulnerabilities chosen was Mozilla Firefox 3.5.0 RC. This particular preview version of the popular browser has the 'Firefox 3.5 escape() Return Value Memory Corruption' vulnerability. This particular vulnerability exploits a memory corruption vulnerability in the Mozilla Firefox browser's JavaScript implementation and is hence specific to the virtualized application. For this vulnerability to be exploited, a user needs to follow a malicious hyper-link, which in turn reconnects to the attacking computer's Metasploit server and allows a remote attacker to exploit the vulnerability.

For our experiment, we used two different types of exploits, namely (i) the `generic/shell_reverse_tcp` exploit, which provides a remote shell connection to the attacker, and (ii) the `windows/patchupvncinject/reverse_tcp_allports` exploit, which tries to connect back to the attacker on all possible TCP ports (1-65535), and then downloads, injects and executes a VNC server DLL in the attacked computer's memory, providing the attacker with a complete remote desktop.

Both exploits were tested in the default virtualization environments of Microsoft App-V and VMware ThinApp for two different scenarios on the attacked workstation, whereby (i) the virtualized application is executed by a user with simple privileges and (ii) the virtualized application is executed by an administrator.

A. Normal User Account

Once an attacker is able to exploit the vulnerability in the virtualized application and gain access, all resources and permissions that are available to the user are also available to the attacker. In the case of the VNC DLL injection attack, an attacker would additionally be able to remotely observe the user's actions. The connection between the attacked workstation and the attacker can be disconnected by closing the virtualized application. This requires a significant amount of time and the process has to be forced to be terminated through the task manager, which is typically not a procedure undertaken by regular users. The alternate approach of opening a remote command line, on the other hand, survives the termination of the virtualized application. The only indicators that there is still a remote command shell in execution are the missing notification that the virtualized application stopped, which is produced by the App-V client after a virtualized application was shut down. In turn, the only possibility to close those connections would be to shut down the App-V client or terminate the command shell process. We achieved similar results in the ThinApp application virtualization environment.

B. Administrative Account

With the virtualized application process being executed utilizing administrative privileges on the host operating system, a potential exploit of the vulnerability results in the execution of malicious code with administrative privileges. The attacker is in turn able to create, change and delete content everywhere on the workstation. We evaluated this particular behavior by creation of content under the system partition's main folders. In addition, the administrative privileges also allow for modification or damaging of the virtualized application in its virtual operating system environment. We note that full deletion was not possible because some elements were still in use in the VNC DLL attack, but possible using the remote command line attack. These changes, however, are only applied for the user and not sytem-wide. We achieved similar results in the ThinApp application virtualization environment.

V. Virtualized Application Security in Sandboxed Environments

The initial evaluation of the default security settings for the two evaluated virtualization environments in Section IV illustrates that security considerations cannot be neglected for virtualized applications. One of the main reasons for the potential of security breaches is that the virtualization environments will typically require some level of interaction with the hosting operating system's file system. In this section, we evaluate a completely sandboxed environment (which, for example, can be achieved using detailed manual configurations in ThinApp). An additional approach we evaluate here is the installation of the application itself in a sandboxed environment, which is focused on providing security. Similar to the virtual operating system approaches, which can be configured for both App-V and ThinApp environments to provide fully sandboxed operation, the Sandboxie application [16] intercepts all default system interactions, e.g., file operations, process creation or registry manipulations, similar to the virtualization environments described in Section II. Though this particular application is targeted at executing locally installed applications or install applications in a sandboxed environment, it can also be used to execute virtualized applications. We additionally note that the Sandboxie application is not geared toward application distribution.

We repeat our evaluations performed for App-V and ThinApp as described in Section IV within the Sandboxie environment (trial version 3.40) for (i) an installation of the Firefox browser into the sandbox and (ii) execution of the virtualized Firefox browser using the single executable generated by ThinApp. We generated the executable using the 'Full' isolation mode in ThinApp according to [12], but were not able to execute it.

Using either approach in a sandboxed environment successfully circumvents the creation and deletion of files outside the sandbox. The permissions of the user executing the application in the sandboxed environment are applicable, e.g., content of all directories and files to which the user has access can be displayed. The Sandboxie environment also is able to intercept the VNC interaction; however, a potential attacker would still be able to monitor the user's actions. Furthermore, the Sandboxie environment successfully protects changes to system settings, such as user management actions.

In order to gain access to any generated files, the user would have to navigate through the file system or use a GUI within the Sandboxie environment. The drawback of such fully sandboxed environments, in other words, is that with the enhanced benefits of additional security, typically additional restrictions on the ease of use are commonplace.

VI. Conclusion

Application virtualization provides several benefits, especially for the manageability of application installations, through the provisioning of a virtualization environment that encompasses application-specific system resources and those of a standardized version of the hosting operating system. As the hosting operating system still provides main functionalities, such as standardized system resources and process management, to a virtualized application, potential vulnerabilities of the virtualized application as well as the virtualized specific resources that it requires can be exploited.

Our evaluation of a vulnerability in the Firefox web browser and its exploitation demonstrates that virtualized applications have similar security risks to traditionally installed applications. If these risks were to be mitigated, typically a negative impact on the ease of use of virtualized applications follow. As virtualized application deployments increase, it is hence an important factor that common security methods are still required to provide security for an IT infrastructure and cannot be neglected.

References

[1] M. Tulloch *et al.*, *Understanding Microsoft Virtualization Solutions: From the Desktop to the Datacenter.* Microsoft Press, 2009.

[2] Microsoft, Inc., "Microsoft application virtualization (app-v) 4.5." [Online]. Available: http://www.microsoft.com/systemcenter/appv/default.mspx

[3] VMware, Inc., "Vmware thinapp 4.03." [Online]. Available: http://www.vmware.com/products/thinapp/

[4] Y. Yu, F. Guo, S. Nanda, L.-C. Lam, and T.-C. Chiueh, "A featherweight virtual machine for windows applications," in *Proceedings of the 2nd international Conference on Virtual Execution Environments (VEE)*, 2006, pp. 24–34.

[5] N. Ruest and D. Ruest, *Virtualization, A Beginner's Guide.* McGraw-Hill, Mar. 2009.

[6] S. T. King and S. W. Smith, "Virtualization and security: Back to the future," *IEEE Security and Privacy*, vol. 6, no. 5, p. 15, Sep. 2008.

[7] R. Perez, L. van Doorn, and R. Sailer, "Virtualization and hardware-based security," *IEEE Security and Privacy*, vol. 6, no. 5, pp. 24–31, Sep. 2008.

[8] S. J. Vaughan-Nichols, "Virtualization sparks security concerns," *Computer*, vol. 41, no. 8, pp. 13–15, 2008.

[9] E. Ray and E. Schultz, "Virtualization security," in *Proceedings of the 5th Annual Workshop on Cyber Security and Information Intelligence Research (CSIIRW)*, Apr. 2009, pp. 1–5.

[10] Microsoft, Inc., *App-V Security Best Practices*, Sep. 2008.

[11] ——, *App-V Security Operations Guide*, Sep. 2008.

[12] VMware, Inc., *ThinApp Users Guide - ThinApp 4.0.3*, 2009.

[13] A. Sabri and K. Shah, "Take your apps virtual with microsoft softgrid," *Microsoft TechNet Magazine*, Aug. 2007. [Online]. Available: http://technet.microsoft.com/en-us/magazine/2007.08.softgrid.aspx

[14] Metasploit LLC, "The metasploit project." [Online]. Available: http://www.metasploit.com/

[15] D. Maynor, *Metasploit Toolkit for Penetration Testing, Exploit Development, and Vulnerability Research.* Syngress, Oct. 2007.

[16] R. Tzur, "Sandboxie 3.4," Sep. 2009. [Online]. Available: http://www.sandboxie.com

Noise Performance of a Finite Uniform Cascade of Two-Port Networks

Shmuel Y. Miller
Ort Braude College
P.O. Box 78, Karmiel, 21982 Israel

***Abstract* - The noise performance of a lumped passive uniform cascade of identical *element* two port networks is investigated. The *N*-block network is characterized in close form based on the eigenvalues of the element two-port *ABCD* transmission matrix. The thermal noise performance is derived and demonstrated in several examples.**

***Kewords* – Cascade, Gain (Ladder), Image Sensor, Interconnect, Ladder, Lumped Network, Noise (Ladder).**

I. INTRODUCTION

The paper considers two-port networks that consist of a cascade of an integer number N of identical two-port networks. This setup has been considered in several areas, including modeling of power lines [1], ladder filters [2], paradoxical infinite ladder-networks [3], ray optics [4], modeling of distributed microwave networks [5], and packaging coupling effects [6]. In the optimization of VLSI interconnections the interconnections are modeled typically as a succession of resistor-capacitor (R-C) segments [7]. In these areas the typical cases involve a small number of underlying cascaded two-port blocks, unless an infinite number is considered as a limiting case. The finite and uniform case is less common, and appears in modeling of distributed microwave elements and cascaded electronic sensors.

The objective in this paper is to obtain the transfer characteristics of a cascade of a finite number of identical R-C blocks. The results serve the noise analysis of distributed R-C interconnections, but are useful as well to other applications, cf. [1]-[7].

The *ABCD* matrix is favored in this setup due to the multiplication property of these matrices in a cascade configuration whereby the product represents the overall equivalent *ABCD* matrix. In this work we refer to any number of two-port cascaded blocks, with the restriction of uniformity (i.e. identical blocks).

Amongst several parameters that are of interest, including input and output impedance, voltage gain, group delay, bandwidth, etc. the focus here will be on the root-mean-square (rms) thermal noise spectral distribution, which is directly related to the real part of the output impedance.

II. NETWORK MODEL

The network comprises a cascade of N identical two-port blocks, as presented in Fig. 1. Each block is characterized by

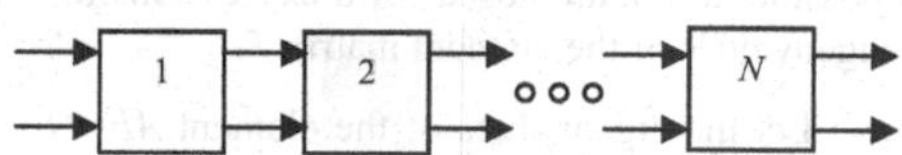

Fig. 1. Two-port cascade of N identical blocks.

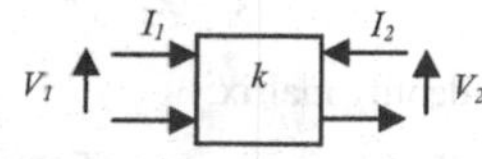

Fig. 2. Voltages and currents per k^{th} two-port block.

an *ABCD* matrix per voltages and currents as defined in Fig. 2. The voltages and currents are related via the *ABCD* matrix as in (1), [8]. The voltage or current subscript ij denotes the block's input-output index by i and the block index by j.

$$\begin{bmatrix} V_{2k} \\ I_{2k} \end{bmatrix} = \begin{bmatrix} A & B \\ C & D \end{bmatrix} \cdot \begin{bmatrix} V_{1k} \\ -I_{1k} \end{bmatrix} \tag{1}$$

Define the transmission matrix T as the *ABCD* matrix, (2).

$$T = \begin{bmatrix} A & B \\ C & D \end{bmatrix} \tag{2}$$

Define the transmission ABCD matrix for the cascade of N blocks as T_N. Then T and T_N are related as in (3).

$$T_N = \begin{bmatrix} A & B \\ C & D \end{bmatrix}^N = T^N \tag{3}$$

The objective is to evaluate T_N explicitly rather then recursively. The T matrix of the element network may be constructed straightforwardly from the two-port voltage-current equations, as demonstrated in the following examples.

A. Example of a resistive ladder element

The voltage divider (Fig. 3a) is characterized by:

$$T = \begin{bmatrix} A & B \\ C & D \end{bmatrix} = \begin{bmatrix} 1 & R_1 \\ 1/R_2 & 1 + R_1/R_2 \end{bmatrix} \tag{4}$$

R_1 R_2 (a) Resistive ladder element R C (b) Low pass filter element

Fig. 3. Examples of a two-port element block

T. Sobh, K. Elleithy (eds.), *Innovations in Computing Sciences and Software Engineering*,
DOI 10.1007/978-90-481-9112-3_50,

B. Example of a low-pass ladder element

The R-C low-pass filter (Fig. 3b) at frequency ω is characterized by:

$$T=\begin{bmatrix} A & B \\ C & D \end{bmatrix}=\begin{bmatrix} 1 & R \\ j\omega C & 1+j\omega RC \end{bmatrix} \tag{5}$$

III. CHARACTERIZATION OF THE N-BLOCK TRNAMISSION MATRIX

It is possible to obtain closed-form expressions for T_N based on the eigenvalues of the element matrix T.

Lemma 1: Let the eigenvalues of the element *ABCD* matrix T be λ_1 and λ_2. Assume distinct eigenvalues. Then

$$T_N=T^N=b_0 I+b_1 T,\quad b_0=\frac{\lambda_1\cdot\lambda_2^N-\lambda_2\cdot\lambda_1^N}{\lambda_1-\lambda_2},\ b_1=\frac{\lambda_1^N-\lambda_2^N}{\lambda_1-\lambda_2} \tag{6}$$

I denotes the 2X2 identity matrix.

Proof: *Invoke* a well-known property of regular functions of a square matrix, based on Caley-Hamilton theorem. This technique is used routinely in solving state-equations of discrete-time linear systems [9], [10]:

$$\lambda_1^N=b_0+b_1\lambda_1,\quad \lambda_2^N=b_0+b_1\lambda_2 \tag{7}$$

The coefficients b_0 and b_1 in (6) result then directly from (7). □

Lemma 2: Let the single eigenvalue of the element *ABCD* matrix T be λ with multiplicity 2. Then

$$T_N=T^N=b_0 I+b_1 T,\quad b_0=(1-N)\cdot\lambda^N,\ b_1=N\cdot\lambda^{N-1} \tag{8}$$

I denotes the 2X2 identity matrix.

Proof: Using the same theory as in the proof of Lemma 1, or performing the limit $\lambda_2\rightarrow\lambda_1$ and applying l'Hôpital's rule yields [9]:

$$\lambda^N=b_0+b_1\lambda,\quad N\lambda^{N-1}=b_1 \tag{9}$$

The coefficients b_0 and b_1 in (8) result then directly from (9). □

The above results are demonstrated in the following examples:

A. Example of a resistive ladder element

Using *Example A* of Section II (Fig. 3a) with $R_1=R$, $R_2=2R$, results in the matrix T (4) with $\lambda_1=0.5$ and $\lambda_2=2$. Substituting in (6) results in:

$$T_N=\frac{2}{3}\cdot\begin{bmatrix} \frac{1}{2}\cdot 2^N+2^{-N} & (2^N-2^{-N})\cdot R \\ (2^N-2^{-N})/(2R) & 2^N+\frac{1}{2}\cdot 2^{-N} \end{bmatrix} \tag{10}$$

B. Example of a low-pass ladder element

Using *Example B* of Section II, the R-C low-pass filter element (Fig. 3b), with ωRC<<1, the matrix T (4) has $\lambda_1\approx\lambda_2\approx 1$, whereas with ωRC>>1, the matrix T (4) has $\lambda_1\approx 0$ and $\lambda_2\approx j\omega RC$. Substituting in (7) and (6) results in (11a) and (11b), respectively:

$$T_N\big|_{\omega RC\ll 1}\approx\begin{bmatrix} 1 & NR \\ j\omega NC & 1+j\omega NRC \end{bmatrix} \tag{11a}$$

$$T_N\big|_{\omega RC\gg 1}\approx(j\omega RC)^{N-1}\cdot\begin{bmatrix} 1 & R \\ j\omega C & 1+j\omega RC \end{bmatrix} \tag{11b}$$

This manifests the low-pass filter operation with cascaded poles.

IV. NOISE PERFORMANCE

The output thermal noise performance is related to the output impedance Z_{out} according to Nyquist's theorem [11]:

$$S_{V_{out}}(\omega)=2kT_0\,\mathrm{Re}[Z_{out}(\omega)] \tag{12}$$

The ambient temperature is T_0 [°K], k the Boltzmann constant, and $S_{V_{out}}(\omega)$ the two-sided spectral density of the output voltage $V_{out}=V_{2N}$.

The output impedance may be derived from the *ABCD* matrix given the input generator impedance Z_g. It is easily shown, using the terminology of (2), that:

$$Z_{out}=\frac{V_2}{I_2}=\frac{AZ_g+B}{CZ_g+D} \tag{13}$$

Thus, the expressions for Z_{out} with Z_g a short or an open-circuit are

$$Z_{out}\Big|_{Z_g=0}=\frac{V_2}{I_2}\Big|_{Z_g=0}=\frac{B}{D} \tag{14a}$$

$$Z_{out}\Big|_{Z_g=\infty}=\frac{V_2}{I_2}\Big|_{|Z_g|\gg 1}=\frac{A}{C} \tag{14b}$$

Taking the real-part of (14) using the entries of the T_N matrix establishes the noise two-sided spectral density up to the constant $2kT_0$.

These results are demonstrated for the low-pass ladder filter. Two cases are considered; a *regular* setup with element values R and C as in (5) and a *normalized* setup with element values R/N and C/N as in (15).

$$T=\begin{bmatrix} A & B \\ C & D \end{bmatrix}=\begin{bmatrix} 1 & R\cdot\frac{1}{N} \\ j\omega C\cdot\frac{1}{N} & 1+j\omega RC\cdot\frac{1}{N^2} \end{bmatrix} \tag{15}$$

Fig.'s (4)–(7) illustrate the real part of Z_{out} (which is directly proportional to the noise voltage spectral density) for values R=1 and C=1, $\omega/2\pi$ ranging from 0.1 to 1.0, and N ranging from 1 to 12. Both the regular and the normalized cases are presented.

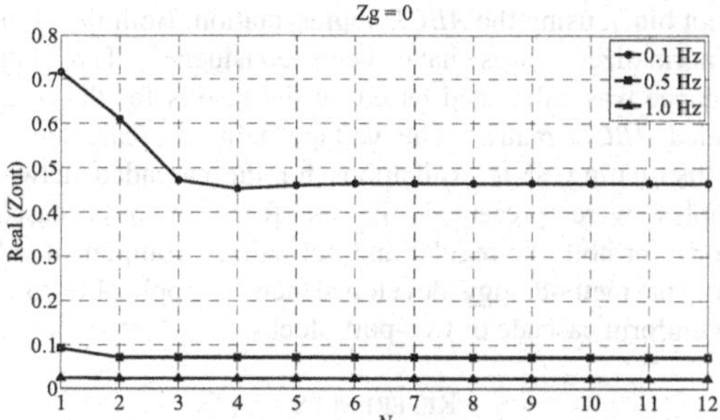

Fig. 4. Real (Zout) with Shortened Generator, regular case

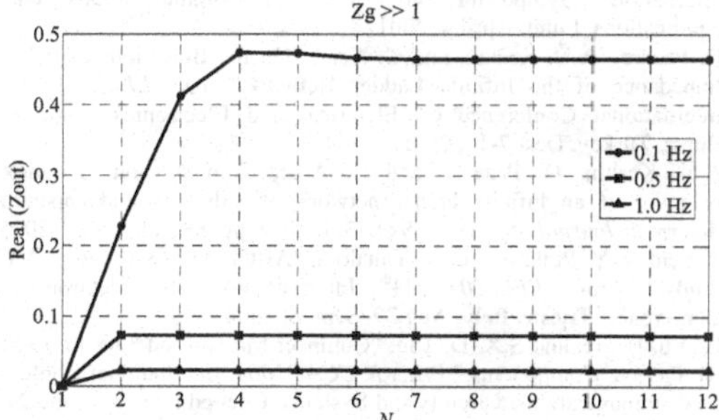

Fig. 5. Real (Zout) with Open Generator, regular case

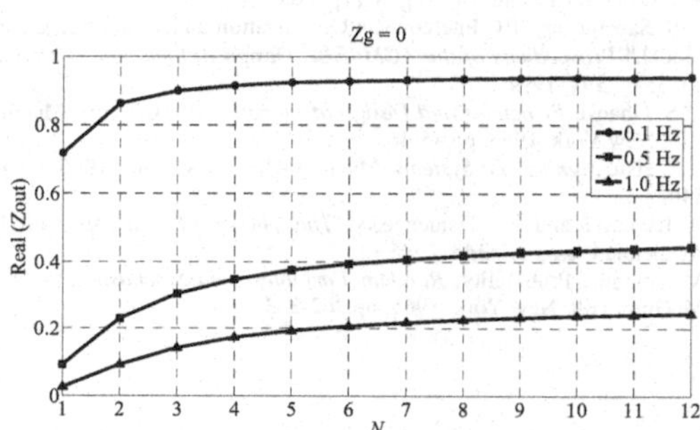

Fig. 6. Real (Zout) with Shortened Generator, normalized case

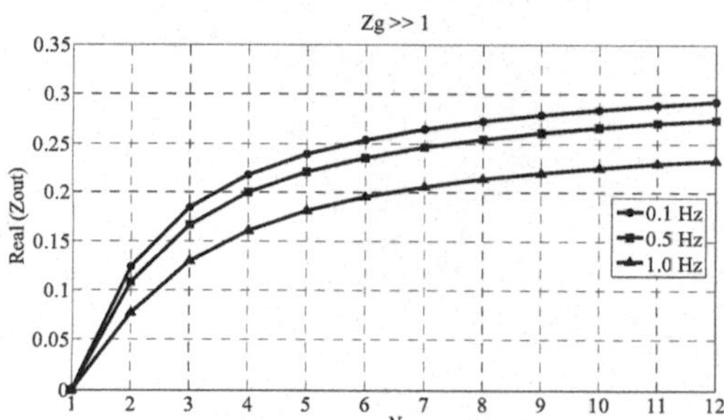

Fig. 7. Real (Zout) with Open Generator, normalized case

The output noise density for the uniform cascaded R-C network increases monotonically with number of stages N in the normalized cases but behaves differently for the regular cases. In all cases the noise level stabilizes towards an asymptote for large enough N. The output noise spectral density decreases monotonically with frequency in all cases, as should be expected with a low-pass ladder network. The noise equivalent bandwidth in the regular case is narrower for the normalized case.

V. Voltage Gain

In many cases it is desirable to evaluate signal to noise power ratio (SNR) rather than just the noise levels. To this end the voltage gain of the cascade network must be evaluated. Given an input voltage level it is possible then to calculate the signal output level and the SNR.

The voltage gain may be easily derived from the definition (1). The basic ABCD input-output relations are:

$$\begin{aligned} V_2 &= AV_1 - BI_1 \\ I_2 &= CV_1 - DI_1 \end{aligned} \tag{16}$$

This leads to:

$$\begin{aligned} V_2/V_1 &= A - B\, I_1/V_1 \\ I_2/(DV_1) &= C/D - I_1/V_1 \end{aligned} \tag{17}$$

Assuming an unloaded output ($|Z_g| \to \infty$), $I_2=0$, thus

$$\begin{aligned} I_1/V_1 &= C/D \\ V_2/V_1 &= A - B \cdot C/D \end{aligned} \tag{18}$$

Finally, only the magnitude of the voltage gain is required for SNR evaluations:

$$A_V = V_2/V_1 \big|_{|Z_L| \to \infty} = \left| A - B \cdot C/D \right| \tag{19}$$

Evaluations of the voltage gain for the uniform cascaded R-C network from section IV are presented next. Both the regular case (Fig. 8) and the normalized case (Fig. 9) are considered.

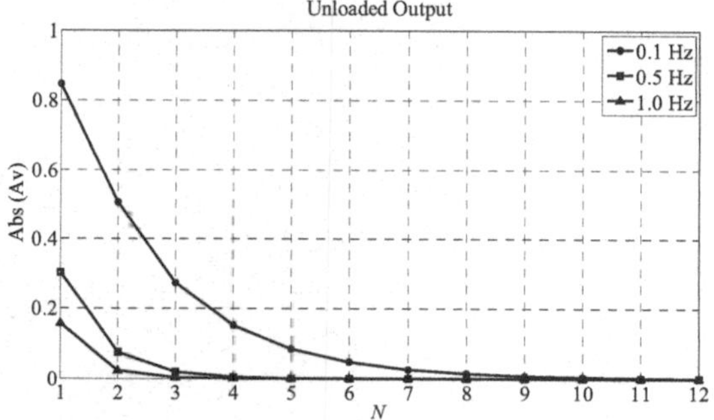

Fig. 8. Abs (A_V) with unloaded output, regular case

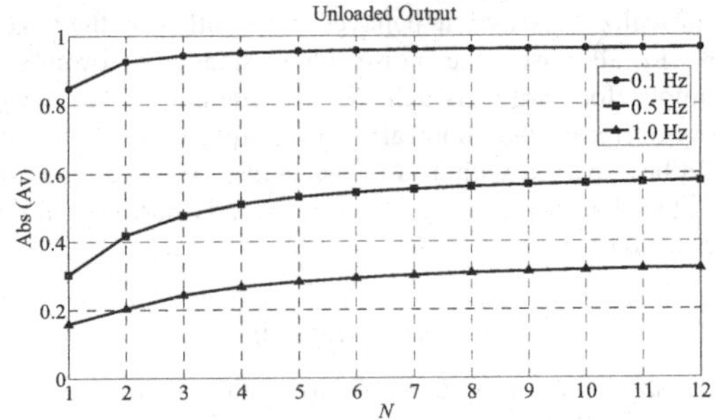

Fig. 9. Abs (A_V) with unloaded output, normalized case

The voltage gain in the regular case decreases with N (asymptotically to zero) in contrast to the normalized case where it increases with N (asymptotically to a fixed positive value). This is obvious since in the regular case the filtering is heavier with increased number of R-C stages, while in the normalized case the fixed total resistance and capacitance are distributed differently as the number of stages increases.

The output SNR for a fixed input signal level (for the R-C cascade example considered above) would decrease with number of cascaded stages in the regular case, since the signal level decreases whereas the noise level reaches a steady value.

In contrast, the SNR in the normalized case would tend to a positive fixed value with increasing number of cascaded stages since both the signal and noise levels reach asymptotically fixed values.

VI. SUMMARY AND CONCLUSIONS

An analysis of the thermal noise of a uniform cascade of two-port networks was performed based on the real part of the output impedance. The uniform finite cascade of two-port element blocks was characterized via the eigenvalues of the element block using the *ABCD* representation. Both the regular and normalized cases have been considered. The output impedance was calculated based on the results for the overall cascaded *ABCD* matrix. The voltage gain was calculated as well, facilitating SNR evaluations for the cascaded network. Examples were presented for an R-C low-pass cascade network, for both the regular and normalized component value cases. The methodology developed here is applicable to any finite uniform cascade of two-port blocks.

REFERENCES

[1] T.C. Banwell, and S. Galli, "A New Approach to the Modeling of the Transfer Function of the Power Line Channel," *Proc. ISPLC2001*, 5th International Symposium on Power-Line Communications and Its Applications, Lund, April 4, 2001.

[2] D. Pazarcı, A.Ü. Keskin, and C. Acar, "On the Behaviour of the Input Impedance of the Infinite Ladder Network," *Proc. ELECO2005*, 4th International Conference on Electrical and Electronics Engineering, Bursa, Turkey, Dec. 7-11, 2005.

[3] A.Ü. Keskin, D. Pazarcı, and C. Acar, Comment on "Paradoxical behavior of an infinite ladder network of inductors and capacitors," *American Journal of Physics*, Vol.73, Issue 9, pp. 881-882, Sept. 2005.

[4] Z. Seidov, Y. Pinhasi, and A. Yahalom, "ABCD Matrix Method: A Case Study," *Proc. FEL2004*, 24th International Free Electron Laser Conference, Trieste, Italy, Aug.29–Sept. 3, 2004.

[5] H. Yu, L. He, and S.X.-D. Tan, "Compact Macro-modeling for On-chip RF Passive Components," *Proc. ICCCAS 2004*, International Conference on Communications, Circuits and Systems, Chengdu, China, June 27-29, 2004.

[6] K.T. Tang, and E.G. Friedman, "Lumped versus Distributed RC and RLC Interconnect Impedances," 43rd *IEEE Midwest Symposium on Circuits and Systems*, Lansing MI, Aug. 8-11, 2000.

[7] S. S. Sapatnekar, "RC Interconnect Optimization under the Elmore Delay Model," *Proceedings of the ACM/IEEE Design Automation Conference*, pp. 387 – 391, 1994.

[8] M.S. Ghausi, *Principles and Design of Linear Active Circuits*, McGraw-Hill, New York, 1965, pp.45-46.

[9] H.P. Hsu, *Signals and Systems*, McGraw-Hill, New York, 1995, pp.439-440.

[10] P. Lancaster,and M. Tismenetsky, *The Theory of Matrices*, 2nd Ed., Academic Press, Orlando, 1985.

[11] A. Papoulis, Probability, *Random Variables, and Stochastic Processes*, McGraw-Hill, New York, 1965, pp.362-363.

Evaluating Software Agent Quality: Measuring Social Ability and Autonomy

Fernando Alonso, José L. Fuertes, Loïc Martínez
Facultad de Informática, Universidad Politécnica de Madrid
Campus de Montegancedo, s/n
28660 – Boadilla del Monte, Madrid (Spain)
e-mail: {falonso, jfuertes, loic}@fi.upm.es

Héctor Soza
Facultad de Ingeniería y Ciencias Geológicas, Universidad Católica del Norte
Avda. Angamos 0610, Antofagasta (Chile)
e-mail: hsoza@ucn.cl

***Abstract*—Research on agent-oriented software has been developed around different practical applications. The same cannot, however, be said about the development of measures to evaluate agent quality by its key characteristics. In some cases, there have been proposals to use and adapt measures from other paradigms, but no agent-related quality model has been investigated. As part of research into agent quality, this paper presents the evaluation of two key characteristics: social ability and autonomy. Additionally, we present some results for a case study on a multi-agent system.**

I. INTRODUCTION

A number of software development paradigms (procedural, object-oriented, agent-oriented, etc.) have been developed throughout computing history. Each paradigm was designed to more efficiently produce software depending on the application type. However, software quality determines how able the software is to satisfy user needs. Several quality measures have been designed so far. In the case of procedural and object-oriented paradigms, these measures have resulted in quality models [1], [2], and an ISO/IEC standard quality model [3]. This standard decomposes software product quality into characteristics, sub-characteristics (attributes) and associated measures.

There has been some research on adapting procedural and object-oriented software measures to evaluate agent-oriented software. This initiative is based on the idea that these concepts have characteristics in common with the agent paradigm, like its modular programming approach, encapsulation, information hiding, etc. [4], [5], [6]. Few studies, though, have developed measures exclusively targeting agent-oriented software [6], [7], and none of them have determined a quality model considering specific characteristics associated with the development and application of an agent.

This paper introduces part of a line of research aiming to evaluate the overall quality of a software agent considering its interactions with the user and other agents and determine the efficiency and quality of its application. Research focuses on analysing the characteristics defining an agent.

A set of measures for evaluating agent social ability and autonomy is presented, considering different attributes associated with these characteristics. Agent social ability is the agent's ability to interact with other agents and humans in order to achieve its design objectives [8]. Agent autonomy means the agent's ability to operate on its own, without the need for any human guidance or the intervention of external elements, and to control its own actions and internal states [4], [7].

This paper is structured as follows: The next section presents some research on agent characteristics measures. In section 3 we discuss agent characteristics and attributes. Section 4 suggests measures for evaluating agent social ability and autonomy attributes. Section 5 presents a case study and Section 6 includes some concluding remarks and discusses future research.

II. RELATED WORK

We have found little relevant research on quality measures related to agent social ability and autonomy.

Dumke, Koeppe and Wille described a set of measures considering product, process and resources to evaluate the performance of agents and bring an empirical criterion into the evaluation [4]. The measure of autonomy of the agent's design considers measuring agent size and complexity.

In a project report Shin outlined the results of adapting some product measurements from the procedural and object-oriented paradigms to agent-oriented software [6]. Shin compared objects and agents, and developed a program to evaluate the measures applied to an example. He proposed that the coupling between objects is a measure for evaluating agent social ability. Moreover, he suggested that agent complexity could be viewed as a way of measuring agent autonomy.

Barber and Martin authored one of the early papers on the issue of measuring agent autonomy [9]. They presented a complete framework for interpreting agent autonomy and delivering an autonomy representation for quantitatively assessing an agent's degree of autonomy. They stated that

T. Sobh, K. Elleithy (eds.), *Innovations in Computing Sciences and Software Engineering*,
DOI 10.1007/978-90-481-9112-3_51, © Springer Science+Business Media B.V. 2010

overall agent autonomy could be measured as the average or sum of the autonomies for all the pursued goals. They expressly stated that such an evaluation is beyond the scope of their study.

Cernuzzi and Rossi proposed a framework for evaluating the agent-oriented analysis and design modelling methods [10]. The proposal takes into consideration qualitative evaluation criteria employing quantitative methods. They evaluated autonomy considering whether or not the modelling technique checks if agents have control over their internal state and their own behaviour.

Huber authored another significant paper on measuring agent autonomy [11]. This work stressed the social aspects of agents and described autonomy as a measure of an agent's social integrity and social dependence. The measure of social dependence is a function of tasks imposed upon the agent by a superior agent, tasks accepted from peers, tasks contracted out to peers (and dependent upon completion) and tasks imposed upon inferior agents (and dependent upon completion). To compute an overall autonomy value for an agent, Huber combines the social integrity autonomy value and the social dependency autonomy value.

Generally, none of the above studies provides specific agent quality measures that could be used to get a global quality measure of the agent. This is the main focus of our research.

III. Software Agent Characteristics and Attributes

In conformance with other key studies of software quality [12], [13], the quality of an agent can be analysed on the basis of its characteristics, sub-characteristics (or attributes) and attribute measures.

It is now an acknowledged fact in the agent-oriented software field that an agent must have the following basic characteristics: social ability, autonomy, proactivity, adaptability, intelligence and mobility (if the agent is mobile) [4], [7]. Agent quality will then be determined by the set of quality attributes for each of the above characteristics, and these attributes can be evaluated by a set of measures.

Agent social ability indicates that the agent is able to interact with other agents, and possibly humans, in order to achieve its design objectives [4].

Agent autonomy is the freedom from external intervention, oversight, or control [14]. Autonomous agents are agents that "are able to work on behalf of their user without the need for any external guidance" [15]. This type of definition fits the concept of autonomy in domains that involve an agent interacting with other agents.

After performing a literature survey of the agent field [4], [5], [6], [16] we propose that agent social ability should consider the attributes of communication, cooperation, and negotiation, defined as follows.

Communication is the reception and delivery of messages by the agent to achieve its goals. Good communication depends on the number of messages invoked in response to a message received by the agent, the number of incoming and outgoing messages received and sent by the agent to maintain a meaningful communication link or accomplish some goals, and the size of the messages sent by the agent during execution [6].

Cooperation is the agent's ability to respond to the services requested by other agents, and to offer services to other agents. Good cooperation depends on the agent's level of collaboration with other agents that require its services, meaning that an agent's collaboration level is measured by its ability to accept or reject services requested by other agents and by its ability to offer services [14].

Negotiation is the agent's ability to make commitments, resolve conflicts and reach agreements with other agents to assure the accomplishment of its goals. Good negotiation depends on agent goal accomplishment, the number of messages sent by the agent when another agent requests a service from it, and the number of messages sent by the agent when it requests a service from other agents [6], [14].

For agent autonomy, on the other hand, we propose the attributes of self-control, functional independence and evolution capability [17], defined as follows.

Self-Control is the level of control that the agent has over its own state and behaviour [4]. Good self-control depends on the complexity of the agent's internal state (evaluated as a function of structural complexity and internal state size) and of its behaviour complexity.

Functional Independence: Agent autonomy is a function of its structural and functional dependence [6], [14]. Functional dependence is related to executive tasks requiring an action that the agent has to perform on behalf of either the user it represents or other agents. A good level of functional independence will indicate that the agent does not have to perform many executive tasks.

Evolution Capability: The evolution of an agent refers to the capability of the agent to adapt to meet new requirements [15] and take the necessary actions to self-adjust to new goals [8]. A good evolution capability depends on its state update capacity, and the frequency of state update [6].

IV. Measures for the Attributes of Social Ability and Autonomy

In this section we present the proposed measures for the agent attributes that define the agent's social ability and autonomy. Some of these measures are based on research within the agent paradigm, others were extracted from other paradigms and adapted to agent technology, and others are new measures proposed here.

The measures used in this research are dynamic measures (i.e. measure the characteristics of the software during execution) and static measures (i.e. examine the source code to measure the characteristics of the software) [18].

To gather valid results in a software product quality evaluation, this evaluation should be conducted in a controlled environment [19], which we will call the benchmark. This assures that the evaluated measures are repeatable and comparable.

A. *Social Ability*

This characteristic considers the attributes of communication, cooperation and negotiation.

The communication attribute can be measured using the following measures.

Response for message measures the average number of messages that are invoked in response to a message received by the agent. To process the incoming message, new messages might be sent to another agent requesting new services. If SM(i) is the number of messages sent in response to the ith message received, and n is the total number of messages received by the agent during one execution of the benchmark, then the value of the average response of messages (RFM) is (1):

$$RFM = \frac{\sum_{i=1}^{n} SM_i}{n} \cdot \qquad (1)$$

An increasing *RFM* value indicates that agent is communicative. A very high value can affect communication with system agents.

Average message size measures the influence of the data size of the messages sent by the agent on its communication. This is an adaptation of a measure described in [6]. Let us define the average message size as the average data size of the messages sent by the agent during its execution, where n is the total number of messages sent by the agent and MB_i is the data size, measured in bytes, of the ith message. AMS is defined as (2):

$$AMS = \frac{\sum_{i=1}^{n} MB_i}{n} \cdot \qquad (2)$$

AMS should not have too high a value, because large message sizes affect communication due to the high message exchange rate between system agents.

Incoming Messages measures the relation of incoming messages to agent communication during its lifetime. Higher values indicate that the agent has more dependent agents requiring its services. This is an adaptation of a measure described in [6]. Let us define the incoming messages (IM) as the total number of incoming messages received by an agent during one execution of the benchmark.

Outgoing Messages measures the relationship between direct outgoing messages and agent communication during its lifetime. Higher values could indicate that the agent is dependent on other agents. This is an adaptation of a measure described in [6]. Let us define the outgoing messages as the total number of outgoing messages sent by an agent (OM) during one execution of the benchmark.

The cooperation attribute can be measured using the following measures.

Services Requests Rejected by the Agent measures the influence of the percentage of rejected agent services requested by other agents on cooperation. Let us define *SA* as the total number of messages requesting a service received and accepted by the agent and *SR* as the total number of messages requesting a service rejected by the agent during its execution. We define the value of the services requests rejected by the agent as the percentage of requests rejected by the agent, when $SA + SR > 0$ (3):

$$SRRA = \frac{SR}{SA + SR} * 100 \cdot \qquad (3)$$

Agent cooperation decreases as the percentage *SRRA* of rejected services is too high.

Agent Services Advertised measures the number of services that the agent advertises on the yellow pages directory in its environment. This is an adaptation of a measure described in [6]. Let us define agent services advertised (ASA) as the quantity of services that the agent provides. These services are usually advertised by the agent on the yellow pages directory in its environment [6]. As S increases, the value of ASA grows, because a low level of offered services is a clear indication of deficient cooperation. If an excess of services is offered, ASA decreases because the agent loses its ability to cooperate, since the number of services it has to deal with increases.

The negotiation attribute can be measured using the following measures:

Agent Goals Achievement determines the negotiating efficiency of agents that use negotiation to accomplish their goals. We define G as the number of objectives achieved by the agent in the benchmark execution time. Then the value of the agent goals achievement (AGA) is (4):

$$AGA = \log_{k+1}(G+1) \cdot \qquad (4)$$

The value of k is equivalent to the maximum possible number of objectives to be achieved by the agent. We find that as the quantity of objectives achieved by the agent increases, the value of *AGA* increases up to the value *1* when $G = k$.

Messages by a Requested Service measures the influence of the number of messages exchanged by the agent doing the negotiation when another agent is requesting services from the agent. Let the messages by a requested service (*MRS*) be the number of messages exchanged by the agent when it receives a service request. A high *MRS* value denotes a low agent negotiation level because a high message exchange rate affects negotiation.

Messages Sent to Request a Service measures the influence of the number of messages exchanged by the agent doing the negotiation when the agent is requesting a service from another agent. Let the messages sent to request a service (*MSS*) be the quantity of messages exchanged by the agent when it requests a service from another agent. A high *MSS* value affects negotiation for the same reasons as above.

B. Autonomy

This characteristic considers the attributes of self-control, functional independence and evolution capability.

The self-control attribute can be measured using the following measures.

Structural Complexity: State structural complexity (SC) is determined by the quantity and complexity of the pointers or references that the agent uses. Let n be the number of pointers and references existing in the agent's internal state and let CP_i be the complexity of the ith pointer or reference. Then the structural complexity is defined as (5):

$$SC = \sum_{i=1}^{n} CP_i \cdot \quad (5)$$

High *SC* values indicate that self-control is low because, an increased number and complexity of the structures referenced by pointers or references may take longer to execute, resulting in a reduction in the agent's autonomy.

Internal State Size measures the agent's variable size. This is an adaptation of a measure described in [6]. Let us define n ($n > 0$) as the total number of variables, and let VB_i be the bytes size of the memory needed to represent the ith variable or agent pointer (if the pointer measures the memory size of the referenced structure), then internal state size (ISS) is (6):

$$ISS = \sum_{i=1}^{n} VB_i \cdot \quad (6)$$

If the value of *ISS* is low, the agent will have less self-control because it will not have all the information required for self-control and to attain its goals.

Behaviour Complexity measures the complexity of the services that the agent offers (only applies to agents that offer services). A service offered by an agent implies performing a series of actions, such as the operations to be executed by the agent to carry out the offered service. The complexity of these services differs depending on the paradigm implementing the agent (object-oriented, knowledge-based system, etc.). Therefore, agent services complexity will be a function of the paradigm implementing the agent [20]. Let us define n ($n > 0$) as the total number of services and let CS_i be the complexity of the ith service then the behaviour complexity (BC) is defined as (7):

$$BC = \sum_{i=1}^{n} CS_i \cdot \quad (7)$$

Very high *BC* values are indicative of low self-control because the increased complexity of implemented services could affect agent autonomy since it could increase the time and effort required to execute its services.

The functional independence attribute can be measured using the following measure

Executive Messages Ratio measures the influence on the agent of the ratio of executive messages (requiring an action) received from the user that the agent represents or other agents (to which it is obliged to respond) to all the received messages (considering the communication actions). Above all, it takes into account FIPA Request messages [21]. Let *MR* be the total number of messages received and let *ME* be the number of executive messages received by the agent during execution. This measure is only applicable when the agent receives messages ($MR > 0$). Then the executive messages ratio (EMR) is defined by (8):

$$EMR = 1 - \frac{ME}{MR} \cdot \quad (8)$$

If the value for *EMR* is high, the agent's autonomy is high because, as it receives few executive messages, it has to execute fewer actions. This affects its autonomy. Having to respond to a high number of executive messages (a low *EMR* value) can penalize the agent's functional independence.

The evolution capability attribute can be measured using the following measures.

State Update Capacity: This static measure is useful for evaluating the software agent's capability to update its state. The agent's state is defined by a set of variables that are dependent on different event occurrences, where the event would change the variable value, and therefore the agent state [6]. This is an adaptation of a measure described in [6]. Let n ($n > 0$) be the number of all executable statements, let m be the number of variables and let S_{ij} be 1 if the ith statement updates the jth variable, and 0 otherwise. Let the state update capacity (SUC) be defined by the mean value of variables updated by agent statements, defined as (9):

$$SUC = \sum_{i=1}^{n} \sum_{j=1}^{m} S_{ij} \cdot \quad (9)$$

The value of *SUC* grows rapidly because each variable is dependent on a growing number of statements with changeable values. This affects the agent's evolution capability.

Frequency of State Update: This measure is useful for evaluating the impact of the state update frequency during the execution of the variable defining the agent state. Depending on what the knowledge is used for, this frequency of change could have a big impact on agent predictability and behaviour [6]. This is an adaptation of a measure described in [6]. Let us define n ($n > 0$) as the number of all executable statements, let m be the number of variables and let us define VC_{ij} as 1 if the ith statement accesses and modifies the jth variable during the execution of the benchmark. Then, we define the frequency of the state update (FSU) inside the agent by equation (10):

$$FSU = \sum_{i=1}^{n} \sum_{j=1}^{m} VC_{ij} \cdot \quad (10)$$

If the *FSU* increases sharply, its evolution capability starts to drop because the knowledge update frequency can become so high as to prevent it from being able to take the appropriate actions to evolve.

The results of each measure are normalized in the interval [0, 1] (where 0 is a poor result for the measure and 1 is a good result).

V. Case Study

To evaluate the introduced measures we have used a multi-agent system with six agent types: three buyers and three sellers [22]. It is an intelligent agent marketplace which includes different kinds of buyer and seller agents that cooperate and compete to process sales transactions for their owners. Additionally, a facilitator agent was developed to act as a marketplace manager. We have used this system to evaluate the functional quality of the buyer and seller agents' social ability and autonomy within the system.

The agents are basic, intermediate and advanced buyers and sellers. They have the same negotiation capacities, but they differ as to how sophisticated the techniques used to implement their negotiation strategies are, ranging from simple, hard-coded logic to forward-chaining rule inference. The seller agents send messages reporting the articles that they have to sell, and the buyers respond stating their willingness to buy and what they offer for the article. The seller agents respond by accepting or rejecting the offer, and, when they receive this message, the buyer agents return a confirmation message.

The social ability study focused on the three types of buyer agents and the three types of seller agents.

Table I shows the values of the communication, cooperation and negotiation measures during the assessment. The values of the social ability measures are found to be generally high. The ASA measure has the same value for all agents because each agent provides the same number of services. Similarly, there is not much difference between the quantity of messages received or sent by each agent, and some of the SRRA measures are the same. For the Basic Buyer and Seller, the value of the AGA measure is low, because they accomplish just one objective for every two of the other agent types.

Table II shows the values for the measure of each attribute, calculated by aggregating the measures for each attribute. Row 5 lists the value of the social ability characteristic for each agent, calculated by aggregating the measures of all the attributes. Finally, the last column shows the value of the system measure, calculated by aggregating the values of the attribute and characteristic measures for all the agents. Thus the bottom right table cell contains the value of the system's overall social ability. The above values are aggregated in each case using the arithmetic mean. Even so, the results could be refined, using a weighted mean with weights elicited from experts using any of the existing weighting techniques. In addition, we can see that advanced agents have a lower, whereas basic agents have a higher social ability value. Finally, the value for system social ability is 85%, that is, the social ability of the agents in this case study is high. *SC* has a very low minimum value. It inherits this value from the basic agents, as a great many, very complex pointers and references are used for these agents, whereas the intermediate and advanced agents have less complex pointers. The results for the other measures applied to all three agents are excellent, highlighting that the properties of these attributes are good for these agents and have a positive impact on their autonomy. We find that the EMR and SC measures are lower because the basic system agents have a lower associated value and the other measures are close to the maximum possible value.

Table III shows the values of the communication, cooperation and negotiation measures during the autonomy assessment. Because all agents have an adequate state update capacity, the evolution capability attribute scores high for all agents, as *SUC* (state update capacity) and *FSU* (frequency of state update) have high values in all cases. This can be attributed to agent programming.

Table III reveals that, unlike the *SC* and *EMR* measures, the *ISS*, *BC*, *SUC* and *FSU* measures have very high values.

TABLE I
MEASURES OF THE SOCIAL ABILITY ATTRIBUTES

	Basic Buyer	Inter. Buyer	Adv. Buyer	Basic Seller	Inter. Seller	Adv. Seller	System
RFM	0.93	0.94	0.98	1.00	0.91	1.00	**0.97**
AMS	0.98	1.00	0.79	0.98	1.00	0.79	**0.92**
IM	0.99	0.96	0.91	1.00	0.99	0.96	**0.97**
OM	0.98	0.92	0.83	1.00	0.98	0.83	**0.92**
SRRA	0.89	0.64	0.44	0.89	0.64	0.44	**0.66**
ASA	0.84	0.84	0.84	0.84	0.84	0.84	**0.84**
AGA	0.50	0.80	0.80	0.50	0.80	0.80	**0.70**
MRS	0.85	0.96	1.00	1.00	1.00	0.89	**0.97**
MSS	1.00	0.89	0.64	1.00	1.00	0.64	**0.85**

TABLE II
VALUES OF SOCIAL ABILITY ATTRIBUTES

	Basic Buyer	Inter. Buyer	Adv. Buyer	Basic Seller	Inter. Seller	Adv. Seller	System
Communication	0.96	0.95	0.88	1.00	0.99	0.89	**0.95**
Cooperation	0.87	0.74	0.64	0.87	0.74	0.64	**0.75**
Negotiation	0.78	0.89	0.81	0.83	0.90	0.81	**0.84**
Social Ability	**0.86**	**0.84**	**0.76**	**0.89**	**0.87**	**0.76**	**0.85**

TABLE III
MEASURES OF THE AUTONOMY ATTRIBUTES

	Basic Buyer	Inter. Buyer	Adv. Buyer	Basic Seller	Inter. Seller	Adv. Seller	System
SC	0.29	1.00	0.96	0.14	1.00	0.96	**0.73**
ISS	0.98	1.00	1.00	1.00	0.00	0.99	**0.99**
BC	0.99	1.00	0.99	1.00	1.00	0.96	**0.99**
EMR	0.73	0.67	0.62	0.70	0.64	0.58	**0.66**
SUC	1.00	0.99	1.00	0.99	1.00	0.98	**0.99**
FSU	0.99	1.00	0.98	1.00	0.98	0.99	**0.99**

TABLE IV
VALUES OF AUTONOMY ATTRIBUTES

	Basic Buyer	Inter. Buyer	Adv. Buyer	Basic Seller	Inter. Seller	Adv. Seller	System
Self-control	0.76	1.00	0.99	0.71	0.99	0.98	**0.91**
Functional Indep.	0.73	0.67	0.62	0.70	0.64	0.58	**0.66**
Evolution Capab.	0.99	0.99	0.99	0.99	0.99	0.99	**0.99**
Autonomy	**0.83**	**0.89**	**0.86**	**0.81**	**0.88**	**0.85**	**0.85**

Table IV shows the values of the measures for the attributes of the autonomy characteristic aggregated using the arithmetic mean of their values. From these results we conclude that the system agents have a very high evolution capability, high self-control and above average functional independence.

Thanks to these measure values, evolution capability is the highest-scoring, and therefore the most important, attribute for this system. According to these results, mean autonomy for this system is 85% (aggregated using the arithmetic mean of attribute values), all agents scoring above 80%, where the autonomy of the basic agents is slightly lower than for the others.

The results of this case study were compared with the opinion of two specialists in the agent field to confirm the reliability of the results.

VI. Conclusions and Future Work

This paper is part of ongoing research aimed at defining the global quality of software agents. To define this overall quality, we first identified relevant software agent characteristics from the literature: social ability, autonomy, proactivity, reactivity, adaptability, intelligence and mobility. For each characteristic, we plan to define a set of attributes and for each attribute, a set of measures.

In this paper, we present a first approximation to a set of measures for the social ability and autonomy characteristics. These characteristics are divided into attributes. Social ability attributes are communication, cooperation and negotiation, and autonomy attributes are self-control, functional independence and evolution capability. We also provide measures for these attributes. We have applied these measures to a typical case study to evaluate the applicability of the proposed measures and the relevance of the identified attributes.

The designed agents show a high social ability (85%). Communication (over 85%) is the highest scoring attribute, whereas values for cooperation are lower (although greater than 60%). The values were 95 % for the communication attribute, 75% for the cooperation attribute, and 84% for the negotiation attribute. Agent social ability for the whole system then was 85%.

The autonomy of the designed agents is high (85%). Two attributes -evolution capability (99%) and self-control (91%)- have very good values, whereas the values for functional independence are much lower (although greater than 60%).

Our future work pursues the ultimate goal of evaluating the global quality of software agents. First, we will have to evaluate the remaining characteristics: proactivity, adaptability, intelligence and mobility. Then we will define an aggregation method for computing the global quality of a software agent, given the results of all the measures of all the attributes of the agent's characteristics. This method will have to deal with the diversity of agent types and multi-agent systems. For this reason, it has to provide ways to adapt the computation process to different situations. What we are actually doing is developing a quality evaluation model for software agents. This model considers agent types, agent characteristics, attributes and measures.

References

[1] J. A. McCall, "An Introduction to Software Quality Metrics", in *Software Quality Management*, J. D. Cooper and M. J. Fisher, Eds. New York: Petrocelli Books, ,1979, pp. 127–142

[2] J. L. Fuertes, "Modelo de Calidad para el Software Orientado a Objetos", Doctoral Thesis, School of Computing, Technical University of Madrid, Madrid, Spain, 2003.

[3] ISO/IEC, Software Engineering- Product Quality- Part 1: Quality Model. International Standard ISO/IEC 9126-1:2001.

[4] R. Dumke, R. Koeppe, and C. Wille, "Software Agent Measurement and Self-Measuring Agent-Based Systems", Preprint No. 11, Fakultät für Informatik, Otto-von-Guericke-Universität, Magdeburg, 2000.

[5] B. Far, and T. Wanyama, "Metrics for Agent-Based Software Development", Proceedings of the *IEEE Canadian Conference on Electrical and Computer Engineering CCECE,* 2003, pp. 1297-1300.

[6] K. Shin, "Software Agents Metrics. A Preliminary Study & Development of a Metric Analyzer", Project Report No. H98010, Dept. Computer Science, School of Computing, National University of Singapore, 2003/2004.

[7] C. Wille, R. Dumke, and S. Stojanov, "Quality Assurance in Agent-Based Systems Current State and Open Problems", Preprint No. 4, Fakultät für Informatik, Universität Magdeburg, 2002.

[8] B. Friedman, and H. Nissenbaum, "Software Agents and User Autonomy", Proceedings of the *First International Conference on Autonomous Agents*, 1997, pp. 466-469.

[9] K. S. Barber, and C. E. Martin, "Agent Autonomy: Specification, Measurement, and Dynamic Adjustment", Proceedings of the *Autonomy Control Software Workshop at Autonomous Agents (Agents'99)*, Seattle, WA, 1999, pp. 8–15.

[10] L. Cernuzzi, and G. Rossi, "On the Evaluation of Agent Oriented Methodologies", Proceedings of the *International Conference on Object Oriented Programming, Systems, Languages and Applications - Workshop on Agent-Oriented Methodologies OOPSLA 02*, Seattle, WA, 2002, pp. 2-30.

[11] M. J. Huber, "Agent Autonomy: Social Integrity and Social Independence", Proceedings of the *International Conference on Information Technology ITNG'07*, Las Vegas, Nevada, 2007, pp. 282-290.

[12] K. Dautenhahn, and C. L. Nehaniv, "The Agent-Based Perspective on Imitation," in *Imitation in Animals and Artefacts*, C. L. Nehaniv and K. Dautenhahn, Eds., Cambridge, CA: The MIT Press, 2002, pp. 1-40.

[13] R. Beale, and A. Wood, "Agent-Based Interaction", *Proceedings of People and Computers IX: Proceedings of HCI'94*, Glasgow, UK, 1994, pp. 239–245.

[14] M. Wooldridge, *An Introduction to Multiagent Systems*, John Wiley & Sons, Inc., 2002.

[15] J. Murdock, "Model-Based Reflection for Agent Evolution", Technical Report GIT-CC-00-34, Doctoral Thesis, Georgia Institute of Technology, Atlanta, 2000.

[16] F. Alonso, J. L. Fuertes, L. Martínez, and H. Soza, "Measuring the Social Ability of Software Agents", Proceedings of the *Sixth International Conference on Software Engineering Research, Management and Applications (SERA 2008)*, Prague, Czech Republic, 2008, pp. 3-10.

[17] F. Alonso, J. L. Fuertes, L. Martínez, and H. Soza, "Towards a set of Measures for Evaluating Software Agent Autonomy", to be published in Proceedings of the *8th Mexican International Conference on Artificial Intelligence (MICAI 2009)*, Guanajuato, Mexico, 2009.

[18] G. M. Barnes, and B. R. Swim, "Inheriting Software Metrics", *J. Object-Orient. Prog.* 6, 7, 1993, 27-34.

[19] ISO/IEC. Software Engineering- Product Quality- Part 4: Quality in Use Metrics. International Standard ISO/IEC TR 9126-4:2004.

[20] S. R. Chidamber, and C. F. Kemerer, "A Metrics Suite for Object Oriented Design", *IEEE T. Software Eng.* 20, 6, 1994, pp. 476-493.

[21] Foundation for Intelligent Physical Agents. FIPA Communicative Act Library Specification, Document Number SC00037J, Geneva, Switzerland, 2002.

[22] J. P. Bigus, and J. Bigus, *Constructing Intelligent Agents using Java*, 2nd ed. New York: John Wiley & Sons, Inc., 2001.

An Approach to Measuring Software Quality Perception

Radosław Hofman[1]
Sygnity Research, Poland

Abstract— *Perception measuring and perception management is an emerging approach in the area of product management. Cognitive, psychological, behavioral and neurological theories, tools and methods are being employed for a better understanding of the mechanisms of a consumer's attitude and decision processes. Software is also being defined as a product, however this kind of product is significantly different from all other products. Software products are intangible and it is difficult to trace their characteristics which are strongly dependant on a dynamic context of use.*

Understanding customer's cognitive processes gives an advantage to the producers aiming to develop products "winning the market". Is it possible to adopt theories, methods and tools for the purpose of software perception, especially software quality perception? The theoretical answer to this question seems to be easy, however in practice the list of differences between software products and software projects hinders the analysis of certain factors and their influence on the overall perception.

In this article the authors propose a method and describe a tool designed for the purpose of research regarding perception issues of software quality. The tool is designed to defeat the above stated problem, adopting the modern behavioral economics approach.

Index terms—.Software, Quality perception, cognitive psychology, behavioral economics.

I. Introduction and Motivation

A. *Motivation*

Software engineering aims to deliver high quality software products. Although a similar goal is common for most of the engineering disciplines, software engineering scientists underline that software products are significantly different from all other human crafted products (1). Intangible software products also seem to be much more complex in the aspect of quality measurement.

On the other hand at every stage of the software production lifecycle, when the software product is presented to individuals (e.g. users), they tend to formulate their own opinion about the quality of the product. Even more, they formulate their opinion in a relatively short time. How is it possible if we consider the fact, that there is no commonly accepted software quality model nor a software evaluation process model? One of the possible answers is a conclusion, that users base their opinion on some other process and different software quality definition than those ones presented in literature.

We have identified the lack of a comprehensive descriptive model explaining the real process of software quality assessment. In consequence we have proposed a theoretical model resulting from cognitive sciences studies (2). In this article we present an approach to set up a scientifically controllable environment for the purpose of software perception investigation. We not only present the theoretical approach but also propose a set of practical solutions for the design of tools supporting such a research activities.

B. *Background*

Software quality has been a subject of study since the 1970's when software development techniques started to be perceived as an engineering discipline. The first quality models were published by McCall(3) and Boehm(4). Successive attempts continue and the most current one is the SQuaRE (Software product QUality Requirements and Evaluation) model developed within the ISO/IEC25000 standards series. This new approach is perceived as the new generation of software quality models(5) and is being used for the decomposition of the end users perspective to software components requirements(6).

The general conclusion about software quality models should observe that there is no commonly accepted model nor is there a commonly accepted evaluation method. On the other hand we conclude that users and customers use some model and method to evaluate software.

The valuation of goods has been studied by economic scientists for centuries (7). Many researchers have also tried to investigate how a personal value grade may be influenced (or fail to be influenced) in the aspect of a cognitive process associated with judgment formulation (compare Lawrence Kohlberg, Max Weber, von Weiser etc.)

The neo-classical economic model of human behavior lays upon assumptions about utility maximization, equilibrium and efficiency. These assumptions correspond with the classical model of human behavior known as *homo economicus*. The concept had appeared in the book considered to be the beginning of the economics science (8). Although discussed assumptions are widely accepted they are just a simplifications made for the purpose of modeling the decision processes or economic behavior. Publications in the last years have put the above assumptions under critic (7). The first publication drawing the attention to limitations of the *homo economicus* concept was the author of this idea Adam Smith. In (9) the author describes the asymmetric reaction to the increase and decrease of wealth. This observation was investigated in the 20th century by Daniel Kahneman and Amos Tversky (10).

[1] EUR ING, Sygnity Research, Poland
also PhD Student Department of Information Systems at The Poznań University of Economics and Polish Standardization Committee Member, email: rhofman@sygnity.pl

T. Sobh, K. Elleithy (eds.), *Innovations in Computing Sciences and Software Engineering*,
DOI 10.1007/978-90-481-9112-3_52,

The economists begrudgingly accepted the counterexamples to neo-classical models based on empirical observation results. The new approach in psychology, cognitive psychology, had proposed a new model of human brain using a metaphor of information processing system (11). Psychologists started to compare their psychological models with the economics ones. Daniel Kahneman and Amos Tversky had published the research results for the heuristics in decision making (12) and the prospect theory (10) considered to be the two most important milestones of behavioral economics (7).

The works of Herbert A. Simon (13), Garry S. Becker (14), George A. Akerlof (15), Michael A. Spence, Joseph E. Stiglitz, and Daniel Kahneman (10) were awarded with the Bank of Sweden Prize in Memory of Alfred Nobel in 1978, 1992, 2001 and 2002 respectively. The prize for Daniel Kahneman was shared with Vernon L. Smith awarded for the research results in experimental economy (16).

Modern experimental psychology, understood as a psychological research area, follows ideas proposed by Wilhelm Wundt, who had established the first laboratory for psychological experiments in the 19th century near Lipsk (Leipzig)(17). Boring concludes, that the psychology scientists were always interested in perception issues which explains the mentioning of this curiosity in literature from the Middle Ages(18). Modern researchers take advantage of the previous achievements especially in the area of rules for scientific control and the usage of structuralized experimentation plans with known factors of strength.

One of the first quality perception models for certain products was proposed by Steenkamp for food quality perception(19). Their research on the model validity was conducted in psychological research paradigm using an independent groups plan.

Experiments are to trace the cause-effect relations between certain values of an independent variable and the resulting level of a dependant variable(s). Tracing such changes in human's attitude and their judgments is methodologically complex due to a relatively high threat from the factors beyond full control of the experimenter. Then one should not only describe investigated phenomenon but also prove the time sequence (cause-effect) and describe the future behavior for the independent variable changes (20).

In the summary of background analysis, described broader in (2), we stress that analyzed areas: software engineering, software quality engineering, behavioral economics and cognitive psychology are in a continuous development stage. There is an ongoing discussion regarding biases and their relation to the customer's experience (21). Some researchers suggest that experienced customers are not prone to biases and the inexperienced customers learn so fast that one should not analyze biases as serious tendencies. Research regarding this subject in the aspect of software products seem to be an important challenge for modern software engineering and behavioral economics.

C. *The software quality perception model*

Software quality psychology is a new research area focusing on the description of cognitive processes associated with the perception of software quality (2). This research area is still being defined and this article is one of the first presenting the experimental evidence supporting this area. First research concentrates on the software quality perception model presented on fig. 1.

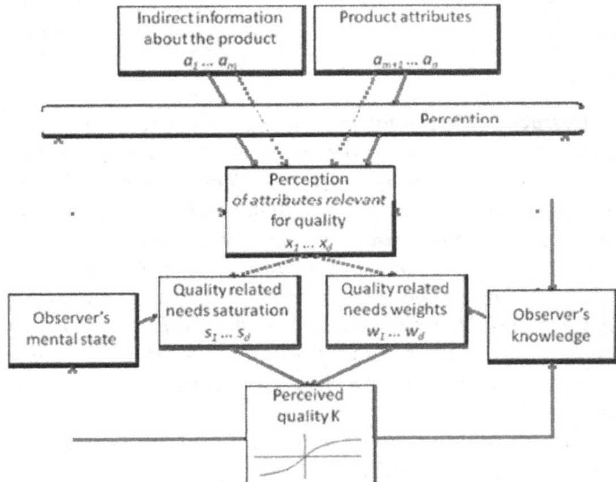

Fig. 1, The software quality perception model

The overall quality grade depends on the knowledge based importance of characteristics and also the current needs saturation. If the observed quality is above expectations then we can expect diminishing marginal increases caused by each "quality unit" (Gossen's law). On the other hand if the observed quality is below expectations then we can expect radical dissatisfaction non proportional to the "quality gap" (positive-negative asymmetry) (22).

Furthermore, both observer's knowledge and the observer's mental state influence the perception of software quality characteristics (e.g. supplies the process with valid or invalid associations etc.). Also both of these structures influence the behavior of the attention filter (perception filter).

The general perceived quality grade is a non linear combination of perceived attributes $K(x,w,s) = \sum_i F_i(s_i, w_i, x_i)$ with an open question what is first: judgments about attributes or the general grade.

II. The Experiment's Requirements

A. *Measuring objectives*

The measurement of perception issues follows the general latent variables measurement models. In consequence one could employ Rash polytomus model (23). In other words, direct answers have to be transformed to obtain the subject's internal feeling about software quality. The problem with this approach regards the lack of an objective reference point. Having two applications we are unable to define their objective quality grade, thus we cannot compare subjects' answers with those grades.

On the other hand it seems more important at this stage to identify the relations between certain variables and subjects' reactions. Measuring such reactions is possible using questionnaires.

Considering what should be measured one has to take into account one of the fundamental assumptions regarding software quality models. These models assume that the overall quality grade consists of several quality characteristics grades. There is no evidence or research results allowing us to propose a function between quality characteristics grades nor a comprehensive set of characteristics representing required dimensions of software product quality. In addition we expect that none of the prescriptive models, described in literature, is adequate for the measurement of actual user's reactions. Therefore we suggest measuring general quality as a general feeling about a product's quality as an ultimate quality grade for this product. Tracing relations between quality grade and quality characteristics grades additionally requires questions to be asked about those grades.

The subsequent decision to be made regards the scale to be used and the form and content of the question to be asked. The decision about the scale affects statistical methods which may be used for the purpose of analyzing the results. We aim to analyze the results among different sets of independent variables thus we need to use at least an interval scale (24). We have decided to refer to subjects' personal feelings about quality thus the question should regard the comparison of the observed application with an ideal object. The ideal object seems to be different for each subject however as we are aiming to measure a personal level of quality needs saturation, we accept these differences. Supporting intuitive decisions of the subjects, we suggest using continuous-like scales, anchored at the ands and at the middle point.

B. Controllable environment

One of the most important issues regarding research, is the need of scientific control. Software products differ in almost every characteristic and these characteristics are interrelated. In consequence an observed effect cannot be related to single cause. Even more, the extent of the possible list of causes is in general unknown.

An alternative approach would use the same application and compare independent variables not associated with the software (e.g. with individual characteristics of subjects). However, in such approach the quality of software is constant. Therefore this approach does not allow the measurement of the perception of quality caused by the quality of the software.

The problem with combining the approaches described above, may be reduced to the general problem of quality modeling and measurement. We have mentioned in the preface that there is no commonly accepted software quality model nor is there an objective evaluation process description. Based on these facts, we have to conclude that the quality of two versions of the same application, cannot be objectively measured. Thus we still have a problem with the large number of independent variables in a comparison of two applications.

On the other hand comparing quality could be achieved if we had a quality order relation between applications. Having the same application we can add a random bug generation function and set the probability of failure. Intuitively we can conclude that, if two applications are identical but one fails more often than the other, it is of lower quality.

Failures of the application have to be realistic and objectively unexpectable. For this reason we have decided to implement typical failures observed in test environments of a chosen sector.

C. Subjects

We have mentioned in the preface that there is an ongoing discussion regarding the relation of biases to the level of subjects' experience. Some authors suggest that subjects learn eagerly (the rise of cognitive structures is observed during the experiment) and others suggest that it is a slow process requiring experience gathered over time.

Having no basis to select one of the above points of view we have referred to real world projects. In the real projects, where important software is to be evaluated, the majority of the evaluation team consists of professional evaluators or key user representatives. In both cases these people are quite experienced and know the domain of use at an expert level. For research regarding the perception for large and critical systems we suggest employing professionals as subjects.

Of course if one wants to investigate the perception of a COTS (commercial off the shelf) product then the selection of subjects should follow their assumption about the target group.

D. Remaining boundaries

The validity of research conducted in a strictly artificial (laboratory) environment is, by assumption, threatened by cofounding. In an artificial environment the effects, which may not occur in the real world, are observable. On the other hand, we have shown possible threats in an approach based on the real world projects observation. A solution to these challenges may be found in a natural field experiments approach (Levitt, et al., 2008).

The proposed TestLab framework is suited to the conduction of such natural field experiments, although it is not only the software, that matters. All communication, procedures and instructions for subjects have to be realistic. It is usually recommended to keep subjects unaware of the real goal of the research to avoid the Hawthorne effect (Henslin, 2008).

An important issue regarding research is the exclusion of cofounding. Cofounding may be a result of some uncontrolled occurrences during the research or systematic differences between compared environments / groups. To avoid these threats we suggest randomly splitting the sample into groups and conduct research simultaneously for these groups / environments which are to be compared. Additionally the researcher should be able to objectively check the homogeneity of the groups.

It is important, especially for longitudinal research, to assure physical separation of groups. An example of omission of this requirement may be found in (Stavrinoudis, et al., 2005). The authors have conducted research among different types of users making them assess the quality of the application in several succeeding weeks. In conclusion the authors state that the objective evaluation of software quality was made, which was thought to be proven by a consensus between individual assessments of the subjects. Regarding experimental psychology knowledge and the research plan proposed by the authors we identify the risk of regression to mean effect, which could have taken place. Without physical separation of subjects the authors were unable to mitigate this risk.

III. PROPOSED APPROACH

A. *Research framework tool*

The authors have decided to prepare a dedicated, realistic environment framework for the research conduction. The tool allows the deployment of application decoys and simulate their real operation. The framework generates pre defined failures according to preset failure probability. Functionality is supplemented with the ability to trace and log user's activities for future analysis and support the survey part of the research.

Based on categorized bug reports for >100 projects we have decided to implement the following failure types in TestLab framework.

1. "Blue screen" - the application fails producing literally a blue screen containing a vast amount of technical information about error in the application. Examplary "Blue screen" is presented on fig 2.,

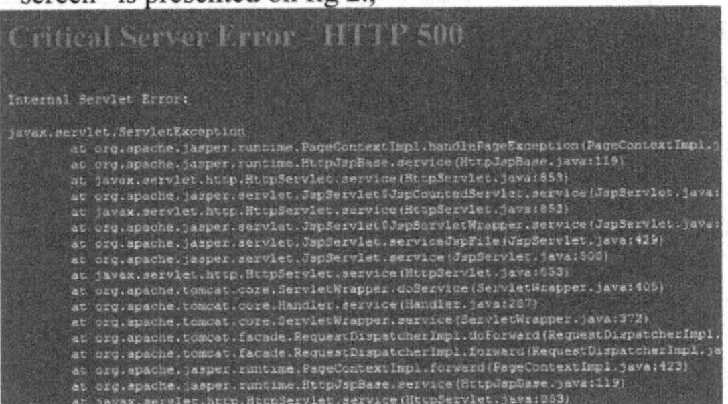

Fig. 2, Exemplary beginning of a "Blue screen"

2. Performance error - after an action is initiated by a user the application waits for 90 seconds before issuing the answer,
3. Data lost error on write - after a completed form is submitted to the application the answer is "you have not completed the form",
4. Data lost error on read – when selecting data (a list of records or a single record) the application returns an empty information set []
5. Data change error on write - after data is submitted to the application it stores truncated data (for example "J" instead of "John"),
6. Data change error on write – this type of failure is similar to the above one, but data are being truncated only during the presentation - when the user requests data for the second time they may receive correct information,
7. Calculation error - the application returns an incorrect calculation result,
8. Presentation error -the application presents the screen as a maze of objects (objects are located in incorrect positions having also incorrect sizes, color sets etc),
9. Static text error – the application randomly swaps static texts on the screen,
10. Form reset error – when this error is generated user is unable to finish filling up a form on the screen – the form is cleared before completion (every 2-10 seconds),
11. Inaccessibility of function – the application disables the possibility of using any of the active controls on the screen (for example after filling a form user cannot submit it),
12. Irritating messages error - the application shows sequential messages about errors but without any real failure – user has to confirm each message by clicking "OK" button

TestLab supports three types of tasks: survey about subject, evaluation task and managers evaluation task. Personal survey allows to gather statistical information about subject's preferences. The evaluation task consist of presentation of evaluation instruction, access to the tested application with a predefined quality level (as discussed above) and the final survey about quality. Managers evaluation task refers to the real life situation where higher management has to prepare their own opinion about software quality but they do not perform actual evaluation. Managers evaluation task presents the evaluation instruction given to subjects and their evaluation reports asking for personal opinion about the quality.

Surveys in TestLab may be constructed using all of typical answer types (singe/multiple choice, free text etc.). Additionally we have implemented a Likert-type scale having the possibility to define bipolar terms at the ends, following Osgood's semantic differential (23). Following the ISO/IEC 25010 draft we have chosen rich functionality, general software quality, compliance with formal rules, efficiency, productivity, satisfaction, learnability, adaptability, reliability, safety and security as the characteristics to be measured besides the question about general quality grade. The ends of the scale are anchored to definitions *Application is the absolute negation of this attribute* [value=1] and *Application is the ideal example of this attribute* [value=11]. In the middle point the neutral anchor is defined as *Application has this quality attribute but not on an exceptional level* [value=6]. The scale is intended to look like a continuous scale (using red color on the negative and green at the positive and with gradient change between). The way of presentation is shown on fig 3.

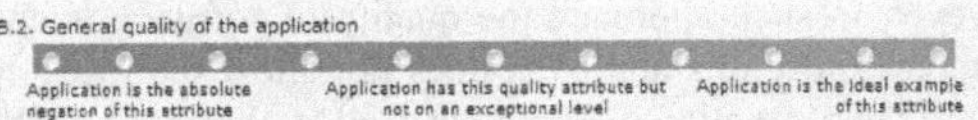

Fig. 3, Scale example for the general quality question

B. *Scenarios*

Tracing the cause-effect relations requires a controllable environment for the analysis as discussed above. Having the environment prepared one needs to develop a formal procedure of conduction to assure a predictable level.

We have mentioned in the previous section, that the internal validity of the experiment may be affected by several occurrences having nothing in common with conducted research. For example if one is investigating the perception of the internet banking applications and, during this time, there were some fraud reports in media, it could have influenced the results. Therefore we have suggested reducing such threats by conduction of the comparable research in the same time but in adjacent rooms. One of the most popular scenarios which could be used is the independent groups plan.

In the independent groups plan there is a requirement to split the sample into independent groups maintaining controllable differences among them. The research is conducted with the respect to these differences. The experiment provides date allowing to analyze relation between a vector of independent variables values and the result.

Evaluation of the software quality perception model requires set of experiments. In each case the subjects have to be prepared to take part in the research and, by the assumption, they have to be unaware of the real goal of the research. This means that after taking part in one of the experiments subjects cannot be assigned to another experiment.

We propose following main scenarios for the purpose of model evaluation:

1. History effect tracing: the subjects will be taking part in the experiment for several periods. In each period they will receive application with a different quality level. Independent groups will receive different "paths" of succeeding versions' quality levels and at the end we will compare the perception of the last version, which will have the same quality level in all groups.
2. Group effect tracing: the subjects will be mixed with figureheads and these figureheads will play roles of people talking positively or negatively about application. To assure the occurrence of the effect we need to make subjects express their opinions before group for example during short "meetings" during the evaluation (the goal is defined as for the evaluation task). At the end we will compare individual surveys completed without any influence of the group.
3. Associations effect: this experiment may be prepared independently or with subjects evaluating the history effect. The subjects will be split into groups and evaluate identical application but in different graphical layouts. Half of the groups will receive application using the graphical layout associated with the previous evaluation task or a pre-test task and the othe group will receive application in different layout. For complete evaluation it is required to analyze the layout for the first group by third group – the subjects who have not seen the first graphical layout. At the end we will analyze the difference in the perception because of the graphical layout association to the previous experience.
4. Manager's perception – the analysis of the manager's perception may be conducted simultaneously to other research scenarios. Managers have to be separated from their groups and rely only on the written reports. At the end we may analyze the same effects which will be analyzed among evaluators and additionally the estimator of manager's opinion about software quality.
5. Attention influence may be investigated when one of the groups will have additional distracter during the evaluation (ability to talk about other subjects, watching a film etc.). At the end we will analyze the relation of the attention possibility to adequate quality assessment.

The above scenarios are the first ones designed for the purpose of software quality perception model evaluation. They should be treated as the general directions which allow to construct several experiments differing in details of the design.

C. Analysis methods

One of the typical approaches to testing statistical importance of the results is testing the null hypothesis approach. Although this method is widely criticized it is at the same time considered as the best possible option (29), (20).

The null hypothesis testing should assume that there is no statistical differences between groups. We may test such hypothesis using the F-test and the ANOVA method (30).

If the null hypothesis is to be rejected on a pre-set confidence level then the effect size may be calculated. Effect size may be estimated using Cohen's *d*, Hedges's *g* etc. (31).

Additionally the experimenter should have designed part of the research for testing the homogenicity of the groups to assure that the observed effect is a result from the independent variables values, not the systematic differences between groups.

D. Compliance

All of the experiments should be conducted with the respect to codes and rules. Regardless of country the experiment is to be led, we suggest using APA Ethics Code (19) as a baseline.

According to section 3.10 (The informed consent) organizations taking part in the research will be asked to agree for experiment having all necessary information provided. Subjects will be asked to take part in an evaluation project, without any extra benefits, and will agree to perform a list of tasks. We have discussed above the need to use deception in experiment to avoid the Hawthorne effect. Information about the experiment and the permission for using the data gathered during the experiment will be issued after the measurements were taken without any consequence on subjects' decisions.

IV. CONCLUSION

Behavioral economics has challenged the neo-classical models showing explicit violations of fundamental assumptions. For several product there have been proposed quality perception models respecting data from the observations. Software engineering is before such e step. Current software quality models assume that the user is perfectly rational, fully informed and aiming to maximize their utility. Are these assumptions true? If one bases on software engineering literature than they conclude that yes they are. However if one aims to understand the actual processes and describe the real observer's perception then the answer is uncertain.

In this article we are summarizing the most important requirements for the research of user's perception of software quality according to the behavioral economics state of the art. Proposed tools, methods and scenarios are not the only ones able to fit into the requirements thus we expect that other approaches will be proposed. However the goal is common – better understanding and predicting the user's perception using a reliable and verifiable model.

Research in the area of software quality perception is a complex challenge. Software quality model and the evaluation process model remains undefined, software projects are incomparable, users' experiences are incomparable. Although we were able to propose a set of assumptions and practical solutions making the reliable research possible.

V. References

1. **IEEE SwEBoK.** *Software Engineering Body of Knowledge.* s.l. : Institute of Electrical and Electronics Engineers, http://www.swebok.org/, 2004.
2. **Hofman, R.** Software quality perception. [book auth.] CISSE2008. *Innovations and Advanced Techniques in Systems, Computing Sciences and Software Engineering.* s.l. : Springer (w przygotowaniu), 2009.
3. **McCall, J., Richards, P. and Walters, G.** *Factors In software quality.* s.l. : Griffiths Air Force Base, NY, Rome Air Development Center Air Force Systems Command, 1977.
4. **Boehm, B., et al.** *Characteristics of software quality.* New York : American Elsevier, 1978.
5. *ISO/IEC SQuaRE. The seconod generation of standards for software product quality.* **Suryn, W. and Abran, A.** 2003. IASTED2003.
6. *SQuaRE based Web Services Quality Model.* **Abramowicz, W., et al.** Hong Kong : International Association of Engineers, 2008. International Conference on Internet Computing and Web Services. ISBN: 978-988-98671-8-8.
7. **Camerer, C. and Loewenstein, G.** *Behavioral Economics: Past, Present, Future (introduction for Advances in Behavioral Economics).* Mimeo : Carnegie Mellon University, 2003.
8. **Smith, A.** *An Inquiry into the Nature and Causes of the Wealth of Nations.* 1776. Chapter IV: Of the Origin and Use of Money.
9. —. *The theory of moral sentiments.* London : A. Millar , 1759.
10. *"Prospect" theory: an analysis of decision under risk.* **Kahneman, D. and Tversky, A.** 47, 1979, Econometrica.
11. **Nęcka, E., Orzechowski, J. and Szymura, B.** *Psychologia poznawcza.* Warszawa : Wydawnictwo Naukowe PWN, 2008.
12. **Tversky, A. and Kahneman, D.** Judgment under Uncertainty: Heuristics and Biases. *Science.* 1974, 185.
13. *Rational choice and structure of environments.* **Simon, H.** 63, 1956, Psychological review.
14. **Becker, G.** Crime and punishment: An Economic Approach. *Journal of Political Economy.* 1968.
15. **Akerlof, G.** The Market for 'Lemons': Quality Uncertainty and the Market Mechanism. *Quarterly Journal of Economics.* 1970, 84.
16. **Nobel Foundation.** Nobelprize.org. *All Laureates in Economics.* [Online] [Cited: 07 27, 2009.] http://nobelprize.org/nobel_prizes/economics/laureates/.
17. **Boring, E.** *A History of Experimental Psychology.* Second Edition. s.l. : Prentice-Hall, 1950.
18. *Who Is the Founder of Psychophysics and Experimental Psychology?* **Khaleefa, O.** 16, 1999, American Journal of Islamic Social Sciences.
19. **Steenkamp, J., Wierenga, B. and Meulenberg, M.** *Kwali-teits-perceptie van voedingsmiddelen deel 1. Swoka.* Den Haag : s.n., 1986.
20. **Shaughnessy, J., Zechmeister, E. and Zechmeister, J.** *Research Methods in Psychology.* Seventh edition. s.l. : McGraw-Hill, 2005.
21. **List, A.** Neoclassical Theory Versus Prospect Theory: Evidence From The Marketplace. *Econometrica.* 2004, 72.
22. **Tversky, A. and Kahneman, D.** Judgement under uncertainty: heuristics and biases. [book auth.] D. Kahneman, A. Tversky and P. Slovic. *Judgement under uncertainty: heuristics and biases.* Cambridge : Cambridge University Press, 1982.
23. **Alagumalai, S., Curtis, D. and Hungi, N.** *Applied Rash Measurement: A book of exemplars.* s.l. : Springer-Kluwer, 2005.
24. **Stevens, S.** Measurement, Psychophisics and Utility. [book auth.] C. Churchman and Ratoosh P. *Definitions and Theories.* New York : Wiley, 1959.
25. **Levitt, S. and List, J.** *Field Experiments in Economics: The Past, The Present, and The Future.* Cambridge : National Bureau of Economic Research Working Paper Series, 2008.
26. **Henslin, J.** *Sociology: a down to earth approach.* nineth edition. s.l. : Pearson Education, 2008. ISBN 978-0-205-57023-2.
27. **Stavrinoudis, D., et al.** Early Estimation of Users' Perception of Software Quality. *Software Quality Journal.* 2005, Vol. 13.
28. **Osgood, C., Suci, G. and Tannenbaum, P.** *The measurement of meaning.* Urbana, IL : University of Illinois Press, 1957.
29. *The earth is round (p<0,05).* **Cohen, J.** 49, 1995, American psychologist.
30. **Ferguson, G. and Takane, Y.** *Statistical Analysis in Psychology and Education.* Sixth Edition. Montréal, Quebec : McGraw-Hill Ryerson Limited, 2005.
31. **Cohen, J.** *Statistical power analysis for the behavioral sciences.* Second Edition. Hillsdale, NJ : Erlbaum, 1988.
32. **American Psychological Association.** Ethical principles of psychologists and code of conduct. [Online] http://www.apa.org/ethics/code2002.html.

Automatically Modeling Linguistic Categories in Spanish

M. D. López De Luise, D. Hisgen, M. Soffer
AIGroup Universidad de Palermo. Mario Bravo 1050. Buenos Aires. Argentina

Abstract— **This paper presents an approach to process Spanish linguistic categories automatically. The approach is based in a module of a prototype named WIH (Word Intelligent Handler), which is a project to develop a conversational bot. It basically learns category usage sequence in a sentence. It extracts a weighting metric to discriminate most common structures in real dialogs. Such a metric is important to define the preferred organization to be used by the robot to build an answer.**

I. INTRODUCTION

Research in conversational bots is programs designed to emulate human conversations. Dated from sixties, they have been developed with several common characteristics: pre-defined tokens and patterns to be matched; lack of handling of linguistics and lack of interpretation of what they are saying. Most of them interact though the computer keyboard. They implement different pattern matching strategies [1][2][4][5][7], Markow chains, neural networks, case logic in most of them. But there are also certain projects that implement language disambiguation parsing, part of speech tagging, and some other NLP (Natural Language Processing)[5] as part of a little linguistics managing.

This paper presents part of a conversational bot project named WIH (Word Intelligent Handler). It implements a bot that processes linguistics to be able to learn and model language usage. This knowledge is stored in a memory named EP-memory and used to construct answers automatically.

One of the oldest work in the area is ELIZA [1][2], a chat that models the behavior of a psychiatrist (the "active listening" strategies of a touchy-feely 1960s Rogerian therapist). Parry is other of the oldest implementations [3], simulates paranoid behavior. Colby subjected PARRY to blind tests with doctors questioning both the program and three human patients diagnosed as paranoid. Reviews of the transcripts by both psychiatrists and computer scientists showed that neither group did better than chance in distinguishing the computer from human patients [4]. PARRY and ELIZA interacted several times, speaking each other.

In 1968 SHRDLU [5] was described in Winograd's dissertation. It handles a small world with certain objects. It can process sentences with something about its context.

Racter (1983), the commercial program attempted to parse text inputs, identify significant nouns and verbs, which it would use to create conversations. It plugs the input from a user into phrase templates that are combined. W. Chamberlain claims that this software is the author of a book [6].

Other known prototypes are ALICE [7], Dr. Sbaitso[8], My-bot [9], SmarterChild [10], all of them available in different formats.

It is also possible to use frameworks like [11][12][13][14] to build a bot using specific technology such as AIML (Artificial Intelligence Markup Language), dictionaries, tagged corpus, etc.

The reason to use complex approaches is the difficulty inherent to language modeling. Structure manipulation frequently involves a specific set of rules that are complemented with a large list of exceptions and specific considerations. The project WIH (Word Intelligent Handler) is intended to process some of the aspects of automatic language generation. Started at the beginning of 2005 [15], it has successfully advanced in the field of automatic categorization of words [16], sentences weighting, automatic summarizations, text profiling among other contributions [17]. This paper is focused on a new module dedicated to model linguistic category usage in humans. It is an important part of the prototype that will be complemented with other two modules that will make the system able to make sentences automatically.

The rest of this paper will present the approach used by WIH to model structures (section II), the implementation in the prototype (section III), statistical analysis of real cases (section IV), conclusions and future work to be done (section V).

II. MAIN APPROACH

Despite the language performs differently according to culture, subject and geographical situation [18], the main hypothesis behind WIH is the existence of a regular basis in the language usage [17]. This makes possible language modeling.

The WIH project is aimed to implement a prototype that learns Spanish language through experiencing dialogs with humans. It is important due the language could change the world perception and interpretation [19].

As can be seen in Fig. 1; the prototype is composed by several modules that interact permanently in order to process different aspects of the modeling.

This work has been performed as part of the WIH project, part of the Artificial Intelligence Group (AIGroup), in the Palermo University. aigroup@palermo.edu.

T. Sobh, K. Elleithy (eds.), *Innovations in Computing Sciences and Software Engineering*,
DOI 10.1007/978-90-481-9112-3_53, © Springer Science+Business Media B.V. 2010

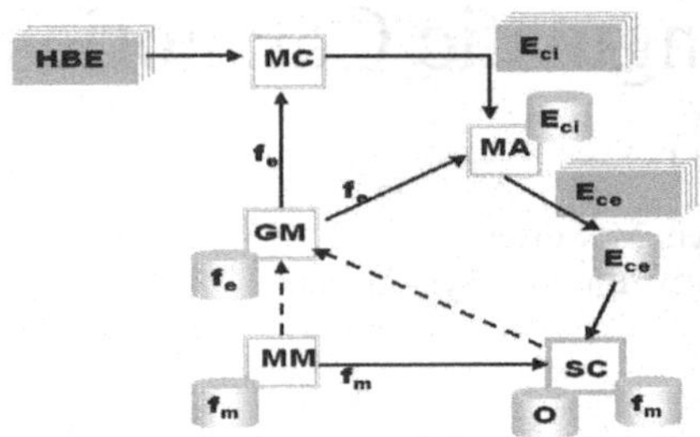

Fig. 1. WIH global architecture.

For instance there is a TLI-module that translates Spanish sentences into an internal representation, which models main sentence characteristics. This internal representation is written as a set of related structures named EBH. The MC-module changes the set of actual EBH to another structure named E_{ci}. This structure models the EBH context within a dialog or text[1]. Finally, the MA-module build a structure named E_{ce} that serves as a complement for the system to find stored information [17]. This paper is focused on the EM-memory which is part of the MA-module.

III. THE PROTOTYPE

The WIH prototype can automatically parse any sentence and derive a related sequence of linguistics categories, each one in correspondence with every word in the input [16][17]. The resulting chain is named *ps* (Parsed Structure). This structure is then saved in the EP-memory taking into account its usage.

Because the parser never stops learning, the first problem registering linguistic category usage is that it should model an endless event. To solve it the input is supposed to be split and analyzed as a finite set of instances as shown in Fig. 2. The input is now a set of linguistic category sequences (denoted with ps, parsed structures) as represented by (1).

$$A = \{A_i\} \qquad (1)$$
$$\# A = M, 1 \le i \le M, M << N$$

Where N is the input size and M is the number of elements in the actual set A. Every A_i has an initial known probability $P(A_i)$ of occurrence in M.

The first time a specific ps_k is processed; there is no previous experience in the EP-memory. Then the related $P(A_k)$ is used as the 'most probable usage' of A_k sequence. The first occurrence is not used to change the memory knowledge but it initializes an instance counter η_k.

ps_1 ps_2 .... ps_M ps_{M+1} ps_{M+2} .... ps_{2M} ps_{2M+1}.....

A_1 A_2 . . . A_M

Fig. 2 Real input are split up into several sets with the same size.

[1] The original Project was designed to process dialogs, WEB pages and text files.

As the system keeps interacting with the environment, it processes more structures, always learning language real usage. Every input updates certain η_k and a global counter η^*. When η^* reaches M, the memory updates its knowledge about structures in the actual set A. The update is performed using (2). P'_k is the new knowledge in EP-memory about ps_k, and $P_k = P(A_k)$ the first time P'_k is calculated.

$$P'_k = \alpha . P_k + \beta . \frac{\eta_k}{N} \qquad (2)$$
$$\alpha + \beta = 1, \alpha > 0$$

The progression of P_k as the memory learns from experience should reinforce learning faster at the beginning from initial knowledge of $P(A_k)$ and stabilizing knowledge after certain number of occurrences. As long as the memory keeps learning it could be changes but the first term in (2) acts as an inertial factor in the learning.

IV. CASE STUDY

In order to visualize the algorithm impact on the linguistic category usage, a dataset with random generated structures was processed. The random structures were built using the following Spanish categories: VERBO (verb), SUSTANTIVO (noun), ADJETIVO (adjective), ADVERBIO_LUGAR (adverb denoting place), ADVERBIO_MODO (adverb denoting manner) , ADVERBIO_TIEMPO (adverb denoting time), PRONOMBRE_DEMOSTRATIVO (demonstrative pronoun), PRONOMBRE_PERSONAL (personal pronoun) and ARTICULO (article). The dataset was processed with the EP-memory to derive its weighting. Every instance x_k in the resulting dataset is composed by a weighting p_k, and a category sequence $\{a_k^i\}$ with random length between 1 and 9. Fig. 3 show an example of a record, where p_k is 0.0184861 and has 4 tokens concatenated as part of the sequence.

Note that samples have been generated randomly, and sequences have not any sense in Spanish, but they all have the same occurrence probability. In consequence, a chain composed by three verbs could be found, despite it is not a possible linguistic construction in Spanish. Part of the database is in Fig. 4.

Because of the implementation of the EP-memory, the samples were organized in files according to the first category in the chain. Within each file the samples always start with the same category. There are 3491 samples generated, all of them saved in a working memory and moved to the EP-memory every 1000 samples (M=20 and N=1000).

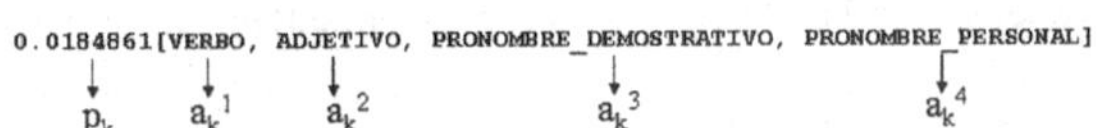

Fig. 3 Sample record x_k with a chain of 4 categories.

```
ADJETIVO.TXT
0.0105003;ADJETIVO
0.0060281;ADJETIVO, ADJETIVO
0.0009980;ADJETIVO, ADJETIVO, ADJETIVO
0.0009980;ADJETIVO, ADJETIVO, ADJETIVO, ADVERBIO_MODO, ADJETIVO
0.0009980;ADJETIVO, ADJETIVO, ADJETIVO, ADVERBIO_TIEMPO
0.0009980;ADJETIVO, ADJETIVO, ADJETIVO, ADVERBIO_TIEMPO, ADVERBIO_LUGAR
0.0009980;ADJETIVO, ADJETIVO, ADJETIVO, VERBO, ADJETIVO, ADJETIVO
0.0009980;ADJETIVO, ADJETIVO, ADVERBIO_LUGAR
0.0009980;ADJETIVO, ADJETIVO, ADVERBIO_LUGAR, ADJETIVO, SUSTANTIVO
0.0009980;ADJETIVO, ADJETIVO, ADVERBIO_MODO
0.0009980;ADJETIVO, ADJETIVO, ADVERBIO_MODO, ADVERBIO_MODO
0.0009980;ADJETIVO, ADJETIVO, ADVERBIO_MODO, ADVERBIO
...
ARTICULO.TXT
0.0123039;ARTICULO
0.0010575;ARTICULO, ADJETIVO
0.0009981;ARTICULO, ADJETIVO, ADJETIVO
0.0009980;ARTICULO, ADJETIVO, ADJETIVO, ADVERBIO_LUGAR
0.0009980;ARTICULO, ADJETIVO, ADJETIVO, ADVERBIO_LUGAR, ADVERBIO_LUGAR
0.0009980;ARTICULO, ADJETIVO, ADJETIVO, ADVERBIO_LUGAR,
        PRONOMBRE_DEMOSTRATIVO, ADVERBIO_TIEMPO
0.0009980;ARTICULO, ADJETIVO, ADJETIVO, ADVERBIO_TIEMPO
0.0009980;ARTICULO, ADJETIVO, ADVERBIO_LUGAR, ADJETIVO
0.0009980;ARTICULO, ADJETIVO, ADVERBIO_LUGAR, PRONOMBRE_DEMOSTRATIVO,
        ARTICULO
0.0009980;ARTICULO, ADJETIVO, ADVERBIO_MODO, ADVERBIO_MODO
...
```

Fig. 4 Some records from the random database.

Fig. 5 and TABLE I show the distribution of the 2853 samples in the EP-memory and Fig. 6 for the 638 samples in the working memory. It can be seen that distribution in both cases are similar, as expected due the random generation process.

The weighting calculated using equation (2) suggests that no special category sequence should be preferred. Since by construction the dataset has no special use of any parsed structure, values should be mostly evenly distributed in the domain. This result are verified the weights shown in Fig. 7.

TABLE I
SAMPLE DISTRIBUTION IN EP-MEMORY

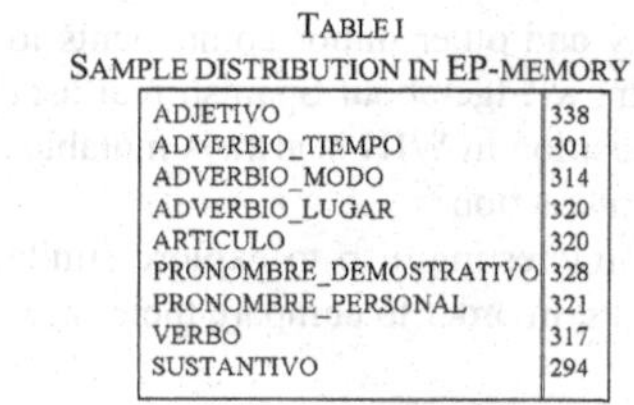

ADJETIVO	338
ADVERBIO_TIEMPO	301
ADVERBIO_MODO	314
ADVERBIO_LUGAR	320
ARTICULO	320
PRONOMBRE_DEMOSTRATIVO	328
PRONOMBRE_PERSONAL	321
VERBO	317
SUSTANTIVO	294

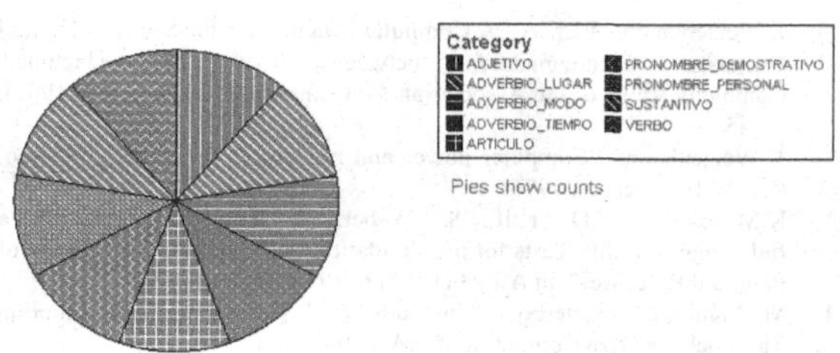

Fig. 5 Sample distribution in EP-memory.

TABLE II
SAMPLE DISTRIBUTION IN WORKING MEMORY

ADJETIVO	73
ADVERBIO_TIEMPO	73
ADVERBIO_MODO	81
ADVERBIO_LUGAR	68
ARTICULO	63
PRONOMBRE_DEMOSTRATIVO	68
PRONOMBRE_PERSONAL	68
VERBO	70
SUSTANTIVO	74

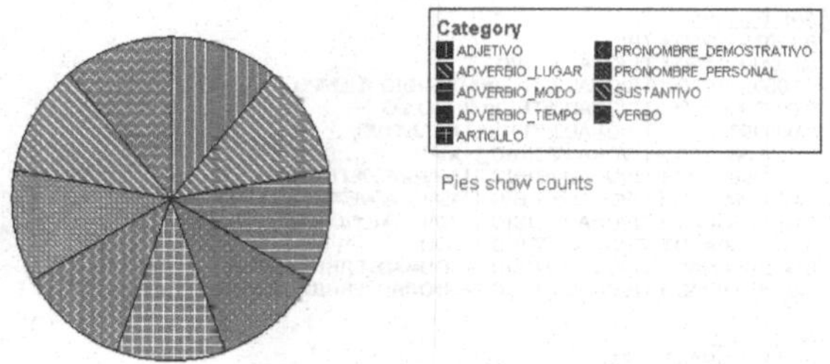

Fig. 6 Sample distribution in working memory.

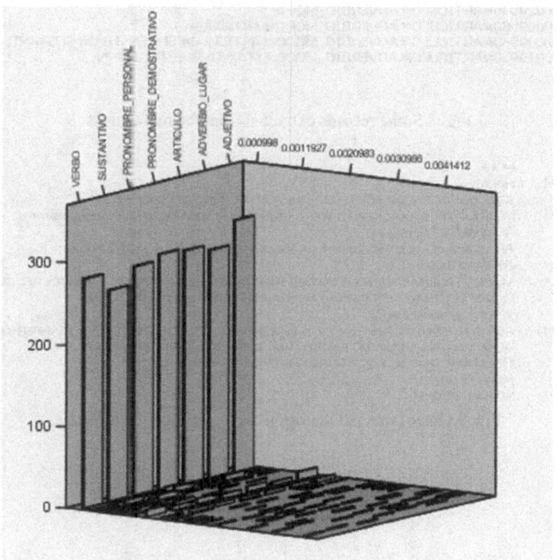

Fig. 7 Weight frequency according to each category in random database.

The bars represent the frequency of structures starting with certain category. Sequences are clustered by the starting category. For instance, the frequency of structures starting with VERBO and weighting 0.000998 (the value of p_0, initial known probability in the test) is near 300. Similar structures with values $p_k > p_0$ have frequencies near zero. As mentioned, this is due the high variation of the structures generated.

In the figure a few cases have a relative higher frequency when p_k =0.0020983. It reflects the reuse of part of the dataset, because the same happens with the rest of the clusters. In real case processing it is expected that higher bars are sparsely spread all over the graphic showing a general disposition.

As a second test, 5 real short dialogs in Spanish were processed by WIH after cleaning previous knowledge in the EP-memory. In Fig. 8 there is an extract of sample data after parsing and processing to extract cathegories. Fig. 9 shows one of the original Spanish dialogs used.

The resulting sp files were learned in a similar way as the randomized dataset. The resulting weight frequencies are summarized in Fig. 10. Category distributions for EP-memory and working memory are shown in TABLE III and TABLE IV respectively.

ADJETIVO.TXT
0.1207585#ADJETIVO
0.0029940#ADJETIVO#ADJETIVO
0.0009980#ADJETIVO#ADJETIVO#ADVERBIO_TIEMPO
0.0009980#ADJETIVO#ADJETIVO#ARTICULO
0.0009980#ADJETIVO#ADJETIVO#SUSTANTIVO
0.0059880#ADJETIVO#ADVERBIO_LUGAR
0.0009980#ADJETIVO#ADVERBIO_LUGAR#ADJETIVO
0.0009980#ADJETIVO#ADVERBIO_LUGAR#ADVERBIO_LUGAR
0.0009980#ADJETIVO#ADVERBIO_LUGAR#PRONOMBRE_PERSONAL
0.0049900#ADJETIVO#ADVERBIO_MODO
0.0019960#ADJETIVO#ADVERBIO_MODO#ADVERBIO_LUGAR
0.0009980#ADJETIVO#ADVERBIO_MODO#ADVERBIO_TIEMPO
...
ARTICULO.TXT
0.1337325#ARTICULO
0.0029940#ARTICULO# ADJETIVO
0.0009980#ARTICULO# ADJETIVO# ADJETIVO
0.0009980#ARTICULO# ADVERBIO_LUGAR
0.0019960#ARTICULO# ADVERBIO_LUGAR# ADVERBIO_LUGAR
0.0009980#ARTICULO# ADVERBIO_LUGAR# ADVERBIO_MODO
0.0029940#ARTICULO# ADVERBIO_MODO
0.0009980#ARTICULO# ADVERBIO_MODO# ARTICULO
0.0009980#ARTICULO# ADVERBIO_MODO# ARTICULO# SUSTANTIVO# SUSTANTIVO
0.0019960#ARTICULO# ADVERBIO_MODO# PRONOMBRE_PERSONAL
...

Fig. 8 Some records extracted from the real dialogs.

U- HOLA
WIH- HOLA
U- SABE DONDE PUEDO CONSEGUIR PASAJES DE AVIÓN ECONÓMICOS?
WIH- SI, SOLO TIENE QUE IR A LA WEB Y BUSCAR EN SU BUSCADOR LAS PALABRAS "PASAJE" Y "AVIÓN".
U- AHÍ SUPONGO QUE ME SALDRÁ LA INFORMACIÓN QUE NECESITO PARA IR A COMPRARLOS
WIH- SI, PERO ADEMÁS TIENE LA POSIBILIDAD DE HACER LA COMPRA A TRAVÉS DEL SITE. CLARO QUE DEBE TENER UNA TARJETA DE CRÉDITO INTERNACIONAL.
U- Y SERÁ SEGURO ESO?
WIH- POR SUPUESTO, EL SISTEMA LE MOSTRARÁ UN CANDADITO EN LA PARTE INFERIOR DE SU PANTALLA CUANDO ESTE EN UNA ZONA SEGURA DE INTERNET. SE SUPONE QUE ALLÍ NO CORRE PELIGRO SU INFORMACIÓN
U- MUCHAS GRACIAS
WIH- NO HAY DE QUE

Fig. 9 One of the real dialogs used to generate the database.

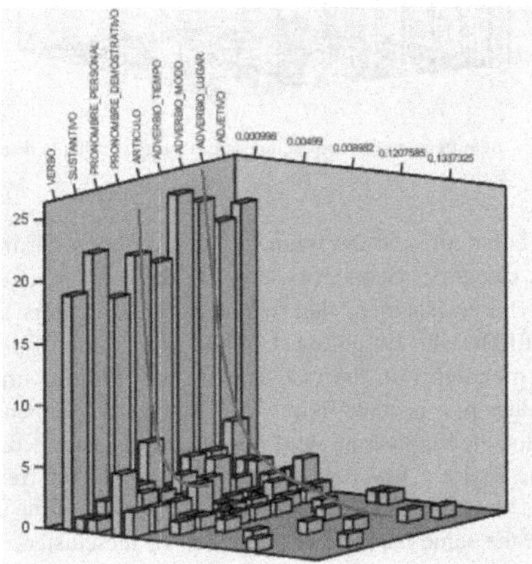

Fig. 10 Weight frequency according to each category in real dialogs.

TABLE III
SAMPLE DISTRIBUTION IN EP-MEMORY. REAL CASES

ADJETIVO	35
ADVERBIO_TIEMPO	39
ADVERBIO_MODO	37
ADVERBIO_LUGAR	39
ARTICULO	32
PRONOMBRE_DEMOSTRATIVO	37
PRONOMBRE_PERSONAL	31
VERBO	29
SUSTANTIVO	33

TABLE IV
SAMPLE DISTRIBUTION IN WORKING MEMORY. REAL CASES

ADJETIVO	66
ADVERBIO_TIEMPO	51
ADVERBIO_MODO	48
ADVERBIO_LUGAR	42
ARTICULO	55
PRONOMBRE_DEMOSTRATIVO	53
PRONOMBRE_PERSONAL	36
VERBO	45
SUSTANTIVO	43

From Fig. 10, it can be seen that highest frequencies are still localized in 0.000998, but they are differently distributed. The graph remarks the use of certain structures specially starting with SUSTANTIVO, ADVERBIO_MODO and ADVERBIO_LUGAR, which have highest weighting. Note the strong change in the general bar distribution since in Fig. 7 they are evenly distributed but in the real cases testing they decrease from highest values describing a slope down curve.

V. CONCLUSION AND FUTURE WORK

An approach to model linguistic category concatenation in Spanish sentences has been presented. From the comparison of random and real test cases it can be seen how specific language structures change the way the system model linguistic usage.

EP-memory is able to model linguistic category usage, and it should be complemented with the learning of context situations were each type of linguistic structure is used. It is being implemented as ER-memory, a module that interacts with EP-memory and other minor components to provide the prototype full knowledge about Spanish real usage. Note that knowledge acquisition in WIH is always mutable and does not require human interaction.

Finally, it is interesting also to explore similar processing in other languages, in order to compare their characteristics.

VI. REFERENCES

[1] J. Weizenbaum. "ELIZA - A Computer Program for the Study of Natural Language Communication between Man and Machine," Communications of the Association for Computing Machinery 9 (1966): 36-45.
[2] J. Weizenbaum. "Computer power and human reason". San Francisco, CA: W.H. Freeman, 1976.
[3] K.M Colby, F.D. Hilf, S. Weber, J. Kraemer. "Turing-Like Indistinguishability Tests for the Validation of a Computer Simulation of Paranoid Processes". in A.I., 3 (1972) pp199-222.
[4] M. Mauldin. "Chatterbots, Tinymuds, And The Turing Test: Entering The Loebner Prize Competition".AAAI-94. 1994
[5] T. Winograd. "Procedures as a Representation for Data in a Computer Program for Understanding Natural Language". Cognitive Psychology Vol. 3 No 1, 1972
[6] W.Chamberlain T. Etter."The Policeman's Beard Is Half Constructed ".(ISBN 0-446-38051-2)
[7] ALICEBOT, alicebot.blogspot.com/
[8] Dr-Sbaitso, download.cnet.com/Dr-Sbaitso
[9] My-bot, webs.uolsinectis.com/stigliano/mybot/
[10] SmarterChild, http://www.pointsincase.com/aim_convos/smarterchild.htm
[11] Colloquis, http://www.colloquis.com/
[12] Pandora Project, http://www.pandorabots.com/
[13] The Personality Forge, http://www.personalityforge.com/
[14] Galaia Project, http://papa.det.uvigo.es/~galaia

[15] M.D. López De Luise, "A Morphosyntactical Complementary Structure for Searching and Browsing". Proceedings of SCSS 2005. Sobh, Tarek; Elleithy, Khaled (Eds.) 2006, XIV, 437 p. ISBN 978-1-4020-5262-0

[16] M.D. López De Luise, J. Ale, "Induction Trees for Authomatic Word Classification". Proceedings of CACIC 2007. 2007.

[17] M.D. López De Luise, "Mejoras en la usabilidad de la Web a través de una estructura complementaria". PhD dissertation. Univ. Nacional de La Plata. Buenos Aires. Argentina. 2008.

[18] M.Bargalló,E. Forgas,C. Garriga,A.Rubio. "Las lenguas de especialidad y su didáctica". J. Schnitzer Eds. Universitat Rovira i Virgili. Tarragona, cap. 1 (P. Schifko, Wirtschaftsuniversität Wien), pp. 21-29. 2001.

[19] L. Wittgenstein. "Tractatus Logico-Philosophicus". Grandes Obras del Pensamiento. Ediciones Altaya, Barcelona, 1997

Efficient Content-based Image Retrieval using Support Vector Machines for Feature Aggregation

Ivica Dimitrovski, Suzana Loskovska and Ivan Chorbev
Department of Computer Science, Faculty of Electrical Engineering and Information Technologies
Skopje, Macedonia

***Abstract*-In this paper, a content-based image retrieval system for aggregation and combination of different image features is presented. Feature aggregation is important technique in general content-based image retrieval systems that employ multiple visual features to characterize image content. We introduced and evaluated linear combination and support vector machines to fuse the different image features. The implemented system has several advantages over the existing content-based image retrieval systems. Several implemented features included in our system allow the user to adapt the system to the query image. The SVM-based approach for ranking retrieval results helps processing specific queries for which users do not have knowledge about any suitable descriptors.**

I. Introduction

An incommensurable amount of visual information is becoming available in digital form in digital archives, on the World Wide Web, in broadcast data streams, art collections, photograph archives, bio-medical institutions, crime prevention, military, architectural and engineering design, geographical information and remote sensing systems and this amount is rapidly growing. The value of information often depends on how easy it can be found, retrieved, accessed, filtered and managed. Therefore, tools for efficient archiving, browsing and searching images are required.

A straightforward way of using the existing information retrieval tools for visual material, is to annotate records by keywords and then to use the text-based query for retrieval. Several approaches were proposed to use keyword annotations for image indexing and retrieval [1]. These approaches are not adequate, since annotating images by textual keywords is neither desirable nor possible in many cases. Therefore, new approaches of indexing, browsing and retrieval of images are required.

Rather than relying on manual indexing and text description for every image, images can be represented by numerical features directly extracted from the image pixels. These features are stored in a database as a signature together with the images and are used to measure similarity between the images in the retrieval process. This approach is known as Content-based Image Retrieval (CBIR).

The aim of CBIR systems is searching and finding similar multimedia items based on their content. Every CBIR system considers offline indexing phase and online content-based retrieval phase. The visual contents of the database images are extracted and described by multidimensional feature vectors in the offline phase. The feature vectors of the database images form the feature database. In the second or online retrieval phase, the query-by-example (QbE) paradigm is commonly used. The user presents a sample image, and the system computes the feature vector for the sample, compares it to the vectors for the images already stored in the database, and returns all images with similar features vectors. The query provided by the user can be a region, a sketch or group of images.

There are several well-known CBIR systems. IBM QBIC retrieves images based on visual image content such as color percentages, color layout, and textures occurring in the images [2]. Virage is basically used for video content based retrieval [7]. Photobook uses an interactive learning agent for retrieval [8]. The VisualSEEk system uses diagramming spatial arrangements of color regions to form a query [3]. MARS (Multimedia Analysis and Retrieval System) introduce relevance feedback into the image retrieval domain [5]. In Blobworld the images are represented by regions that are found with Expectation-Maximization-like (EM) segmentation process [4].

The quality of response depends on the image features and the distance or similarity measure used to compare features of different image [1]. Regarding the features, different approaches are used but the most common for image content representation are color, shape and texture features. Each extracted feature characterizes certain aspect of the image content. Multiple features are usually employed in many CBIR systems to provide an adequate description of image content. The idea behind these approaches is to employ as many image features as possible, in the hope that at least one will capture the unique property of the target images. It is very challenging problem to measure the image similarity from various individual features similarities because different features are defined in different spaces which are not directly comparable. Research in feature aggregation is aimed to address this problem [10]. Feature aggregation is a critical technique in content-based image retrieval systems that employ multiple visual features to characterize image content.

In this paper we present efficient content-based image retrieval system which uses Support Vector Machines (SVM) to fuse the different image features. The implemented system has several advantages over the existing content-based image retrieval systems. Several implemented features of our system allow the user to adapt the system to the query image. The SVM-based approach for feature aggregation allows flexible query formulations and helps processing specific queries for which the users have no knowledge about any suitable descriptors. For the experiments, public image database is used and the retrieval performance of the aggregation scheme is analyzed in details. The rest of the paper is organized as follows. Section

T. Sobh, K. Elleithy (eds.), *Innovations in Computing Sciences and Software Engineering*,
DOI 10.1007/978-90-481-9112-3_54, © Springer Science+Business Media B.V. 2010

2 introduces large number of image descriptors that we have implemented in our content-based image retrieval system. In Section 3 we describe the feature aggregation scheme and the SVM-based approach for ranking retrieval results. In Section 4 we describe the basic characteristics of the image database used in the experiments. Section 5 presents the retrieval metrics. Section 6 presents the experimental results, and Section 7 concludes the paper.

II. Features and Associated Distance Measures

In content-based image retrieval systems a set of features is used to help the user find visually similar images to presented query image. The word similar has different meaning for different groups of users. Furthermore, the users usually have different criteria of similarity. To satisfy user's different needs different descriptions are required because different features describe different aspects of the image content.

Features can be grouped into the following types: color features, texture features, local features, and shape features. The distance function used to compare the features representing an image obviously has a big influence on the performance of the system. In our system the distance functions were selected according to previous research and experiments concerning their influence in the retrieval process [8], [9].

Table 1 gives an overview of the features implemented in our system. The distance functions for each image feature are presented in Table 1, too.

TABLE I
FEATURES AND THEIR ASSOCIATED DISTANCE MEASURES

Feature	Distance function
Color histogram	Jensen-Shannon divergence
Color moments	Euclidean distance
Tamura histogram	Jensen-Shannon divergence
SIFT histogram	Jensen-Shannon divergence
MPEG 7: Edge histogram descriptor	MPEG7-internal distance
MPEG 7: Color structure descriptor	MPEG7-internal distance
MPEG 7: Color layout descriptor	MPEG7-internal distance
MPEG 7: Dominant color descriptor	MPEG7-internal distance
MPEG 7: Region-based descriptor	MPEG7-internal distance

A. *Color Histogram*

The color histogram represents the color content of an image. It is robust to translation and rotation. A histogram is the distribution of the number of pixels in an image. Color histogram is a global property of an image and it does not consider the spatial information of pixels. Therefore, different images may have similar color distributions. Large image database increases the probability two images to have same histogram.

To reduce the computation time, we quantized the 256x256x256=16777216 color images into 8x8x8=512 color images in RGB color space. Since R, G and B channels have same distance in its color space the quantization is done into same levels. The resulting histogram has 512 bins. In accordance to [9], we use Jensen-Shannon divergence to compare the color histograms.

B. *Color Moments*

Color moments are compact representation of the color [2]. This descriptor is very suitable for images that contain only one object. It has been shown that most of the color distribution information is captured by three low-order moments. The first-order moment captures the mean color, the second-order moment captures the standard deviation, and the third-order moment captures the color skewness. The best results are obtained in combination with HSV color space. We extract the three low-order moments for each color planes. As a result, we obtain only nine parameters to describe the color image.

C. *Tamura Histogram*

Tamura proposes six texture features: coarseness, contrast, directionality, line-likeness, regularity, and roughness [11]. Experiments show that the first three features are very important in the context of human perception [11]. So, we use coarseness, contrast, and directionality to create a texture histogram. The histogram consists of 512 coefficients.

D. *SIFT Histogram*

Many different techniques for detecting and describing local image regions have been developed [12]. The Scale Invariant Feature Transform (SIFT) was proposed as a method of extracting and describing keypoints which are reasonably invariant to changes in illumination, image noise, rotation, scaling, and small changes in viewpoint [12].

For content based image retrieval good response times are required and this is hard to achieve using the huge amount of data obtained by local features. A typical image of 500x500 pixels will generate approximately 2000 keypoints. The dimension of this feature is extremely high because the size of the keypoint descriptor is 128 dimensional vector.

To reduce the dimensionality we use histograms of local features [9]. With this approach the amount of data is reduced by estimating the distribution of local features for every image. The key-points are extracted from all database images, where a key-point is described with a vector of numerical values. The key-points are then clustered in 2000 clusters. Afterwards, for each key-point we discard all information except the identifier of the most similar cluster center. A histogram of the occurring patch-cluster identifiers is created for each image. This results in a 2000 dimensional histogram per image.

E. *MPEG 7 Visual Descriptors*

The Moving Picture Experts Group (MPEG) has defined several visual descriptors in their MPEG-7 standard. An extensive overview of these descriptors can be found in [13]. The MPEG-7 standard defines features that are computationally inexpensive to obtain and compare and strongly optimizes the features with respect to the required storage memory. In our research we used the following MPEG 7 descriptors: Color Structure Descriptor [19], Color Layout Descriptor [15], Edge Histogram Descriptor [14],

Dominant Color Descriptor [18] and Region Shape Descriptor [16].

III. Feature Aggregation

Very often, one visual feature is not sufficient to describe different aspects of the image content. A general CBIR system usually requires multiple features to adequately characterize the content of images. Furthermore, it is expected that a proper combination of different visual features could result in improved performances. In CBIR systems using multiple features, the relevant images are ranked according to an aggregated similarity of multiple feature descriptors computed as:

$$\frac{\sum_{i=1}^{n} d_i}{n}$$

where d_i, (i=1, 2, ..., n) is i-th feature distance between the query image and an image in the database.

But, before using multiple features it is necessary to understand the impact of the individual features on the retrieval results. To get a higher system performance, methods for multiple features combination are proposed [10]. The basic method uses equal weights assuming that different features have same importance during the search. But in most cases, they don't have the same importance. The general idea is to assign higher weights to a feature that is more important for the query image. Weights of the features are usually generated from the query image and the images from the user's relevance feedback based on information theory concepts [21].

A. *Normalization of the Distances*

The distances for each feature vary within a wide range. To ensure equal emphasis of each feature within the feature aggregation scheme we apply normalization of the distances. The distance normalization process produces values in the range [0, 1].

For any pair of images I_i and I_j we compute the distance d_{ij} between them:

$$d_{ij}=distance\_function(F_{Ii},F_{Ij})$$

where F_{Ii} and F_{Ij} are the features of the images I_i and I_j for i, j=1, ..., N, where N is the number of images in the database.

For the sequence of distance values we calculate the mean μ and standard deviation σ. We store the values for μ and σ in the database to be used in later normalization of the distances d_i (Figure 2). After a query image Q is presented we compute the distance values between Q and the images in database. We normalize the distance values as follows:

$$d_{QI_{norm}} = \frac{1}{2}\left(1+\frac{d_{QI}-\mu}{3\sigma}\right)$$

The additional shift of ½ will guarantee that 99% of the distance values are within [0, 1]. For the remaining distances we simply set 1. These images will not affect the retrieval performance because of their dissimilarity with the query image. We convert the distance values into similarity values using (1-d_{QI}). At the end of this normalization all similarity values for all features have been normalized to the same range [0, 1] and value 1 means exact match and 0 denotes maximum dissimilarity.

B. *Scoring of Distances using Relevance Feedback and SVM*

The problem of image retrieval could be considered as classification problem. For a query image q, the images from the database have to be classified to be either relevant (denoted by +1) or irrelevant (denoted by −1).

We want to classify the images into two categories "relevant" and "irrelevant" on the basis of the distances between their features. To construct the training dataset for the classifier we use relevance feedback technique.

The concept of relevance feedback was introduced into CBIR from text-based information retrieval in the 1990s [22]. With relevance feedback, a user can label a few images as new examples for the retrieval engine if he is not satisfied with the retrieval result. Actually, these new images refine the original query which enables the relevance feedback process to overcome the gap between high-level image semantics and low-level image features.

In our implementation, after presenting the initial results obtained from the feature aggregation technique the system prompts the user to select a set of relevant and irrelevant images from the displayed results. For the query image q and each selected image q_n in the relevance feedback cycle, the distance vector $D(q_n,q)$ = $(d_1(q_n,q),...,d_m(q_n,q))$ is calculated, where m is the number of image features (in our case this number is nine, because we use nine different image features). This leads to n distance vectors, where n is the number of selected images during the relevance feedback cycle. These distance vectors are then labeled according to the relevance: those $D(q_m,q)$ where q_m is relevant with respect to q are labeled +1 (relevant) and the remaining ones are labeled with the class label −1 (irrelevant).

The constructed training set can be used to train a classifier that will be able not only to classify distance vectors of unseen images to an image class from the database, but additionally return some score or confidence with which the database images can be ranked.

Relevance feedback is an approach designed to learn from users behavior through feedback and in an interactive manner. There are several factors to be considered in designing relevance feedback. The most important are: small training data and singularity.

Singularity is often an issue in CBIR systems with relevance feedback and arises when the number of training samples is smaller than the dimension of the feature vector. We eliminate this problem by taking into account only the distances of the individual features. To eliminate the small training data problem we considered the approach proposed in [23]. The researchers in the paper report the use of long term learning in CBIR systems. In this method, a matrix is generated from the image database which contains the semantic relationship between each image in the database. It may be viewed as an NxN table where N is the number of images in the database. The table stores a semantic score for each image against each of the other images. The semantic score is calculated by the users through the retrieval feedback cycles. Before constructing the training dataset we scan the semantic matrix and select and add to the training dataset the images that are semantically relevant to the images from the current relevance feedback cycle.

Since dividing given distances into "relevant" and "irrelevant" is a two-class problem, we employ a support vector machine for classification. Considering the distance vectors D, as described above as feature vectors, we rank the images using the distances to the separating hyper plane [24].

IV. BENCHMARK DATABASE FOR CBIR

We evaluate the methods on public image database called WANG. This database was created by the group of professor Wang from the Pennsylvania State University [20]. The WANG database is a subset of 1,000 images of the Corel stock photo database which have been manually selected and divided into 10 classes of 100 images each.

Some example images from this database are shown in Figure 1.

Figure 1. Example images from the WANG database.

V. RETRIEVAL METRIC

Let denote the database images by $\{x_1, \ldots, x_i, \ldots, x_N\}$ and each image is represented by a set of features. To retrieve images similar to a presented query image q, the system compares each database image x_i with the query image by an appropriate distance function $d(q, x_i)$. Then, the database images are sorted to fulfill the following distance relation $d(q, x_i) \leq d(q, x_{i+1})$ for each pair of images x_i and x_{i+1} in the sequence $(x_1, \ldots, x_i, \ldots, x_N)$.

Several performance measures based on the precision P and the recall R have been proposed for CBIR systems evaluation [17]. Precision and recall values are usually represented by a precision-recall-graph $R \rightarrow P(R)$ summarizing $(R, P(R))$ pairs for varying numbers of retrieved images. The most common approach to summarize this graph into one value is the mean average precision (*MAP*). The average precision *AP* for a single query q is the mean over the precision scores after each retrieved relevant item:

$$AP(q) = \frac{1}{N_R} \sum_{n=1}^{N_R} P_q(R_n)$$

where R_n is the recall after the n-th relevant image was retrieved. N_R is the total number of relevant documents for the query. The mean average precision *MAP* is the mean of the average precision scores over all queries:

$$MAP = \frac{1}{|Q|} \sum_{q \in Q} AP(q)$$

where Q is the set of queries q. An advantage of the mean average precision is that it contains both precision and recall oriented aspects and is sensitive to the entire ranking.

VI. EXPERIMENTAL RESULTS

For the evaluation of the different features on the WANG database a leaving-one-out approach has been followed. Every image was used as a query and the remaining 99 images from the same class as the current query image were considered relevant and the images from all other classes were considered irrelevant.

The experimental results for the SVM scoring distances method were performed automatically with simulated user feedback. Each query was performed and all relevant images retrieved among the top 20 results were added to the set of positive samples and all non relevant images among these were added to the set of negative samples. We also add these images in the semantic matrix. With this approach we have effectively simulated a user who is judging each of the twenty top ranked images regarding its relevance. This procedure was repeated three times.

For the selected features and aggregation methods we report the mean average precision and complete PR graph.

Table 2 summarizes the result for the *MAP* on the selected database. Figure 2 shows the corresponding PR graphs for the selected features and aggregation methods. It shows that different features perform differently on the selected database. The color histogram and color structure descriptor are most suitable for the selected database (mean average precision approximately equals to 50%). In general all color descriptors (color layout, color moments and dominant color descriptor) gave satisfactory results with mean average precision approximately equals to 40%. The rest of the features didn't perform well for the selected database and there is an obvious need for aggregation.

The results in Table 2 show that the performance was improved by adding more features in the retrieval process. Furthermore, the best results were obtained by using SVM-based approach for ranking retrieval results. Compared with the basic feature aggregation method the performance increases by 28%.

VII. CONCLUSIONS

This paper describes a content-based image retrieval system for aggregation and combination of different image features. For it, we have implemented and tested various feature extraction algorithms. The CBIR system supports query by image retrieval. The query interface supports inclusion of more than one feature in the retrieval process.

Using one feature is not good enough to retrieve target images in all cases. To get a better retrieval performance feature aggregation is necessary. The feature aggregation provide improvement over the individual features, but to improve precision the salient features are to be determined and assigned higher weights.

We use relevance feedback technique to determine and capture more precisely the query concept presented by the user. With the proposed method based on semantic matrix and SVM for ranking retrieval results we achieved very high *MAP* of 85.23%.

The implemented system has several advantages over the existing content-based image retrieval systems. The diversity of the implemented features included in our system allows the user to adapt the system to the query image. The semantic matrix and SVM based approach for ranking retrieval results allows flexible query formulations and helps processing specific queries for which users have no knowledge about any suitable descriptors.

TABLE II
MEAN AVERAGE PRECISION [%] FOR EACH OF THE FEATURES

Feature	MAP (%)
Color histogram	51.24
Color moments	36.76
Tamura histogram	34.61
SIFT histogram	48.94
MPEG 7: Edge histogram descriptor	40.23
MPEG 7: Color structure descriptor	48.37
MPEG 7: Color layout descriptor	42.39
MPEG 7: Dominant color descriptor	40.21
MPEG 7: Region-based descriptor	23.25
Feature aggregation	57.25
SVM scoring distances	85.23

REFERENCES

[1] R. Datta, D. Joshi, J. Li, and J. Z. Wang, "Image Retrieval: Ideas, Influences, and Trends of the New Age", *ACM Transactions on Computing Surveys*, 40(5), 2008.

[2] C. Faloutsos, R. Barber, M. Flickner, J. Hafner, W. Niblack, D. Petkovic, and W. Equitz, "Efficient and Effective Querying by Image Content", *Journal of Intelligent Information Systems*, Vol. 3, No. 3/4, pp. 231–262, 1994.

[3] J. R. Smith, and S. F. Chang, "VisualSEEk: a Fully Automated Content-Based Image Query System", in *ACM Multimedia*, Boston, MA, 1996.

[4] C. Carson, S. Belongie, H. Greenspan, and J. Malik, "Blobworld: Image Segmentation Using Expectation-Maximization and its Application to Image Querying", *IEEE Transactions on Pattern Analysis and Machine Intelligence*, Vol. 24, No. 8, pp. 1026–1038, 2002.

[5] T. Huang, S. Mehrotra, and K. Ramchandran, "Multimedia Analysis and Retrieval System (MARS) project", *Proc of 33rd Annual Clinic on Library Application of Data Processing-Digital Image Access and Retrieval*, 1996.

[6] A. Pentland, R. W. Picard, and S. Sclaroff, "Photobook: Content-based manipulation of image databases", *International Journal of Computer Vision*, 18(3), pp. 233-254, 1996.

[7] J. Bach, C. Fuller, A. Gupta, A. Hampapur, B. Gorowitz, R. Humphrey, R. Jain, and C. Shu, "Virage image search engine: an open framework for image management", in *Proceedings of the SPIE, Storage and Retrieval for Image and Video Databases IV*, San Jose, CA, pp. 76-87, 1996.

[8] H. Eidenberger, "Distance measures for MPEG-7-based retrieval", *Proceedings of the 5th ACM SIGMM international workshop on Multimedia information retrieval*, pp. 130-137, Berkeley, California, 2003.

[9] T. Deselaers, D. Keysers, and H. Ney, "Features for Image Retrieval: An Experimental Comparison", *Information Retrieval*, vol. 11, issue 2, The Netherlands, Springer, pp. 77-107, 2008.

[10] J. Zhang, and L. Ye, "An Unified Framework Based on p-Norm for Feature Aggregation in Content-Based Image Retrieval", *Ninth IEEE International Symposium on Multimedia*, pp. 195-201, Taichung, 2007.

[11] H. Tamura, S. Mori, and T. Yamawaki, "Textural Features Corresponding to Visual Perception", *IEEE Transaction on Systems, Man, and Cybernetics*, 8(6), pp. 460–472, 1978.

[12] D. G. Lowe, "Distinctive Image Features from Scale-Invariant Keypoints", *International Journal of Computer Vision*, 60(2), pp. 91-110, 2004.

[13] J. M. Martinez, *Overview of the MPEG-7 Standard, v 6.0, MPEG Requirements Group*, ISO/MPEG N4674, 2002.

[14] D. K. Park, Y. S. Jeon, and C. S. Won, "Efficient use of local edge histogram descriptor", in *International Multimedia Conference, ACM workshops on Multimedia*, pp. 51–54, Los Angeles, California, United States, 2000.

[15] E. Kasutani, and A. Yamada, "The MPEG-7 color layout descriptor: a compact image feature description for high-speed image/video segment retrieval", in *International Conference on Image Processing*, Vol. 1, pp. 674–677, Thessaloniki, Greece, 2001.

[16] M. Bober, "MPEG-7 visual shape descriptors", *IEEE Transactions on Circuits and Systems for Video Technology*, 11(6), pp. 716–719, 2001.

[17] H. Muller, W. Muller, D. McG. Squire, S. Marchand-Maillet, and T. Pun, "Performance Evaluation in Content-Based Image Retrieval: Overview and Proposals", *Pattern Recognition Letters* (*Special Issue on Image and Video Indexing*), 22(5), pp. 593–601, 2001.

[18] K. M. Wong, and L. M. Po, 2004, "MPEG-7 dominant color descriptor based relevance feedback using merged palette histogram", *International Conference on Acoustics, Speech, and Signal Processing Proceedings*, Volume 3, 2004.

[19] D. S. Messing, P. van Beek, and J. H. Errico, "The MPEG-7 colour structure descriptor: image description using colour and local spatial information", in *International Conference on Image Processing*, vol.1, pp. 670-673, Thessaloniki, Greece, 2001.

[20] J. Z. Wang, J. Li, and G. Wiederhold, "SIMPLIcity: Semantics-sensitive Integrated Matching for Picture Libraries", *IEEE Trans. on Pattern Analysis and Machine Intelligence*, vol. 23, no.9, pp. 947-963, 2001.

[21] T. Deselaers, T. Weyand, and H. Ney, "Image Retrieval and Annotation Using Maximum Entropy", *CLEF Workshop 2006*, Alicante, Spain, 2006.

[22] J. Rocchio, "Relevance feedback in information retrieval", *In the SMART Retrieval System: Experiments in Automatic Document Processing*, pp. 313-323. Prentice-Hall, Englewood Cliffs, NJ, USA, 1971.

[23] J. Fournier, and M. Cord, "Long-term similarity learning in content-based image retrieval", *International Conference on Image Processing*, Volume: 1, pp. I-441- I-444, 2002.

[24] N. Cristianini, and J. Shawe-Taylor, *An Introduction to Support Vector Machines (and Other Kernel-Based Learning Methods). Cambridge University Press*, 2000.

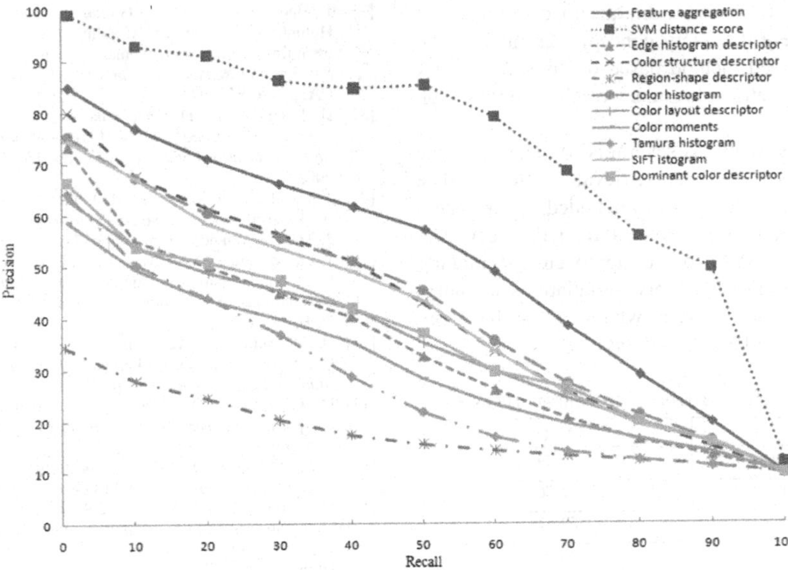

Figure 2. PR graphs for each of the selected features.

The Holistic, Interactive and Persuasive Model to Facilitate Self-care of Patients with Diabetes

Miguel Vargas-Lombardo [#*1], Armando Jipsion [*2], Rafael Vejarano [*3], Ismael Camargo [*4], Humberto Álvarez [*5]
Elena Villalba Mora [+6], Ernestina Menasalva Ruíz [+7]

[1#] *Senacyt-Ifarhu Panama,* [*2,3,4,5,] *Technological University of Panama, Panama.*
PTY 36366 P.O. BOX 025207, Miami, FL 33102-5207
miguel.vargas@utp.ac.pa, armando.jipsion@utp.ac.pa, rafael.vejarano@utp.ac.pa, ismael.camargo@utp.ac.pa, humberto.alvarez@utp.ac.pa

[+6,7] *Polytecnical University of Madrid,* Madrid, Spain.
villalba.elena@cdti.es, emenasalvas@fi.upm.es

Abstract—

The patient, in his multiple facets of citizen and user of services of health, needs to acquire during, and later in his majority of age, favorable conditions of health to accentuate his quality of life and it is the responsibility of the health organizations to initiate the process of support for that patient during the process of mature life. The provision of services of health and the relation doctor-patient are undergoing important changes in the entire world, forced to a large extent by the indefensibility of the system itself. Nevertheless decision making requires previous information and, what more the necessity itself of being informed requires having a "culture" of health that generates pro activity and the capacity of searching for instruments that facilitate the awareness of the suffering and the self-care of the same. Therefore it is necessary to put into effect a ICT model (hiPAPD) that has the objective of causing Interaction, Motivation and Persuasion towards the surroundings of the diabetic Patient facilitating his self-care. As a result the patient himself individually manages his services through devices and AmI Systems (Ambient Intelligent).

Keywords—
ICT, Emotional Design, Captologic, Patient diabetic, self-Care

I. INTRODUCTION

For [1],[2],[3], in spite of innumerable studies and seminaries the problems of the diabetic patient are centered services such as:

• Related to the administration: insufficient means, shortage of personnel, lack of sensitivity to the subject, little coordination among estates, mobility of the sanitary personnel.
• Centered on the patient: lack of interest, difficulties of understanding, real or functional illiteracy, serious economic problems, self-care, etc.
• Attributable to the equipment: lack of coordination, delegation of functions of the doctor in the nurse, lacks of authentic equipment, etc.
• Due to the professionals themselves, basically caused by an inadequate pedagogical preparation.

Throughout the years, responses have been getting worse, so that to a great extent they are centered more in external causes (the sanitary administration, the characteristics of the patient) and more responsibility of the sanitary personnel is recognized, at the present time those that predominate are those that can be denominated internal (those of the equipment and the professional himself) of course without denying the evident reality that the medium is, sometimes, authentically hostile. In order to guide the patient in this process, the traditional education based on the transmission of knowledge and on memory is of little practical utility and other didactic resources are needed that are based on the creation on conditions that facilitate the personal discovery on the part of the patient.

On the other hand, the inoperability of the health systems, that at the present time lack the best strategies and resources to facilitate medical services of quality to the population, is an authentic sample of the necessity of new strategies [3]

The diabetic patient must perceive some immediate benefit of what is proposed to him, since otherwise the changes of conduct will hardly remain for a reasonable time.

The relationship must be based on the motto "I win, you win", instead of "I win you lose" as it often happens. The loss of some liberties (to eat without any type of limitations, not to habitually control hair glycemia, and other.) must be accompanied by some immediate benefit (to wear a size less in pants, to be able to have a small treat when the sugar level is good, etc.) in order to avoid feelings of frustration.

The hiPAPD model will offer services of health with the objectives of conciliating the collaboration relationships in the Patient contexts, Relatives of the Patient, Friends of Patient, Medical, sanitary Personnel and Society. Also to facilitate the self-care of the diabetic Patient, by relating the Patient to

T. Sobh, K. Elleithy (eds.), *Innovations in Computing Sciences and Software Engineering*,
DOI 10.1007/978-90-481-9112-3_55, © Springer Science+Business Media B.V. 2010

devices and software tools (www.cuidandotudiabtes.org) those are ubiquitously at his disposition, see figure 1.

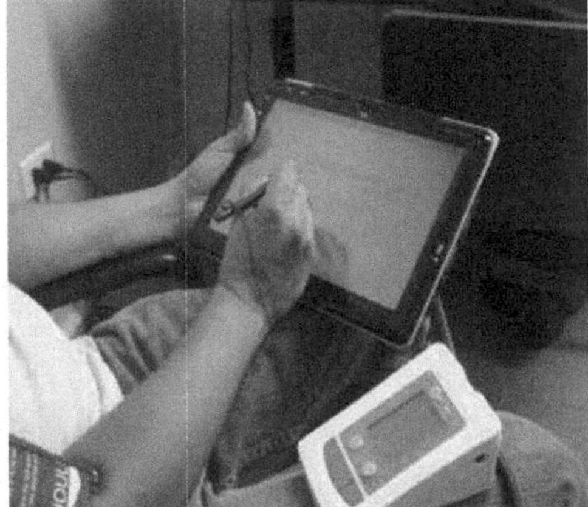

Fig. 1. Interaction and Captology in action for the patient

This way, the medical processes must be centered on the patient by offering ICT systems (see figure 2), to facilitate the organization and the reorganization of the patient in connection to the medical system, approaching him to the services, and making possible a symmetrical relation between patient and the professionals of health.

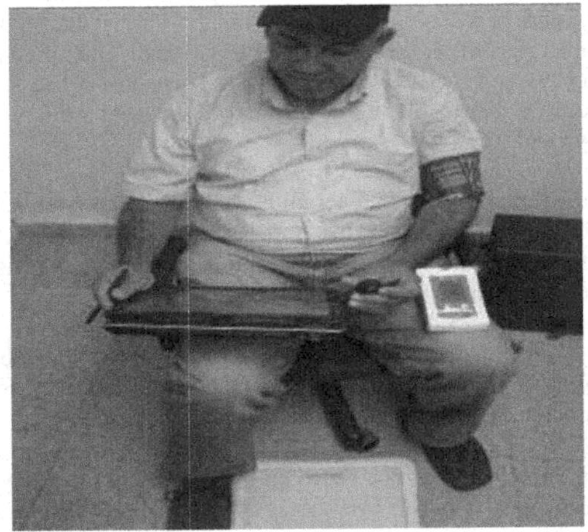

Fig. 2. ICT for managing patient self-care

The paper is organized in the following way; in section one, the cognitive Psychological connotations and its application to the design context, the medical design and of the patient. In the second section the characteristics of the Emotional Design which is a component of the hiPAPD model are exposed. Section three continues with the presentation of the Captology model, this being another component of the hiPAPD model. In the fourth section the properties and characteristics of the hiPAPD model are defined. In order to culminate the presentation of this paper the future conclusions and works are exposed.

II. COGNITIVE PSYCHOLOGY

Cognitive psychology is one of the many disciplines that contribute to the area of human-computer Interaction, for the design as well as for the evaluation of interfaces. In fact, the relationships are mutual. On one hand, specialists in computation resort to psychology as a guide for the design of more and more interactive interfaces, where sensations, perceptions, motor controls and cognitive aspects in general, have much incidence. Appropriate conditions to represent a model that facilitates interaction of diabetic patients with the medical equipment more and more oriented to interact with the patients without the approach of third persons (Doctors and sanitary personnel) in their family surroundings, but still dependent on the computer, for example (Pedometer, Weight Scale, Measurer of Blood Pressure.) of IEEE 802.15.1 technologies.

The relationships between psychology and HCI, is interesting to mention a point of view that has allowed us to clarify concepts on HCI. For Liam Bannon [4] suggests that "For a process to be totally automatic, it will need human intervention". Traditionally, the "human factors" tried to harmonize tasks, capacities and performance of machines and men. That is to say, the computer and man operate as of internal representations of symbolic character, the information is stored in memory systems and both execute processes, such as codification, storage, recovery, organization and transformation of the information. At the same time, computer scientists greatly contributed to fix the metaphor, using words such as “intelligence", "memory", "language", when they talked about computers, establishing a parallelism with the equivalent human phenomena.

Therefore, these are the elements to which we will resort to educate, to become aware, and to motivate the self-care of the diabetic patient, all this through a model based on the Ubiquity, Motivation, Interaction and Persuasion of the AmI surroundings.

III. EMOTIONAL DESIGN

For Norman [5]human beings are without a doubt, the most complex of all the animals and have cerebral structures of an agreed complexity. The model of Emotional Design of Donald Norman [5], consists of three levels of processing: Visceral, Conductive and Reflexive, see figure ( ). These levels can be defined as follows:

Visceral Level: it is fast, it makes fast judgments about what is good or bad, safe or dangerous, and sends appropriate signals to the muscles (the motor system) and alerts the rest of the brain. Thus the affective processing begins. They are signals that are biologically determined and can be inhibited or intensified through signals of control coming from superior levels.

The conductible level is the location in which almost all human behavior is carried out. In the conductible level he is not conscious, and therefore we can satisfactorily drive an automobile at a conductible level whereas, in the reflexive, we are thinking in a conscious way about something different. His actions can be intensified or inhibited through the reflective layer and at the same time, it can intensify or inhibit the visceral layer.

The superior layer is the reflexive thought. This level does not have direct access neither to the sensorial input nor to the control of behavior. Rather it watches, reflects and tries to influence in the conductible level. Also the use of metaphors is contemplated to induce the use of interfaces. See figure 3.

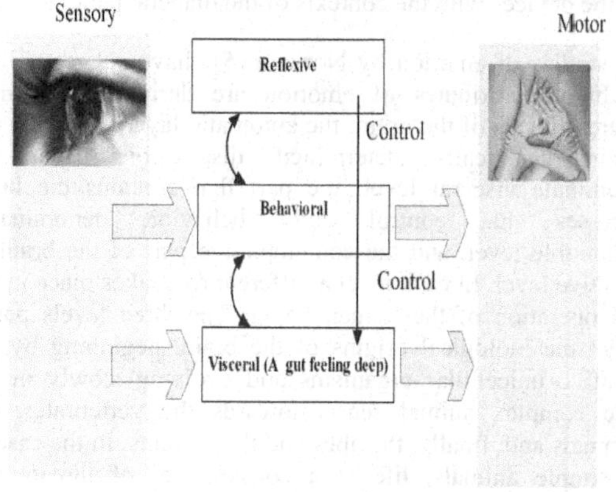

Fig.3. Emotional Design Model, D. Norman

IV. Technology Persuasive

Briefly, a computer is an interactive technological tool that changes the attitudes of a person or their behavior BJ. Fogg [6], [7], [8] see figure 4.

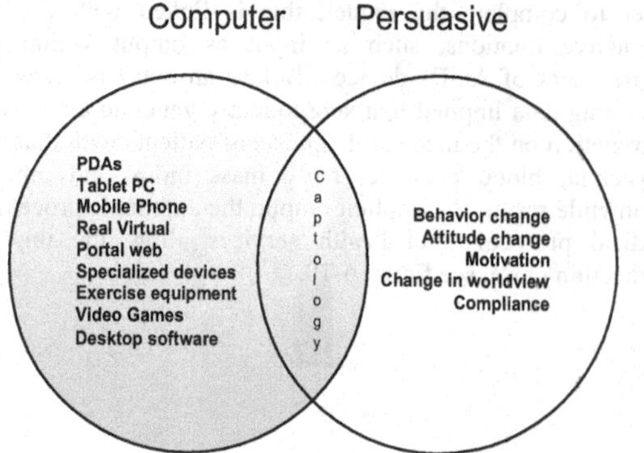

Fig.4. Persuasive or Captology Model, BJ FOGG

This definition works well in many cases, but a more complete definition and that gives a better understanding of persuasive computation is to obtain the change of attitude in the persons who take possession of the new technologies.

Captology influences in the design, the investigation and the interactive analysis of computer science technologies intentionally created to change the attitudes or behavior of the people, an aspect that is reached in our investigation through the use of this model and the proposal of Professor Norman, taking both models to the context of the diabetic patient. These technologies include Web Portals, PDA, mobile Telephones, and Video Games and in a more ample context the software services from the desk: Forums, Chat, Virtual Communities, Personal and Social Networks, etc.

Both D. Norman and B.J. FOGG models are the nucleus of our hiPAPD model, whose goal is the development of modern graphic interfaces and software able to facilitate the self-care of the Diabetic Patient.

V. Holistic, Interactive and Persuasive to facilitate the Self-care of patients with diabetes (iPAPD)

In the hiPAPD model, the Patient contexts, Relatives of the patient, Friends of the patient, Doctors, Sanitary Personnel and Society have been conjugated, which interact jointly and systematized to educate, to guide, to facilitate and to support the management of self-care of the patient with diabetes. We describe the model through seven adjacent layers, see figure 5; which are clearly identified by the Patient with diabetes.

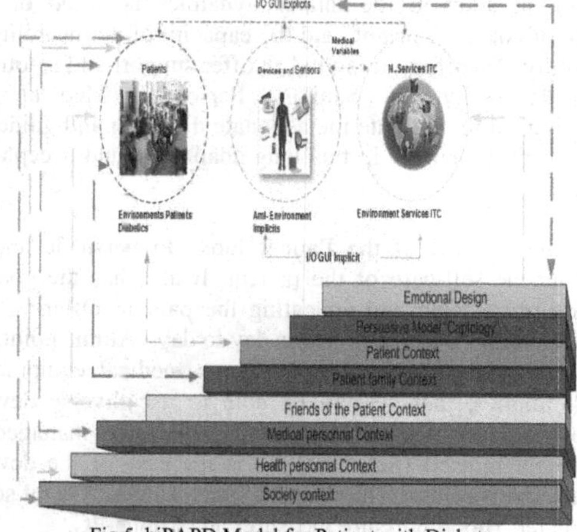

Fig.5. hiPAPD Model for Patient with Diabetes

In the most external layer of the (hiPAPD) model appears the context Society, which occupies an important position for the establishment of ties collaboration, education, prevention of diabetes. The social support groups directed to diabetic people constitute a powerful and constructive form of permitting people to help themselves as well as helping others. The use of group intervention in the diabetic patient is highlighted in educational programs.

Within the layer of the Sanitary Personnel are the management, support and follow-up of the diabetic patient, the managing of the essential medical services to guarantee his care. In the following layer the context of the Medical Personnel, who will have to offer medical services for the prioritized attention and the diagnosis of diabetic suffering, including the follow-up and the evolution of the chronic suffering of diabetes in the Patient´s. Later, in the context layer, Friends of the Patient, have as a goal to offer external support as he would offer the relative of the patient. In this context the conformation of support groups for the diabetic patient is possible whose purpose is the education and the motivation of the patient. This conformation is of groups with the same medical or similar condition, which favors social support, recognition and knowledge of new experiences on this suffering by the groups of diabetic patients, enriching the common support and motivation among patients.

The layer nearest to the Patient is the context Relatives of the Patient. The diabetic suffering of a family member supposes the modification and later readjustment of the family system, more or less deep, based on the type of diabetes. Depending on the conceptions on health of the family, the disease and the resources that they have to face this, a family disorganization takes place, secondary to the impact of the diagnosis. The degree of disorganization depends on two variables: the type of disease, that includes characteristics such as pain, incapacity, treatment, evolution and ideology (social and family), in addition the family dynamics is based on the degree of cohesion or not, and the capacity of permeability of the family. Therefore, it is vital to offer support and resources as well as by the Sanitary Personnel, Medical and technological to facilitate the adequate direction and guides to accompany the family in this long adaptation and acceptance process.

The layer context of the Patient looks to persuade and to motivate the self-care of the patient. It also has the goal of guiding, instructing and educating the patient. Offering him new technologies to facilitate his day to day. At this point, the patient is offered medical noninvasive medical equipments, which implies, that he will be able to use diverse devices without support of third users, being able to be managed by the patient himself (Self-care), as is the case of the devices digitals and wireless: Glucometer (Sugar tester), Weight scale, Pedometer, Blood pressure measurer and Tablet PC.

All these technologies are easily usable by the Relatives of the Patient, Family of Patient, Friends of the Patient, Doctors, Sanitary Personnel and Society. To obtain an effective synchronization of the contexts, the model (hiPAPD) is based on Persuasive Technology, which emphasizes on the capacity of the computers and software services to persuade the people to its use, looking forward to achieve a Change in Attitude, of Vision of the world and Motivation [6],[9],[7] . For the Professor B.J. Fogg [6], [9] computation is an interactive technological tool that changes the attitudes of many persons and their behavior. In the same manner, on these aspects it has been proposed as the nucleus of the model of Emotional Design [5]. The framework of Emotional Design sustains the recognition of the most complex characteristics of the brain structures of human beings, and in the approach of the design centered in the users to offer interfaces of high quality and usability to facilitate the interaction of the software services and the devices with the contexts of the diabetic patient.

The studies of emotion by Norman [5] have suggested that the human attributes of emotion are derived from three different levels of the brain: the automatic layer of systems of certain genetically determined dispositions, that we denominate visceral level; the part that contains the brain processes that control daily behavior, denominated conductible level, and the contemplative part of the brain or reflective level. In each level a different role takes place in the total operation of the human being. The three levels partly reflect the biological origins of the brain, beginning by the primitive unicellular organisms and evolving slowly in the more complex animal sense, towards the vertebrates, the mammals and, finally, the apes and the humans. In the case of the simple animals, life is a constant set of threats and opportunities, and an animal must learn the way to react adequately one way and others. The basic cerebral predispositions, therefore, are in fact mechanisms of answers that analyze a situation and react.

To complete the relation models conducted explicitly by input and output generated by patients and his environment, those are managed by systematizing the graphical interfaces that hide the processes and action taken by patient's activities. In order to complete the model, this is linked with implicit interactive relations, such as input as output within the environment of AmI's devices. Before an entry is stored by extracting data implied that subsequently generate a mainstay information on the medical diagnosis of patients with diabetes (glycemia, blood pressure, body mass index and others), meanwhile rest of the implicit output, the automatic process of medical protocols and health services allow the implicit connection close, see figure 6-10.

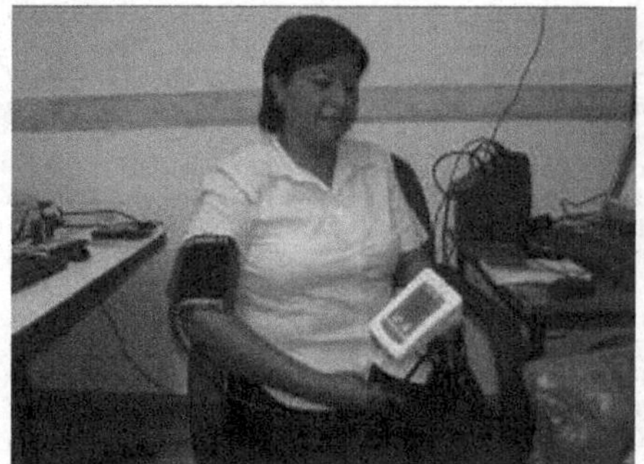

Fig. 6. More patients interacting with devices

Fig.7. Full Interaction with the devices and software

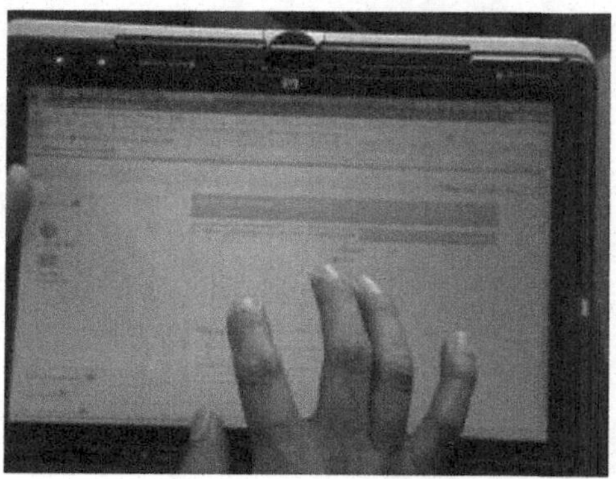

Fig.8. Interaction and Persuasive of the software and Patient, www.cuidandotudiabetes.org

Fig. 9 The Portal cuidandotudiabetes.org, use the tool MiAutocuidado (My Self-care)

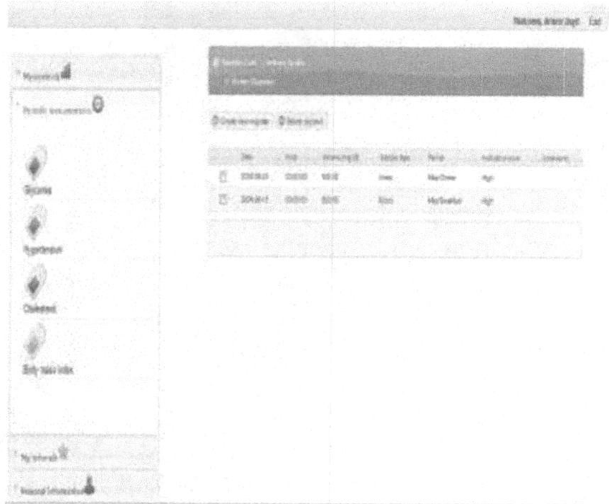

Fig. 10. The Components Tool of cuidandotudiabetes.org, see tool MiAutocuidado (My Self-care)

VI. Conclusions

This model arises from the restlessness of technologists and doctors, worried about the necessity of quality systems for health. The proposed model is the first link in a long chain of necessities to take care of. The main objective of the hiPAPD model is to accompany and satisfy the medical services of a great number of diabetic patients. This aspect is reached through software tools and devices such as: sugar testers, weight scales and measurer of blood pressure integrated on movable networks. The ubiquity of the hiPAPD model is obtained through the Web Portal cuidandotudiabetes.org, whose goal is the permanent self-care of the diabetic Patient.

It is the intention of the hiPAPD model to be a reference for the establishment of e-health systems. In the same manner, work will continue to purify the hiPAPD model jointly with the principal actors of the model Diabetic Patient, Relatives of the Patient, Friends of the Patient, Doctors, Sanitary Personnel and Society.

REFERENCES

[1] D. Bloise, *et al.*, "Education of Diabetic patient," *Pickup Jc, Williams G, editors, TextBook of Diabetes, Oxford: Blackwell Science,* vol. 78, pp. 1-11, 1997.

[2] A. Lacroix and J.-P. Assal, "L' education thérapeutique des pacients," *Nouvelles approches de la maladie cronique, Paris: Vigot* 1998.

[3] Ministerio-de-Sanidad-y-Política-Social., "Estrategia en diabetes del Sistema Nacional de Salud," *Ministerio de Sanidad y Politica Social, CENTRO DE PUBLICACIONES Paseo del Prado, 18. 28014 Madrid NIPO: 351-07-003-4, Depósito Legal: M-19388-200* 2007.

[4] L. Bannon, *From Human Factors to Human Actors: The Role of Psychology and Human-Computer Interaction Studies in Systems Design* 1991.

[5] D. Norman, "Emotional Designed," *Paidos, Spain,* 2003.

[6] B. J. Fogg, "Persuasive Computers: Perspectives and Research Directions," *ACM, CHI 98, Los Angeles CA USA* 1997.

[7] B. J. Fogg, ""What Makes A Web Site Credible? A Report on a Large Quantitative Study"," *Proceedings of ACM CHI 2001 Conference on Human Factors in Computing Systems, v. 1, 61-68. New York: ACM Press.,* 2001.

[8] B. J. Fogg, *et al.*, ""Elements that Affect Web Credibility: Early Results from a Self-Report Study"," *Proceedings of ACM CHI 2000 Conference on Human Factors in Computing Systems, v.2, New York: ACM Press,* 2000.

[9] B. J. Fogg, ""Stanford-Makovsy Web Credibility Study 2002: Investigating What Makes Web Sites Credible Today," *Stanford Research Institute • Menlo Park, California,* 2002.

Jawi Generator Software Using ARM Board Under Linux

O. N. Shalasiah, S. M. F. Rohani, H. Zulkifli
School of Computer and Communication Engineering
Universiti Malaysia Perlis
02000 Kuala Perlis, Perlis. MALAYSIA

Abstract-**Jawi knowledge is becoming important not just to adult but also to growing children to learn at the initial stage of their life. This project basically is to study and develop Embedded Jawi Generator Software that will generate and create Jawi script easily. The user could choose and enter Jawi scripts and learn each of the script. The sum of scripts was from alif until yaa, approximately about 36 scripts with the colorful button. The system also should b creating as an interactive system that will attract users especially kids. This Jawi Generator Software developed using java language in a Linux operating system (fedora). This software will be running on UP-NETARM2410-S Linux. Later the performances of Jawi Generator System are investigate for its accuracy in displaying of the words, and also board performances.**

I. Introduction

Today, the Jawi script is mainly used for Islamic religious documents and texts. There are factor that threatened the usages of Jawi. One dominant factor is the growing reluctance among local publishers to publish religious books for the public mainly in Jawi. So, in order to improve the standard of Jawi script, Jawi Generator Software will help user to learn this script. This system can be used by beginner user and researcher who want to learn the Jawi script. It provides a computer aided instructional products and services for the study of Jawi writing and spelling. This software will generate the Jawi scripts [1], using the interface builds up, with the suitable size, and combines it into a word. User needed to press signed buttons at the interface; in order to display the Jawi font and combine it together [2]. Later the performances of Jawi Generator System are investigated for its accuracy or achievement in displaying of the words and board performances itself.

Nowadays, there were some similar applications that already existed in Malaysia, but most of them were online application software such as ejawi.net online converter and also jawinet.8k.com. All those applications seem very complicated for the beginner user like kids, who even don't know yet what "alif" and "baa" is. This study will find another alternative method in order to create a Jawi Generator Software for the beginner user, because the software is really simple, and user friendly where the script button provided in Malay language.

Besides that, this study also is an alternative way to implement Jawi Generator Software in the open source environment, which is Linux Fedora and also may be tested in an embedded board which is UP-NETARM 2410 S Linux which is has been developed in Red Hat 9 environment. This board is actually a product from Beijing Universal Pioneering Technology Co., Ltd (Up-tech). This organization is a famous provider of software and solutions to the embedded system products, project outsourcing and technical services [3]. In additional, this board is a combination of computer hardware and software, either in fixed in capability or programmable, that is specifically designed for a particular kind of application device. Furthermore, Linux is latest free and open source software, also stable and easy to find in websites. In this study, Fedora is used because it is a Redhat Package Manager (RPM)-based, general purpose operating system built on top of the Linux kernel, developed by the community-supported Fedora Project and sponsored by Red Hat [4].

This Jawi Generator Software also been developed using java programming language. Java is a programming language originally developed by James Gosling at Sun Microsystems and released in 1995 as a core component of Sun Microsystems' Java platform. The language derives much of its syntax from C and C++ but has a simpler object model and fewer low-level facilities. Java applications are typically compiled to bytecode (class file) that can run on any Java Virtual Machine (JVM) regardless of computer architecture. The original and reference implementation Java compilers, virtual machines, and class libraries were developed by Sun from 1995. As of May 2007, in compliance with the specifications of the Java Community Process, Sun relicensed most of their Java technologies under the GNU General Public License. The others also developed alternative implementations of these Sun technologies, such as the GNU Compiler for Java and GNU Classpath [5].

In addition, some low-end consumer products use a very inexpensive microprocessor and limited storage, with the application and operating system are both part of the program. The program is written permanently into the system's memory in this case, rather than being loaded into RAM (random access memory) like programs on a personal computer [6]. This study basically will be implemented on UP-NETARM 2410-S Linux; in order to test the Jawi Generator Software on the board.

T. Sobh, K. Elleithy (eds.), *Innovations in Computing Sciences and Software Engineering*,
DOI 10.1007/978-90-481-9112-3_56,

II. OBJECTIVES

- To study about java in Embedded Linux System; using UP-NETARM 2410-S Linux
- To design an Embedded Jawi Generator Software using java language
- To develop an Embedded Jawi Generator Software using java language

III. METHODOLOGY

A. System Design

The first stage of the project is to design a Jawi Generator Software. This software built using java programming language [7]. This software has a simple and user friendly interface.

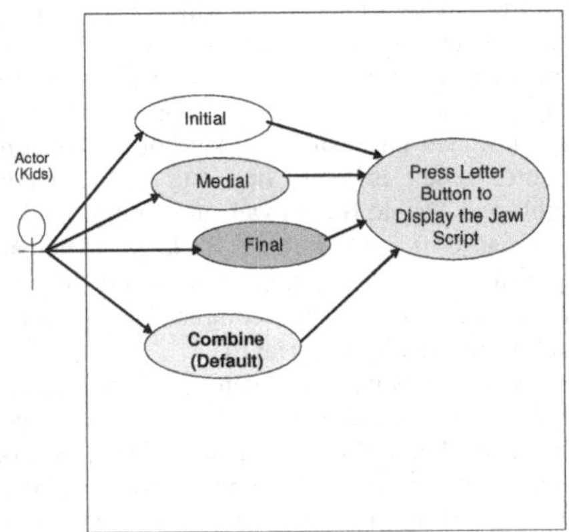

Fig. 1. Use Diagram of the system

Figure 1 above shows about the use diagram of the system. From the system use diagram, the actor is a user who will use Jawi Generator Software. The diagram shows that the user can choose initial, medial, final, and combine button for the optional. The default option of this system is combine option. The system displayed the selected script after pressing the script button.

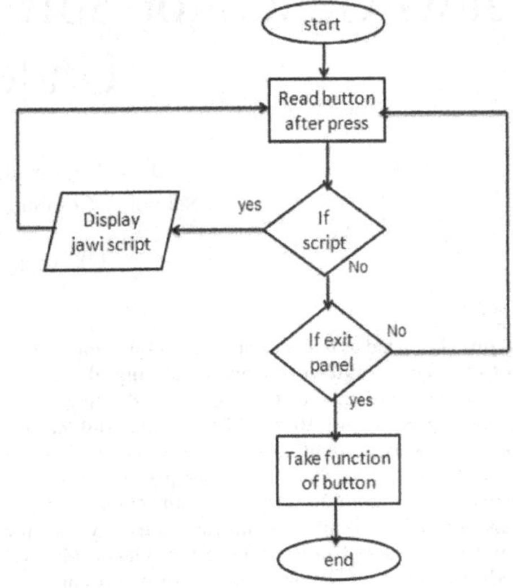

Fig. 2. Flowchart of the system

Figure 2 shows about the flow process of the system, which is starting from reading the button after pressed until take the function of the button.

B. Operating System

In this Jawi Generator Software, the operating system that used is Linux. The particular distribution currently used is a version of Fedora. Fedora was chosen because it is well documented and packaged for the ease of use, and its current widespread popularity makes it relatively easy to and answers to common problems [8]. Fedora also is a Linux based operating system that provides users with access to the latest free and open source software, in a stable, secure and easy to manage form.

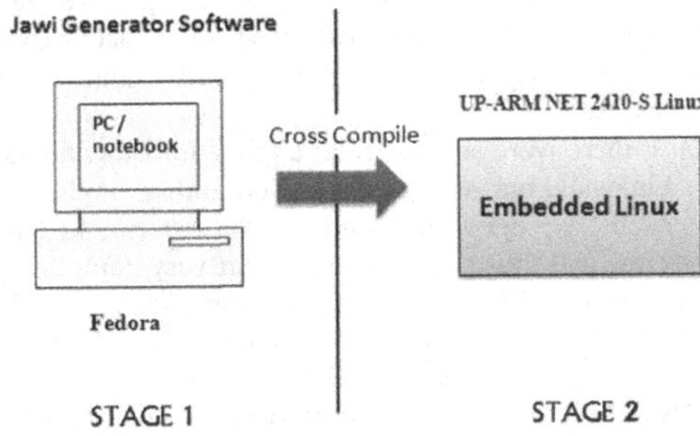

Fig. 3. Block Diagram of the Operating System

Figure 3 describe about the block diagram of the operating system. The operating system basically divided in two stages, which is stage 1 and stage 2. Stage 1 is a system developing process, and stage 2 is a software testing process in the board. The system in the first stage should be cross compile before transfer it to the board in the second stage. The cross compilation involved here [9].

C. System Test

Testing may be occurring on several levels as the project develops. Each task that has been down must be checked. After the project successfully been integrated, it must now be tested to locate any bugs that were committed during the previous phases. Test suites against integrated models must be developed and executed. Besides that, the project as whole must be reviewed for the completeness, accuracy, and ease of use. After compiling the system, testing has been done on users for the first stage of the testing process. The chosen users were one of the cafeteria's daughters and one of the Indian girls.

The kid is in standard one and before using this system interface, this child doesn't have enough knowledge about Jawi, only a basic knowledge by memorizing it during Quran extra class once in a week. Fortunately, after use this system, this kid is able to spell and write her own name. The second user that had been chosen is one of non-Muslim students. She had given a positive improvement after using this Jawi Generator Software twice. Her improvement about Jawi can be seen when she is able to combine this Jawi script into words and sentences as well. For the future improvement of this project, simple questionnaires had been given to those users, in order to investigate their thought and opinion about this Jawi Generator Software.

The second stage is testing should be done on the Linux embedded system, after embed the Jawi Generator Software into the board.

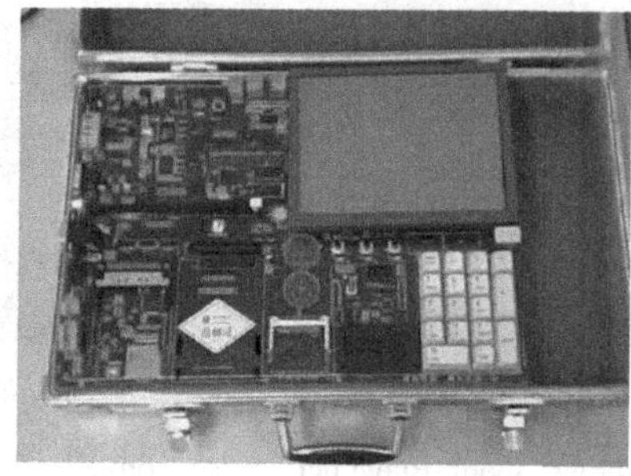

Fig. 4. Screenshot of UP-ARMNET 2410-S Linux

Figure 4 describe about the screenshot of UP-NETARM 2410-S Linux board that used in the second stage of the project. The software that already built will be embedding into this board. The core module of this board is SAMSUNG S3C2410 micro processor based on ARM 920T kernel, 64MB Nand Flash, 64MB SDRAM, and the system also works steadily under the frequency of 202MHZ.

IV. CURRENT RESULT

The system interface of Jawi Generator Software was performed as the system output. The user could choose and enter Jawi scripts that they want to display from the colorful interface. The sum of the scripts was from 'alif' until 'yaa', approximately about 36 scripts with the colorful button. The system had been created as a colorful interface that will attract users especially kids.

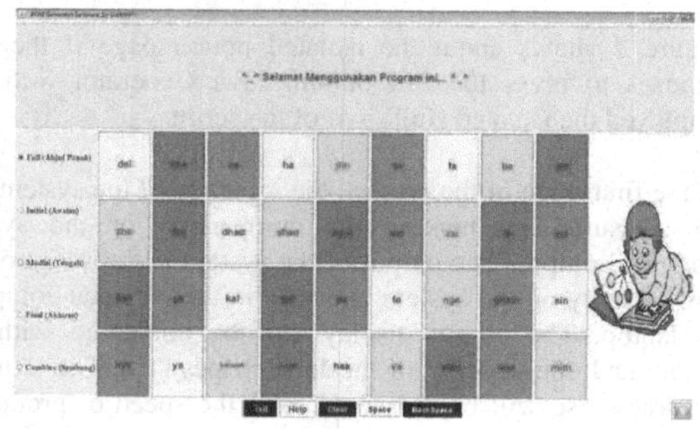

Fig. 5. Jawi Generator interface.

Figure 5 describes about the interface when the Jawi Generator Software has been compiling. This interface is an initial menu pop-up after the compilation process. At this initial menu interface, user can choose to press the buttons. The optional buttons are combine, initial, medial, and final button. The default option is combine button; if the user doesn't choose any button yet.

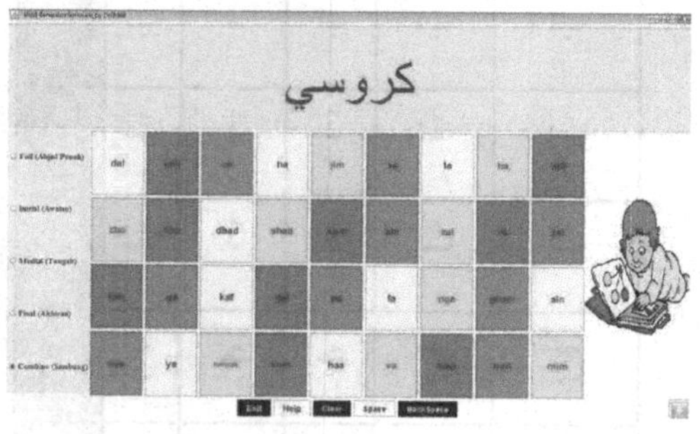

Fig. 6 Combine option page

Figure 6 describes about the combine option page where the default option is if the user doesn't choose any button previously in the main menu interface. The system displayed the jawi script in the combine mode, which is automatically combining it together into a word.

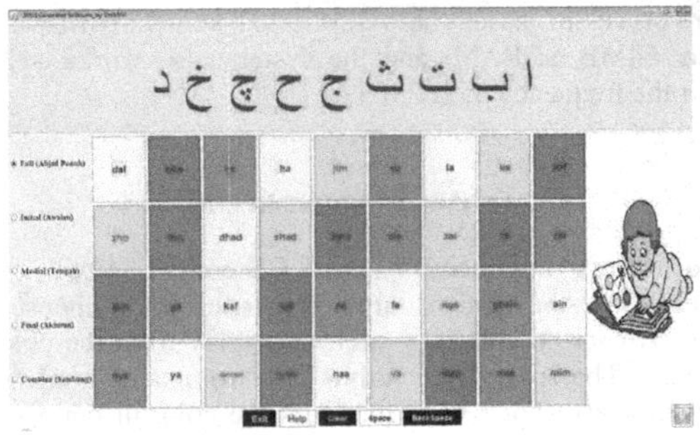

Fig. 7. The isolated option page.

Figure 7 shows about the isolated option page if the user chooses to press the full button. Jawi Generator Software displayed the isolated (full) part of the script.

In the first stage of the project, the accuracy of the system will be measured by making the comparison of the system graphical output. The output of the system is the script of the Jawi display on the system interface in the personal computer or laptop. The output display will be compared with the theoretical output script of the Jawi shapes [10]. The terms of accuracy also will be measured from the speed of producing the output.

TABLE I.
SAMPLE OF JAWI SCRIPTS

Character	Isolated	Initial	Medial	Final	Name
ا	ا			ـا	alif
ب	ب	بـ	ـبـ	ـب	ba
ت	ت	تـ	ـتـ	ـت	ta
ث	ث	ثـ	ـثـ	ـث	tsa
ج	ج	جـ	ـجـ	ـج	jim
ح	ح	حـ	ـحـ	ـح	hha

Table 1 show about the sample of Jawi script. Jawi scripts are divided into initial, medial, final and isolated part [11]. The system built will be compared with this theoretical script in terms of shape accuracy.

V. RELATED WORK

In addition, the similar application with this Jawi Generator Software is Ejawi™ Online 2.2, which is Roman Alphabets to Old Malay (Jawi) Script Online Converter [12]. This converter has an ADD-ON keyboard Jawi that is very compatible and sophisticated. This converter gives benefits to people especially an adult. The function looks similar with this Jawi Generator Software but its function looks like more complicated for the kids usage compared with this project.

The scopes of this project are simple and 'ease learning' which is suitable to the kids, who want to learn jawi script from the beginning. This Jawi Script Online Converter also can be only used if the users have the internet connection, because it is online software. The other existing online software that quite similar is Jawinet Website at the jawinet.8k.net [13]. This software also one of the online learning software, and its limitation is users need to have the connection with the internet in order to learn jawi. But it seems like the website is not maintained very well since the last update of the system was year 2000.

Furthermore, the other similar applications with this project are "Doktor Jawi" which is learning application in a set of book and cdrom [14], "Jawi Writer" which is a product from GTi Technologies Sdn Bhd [15], and also "Pandai Jawi" which is can be found at Malaysia Kedaidbp website [16]. All these three applications were learning application in cdrom which is mean users need to have cdrom player in order to learn Jawi scripts.

Fig. 8. Ejawi.net online converter.

Figure 8 shows about Ejawi.net online converter which is roman alphabets to jawi scripts converter. This converter is an online converter, which is the limitation is needed the internet connection if the user want to learn Jawi script.

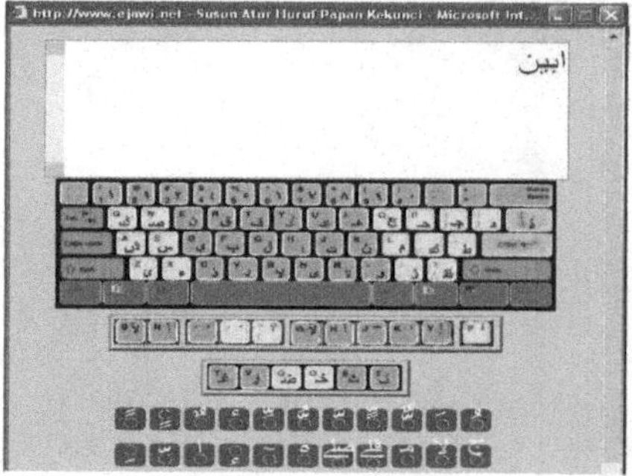

Fig. 9. ADD-ON Keyboard Jawi

Figure 9 describe the ADD-ON keyboard jawi script, which is included in Ejawi.net online converter. This ADD-ON keyboard has an interface buttons looks like the keyboard button. This interface also operates looks like Jawi Generator Software but the different is it more complicated interface, suitable for adult user.

VI. Conclusion & Future Work

In order to improve the performance of Jawi Generator Software, this project should make an improvement or revolution in many aspects, such as, it will be providing more attractive learning if the system has included with the sound in each button. This sound is a guide on how to pronounce the Jawi script based on the right pronunciation and 'baris'. The application of free dictionary also should be attached in order to make guidance for the user while using this system.

Jawi Generator Software should have an auto corrector or auto detector; which is will detect the wrong spelling and grammar while combining the letter. Besides that, this system should be upgraded in the main operation including, auto clear, the main screen / text box, and also there will be another choice in 'Combo Box' concept; this combo box will provide the choices of changing the different displayed font size.

Looking further ahead, Jawi Generator Software will be embedding into the board which is running in SBC TS7200 and UP-NET ARM 2410-S Linux. The performance analysis and comparison in both embedded platform will be done, in terms of system output, speed of producing the output, and also performances of the board itself.

Acknowledgment

We would like to thank to all lecturers and students of School of Computer and Communication, Universiti Malaysia Perlis, Malaysia for their moral support. We also would like to thank to R&D Department of Universiti Malaysia Perlis for the finance support from the short term grant.

References

[1] [Daniel Liang Y., "Creating User Interface". Introduction to Java™ Programming Comprehensive Version Fifth Edition, pp.446-482, October 2008.

[2] http://www.alanwood.net/unicode/arabic-supplement.html, October 2008

[3] http://www.up-tech.com/eng/company/index.asp, November 2008

[4] http://en.wikipedia.org/wiki/Fedora_(operating_system), June 2009

[5] Jon Byous, *Java technology: The early years*, Sun Developer Network, October 2009

[6] http://www.embeddedarm.com/, November 2008

[7] http://java.sun.com/developer/onlineTraining/, December 2008

[8] https://fedoraproject.org/, January 2009

[9] http://landley.net/writing/docs/cross-compiling.html, February 2009

[10] http://homepage3.nifty.com/tao/jawi-study/unicode_chart.html, March 2009

[11] http://wazu.jp/gallery/Fonts_Arabic.html, May 2009

[12] http://www.ejawi.net/converter.php, May 2009

[13] http://jawinet.8k.com/index.html, June 2009

[14] www.doktorjawi.com/, July 2009

[15] www.gtitec.com.my/jawi.htm, August 2009

[16] www.kedaidbp.my/cms/articles.php?lng=en&pg=362, September 2009

Efficient Comparison between Windows and Linux Platform Applicable in a Virtual Architectural Walkthrough Application

P. Thubaasini, R. Rusnida and S. M. Rohani
School of Computer and Communication
Universiti Malaysia Perlis
Kuala Perlis, Malaysia

Abstract-This paper describes Linux, an open source platform used to develop and run a virtual architectural walkthrough application. It proposes some qualitative reflections and observations on the nature of Linux in the concept of Virtual Reality (VR) and on the most popular and important claims associated with the open source approach. The ultimate goal of this paper is to measure and evaluate the performance of Linux used to build the virtual architectural walkthrough and develop a proof of concept based on the result obtain through this project. Besides that, this study reveals the benefits of using Linux in the field of virtual reality and reflects a basic comparison and evaluation between Windows and Linux base operating system. Windows platform is use as a baseline to evaluate the performance of Linux. The performance of Linux is measured based on three main criteria which is frame rate, image quality and also mouse motion.

I. Introduction

Virtual reality (VR) is the simulation of a real or imagined environment that can be experienced visually in the three dimensions of width, height, and depth and that may additionally provide an interactive experience visually in full real-time motion with sound and possibly with tactile and other forms of feedback [1]. Here real time means that the computer is able to detect a user's input and modify the virtual world instantaneously. The real-time aspect of such systems revealed to be very appreciated by the users as it enabled them to show, in much more details and realism, their designs to others [2]. The simplest form of virtual reality is a three dimensional (3D) image that can be explored interactively at a personal computer, usually by manipulating keys or the mouse so that the content of the image moves in some direction or zooms in or out [1]. The key technique of VR includes modeling technique of dynamic environment, 3D graphics real-time rendering technique, application system developing tool and system inheritance system.

VR technologies address a wide range of interaction and immersion capabilities. Interaction varies learner control during the VR experience. Immersion varies from first person, second person, or third person experiences and in physical, perceptual, and psychological options. Often, the term virtual environment (VE) is used instead of just virtual reality to stress that there is no ambition to remodel the universe. VE are realistic representations of some physical basis at all (e.g. 3D databases). It may also be an abstract representation of some physical simulation (e.g. molecular structure) [3].

Virtual reality environments have huge application in visualization industry, starting from simulation to games. One of the most obvious applications of virtual reality was the so familiar architectural walkthrough in which this project is focused on. An architectural walkthrough is a computer-based, interactive system that can simulate the visual experience of moving through a 3D model of a building by displaying rendered images of the model as seen from a hypothetical observer viewpoint under interactive control by the user [4]. It allows user to navigate a virtual architecture as if in the real world. Walkthroughs, as they are commonly called, are not only valuable for conveying information about a building, structure or large scale environment, they are also relatively easy for almost anyone to produce at a simplistic or amateur level. Typically in walkthrough animations, structural and environmental objects such as walls, columns, doorways, buildings, and trees remain stationary while the camera moves through the scene. Walkthroughs and flythroughs differ in technique. A walkthrough is used to show the actual point of view of a person walking through a scene and is generally shot at or slightly below eye level. Flythroughs are not as narrowly structured as walkthroughs and can be made from any point of view desired and at any speed and camera angle [5].

Another reason that 3D animation walkthroughs have come into popular use in business and industry is that they are fairly inexpensive to produce especially when it deals with open source platform. This project emphasizes on using Linux as an approach to create the virtual architectural walkthrough. The use of Linux for virtual reality has become a popular topic to debate. Linux is gaining popularity and functionality in the virtual reality community. However, the demands of hard VR applications have produced a niche market of very powerful operating systems. While the performance of popular VR operating systems is good, the cost is high. Users of popular VR operating systems must pay for the development environment, compilers, technical support, and the operating system including royalties. Linux provides the benefit of being open source and also is generally less expensive than proprietary software. There also is a large Linux user community that is extremely helpful in answering

T. Sobh, K. Elleithy (eds.), *Innovations in Computing Sciences and Software Engineering*,
DOI 10.1007/978-90-481-9112-3_57, © Springer Science+Business Media B.V. 2010

questions that arise. The decision of whether or not to use Linux in VR is a difficult one without actual data and facts. Therefore this research is done in order to determine and evaluate the performance of Linux applicable in an architectural walkthrough.

II. Software and Hardware Specifications

The architectural walkthrough application system is implemented in C++ using OpenGL and GLUT libraries. The performance tests were run on a desktop system which consists of dual operating system; Windows and Linux. The output is displayed through a high resolution monitor while user will interact with the walkthrough application using mouse and keyboard. The specifications used for the delivery platform PC are as listed as below:-

- Intel® Core™ 2 Duo CPU T6500 @ 2.10GHz
- 4GB of RAM.
- A fast 3D NVIDIA GEFORCE graphic card supporting 1024x768x16-bit color with 512 MB of memory.
- OpenSUSE Linux 11.1 and Windows XP operating system.

III. Design and Implementation

Architectural walkthrough is huge task that is usually broken into smaller bites. These bites or phases can be summarized by the figure below:-

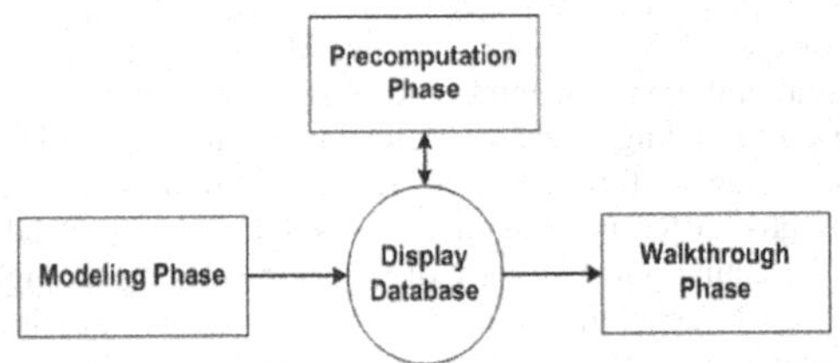

Fig. 1. Architectural Walkthrough Development Task.

A. *Modeling Phase*

Modeling is a process of constructing a virtual 3D graphics object (computer model or model) from a real object or an imaginary entity. Creating graphics models requires a significant amount of time and effort. Modeling tools make creating and constructing complex 3D models fast and easy. A graphics model includes geometrical descriptions (particles, vertices, polygons, etc.) as well as associated graphics attributes (transparencies, colors, shadings, materials, etc.) which can be saved in a file using a standard (3D model) file format. Modeling tools help create virtual objects and environments for CAD (computer-aided design), visualization, virtual reality, simulation, education, training and entertainment [6].

Apparently, in the graphic developing environment, it is difficult to create complicated 3D models by encoding directly into advanced languages proposed in this research. Therefore a new modeling way has been found to solve the difficulty of creating and fetching 3D models in VR system. The solution is to create complicated models by using AutoCAD (DWG and its ASCII equivalent, DXF) and have the model files exported to 3DS-format and fetched into Linux in which real-time rendering effects are attainable. After analyzing 3DS file data structure, an arithmetic is put forward of how to read 3DS files in Linux so that both advantage of 3D modeling by AutoCAD software and real-time rendering in Linux are combined together. The overall process of modeling is as shown in the diagram below:-

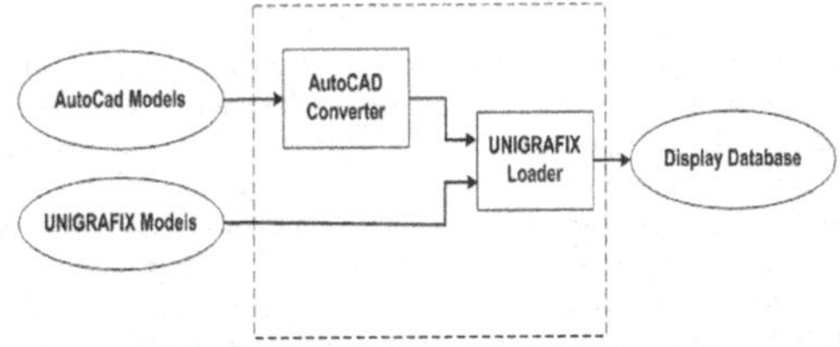

Fig. 2. Modeling Phase Diagram.

The modeling phase can be summarized by the following four steps:-

1. Construct a building model from CAD floor plans and elevations.
2. Implement a converter that extracts geometrical and surface attribute information embedded in the CAD files.
3. Transform the attributes into a format suitable for 3D object modeling.
4. Detect and correct anomalies and fix remaining modeling errors with interactive tools.

B. *Precomputation Phase*

The overall process of precomputation is as shown in the diagram below:-

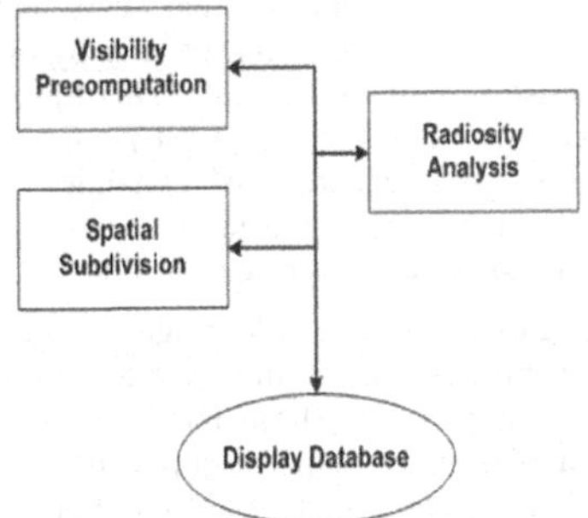

Fig. 3. Precomputation Phase Diagram.

Calculations that do not depend on observer viewpoint are done off-line before the user begins an interactive walkthrough. Increased storage space is traded for reduced real-time computation, accelerating frame rates during the walkthrough phase [6].

C. *Walkthrough Phase*

The walkthrough phase diagram is as shown in figure below:-

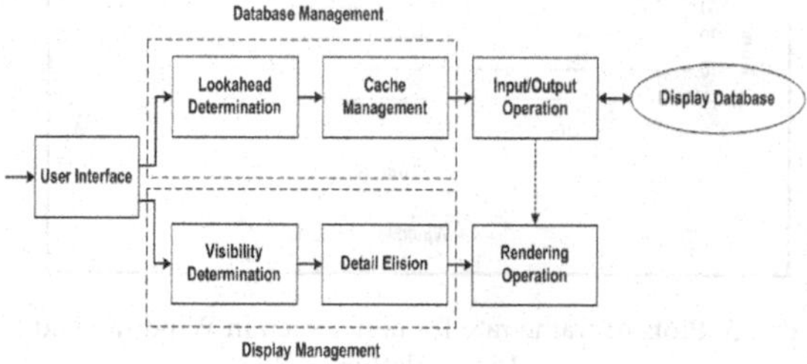

Fig. 4. Walkthrough Phase Diagram

Once all the pre-computation work is done, it starts on with the walkthrough phase. This phase can be summarized by the following steps:-

1. Simulate the observer moving through the model.
2. Render the model as seen from the observer viewpoint at interactive frame rates as the user moves the viewpoint through the model.

IV. Performance Targets

A. *Frame Rate*

Frame rate can be defined as the measurement of frequency (rate) at which an imaging device produces unique consecutive images called frames [7]. In order to maximize user performance and comfort, any VR system as well as the platform used to run the system must satisfy the real-time requirement, which means maintaining a constant frame rate that is above a certain threshold. The ability of accelerating the frame rate is certainly one of the most important criteria for evaluating the performance of a software platform. Maintaining a constant frame rate is also very important. Especially when the mean frame-time is high, fluctuations in frame-rate can influence the performance of VR tasks. High and constant frame rates are both important. VR users may feel sick, lose immersive feeling and lose hand-eye coordination during performing a VR task without satisfying either of these two requirements. Therefore, both fast frame-rate and constant frame time management should be considered for any VR system [8]. The VR system developed is simulated in two different platform; Windows and Linux. The frame rate result obtain in Windows platform is used as a baseline to evaluate the frame rate performance in Linux.

B. *Image Quality*

Image quality is a characteristic of an image that measures the perceived image degradation (typically, compared to an ideal or perfect image) [9]. In virtual reality community, when talk about the image quality, it is always referred to 'realistic' as one of the main criteria. In a VR system, the user's perception of engagement and being in a 'real' world should be as natural as possible. It involves how accurate the geometric models and fine textures resemble real objects and how well it captures many of the effects of light interacting with objects [8]. In this performance evaluation research, we are mainly concerned on how well does Linux preserve image quality. For a comparison, the developed virtual architectural walkthrough system is also being simulated on Windows system.

C. *Mouse Motion*

Mouse motion can also be considered as one of the most important aspects in evaluating the performance of a platform. The user must be able to move around the virtual architectural walkthrough without jerkiness in display when using a mouse. The representation of the self/presence and behavior manifest in the VR should be faithful to the user's actions. Response time between mouse movement and update of the VR display should be less than 200 ms to avoid motion sickness problem. Mouse movement events are created each time the mouse moves. The movement per event can be captured by determining how far the mouse moved as an offset from the last event.

V. Evaluation Methods

A. *Frame Rate*

The frame rate measurement data for this research is done in two modes; full screen and half screen. The following source code is included in the OpenGL program in order to calculate the frame rate:-

```
void FPS()
{
static float fps          = 0.0f;
static float previousTime = 0.0f;
static char strFPS[20]   = {0};
float currentTime = (GetTickCount() * 0.001f);

 ++fps;
if( currentTime - previousTime > 1.0f )
{
  previousTime = currentTime;
  sprintf(strFPS, "FPS: %d", int(fps));
     SetWindowText(hWnd, strFPS);
  fps = 0.0f;
}
```

The current time in seconds (milliseconds * .001 = seconds) is obtained through the equation written in line 6 of the source code above. *GetTickCount* is a function in the Windows API which takes no (void) parameters and returns the time since the system was started. With each pass of the loop, the FPS function is run to increase the fps variable by one to increase the current frame per second. After the FPS counter increment, the elapsed time is calculated by subtracting the previous time from the current time. If the elapsed time is greater than or equal to 1000ms (one second), then it has been clocked one second's worth of frame updates, which allows an accurate display of FPS by saving the current time to the previousTime variable. Finally, the fps variable is reset to 0.

B. Image Quality

The quality of an image should be measured locally and globally. Since the change of each pixel value effects the quality of the image and the overall quality is dependent on the total number of pixels that were changed, the total number of pixels that were changed should hence be used in evaluating the quality of an image. Imatest software tool is used as an approach to measure the image quality of each platform. Imatest is a product of the Imatest LLC. It is a capable software package for measuring the key image factors such as sharpness, noise dynamic range, color accuracy, distortion, uniformity, chromatic aberration, veiling and much more. Every screenshots from the VR system is captured using an image capturing software tool. The image file obtain is then simulated in Imatest in order to measure its image quality.

C. Mouse Motion

Evaluation on mouse motion in Linux is done mainly to identify and compare the speed of motion with Windows base operating system. Mouse movement events are created each time the mouse moves. The movement per event can be captured by determining how far the mouse moved as an offset from the last event. The time difference between two events is determined first in order to obtain the speed measurement. This means, each time a distance is sampled, the time interval of that particular sample is determined too. The following equation is used in order to determine the speed of the mouse motion:-

$$Speed = \frac{Distance\ moved}{Time\ taken} \quad (1)$$

VI. Experiments and Results

A. Frame Rate

The process of measuring frame rate in the VR system is done in two different modes; full screen and half screen. The measurements are taken in a 30 seconds duration time. The overall frame rate for both half screen and full screen in Windows and Linux are plotted in a form of graph as shown in figure 1 and figure 2:-

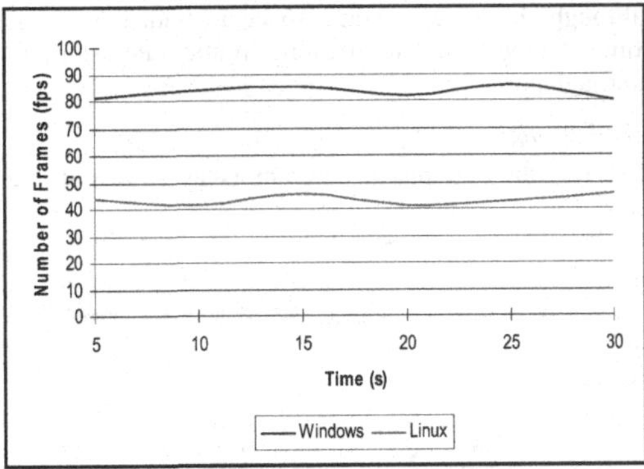

Fig. 5. Plots of frame rate for half screen in Windows and Linux platform

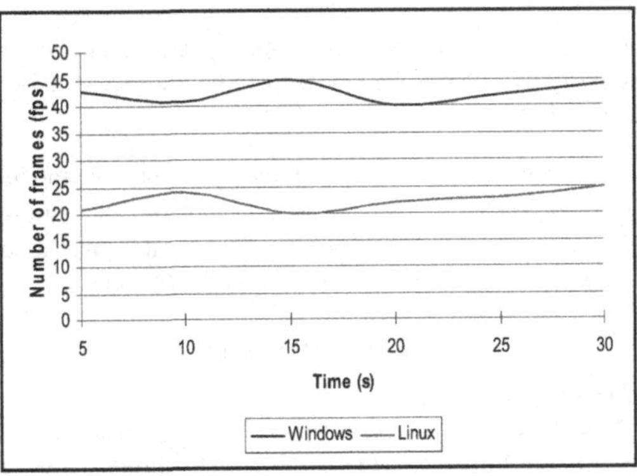

Fig. 6. Plots of frame rate for full screen in Windows and Linux platform

Table below shows an average fps (frame per second) reading in full screen and half screen for both Windows and Linux operating system:-

TABLE I.
AVERAGE FRAME RATE IN WINDOWS AND LINUX PLATFORMS

Platform	Average Frame Rates (fps)	
	Full Screen	Half Screen
Windows	42 fps	83 fps
Linux	21 fps	43 fps

From the result obtained, it is clearly proved that the frame rate performance in Windows is much better compare to Linux for both half and full screen.

B. *Image Quality*

Figure 3 and 4 represent screenshots of the virtual architectural walkthrough application captured from two different platforms.

Fig. 7. A screenshot of the virtual architectural walkthrough application in Linux platform.

Fig. 8. A screenshot of the virtual architectural walkthrough application in Windows platform.

From the result obtained, it shows that the texture, lighting effect and also color resolution is much higher in Linux platform compare to Windows. This concludes that the image quality in Linux is better than in Windows.

C. *Mouse Motion*

The speed of the mouse motion is tracked every 6 seconds. Table II and III shows the data capture in Windows and Linux platform in order to obtain the speed in each platform. Each table consists of distance (cm), time (s) and speed (cm/s).

TABLE II
SPEED DATA CAPTURE IN WINDOWS PLATFORM

Distance (mm)	Time (s)	Speed (mm/s)
1300	06	216.67
1200	12	200.00
1450	18	241.67
1340	24	223.33
1300	30	216.67
1250	36	208.33
1340	42	223.33
1400	48	233.33
1270	54	211.67
1340	60	223.33
1360	66	226.67
1420	72	236.67
1230	78	205.00

TABLE III
SPEED DATA CAPTURE IN WINDOWS PLATFORM

Distance (m)	Time (s)	Speed (m/s)
560	06	93.33
610	12	101.67
550	18	91.67
540	24	90.00
670	30	111.67
710	36	118.33
760	42	126.67
510	48	85.00
446	54	74.33
620	60	103.33
700	66	116.67
670	72	111.67
540	78	90.00

Table IV shows the average speed reading for both Windows and Linux platform:-

TABLE IV
AVERAGE SPEED READING

Platform	Average Speed (mm/s)
Windows	220.51
Linux	101.10

Based on the result obtained, it clearly shows that the Windows platform performs better in terms of mouse movement criteria compare to Linux.

VII. Conclusion

This paper has presented a design and performance evaluation framework for two different platforms applicable in a virtual architectural walkthrough. The key contributions of this paper are performance targets to measure and evaluate a virtual walkthrough, performance methods as well as evaluation results to compare the performance of the particular VR system in two different platforms; Windows and Linux. Besides that, this article discusses a new method of designing 3D modeling for VR system, which is using the professional 3D modeling software as an assistant modeling tool to create 3D models and have the 3D model exported into a 3DS-format file so that it can be fetched in OpenGL. Based on the objectives set, this research has the potential of saving in the government as well as in private sectors not only in terms of money but also visual quality mainly because the use of open source software (OSS). There is a growing community of users around the world and, because of its Open Source free availability; there are also a growing number of contributors expanding its capabilities.

Acknowledgment

We would like to thank all lecturers and reviewers for their helpful comments. This project was partially supported by School of Computer and Communication Engineering at University Malaysia Perlis, Malaysia. Furthermore, we thank all users for their feedback.

References

[1] http://www.openchannelsoftware.com/discipline/Visualization_and_Virtual_Reality/

[2] Grigore C. Burdea and Philippe Coiffet, "Virtual Reality Technology", Prentice Hall, pp. 2-13, 2003.

[3] Alexei Sourin, "From a small formula to virtual worlds," *Computer Graphics,* Prentice Hall, pp. 202-212, 2005.

[4] http://www.cs.nps.navy.mil/people/faculty/capps/4473/projects/architect/main.html.

[5] Clark A. Cory, W. Scott Meador and William A. Ross, "3D animated walkthroughs for architecture, engineering and construction applications," International Conference Graphicon, 2001.

[6] Chunyang Chen, "Foundations of 3D graphics programming using JOGL and Java3D", Springer, 2008.

[7] http://en.wikipedia.org/wiki/Frame_rate

[8] P.Yuan and M.Green, "A framework for performance evaluation of real-time rendering algorithms in virtual reality", University of Alberta, Edmonton, Canada

[9] http://en.wikipedia.org/wiki/Image_quality

Simulation-Based Stress Analysis for a 3D Modeled Humerus-Prosthesis Assembly

S. Herle[1], C. Marcu[1], H. Benea[2], L. Miclea[1], R. Robotin[1]
[1]Department of Automation, Technical University of Cluj-Napoca, Romania
C. Daicoviciu 15, 400020 Cluj-Napoca, Romania
{Sorin.Herle, Cosmin.Marcu, Liviu.Miclea, Radu.Robotin}@aut.utcluj.ro
[2]"Iuliu Hatieganu" University of Medicine and Pharmacy, Romania,
V.Babes 8, 400012 Cluj-Napoca, Romania
beneahorea@yahoo.com

***Abstract*- The development of mechanical models of the humerus-prosthesis assembly represent a solution for analyzing the behavior of prosthesis devices under different conditions; some of these behaviors are impossible to reproduce in vivo due to the irreversible phenomenon that can occur. This paper presents a versatile model of the humerus-prosthesis assembly. The model is used for stress analysis and displacement distributions under different configurations that correspond to possible in vivo implementations later on. A 3D scanner was used to obtain the virtual model of the humerus bone. The endoprosthesis was designed using 3D modeling software and the humerus-prosthesis assembly was analyzed using Finite Element Analysis software.**

I. Introduction

The development of a durable endoprosthesis with a good rate of integration represents a major goal for both physicians and bioengineers.

The prosthesis devices used today have problems related to the osseointegration, especially in the long term. The possible complications that may occur are related to pathological, surgical or design factors [1],[2],[3]. Bone is a living tissue, which continuously rebuilds its structure according to the direction of the loads exerted on it. The insertion of a metal prosthesis into the medullar canal will disturb the load equilibrium in the bone. If a reduced load is encountered at the interface of the bone with the prosthetic device (which means that the prosthetic device is not well fixed) this will cause atrophy of the bone, and in time the loss of the prosthesis. A lack in osseointegration can also be related to an increased stress at the contact surface of the prosthetic device with the bone. This increased stress will reduce the capacity of the bone to grow and to integrate the prosthesis.

Because endoprostheses are affected by these mechanical factors, together with other, chemical and thermal factors, suitable materials are required to achieve biocompatibility and durability. Titanium alloy and cobalt alloy are the most often used materials for these prostheses. Even if these materials are biocompatible, there still remains the problem of interfacing the endoprosthesis and the bone in order to increase the osseointegration and to reduce the rate of failure. To solve this problem, materials like hydroxyapatite, chitosan and collagen fibers are used at the interface of the bone with the prosthetic device.

To find the best solution for prosthesis development, it is important to use noninvasive methods. Therefore mathematical models of prostheses are developed and used to analyze behaviors under different conditions (applied forces, materials used for prosthesis and coating materials for osseointegration). The most often used computer based method is finite element analysis.

In this paper we focus on the analysis of behaviors of the healthy humeral bone and the humeral bone with an endoprosthesis. The force and stress distribution into the bone-prosthesis assembly will be analyzed when the prosthesis is made of titanium alloy and cobalt alloy, respectively. The analysis will be performed in the absence, as well as in the presence of interfacing materials (hydroxyapatite and collagen fibers) that coat the prosthesis.

II. Modeling the Humeral Endoprosthesis

Analysis of forces and stress distribution along the healthy humerus and humerus-prosthesis assembly in vitro requires models of humerus and humeral endoprosthesis.

A. Humerus 3D model

It is known that the bone is a non-isotropic material. However, to simplify the modeling, we consider the bone as an isotropic material. If e.g., the humerus model is obtained using 3D scanning and digital reconstruction, then the model can be considered very close to the natural bone. Using the finite element method, a series of analyses can be made such as deformations, elastic strain and stress when an external force is applied to the bone.

Due to the complex form of the bone, its model is almost impossible to design using 3D design software. Therefore, we used a 3D scanner and reconstructed the bone model from cross sections of the bone. The scanner model is 3D Kreon Zephyr KZ 50 capable to identify 30000 points per second with a vertical resolution of 5 μm. The initial result from the scanner was a cloud of points which has been processed and prepared for the next operation. The next operation consisted in building the mesh using a triangulation method having as input the cloud of points from the previous operation. Then as a last operation the bone surfaces were built based on the previous mesh.

T. Sobh, K. Elleithy (eds.), *Innovations in Computing Sciences and Software Engineering*,
DOI 10.1007/978-90-481-9112-3_58,

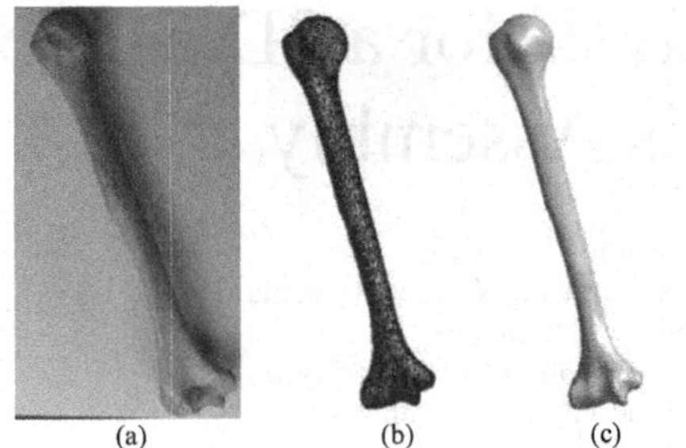

(a) (b) (c)

Figure 1. Steps in 3D bone reconstruction: (a) real bone, (b) the mesh, (c) 3D model of the bone

Fig. 1 presents the real bone, the mesh from cloud of points and the final 3D model used in analyses.

B. Modeling the humeral endoprosthesis

The design of the humerus prosthesis implies some constrains regarding its shape and material.

From the material point of view, in case of an endoprosthesis the most often used materials are cobalt-chrome alloys and titanium-aluminum- vanadium (Ti6Al4V) alloy.

Due to the patient-to-patient variation of the humerus bone, the humerus endoprostheses must be personalized in shape and dimensions.

In the design stage we considered a prosthesis made by Solar company [4] starting from the premise that the study presented in this paper wants to show the design and implementation of some virtual models which can be used in analysis of the mechanical behavior of the humerus-prosthesis assembly. The shape and dimensions used for the particular case of the designed model are presented in Fig. 2. Fig. 3 illustrates different views of the prosthesis model used later for the analysis.

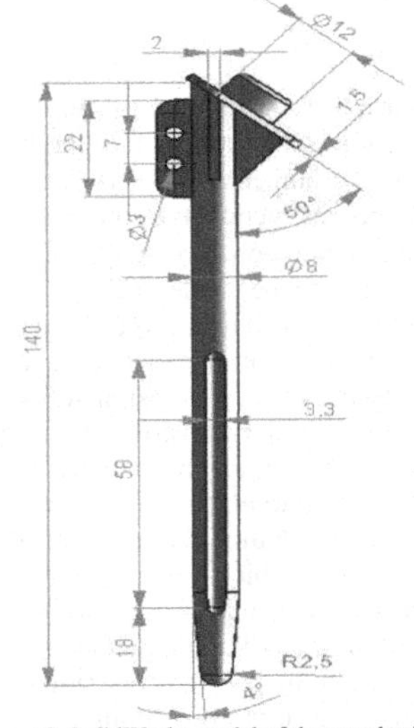

Figure 2. SolidWorks model of the prosthesis

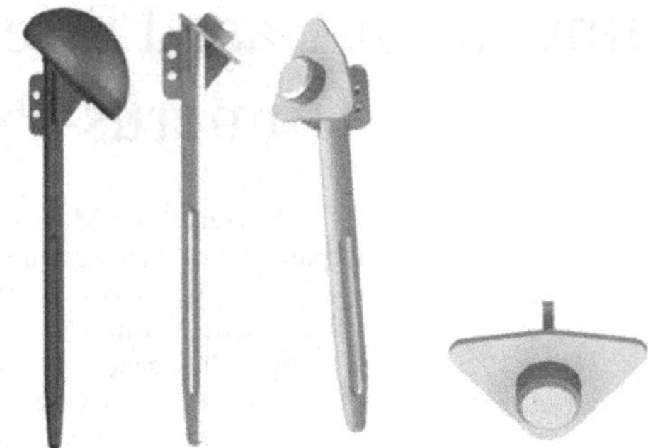

Figure 3. Different views of the SolidWorks endoprosthesis model

The endoprosthesis model has two components forming an assembly: the prosthesis head and the prosthesis tail.

C. Creating the humerus-prosthesis assembly model

To build the humerus-prosthesis assembly, the humerus model has been cut in order to respect the external surface of the prosthesis. We established coincidence and concentricity links between contact surfaces in order to obtain a correct analysis when imported in the Ansys software.

Considering the X-Ray photograph presented in Fig. 4a which illustrates the placing mode of the prosthesis in the humerus, we realized the humerus-prosthesis assembly presented in Fig. 4b.

During surgery, the humerus is processed in order to fix the endoprosthesis. The humeral head is cut and the humerus bone is prepared by manually milling the fixing channels. In our case, the 3D model of the humerus was processed in order to obtain the correct assembly with the modeled endoprosthesis.

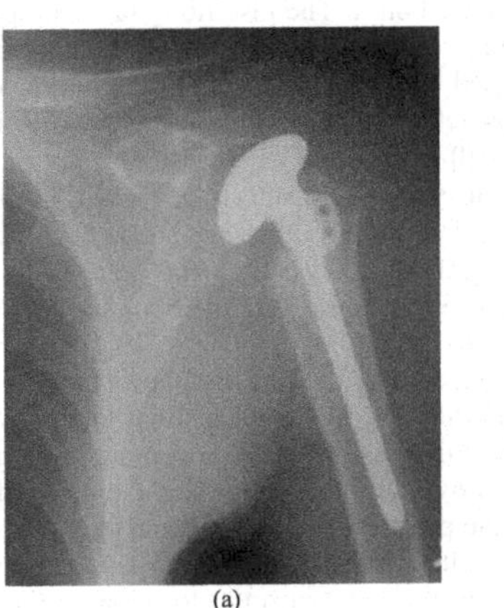

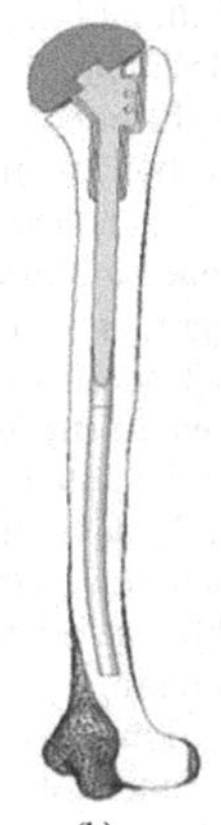

(a) (b)

Figure 4. (a) X-Ray picture of the prosthesis fixed into the humerus, (b) Humerus-Prosthesis assembly

III. Analysis of Mechanical Properties

One method widely used to analyze the mechanical properties analyses of a material is finite element analysis. The drawback of this method is the computational load due to the large number of equations that must be solved. The solving time of the analysis depends on the model complexity and on the computer performance. For all the analyses made we considered that the humerus and the prosthesis are isotropic and elastic materials. The properties of materials used for analyses were: Young Modulus, Poisson's Ratio, Density, Tensile Yield Strength, Compression Yield Strength, Ultimate Yield Strength, Thermal expansion, Thermal conductivity and Specific heat. Table 1 presents the values of these properties for different materials used in simulations and analyses [6-11].

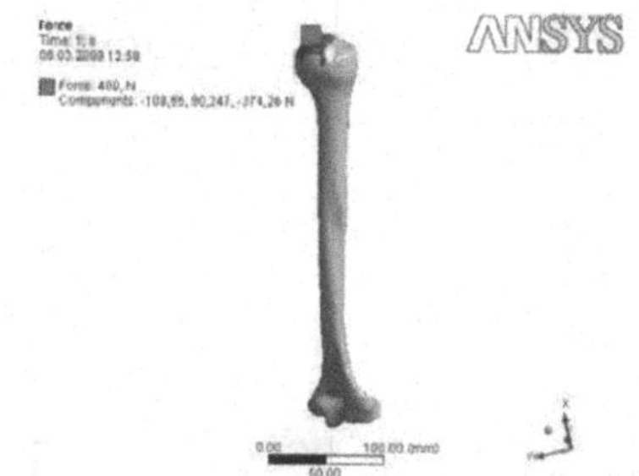

Figure 5. A force of 400 N acting on the humeral head

The distributions of Equivalent Stress (Von Mises), Total Deformation and Equivalent Elastic Strain are illustrated in Fig. 6, Fig. 7 and Fig. 8.

Table 1. Mechanical properties of materials

Properties	UM	Trabecular bone	Cortical bone	Hydroxy-apatite	Collagen fibers	Composite material (HAP+collagen)	Prosthesis Co-28Cr-6Mo alloy	Prosthesis Ti-6Al-4V alloy
Young Modulus	N/m^2	$3*10^9$	$14.2*10^9$	$114*10^9$	$54,3*10^6$	$3*10^9$	$2,08*10^{11}$	$123*10^9$
Poisson's Ratio	-	0.12	0.3	0.28	0.35	0.315	0,3	0.3
Density	kg/m^3	800	2100	3156	2000	2578	8300	4429
Tensile Yield Strength	N/m^2	$7.4*10^6$	$0.15*10^9$	-	$8,5*10^6$	-	-	$827*10^6$
Compression Yield Strength	N/m^2	$12.52*10^6$	$182*10^6$	-	-	-	-	-
Ultimate Yield Strength	N/m^2	$5*10^6$	$100*10^6$	-	$2,5*10^7$	-	-	$1,05*10^9$
Thermal expan.	/Kelvin	$27.5*10^{-6}$	$27.5*10^{-6}$	$17*10^{-6}$	$6*10^{-4}$	$1.129*10^{-6}$	-	$9*10^{-6}$
Thermal conductivity	W/m*K	0.38	0.38	-	-	-	-	6,7
Specific heat	J/Kg*K	1260	1260	-	3900	-	-	586

In this study we considered a subject with a mass of 80 Kg in handstand position. This means that a force of approximately 400 N acts on each upper limb. The behavior of the humerus and humerus-prosthesis assembly will be analyzed using three parameters: Equivalent Stress (Von Mises), Total Deformation and Equivalent Elastic Strain.

Seven scenarios were analyzed: (1) healthy humerus, (2) humerus and uncoated Ti-6Al-4V alloy prosthesis, (3) Humerus and Ti-6Al-4V alloy prosthesis coated with Hydroxyapatite, (4) Humerus and Ti-6Al-4V alloy prosthesis coated with one layer of Hydroxyapatite and one layer of Collagen fibers, (5) Humerus and Ti-6Al-4V alloy prosthesis coated with one layer of composite material (HAP and Collagen fibers), (6) Humerus and Co-28Cr-6Mo alloy prosthesis coated with one layer of Hydroxyapatite and one layer of Collagen fibers, (7) Humerus and Co-28Cr-6Mo alloy prosthesis coated with one layer of composite material (HAP and Collagen fibers).

Scenario 1 Healthy humerus

A force of 400 N was applied on the humeral head as illustrated in Fig. 5.

The Equivalent Stress is distributed along the bone with a peak value on the Medial Epicondyle. The Total deformation distribution has a maximum on the humeral head and is insignificant on the distal part of the bone.

The Equivalent Elastic Strain is distributed along the bone with a maximum on the Medial Epicondyle as can be seen in Fig. 8.

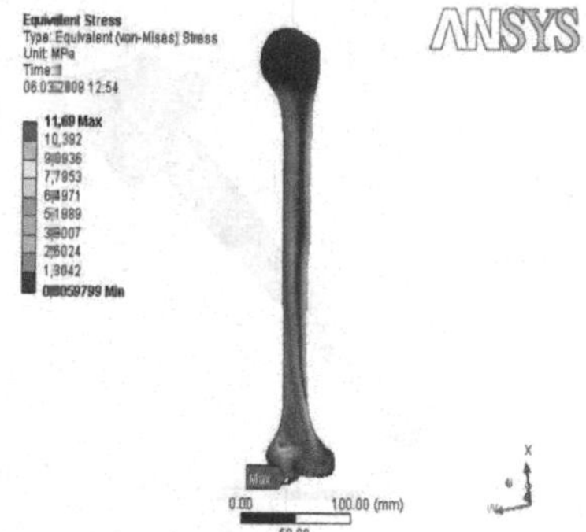

Figure 6 The Equivalent stress on healthy humerus

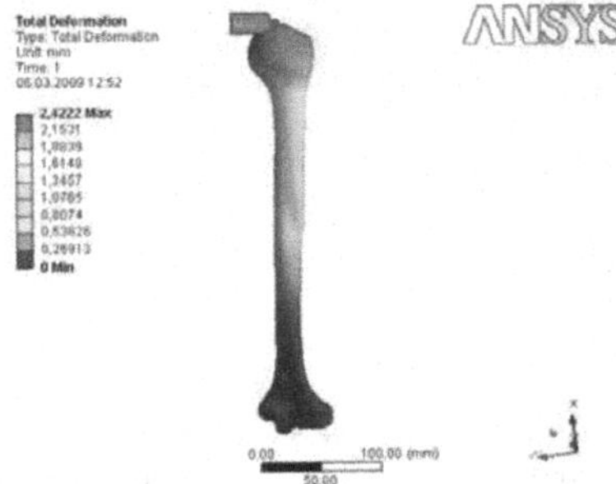

Figure 7 Total deformation distribution on healthy humerus

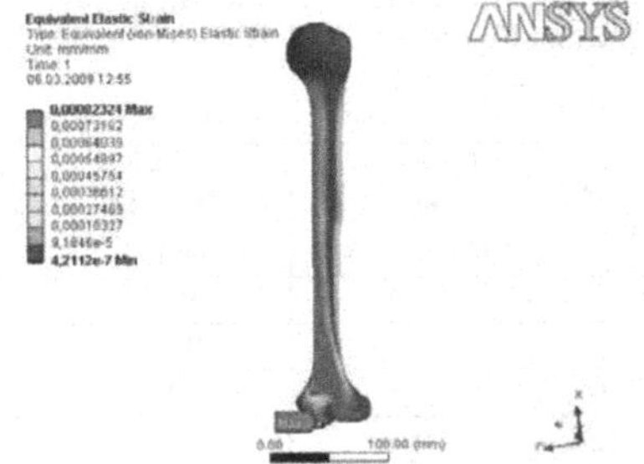

Figure 8 The Equivalent Elastic Strain distribution on healthy humerus

Scenario 2 Humerus and uncoated Ti alloy prosthesis

The same force of 400 N was applied on the ball of the prosthesis. Unlike the case of healthy bone, in this case the Equivalent Stress is concentrated on the neck of the prosthesis as can be seen in Fig 9. This happens because the anatomy of the bone was modified.

The Total deformation has the same distribution like in scenario 1, with a maximum value on the ball of the prosthesis. The value of the total deformation is smaller than in the first scenario.

The Equivalent Elastic Strain is concentrated at the surface contact between the bone and the neck of the prosthesis.

Figure 9 The Equivalent stress distribution on the uncoated prosthesis

Scenario 3 Humerus and Ti alloy prosthesis coated with hydroxyapatite

The prosthesis's stem was covered with a 2 mm hydroxyapatite layer. For the same force of 400 N applied on the ball of the prosthesis, the Equivalent Stress is concentrated on the neck of the prosthesis, like in previous scenario, but a 10% diminution was encountered. This fact confirms that the presence of the hydroxyapatite as an interface between bone and prosthetic device is a benefit. The total deformation was smaller than in previous scenario with more than 50%. Also the Equivalent Elastic Strain was three times smaller than in previous scenario, with a distribution similar to that of a healthy humerus.

Scenario 4 Humerus and Ti alloy prosthesis coated with two layers of hydroxyapatite an collagen fibers

For this scenario the stem of the prosthesis was covered with 1 mm hydroxyapatite layer. Over this layer a second layer of collagen with a thickness of 1 mm was added. The values of the three parameters: Equivalent Stress, Total Deformation and Equivalent Elastic Strain were higher than in the case of prosthesis coated with a 2 mm hydroxyapatite layer. The distribution of the equivalent elastic strain is concentrated into the collagen layer, as can be seen in Fig. 10.

Scenario 5 Humerus and Ti alloy prosthesis coated with two millimeters of composite material

A layer of hydroxyapatite and collagen fibers in composite material with a thickness of 2 mm was considered as interface between bone and prosthesis. The maximum value of Equivalent Stress determined after simulation was higher than in the scenarios were prosthesis was coated with hydroxyapatite. The Equivalent Stress was distributed in the coating layer, in the neck area of the prosthesis. The Total Deformation distribution was similar with that encountered in previous two scenarios, but the value of it was smaller. The Equivalent Elastic Strain has a maximum value in the coating layer.

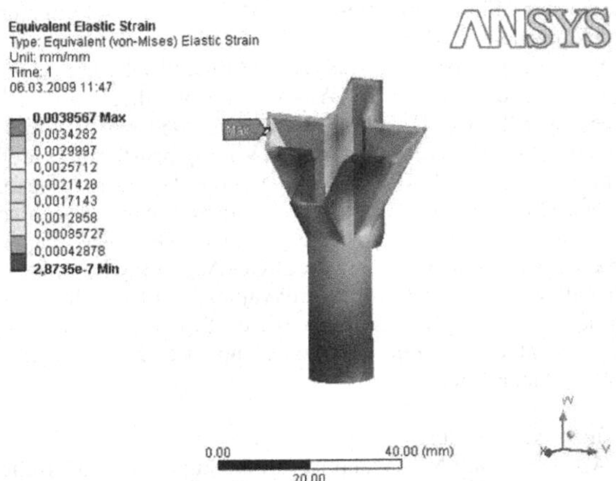

Figure 10 The Equivalent Elastic Strain distributions on collagen layer

Scenario 6 Humerus and Co alloy prosthesis coated with two layers of hydroxyapatite an collagen fibers

For this scenario the stem of the prosthesis made of Co-28Cr-6Mo alloy, was covered with a 1 mm thick hydroxyapatite layer. Over this layer a second layer of collagen with a thickness of 1 mm was added. The maximum value of Equivalent Stress was higher than in the case of Ti alloy prosthesis coated with the same two layers, but the maximum value of Total Deformation was 20% smaller. The maximum value and the distribution of the Equivalent Elastic Strain is comparable with the case of Ti alloy made prosthesis.

Scenario 7 Humerus and Co alloy prosthesis coated with 2 mm of composite material

A 2mm layer of hydroxyapatite and collagen fibers in composite material was considered as interface between bone and prosthesis The maximum value of Equivalent Stress determined after simulation was higher than in the scenarios were prosthesis was made on Ti alloy coated with the same layer of composite material.

The Total Deformation distribution was similar with that encountered in Scenario 5, but the value of it was smaller. Like in the previous scenario, the maximum value and the distribution of the Equivalent Elastic Strain is comparable with the case of Ti alloy made prosthesis.

To summarize the results, Table 2 presents the maximum value and the location for Equivalent Stress (Von Mises), Total Deformation and Equivalent Elastic Strain, in the seven scenarios described above.

Table 2. Maximum values of mechanical parameters

Scenario		Equivalent Stress		Total Deformation		Equivalent Elastic Strain	
No.	Description	max. value [MPa]	localization	max. value [mm]	localization	max. value [mm/mm]	localization
S1	Humerus (H)	11,69	Medial Epicondyle	2,4222	Head	0,00082324	Medial Epicondyle
S2	H + Ti alloy prosthesis (TiP)	185,2	prosthesis proximal	1,7163	prosthesis head	0,0033365	bone-prosthesis interface
S3	H+TiP+Hydroxyapatite (HPA) 2 mm	167,34	prosthesis proximal	0,87227	prosthesis head	0,0014287	bone-prosthesis interface
S4	H+TiP+HPA 1mm + Colagen fibers (CF)1mm	297,19	prosthesis proximal	1,3527	prosthesis head	0,0038567	colagen layer
S5	H+TiP+composit material HPA and colagen(CM) 2mm	368,48	coating layer	0,54623	prosthesis head	0,00090898	bone-prosthesis interface
S6	H+Co alloy prosthesis (CoP) +HPA 1mm +CF 1mm	385,5	prosthesis porous layer	1,12	prosthesis head	0,0033706	colagen layer
S7	H+CoP+ CM 2mm	392,92	coating layer	0,49459	prosthesis head	0,00085113	Medial Epicondyle

Using collagen fibers as an interface between the prosthetic device and the bone increases the stress as can be observed in Fig. 11. This happens due to the mechanical properties of the collagen which are worse than those of the other components of the humerus-prosthesis assembly.

The Total deformation has a maximum in the healthy bone as can be observed in Fig.12. This means that from this point of view any solution described by the scenarios 2 to 7 is feasibleness. However the cobalt alloy prosthesis covered with composite material is recommended due to the smallest deformation encountered when the same forces was applied.

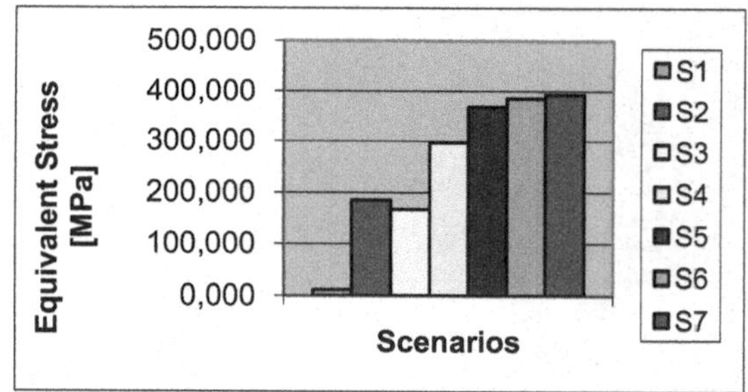

Figure 11 The maximum value of Equivalent Stress in the scenarios considered

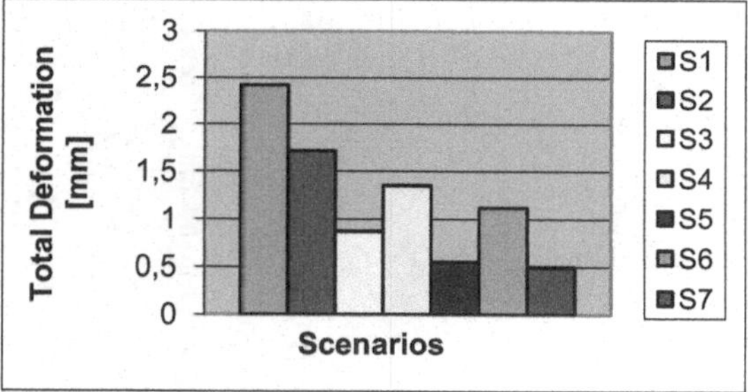

Figure 12 The maximum value of Total deformation in the scenarios considered

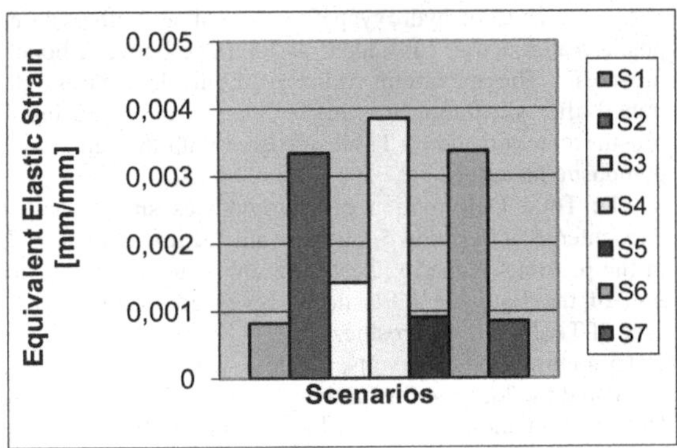

Figure 13 Maximum Equivalent Elastic Strain in the scenarios considered

Analyzing the values in Fig. 13 we can observe that the maximum equivalent elastic strain has comparable values for the healthy bone and the humerus-prosthesis assembly when the interface between bone and prosthesis is the composite material made of hydroxyapatite and collagen fibers.

IV. Conclusion

The developed models can be used to study mechanical phenomena in the bone-prosthesis assembly. These models are very important because they allow determining maximum values of parameters like tensile yield strength, compression yield strength, ultimate yield strength, etc. Making tests in vivo, is almost impossible because if they are not conducted very carefully they can generate harmful irreversible phenomena, i.e. breaking of the bone or prosthesis elements. By means of these models we can analyze different materials in a practical fashion and we can determine which solution is a best fit for a certain case.

One important characteristic of the models presented in this paper is their versatility. This is very important because of the variable dimensions and shape of the human humerus, which can vary from person to person.

Analyses presented in this paper revealed the fact that there is no ideal solution for prostheses coating.

Each solution has advantages and disadvantages, and the decision to choose a particular solution depends on factors related to patient and surgical conditions.

Using the models developed in this paper, it is also possible to analyze other materials.

We intend to analyze in the future materials like chitosan, which is used as interface between prosthesis device and the bone.

References

[1] R. Oosterom, F.C.T. van der Helm, J.L. Herder, H.E.N. Bersee, "Analytical study of the joint translational stiffness in total shoulder arthroplasty", The 4th Meeting of the international shoulder group, Cleveland, OH, 2002.

[2] I. Wakabayashi, E. Itoi, H. Sano, Y. Shibya, R. Sashi, H. Minagawa, "Mechanical environment of the supraspinatus tendon: A two dimensional finite element model analysis", Journal Shoulder Elbow Surgery, Vol 12, pp. 612-617, 2003.

[3] R.E. Debski, J.A. Weiss, W.J. Newman, S.M. Moore, P.J. McMahon, Stress and strain in the anterior band of the inferior glenohumeral ligament during a simulated clinical examination, Journal Shoulder Elbow Surgery, Vol 14, Issue 1, Suppl 1 , pp. S24-S31, 2005.

[4] ****, Zimmer M/L taper hip prosthesis with kinectiv technology, Zimmer. Inc. 2007.

[5] A. Borzacchiello, L. Ambrosio, L. Nicolais, E. J. Harper, K. E. Tanner, W. Bonfield, Journal of Materials Science-Materials in Medicine 9, pp. 835-838, 1998.

[6] A. Odgaard, , F. Linde, The underestimation of Young's modulus in compressive testing of cancellous bone specimens, Journal of Biomechanics 24, pp. 691-698, 1991.

[7] D. E. Grenoble, J. L. Katz, K. L. Dunn, R. S. Gilmore, K. L. Murty The elastic properties of hard tissues and apatites, J. Biomed. Mater. Res., 6(3), pp. 221-223, 1972.

[8] R. Martens, R. Van Audekercke, P. Delport, P. Demeester, J. C. Mullier, The mechanical characteristics of cancellous bone at the upper femoral region, Journal of Biomechanics 16, pp. 971-983, 1983.

[9] B. K. Hoffmeister, D. P. Johnson, J. A. Janeski, D. A. Keedy, B. W. Steinert, A.M. Viano, S.C. Kaste, Ultrasonic characterization of human cancellous bone in vitro using three different apparent backscatter parameters in the frequency range 0.6-15.0 MHz, IEEE Transactions on ultrasonics, ferroelectrics, and frequency control, vol. 55, no. 7, 2008.

[10] S. Pal, Mechanical properties of human bone, Biomechanics, Ed. John Wiley and sons, New Delhi, 1989.

[11] O. Babushkin, T. Linback, A. Holmgren, J. Li, L. Hermansson, Thermal expansion of hot isostatically pressed hydroxyapatite, Journal of Material and Chemistry, pp. 413, 1994.

Chaos-Based Bit Planes Image Encryption

Jiri Giesl
Department of Applied Informatics
Tomas Bata University
Nad Stranemi 4511, Zlin 760 05, Czech Republic
jgiesl@fai.utb.cz

Tomas Podoba
Department of Applied Informatics
Tomas Bata University
Nad Stranemi 4511, Zlin 760 05, Czech Republic
podoba@fai.utb.cz

Karel Vlcek
Department of Applied Informatics
Tomas Bata University
Nad Stranemi 4511, Zlin 760 05, Czech Republic
vlcek@fai.utb.cz

***Abstract*— Bit planes of discrete signal can be used not only for encoding or compressing, but also for encrypting purposes. This paper investigates composition of bit planes of an image and their utilization in the encryption process. Proposed encryption scheme is based on chaotic maps of Peter de Jong and it is designed for image signals primarily. Positions of all components of bit planes are permutated according to chaotic behaviour of Peter de Jong's system.**

I. Introduction

Many areas of research presume possibility of prediction and repetition of experiments. However, there were found very simple deterministic systems which cannot be predicted nor repeated. Even a minimal divergence in initial conditions or control parameters can cause a large scale alternations and different outcome of those systems. Chaos theory belongs to the field of nonlinear dynamics, which is part of dynamical systems. There are exist two types of dynamical systems – stochastic and deterministic. When the system is described by mathematic formulas, chaotic behaviour of that system is called as deterministic chaos. Dynamical systems are very often expressed by discrete maps or differential equations which represent behaviour of system in short time period. These systems produce chaotic behaviour but they are still deterministic, thus they can be utilized in many science disciplines. One of these disciplines is cryptography. Simple chaotic system can be used for design of cryptographic system with very efficient properties and resistance against unauthorized reading and some types of attack.

During the past decade a large number of chaos-based encryption systems have been proposed. Some schemes are based on generation of the encryption key [1,2] which is then used for the rearranging and modifying pixels of an image. Other algorithms uses two-dimensional maps, because of two-dimensional character of an image [3,4], or S-box algebraic operations [5,6]. Most of those schemes belong to the block ciphers; only a few of them were designed as stream ciphers [7] which provide efficient way for the real-time processing.

In our previous research work, we proposed an image encryption scheme [8] with high security. That algorithm lies in permutation of pixels positions and modification of their values done by XOR operation. Modification of values is necessary because pure position permutation is not sufficient in terms of security. That process can be revealed by the system of fuzzy ergodic matrices very easily [9]. However, bit planes offer new way of encrypting – permutation of positions of components among bit planes can replace modification process. The main purpose of this work is to propose encryption scheme without XOR operation.

The remainder of this paper is organized as follows. Section 2 provides methods used for the encryption purposes. Section 3 presents the experimental results and some security analyses. In Section 4 the performance of proposed scheme is evaluated and finally Section 5 concludes this paper.

II. Methods

A. *Chaos and strange attractors*

The behaviour of the chaotic dynamical system takes place to a set of states, which is called an attractor. There are several types of an attractor – a point, a curve, a manifold or a complicated set with a fractal structure which is called strange attractor [12]. The fixed points of strange attractor are locally unstable but the system is globally stable. Strange attractors can be generated in several ways such as by quadratic (1) or trigonometric (2) maps. Control parameters a,b,c,d,e,f,g,h,i,j,k,l define behaviour of the chaotic system.

$$\begin{aligned} x_{n+1} &= a+b\cdot x_n+c\cdot x_n^2+d\cdot x_n y_n+e\cdot y_n+f\cdot y_n^2 \\ y_{n+1} &= g+h\cdot x_n+i\cdot x_n^2+j\cdot x_n y_n+k\cdot y_n+l\cdot y_n^2 \end{aligned} \qquad (1)$$

T. Sobh, K. Elleithy (eds.), *Innovations in Computing Sciences and Software Engineering*,
DOI 10.1007/978-90-481-9112-3_59,

$$x_{n+1} = a \cdot \sin(b \cdot y_n) + c \cdot \cos(d \cdot x_n)$$
$$y_{n+1} = e \cdot \sin(f \cdot y_n) + g \cdot \cos(h \cdot x_n) \quad (1)$$

Strange attractor can be revealed after several iterations of a map (1) or (2). When the strange attractor is represented geometrically, it is obvious that fixed points are locally unstable but the system is globally stable.

Necessary condition of the chaotic behaviour of the strange attractor is that the Lyapunov exponent of one map is positive and the magnitude of the negative exponent hat to be greater than the positive one. The positive exponent corresponds to the expansion; the negative exponent corresponds to the contraction of the system.

Suppose that $x_{n+1} = f(x)$. The Lyapunov exponent Λ is then determined as (3).

$$\Lambda = \lim_{n \Rightarrow \infty} \left(\frac{1}{n} \cdot \sum_{i=0}^{n-1} \ln |f'(x_i)| \right) \quad (3)$$

Strange attractors are markedly patterned, having fixed geometric structures, despite the fact that the trajectories moving within them appear unpredictable. One of the strange attractors with predefined control parameters is shown in Figure 1. This attractor was found by Peter de Jong and this dynamical system is used for the encryption purposes in our algorithms.

Figure 1. Example of Peter de Jong attractor

B. Bit planes

Decomposition of an image into different planes (bit planes) plays an important role in image processing. The most useful area is image compression, where some planes can be suppressed and then preserved planes may be used in conjunction to create compressed image.

It is possible to decompose an image into 8 planes, if an 8-bit image is at the disposal. Significance of planes rises with the index of that plane. Plane indexed as 0 contains the least significant bit (LSB) of pixels; otherwise plane indexed as 7 contains the most significant bit (MSB). Figure 2 shows decomposition of an image into 8 different bit planes.

Figure 2. Decomposition of an image into bit planes

C. Image encryption scheme

Suppose the three-dimensional matrix P which contains the bit values $p_{x,y,z} \in P$ of an image, where $x \in (0,1,2,...W)$ and $y \in (0,1,2,...H)$, W and H represents the width and the height of the matrix/image and $z \in (0,1,2,...7)$ represents index of the plane. Components $p_{x,y,z}$ of the bit planes are the input data for the encryption algorithm.

Chaotic system of Peter de Jong is used for the encryption purposes here. Original chaotic system consists of two maps, which can be used for the positions permutation. However, matrix has three-dimensional character; hence the chaotic system has to be extended to 3D version (4). Third map can be used for the positions permutation among bit planes.

$$x_{n+1} = \sin(a \cdot y_n) - \cos(b \cdot x_n)$$
$$y_{n+1} = \sin(c \cdot y_n) - \cos(d \cdot x_n) \quad (4)$$
$$z_{n+1} = \sin(e \cdot z_n) - \cos(f \cdot y_n)$$

Idea of the encryption process is to encrypt each bit component separately. The control parameters a,b,c,d,e,f in the chaotic system (4) play the role of the encryption keys here. Define b_A as the bit component at coordinates (x_x, y_y, z_z). Positions x_x, y_y and z_z are put into (4) as initial conditions of the appropriate maps. Resultant values x_k, y_k and z_k are at the disposal after k-th iteration of the chaotic system and the quantization of the resultant values. The second bit component b_B at coordinates (x_k, y_k, z_k) must be found. The component b_B is then swapped with the component b_A as illustrated in Figure 3.

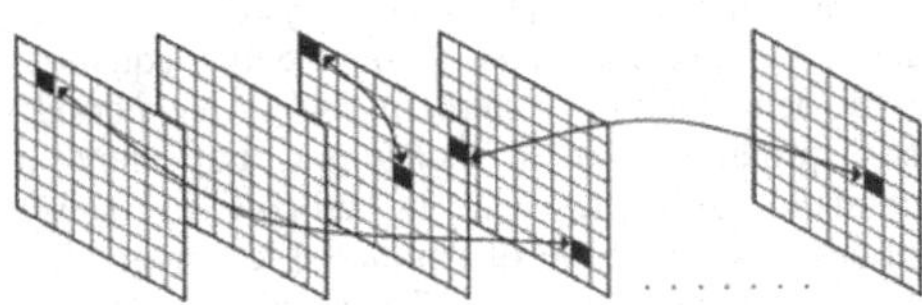

Figure 3. Swapping of components among bit planes

This process must be done for every bit component in the matrix P and can be done m times in order to increase the security of encrypted image. Flowchart of the encryption process is drawn in the Figure 4.

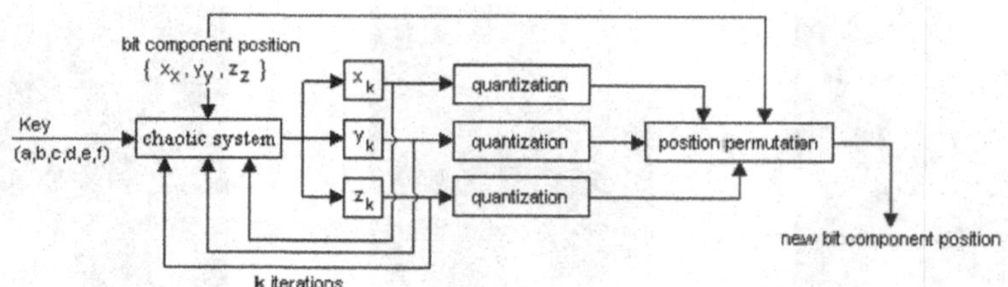

Figure 4. Flowchart of the encryption process

III. Experimental Results And Security Analyses

The encryption scheme described above was experimentally tested on some images of 256x256 pixels size. Original images were encrypted by the keys (6). These keys are the control parameters of the chaotic system.

$$\{a = 1.4, b = -2.3, c = -2.4, d = -2.1, e = 1.2, f = 1.6\} \quad (6)$$

The encrypted image was then decrypted by the keys (7). First control parameter has a minimal divergence from that parameter in (6).

$$\{a = 1.40001, b = -2.3, c = -2.4, d = -2.1, e = 1.2, f = 1.6\} \quad (7)$$

Figure 5 and Figure 7 shows original, encrypted and incorrectly decrypted image and Figure 6 and Figure 8 shows distribution of pixel values of appropriate image. It is obvious that distribution of pixels of original images was significantly modified and original images become illegible. Figure 5(c) and Figure 7(c) illustrates that even a slight change in decryption keys will cause illegibility and indeterminateness of the reconstructed image. That is the greatest contribution of encryption schemes based on chaos.

The similarity between the original image and its encrypted form can be proof of efficient confusion and diffusion properties of this encryption scheme. That similarity can be expressed by the cross-correlation. Cross-correlation is a standard method of estimating the degree to which two series are correlated. Consider two series x_i and y_i where $i = 1,2,\ldots,N$ and $E(x)$, $E(y)$ are the means of the corresponding series according to (8).

$$E(x) = \frac{1}{N} \cdot \sum_{i=1}^{N} x_i \quad (8)$$

The cross correlation r at delay d is defined as:

$$r(d) = \frac{\sum_i (x_i - E(x)) \cdot (y_{i-d} - E(y))}{\sqrt{\sum_i (x_i - E(x))^2} \cdot \sqrt{\sum_i (y_{i-d} - E(y))^2}} \quad (9)$$

Cross-correlation can be used as a measure of similarity of two images that differ only by a shift. Cross-correlation was computed from the delay $d = 0$ to $d = 127$. The denominator in the expression (9) normalizes the correlation coefficients such that $-1 \le r(d) \le 1$. This bound indicates maximum correlation and $r(d) = 0$ indicates no correlation. A high negative correlation indicates a high correlation in the case of inversion of one of the series [13].

Figure 9 shows cross-correlation of original "Lena" image and its encrypted form and Figure 10 cross-correlation of encrypted image and incorrectly decrypted image by keys (7). It is obvious that correlation value does not exceed ±0.01. That means very low correlation and very low similarity of the images.

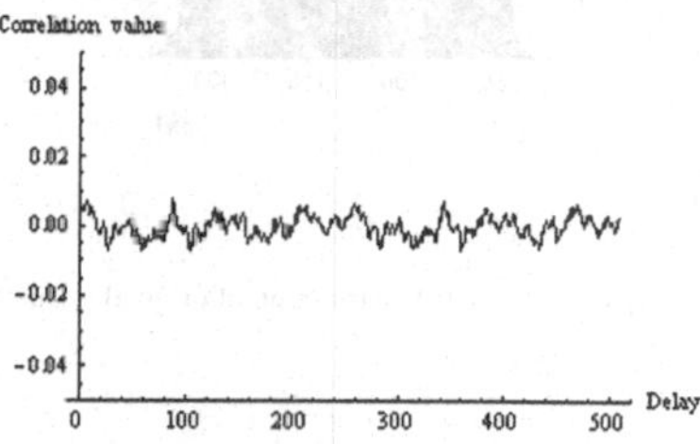

Figure 9. Cross correlation of original and encrypted image

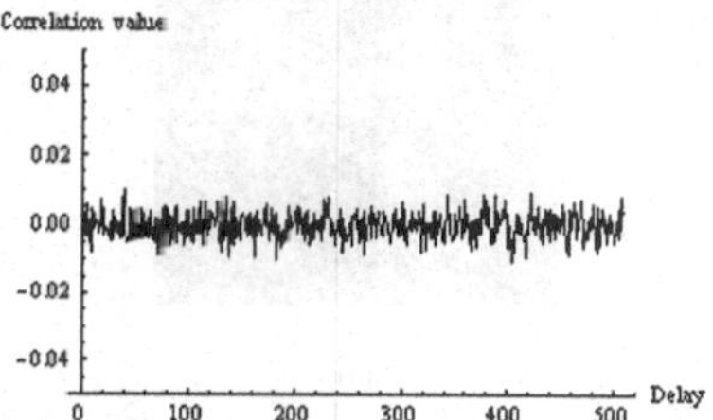

Figure 10. Cross correlation of encrypted and incorrectly decrypted image

In general, adjacent pixels of the most plain-images are highly correlated. One of the requirements of an effective image encryption process is to generate encrypted image with low correlation of adjacent pixels. Correlation between two horizontally, vertically and diagonally adjacent pixels of the original and the encrypted image was analyzed. Each pair of adjacent pixels of the original image was chosen and correlation coefficient was computed according (9). Then the same process was done for the encrypted image. Correlation coefficients in different directions of adjacent pixels are listed in Table 1.

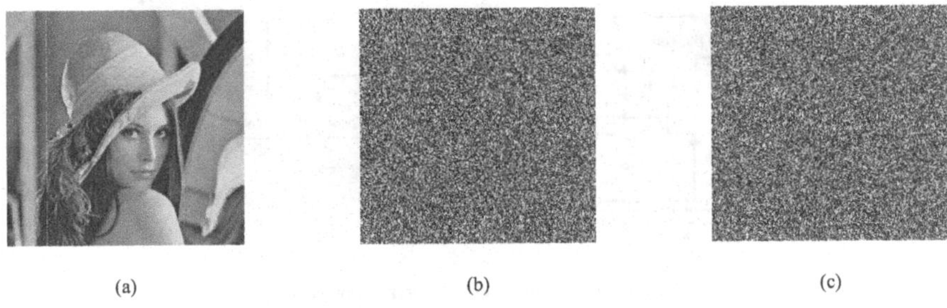

(a) (b) (c)

Figure 5. (a) original "Lena" image, (b) encrypted image, (c) incorrectly decrypted image

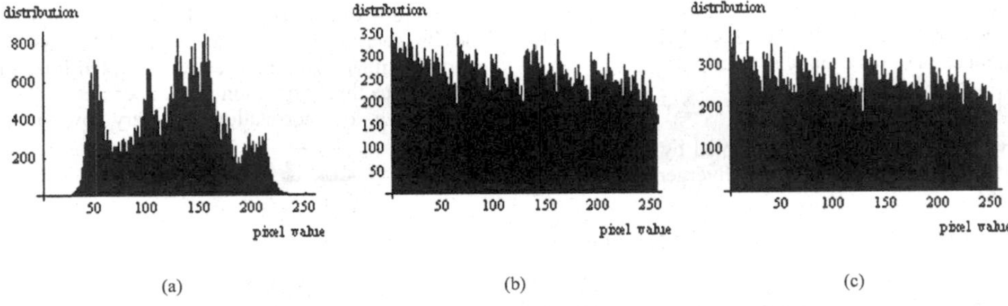

(a) (b) (c)

Figure 6. (a) distribution of original image, (b) distribution of encrypted image, (c) distribution of incorrectly decrypted image

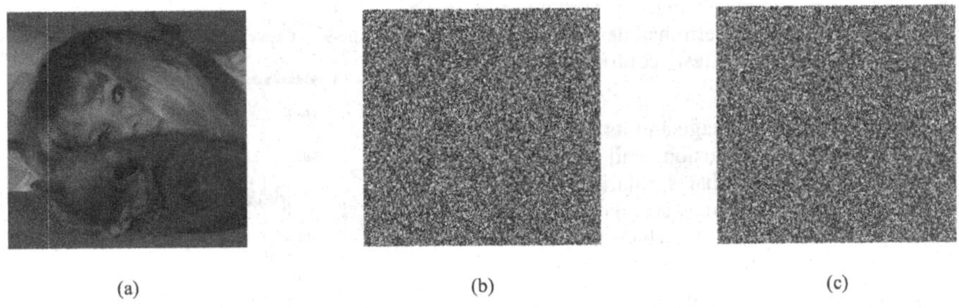

(a) (b) (c)

Figure 7. (a) original "Petra" image, (b) encrypted image, (c) incorrectly decrypted image

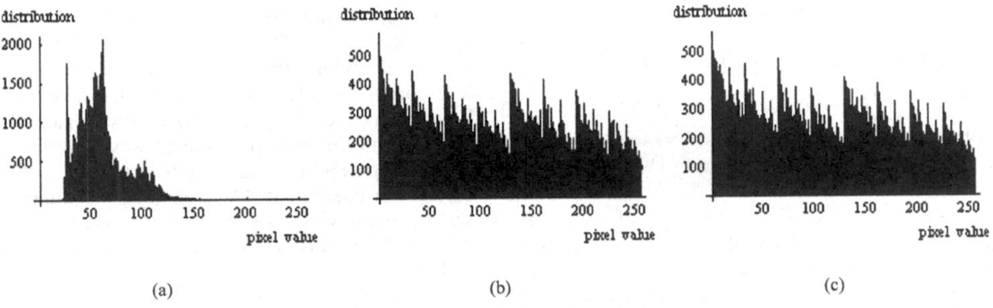

(a) (b) (c)

Figure 8. (a) distribution of original image, (b) distribution of encrypted image, (c) distribution of incorrectly decrypted image

TABLE I. CORRELATION COEFFICIENTS OF ORIGINAL/ECRYPTED IMAGE

Direction of adjacent components	Original image	Encrypted image	Encrypted image by [8]	Encrypted image by [10]	Encrypted image by [11]
Horizontal	0.942755	0.000693	0.001522	0.005776	-0.014200
Vertical	0.970970	-0.001209	0.001866	0.028434	-0.007400
Diagonal	0.920081	0.003781	-0.003903	0.020662	-0.018300

As can be seen, every encryption scheme [8,10,11] can effectively de-correlate adjacent pixels in the original image. The correlation coefficients are very low when the proposed encryption scheme is used. Thus, proposed scheme has efficient permutation and diffusion properties.

Sensitivity of decryption keys is very high as it was shown in Figure 7. This statement can be proved from the cross correlation view by simple experiment. Take parameter a of decryption keys (7) and compute cross-correlation values between original and decrypted bit plane from $a = 1.399999999$ to $a = 1.400000001$ by step 0.000000000001. It is obvious that the cross correlation will be maximal when the parameter is set to $a = 1.4$ (this value is correct). Figure 11 shows dependency of correlation values on different values of parameter a. The peak located in the middle of the plot signifies correct value of the parameter a and thus maximal correlation between original and decrypted bit plane (this peak reaches value 1, which is beyond the figure).

However, correlations are very low when other values from the interval of the parameter are used. Only if we are getting very close to that correct value, the correlations are ascended suspiciously. However, they are still very low. This experiment shows that even close neighbourhood of the correct decryption key cannot reconstruct bit plane neither to its approximately form.

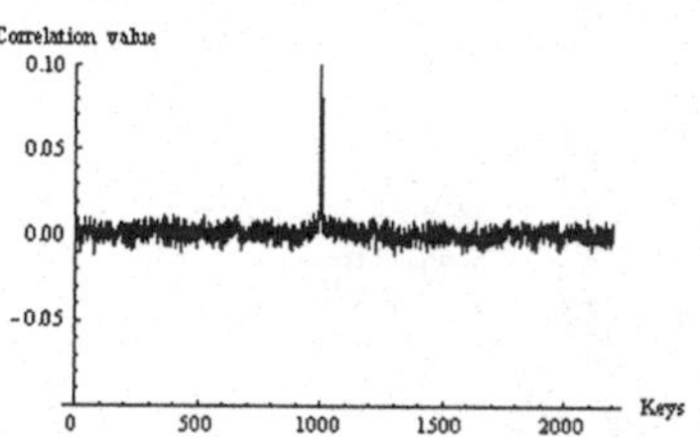

Figure 11. Cross correlation of original and decrypted coefficients by different keys

IV. CONCLUSION

Proposed encryption scheme uses decomposition of an image into bit planes. These bit planes are then encrypted by the chaotic system of Peter de Jong. Coordinates of components of bit planes become initial conditions of the appropriate map of chaotic system. Coordinates are permutated after several iterations of that system; however bits themselves are not modified directly. Modification of them lies in the permutation of bits among bit planes and pixel values of an image are changed in that way. Cross-correlation analysis shows that this encryption algorithm is sufficient for the practical usage in terms of security, especially for the archiving and storage purposes.

ACKNOWLEDGMENT

We would like to thank Petra Stalmachova for providing her photo and Pavel Ondrusz for the aid with graphic work on some figures.

REFERENCES

[1] Fu, Ch., Zhang, Z., Chen, Z., Wang, X. An Improved Chaos-Based Image Encryption Scheme. ICCS 2007, Springer-Verlag, Berlin, 2007.

[2] Fu, Ch., Zhang, Z., Cao, Y. An Improved Image Encryption Algorithm Based on Chaotic Maps. ICNC 2007.

[3] Mao, Y., Chen, G. Chaos-Based Image Encryption. Springer-Verlag, Berlin, 2003.

[4] Zhai, Y., Lin, S., Zhang, Q. Improving Image Encryption Using Multi-chaotic Map, Workshop on Power Electronics and Intelligent Transportationi System, 2008.

[5] He, X., Zhu, Q., Gu, P. A New Chaos-Based Encryption Method for Color Image, Springer-Verlag, Berlin, 2006.

[6] Asim, M., Jeoti, V. Hybrid Chaotic Image Encryption Scheme based on S-box and Ciphertext Feedback. ICIAS 2007.

[7] Hossam, A., Hamdy, K., Osama, A. An Efficient Chaos-Based Feedback Stream Cipher (ECBFSC) for Image Encryption and Decryption. Informatica 31, 2007.

[8] Giesl, J., Vlcek, K., Image Encryption Based on Strange Attractor, ICGST-GVIP Journal. 2009, vol. 9, is. 2, pp. 19-26. ISSN 1687-398.

[9] Zhao., X-y., Chen, G., Zhang, D., Wang, X-h., Dong, G-c. Decryption of pure-position permutation algorithms. JZUS, Hangzhou, 2004.

[10] Mao, Y., Chen, G. Chaos-Based Image Encryption. Springer-Verlag, Berlin, 2003.

[11] Gao, T., Chen, Z. A new image encryption algorithm based on hyper-chaos, ScienceDirect, 2007.

[12] Sprott, J.C. Chaos and Time-Series Analysis, Oxford University Press, 2003, ISBN 978-0-19-850840-3.

[13] Bourke, P. Cross Correlation [online]. Available at WWW: http://local.wasp.uwa.edu.au/~pbourke/miscellaneous/correlate/ , 2006.

FLEX: A Modular Software Architecture for Flight License Exam

Taner Arsan, Hamit Emre Saka, Ceyhun Sahin
Kadir Has University
Department of Computer Engineering
Cibali 34230 Istanbul, Turkey

Abstract - **This paper is about the design and implementation of an examination system based on World Wide Web. It is called FLEX-Flight License Exam Software. We designed and implemented flexible and modular software architecture. The implemented system has basic specifications such as appending questions in system, building exams with these appended questions and making students to take these exams. There are three different types of users with different authorizations. These are system administrator, operators and students. System administrator operates and maintains the system, and also audits the system integrity. The system administrator can not be able to change the result of exams and can not take an exam. Operator module includes instructors. Operators have some privileges such as preparing exams, entering questions, changing the existing questions and etc. Students can log on the system and can be accessed to exams by a certain URL. The other characteristic of our system is that operators and system administrator are not able to delete questions due to the security problems. Exam questions can be inserted on their topics and lectures in the database. Thus; operators and system administrator can easily choose questions. When all these are taken into consideration, FLEX software provides opportunities to many students to take exams at the same time in safe, reliable and user friendly conditions. It is also reliable examination system for the authorized aviation administration companies. Web development platform – LAMP; Linux, Apache web server, MySQL, Object-oriented scripting Language – PHP are used for developing the system and page structures are developed by Content Management System – CMS.**

I. Introduction

Private pilot license examinations are very important issues in civil airways companies. There are a lot of payloads and overheads such as registering students in to the classrooms, preparing the examinations by selecting most convenient question types, managing the operators, students, instructors and also the whole program. On the other hand, the people who want to have a flight license are responsible to find a way to prepare themselves to the flight license examination as FAA Private Pilot Written Exam in the US or Turkish Airlines Flight License Examination in Turkey. In general, airways companies use traditional methods to prepare the questions and to manage all the exam procedures. On the other hand, civil airways academy needs information management software, but unfortunately the cost of such software is extremely high and it is not easy to integrate such software to their system.

In this paper, modular software architecture [1,2] for Flight License Exam (FLEX) is introduced as a total solution for airways companies. This system is also a successful application of LAMP architecture and Content Management Systems (CMS) for commonly used traditional methods. All software tools and platforms including operating system are open source and free of charge. On the other hand, FLEX software only needs a web browser with JavaScript support on the client side. The details of the modules are given in Section II. The rest of this paper is organized as follows. In Section III, the reasons of why a company prefer FLEX. We introduce the technologies of FLEX; LAMP choice and CMS in Section IV and we give complete system architecture of FLEX software in Section V. We conclude the paper with research contributions in Section VI.

II. A Modular Software Architecture for Proposed Flight License Exam FLEX System

FLEX is modular and flexible software architecture for flight license examination and it is introduced as a total solution for airways companies. FLEX includes common and company oriented modules such as user management, department management, lecture management, topic management, registration management, question management, and examination management. These modules have interconnection with each other and have to work efficiently to compose an examination which is the main goal of the system. There are three types of user in FLEX Software. These are System Administrator, Operator and Student as shown in Fig.1.

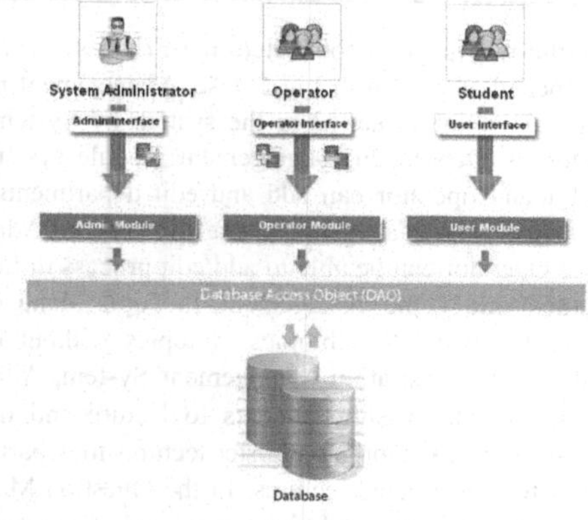

Fig.1. Modules of FLEX System

T. Sobh, K. Elleithy (eds.), *Innovations in Computing Sciences and Software Engineering*,
DOI 10.1007/978-90-481-9112-3_60, © Springer Science+Business Media B.V. 2010

System Administrator can add a new user (student and operator), edit an existing user, add/edit department, add/edit lecture, add/edit topic, register lecture to department, register topic to lecture, register student to lecture, add/edit question and add/edit exam. The only difference between system administrator and operator is in adding new user part. Operator can only add student to the system. Students can only take exams from their own account as usual. Account types and privileges are shown in Table I.

TABLE I
ACCOUNT TYPE AND PRIVILEGES

PROCESS DESCRIPTION	ACCOUNT TYPE		
	ADMIN	OPERATOR	STU.
Create New Account	+	-	-
Create New Account Type	+	-	-
Activate/Deactivate User Accounts	+	-	-
Authorizing/Authority Management	+	-	-
Create New Class	+	+	-
Change Class Specs	+	+	-
Change Class Capacity	+	+	-
Create New Process	+	-	-
Change Existing Process	+	-	-
Register Student to a Class	+	+	-
Create Category / Sub Category	+	+	-
Create New Topic / Sub Topic	+	+	-
Change Existing Topic Explanation	+	+	-
Change Relations between Topics	+	+	-
Create Exam	-	+	-
Change Type of Existing Exam	-	+	-
Change Category of Existing Exam	-	+	-
Create Question	-	+	-
Change type of Question	-	+	-
Change related type of Question	-	+	-
Change Difficulty Level of the Question	-	+	-
Activate / Deactivate the Question	-	+	-
Create the Answer	-	+	-
Change the type of Existing Answer	-	+	-
Change the spec of Existing Answer	-	+	-
Create Exam by Existing Questions	-	+	-
Take Assessment	-	-	+
Create Student Report	-	+	+

When the web page is connected, the FLEX system login page is opened as shown in Fig.2. User Management makes students and operators added to the system by System Administrator. In Department Management module system administrator and operator can add and edit departments. Not only in Department Management, but also System Administrator and Operator can be able to add/edit process in Lecture Management and Topic management. In Topic Management module user can create subtopics of topics without limits. Furthermore in Registration Management System, Administrator and Operator assign students to lecture and departments, also Administrator can register lectures to departments and topics to their related lectures. In the Question Management module, System Administrator and Operator can add/edit questions to system's topics and subtopics optionally. System does not consist of basic question types. System allows you to choose multiple choices, multiple select and true/false questions. The other module of our system, Examination Management is a module where System Administrator or Operator creates and edits exams. Optionally, system administrator or operator can create exams in two ways; automatically and manually. If system administrator or operator wants to create examination automatically, choosing the topics and subtopics of lectures is adequate. The system develops exams surely. In manually, System Administrator or Operator has to choose questions.

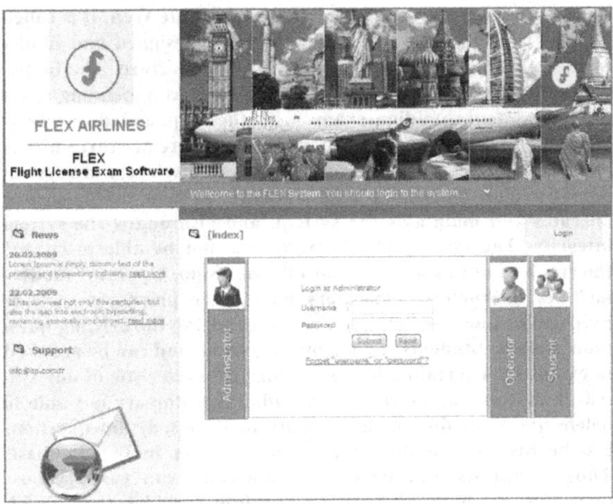

Fig.2. FLEX System Login Page.

On the other hand, our systems most powerful user, students, they can take exams easily which assigned by System Administrator and Operators. After examination, students can see their results immediately. Also, the system reports the results of examination to the System Administrator and Operator.

Furthermore, it is not important to forget password in our system, with two click and users own registered mail address, they can reach their new passwords and user can change their password whether they want.

When all these are taken in to consideration, our examination system makes developing online exams easy and secure.

III. WHY FLEX SYSTEM SHOULD BE PREFERRED

There are numerous factors making FLEX system preferable. These factors are security, modularity, flexibility, being user friendly and being web based.

A. Security

There are numerous security vulnerabilities in the systems that are used in the market. All of the security arrangements known and often used have been applied to the every part of the system from beginning to end. Security processes and character restrictions have been done for all the input fields (to block methods like SQL injection.). On the stage of recording important data such as code, MD5 encryption has been used. Besides, for all the processes that have been done on the system controls are provided both on the client and server side.

B. Modularity

Our system consists of a modular structure. This modular structure provides facilities such as adding new properties to the system and changing it arbitrary.

C. Flexibility

Proposed and implemented system has a flexible structure. So that it can be adapted to every type of industrial applications. The other advantage of the system is to be developable and modifiable.

D. User Friendly

Although the implementation of the system is not an easy task and therefore it is a huge software architecture, it is user friendly, so that means it can be used easily.

E. Web based

In contrast to the most of the desktop application systems used in the market our system is web based. Our system is also supported by Internet Explorer and Firefox. The other advantage is you don't have to download anything to your company's computer when you are using FLEX. You can reach to system from Internet and control it.

IV. FLEX TECHNOLOGIES

We are implementing our projects on open source software platform known as the LAMP architecture [10]. The LAMP architecture has become very popular as a way of deploying inexpensive, scalable, secure web applications [11].

A. LAMP Architecture

As shown in Fig.3, LAMP is an open source Web development platform that uses Linux as operating system, Apache as Web server, MySQL as relational database management system and PHP as the object-oriented scripting language (Sometimes Perl or Python is used instead of PHP). This combination of software allows one to build and customize a

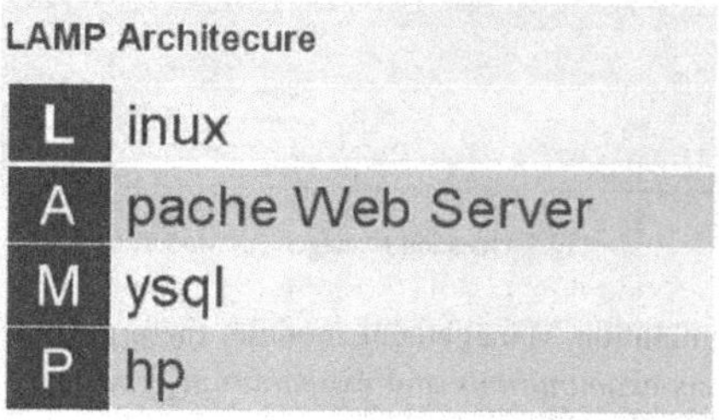

LAMP Architecure

L inux

A pache Web Server

M ysql

P hp

Fig.3. LAMP Architecture.

high performance and cutting edge web server. All that is required is a decent computer and a willingness to learn.

Linux is an open source and constantly evolving operating system which allows the administrator full control over almost every system aspect. In recent years, Linux has proven itself to be a production level competitor in the OS world. Popular choices for the Linux distribution are Red Hat, Debian, and Slackware.

Apache 1.3.x, a powerful and well documented webserver application, handles the actual web page serving [3]. Everything you see in your web browser came from the Apache webserver. Although Apache 2.0 is available for use, Apache 1.3.x is still the standard for LAMP servers. With internals that have been tested and perfected, Apache 1.3.x proves to be the best WWW server available today.

MySQL is a database server that holds content for many things. For example, one could store website member information in a MySQL database for use on a website. A database server allows a webmaster to keep data organized and accessible. Database driven websites are now becoming more prevalent as users demand dynamic and customizable websites. The most popular open source database server is MySQL [4, 5].

PHP is a relatively new server side programming language which allows webmasters to easily add dynamic pages to their website [6-9]. PHP is extremely versatile, as it can do everything from printing database data to a webpage to declaring browser cookies. Bear in mind all of these applications are open source and free for your use - you are free to experiment and modify."

The key to the idea behind LAMP, a term originally coined by Michael Kunze in the German magazine in 1998, is the use of these items together. Although not actually designed to work together, these open source software alternatives are readily and freely available as each of the components in the LAMP stack is an example of Free or Open Source Software (FOSS).

LAMP has become a development standard [10-13]. Today, the products that make up the LAMP stack are included by default in nearly all Linux distributions, and together they make a powerful web application platform. Because the platform has four layers, LAMP is sometimes referred to as a LAMP stack. Stacks can be built on different operating systems. Developers that use these tools with a Windows operating system instead of Linux are said to be using WAMP; with a Macintosh system, MAMP; and with a Solaris system, SAMP.

B. CMS - Content Management System

We have developed page structures by content management system. By using only a single index.php file we have enhanced all pages on it. Because of this feature, we have had to account for creating extra codes for the invariable parts of every page. We implement this application by dividing the page into two main pieces as top and main. And by making changes in the index.php file, for every page, in the top or main parts, we have created new pages. Now it is time to explain what content management system is. Firstly we start with what content is. Content is in essence, any type or unit of digital information. It can be text, images, graphics, video, sound, documents, records etc or anything that is likely to be managed in an electronic format. Content Management is effectively the management of the content described above, by combining rules, process and/or workflows in such a way that it's electronic storage is deemed to be 'managed' rather than 'unmanaged'.

CMS is a computer application used to create, edit, manage, search and publish various kinds of digital media and electronic text.

CMS is frequently used for storing, controlling, versioning, and publishing industry-specific documentation such as news articles, operators' manuals, technical manuals, sales guides, and marketing brochures. The content managed may include computer files, image media, audio files, video files, electronic documents, and Web content. These concepts represent integrated and interdependent layers. There are various nomenclatures known in this area: Web Content Management, Digital Asset Management, Digital Records Management, Electronic Content Management and so on. The bottom line for these systems is managing content and publishing, with a workflow if required.

V. Complete System Architecture of FLEX

In this paper, our goal is to design and implement a modular and flexible software architecture system for flight license examination. Our design goals are to provide fast reliable, safe examination system, to compete with our rivals, to provide the best web based examination system, to reduce complexity of similar examination systems in the market, to obtain 100% customer satisfaction, to assure ease of access due to web based applications, to provide best software state of the art, to develop a flexible application that can be easily improved, and to develop a user friendly software application.

Implemented software includes modules such as user management, department management, lecture management, topic management, registration management, question management, and examination management as shown in Fig.4.

In User Management module, there are two entities such as *account_types* that is used to store and manage the account types and *users* entity that is used to store and manage the user accounts and the relevant information. Authorizing can be handled in two different ways: a user's authorities/privileges also can be defined, even if it is defined by the account type.

In Department Management module, there is an entity called as *departments* and that is used to store and manage the departments and the relevant information.

In Lecture Management module, there is an entity called as *lectures* and that is used to store and manage the lectures and the relevant information. This module can be interpreted as course management module as in the traditional course management.

In Topic Management module, there is an entity called as *topics* and that is used to store and manage the topics and the relevant information.In Registration Management module, there are several entities such as *r_topics_to_lectures that is used to assign the topics to the related lectures, r_lectures_to_department that is used to assign the lectures to the related departments, r_students_to_departments and r_students_to_lectures,* that are used to register the students to the departments or the lectures.

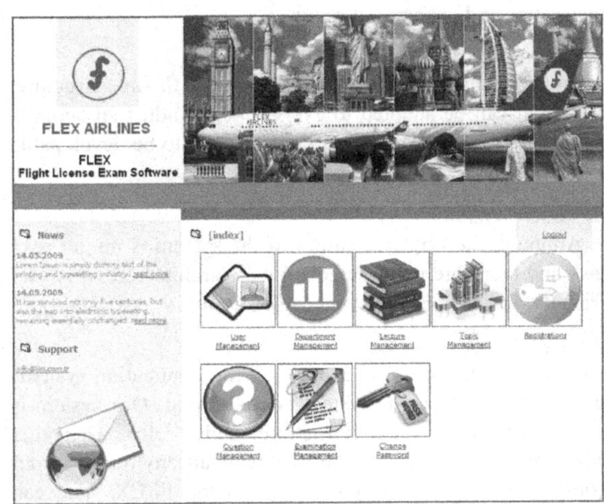

Fig.4. FLEX System Main Menu.

In Question Management module, there are two entities such as *questions entity* that is used to store and manage the questions and relevant information and *question_types that is used to define question types*. Question Management is one of the most important modules in FLEX system, because preparing questions is the main goal of this software. Question Management module of FLEX system is shown in Fig.5.

Question Management

1st Filter: Last added 25 Topics || All Topics
2nd Filter: All || Active || Deactive || Locked

ID	Name	Description	Status
91	Technique	Urgency Procedures	Active
90	[illegible]	Urgency Procedures	Active
89	Standard words and phrases	General Operating Procedures II	Active
88	Transmission technique	General Operating Procedures II	Active
87	Transmission of time	General Operating Procedures	Active
86	Transmission of numbers (including level information)	General Operating Procedures	Active
85	Transmission of letters	General Operating Procedures	Active
84	Categories of messages	Introduction to VFR Communications	Active
83	Q-code groups commonly used in RTF air-ground communications	Introduction to VFR Communications	Active
82	Air Traffic Services abbreviations	Introduction to VFR Communications	Active

Fig.5. Question Management Module.

In Examination Management module, there are three entities such as *examinations* and *examination_types* that are the entities that all of the information related with examinations are stored in, and *examination_results* that is used to store the answers given by the students and their results with the related examinations. Examination Management is another most important module in FLEX system. Examination Management module of FLEX system is shown in Fig.6.

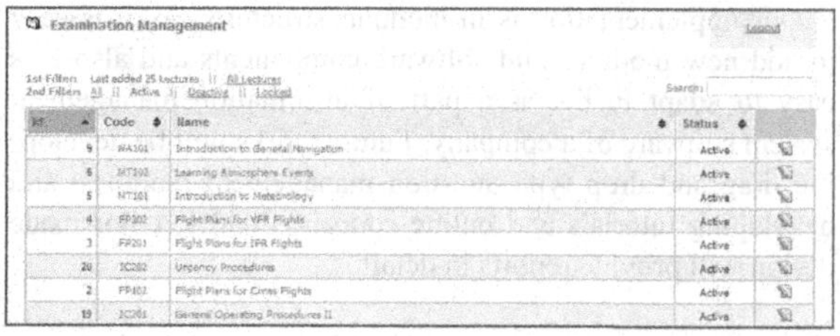

Fig.6.Examination Management Module.

There are also two entities which are related with CMS in the system: *pages* and *displayxref*. *Pages* entity is used to define the pages and the page structures, and *displayxref* is used to relating page-parts to pages.

Entity-Relationship diagram of the system or in other words "Complete Software Architecture Diagram of the System" is given in Fig.7.

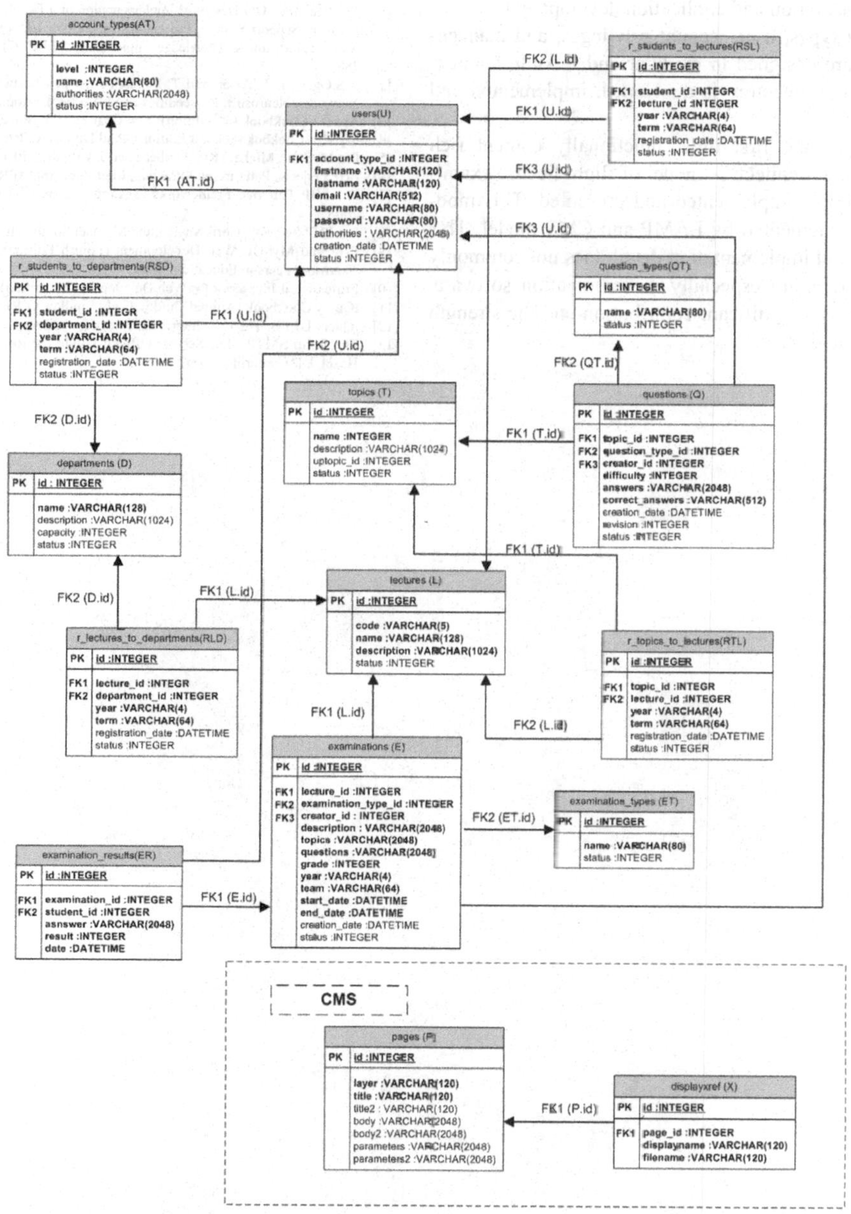

Fig.7. Entity-Relationship Diagram of Flight License Exam – FLEX System.

VI. CONCLUSIONS

In this paper, Modular software architecture for Flight License Exam (FLEX) is proposed, developed, implemented and presented in detail as a total solution. We believe to have successfully applied the current object-oriented software engineering principles, techniques and methodology to implement a ***flight license exam software architecture***.

LAMP architecture and Content Management System is used for implementation and application development.

User account types, user account privileges, and management modules are designed in modular and flexible manner. A novel system architecture is developed, implemented and discussed.

A new, maybe the first time, functionally content rich complete software architecture model of flight license examination is developed, implemented and presented. This modular model is implemented by LAMP and CMS model. This level of design and implementation detail does not commonly appear in the literature especially in examination software. We believe this is a significant contribution and the strength of our implementation.

Our implementation is in modular structure. So, it is easy to add new modules and software components and also it is easy to adapt FLEX as a part of information management system software of a company. Future works will be developing drag and drop type question management modules, and developing tutorials and online courses. Finally, tailor made design will provide reports in detail.

REFERENCES

[1] W. Pree et al., OO Design & Implementation of a Flexible Software Architecture for Decision Support System, Proceedings of the 9th International Conference on Software Engineering & Knowledge Engineering (SEKE'97) Madrid, Spain, 1997, 382-388.

[2] A.S.Ogrenci, T. Arsan and T. Saydam An Open Software Architecture of Neural Networks: Neurosoft, Proceedings of SEA2004, Boston,MA. November 2004.

[3] Apache Cookbook (2nd edition), Ken Coar & Rich Bowen, O'REILLY, 2008.

[4] MySQL Cookbok (Second Edition), Paul Dubois, O'REILLY, 2007.

[5] Pro MySQL, Michael Kruckenberg and Jay Pipes, APRESS, 2005.

[6] PHP Objects, Patterns, and Practice, Matt Zandstra, APRESS, 2008.

[7] Pro PHP Patterns, Frameworks, Testing and more, Kevin McArthur, APRESS, 2008.

[8] Pro PHP Security, Chris Snyder and Michael Southwell, APRESS, 2005.

[9] PHP and MySQL Web Development (Fourth Edition), Luke Welling and Laura Thomson, Pearson Education, 2009.

[10] Professional Javascript for Web Developers (2nd edition), Nicholas C. Zakas, 2009.

[11] jQuery Cookbook (Animal Guide), Cody Lindley, O'REILLY, 2009.

[12] jQuery UI 1.6: The User Interface Library for jQuery, Dan Wellman, 2009.

[13] The Exim SMTP Mail Server: Official Guide for Release 4 (2nd edition), Philip Hazel, UITCambridge, 2007.

Enabling and Integrating Distributed Web Resources for Efficient and Effective Discovery of Information on the Web

Neeta Verma[1], Pechimuthu Thangamuthu[2], Alka Mishra[3]
NIC, Department of Information Technology, New Delhi, India
(1. neeta@nic.in, 2. tpmuthu@nic.in, 3. amishra@nic.in)

Abstract: **National Portal of India [1] integrates information from distributed web resources like websites, portals of different Ministries, Departments, State Governments as well as district administrations. These websites are developed at different points of time, using different standards and technologies. Thus integrating information from the distributed, disparate web resources is a challenging task and also has a reflection on the information discovery by a citizen using a unified interface such as National Portal. The existing text based search engines would also not yield desired results [7].**

Couple of approaches was deliberated to address the above challenge and it was concluded that a metadata replication based approach would be most feasible and sustainable. Accordingly solution was designed for replication of metadata from distributed repositories using services oriented architecture. Uniform Metadata specifications were devised based on Dublin core standard [9]. To begin with solution is being implemented among National Portal and 35 State Portals spread across length and breadth of India. Metadata from distributed repositories is replicated to a central repository regardless of the platform and technology used by distributed repositories. Simple Search Interface has also been developed for efficient and effective information discovery by the citizens.

KEYWORDS: metadata repository, web resources, information discovery, metadata replication service

I. INTRODUCTION

The National Portal of India [1] a Citizen centric government portal integrates information from various ministries, departments, state and district level portals. It provides a single window access for all citizen centric information and services provided by the government. As volume of the content repository grows, there is a need for search service to facilitate citizens to find relevant information quickly and efficiently. Already existing text based search solutions could crawl only at the surface level [6] [7] and cannot index the content at deeper levels. Web portals developed content management systems pose a further challenge in this regard. This paper discusses the challenges of integrating distributed, disparate web resources and suggests possible solution and their implementation in the context of state portals.

Remaining sections of the paper are organized as follows. In the beginning of this paper the challenges of information discovery on the web are discussed in detail. Later in section [III] possible solutions for searching information on distributed web resources are discussed. The role of metadata for describing web resources and their management has been discussed in section [IV]. In sections [V, VI] the detailed architecture of syndicating metadata to National Portal Metadata repository using Metadata Replication Service and Meta data consolidator has been provided. The section [VII] covers the consolidated Metadata data storage and search service over the repository. The final section [VIII] concludes the paper and future work on this project is described.

II. INFORMATION DISCOVERY CHALLENGES ON THE WEB

Web portals display information gathered from distributed data sources of specific domain. Search engine integrated to a portal or an open web search engines like Google, Yahoo can search web documents and give results only based on the availability of relevant text on the webpage and its related link to other web pages or documents. In the world of dynamic web, information on the web page is generated using programming interface without enough Meta data for search engines. Moreover the actual data record is stored in database or some content repository which can be retrieved for display on web page using certain programming interfaces and database search queries. Search engine are not able to reach up to the lower level web (deep web [7]) for indexing. If the web resource is relocated or its metadata modified the search index is not updated instantly. Therefore, the search result based on that index would give link to inaccurate or unavailable web contents.

III. POSSIBLE SOLUTIONS

A. Directory based search

Search modules have to be implemented at remote web portals and integrated with National Portal of India based on information category. At National Portal level a directory has to be implemented for search. In this approach user has to decide the search category for desired search item.

B. Federated search

In this approach search request is routed to the desired remote search services which are defined at remote web portals. The global search service has to be implemented with adequate search routing mechanism to transfer the user search

T. Sobh, K. Elleithy (eds.), *Innovations in Computing Sciences and Software Engineering*,
DOI 10.1007/978-90-481-9112-3_61,

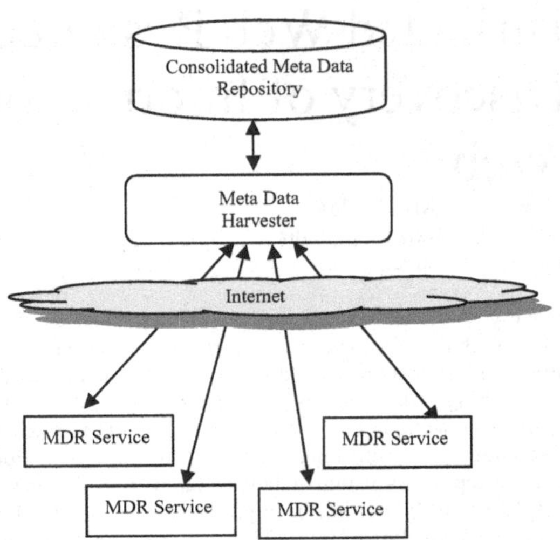

Fig. 1: Integral view of MDR service and consolidated metadata repository

request to respective remote search services. However the quality and accuracy of search result depends to the method of search routing and the quality of remote search service.

C. *Consolidated Metadata repository based search*

In this method the remote web portals are enabled for metadata and replicated to common metadata repository using web services as given in "Fig. 1." A search interface can be implemented based on the consolidated metadata repository for accurate search result. The integrity between consolidated metadata repository and remote web portals has to be maintained for metadata validity at consolidated repository.

IV. METADATA CREATION AND MANAGEMENT FOR WEB RESOURCES

Metadata is information in a structured format for describing a web resource. A web resource may be a publication such as a report or journal, a web page about a particular topic or service, documents, interactive forms or a multimedia objects such as graphics, images, animation, audio and video clips. Good quality metadata improves the efficiency of searching, making it much easier to find something specific and relevant.

Metadata specifications as given in Table I was defined for government web space; International Standard of Dublin core metadata standard [9] was used to define metadata specifications.

Since state portals are in the process of major revision/ redevelopment under the Mission Mode Project of National E-Governance Programme (NeGP) of government India. A comprehensive State Portal Framework has been developed [2]

TABLE I

METADATA SPECIFICATIONS: LIST OF ATTRIBUTES

DC.Creator.DeptName	DC.Publisher.DeptName
DC.Creator.OrgName	DC.Publisher.Email
DC.Creator.Email	DC.Publisher.Address
DC.Coverage.Spatial	DC.Publisher.Phone
DC.Coverage.Temporal	DC.Relation
DC.CoverageJurisdiction	DC.Source
DC.Description	DC.Title
DC.Date.Created	DC.TitleAlternate
DC.Date.Published	DC.Subject.Keywords
DC.Date.Modified	DC.Subject.Classification
DC.Format	DC.Type
DC.Language	DC.Identifier
DC.Publisher.OrgName	

to guide the development, operation and management of state portals using the best practices. Creation of metadata and its management is a part of web content management, therefore all web contents are associated with a metadata set and follows the same life cycle of web content. States have been advised through the state portal framework to generate metadata of each piece of information published on the state portal. Metadata Specifications have also been communicated to them to follow to bring a degree of standardization. As per the frame work defined for state portals [2], they have advised to use some sort of Content Management System, and provide standard based access to state level metadata repository.

V. METADATA REPLICATION SERVICE

Metadata Replication Service is a web service defined as integral part of a Web source which replicates metadata to Common Metadata Repository to be used by National Portal of India [1] level to begin with. This metadata repository can be subsequently used for many other basic and value added services. The "Fig. 2." shows the logical flow of Metadata Replication Service implemented with necessary functionalities for fetching metadata from web content repositories using CMS-SDK and MDR-CMS-API.

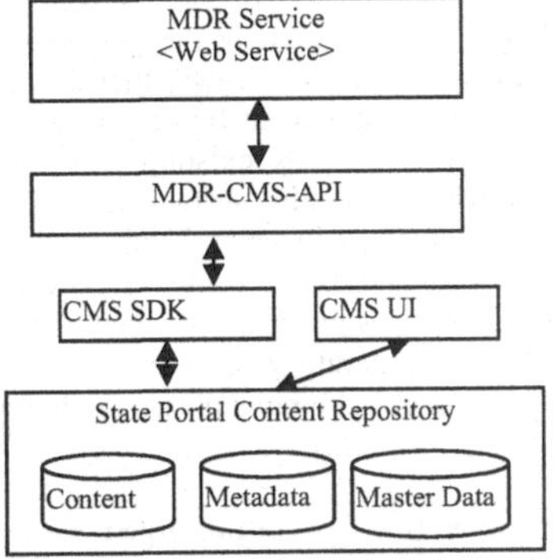

Fig. 2: Metadata Replication Service Architecture

On top, the web service interface provides necessary interfaces for harvester to harvest metadata over internet. Using the CMS-UI (Content Management System- User Interface), portal contents are created by content contributors for state portal.

Procedure for retrieving Metadata from CMS and sending response with metadata dataset is given below.

i. Connect to CMS
ii. Extract start time and end time from request
iii. Retrieve data for 'start time' to 'end time'
iv. Send data, start time, end time

MDR service functionalities

Based on our studies and experiences, the following are some of the essential functionalities of MDR services which are described below.

a. It should implemented as web service with a well defined WSDL [5] compliant standard interface.
b. Provide metadata of published content from the content repository of State Portal, for following events occurring in the given time period
   i. New web page is published
   ii. Metadata of published web pages is modified
   iii. Web page is exited or deleted
c. Normalized metadata extracted from content repository, based on defined standard metadata schema (this include attribute names, data type, number of attributes, valid values, max allowed length, data range etc.).
d. Provide metadata of given web pages from the content repository of State Portal.
e. Provide status of MDR service, indicating it's availability and normal functioning.
f. Provide information about metadata validation errors (if any).
g. Maintain time up to which metadata is propagated to "consolidated metadata repository".
h. It should be deployed on a highly available infrastructure.
i. It should provide message level authentication based on user-id and password.
j. Ensure that metadata is kept for sufficient time such that request for metadata can be satisfied as and when they come.
k. Provide required error logging, activity logging and email notifications for errors.

VI. METADATA HARVESTING AND CONSOLIDATION

A detailed overview about creating metadata for web resources and procedure for disseminating the metadata as web service has been described in previous chapters. This chapter covers how metadata replication services are accessed for harvesting metadata from state portals web resources and integrating them with National Portal of India content repository. The Harvester application pulls metadata from Metadata Replication Service over internet.

Functionalities of Metadata Harvester

Following are some of essential functionalities of metadata harvester application defined in the scope of this project.

a. Retrieve metadata of published content on State Portal's using MDR services at configurable periodicity.
b. Metadata should be retrieved for following events
   i. New web page is published
   ii. Metadata of published web pages is modified
   iii. Web page is exited or deleted
c. Validate retrieved metadata
d. Normalize metadata based on defined standard metadata schema (this include attribute names, data type, number of attributes, valid values, max allowed length, data range etc.).
e. Store retrieved metadata into consolidated metadata repository.
f. Monitor the status of MDR services at configurable periodicity
g. Maintain list of MDR services or State Portals from which metadata to be consolidated
h. Maintain time up to which metadata is received from each MDR service

The integral view of metadata harvester and Replication service is show in "Fig. 3."

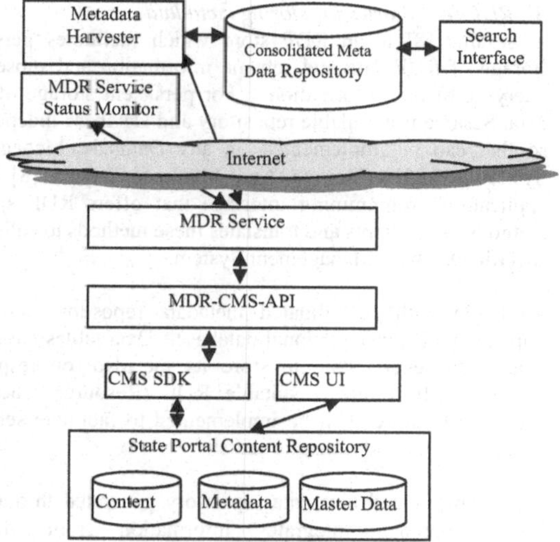

Fig. 3: Metadata Harvester and MDR Service an integral

VII. Metadata Repository Storage

This section focuses on metadata repository storage for storing them in a suitable repository to provide effective content search and virtually integrating state specific web contents with the content repository of National Portal of India. Different data repository types were studied and deliberated. Some of the important store types which were considered are discussed.

A. RDBMS based Metadata Repository

Relational database can be used as metadata store for storing the harvested metadata from various state portal metadata replication services. Data tables can be created based on the content category. As the table schema is unique for all state portals, the data tables can be created for every state to store its metadata on respective category. The metadata in XML format can also be directly serialized in to database table for every state. But due to the processing overhead on xml content for consolidated search, serializing xml content in to data table has not been considered.

A. XML repositories for metadata storage

An XML (eXtended Markup Language) repository is a system for storing and retrieving XML [5] data. This data is usually in the form of XML documents and their associated Document Type Definitions (DTDs) or XML Schemas. Because XML data lends itself to a hierarchical structure rather than a relational structure, it may be difficult to store XML data in traditional relational database systems. The repository itself may be a relational database system, but it is more likely to be a custom storage system built exclusively for XML (or hierarchical) data.

B. RDF repositories for storing metadata

Sesame [8] is an RDF store which facilitates persistent storage of RDF data and schema information and subsequent querying of that information. For persistent storage of RDF data, Sesame is a scalable repository and Database independent so that can be implemented on any Database Management System. SAIL (Storage And Inference Layer) [8] is an application programming interface that offers RDF specific methods to its clients and translates these methods to calls to its specific Database Management System.

To begin with consolidated metadata repository has been implemented using relational database. Data tables have been created for every state to store its metadata on respective category. In future a suitable RDF (Resource Document Framework) store shall be implemented to facilitate semantic data repository and semantic search.

Thus consolidated metadata repository generated through the above approach integrates information from different distributed, disparate web resources to facilitate unified, single window access to government information and services at various levels of administration right from central, state, districts and can be further extended to panchayats in Villages of India.

VIII. Conclusion and Future Work

The web service based metadata replication service described in this paper along with metadata specifications, and the extended metadata set Web Resource Metadata Specification (WRMS) in Table I facilitated state portals to disseminate metadata to Consolidated Metadata Repository of National Portal of India [1]. The consolidated metadata repository [VI, V] empowers the National Portal for discovering citizen centric information efficiently by its users.

As described in section IV the MDR service can be enhanced using protocol like OAI-PMH for metadata harvesting so that other metadata consolidation service can utilize this service. The consolidated metadata repository discussed in sections [VI, V] can be enhanced based on RDF schema or Ontology for discovering information semantically. This search component of National Portal of India will be implemented as web service and integrated with other government department portals.

Acknowledgement

The National Portal of India (India.gov.in) is a reflection of contribution from a large number of people, and we wish to thank them for their important efforts and sage advice. Writing this paper, would not have been possible without the responsiveness, commitment and support provided by the Data Centre and Web Services Division at National Informatics Centre, Government of India.

Further, the views endorsed in this paper are purely of those in their personal capacity and nowhere reflect the views of the organisations/departments namely National Informatics Centre.

References

[1] National Portal of India, NIC, Department of Information Technology, India, [http://india.gov.in]

[2] Neeta Verma, Alka Mishra, T. Pechimuthu, "State Portal Frame work", NIC, Department of Information Technology, India, [http://spf.india.gov.in], "unpublished"

[3] Neeta Verma, Alka Mishra (2008),"Portal Content Framework", NIC, Department of Information Technology, India , [http://india.gov.in/cfw/] "unpublished"

[4] Rakhi Tripathi, Dr. M.P. Gupta and Jaijit Bhattacharya (2007) "Selected Aspects of Interoperability in One-stop Government Portal of India" Indian Institute of Technology Delhi, Hauz Khas, New Delhi-110016, India

[5] "XML, XML schema, SOAP, WSDL" , [http://w3cSchools.com]

[6] Brooks, Terrence A. (2003), "Web Search: how the Web has changed information retrieval" Information Research, 8(3) paper no. 154 [http://InformationR.net/ir/8-3/paper154.html]

[7] Michael K. Bergman , "The Deep Web: Surfacing Hidden Value",vol. 7, no. 1, August, 2001 [http://dx.doi.org/10.3998/3336451.0007.104]

[8] Jeen Broekstra, Arjohn Kampman, and Frank van Harmelen "Sesame: A Generic Architecture for Storing and Querying RDF and RDF Schema"

[9] "Dublin Core Metadata Initiative" , [http://dublincore.org/]

Translation from UML to Markov Model: A Performance Modeling Framework

Razib Hayat Khan
Norwegian University of Science & Technology (NTNU)
7491, Trondheim, Norway

Poul E. Heegaard
Norwegian University of Science & Technology (NTNU)
7491, Trondheim, Norway

Abstract- **Performance engineering focuses on the quantitative investigation of the behavior of a system during the early phase of the system development life cycle. Bearing this on mind, we delineate a performance modeling framework of the application for communication system that proposes a translation process from high level UML notation to Continuous Time Markov Chain model (CTMC) and solves the model for relevant performance metrics. The framework utilizes UML collaborations, activity diagrams and deployment diagrams to be used for generating performance model for a communication system. The system dynamics will be captured by UML collaboration and activity diagram as reusable specification building blocks, while deployment diagram highlights the components of the system. The collaboration and activity show how reusable building blocks in the form of collaboration can compose together the service components through input and output pin by highlighting the behavior of the components and later a mapping between collaboration and system component identified by deployment diagram will be delineated. Moreover the UML models are annotated to associate performance related quality of service (QoS) information which is necessary for solving the performance model for relevant performance metrics through our proposed framework. The applicability of our proposed performance modeling framework in performance evaluation is delineated in the context of modeling a communication system.**

I. INTRODUCTION

Communication systems are complex systems. To meet functional requirements are obviously important while designing applications for communication system, but they are not the only concern. Performance evaluation to meet user requirement is another important factor. Performance evaluation is the degree to which a system meets its objectives and satisfies user expectation which is important in many cases and is critical in some real-time applications. It is necessary to take into account the performance issues earlier in the system development lifecycle and treating these as an essential part of the system development process. Therefore finding a way to extract performance model from design model at early stage of system development process and solves the model for relevant performance metrics is a key issue in the perspective of system performance engineering so that developers will be able to make informed decisions within the design process as well as readily explore 'what-if' scenarios and assessing the implication of changing logic in execution of application by considering all the dynamics, interaction among the system components as well as considering the system's execution environment (i.e. the deployment of network resources, network technology and network topology) and workload factors of the system which all have greater impact on a system's performance. To consider all the above issue, our proposed framework utilizes UML collaboration [1], activity [1] and deployment diagram [1] as UML is the most widely used modeling language which models both the system requirements and qualitative behavior through different notations. Collaboration and activity diagram will be specified capturing system dynamics and interaction among service components as reusable specification building blocks [2] by highlighting component's behavior. To compose the overall activity of the system in the form of collaboration events identified as input and output pins on the activities that are connected together [2]. Deployment diagram will identify the system components, the process executes on the each component as well as to consider the execution platform and network topology of the system. A mapping is delineated between system components and collaborations thereafter to show how the service is defined by the joint behavior of the system component. Moreover the UML models are annotated incorporating performance related information. By the above specification style of UML, probable state and the performance parameters for triggering the change of the states of the performance model will be generated and solved by our proposed performance modeling framework.

Markov model [3], queuing network [3] and stochastic petrinet [3] are probably the best studied performance modeling techniques. Among all of them, we will choose Markov model [3] as the performance model generated by our proposed framework due to its modeling generality, its well-developed numerical modeling analysis techniques, its ability to preserve the original architecture of the system, to facilitate any modification according to the feedback from performance evaluation and the existence of analysis tools.

The objective of this paper is to provide an extensive performance modeling framework that provides a translation process to generate performance model from system specification description captured by the UML behavioral diagram [1] and solves the model for relevant performance metrics to validate against the performance requirements at the early stage of system development life cycle.

The rest of this paper is organized as follows: section 2 focuses on related work, section 3 presents our approach of specifying UML technique for performance modeling, section 4 describes our performance modeling framework and section 5 delineates conclusion with future work.

T. Sobh, K. Elleithy (eds.), *Innovations in Computing Sciences and Software Engineering*,
DOI 10.1007/978-90-481-9112-3_62, © Springer Science+Business Media B.V. 2010

II. RELATED WORK

Related work includes a number of efforts are made generating a performance model from the system specification. Kähkipuro developed a performance modeling framework to generate queuing network with simultaneous resource possessions from the high level UML notations so that model can be solved for the relevant performance metrics [4]. Lopez-Grao *et al.* proposed a conversion method from annotated UML activity diagram to stochastic petrinet model [5]. Trowitzsch and Zimmermann proposed the modeling of technical systems and their behavior by means of UML and for the resulting models a transformation into a Stochastic Petri Net was established [6]. Abdullatif and Pooly presented a method for providing computer support for extracting Markov chains from a performance annotated UML sequence diagram [7]. The framework in this paper is the first known approach that introduces a new specification style utilizing UML behavioral diagrams as reusable specification building block that is used for generating performance model. The main focus here is to introduce reusable building blocks, from which systems can be composed and performance model will be generated. These building blocks are collaborations, which mean that one building block describes the behavior of several system components. This makes it easier to reuse complete services, since all interactions necessary to coordinate behavior among components can be encapsulated [8].

III. UML TECHNIQUE OF PERFORMANCE MODELING

In this paper we utilize UML 2.2 collaboration, activity and deployment diagram to be used for generating performance model from system design specification. We outline a specification style using UML 2.2 collaboration and activity diagram which is the part of the tool suite Arctis [8]. Arctis focuses on the Collaboration and activity as reusable specification building blocks describing the interaction between system components as well as internal behavior of the components [2]. To mention the overall behavior of the system by composing the reusable building blocks the events are identified as input and output pins on the activities that are connected together [2]. Deployment diagram is another integral part of our proposed framework that specifies a set of constructs that can be used to define the execution architecture of the systems that represent the assignment of software artifacts to the system components or nodes [1]. As an example, we utilize a system description where users are equipped with cell phone or PDA wants to receive weather information of the current location using his/her hand held device. The user request is first transferred to location server through base transceiver station to retrieve location information of the user. The location information is then transferred to weather server for retrieving the weather information according to the location of the user.

Fig.1 shows the UML collaboration which focuses on the formulation of building block declaring the participants as collaboration role and connection between them [2]. User service request is generated from user's hand held device. The users are part of the environment and therefore labeled as <<external>>. User service request is transferred between the mobile terminal (MT) and Base Transceiver Station (BTS) is highlighted by collaboration *t*. BTS interacts with the location server (LS) for retrieving user location information by using collaboration *l*. The location server retrieves the desired information from databases using collaboration use *d1*. Then BTS interacts with the weather server (WS) for weather information by using collaboration *w* according to the location information of user supplied by the location server. The weather server retrieves the desired information from databases using collaboration use *d2*.

While UML collaboration describes the structural aspect of the composed service the internal behavior of the collaboration is described by the UML activity [2]. Hereby collaborations of Fig.1 are modeled by a call behavior action referring to the activity [9]. To deliver the requested information to the user through his/here mobile terminal, BTS participates in the collaboration *Request Location Info* together with the location server and *Request Weather info* together with weather server. These are specified by the collaboration *l: Request Location Info and w: Request Weather info* where the BTS plays the role client and the location server and weather server play the role server. The behavior of the collaboration is described by the UML activity in Fig. 3 where activity is divided into two partition one for each collaboration role (Client & Server) [2]. The activity is started on the client side when the user request is provided as parameter *u_req* at the input pin. The *u_req* directly sent to the location server where it is converted into a database request by the call operation action *processing*.

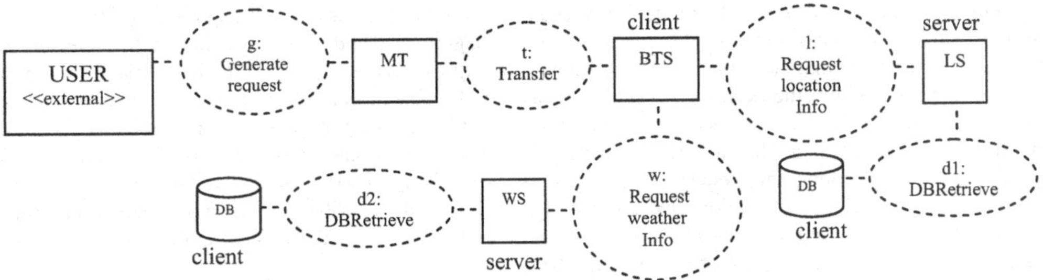

Fig.1: Collaboration Diagram

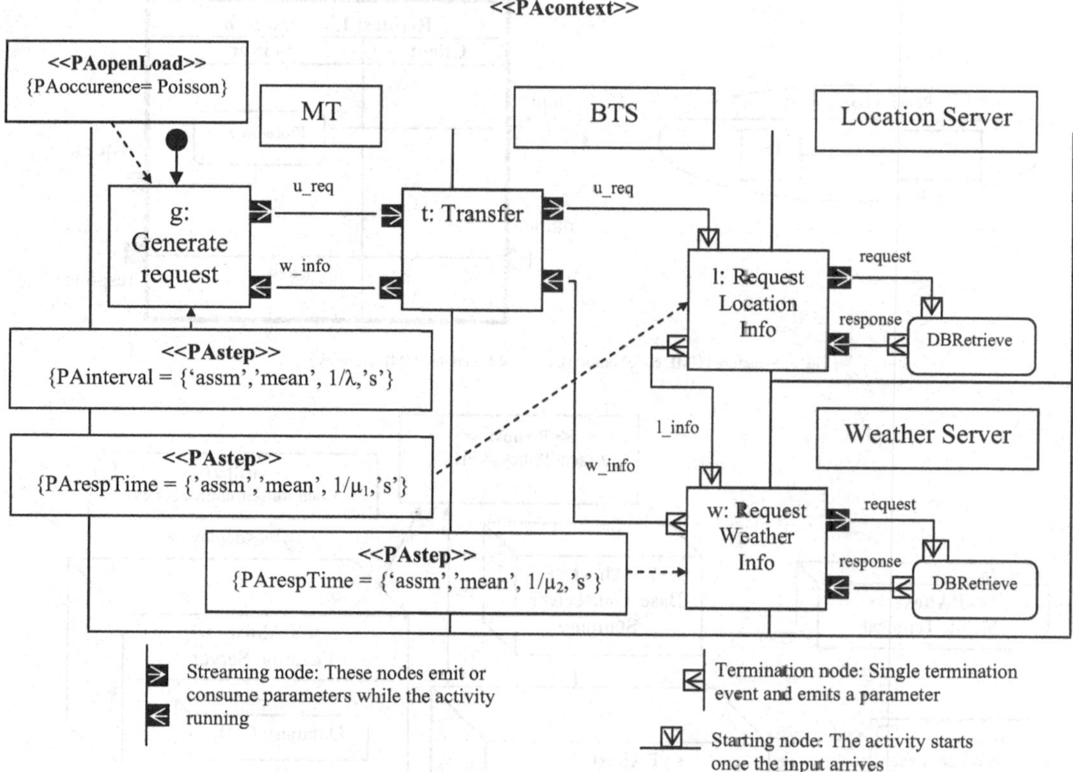

Fig. 2: System activity to couple the collaboration

After that it is the task of the collaboration between the server and the database to provide the stored information. To get the information the request leaves the activity *Request Location info* and the server waits for the reception of response. This is modeled with the input and output pins *request* and *response*. After getting the response, the result is delivered to the corresponding output pin in the client side and the activity is terminated. Here we describe the behavior of collaboration *Request Location info*. Likewise we can describe the behavior of *Request Weather info* through activity partition of client and server where location information of user is forwarded by the client to request server for retrieving the weather information of that particular user location.

We use activity in Fig.2 to describe how the events of the individual collaborations between the system components are coupled with each other so that the desired overall system behavior is obtained [2]. The initial node (●) marks the starting of the activities. The activity is started on the client side. When a user service request is generated via mobile terminal, *g: Generate request* will transfer the user service request as parameter *u_req* to the BTS via collaboration *t: Transfer*. Once arrived at the BTS request for location information is forwarded to the location server represented by activity *Request location info*. Location server makes a database request which is modeled by *d1: DBRetrieve* and terminates with result *l_info* (Location information). After getting the location information, request for weather information according to user current location is forwarded by the BTS to the weather server represented by activity *Request weather info*. Weather server makes a database request which is modeled by *d2: DBRetrieve* and terminates with result *w_info* (Weather information). After that, the final result is transferred to the user hand held device by BTS via collaboration *t: Transfer*. The structure of collaborations as well as the way to couple them facilitates the reuse of activities. For example both the collaboration *d1* and *d2* are identical and can be instantiated from single collaboration type. Moreover the collaboration *l* and *w* have very similar behavior and can be based on the same UML template. Thus, systems of a specific domain can often be composed of reoccurring building blocks by reusing them [2].

The deployment diagram of the overall system is shown in Fig.4 highlighting the physical resources of our system such as Mobile terminal, Base transceiver station, Location server, Weather server. Service request is deployed on the user's mobile terminal which then transferred by the base transceiver station to the location server where process for retrieving the location information of user is deployed. After that, process for retrieving the weather information of the user location is deployed in weather server.

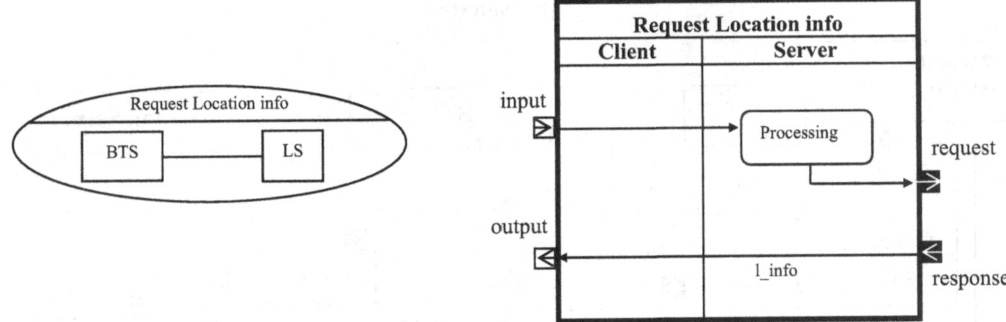

Fig. 3: Structure (UML collaboration), Internal Behavior (UML Activity)

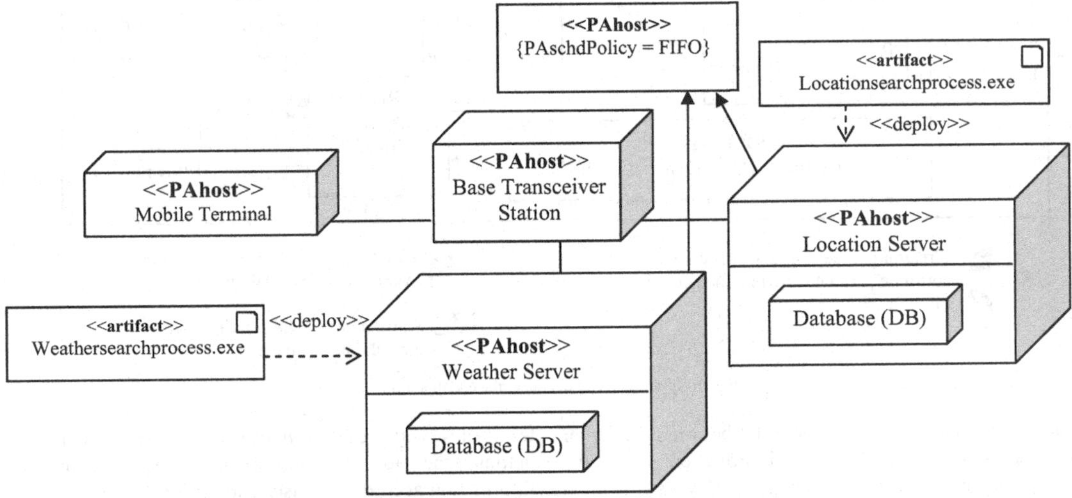

Fig.4: Deployment Diagram

IV. STEPS FOR BUILDING & EVALUATING THE PERFORMANCE MODEL (CTMC) FROM PROPOSED MODELING FRAMEWORK

Here we describe how performance model will be generated and evaluated by our proposed framework shown in Fig.9 by utilizing the above specification style of UML. Steps 1 and 2 are the part of the tool suite Arctis [8] and other steps are the extensions we needed generating the performance model by our proposed framework. The steps are as follows:

1) Construction of collaborative building block: This step defines the formulation of the building blocks in form of collaboration as major specification unit of our framework shown in Fig.1. The structure of the building block is defined by the UML collaboration shown in Fig.3. The building block declares the participants as collaboration role and connection between them. The internal behavior of the building block is described by a UML activity shown in Fig.3. It is declared as the classifier behavior of the collaboration and has one activity partition for each collaboration role in the structural description.

2) Composition of building blocks: For composition of building blocks, UML collaboration and activities are used complementary to each other. UML collaborations alone do not specify any behavior but only show how functionality may be decomposed. Therefore a UML activity is attached to a UML collaboration which focuses on the behavior of collaborations as well as how behaviors of subordinate collaboration are composed. The activity in Fig.2 and the collaboration in Fig.1 show how reusable specification building blocks in form of collaboration can be composed.

3) Designing the deployment diagram and stating relation between system component and collaboration: Developing deployment diagram can be used to define the execution architecture of systems by identifying the system component and the assignment of software artifacts to those identified system components [1]. For our defined scenario the Identified system components are Mobile terminal, Base transceiver station, Location server and Weather server shown in Fig.4. The artifact locationsearchprocess.exe is deployed on the location server and artifact weathersearchprocess.exe is deployed on the weather server. In our mentioned scenario we consider single instance of location server and weather server.

After designing the deployment diagram the relation between system component and collaboration will be delineated describing the service delivered by the system. The service is delivered by the joint behavior of the system components which may be physically distributed. The partial behavior of the component utilized to realize the collaboration is represented by the collaboration role [10]. In our scenario description identified system components are Mobile terminal, Base Transceiver station, Location server, Weather server. The behavior of the components Mobile terminal, Base Transceiver station, Location server, Weather server is represented by collaboration roles MT, BTS, LS & WS to utilize the collaboration *t: transfer, l: request location info, w: request weather info*. Here it is a one to one mapping between the system components and collaboration roles shown in Fig.5.

4) Annotation of source models: Performance information is incorporated to the UML activity diagram in Fig.2 and deployment diagram in Fig.4 according to the UML Profile for Schedulability, Performance and Time [11] to enable system performance to be evaluated by performance model solver for relevant performance metrics through our proposed framework. We use the stereotype PAcontext, PAopenLoad, PAhost, PAstep and the tag value PAoccurence, PAschdPolicy, PArespTime and PAinterval. A PAcontext models a performance analysis context. A PAopenLoad is modeled as a stream of requests that arrive at a given rate in predetermined pattern with PAoccurence. A PAhost models a processing resource with tags PAschdPolicy defining the policy by which access to the resource is controlled. A PAstep models a scenario step with tags PArespTime defining a step's response time and PAinterval defines time interval between successive repetitions of a step.

5) State marking and Reachability graph: Here we will describe how the probable states of the performance model will be generated. While generating the probable states for our performance model we consider only those participants which have greater impact on the system performance and the states of the system will be generated based on the status of these participants shown by their internal behavior. For our example scenario, we will consider the participants location server and weather server as limiting factor for the system performance and the performance model states will be generated from location server and weather server status. The status of these servers is defined by their internal behavior through collaboration *request location info* and *request weather info*. The status of the both the servers are defined as idle, processing. When a step (annotated as <<PAstep>> in Fig.2) will be executed the status of the servers will be marked as performance model state as a whole from where a new state may be generated with a transition rate or return back to a already marked state with a transition rate mentioned in the annotated UML model in Fig.2. The states of the performance model are shown in Table.1 based on the status of both the servers as a whole. The states are: (idle, idle), (processing, idle), (idle, processing), (processing, processing) where the first part defines the status of the location server and second part defines the status of the weather server. If we assume initial marking such as the status of the location server and weather server is idle that means participants have no user request to process then we can derive all the reachable markings of the performance model from the initial marking according to the arrival or departure of requests by following the interaction among the participants shown in the composition of building block through UML activity diagram in Fig.2. If we now construct the reachability graph with each of this reachable marking as a node and each edge between the nodes leveled with the trigger of their change by transition rate, we have a state transition diagram of the performance model. Here if we assume system is stable, both servers buffer capacity are null and servers can process one request at a time, the state transition diagram is shown in Fig.6 where system states are generated from location server and weather server status shown in Table.1 where idle means no job is in the servers to process and processing means 1 job (number of job in the location server & weather server is mentioned by N & M & here highest value of N=M=1 in Fig.6) is processed by the servers.

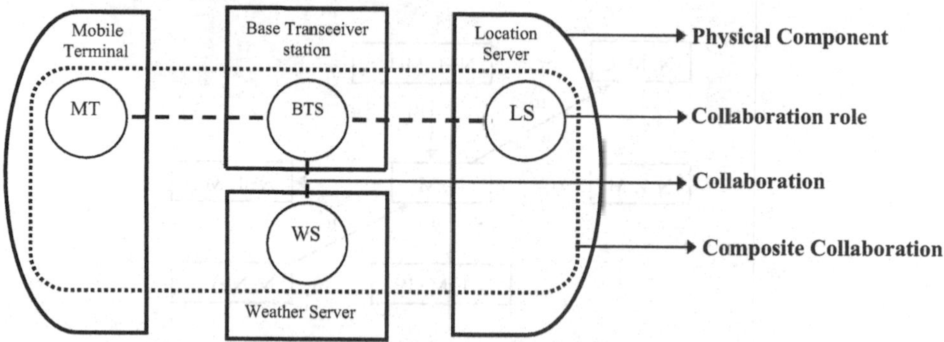

Fig.5: Relation between system components and collaborations

TABLE1
STATES OF PERFORMANCE MODEL BASED ON THE STATUS OF LOCATION SERVER & WEATHER SERVER

Location Server	Weather Server
Idle	Idle
processing	Idle
Idle	Processing
processing	Processing

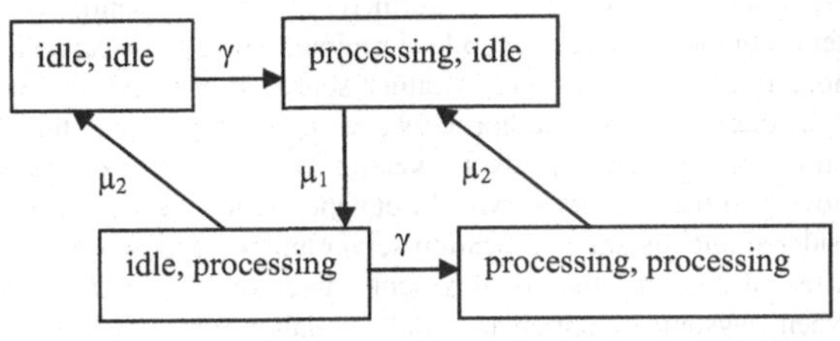

Fig.6: State transition diagram of the Markov model when number of request or job arrived and serviced by the system is 1

if we assume the system is stable, both servers buffer capacity is infinite, follow Poisson arrival pattern & FIFO (First In First Out) scheduling policy and servers can process one request at a time, the state transition diagram is shown in Fig.7 (where (N, M) >1 to infinity) which shows more states than the states generated from the status of both the servers. So if N=M=1 then the state transition diagram will be mentioned in Fig. 6 which just reflect the internal behavior of the servers showing the change of system states mentioned in Table.1. If (N, M) > 1 the state transition diagram will be mentioned in Fig.7 highlighting more additional states including the states shown in Tab.1 & Fig.6 where the states will be marked by the total number of job N & M in the server where 1 job will be processed by the servers and other remaining N-1 & M-1 job will be waiting in the buffer of location server and weather server for being processed. The generalized state transition diagram of our performance model is shown in Fig. 8 including the boundary sates.

6) Generating the performance model: From the mentioned reachability graph and annotated UML structure probable states (based on the value of N & M) and transition rate of the trigger of the change between states will be found based on which performance model will be generated which can further be used as the input for the performance model solver.

7) Solving the performance model: The generated performance model will be solved by the SHARPE [12] performance model solver to generate performance result. Some of the performance evaluation result generated by the tools is shown in the graph form in Fig.10:

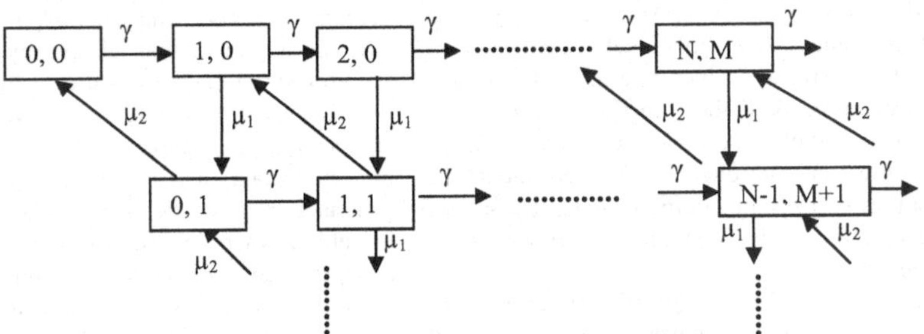

Fig. 7: state transition diagram of the Markov model

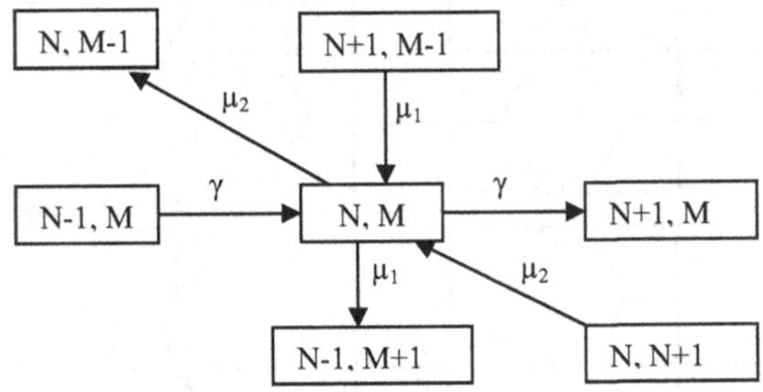

Fig. 8: Generalized state transition diagram of the Markov model

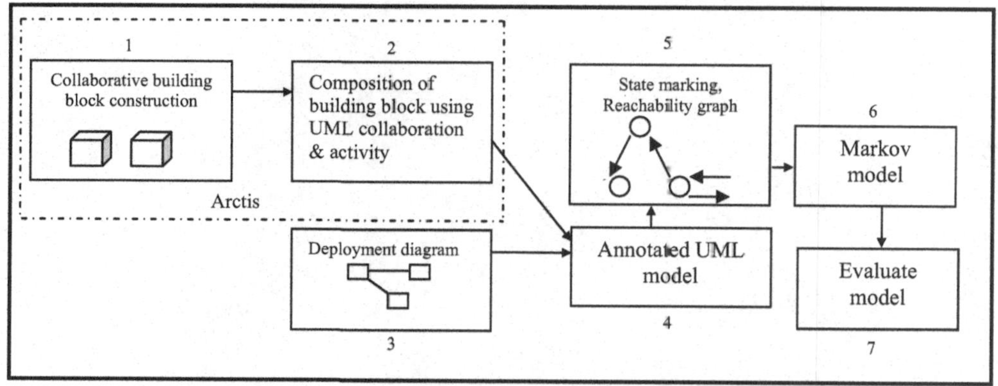

Fig. 9: Proposed Performance modeling framework

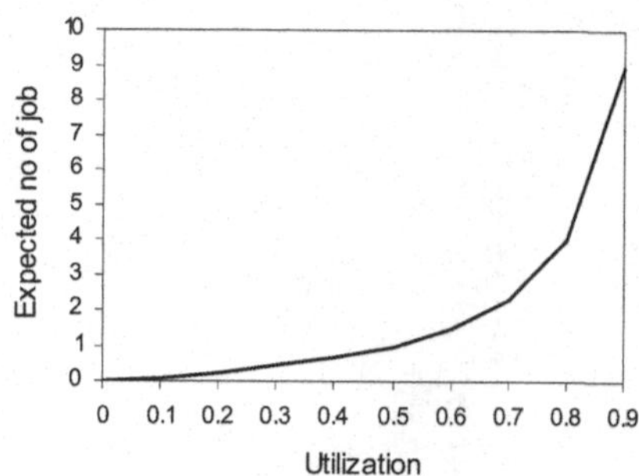

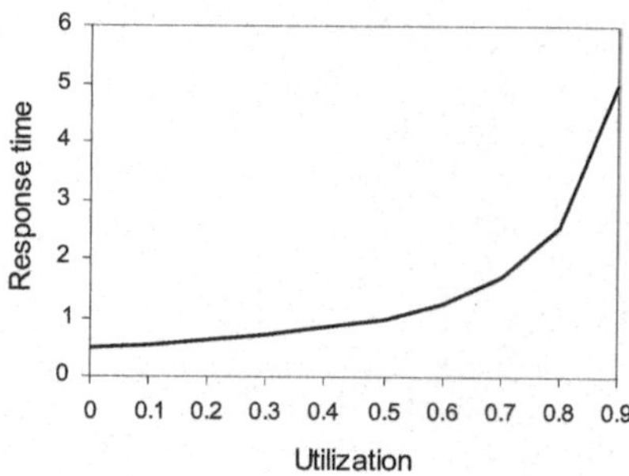

Fig.10: Expected number of jobs & Average response time vs. Utilization

V. CONCLUSION

In this paper our main contribution is delineated as presenting a performance modeling framework of a system by introducing a new specification style utilizing UML collaboration and activity diagram as reusable specification building blocks to capture the system dynamics, while UML deployment diagram identifies the physical resources or components of the system. This specification style later generates the probable states based on which our performance model will be generated and solved by our performance modeling framework for relevant performance metrics captured by the annotated UML models. However the size of the underlying reachability set is major limitation for large and complex system. Further work includes automating the whole process of translating from our UML specification style to generate a performance model and the way to solve the performance model through our proposed framework as well as tackling the state explosion problems of reachability marking for large system.

REFERENCES

[1] OMG UML Superstructure, Version-2.2

[2] F. A. Kraemer, P. Hermann, "Service specification by composition of collaborations-an example", Proceedings of 2006 WI-IAT workshops, Hong kong, p. 129-133, IEEE, 2006

[3] K. S. Trivedi, "Probability and Statistics with Reliability, Queuing and Computer Science application", Wiley-Interscience publication, ISBN 0-471-33341-7

[4] P. Kåhkipuro, "UML based performance modeling framework for object-oriented distributed system", lecture notes in Computer science, Springer.

[5] J. P. Lopez, J. Merseguer, J. Campos, "From UML activity diagrams to SPN: application to software performance engineering", ACM SIGSOFT software engineering notes, NY, USA, 2004

[6] J. Trowitzsch, A. Zimmermann, "Using UML state machines and petri nets for the quantitative investigation of ECTS", Proceeding of the 1st international conference on performance evaluation methodologies and tools, ACM, USA, 2006

[7] Abdullatif, R. Pooly, "A computer assisted state marking method", International Journal of Simulation, Vol. 8, No. 3, ISSN – 1473-804x

[8] F. A. Kramer, "ARCTIS", Department of Telematics, NTNU, http://arctis.item.ntnu.no.

[9] F. A. Kramer, "Engineering Reactive Systems: A Compositional and Model-Driven Method Based on Collaborative Building Blocks", Doctoral thesis, NTNU, Norway, 2008

[10] F. A. Kramer, R. Bræk, P. Herrmann, "Synthesizes components with sessions from collaboration-oriented service specifications", Proceedings of SDL 2007, V-4745, Lecture notes of Computer Science, p.166-185.

[11] OMG 2005. UML Profile for Schedulability, Performance, and Time Specification. Version – 1.1

[12] K. S. Trivedi, R. Sahner, " SHARPE: Symbolic Hierarchical Automated Reliability / Performance Evaluator", Duke Univerisyt, Durham, NC.

A Comparative Study of Protein Sequence Clustering Algorithms

A. Sharaf Eldin, S. AbdelGaber, T. Soliman, S. Kassim, and A. Abdo*
*Teaching Assistant at the Faculty of Computer and Information Sciences, Helwan University, Egypt.
amanyabdo_80@yahoo.com

Abstract- **In this paper, we survey four clustering techniques and discuss their advantages and drawbacks. A review of eight different protein sequence clustering algorithms has been accomplished. Moreover, a comparison between the algorithms on the basis of some factors has been presented.**

I. Introduction

There is an increasing demand for the development of automatic and accurate techniques for protein sequences comparison, classification, and functional prediction. Successful methods for the categorization of protein sequences have been developed.

Protein Databases

Five types of protein databases are available for use: sequence, motifs (i.e. PROSITE [1], PRINTS [2], [3], and BLOCKS [4]), domains (i.e. Pfam [5], SMART [6], ProDom [7], and COGS [8]), integrated domains and motifs (i.e. InterPro [9], and CDD [10]), and structure protein databases (i.e. PDB [11], [12], MMDB [13], FSSP [14], SCOP [15], and CATH [16]).

Examples of protein sequence databases are, which are the focus of this study are: Entrez [17], SWISS-PROT [18], TrEMBL [18], PIR [19,20], and PRF [21].

Protein Sequence Similarity

Pairwise sequence alignment is concerned with comparing two amino acid sequences – finding the global and local "optimum alignment" of the two sequences. Global alignments are most useful when the sequences in the query set are similar and of roughly equal size. A general global alignment technique is called the Needleman-Wunsch algorithm [22] and is based on dynamic programming. Local alignments are more useful for dissimilar sequences. The Smith-Waterman [23], FASTA [24] and BLAST [25] are local alignment algorithms. Multiple sequence alignment is an extension of pairwise alignment to incorporate more than two sequences at a time. The CLUSTAL [26] family of programs and Profile Hidden Markov Models (HMMs) [27, 28] are the most successful solutions of multiple sequence alignment.

The paper is organized as follows: Section two surveys clustering methods and eight algorithms applied in protein sequence clustering. Section three presents the desirable clustering factors and the comparison between the algorithms in terms of these factors. Finally, section four concludes the paper and presents future work.

II. Clustering Methods and Algorithms

Clustering Methods

Clustering methods that have been widely used in protein clustering are classified into: Hierarchical, Partitioning, Incremental, Density-based, Graph-based, Grid-based, and Model-based techniques. Categorization of clustering methods is neither straightforward, nor canonical. In reality, methods sometimes overlap. In the current paper, a concentration on the first four techniques is illustrated, given a clarification of a set of algorithms on each.

Hierarchical clustering algorithms partition the objects into a tree of nodes. There are two major methods under this category: one is the agglomerative method, which forms the clusters in a bottom-up fashion until all data instances belong to the same cluster. The other is the divisive method, which splits up the data set into smaller clusters in a top-down fashion until each cluster contains only one instance. Many protein sequence clustering algorithms has been implemented, based on agglomerative clustering, such as: ProtoMap [29], ProtoNet [30], CluSTr [31], CLICK [32], and SYSTERS [33]. Hierarchical clustering algorithms output a hierarchy, a structure that is more informative than the unstructured set of clusters returned by partitioning clustering. Hierarchical clustering does not require a user to pre-specify the number of clusters. Almost all of the agglomerative clustering algorithms require much time to compare the sequences because they perform 'all-against – all' comparison. Also, some of these algorithms are based on the graph theory method, which requires additional time to process the graph.

Partitioning methods are based on the philosophy that objects are partitioned from the beginning into a fixed number of clusters and during the clustering process; they change clusters based on their similarity to the closest

T. Sobh, K. Elleithy (eds.), *Innovations in Computing Sciences and Software Engineering*,
DOI 10.1007/978-90-481-9112-3_63, © Springer Science+Business Media B.V. 2010

cluster. K-means [34], K-medoids, K-modes, and PAM are typical examples of partitioning clustering algorithms. CLARA and CLARANS are improved versions of PAM designed for large data sets [35]. An example of protein sequence clustering algorithms based on partitioning clustering is the scalable algorithm for clustering protein sequences [36]. Reference [37] also enhanced four partitioning clustering algorithms based on existing ones for clustering protein sequences. One of the main advantages of partitioning algorithms is that they are conceptually simple. Also, partitioning algorithms may be computationally faster than hierarchical clustering if the number of required clusters is small. However, they suffer from a number of drawbacks, such as creating a flat set of clusters without any explicit structure that would relate clusters to each other and fixing number of clusters can make it difficult to predict what number of clusters should be.

Incremental clustering is an approach for scaling up a clustering algorithm by reducing its runtime such that it can be applied to larger databases. This reduction in runtime can be achieved by applying the clustering algorithm to only a summary of the database instead of the whole database. The Leaders-SubLeaders algorithm [38] is an example of the incremental algorithms designed to cluster protein sequences. A drawback of incremental clustering algorithms is that they are dependent on the order of input data.

Density-based approaches use a local density criterion; clusters are subspaces in which the objects are dense and are separated by subspaces of low density. The key idea is that for each point of a cluster the neighborhood of a given radius has to contain at least a minimum number of points.

Density-based algorithms have advantages over partitioning and hierarchical methods in discovering clusters of arbitrary shapes and sizes. Also, unlike partitioning methods, the number of clusters is automatically determined. Drawbacks of density-based clustering include time inefficiency and parameters that characterize the density are problem-specific and must be chosen manually. SEQOPTICS [39] is an example of the density-based algorithms developed for the clustering of protein sequences. SEQOPTICS proved its value only for small data sets.

Protein sequence clustering algorithms

In this section a review of eight clustering algorithms; primarily developed for clustering protein sequences is presented:

Hierarchical Clustering

ProtoMap

ProtoMap offers an automatic clustering of all protein sequences in SWISS-PROT database, into groups of related proteins. In this work, the protein space is represented as a weighted graph whose vertices are the sequences. Combinations of Smith-Waterman, FASTA, and BLAST with two different scoring matrices (BLOSUM 50, BLOSUM 62 [40], [41]) have been used to determine the similarity between protein sequences. The resulting clusters are iteratively merged in agglomerative hierarchical clustering, using an average-link.

ProtoMap has been applied to SWISS-PROT Release 36, which contains 72613 protein sequences. A Web-based interface of this tool is available, which allows browsing the clusters both textually and graphically. ProtoMap maintains Swiss-Prot annotations and keywords. It also provides individual protein pages linking each protein to all clusters containing it. Each cluster also has a summary page with some additional information such as PROSITE families and taxonomy. Moreover, ProtoMap provides a graphical display of cluster relationships as well as a tree-like representation.

ProtoNet

ProtoNet is an automatic hierarchical clustering of the SwissProt and TrEMBL (~ one million protein sequences) protein databases. The clustering process is based on an all-against-all BLAST similarity search. The similarities' E-score is used to perform a continuous bottom-up clustering process by joining at each step the two most similar protein clusters, resulting in a hierarchy of protein clusters at various degrees of biological granularity.

ProtoNet can be used to assess the function of novel protein sequences. It also provides detailed information in the cluster level, as it shows a graphical representation of the sequence of merges taking place for the creation of this cluster and subsequent clusters. ProtoNet provides motif and domain information taken from PFAM, Prints, ProDom, Prosite, and SMART.

ClusTr

ClusTr is a protein sequence clustering algorithm. The algorithm starts by building a similarity matrix of "all-against-all" protein sequences (using Smith-Waterman score). A Monte-Carlo simulation is performed to assess a statistical significance of the Smith-Waterman scores, yielding Z-values. Clusters are built using a single linkage algorithm for different levels of protein similarity. The CluSTr data is stored in a relational database (Oracle). Multiple users have direct access to the database via Java servlets.

CluSTr data is updated incrementally in a synchronized manner with weekly releases of SWISS-PROT + TrEMBL ('new against new' and 'new against current'). Only a subset "CluSTr Slim"of all clusters in CluSTr is available via the web interface.

CLICK

The authors represented the input data as a weighted similarity graph; edge weights are derived from the similarity values (The E-value of the similarity between every two proteins as computed by BLAST). The algorithm used graph-theoretic and statistical techniques to identify tight groups of highly similar elements (kernels). Also, a minimum weight cut algorithm has been used to split the graph into subgraphs.

The CLICK program was written in C programming language and executed on an SGI ORIGIN200 machine utilizing one IP27 processor. The implementation used linear space and stored the similarity graph in a compact form by using linked adjacency lists. The running times were approximately linear in the number of sequences, and ranged from few seconds for a data set of 500 elements, to seven minutes for a data set of 10,000 elements.

SYSTERS

The SYSTEmatic Re-Searching (SYSTERS) algorithm is designed to identify a set of similar sequences without ranking them. SYSTERS consists of three main procedures: SYSTERS1 (set-theoretical clustering) started with a database search, iterated the BLAST (with BLOSUM 50) and produced a cluster of sequences related to a query. SYSTERS 2 (single linkage clustering) changes the set-theoretical point of view to a graph oriented perspective. SYSTERS 3 (hierarchical clustering): employed the self-structuring properties of the data to find a reasonable partitioning into superfamily and family clusters without relying on an arbitrarily chosen threshold. The complete cluster set of SYSTERS clusters is derived by a script written in Perl. The clustering routines are implemented in C++, using the LEDA library for the processing and visualization of the sequence graphs.

SYSTERS was tested on the SWISS-PROT Rel. 34 and the PIR1 databases Rel. 51.The tests showed that the runtime for clustering 59,021 sequences took roughly five days on a workstation cluster consisting of eight SUN Ultra workstations.

Partitioning Clustering

A scalable algorithm for clustering protein data sequences

This approach does not require an 'all - against –all' analysis, and uses a near linear complexity k-means based clustering algorithm. The key idea is to find a set of features that capture the sequential nature of the various data sequences. These frequent subsequences, often called "motifs". Then, project each data sequence into a new space whose dimensions are these features, and then use a traditional vector-space k-means based clustering algorithm to find the clusters of data sequences. The experiments were run on a Linux machine with 4 GB of memory utilizing 550 MHz Pentium III CPU. No tool or database resulting from this interesting work has been made available to the scientific community.

Incremental Clustering

Leaders-SubLeaders

In this algorithm, the first pattern is selected as the leader of a cluster and the remaining patterns are classified depending on the existing leaders or may become a leader of a new cluster. The SIM tool was used with PAM 250 scoring matrix [41] to compute the similarity between protein sequences. The data set considered has totally 2565 sequences. The experiments were done on Intel pentium-4 processor based machine having a clock frequency of 1700 Mhz and 512 MB RAM. The leaders and leaders-subleaders require only one and two database scans respectively. The time complexity for these algorithms is O(n). The results of this algorithm are given based on a small data set.

Density-Based Clustering

SEQOPTICS

SEQOPTICS is an extension of the OPTICS algorithm (Ordering Points to Identify the Clustering Structure). SEQOPTICS was implemented in the following steps. First, data sets are created by extraction of a collection of protein sequences from one or more families in public databases, and then the sequences are mixed and randomized. Second, a matrix of pairwise distances between the proteins is computed. A normalized form of the Smith-Waterman score with BLOSUM 50 scoring matrix is used. Then the OPTICS algorithm is adopted to execute the clustering and the clustering structure is graphically presented. A reachability distance plot is made for each data set. Four data sets are extracted from different protein repositories (Pfam, Swiss-

Prot, and NCBI) for testing. The whole data set contains 1097 sequences. SEQOPTICS has proved its value for handling small data sets.

III. ALGORITHMS' COMPARISON

A general set of factors, which are common across all clustering algorithms is used in the comparison. A brief description of these factors is clarified as follows:

- Clustering method: partitioning, hierarchical, incremental, or density-based clustering.
- Linkage strategy: single, complete, or average linkage.
- Time Complexity: The time required to run an algorithm.
- Robust to outliers: The sensitivity of an algorithm to relatively distant sequences.
- Limited number of clusters: Most of the partitioning clustering algorithms require the user to specify the number of clusters before performing the clustering.
- Availability: The programming language used to implement the tool.
- Data Source: The database (s) source of the sequences that the algorithm is tested on.
- Number of sequences: The total number of sequences that have been clustered by the algorithm.
- Similarity measure: The three popular similarity measures: Smith waterman, BLAST, and FASTA are the most commonly used ones, but there are other tools available.
- Scoring Matrix: This matrix may be one of the series of BLOSUM or PAM. The BLOSUM series include BLOSUM 62, BLOSUM 50, BLOSUM 45, and BLOSUM 80. The PAM series include PAM 1, PAM 30, PAM 120, and PAM 250.
- Hierarchy produced: is the tool produces a hierarchy of clusters for super families, families, and sub families.
- Order independence: A clustering algorithm should not be sensitive to the ordering of the input objects.
- Suitable for large Data Set: If the algorithm succeeded to cluster to cluster many thousands of sequences in a proper time, then it is suitable to be applied on large data sets.

In the Table I, we present a comparison between the clustering algorithms reviewed in the previous section in terms of the above factors.

IV. CONCLUSION

In this paper, we investigated in the problem of clustering protein sequences. We reviewed the issues of protein sequence databases including sequence similarity search, protein sequence alignment and scoring matrices. A survey and a comparison of eight protein sequence clustering algorithms have been accomplished. Partitioning and Hierarchical clustering methods are the most time consuming ones. While incremental and density-based approaches proved their value for small data sets.

Due to the large size of protein sequence databases, there is an urgent need to develop protein sequences clustering algorithms that could enhance the computation time. Moreover, clustering algorithms are needed to annotate new protein sequences in an efficient time.

References

[1] Hofmann K, Bucher P, Falquet L, Bairoch A. "The PROSITE database, its status in 1999". Nucleic Acids Res vol. 27, No. (1): pp. 215-219, 1999.

[2] Attwood TK, Croning MD, Flower DR, Lewis AP, Mabey JE, Scordis P, et al." PRINTS-S: the database formerly known as PRINTS". Nucleic Acids Res vol. 28, No. (1): pp. 225-227, 2000.

[3] Attwood TK, Flower DR, Lewis AP, Mabey JE, Morgan SR, Scordis P, et Al. "PRINTS prepares for the new millennium". Nucleic Acids Res vol 27, No. (1): pp 220-225, 1999.

[4] Henikoff S, Henikoff JG, Pietrokovski S."Blocks+: A Non-Redundant Database of Protein Alignment Blocks Derived from multiple compilations". Bioinformatics vol. 15, No. (6): pp. 471-479, 1999.

[5] Bateman A, Birney E, Durbin R, Eddy SR, Howe KL, Sonnhammer EL."The Pfam protein families database". Nucleic Acids Res vol. 28, No. (1): pp. 263-266, 2000.

[6] Letunic I, Copley RR, Pils B, Pinkert S, Schultz J, Bork P. "SMART 5: domains in the context of genomes and networks". Nucleic Acids Res. Vol. 34, No. (1): pp. 257-60, 2006.

[7] Catherine Bru, Emmanuel Courcelle, et. Al." The ProDom database of protein domain families: more emphasis on 3D". Nucleic Acids Res. Vol. 33, No. (1): pp. 212-215, 2005.

[8] Tatusov RL, Natale DA, Garkavtsev IV, et. Al."The COG database: new developments in phylogenetic classification of proteins from complete genomes". Nucleic Acids Res. Vol. 29, No. (1): pp. 8-22, 2001.

[9] Hunter S., Apweiler R., Attwood K., et. Al."InterPro: the integrative protein signature database". Nucleic acids research vol. 37, No. (1): pp. 211–215, 2009.

[10] Marchler-Bauer A, Anderson JB, Chitsaz F, et. Al." CDD: specific functional annotation with the Conserved Domain Database".Nucleic Acids Res Vol. 37, No. (1): Pp. 5-10, 2009.

[11] Bernstein FC, Koetzle TF, Williams GJ, Meyer EF, Jr., Brice MD, Rodgers JR, et Al." The Protein Data Bank. A computer-based archival file for macromolecular structures". Eur J Biochem Volume 80, No. (2): Pp. 319-24, 1977.

[12] Berman HM, Westbrook J, Feng Z, Gilliland G, Bhat TN, Weissig H, et Al." The Protein Data Bank". Nucleic Acids Res Vol. 28, No. (1): Pp. 235-42, 2000.

[13] Yanli Wang, Kenneth J. Addess, Jie Chen, Lewis Y. Geer, Jane He,et. Al. "MMDB: annotating protein sequences with Entrez's 3D-structure database". Nucleic Acids Research Vol. 37, No. (1): Pp. 298-300, 2007.

[14] Holm L, Sander C." Touring protein fold space with Dali/FSSP". Nucleic Acids Res Vol. 26, No. (1): Pp. 316-319, 1998.

[15] Lo Conte L, Ailey B, Hubbard TJ, Brenner SE, Murzin AG, Chothia C. "SCOP: a structural classification of proteins database". Nucleic Acids Res Vol. 28, No. (1): Pp. 257-259, 2000.

[16] FM, Lee D, Bray JE, Sillitoe I, Todd AE, Harrison AP, et Al. "Assigning genomic sequences to CATH". Pearl Nucleic Acids Res Vol. 28, No. (1): Pp. 277-282, 2000.

[17] Schuler GD, Epstein JA, Ohkawa H, Kans JA." Entrez: molecular biology database and retrieval system". Methods Enzymol Vol. 62: Pp. 141-266, 1996.

[18] Bairoch A, Apweiler R." The SWISS-PROT protein sequence database and its supplement TrEMBL in 2000". Nucleic Acids Res Vol. 28, No. (1): Pp. 45-8, 2000.

[19] McGarvey PB, Huang H, Barker WC, Orcutt BC, Garavelli JS, Srinivasarao GY,et al." PIR: a new resource for bioinformatics".Bioinformatics Vol. 16, No. (3): Pp. 290-291, 2000.

[20] Winona C. Barker, John S. Garavelli, et. Al."The PIR-international protein sequence database". Nucleic Acids Res Vol. 27, No. 1: pp. 39-43, 1999.

[21] Shu-ichi Hashimoto, Hirofumi Nishizumi, Reiko Hayashi, Akio Tsuboi, Fumikiyo Nagawa, Toshitada Takemoril and Hitoshi Sakano. "Prf, a novel Ets family protein that binds to the PU.1 binding motif, is specifically expressed in restricted stages of B cell development". International Immunology Vol. 11, No. (9): Pp. 1423-1429, 1999.

[22] Saul B. Needleman and Christian D. Wunsch. "A General Method Applicable to the Search for Similarities in the Amino Acid Sequence of Two Proteins". J. Mol. Biol. Vol. 48: Pp. 443-453, 1970.

[23] Smith TF, Waterman MS." Identification of Common Molecular Subsequences". Journal of Molecular Biology Vol. 147: Pp. 195–197, 1981.

[24] William R. Pearson and David J. Lipman. "Improved tools for biological sequence comparison". Proc. Natl. Acad. Sci. USA, Biochemistry, Vol. 85: Pp. 2444-2448, 1988.

[25] Stephen F. Altschul, Warren Gish, Webb Miller, Eugene W. Myers and David J. Lipman."Basic Local Alignment Search Tool". J. Mol. Biol. Vol. 215: Pp. 403-410, 1990.

[26] John M. Walker. "The Clustal Series of Programs for Multiple Sequence Alignment". Humana Press, DOI: 10.1385/1-59259-890-0:493, Pp. 493-502, 2005.

[27] Rabiner, L.; Juang, B."An introduction to hidden Markov models". ASSP Magazine, IEEE Vol. 3, No.1: Pp. 4 – 16, 1986.

[28] A. Krogh. "An introduction to hidden Markov models for biological sequences". chapter 4, Computational methods in molecular biology, Book, Feb 1999.

[29] G. Yona, N. Linial, and M. Linial." ProtoMap: automatic classification of protein sequences and hierarchy of protein families". Nucleic Acids Research Vol. 28, 2000.

[30] Ori Sasson, Avishay Vaaknin, Hillel Fleischer." ProtoNet: hierarchical classification of the protein space". Nucleic Acids Research Vol. 31, No. (1): Pp. 348–352, 2003 .

[31] E.V. Kriventseva, W. Fleischmann, E.M. Zdobnov, and G. Apweiler.]" CluSTr: a database of clusters of SWISSPROT+ TrEMBL proteins". Nucleic Acids Research Vol. 29, 2001.

[32] R. Sharan, and R. Shamir." CLICK: A clustering algorithm with applications to gene expression analysis". Proc.Of International Conference on Intelligent Systems for Molecular Biology (ISMB), Pp. 307-316, AAAI Press, Menlo Park, CA.2000.

[33] A. Krause. "Large scale clustering of protein sequences". Ph.D. Dissertation, Berlin, 2002.

[34] FAHIM A.M., SALEM A.M., et. Al."An efficient enhanced k-means clustering algorithm". Journal of Zhejiang University SCIENCE A, Vol. 7, No. (10): Pp. 1626-1633, 2006.

[35] Zhexue Huang."Extensions to the k-Means Algorithm for Clustering Large Data Sets with Categorical Values". Jornal of Data Mining and Knowledge Discovery Vol. 2, No.(3): pp. 283-304, 1998.

[36] V. Guralnik, and G. Karypis. "A scalable algorithm for clustering protein sequences". Proc. Of 1st IEEE conference On Data Mining, 2001.

[37] Sondes Fayech, Nadia Essoussi and Mohamed Limam. "Partitioning clustering algorithms for protein sequence data sets". BioData Mining VOL 2, NO (3), 2009.

[38] P. A. Vijaya, M. Narasimha Murty and D. K. Subramanian." An efficient incremental protein sequence clustering algorithm". ICPR Vol. 2: Pp. 447-450, 2004.

[39] Yonghui Chen, Kevin D. Reilly, Alan P. Sprague, Zhijie Guan. "SEQOPTICS: A Protein Sequence Clustering Method". BMC Bioinformatics Vol. 7 (Suppl 4):S10, 2006.

[40] Kun-Mao Chao and Louxin Zhang. "Sequence Comparison Theory and Methods", book, part II. Chapter: "Scoring matrices". Vol. 7: Pp. 149-172, 2009.

[41] W. John Wilbur. "On the PAM Matrix Model of Protein Evolution". Mol. Biol. Vol. 2, No.(5): Pp. 434-447, 1985.

TABLE I

COMPARISON BETWEEN PROTEIN SEQUENCE CLUSTERING ALGORITHMS

Clustering Method	Partitioning	Hierarchical					Incremental	Density-Based
Example of an Algorithm	A Scalable Algorithm	CLICK	CluSTr	ProtoMap	ProtoNet	SYSTERS	Leaders-SubLeaders	SEQOPTICS
Linkage strategy	-	Average	Single	Average	Average	Single	-	-
Time Complexity	Near-linear to r	Fast	Fast	-	Fast	O (n2)+ 2k * f(r, d)+ O (rd + r2 log r)	O(n)	O(n2L2)
Robust to outliers	-	-	-	No	Yes	Yes	Yes	Yes
Limited number of clusters	Yes	No	No	No	No	No	No	No
Availability	-	C	JAVA, Oracle	JAVA	JAVA	PostgreSQL, Perl C++	Pseudo code	JAVA
Data Source	Swiss-Prot	DS1 (72'623 from the ProtoMap), DS2(117'835 from SYSTERS)	80'000 from Swiss-Prot and 351'834 from TrEMBL	Swiss-Prot	SwissProt and TrEMBL.	101'602 from Swiss-Prot and 636'825 from TrEMBL	1609 of HLA protein family, 227 of AAA protein Family, 629 of Globins protein family.	Pfam, Swiss-Prot, and NCBI
Number of Sequences	53632 sequences	190'458 sequences	341'834 sequences	80'000 sequences	One million proteins	738'427	2465 sequences	1097 sequences
Similarity measure	-	BLAST	SmithWaterman, MonteCarlo	SmithWaterman, BLAST, FASTA	BLAST	BLAST	SIM	Normalized SmithWaterman
Scoring Matrix	-	-	-	BLOSUM 50, BLOSUM 62	-	BLOSUM 50	PAM 250	BLOSUM 50
Hierarchy produced	No	No	Yes	Yes	Yes	Yes	Yes	No
Order Independence	Yes	Yes	Yes	Yes	Yes	Yes	No	Yes
Suitable for large DS	Yes	Yes	Yes	Yes	Yes	Yes	Yes	No

OpenGL in Multi-User Web-Based Applications

K. Szostek, A. Piórkowski
Department of Geoinfomatics and Applied Computer Science,
AGH University of Science and Technology, Cracow, Poland.
{szostek, pioro}@agh.edu.pl

Abstract — **In this article construction and potential of OpenGL multi-user web-based application are presented. The most common technologies like: .NET ASP, Java and Mono were used with specific OpenGL libraries to visualize tree-dimensional medical data. The most important conclusion of this work is that server side applications can easily take advantage of fast GPU and produce efficient results of advanced computation just like the visualization.**

Index Terms — **server-side visualization, 3D, OpenGL**

I. Introduction

Server-side solutions became more popular because of high computation power, large data storage space and security. Advanced computation of seismic field modeling [1] or Web-based DICOM viewing service [2] are examples of server-side applications which take advantage of this solution. Web-based DICOM viewer had been also described in [3]. Furthermore, graphic hardware (GPU) can increase their performance even hundred times [4]. Possibilities of DICOM data visualizations were presented in [5], [6] and [7]. Three-dimensional data, like results of computed tomography (CT)(Fig 1.) or 3D seismic survey can be visualized in real-time using OpenGL technology. These visualizations, parallel to conventional presentation methods, like presented in [2], can improve understanding complex 3D data.

II. Visualization Tools and Technique

A. OpenGL

OpenGL is a set of libraries and extensions that enables programmer to take advantage of graphic hardware [8]. These libraries were originally designed to provide users with high quality computer graphics in real-time, but today, thanks to the extensions, graphic hardware can be also used to solve complex mathematic or physic problems.

OpenGL creates or *renders* visualization in *contexts*. This contexts must be initialized in system's graphic context prior to any OpenGL's function calls. What is more, there can not be more than one active render context. All of OpenGL's functions have to be called from the thread having active context, which means that only one thread can work with one context. Otherwise, context must be switched between threads, which is unfortunately slow and mostly discourage.

All the rendering occurs in *frame buffer*, which is usually the monitor display. OpenGL's extension allows to render directly into graphic's memory via *framebuffer object* (FBO), which is faster than frame buffer.

The Shader technology, an extension of OpenGL, may be useful to provide visualization with higher quality and to modularize server application. Advanced computation are also available through this technology. In this work Shader technology is omitted.

OpenGL libraries works with almost any programming language. For most of them there are OpenGL wrappers, like Tao Framework [9] or OpenTK [10] for MS .NET or Mono, Java 3D, Java OpenGL (JOGL) [11] or Lightweight Java Game Library (LWJGL) [12] for Sun Java. These libraries are usually very similar in use and code may be easly and fast reused.

To construct OpenGL server application Tao Framework, JOGL and LWJGL were used as they are very similar. OpenTK, based on Tao Framework, and Java 3D were omitted because they provide different approach to OpenGL application construction.

B. DirectX and XNA

DirectX and XNA are sets of tools and libraries from Microsoft. These tools are omitted because of their commercial character and limit of language and platform options.

C. Volume render

Volume render is a method of visualization of three-dimensional data. OpenGL with extensions includes tools to compose 3D texture, which can be sampled by planes parallel to view to display 3D data (Fig 2.). Depending on *transfer function* these planes have applied opacity to present chosen part of data.

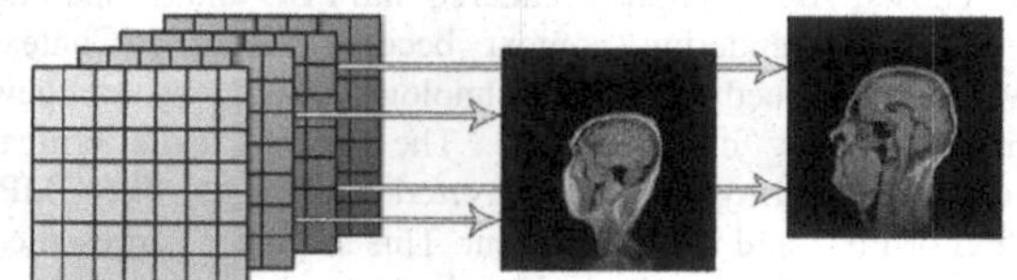

Fig 1. Example of 3D data.

T. Sobh, K. Elleithy (eds.), *Innovations in Computing Sciences and Software Engineering*,
DOI 10.1007/978-90-481-9112-3_64, © Springer Science+Business Media B.V. 2010

This method was chosen because of its popularity, simplicity and possibility of Shader technology application. Shader technology may be used to define custom transfer function and to improve quality of visualization. [5] [6] Different approach of visualization was presented in [7].

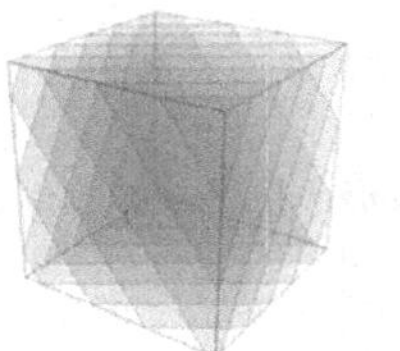
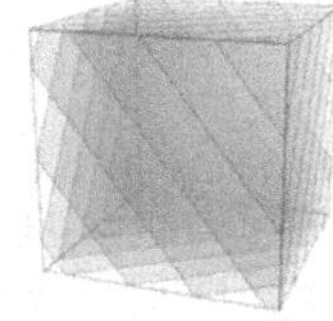

Fig 2. Box of 3D data sampled by planes in volume render.

III. WEB-BASED VISUALIZATION APPLICATION

A. Concept

General idea of OpenGL multi-user web-based application is to provide high quality visualization of 3D data to thin client architecture via web browser. The server application has to be able to produce series of visualization for multiple clients requests at one time. Method of visualization may vary depending on type of 3D data.

B. Hardware and software requirements

In order to take full advantage of OpenGL application, graphic hardware must support 3D texturing and Shader technology. Its amount of memory should be above average, because 3D data may be very large. Server's operating system must run in graphic mode as the graphic context is required.

C. Construction of application

The first request received by server application initializes OpenGL rendering context and FBO. Then 3D data are loaded from files (or one prepared file) and 3D texture is created. The visualization is ready to be rendered and the application can now receive more requests.

Then the process enters critical section. This prevents other request from calling OpenGL's function or changing active context. The context is set as active and visualization's parameters sent by client, e.g. eye-view position, are applied. The chosen visualization is rendered into FBO and copied into byte array. Rendering context become inactive. Context switching is forced by server technology, which may start new thread for new client request. The process exits critical section. Byte array is then converted into image, like BMP, JPEG or PNG and is sent to client. This sequence is presented on figure Fig 4. Analogical and more general model of communication was described in [13].

D. The applications

Application's interface is a web page, written in HTML and JavaScript (Fig 3.). It provides user with control buttons and visualization.

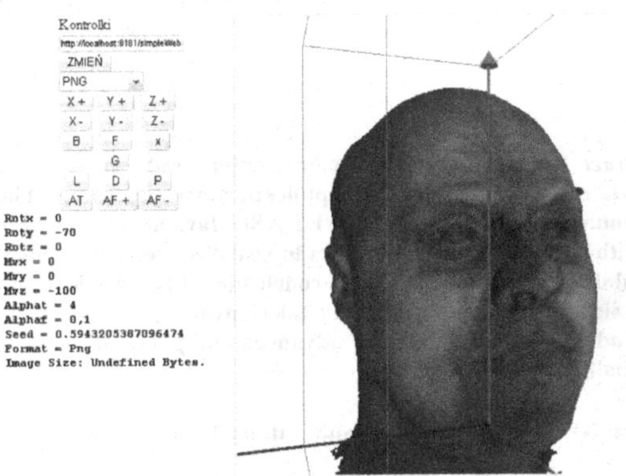

Fig 3. Web page interface with example visualization of CT images

User sends request each time he clicks any of the control button. Results of the requests are displayed next to this controls.

IV. PRELIMINARY TESTS

A. Operating systems

The application was preliminarily tested on two operating systems: MS Windows XP (SP3), and Linux (Fedora Core 10, kernel: 2.6.27.21-170.2.56.fc10.i686). There were few changes made on systems to allow running OpenGL server application and operate on large amount of data.

Windows Server 2008 and its security solution causes problems to OpenGL server application. This OS was omitted in this paper, but will be examined in future.

B. Software environment

Internet Information Services (IIS), version 5.1 for Windows XP and version 7.0 for Windows Server 2008 to run ASP .NET server application and Apache Tomcat, version 6.0.18 for Sun Java SE (1.6.0_14) were installed.

The application was written in ASP and C# for .NET Framework, version 2.0 and Mono, version 2.4; and in Java language. The Tao Framework, version 2.1.0, JOGL, version 1.1.1a and LWJGL, version 2.1.0 OpenGL's wrappers were used.

In Mono and Java libraries few issues were found and reported as bug.

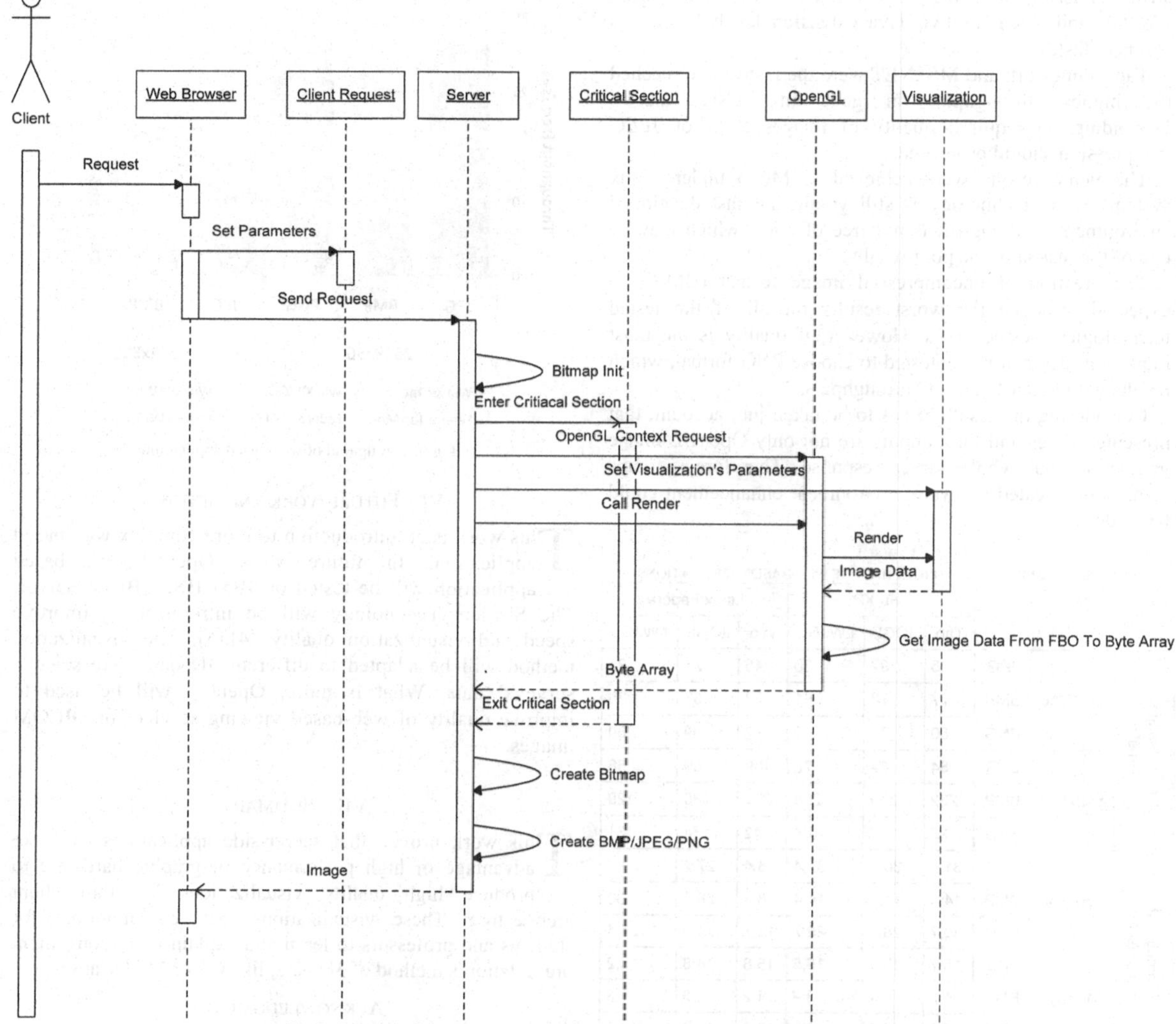

Fig 4. Sequence diagram of request handling by constructed web-based applications.

C. Hardware environment

The tests were performed using two computers. The server machine was single computer (laptop) which has following parameters:

- Intel Pentium III Xeon, 2500 MHz,
- 3072 MB RAM,
- NVIDIA Quadro FX 1600M (512 MB).

The second computer, known as thin client, was standard PC which has following parameters:

- Intel Pentium 4, 1600 MHz,
- 640 MB RAM.

It has MS Windows XP Professional SP3 installed.

D. The tests

Created applications were tested using JMeter 2.3.2 installed on the client side. Minimal response for single user and throughput for 30 users were examined. Tests were done for resolutions 256x256 and 512x512, for three common image file formats (BMP, JPEG and PNG). The results are presented in Table I and figures Fig 5. and Fig 6.

V. Discussion

The shortest time of response was reached in Java and LWJGL under control of Linux Fedora Core 10. This solution seems to be the most promising for future work, which may be surprising, because LWJGL is not just an OpenGL's wrapper. It has some additional classes and mechanisms. As we can read on the official web site of the project: *"The whole point of LWJGL was to bring the speed of*

Java rendering into the 21st century" [12]. Comparing LWJGL and JOGL as two Java extension LWJGL was, as claimed, fastest.

Tao Framework and MS .NET were the fastest and reached the highest throughputs in generating PNG images. Depending on required quality of images PNG or JPEG compression should be chosen.

The worst results were achieved in Mono under Linux system. Mono technology is still young but fast developed environment. Although it is not free of bugs, which may be one of the reason of the poor results.

The creation of uncompressed image format (BMP), as expected, produce the worst results for all of the tested technologies, besides Java. However, if quality is the most important factor, it is suggested to choose PNG format, which results with better times and throughputs.

Considering the results it has to be taken into account, that presented times and throughputs are not only OpenGL image generation, but whole server response. Therefore, perhaps some sophisticated software environment enhancement could be made.

TABLE I
TIME PERFORMANCE AND THROUGHPUT OF WEB-BASED APPLICATIONS

			Win XP			Linux Fedora		
			Tao	JOGL	LWJGL	Tao	JOGL	LWJGL
Response time [ms]	256x256	JPG	35	32	30	45	24	23
		BMP	77	73	81	122	38	36
		PNG	50	74	70	92	59	60
	512x512	JPG	84	84	79	109	69	66
		BMP	232	269	268	262	130	129
		PNG	97	167	165	142	134	131
Throughput [req./sec]	256x256	JPG	31,3	30,4	31,4	15,4	27,2	29,7
		BMP	14,4	14,2	14,4	8,3	28,1	30
		PNG	30,7	26,3	26,7	13,7	24,9	27,4
	512x512	JPG	15,7	15,4	15,5	15,8	14,3	15,2
		BMP	4,2	4	3,9	4,2	13	13
		PNG	15,6	9,6	9,2	10,8	10,8	10,6

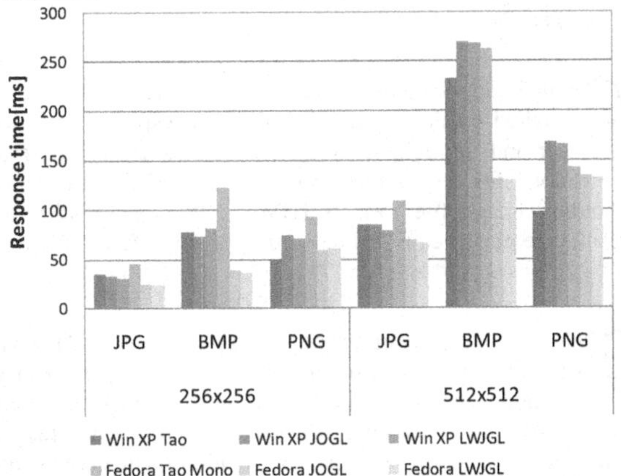

Fig 5. Time performance of web-based applications

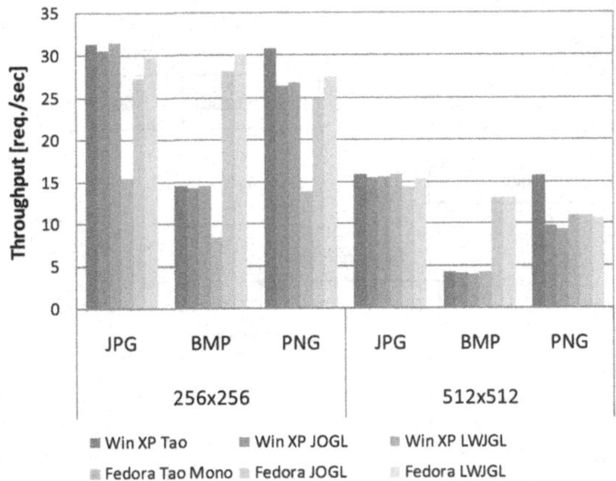

Fig 6. Throughput of web-based applications

VI. FUTURE WORK AND OPTIONS

This work is an introduction to more complex web-based application. In future work OpenGL web-based application will be tested on IBM HS21 Blade Server. The Shaders Technology will be introduced to improve speed and visualization quality [4],[5]. The visualization method will be adapted to different 3D data, like seismic surveys' data. What is more, OpenGL will be used to improve quality of web-based viewing service for DICOM images.

VII. SUMMARY

This work proved that server-side applications can take advantage of high performance of graphic hardware to produce high quality visualizations for thin client architecture. These visualizations may be important for students and professors to learn and explain more convenient presentation's method of 3D data, like CT or MRI scans.

ACKNOWLEDGMENT

This work was financed by the AGH - University of Science and Technology, Faculty of Geology, Geophysics and Environmental Protection as a part of statutory project number 11.11.140.561.

REFERENCES

[1] A. Kowal, A. Piórkowski, T. Danek, A. Pięta, "Analysis of selected component technologies efficiency for parallel and distributed seismic wave field modeling," in Innovations and Advances in Computer Sciences and Engineering, Springer, 2010.

[2] A. Piorkowski, L. Jajesnica, K. Szostek, "Creating 3D Web-Based Viewing Services for DICOM Images", in Computer Networks, 16th Conference, CN 2009, Wisla, Poland, June 16-20, 2009, Communications in Computer and Information Science, Springer Berlin.

[3] J. Fernandez-Bayó, O. Barbero, C. Rubies, M. Sentís, L. Donoso, "A DICOM Web Server and a DICOM Java Viewer," in Distributing Medical Images with Internet Technologies, RadioGraphics, 2000.

[4] T. Danek, "Seismic wave field modeling with graphics processing units," in Lecture Notes in Computer Science, vol. 5545, 2009.

[5] O. Kuttera, R. Shamsb, N. Navaba, "Visualization and GPU-accelerated simulation of medical ultrasound from CT images,"in Computer methods and programs in biomedicine 94, Elsevier, 2009.

[6] J. Krüger and R. Westermann, Acceleration Techniques for GPU-based Volume Rendering, Computer Graphics and Visualization Group, Technical University Munich, 2003.

[7] P.N. Ancuta, "3D Object Modeling and Visualization Software for Surgery Preoperative Plan," in 6th Workshop on European Scientific and Industrial Collaboration on promoting Advanced Technologies in Manufacturing, WESIC'08, 2008.

[8] The OpenGL Graphics System: A Specification (Version 3.1 - March 24, 2009) [@:] http://www.opengl.org

[9] The Tao Framework documentation, [@:] http://www.taoframework.com/about

[10] The Open Toolkit Manual, [@:] http://www.opentk.com/doc

[11] J.X. Chen and E.J. Wegman, Foundations of 3D Graphics Programming Using JOGL and Java3D, Springer Verlag, New York, 2006.

[12] Home of the Lightweight Java Game Library. [@:] www.lwjgl.org/

[13] C. W. Arnold, A. A. T. Bui, C. Morioka, S. El-Saden, and H. Kangarloo, "A Prototype Web-based Reporting System for Onsite-Offsite Clinician Communication," in Radiographics July 2007 27:1201-1211

Testing Task Schedulers on Linux System

Leonardo Jelenković, Stjepan Groš, Domagoj Jakobović
University of Zagreb, Croatia
Faculty of Electrical Engineering and Computing

***Abstract* – Testing task schedulers on Linux operating system proves to be a challenging task. There are two main problems. The first one is to identify which properties of the scheduler to test. The second problem is how to perform it, e.g., which API to use that is sufficiently precise and in the same time supported on most platforms. This paper discusses the problems in realizing test framework for testing task schedulers and presents one potential solution. Observed behavior of the scheduler is the one used for "normal" task scheduling (SCHED_OTHER), unlike one used for real-time tasks (SCHED_FIFO, SCHED_RR).**

I. Introduction

Starting from Linux kernel version 2.6.23 task scheduler was changed from *O(1)* [1] to *Completely Fair Scheduler* (CFS) [2]. This caused a lot of discussion in the Linux community [3]. Arguments used to support the claim that "*this* scheduler is better than *the other*" varies from (subjective) user experience in everyday activities to (objective) results of some benchmarking programs. Opinion of the authors of this paper is that benchmarking programs currently used are too hard on scheduler, putting it in atypical working environment and testing only some of it's property. Therefore, more systematic approach is necessary. One such attempt will be presented in this paper. Identification activity of important scheduler properties can start with most discussed properties: scheduler efficiency, behavior under heavy loads and scheduling interactive tasks.

Testing for efficiency

Efficiency, in scheduler context, represents the ability of a system to perform more operations, to complete more tasks in less time using less system resources. For example, if a collection of jobs under some scheduler completes in less time than with second scheduler, then the first one is more efficient. To be efficient, scheduler should have small overhead and better scheduling decisions. Basic benchmarking of scheduling efficiency could be performed with collection of predefined tasks. Tasks may be independent, they can have dependencies (e.g., preceding-successor ordering), or they can use the same resources and synchronize themselves [4]. The benchmark could end when all tasks finish their jobs, or when predefined time elapses, in which case task's progress can be used for evaluation.

An example of extreme test for scheduler efficiency can be done with a set of tasks that exchange a token in a circular pattern [5]. Implementation of this benchmark could use pipes, messages or some synchronization mechanisms. Most of the time system will run in scheduler, because passing a token is a very short activity which is followed by activating next task that has received the token. This kind of tests will measure scheduler ability to switch between tasks.

Testing efficiency requires ability to start and simultaneously run a set of various tasks. E.g, tasks can communicate or not, continuously run or have sleep periods, have high priority, etc.

Testing for interactivity

Interactivity testing considers system's response times to user commands, input/output events, interactive applications, multimedia applications and similar. All those activities behave in a similar pattern: most of the time they do not require system attention (processing), but when they do, they should be processed as soon as possible. E.g., user may be annoyed by delayed reaction on his activities, like typing commands in shell, or using graphic interface. Multimedia applications may not have required quality if they experience long delays (sound might have pauses, video may skip frames). For desktop computers, which are mostly used by single user (at a time), scheduler should put precedence to user requests, and boost priority of foreground application when needed. For example, Microsoft Windows operating systems have a fairly simple scheduler [6], oriented toward single user systems[1] that satisfies requirements of foreground applications. Background applications get unused time, or at least bits of processor's time to avoid task starvations [7].

Testing for interactivity could be done with user who uses interactive applications in different working environments (e.g., different system loads). One problem with such approach is in quantification: how good or bad is the scheduler, how to compare schedulers, how scheduling changes with load? Another problem is in test repetition: how to repeat certain conditions that lead to particular system behavior.

Another way of testing interactivity is to eliminate the user from the test – construct test framework that will quantify scheduler behavior with synthetic interactive applications. Those tests might be more objective, but may also be too synthetic, i.e. they might miss to test some important scheduler behavior that occurs in real usage scenarios.

Synthetic tests can be used to evaluate several scheduler behaviors. The first one is regarding delays from events occurrence and start of their processing (in associated tasks). The second is in event processing durations (which can be interrupted and further delayed). Number of events processed too late may be indicator that scheduler is not performing as expected or system is not in normal state (e.g., heavy loaded).

Tasks used for interactivity testing could be modeled as periodic tasks, i.e. the ones that act on periodic events. Period length and event processing time could be test parameters. Many events in real systems do not arrive periodically but are

1 "Single-user system" in this context is used to describe system usage scenarios, not capabilities. System could have "multi-user" capabilities, but if in tested scenario is used only by single user, scheduler behavior will be evaluated as for single-user system.

T. Sobh, K. Elleithy (eds.), *Innovations in Computing Sciences and Software Engineering*,
DOI 10.1007/978-90-481-9112-3_65,

aperiodic or sporadic. Still, using a periodic task or several with different periods such events can be simulated. In the end, system's reaction time is important for tests and that property should be investigated, not event occurrence patterns. Environment modeling can be extended with background tasks simulating different system loads.

Testing under different loads

Testing scheduler behavior under different system loads involves changing load and repeating tests. Since tests must be repeatable, even background load should be carefully modeled. Tasks for background load (*worker* tasks) could continuously consume all computing power when scheduled or use only part of given computing time. In a simple implementation this could be achieved with adding sleep interval that follows working interval. With duration of work and sleep intervals various background loads can be modeled. Other types of background tasks may include a set of tasks that intensively use scheduler, such as token passing tasks or even interactive tasks.

Background tasks priority can be lower, equal or even higher than priority of testing tasks.

Testing for scalability

Since multiprocessor systems have gone mainstream (as real multiprocessor or as multi-core) and are present in almost any new computer system, it is important to look into scheduler behavior in this environment. Testing schedulers for scalability requires no special changes in the test framework, but just adequate test parameters and appropriate result interpretation.

Scheduler must be aware of hardware characteristics and try to exploit them for achieving maximal performance. As an example, it is a common practice to associate tasks with particular processor, trying to exploit data already present in processors caches across successive task run time (interrupted by kernel calls and other tasks). However, if this is implemented by multiple run-queues, one for each processor, periodic balancing could be needed, preventing starvation and obtaining fair share of computing time for all tasks in system.

Testing for fairness

On a single-user systems, scheduler must satisfy requirements of a single user. Application currently used by the user (foreground application) is usually most important for user at that time, and should receive maximum system's attention. Scheduler should be aware of foreground application and raise its priority when it comes to foreground.

On multi-user systems scheduler must be fair. Fairness can be defined per user or per task. In *per user* concept, fair scheduler will balance different user's tasks execution times so that they distribute available computing time equally. In *per task* concept, all tasks should get fair (equal) amount of computing time. However, neither all users nor all tasks are equal. Some may be more important than other (e.g., "root" compared to a normal user). Differentiation is achieved trough different task (or/and user) priorities. For example, on UNIX like systems priority for non-real-time tasks is called *nice level*. The lower *nice* value is, a higher priority the task has. Values for nice are in range from -20 to 19. If the first task has nice of n and the second $n+1$, than the first task should receive more computing power than the second, e.g. 10% more [8]. Scheduler must take into account tasks priorities and accordingly distribute available computing power.

To test for fairness, test application should create task set, run it for some time, and compare tasks advancements. If tasks have same priorities, advancements should be similar, otherwise, task priorities should be seen in tasks progress.

II. TEST FRAMEWORK ARCHITECTURE

Scheduler testing should be performed with specific tasks. In a test framework it must be possible to define various tasks types. One way to achieve it, is to define generic properties which in combination define particular task type.

In a single test a collection of tasks can be used, some with same and some with different properties. Tasks with same properties can be grouped together and create a *task group*. Proposed configuration file skeleton is shown in Fig. 1.

```
global {
   test_name = "example";
   duration = 60 s;
   run = interactive[1], background[3];
}
tasks {
   interactive {
      #definition of task properties
   }
   background {
      #definition of task properties
   }
} # comment from # to end of line
```

Fig. 1. Test configuration skeleton

Besides test name and duration, *global* section must define which tasks to create and run. For that purpose, group names and number of tasks to create are used, as shown in Fig. 1 with the *run* keyword. Task group properties are defined within *tasks {}* section, separately for each task group.

Defining worker tasks

Worker tasks come in two categories: in one are those that use all computing time, and in the other one are those that don't. Modeling the first group is done with a simple program loop, that will consume given computing time (processor's time). However, in order to measure task progress a number of finished loops can be counted. If a processing within the loop is too simple, a number of completed loops will be very large. It is preferred that the processing within single loop take measurable amount of time, e.g., one millisecond. In that way loop count will directly measure computing time a task had spent. Creating such job could be done by an inner loop that performs some simple operations a number of times. Since computing power differs across different processors, number of inner loop iterations (e.g., *loops_per_ms*) can be calculated in advance, before test is started. This could be performed in several ways.

The first approach could be to guess a number of iterations based on some system property, e.g., processor's speed. Execution of the calculated number of iterations should then be timed. Based on execution time, iterations could be corrected (even several times). However, some measurements must be invalidated if timings are significantly longer – they are probably caused by task switch. Time measuring should be done with precise system calls, such as *clock_gettime()* [9].

In the second approach the same loop can be run for extended period of time. Then, using consumed *user time* retrieved from the system (e.g., with *getrusage()*) number of iterations that will yield a required time period for one inner loop can be calculated.

Both approach were tested and conclusion is that the second approach has a small advantage as it's results are little more consistent across several executions. But absolute accuracy is actually not needed. For comparing task progression its only necessary that jobs within iterations are the same, so that completed iterations can be used for comparison. Number of iterations only approximates task computation time, and its accuracy is less important for worker tasks. In test framework, although both methods were implemented, second approach is preferred. Before executing a test, a number of iterations for inner loop that will consume one millisecond time is defined in an environment variable and is used in the tests.

Defining worker tasks that don't work all time, require defining *working time* and *sleeping time* within single iteration [10].

Both worker task types can be in simplified form described with a pseudo code in Fig. 2.

```
worker_task {
    for iter = 0 to inf do {
        work(working_time);
        sleep(sleeping_time);
    }
}
```

Fig. 2. Worker tasks

Sleeping can be achieved in a number of different ways. System call *clock_nanosleep()* is chosen because of its high resolution. If a code like the one in Fig. 2 is used in test with more than one task from same task group then all the tasks will try to start execution at the same time, and then sleep at the same time, at least at the start of the test. Later they will probably desynchronize. However, it would be a good idea to desynchronize them intentionally at the start, with a randomization of their first working time duration.

Defining interactive tasks

As described before, interactive tasks can be modeled by periodic tasks. Periodic activity may be modeled by periodic signals sent to tasks, or tasks can suspend themselves until time of the next event (which can be precalculated). Both methods are used in real interactive applications, hence both should be used (separately) and tested.

Fig. 3 shows proposed implementation of interactive tasks using signal and sleep method.

Implementing periodic signals can be done in several different ways. A one solution is to use system call *setitimer()* which periodically sends signal to the calling task. With system call *pause()* task stops itself until signal is received. In signal handler function, times of start and end for event processing should be saved for later analysis (or analysis could be started in handler function).

```
interactive_task{
    if (interactive_signals_defined()) {
        set_signal_handler(signal_handler_function);
        create_periodic_timer(period);
    }
    if (interactive_sleep_defined())
        start_time = get_time();
    for iter = 0 to inf do {
        if (interactive_signals_defined())
            pause();
        if (interactive_sleep_defined()) {
            signal_handler_function();
            sleep_until(start_time + iter * period);
        }
    }
}
signal_handler_function() {
    save_start_time;
    simulate_event_processing;
    save_end_time;
}
```

Fig. 3. Interactive tasks with signal and sleep method

Without signals, interactive task should be delayed until next event occurrence. Clock used in *get_time()* and *sleep_until()* should be real time clock (or monotonic clock). Parameter to *sleep_until()* is absolute time, not relative. Relative waiting could result in prolonged periods due to eventual task switching. System calls that give required functionality and don't use signals are *clock_gettime()* and *clock_nanosleep()*.

For both implementations, "interactivity ratio" can be defined by defining period and event processing times. Real interactive tasks have period that is usually much longer than processing time.

Defining collaborative tasks

Collaborative (communicating) tasks represents tasks that communicate, exchange data or synchronize themselves, like token-passing communication. Collaborative tasks use scheduler more extensively than other task types, because scheduler is invoked much more frequently. Besides token-passing collaboration, another collaborative tasks widely used in multitasking applications are the ones that use shared resource protected by critical section mechanisms. Similar widely used task collaboration is with "barrier type" synchronization. In this synchronization all task are blocked at certain point in program until all other tasks reach the same point. Only then all tasks are released and may continue until next synchronization point.

All mentioned tasks have a start part, and an end part, as shown in Fig. 4.

```
cooperative_task {
    for iter = 0 to inf do {
        if (token_pass_defined()) {
            token_pass_wait();
            token_pass_process();
            token_pass_send();
        }
        if (critical_section_defined()) {
            critical_section_enter();
            critical_section_process();
            critical_section_leave();
        }
        if (barrier_defined()) {
            barrier_wait();
        }
    }
}
```

Fig. 4. Collaborative tasks

Defining additional task properties

Each task, even within the same task group, can have different priority. The simplest priority assignment is to set same priority to all tasks. A bit more complex assignment is to give priorities in a sequential order, e.g., first task gets priority p, the second $p+1$, the third $p+2$, etc. The priorities of the tasks and the assignment policy is a task group property (that is defined in the configuration file).

Single task can be represented by a thread in multi-threaded process, or as a separated process (with only one thread). Some systems may handle threads and processes in different way and the test framework, as specified here, support the evaluation of this difference (e.g., switching between threads from the same process might be faster than between threads from different processes).

Defining universal task

Universal task description should be able to describe all previous task types with their properties, as well as priority and representation (thread/process). Fig. 5 shows universal task code that includes all the behaviors from the previously discussed task types. Functions defined in the previous figures are not repeated since they are the same.

```
universal_task {
   initializations();
   for iter = 0 to inf do {
      iteration_specific();
      work(working_time);
      sleep(sleeping_time);
   }
}
initializations() {
   set_task_priority();
   if (interactive_signals_check()) {
      set_signal_handler(handler_function);
      create_periodic_timer(period);
   }
   if (interactive_sleep_check()) {
      start_time = get_time();
   }
   sync_start_for_all_tasks();
}
iteration_specific() {
   # per type processing, as in Fig. 3 and Fig. 4
}
```

Fig. 5. Universal task behavior

With the appropriate values of the task properties, various task types can be defined. E.g., for interactive tasks properties *working_time*, and *sleeping_time* should be set to zero.

An example of a task definition, including all the properties, of which are some commented out, is shown in Fig. 6.

```
tasks {
   example_task {
      working_time = 50 ms; # zero if not defined
      sleeping_time = 20 ms;
      priority = 5; # or e.g. "sequential[3, 16];"
      task_type = PROCESS; # (default) or THREAD
      #specific = INTERACTIVE_SIGNALS[250 ms,5 ms];
      #specific = INTERACTIVE_SLEEP[150 ms, 15 ms];
      #specific = TOKEN_PASS[MSG, 5 ms];
      #specific = CRITICAL_SECTION[5 ms];
      #specific = BARRIER;
   }
}
```

Fig. 6. Universal task definition

Proposed task definitions, both as in definition file and as task behavior defined with pseudo code, allow definition not of just previously mentioned task types, but also a task with mixed properties.

III. SELECTING AND DEFINING TESTS

In the previous sections test conditions and scheduler properties that should be tested are defined. Also, test framework structure and configurations are presented. In this section few examples of concrete configurations are presented.

First test, as shown in Fig. 7, consists of a set of worker tasks with same priorities.

```
tasks {
   worker {
      working_time = 10 ms;
      priority = 5;
   }
}
global {
   test_name = "worker tasks";
   duration = 60 s;
   run = worker[10];
}
```

Fig. 7. Test configuration with worker type tasks

Using configuration from Fig. 7, test framework will create 10 tasks *(worker[10])* and run them for one minute (*duration = 60 s*). At the test's end, various statistic are reported, e.g., the number of iterations completed, used "user" and "system" times, number of context switches that were performed on task, task priority, task identification number like process and/or thread id, etc. (see Fig. 8). For a given test, comparing iteration numbers from all tasks should give us a measure of the scheduler fairness. Also, different schedulers could be used on same system, they can be compared for efficiency (comparing iterations).

The tests were performed on *Ubuntu* distribution with Linux kernel 2.6.31 (x86_64), with one to four processors (cores) set to constant (maximal) processor's frequency (and hyper-threading ability switched off). Test results for configuration from Fig. 7 (not given here in raw form) showed that scheduler is satisfactory fair in distributing available computing time. When only one processor was activated, tasks got almost the same computing time (numbers of iterations are very close). When more processors are activated, tasks iterations are mostly close to mean value. However, few tasks may have significantly lower or higher values for iteration, with a deviation of up to 25 percent (from several experiments). Since tasks are independent, with four processors number of iterations was four time larger – compared to test with single processor.

When processors' speed was set to "on demand" and hyper-threading ability was activated (default settings!), test showed major progress difference between tasks, indicating scheduler is not yet appropriately adapted for such hardware environment (in respect to fairness).

Changing priorities assignment to sequential will show how initial task priority contribute to given computing time. If the configuration from Fig. 7 is modified by changing line 4 to:

priority = sequential[1-10];

then the first created task will get priority of one and the last one will got the priority ten. The result from a single execution of the test is presented in Fig. 8 and Fig. 9. Repeating the tests shows similar results.

TN	Name	PID	NICE	ITERS	UTIME(C)	UTIME	STIME	CW(v/i)
0	sample	2352	10	5454	54.540000	55.260000	0.000000	1/1740
1	sample	2353	11	4487	44.870000	45.400000	0.000000	1/1335
2	sample	2354	12	3195	31.950000	32.280000	0.000000	1/1062
3	sample	2355	13	2489	24.890000	25.460000	0.000000	1/892
4	sample	2356	14	2064	20.640000	21.200000	0.000000	1/924
5	sample	2357	15	1554	15.540000	15.730000	0.000000	1/749
6	sample	2358	16	1395	13.950000	14.360000	0.000000	1/840
7	sample	2359	17	1169	11.690000	11.870000	0.000000	1/723
8	sample	2360	18	1099	10.990000	11.140000	0.000000	1/770
9	sample	2361	19	673	6.730000	6.920000	0.000000	1/641

'sample': iter_sum=23579 (235.79 s), avg=2357, stdev=1575

Fig. 8. Test results for worker tasks with different priorities

Column *UTIME(C)* presents calculated run time based on iterations completed and assuming accurate inner loop timings. Columns *UTIME* and *STIME* present data for "user" and "system" time respectively, collected using *getrusage()* system call. Difference between *UTIME(C)* and *UTIME* comes from inaccuracy from both inner loop calibration and inaccuracy of the statistic collected by the system (kernel). The last two columns *CW(v/i)* contain numbers of context switches performed on task, both voluntary (when task blocks itself, like blocking on semaphore) and involuntary (task was switched by scheduler).

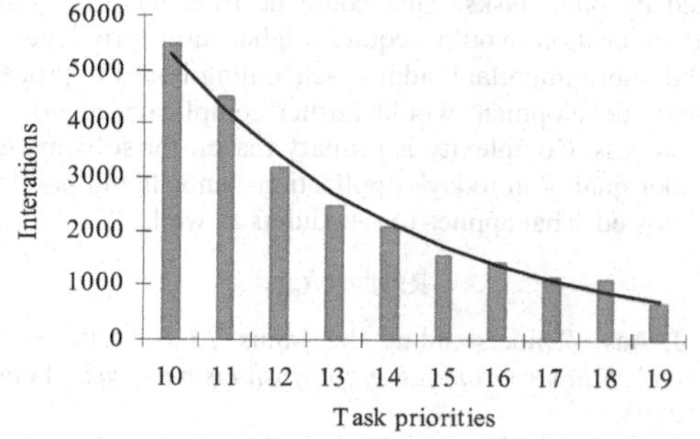

Fig. 9. Priority and progress relation

Bars in the Fig. 9 show the number of iterations achieved by all tasks. Since each task has different priority, each task progress was different. Comparing tasks with priority difference of one and their iterations, an average ratio of 1.25 was calculated in favor of higher priority task (lower "nice" number). Line above bars in Fig. 9 shows trend-line if ratio is to be exactly 1.25. The results show good conformity with trend-line. However, not all tests gave such results. Tests with shorter period on multiprocessor have larger deviations from trend-line, although globally the same ratio is followed.

Introducing sleep time into previous configuration, tests become less intensive on the scheduler, but the relative results are similar: fairness and respect for different priorities didn't change.

Tests with collaborative tasks can show several scheduler properties. With tasks that intensively collaborate, context switching ability can be measured. The example configuration for such test is shown in Fig. 10.

```
tasks {
    token_pass {
        working_time = 0 ms;
        priority = 5;
        specific = TOKEN_PASS[MSG, 0 ms];
    }
}
```

Fig. 10. Token pass task

Section *global* is not shown in the Fig. 10 because it is similar to the same section given in the Fig. 7. Working time is set to zero both for task iteration and token processing, forcing task to block immediately after passing token on (messages were used for passing token). Number of instructions task perform in single iteration before it's switched is almost negligible compared to task switching time and scheduler activity, which are in focus.

With critical section and barrier synchronizations, scheduler can also be tested in extreme conditions, putting all working times to zero. However, those tests are also suitable for evaluating possible gains from multiprocessor systems when a job can be executed by collaborative tasks. Also, with proper distribution of tasks across multiprocessor, scheduler can help in improving performance of such applications. For example, when collaboration can be defined by critical section synchronization, and at some point in application execution only two nonblocked tasks are present on the same processor (one as active and second as a ready task), it would be desirable that the scheduler moves the second task to another processor. It could be that first (active) task has just exit critical section and unblocked second one (that is scheduled on same processor). First task could spend a majority of its current time slice in noncritical section, further delaying second task from executing its critical section, and releasing other task that could run on different processor. This switch should be done regardless of other tasks in system (tasks from other applications). However, such scheduler behavior shouldn't be coded per situation basis, otherwise, a lot of heuristic can also be coded in scheduler, who could became more complex, slower and possibly not work for all situations. But still, since multiprocessors are reality, some simple heuristic regarding scheduling a multi-task application should be applied if possible.

Interactivity behavior can be tested with previously defined interactive task. Two main parameters define interactive task: period in which event recur, and event processing time. In Fig. 11 definitions of two tasks were present: first one activated with signal and second one which is waked on timer expiration.

```
tasks {
    interactive_signal {
        specific = INTERACTIVE_SIGNALS[150 ms, 5 ms];
    }
    interactive_sleep {
        specific = INTERACTIVE_SLEEP[100 ms, 15 ms];
    }
}
```

Fig. 11. Token pass task

Tests on low loaded system, with configuration as in Fig. 11, showed very good scheduler interactivity behavior. Also, shortening period (even down to 1 millisecond on tested system) didn't increase reaction delay. Loading system with moderate "background", reactions becomes little slower, but as long as their period is long enough (at least 10 milliseconds) and background tasks have lower priority, reactions are tolerable.

With heavier system loads overall delay in event processing grows. It depends on application if this longer delays (e.g., 10 to 20 milliseconds) are still acceptable. In example, if user uses multimedia application to play music while working on something else, regardless of that work, music should be played without degradation in quality. Since music player uses only small percent on computing power, scheduler should give him processor's time as soon as requests is made.

IV. Conclusion

Evaluating most active part of an operating system – its task scheduler – is a challenging problem. First, the required scheduler behavior must be defined for all (most) usage scenarios. Second, methods for testing scheduler in those scenarios, methods that are also realizable within given system and its interfaces, must be designed and implemented. Limitations from both: used interfaces and simplifications, must be considered when analyzing test results.

In this paper, an attempt to define required scheduler behavior is presented and elaborated. Based on the presented ideas the test framework is designed and using test framework different basic tests are defined and performed, with brief comments of obtained results.

On the implementation side several problems were encountered. Interface used in the test framework is chosen to be compatible with most Linux based systems. However, precision of those interfaces, as well as behavior, slightly changes across different kernel versions.

The first implementation problem was how to create simulated work with precisely timed execution (determine number of loop iterations that give required duration). Timing is only required for creating tasks with given work/sleep ratio, for defining work time for collaborative and interactive tasks. Timing simple loops showed to be unreliable method since it can be interrupted by the scheduler for a short or even longer time (e.g., task switching). Using longer loop and collecting used "user" time from system relies on imprecise system interface. However, the later approach turned out to be more consistent in repeated tests and is thus preferred method. Based on test experiences, its accuracy its approximately within 10%, which is satisfactory for tests.

The next problem was how to implement "sleep" period. On some systems the interface used (*clock_nanosleep*) showed to be quite accurate. On the others, it wasn't so accurate, probably due to a different time slice and a minimal sleep period. On those systems, if test results are to be meaningful and sleeps are required, longer periods should be used.

Time measurement interfaces suffer from the same problems as implementation of sleep – somewhere are accurate down to 1 millisecond and below, somewhere lower bound is higher.

The test framework was built for scheduler testing only and could be inadequate for other system tests, like performance evaluation. It should be noted that simple program changes (e.g., type and scope of a variable) can noticeably change loop number a task can execute within same time period. Utilized simulated work in (inner) loop includes simple logic operations on integer numbers, and may not relate for real tasks that perhaps use float point arithmetic or are memory intensive. However, approximate comparison between different systems, from performance perspective, can be made (using the same number of inner loop iterations – bypassing calibration).

Based on tests performed during and after building test framework, the results roughly follow expectations. On multiprocessor, fair division of computing time its harder to achieve. Interactive application are treated better than expected (based on past experience), but that could be in part because of the tested system (newer kernel and hardware).

Future work will include extensive testing with the constructed framework on more diverse hardware/software systems, creation of test configuration that more accurately model real working scenarios and test particular scheduler property or more of them simultaneously.

Someone could ask why putting such effort on building and testing schedulers since programmer can significantly influence application scheduling by setting appropriate priority and scheduling policy. E.g., for an interactive application, a real-time scheduling could be chosen, removing problems possibly caused by other tasks. That could be true, but first, running such application would require higher user privileges, and second, more important, adding scheduling issues to process of software development would further complicate already complex process. Complexity is primary reason for software errors and poor quality in today's applications, and should not be further boosted. That applies to schedulers as well.

References

[1] J. Aas, "Understanding the Linux 2.6.8.1 CPU Scheduler," *Silicon Graphics, http://joshaas.net/linux/*, February 2005.

[2] I. Molnar, "Completely Fair Scheduler," *http://kerneltrap.org/node/8059*, April 2007.

[3] J. Andrews et al, "Additional CFS Benchmarks," *http://kerneltrap.org/Linux/Additional_CFS_Benchmarks*, September 2007.

[4] L. Budin, "Operating systems," *Element Zagreb*, in press.

[5] "Pipe-test", http://kerneltrap.org/node/14745.

[6] Win32 thread scheduling, *http://msdn.microsoft.com/en-us/library/ms685096(VS.85).aspx*, October 2009.

[7] B. Hunjadi, "Process scheduling in Win32 environment," *undergraduate thesis (in Croatian), FEE&C – University of Zagreb*, June 2009.

[8] J. Andrews et al, "Linux: History Of Nice Levels," *http://kerneltrap.org/node/11778*, July 2007.

[9] The Single UNIX Specification (man pages), *http://www.opengroup.org/onlinepubs/009695399/*.

[10] Con Kolivas, "Ten percent test," *http://lkml.org/lkml/2007/4/5/384*, April 2007.

Automatic Computer Overhead Line Design

Lucie Noháčová, Karel Noháč

University of West Bohemia, Pilsen, 30614, Czech Republic

***Abstract* — Approach to design of outer electric lines has changed in last years very significantly. Especially new demands in branch reliability should designer keep in mind. These new requests are basis of new European and national standards. To simplify design layout, automate verification of all rules and limitations and minimize mistakes computer application was developed to solve these tasks. This article describes new approach to this task, features and possibilities of this software tool.**

***Index Terms* — Power engineering, Overhead Line Design, Software Application**

I. Introduction

Design of outer electric lines is very complex problem, which contains solving questions not only in branch electric network, but also in branches mechanical dimensioning, geodetic measurement, reliability optimalization and environment consideration. Because of that a computer tool aiding to deal common tasks in main steps of design was developed and programmed.

Application "Electric Line Design" integrates these steps:

- Import of measured data of terrain in three dimension coordinate system, with possible additional information, like point name, comment of height point
- Graphical interactive pylon positioning, including selection of pylon and wire type, choice of basic horizontal wire stress and many other parameters
- Calculation of wire stress in different temperature and overload conditions for verification of maximal possible wire stress limitation and maximal pylon interval to keep distance between wires over minimal adequate value according to supposed conditions
- Calculation of wire stress, wire height and other parameters of wire shape between pylons to respect minimal distance of wire to every terrain important points
- Calculation of installation table of wire stress and deflection for demanded spectrum of temperatures
- Graphical export of created design in form suitable for many CAD applications to simplify project documentation

II. Application Description

Described application was developed in Borland® Delphi® for Microsoft® Windows™ Version 10 Turbo Explorer Edition.

Application is intended for use in Czech Republic, and is therefore almost whole written with captions, input and output text and help in Czech language.

Application layout includes two main windows: Starting window and graphical design windows plus few additional windows.

Starting window allows basic computation parameters management, file operations including data import and launching other parts of application:

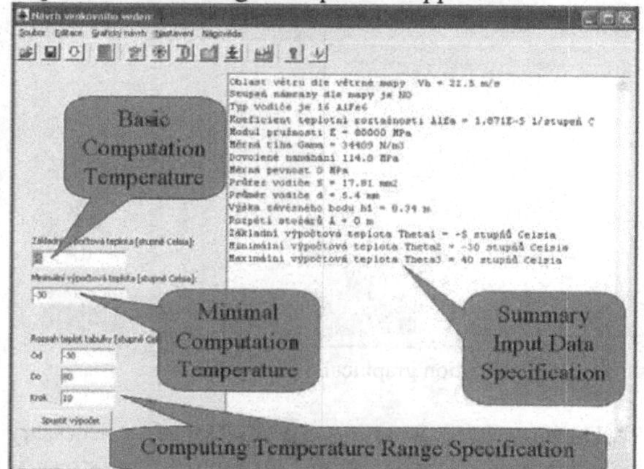

Fig. 1. Application start window

Imported 3D terrain data must be in ASCII file format, position and format of data are arbitrary adjustable in application configuration file. File containing point number, 3D coordinates and point name can for example have following format:

```
201 -909.256  611.315  303.395 meadow
202 -951.106  627.228  303.752 point
203 -982.338  639.393  303.961 ditch
. . .
```

This format is well suitable for import of raw data obtained from special terrain measurement equipment and is fully adjustable. From basic window also editor of all tabular input data can be started. Here database of usual wire and pylon parameters, frost area parameters and wind area parameters can be changed and new elements in database added. For example pylon parameter editing looks following (includes pylon

T. Sobh, K. Elleithy (eds.), *Innovations in Computing Sciences and Software Engineering*, DOI 10.1007/978-90-481-9112-3_66, © Springer Science+Business Media B.V. 2010

description, high, attachment type, wire distance in horizontal and vertical direction):

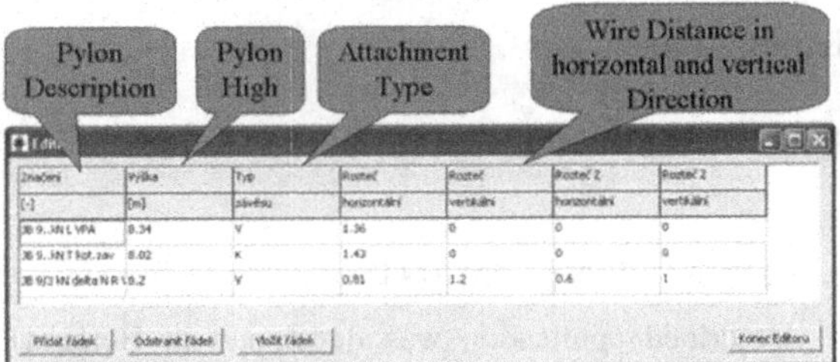

Fig. 2. Tabular input data editor

Graphical design window allows almost all other operations: Pylon type and position management, wire type and basic stress selection, line refraction angle value choice, wind area and frost area selection, distance marker adjust, temperatures and conditions for stress limit computation and for displaying selection, graphical scales adjust and remaining parts of application launch:

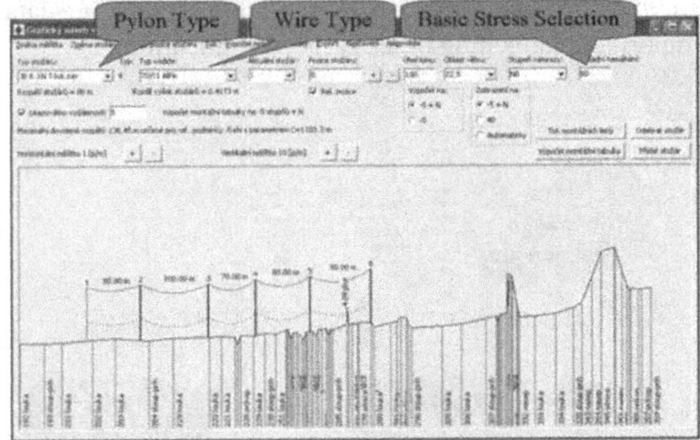

Fig. 3. Application graphical design window

During line creation progress all necessary calculations are made. When maximum wire stress is exceeded, then specified basic stress is showed in red box. At the same time information message about error reason is showed in window.

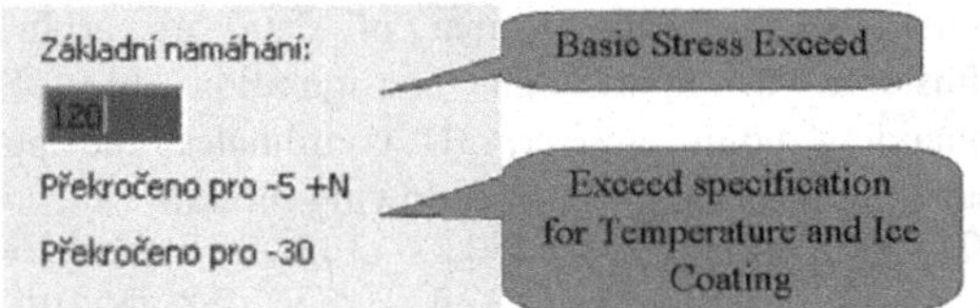

Fig. 4. Error announcement in value edit box

Here exceeding for temperature -5 °C plus overload and for -30 °C is showed.

Similarly if maximum pylon span is exceeded and so wire deflection is bigger than allowed for current pylon and minimal wire distances, than wire is painted in red.

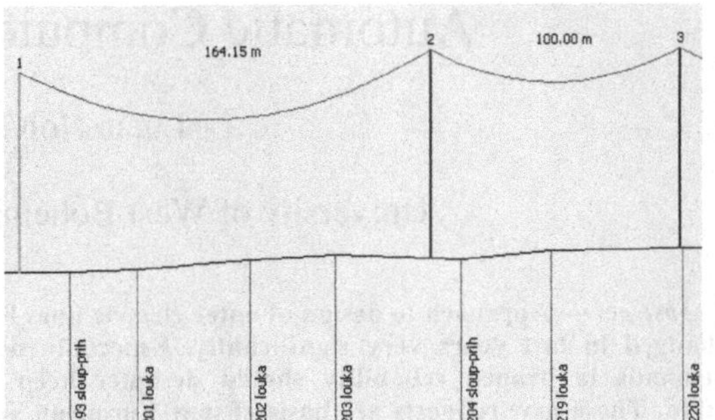

Fig. 5. Error red color announcement in graphical display window

Adequately in generated calculation report all forbidden values of stress are marked with triple exclamation marks following:

```
------------------------------
Teplota        Mech. namáhání
Temperature          Wire stress
[stupně C]     [MPa]
------------------------------
-30            116.32 !!!
-20            104.08
-10            92.433
0              81.589
10             71.764
   . . .
80             34.599
------------------------------
-5 + N         110.00 !!!
------------------------------
```

And of course also in installation tables are improper values recognizable by red color:

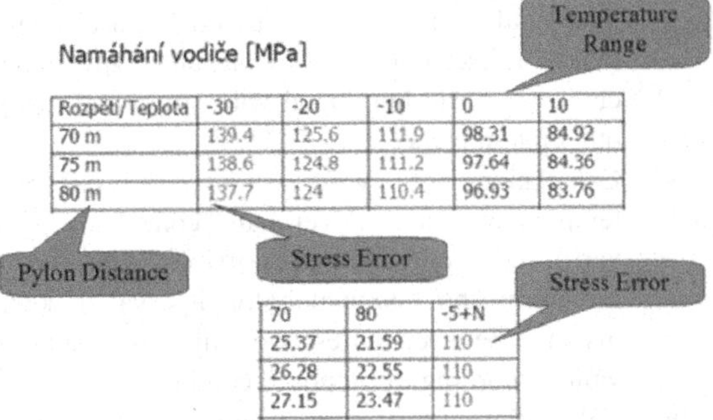

Namáhání vodiče [MPa]

Rozpětí/Teplota	-30	-20	-10	0	10
70 m	139.4	125.6	111.9	98.31	84.92
75 m	138.6	124.8	111.2	97.64	84.36
80 m	137.7	124	110.4	96.93	83.76

70	80	-5+N
25.37	21.59	110
26.28	22.55	110
27.15	23.47	110

Fig. 6. Error announcement in installation tables

Finally application can create export of line layout for CAD (for example AutoDesk AutoCAD, Bentley Microstation and even some free CAD systems and viewers) in DXF format. This is very suitable to use this feature for easy project documentation making. Exported line and terrain data in Solid Edge tools show next pictures:

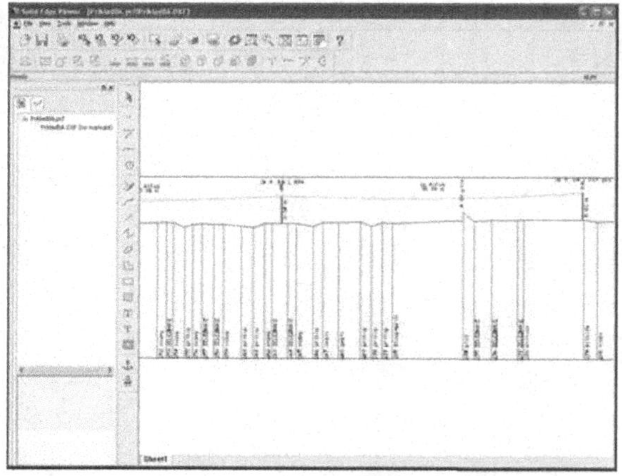

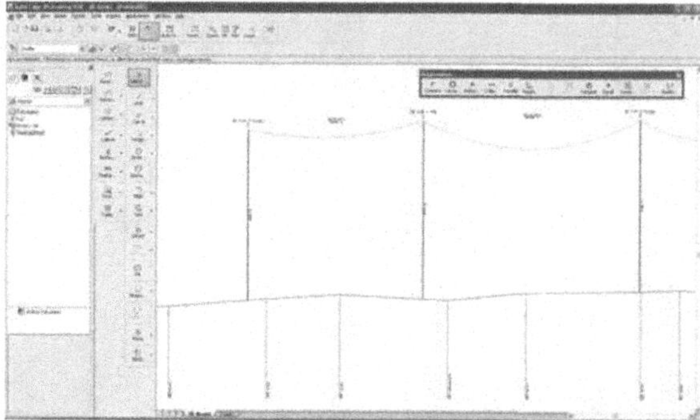

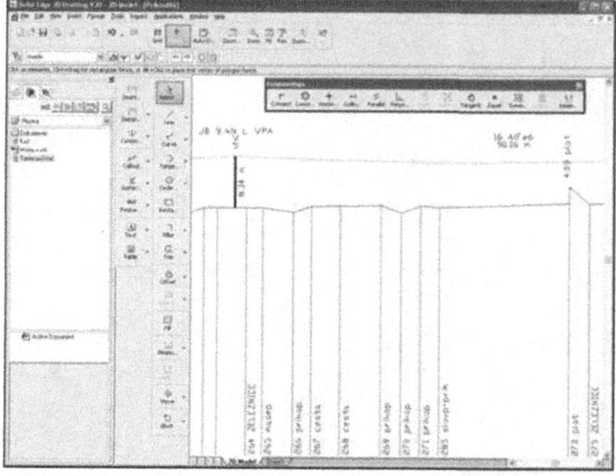

Fig. 7. Exported data displayed in Solid Edge CAD system

Beside that application includes internal interactive help system with description of all major features, using principles and parameters customizations.

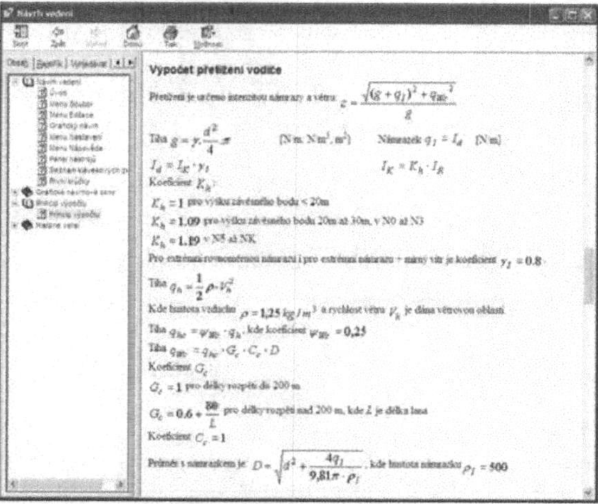

Fig. 8. Internal help system using example - wire stress computation explanation

IV. SUMMARY AND CONCLUSION

New application for line design makes construction, verification calculation, project documentation and installation data table creating easier and faster. Beside that it reduces possible mistakes in respecting all new standards.

V. ACKNOWLEDGEMENT

This paper was written under solving science project 2A-TP/051.

REFERENCES

Papers from Conference Proceedings (Published):

[1] Nohá K., Nohá ová L.: "Overview of today possibilities of computer simulation in power engineering", article of 6th International Conference" "*Control of power systems 2004*", Štrbské Pleso, Slovak Republic, 16.-18. 6. 2004, Slovak University of Technology in Bratislava, ISBN: 80-227-2059-3, pp. 1-8

[2] Czech and European standards associated with overhead line design SN EN 50341-1, SN EN 50423-1, NNA - SN EN 50423-3

[3] L. Nohá ová, K. Nohá , "Some cases of distributed resources connected to the distribution network" article in 13th International Expert Meeting *"Power Engineering 2004"*, Maribor, Slovenia Republic 2004

[4] Martínek Z., T ma I., Muhlbacher J. "Analysis of Complex Networks in the Power System". 13. Mednarodno posvetovanje Komunalna energetika, 18. to 20. 5. 2004 Maribor, Slovenija, ISBN 86-435-0618-4, 13. International Expert Meeting

[5] Nohá K., Nohá ová L., "New Application Solution for Electric Line Design " article of 5th International Expert Meeting "Environmental Impacts of Power Industry 2008". Pernink, Czech Republic 2008, University of West Bohemia, Pilsen

Building Test Cases through Model Driven Engineering

Helaine Sousa[1], Denivaldo Lopes[1], Zair Abdelouahab[1], Slimane Hammoudi[2], Daniela Barreiro Claro[3]
(1) Federal University of Maranhão – UFMA, Brazil
(2) Ecole Supérieure de l'Ouest – ESEO, France
(3) Federal University of Bahia – UFBA, Brazil
{helainecss, dlopes, zair}@dee.ufma.br, shammoudi@eseo.fr, dclaro@ufba.br

***Abstract*- Recently, Model Driven Engineering (MDE) has been proposed to face the complexity in the development, maintenance and evolution of large and distributed software systems. Model Driven Architecture (MDA) is an example of MDE. In this context, model transformations enable a large reuse of software systems through the transformation of a Platform Independent Model into a Platform Specific Model. Although source code can be generated from models, defects can be injected during the modeling or transformation process. In order to delivery software systems without defects that cause errors and fails, the source code must be submitted to test. In this paper, we present an approach that takes care of test in the whole software life cycle, i.e. it starts in the modeling level and finishes in the test of source code of software systems. We provide an example to illustrate our approach.**

I. Introduction

The complexity in the development, maintenance and evolution of software systems is managed by Model Driven Engineering (MDE). However, errors can be injected during the software development process. In spite of test cases can be applied to find errors in a software system, the manual creation of test cases can result in the involuntary injection of errors that make the tests inefficient.

Model Driven Engineering (MDE) provides quick answers to meet new requirements both functional and non-functional and to adapt new technologies to legacy systems, enabling the integration between different technologies [11]. These proposals represent a significant step forward for the development of software systems. However, such proposals remain to be done on the use of Model-Driven approaches (MDx). For example, the use of MDx in the software testing process remains a challenge for the academy and software industry.

The Model Driven Testing (MDT) is another MDx example and its aim is to automate the software testing, significantly reducing test efforts during the course of development of software systems [13, 16].

Model Transformations can be used to create test models for metamodel verification and the source code, then contributing to greater viability, productivity, reliability and effectiveness, as well as provide a link between the source and other development artifacts.

This paper presents an approach for supporting the automated generation of test cases. A metamodel for creating platform independent test allows the development of test models that are transformed in test source code that can be applied to inspect a specific software system. This metamodel for platform independent test provides support to functional test, unit-test and integration test. Another metamodel for platform specific test based on xUnit is provided.

This paper is structured in the following way. Section II provides an overview of the theoretical foundation about related subjects to this research. Section III describes our proposed approach for automatic generation of test cases. Section IV provides an illustrative example of our approach. Finally, section V provides a conclusion and future directions of our research work.

II. Overview

Before presenting our proposed solution for automatic generation of test cases, we need to discuss some important concepts around this proposal.

A. *Software Test*

Test is a crucial activity in the Software Verification & Validation process. This process involves high costs and it is heavily dependent on automation. The lack of reliability in the tests can invalidate an entire Software Verification & Validation process. The tests must be continuously maintained and implemented throughout the software lifecycle [4].

The testing process could reduce significantly the occurrence of defects during the lifetime of software, minimizing risks to a business and ensuring that the customer's requirements are achieved.

B. *Model Driven Architecture (MDA)*

MDA is an initiative of Object Management Group (OMG) that promotes the use of models to manage the complexity in the software development, maintenance and evolution [15]. MDA promotes interoperability and portability of software systems. So this initiative emerged to meet the new challenges posed by the integration of platforms, while preserving their investments in existing business based on existing platforms and future technologies [4].

These initiatives include the code generation from a model, or approaches in which the system specification is made independently of platform and, for each specific platform, such

T. Sobh, K. Elleithy (eds.), *Innovations in Computing Sciences and Software Engineering*,
DOI 10.1007/978-90-481-9112-3_67, © Springer Science+Business Media B.V. 2010

as a specification can be automatically converted into a corresponding implementation. MDA proposes to increase the productivity and the reuse through the separation of concerns and abstraction [6, 14].

C. *Model Driven Testing (MDT)*

Model Driven Testing (MDT) has recently emerged as a necessary feature for the success of MDA [5, 8, 12, 13]. The MDT promoters claims that it provides some benefits such as reduction of overall testing time by supporting the reuse of many common testing functions, enhancement of test quality, management of complexity by offering a systematic approach for test suite, drastic reduction of test maintenance costs, because implementation changes are captured in the model [4].

Tools of Model-Driven Testing help developers to perform the following tasks: create and edit models of software components, simulate models, generate test suites for software components, run test suites against the software components, create templates for test execution directives and test proxies, translate test suites to create scripts for legacy test drivers and review both the test suites and their execution trace.

The aim of MDT is to provide some benefits for software testing. However, few researches were done in order to demonstrate how MDT will perform these benefits.

D. *UML 2.0 Testing Profile (U2TP)*

U2TP is a language for designing, visualizing, specifying, analyzing, constructing, and documenting the artifacts of test systems [8, 16].

This approach can be applied to test systems in various application domains; this language can be used for the manipulation of test artifacts or in an integrated manner with UML for manipulating system and test artifacts. U2TP was initially designed to interact with the UML version 2.0. It is defined using a metamodeling approach and makes direct use of the UML concepts, extends them and adds new concepts. It conforms to the MOF metamodel.

III. AN MDE APPROACH FOR GENERATING TEST CASES

This paper proposes a solution to automate the generation of test source code and its aim is to test the source code created through model transformations providing more quality.

Figure 1 illustrates our proposed approach to create platform independent test cases (conforms to Metamodel for Test - MT) and generate a model conform to xUnit metamodel. Afterwards, this test model conforms to xUnit can be transformed in a source-code conforms to JUnit platform. The Test model conforms to MT makes reference to the PIM (i.e. a model of a system).

This proposed approach provides the foundation to automatically generate the test source code for a software system. In this case, both source code of testing and source code of software system are concomitant created. So, the test phase is started in conjunction with the design phase in a development process according to MDE.

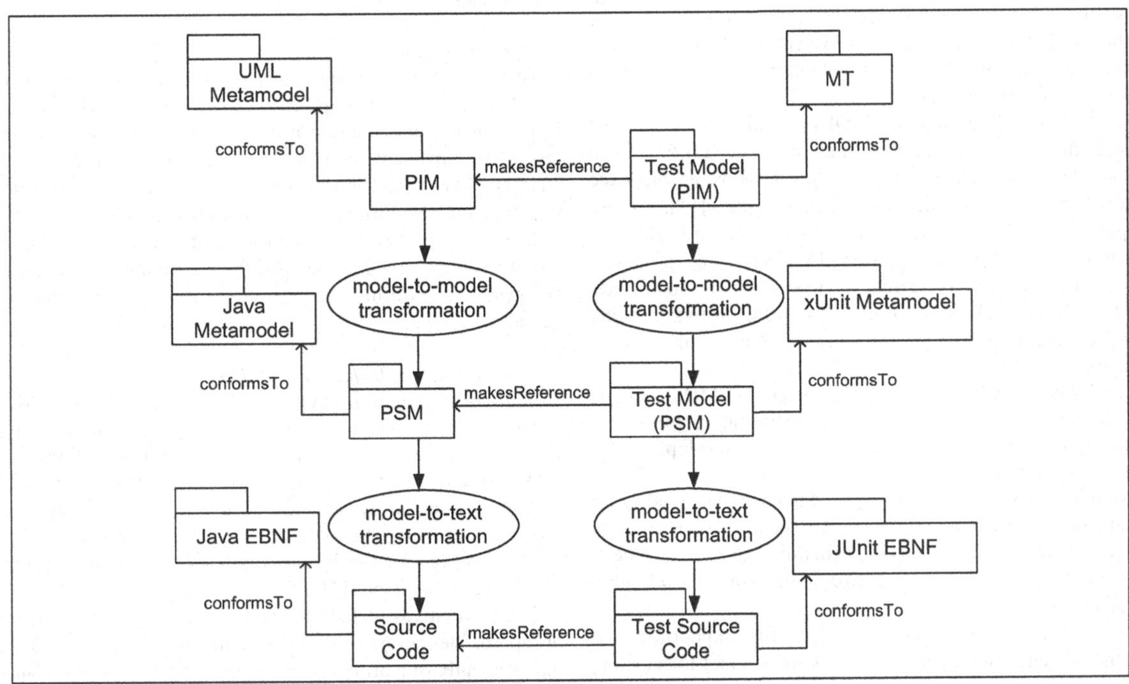

Figure 1: Proposed Approach to Generate Test Cases

A. Proposed Methodology

A methodology is proposed to complement our approach. The aim of methodology is provide reliable software systems. The methodology is illustrated in Figure 2.

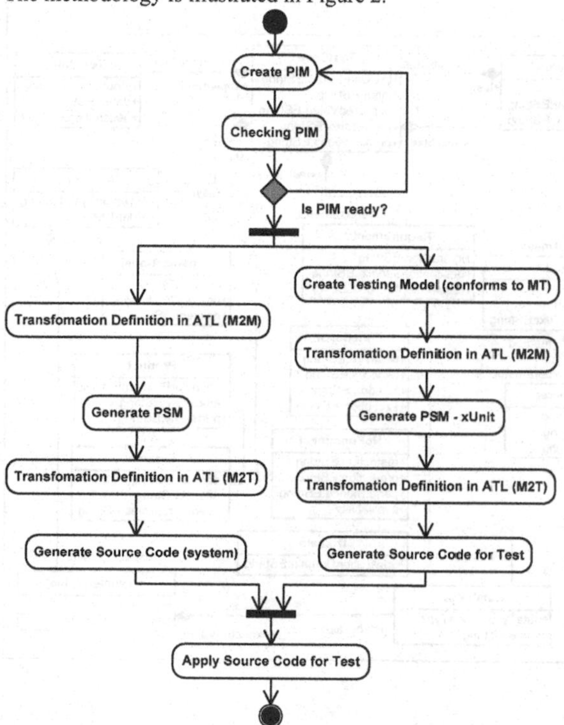

Figure 2: Methodology to Generate Test Case.

The initial action is the creation of a PIM. This PIM is used in the source code generation for a particular software system as well for generating the test source code. This test source code is used to test the source code of a particular software system generated from this PIM. Once the PIM has been created, we move to next action, which verifies the created PIM. If the PIM is not correct, it will be created again. If it is correct, the flow of activities will fork into two actions: the source code generation and test source code generation.

In the set of actions to generate the source code for a particular software system, a model-to-model transformation in Atlas Transformation Language (ATL) [1] generates the PSM. Afterwards, this PSM is transformed in source code of a particular software system using a model-to-text transformation in ATL [1]. Once the source code for a particular software system and the test source code are created, the last code can be used to test the first code.

B. Proposed Metamodels

Two metamodels are proposed to ensure the quality in the software system through the automatic test case generation that provides a planning of test. These metamodels are the basis for automatic generation of test cases of specific software.

B.1 Metamodel for Test (MT)

Metamodel for Test (MT) is based on the functional testing (or black-box). In this technique, input data are provided, the test runs and the result is compared to an expected result previously known [10]. Levels of Module Testing (or Unit Testing) and Integration Testing were used to inspire the creation of our test metamodel. At the level of Unit Testing or Module Test, the units are individually tested through their functional or non-functional requirements and classes through assertions. This level of test is a process where the smaller units of software are tested. The Integration Test is added in our metamodel to enable the search for faults inserted by the internal integration of modules or system units [3].

In order to create our test metamodel, we studied three types of approaches for integration testing, *Big-Bang*, *TopDown* and *Bottom-up*. After a detailed survey on the approaches to integration test, the approach *TopDown* was chosen because consists in separating the system built in small segments, facilitating the test efforts in case of possible errors. The test begins with the high-level system components, and integration takes place from top to bottom in a component hierarchy starting from a module or a main control component. The modules or components subject to the component or control module is incorporated to the main structure in a manner "depth-first" or "breadth-first" [9].

Figure 3 presents the MT that has the following main elements. *ModelTest* contains *ModuleTest* and *IntegrationTest*. *ModuleTest* acts as a container for *TestSuite* and *TestCase*. A *TestCase* can have *Assertions* that are conditions that should hold true after executing the *TestCase*. *Assertions* can be of different types which are specified by its attributes.

TestCase contains one or more *TestClass*, *Assertion* and *Requeriments*. *TestClass* has zero or one *Attribute* and/or *Method*. An *Attribute* can be classified by *Type* whose expected value is of type *SimpleType* or *ComplexType*. *SimpleType* is atomic and does not contain any other data values. *ComplexType* contains other values, i.e. it acts as data structures. In *ModuleTest*, modules or components are tested separately. In the *TestIntegration*, module integration is tested. *TestIntegration* has the element *TopDownIntergration* and this last contains *ControlModule* element. *ControlModule* starts the hierarchy of tests.

B.2 xUnit Metamodel

xUnit Metamodel has structures of tests used to write and perform repetitive software test [7]. xUnit is an open source framework that facilitates the source code creation for the automated unit test. It verifies that each method of a class works as expected showing possible errors or failures [7]. Our proposed metamodel for xUnit is based on [5].

Figure 4 illustrates the fragment of the proposed metamodel. The main element of our xUnit metamodel is *xUnitModel* that

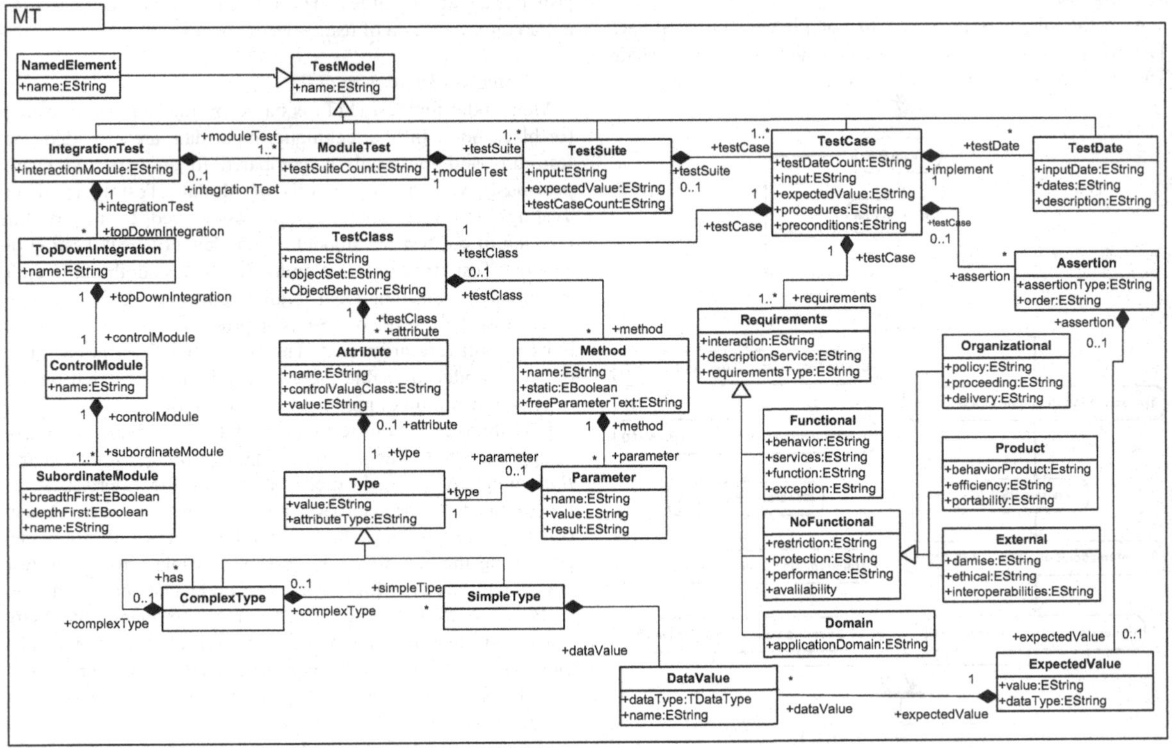

Figure 3: Metamodel for Test (MT).

contains the *TestSuite* element. *TestSuite* acts as a container for *TestCase*. A *TestCase* has *Assertions* and *TestClass*. *TestClass* has *Attributes* and *Methods*. An *Assertion* has a relationship with a *Method* and has an *ExpectedValue*. An *Attribute* can be a *SimpleAttribute* or a *ComplexAttribute*.

IV. PROTOTYPING

A prototype is provided in order to demonstrate our approach developed using EMF [2]. Firstly, a model is created using the EMF wizard (Create Model). After, a model type is chosen, i.e. EMF model (Defining model in EMF). The next step consists in generating metamodel in the tree format (generating Metamodel in tree in Ecore). Once the metamodel is created, a plug-in based on this metamodel can be generated. In order to create this plug-in, a *genmodel* is generated from this metamodel. After the EMF framework is used to generate the source code for this plug-in.

Before using this plug-in, it must be installed in the Eclipse. The process of using this plug-in consists in creating a Model Project. A new wizard is generated in conjunction with this plug-in and it is used to create a model conforms to this metamodel (select Example EMF Model Creation Wizards). The wizard is used to create a model in the form of tree (select a model object to create a model in tree). A model is edited through the creation of *child* and *sibling* elements. To complete the edition of a model, values are assigned to the properties of each element model. Once a model is complete, it is validated using the EMF plug-in that checks the conformity of the model with its metamodel. Finally, the model is used to generate a test source code.

Figure 5 illustrates a fragment of the MT, and Figure 6 illustrates a fragment of the xUnit metamodel. EMF provides some functionality that allows the creation of plug-ins in Eclipse [2], for editing models conform these metamodels. Once a plug-in based on metamodel is created, we can modify and extends this plug-in introducing the functionalities described in our approach.

A. Illustrative Example

In order to illustrate the functionalities of our prototype, a case study is provided. It consists in a simple Student Academic Information System that helps a student to subscribe to a course and a professor to register marks and obtain Grade

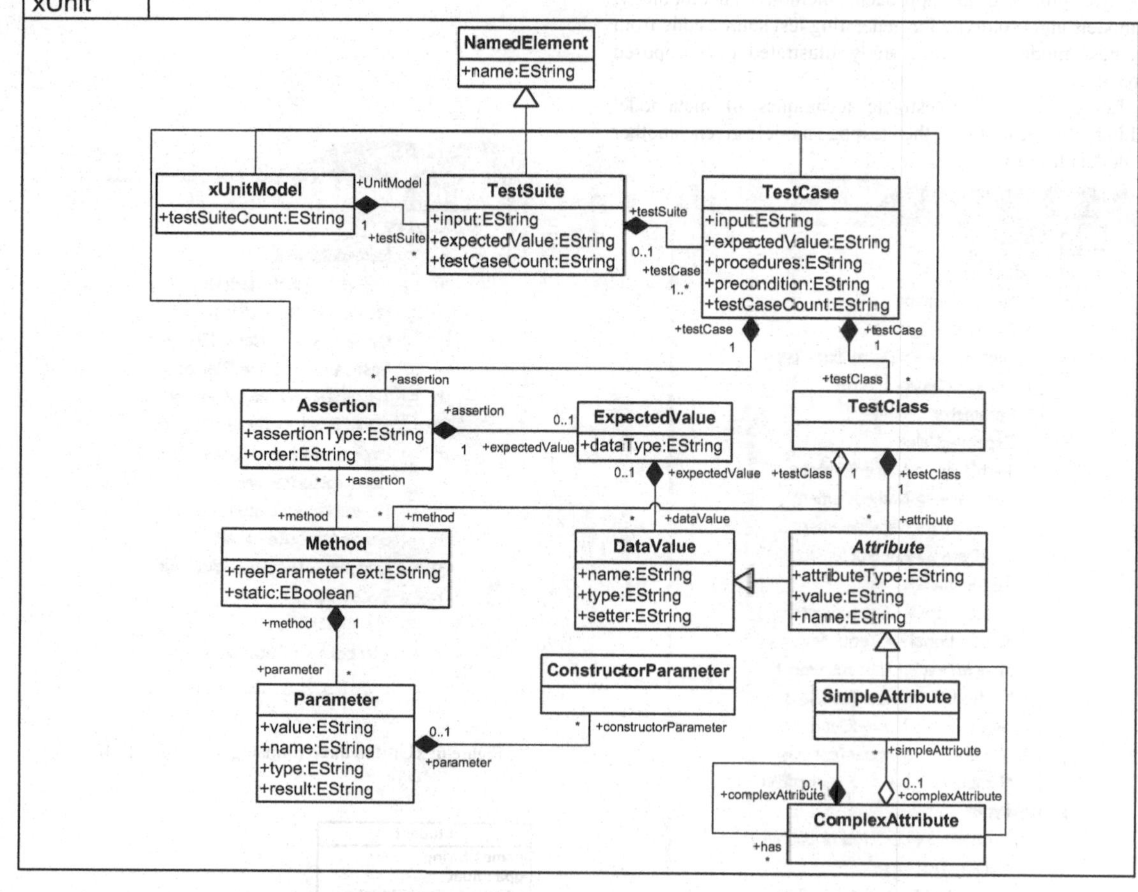

Figure 4: xUnit Metamodel.

Point Average (GPA). Figure 7 illustrates a class diagram for this student academic information system.

In this Information System, we consider two features: Enrollment of students in a particular course and Registration of remarks of a student for a particular discipline. To make the enrollment of a student you need to verify that this student is already registered in the system and if there are places available for the desired course. Moreover, the system should verify if a student is registered in a course, before a mark is given by the professor for this student. Once the registration of remarks is done, the student's GPA is calculated. If this student obtains GPA greater than or equal to 7, this student is approved. If this student obtains GPA less than 7, this student is disapproved.

Figure 8 illustrates the test model conforms to MT in the form of three. This testing model makes reference to the class diagram of the student academic information system. This testing model contains the description of testing the functionality provided by this system.

Figure 9 illustrates the test model conform to xUnit metamodel generated through our approach. It is created from the test model presented in Figure 8 through a transformation definition in ATL.

Once the PIM for the Student Academic Information System is created, our prototype allows to edit the test model conform to MT. Afterwards, we can use a transformations model-to-model to generate the test model conforms to xUnit. Afterwards, a transformation model-to-text generates the test source code in a specific platform such as JUnit.

V. CONCLUSIONS

A Model Driven approach provides techniques to test the code generated by model transformations. Model-Driven Testing is gaining support in the software industry. In this paper, we proposed an approach, including methodology, metamodels and prototype for generating test source code from a business model. The case study illustrated our proposed approach.

In future, we will investigate techniques of metamodel matching for generating the testing model given another metamodels for test.

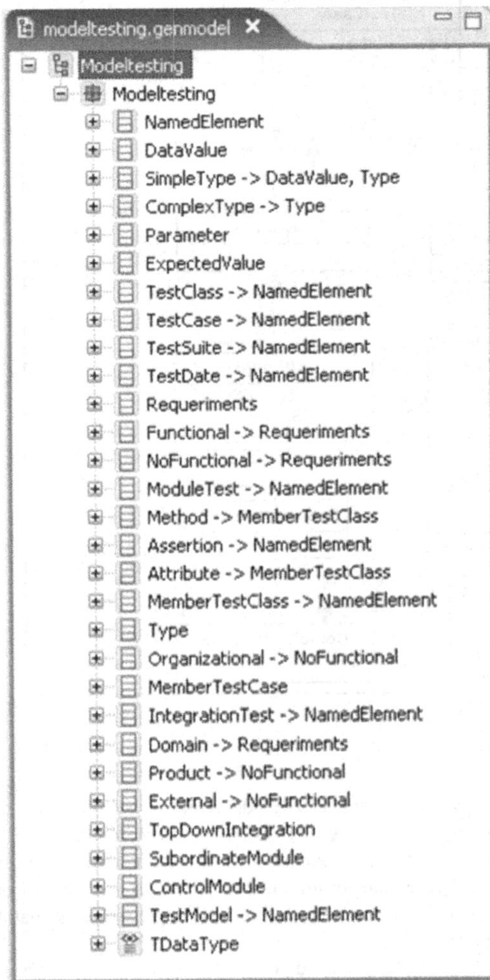

Figure 5: MT in tree format (*genmodel* of EMF)

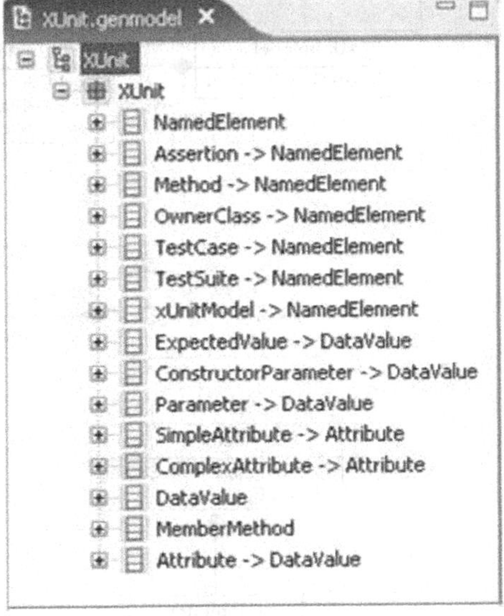

Figure 6: xUnit in three format (*genmodel* of EMF)

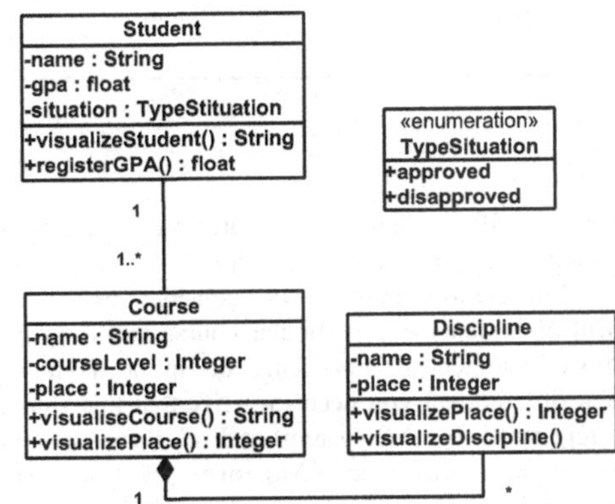

Figure 7: Class Diagram for the Student Academic Information System.

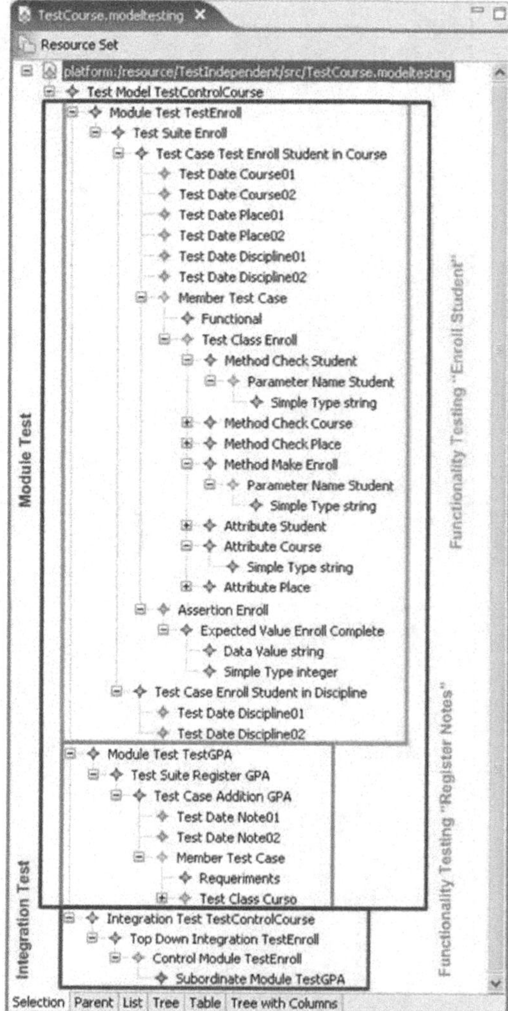

Figure 8: Test Model for testing the student academic information system (conforms to MT)

ACKNOWLEDGMENT

The work described in this paper is supported by FAPEMA, CAPES and CNPq.

REFERENCES

[1] ATLAS group LINA & INRIA Nantes. *ATL - ATLAS Transformation Language: ATL User Manual*, 2006.

[2] Dave Steinberg, Frank Budinsky, Marcelo Paternostro, Ed Merks, *EMF: Eclipse Modeling Framework*, Addison-Wesley Professional, 2 edition, 2008.

[3] Márcio Eduardo Delamaro, José Carlos Maldonado, Mário Jino, *Introduction to Software Testing*, Campus, 2007.

[4] IBM Haifa Research Laboratory. *Overview Model-driven Testing Tools*, Accessed on 10/15/09, Available at http://www.haifa.ibm.com /projects/verification/mdt/public.html.

[5] A. Z. Javed, P.A. Strooper, G. N. Watson, "Automated Generation of Test Cases Using Model-Driven Architecture", Second International Workshop on Automation of Software Test (AST '07), 2007.

[6] Denivaldo Lopes, Slimane Hammoudi, José de Souza, and Alan Bontempo, "Metamodel Matching: Experiments and Comparison", IEEE International Conference on Software Engineering Advances, 2006.

[7] Gerard Meszaros, *xUnit Test Patterns: Refactoring Test Code*, Pearson Education, 2007.

[8] OMG, *UML Testing Profile*, Version 1.0, Document Number: formal/05-07-07, 2005.

[9] Shari Lawrence Pfleeger, *Software Engineering: Theory and Practice*, Prentice-Hall, 2004.

[10] Ian Sommerville, *Software Engineering*, 8th edition, Addison-Wesley, 2007.

[11]Douglas C. Schmidt, "Model-Driven Engineering", *IEEE Computer*, vol. 39, no. 2, pages 25-31, February 2006.

[12] Sebastian Wieczorek, Mathias Fritzsche, Joachim Schnitter, "Enhancing Test Driven Development with Model Based Testing and Performance Analysis", Testing: Academic & Industrial Conference – Practice and Research Techniques, 2008.

[13] Pedro Santos Neto, Rodolfo F. Resende, Clarindo Pádua, An Evaluation of a Model-Based Testing Method for Informaiton System, Proceedings of ACM Symposium on Applied Computing, p. 770-776, 2008.

[14] Nuo Li,Qin-qin Ma, Ji Wu, Mao-zhong Jin, Chao Liu, "A Framework of Model-Driven Web Application Testing", 30th Annual International Computer Software and Applications Conference, p. 157-162, 2006.

[15] OMG. MDA Guide Version 1.0.1, Document Number: omg/2003-06-01, 2003.

[16] Paul Baker, Zhen Ru Dai et al, Model-Driven Testing: Using the UML Testing Profile, 1rst edition, Springer, 2007.

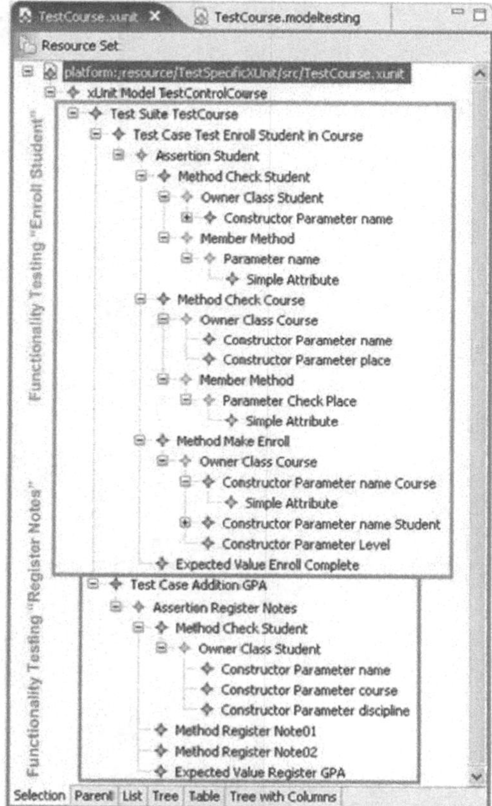

Figure 9: xUnit Model for testing the student academic information system (conforms to xUnit metamodel)

The Effects of Educational Multimedia for Scientific Signs in the Holy Quran in Improving the Creative Thinking Skills for Deaf Children

Sumaya Abusaleh, Eman AbdelFattah, Zain Alabadi, Ahmad Sharieh

Computer Science and Engineering Department
University of Bridgeport
Bridgeport, CT 06605
sabusale@bridgeport.edu, eman@bridgeport.edu

***Abstract*- This paper investigates the role of the scientific signs in the holy Quran in improving the creative thinking skills for the deaf children using multimedia. The paper investigates if the performance made by the experimental group's individuals is statistically significant compared with the performance made by the control group's individuals on Torrance Test for creative thinking (fluency, flexibility, originality and the total degree) in two cases:**

1. **Without considering the gender of the population.**
2. **Considering the gender of the population.**

Keywords: Scientific Signs, Creative Thinking Skills, Deaf Children, Multimedia Components, Gestures, Hearing-Impaired Students, Fluency, Flexibility, Originality, Total Degree.

I. INTRODUCTION

Creative thinking is one of the important needs to develop through our life because it's one of the things that humans will ever have a monopoly on. Several methods have been identified for producing creative results. Here are the five classic ones: Evolution, Synthesis, Revolution, Reapplication, and Changing Direction. With Synthesis method, two or more existing ideas are combined into a third, new idea [1].

Multimedia applications may be used for such diverse purposes as entertainment, education, commerce, communications (e.g. video-conferencing), and even art. For educational process Multimedia applications are very important issue. By using multimedia component in a systematic and structure manner we can get greater understanding and improve the traditional ways in education.

The most advantage of using multimedia is an increased naturalness of interaction. This naturalness can stem from different sources [2]. Furthermore, some argue that redundancy, either in terms of multiple output media or multiple input devices, can make interaction more natural [3, 4]. A Testple in our paper we use multimedia components (video, animation, pictures, gestures) as a mean of communication for deaf children to explain the meaning of verses of the Quran and explain the scientific signs in the selected verse. Second, new types of media and media combinations can improve naturalness through an increased depth in the information that is communicated to the user, for Testple using gestures to explain the scientific terms information about human body. This allows the users to take advantage of the ability to attend to more than one stimulus at a time [5, 6].

In this paper we apply the Synthesis method through combining the scientific signs of the Quran in the human body and multimedia components such as: sound, video, text, animation, pictures, and gestures that are useful for deaf children.

II. EARLIER STUDIES

Rangel [7] created the digital video dictionary and aimed through it at improving the skills of fluency for the hearing-impaired students, letting them acquire new vocabularies and improving their reading and writing skills. This program included texts, pictures and video animations. Through this study, each student took part in building the dictionary on the computer through his/her journalistic interviews. This program was applied on a sample of hearing-impaired people consisted of 12 students where pre and post measures were made. The following results were reached in this program: the dictionary reduced the anxiety when reading and writing among hearing-impaired students, allowed them to effectively participate in improving the fluency skill, gave them the opportunity to acquire new communications skills and enhanced their self-confidence in using the modern technology in education.

Abdulmutaleb [8] had a study for the students of the elementary stage. This study aimed at discovering the relation between the creative thinking abilities of the hearing-impaired students and their chronological and mental age. The study consisted of 400 students (males and females). The researcher used Torrance Test for creative thinking (B) and the photographed cleverness test for measuring the skills of fluency, flexibility and originality. The results showed that there were statistically indicated differences between the classes. Those differences were in the side of the upper classes in the skills of creative thinking.

Kaplan [9] has a study which aimed at following up the effectiveness of technology (computer) in developing knowledge experiences of the hearing-impaired people. This

T. Sobh, K. Elleithy (eds.), *Innovations in Computing Sciences and Software Engineering*,
DOI 10.1007/978-90-481-9112-3_68, © Springer Science+Business Media B.V. 2010

study consisted of a sample of school students (the first and the eighth classes). The researcher employed many suggested computer programs on that sample to know the importance of using technology in developing the knowledge experiences of the hearing-impaired people. The study reached to the confirmation that the technology methods positively affect in enriching the developing of knowledge experiences of the hearing-impaired people. This study also came up with many recommendations contributing in building computer programs within the criteria that goes with the nature of the hearing-impaired people.

Passing and Eden [10] has a study aimed at following up the effectiveness of the computers in developing the creative thinking of the hearing-impaired children. This study comprised 60 students divided into two groups. The first group consisted of 44 students which was also divided into two groups; the control and the experimental ones. The second group consisted of 16 normal children represented a second control group. The experimental group was subject to the three dimensions computer games. As for the first control group, it was subject to two dimensions computer games while the second control group was not subject to any training program. The program lasted for three months. The two researchers used Torrance Test for creative thinking; the shape picture as pre and post tests for the two groups. The results indicated that there were statistically- indicated differences in the side of the performance of the experimental group. The results also showed that there was a slight difference in the ability of creative thinking in comparison with the normal children representing the second control group.

There are several multimedia programs that present the scientific signs in the Quran. The photographed science of the Holy Quran [11] is a program that presents some verses and explains the scientific signs in the Holy Quran in the following fields: food, natural phenomenon and space. This program is supported by pictures, videos and texts. Another program is The series of scientific miracles in the Holy Quran [12]. This video program dealing with aspects of the scientific signs of the human, animal, plants, astronomy, earth, sea, health and insects.

Although there are several reported approaches in the literature that handles using multimedia for targeting the deaf children, none of these approaches using the scientific signs of the Holy Quran as the main tool for improving creative thinking skills (fluency, flexibility, originality and total degree).

III. METHODOLOGY

For achieving the goals of this study, a sample was taken from Al-Rajaa School in Jordon for deaf children. The number of this sample was 60 students (males and females). They were all divided randomly into two groups; one of which was the control group and the other was the experimental one. The number of each group was 30 students. The computerized program of the scientific signs in the Holy Quran was employed for the individuals of the experimental group for eight weeks. The same program was employed as a script for the individuals of the control group. To measure the role of the computerized program of the scientific signs in the Holy Quran, the Torrance Test for the creative thinking was employed for the two groups prior to implementing the program as a preceding-test, and as a subsequent test after its being employed for the two groups.

To answer the questions introduced in the study, the averages and the measuring curves of the performance made by the two groups were calculated according to the results emerged from both the preceding and the subsequent tests.

To know whether there is a statistically-indicated difference on the point ($0.05 \geq \infty$) between the averages of the two groups of the study, the Analysis of Covariance (ANCOVA) was employed [13].

IV. IMPLEMENTAION

An Object Oriented approach was used to implement the multimedia program used for improving the skills for the deaf children. Figure 1 shows the subsystems used in the Quran scientific signs program and Figure 2 shows the UML class diagram for the same program. The following software tools were used in the development phase: Macromedia Director v8.5, Macromedia Falsh 5.0, Sound Recorder, Movie Maker, VCD Cutter v3.0, Image Styler v7.0, Jasc Animation Pro v7.0, Quick Time v5.0.1, Real One Player 2.0, and SPSS 13.0.

V. STATISTICAL ANALYSIS

The first question we are addressing in this study is there any statistically-indicated difference between the performance of the experimental group individuals and the performance of the second control group individuals according to Torrance Test for creative thinking in which the implementation of the computerized Holy Quran is referred. The averages and measuring curves are calculated on the dimensional measurement of all experimental and control group individuals. The results are shown in Table 1.

As shown in table 1, the average of the experimental group on the skill of fluency is (12.19) while the average of the control group on the same skill is (10.89). The average of the performance of the experimental group on the flexibility skill is (10.00) while the performance of the control group on the same skill is (8.38). It is also shown in the table that the average of the performance of the experimental group on the skill of originality is (5.39) while the average of the performance of the control group on the same skill is (4.43). As for the total degree, the average of the performance of the experimental group reached (27.58) and the average of the performance of the control group on the total degree reached (23.71).

It is noticeable that there is a difference between the average of the performance of the experimental and the control groups. To verify this statistically, ANCOVA was used. Table 2 shows the result of ANCOVA in the performance of the experimental and control groups on the creative thinking test for the fluency, flexibility, originality and total degree skills.

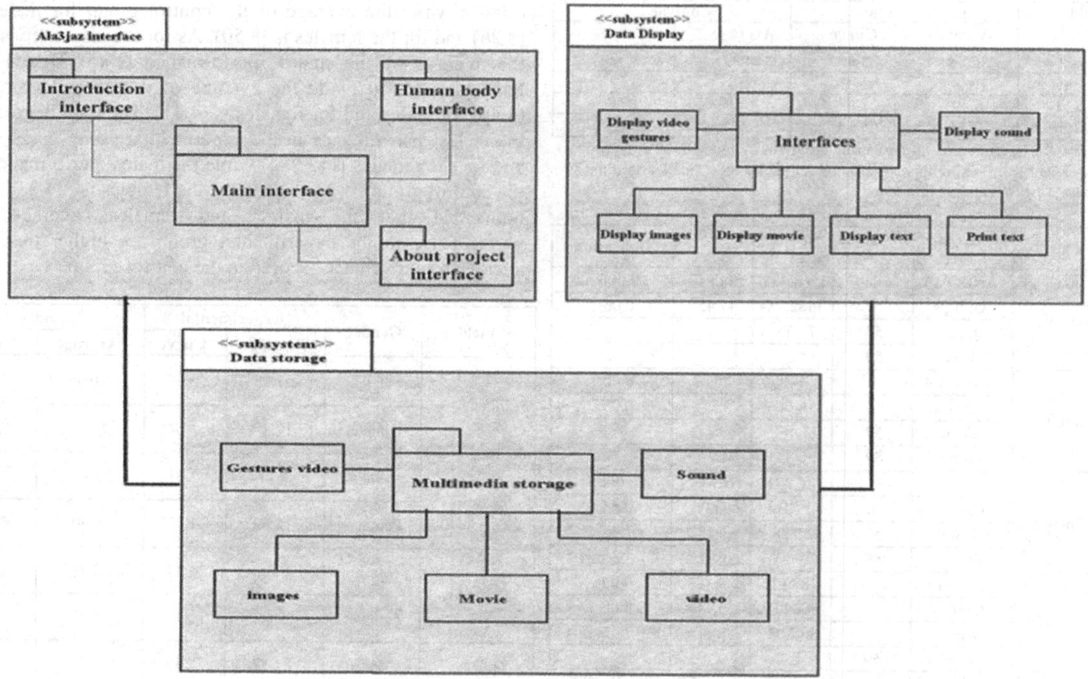

Figure 1: The subsystems used in the scientific signs of the Quran program

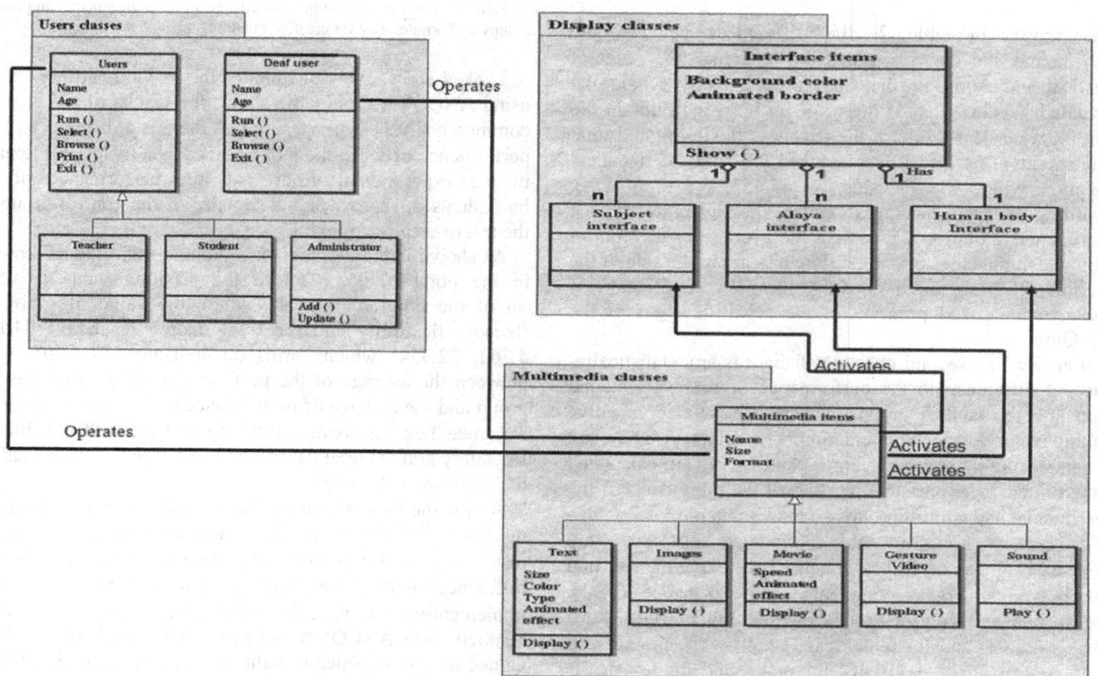

Figure 2: UML class diagram for the scientific signs of the Quran program.

Field	Experimental		Control	
	Average	Curve	Average	Curve
Fluency	12.19	3.65	10.89	3.58
flexibility	10.00	2.03	8.38	2.57
Originality	5.39	2.08	4.43	1.71
total degree	27.58	5.10	23.71	3.82

Table 1: The averages and measuring curves calculated on the dimensional measurement of all experimental and control group individuals according to Torrance Test for creative thinking

Field	Difference Source	Freedom degrees	Squares average	F	Indication
Fluency	ANCOVA	1	1764.382	24.042	0.000
	Groups	1	3482.784	47.457	0.00
	Error	57	73.38		
	Total	59			
Flexibility	ANCOVA	1	114.096	36.03	0.00
	Groups	1	16.96	5.316	0.00
	Error	57	3.46		
	Total	59			
Originality	ANCOVA	1	36.221	9.715	0.000
	Groups	1	1.516	0.406	0.54
	Error	57	3.728		
	Total	59			
Total degree	ANCOVA	1	3829.767	34.183	0.00
	Groups	1	3934.033	35.114	0.00
	Error	57	112.03		
	Total	59			

Table 2: The results of ANCOVA of the performance of the experimental and control groups on Torrance Test for creative thinking: (fluency, flexibility, originality and total degree).

As shown in table 2, the differences between the experimental and control groups did not reach the point of statistical indication in the field of originality where the calculated F value (0.406) does not form an indicator in the point (0.05) or less while in the (fluency, flexibility and total degree fields), the differences reached the point of statistical indication where the F value is (47.457, 5.316, 35.114). According to the averages table, the average of the experimental group is higher than the average of the control group which indicates that the differences are in the side of the experimental group and assures that there is a significant role of the computerized program of the scientific signs of the Holy Quran.

To answer the second question if there is any statistically-indicated difference in the performance of the experimental group and the control group on Torrance Test for creative thinking which forms the interaction between the program and the gender, the interactive averages and curves are calculated on the dimensional measurement for all the individuals of the experimental and control groups as shown in table 3.

The results shown in table 3 indicate that there are differences in the averages of the two experimental and control groups. The average of the performance of the experimental and control groups on the skill of fluency for males is (12.08) and for females is (12.30) while the average of the control group is (10.46) for males and for females is (11.32). As for the flexibility skill, the average of the performance of the males is (9.91) and for the females is (10.09) while the average of the control group for males is (8.26) and for the females is (8.50). As for the originality skill, the average of the males' performance is (5.33) and the females is (5.45) while the average of the control group is (4.46) for males and for females is (4.41). The total degree for the males' performance in the experimental group is (27.32) and for the females is (27.84) while the males' performance in the control group is (23.19) and for the females is (24.23). It is noticeable that the males' and females' averages of performance in the experimental group are higher than the average of performance scored in the control group.

Field	Gender	Experimental		Control	
		Average	Curve	Average	Curve
Fluency	Males	12.08	3.54	10.46	2.34
	Females	12.30	3.04	11.32	2.95
Flexibility	Males	9.91	2.33	8.26	2.74
	Females	10.09	1.75	8.50	2.51
Originality	Males	5.33	2.57	4.46	1.68
	Females	5.45	1.73	4.41	1.78
Total degree	Males	27.32	7.90	23.19	6.24
	Females	27.84	4.85	24.23	6.75

Table 3: Interactive averages and curves for the experimental and control groups on Torrance Test for creative thinking.

Table 4 shows the indication of the previous differences by using ANCOVA. This table shows the results of the bilateral common analysis to make sure that there is a difference in the performance between the individuals of the males and females in the experimental group and the performance of the individuals of the males and females of the control group on the test of creative thinking.

As shown in table 4, there are statistic-indicated differences in the point (0. 05 ≥ ∞) to the program value (0. 05 ≥ ∞) of the program variable, where the value of F for the fluency, flexibility and the total degree reached (44.169, 4.762, 32.434) which forms an indicator on (0.05 ≥ ∞) between the average of the performance of the experimental group and the average of performance of the control group on Torrance Test for creative thinking and the skills of fluency, flexibility and the total degree. This difference is in the side of the experimental group.

As for the skill of originality, the differences do not reach the point (0.05 ≥ ∞) of the statistical indication while the results in table 4 indicated that there is no statistical indication difference on the point (0.05 ≥ ∞) to gender variable upon implementing the program where the value of F which resulted from ANCOVA is (0.611, 0.34, 0.15, 0.73). Those values are not statistically-indicated ones on the point (0. 05 ≥ ∞) between the average of the performance made by the males' individuals of the experimental group and the average of the performance made by the females' individuals in the same group on Torrance Test for creative thinking. When comparing the averages from table 3, we notice that the average of the performance between the males and females is close.

As for the interacting between the gender and the experimental treatment variables, the statistical value of F reached between the skills of creative thinking and the total degree and between the gender variable is (0.30, 0.091, 0.28, 0.32) and all of which are not statistically-indicated difference on the point ($0.05 \geq \infty$). Thus, there is no relation between the skills of creative thinking and the total degree and between the genders variable on the performance of the sample individuals upon implementing the creative thinking Test.

Field	Difference source	Freedom degrees	Square average	F	Indication
Fluency	ANCOVA	1	1608.762	21.939	0.000
	Groups	1	3238.862	44.169	0.000
	Gender	1	44.835	0.611	0.58
	Groups × Gender	1	22.070	0.30	0.58
	Error	55	73.32		
	Total	59			
Flexibility	ANCOVA	1	108.045	30.349	0.000
	Groups	1	15.137	4.762	0.300
	Gender	1	1.242	0.34	0.55
	Groups × Gender	1	325	0.091	0.76
	Error	55	3.56		
	Total	59			
Originality	ANCOVA	1	35.899	11.353	0.001
	Groups	1	1.137	0.359	0.57
	Gender	1	0.49	0.15	0.69
	Groups × Gender	1	0.91	0.28	0.59
	Error	55	3.16		
	Total	59			
Total degree	ANCOVA	1	3580.230	31.875	0.00
	Groups	1	3642.991	32.434	0.00
	Gender	1	82.452	0.73	0.51
	Groups × Gender	1	36.687	0.32	0.57
	Error	55	112.32		
	Total	59			

Table 4: The results of ANCOVA in the performances between the average of the training program and gender is shown according the creative thinking (fluency, flexibility, originality and total degree).

VI. BENEFITS OF USING THE SYSTEM

Using the system developed in this research in educating the deaf children has the following advantages:

1. This system increases the opportunities and the possibilities of communication and interactions between the deaf children and the computer. They can start or stop the show anytime and can also move to any piece of information they want to repeat any part of it.
2. The program presented the scientific signs in the human body in a very interesting and flexible manner. The pictures and videos accompanied by it enable the user to build his / her actual imagination from what s/he learnt. It also compensates the deaf children through using the visual effects.
3. The educational program opens the door for everyone to interact and work in accordance with his / her ability.
4. The program also contributes in raising enthusiasm among users and motivating their interest for the subjects introduced in this program especially the deaf ones as it creates positive attitudes for them towards the computers.
5. The computerized educational program will organize the possibilities of deaf user learning as part of persons with little abilities.
6. The program saves teachers' time and effort in explanation. This time and effort can be utilized in helping the deaf user individually.
7. The usage of voice in this project increases children's interaction with the program. It also helps the partially deaf persons to utilize their ability to understand what is said or mentioned in the program.
8. The program helps children getting rid of fear, hesitation and shame during the learning process where the show can be repeated more than one time as well as enabling them to understand missed or implicit information. This method is better than saying the information in the traditional way by the teacher as many students become hesitant in asking the question.
9. The program contributes in developing the ability of the deaf people for the scientific terms and concepts where they face problems in understanding those terms.

V. CONCLUSIONS

The children with hearing difficulties are considered to be one of the most important categories in the society that needs to have its linguistic skills developed and to have its understanding of the scientific terms improved. This development and improvement can't be achieved without directly connecting this category with the heard universe.

This research paper discusses the influences of the scientific signs in the Holy Quran in improving the skills of creative thinking for the deaf children. The system used in this research is unique in using the scientific signs in the Holy Quran to serve the people of hearing difficulties as a category that requires special educational, psychological and social needs.

Since a computer-based learning has many features one of which is creating a simultaneous feedback, this system serves both students and teachers in providing the mutual reaction between the user and the computer. This program also contributes in increasing the learners' self-confidence and developing a positive self-conception and provides an educational environment closer to the real educational situation.

The results showed that there are statistically-indicated differences on the point ($0.05 \geq \infty$) between the averages of the students' performance according to the Torrance Test and skills: (fluency, flexibility and the total degree). Those differences referred to the employment of the computerized system of the Holy Quran. The results are in the side of the experimental group on the skills of fluency, flexibility and the total degree while the differences between the two groups in the skill of originality are less than the point ($0.05 \geq \infty$).

Also, the results showed that there are no statistically-indicated differences on the point ($0.05 \geq \infty$) between the averages of the males' and females' performances according to the Torrance Test for creative thinking and its three skills. The results also showed that there is an interaction between the computerized program of the Holy Quran and the gender factor of the creative thinking and its three skills on the point ($0.05 \geq \infty$).

REFERENCES

1. Jarwan, Fathi., (2004), Talent and thought and creativity, Amman, Dar AL-feker for Printing and Publishing.
2. Takebayashi, Y. 1992. Integration of Understanding and Synthesis Functions for Multimedia Interfaces. In *Multimedia Interface Design*. Blattner, M. M. and Dannenberg, R. B. (eds), ACM Press, Addison-Wesley Publishing Company, New York
3. Coutaz, J., Nigay, L., Salber, D., Blandford, A., May, J. and Young, R. M. 1995. Four easy pieces for assessing the usability of multimodal interaction: the CARE properties. In *Human-Computer Interaction: Interact '95.* Nordby, K., Helmersen, P., Gilmore, D.J. and Arnesen, S. A. (eds), Champing & Hall.
4. Marmolin, H. 1991. Multimedia from the Perspectives of Psychology. In *Multimedia Systems, Interaction and pplications. 1st Eurographics Workshop*, Stockholm, Sweden, April 18/19, L. Kjelldahl (ed), Springer Verlag.
5. Alty, J. 1991. Multimedia - What is It and How do we Exploit it? In *HCI '91.*
6. Bearne, M., Jones, S. and Sapsford-Francis, J. 1994. Towards usability guidelines for multimedia systems. *Proceedings of Multimedia '94* San Francisco, Oct. 1994, ACM, New York, pp. 105-110
7. Rangel, F.(2001), Integrating Technology Into Literacy for Hearing-impaired Student, Digital Video Dictionaryments/ Techerp/Tech02.Html
8. Abdel-Mutaleb, Saed 2000 the Abilities and Indications of Creative Thinking for the Hearing-impaired and Mute Students. The First Episode of the Primary Education. Unpublished Master thesis, Faculty of Qualities Educational , Al-Mansoora University. Egypt.
9. Kaplan, H. (2003), National Center to Improve The Quality of Technology, Media And Materials: Http://Www.Lidea.Uogon./Edu/~Ncite/Docu
10. Passing, D.& Eden, S. (2000), Improving The Flexible Thinking in Hearing-impaired And Hard of Hearing Children With Virtual Reality Technology, American Annals of The Hearing-impaired, Vol. 145.
11. Future soft (CD).Egypt
12. Al-Turath center for Computer Research.(CD's-part1,Part2,Part3). Jordan.
13. McDonald, J.H. (2009), Handbook of Biological Statistics, Sparky House Publishing, Baltimore, Maryland, pp. 232-237.

Parallelization of Shape Function Generation for Hierarchical Tetrahedral Elements

Sara E. McCaslin
The University of Texas at Tyler
3900 University Blvd.
Tyler, TX 75799
Sara_McCaslin@uttyler.edu

***Abstract*-Research has gone into parallelization of the numerical aspects of computationally intense analysis and solutions. Recent advances in computer algebra systems have opened up new opportunities for research: generating closed-form, symbolic solutions more efficiently by parallelizing the symbolic manipulations.**

I. INTRODUCTION

Computers have proven a powerful tool in engineering, beginning in 1910, although it must be admitted that the term had a slightly different meaning. Richardson referred to the use of "computers" for iterative calculations in the finite difference method as applied to calculating stresses in a dam, and his computers, as it turns out, were actually young high school students who performed iterative calculations for [1].

Numerical methods, such as the finite different method, have successfully been used many years to perform analysis and simulation. Much research has gone into improving the efficiency of these methods, and finding better ways to harness modern computing power to deal with increasingly complex systems.

Along with the increase of speed, memory, and processing capabilities, there have been significant improvements in computer algebra systems (CAS). Systems such as *Mathematica*, *Matlab,* and *Maple* make it possible to obtain closed-form, exact/symbolic solutions to problems that simply were not possible even thirty years ago.

Symbolic solutions have been a topic of interest to researchers in various fields of science and engineering, and have often been found more computationally efficient than the standard numerical approach. However, limitations still exist as the complexity of the solutions increases. Typical limitations include the memory needed to obtain successfully obtain the solution, and the excessive amount of time that some solutions require.

Parallelization of the symbolic solution generation step can aid with the time and memory issues. However, with limited resources may not have ready access to high performance computing systems, and must limit their work to problems that can be solved on a desktop or workstation.

Many engineers and scientists do not have the necessary specialized programming background to successfully (and efficiently) write source code implementing parallelization [2], and this need has been identified as a serious lack in the scientific community.

With these two points in mind, a general methodology for quickly applying parallel processing symbolic solution generation would be beneficial to researchers, especially if it focused on a very-high level language (VH-LL) symbolic manipulator that would likely be used by non-computer scientists. A first step toward this goal would be the parallelization of a straight-forward, yet time-intensive, portion of a closed-form solution using a computer algebra system that supports parallelization.

II. SOFTWARE

Various CAS packages have been used to generate symbolic solutions, including *Mathematica*, *Maple*, and *MATLAB*, as well as the the older *REDUCE*, *DERIVE*, *ALTRAN*, and *MACSYMA* [3]. Currently, there are several VH-LL CAS packages that support parallel computing. *MATLAB*, for example, supports built-in parallelization with certain add-in toolboxes combined with the Parallel Computing Toolbox, but the Symbolic toolbox is not included [4]. It does, however, allow a level of abstraction similar to *Mathematica* [5]. *Maple 13* also provides a high-level multithreaded programming model, but it is not automated as *Matlab* or *Mathematica* [6, 7].

Mathematica 7 was chosen for this research project because (1) it is considered the most widely employed computer algebra system for structural applications such as finite element analysis [3] (on which the test case is based), (2) it has been used specifically for generating shape functions for finite element applications [8], (3) has been successfully used to generate closed-form solutions for isoparametric tetrahedral elements [9, 10], and (4) it readily lends itself to multi-core machines (as opposed to clusters) [11] which makes this research of interest to those with limited funding or resources.

The newest version of *Mathematica* can attempt automatic parallelization of its built-in mathematical capabilities and provide the user with feedback regarding whether or not parallelization was possible [12, 13], which will aid those inexperienced in parallelization in determining whether a section of script can be evaluated in parallel. It makes available commands for parallelizing the development of tables, command onto a list of variables, and do loops, just as many other parallel CAS packages do.

T. Sobh, K. Elleithy (eds.), *Innovations in Computing Sciences and Software Engineering*,
DOI 10.1007/978-90-481-9112-3_69, © Springer Science+Business Media B.V. 2010

For parallelization to be possible the programmer must still make changes to the original solution. By using a parallel CAS to generate the shape functions, rather than a typical language that supports parallel processing, a two-fold objective is achieved: the programmer can focus on the symbolic aspects of the code rather than on the complicated details of more machine-dependent, low-level parallel implementations, and symbolic, rather than merely numeric, results can be achieved using built in-functions. Most research has focused on obtaining numerical results using parallel processing, instead of symbolic results, which makes this approach different.

III. TEST CASE

In order to explore the possibilities in the area of research, a simple test case was chosen: generating the shape functions of hierarchical tetrahedral elements with p-levels ranging from 4 to 20 as part of obtaining closed-form solutions for finite element applications.

Closed-form solutions have been successfully used in finite element analysis to improve efficiency over methods using numerical approximations [8, 9], most recently for obtaining the closed-form stiffness matrices for hierarchical straight-sided tetrahedral elements through the fourth order [10]. The first stage of developing closed-form solutions for hierarchical elements involves the generation of the element shape functions.

The shape functions for tetrahedral elements are described in terms of local coordinates, called volume or natural coordinates and indicated by L, as shown in Fig. 1.

To map from the local coordinates to global coordinates, the transformation shown in (1) is used. Local coordinates L_i (i=1, 2, 3, 4) are mapped to global coordinates of any point within the element represented $\{x, y, z\}$ based on the global coordinates of the vertices of the tetrahedral element $\{x_i, y_i, z_i\}$ (i=1, 2, 3, 4).

$$\begin{Bmatrix} x \\ y \\ z \\ 1 \end{Bmatrix} = \begin{bmatrix} x_1 & x_2 & x_3 & x_4 \\ y_1 & y_2 & y_3 & y_4 \\ z_1 & z_2 & z_3 & z_4 \\ 1 & 1 & 1 & 1 \end{bmatrix} \begin{Bmatrix} L_1 \\ L_2 \\ L_3 \\ L_4 \end{Bmatrix} \tag{1}$$

Shape functions are expressed in terms of the local coordinates. For this research, Szabo and Babuska hierarchical shape functions [14] as described by Adjerid et al. [15] were used to automatically generate the shape functions for p-levels 4 through 20.

Hierarchic elements are also based on a complete set of polynomials, as illustrated in Fig. 2 by Pascal's pyramid through p-level 4, the lowest-order polynomial level generated for this research. Babuska, Szabo, and Katz [16] introduced a family of hierarchic elements, used in this research, with the property that polynomial p is a subset of polynomial $p + 1$. What makes this type of shape function extremely practical for finite element applications is that the stiffness matrix, equivalent nodal loads, and error estimation terms posses this same property.

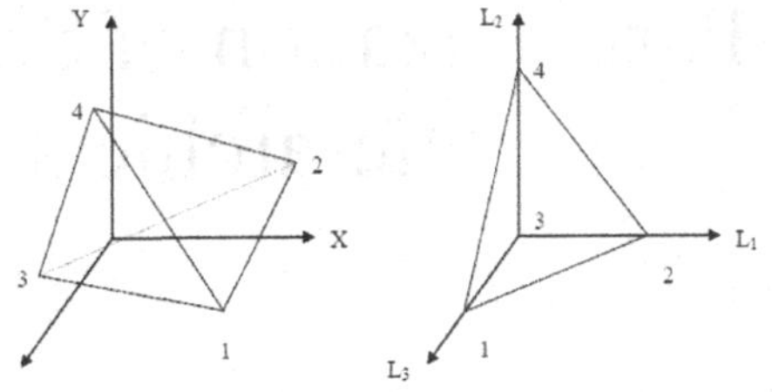

Fig. 1. Global coordinates and local coordinates.

For hierarchical tetrahedral elements, there are four nodal shape functions and three types of modes: edge, face, and internal. The edge modes are always associated with mid-side edge nodes, while the face modes are associated with the center of the face; the internal modes, or bubble nodes, are located at the centroid of the element.

The shape functions are based on Legendre polynomials, and are generated using (2) through (8).

$$\varepsilon_k(t_1,t_2) = \frac{-8\sqrt{4k+2}}{k(k+1)} P_i'(t_2 - t_1) \tag{2}$$

$$F_{r_1,r_2}(t_1,t_2,t_3) = P_{r_1}(t_2 - t_1)P_{r_2}(2t_3 - 1) \tag{3}$$

$$B_{r_1,r_2,r_3}(t_1,t_2,t_3) = P_{r_1}(t_2 - t_1)P_{r_2}(2t_3 - 1)P_{r_4}(2t_4 - 1) \tag{4}$$

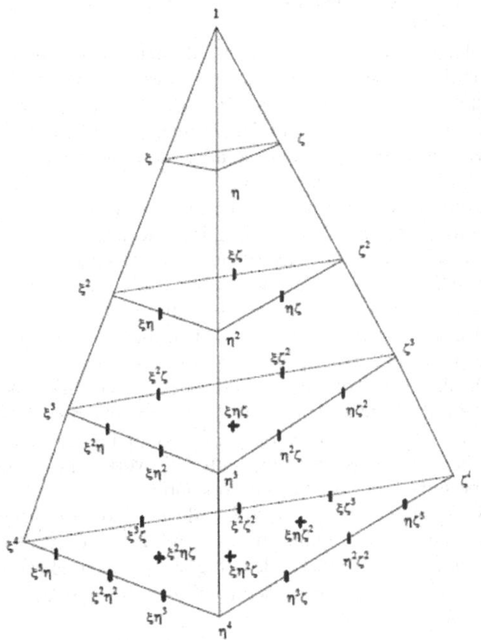

Fig. 2. Pascal's triangle through p-level 4.

Nodal shape functions (4 nodes)

$$\varphi_i^1 = L_i \text{ where } i = 1, 2, 3, 4 \quad (5)$$

Edge Modes (6 (*p*-1) nodes)

$$\varphi_i^2 = L_{j_1} L_{j_2} \varepsilon_k \left(L_{j_1}, L_{j_2}\right) \quad \text{where } k = 1, 2, \ldots p\text{-}1$$

$$j_1 = \begin{cases} 1 + j \bmod 3, 1 \le j \le 3 \\ 1 + j \bmod 4, 4 \le j \le 6 \end{cases} \text{and}$$

$$j_2 = \begin{cases} 1 + (j+1) \bmod 3, 1 \le j \le 3 \\ 4, 4 \le j \le 6 \end{cases} \quad (6)$$

Face Modes (2 (*p*-1) (*p*-2) nodes)

$$\varphi_i^3 = L_{j_1} L_{j_2} L_{j_3} F_{r_1, r_2} \left(L_{j_1}, L_{j_2}, L_{j_3}\right)$$

$$j_1 = 1 + j \bmod 4,\ j_2 = 1 + j_1 \bmod 4,\ j_3 = 1 + j_2 \bmod 4$$

$$k = 3, 4 \ldots p \text{ and } r_1 + r_2 = k - 3 \quad (7)$$

Bubbles Modes ((*p*-1) (*p*-2) (*p*-3)/6 nodes)

$$\varphi_i^4 = L_1 L_2 L_3 L_4 B_{r_1, r_2, r_3} \left(L_1, L_2, L_3, L_4\right)$$

$$\text{where } k = 4, 5, \ldots p \text{ and } r_1 + r_2 + r_3 = k - 4 \quad (8)$$

For *p*-levels 5 through 20, the number of edge, face, and bubble nodes for each p-level are shown in Fig. 3. Note that the bubble node count increases with *p*-level more quickly than any other type of node, and also has the most complex representation.

Fig. 3 summarizes the number of nodes required for each *p*-level, and showing a quadratic relation between p-level and total nodes required. Note that *p*-level 5 required a total of 56 nodes, *p*-level 10 required 386, and *p*-level 30 required 5456 nodes. This graph makes it easy to see why the level of complexity of the calculations increases with *p*-level.

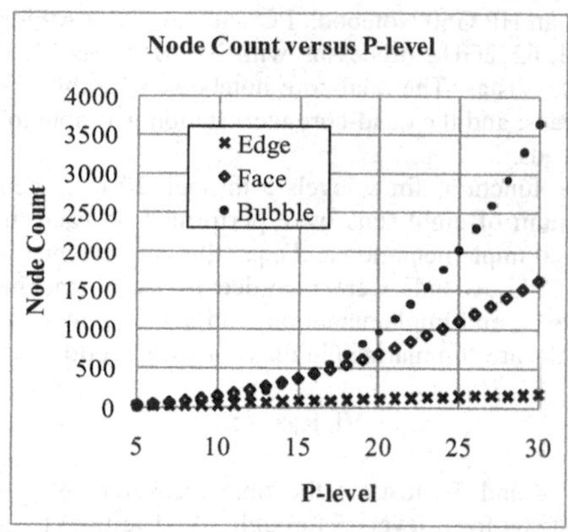

Fig. 3. Node count for each type of node versus *p*-level.

IV. Serial Generation

The serial approach to generating these shape functions is very straightforward, and can closely follow the equations given. An single shape function array is sized based on the number of nodes required for the *p*-level, and each type of node is generated in succession, beginning with vertex nodes, and followed by edge, face, and bubble nodes. The time required for generating a full set of shape functions increases with p-level. The general algorithm is given below.

1. Calculate the total number of nodes required based on the *p*-level
2. Initialize node count to 0
3. Create a shape function vector (list) called *nn* sized to hold the total number of nodes required
4. Use a for loop to create the four vertex nodes (5) incrementing the node count each time and placing them individually in the *nn* vector
5. Create the edge nodes, (6)
   a. Iterate over *j* and *k*
   b. Calculate j_1 and j_2
   c. Increment the node count
   d. Add the new shape function generated and simplified to the *nn* vector at position node count
6. Create the face nodes (7)
   a. Iterate over *j* and *k*
   b. Calculate j_1, j_2 and j_3
   c. Iterate over possible values for r_1 and r_2 that sum to $k-3$
   d. Increment the node count when an acceptable combination of r_1, r_2 and r_3 has been found
   e. Add the new shape function generated and simplified to the *nn* vector at position node count
7. Create the bubble nodes (8)
   a. Iterate over *j* and *k*
   b. Iterate over possible values for r_1, r_2 and r_3 that sum to $k-4$
   c. Increment the node count when an acceptable combination of r_1, r_2 and r_3 has been found
   d. Add the new shape function generated and simplified to the *nn* vector at position node count

The shape function generation script was implemented in *Mathematica* 7, making possible the efficient generation of symbolic solutions because of built-in mathematical capabilities, such as matrix and list manipulation, simplification, and programming constructs such as loops and decision structures. The total seconds of CPU time needed to generate and simplify the shape functions for each *p*-level is recorded using TimeUsed [17], and the system cache is cleared each time a set of shape functions is generated.

V. Parallel Generation

Computer systems which support parallelization can run multiple computing tasks at the same time to solve problems in less time. This can make it feasible for researchers to solve larger problems, as well as, problems that would be impossible otherwise. If each processor has its own memory, then problems requiring too much memory for one processor can then be solved [18, 19].

In order for a parallel system to be able to run a program faster than it would with a single-processor, the program must be parallelized. This means that the program is setup to have more than one task (which could include one or more instructions) running simultaneously. Serial code, on the other hand, indicates that each command is executed one at a time. Because of these differences, writing parallel code requires a vastly different approach from writing serial code [18].

The first instinct for some programmers without extensive experience in parallelization would be to use four threads to calculate the vertex, edge, face, and bubble nodes simultaneously. However, as the script currently stands, all four sections of code depend on the node count variable and the *nn* shape function list.

One solution (of many) would be to let each type of node have its own list: a list of vertex nodes, a list of edge nodes, a list of face nodes, and a list of bubble nodes and simply combine the lists into one after the script has finished generating the shape functions. Each type of node could also have its own node count variable. This removes a major source of interdependence that would prevent parallelization.

The next issue is one of efficiency: is it really the best approach to use one thread for each type of node we are generating? The vertex nodes are generated so quickly that their processing time is extremely small compared to that of the other types of nodes. Trying to calculate vertex nodes them in parallel with edge nodes (which are always more in number and complexity) would be a poor use.

A better approach would be to parallelize the generation of edge, face, and bubble nodes separately, so that all expression sent to the concurrent threads take about the same amount of time to process [20]. This achieves better load balancing. The first attempt at a parallel approach took this form, using the same equations as the serial approach but without including any details of how to achieve it using code:

1. Distribute the functions for ε, F, and β, (2) – (4)
2. Generate vertex nodes in parallel and store them in list nv
3. Generate edge nodes in parallel using available threads iterating over j and k, and store the resulting list in ne
4. Append list ne to list nv
5. Generate face nodes in parallel using available threads, and store them in list nf
6. Append list nf to list nv
7. Generate bubble nodes in parallel using available threads, and store them in list nb
8. Append list nb to list nv

Now the script is ready for the programmer to focus on the details of parallelizing the node generation for each node type. First, all functions used in shape node generation and the volume coordinates that are common to all the shape functions must be distributed to all threads using the DistributeDefinitions command [22]. This command "distributes" the current definitions of variables and functions to all kernels, with each kernel maintaining its own independent local copy [20].

Generation of the edge nodes requires no nested loops: observation of (6) shows that the equations must be generated while iterating over j and k. This section of script can be easily modified for use with the ParallelTable command, which builds a table while parallelizing the procedure as much as possible with available threads [23], for which Mathematica allocates on parallel kernel per core [20] Note that only two iterators are required in order to generate the edge nodes.

Face node generation, as found in (7), requires nested loops to find pairs of r_1 and r_2 that sum to k-3, while also iterating through values of both j and k. The ParallelTable command can also be used although care must be taken because of this dependency: j_3 depends on j_2 which depends on j_1. Processing the data required four iterators.

Bubble node generation, as found in (8), faces the same challenged: it also requires nested loops to find triples of r_1, r_2 and r_3 that sum to k-4, while also iterating through values of both j and k. A total of four iterators are required, and ParallelTable works for this section of code.

The second revision of the algorithm takes into account the need to perform simplification on the resulting shape functions stored in *nn* to reduce their length, which can quickly become excessive. This command makes use of ParallelMap [24] so that two or more shape functions can be simplified in parallel. After the serial and parallel scripts were finalized, they were tested to compare their efficiency as discussed in the next section.

V. Testing Method

As discussed, CPU seconds required to generate each p-level was recorded. Scripts were implemented on a Dell PC 690 precision workstation with a quad-core Intel Xeon 1.86GHz processors and 4 GB SDRAM running Windows XP, and an HP G60 Notebook PC with an AMD Athlon Dual-Core QL-62 2GHz processor with 3 GB of RAM, running Windows Vista. The dual-core notebook was able to launch two threads, and the quad-core workstation was able to launch four threads.

Shape functions for p-levels 5 through 20 were generated. A minimum of eight runs were performed on each machine, for a serial implementation and a parallel implementation.

The CPU seconds were recorded for each machine type, run, p-level, and implementation, and subsequently averaged. The results are summarized in the following section.

VI. Results

Figs. 4 and 5 illustrate the time measurements taken on both systems for p-levels 5 through 20. The time to generate the shape functions increases exponentially with p-level for both the serial and parallel computations. Parallelization reduces the time required, but retains this exponential relationship.

By *p*-level 20, the maximum serial processing time on the dual-core notebook was nearly 80 CPU seconds, and on the quad-core workstation nearly 50. When parallelization was used, the dual core notebook took less than 20 CPU seconds and the quad-core workstation took less than 2 CPU seconds.

Note that the CPU times were averaged over a eight runs on both systems for all *p*-levels from 5 to 20. While the dual-core notebook consistently required more time for both the serial and parallel implementations, it can be noted that both the notebook and workstation demonstrated the same exponential relationships between *p*-level and processing time.

A speed- up ratio, defined as the ratio of serial processing time to parallel processing time, was calculated for each *p*-level on both implementations to measure the level of efficiency achieved by using parallelization.

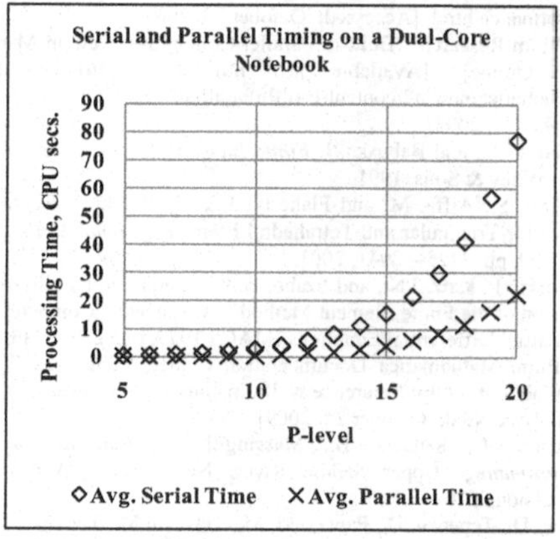

Fig. 4 Serial and parallel shape function generation timing versus *p*-level on a dual processor laptop.

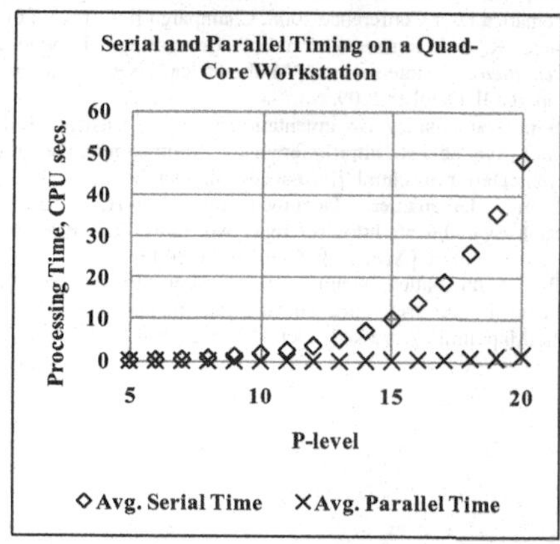

Fig. 5 Serial and parallel shape function generation timing versus *p*-level on a quad-core workstation.

Fig. 6 shows the ratios achieved on the dual-core notebook. Note that the maximum speed-up ratio achieved was slight over 7.26, with a minimum ratio of 3.4. Fig, 6 shows the same data for the quad-core workstation. The maximum speed-up ratio achieved was 73.5, and the minimum was 17.5 for *p*-level 5. For the workstation, Figs. 6 and 7 appears to converge at a speed-up ratio around 32 for the quad-core workstation and 3.5 for the dual-core notebook.

Both systems show some unusual outliers between *p*-levels 5 and 9. Looking at Fig. 3, it is apparent that within this range the count of edge, face, and bubble nodes are close to the same, but beyond *p*-level 10 there is a definite divergence between the node count of different types of nodes. Considering the complexity of the face and bubble shape function expressions, this combination of node counts and complexity could account for these outliers.

Note that above *p*-level 10, both the notebook and the workstation show a similar relationship between *p*-level and speed-up ratio.

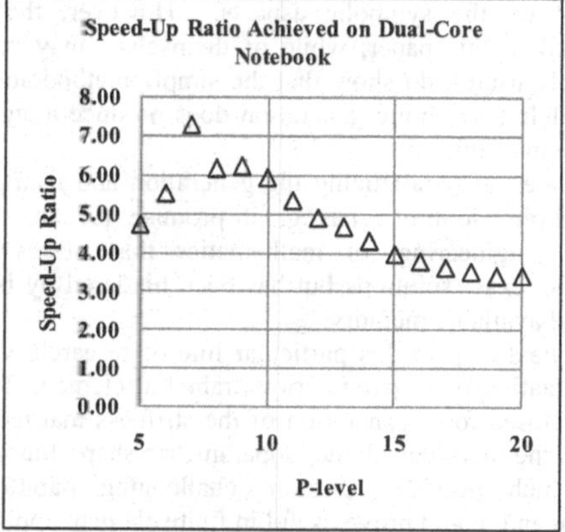

Fig. 6 Speed-up ratios for dual-core notebook.

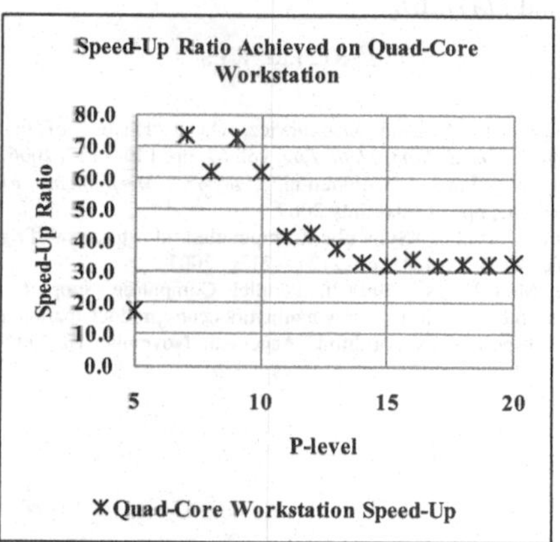

Fig. 7 Speed up ratios for quad-processor workstation.

VII. Conclusions

Parallelization of the generation of hierarchical tetrahedral element shape functions for *p*-levels 5 through 20, using *Mathematica*'s parallelization support, showed considerable time savings in terms of CPU seconds when compared to serial processing. At *p*-level 20, the dual-processor laptop achieved a speed-up ratio of 3.4 and the quad -processor workstation achieved 33.9 when compared to serial processing.

Data sharing between parallel threads was achieved by separately parallelizing the edge, face, and bubble node shape function generation and providing each with its own vector array. After each type of nodal shape function (bubble, edge, face) has been generated, it is appended to a main vector array that will hold the entire set of shape functions. The Simplification command is then parallel mapped to the entire array.

Most parallelization research in science and engineering has focused on numerical aspects of simulation and analysis, and not on the symbolic aspects. However, the results presented in this paper, while of themselves may not seem extremely useful, do show that the simple methodology used to parallelize symbolic generation does produce a significant increase in efficiency.

The idea of parallelizing the generation and manipulation of symbolic solutions has great promise for any area of science, engineering, or mathematics that makes use of symbolic, exact solutions but has been hindered by issues of time and available memory.

The next step in this particular line of research would be parallelization of isoparametric tetrahedral element, followed by the closed-form generation of the stiffness matrices based on both the hierarchical and isoparametric shape functions [9, 10], which provides a more challenging parallelization problem and would prove useful in finite element applications. Future work should also include comparisons in speed gains achieved with equivalent serial and parallel scripts in both *Maple* and *MATLAB*.

References

[1] Samuelsson, A., and Zienkiewicz, O.C., "History of the Stiffness Method," *Int. J. Num. Meth. Eng*, vol. 67, pp. 149 – 157, 2006.

[2] Thilmay, J.,,ed. "Computing," *ASME Mechanical Engineering Magazine*, pp. 14 – 16, July 2009.

[3] Pavlovic, M.N., "Symbolic Computation in Structural Engineering," *Comp. Struc.*, vol. 81, pp. 2121 – 2136, 2003.

[4] The MathWorks, "Built-In Parallel Computing Support," [Online]. Available at: http://www.mathworks.com/products/parallelcomputing /builtin-parallel-support.html. [Accessed: November 16, 2009].

[5] The MathWorks, "Parallel Computing Toolbox 4.2," [Online]. Available at: http://www.mathworks.com/products/parallel-computing/. [Accessed: November 16, 2009].

[6] Maplesoft, "Maplesoft Online Help: Task Programming Model," [Online]. Available at: http://www.maplesoft.com/support/help/AddOns /view.aspx?path=TaskProgrammingModel. [Accessed: November 16, 2009].

[7] MaplePrimes, "The Parallel Programming Blog," [Online]. Available at: http://www.mapleprimes.com/blog/dohashi/parallelprogrammingblog [Accessed: November 16, 2009].

[8] Yew, C.K., Boyle, J.T., and Mackenzie, D., "A Computer Algebra Based Finite Element Development Environment," *Advances in Engineering Software*, vol. 32, p. 913 – 925, 2002.

[9] Shiakolas, P.S., Lawrence, K.L., and Nambiar, R.V. "Closed-Form Expressions for the Linear and Quadratic Strain Tetrahedral Finite Elements," *Comput. Struct.*, vol. 50, pp. 743 – 747, 1994.

[10] McCaslin, S.E., Shiakolas, P.S., Dennis, B.H., Lawrence, K.L, "Closed-form matrices for higher order tetrahedral elements," Proceedings of the 12th International Conference on Civil, Structural and Environmental Engineering Computing, Madeira, Portugal, September 2009.

[11] Bruhnke, M., Hahn, T., "A Simple Way to Distribute Mathematica Evaluations," Cornell University Library, arXiv.org, [Online]. [Available at: http://arxiv.org/abs/0902.1885v1], 2009.

[12] Wolfram Research, "Key Capabilities of Mathematica," [Online]. Available: http://www.wolfram.com/products/mathematica/overview/ performance.html. [Accessed: October 25, 2009].

[13] Wolfram Research, "Built-in Parallel Computing: New in Mathematica 7," [Online]. [Available at]: http://www.wolfram.com/products/ mathematica/newin7/content/BuiltInParallelComputing. [Accessed: October 25, 2009].

[14] Szabo, B.A., and Babuska, I. *Finite Element Analysis*. New York, NY: John Wiley & Sons, 1991.

[15] Adjerid, S., Aiffa, M. and Flaherty, J.E. "Hierarchical Finite Element Bases for Triangular and Tetrahedral Elements, *Comp. Meth. Appl. M.*, vol. 190, pp. 2925 – 2941, 2001.

[16] Babuska, I., Katz, I.N., and Szabo, B.A. "Hierarchic Families for the P-Version of the Finite Element Method," Advances in Computer Methods for Partial Differential Equations IMACS 1979, pp. 272 – 286, 1979.

[17] Wolfram Mathematica Documentation Center, "TimeUsed," [Online]. Available at: http://reference.wolfram.com/mathematica/ref/TimeUsed. html. [Accessed: October 25, 2009].

[18] Mattson, T., Sanders, B., Massingill, B., *Patterns for Parallel Programming*, Upper Saddle River, New Jersey: Addison-Wesley Professional, 2004.

[19] Petcu, D., Tepeneu, D., Paprzycki, M., Tetsuya, M., Tetsuya, I., "Survey of Symbolic Computations on the Grid," 3rd International Conference: Science of Electronic Technologies of Information and Telecommunications, Tunisia, March 2005.

[20] Maeder, R., "Enhancements in Parallel Computing," International Mathematica User Conference 2008, Champaign Il, October 2008.

[21] Maeder, R., "Mainstream Parallel Computing: Experience with *Mathematica* 7," International Mathematica User Conference 2009, Champaign Il, October 2009.

[22] Wolfram Mathematica Documentation Center, "DistributeDefintions," [Online]. Available at: http://reference.wolfram.com/mathematica/ref/ DistributeDefinitions.html. [Last accessed: October 25, 2009].

[23] Wolfram Mathematica Documentation Center, "ParallelTable," [Online]. Available at: http://reference.wolfram.com/mathematica/ref/ ParallelTable.html. [Accessed: October 25, 2009].

[24] Wolfram Mathematica Documentation Center, "ParallelMap," [Online]. Available at: http://reference.wolfram.com/mathematica/ref/ ParallelMap.html. [Accessed: October 25, 2009].

Analysis of Moment Invariants on Image Scaling and Rotation

Dongguang Li

School of Computer and Security Science, Edith Cowan University, Australia
E-mail: d.li@ecu.edu.au

***Abstract*—Moment invariants have been widely applied to image pattern recognition in a variety of applications due to its invariant features on image translation, scaling and rotation. The invariant properties are strictly invariant for the continuous function. Normally, images in practical applications are discrete. Consequently, the moment invariants may change over image geometric transformation. To address this research problem, an analysis with respect to the variation of moment invariants on image geometric transformation is presented in this paper, i.e., scaling and rotation. The guidance is also provided for minimizing the fluctuation of moment invariants.**

Keywords-Pattern recognition, Hu's moment invariant, Image transformation, Sapatial resolution

I. Introduction

Moment invariants are firstly introduced by Hu[1]. In[1], Hu derived six absolute orthogonal invariants and one skew orthogonal invariant based upon algebraic invariants, which are not only independent of position, size and orientation but also independent of parallel projection. The moment invariants have been proved to be the adequate measures for tracing image patterns regarding the images translation, scaling and rotation under the assumption of images with continuous functions and noise-free. Moment invariants have been extensively applied to image pattern recognition[2-5], image registration[6] and image reconstruction. However, the digital images in practical application are not continuous and noise-free, because images are quantized by finite-precision pixels in a discrete coordinate. In addition, the noise may be introduced by various factors such as camera. In this respect, errors are inevitably introduced during the computation of moment invariants. In other words, the moment invariants may vary with image geometric transformation. But how much are the variation? To our knowledge, this issue has never been quantitatively studied for image geometric transformation.

Salama[7] analyzed the effect of spatial quantization on moment invariants. He found that the error decreases when the image size increases and the sampling intervals decrease, but does not decrease monotonically in general. Teh[8] analyzed three fundamental issues related to moment invariants, concluding that: 1) Sensitivity to image noise; 2) Aspects of information redundancy; and 3) Capability for image representation. Teh declared that the higher order moments are the more vulnerable to noise. Computational errors on moment invariants can be caused by not only the quantization and pollution of noise, but also transformations such as scaling and rotation. When the size of images are increased or decreased, the pixels of images will be interpolated or deleted. Moreover, the rotation of images also causes the change of image function, because it involves rounding pixel values and coordinates[9]. Therefore, moment invariants may change as images scale or rotate.

This paper quantitatively analyzes fluctuation of moment invariants on image scaling and rotation. Empirical studies have been conducted with various images. The major contributions of this paper include the findings the relationship among the image scaling, rotation and resolution, and the guidance of minimizing the errors of moment invariants for image scaling and rotation.

The rest of paper is organized as follows: Section II describes seven Hu's moment invariants. Section III discusses the variation of moment invariants when images scale and rotate. Section IV analyzes the relationship between moment invariants and computation. Finally, section V concludes the paper.

II. Moment Invariants

Two-dimensional (p+q)th order moment are defined as follows:

$$m_{pq} = \int_{-\infty}^{\infty}\int_{-\infty}^{\infty} x^p y^q f(x,y)dxdy \qquad (1)$$
$$p,q = 0,1,2,\cdots$$

If the image function f(x,y) is a piecewise continuous bounded function, the moments of all orders exist and the moment sequence $\{m_{pq}\}$ is uniquely determined by f(x,y); and correspondingly, f(x,y) is also uniquely determined by the moment sequence $\{m_{pq}\}$.

One should note that the moments in (1) may be not invariant when f(x,y) changes by translating, rotating or scaling. The invariant features can be achieved using central moments, which are defined as follows:

$$\mu_{pq} = \int_{-\infty}^{\infty}\int_{-\infty}^{\infty} (x-\bar{x})^p (y-\bar{y})^q f(x,y)dxdy \qquad (2)$$
$$p,q = 0,1,2,\cdots$$

Where $\bar{x} = m_{10}/m_{00}$ and $\bar{y} = m_{01}/m_{00}$, which are the centroid of the image f(x,y).

The centroid moments μ_{pq} computed using the centroid of the image f(x,y) is equivalent to the m_{pq} whose center has been shifted to centroid of the image. Therefore, the central moments are invariant to image translations.

T. Sobh, K. Elleithy (eds.), *Innovations in Computing Sciences and Software Engineering*,
DOI 10.1007/978-90-481-9112-3_70,

Scale invariance can be obtained by normalization. The normalized central moments are defined as follows:

$$\eta_{pq} = \frac{\mu_{pq}}{\mu_{00}^{\gamma}}, \quad \gamma = (p+q+2)/2, \ \mathrm{p+q} = 2,3,\cdots \quad (3)$$

Based on normalized central moments, Hu[1] introduced seven moment invariants:

$$\phi_1 = \eta_{20} + \eta_{02}$$

$$\phi_2 = (\eta_{20} - \eta_{02})^2 + 4\eta_{11}^2$$

$$\phi_3 = (\eta_{30} - 3\eta_{12})^2 + (3\eta_{21} - \mu_{03})^2$$

$$\phi_4 = (\eta_{30} + \eta_{12})^2 + (\eta_{21} + \mu_{03})^2$$

$$\phi_5 = (\eta_{30} - 3\eta_{12})(\eta_{30} + \eta_{12})[(\eta_{30} + \eta_{12})^2 - 3(\eta_{21} + \eta_{03})^2] + (3\eta_{21} - \eta_{03})(\eta_{21} + \eta_{03})[3(\eta_{30} + \eta_{12})^2 - (\eta_{21} + \eta_{03})^2]$$

$$\phi_6 = (\eta_{20} - \eta_{02})[(\eta_{30} + \eta_{12})^2 - (\eta_{21} + \eta_{03})^2] + 4\eta_{11}(\eta_{30} + \eta_{12})(\eta_{21} + \eta_{03})$$

$$\phi_7 = (3\eta_{21} - \eta_{03})(\eta_{30} + \eta_{12})[(\eta_{30} + \eta_{12})^2 - 3(\eta_{21} + \eta_{03})^2] - (\eta_{30} - 3\eta_{12})(\eta_{21} + \eta_{03})[(3(\eta_{30} + \eta_{12})^2 - (\eta_{21} + \eta_{03})^2]$$

The seven moment invariants are useful properties of being unchanged under image scaling, translation and rotation.

III. MOMENT INVARIANTS AND IMAGE TRANSFORMATION

Image geometric transformation is a popular technique in image processing, which usually involves image translation, scaling and rotation. The translation operator maps the position of each pixel in an input image into a new position in an output image; the scale operator is used to shrink or zoom the size of an image, which is achieved by subsampling or interpolating to the input image; the rotation operator maps the position of each pixel onto a new position by rotating it through a specified angle, which may produce non-integer coordinates. In order to generate the intensity of the pixels at each integer position, different interpolation methods can be employed such as nearest-neighbor interpolation, bilinear interpolation and bicubic interpolation.

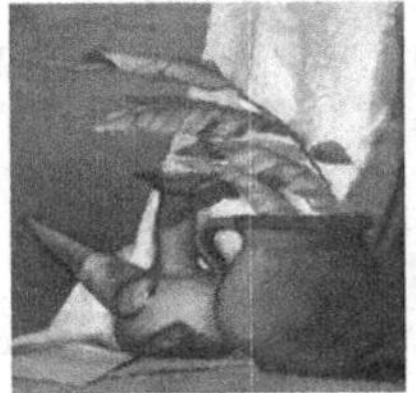

Image A Image B

Figure 1. Images for experiments

From the description in last paragraph, we can see that translation only shifts the position of pixels, but scaling and rotation not only shift the position of pixels but also change the image function itself. Therefore, only the scaling and rotation cause the errors of moment invariants. We employ two images with 250 x 250 resolutions to study what extent the image scaling and rotation can impact the moment invariants, One is a complex image without principal orientation (image A); the other is a simple image with principal orientation (image B). Figure 1 shows the two images.

A. Moment Invariants and Image Scaling

As described above, image scaling may cause change of image function, so the moment invariants may also change correspondingly. Therefore, it is very necessary to study the relationship between moment invariants and image scaling. We conduct the research by computing seven moment invariants on image A and image B with resolution from 10x10 to 500x500 in 10 increments. The Figure 2(a), (b) separately shows the results of moment invariant for image A and B. From the diagrams we see that the resolution of 130x130 is the threshold for image A. The values have apparent fluctuations when the resolution less than the threshold but stability when the resolution more than the threshold. Correspondingly, the threshold of image B is 150x150.

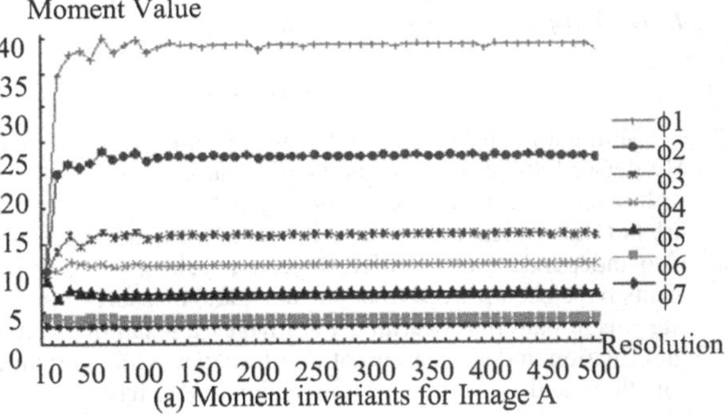

(a) Moment invariants for Image A

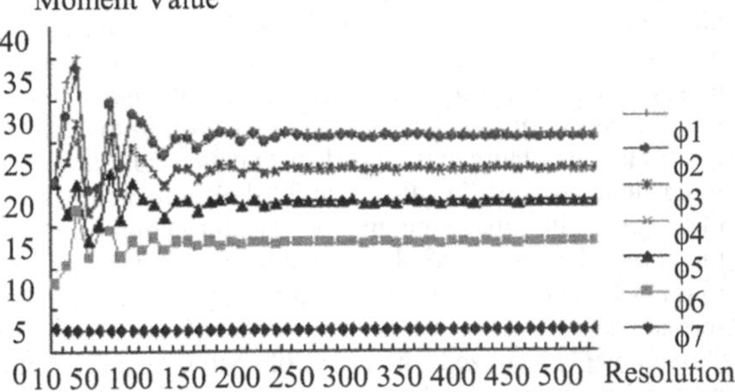

(b) Moment invariants for Image B

Figure 2. Moment invariants on image scaling

The equation (4) is used to measure the fluctuation a series of data x.

$$R = \frac{\max(\mathrm{x}) - \min(\mathrm{x})}{|\,\mathrm{mean}(\mathrm{x})\,|} \times 100\% \quad (4)$$

Where, max(x), min(x) and mean(x) separately note the maximum, minimum and mean in data x. The data in Figure 2(a) are divided into two groups by the threshold 130x130 to separately compute the fluctuation by equation (4). The results are displayed in table 1. The maximum of fluctuation comes up to 124.38% in $\phi 5$ when resolution of image less than threshold. But it decreases to 5.68% in $\phi 5$ when resolution of image greater then threshold.

Table 1. fluctuation ratio on image A

moment invariants	Resolution <Threshold	Resolution ≥Threshold
$\phi 1$	0.58%	0.04%
$\phi 2$	47.02%	1.06%
$\phi 3$	60.25%	1.41%
$\phi 4$	88.26%	1.40%
$\phi 5$	124.38%	5.68%
$\phi 6$	84.43%	1.84%
$\phi 7$	102.94%	2.59%

B. *Moment Invariants and Image Rotation*

Since the rotation of an image can change the function of the image more or less, the moment invariants keep changing as the image is rotated. In order to investigate the fluctuation of moment invariants result from the image rotation, we conduct the two kinds of experiments, i.e., one kind is the different images (A, B) with the same resolution; another is the different resolutions of the same image. Each input image is rotated from 1° to 360° in 1° increments.

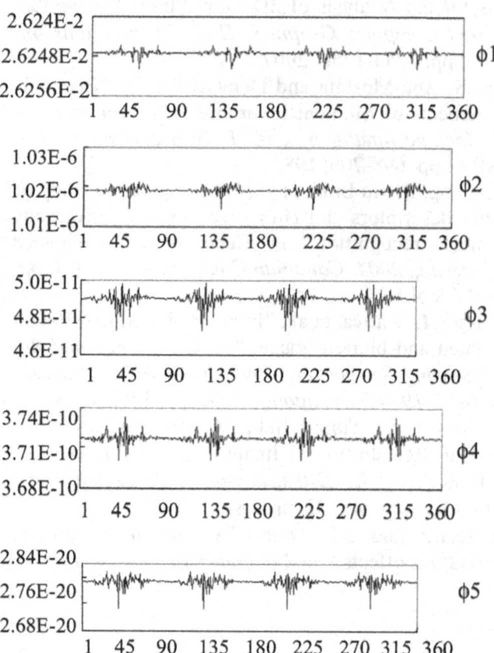

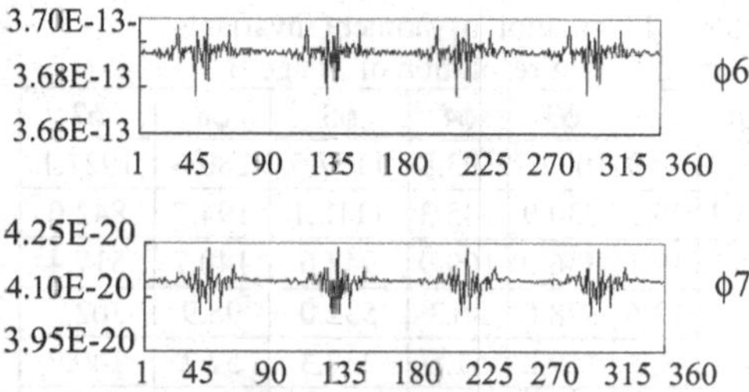

Figure 3. Moment invariants on Image B rotated from 1° to 360° in 1° increments

Figure 3 display the results of moment invariants for image B rotated from 1° to 360°, it shows the fluctuation of moment invariants becomes strong when the rotated angle near to 45,135, 225 and 315 degrees, while becomes weak as the rotated angle near to 90,180, 270 and 360 degree.

In section III A, we know the threshold of resolution on Image B is 150x150. Does the same image have same threshold between scaling and rotation? In order to answer this question, we produce a series of images with resolutions from 60x60 to 330x330 in 30 increments using the same original image, and compute the moment invariants for each image rotated from 1° to 360°. Then, the fluctuation is computed by equation (4) for each 360 images. Figure 4 shows the trend of fluctuation of moment invariants. From the diagram, we can see that the threshold is different between image scaling and image rotation. The threshold of image rotation on Image B is not 150x150 but 240x240.

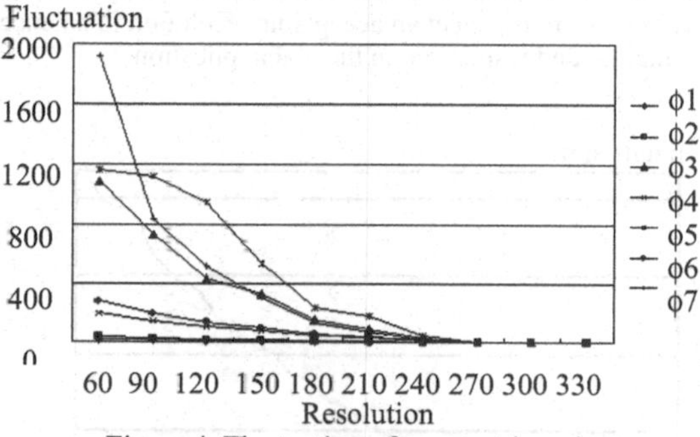

Figure 4. Fluctuation of moment invariants on Image B with different resolution

Table 2 shows the values of fluctuation for seven moment invariants on different resolution from 60x60 to 330x330. We can see that the fluctuation decreases as the image spatial resolution increases. The fluctuation almost comes up to 1921.1% when the resolution is only 60x60, but rapidly decreases to 1.1% when the resolution is 270x270. The fluctuation obviously decreases as the resolution increases until to the threshold. However, the fluctuation does not monotonically decrease any more when the resolution greater than 270x270.

Table 2. Fluctuation of moment invariants on different resolution of Image B

resolution	ϕ1	ϕ2	ϕ3	ϕ4	ϕ5	ϕ6	ϕ7
60x60	18.7	39.9	1084.7	193.8	1157.5	280.6	1921.1
90x90	13.3	26.5	730.9	145.3	1118,1	194.7	842.0
120x120	10.7	19.1	436.0	109.9	947.6	140.7	517.4
150x150	7.4	13.6	328.0	86.3	532.0	98.9	302.1
180x180	4.5	8.2	159.2	51.5	237.3	57.7	140.0
210x210	3.2	5.6	88.1	36.2	179.3	38.9	75.5
240x240	1.1	1.9	21.4	12.3	46.2	12.8	19.7
270x270	0.2	0.3	1.8	0.4	2.9	0.5	1.1
300x300	0.2	0.5	1.4	0.3	2.0	0.5	1.3
330x330	0.1	0.3	1.9	0.2	1.2	0.2	1.7

IV. Moment Invariants and Computation

From section III, we can get the conclusion: The higher the resolution is, the lower the fluctuation is. However, the computation of moment invariants will increase when the resolution increases. As a consequence, the research of relationship between the resolution of images and computation is necessary.

We calculate the computation of moment invariants for the resolutions from 10x10 to 1500x1500 in 30 increments on a PC (CPU P4 2.0G, RAM 1G). Figure 5 shows the results. From the diagram, we can see that the relationship between the resolution and the computation is non-linear. Therefore, we must select an acceptable resolution to balance computation and resolution on the real application.

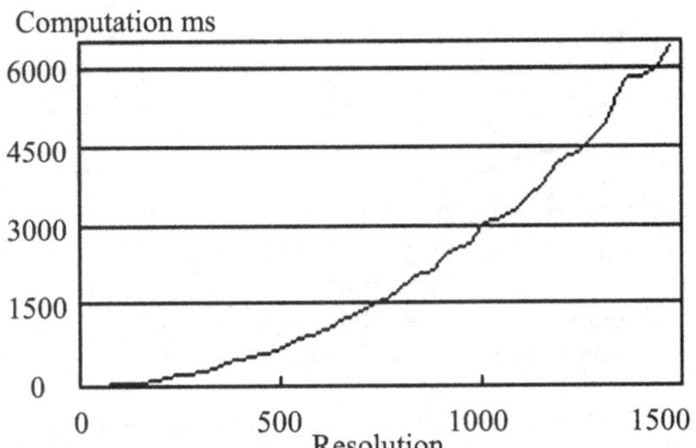

Figure 5. Computation of moment invariants for different resolution

V. Conclusion

This paper has presented an analysis of fluctuation of Hu's moment invariants on image scaling and rotation. Our findings may be summarized as follows: (1) the moment invariants change as images scale or rotate, because images are not continuous function or polluted by noise; (2) the fluctuation decreases when the spatial resolution of images increases. However, the change will not remarkably decrease as resolution increases if the resolution greater than the threshold; (3) the computation increases quickly as resolution increases.

From the experimental studies, we find that the choice of image spatial resolution is very important to keep invariant features. To decrease the fluctuation of moment invariants, the image spatial resolution must be higher than the threshold of scaling and rotation. However, the resolution cannot be too high, because the computation will remarkably increase as the resolution increases. Therefore, the choice of resolution must balance computation and resolution on the real application

VI. Acknowledgement

Mr Z. Huang, as a visiting fellow at ECU, helped with digital image preparation.

References

[1] Hu Ming-Kuei, "Visual pattern recognition by moment invariants," *Information Theory, IRE Transactions,* vol. 8, pp. 179-187, 1962.

[2] M. Schlemmer, M. Heringer, et al., "Moment Invariants for the Analysis of 2D Flow Fields," *Visualization and Computer Graphics, IEEE Transactions on,* vol. 13, pp. 1743-1750, 2007.

[3] Yaser S. Abu-Mostafa and Demetri Psaltis, "Recognitive Aspects of Moment Invariants," *Pattern Analysis and Machine Intelligence, IEEE Transactions on,* vol. PAMI-6, pp. 698-706, 1984.

[4] Chen Qing, Petriu Emil, et al., "A comparative study of Fourier descriptors and Hu's seven moment invariants for image recognition," in *Electrical and Computer Engineering, 2004. Canadian Conference on*, 2004, pp. 103-106 Vol.1.

[5] J. Flusser, B. Zitova, et al., "Invariant-based registration of rotated and blurred images," in *Geoscience and Remote Sensing Symposium, 1999. IGARSS '99 Proceedings. IEEE 1999 International*, 1999, pp. 1262-1264.

[6] Jan Flusser and Tomas Suk, "A Moment-based Approach to Registration of Images with Affine Geometric Distortion," *IEEE transaction on Geoscience and Remote Sensing,* vol. 32, pp. 382-387, 1994.

[7] G. I. Salarna and A. L. Abbott, "Moment invariants and quantization effects," in *Computer Vision and Pattern*

Recognition, 1998. Proceedings. 1998 IEEE Computer Society Conference on, 1998, pp. 157-163.

[8] CHO-HUAK TEH and ROLAND T. CHIN, "On Image Analysis by the Methods of Moments," *IEEE Transactions on Pattern Analysis and machine Intelligence,* vol. 10, pp. 496-513, 1988.

[9] Rafael C. Gonzalez and Richard E. Woods, *Digital Image Processing(Third Edition)*: Prentice Hall, 2007.

A Novel Binarization Algorithm for Ballistics Firearm Identification

Dongguang Li
School of Computer and Security Science, Edith Cowan University, Western Australia
e-mail: d.li@ecu.edu.au

***Abstract*—The identification of ballistics specimens from imaging systems is of paramount importance in criminal investigation. Binarization plays a key role in preprocess of recognizing cartridges in the ballistic imaging systems. Unfortunately, it is very difficult to get the satisfactory binary image using existing binary algorithms. In this paper, we utilize the global and local thresholds to enhance the image binarization. Importantly, we present a novel criterion for effectively detecting edges in the images. Comprehensive experiments have been conducted over sample ballistic images. The empirical results demonstrate the proposed method can provide a better solution than existing binary algorithms.**

Keywords-Ballistics, forensics, image processing,binarization

I. INTRODUCTION

The identification of ballistics specimens from imaging systems is of paramount importance in criminal investigation[1, 2]. The characteristic marks on the cartridge and projectile of a bullet fired from a gun can be recognized as a fingerprint for identification of the firearm[3]. Traditional methods for the identification of these marks are based on incident light microscopy[4]. However, the assessment by the ballistician of the similarity between comparable marks on respective ballistics specimens from crime scenes and test firings is based on the expertise and experience. In this regard, the traditional methods of matching marks have some inherent difficulties and entail an element of subjectivity[5]. Therefore, the development of automatic firearm identification is highly demanded by real applications.

Several ballistics identification systems have been available in both a commercial form and a beta-testing state. The two major international ballistics imaging systems are manufactured by the IBIS Company in Montreal, QC, Canada, and the FBI (Drugfire) in USA. A Canadian company called Walsh Automation has also developed a commercial system called "Bulletproof", which can acquire and store images of projectiles and cartridge cases by searching the image database for particular striations on projectiles. However, it is required to match the impressed markings or striations by user on the projectiles. This kind of limitation makes the system very difficult to use. Our previous work[6-8] has developed a novel identification system called Fireball Firearm Identification System. This system is able to identify, store, and retrieve the images of cartridge case heads. It also can obtain position metrics for the firing-pin impression, ejector mark, and extractor mark. The limitation of this system is that the position and shape of the impression images need to trace manually by the user. The FireBall system needs further development and improvement.

To implement the automatic identification of cartridge, we need to binarize the image before extracting its features. The binarization is a key step in image preprocessing. The quality of the final result of identification is heavily dependent on the quality of the binary output[9-12]. Until now, various binarization techniques have been proposed. There is no fit-in-all method that can be applicable to different kind of images, even is 'good' for some certain type of images. Meanwhile, the performance of binarization is very sensitive to the choice of the parameter values, i.e., threshold or threshold surface. Mehmet[13] categorizes the thresholding methods into six groups according to the information they are exploiting: histogram shape-based thresholding methods; clustering-based thresholding methods; entropy-based thresholding methods; thresholding based on attribute similarity; spatial thresholding methods and locally adaptive thresholding. We can also divide those thresholding methods into two categories, i.e., global thresholding and local thresholding. If only one threshold is used for the entire image then it called global thresholding. On the other hand, if a few thresholds are used for the entire image and each threshold based upon a part of the image, then it called local thresholding.

The global thresholding algorithm works well in situations where there is a reasonably clear valley between the modes of the histogram related to objects and background. Otsu[14] is a good global thresholding algorithm. Unfortunately, it is not easy to find a right global thresholding when an image has noise or uneven illumination or poor contrast.

The local thresholding methods choose variable thresholds based on the local information in an image[15-18]. They overcome the drawbacks of global thresholding algorithms. In this paper, we utilize various local thresholding algorithms to binarize cartridge images in ballistic imaging system, such as Chow and Kaneko[15], Yanowitz and Bruckstein[17]. However, we can hardly get the satisfactory results because the images we process have not only uneven illumination and poor contrast, but also complex and noisy.

In this paper, we propose a new algorithm for the cartridge binarization, which combines the global thresholding and local thresholding. We utilize the global and local thresholds to enhance the image binarization. Importantly, we present a novel criterion for effectively detecting edges in the images. The experiment results

T. Sobh, K. Elleithy (eds.), *Innovations in Computing Sciences and Software Engineering*,
DOI 10.1007/978-90-481-9112-3_71, © Springer Science+Business Media B.V. 2010

indicate that the proposed algorithm performs better than those with the existing algorithms.

The proposed algorithm has the following advantages: 1. Edges detecting is more accurate due to the edges enhancement operator that enhances edges and depress the non-edges. 2. Reduce the false objects benefit from the combination of the local thresholding and global thresholding; 3. Reduce noisy points by removing small size blocks in the output image.

The rest of this paper is organized as follows: Section II, introduces the existing algorithms, which are used in comparative studies. The binarization algorithm is described in Section III. Experimental results are presented in Section IV. Section V concludes the paper.

II. MAJOR BINARIZATION TECHNIQUES

In order to make a comparison with the proposed algorithm, we discuss one classical global thresholding Otsu[14] and two threshold algorithms, i.e., Chow and Kaneko[15], Yanowitz and Bruckstein[17].

Otsu is a typical and popular global thresholding algorithm. It divides the image into two parts (namely foreground and background) by threshold. The basic idea of Otsu aims to find an optimal threshold that gives the best separation between the two classes in terms of their intensity values. In order to obtain an optimal threshold, the algorithm tests all possible thresholds from one to maximum intensity, in order to find the maximum variance between the two classes.

Chow and Kaneko[15] propose another algorithm to divide the image into nonoverlaping cells of equal area forming a regular grid, and then determine the (sub)histograms of the grey levels of pixels in each cell. This method was further studied and developed by Nakagawa and Rosenfeld[8]. The sub-histograms that are judged to be bimodal are used to determine local threshold values for the corresponding cell centers, while the local thresholds are interpolated over the entire image to yield a threshold surface. It can work well when the objects of interest and the background occupy regions of reasonably comparable size in a cell. Otherwise, the method often fails because the cell only contains objects or background pixels.

Yanowitz and Bruckstein[17] use edges and gray level information to obtain threshold surface. The algorithm computes the gray level gradient magnitude from a smooth version of the original image. The gradient values are then thresholded and thinned by local maxima that direct thinning process. Locations of these local gradient maxima are taken as boundary pixels between object and background. The corresponding gray levels in the image are taken as the local thresholds. The sampled gray levels are then interpolated over the entire image to obtain an adaptive threshold surface. The algorithm has made a great improvement compared with that of Chow and Kaneko[7]. The efficiency is however dependent on the correct detection of edges in the image. Consequently, it may yield "ghost" objects and stains in the segmented image when edges are mistakenly detected.

III. ALGORITHM

A. *Algorithm*

The algorithm based upon the global thresholding and local thresholding. The pixels in the image have been divided into two categories, namely edge pixels and non-edge pixels. The global threshold has been adopted to the non-edge pixels. Correspondingly, the local thresholds have been used to the edge pixels. In order to remove the noisy points, the size of each object in binary image has been measured. The objects whose size is less than the size of 1/3000 of entire image will be removed.

The algorithm is detailed as follows:

1. Smooth the original image by the Median Filter with 5×5 size. It aims to reduce the noise that may produces by camera, lighting conditions, etc.

2. Stretch the smoothed image from step 1. This step is important because the low contrast image due to the foreground and the background of cartridge made by same materials is harmful to the subsequent process.

3. Detect the edges in stretched image using Sobel operator, then enhance the edges and depress the non-edges, and finally generate an edge binary image by binarizing the enhanced and depressed image.

4. Compute the global threshold in stretch image by Otsu algorithm[14], and compute the local thresholds to the pixels on the edge image.

5. Binarize the stretched image using global threshold in non-edge pixels and local thresholds in edge pixels.

6. Removing the noisy blocks and obtain a satisfactory binary image. The binary image from step 5 may contain some noisy blocks due to the noisy original image or rough surface of cartridge. The size of these blocks is small. We can clear them by removing small-size blocks.

B. *Illustrating Examples*

1) *Smooth the original image.*

For practical applications, the quality of the image acquired by camera can be noised by many factors such as the lighting conditions, the materials of the cartridge, the original texture on the surface of cartridge and cameras itself. Strong noise would lead the difficulties in binarization and even get wrong results. Low-pass filter operation is a good way to reduce the noisy effects mentioned above. We test conventional low-pass filters both on spatial domain (Averaging Filter and Median Filter) and on frequency domain (Ideal Low-pass Filter, Butterworth Low-pass Filter and Gaussian Low-pass Filter). After comparing those filters mentioned above, we find that the Median Filter can not only reduce the noise, but also keep the sharp edges. Science sharp edges are important for subsequent process, we decide to select the Median Filter with 5×5 size.

2) *Gray stretch.*

From the Figure 1(a), the foreground letters and background almost have the same gray. The low contrast may result from the foreground and the background made by same materials. We binarize the image using Otsu algorithm[14] and get the result in Figure 1(e). We can hardly get the useful information from the Figure 1(e). By analyzing the histogram of the image Figure 1(c), we can find that the gray value in all pixels concentrates in a narrow range, which is very disadvantageous to binarize the image. In other words, we prefer that the gray value in enhanced image covers all available gray space, rather than mainly distributing in a narrow range. In order to enhance the contrast of the image, we perform a contrast enhancement in equation (1) to expand the gray range.

$$f(x) = \begin{cases} 0 & x < x_1 \\ \dfrac{y_2 - y_1}{x_2 - x_1}(x - x_2) + y_2 & x_1 \le x \le x_2 \\ 255 & x > x_2 \end{cases} \qquad (1)$$

where x1 denotes the minimum gray value, x2 denotes the maximum gray value, x denotes the gray value in original image, and f(x) denotes the gray value in processed image.

The example is given in Figure 1. The original image is shown in Figure 1(a). The image in Figure 1(b) has been enhanced and the contrast has a great improvement. This can also be evidenced by the change of the histogram. The distribution of the histogram in Figure 1(d) is wider than that in Figure 1(c). The image in Figure 1(f) is the result binarized on image Figure 1(b) using OTSU algorithm[14]. Figure 1(f) has more information than Figure 1(e), but it still doesn't include enough information.

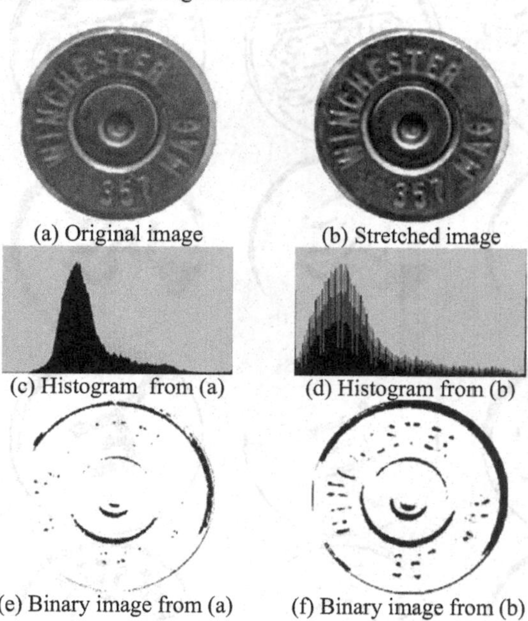

(a) Original image (b) Stretched image

(c) Histogram from (a) (d) Histogram from (b)

(e) Binary image from (a) (f) Binary image from (b)

Figure 1. Gray stretch

3) Compute the global and local thresholds.

In previous section, we employ the gray stretch to enhance the image, and then binarize the enhanced image. We find that the binarized image in Figure 1(f) is still unsatisfactory. The use of global threshold cannot meet our requirements. Meanwhile, it is also difficult to find local thresholds that are used to binarize images. Yanowitz and Bruckstein[17] take pixels with local gradient maxima as boundary pixels between object and background. The corresponding gray levels in the image are taken as local thresholds. This is verified by the experiments over cartridge images. Apparently, neither global nor local thresholding algorithm can fully solve our problems.

After extensive experiments, we find the 'good' results are obtained using the global thresholding to non-edge pixels and using the local thresholds to edge pixels. The global threshold can be obtained by Otsu algorithm, while local threshold in each pixel is the mean gray value with neighborhood with size 5×5.

The popular edge detection methods are based on gradient or zero crossing. The gradient method detects the edges by computing value in the first derivative of the image. The zero crossing method searches for zero crossings in the second derivative of the image to find edges. For detection of edge, various detection operators can be used. Most of these are applied with convolution masks and most of these are based on differential operations. We adopt Sobel operator as a mask of edge detector. Sobel operators include vertical, horizontal, 45 degree and 135 degree directions operation masks. In our experiments, the Sobel operators are used to extract edges of letters on the images of cartridge head. Because the letters on the image almost have a 45 or 135 degree direction, so we use 45 and 135 degree mask (shown in Figure 2 with 3×3 window).

-2	-1	0
-1	0	1
0	1	2

0	-1	-2
1	0	-1
2	1	0

Figure 2. Sobel mask 45 and 135 degree direction

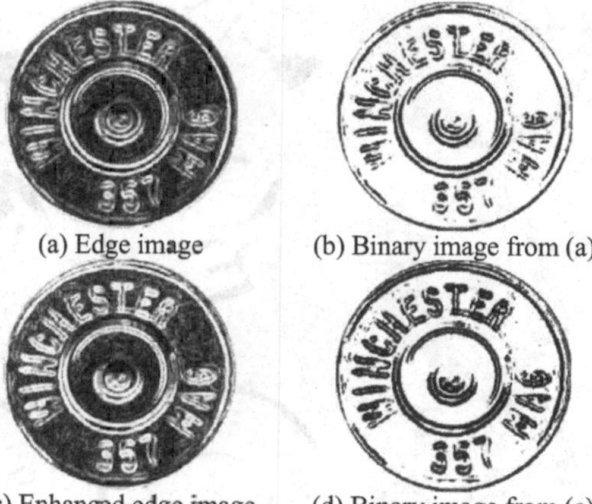

(a) Edge image (b) Binary image from (a)

(c) Enhanced edge image (d) Binary image from (c)

Figure 3. Edge images

The edge image obtained by convolving the images with the Sobel masks is shown in Figure 3(a). Its binary image in Figure 3(b) has noncontinuous edges due to the low contrast between the edges and the background, which needs further refinement.

In order to improve the accuracy of edge, we present a novel criteria for effectively identifying the edges, detailed in equation (2).

$$f_1(x,y) = f(x,y) \times \frac{\text{gradient(x , y)}}{\text{AvgGradien t(x, y)}} \qquad (2)$$

where f(x,y) denotes the input image, gradient(x,y) presents the gray value of pixel, and the AvgGradient(x,y) is the mean gray of input image. It is clear that the gradient(x,y) of pixels in edges is greater than AvgGradient(x,y), so we can find gradient(x,y)/AvgGradient > 1. Similarly, the gradient(x,y) of pixels in non-edges is smaller than AvgGradient(x,y), i.e., gradient(x,y)/AvgGradient < 1. Based on equation (2), the gray values in edge pixels will be increased, while the gray values in non-edge pixels will be decreased.

Figure 3(c) is the enhanced image operated by equation (2). Compared with Figure 3(a), the enhanced image has a great improvement. Correspondingly, Figure 3(d) is better than Figure 3(b).

4) Binarization.

By comparing edge image in Figure 3(d) with original image in Figure 1(a), we find the foreground pixels in Figure 1(a) almost close black pixels in Figure 3(d), while the background pixels in Figure 1(a) almost near white pixels in Figure 3(d). Therefore, we take Figure 3(d) as a mask of thresholding selection. The pixels in the neighborhood with size 5×5 of black pixel adopt the local threshold that is the mean gray value of its neighborhood with size 5×5, while the global thresholding is adopted in the remaining pixels. The steps of binarization are detailed as follows:

1. Compute the global threshold of the input image f(x,y) in Figure 1(b) by Otsu algorithm[14].
2. Declare a w×h threshold array T(x,y), where w and h are separately the width and height of input image.
3. Obtain the edge binary image g(x,y) based upon the algorithm in last Section.
4. Scan the edge binary image g(x,y). If the gray value of pixel in g(x,y) is 1 (black point), the pixels in its neighborhood with size 5×5 use the local thresholding, which is a gray mean of this neighborhood pixels, and save this threshold into corresponding elements of T(x,y). On the other hand, if the value of pixel in g(x,y) is 0 (white point), save the global thresholding into the corresponding element of T(x,y). Thus, we can get the threshold surface that includes threshold of each pixel in input image f(x,y).
5. Binarize the input image f(x,y) depend upon the thresholds in array T(x,y) and obtain the binary image.

Figure 5. Results of experiments

5) Remove noisy block.

Normally, images may contain some noisy. For example, Figure 4(a) contains some noisy blocks. We need to filter the noisy embedded in images. For our ballistics Images, we find the size of noisy blocks is less than 1/3000 of the entire input image, while the size of objects is greater than 1/1000 of the entire input image. So we remove the blocks whose size is less than 1/3000 of the entire input. The results are illustrated in Figure 4(b).

(a) Binary image (b) Remove small size blocks

Figure 4. Binary image

IV. EXPERIEMENTS

A. Smaple Images

We choose four typical cartridges images, shown column 1 in Figure 5. Every image size is 300×300 pixels. In Figure 5, images in row 1 has a complex signs and letters with a rim fire; images in row 2 has a simple letter T in center and also has a rim fire, which almost has a same gray between the letter and the background; images in row 3 is blur due to the incorrect focus of camera; images in row 4 has so many letters at the outer with a center fire.

B. Results and discussion.

In order to make a comparison with the proposed algorithm, we compare performance of the proposed algorithm with those of Otsu[14], Chow and Kaneko[15] and Yanowitz and Bruckstein[17]. The Otsu is a typical adaptive global thresholding algorithm, while the other two methods are the local thresholding. Figure 5 shows the results of these algorithms. The column 2, 3, 4, 5 are separately the results of Otsu, Chow and Kaneko, Yanowitz and Bruckstein and proposed algorithm. The proposed algorithm performs better than the others

V. CONCLUSION

The binarization is of great importance for identification of cartridges. In this paper, we propose a novel binary algorithm for cartridge images. The criteria proposed can increase the efficiency of edge detection. The experimental results demonstrate that the proposed algorithm can provide a better solution to the noisy and low illumination ballistics images.

VI. ACKNOWLEDGEMENT

The ballistics specimens were provided by Australia Police. Mr Z. Huang , as a visiting fellow, helped with digital image acquisition.

REFERENCES

[1] D.G. Li, "Ballistics Projectile Image Analysis for Firearm Identification," *IEEE Transactions on Image Processing,* vol. 15, pp. 2857-2865, 2006.

[2] R. M. C.L. Smith, Evans. P,, "Linescan Imaging for the positive identification of ballistics Specimens," *Proceedings of the IEEE International Carnahan Conference on Security Technology,* pp. 269-275, 2000.

[3] E.Springer, "Toolmark Examinations-A Review of its Development in the Literature," *Journal of Forensic Sciences,* vol. Vol.40,No.6, pp. 964-968, 1995.

[4] R.G. Nichols, "Firearm and Toolmark Identification Criteria:A Review of the Literature," *Journal of Forensic Sciences,* vol. Vol.42,No.30, pp. 466-474, 1997.

[5] R. J. G. M. S. Bonfanti "Visualisation by confocal microscopy of traces on bullets and cartridge cases," *Sci. Justice,* vol. vol. 40,no. 4, pp. 241-256, 2000.

[6] J. M. C. C.L. Smith, "Optical Imaging Techniques for Ballistics Specimens to Identify Firearms," in *Proc. 29th Annu. int. Conf. Security Technology,* 1995, pp. 275-289.

[7] C. L. Smith, "Fireball: a forensic ballistics imaging system," in *Security Technology, 1997. Proceedings. The Institute of Electrical and Electronics Engineers 31st Annual 1997 International Carnahan Conference on,* 1997, pp. 64-70.

[8] A. C. W. D. G. Li, "Ballistics firearms identification based on images of cartridge case and projectile," *presented at the SPIE Enabling Technologies for Law Enforcement and Security Symposium Boston,MA,* 1998.

[9] R. E. W. Rafael C. Gonzalez, "Digital Image Processing(Third Edition)," in *Pearson Education.Inc,* 2008.

[10] M. Kamel, "Extraction of Binary Character Graphics Images from grayscale Document Images," *CVGIP-Graphical models and Image processing,* vol. 55, pp. 203-217, 1993.

[11] Y. Ohta, "Color Information for Region-Segmentation," *Computer Graphics and Image Processing,* vol. 13, pp. 222-241, 1980.

[12] D.G. Li, "Image processing for the positive identification of forensic ballistics specimens," in *Information Fusion, 2003. Proceedings of the Sixth International Conference,* 2003, pp. 1494-1498.

[13] S. Mehmet and S. Bulent, "Survey over image thresholding techniques and quantitative performance evaluation." vol. 13: SPIE, 2004, pp. 146-168.

[14] N. Otsu, "Threshold Selection Method from Gray-Level Histograms," *IEEE Transcations on Systems Man and Cybernetics,* vol. 9, pp. 62-66, 1979.

[15] T. K. C.K. Chow "Automatic boundary detection of the left ventricle from cineangiograms," *Comput. Biomed. res. 5,* pp. 388-410, 1972.

[16] Y. Nakagawa and A. Rosenfeld, "Some experiments on variable thresholding," *Pattern Recognition,* vol. 11, pp. 191-204, 1979.

[17] S. D. Yanowitz and A. M. Bruckstein, "A new method for image segmentation," in *Pattern Recognition, 1988., 9th International Conference on,* 1988, pp. 270-275 vol.1.

[18] Bernsen J, "Dynamic Thresholding of Gray- level Images," *Proc of the 8th Int Conf on Pattern Recognition, Paris,France,* 1986.

A Schema Classification Scheme for Multilevel Databases

Tzong-An Su and Hong-Ju Lu
Department of Information Engineering and Computer Science
Feng Chia University
Taichung Taiwan

Abstract- **Multilevel secure (MLS) database models provide a data protection mechanism different from traditional data access control. The MLS database has been used in various application domains including government, hospital, military, etc. The MLS database model protects data by grouping them into different classification and creates different views to the users of different clearance levels. Previous models have focused on data level classification like tuples and elements. In this study, we introduce a schema level classification mechanism, i.e. attribute and relation classification. We first define the basic model, and then give definitions of integration properties and operations of database. The schema classification scheme will reduce semantics inferences and thus prevent users from compromising the database.**

I. I. INTRODUCTION

Data security has become an important topic in recent years. Various mechanisms to protect digital data have been developed and implemented. Access control is one of the mechanisms in managing private data. By allowing or denying the ability of data access, access control provides a great way in security management. For example, one should not be allowed to enter a company unless he/she shows his/her identification card to the guard. However, traditional access control cannot satisfy organizations which have high data protecting requirements, e.g. government, military, hospital, etc. In such organizations data access may be classified by hierarchy levels. In order to support applications in such organizations, the notion of multilevel security (MLS) had been proposed.

Multilevel secure (MLS) database is one of the applications from multilevel security. In that, each piece of data has a classification level c and each user has a clearance level u. Only when $u \geq c$, the user can access the data. Figure 1 gives an example of a database relation with predefined secure levels[1].

Relation SOD

Starship	C_S	*Objective*	C_O	*Destination*	C_D	*TC*
Enterprise	U	Exploration	U	Talos	U	U
Voyager	S	Spying	S	Mars	S	S
Enterprise	U	Spying	TS	Talos	U	TS

Figure 1 Multilevel Relation *SOD*

[1] Top Secret (TS) > Secret (S) > Confidential (C) > Unclassified (U).

This figure shows a classic example of multilevel relation, where classification information are specified both on each tuple and each data element [4]. Note that "C_S" represents the classification level attribute of attribute "***Starship***" and "***TC***" is the tuple/record classification attribute.

While traditional MLS databases have succeeded in many application areas, still we found some problems with it. Consider the following customer profile relation.

Relation PROFILE

Name	C_N	*Phone*	C_P	*Balance*	C_B	*TC*
B. Smith	U	2129197788	U	200000000	S	U
A. Canon	S	4163211234	S	100000000	S	S

Figure 2 Multilevel Relation *PROFILE*

When a user with clearance level U queries this table, the result he gets is shown in Figure 3.

Relation PROFILE

Name	*Phone*	*Balance*
B. Smith	2129197788	Null

Figure 3 Query Result of a *U*-user for Relation *PROFILE*

Curiosity is an intrinsic nature of human beings; the revelation of the attribute "Balance" might trigger users to steal that information. We believe that the attribute should be hidden from those *U*-users just as those real data. This actually gives rise to the need of schema classification of a database. In this paper, a new scheme is proposed for this reason to support classification in schema level, including classification both on relations and attributes.

II. RELATED WORKS

Various MLS database models have been proposed. The Hinke and Schaefer model [5] first proposed to support classification at attribute level (or column level); the I.P. Sharp model [6] then proposed to support classification at relation level; the TRW model [7] also was proposed to support classification at tuple-level. The SeaView Model [8, 9] supports classification not only at the tuple-level but also at element-level; as a project of U.S DoD, the SeaView Model satisfies trusted database system in class A1 [10].

Polyinstantiation is known as an inevitable part of multilevel secure database [12]. It can be defined as creation of different views from shared resources/objects to different subjects. In database applications, data entities can be

T. Sobh, K. Elleithy (eds.), *Innovations in Computing Sciences and Software Engineering*,
DOI 10.1007/978-90-481-9112-3_72, © Springer Science+Business Media B.V. 2010

considered as shared resources. From the example of Figure 1, relation SOD has tuples with the same key value (Enterprise), but different TC values; these tuples represent a single entity, and are called polyinstantiation tuples [13] of an entity. These polyinstantiation tuples are created due to different views from *U*-users and *TS*-users.

The LDV approach [14-16] achieved multilevel security in database by using Lock Data Views policy of operation systems; one of features of LDV is that while there are polyinstantiation tuples, only one tuple per secure class would be exist in an entity. The Belief-Consistent Model (BCMLS) [17] first considered the semantics of data [18], by using true/false label representing the correctness of data to increase database completeness. Last, the Multilevel Relational (MLR) Data Model [19] is a redesign of SeaView model proposed by the same authors. It takes the adventure of previous models and first gave formal definition of operations and integrity properties; also, it is the first model using mathematical proof to show that the MLR model satisfied soundness, completeness, and security property.

III. DATA MODEL

A. Basic Model

In this paper, we limit our investigation to the schema classification. It does not include data classification which will be integrated into this result later. Since data classification is not involved, there is no polyinstantiation issue. The goal of this research then is to propose a schema classification scheme to reduce the inference problems from the semantics of the schema. We begin with the definition of databases in our data model.

- **Definition 1** A relation scheme is denoted by $R(A_1, A_2, \ldots, A_n)$, where each A_i is a data attribute over domain D_i.
- **Definition 2** A relation instance, denoted by $r(A_1, A_2, \ldots, A_n)$, is a set of distinct tuples of the form $(a_1, a_2, \ldots, a_n)$, where each $a_i \in D_i$.

Definition 1 and 2 described the scheme of relation and relation instance. Figure 4 gives an example of a relation where "Starship", "Objective", Destination" represents the names of attributes. As Figure 4 shows, relation scheme defines relation name and all attributes in a relation, and relation instance stores all of the data in it.

A relation scheme example of SOD

Starship	*Objective*	*Destination*

A relation instance example of SOD

Enterprise	Spying	Rigel

Figure 4 Example of relation scheme and relation instance

To support the schema classification, we also define a system-wide relation to store classification information of all relations and attributes in a database.

- **Definition 3** A schema configuration relation of all relations in a database, denoted by $R_S(RN, C_{RN}, AN, C_{AN})$, contains an instance $r_S(RN, C_{RN}, AN, C_{AN})$ including a set of distinct tuples of the form (rn, c_{rn}, an, c_{an}), where "rn" is a relation name and "an" is an attribute belonging to "rn", and $c_{rn}, c_{an} \in \{L \ldots H\} \cup$ null, representing classification level of rn and an respectively. As a system relation, this relation has no key attribute, and it can not be access and updated by subjects.

As definition 3 shows, schema configuration relation is a system relation, and it could be access or update only by database administrator. In R_S, RN represents the name of relation, and AN represents the name of attribute in relation RN, C_{RN} and C_{AN} both represents the classification of relation and attribute, respectively. Figure 5 gives an example of schema configuration relation, where classification level TS > S > U.

Relation SOD

Starship	*Objective*	*Destination*

Schema configuration relation R_S

RN	*C_{RN}*	*AN*	*C_{AN}*
SOD	U	Destination	U
SOD	U	Objective	S
SOD	U	Starship	U

Figure 5 Example of schema configuration relation

In this example, the classification of relation "SOD" is U, and the classification of attribute "Destination", "Objective", and "Starship" is U, S, U, respectively.

The following definition explains the database state.

- **Definition 4** A database is a collection of relations and contains a schema configuration relation. A database state is a collection of all relation instances of a database at a particular time.

B. Integrity Properties

A database model must support consistency, correctness, and availability of any database. To enforce these requirements, there are integrity constraints associated with a database model. We first list integrity properties from traditional database systems which are all applicable to our database model.

- **Property 1** [Domain Integrity (DI)] The value of each attribute must be derived from some specific set of values or within some specific range.
- **Property 2** [Key Integrity (KI)] Keys are attributes or sets of attributes in a relation that uniquely identify a tuple within a relation instance.
- **Property 3** [Entity Integrity (EI)] The value of any attribute in a primary key can not be NULL.
- **Property 4** [Referential Integrity (RI)] The value of a foreign key in the referencing relation must match the value of one primary key in the referenced relation.

Other than the four integrity properties above, we have to add one more below to support our schema classification.

- **Property 5** [Schema Integrity (SI)] Schema configuration relation instance r_s of schema configuration relation R_s satisfies schema integrity if and only if for $t_s, t_1, t_2 \in r_s$:

(1) if $t_1[RN] = t_2[RN]$ then $t_1[C_{RN}] = t_2[C_{RN}]$; and

(2) $t_s[C_{AN}] \geq t_s[C_{RN}]$.

This property says that each tuple with the same relation name in R_S will have the same classification for the relation name attribute; also, the classification level of an attribute of a relation is always greater than or equal to the level of that relation. The schema configuration relation R_S in Figure 5 gives an example of SI.

C. Database Operations

In this database model, we allow operations to support schema classification. These operations include CREATE RELATION to create and specify the classification of a relation and its attributes, ADD ATTRIBUTES to add attributes to some relation, INSRT to insert a data entity, DELETE to delete an entity, UPDATE to change values of attributes, and SELECT to query data. The following gives a description of each operation.

1) CREATE RELATION

- **Syntax:** A CREATE RELATION statement executed by a *c*–subject (user classified at *c* level) has the following general form[2]:

```
CREATE RELATION R   :CR (
    Aj1          :CAj1     Dj1
   [,Aj2         :CAj2     Dj2]
    . . .
)
```

- **Symbol Explanation:** R is the relation name, $1 \leq j1, j2, \ldots \leq n$; $A_{j1}, A_{j2} \ldots$ is data attribute; C_R is the classification of R, $C_{Aj1}, C_{Aj2} \ldots$ represent the classification attribute of attribute $A_{j1}, A_{j2} \ldots$ respectively; $D_{Aj1}, D_{Aj2} \ldots$ is the parameter of each attribute (i.e. primary key).

- **Semantics:** A CREATE RELATION operation will create a relation stored in database, and create correspond tuples in schema configuration relation R_s.

(1) If $C_R \leq c$, $C_{Aj1} \leq c$, $C_{Aj2} \leq c$... etc, then the relation is created in the form of $(A_{j1}, A_{j2}, \ldots)$, and

(2) In schema configuration relation instance $r_s \in R_s$, tuples $t_1 \in r_s$, $t_2 \in r_s \ldots$ is created where $t_1[RN, C_{RN}, AN, C_{AN}] = (R, C_R, A_{j1}, C_{Aj1})$, $t_2[RN, C_{RN}, AN, C_{AN}] = (R, C_R, A_{j2}, C_{Aj2}) \ldots$ etc.

The statement is permitted if and only if

(3) There doesn't exist $C_R > c$ or $C_{Aji} > c$ $(1 \leq i \leq n)$; and

(4) Database state satisfies SI after operation.

[2] In this paper, [] represents optional clause, and ... represents repetition clause.

- **Commentary:** Compare to traditional database model, this statement not only can be use to specify the relation name and attribute name with their parameter; users can also specify each classification of relation of attributes. The only constrain is the classification level must less or equal than subject whom query. In addition, this statement usually rename to CREATE TABLE on implementation.

2) ADD ATTRIBUTES

- **Syntax:** An ADD ATTRIBUTES statement executed by a *c*–subject (user classified at *c* level) has the following general form[3]:

```
ADD ATTRIBUTES R     (
    Aj1          :CAj1     Dj1
   [,Aj2         :CAj2     Dj2]
    . . .
)
```

- **Symbol Explanation:** R is the relation name, $1 \leq j1, j2, \ldots \leq n$; $A_{j1}, A_{j2} \ldots$ is data attribute; $C_{Aj1}, C_{Aj2} \ldots$ represent the classification attribute of attribute $A_{j1}, A_{j2} \ldots$ respectively; $D_{Aj1}, D_{Aj2} \ldots$ is the parameter of each attribute (e.g. TYPE).

- **Semantics:** An ADD ATTRIBUTES operation will add attributes to a relation stored in database, and create corresponding tuples in schema configuration relation R_s.

(5) If $C_R \leq c$, $C_{Aj1} \leq c$, $C_{Aj2} \leq c$... etc, then the relation R is modified as $(B_{j1}, B_{j2}, \ldots A_{j1}, A_{j2}, \ldots)$, where $B_{j1}, B_{j2}, \ldots$ are existing attributes of R, and

(6) In schema configuration relation instance $r_s \in R_s$, tuples $t_1 \in r_s$, $t_2 \in r_s \ldots$ is created where $t_1[RN, C_{RN}, AN, C_{AN}] = (R, C_R, A_{j1}, C_{Aj1})$, $t_2[RN, C_{RN}, AN, C_{AN}] = (R, C_R, A_{j2}, C_{Aj2}) \ldots$ etc.

The statement is permitted if and only if

(7) There doesn't exist $C_R > c$ or $C_{Aji} > c$ $(1 \leq i \leq n)$; and

(8) Database state satisfies SI after operation.

- **Commentary:** This operation is used to add attributes to existing relations. The purpose is to prevent higher clearance users from create a similar relation as an existing one. The only constrain is the classification levels of attributes must less than or equal to that of users.

3) INSERT

- **Syntax:** An INSERT statement executed by a c-subject has the following general form:

```
INSERT
INTO    R[(Aj1[, Aj2]. . . )]
VALUES  (aj1[,aj2]. . . )
```

- **Symbol Explanation:** R is the relation name, $1 \leq j_1, j_2, \ldots \leq n$, assumes R has data attributes $A_1, \ldots, A_n$; than $a_{j1}, a_{j2}, \ldots$ is the data value of $A_1, \ldots, A_n$.

  In this statement, values must specify in appropriate domain, i.e. $a_{j1} \in D_{j1}, a_{j2} \in D_{j2} \ldots$ etc.

- **Semantics:** A INSERT operation will insert at most one tuple t in relation R. The tuple to be inserted is constructed by the following rule:

  For all $1 \leq i \leq n$:

  (9) If A_i appears in INTO clause, then $t[A_i] = (a_i)$;

  (10) If A_i does not appears in INTO clause, then $t[A_i] = (null)$;

  The statement is permitted if and only if

  (11) There doesn't exist tuple $t' \in r$ such that $t'[A_1] = a_1$ assume A_1 is the primary key; and

  (12) $C_{Aji} \leq c$, $1 \leq j_1, j_2, \ldots \leq n$ and

  (13) Database state satisfies DI, KI, EI, and RI after operation.

- **Commentary:** The INSERT statement inserts a tuple into database. In our model, the value of data could be null. Furthermore, in access level c such that $c < t_s[C_{AN}] \wedge t_s[AN] = A_i$ means c-subject cannot observe attribute A_i; so if A_i appears in INTO clause of this situation, operation will be denied.

4) DELETE

- **Syntax:** A DELETE statement executed by a c-subject has the following general form:

  DELETE
  FROM R
  [**WHERE** p]

- **Symbol Explanation:** R is the name of relation, assumes relation R has data attributes $A_1, \ldots, A_n$; p represents a condition rule of data attributes.

- **Semantics:** For all tuples $t \in r$ satisfied by p, tuple t is deleted.

  The statement is permitted if and only if

  (14) $C_R \leq c$, and for all A_i in p, $C_{Ai} \leq c$

  (15) Database state satisfies RI after operation.

- **Commentary:** The DELETE statement deletes only tuples observed by c-subject.

5) SELECT

- **Syntax:** A SELECT statement executed by a c-subject has the following general form:

  SELECT B_1,[B_2]...
  FROM R_1,[R_2]...
  [**WHERE** p]

- **Symbol Explanation:** $R_1, R_2, \ldots$ is the name of relation; $B_1, B_2, \ldots$ is the name of attribute in $R_1, R_2, \ldots$ respectively; * means all data attributes; p represents a condition rule of data attributes.

- **Semantics:** In relation specified in FROM clause, only tuples $t \in r_1, r_2, \ldots$ will be consider by p. Tuples satisfy p will be selected based on the attributes specified in SELECT clause, but only relations satisfied $t_s[RN, C_{RN}]$ and $c \geq c_i$ $(1 \leq i \leq n)$ will be considered, and attributes $A_i \in R_1, R_2, \ldots$ satisfy $t_s[RN, AN, C_{AN}] = (R, A_i, c_i)$ and $c \geq c_i$ $(1 \leq i \leq n)$ will be output.

- **Commentary:** SELECT statement displays the data satisfies condition p and authorized to the user.

6) UPDATE

- **Syntax:** An UPDATE statement executed by a c-subject has the following general form:

  UPDATE R
  SET $A_{j1} = a_{j1}$ [, $A_{j2} = a_{j2} \ldots$]
  WHERE p

- **Symbol Explanation:** R is the relation name; $A_{j1}, A_{j2}, \ldots 1 \leq j_1, j_2, \ldots \leq n$, are attributes of R; $a_{j1}, a_{j2}, \ldots$ are the data values to be set to $A_{j1}, A_{j2}, \ldots$

  In this statement, values must specify in appropriate domain, i.e. $a_{j1} \in D_{j1}, a_{j2} \in D_{j2} \ldots$ etc.

- **Semantics:** An UPDATE operation will set new values to those attributes specified in the SET clause if p condition is satisfied. For all $1 \leq i \leq n$:

  The statement is permitted if and only if

  (16) $C_R \leq c$, and $C_{Aji} \leq c$, $1 \leq j_1, j_2, \ldots \leq n$ and

  (17) Database state satisfies DI, KI, and EI after operation.

- **Commentary:** The UPDATE statement changes values of some attribute specified, but only those authorized relations and attributes can be modified by the user.

IV. CONCLUSION

In this paper, we defined a new multilevel database model to support classification of relations and attributes in database. According the requirements of database model design, we first defined the basic model and proposed a schema configuration relation to store all classification information of relations and attributes; second we defined a set of integrity properties including SI, KI, EI, DI, and RI to constrain database; we also defined operations serve to user queries including CREATE RELATION, ADD ATTRIBUTES, INSERT, DELETE, UPDATE, and SELECT. By classifying schema of a database, which can hide attributes and relations to those unauthorized users, thus, we can reduce lots of curiosity from users and therefore could reduce unauthorized attempts to steal information from the database.

V. REFERENCES

[1] D. E. Bell, and L. J. LaPadula, "Secure Computer Systems: Mathematical Foundations," 01 Nov 1973, 1973.

[2] D. Bell, and L. La Padula, "Secure Computer System: Unified Exposition and Multics Interpretation, MTR-2997," *MITRE Corp., Bedford, MA*, 1976.

[3] K. Biba, "Integrity considerations for secure computer systems," Storming Media, 1977.

[4] X. Qian, and T. Lunt, "Tuple-level vs. element-level classification," in Results of the Sixth Working Conference of IFIP Working Group 11.3 on Database Security on Database security, VI : status and prospects: status and prospects, Simon Fraser Univ., Vancouver, British Columbia, Canada, 1993.

[5] T. Hinke, and M. Schaefer, *Secure Data Management System*: Defense Technical Information Center, 1975.

[6] C. C. C. OTTAWA, and M. Grohn, "A Model of a Protected Data Management System," 1976.

[7] T. Hinke, C. Garvey, N. Jensen *et al.*, "Al secure DBMS design."

[8] D. E. Denning, T. F. Lunt, R. R. Schell *et al.*, "The SeaView security model." pp. 218-233.

[9] T. F. Lunt, D. E. Denning, R. R. Schell *et al.*, "The SeaView Security Model," *IEEE Trans. Softw. Eng.*, vol. 16, no. 6, pp. 593-607, 1990.

[10] D. Tcsec, *Trusted computer system evaluation criteria*, Technical Report 5200.28-STD, US Department of Defense, 1985.

[11] S. Jajodia, and R. Sandhu, "Toward a multilevel secure relational data model," *SIGMOD Rec.*, vol. 20, no. 2, pp. 50-59, 1991.

[12] T. F. Lunt, "Polyinstantiation: an inevitable part of a multilevel world." pp. 236-238.

[13] A. Galinovic, and V. Antoncic, "Polyinstantiation in Relational Databases with Multilevel Security." pp. 127-132.

[14] P. Dwyer, E. Onuegbe, P. Stachour *et al.*, "Query processing in LDV: a secure database system." pp. 118-124.

[15] D. O'Brien, "The LDV approach to polyinstantiation." pp. 239-240.

[16] P. D. Stachour, and B. Thuraisingham, "Design of LDV: a multilevel secure relational database management system," *Knowledge and Data Engineering, IEEE Transactions on,* vol. 2, no. 2, pp. 190-209, 1990.

[17] N. Jukic, S. V. Vrbsky, A. Parrish *et al.*, "A belief-consistent multilevel secure relational data model," *Information Systems,* vol. 24, no. 5, pp. 377-400, 1999.

[18] M. Pranjic, K. Fertalj, and N. Jukic, "Importance of semantics in MLS database models." pp. 51-56 vol.1.

[19] R. Sandhu, and F. Chen, "The multilevel relational (MLR) data model," *ACM Trans. Inf. Syst. Secur.*, vol. 1, no. 1, pp. 93-132, 1998.

[20] H. Garcia-Molina, J. D. Ullman, and J. Widom, *Database Systems: The Complete Book*: Prentice Hall Press, 2008.

[21] J. Goguen, and J. Meseguer, "Security policies and security models," *Proceedings of the 1982 Symposium on Security and Privacy*, pp. 11–20, 1982.

Memory Leak Sabotages System Performance

Nagm Mohamed

I. INTRODUCTION

This refers to the inability of a program to release the memory-or part it-that it has accessed to perform certain task(s) in computer systems [1]. The unintended consequences of such behavior are manifested in forms of diminishing performance at best. In worse case scenarios, memory leaks could lead the computer system to freeze and/or complete application failure. Memory leaks are particularly disastrous in limited memory embedded systems and client-server environments where applications share memories across multiple-user platforms. It is up to operating system designers to make sure that the currently running applications release memory after program termination. This work accesses and quantifies the impact of memory leak in system performance.

II. MEMORY LEAK SHOWCASE

A practical example to showcase the impact of memory leak in embedded systems is an elevator operation which is illustrated by figure 1. When a user gets into the elevator and presses a floor button, the system responds by allocating some memory to save the requested floor number. This entry is used to initiate the program that controls the elevator operation. The decision making snippet checks to see whether the requested floor is where the elevator is located at that time. If that is not the case, the elevator motor is instructed to gear towards the requested floor. After arriving to the floor, the program frees the acquired memory that has been used to save the floor number. The elevator status then becomes ready to serve the next request.

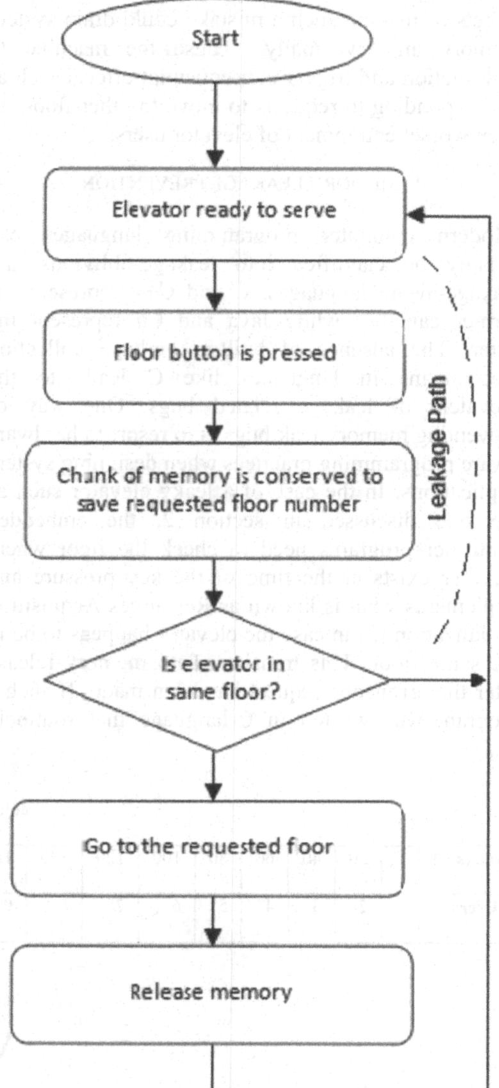

Figure 1: Flowchart depicting the operation of a leaky elevator

T. Sobh, K. Elleithy (eds.), *Innovations in Computing Sciences and Software Engineering*,
DOI 10.1007/978-90-481-9112-3_73, © Springer Science+Business Media B.V. 2010

On the other hand, if the requested floor number is pressed while the elevator is physically in the required floor, an instance of memory leakage is spotted (provided that the seized memory was not released after such an inadvertent request). While this does not happen occasionally, since users normally do not request the floor they are in, the accumulated effects of making such a mistake could drain system memory and eventually cause the machine to malfunction and trigger consequential effects such as not responding to requests to move to other floors or even worse: entrapment of elevator users.

III. MEMORY LEAKAGE PREVENTION

Modern computer programming languages can broadly be classified into leakage-oblivious and leakage-aware languages. C and C++ represent the former category while Java and C# represent the latter. The absence of built-in garbage collection mechanisms in languages like C leads to the prevalent of leakage related bugs. One way of preventing memory leak bugs is to resort to hardware –ware programming practices when designing system applications. In the case of a leaky elevator such as the one discussed in section 2, the embedded controller programs need to check the floor where elevator exists at the time of the key pressure and implements what is known as Resources Acquisition Initialization [2] in case the elevator happens to be in the same floor. This translates into memory release after the erroneous request has been made. If such a program was written in C-language that routinely executes **Takeme_2_Floor()** function, then applying RAI approaches would require freeing memory statically [3] at the end of the function as shown below:

```
#include <stdlib.h>
 Void Takeme_2_Floor( int n)
     {
       int* array = calloc(n, sizeof(int));  /*Allocates
some space for floor number */
       do_something();
       free(array); /* Frees the allocated space if
elevator in same floor */
     }
```

The computer industry tackles the leakage obliviousness by devising sophisticated debuggers such IBM Rational Purify [4].

IV. EXPERIMENTS AND RESULTS

This work examines the operation of an application server that handles the workload of ten clients running in client-server architecture that executes an elevator embedded program. HP Mercury LoadRunner [5] simulator is used as a vehicle for work emulation and memory leak detection. Multiple load scenarios were developed to mimic a real load environment. Virtual users were scheduled to load-stress the system gradually. Once the maximum load has been applied, the load was sustained for some duration in search for memory leakage. The load was then set to vanish gradually. This is illustrated in Table-1 and figure 2 below.

Table-1: User scheduling

Time (sec)	0	20	40	60	80	100	120	140	160	180	200	220	240	260	280	300	320	340	360	380
V-Users	1	2	3	4	5	6	7	8	9	10	10	10	10	10	10	8	6	4	2	0

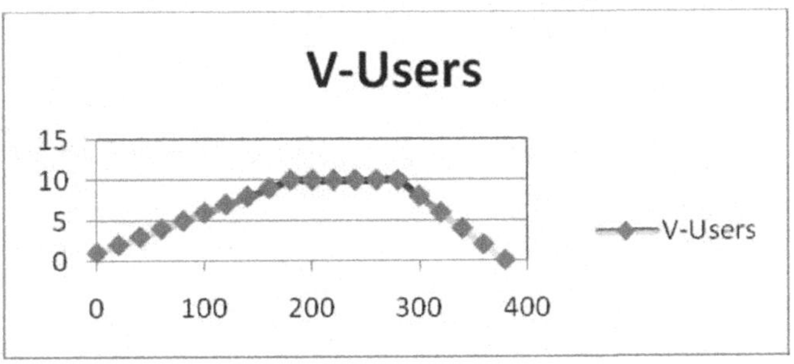

Figure 2: Interactive users schedule graph

The system performance was then measured in terms of average response time and throughput. This has been documented in Table-2, Table-3 and illustrated graphically in Figures 3 and 4 respectively. The sets of test outcomes given by the second rows of the two tables and the blue graphs in the figures represent the leaky scenario. This memory leak is detected when memory usage continues to increase substaintially as shown in figure 5 in form of 'Memory Usage1'. The performance degradation is quite obivious.

Table-2: Average Response time

Elapsed Time (hours)	0	0.5	1	1.5	2	2.5	3	3.5	4	4.5	5
Average Reponse Time1(sec)	7	7	7	7.1	7.1	20	35	37	55	65	58
Average Response Time2 (sec)	7	7	7	7.2	7.3	8.9	8.1	7.9	7.5	7.7	7.8

Table-3: Throughput

Elapsed Time (in hours)	0	0.5	1	1.5	2	2.5	3	3.5	4	4.5	5
Byte/Second 1	10230	34051	64140	83071	102019	20312	10937	799	9091	2040	5037
Byte/Second 2	10192	33101	43233	51332	59603	31220	33037	2660	12371	2210	5119

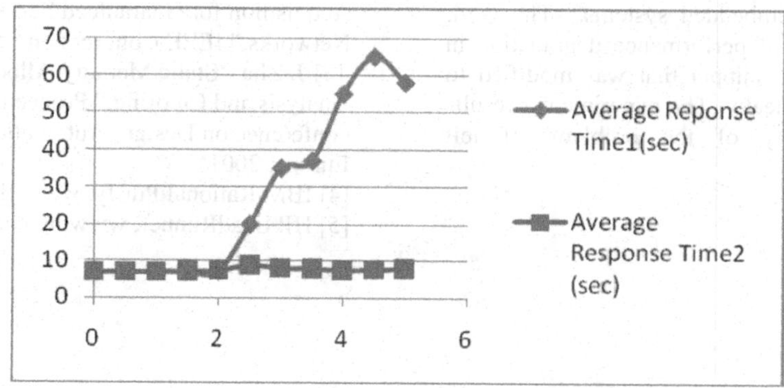

Figure 3: Average respone time in second over 5-hour run

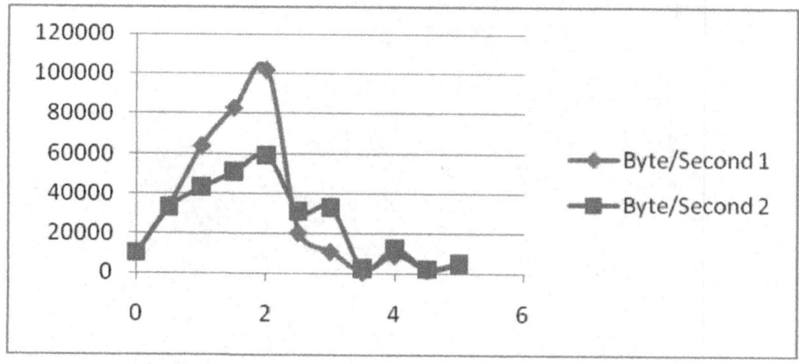

Figure 4:Throughput in terms of bytes per second over 5-hour run

When the source of memory leak was resolved programmatically- by freeing seized memory- and same test scenarios were rerun, the test outcomes reflect enhancement in the chosen metrics as depicted by the brown graphs in Figures 3 and 4. This improvement is achieved as the memory usage shows stability along the experiment lifetime (Memory Usage2 in figure 5).

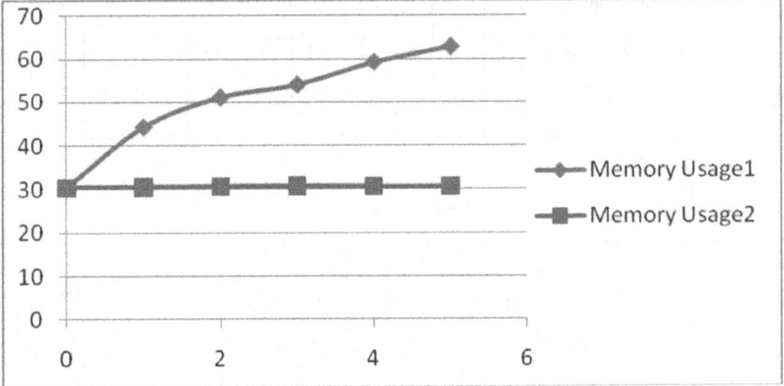

Figure 5: Contrasting the memory usage in leaky program (usage1) with a non-leaky program (usage 2) in 4-hour simulation experiment

V. CONCLUSION

This work highlighted the impact of memory leakage in performance hindrance. It defines the concept, the root causes and offered a glimpse of combating memory leakage in embedded systems. The work quantified the levels of performance degradation in an elevator controller snippet that was modified to intentionally become leaky. The experimental results reflected the severity of the problems if left undetected.

REFERENCES

[1] C. Erickson, "Memory Leak Detection in Embedded Systems," Linux Journal, Sept 2002

[2] J. CH and P. Wang, "Cost-Aware Resource Acquisition for Guaranteed Service in P2P Networks," IEEE Congress on Service, Part-II, 2008

[3] J. Zhu, 'Static Memory Allocation by Pointer Analysis and Coloring," Proceedings of the conference on Design, Automation and Test in Europe, 2001

[4] IBM Rational Purify, www.IBM.com

[5] HP LoadRunner, www.hp.com

Writer Identification Using Inexpensive Signal Processing Techniques

Serguei A. Mokhov
Computer Science
and Software Engineering,
Concordia University, Montreal, Canada,
Email: mokhov@cse.concordia.ca

Miao Song
Graduate School,
Concordia University,
Montreal, Canada,
Email: m_song@cse.concordia.ca

Ching Y. Suen
Centre for Pattern Recognition
and Machine Intelligence,
Concordia University, Montreal, Canada,
Email: suen@cenparmi.concordia.ca

***Abstract*—We propose to use novel and classical audio and text signal-processing and otherwise techniques for "inexpensive" fast writer identification tasks of scanned hand-written documents "visually". The "inexpensive" refers to the efficiency of the identification process in terms of CPU cycles while preserving decent accuracy for preliminary identification. This is a comparative study of multiple algorithm combinations in a pattern recognition pipeline implemented in Java around an open-source Modular Audio Recognition Framework (MARF) that can do a lot more beyond audio. We present our preliminary experimental findings in such an identification task. We simulate "visual" identification by "looking" at the hand-written document as a whole rather than trying to extract fine-grained features out of it prior classification.**

***Index Terms*—writer identification, Modular Audio Recognition Framework (MARF), signal processing, simulation**

I. Introduction

A. Problem Statement

Current techniques for writer identification often rely on the classical tools, methodologies, and algorithms in handwriting recognition (and in general in any image-based pattern recognition) such as skeletonizing, contouring, line-based and angle-based feature extraction, and many others. Then those techniques compare the features to the "style" of features a given writer may have in the trained database of known writers. These classical techniques are, while highly accurate, are also time consuming for bulk processing of a large volume of digital data of handwritten material for its preliminary or secondary identification of who may have written what.

B. Proposed Solution

We simulate "quick visual identification" of the handwriting of the writer by looking at a page of hand-written text as a whole to speed up the process of identification, especially when one needs to do a quick preliminary classification of a large volume of documents. For that we treat the sample pages as either 1D or 2D arrays of data and apply 1D or 2D loading using various loading methods, then 1D or 2D filtering, then in the case of 2D filtering, we flatten a 2D array into 1D prior feature extraction, and then we continue the classical feature extraction, training and classification tasks using a comprehensive algorithm set within Modular Audio Recognition Framework (MARF)'s implementation, by roughly treating each hand-written image sample as a wave form as in e.g. in speaker identification. We insist on 1D as it is the baseline storage mechanism for MARF and it is less storage consuming while sufficient to achieve high accuracy in the writer identification task.

This approach is in a way similar to the one where MARF was applied to file type analysis for forensic purposes [1] using machine learning and assuming each file is a sort of a signal on Unix systems as compared to the traditional `file` utility [2], [3].

C. Introduction to MARF

Modular Audio Recognition Framework (MARF) is an open-source collection of pattern recognition APIs and their implementation for unsupervised and supervised machine learning and classification written in Java [4], [5], [6], [7], [8], [9]. One of its design purposes is to act as a testbed to try out common and novel algorithms found in literature and industry for sample loading, preprocessing, feature extraction, and training and classification tasks. One of the main goals and design approaches of MARF is to provide scientists with a tool for comparison of the algorithms in a homogeneous environment and allowing the dynamic module selection (from the implemented modules) based on the configuration options supplied by applications. Over the course of several years MARF accumulated a fair number of implementations for each of the pipeline stages allowing reasonably comprehensive comparative studies of the algorithms *combinations*, and studying their *combined* behavior and other properties when used for various pattern recognition tasks. MARF is also designed to be very configurable while keeping the generality and some sane default settings to "run-off-the-shelf" well. MARF and its derivatives, and applications were also used beyond audio processing tasks due to the generality of the design and implementation in [10], [11], [12], [13], [14] and other unpublished or in-progress works.

1) Classical Pattern Recognition Pipeline: The conceptual pattern recognition pipeline shown in Figure 1 depicts the core of the data flow and transformation between the stages of the MARF's pipeline. The inner boxes represent most of

T. Sobh, K. Elleithy (eds.), *Innovations in Computing Sciences and Software Engineering*,
DOI 10.1007/978-90-481-9112-3_74,

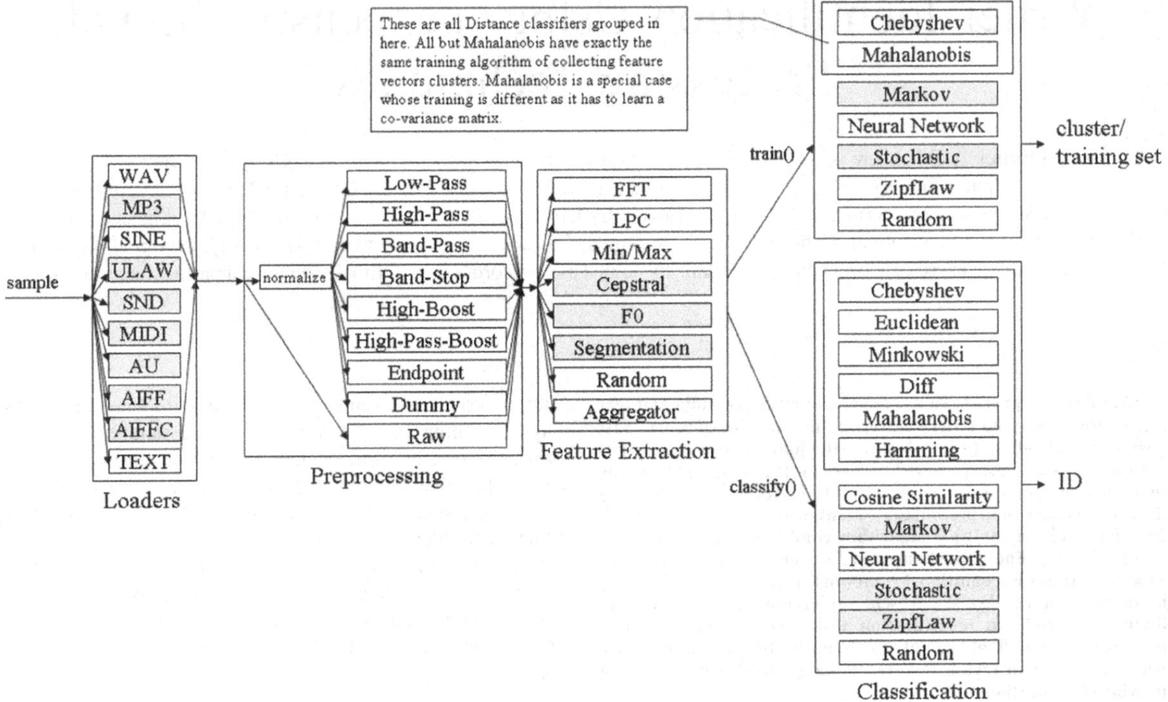

Fig. 1. MARF's Pattern Recognition Pipeline

the available concrete module implementations or stubs. The grayed-out boxes are either the stubs or partly implemented. The white boxes signify implemented algorithms. Generally, the whole pattern recognition process starts by loading a sample (e.g. an audio recording in a wave form, a text, or image file), preprocessing it (removing noisy and "silent" data and other unwanted elements), then extracting the most prominent features, and finally either training of the system such that the system either learns a new set of a features of a given subject or actually classify and identify what/how the subject is. The outcome of training is either a collection of some form of feature vectors or their mean or median clusters, which a stored per subject learned. The outcome of classification is a 32-bit unique integer usually indicating who/what the subject the system believes is. MARF designed to be a standalone marf.jar file required to be usable and has no dependencies on other libraries. Optionally, there is a dependency for debug versions of marf.jar when JUnit [15] is used for unit testing.

2) Algorithms: MARF has actual implementations of the framework's API in a number of algorithms to demonstrate its abilities in various pipeline stages and modules. There are a number of modules that are under the process of implementation or porting from other project for comparative studies that did not make it to this work at the time of its writing. Thus, the below is an incomplete summary of implemented algorithms corresponding to the Figure 1 with a very brief description:

- Fast Fourier transform (FFT), used in FFT-based filtering as well as feature extraction [16].
- Linear predictive coding (LPC) used in feature extraction.
- Artificial neural network (classification).
- Various distance classifiers (Chebyshev, Euclidean, Minkowski [17], Mahalanobis [18], Diff (internally developed within the project, roughly similar in behavior to the UNIX/Linux `diff` utility [19]), and Hamming [20]).
- Cosine similarity measure [21], [22], which was thoroughly discussed in [23] and often produces the best accuracy in this work in many configurations (see further).
- Zipf's Law-based classifier [24].
- General probability classifier.
- Continuous Fraction Expansion (CFE)-based filters [25].
- A number of math-related tools, for matrix and vector processing, including complex numbers matrix and vector operations, and statistical estimators used in smoothing of sparse matrices (e.g. in probabilistic matrices or Mahalanobis distance's covariance matrix). All these are needed for MARF to be self-contained.

II. METHODOLOGY

To enable the experiments in this work and their results we required to do the alteration of the MARF's pipeline through its plug-in architecture. We outline the modifications and the experiments and conducted using a variety of options.

A. Modified MARF's Pipeline

There are slight modifications to the pipeline that were required to MARF's original pipeline in order to enable some of the experiments outlined below for the writer identification tasks. Luckily, due to MARF's extensible architecture we can do those modifications as plug-ins, primarily for sample loading and preprocessing, that we plan on integrating into the core of MARF.

1) Loaders: We experiment with a diverse scanned image sample loading mechanisms to see which contribute more to the better accuracy results and the most efficient. There is a naive and less naive approach to do so. We can treat the incoming sample as:

- an image, essentially a 2D array, naturally
- a byte stream, i.e. just a 1D array of raw bytes
- a text file, treat the incoming bytes as text, also 1D
- a wave form, as if it is encoded WAVE file, also 1D

Internally, regardless the initial interpretation of the scanned hand-written image samples, the data is always treated as some wave form or another. The initial loading affects the outcome significantly, and we tried to experiment which one yields better results, which we present as options. For this to work we had to design and implement `ImageSampleLoader` as an external to MARF plug-in to properly decode the image data as image and return a 2D array representation of it (it is later converted to 1D for further processing). We adapt the `ImageSample` and `ImageSampleLoader` previously designed for the `TestFilters` application of MARF for 2D filter tests. The other loaders were already available in MARF's implementation, but had to be sub-classed or wrapped around to override some settings. Specifically, we have a `ByteArrayFileReader`, `TextLoader`, and `WAVLoader` in the core MARF that we rely upon. For the former, since it does not directly implement the `ISampleLoader` interface, we also create an external wrapper plug-in, `RawSampleLoader`. The `TextLoader` provides options for loading the data as uni-, bi-, and tri-gram models, i.e. one sample point consists of one, two, or three characters. The `WAVLoader` allows treating the incoming sample at different sample rates as well, e.g. 8000 kHz, 16000 kHz, and so on. We had to create a `TIFFtoWAVLoader` plug-in for this research work to allow the treatment of the TIFF files as WAV with the proper format settings.

2) Filters: The Filter Framework of MARF and its API represented by the `IFilter` interface has to be invoked with the 2D versions of the filters instead of 1D, which is a sufficient default for audio signal processing. The Filter framework has a 2D API processing that can be applied to images, "line-by-line". The 2D API of `IFilter` returns a 2D results. In order for it to be usable by the rest of the pipeline, it has to be "flattened" into a 1D array. The "flattening" can be done row-by-row or column-by-column; we experiment with both ways of doing it. Once flattened, the rest of the pipeline process functions as normal. Since there is no such a default preprocessing module in the core MARF, we implement it as a preprocessing plug-in in this work, which we call `Filter2Dto1D`. This class implements `preprocess()` method to behave the described way. This class in itself actually does not do much, but instead the FFT-based set of filters is mirrored from the core MARF to this plug-in to adhere to this new implementation of `preprocess()` and at the same time to delegate all the work to the core modules. Thus, we have the base `FFTFilter2Dto1D`, and the concrete `LowPass2Dto1D`, `HighPass2Dto1D`, `BandStop2Dto1D`, and `BandPass2Dto1D` FFT-based filters. The CFE-based filters require further testing at this point and as such were not included in the experiments.

3) Noise Removal: We employ two basic methodologies of noise removal in our experiments: (1) we either remove the noise by loading the "noise" sample, a scanned "blank" sheet with no writings on it. Subtracting the frequencies of this noise sample from the incoming samples gives us the net effect of large noise removal. This FFT sample-based noise remover is only effective for the 2D preprocessing operations. Implementation-wise, we implement it in the `SampleBasedNoiseRemover` preprocessing plug-in class. (2) We compare that to the default noise removal in MARF that is constructed by application of the plain 1D low-pass FFT filter.

B. `WriterIdentApp`

We provide a testing application, called `WriterIdentApp`, to do all the experiments in this work and statistics gathering. The application is a writer-identification-oriented fork of `SpeakerIdentApp` present within MARF's repository [5] for speaker identification task. The application has been amended with the options to accept the four loader types instead of two, noise removal by subtraction of the noise sample, and the 2D filtering plug-ins. The rest of the application options are roughly the same as that of `SpeakerIdentApp`. Like all of MARF and its applications, `WriterIdentApp` will be released as open-source and can be made available to the willing upon request prior that.

C. Resolution

We vary the resolution of our samples as 600dpi, 300dpi, and 96dpi in our experiments to see how it affects the accuracy of the identification. The samples are both grayscale and black-and-white.

III. Testing, Experiments, and Results

The handwritten training samples included two pages scanned from students' quizzes. The testing performed on the another, third page of the same exam for each student. The total number of students's exams in class studied is 25.

A. Setup

In the setup we are testing multiple permutation of configurable parameters, which are outlined below.

1) Samples: The samples are scanned pages letter-sized as uncompressed TIFF images of the following resolutions and color schemes:

- 600 dpi grayscale, black-and-white
- 300 dpi grayscale, black-and-white
- 96 dpi grayscale, black-and-white

2) Sample Loaders:

- Text loader: unigram, bigram, trigram
- WAVE loader: PCM, 8000 kHz, mono, 2 bytes per amplitude sample point
- Raw loader: byte loader (1-byte, 2-byte, 4-byte per sample point)
- TIFF Image 2D loader

Byte loader and text loader are similar but not identical. In Java characters are in UNICODE and occupy physically two bytes and we use a character-oriented reader to do so. In the byte loader, we deal with the raw bytes and our "ngrams" correspond to the powers of 2.

3) Preprocessing:

- 1D filtering works with 1D loaders, and low-pass FFT filter acts as a noise remover
- 2D filtering covered by a plug-in with 2D FFT filters and noise sample subtraction
- Flattening of the 2D data to 1D by row or column

4) Feature Extraction and Classification: The principle fastest players in the experimentation so-far were primarily the distance and similarity measure classifiers and for feature extraction FFT, LPC and min/max amplitudes. All these modules are at their defaults as defined by MARF [5], [7], [6], [8], [9].

B. Analysis

Generally, it appears the 2D versions of the combinations produce higher accuracy. The text-based and byte-based loaders perform at the average level and the wave form loading slightly better. The black-and-white images at all resolutions obviously load faster as they are much smaller in size, and even the 96 dpi-based image performed very well suggesting the samples need not be of the highest quality. Algorithm combinations that had silence removed after either 1D or 2D based noise removal contributed to the best results by eliminating "silence gaps" (in the image strings of zeros, similar to compression) thereby making samples looking quite distinct. The noise-sample based removal, even eliminates the printed text and lines of the handed-out exam sheets keeping only hand-written text and combined with the silence removal pushes the accuracy percentage even higher.

The experiments are running on two major hardware pieces: a Dell desktop and a server with two 2 CPUs. Run-time that it takes to train the system on 50 600dpi grayscale samples (35Mb each) is varied between 15 to 20 minutes on a Dell Precision 370 workstation with 1GB of RAM and 1.5GHz Intel Pentium 4 processor running Fedora Core 4 Linux. For the testing samples, it takes between 4 and 7 seconds depending on the algorithm combination for the 35Mb testing samples. All the sample files were read off a DVD disk, so the performance was less optimal than from a hard disk. In the case of the server with two Intel Pentium 4 CPUs, 4GB of ram and the four processing running it takes 2-3 times faster for the same amount. 96dpi b/w images take very fast to process and offer the best response times.

IV. Conclusion

As of this writing due two numerous exhaustive combinations and about 600 runs per loader most of the experiments and some testing are still underway and are expected to complete within a week. The pages with the list of resulting tables are obviously not fitting within a 6-page conference paper, but will be made available in full upon request. Some of the fastest results have come back entirely, but for now they show disappointing accuracy performance of 20% correctly identified writiers in our settings, which is way below expected from our hypothesis. Since the results are incomplete, the authors are reviewing them as they come in and seek the faults in the implementation and data. The complete set of positive or negative outcomes will be summarized in the final version of the article.

A. Applications

We outline possible applications of our quick classification approach:

- Students' exams verification in case of fraud claims to quickly sort out the pages into appropriate bins
- For large amount of scanned checks (e.g. same as banks make available on-line). Personal checks identification can be used to see if the system can tell they are written by the same person. In this case the author used his personal check scans due to their handy availability.
- Quick sorting out of hand-written mail.
- Blackmail investigation when checking whether some letters with threats were written by the same person or who that person might be by taking sample handwriting samples of the suspects in custody or investigation.

B. Future Work

- Further improve recognition accuracy by investigating more algorithms and their properties.
- Experiment with the CFE-based filters.
- Automation of training process for the sorting purposes.
- Export results in Forensic Lucid for forensic analysis.

C. Improving Identification Accuracy

So far, we did a quick way of doing writer authentication without using any common advanced or otherwise image processing techniques, such as contouring, skeletonizing, etc. and the related feature extraction, such as angles, lines, direction, relative position of them, etc. We can "inject" those approaches into the available pipeline if we can live with slower processing speeds due to the additional overhead induced by the algorithms, but improve the accuracy of the identification.

ACKNOWLEDGMENTS

This work is partially funded by NSERC, FQRSC, and Graduate School and the Faculty of Engineering and Computer Science, Concordia University, Montreal, Canada.

REFERENCES

[1] S. A. Mokhov and M. Debbabi, "File type analysis using signal processing techniques and machine learning vs. `file` unix utility for forensic analysis," in *Proceedings of the IT Incident Management and IT Forensics (IMF'08)*, O. Goebel, S. Frings, D. Guenther, J. Nedon, and D. Schadt, Eds. Mannheim, Germany: GI, Sep. 2008, pp. 73–85, LNI140.

[2] I. F. Darwin, J. Gilmore, G. Collyer, R. McMahon, G. Harris, C. Zoulas, C. Lowth, E. Fischer, and Various Contributors, "`file` – determine file type, BSD General Commands Manual, file(1)," BSD, Jan. 1973–2007, man file(1).

[3] ——, "`file` – determine file type," [online], Mar. 1973–2008, ftp://ftp.astron.com/pub/file/, last viewed April 2008.

[4] S. Mokhov, I. Clement, S. Sinclair, and D. Nicolacopoulos, "Modular Audio Recognition Framework," Department of Computer Science and Software Engineering, Concordia University, Montreal, Canada, 2002–2003, project report, http://marf.sf.net, last viewed April 2008.

[5] The MARF Research and Development Group, "The Modular Audio Recognition Framework and its Applications," [online], 2002–2009, http://marf.sf.net, last viewed October 2009.

[6] S. A. Mokhov, "Experimental results and statistics in the implementation of the modular audio recognition framework's API for text-independent speaker identification," in *Proceedings of the 6th International Conference on Computing, Communications and Control Technologies (CCCT'08)*, C. D. Zinn, H.-W. Chu, M. Savoie, J. Ferrer, and A. Munitic, Eds., vol. II. Orlando, Florida, USA: IIIS, Jun. 2008, pp. 267–272.

[7] ——, "Introducing MARF: a modular audio recognition framework and its applications for scientific and software engineering research," in *Advances in Computer and Information Sciences and Engineering*. University of Bridgeport, U.S.A.: Springer Netherlands, Dec. 2007, pp. 473–478, proceedings of CISSE/SCSS'07.

[8] ——, "Choosing best algorithm combinations for speech processing tasks in machine learning using MARF," in *Proceedings of the 21st Canadian AI'08*, S. Bergler, Ed. Windsor, Ontario, Canada: Springer-Verlag, Berlin Heidelberg, May 2008, pp. 216–221, LNAI 5032.

[9] ——, "Study of best algorithm combinations for speech processing tasks in machine learning using median vs. mean clusters in MARF," in *Proceedings of C3S2E'08*, B. C. Desai, Ed. Montreal, Quebec, Canada: ACM, May 2008, pp. 29–43, ISBN 978-1-60558-101-9.

[10] ——, "On design and implementation of distributed modular audio recognition framework: Requirements and specification design document," [online], Aug. 2006, project report, http://arxiv.org/abs/0905.2459, last viewed May 2009.

[11] S. A. Mokhov, L. W. Huynh, and J. Li, "Managing distributed MARF with SNMP," Concordia Institute for Information Systems Engineering, Concordia University, Montreal, Canada, Apr. 2007, project Report. Hosted at http://marf.sf.net, last viewed April 2008.

[12] S. A. Mokhov, "Towards security hardening of scientific distributed demand-driven and pipelined computing systems," in *Proceedings of the 7th International Symposium on Parallel and Distributed Computing (ISPDC'08)*. Krakow, Poland: IEEE Computer Society, Jul. 2008, pp. 375–382.

[13] S. A. Mokhov, L. W. Huynh, J. Li, and F. Rassai, "A privacy framework within the java data security framework (JDSF): Design refinement, implementation, and statistics," in *Proceedings of the 12th World Multi-Conference on Systemics, Cybernetics and Informatics (WM-SCI'08)*, N. Callaos, W. Lesso, C. D. Zinn, J. Baralt, J. Boukachour, C. White, T. Marwala, and F. V. Nelwamondo, Eds., vol. V. Orlando, Florida, USA: IIIS, Jun. 2008, pp. 131–136.

[14] S. A. Mokhov, L. Wang, and J. Li, "Simple dynamic key management in SQL randomization," 2009, unpublished.

[15] E. Gamma and K. Beck, "JUnit," Object Mentor, Inc., 2001–2004, http://junit.org/.

[16] S. M. Bernsee, *The DFT "à pied": Mastering The Fourier Transform in One Day*. DSPdimension.com, 1999-2005, http://www.dspdimension.com/data/html/dftapied.html.

[17] H. Abdi, "Distance," in *Encyclopedia of Measurement and Statistics*, N. Salkind, Ed., Thousand Oaks (CA): Sage, 2007.

[18] P. Mahalanobis, "On the generalised distance in statistics." Proceedings of the National Institute of Science of India 12 (1936) 49-55, 1936, http://en.wikipedia.org/wiki/Mahalanobis_distance.

[19] D. Mackenzie, P. Eggert, and R. Stallman, "Comparing and merging files," [online], 2002, http://www.gnu.org/software/diffutils/manual/ps/diff.ps.gz.

[20] R. W. Hamming, "Error Detecting and Error Correcting Codes." Bell System Technical Journal 26(2):147-160, 1950, http://en.wikipedia.org/wiki/Hamming_distance.

[21] E. Garcia, "Cosine similarity and term weight tutorial," 2006, http://www.miislita.com/information-retrieval-tutorial/cosine-similarity-tutorial.html.

[22] A. Kishore, "Similarity measure: Cosine similarity or euclidean distance or both," Feb. 2007, http://semanticvoid.com/blog/2007/02/23/similarity-measure-cosine-similarity-or-euclidean-distance-or-both/.

[23] M. Khalifé, "Examining orthogonal concepts-based micro-classifiers and their correlations with noun-phrase coreference chains," Master's thesis, Concordia University, Montréal, Canada, 2004.

[24] G. K. Zipf, *The Psychobiology of Language*. Houghton-Mifflin, New York, NY, 1935, http://en.wikipedia.org/wiki/Zipf%27s_law.

[25] S. Haridas, "Generation of 2-D digital filters with variable magnitude characteristics starting from a particular type of 2-variable continued fraction expansion," Master's thesis, Concordia University, Montréal, Canada, Jul. 2006.

Software Artifacts Extraction for Program Comprehension

Ghulam Rasool, Ilka Philippow
Software Systems/Process Informatics Group
Technical University of Ilmenau Germany
Ghulam.rasool|ilka.philippow@tu-ilmenau.de

Abstract -**The maintenance of legacy software applications is a complex, expensive, quiet challenging, time consuming and daunting task due to program comprehension difficulties. The first step for software maintenance is to understand the existing software and to extract the high level abstractions from the source code. A number of methods, techniques and tools are applied to understand the legacy code. Each technique supports the particular legacy applications with automated/semi-automated tool support keeping in view the requirements of the maintainer. Most of the techniques support the modern languages but lacks support for older technologies. This paper presents a lightweight methodology for extraction of different artifacts from legacy COBOL and other applications.**

Keywords: Code analysis, Software maintenance, Reverse engineering, Program comprehension.

I. INTRODUCTION

Program comprehension is the vital activity which facilitates reuse, inspection, maintenance, code understanding, restructuring, refactoring, reverse engineering and reengineering of existing legacy applications. Automated program understanding is active, dominant and ongoing research area. Program understanding research includes the empirical research and technology research [1]. The empirical research focuses on understanding cognitive processes which are used by the engineers while understanding programs and technology research has a focus on developing semi-automated tool support to aid in program comprehension. The top-down, bottom-up, integrated and as needed comprehension techniques are used by the engineer to build different hypotheses and to develop the mental model of program structure. Most of the program comprehension techniques are limited so far to modern programming languages, while lacking similar capabilities for older technologies like COBOL, PASCAL and FORTRAN etc. The survey reports in [2 3 4 5 6] show that older technologies are still not dead and reflect the attention of research community towards these legacy applications. The comprehension of these applications is time consuming task. The fifty to ninety percent of the time, depending upon the system under consideration is spent on program understanding [28 29].

Rapid legacy application understanding, in which fast comprehension is more important than highly accurate or detailed understanding, plays an important role in the planning, feasibility assessment and cost estimating phases of system renovation projects [7]. The Skills and Experience of the programmer with different programming languages, available documentation and expert knowledge play very important role in early program comprehension. It is more important to understand what the legacy system does rather than how it's various components works. The major riddles during the extraction of different artifacts for program comprehension are how can we search a particular artifact in a legacy software system with optimal method by reducing time and cost? How can we obtain detailed information and comprehend the legacy system when documents and expert knowledge is not available? Which statements and functions relate to GUI and architecture components? Does the system contain reusable artifacts and how we can ensure the quality of the reusable artifacts? How to develop a good theoretical understanding and build a mental model for the legacy application? The last but not least how we can convey the benefits of program comprehension techniques to the stakeholder while minimizing business risks of program comprehension techniques to the industrial applications?

Maintenance is the one of most important activity supported by the comprehension. The maintenance cost of software is increasing with respect to time and the use of program comprehension methods and techniques is gaining more and more attention in the field of legacy and embedded applications. A major challenge to software maintenance is to keep documented specifications and other artifacts consistent and up to date as changes are made in the source code.

There are a number of open source and commercial comprehension tools that can help in program comprehension but most of tools are language specific and specially lack support for old languages. The lexical and syntactic tools are used for extraction of patterns from legacy applications. The syntactic tools have advantage of high precision in pattern matching in comparison with lexical tools. The major limitation in these tools is their robustness ability i.e. the source code should be free of errors. It must be syntactically and semantically correct, and language variants are not tolerated Lexical analysis provides a level of language independence here, and makes the system easier to adapt to new languages and dialects but has problem of accuracy. We used the abstraction methodology to design the innovative vocabulary of our tool which is generic in the nature that similar specifications are used to match desired patterns of source code written in different programming languages [27].The capabilities of program comprehension tools are

T. Sobh, K. Elleithy (eds.), *Innovations in Computing Sciences and Software Engineering*,
DOI 10.1007/978-90-481-9112-3_75, © Springer Science+Business Media B.V. 2010

measured based on their extraction, analysis and presentation features. The extraction step is the most important and primary step which is required for analysis and presentations steps. So, we have applied our custom build tool DRT [8] for rapid extraction of different artifacts from legacy COBOL, PASCAL and other applications. The analysis and presentation steps are still not supported by our tool.

II. PROGRAM COMPREHENSION APPROACHES

Many program comprehension approaches generate too much or not enough information and the maintainer has to judge itself the level of information according to his goals. Different approaches are used at different level of abstraction for program comprehension according to the requirement of the maintainer. The maintainer has to address different set of questions during the legacy application understanding and maintenance.

TABLE 1
PROGRAM COMPREHENSION APPROACHES

Method	Description
Formal Concepts Analysis	Constructs all possible concepts sharing common features. It represents the concepts using lattice representation [10].
Cluster analysis Techniques	It partitions the set of items in a series of disjoint clusters, by means of numeric distance between items indicating how many features they share [11].
Visualization Techniques	They visualize the applications using graphs, views and UML diagrams [12].
Dynamic analysis Techniques	Dynamic analyses techniques typically comprise the analysis of a system's execution through interpretation (e.g., using the Virtual Machine in Java) or instrumentation [13].
Filtering Techniques	Techniques Use merging, pruning and slicing techniques to comprehend the program [14].
Metrics trace Techniques	Analyses the traces of legacy applications to determine the complexity and the quality of the code [15].
Static analysis techniques	Obtain information through static analysis from source code and documentation with lexical and syntactic tools [16].
Heuristics Techniques	Use of heuristics for probabilistic ranking or sampling [17]
Querying Techniques	These techniques provide mechanism to extract program artifacts and the semantic relationship between those artifacts [18].
Features locating techniques	These techniques need to locate the code that implements a specific feature of a program in order to fix a problem or add an enhancement [19].
Multiple Traces.	These techniques measures to what extent multiple traces use same set of routines [20].
Fact Collection Method	FCM are used in studies that have a large number of subjects and as a complement to other methods for tracing cognitive processes, such as user log files [21].
Association rule mining	These techniques inputs data extracted from code and derives association rules. Rules are then processed to abstract programs into groups containing interrelated entities. [22].
Web Mining Techniques.	Web mining techniques use the web as a large graph, where each node represents a page and each edge represents a hyperlink [23].
Ontology Based approaches	The ontological representation unifies information from various sources, and therefore reduces the maintainers' comprehension efforts [24].
Design pattern base approaches.	These techniques use design patterns for program comprehension [25].

It is very difficult to understand how a program works before modifying it in large legacy applications. According to our literature survey, more than 16 techniques are used for program comprehension as mentioned in table1. Unfortunately, many of these approaches rely on features such as scope rules, return types, and parameter passing, available in languages like C/C++, PASCAL but many data-intensive business programs are written in languages like COBOL that do not have these features. As a result, these class extraction approaches have not been applied successfully to COBOL systems, as was also observed by Cimitile et al. [9]. Automated tools play very important role in program comprehension approaches, but these tools require human interaction at some stages to extract different artifacts from legacy applications.

III. METHODOLOGY FOR COMPREHENSION

Our approach starts with analyzing source code and documentation related with the legacy application. Based on this information and keeping in view certain hypotheses about the structure of the system, we build the domain model about the architecture of the legacy application. Fig 1 shows the possible source of information for developing the domain model. The domain model shows the relationship between different entities of legacy application. The domain model information is given to our tool which matches the domain model entities with information available in the source code. The domain model can be refined after matching different patterns available in the source code.

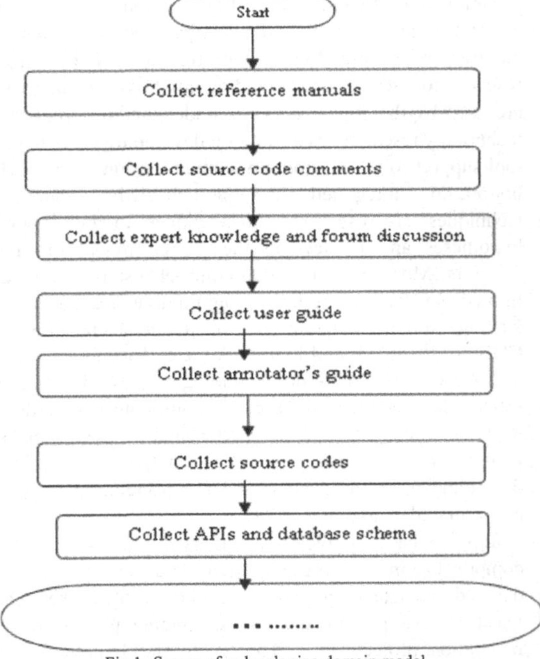

Fig 1. Sources for developing domain model

The abstract pattern definitions can be used to map entities of domain model with different entities available in the source code to extract different artifacts used for program comprehension.

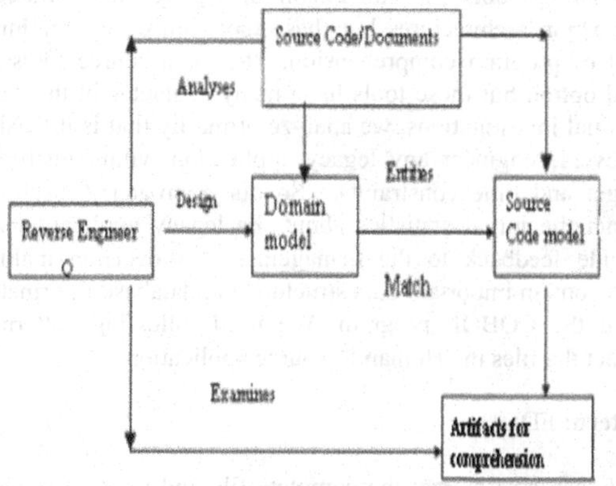

Fig. 2. Comprehension Methodology

The approach is represented in the block diagram as shown in fig 2. The comments in the source code give useful clues about the GUI components. We have extracted comments from the COBOL legacy code which are very helpful for building the domain model as shown in fig 3.

IV EXPERIMENTAL EXAMPLES

We have performed experiments on the following examples:

A. *EXAMPLE 1*

We have evaluated our approach for extraction of different artifacts which are used for understanding legacy COBOL applications. The structure of COBOL program consists of four main divisions which are further divided into different sections. The pattern **a** is used to extract the main four divisions of COBOL program. Similarly the patterns b, c, d and e are used to extract the contents of identification, environment, data and procedure divisions from the legacy COBOL source code respectively. Pattern f and e used to extract the different file structures and open COBOL file statement. Further, we can define different pattern definitions according to our requirements to extract procedure calls, file structures, record structures, data types, comments and other artifacts from source code. Table 2 shows the pattern definitions and results extracted from Client Messaging (Messaging software in COBOL) [26].

a: COBDIV-IDENTIFICATION DIVISION|ENVIRONMENT DIVISION|DATA DIVISION|PROCEDURE DIVISION.

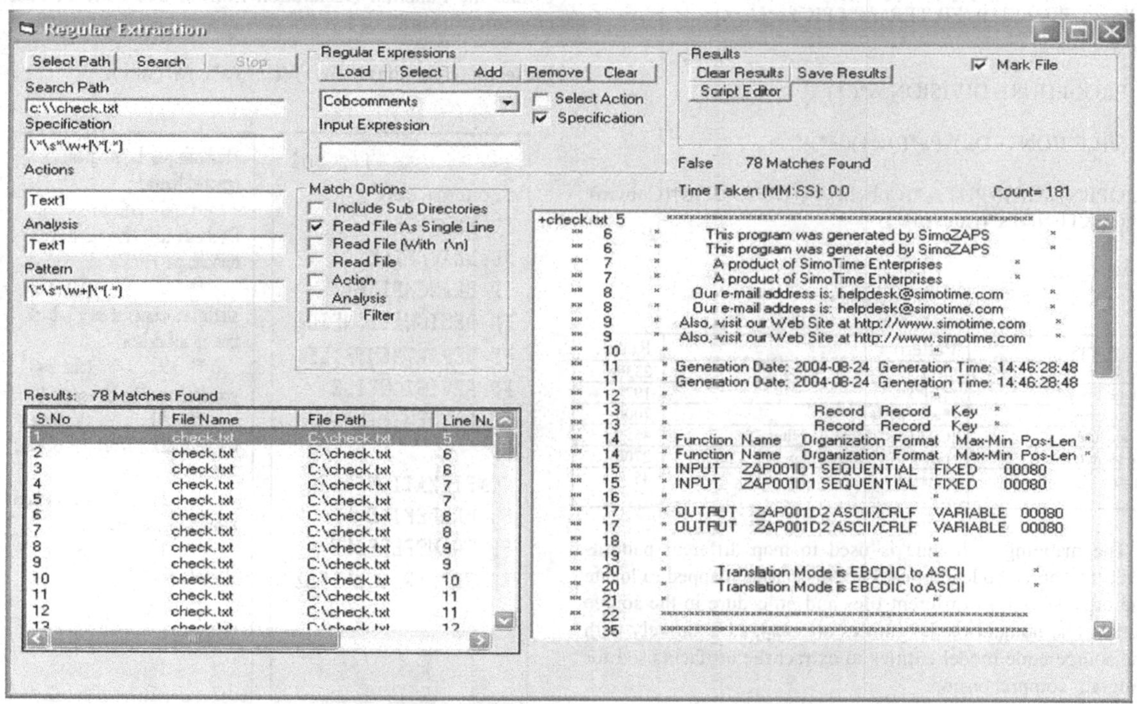

Fig 3. Extracted Comments from legacy COBOL Code

b: (IDENTIFICATION DIVISION.)\s*PROGRAM- ID.\s*(\w)+\.\s* ((AUTHOR.)\s*(\w)+\.\s*)?((INSTALLATION.)\s*(\w)+\.\s*)?((DATE-WRITTEN.)\s*((0[1-9]|1[012])[- /.](0[1-9]|[12][0-9]|3[01])[- /.](19|20)\d\d)\.\s*)?((DATE-COMPILED.)\s*((0[1-9]|1[012])[- /.](0[1-9]|[12][0-9]|3[01])[- /.](19|20)\d\d)\.\s*)?((SECURITY.)\s*(\w)+\.\s*)?((REMARKS.)\s*(\w)+\.\s*)?

c: (([a-zA-Z][a-zA-Z0-9-$]*))\.\s*(WITH\s*DEBUGGING\s*MODE\s*\.)?)(OBJECT-COMPUTER.\s*(([a-zA-Z][a-zA-Z0-9-$]*))\.\s*))(SPECIAL-NAMES.\s*(CURRENCY SIGN)\s*(IS)\s*\'\$\'\s*(DECIMAL-POINT)\s*(IS)\s*(COMMA)\s*\.)?))?\s*((INPUT-OUTPUT SECTION.)\s*((FILE-CONTROL)\s*(SELECT\s*(([a-zA-Z][a-zA-Z0-9-$]*))\s*(ASSIGN TO)\s*(([a-zA-Z][a-zA-Z0-9-$]*))\s*(\.)?\s*)*\s*(ORGANIZATION)\s*(IS)\s*(SEQUENTIAL|RELATIVE|INDEXED)\s*ACCESS\s*MODE\s*IS\s*(SEQUENTIAL|RANDOM| DYNAMIC)\s*RECORD\s*KEY\s*IS\s*(([a-zA-Z][a-zA-Z0-9-$]*))\s*(WITH DUPLICATES)?\s*(ALTERNTIVE\s*RECORD\s*KEY\s*IS\s*(([a-zA-Z][a-zA-Z0-9-$]*))\s*(WITH DUPLICATES)?)*\s*FILE\s* STAUS\s*IS\s* (([a-zA-Z][a-zA-Z0-9-$]*))(\,\s*(([a-zA-Z][a-zA-Z0-9-$]*)))*\.)?)

d: (DATA DIVISION.)\s*((FILE SECTION.)\s*((FD|SD)\s* (([a-zA-Z][a-zA-Z0-9-$]*))\.\s*((IS)\s*(EXTERNAL |GLOBAL))?\s*((([0]?[1-9]|[1-4][0-9]|66|77|88))\s*((([a-zA-Z][a-zA-Z0-9-$]*))|(FILTER))\s*(PIC)\s*[A-Z]\(\d+\)\.)+)*)

e: PROCEDURE DIVISION.\s*(.*)

f: (FILE-CONTROL)\.(\s*((\w+)(\s*))*\.)

g:(OPEN)\s*(((INPUT)\s*(Cobvrn)+)|((OUTPUT)\s*(Cobvrn)+)|((EXTEND)\s*(Cobvrn)+))+

TABLE 2
ARTIFACTS FROM CLIENT MESSAGING

Artifacts	Pattern	Result
LOSC	^(.*)	23396
Blank lines	^[\s]*$	197
Comments	*\s*\w+|*(.*)	7000
Procedures	(CALL)\s*(Identifier| literal)	455
Go to statements	(GO TO)\s*(Identifier)	2700
Files	FD\s+\w+	45

The mapping technique is used to map different patterns with the source code entities. Patterns can be mapped to locate the organization of different files and procedure in the source code. The domain model entities are mapped iteratively with the source code model entities to extract the artifacts used for program comprehension.

B. EXAMPLE 2

In another example, we analyzed the Human Resource Program developed in COBOL. The industry has different commercial tools for conversion of legacy code into new application architectures but these tools are costly for initial level of program comprehension. The open source tools are good option but these tools have many obstacles in their use. In initial investigations, we analyze primarily that is it feasible to reverse engineer any legacy application within justifiable budget and time constraints. So our approach is useful to extract the initial statistics about the legacy application and provide feedback to the management for decision making. Files contain important data structure and database information about the COBOL program. We used following pattern to extract the files the Human Resource application.

Pattern: FD\s+\w+

We can also extract the complete file and record structures from the source code of COBOL by different pattern specifications. These specifications further may be used for recovering the ERD model of COBOL applications. Our pattern specifications use abstraction at each level to investigate the required information used for program comprehension. The functions are basic building block of Pascal programs. The following pattern specification is used to extract the Function Declaration from source code of Pascal program (File utilities).

Pattern: ((function)\s*(\w+)\((.*)\)\s*(:)\s*(\w+))

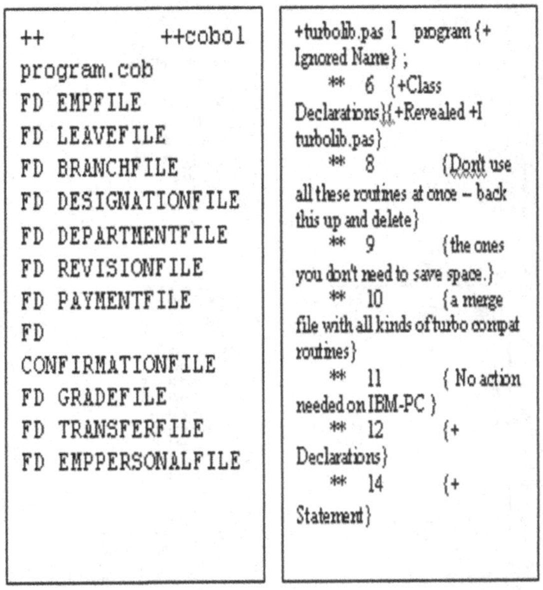

```
++            ++cobol
program.cob
FD EMPFILE
FD LEAVEFILE
FD BRANCHFILE
FD DESIGNATIONFILE
FD DEPARTMENTFILE
FD REVISIONFILE
FD PAYMENTFILE
FD
CONFIRMATIONFILE
FD GRADEFILE
FD TRANSFERFILE
FD EMPPERSONALFILE
```

```
+turbolib.pas 1   program {+
Ignored Name} ;
    **  6  {+Class
Declarations}{+Revealed +I
turbolib.pas}
    **  8          {Dont use
all these routines at once – back
this up and delete}
    **  9          {the ones
you don't need to save space.}
    **  10         {a merge
file with all kinds of turbo compat
routines}
    **  11         { No action
needed on IBM-PC }
    **  12         {+
Declarations}
    **  14         {+
Statement}
```

Fig 4. Artifacts Recovered from COBOL and PASCAL Applications

V. CONCLUSIONS

The presented methodology is lightweight, iterative, scalable, and customizable and can be used for procedural as well as object oriented applications. The major focus is to extract artifacts from old legacy applications which are still not dead. The technique is useful at initial level of program comprehension to extract different artifacts from legacy applications which combine the domain knowledge and tool support for program comprehension. The extracted artifacts can be visualized for better program comprehension. We are extending the vocabulary of different patterns to support the languages having mix-mode code in their syntax. The patterns of our technique can be used by the other lexical pattern matching techniques and tools. The techniques will be extended to extract different design patterns from the legacy applications.

REFERENCES

[1] M. Storey, "Theories, tools and research methods in program comprehension past, present and future", Software Quality Journal pp.187–208, 2006.

[2] F. Zoufaly, "Issues and Challenges facing legacy Systems",http://www.developer.com/mgmt/article.php/1492531 [Accessed on 4th October, 2009).

[3] IBM Executive Brief, Legacy Transformation: Finding New Business Value in Older Applications, 2005. http://www306.ibm.com/software/info/features/bestofboth

[4] Research Triangle Institute Report: Accessed on [12thNov,2008]http://www.nist.gov/public_affairs/releases/n02-10.html

[5] Capers Jones, Geriatric Issues of Aging Software, Vol. 20 No 12, pp.1-13, Dec 2007.

[6] IBM Executive Brief, Legacy Transformation: Finding New Business Value in Older Applications, 2005. http://www306.ibm.com/software/info/features/bestofboth.

[7] T. Kuipers, "Techniques for Understanding Legacy Software Systems", A PhD Thesis, University of Amsterdam Nederland, February 2002.

[8] G. Rasool, N. Asif, "A Design Recovery Tool", International Journal of Software Engineering, ISSN (1815-4875), Vol. 1, pp. 67-72 , May 2007.

[9] A. Cimitile, A. De Lucia, G. A. Di Lucca, and A. R. Fasolino, Identifying objects in legacy systems using design metrics, Journal of Systems and Software, Vol. 44, No. 3, pp.199–211, 1999.

[10] M. Janota and G. Botterweck, "Formal Approach to Integrating Feature and Architecture Models," In Procs of Fundamental Approaches to Software Engineering (FASE 2008) Budapest, Hungary, 2008.

[11] K Angelopoulos Miannis, T. Christos, "Data mining source code to facilitate program comprehension" , In Procs of 12th IEEE International Workshop on Program Comprehension, 24-26 June, 2004, Bari, Italy ,pp. 214-223.

[12] M. J. Pacoima, "Software Visualization for Object-Oriented Program Comprehension", In Procs of the 26th International Conference on Software Engineering", pp. 63 - 65, 2004.

[13] A. Hamou-Lhadj, "Techniques to Simplify the Analysis of Execution Traces for Program Comprehension", PhD Thesis pp.78

[14] A. Marcus, L. Feng, J. I. Maletic, "3D representations for software visualization", In Procs of the 2003 ACM symposium on Software visualization ,pp. 27 - ff , 2003 .

[15] H. M. Sneed, "Understanding software through numbers: A metric based approach to program comprehension", In Journal of Software Maintenance and Evolution: Research and Practice, Vol 7 ,Issue 6, pp. 405 – 419, 30, Oct 2006.

[16] T. Eisenbarth, R. Koschke, D. Simon, "Aiding program comprehension by static and dynamic feature analysis, In Procs of IEEE International Conference on software maintenance , pp. 602-611, 2001 .

[17] Bradley L. Vinz, Letha H. Etzkorn, "Improving program comprehension by combining code understanding with comment understanding", In Journal of Knowledge-Based Systems , Vol 21, Issue 8 pp. 813-825, 2008.

[18] M. Verbaere, M. W. Godfrey, T. Girba, "Query Technologies and Applications for Program Comprehension", In Procs of the 16th IEEE International Conference on Program Comprehension - Vol 00 ISBN: 978-0-7695-3176-2, pp. 285-288, 2008.

[19] N. Wilde., M. Buckellew , H. Page , V. Rajilich , L. Pounds "A comparison of methods for locating features in legacy software", In Journal of Systems and Software Vol 65, Issue 2, 15, Pages 105-114, February 2003.

[20] C. Andy Zaidman, D. Holten, L. Moonen, A. van Deursen, Jarke J. van Wijk , "Execution trace analysis through massive sequence and circular bundle views", In Journal of Systems and Software,Vol 81, Issue 12, pp. 2252-2268, December 2008.

[21] A Tjortjis, C. Sinos, L. Layzell, P. "Facilitating program comprehension by mining association rules from source code",. In Procs of 11th IEEE International Workshop on Program Comprehension, pp. 125- 132, 10-11 May 2003.

[22] Thomas D. LaToza, D. Garlan, James D. Herbsleb, Brad A. Myers "Program Comprehension as Fact Finding", In Procs of the 6th joint meeting of the European software engineering conference and the ACM SIGSOFT symposium on The foundations of software engineering, Dubrovnik, Croatia, pp. 361-370, 2007.

[23] A. Zaidman, B. Du Bois, and S. Demeyer, "How Webmining and Coupling Metrics Improve Early Program Comprehension", In Procs of the 14th IEEE International Conference on Program Comprehension (ICPC'06) pp.74-78, 26 June 2006.

[24] Y. Zhang, R. Witte, J. Rilling, and V. Haarslev, "Ontology-based Program Comprehension Tool Supporting Website Architectural Evolution", In Procs of 8th IEEE International Symposium on Web Site Evolution (WSE 2006), pp.41-49, Philadelphia, PA, USA, September 23-24, 2006.

[25] J. Ka-Yee Ng, Y. Gueheneuc, "Identifcation of Behavioral and Creational Design Patterns through Dynamic Analysis", In Procs of the 3rd International Workshop on Program Comprehension through Dynamic Analysis (PCODA'07), pp- 34-42, 2007.

[26] http://www.cobug.com/cobug/docs/codesamples0020.html [Accessed on 28 December 2008]

[27] G. Rasool, N. Asif, " Software Artifacts Recovery Using Abstract Regular Expressions", In Procs of 11th IEEE Multitopic Conference , pp. 1-6, 28-30 December 2007 Lahore, Pakistan.

[28] H. Muller, K. Wong, S. Tilley, "Understanding Software Systems Using Reverse Engineering Technology", In Procs of 62nd Congress of "L'Association Canadiene Francaise pour l'Avancement des Sciences (AFCAS)", Montreal Canada, May 16-17, 1996.

[29] T.M. Pigoski, Practical Software Maintenance: Best Practices for Managing your Software Investment, Wiley Computer Publishing, 1996.

Model-Driven Engineering Support for Building C# Applications

Anna Derezińska, Przemysław Ołtarzewski
Institute of Computer Science, Warsaw University of Technology
A.Derezinska@ii.pw.edu.pl

Abstract – **Realization of Model-Driven Engineering (MDE) vision of software development requires a comprehensive and user-friendly tool support. This paper presents a UML-based approach for building trustful C# applications. UML models are refined using profiles for assigning class model elements to C# concepts and to elements of implementation project. Stereotyped elements are verified on life and during model to code transformation in order to prevent creation of an incorrect code. The Transform OCL Fragments into C# system (T.O.F.I.C.) was created as a feature of the Eclipse environment. The system extends the IBM Rational Software Architect tool.**

Keywords: MDA, UML, OCL, C#, model transformation, code generation, Eclipse, IBM Rational Software Architect

I. Introduction

Modeling at various levels of abstraction is viewed as an essential part of model-driven engineering approaches (MDE) [1]. The availability of good modeling tools can help to achieve this goal.

Model transformations are becoming more and more important in software development, particularly as a part of MDE. There are different kinds of model transformations [2,3]. According to the taxonomy given by Mens and van Gorp in [3] code generation can be treated as a vertical, exogenous model transformation. In a vertical transformation the source and target models reside at different abstraction levels. Exogenous transformations are transformations between models using different notations.

However, inconsistencies in models could make automatic code generation hardly possible negating MDE idea [4]. Moreover, only 15.6% of different solutions for UML model consistency management are suitably integrated with a CASE tool [4]. Therefore, developing a model-to-code transformation, we should assist a user in precise mapping between concepts of two abstraction levels and in verification of the model refinement and code generation process.

To solve these problems a Transform OCL Fragments into C# system (T.O.F.I.C.) was designed and implemented [5]. The approach is developed in accordance to Model Driven Architecture (MDA) [6,7], which is the leading MDE proposal. A UML model can be refined towards a model consistent to a given programming language, and then transformed into a target code. Code specific features are encapsulated in UML profiles [8].

End users may also want to enhance their models with more precise specifications, like class invariants, operations pre- and post-conditions. The T.O.F.I.C. system supports this features via transformation of a class model combined with OCL queries [9].

The system was implemented in full integration with an existing CASE tool - IBM Rational Software Architect [10]. The extension mechanisms of RSA were used as well as extensions of the standard development platform Eclipse Modeling Framework (EMF) [11,12] on that RSA is based. The current T.O.F.I.C. system version facilitates C# code generation from a refined UML class model and OCL constraints, and is a working prototype.

The rest of the paper is structured as follows: Section 2 describes briefly background and principles of the approach. Section 3 presents tool requirements. Technology and system architecture are discussed in Section 4. In Section 5 we present the basic steps of model-driven development using the tool. Finally, we make conclusions and suggest some future work.

II. MDA Vision at Work

This section describes basic MDA models and their relations (A) and other background of the approach (B). Next, the main principles of realization of MDA ideas are presented (C).

A. *MDA basic concepts*

The Object Management Group (OMG) developed a variety of standards focused on object-oriented systems and system modeling. OMG standards provide a foundation for Model Driven Architecture (MDA) [6]. MDA is an architectural framework that stimulates a software development approach by different detailed specifications. The key features are separation of different abstraction levels extracting conceptual models and descriptions based on virtual or specific technological platforms, as well as, integration of different solutions.

MDA recognizes several fundamental abstract levels, so called viewpoints, with corresponding models. Computation Independent Viewpoint deals with algorithmic issues and system requirements, regardless of structures and system processing. At the next abstract levels Platform Independent Models (PIMs) are developed. Their specification is relative to a set of features of different platforms and should be these features independent. Characteristics of a technological platform can be summarized building a Platform Description Model (PDM). Merging of the appropriate PIM with one of available PDMs gives a Platform Specific Model (PSM). It expresses the PIM model in terms of details of the target

T. Sobh, K. Elleithy (eds.), *Innovations in Computing Sciences and Software Engineering*,
DOI 10.1007/978-90-481-9112-3_76, © Springer Science+Business Media B.V. 2010

platform. The models can be further transformed to lower abstract levels and merged with another platform depended details. Relations between models are shown in Fig. 1.

B. Background

There are two main directions of research dealing with execution of models. In the first one, a model is run directly using a kind of virtual machine supporting abstracts of a modeling notation. The OMG developed Foundation Subset for Executable UML Models (FUML) [13] that defines a basic virtual machine for the subset of the Unified Modeling Language. The second direction tends to transformation of models into executable languages, mostly the known general purpose languages. In the later case, we can use the existing environments supporting further program development.

Numerous tools address the problem of model to code transformation for the commonly used languages, like Java, C++, C#, e.g. [10]. They mainly take only class models as a source, but code generation from behavioral models, especially statecharts, is also supported [14]. However, the most of the model to code transformations deal with general, may be incomplete, class models. Therefore the models and their transformations cannot be precisely verified, and an ambiguous or incorrect code can be generated. Even restricting to a class model, modeling concepts are comprehend and transformed in various ways, as for example an association [15]. PIM models that are the targets of an automatic transformation process [16] require also further user-controlled refinement in order to conform to platform dependant requirements.

One of MDE-based approaches is a code generation process that introduces an intermediate model level between UML models and code generations [17]. The simplified meta-model of the intermediate level is intended to simplify further transformation to a desired programming language.

A solution that provides the closest functionality to the proposed approach is Rational Modeling Extension for .NET [18]. However its usage has several limitations, including possibility of full modeling C# concepts or modification capabilities. The main drawback is weakness of validation facilities that are the crucial requirement for refinement of inconsistent models and generation of a trustful code.

C. Principles of the approach

The approach presented in this paper is realized according to MDA concepts (Fig. 1). It is based on gradual model refinement and model to code transformation. The main idea was the enhancement of general purpose UML models with features targeted to a selected programming language (C# in the discussed case). A refined UML model (Fig. 2) was a source for further model to code transformation. Therefore the model can be verified before and during transformation in order to preserve consistency between input model and the generated code and to check correctness of the output.

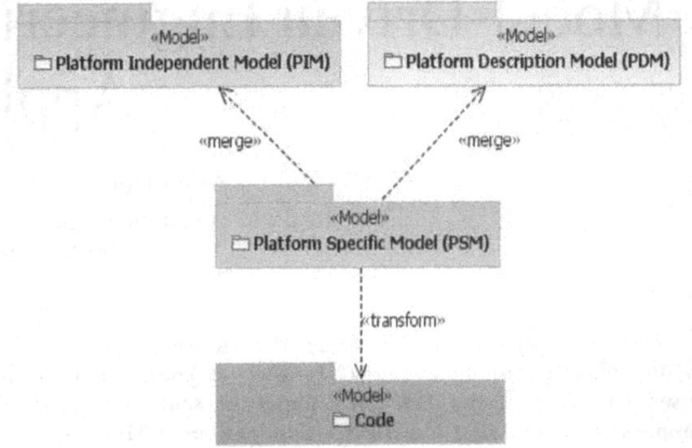

Fig. 1. Model relations in OMG MDA

Two kinds of refined models were distinguished: a code model and a mapping model. A code model consists of UML elements corresponding to elements of the target programming language. Mapping model depicts a structure of directories and files of compilation units. It defines also relations between compilation units from a mapping model and corresponding elements of a code model. Code and mapping models constitute input data for code generation.

These models can be introduced in UML using profiles. Profiles are the primary mechanism for defining domain-specific UML variant [1]. A UML profile describes how UML model elements are extended to support usage in a particular domain. UML model elements are extended using stereotypes and tagged values that define additional properties associated with the elements. However, the UML profile definition does not provide a means for precisely defining semantics associated with extension. To cope with this problem stereotypes were defined with their correctness constraints. The constraints help to verify whether a given stereotype can be related to a particular UML model element in a certain model context.

Two profiles were created. The first profile - *CSharpCodeProfile* is responsible for mapping of UML meta-model elements (in the current system version – only UML class elements) to corresponding constructions of the target language (currently C#). Apart from classes, methods and fields, appropriate stereotypes can specify that given model

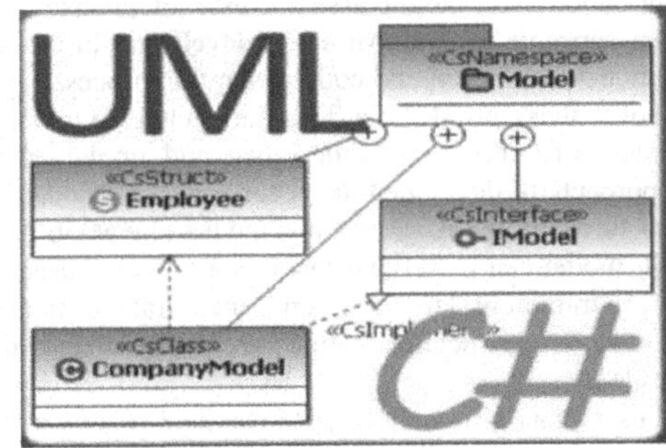

Fig. 2. UML model refined for C # target

elements should be recognized as C# properties, indexers, delegates, namespaces etc. For example, a stereotype «CsNamespace» can be added to a package defining a naming scope in terms of C#.

The second profile - *CSharpMapProfile* is used for modeling a file structure of an implementation project. It includes stereotypes identifying a main project directory, secondary directories, implementation units, etc. A main project directory creates a root element of the map model. A compilation unit can be mapped to an element of a code model element using «CsMap» stereotype.

Finally, CSharpPrimitiveTypesLibrary includes primitive types of C# language. The types can be associated to model elements (attributes, operation return types, parameters). They can be also used in OCL expressions. The library together with developed profiles constitutes a PDM in the MDA sense (Fig. 1).

In Fig. 3 and 4 exemplary class diagrams are presented. The first model, without stereotypes, can be treated as a PIM. The next one presents a code model. It is the same model after refinement using stereotypes from CSharpCodeProfile and types from CSharpPrimitiveTypesLibrary. The refined model represents PSM according to MDA.

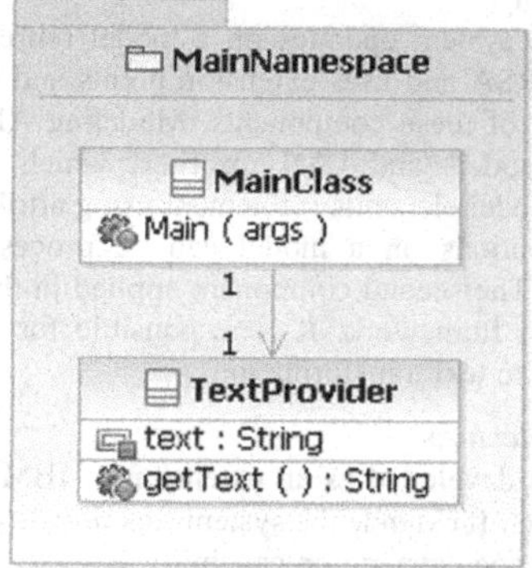

Fig. 3. PIM - class model

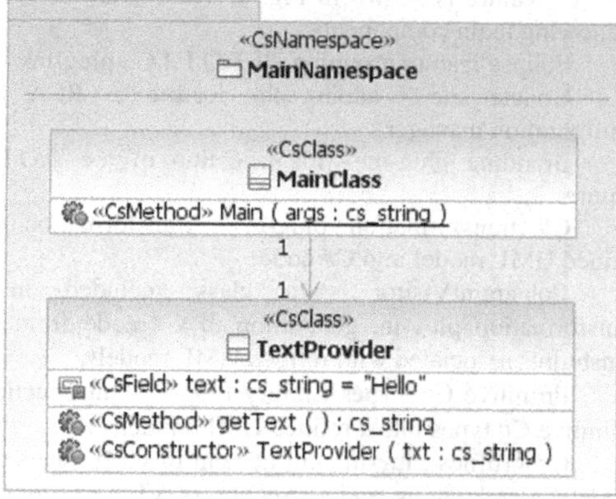

Fig. 4. PSM - C# code model

An exemplary structure of an implementation project is defined by a mapping model shown in Fig. 5. Two implementation units are mapped with «CsMap» stereotype to corresponding classes from the code model.

III. System Requirements

The main motivation for creation of the T.O.F.I.C. system was supporting of MDE ideas. This project was also motivated by:

- modeling with C# target, supporting convenient refinement towards C# applications,
- verification of a model refined for a target programming language, a facility scarcely supported by available environments,
- secure generation of a documented code allowing developers to concentrate on problem solving,
- utilization of the extension mechanisms offered by a CASE tool.

Analysis of the main system features and investigation of existing tools finished with conclusions that a high quality tool should meet the following goals:

1) UML modeling – creating of UML class diagrams with OCL constraints associated to model elements,

2) C# modeling – modeling elements of C# language and code structure using UML notation,

3) Modeling of file and directory structures – modeling of file trees and C# compilation items using refined elements of UML class model,

4) Model refinement – step by step gradual model refinement towards a final source code generation,

5) Verification of refined UML class model elements – checking if selected model extracts with associated OCL constraints can be a source for correct C# code generation,

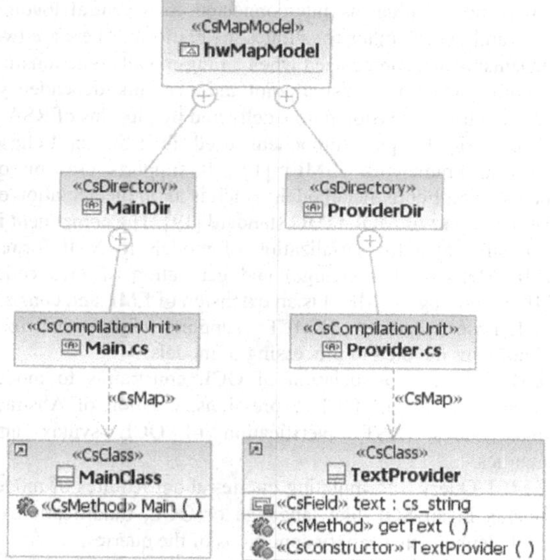

Fig.5. Mapping model.

6) Verification of files and directories – checking if a structure of created file trees and compilation items is correct,

7) Verification of OCL constraints – checking whether input OCL expressions (like class invariants, operation pre- and post-conditions) are syntactically and semantically correct,

8) Code generation – C# code generation based on dedicated UML class model elements and associated OCL constraints,

9) Selective code generation – code generation based only on selected UML model elements,

10) Complete code generation – all permitted C# constructions can be generated based on a refined UML model,

11) Correctness of generated code – a target C# code generated should be correct,

12) Error detection – a user is informed about detected errors in UML models, OCL constraints and during C# code generation,

13) Easy tool comprehension – understandable principles of tool exploitation,

14) Consistency with OMG specifications – support of current UML and OCL specifications,

15) Code readability – the appropriate structure of the generated code,

16) Intuitive user interface – ergonomic and easy to learn user interface, similar to other tools,

17) Compatibility and integration – integration with a given CASE tool, utilization and extension of its functionality.

IV. T.O.F.I.C. SYSTEM

In this section we present the main technology used in the system (A) and its architecture (B).

A. Technology

Extension mechanism of IBM Rational Software Architect [10] is based on capabilities supplied by the Eclipse platform [11]. A net of plug-ins interconnected to a central loading kernel and to each other constitutes the platform. There are two mechanisms that can be used when a plug-in calls functionality of another one: an extension point and a runtime dependency. T.O.F.I.C uses extension points delivered by plug-ins of RSA.

The basic Eclipse component used in RSA is Eclipse Modeling Framework (EMF) [12]. It supports creation of models using Ecore metamodel, which is an implementation of EMOF – a part of MOF OMG standard [19]. The component is responsible also for serialization of models to XMI format (XML Metadata Interchange) and generation of Java code. EMF Technology (EMFT) is an extension of EMF and consists of Eclipse features. EMFT supports following four technologies devoted to processing of models:

EMFT OCL – association of OCL constraints to model elements, parsing of OCL expressions, creation of Abstract Syntax Trees (AST), verification of OCL syntax and semantics,

EMFT Query – formulating queries about features of model elements in an SQL-like language or OCL, modification of model elements that satisfy conditions of the queries,

EMFT Transformation – processing of transactions in EMF model, parallel execution of various threads realizing read and write operations on the same model,

EMFT Validation – definition of constraints consistent with EMF, live and batch validation of constraints, support for a creator of parsers for constraints languages, declaration of an order in which model elements are verified.

Basing on EMF component, an Eclipse UML component was created in order to simplify model manipulation at higher level. Therefore a developer can create tools operating on UML models preserving consistency with the internal Ecore representation. Creation of a user interface is supported by two Eclipse components Graphical Editing framework GEF and Graphical Modeling Framework GMF.

IBM RSA uses EMF, EMFT, GEF and GMF components of Eclipse in its features and makes available for developers via its application interfaces. A developer can use several components to extend a system:

- Modeling API,
- Patterns framework,
- Transformation framework,
- Compare and merge framework,
- Reusable Asset Specification API,
- Plugets API.

The T.O.F.I.C. system operates on a model representation created by IBM RSA and uses extension points and packages delivered by two of these components. Modeling API assists creating UML models and UML profiles, which comprise stereotypes for model elements refinement using attributes and constraints. Operations on a model can be processed in a transitional way. The second component applied in the system is Transformation framework. It is responsible for model to model and model to text transformation.

B. System Architecture

T.O.F.I.C. was developed as an extension of IBM Rational Software Architect. It extends the system functionality with C# modeling and C# code generation capabilities.

T.O.F.I.C. was implemented as a feature of Eclipse platform available via an update site. A general structure of the T.O.F.I.C. feature is shown in Fig. 6. The feature consists of the following main components:

- Eclipse feature grouping all T.O.F.I.C. plug-ins,
- Update site - adding the feature to RSA using configuration manager,
- Branding plug-in - identification of the T.O.F.I.C. feature,
- C# transformation plug-in - transformation of a refined UML model into C# code,
- ConstraintVisitor - a class included in C# transformation plug-in, generation of C# code from OCL constraints associated with refined UML models,
- Primitive C# Types Library Plug-in - introduction of primitive C# types into a refined UML model,
- C# Profiles Plug-in - refinement of UML elements to model C# code items, and a structure of a file tree and a C# project catalogue,

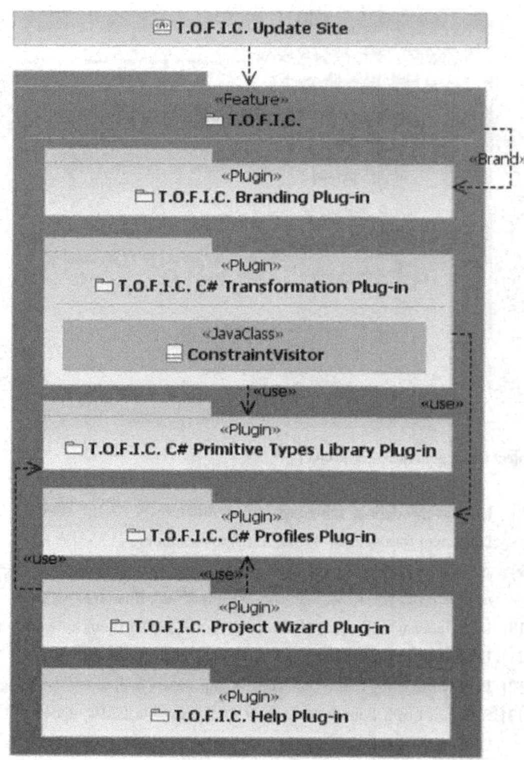

Fig. 6. System architecture.

- Project Wizard Plug-in - creation of an UML project adapted for C# modeling,
- Help Plug-in - extension of the Eclipse help system with T.O.F.I.C. users guide.

V. APPLICATION OF THE SYSTEM

This section describes how a user can work with T.O.F.I.C.

A. Basic activity flow

The system can be used for developing a model, refining it and building a C# application. The whole process consists of the following steps:

1) Project creation

A user creates a C# model project using the project creator. The names for a project, a code model and a map model are provided. T.O.F.I.C. generates the project using appropriate UML profiles and libraries. The project includes two models with «CsCodeModel» and «CsMapModel» stereotypes, and primitive types of UML and CSharp. In Fig. 7 the structure of a project is shown at the left hand side.

2) UML modeling

The user models a code structure using IBM RSA diagram editors. The UML diagrams are created. Class elements can be annotated with OCL constraints.

3) C# implementation structure creation

The user creates a structure of implementation project using UML class diagrams.

3) C# modeling

Available stereotypes and primitive types are used for gradual refinement of model elements. Relations between a map model and a code model are built (Fig. 5).

Steps 2) 3) and 4) can be fulfilled in sequel or in parallel. A general UML model can be created, further accompanied with stereotypes. On the other hand, stereotyped elements can be also created at the initial step, according to the user needs.

4) Transformation configuration

Having a completed model, the user creates an empty Eclipse project. A new configuration is build using the transformation management menu. The root element of the map model constitutes a source element of the transformation. The Eclipse project states as a transformation target element.

5) Code generation

Next, the user run the configured transformation and the corresponding C# code structures are created (Fig. 7).

The help system can assist in solving problems at any stage of project development.

B. Model verification

Proposed profiles include stereotypes with their correctness constraints. The constraints check dependencies between elements of a code model in accordance to the specification of C# language [20]. They verify also a correct structure of file and directory trees in a mapping model. Verification rules of each constraint are implemented in a dedicated Java class. A constraint has an associated key of an error message generated in case the constraint is broken. Error messages are stored in an appropriate file of the profile properties.

Preservation of constraints can be verified on user demand. Selected model elements are validated, as well as all elements included in the selected ones. Some stereotype constraints are also checked automatically after modification of a model. Model verification is also performed before model to code transformation.

VI. CONCLUSIONS

The paper presented the environment for building C# applications using MDA paradigm. The T.O.F.I.C. system is an extension of IBM Rational Software Architect. It can be used for modeling of C# code and project structure. The gradual refinement of meaning of model elements is made by utilization of dedicated UML profiles and a library of primitive types. A refined model is transformed into C# code. The system is easy to use thanks to full integration with the CASE tool, its modeling policies and interfaces, which are known to a user.

The main advantage of the system is its capability to precise modeling of detailed concepts of the desired programming language. The refinement process can be verified beginning from the early stages of system modeling.

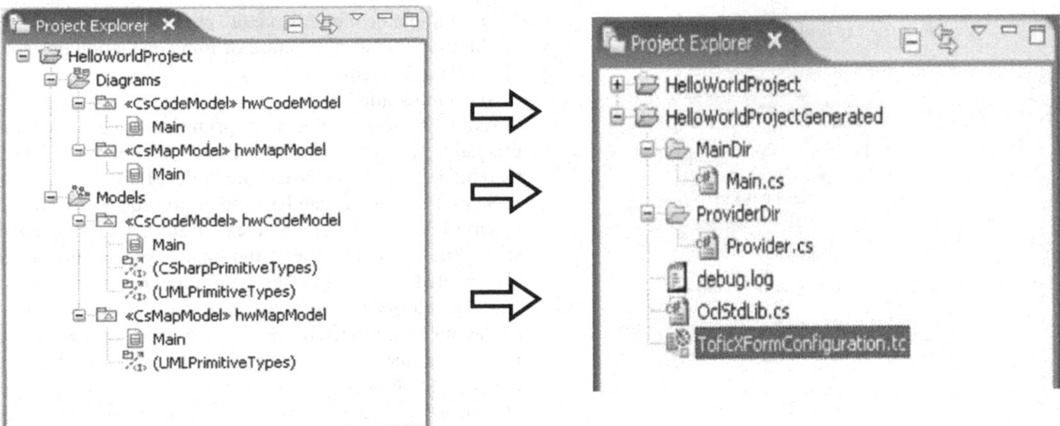

Fig. 7. Structure of a T.O.F.I.C. project and a generated C# project

The T.O.F.I.C. system is still under development. The working prototype will be extended with new functionality. The CSharpCode profile will comprise comprehensive set of C# language grammar constraints. The code will be generated for more language constructions expressed by appropriate stereotypes. Further development of the T.O.F.I.C system should take into account new versions of RSA environment and C# compiler. Another direction of T.O.F.I.C. development is extension of the OCL processing.

REFERENCES

[1] R. France, B. Rumpe, "Model-driven Development of complex software: A research roadmap", *Future of Software Engineering at ICSE'07*, IEEE Soc., 2007, pp. 37-54.

[2] K. Czarnecki, S. Helsen, "Feature-based survey of model transformation approaches", *IBM System Journal*, Vol. 45, No 3, 2006, pp. 621-645.

[3] T. Mens, P. van Gorp, "Taxonomy of model transformation", *Proceedings of the International Workshop on Graph and Model Transformation (GraMoT 2005)*, Tallin, Estonia, Sept. 2005, *ENTCS*, Vol. 152, March 2006, Elsevier, 2006, pp. 125-142.

[4] F. J. Lucas, F. Molina, A. Toval, "A systematic review of UML model consistency management", *Journal of Object Technology*, 2009, in press.

[5] P. Ołtarzewski, "T.O.F.I.C. Extending IBM Rational Software Architect with UML model refinement and C# code generation", Bach. Thesis. Inst. of Comp. Science, Warsaw Univ. of Technology 2008 (in polish).

[6] MDA home page, http://www.omg.org/mda/

[7] S. Frankel, *Model Driven Architecture: Appling MDA to enterprise computing*, Wiley Press, Hoboken, NJ, 2003.

[8] Unified Modeling Language Superstructure v. 2.1.2 (2007). OMG Document formal/2007-11-02, http://www.uml.org

[9] A. G. Kleppe, J. Warmer, *The Object Constraint Language: Getting your models ready for MDA*, Addison-Wesley 2nd ed, Boston MA, 2003.

[10] IBM Rational Software Architect, http://www-306.ibm.com/software/rational

[11] Eclipse Open Source Community, http://www.eclipse.org

[12] Eclipse Modeling Framework (EMF), http://www.eclipse.org/modeling/emf

[13] Semantics of a Foundation subset for executable UML models (FUML) 2008, http://www.uml.org

[14] R. Pilitowski, A. Derezinska, "Code Generation and Execution Framework for UML 2.0 Classes and State Machines", T. Sobh (Ed.) *Innovations and Advanced Techniques in Computer and Information Sciences and Engineering*, Springer, 2007, pp. 421-427.

[15] G. Gonzola, C. R. del Castillo, J. Llorens, "Mapping UML associations into Java code", *Journal of Object Technology*, vol. 2 , no 5, September-October 2003, pp135-162.

[16] O. Nikiforowa, N. Pavlova, "Development of the tool for generation of UML class diagram from two-hemisphere model", *Proc. of Inter. Conf. on Soft. Eng. Advances*, ICSEA, Oct. 26-21 Malta, 2008, pp. 105-112.

[17] T. Haubold, G. Beier, W. Golubski, "A pragmatic UML-based meta model for object-oriented code generation", *Proc. of 21st Inter. Conf. on Soft. Eng. & Knowledge Eng. SEKE'09*, 2009, pp. 733-738.

[18] L. K. Kishore, D. Saini, "IBM Rational Modeling Extension for Microsoft .NET", http://www.ibm.com/developerworks/rational/library /07/0306_kishore_saini/

[19] Meta Object Facility (MOF), OMG specification, http://www.omg.uml

[20] C# 2.0 specification http://msdn.microsoft.com/en-us/library/ ms228593(VS.80).aspx

Early Abnormal Overload Detection and the Solution on Content Delivery Network

Cam Nguyen Tan
Department of IT, HCM UNS
camnguyentan@gmail.com

Son Dang Truong
University Of Technical Education HCM
sontruongdang@gmail.com

Tan Cao Dang
Department of IT, HCM UNS
tan@hcmuns.edu.vn

***Abstract*-From articles of H. Yu Chen about early detection of network attacks [1], the authors applied his approach to Early Abnormal Overload Detection (EAOD) on Content Delivery Network (CDN) and suggested solutions for the problem, to limit abnormal overload to be occurred on a large network, ensuring users always being accessed to desired resources. Early overload detection mechanism are based on three levels: at each router, in each autonomous system domain (AS domain) and on inter-autonomous domains (inter-AS domains). At each router, when abnormal load exceeds a threshold, it will notify to a server that contains the Change Aggregation Tree (CAT) in the autonomous domain. Each node of the tree is an overloaded router above. On inter-AS domains, the CAT servers exchange information with each other to create global CAT. Based on the height and shape (dense) of the global CAT tree, the overload can be determined on which destination network and which user network caused this overload. Next, the administrator decided to move the content (as a service) which causes overload, to a user network. By this way, it prevents overload on intermediate and destination networks. This approach asks the cooperation among network providers.**

***Keyworks*:** Early abnormal Overload Detection, CDN, Overload

I. INTRODUCTION

CDNs boost rapidly Internet development. When the number of user requests to a particular content in a CDN increases suddenly, overload can occur in the intermediate or destination network. Currently, there are two major approaches to solve this problem: at the server that has content [2] or at the network that contains server [3]. However, limitation of the general solution is the overload happen before being detected. It's too late.

This paper refers to a distributed early overload detection method. It is able to detect which content network causes overload. On that basis the network administrators can actively transfer the content to near by user network.

II. THE RELATED RESEARCH RESULTS

The researches about network overload detection have been implemented with many different approaches and many specific results:

The approach to solve the problem at the local area network was done by the F5 company [3]. They implemented the system to detect overload and to balance the load by moving it to other servers in the same cluster. This approach is simple, easy to deploy, just configure in network where the content is contained on. However, this approach encounters a number of limitations such as only solve the overload network in the same cluster server. When there is overload in all servers in this cluster the overloaded is considered as happen on the load balancing device, the user can not access any more to the desired content.

In 2003, Matt Welsh and David Culler [2] offered a different model to solve the overload problem for Internet servers. The authors built the overload control system SEDA. It based on classification of data streams to the server and control the response time for each request. Results were showed very good when applied to the Arashi mail system. The advantage of this approach is simple, just deployed on the network containing the Internet server. The main limitation of this approach is only for single server and do not detect the overload earlier.

In 2007, C. Yue and H. Wang [4] proposed solutions of reducing load for e-commercial websites through protecting customer rights of the site. This approach is simple, but narrowly because it is applicable only to commercial websites. This approach only solves the overload on the server containing the website. This method is limited in the early overload detection before overload occurs.

In 2005, Gerhard Munz, et al, [5] offered a model to detect overload, called DIADEM Firewall to detect and control overloading at the web server. Strength of this solution rooted in collecting information about load of external network so that overload will be detected earlier before occurring on the destination network.

T. Sobh, K. Elleithy (eds.), *Innovations in Computing Sciences and Software Engineering*,
DOI 10.1007/978-90-481-9112-3_77,

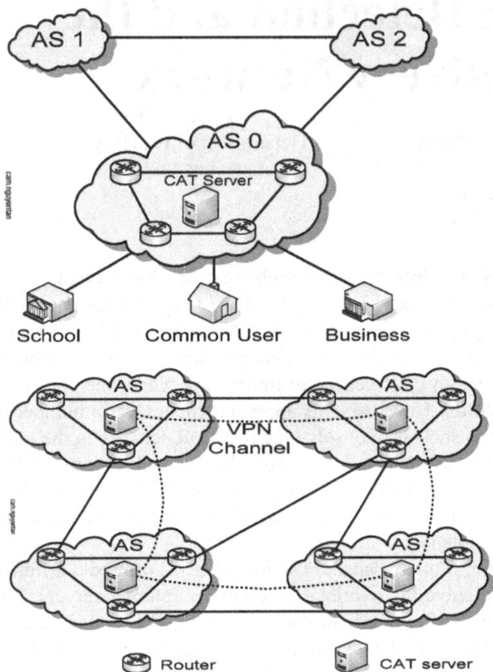

Fig. 1, The early abnormal overload detection system.

The EAOD problem and the early attack detection problem have the similarity. The early attack detection model detects the abnormal data stream on the destination network. This model can also be applied for the early overload detection model.

In 2005, Kim Yoohwan and et al offered the PacketScore model based on a statistical model [6] to control overload by DDOS attacks caused. Considering the flow of network packets to the network containing the information, this model classifies the data streams in two groups: attack streams and valid streams. Suspected attack stream will be removed. However, this method is a local solution at each router, lack of information on the domain and inter-autonomous domains.

In 2007, H. Yu Chen and et al gave the early DDOS attack detection model [1] by analyzing the rate of incoming and outgoing packets at a router between the continuous time slots. This model is only 1% false alarming.

Article about Early Abnormal Overload Detection is based on the idea of the early DDOS attack detection model above, but is improved and applied to build the early overload detection system at the destination network. By collecting information on packet stream at all routers on the network, the system can identify the router which has alert about overload state. Based on the distribution and number of alert routers, the system will determine which network is overloaded and which network causes the overload. Finally, network administrator moves content from the overload network next to the user network that causes the overload. From this moment accesses to the content will be redirected to this new position. The results are: the load on the old network is decreasing and the accessing to required content is still being met.

III. Early Abnormal Overload Detection System

A. *Early Abnormal Overload Detection Mechanisms*

The system detects overload by monitoring changes in abnormal network traffic at the routers on inter-domains. At each router on the network, if there was any abnormal increasing of the network traffic, it sends an alert message to the CAT server. The alarm information in each domain will be collected by the CAT server and it builds a picture of overload ability as a tree (called a CAT subtree). On the inter-autonomous domains, a similar structure called the Global CAT tree was constructed by CAT subtrees that was collected from the autonomous domains. Specifically, in each CAT server, two things have been done: (1) Posting CAT subtrees to another CAT server in the inter-domain, (2) Getting CAT subtrees from another CAT servers and built global CAT tree. Based on the height of the global CAT tree and dense rate of alert routers, the CAT server can know the overload occurred on inter-domains or not and the level of overload. Based on position of the root of the global CAT tree, the CAT server can know which the destination network causes the overload.

Fig. 1 describes the structure of the early overload detection system. The system is deployed on that inter-domain environment (domains AS: AS0, AS1, AS2). Each domain has a CAT server. The CAT server can exchange information with each other through a VPN protocol. In this example, the AS0 domain has a server, it manages alert message from four routers in the domain. The routers can be connected to the user network.

The architecture of the EAOD system was divided into three levels:

The router level: it works as a sensor, monitors network traffic through it. The sensor is operating under an algorithm [1], detecting abnormalities, if any, and sending alarm information to the CAT server when abnormal can lead to overload.

The domain level: based on alarm information received from a router in AS domain, the CAT server built into the structured database (called CAT subtree). It shows status and direction of the packet stream capable causing overload, passing through the domain. At the CAT server of each domain, the CAT subtree was built using algorithm 2 from [1].

Fig. 2 describes the CAT subtree that has R0 as the root. The tree is built based on the alert messages from nine routers.

The inter-domains level: the CAT server receives the current global CAT trees from other CAT servers, and then adds its CAT subtree into received global CAT trees to build a larger global CAT tree. If global CAT tree is large enough (about the height and density) to exceed a threshold, the system raises an overload alert on that inter-domain. If the global CAT tree is

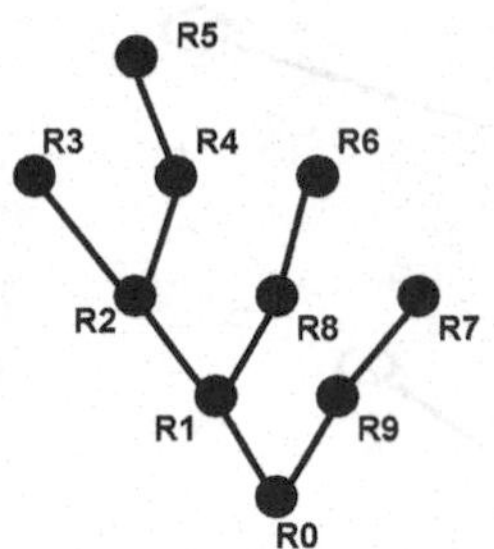

Fig. 2, The CAT subtree.

not large enough, the CAT server will send the global CAT tree to other CAT server. The process will be repeated until the global CAT tree large enough to exceed the alert threshold, or the defined time has expired and rebuilding a new global CAT tree. The global CAT tree was built using Algorithm 3 from [1].

Global CAT tree shows status of data stream which causes the overload and determines the overloaded network on inter-domains, and knows which network cause the overload.

Fig. 3 describes the global CAT tree that was constructed over multiple AS domains.

B. Early Abnormal Detection At Each Router

At each router, to detect the data stream caused abnormal overload, the system need to determine abnormal packet increasing and abnormal convergence of packet stream. When it is detected router raises an alert to CAT server.

Call $t_1, t_2, \ldots, t_m$ is the time separately, called the time slots (windows size)

x (t_m, i): number of packets going into port i in the time slot t_m.

The average number of packets estimated in the past, went to port i, at the time t_m.

$$\overline{X}(t_m, i) = (1-\alpha).\overline{X}(t_{m-1}, i) + \alpha.X(t_m, i). \quad (1)$$

With 0< α <1, if α is higher to 1, X becomes to the value of the current time slot.

S_{in} (t_m, i): the difference between the number of packet at current time slot and the above average in port i, at time t_m (Difference = | Current - Average |).

$$S_{in}(t_m, i) = max\{0, S_{in}(t_{m-1}, i) + x.(t_m, i) - \overline{X}(t_m, i)\}. \quad (2)$$

DFA (Deviation from Average): compared with the average deviation.

DFA_{in}(t_m, i): compared with the average deviation of the traffic to port i, at time t_m.

$$DFA_{in}(t_m, i) = S_{in}(t_m, i) / \overline{X}(t_m, i). \quad (3)$$

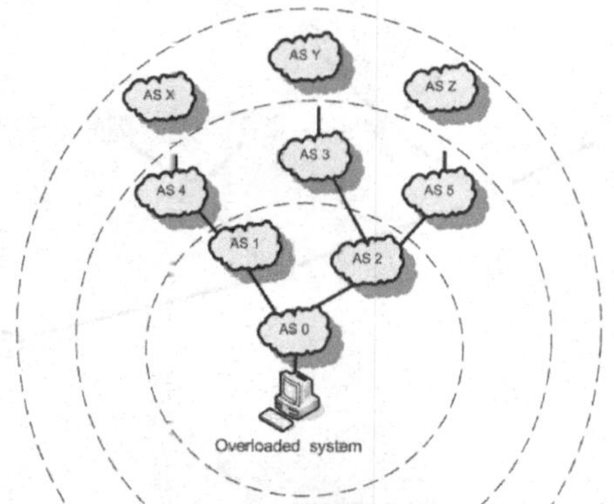

Fig. 3, The development of the global CAT tree through multi domains.

If DFA exceeds the threshold β, the router sends an alarm to the CAT server. Usually $2 \leq \beta \leq 5$

It is similar to the packets from the router.

y (t_m, i): number of packets from the router at port i, at time t_m

The average number of packets in the past, go out of port i, at time t_m.

$$\overline{Y}(t_m, i) = (1-\alpha).\overline{Y}(t_{m-1}, i) + \alpha.Y(t_m, i). \quad (4)$$

S_{out} (t_m, i): the difference between the number of outgoing packet at current time slot and the above average in port i, at time t_m (Difference = | Current - Average |).

$$S_{out}(t_m, i) = max\{0, S_{out}(t_{m-1}, i) + Y.(t_m, i) - \overline{Y}(t_m, i)\}. \quad (5)$$

DR (Deviation ratio): the rate of out /in packets at each router at the time t_m.

$$DR(i_{in}, i_{out}) = S_{out}(t_m, i_{out}) / S_{in}(t_m, i_{in}). \quad (6)$$

At each router, the system monitors the difference and the number of packets in a time slot at each I/O ports. There are many different situations for the difference between incoming packets and outgoing packets at the same router. We classify traffic patterns corresponding to the suspicious traffic at all I/O ports of the router. Each router has m incoming ports, n outgoing ports. We have 2^{m+n} traffic patterns. [1]

When the router detects DFA_{in} exceeded threshold β, router calculates the deviation between the incoming packets and outgoing packets at the same router, if the DR value closes to 1, the router believes that an abnormal situation was happen and sends an alert to the CAT server. Conversely, routers only send a normal report.

More detail in Algorithm 1 from [1] for local change detection at the router level.

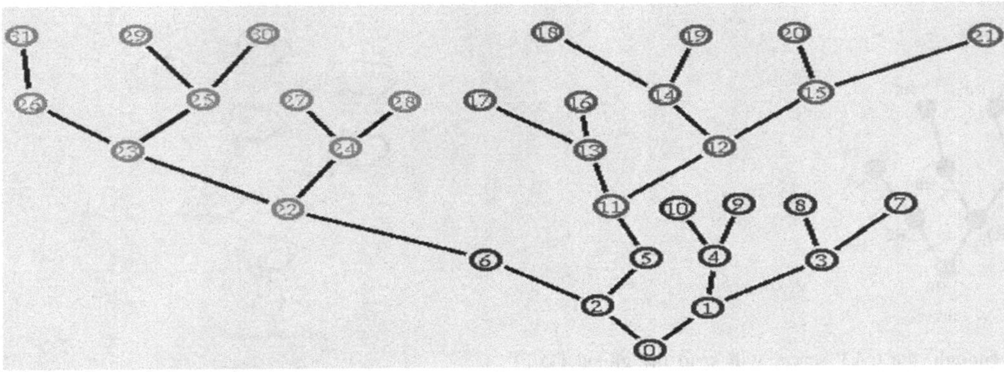

Fig. 4, Distribution of routers in the experiment.

Algorithm 3: **Global CAT tree construction and detection decision.**

Input: CAT subtree reports from participating domain servers, the server detection threshold θ, dense rate γ.
Output: The global CAT tree over multiple AS domains. Raise the alert for an imminent overload.

```
Procedure:
Construct the local CAT sub-tree (Algorithm 2) periodically.
Receiving sub-trees from other CAT servers
If local subtree exists, Then Check the superflow ID
    If this domain is the destination domain, Then Set distance r = 1
      Merge subtrees from domains at distance r to the current global tree
      r ← r + 1
            While{there are un-checked subtrees}, generate the CAT profile, CAT dense
                    If CAT profile>=θ and CAT dense>=γ then raise an alert for overload
    Else Check the root router position
       If root router is connected to other domain.
         Then Sent the global CAT tree to the destination domain server
Else Raise an attack alert based on the global tree merged
```

C. Early Abnormal Detection in Autonomous System Domain

In each domain, the system builds a subtree CAT in CAT server. Different subtrees are generated in multiple network domains. The global CAT tree is generated by merging all subtrees. The router reports the identifier of a super flow causing the traffic surge. Since all routers are under the same ISP authority and work cooperatively, each router knows their immediate neighbors. Using the reported status information, the CAT server detects the overload traffic based on the CAT tree constructed.

The alert message provides the upstream and downstream router identifier list to CAT server. Based on this information, the CAT server includes the alerting routers into the CAT subtree keeping the relative order among alert routers.

To indicate the location of a suspicious flow, the router identifier must be sent. We need to identify the super flow identifier of the n-bit prefix of the destination IP addresses. To construct the CAT, the status report provides the upstream and downstream router identifiers instead of router I/O port numbers. Using the reported status information, the domain server constructs the CAT tree gradually after receiving the alert reports from the routers in domain.

The output of Algorithm 2 is a single-domain CAT subtree. The CAT tree is specified by a hierarchical data structure. The root node carries the super flow ID, the router list the super flow passed through, root node ID, and the count of child nodes at the next level. See more detail on Algorithm 2 from [1].

D. Early Abnormal Detection On Inter AS Domains

The r is the distance from a domain to the destination AS domain (containing the content). Firstly, the system merges the subtrees from AS domains located in 1-hop distance (r = 1) to form a partial global tree. Next, it merges the subtrees from domains at 2-hop distance. The merging process repeats with distances r = 3, 4,…, until all subtrees are merged into the final global CAT tree or until the global CAT tree size exceeds the threshold. The overload detection can be completed before all the CAT subtrees included in the CAT tree.

We modified Algorithm 3 from [1] by adding the dense rate γ (CAT dense) as the additional criteria besides CAT tree height criteria to launch an overload alert or not. Dense rate is the ratio between the alert routers and total routers in the domain.

$$CAT\ dense = the\ number\ of\ alert\ router\ /\ the\ total\ of\ router. \quad (7)$$

E. Load Reducing

There are two ways for load reducing: move the content to user network and move the content to the intermediate network. The content is divided according to the following cases: 1) a digital content in a service on a server, 2) a service on a server, 3) multiple services on a server, 4) a service placed on multiple servers. Virtual servers allow cloning, copying, moving from one physical server to other physical server, this allows us to move a virtual server (contains content that cause overload) to near the user network when necessary. The network administrators should coordinate each with another to select the physical server to host virtual server and add to local DNS its new IP address.

IV. Testing And Evaluation

This paper mainly focuses on early abnormal overload detecting in CDN. We choose NS2 [7] to deploy the experiment, because it allows to modifying source code to add new module. It allows to tracing packet through over each router object. It allows to creating graph from trace file.

Experiment model consists 32 routers were simulated over 3 AS domains. The link bandwidth among the network domains was set at 100 Mbps. We use NS2 to create packet streams from the user network and generate different scenarios of abnormal packet increasing. To evaluate the method of the early abnormal overload detection we use different values of three parameters: time slot, the height of the global CAT tree and dense rate.

The various values of time slot are used: 100ms, 200ms, 300ms, 400ms, 500ms, 600ms, 700ms, 800ms, 900ms, 1000ms. As results in Fig. 5, the system detects well the overload when time slot is set as 500ms. System has total of 17/32 alert routers and only 7/32 false alert routers on inter-domains. The false positive alarm number increases steadily with increasing window size.

The various values of height threshold of the global CAT tree are set from 1 to 15 to check the accuracy of the system. According to the results in Fig. 6, the system detects a possible overload when we set height threshold of global CAT tree under 7. If the threshold is more height, the detection rate is deceased. If the threshold is more height, it is very difficult to reach to the abnormal status, so that the system can not raise the alert. Fig. 7 shows the false positive alarm rate against the height global CAT tree threshold θ. The number of alert generated by random fluctuation in normal traffic is small and negligible. With the height global CAT tree threshold is more than 4, the false positive rate drops to less than 1%. Thus,

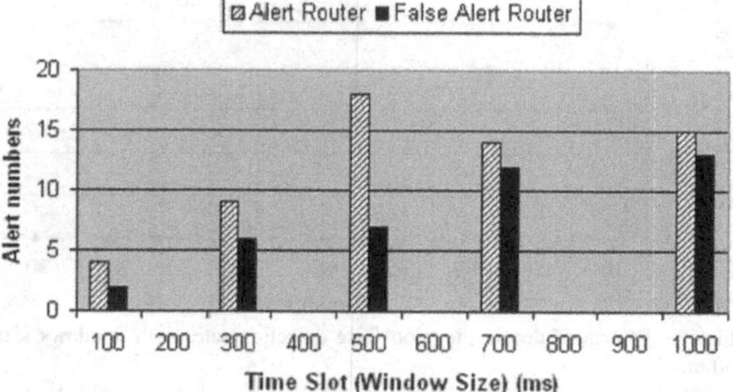

Fig. 5, The router alert number using various windows size.

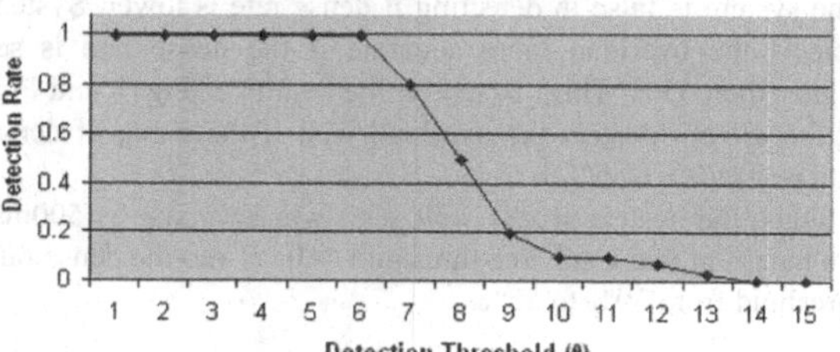

Fig. 6, Effects of server threshold on detection rate with dense of 54.8%.

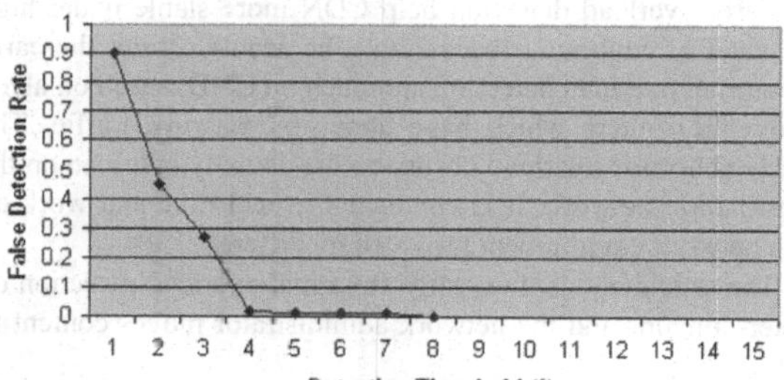

Fig. 7, Effects of server threshold on false detection rate with dense of 54.8%.

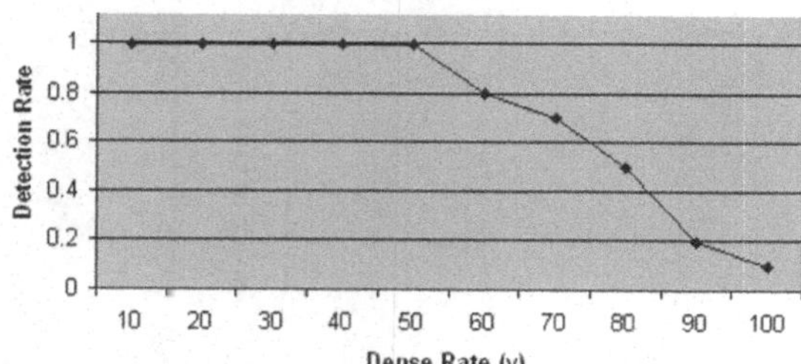

Fig. 8, Effects of dense rate γ on detection rate, with windows size 500ms.

based on the results of Fig. 6 and Fig. 7, the system detects the overload well if the value of height global CAT tree threshold is $4<\theta<7$.

The system detects the overload, if height global CAT tree exceeds threshold θ and CAT tree dense exceeds rate γ. The experiment was tested with different values of dense rate γ. According to the results in Fig. 8, the system detects the overloaded very well with dense rate less than 55%.

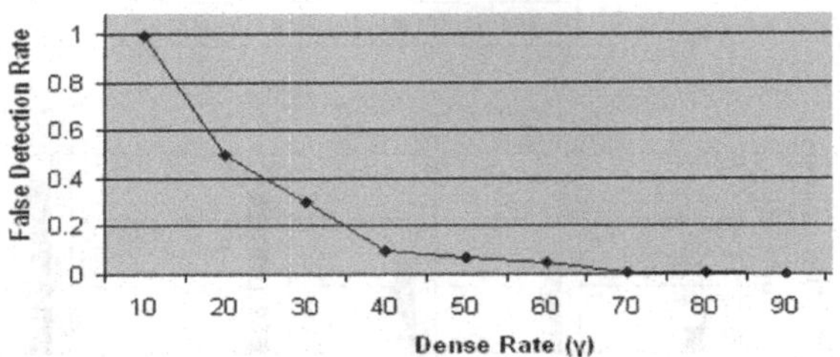

Fig. 9, Effects of dense rate γ on false detection rate, with windows size 500ms.

Fig. 9 is the result of false detection depends on the dense γ. The system is false in detecting if dense rate is lower. System detects the overload more accurate if the dense rate is set higher than 35%. Thus, based on the results of Fig. 8 and Fig. 9, the system detects the overload well if the value of dense rate is 30% < γ <55%.

Thus, the system works well with windows size is 500ms, the height global CAT tree threshold 4<θ<7, and the dense rate threshold from 30% to 55%.

V. CONCLUSION

Early overload detection help CDN more stable under high demand of continuous accessing. The article set out the early abnormal overload detection approach on CND, based on alerts from the routers which have abnormal network traffic. The early abnormal overload occurs before actually overload on the destination network. It is conducted in real time and work on the network environment provided by different ISPs.

The article only solves early abnormal overload detection on inter-domains and the network administrator moves content to near the user network. In the future, the system can be improved to be able to transfer content to near the user network when the overload occurs and able to choose right time slots automatically.

ACKNOWLEDGMENT

We would like to thank the members of the Grid Research Group, University of Natural Science Ho Chi Minh City, Viet Nam, who have contributed useful comments to complete this article.

REFERENCES

[1] H Yu Chen, Kai Hwang, and Wei-Shinn Ku, "Collaborative Detection of DDoS Attacks over Multiple Network Domains", *IEEE Transactions on Parallel and Distributed Systems,* 2007.

[2] M. Welsh and Culler D., "Adaptive Overload Control for Busy Internet Servers", Proc. Fourth USENIX Conf. Internet Technologies and Systems (USITS '03), Mar. 2003.

[3] F5 network solution company, *www.f5.com,* August, 2009.

[4] C. Yue and H. Wang, "Profit-Aware Admission Control for Overload Protection in E-Commerce Web Sites", *Proc.* 15th IEEE Int'l Workshop Quality of Service, June 2007.

[5] G Münz and et al, "*DIADEM* Firewall: Web Server Overload Attack Detection and Response", Broadband Europe (BBEurope), Bordeaux, France, December, 2005.

[6] Y. Kim, W.C. Lau, M.C. Chuah, and H.J. Chao, "PacketScore: Statistics-based Overload Control against Distributed Denial-of-Service Attacks", IEEE , 2004.

[7] Kavin Fall, Kannan Varadhan, "The ns Manual: The VINT Project, A Collaboration between researchers at UC Berkeley, LBL, USC/ISI, and Xerox PARC", http://www.isi.edu/nsnam/ns/ , February 10, 2009.

[8] H. Jamjoom, J. Reumann, and K. G. Shin, "QGuard: Pro-tecting Internet servers from overload", Technical Report CSE-TR-427-00, University of Michigan Department of Computer Science and Engineering, 2000.

[9] Guillaume Pierre and Maarten van Steen, "Globule: A Collaborative Content Delivery Network", IEEE Communications Magazine, 2006.

ECG Feature Extraction using Time Frequency Analysis

Mahesh A Nair, Member, IEEE
Electronics Engineering Department, Higher Colleges of Technology,
Abu Dhabi, UAE
Email : mnair@hct.ac.ae

Abstract-**The proposed algorithm is a novel method for the feature extraction of ECG beats based on Wavelet Transforms. A combination of two well-accepted methods, Pan Tompkins algorithm and Wavelet decomposition, this system is implemented with the help of MATLAB. The focus of this work is to implement the algorithm, which can extract the features of ECG beats with high accuracy. The performance of this system is evaluated in a pilot study using the MIT-BIH Arrhythmia database.**

Keywords: **ECG Beat Feature Extraction, MIT-BIH database, Pan Tompkins, Wavelets**

I. Introduction

The Electrocardiogram (ECG) is easily recorded using surface electrodes placed on the chest. From the signal, the heart rate (BPM) is determined by identifying the R-waves per time. Alteration of ECG wave-shape is a possible indication of the presence of cardiovascular disease. Thus, the proper detection and feature extraction of the ECG signal improves patient diagnosis. This paper presents an automatic system to extract the features of the ECG beats.

A. ECG Pattern

The ECG wavelet begins when the SA node (the natural pacemaker) fires and the action potential propagate through the atria and causes contraction of atria.

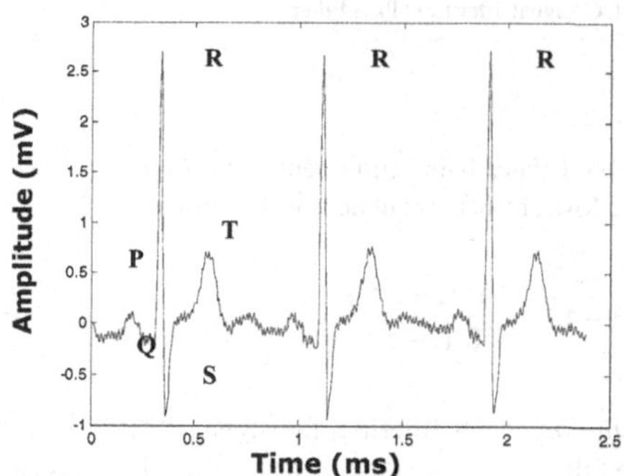

Fig.1. A normal ECG Waveform with P, Q, R, S and T waves indicated. R peaks of a normal ECG happens at equal interval of time.

This displays as the P wave of ECG, which is 0.1/0.2 mV and 60 – 80ms wide. This action potential reaches the ventricles through the HIS bundle, which is displayed as the PQ segment. When the impulse reaches the ventricles, the QRS wave of ECG (1mV and 80ms) occurs and results in contraction of the ventricle. The ST segment (100-120ms) following the QRS represents the duration between ventricular contraction and relaxation. Finally, the re-polarization causes T wave (0.2mV, 120 ms) [4]. P wave and T wave are weaker compared to QRS complex and hence more difficult to detect. The ECG signal is a combination of three different wavelets happening in sequential intervals of time.

B. Objectives

There are different types of ECG feature extraction methods available. Most use time based analysis for ECG detection usually based on signal derivatives. For better performance, the detection algorithm makes use of a time frequency analysis of the ECG wavelet using Short Term Fourier Transform or Wavelet Transform.

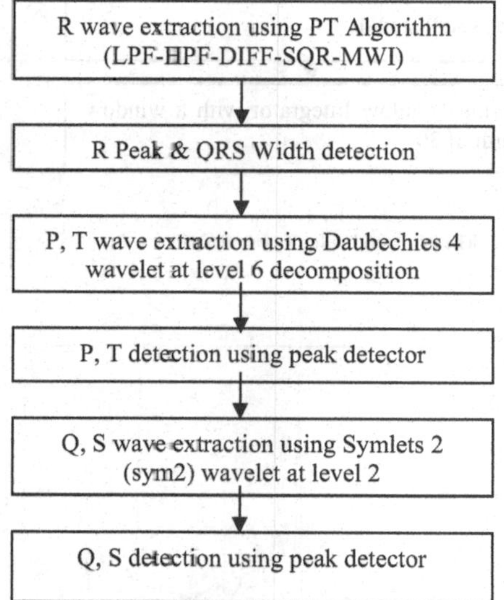

Fig. 2. The feature extraction process.

T. Sobh, K. Elleithy (eds.), *Innovations in Computing Sciences and Software Engineering*,
DOI 10.1007/978-90-481-9112-3_78,

The main objective of this study is to implement an automatic ECG beat detection system by combining Pan Tompkins (PT) algorithm and a wavelet decomposition in order to increase the accuracy of detection. Compared to the work done by Mahmoodabadi et. al [10] which makes use of Daubechies wavelet to extract all features of ECG, this method gives more accurate results as a combination of two well accepted algorithms with proven accuracy.

II. METHODOLOGY

The proposed method extracts the following features from an ECG Signal: R-Peak, P and T wave, Q and S troughs.
As shown in "Fig. 2", the R peaks are first extracted from the moving window integration results using a PTR algorithm. This algorithm detects the peaks and troughs of a given signal, for a specified period of time [6]. A work by Jung and Tompkins [7], uses Daubechies d6 and d7 wavelet for P and T detection. This system extracts P and T waves accurately with db4 wavelet at level 6.

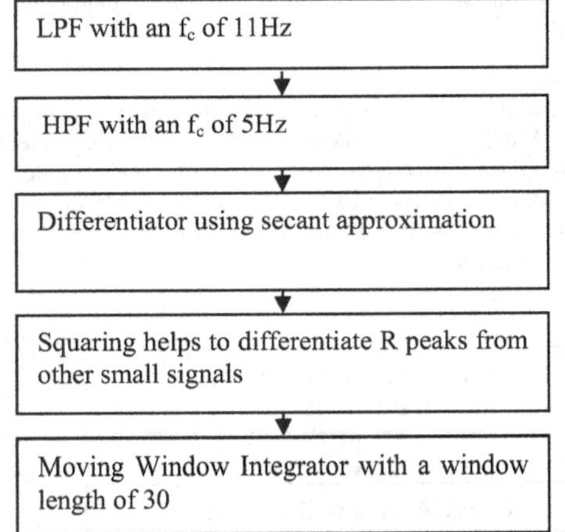

Fig. 3. The PT algorithm for R peak detection

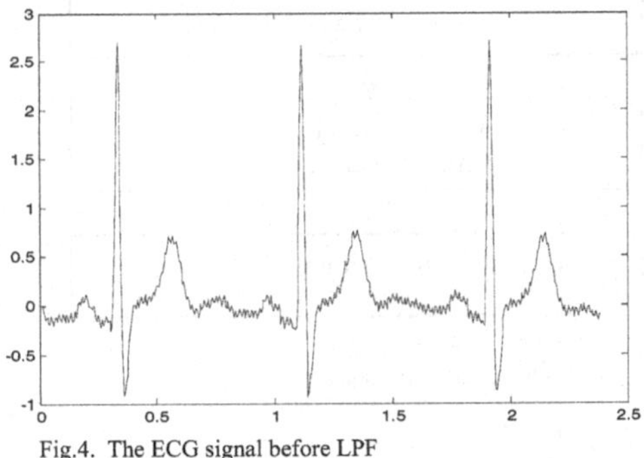

Fig.4. The ECG signal before LPF

A. R wave detection

In this system R wave detection is done using a MATLAB implementation of Pan-Tompkins algorithm [8]. PT algorithm uses a dual threshold technique to find missed beats and thereby reduce false negatives. This technique does not work if the heart beat is irregular.

Pan-Tompkins algorithm is a well-accepted method for R peak detection. "Fig. 3" shows the different stages for R peak detection. R peak is an important part of the ECG as it is the strongest signal and other waves are located on both the sides of R the Peak. If R peak can be located precisely, the process of feature extraction becomes easier [2].

Pan-Tompkins algorithm has a sampling rate of 200S/s and uses a LPF and HPF cascaded to make a band pass filter.

1) Low Pass Filter: The recursive LPF used in PT algorithm has integer coefficients to reduce computational complexity [4]. Equation (1) shows the transfer function of LPF.

$$H(z) = \frac{1}{32}\frac{(1-z^{-6})^2}{(1-z^{-1})^2} \tag{1}$$

"Fig. 4" and "Fig. 5" shows the signal at the input and output of LPF.

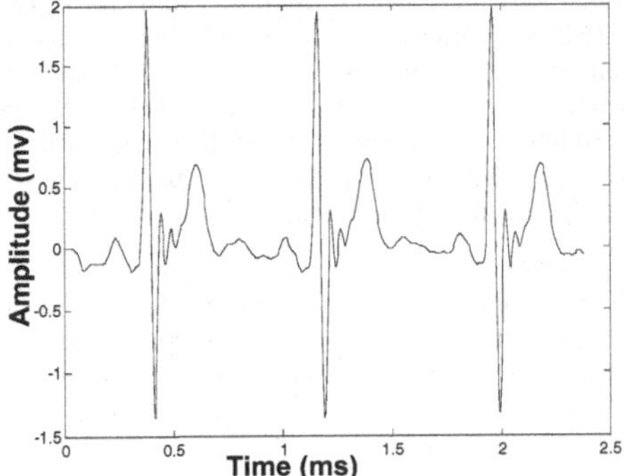

Fig.5. ECG signal after Low Pass Filter

2) High Pass Filter: It is implemented as an all pass –low pass filter. The low cut-off frequency of this signal is 5Hz.

$$H(z) = z^{-16} - \frac{1}{32}\frac{(1-z^{-32})}{(1-z^{-1})} \tag{2}$$

3) Differentiation: After filtering, the signal is differentiated to provide the QRS complex slope information. The derivative procedure suppresses the low frequency components of the P and T wave, and provides a large gain to the High Frequency components arising from the high slope of the QRS complex [4].

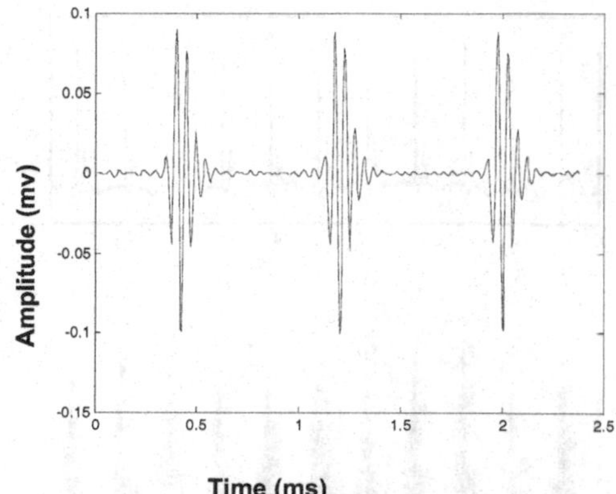

Fig. 6. The ECG signal after High Pass Filter

Differentiation is achieved using the secant approximation method and it approximates an ideal derivative in the range of DC to 30Hz, where we have the ECG information and suppresses the high frequency noise.

$$y(n)=\frac{1}{8}[2x(n)+x(n-1)-x(n-3)-2x(n-4)] \quad (3)$$

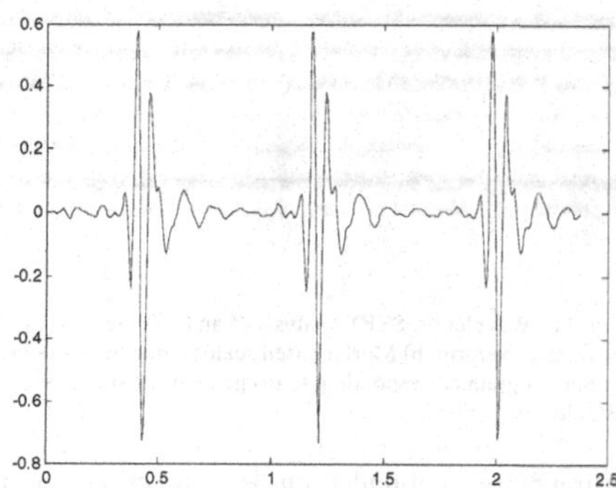
Fig. 7. The signal after differentiator

4) *Squaring:* The squaring operation makes the result positive, emphasizes the large differences from the QRS complex and suppresses the small differences of the P and T wave. It is obvious from the plots that QRS complex is comparatively high in frequency compared to the P and T waves of the ECG. Moreover, the squaring function enhances the QRS complex.

$$y(n)=[x(n)]^2 \quad (4)$$

5) *Moving Window Integration:* It is obvious from "Fig. 7" that the output from a derivative based operation exhibit multiple peaks within the duration of the single QRS peak. The PT algorithm performs a smoothing of these peaks with the help of a moving window integration filter as given in (5)

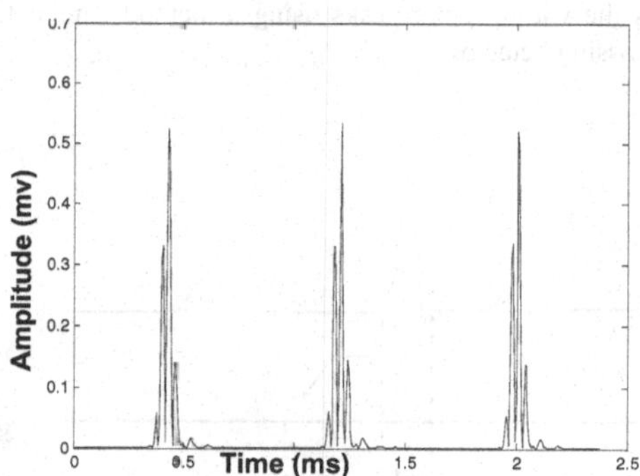

Fig. 8. The signal after squaring

$$y(n)=\frac{1}{N}[x(n-(N-1))+x(n-(N-2))+....x(n)] \quad (5)$$

A too large window size will result in the merging of QRS and T waves and if it is too narrow, some of the QRS complexes may produce several peaks in the integration waveform. For a sample rate of 200 Samples/s, the best window size is 30 samples wide (150ms). "Fig. 9" shows the result of MWI.

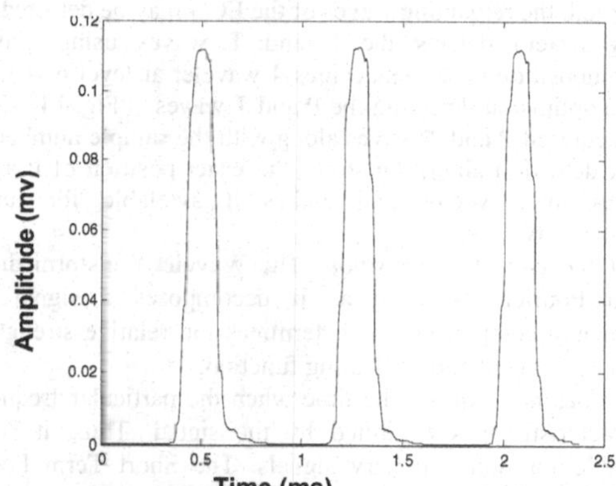

Fig. 9. The signal after Moving Window Integration. Width of these waves is width of QES complex and the Window size.

6) *R peak detection and RR interval:* From the output of Moving Window Integration filter, the R peaks are detected using the Peak detector algorithm [6]. Once the R peaks are obtained, the RR interval can be calculated by taking the average distance between them.

7) *QRS Complex:* The width of the QRS complex is calculated by using a function called "PWidth" which is applied to the signal shown in "Fig. 8". The 'PWidth' function returns the width of the peaks using a method similar to the zero crossing detector.

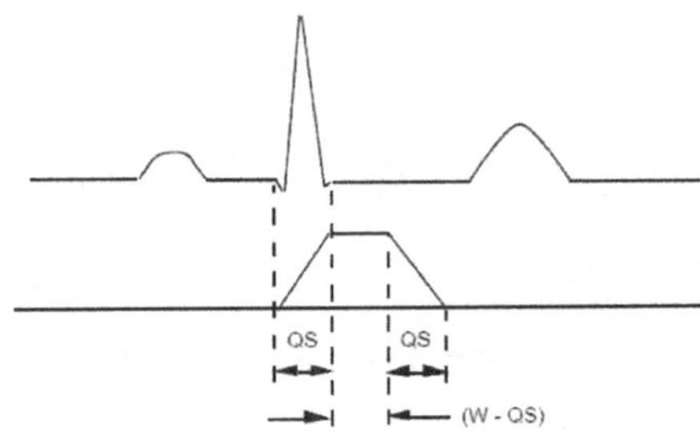

Fig. 10. Moving Window Integration result compared with QRS complex, PT Algorithm [4]

According to the Pan Tompkins algorithm, the width of the signal shown in "Fig. 9" is a combination of QRS + (W - QRS) + QRS. (Refer "Fig. 10"). Therefore subtracting W (the width of the window), from the signal width obtained in "Fig. 9" will give the QRS width.

B. P and T wave detection

PT algorithm accurately detects R peak and RR interval by reducing interference of other bio-potential signals from the body like EMG, and the AC line interference. It also suppresses the P and T waves. However, with the R peak detected, the remaining waves of the ECG may be detected. This system detects the P and T waves using wavelet decomposition. The Daubechies-4 wavelet at level 6 is found to be optimal at detecting the P and T waves. "Fig. 14" shows the acquired P and T waves along with the sample numbers. A peak detection algorithm stores the exact position of P and T waves in a vector and makes it available for further calculations.

1) Wavelet Decomposition: The Wavelet transform differs from Fourier transform as it decomposes a signal into frequency component and determines the relative strength of each component and its Scaling function.

It does not indicate the time when the particular frequency characteristic was exhibited by the signal. Thus, it is not suitable for non-stationary signals. The Short Term Fourier Transform (STFT) moves a fixed duration window over the time function and extracts the frequency content in that interval.

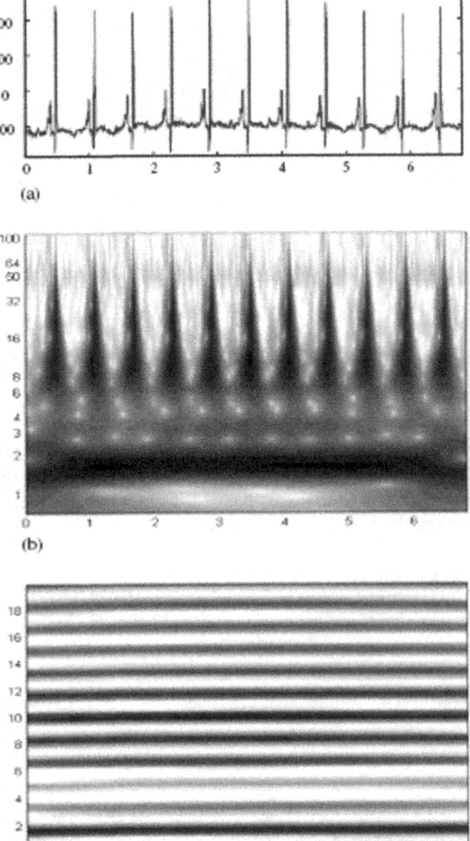

Fig. 11. Wavelet vs. STFT analysis of an ECG signal [12]
a) ECG waveform, b) Morlet based scalogram corresponding to (a), c) Spectrogram corresponding to (a) generated using 3.4s Hanning Window.

Wavelet transform is founded on basis functions formed by dilation and translation of a prototype function. These basis functions are short duration - high frequency and long duration - low frequency functions. They are most suitable for representing short bursts of high-frequency signals like ECG signals [5]. Even though STFT is also a time and frequency analysis, signal representation is superior in case of wavelet transform as it is a multi-resolution analysis. A detailed comparison of STFT and wavelets has been done by Vetterli et.al [9].

Incase of DWT, filters of different cut-off frequencies are used to analyze the signal at different scales. The signal is passed through a series of high pass and low pass filters to analyze high and low frequencies respectively.

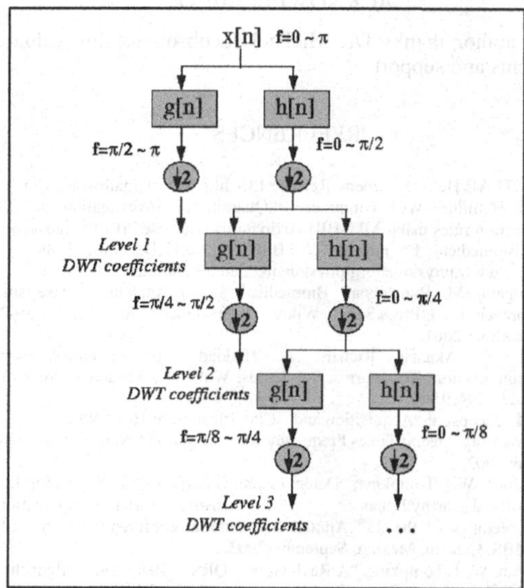

Fig. 12. Wavelet decomposition [13]

The resolution of the signal is changed by the filtering operations and the scale is changed by up sampling and down sampling operations.

Wavelet Transforms can be classified mainly into two: Continuous Wavelet Transform (CWT) and Discrete Wavelet Transform (DWT). The CWT has a variable window width related to the scale of observation and this allows isolation of high frequency features. Equation (2.6) defines the wavelet transform of a continuous signal x(t).

$$T(a,b) = \frac{1}{\sqrt{a}} \int_{-\infty}^{+\infty} x(t)\psi^{*}\left(\frac{t-b}{a}\right)dt \qquad (6)$$

Where ψ*(t) is the complex conjugate of analyzing wavelet function ψ (t), "a" is the dilation parameter of the wavelet and "b" is the location parameter of the wavelet.

"Fig. 12" illustrates this procedure where x[n] is the original signal to be decomposed and h[n] and g[n] are low pass and high pass filters respectively. After each filter stage, the signal has half time resolution and double frequency resolution. This procedure continues until two samples are left. The DWT of the original signal is then obtained by concatenating coefficients of all stages. The Daubechies wavelet used here are family of orthogonal wavelets defining discrete wavelet transform. The P and T waves of the ECG is clearly extracted at level6 of Debauchies4 (db4) wavelet as in "Fig. 14".

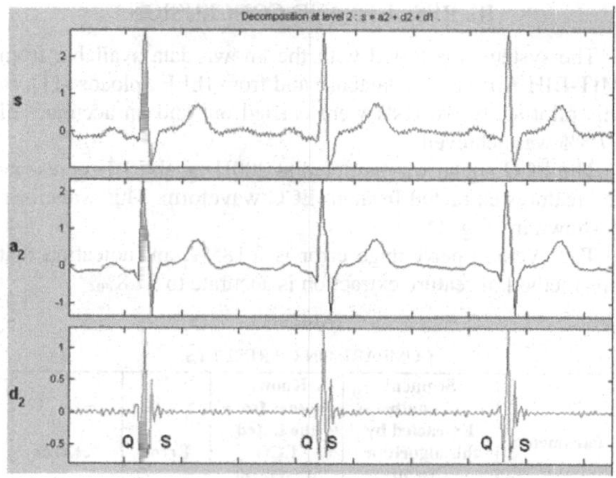

Fig. 13. Using Sym2 wavelet at Level 2 the Q and S waves are extracted from the ECG wave.

C. *Q and S wave detection*

We have so far detected P, T and R waves. For detecting Q and S waves, the system uses Sym2 wavelet at level2. It is found that the Sym2 wavelet brings out the Q and S wave very clearly as shown in "Fig. 13". The troughs detecting algorithm with refractory fetches the exact location of the Q and S wave from the decomposed signal and makes it available for further calculations. The vector having the positions of S wave is subtracted from the vector having the positions of T wave to obtain the ST segment.

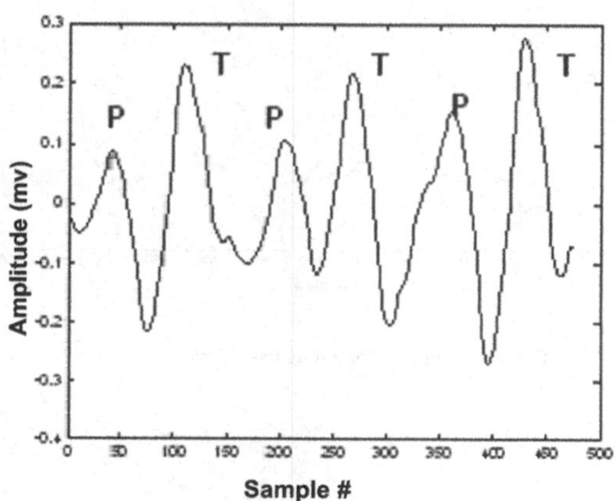

Fig. 14. P and T waves from wavelet decomposition (using Daubechies4 wavelet at level6). The position of the peaks of P and T waves are determined by Peak detector algorithm.

III. RESULTS AND CONCLUSION

The system was tested with the known data available from MIT-BIH Arrhythmia database and from IEEE uploads [11]. In this pilot study, 10 tests were carried out and an accuracy of 97.8% was achieved.

The ECG signal was sampled at 200Hz. Table3.1 represents the features extracted from an ECG waveform. This waveform is shown in "Fig. 15"

The average percentage error is 2.185%, an indication that this method of feature extraction is accurate to 97.8%.

TABLE I

COMPARISON OF RESULTS

Parameter	Segment Length Extracted by this algorithm (No. of Samples)	Known Values from the tested ECG waveform "Fig. 15"	Error	%Error
RR interval	158.0	158.5	0.5	0.32
QRS complex	15.0	14.5	0.5	3.3
PQ segment	16.6	16.6	0.0	0
PT segment	66.6	70.8	4.2	6.3
ST segment	46.3	45.8	0.5	1.0

The error is calculated by comparing the segment lengths obtained from this method with the actual lengths of the ECG signal used for the process.

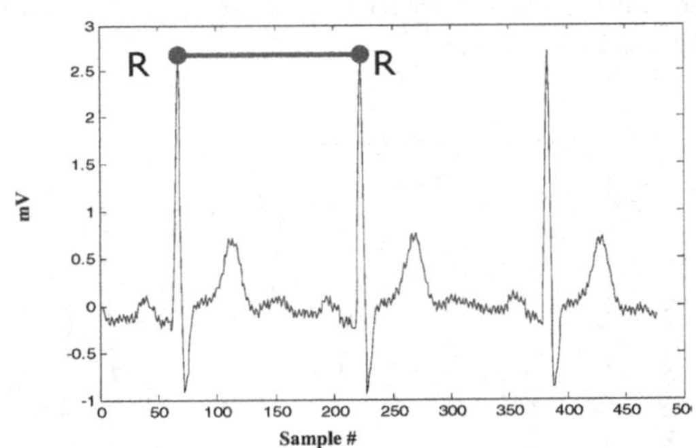

Fig. 15. The waveform used for testing this algorithm

ACKNOWLEGMENT

The author thanks Dr. Michael Jacobson for his valuable comments and support.

REFERENCES

[1] MATLAB Help Document, Release 13, http://www.mathworks.org

[2] P. S. Hamilton, W. J. Tompkins: "Quantitative Investigation of QRS detection rules using MIT-BIH Arrhythmia database" IEEE Transactions on Biomedical Engineering, Vol.BME-33, No.12,December 1986.

[3] http://www.physionet.org/physiobank/ database/mitdb/

[4] Rangaraj M. Rangayyan: Biomedical Signal Analysis-A case study approach, IEEE Press Series, Wiley Interscience Inc., pp 19-20, December 2001.

[5] Ali. N. Akansu, Richard A. Haddad: Multi-resolution signal decomposition -Transforms, Sub bands, Wavelets, Academic Press Inc., pp 292-296, 1992.

[6] M.L. Jacobson: "Acquisition and Classification of Heart Rate Variability using Time- Frequency Representation" Napier University, May 2003.

[7] Y. Jung, W.J. Tompkins: "Detecting and classifying life threatening ECG Ventricular arrhythmias using wavelet decomposition", Proceedings of the 25th Annual International conference on the IEEE EMBS, Cancun, Mexico, September2003.

[8] J. Pan, W. J. Tompkins: "A Real-Time QRS detection algorithm", IEEE Transaction Biomedical Engineering, Vol. BME-32, No.3, March 1985.

[9] M. Vetterli, C. Herley: "Wavelet and Filter Banks: Theory and Design", IEEE, Vol. 40, No.9, Sept 1992.

[10] S. Z Mahmoodabadi, A. Ahmadian, M.D. Abolhasani: "ECG Feature Extraction using Daubechies wavelet", IASTED International conference Visualization, Imaging, and image processing, September 2005, Benidorm, Spain.

[11] ftp://ftp.ieee.org/uploads/press/rangayyan

[12] Paul S Addison:" Wavelet transforms and ECG –a review", Institute of Physics Publishing, Physiol.Meas. 26(2005) R155-R99.

[13] Roby Polikar, Wavelet Tutorial: http://users.rowan.edu/~polikar/WAVELETS/WTpart4.html

Optimal Component Selection for Component-Based Systems

Muhammad Ali Khan[(a)], Sajjad Mahmood[(b)]
(a) Preparatory Year Mathematics Program, (b) Information and Computer Science Department
King Fahd University of Petroleum and Minerals, Dhahran 31261, Saudi Arabia
malikhan@kfupm.edu.sa, smahmood@kfupm.edu.sa

Abstract- **In Component-based Software (CBS) development, it is desirable to choose software components that provide all necessary functionalities and at the same time optimize certain nonfunctional attributes of the system (for example, system cost). In this paper we investigate the problem of selecting software components to optimize one or more nonfunctional attributes of a CBS. We approach the problem through the lexicographic multi-objective optimization perspective and develop a scheme that produces Pareto-optimal solutions. Furthermore we show that the Component Selection Problem (CSP) can be solved in polynomial time if the components are connected by serial interfaces and all the objectives are to be minimized, whereas the corresponding maximization problem is NP-hard.**

I. INTRODUCTION

The extensive use of software has placed new expectations on software industry [1] and there is an ever growing push towards software reuse. Component-based software (CBS) development is an approach that aims to move the software industry away from developing each system from scratch. It focuses on integrating existing *off-the-shelf components* to build a software system, with a potential benefit of delivering quality system by using quality components. The success of CBS [2, 3, 4] depends on the ability to select suitable components. An inappropriate component selection can lead to adverse effects, such as introducing extra cost, in integration and maintenance phases [3].

Nonfunctional aspects play a significant role in determining software quality. Given the fact that lack of proper handling of nonfunctional aspects [5] of a software application has led to a series of software failures (e.g. [6]), nonfunctional attributes such as reliability, security and performance should be considered during the component selection phase of CBS development. Its importance for CBS development is further highlighted as component selection is a complex and risk prone process. We believe that for CBS to become part of mainstream software engineering culture there is a need for component selection approaches that take into consideration the nonfunctional aspects of a system.

In this paper, we present a component selection approach that qualifies nonfunctional attributes of the system and helps system analysts to evaluate the suitability of a component for a software application. The *component selection problem* (CSP) is represented as a multi-objective optimization problem on a clustered graph, with nonfunctional attributes formulated as objective functions. We use metrics to quantify contributions of components and their associated interfaces to each objective function. A lexicographic optimization algorithm is proposed that generates Pareto-optimal solutions for CSP.

Our approach is more general compared to existing component selection techniques (for example, [7, 8, 9, 10]), as we make no assumptions regarding the nature of interfaces and our lexicographic procedure can optimize any number of nonfunctional objectives. Furthermore, we analyze the computational complexity of component selection in detail, pointing out both polynomially solvable and NP-hard instances.

The rest of this paper is organized as follows. Section II reviews related literature. In Section III, we model CSP as an optimization problem. Section IV describes the lexicographic multi-objective framework for solving CSP while Section V deals with computational complexity of the problem. We conclude the paper by outlining our contributions and future work in Section VI.

II. RELATED WORK

Most component selection approaches are based on system functionalities or system architecture [9]. Considerably less attention has been devoted to component selection based on desired nonfunctional system attributes.

Lee et al. [11] have presented a component identification algorithm with focus on high cohesion and low coupling values. For the component identification process, at first,

T. Sobh, K. Elleithy (eds.), *Innovations in Computing Sciences and Software Engineering*,
DOI 10.1007/978-90-481-9112-3_79, © Springer Science+Business Media B.V. 2010

architecture design is analyzed to identify the architecture layers and subsystems. In the next step, the subsystem dependencies are determined using sequence diagrams. The subsystems are re-organized to make subsystem dependency less complex. This re-organization of subsystems is performed by re-arranging classes among subsystems. After subsystems are re-organized, the clustering algorithm is used to identify components. In [7] an approach has been proposed which assists in selecting components by using a clustering algorithm based on a set of predefined rules and heuristics.

Simulation composability is another well-known approach to adaptable component selection. In [12] it is shown that the complexity of optimal selection of adaptable components varies from polynomial to NP-complete, and even exponential depending on our assumptions.

Haghpanah et al. [9] have formulated component selection in terms of a series of feature subset selection problems. However, they point out that incorporating nonfunctional requirements into their solution framework remains a challenge.

Our work is motivated by the need for a general component selection scheme that achieves the optimal trade-off among nonfunctional attributes of a system. The same problem has been considered by Sedigh-Ali and Ghafoor [8]. One of the limitations of their graph-theoretic model is that it only applies when all components are linked by serial interfaces. Furthermore, the problem was formulated only to optimize three specific nonfunctional attributes (cost, reliability and complexity). We also use a graph-based representation for component selection but contrary to [9], we do not assume serial interfaces and our lexicographic multi-objective optimization technique works for any number of nonfunctional attributes.

Recently, Vescan et al. [10] have formulated the component selection as a multi-objective problem. They use an evolutionary computation technique to select a set of components which can satisfy a given set of functional requirements while minimizing the costs associated with component selection. One of the limitations of their work is that component compatibilities and integration effort are not considered. We address this issue in the present work.

III. Problem Formulation

In this section we describe a general instance of the component selection problem using clustered graphs.

A. Assumptions

Suppose we want to develop a CBS with p system functionalities labeled 1, 2, … , p. We assume that for each required functionality i a set C_i of candidate components is available, each providing the same level of functionality i. We further assume that the sets C_i are pairwise disjoint, that is $C_i \cap C_j = \emptyset$ for $i \neq j$. Thus a candidate component can provide a single functionality only. We would like to emphasize that these assumptions are not oversimplifying and are standard in CBS literature [8] as they can be reasonably satisfied by choosing components of suitable granularity. Unlike in [8] we assume nothing regarding the nature of interfaces between components (although later on we shall see that the type of interfaces has a significant impact on the computational complexity of the problem). Finally let n be the total number of candidate components.

B. Representation

We represent the problem as a clustered graph $G = (X, E)$ with node set X and edge set E. Let $|X| = n$ and $|E| = m$ where $|X|$ denotes the number of elements in set X. A node x corresponds to a candidate component and the node set is partitioned into p clusters $C_1, C_2, \ldots, C_p$, one for each set of candidate components. An interface between two components x and y is represented by an undirected edge (x, y). We say that cluster C_i and C_j are *adjacent*, denoted by $C_i \sim C_j$, if components (nodes) in C_i and C_j are linked by interfaces (edges). We define an *induced subgraph* s of G as a subgraph containing all edges between its nodes [13, p. 49].

This graphical representation is similar to the ones given in [8] and [14] but is more general. The nonfunctional attributes of a CBS depend on the nonfunctional attributes of its components (nodes) and their interfaces (edges). Examples of such attributes include cost, reliability, response time and complexity of the system [15, p. 160]. We would obviously like to maximize the first two while minimizing the later two. A nonfunctional attribute can be quantified by defining a suitable metric.

Suppose that we are interested in optimizing the nonfunctional metrics $F_1, F_2, \ldots, F_r$. and numerical values of all metrics of interest are known for every component and likewise for every interface. Since we are formulating component selection as an optimization problem, we shall call $F_1, F_2, \ldots, F_r$ the *objective functions* or simply *objectives*, each to be maximized or minimized.

Let the metric $f_k(x)$ denote the contribution of component (node) x, if selected in a feasible solution s, to the kth objective function F_k and $f_k(x,y)$ the corresponding contribution of the interface (edge) (x, y). The component level metrics describe the role of each component in the system, while the interface level metrics encompass the effect of integrating individual components. For instance if F_k represents the cost objective then $f_k(x)$ is the cost of acquiring component x. Whereas $f_k(x, y)$ can be interpreted as the cost of acquiring middleware or the cost of developing the integration code internally for components x and y.

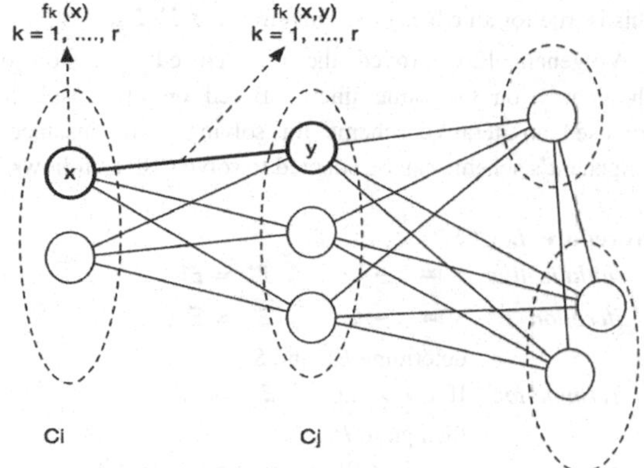

Fig. 1. An instance of the component selection problem

We remark that the values of component level metrics can be found through a variety of sources such as vendor specifications, black-box testing, simulation and extrapolating the market data [8]. The same applies to interface metrics if the integration code is obtained as middleware. For internally written integration code white-box testing can be used.

C. *Statement of Problem*

We can now state the component selection problem (CSP) as a multi-objective optimization problem (MOP) that asks for an induced subgraph s of G containing exactly one node (component) from each cluster C_i such that all the objectives $F_1, F_2, \ldots, F_r$ are optimized.

A typical instance of the component selection problem is shown in Fig. 1. Our approach to solving CSP is described in the next section.

IV. SOLVING COMPONENT SELECTION PROBLEM AS MOP

Compared to single objective optimization problems, solving MOPs require more sophisticated techniques as we try to strike an optimal balance among different objective functions. Instead of looking for a single optimum we have to search for the *Pareto front* (also known as *Pareto set*) which is the set of non-dominated solutions that cannot be improved in one objective without worsening another [16, p. 19]. Several methods are known to achieve this such as lexicographic multi-objective optimization (LMO), aggregate objective function (AOF) method, goal programming (GP) and evolutionary multi-objective optimization (EMO). Although evolutionary algorithms have been preferred in recent literature on component selection [9, 10], we adopt LMO based on following grounds:

- Evolutionary algorithms (EAs) are problem independent and thus provide little insight into the nature and complexity of the problem. Furthermore theories explaining how EAs perform are few and only recently some progress has been made on rigorously analyzing the computational complexity of EAs [17].
- Goal programming is attractive for its ease of implementation. However it is known to produce solutions that are not Pareto efficient [18].
- Despite the fact that AOF method is probably the most intuitive multi-objective optimization method it suffers from several drawbacks. Firstly by combining different objective functions into a single AOF the multi-objective nature of the problem is lost. Secondly most AOF techniques such as the weighted-sum method tend to be highly subjective. Last but not the least AOF methods fail when the Pareto front is concave [19].
- An LMO scheme orders the solution vectors lexicographically according to a priority ranking of objectives. The LMO optimizes a first objective and then as far as a choice remains a second one and so on. The kth objective in the ranking is considered only after the prior $k-1$ objectives have been successively optimized. LMO is subjective as it depends on a priority ranking. However, this approach lends itself to component selection problem as nonfunctional software attributes are always subject to stakeholder's priorities. A domain expert plays an important role in assessing the relative importance of nonfunctional attributes of interest and can prioritize the objectives accordingly. Moreover, LMO always produces Pareto-optimal solutions [16, p. 135], it is fast and allows a rigorous computational complexity analysis (refer to Section V for details).

In this paper, our proposed LMO solution is inspired by Volgenant's work [20]. We have selected Volgenant method as it is particularly suitable for shortest path type problems; and many special instances of component selection problem are multi-objective variants of the shortest path problem.

A. *The Lexicographic Approach*

All objectives considered in this paper are *sum objectives*. A sum objective F can be expressed mathematically as $F = \sum_s f$, where $\sum_s f$ is the sum of contributions to the objective F of all components and interfaces occurring in a feasible solution s. Many objectives that do not appear to be sum objectives can be represented in this way. For instance an objective of the form $F = \prod_s f$, where every $f > 0$, can be transformed into an equivalent sum objective

$$\log(F) = \Sigma_s \log(f).$$

We point out that restricting to sum objectives does not result in a significant loss of generality as most nonfunctional software attributes fall in this category (e.g., cost, response time and complexity are sum objectives while reliability can also be expressed as a sum objective).

Recall that an instance of CSP consists of a clustered graph $G = (X, E)$ with node set X partitioned into p clusters $C_1, C_2, \ldots, C_p$, edge set E and a series of (sum) objective functions $F_1, F_2, \ldots, F_r$, each to be maximized or minimized. A feasible solution is an induced subgraph s of G containing exactly one node from each cluster. For each component (node) x the values $f_1(x)$, $f_2(x)$, …, $f_r(x)$ are known and likewise for each interface (edge) (x, y).

Let F be an objective of interest (one of $F_1, F_2, \ldots, F_r$) for the above CSP instance Let $S(E)$ denote the set of feasible solutions and $S^*(E)$ the set of optimal solution over the edge set E for the objective function F. We introduce the quantities

$$\delta(x, y) = \begin{cases} 1 & \text{if the egde } (x, y) \text{ does not occur in any optimal solution of objective } F \\ 0 & \text{otherwise} \end{cases}$$

If $\delta(x, y) = 0$ then the optimal value of objective function F remains unchanged under the additional constraint that (x, y) must occur in an optimal solution. We now define

$$E^* = \{(x, y) \mid \delta(x, y) = 0\}.$$

We observe that E^* is the union of edge sets of all optimal solutions of F. Let G^* be the graph with edge set E^* and node set X^* consisting of end nodes of edges in E^*. Then G^* is also a clustered graph with p clusters. We further note that G^* is completely determined by its edge set E^* so it suffices to consider E^* only.

The next theorem shows that for any objective F the set of optimal solutions over E is equal to the set of feasible solutions over E^*.

Theorem 1 For a given objective F we have $S^*(E) = S(E^*)$.

Proof. Suppose an optimal solution $s^* \in S^*(E)$ contains an edge (x, y) with $(x, y) \notin E^*$. Then $\delta(x, y) = 1$ and the solution s^* can be improved by replacing the edge (x, y) with a better alternative. This contradicts the optimality of s^*. Thus s^* only contains edges from E^*.

Conversely assume that a feasible solution $s \in S(E^*)$ contains an edge (x, y). Then $(x, y) \in E^*$ and so $\delta(x, y) = 0$. This is true for all edges of s. Therefore $s \in S^*(E)$.

Volgenant [20] proved the directed edge version of Theorem 1 on the same lines. Based on this result he proposed an iterative scheme for solving LMO instances. Volgenant's scheme can be adapted to solve CSP as follows:

Procedure: *Lex CSP*

Initialization	$k := r + 1;$	$E^*_k := E;$
Iteration	$k := k - 1;$	$E_k := E^*_{k+1}$
	determine E_k^* and $S^*(E_k)$	
Termination	If $k > 1$ and $\lvert S^*(E_k)\rvert > 1$	
	then go to *Iteration*	
	else the CSP instance has been solved.	

It must be noted that the objectives should be arranged in ascending order of priority with F_r being the most important. The procedure starts with the edge set E and successively reduces it ($E \supseteq E_r^* \supseteq E_{r-1}^* \supseteq \cdots \supseteq E_1^*$) until either all objectives are optimized ($k = 1$) or there is only one solution left ($\lvert S^*(E_k)\rvert = 1$).

B. *Optimizing Individual Objectives*

Every iteration of the above procedure corresponds to maximizing or minimizing a single objective F over an undirected clustered graph $G = (X, E)$ with node clusters $C_1, \ldots, C_p$. We can formulate this single objective optimization problem as a {0, 1}-integer linear program (ILP) by introducing the variables

$$u(x) = \begin{cases} 1 & \text{if node } x \text{ is selected} \\ 0 & \text{otherwise} \end{cases}$$

$$v(x, y) = \begin{cases} 1 & \text{if edge } (x, y) \text{ is selected} \\ 0 & \text{otherwise} \end{cases}$$

The linear programing relaxation of the resulting ILP can be solved by a suitable branch and bound algorithm.

V. Computational Complexity And NP-hardness

The run time complexity of *Lex CSP* procedure developed in Section III depends on how fast the quantities δ and the edge set E_k^* can be determined during an iteration.

Using the notation of [20] let $T(n, m)$ be the time to solve a single objective CSP on n nodes and m edges. Given an edge (x,y) we can calculate $\delta(x,y)$ by solving the single objective CSP under the restriction that (x,y) must appear in an optimal solution. The restricted problem can be solved in time $T(n-2, m-1)$ as two nodes and one edge have been fixed. If the optimal objective value of the restricted problem is the same as the original problem then $\delta(x,y)=0$; otherwise $\delta(x,y)=1$. Hence the set E_k^* can be determined in time $T(n,m)+O(m)T(n-2,m-1)$. For most practical applications the complexity is dominated by the term $T(n,m)$. The running time of *Lex CSP* is therefore $O(r)T(n,m)$ where r is the number of objectives.

A. The Case of Serial Interfaces

The run time $T(n,m)$ strongly depends on the nature of component interfaces; and also on whether the objective is being maximized or minimized. An important special case of CSP occurs when the components are connected by serial interfaces [8] (see Fig.2.).

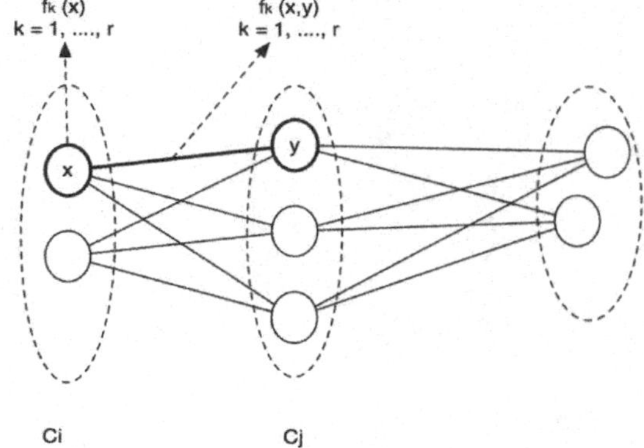

Fig. 2. Component selection problem with serial interfaces

Under this assumption the single objective minimization CSP reduces to a variant of all pairs shortest path problem that can be solved by a Floyd-Warshall type algorithm in time $T(n,m)=O(n^3)$. Thus if all objectives are to be minimized, the *Lex CSP* procedure solves the multi-objective CSP in time at most $O(rn^3)$.

The single objective maximization CSP is much harder to solve as it is equivalent to the all pairs longest path problem which is known to be NP-hard.

Therefore we conclude that the multi-objective minimization CSP can be solved in polynomial time if the components are connected through serial interfaces; while the corresponding maximization CSP is NP-hard.

VI. Concluding Remarks

In this paper, we have presented a new technique for component selection that guides system analysts through a process of identifying suitable components that optimize one or more nonfunctional attributes of a CBS. We formulate component selection as a lexicographic multi-objective optimization problem, with an aim to optimize nonfunctional objectives, and present an efficient solution scheme. The proposed model guides selection by identifying components that will collectively achieve the best tradeoff among the metrics desired for the system. This technique results in a quality management method that can alleviate concerns regarding uncertainty in the cost and quality of a component-based system. The complexity of component selection problem has also been examined extensively.

In future, there is a need to have an integrated requirements analysis and component selection process that analyzes both functional and nonfunctional system requirements and extends the presented technique to select optimal set of components. We also plan to conduct an empirical study to better understand the benefits and limitations of our component selection process for a CBS.

Acknowledgment

The authors would like to thank King Fahd University of Petroleum and Minerals, Dhahran, Saudi Arabia for continuous support in research.

References

[1] S. Mahmood, R. Lai, Y. S. Kim, J. H. Kim, S. C. Park and H. S. Oh, "A survey of component based system quality assurance and assessment," *Information and Software Technology*, vol. 47, pp. 693 – 707, 2005.

[2] N. A. Maiden and C. Ncube, "Acquiring COTS software selection requirements," *IEEE Software*, vol. 15, pp. 46 – 56, 1998.

[3] K. R. P. H. Leung and H. K. N. Leung, "On the efficiency of domain based COTS product selection method," *Information and Software Technology*, vol. 44, pp. 703 – 715, 2002.

[4] C. Alves and A. Finkelstein, "Investigating conflicts in COTS decision making," *International Journal of Software Engineering and Knowledge Engineering*, vol. 13, pp. 1 – 21, 2003.

[5] L. M. Cysneiros and J. C. S, Leite, "Nonfunctional requirements: from elicitation to conceptual models," *IEEE Transactions on Software Engineering*, vol. 30, pp. 328 - 350, 2004.

[6] A. Finkelstein and J. Dowell, "A comedy of errors: the London ambulance service case study," *Proc. of Eight International Workshop on Software, Specification and Design*, pp. 2 - 5, 1996.

[7] H. Jain, N. Chalimeda, N. Ivaturia and B. Reddy, "Business component identification: a formal approach," *Proc. of Fifth International Conference on Enterprise Distributed Object Computing*, pp. 183 - 187, 2001.

[8] S. Sedigh-Ali, and A. Ghafoor, "A graph-based model for component-based software development", *Proc. of the 10th IEEE Workshop on Object-Oriented Real-Time Dependable Systems*, 2005.

[9] N. Hagpanah, S. Moaven, J. Haibibi, M. Kargar and S. H. Yaganeh, "Approximation algorithm for software component selection problem," *Proc. of 14th Asia Pacific Software Engineering Conference*, pp. 159 - 166, 2007.

[10] A. Vescan, C. Grosan and H. F. Pop, "Evolutionary algorithms for the component selection problem," *Proc. of 19th International Conference on Database and Expert Systems Application*, pp. 509 - 513, 2008.

[11] J. K. Lee, S. J. Jung, S. D. Kim, W. H. Jang and D. H. Ham, "Component identification method with coupling and cohesion," *Proc. of Eight Asia Pacific Software Engineering Conference*, pp. 79 - 86, 2001.

[12] R. G. Bartholet, D. C. Brogan and P. F. Reynolds, "The computational complexity of component selection in simulation reuse," *Proc. of the 2005 Winter Simulation Conference*, pp. 2472 - 2481, 2005.

[13] J. Gross and J. Yellen, *Graph Theory and its Applications*, FL: CRC Press Inc., 1999.

[14] S. Krishnamurthy and A. Mathur, "On the estimation of reliability of a software system using reliabilities of its components," In *Proc. of the 8th Int'l Symp. on Software Reliability Eng. (ISSRE '97)*, 1997.

[15] L. Chung, B.A. Nixon, E. Yu and J. Mylopoulos, *Non-functional Requirements in Software Engineering*, Kluwer International Series in Software Engineering Vol. 5, Kluwer Academic Publishers, 2000.

[16] M. Ehrgott, *Multicriteria Optimization*, Lecture Notes in Economics and Mathematical Systems (no. 491), Berlin: Springer-Verlag, 2000.

[17] P. S. Oliveto, J. He, and X. Yao, "Time complexity of evolutionary algorithms for combinatorial optimization: A decade of results," *International Journal of Automation and Computing*, vol. 4, pp. 281-293, 2007.

[18] Caballero R., L. Rey and F. Ruiz, "Determination of Satisfying and Efficient Solutions in Convex Multiobjective Programming," *Optimization,* vol. 37, no. 2, pp. 125-137, 1996.

[19] I. Das and J. E. Dennis, "A closer look at drawbacks of minimizing weighted-sums of objectives for Pareto set generation in multicriteria optimization problems," *Structural Optimization* vol. 14, pp. 63–69, 1997.

[20] A. Volgenant, "Solving Some Lexicographic Multi-objective Combinatorial Problem," *European Journal of Operational Research*, vol. 139, no. 3, pp. 578-584, 2002.

Domain-based Teaching Strategy for Intelligent Tutoring System Based on Generic Rules

Dawod Kseibat, Ali Mansour, Osei Adjei, Paul Phillips
Dawod.kseibat@beds.ac.uk, Ali.Mansour@beds.ac.uk, Osei.Adjei@beds.ac.uk, Paul.Phillips@beds.ac.uk
Department of Computer Science and Technology
University of Bedfordshire, UK

Abstract - **In this paper we present a framework for selecting the proper instructional strategy for a given teaching material based on its attributes. The new approach is based on a flexible design by means of generic rules. The framework was adapted in an Intelligent Tutoring System to teach Modern Standard Arabic language to adult English-speaking learners with no pre-knowledge of Arabic language is required.**

I. INTRODUCTION

An Intelligent Tutoring System (ITS) can be defined as educational software containing some artificial intelligence components. An ITS should be capable of emulating teacher's behaviour in all aspects relating to supporting learners as they acquire knowledge [2]. The goal of ITSs is to engage the learner in a continuous reasoning activity and interact with them based on the understanding of their behaviour. ITSs are computer-based instructional systems that employ theories from education, computer science [3]. The interaction between education, computer science and psychology is presented in Fig 1.

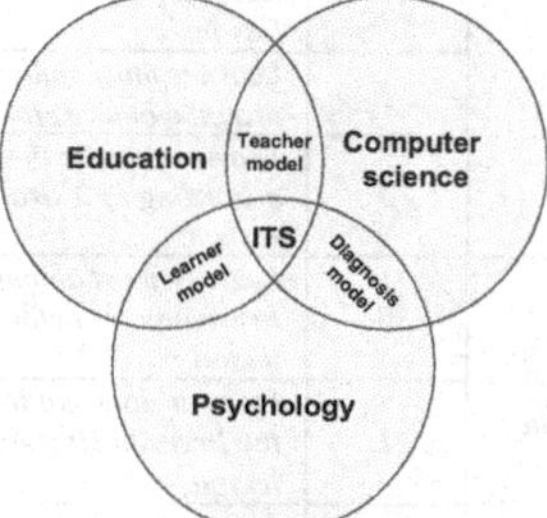

Fig. 1. The Interactions of Intelligent Tutoring Systems (ITSs)

While existing ITSs vary in their structures, they typically consist of at least three basic components or subsystems. Hartley and Sleeman [2] described the requirements of ITS for the first time in 1973 [4]. ITSs rely on: 1) the Domain model, or Domain knowledge, that contains the expertise of the human teacher in certain knowledge domain, 2) the Learner model that contains the student knowledge and behaviour, and 3) the Pedagogical model that controls the learning process and provides teaching and learning aims, curriculum content and the approach to delivery. The interactions between the learners and the ITS is provided via a user interface. Fig 2 shows the subsystems of ITS. Although ITSs are becoming more common and increasingly effective they are still expensive to build [5, 6]. Moreover despite the fact that there are many authoring systems commercially available for computer aided instruction nevertheless they lack the sophistication and the intelligence necessary for such systems. Hence, different modes of teaching should be presented by the tutoring system in order to provide significant learning experiences for each group of learners.

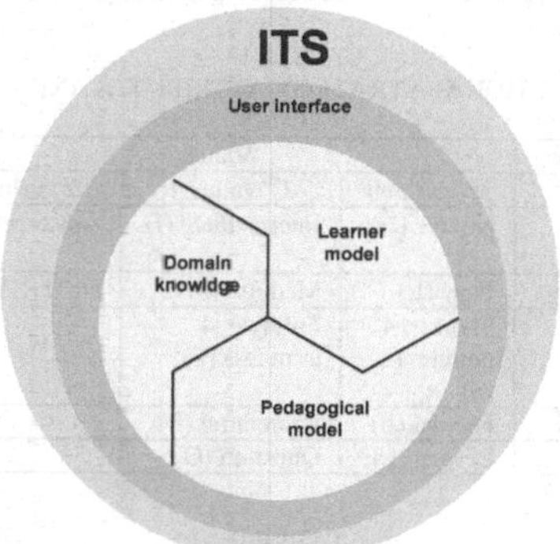

Fig. 2. Subsystems of ITS

II. DESIGN OF INSTRUCTIONAL STRATEGIES

The teaching of the learning materials is based on differentiated instruction strategies design which can be interactively adjusted by the teacher during runtime. The system selects the proper instructional strategy for teaching certain lessons/questions based on their attributes as presented in Fig III. The attributes set (**x**) includes pedagogical parameters from learning materials. The complete list of these attributes and their initial values are presented in Tables I and 2 respectively. Based on the design of the instructional strategies, each combination of these attributes is mapped into a certain instructional strategy.

Two groups of different instructional strategies were developed in this system. Each group contains different strategies and each strategy is pre-defined by the partition of the input space, i.e. of the attributes themselves. The first

T. Sobh, K. Elleithy (eds.), *Innovations in Computing Sciences and Software Engineering*,
DOI 10.1007/978-90-481-9112-3_80, © Springer Science+Business Media B.V. 2010

group is concerned with providing the proper instructional strategies for lessons (see table III).

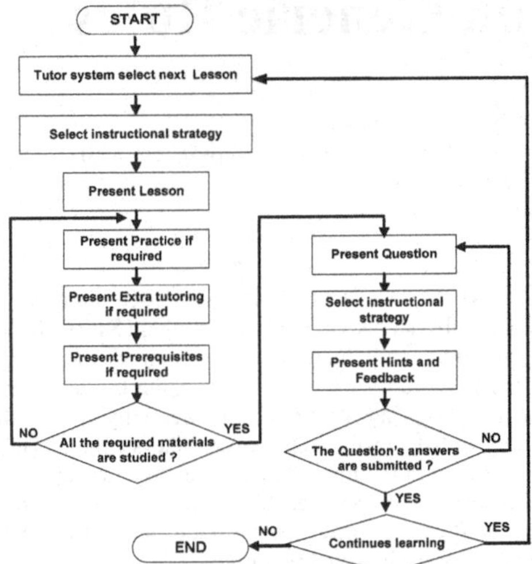

Fig. 3. The selection process of the Instructional strategy

TABLE I
INSTRUCTIONAL STRATEGY ATTRIBUTES AND THEIR VALUES

Attributes	Values		
	1st value=0	2nd value=1	3rd value=2
Learning level	Novice (N)	Intermediate (I)	Advanced (A)
Difficulty	Easy (E)	Medium (M)	Hard (H)
Time	Short (< 4 minutes) (S)	Full (>= 4 minutes) (F)	
Category	Factual (F)	Procedural (P)	
Type	Lesson (L)	Question (Q)	

TABLE II
THE INITIAL VALUES OF THE STRATEGY FILE

Instructional strategies	Learning level (ll)	Difficulty (diffcu)	Time (time)	Category (cat)
1	A	E /M /H	S/ F	F/ P
2	I	E / M /H	S/ F	F
3	I	E / M /H	S/ F	P
4	N	E / M /H	S/ F	F/ P
5	I / A	M /H	S/ F	F/ P
6	I /A	E	F	F/ P
7	I / A	E	S	F/ P
8	N	E / M /H	S/ F	F/ P

The second group is concerned with providing the proper instructional strategies for questions (see Table IV). Three features (activities) which control the actions of each instructional strategy are embedded in the design of each group. For the first group, strategies 1 to 4, these features can be described as follows:

1. **Practice**. The process of the learner going through (studying) the practice content related to a certain lesson.
2. **Prerequisites**. The process of completing all the lessons' prerequisites by the learner. Prerequisites are different lessons that precede the given lesson.
3. **Extra tutoring**. Extra tutoring is a mechanism for providing additional education by providing further explanations and other curriculum activity for the learner.

For the second group, strategies 5 to 8, these features can be described as follows:

1. **Hint**. Short statement in a form of a clue or tip presented to the learner according to a certain strategy to provide help in answering a question.
2. **Feedback**. One statement or more presented to the learner according to a certain strategy to provide some help in answering a question.
3. **Time**. The time allowed by the system to answer a question.

TABLE III
LESSONS STRATEGIES AND THEIR FEATURES

	Strategies	Practice	Prerequisites	Extra tutoring
1	Strategy 1	2	0	0
2	Strategy 2	2	2	2
3	Strategy 3	1	1	2
4	Strategy 4	1	0	2

Table III key

Features	*Values*	*Description*
Practice	*0*	*Learner does not have to study the lessons' practice before starting a new lesson.*
	1	*Learner must study the lessons' practice before starting a new lesson.*
	2	*Learner studies the lessons' practice according to a strategy guided by the system.*
Prerequisites	*0*	*Learner must complete all the Prerequisites before starting this lesson.*
	1	*Learner does not have to complete all the Prerequisites before starting this lesson.*
	2	*Learner must study Prerequisites according to strategy guided by the system.*
Extra tutoring	*0*	*Learner does not have to study extra before starting a new lesson.*
	1	*Learner must study extra tutoring before starting a new lesson*
	2	*Apply extra tutoring to the learner according to strategy guided by system.*

TABLE IV
THE QUESTIONS STRATEGIES AND THEIR FEATURES

	Strategies	Time	Feedback	Hints
1	Strategy 5	1	1	1
2	Strategy 6	0	1	0
3	Strategy 7	0	1	1
4	Strategy 8	0	0	1

Table IV Key

Features	*Values*	*Description*
Time	*0*	*Learner has unlimited time to answer the given question.*
	1	*Learner must answer the given question within a given time guided by the system.*
Feedback	*0*	*The system provides feedback to the learner.*
	1	*The system provides feedback to the learner according to a strategy guided by the system.*
Hints	*0*	*The system provides Hints to the learner.*
	1	*The system provides Hints to the learner according to a strategy guided by the system.*

In the presented framework, the features in each instructional strategy can be easily modified, making it flexible and convenient. The features of all the instructional strategies are stored in the file called "Features". In the file, each row represents a lesson/question strategy and each column represents a lesson/question strategy feature. The value of each feature in each row is represented as character with a fixed width of 1 byte. Table V represents the initial internal structure of the 'Features' file.

TABLE V
THE INTERNAL STRUCTURE OF THE FATURES FILE

Instructional Strategies	Feature 1	Feature 2	Feature 3
1	2	0	0
2	2	2	2
3	1	1	2
4	1	0	2
5	1	1	1
6	0	1	0
7	0	1	1
8	0	0	1

The structure of the 'Features' file is evident from its usage. The Course manager is responsible for extracting particular information from the file and converting it into a format understandable by the user.

III. SELECTING INSTRUCTIONAL STRATEGIES

This process is based on a set of rules that are responsible for selecting the proper instructional strategy for certain learning materials: lessons or questions. The design of these rules is based on a "generic" design in which the teacher, who has no experience in programming languages, can adjust the prediction process during run time. He/She can modify the feature of each instructional strategy through a special teacher interface as presented in Fig 4. This will reduce the cost and effort involved in developing and maintaining the system. The modification process is done by altering the features of the instructional strategy(s). The selection process involves the following three steps:

1. Connecting a certain set of learning materials' attributes to a certain instructional strategy and storing this information in a "Strategies" file (see Table II). The information is used by the system in the selection process (step 3) of the proper instructional strategy for certain learning materials' attributes. In the Strategies file, each row represents an instructional strategy and each column represents an input's attribute. The value of each attribute in each row is represented as character with fixed width of 1 byte.
2. Generating a new set of patterns each with 4 inputs (attributes): learning level, difficulty, time, category and type, and one output (instructional strategy) using teacher interface. A set of generic rules was developed to perform the "*generation*" process based on any changes done on the contents of Strategies file. These rules are used to built a variable "***Sentence***" that is embedded in the design of MySQL query as follows:
   Update "Strategy" Where Sentence
   The general form of these rules can be described as follows:

   IF (Input attribute $_{k}$ = Input attribute's value $_{k,1}$ and/or Input attribute's value $_{k,2}$ and/or Input attribute's value $_{k,J}$) then ***sentence=sentence+" ('attribute value*** $_{k,1}$ ***' and/or 'attribute value*** $_{k,1}$ ***' and/or 'attribute's value*** $_{k,J}$ ***') "* endif**

3. Selecting the proper instructional strategy based on the collected combination of attributes for the current learning materials: Lesson or Question as described by the following MySQL query:
   Select "instructional strategy" from "Strategies" Where "attributes"

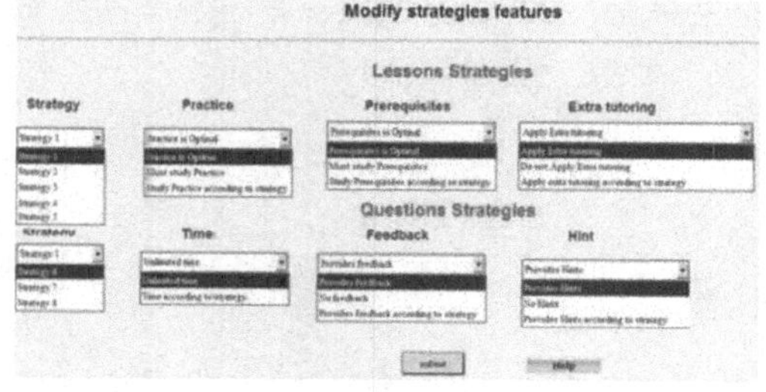

Fig. 4. The modification of the Instructional strategy

IV. THE CURRICULUM DESIGN

The system is restricted to tutoring a small subset of the Arabic language. Given a Lesson (L), there is a Lesson's Practice (R), Lesson's Extra tutor (Ex), n prerequisites (Pr_1,

$Pr_2, \ldots, Pr_n$), and Lesson's Question (Q). Each Question has two-level on-demand hints (H_1, H_2) and two-level on-demand Feedback (F_1, F_2).

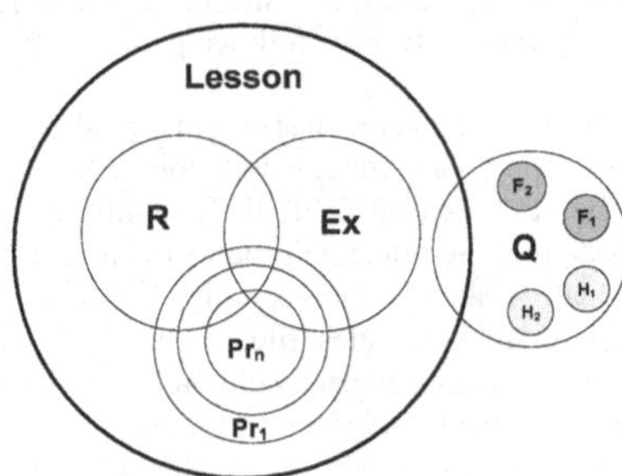

Fig. 5. The system courseware

The courseware is presented in the form of different Lessons, Questions, Practices, Extra tutoring, and Exams (see Fig 5). The Lesson is a period of teaching of certain learning materials in which learners are taught about a particular language subject or taught how to perform a particular activity. The Question is presented to the learner in order to make an assessment and examine his status of comprehension. Two types of questions, selection type, or supply type, can be used. Practice is a connection between lessons and Questions. The learner develops skills in practical manner such as grammar or listening. Extra tutoring provides extra teaching materials to the leaner. Exam is a set of questions designed to determine the learner's knowledge or skills at a certain learning level. Lessons, Questions, Practices and exams take the form of text and may include multimedia elements (picture, audio, and video).

V. CONCLUSION

In this paper an enhanced new framework for selecting the proper instructional strategy for a given teaching material based on its attributes (domain based) is presented. This framework is an enhancement of the design presented by Kseibat *et al.* [1]. The implemented approach is flexible since it accommodates different styles of instructional strategies. The selection process is based on generic rules which can be modified by the teacher during a learning session through a special teacher's interface. Such a feature has the advantages of reducing time and the cost required for building ITSs. The prototype of the proposed system was developed using PHP and MySQL.

REFERENCES

[1] Kseibat, D., Mansour, A., Osei Adjei, O., Onley, P., (2007), "A Prototype for the Design of Intelligent Tutoring Systems for Teaching Modern Standard Arabic Language", IASK, E-Activity and Leading Technologies, 2-6 DEC, Porto, Portugal.

[2] Hatzilygeroudis, I., Prentzas, J., (2004), "Using a hybrid rule-based approach in developing an intelligent tutoring system with knowledge acquisition and update capabilities", Expert Systems with Applications, Vol 26, pp. 477–492.

[3] Tuaksubun, C., Mungsing, S., (2007), "Design of an Intelligent Tutoring System that Comprises Individual Learning and Collaborative Problem-Solving Modules", fourth International Conference on eLearning for Knowledge-Based Society, November 18-19, Bangkok, Thailand.

[4] Hartley, J., Sleeman, D., (1973), "Toward more intelligent teaching systems", International Journal of Man-Machine studies, pp. 215-236.

[5] Gardner, H., (2006), "Multiple Intelligences: New Horizons in Theory and Practice", Basic books, USA.

[6] Koedinger, K., Anderson, J., Hadley, W., Mark, M., (1997), "Intelligent tutoring goes to school in the big city", Journal of Artificial intelligence in Education,

[7] Murray, Ainsworth, & Blessing (eds.) (2003), Authoring Tools for Adv. Tech. Learning Env., Kluwer Academic Publishers, Printed in the Netherlands. pp.493–546.

Parallelization of Edge Detection Algorithm using MPI on Beowulf Cluster

Nazleeni Haron
Universiti Teknologi PETRONAS
nazleeni@petronas.com.my

Ruzaini Amir
Universiti Teknologi PETRONAS

Izzatdin A. Aziz
Universiti Teknologi PETRONAS
izzatdin@petronas.com.my

Low Tan Jung
Universiti Teknologi PETRONAS
lowtanjung@petronas.com.my

Siti Rohkmah Shukri
Universiti Teknologi PETRONAS

Abstract—**In this paper, we present the design of parallel Sobel edge detection algorithm using Foster's methodology. The parallel algorithm is implemented using MPI message passing library and master/slave algorithm. Every processor performs the same sequential algorithm but on different part of the image. Experimental results conducted on Beowulf cluster are presented to demonstrate the performance of the parallel algorithm.**

Keywords-component; Beowulf Cluster, Edge detection, MPI, Parallel Programming.

I. INTRODUCTION

Image processing is widely used in many applications such as medical imaging, scientific visualization, geo-visualization etc. in order to illustrate critical information. One of issues faced in this area is the size of the images is very large yet the processing time has to be very small. Therefore, there has been an increasing interest in the developing and the use of parallel algorithms in image processing. Many algorithms have been developed for parallelizing different image processing areas on different parallel architectures [1].

In this paper, we present an approach to parallelize edge detection which is one form of image processing in the areas of feature detection and feature extraction. Edges play quite an important role in many applications of image processing, in particular for machine vision systems that analyze scenes of man-made objects under controlled illumination conditions.

Edge detection refers to algorithms which aim at detecting sharp changes in image brightness in order to capture important events and changes in properties of the world. Thus, applying an edge detector to an image may significantly reduce the amount of data to be processed and may therefore filter out information that may be regarded as less relevant, while preserving the important structural properties of an image. If the edge detection step is successful, the subsequent task of interpreting the information contents in the original image may therefore be substantially simplified [2].

In this paper we propose a parallel algorithm design for edge detection that can work on parallel machines or cluster of workstations. The proposed parallelization scheme is meant to reduce the computation time of the edge detection operation.

This paper is organized as follows: Section 2 gives a brief introduction on the Sobel edge detection algorithm. section 3 describes the parallel design while section 4 presents the the parallel programming paradigms, section 5 potrays the implementation of the algorithm. Section 6 prsents some insights on Beowulf cluster, section 7 discusses the experimental results and finally, section 8 outlines some conclusions.

II. EDGE DECTECTION ALGORITHM

We choose Sobel edge detection algorithm in this research [3]. This is because it is one of the most widely used algorithms for edge detection.

The Sobel operator performs a 2-D spatial gradient measurement on an image. Typically it is used to find the approximate absolute gradient magnitude at each point in an input grayscale image. The Sobel edge detector uses a pair of 3x3 convolution masks. One mask is used to calculate the gradient in the x-direction (columns) and the other is to estimate the gradient in the y-direction (rows) as shown in Fig. 1. The mask is going to be slid over the image, manipulating a square of pixels at a time. The actual Sobel masks are shown in Fig. 1.

-1	0	+1
-2	0	+2
-1	0	+1

Gx

+1	+2	+1
0	0	0
-1	-2	-1

Gy

Fig. 1. Sobel masks

T. Sobh, K. Elleithy (eds.), *Innovations in Computing Sciences and Software Engineering*,
DOI 10.1007/978-90-481-9112-3_81,

The GX mask is used to determine the edges in the horizontal direction while the GY mask is to identify the edges in the vertical direction. The resulting output will be calculated from the magnitude of the gradient that will determine the edges in both directions.The magnitude of the gradient are calculated using the formula:

$$|G| = \sqrt{Gx^2 + Gy^2}$$

An approximate magnitude can be calculated using:

$$|G| = |Gx| + |Gy|$$

Fig. 2 shows three items namely the input image in form of boxes of pixels (each pixel is labeled as $a_{rowcolumn)}$, the mask and the output image. Each pixel value in output image is calculated using the mask coefficients in a weighted sum of the value of pixels and its neighbours.

For example, when a mask is placed on the input image and pixel (b_{22}) is derived by such calculation as follows:

$$b_{22} = (a_{11}*m_{11}) + (a_{12}*m_{12}) + (a_{13}*m_{13}) + (a_{21}*m_{21}) + (a_{22}*m_{22}) + (a_{23}*m_{23}) + (a_{31}*m_{31}) + (a_{32}*m_{32}) + (a_{33}*m_{33})$$

Input Image

a_{11}	a_{12}	a_{13}	...	a_{1n}
a_{21}	a_{22}	a_{23}	...	a_{2n}
a_{31}	a_{32}	a_{33}	...	a_{3n}
⋮	⋮	⋮	...	⋮
a_{n1}	a_{n2}	a_{n3}	...	

Mask

m_{11}	m_{12}	m_{13}
m_{21}	m_{22}	m_{23}
m_{31}	m_{32}	m_{33}

Output Image

b_{11}	b_{12}	b_{13}	...	b_{1n}
a_{21}	b_{22}	b_{23}	...	b_{2n}
b_{31}	b_{32}	b_{33}	...	b_{3n}
⋮	⋮	⋮	...	⋮
b_{n1}	b_{n2}	b_{n3}	...	

Fig. 2. Calculation of pixel value in Output Image

Based on the above operation, it can be inferred that edge detection is quite a trivial task, but it still adds to the overall computation time if it were to be operated on big-sized images. Therefore finding means to accelerate the process can contribute to faster overall image processing time.

III. Parallel Algorithm Design

We have adopted Foster's design methodology in designing the parallel algorithm [4]. The proposed four-step process encourages the development of scalable parallel algorithms by delaying machine-dependent considerations to later steps. The four design steps consist of partitioning, communication, agglomeration and mapping.

A. *Partitioning*

Partitioning is the process of dividing the computation and data into pieces [5]. There are two options on how partitioning can be done; domain or functional decomposition. The main goal of decomposition is to identify as many primitive tasks as possible because it determines the upper bound on the parallelism we can exploit [5]. Domain decomposition is a data-centric approach in which the data will first be divided into pieces and then will be associated with the computations on the data. Functional decomposition is the opposite strategy where computations will be first divided into pieces and will be associated with the relevant data.

Since the ultimate aim for edge detection algorithm is to detect edge in every part of the image so we have chosen domain decomposition by breaking the image into smaller elements (pieces) and associating a primitive task with each of these elements. The primitive task in this case is calculating the gradient for each pixel in the image. We have chosen this approach because equal load can be distributed to each node since all nodes will be performing the same number of calculation. The best decomposition design is when the resulting primitive tasks are roughly the same size [5].

B. *Communication*

This step is taken in order to determine the communication pattern between the primitive tasks. There are two types of communication patterns that exist in any parallel algorithms: local and global [5]. Local communication exists when a primitive task requires values from only a small number of other primitive tasks in order to perform a computation. On the contrary, global communication exists when a primitive task requires values from significant number of primitive tasks.

In this case, only local communication pattern exists. This is because each primitive task only needs values from a small number of other tasks in order to perform a communication. For example as shown in Fig. 2, in order to calculate the gradient for a22, the information needed is only from the surrounding pixels. The best communication structure for any parallel algorithm is when the communications operations are balanced among the tasks, each task communicates with small number of neighbours and task can perform their communications and computations concurrently.

C. *Agglomeration*

Agglomeration is the process of grouping primitive tasks into larger task in order to improve performance or simplify programming. We have chosen rowwise block-striped decomposition in order to agglomerate the primitive tasks. The reasons being are because it is easy to distribute rows among nodes and it is much simpler to output the result matrix in row order. In addition, we are leveraging on the natural mechanism of edge detection algorithm where half of the execution is conducted row by row on an image. By choosing this mechanism, we can also ensure that the tasks will have similar computational and communication costs.

The example of agglomeration using rowwise block-striped decomposition is shown in Fig. 3. In this case, every primitive task for each row will be grouped together to form one larger task. Fig. 3 depicts 9 rows are divided among three processors. The number of rows is computed by dividing the image height with number of processors involved. Fig. 4 shows the example of rowwise block-striped decomposition on Lena image involving four processors. As such, the combination of several primitive tasks can aid to eliminate communications or at least reduce the communication overhead as well as increasing the locality of the algorithm.

Row 1
Row 2
Row 3
Row 4
Row 5
Row 6
Row 7
Row 8
Row 9

Fig. 3. Rowwise block-striped decomposition on image

Fig. 4. Example of Rowwise block-striped decomposition on Lena Image

D. Mapping

Mapping is the process of assigning task to processors. The goals are to maximize processor utilization and minimize interprocessor communication. We have referred to decision tree in [5] in order to determine the best mapping strategy. Based on our parallel edge detection algorithm, the number of tasks is static and communication pattern among the tasks is regular. The time needed to perform each task (to detect edge for each part of the image) is roughly the same because each task performs the same computation. Hence, the good mapping strategy is to have one task per processor, agglomerating primitive tasks so that computational workloads are balanced and communication among the nodes is minimized.

IV. Parallel Programming Paradigm

It has been proven that tasks accomplished through parallel computation results in faster execution as compared to a computational processes that runs sequentially [6]. MPI was chosen due to the fact it is designed for high performance computing on parallel machines or cluster of workstations [7].

Choosing the best parallel programming paradigm is actually an imperative concern when it comes to parallelization of an application or algorithm. There are a few parallel programming paradigms available such as MPI, OpenMP and Parallel Virtual Machine (PVM).

We have chosen MPI as the paradigm of choice due to the nature of our problem, the hardware components and the network setup that we have in the laboratory [8]. MPI consists of specifications for message passing libraries that can be used to write parallel programs. This message passing paradigm not only can be employed within a node but also across several nodes in a cluster. This is the advantage of MPI over OpenMP. Unlike OpenMP, MPI is also viable for wide range of problems. Besides that, MPI offers the user's complete control over data distribution and process synchronization. This feature is vital in order to ensure optimum performance of the parallelization. PVM may be more suitable for heterogeneous network setup and although MPI does not have the concept of a virtual machine, MPI does provide a higher level of abstraction on top of the computing resources in terms of the message-passing topology.

V. Parallel Edge Detection Implementation

The parallel edge detection is implemented using master/slave algorithm. In this algorithm, values of each pixel per row will be distributed to multiple cluster nodes (slaves) and the gradients are calculated concurrently. To ensure load balancing, each node of the cluster performs gradient calculation for equal number of rows. After generation for all rows, they are sent to the master node using the appropriate MPI routines. When the master node receives rows from all slaves, it will construct the image based on the info on lower and upper bound given to each slave earlier.

The following pseudocode illustrates the proposed parallel edge detection algorithm for each slave.

```
Begin
Local variables
m = node identifier
p = cluster size
r = image region size
i = image height
l = lower bound
u = upper bound
Initialize MPI
Get the node/process identifier, m
Get how many total nodes/processors, p
Determine the amount of the image each node will
process
    r = i /p
Determine the lower bound where each node starts
processing
    l = m * r
Determine the upper bound where each node stops
processing
    u = l + r

If more than l and less than u
   Read the portion of the image
   Apply filter matrix to the portion to the current pixel
     to the left neighbour
     to the right neighbour
     to the above neighbor
     to the below neighbor
   Record new pixel, x
 end if
Send x to master

End
```

VI. BEOWULF CLUSTER

Beowulf cluster is an ensemble of low cost off-the-shelf computers that is integrated by an interconnection of network and is operated within a single administration domain [9]. Due to its low cost set up and ease to maintain reasons, it has become the best alternative for the commercial parallel and high performance computers since it can also offer similar performance with the right set up. It can run widely available low cost and no cost software to manage its system resources and to coordinate the parallel executions.

VII. PERFORMANCE ANALYSIS

A. Experimental setup

The experiment was conducted on a Beowulf cluster consists of 10 SGI machines. Each of the machines consists of off-the-shelf Intel i386 based dual P3-733MHz processors with 512MB memory Silicon Graphics 330 Visual Workstations. These machines are connected to a Fast Ethernet 100Mbps switch. The head node performs as master node with multiple network interfaces. The rest are all compute nodes working as slaves. Although these machines are considered to be superseded in terms of hardware and performance as compared to the latest version of high performance computers, what's important in this research is the parallelization of the algorithm and how jobs are disseminated among processors.

B. Results

The main goal of parallelization is to gain a good speedup. A good speedup means to be nearly n times faster with n processors.

Speedup is the ratio between sequential execution time and parallel execution time and can be calculated using the formula below:

$$Speedup = \frac{sequential\ execution\ time}{parallel\ execution\ time}$$

Sequential execution time is the time taken for a processor to perform the required computation. Parallel execution time is the total duration after all the processors have finished performing the computation. The efficiency of a parallel program is a measure of processor utilization and is calculated using the formula below:

$$Efficiency = \frac{Sequential\ execution\ time}{processors\ used \times Parallel\ execution\ time}$$

Table 1 and 2 present the results of running parallel edge detection algorithm on the distributed memory cluster using two image sizes. Table 1 shows the results of running parallel edge detection algorithm on 640 X 480 pixels image while Table 2 depicts the results for 2592 x 3872 pixels image size.

TABLE I.
RESULTS OF PARALLEL EXECUTION TIME, SPEEDUP AND EFFICIENCY FOR IMAGE SIZE : 640 X 480 PIXELS

Number of processors	Execution time (seconds)	Speedup	Efficiency
1	0.1486	-	-
2	0.1007	1.476	0.7378
4	0.0608	2.444	0.611
6	0.0451	3.295	0.5492
8	0.0355	4.186	0.5232
10	0.0302	4.921	0.4921

TABLE II.
RESULTS OF PARALLEL EXECUTION TIME, SPEEDUP AND EFFICIENCY FOR IMAGE SIZE : 2592 X 3872 PIXELS

Number of processors	Execution time (seconds)	Speedup	Efficiency
1	0.1513 (Sequential)	-	-
2	0.1146	1.320	0.6601
4	0.0674	2.245	0.5612
6	0.0472	3.206	0.5343
8	0.0359	4.214	0.5268
10	0.0311	4.865	0.4865

As shown in Table 1 and Table 2, it was expected that by increasing the number of processors, the total execution time is reduced significantly. In addition, we can deduce that the efficiency of the parallel computation decreases as the number of processors increases. The utilization of the processors decreases when the numbers of processors increases since the tasks computed by each processor are getting lesser.

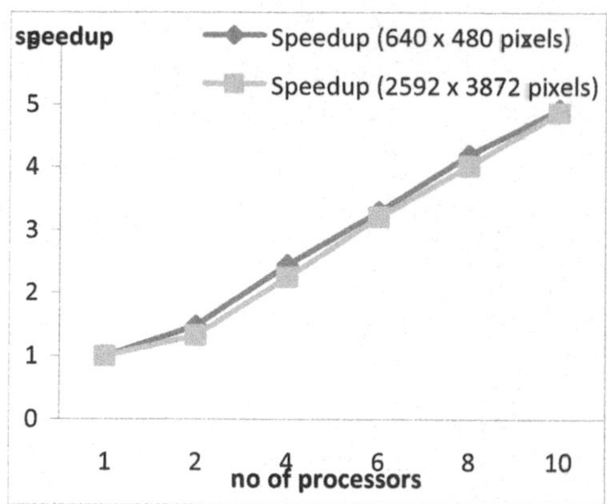

Fig. 5. Speedup results

Fig. 5 shows the speedup results against number of processors for both image sizes. Both gain good speedups using 6 to 8 number of processors. However, both reached saturation point at 10 processors and is predicted to have less difference in speedup as number of processors increases.

Therefore to determine the cause of such speedup we use The Karp-Flatt Metric [9] which is called experimentally determined serial fraction, *e* and calculated using formula below:

$$e = \frac{\dfrac{1}{speedup} - \dfrac{1}{no.\_of\_processors}}{1 - \dfrac{1}{no.\_of\_processors}}$$

Fig. 6 depicts the serial fraction obtained for both type of image size and it shows that the experimentally determined serial fraction is steadily increasing as the number of processors increases. Based on [10], it can be inferred that the principal reason for smaller gap in speedup is due to parallel overhead. The parallel overhead is actually due to time spent in process startup, communication and synchronization between the master and other compute nodes or slaves.

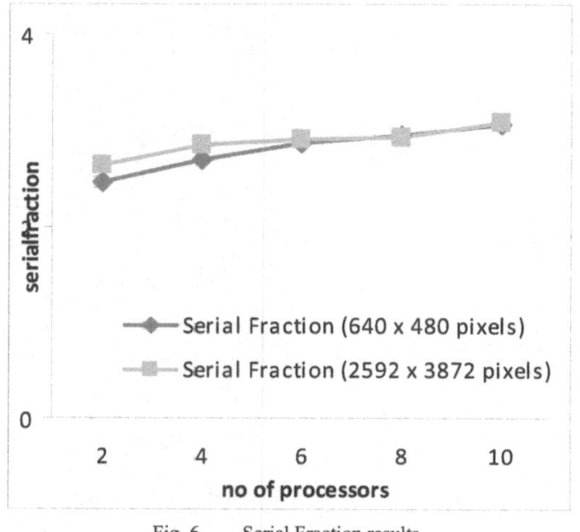

Fig. 6. Serial Fraction results

VIII. CONCLUSION

In this paper we have presented a design of parallel edge detection algorithm using Foster's methodology. The methodology consists of four steps namely partitioning, communication, agglomeration and mapping. In the partitioning stage, we have chosen domain or data decomposition approach where we break the image into smaller pieces and each piece is associated with one primitive task. The primitive task identified for edge detection algorithm is calculating the gradient for each pixel of the image. In addition, we have identified that only local communication exists in this parallel algorithm, since the primitive task requires values from only its neighboring pixels. We have chosen rowwise block-striped decomposition in order to agglomerate tasks. The reason being is because it is easy to distribute rows among compute nodes (slaves) as well as due to the nature of edge detection mechanism where the computation is carried row by row in an image. Mapping is the process of assigning tasks to each processor. We have assigned each agglomerated task to each processor. In other words, each row of the image will be assigned to one processor (node/slave) for computation. Prior to that, the input image will be broken down into different pieces by dividing image height with number of processors. It will result in how many rows each processor will work on.

The parallel algorithm was then implemented using MPI libraries. The parallelization of the algorithm was fully distributed as every processors performs the same sequential algorithm but on the different part of the image. Our parallel algorithm was evaluated on distributed memory Beowulf cluster. The results achieved were satisfactory if compared to those obtained by the sequential version of the algorithm. As future work, we plan to investigate the potential of functional decomposition in the edge detection algorithm in order to gain more parallelism.

REFERENCES

[1] C. Nicolescu, P. Jonker, "A data and task parallel image processing environment", Journal of Parallel Computing, volume 28, 2002, pp. 945-965

[2] Vincent, O. R., Optimization of network bandwidth using image compression. *Proceedings of the* National Conference on advanced Data Computing Communications and Security, Kadi, India, 2007.

[3] Sobel, I., Feldman, G., "A 3x3 Isotropic Gradient Operator for Image Processing", unpublished but often cited, orig. in Pattern Classification and Scene Analysis, Duda, R. and Hart, P., John Wiley and Sons,'73, pp 271-2.

[4] I. Foster, Designing and Building Parallel Programs:Concept and Tools for Parallel Software Engineering. Reading, MA : Addison-Wesley, 1995.

[5] M. J. Quinn, Parallel Programming in C with MPI and OpenM*P*, New York, McGraw-Hill, 2004.

[6] S. G. Aki, S. D. Bruda, "Improving A Solution's Quality Through Parallel Processing", The Journal of Supercomputing, Volume 19, Issue 2, 2001.

[7] MPI Retrieved on May, 17 2008 from http://www-unix.mcs.anl.gov/mpi/

[8] D. Adhipta, I. A. Aziz, L. T. Jung, N. S. Haron .Performance Evaluation on Hybrid Cluster: The Integration of Beowulf and Single System Image, Proceedings of ICTS, Jakarta, August 2006.

[9] T. Sterling , E. Lusk , W.Gropp, Beowulf Cluster Computing with Linux, MIT Press, Cambridge, MA, 2003 .

[10] A. H. Karp, H. P. Flatt, "Measuring parallel processor performance". Communications of the ACM, vol. 33(5), pp 539-543, May 1990.

Teaching Physical Based Animation via OpenGL Slides

Miao Song
Graduate School,
Concordia University,
Montreal, Canada,
Email: m_song@cse.concordia.ca

Serguei A. Mokhov
Computer Science
and Software Engineering,
Concordia University, Montreal, Canada,
Email: mokhov@cse.concordia.ca

Peter Grogono
Computer Science
and Software Engineering,
Concordia University, Montreal, Canada,
Email: grogono@cse.concordia.ca

***Abstract*—This work expands further our earlier poster presentation and integration of the OpenGL Slides Framework (OGLSF) – to make presentations with real-time animated graphics where each slide is a scene with tidgets – and physical based animation of elastic two-, three-layer softbody objects. The whole project is very interactive, and serves dual purpose – delivering the teaching material in a classroom setting with real running animated examples as well as releasing the source code to the students to show how the actual working things are made.**

***Index Terms*—education, presentation, softbody, real-time, frameworks, OpenGL, physical-based modeling**

I. Introduction

It is very helpful for effective teaching of computer graphics (CG) techniques [1], [2], [3], especially advanced topics such as real-time physical based animation of softbody objects, with a real working code on hand that can be demonstrated in a classroom and then given out to students for learning purposes and extension for their course work. It is reasonable to assume, in subjects like CG, teaching may be less effective if the examples are not visualized in class for the students. On top of that, it can be a nuisance for the instructor presenting the concepts and switching between the presentation power-point-like slides and the demo especially if it is complex and highly interactive with a lot of variable parameters to tweak. As a result, for the cases like the one briefly described, we argue that it is more effective *and* efficient to combine the OpenGL CG programs with OpenGL presentation slides in one teaching unit. There the traditional power-points and various techniques can be exemplified at run-time at the same time and the source code can be released to the students later to follow the examples through at all angles. For this purpose we integrated the physical-based softbody simulation system [4], [5], [6] with the OpenGL slides presentation framework (OGLSF) [7], [8] that compose in a small demo that we discuss throughout this work.

Organization

In Section II we discuss the background and the related work done that contribute to the creation of this teaching unit, specifically we discuss the properties of the OGLSF in Section II-A and the Softbody Simulation System in Section II-B. We then describe a brief methodology and layout in Section III. Afterwards, we conclude in Section IV describing our achievement, the limitation of the approach in Section IV-A, and the future work items in Section IV-B. All the sections are illustrated with the actual screenshots from the said OpenGL softbody system presentation slides and referenced where appropriate.

II. Related Work

The major pieces of the related work that contribute to this works, are two frameworks alongside with their implementation, put together with other items, to eventually form a teaching module for computer graphics. Here we extrapolate from our previous poster presentation [9] on this topic with more details on the actual design and implementation of the physical-based softbody animation techniques in an OpenGL power-point-like presentation tool with the demonstrated results. We describe the two CG systems in this section in some detail for the unaware reader.

A. OpenGL Slides Framework (OGLSF)

OGLSF gives ability to make slides, navigate between them using various controls, and allow for common bulleted textual widgets – the *tidgets*. It also allows to override the control handling from the main idle loop down to each individual (current) slide. All slides together compose a concrete instance of `Presentation`, which is a collection of slides that uses the Builder pattern to sequence the slides. Each slide is a derivative of the generic `Slide` class and represents a scene with the default keyboard controls for the tidgets and navigation. It is understood that the tidgets can be enabled and disabled to allow the main animation to run unobstructed [7], [8], [9]. Each scene on the slide is modeled using traditional procedural modeling techniques [10] and is set as a developer or artist desires. It can include models and rendering of any primitives, complex scenes, texturing, lighting, GPU-based shading, and others, as needed and is fit by the presenter [7], [8]. The main program delegates its handling of the callback controls for keyboard, mouse, and idle all the way down to the presentation object that handles it and passes it down to each current slide [7], [8], [9].

T. Sobh, K. Elleithy (eds.), *Innovations in Computing Sciences and Software Engineering*,
DOI 10.1007/978-90-481-9112-3_82, © Springer Science+Business Media B.V. 2010

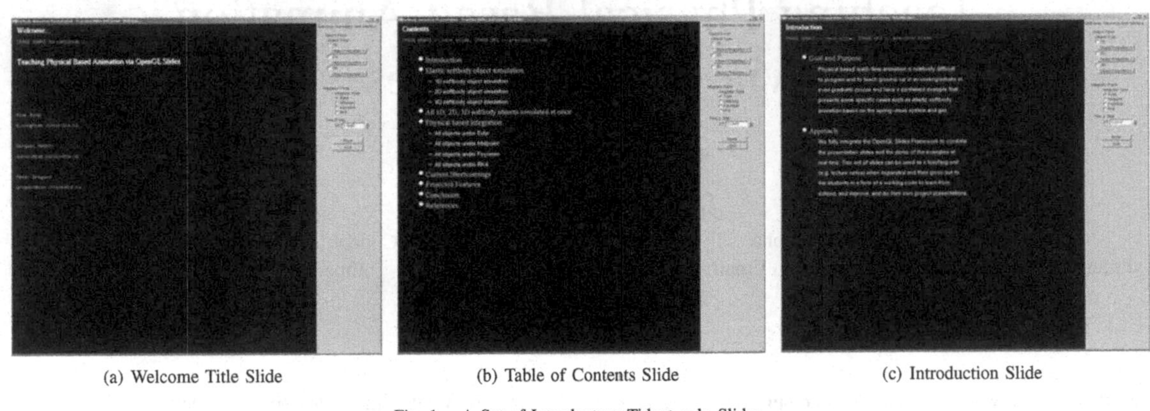

(a) Welcome Title Slide (b) Table of Contents Slide (c) Introduction Slide

Fig. 1. A Set of Introductory Tidget-only Slides

B. *Softbody Simulation Framework and System*

The Softbody Simulation System's main goal is to provide real-time simulation of a variety of softbody objects, founded in the core two- or three- layer model for objects such as human and animal's soft parts and tissue, and non-living soft objects, such as cloth, gel, liquid, and gas. Softbody simulation is a vast research topic and has a long history in computer graphics. The softbody system has gone through a number of iterations in its design and development. Initially it had limited user interface [4], [5]. Then the fine-grained to high-level level-of-detail (LOD) GLUI-based [11] user interface has been added [6], GPU shading support was added [12] using the OpenGL Shading Language [13], a curve-based animation was integrated, and software engineering re-design is constantly being applied. The example of the common visual design of the LOD interactivity interface is summarized in Figure 2. The LOD components are on the right-hand-side, expanded, and the main simulation window is on the left (interactivity with that window constitutes for now just the mouse drag and functional keys). Following the top-down approach configuration parameters, that assume some defaults, were reflected in the GUI [9].

The core framework's design is centered around common dimensionality (1D, 2D, and 3D) of graphical objects for simulation purposes, physics-based integrators, and the user interaction component. The `Integrator` API of the framework as of this writing is implemented by the well-known Explicit Euler, Midpoint, Feynman, and Runge-Kutta 4 (RK4)-based integrators for their mutual comparison of the run-time and accuracy. The system is implemented using OpenGL [14], [15] and the C++ programming language with the object oriented programming paradigm [9].

This elastic object simulation system has been designed and implemented according to the well known architectural pattern, the model-view-controller (MVC). This pattern is ideal for real-time simulation because it simplifies the dynamic tasks handling by separating data (the model) from user interface (the view). Thus, the user's interaction with the software does not impact the data handling; the data can be reorganized without changing the user interface. The communication between the model and the view is done through the controller. This also closely correlates to the OpenGL state machine, that is used as a core library for the implementation [5], [9].

III. METHODOLOGY

The methodology consists of the design and implementation modification required for the integration followed by making the actual presentation slides. The source code of the presentation is a part of the learning material along the actual content of the material presented and is prepared as such. Separately, both frameworks and implementing systems define the `main()` function, which cannot be included into any of the libraries (both can be compiled into the library files to be linked into other projects) because of the linker errors when the object code from the two or more systems is combined into a single executable. We therefore started a new application with a new `main()`, the SoftBodyPresentation.cpp. Additionally, both frameworks have to declare their own namespaces, which both have not done in the past, similarly to CUGL [16] because there are some common names of variables, classes, or functions that clash on compilation. This is an overall improvement not only for this work, but also for any similar type of integration with other projects (cf. Section IV-B). Thus, we declared the namespaces `softbody:` and `slides:` and move the clashing variables under those namespaces. Most of the main code from SoftbodySimulation.cpp application is encapsulated into a generic `SoftbodySimulationSlide` class that includes the default configuration of the softbody simulation parameters [9] this class is inherited by the slides that do the actual simulation of softbody objects. Furthermore, the concrete slides that inherit from `SoftbodySimulationSlide` are broken down into some preset distinct configuration defaults and accompanying tidgets. They override the `animate()` method (the "idle" function) as well as the state LOD pa-

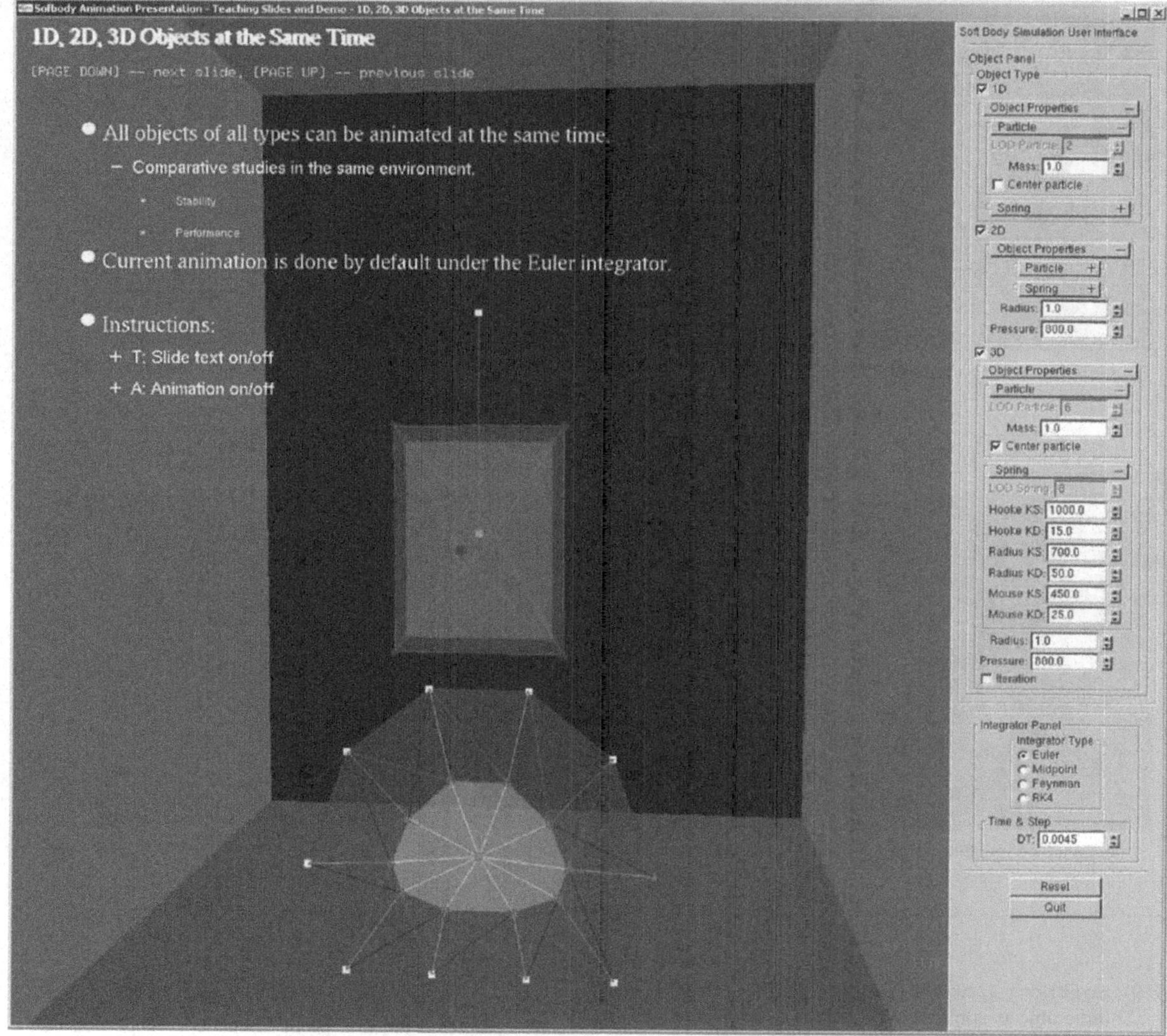

Fig. 2. Three Types of Softbody Objects Simulated Together on a Single Slide Scene

rameters per an example slide.

For the presentation in this work the demonstration slides currently include the following:

1) `TitleSlide` – a typical title slide with the lecture/presentation title and the presenter information (see Figure 1(a)).
2) `TOCSlide` – a tidget table of contents of the presentation (see Figure 1(b)).
3) `IntroductionSlide` – a tidget introduction of the material (see Figure 1(c)).
4) `SoftbodySimulationSlide1D` – a slide featuring the 1D elastic object configured by default encased in the `ViewBox`, see Figure 3(a).
5) `SoftbodySimulationSlide2D` – a slide featuring the 2D softbody object configured by default, see Figure 3(b).
6) `SoftbodySimulationSlide3D` – a slide featuring the 3D softbody object configured by default, see Figure 3(c).
7) `SoftbodySimulationSlideAllD` – a slide featuring all types of softbody objects configured by default, as shown in Figure 2, included into the slide environment.
8) `SoftbodySimulationSlideAllEuler` – all three objects configured by default to animate under the Explicit Euler integrator, see Figure 4(a).

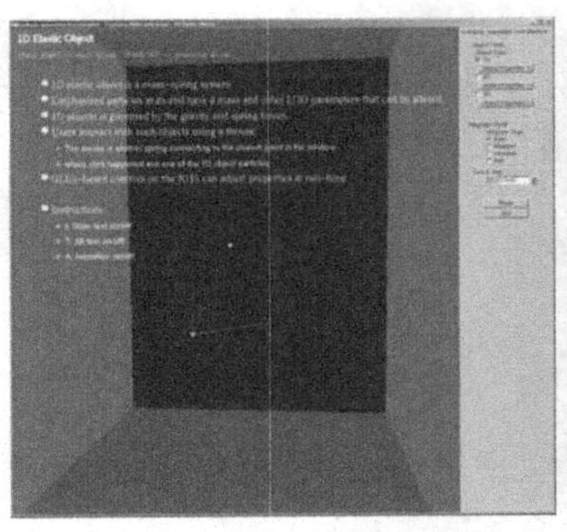

(a) 1D Elastic Object Simulation Slide

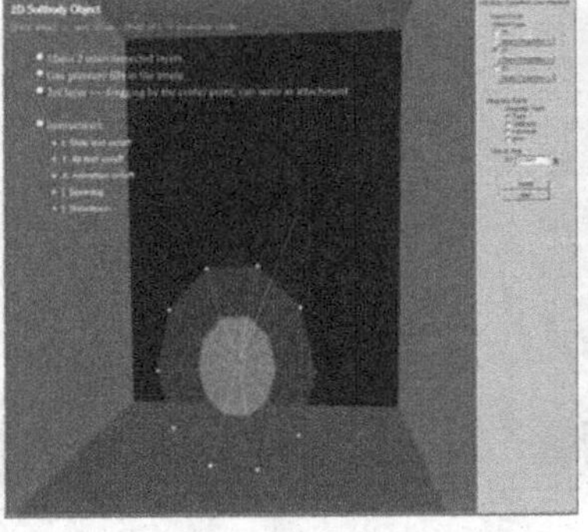

(b) 2D Elastic Object Simulation Slide

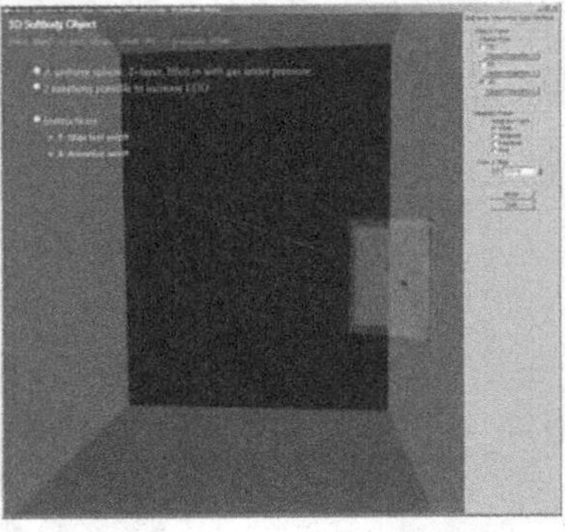

(c) 3D Elastic Object Simulation Slide

Fig. 3. Simulation of Single 1D, 2D, and 3D Softbody Elastic Objects Slides

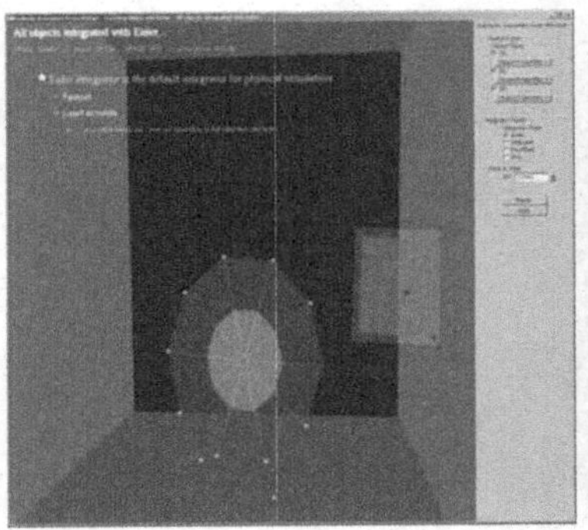

(a) Simulation with Euler Integrator Slide

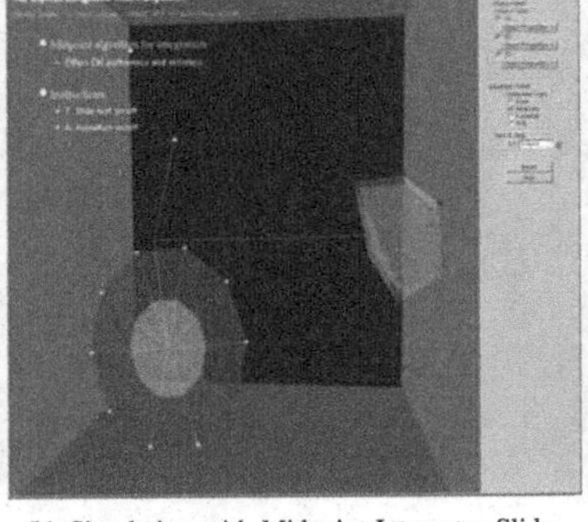

(b) Simulation with Midpoint Integrator Slide

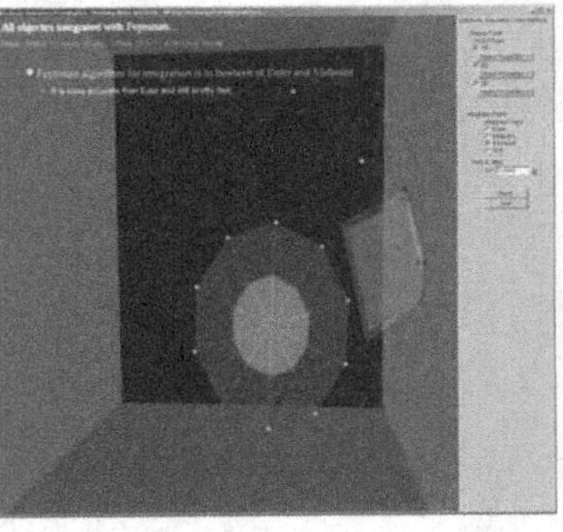

(c) Simulation with Feynman Integrator Slide

Fig. 4. Simulation of all Softbody Object Types with Various Integrators Slides

9) `SoftbodySimulationSlideAllMidpoint` – all three objects configured by default to animate under the Midpoint integrator, see Figure 4(b).
10) `SoftbodySimulationSlideAllFeynman` – all three objects configured by default to animate under the Feynman integrator, see Figure 4(c).
11) `SoftbodySimulationSlideAllRK4` – all three objects configured by default to animate under the RK4 integrator, see Figure 5.
12) `ShortcomingsSlide` – a slide describing the limitations of the approach (cf. Section IV-A, see Figure 7(a)).
13) `ProjectedFeaturesSlide` – a summary of some projected features for the future work (cf. Section IV-B, see Figure 7(b)).
14) `ConclusionSlide` – a preliminary conclusions slide (cf. Section IV, see Figure 6).
15) `ReferencesSlide` – the list of references, see Figure 7(c).

IV. Conclusions and Future Work

We completed the first proof-of-concept integration of the softbody simulation system and OGLSF frameworks. We made a number of slides in a OpenGL-based softbody presentation typically found in lab/tutorial like presentations, which are to be extended to a full lecture-type set of slides. This milestone significantly advances our contribution to a good CG teaching module, suitable for use by instructors to present the material in class as well as for learning by providing its source code to the students for study and extension to demonstrate their CG projects at the end of a semester.

We have encountered some integration difficulties due to the frameworks' original design and implementation consideration, that we do not discuss here, but rather discuss and generalize at length in our follow up software engineering work in [17].

We further discuss the limitation of the proposed approach as well as the future (and ongoing) work on these and the related projects.

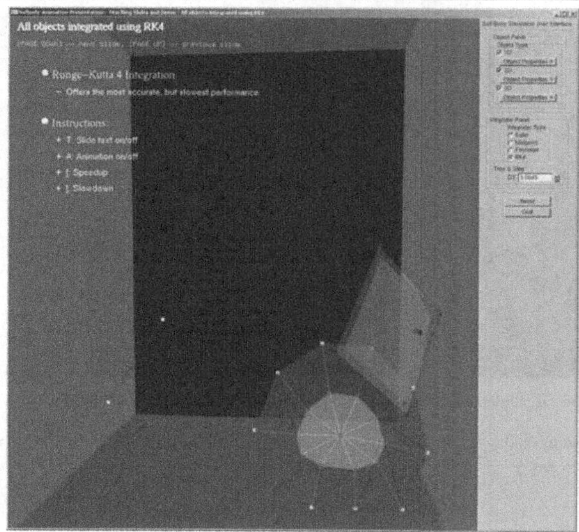

Fig. 5. Simulation with Runge-Kutta 4 Integrator Slide

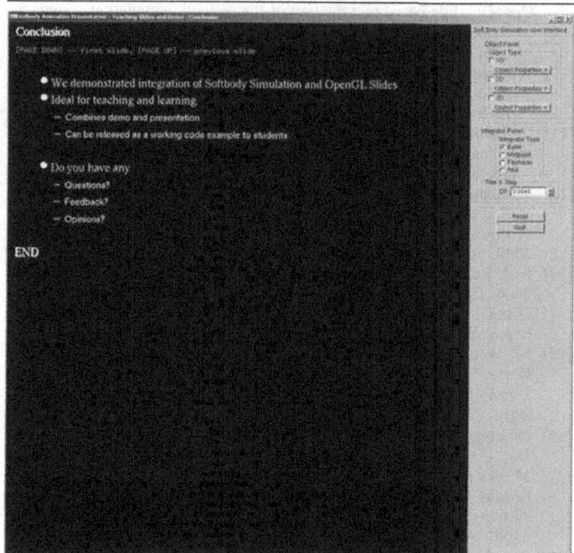

Fig. 6. Conclusion OpenGL Slide Example

A. Limitations

There are some assumptions and limitations to the approach described here; thus, it is not an all-in-one solution, but rather for a specific purpose presentations.

- Assumes the CG topics taught are renderable at real-time, like this softbody simulation.
  - One can presumably also render images that were premade offline, but then what is the point? (Unless one is to demonstrate the texture mapping, etc. of course).
  - One can play AVI and HD movies in OpenGL, but again not as a primary learning source, though may be necessary at times (e.g. to teach how to play such things when/if needed).
- Not suitable for presentation in online conferences, so have to make screenshots (not a big deal, but ideally, at least the screenshots should be taken automatically).
- May be hardware dependent.
  - Though today's commodity hardware should generally be good enough, but one own's laptop and the PC in a classroom may have enough differences to distort the presentation or render it unacceptably.
- Tedious to compose and debug – need to be a programmer.
  - A proposal to load import info from XML or text is made.
  - Has to be done well in advance before the teaching session.
  - Assumption is made the instructors and the students are able to do C++ or OpenGL programming in a CG programming course.
- Rendering is resolution-sensitive – tidgets may have various spacing or stretch, not matching the softbody object being displayed in the scene.
- Rendering is an issue (not supported, or tedious/difficult) for now for math (formulas), source code, highlighting – can only be done as images.

B. Future Work

Aside from addressing some of the limitations from the previous section, there are a number of immediate items for the future work:

- Port the source code fully to Linux and MAC OS X. Currently it only compiles properly under WINDOWS XP 32-BIT under Visual Studio 2005.
- Release our code and documentation as open-source implementation either a part of the Concordia University Graphics Library [16] and/or as part of a Maya [18] plug-in and as a CGEMS [2] teaching module.
- Allow advanced interactive controls of the scenes and slides by using haptics devices [19] with the force feedback, head-mounted displays and healthcare virtual reality systems [20].
- Integrate stereoscopic effects into the presentation of soft-body objects (under way) with another open-source plug-in project under development that implements OpenGL-based stereoscopic effects [21], [22], [20].
- While working on this and other integration efforts, take down and formalize software engineering requirements for systems like ours to simplify the future development and integration process of academic and open-source OpenGL and CG frameworks and systems for physical based animation and beyond [17] (in progress).

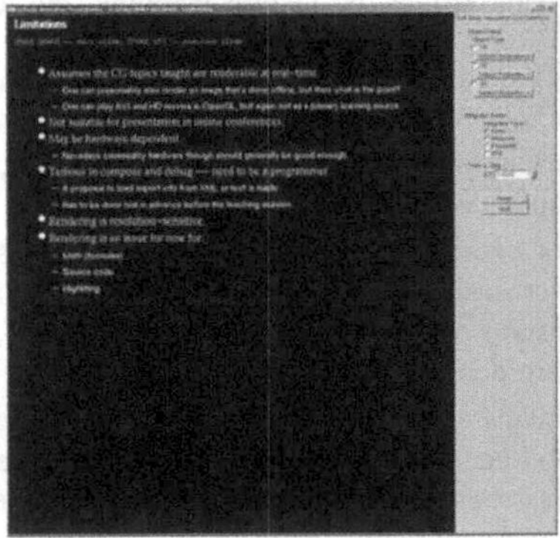

(a) Limitations OpenGL Slide Example

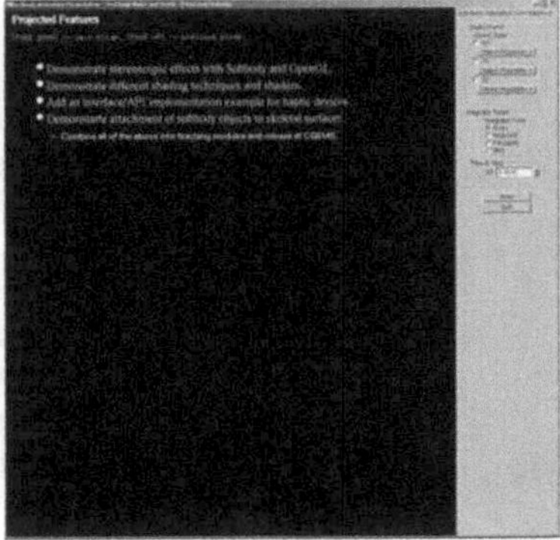

(b) Projected Features OpenGL Slide Example

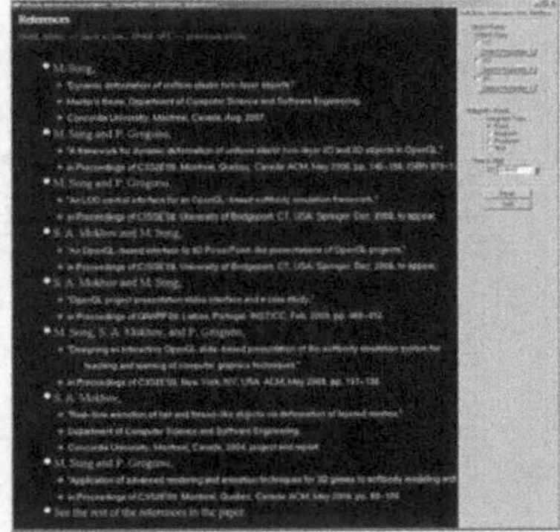

(c) References OpenGL Slide Example

Fig. 7. Concluding Slides

- Provide automatic loading and display of the softbody simulation source code on the slides with breakdown onto multi-page slides.
- Demonstrate different softbody shading techniques and shaders via the OpenGL slides. We already implemented the first draft version of a vendor-independent API for shader use within the softbody system and provided two implementations of that API – one that loads GLSL vertex and fragment shaders and the other that loads the cross-vendor assembly language for shaders.
- Demonstrate attachment of softbody objects to skeletal surfaces via the slides.

Acknowledgments

This work is partially funded by NSERC, FQRSC, and the Faculty of Engineering and Computer Science, Concordia University, Montreal, Canada.

References

[1] D. Tenneson, A. M. Spalter, J. Kumar, I. Medvedev, and A. van Dam, "The Graphics Teaching Tool (GTT)," [online], Brown University, 2003 – 2008, http://graphics.cs.brown.edu/research/gtt/.

[2] J. Jorge, F. Hanisch, F. Figueiredo, and R. Schauer, "CG Educational Materials Source (CGEMS)," [online], 2008–2009, http://cgems.inesc.pt/.

[3] J. O. Talton, "Teaching graphics with the OpenGL Shading Language," *ACM SIGCSE Bulletin archive*, vol. 39, no. 1, Mar. 2007.

[4] M. Song, "Dynamic deformation of uniform elastic two-layer objects," Master's thesis, Department of Computer Science and Software Engineering, Concordia University, Montreal, Canada, Aug. 2007.

[5] M. Song and P. Grogono, "A framework for dynamic deformation of uniform elastic two-layer 2D and 3D objects in OpenGL," in *Proceedings of C3S2E'08*. Montreal, Quebec, Canada: ACM, May 2008, pp. 145–158, ISBN 978-1-60558-101-9.

[6] ——, "An LOD control interface for an OpenGL-based softbody simulation framework," in *Proceedings of CISSE'08*. University of Bridgeport, CT, USA: Springer, Dec. 2008, to appear.

[7] S. A. Mokhov and M. Song, "An OpenGL-based interface to 3D PowerPoint-like presentations of OpenGL projects," in *Proceedings of CISSE'08*. University of Bridgeport, CT, USA: Springer, Dec. 2008, to appear.

[8] ——, "OpenGL project presentation slides interface and a case study," in *Proceedings of GRAPP'09*. Lisboa, Portugal: INSTICC, Feb. 2009, pp. 409–412.

[9] M. Song, S. A. Mokhov, and P. Grogono, "Designing an interactive OpenGL slide-based presentation of the softbody simulation system for teaching and learning of computer graphics techniques," in *Proceedings of C3S2E'09*. New York, NY, USA: ACM, May 2009, pp. 131–136.

[10] Wikipedia, "Procedural modeling — Wikipedia, The Free Encyclopedia," [online; accessed 28-November-2009], 2009, http://en.wikipedia.org/w/index.php?title=Procedural_modeling&oldid=326319778.

[11] P. Rademacher, N. Stewart, and B. Baxter, "GLUI - A GLUT-based user interface library, version 2.35," [online], 1999–2006, http://glui.sourceforge.net/.

[12] M. Song and P. Grogono, "Application of advanced rendering and animation techniques for 3D games to softbody modeling and animation," in *Proceedings of C3S2E'09*. Montreal, Quebec, Canada: ACM, May 2009, pp. 89–100.

[13] R. J. Rost, *OpenGL Shading Language*. Pearson Education, Inc., Feb. 2004, ISBN: 0-321-19789-5.

[14] OpenGL Architecture Review Board, "OpenGL," [online], 1998–2009, http://www.opengl.org.

[15] M. Woo, J. Neider, T. Davis, D. Shreiner, and OpenGL Architecture Review Board, *OpenGL Programming Guide: The Official Guide to Learning OpenGL, Version 1.2*, 3rd ed. Addison-Wesley, Oct. 1999, ISBN 0201604582.

[16] P. Grogono, "Concordia University Graphics Library (CUGL)," [online], Dec. 2005, http://users.encs.concordia.ca/~grogono/Graphics/cugl.html.

[17] M. Song, S. A. Mokhov, and P. Grogono, "Deriving software engineering requirements specification for computer graphics simulation systems through a case study," Dec. 2009, submitted for publication to SERA'2010.

[18] Autodesk, "Maya," [digital], 2008–2009, autodesk.com.

[19] M. Song and P. Grogono, "Are haptics-enabled interactive and tangible cinema, documentaries, 3D games, and specialist training applications our future?" in *Proceedings of GRAPP'09*. Lisboa, Portugal: INSTICC, Feb. 2009, pp. 393–398.

[20] M. Song, S. A. Mokhov, A. R. Loader, and M. J. Simmonds, "A stereoscopic OpenGL-based interactive plug-in interface for Maya and beyond," in *Proceedings of VRCAI'09*. New York, NY, USA: ACM, 2009, to appear.

[21] A. R. Loader, S. A. Mokhov, and M. Song, "Open Stereoscopic 3D Plugin Collection," SourceForge.net, 2008–2009, http://sf.net/projects/stereo3d, last viewed November 2009.

[22] A. R. Loader, "Making space," Master's thesis, Department of Design and Computation Arts, Concordia University, Montreal Canada, 2008.

Appraising the Corporate Sustainability Reports – Text Mining and Multi-Discriminatory Analysis

J. R. Modapothala, B. Issac and E. Jayamani
Swinburne University of Technology (Sarawak Campus), Malaysia
{jmodapothala, bissac, ejayamani}@swinburne.edu.my

Abstract—**The voluntary disclosure of the sustainability reports by the companies attracts wider stakeholder groups. Diversity in these reports poses challenge to the users of information and regulators. This study appraises the corporate sustainability reports as per GRI (Global Reporting Initiative) guidelines (the most widely accepted and used) across all industrial sectors. Text mining is adopted to carry out the initial analysis with a large sample size of 2650 reports. Statistical analyses were performed for further investigation. The results indicate that the disclosures made by the companies differ across the industrial sectors. Multivariate Discriminant Analysis (MDA) shows that the environmental variable is a greater significant contributing factor towards explanation of sustainability report.**

I. Introduction

The practice of disclosing company's sustainability reports to variety of stakeholders is now widely accepted and is done by companies across a wide range of industrial sectors. The publication of such voluntary sustainability reports are attracting scrutiny from the state (governments), business and investment community, and civil society [1] – [2]. Also, reporting companies have to meet the different requirements of wider stakeholder groups.

In order to increase and improve environmental and sustainability reporting, efforts are made in improving the guidelines and standards. Due to the diversity that exists, there is a wide disparity in the report content. Credibility, continuity and comparability of the reports are of major concern [3]. In order to implant a standardized approach towards sustainability reporting, Global Reporting Initiative (GRI) has initiated its efforts towards providing guidelines and a more standardized approach to reporting.

The paper is organized as follows. Section 2 is literature review, section 3 is research objectives and hypothesis, section 4 is methodology, section 5 is results and discussion and section 6 is limitations and conclusion.

II. Literature Review

The growing importance of stakeholder's perception is widely recognized by the companies and could be observed in various ways, via investments, sales, governmental pressure and ultimately the size of future business profits. It is argued by Grey et al., that net benefit can be achievable by the companies provided they communicate through these separate reports [4]. Furthermore, it gives a dynamic corporate competition in providing good environmental performance or resource productivity [5] – [7]. On the same note, Schuster observed that environmental reporting as an important information tool within the industrial sector [8].

Livesey and Kearins and Milne et al. conducted studies on analyzing the language used in corporate organizations [9]-[11]. A similar study was conducted focusing on the language and images used to construct meanings, and the context in which the reports emerged, the traces of the organization's reporting developments with all of the organization's reports since 1993 through 2003 [12].

Studies on current voluntary corporate environmental reports meeting the requirements of the Global Reporting Initiative GRI 2000 sustainability reporting guidelines and ISO 14031 environmental performance evaluation standard were of great inspiration. [13]. Metrics were also used in analyzing the corporate environmental reports in view of environmental sustainability and application of taxonomies [14].

Rao et al., conducted their research on Small and Medium-size Enterprises (SMEs) applied exploratory analysis and a structural equation model to bring out statistically significant linkages between five latent constructs: environment management indicators, environment performance indicators, environmental performance, business performance and competitiveness [15]. As a strategy, corporate sustainability integrates long-term economic, social and environmental aspects of the business while maintaining global competitiveness [16] and green brand equity [17].

From time to time, various methods of reporting were promulgated by different agencies which includes, ISO 14031 (1999) [18] and Global Reporting Initiative (2000, 2002) as in [19]. The most prominent reporting guidelines are the Global Reporting Initiative (GRI) Sustainability Reporting Guidelines on Economic, Environmental and Social Performance (GRI, 2000), promulgated in June 2000. These guidelines are generally accepted as current 'best practice' reporting.

Though there are several studies made on environmental reports and Corporate Social Responsibility (CSR), diminutive research effort is made into what types of indicator are being used in Corporate Environmental Reports (CERs). Lober et al. [20] examined types of company reports and, in a generalized, anecdotal manner, looked at types of information provided in CERs. Noci [21] made a deep emphasis on CERs issued by Italian firms and Italy-based multinationals. Prior studies on metrics were done on environmental reporting in SME's [22],

T. Sobh, K. Elleithy (eds.), *Innovations in Computing Sciences and Software Engineering*,
DOI 10.1007/978-90-481-9112-3_83, © Springer Science+Business Media B.V. 2010

internet technologies [23], and text mining approach on selected 10-variables [24].

TABLE I
SELECTED VARIABLES – MEAN AND STANDARD DEVIATION

	Organizational Performance		Environmental Performance		Social Performance		Economic Performance	
Sector	**Mean**	**S.D**	**Mean**	**S.D**	**Mean**	**S.D**	**Mean**	**S.D**
Automobile	2.21	1.25	1.70	0.75	1.58	0.81	0.88	0.59
Banks	2.03	1.23	0.83	0.52	1.42	0.93	1.00	0.68
Beverages	1.53	0.96	1.11	0.59	1.23	0.78	0.73	0.44
Chemicals	2.00	1.03	1.44	0.64	1.58	0.77	0.88	0.51
Construction	1.94	1.21	1.16	0.65	1.33	0.84	0.78	0.71
Diversified Industries	2.12	1.34	1.37	0.68	1.66	0.85	1.00	0.84
Electricity	2.20	1.25	1.57	0.81	1.54	0.94	1.02	0.74
Electronic-electric Equipment	1.86	1.23	1.26	0.55	1.36	0.82	0.66	0.48
Food Producers	1.94	1.17	1.18	0.53	1.37	0.78	0.79	0.54
General Retailers	2.13	1.10	1.18	0.58	1.52	0.80	0.86	0.46
Household Textiles	1.88	1.17	1.23	0.55	1.41	0.82	0.84	0.68
Insurance	2.01	1.24	0.83	0.43	1.58	0.98	0.87	0.53
IT Hardware	2.21	1.17	1.46	0.72	1.84	0.83	0.92	0.51
Leisure Entertain-ment Hotels	1.85	1.22	1.01	0.47	1.27	0.71	0.71	0.44
Media and Photography	2.38	1.34	1.19	0.58	1.62	0.83	0.85	0.43
Mining	2.06	1.09	1.25	0.60	1.75	0.78	0.82	0.52
Multi-utilities	1.66	1.41	1.10	0.91	1.10	1.04	0.74	0.56
Oil and Gas	2.05	1.11	1.40	0.65	1.64	0.79	0.92	0.51
Pharma-ceutical	2.01	1.29	1.25	0.56	1.53	0.94	0.87	0.91
Real Estate	1.85	1.18	1.04	0.55	1.29	0.75	0.73	0.54
Specialty Other Finance	2.09	1.48	1.33	0.76	1.57	0.94	1.04	1.02
Steel	1.55	1.04	0.86	0.56	1.06	0.79	0.69	0.57
Support Services	1.55	1.04	0.86	0.56	1.06	0.79	0.69	0.57
Tele-communicat-ions	2.31	1.36	1.05	0.67	1.59	0.99	0.92	0.72
Transport	1.80	1.20	1.01	0.53	1.16	0.83	0.67	0.70
Water	1.93	1.09	1.09	0.51	1.15	0.67	0.77	0.50
Total	**1.94**	1.20	**1.16**	0.66	**1.41**	0.87	**0.83**	0.63

Every organization accumulates huge volumes of data from a variety of sources on a daily basis. Data mining is an iterative process of creating predictive and descriptive models, by uncovering previously unknown trends and patterns in vast amounts of data from across the enterprise, in order to support decision making. Text mining applies the same analysis techniques to text-based documents. The knowledge gleaned from data and text mining can be used to fuel strategic decision making.

TABLE II
SELECTED VARIABLES FISHER'S LINEAR DISCRIMINANT

	Fisher's Linear Discriminant Functions				
Sector	**Org.**	**Env.**	**Soc.**	**Eco.**	**(Constant)**
Automobile	-0.03	5.36	-0.59	-0.32	-7.17
Banks	0.75	-0.24	0.72	0.95	-4.91
Beverages	-0.32	2.92	0.35	0.18	-4.92
Chemicals	-0.26	3.74	0.50	-0.16	-6.01
Construction	0.48	2.47	-0.01	-0.14	-5.10
Diversified Industries	-0.12	2.94	0.68	0.25	-5.84
Electricity	0.06	4.60	-0.90	0.70	-6.60
Electronic-electric Equipment	0.21	3.22	0.34	-0.87	-5.42
Food Producers	0.38	2.48	0.17	-0.16	-5.14
General Retailers	0.54	1.85	0.63	-0.29	-5.28
Household Textiles	0.01	2.87	0.29	0.12	-5.29
Insurance	0.51	-0.64	2.18	-0.34	-5.08
IT Hardware	-0.28	2.97	1.69	-0.80	-6.32
Leisure Entertainment Hotels	0.62	1.69	0.32	-0.37	-4.76
Media and Photography	0.99	1.38	0.84	-0.86	-5.56
Mining	-0.14	1.87	2.17	-1.07	-5.75
Multi-utilities	0.31	3.00	-0.80	0.50	-4.91
Oil and Gas	-0.25	3.26	0.83	-0.12	-5.92
Pharmaceutical	0.10	2.53	0.67	-0.13	-5.40
Real Estate	0.51	1.84	0.34	-0.29	-4.80
Specialty Other Finance	-0.02	2.92	0.15	0.78	-5.70
Steel	0.44	1.51	-0.09	0.37	-4.33
Support Services	0.44	1.51	-0.09	0.37	-4.33
Telecommunication	0.99	0.50	0.96	-0.28	-5.30
Transport	0.72	2.06	-0.26	-0.23	-4.73
Water	0.91	2.47	-1.04	0.33	-5.01

Though there were attempts made earlier in evaluating CERs, it had a limited emphasis on the variables and small sample size. Hence, this study is made to provide a detailed

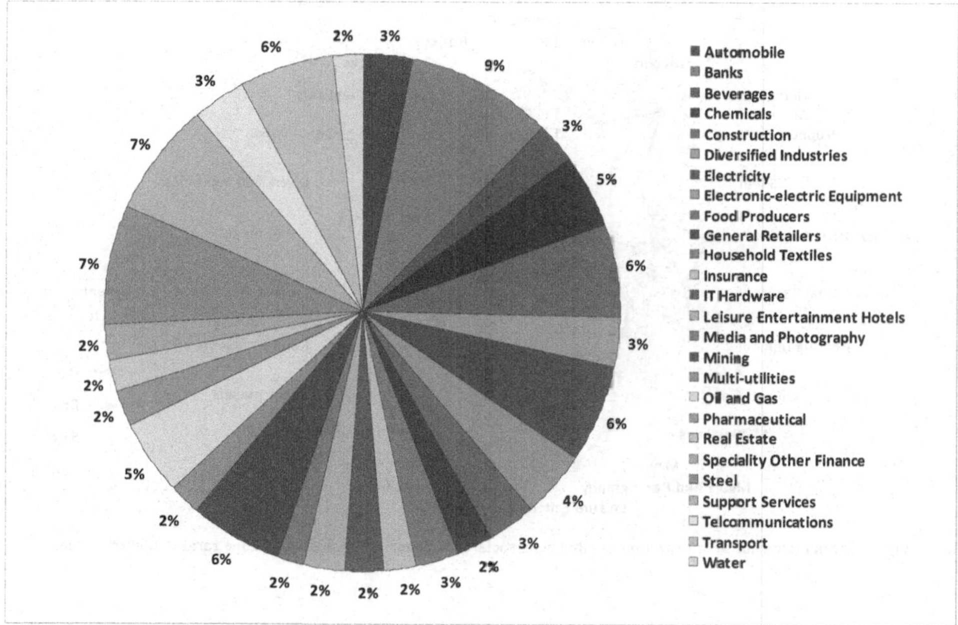

Fig. 1. Sustainability Reports used for the Statistical Analysis (N=2235)

analysis on CERs using GRI sustainability reporting guidelines (2000), with a very large sample and wide demographics.

III. Research Objectives and Hypothesis

The overall objective of the study is to examine and analyze systematically the CERs of all the possible sectors in a global perspective. To perform a greater reliable and robust approach, text mining approach is used to perform on a larger data sample. The research objectives are:

1. To construct a text mining and knowledge recovery model for generating frequencies and scorecard for the sustainability reports.
2. To examine which of the selected variables i.e., organizational, environmental, social performance and economic are most preferred among all the sectors.

Prior studies suggest that the motivation to report would be higher in the sectors with high environmental pressures compared with sectors with low environmental pressures. [25] - [27]. On the contrary KPMG identified the growing desire of low-environment-impact firms to report. Though these studies highlighted the significance of industry based disclosure, little emphasis is made on the aspects they disclose and of their correlation. The hypotheses used are: *Hypothesis 1 – 3:* The extent of reporting of the selected variables i.e., organizational (H1), social (H2) and environmental (H3) among the various nature of business is similar. *Hypothesis 4:* To determine which control variables discriminate between two or more naturally occurring groups.

IV. Methodology

The assessment technique used in the present study is adapted from questions based on GRI sustainability reporting guideline on organization, economic, environmental, and social performance by Denis et al. [28] using modified criteria that meet the requirement of effective text mining. Only selected variables were used in this study.

The data for the study i.e., CERs were extracted from Corporate Register website [29], which is a world directory of published corporate environmental and social reports. To select the relevant data for the study, judgmental sampling was applied in this study. In each of the available categories from the website, where the reports are less than 30 numbers were not considered. All the reports that were under year 2008 category were considered for the initial analysis (of text mining). Thus, the initial sample for the study is 2650 CER documents (inclusive of foreign language).

Text/data mining and extraction was done by writing a customized Java program. The different criteria that need to be checked were broken down into appropriate keywords. The basic idea was to search for keywords or related words in the reports that were to be analyzed and to check the presence or strength of these keywords. The keywords selected should be appropriate and even strong synonyms can be used for searching. A better approach would be to have the first level search with real keywords and second level searches with synonyms from a dictionary file. The first level searches could be given a higher score weight and second and third level (if any) searches given lower weights.

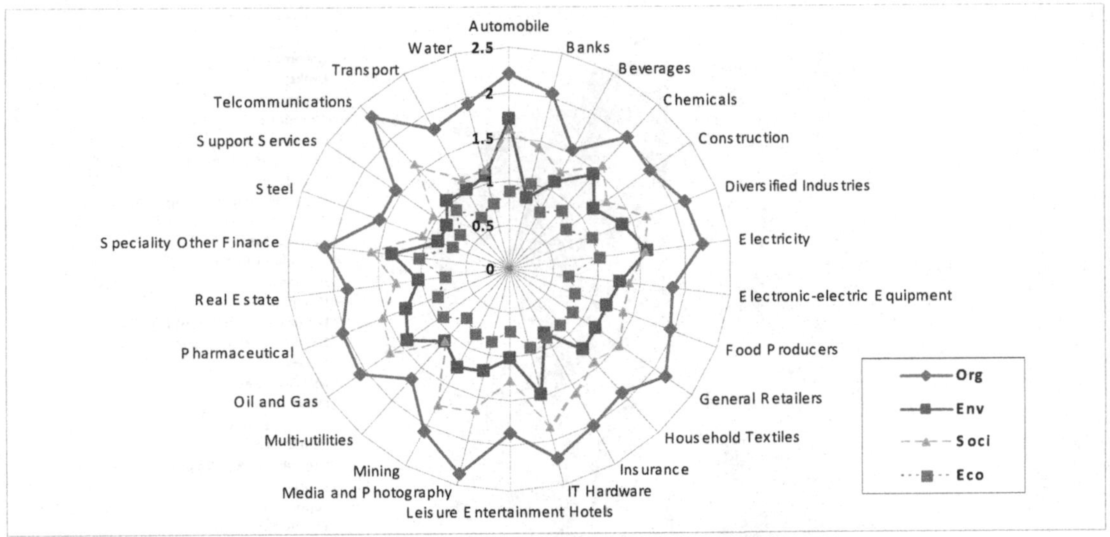

Fig. 2. Mean preference of organization, environment, social and economic variables among the various industrial sectors

TABLE III
BOX'S M TEST RESULTS

	Box's M	812.982
F	3.178	2.246
	250	110
	7.193E5	449035.606
	.000	.000

TABLE IV
WILK'S LAMBDA – MDA

Test of Function(s)	Wilks' Lambda	Chi-square	Df	Sig.
1 through 4	.681	852.207	100	.000
2 through 4	.866	320.385	72	.000
3 through 4	.945	124.649	46	.000
4	.978	49.206	22	.001

TABLE V
STANDARDIZED CANONICAL DISCRIMINANT FUNCTION COEFFICIENTS

	Function			
	1	2	3	4
avg_org	-.643	-.555	-.258	**1.719**
avg_env	**1.600**	-.412	.038	-.044
avg_soc	-.374	**2.031**	-.306	-.650
avg_eco	-.192	-.679	**1.341**	-.478

The keyword frequency count done is then scaled between 0 and 10. The reason for scaling is that it takes range of values and then maps it to a score. So the possible error in the frequency count is lessened.

V. RESULTS AND DISCUSSION

After executing the simulated program, the environmental reports that are in foreign languages, i.e., other than English are excluded for analysis. An elimination criterion, with a total frequency of 'less than 10' is applied. Thus the sample size for further statistical analysis is reduced to 2235. Exploratory and confirmatory analyses were performed on the said data.

In the present study, around 26 sectors were chosen after applying the elimination criteria. The major contribution towards the number of reports (greater than 100) have come from banks, support services, steel, mining, electricity, construction, transport, oil and gas and chemical sectors. Overall sectoral composition of contribution of reports is shown in fig. 1.

It is observed that organizational performance variable (1.94) is most addressed followed by social (1.41), environmental (1.16) and economic performance (0.83) respectively as shown in table 1. One-way ANOVA is performed to find whether the preference of organization, environment, social, and economic variables differ from the industrial sectors. The findings show that all the variables are significant at 0.05 level significance, null hypotheses (H1) (H2), and (H3) are rejected. This indicates that, variables selected differ among the various industrial sectors (see fig. 2).

The goal of MDA (Multivariate Discriminant Analysis) is to classify cases into three or more categories using continuous or dummy categorical variables as predictors. Upon performing MDA, it extracted four functions with canonical correlation as 'moderate to weak' i.e., for function-1 (0.462), function-2 (0.291), function-3 (0.183), and function-4 (0.148). Wilks Lambda test is significant for all the variables. As the Wilk's Lambda in table 4 is smaller, the more important is the

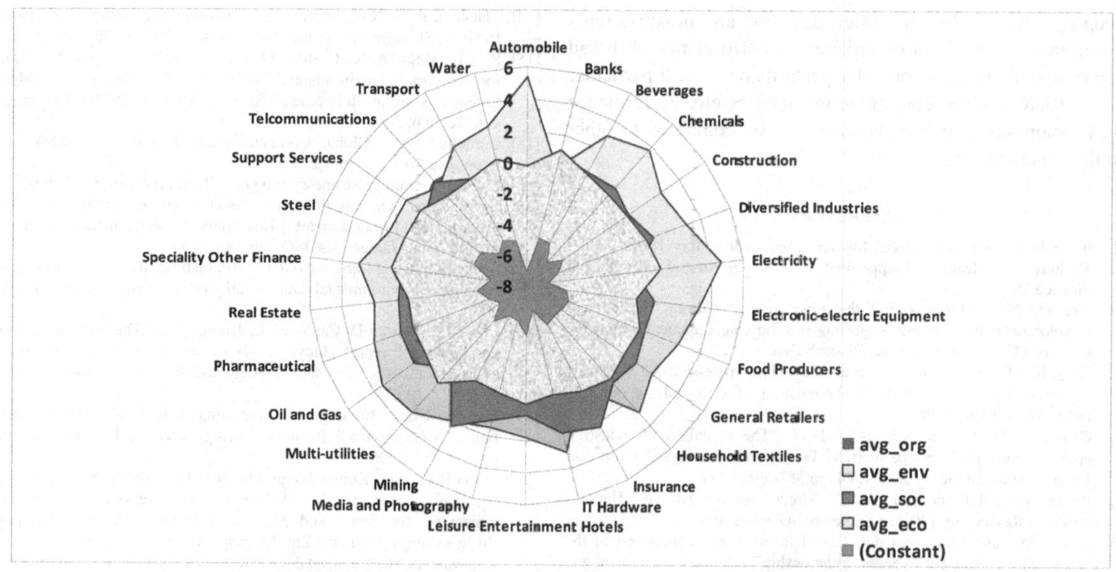

Fig. 3. Graphical view of fisher linear discriminant across all categories

independent variable to the discriminant function. Box's M Test as in table 3, is sensitive in meeting the assumption of multivariate normality. The result indicates that groups do differ in covariance matrices, violating the assumption of Multivariate Discriminant Analysis (MDA). The contribution of a variable to the discriminant function in the context of the other predictor variables is explained in table 5. Organisation variable contributes 1.719 in function-4, environmental variable contributes 1.60 in function-1, social variable contributes 2.031 in function-2, and economic variable contributes 1.341 in function-3.

Eigen values indicate that, function-1 contributes predominantly with 64.5% followed by function-2 (22%), function-3 (8.2%), and function-4 (5.3%) respectively. This is also confirmed from the structure matrix that environmental variable has greater correlation in function-1, followed by social variable in function-2, economic variable in function-3, and organization variable in function-4. This indicates that the environmental variable has a greater significant factor in contributing towards the explanation of sustainability report.

The Fisher coefficients are extracted to compute a discriminant score for each dimension and the case is classified in the group generating the highest score as seen in table 2. The graphical lay out of the fisher linear discriminant is depicted in fig. 3. The classification results indicate 10.7% of the cases that are correctly classified. All the three cases (industries) are equally evaluated with similar scoring, thereby proves a satisfactory discriminant analysis. The low score of prediction could be because of the low percent of sectoral reports available (i.e., below 9%).

VI. Limitations and Conclusion

The data mining on the qualitative reports done can be improved by making the search more intelligent. In spite of large sample, the sector-wise composition of reports is below 10%.

Banking sector contributed major sustainability reports during 2008. By using one-way ANOVA, it is found that all the variables selected are preferred differently across various industrial sectors. Organizational variable is widely reported followed by social, environmental and economic factors. In order to determine which control variables discriminate between two or more naturally occurring groups; MDA was performed. The findings are very interesting and significant, as environmental variable has greater significant contributing factor towards explanation of sustainability report. The predictions are of low score, due to the lower composition of the industrial sector.

On a general note, reporting on sustainability performance is an important way for organizations to manage their impact on sustainable development. The challenges of sustainable development are many, and it is widely accepted that organizations have not only a responsibility but also a great ability to exert positive change on the state of the world's economy, and environmental and social conditions. Reporting leads to improved sustainable development outcomes because it allows organizations to measure, track, and improve their performance on specific issues. Organizations are much more likely to effectively manage an issue that they can measure. As well as helping organizations manage their impacts, sustainability reporting promotes transparency and accountability. This is because an organization discloses information in the public domain. In doing so, stakeholders (people affected by or interested in an organization's operations) can track an organization's performance on broad themes – such as environmental performance - or a particular issue - such as labor conditions in factories etc. Performance can be monitored year on year, or can be compared to other similar organizations.

REFERENCES

[1] Bayon R. Reporting goes global. Environmental Finance May: 16–18. 2002.

[2] Mathias A. Meacher disappointed by UK reporting. Environmental Finance May: 10. 2002.

[3] Gee D. 2001. Business and the Environment: Current Trends and Developments in Corporate Reporting and Ranking,Technical Report 54. European Environment Agency:Copenhagen.

[4] Gray, R. "The Greening of Accountancy – the Profession After Peace", Research Report 17, Chartered Association of Certified Accountants (ACCA): London, 1990.

[5] Characklis G. W. and Richards, D. J. "The evolution of industrial environmental performance metrics: Trends and challenges," Corporate Environmental Strategy, vol.6, no.4, pp.387-398, 1999.

[6] Porter, M. and Linde van der, C. "Green and competitive," Harvard Business Review, pp.120-134 September-October, 1995.

[7] Porter, M. and Linde van der, C. "Toward a new conception of the environment: Competitiveness relationship." Journal of Economic Perspectives, vol.9, no.4, pp.Green and competitive," Harvard Business Review, pp.120-134 September-October, pp.97-118.

[8] Schuster, A. "Die Erstellung Einer Okobilanz unter Berucksichtigung des Kosten – Nutzen Effektes, magisterrerum socialium oeconomicarumque." Sozial-undWirtschafts-wissenschaftliche Fakultat der Universitat Wien, Wien, 2000.

[9] Livesey, S. "The discourse of the middle ground: Citizen Shell commits to sustainable development". Management Communication Quarterly, vol.15, no.3, pp.313–349, 2002.

[10] Livesey, S. M. and Kearins, K. "Transparent and caring corporations? A study of sustainability reports by The Body Shop and Royal Dutch/Shell," Organization and Environment, vol.15, no.3, pp.233–258,2002.

[11] Milne, M. J., Kearins, K. and Walton, S. "Creating adventures in Wonderland: The journey metaphor and environmental sustainability," Organization, 2006

[12] Milne, M. J., Tregidga, H. and Walton, S. "Playing with magic lanterns: the New Zealand Business Council for Sustainable Development and corporate triple bottom line reporting," Proceedings of 4th APIRA Conference, Singapore, 2004.

[13] Mohardt, J. E. "Scoring corporate environmental and sustainability reports using GRI 2000, ISO 14031 and other criteria," Corporate Social Responsibility and Environmental Management, vol.9, pp.215-233, 2002.

[14] Marshall, R. S. "Corporate environment reporting: What's in a metric?" Business Strategy and the Environment, vol.12, pp.87-106, 2003.

[15] Rao, P., Singh, A. K., Castillo, O., Intal Jr., S. P. and Sajid, A. "A metric for corporate environmental indicators…for Small and Medium Enterprises in the Philippines," Business Strategy and the Environment, vol.17, No.6, 2006.

[16] Cornelius PK. Global Competitiveness Report, 2002–2004, World Economic Forum: Geneva, 2003.

[17] Davis J. Journal of Business Strategy, vol.12, no.4, pp.14–17, 2001.

[18] International Organisation for Standardization (ISO). ISO 14031 Environmental Management – Environmental Performance Evaluation – Standards and Guidelines. ISO: Geneva, 1999.

[19] Global Reporting Initiative (GRI), Sustainability Reporting Guidelines on Economic Environmental and Social Performance, Boston, MA: GRI, 2000.

[20] Lober DJ, Bynum D, Campbell E, Jacques M. "The 100 plus corporate environmental report study: A survey of an evolving environmental management tool," Business Strategy and the Environment, vol.6, no.3, pp.57–73, 1997.

[21] Giuliano Noci, "Environmental reporting in Italy: Current practice and future developments," Business Strategy and the Environment, vol.9, pp.211–223, 2000.

[22] Purba Rao, Alok Kumar Singh, Olivia la O' Castillo, S. Ponciano Intal Jr., and Ather Sajid, "A metric for corporate environmental indicators…for Small and Medium Enterprises in the Philippines," Business Strategy and the Environment, vol.17, no.6, 2006.

[23] R. Isenmann, "Customized corporate environmental reporting by internet-based push and pull technologies", Eco-Management and Auditing, vol.8, pp.100-110, 2001.

[24] J. Modapothala and B. Issac, Evaluation of Corporate Environmental Reports using Data Mining Approach, International Conference on Computer Engineering and Technology, Singapore, 2009.

[25] Martin AD, Hadley DJ. Corporate environmental non-reporting – a UK FTSE 350 perspective. Business Strategy and the Environment in press, 2006.

[26] Clemens B. "Changing environmental strategies over time: An empirical study of the steel industry in the United States," Journal of Environmental Management, vol.61, pp.1–11, 2001.

[27] Kolk A. "Trends in sustainability reporting by the Fortune Global 250," Business Strategy and the Environment, vol.12, pp.279–291, 2003.

[28] Dennis M. Hussey, Patrick L. Kirsop, and Ronald E. Meissen, "Global Reporting Initiative Guidelines: An Evaluation of Sustainable Development Metrics for Industry," Environmental Quality Management, Autumn, pp.1-20, 2001

[29] Online Corporate Register, [Online]: www.corporateregister.com [Accessed 30 March, 2009].G. O. Young, "Synthetic structure of industrial plastics (Book style with paper title and editor)," in *Plastics*, 2nd ed. vol. 3, J. Peters, Ed. New York: McGraw-Hill, 1964, pp. 15–64.

A Proposed Treatment for Visual Field Loss caused by Traumatic Brain Injury using Interactive Visuotactile Virtual Environment

Attila J. Farkas, Alen Hajnal, Mohd F. Shiratuddin and Gabriella Szatmary

***Abstract* - In this paper, we propose a novel approach of using interactive virtual environment technology in Vision Restoration Therapy caused by Traumatic Brain Injury. We called the new system Interactive Visuotactile Virtual Environment and it holds a promise of expanding the scope of already existing rehabilitation techniques. Traditional vision rehabilitation methods are based on passive psychophysical training procedures, and can last up to six months before any modest improvements can be seen in patients. A highly immersive and interactive virtual environment will allow the patient to practice everyday activities such as object identification and object manipulation through the use 3D motion sensoring handheld devices such data glove or the Nintendo Wiimote. Employing both perceptual and action components in the training procedures holds the promise of more efficient sensorimotor rehabilitation. Increased stimulation of visual and sensorimotor areas of the brain should facilitate a comprehensive recovery of visuomotor function by exploiting the plasticity of the central nervous system. Integrated with a motion tracking system and an eye tracking device, the interactive virtual environment allows for the creation and manipulation of a wide variety of stimuli, as well as real-time recording of hand-, eye- and body movements and coordination. The goal of the project is to design a cost-effective and efficient vision restoration system.**

Keywords: restoration, stroke, therapy, vision, visuotactile, virtual environment

I. Introduction

THIS research investigates the possibilities for incorporating a 3D interactive virtual environment (VE) system or the Interactive Visuotactile Virtual Environment (IVVE) as part of treatments for restoring visual field following traumatic brain injury (TBI). The proposed treatment approach consists of creating an interactive stimulus set around transitional areas at the interface of intact and damaged visual field regions. Current conventional treatments only involve presentation of two-dimensional (2D), or one-dimensional stimulus arrays to the patient. We propose a new treatment approach whereby real-time 3D virtual space with the presence of 3D virtual objects (Fig.1.) will be presented using the IVVE system. We believe that these 3D stimuli simulate real life situations more closely and more effectively and most likely give rise to cross-modal interaction between the senses serving hand-eye coordination, hypothetically enhancing the rehabilitative effect.

A. J. Farkas, and A. Hajnal are with the Department of Psychology, University of Southern Mississippi, Hattiesburg, MS 39406 USA (corresponding author phone: 601-266-4617; fax: 601-266-5580; e-mail: alen.hajnal@usm.edu).

M. F. Shiratuddin is with the School of Construction, The University of Southern Mississippi, Hattiesburg, MS 39406 USA.

G. Szatmary is with the Department of Neurology, Hattiesburg Clinic, Hattiesburg, MS 39402 USA.

Vision Restoration Therapy

Vision Restoration Therapy (VRT) is a noninvasive procedure developed to restore functionality of damaged neural pathways and cortical regions by exploiting the natural plasticity of the central nervous system. VRT is implemented to restore visual field defects that arise as a result of stroke and other traumatic brain injuries. Traditionally, these visual field deficits were considered untreatable. However, recent advancements in computer technologies have allowed the advent of VRT that can be performed using a desktop Personal Computer (PC) in the privacy of the patient's home and comfort. The downside of the currently administered therapy is its cost and duration of recovery; the training includes daily one-hour sessions for the duration of six months. Despite the early promising results [1], [2], more recent outcomes have not been convincing [3]. The major criticism of VRT is the lack of control for eye fixation [4], [5]. By definition, the visual field can be mapped onto appropriate neural substrates only if the eyes are fixated, that is, stationary. As soon as fixation is not maintained, any recovery that occurs is considered compensatory, and not truly indicative of any neurological restoration of actual brain cells [6].

Advantages of Visuomotor Restoration over Visual-only Restoration

Even though very little restorative effect has been shown by the mostly passive psychophysical training procedures included in VRT, so far, no attempt has been made to directly

T. Sobh, K. Elleithy (eds.), *Innovations in Computing Sciences and Software Engineering*,
DOI 10.1007/978-90-481-9112-3_84,

train the visual system simultaneously with the motor system, whereas in real life, the two systems are continuously integrated. The separation of perceptual and motor systems is a matter of scientific convenience that does not reflect actual behavior in real space and time. Another drawback of existing VRT techniques is that they are restricted to a 2D visual field. Integrated sensorimotor training in 3D space holds the promise of proving VRT more effective in 3D, since it is closer to real life situations and activities that ultimately have to be served by any post-TBI rehabilitation treatment. It is a well established fact in skill acquisition research that decision making in healthy individuals who use action and perception jointly is superior to apprehension based on perception only [7]. To date, stimulation of both visual and motor pathways during recovery of visual function in a 3D environment that resembles everyday locations, tasks and events has not been incorporated into any of the restorative training procedures. Our research aims to fill this gap.

Rationale for using 3D Interactive Virtual Environment Technology in Vision Restoration Therapy

A 3D interactive VE has several properties, which makes it a valuable treatment tool. Firstly, objects in a 3D virtual space can be easily manipulated in real-time. Using this feature one can adjust the distance and shape of objects presented to a combined field of anopic and intact areas (Fig. 1).

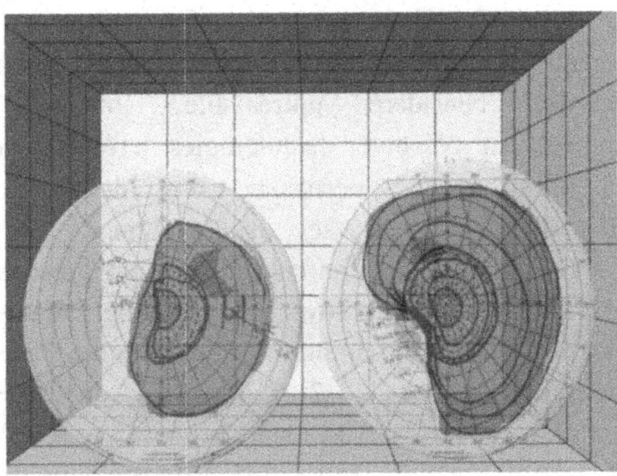

Fig. 1. The two distinct dark areas represent the anopic portion of the visual field of the left and right eye, respectively.

Secondly, in a 3D interactive VE, not only the shape of the stimulus can be modified, but we can also add information about distance, depth, and illumination; hence making it not only interactive but also information rich. The additional information about objects may further stimulate the visual processing via cross-modal interaction, for example when completing figures with missing or occluded areas.

Thirdly, the 3D interactive VE can be programmed to use tactile information to establish the interaction between a user and the 3D objects. By giving patients the opportunity to interact with the VE to fit their visual abilities, we could gain insight about how the loss of the visual field distorts the perceived visuomotor space. As a result of this mapping process, individualized treatment stimuli can be generated specifically to fit the needs and represent the damaged visual areas for each patient. Patients would be given a personalized treatment, tailored exactly to their visual field deficits.

Use of VE Technologies in Sensorimotor Rehabilitation

VE technologies have been used at many academic research levels to assist various motor rehabilitation efforts of stroke patients [8], [9]. However, due to high initial cost of investment and maintenance, and also the requirement of a highly qualified technician or operator, many of the VE systems are simply impractical and not viable for treatment purposes, and in the commercial world.

The recent advancement in video games software and hardware technologies have opened up a new avenue that can make 3D interactive VE more affordable and yet practical for patients' rehabilitation process. Video game consoles such as the Nintendo Wii have been used in motor rehabilitation after stroke [10], [11]. The Nintendo Wii, for example, uses a wireless motion sensing controller called the Wiimote that allows for more natural interactions with the video games. A user simply uses hand or body gestures or motions to perform specific interactions, for example in a bowling game a user simply swings the Wiimote as if one is throwing a bowling ball. In this research, we propose the use of the Nintendo Wii video game console as the enabling technology. The Wiimote itself coupled with specially designed game-like VE can instigate not only visual recovery, but also improve hand-eye coordination. We believe that using such techniques can increase the level of recovery of patients going through the rehabilitation treatments as they involve a more active approach that can stimulate the visual cortex and involve motor control.

An Exemplary Pilot Treatment Procedure for Vision Restoration Therapy using 3D Interactive VE

A basic task for the patient would be to move a virtual 3D object starting from the anopic area until it can be identified. Depending on the severity and extent of the visual field deficit, identification would occur when a considerable portion of the object is still "occluded" by the anopic area. This is the basic procedure that will be used to map out the whole visual field. The reconstructed 3D visual field will contain the intact and anopic areas in the form of "optical tunnels" (Fig. 2) through the VE. Since the perceptual space is warped [12], we anticipate our empirical mapping procedure to reflect this by generating "curvy" optical tunnels.

The Main Stages of the Treatment Procedure

The first step is to map out the visual field identifying the transitional areas between intact and anopic regions. We will be able to recreate the perceived 3D environment as a topography of the patient's visual perception (Fig. 2). This procedure is usually preceded by the mapping out of the 2D visual field that is routinely performed as part of standard neuro-ophthalmologic clinical diagnosis using the Humphrey Field Analyzer [13], [14]. During the Humphrey perimetry test the patient fixates the central visual field without moving their eyes, and is asked to respond as quickly as possible to a series of visual stimuli, usually small dots or straight lines presented on the inner side of a hemi-sphere. After the assessment of the two dimensional visual field, we plan to continue testing in order to map out the whole three-dimensional visual space. Instead of these stimuli, we propose to use pictures of real objects as stimuli in a virtual environment.

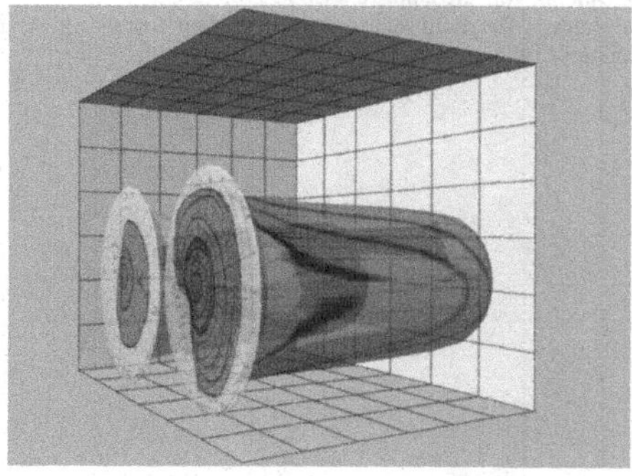

Fig. 2. The representation of the "optical tunnel" in a sample affected visual space. Darkened volumes are representative of damaged visual field areas. The "optical tunnel" is curved due to the warped nature of perceived space.

In this next step, the object is placed at the boundary between an intact and anopic area, so that only a small, unrecognizable portion of the object is visible. The patient is asked to slowly move the object towards the intact area until it becomes identifiable. This distance is recorded on each trial and will serve to map out the boundaries of the visual field deficit in the three-dimensional space. On each new trial a different object will be presented at one of many distances and eccentricities. A hypothetical sample three dimensional anopic area is represented as a complex group of warped "optical tunnels" (Fig. 2).

In the next step, an object is placed inside the intact area (Fig. 3 and Fig. 4) consisting of two components. One part of the object will represent the portion that allowed the patient to reliably identify it (depicted as non-occluded areas in Fig. 3 and Fig. 4) during the mapping phase of the treatment; the other part will be the unnoticed portion (depicted as occluded areas in Fig. 3 and Fig. 4). The two elements will be clearly visible to the patient, and the task will be to move the two pieces closer in a 3D virtual space to fit them together as two pieces of a puzzle in order to complete the whole object.

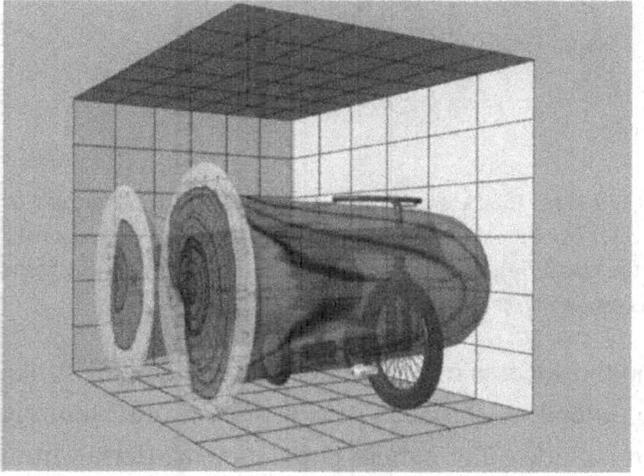

Fig. 3. The presentation of an object (such as a bicycle) to a hemianopic visual field. As a consequence of the visual deficit parts of the object will not be detected (darkened area).

The idea of this task is to project the incomplete object onto the intact areas, so the patient can detect the actual extent of his or her deficits. More specifically, the patient will receive direct feedback about the nature of distortion and the size of the unnoticed area. This procedure will be repeated until the size of the unnoticed area shrinks to a satisfactorily low level.

The vision restoration therapy is concluded by repeating the Humphrey perimetry test. A comparison with the pretest Humphrey results will be an objective indicator of how much actual visual restoration was achieved.

We plan to start collecting data on a sample of patients with acute stroke that occurred not more than 3 months ago in order to increase the chances of visual field recovery.

CONCLUSION

The goal of our project is to offer a novel approach to sensorimotor rehabilitation of stroke patients using 3D interactive VE technology.

Traditional methods rely on passive psychophysical techniques using 2D meaningless stimuli and involve training only visual perception. We plan to create an active restorative procedure that involves physical interactions with meaningful stimuli in simulations of functional behavioral tasks. We hope to adapt the Wii video game console for this purpose and use it as an interactive tool in a 3D interactive and immersive VE.

Fig. 4. The blocked areas (black area in the inset) and the visible areas (the front of the bicycle) from a side view. The apparent left-right reversal of the anopic areas of the visual field and the occluded part of the object is due to the way the image is projected on the retina.

Depending on the success of our proposed technique for stroke patients, we intend to broaden the scope of our training procedures to include other patient populations suffering from traumatic brain injuries and other neurological sensorimotor disorders.

REFERENCES

[1] E. Kasten, and B.A. Sabel, "Visual field enlargement after computer training in brain-damaged patients with homonymous deficits: an open pilot trial," *Restor. Neurol. Neurosci.*, vol. 8, pp. 113–27, 1995.

[2] E. Kasten, H. Strasburger, and B.A. Sabel, "Programs for diagnosis and therapy of visual field deficits in vision rehabilitation," *Spat. Vis.*, vol. 10, pp. 499–503, 1997.

[3] J. Reinhard, et al., "Does visual restitution training change absolute homonymous visual field defects? A fundus controlled study," *Br. J. Ophthalmol.*, vol. 89, pp. 30–35, 2005.

[4] J.C. Horton, "Vision restoration therapy: confounded by eye movements," *Br. J. Ophthalmol.*, vol. 89, pp. 792–794, 2005.

[5] G.T. Plant, "A work out for hemianopia," *Br. J. Ophthalmol.*, vol. 89, p. 2, 2005.

[6] A.R. Lane, D.T. Smith and T. Schenk. "Clinical treatment options for patients with homonymous visual field defects." *Clin. Ophthalmol.,* vol. 2(1), pp. 93–102, 2008.

[7] R.R. Oudejans, and C.F. Michaels, "The relevance of action in perceiving affordances: perception of catchableness of fly balls," *J. Exp. Psychol. Hum. Percept. Perform.*, vol. 22(4), pp. 879-891, 1996.

[8] J.C. Stewart, et al., "Pilot trial results from a virtual reality system designed to enhance recovery of skilled arm and hand movements after stroke," *Virt. Rehabil.*, p. 11-17, 2006.

[9] P.L. Weiss, and N. Katz, "The potential of virtual reality for rehabilitation," *J. Rehabil. Res. Dev.*, vol. 41(5), pp. vii-x, 2004.

[10] R.S. Leder, et al., "Nintendo Wii remote for computer simulated arm and wrist therapy in stroke survivors with upper extremity hemipariesis," *Virt. Rehabil.*, pp. 74-74, 2008.

[11] J. Decker, H. Li, D. Losowyj, and V. Prakash, "Wiihabilitation: rehabilitation of wrist flexion and extension using a wiimote-based game system," *Governor's School of Engineering and Technology Research Journal*, Retrieved on October 11, 2009 from http://www.osd.rutgers.edu/gs/09papers/Wii.pdf

[12] J.M. Foley, N.P. Ribeiro-Filho, and J.A. Da Silva, "Visual perception of extent and the geometry of visual space," *Vis. Res.*, vol. 44(2), pp. 147-156, 2004.

[13] P.J. Muirhead, and A.W. Johnston, "Reproducibility of central field results using the Humphrey Field Analyser in normal subjects," *Clin. Exp. Optom.*, vol.73(5), pp. 164-167, 1990.

[14] M.J. Haley, "The field analyser primer." San Leandro, CA: Allergan Humphrey, 1986.

Adaptive Collocation Methods for the Solution of Partial Differential Equations

Paulo Brito
Dept. of Chemical and Biological Technology, School of Technology and Management, Polytechnic Inst. of Bragança
Campus de Santa Apolónia, Apartado 1134
5301-857 Bragança - Portugal
paulo@ipb.pt

António Portugal
Dept. of Chemical Engineering, Faculty of Sciences and Technology, University of Coimbra
Pólo II, Rua Sílvio Lima
3030-790 Coimbra - Portugal
atp@eq.uc.pt

Abstract—**An integration algorithm that conjugates a Method of Lines (MOL) strategy based on finite differences space discretizations, with a collocation strategy based on increasing level dyadic grids is presented. It reveals potential either as a grid generation procedure and a Partial Differential Equation (PDE) integration scheme. It copes satisfactorily with a example characterized by a steep travelling wave and a example that presented a forming steep shock, which demonstrates its versatility in dealing with different types of steep moving front problems, exhibiting features like advection-diffusion, widely common in the standard Chemical Processes simulation models.**

Keywords-Partial Differential Equation; Numerical Methods; Adaptive Methods; Collocation Methods; Dyadic Grids

I. INTRODUCTION

One can state that the main purpose of science is to contribute for the understanding of the physical phenomena that surround us. Therefore, in order to achieve this goal, scientific researchers apply the so called scientific method that can be resumed as:

- Use of experience and data available for recognition of problems that need to be solved.
- Formulation of hypothesis that potentially would solve the problem detected.
- Gathering of information in order to test the hypothesis formulated.
- Confirmation or rejection of the hypothesis formulated by the analysis of former or new data obtained.

The generally explanatory hypothesis can be simply a model, or more precisely, a mathematical model, that resume the observed phenomena on more easily treatable relations between abstract entities trough mathematical operations. In the field of mathematical models, one can narrow even more the scope of interest to problems defined over space-time continuous domains, where phenomena are not only affected by the values of the variables that define its state, but also by the gradients of these variables in relation to the independent coordinates. In the latter case, the mathematical models are necessarily constituted by differential (or integral) equations defined on multidimensional domains, i.e., partial differential equations (PDE's). However, the process of constructing a suitable model, or modelling, has to be complemented with the not less important task of solving it efficiently.

II. NUMERICAL METHODS

It is clear that it is not always possible to solve mathematical problems using analytic procedures. In these cases (usually non-linear problems), one has to resort to numerical analysis, the study of algorithms, i.e. sequential operation schemes that generally imply a discretization of continuous defined problems. These schemes can be applied in the solution of a variety of mathematical problems, such as optimization, calculation of integrals, interpolation, resolution of algebraic or differential equations, etc. Our interest resides on the numerical methods for the solution of time dependent partial differential equations (or systems of equations) defined over one- or multidimensional space domains. These schemes usually imply the construction of discrete grids that cover the total domain, and the approximation of the continuous solution by basis functions. The most important classes of numerical methods developed for the solution of PDE's differ between each other by the type of basis functions chosen, e.g.:

- Finite Differences (FD) – Taylor expansion series.
- Finite Elements (FE) – Interpolating polynomials.
- Spectral – Orthogonal Functions.

A. Method of Lines

However, our interest reside in a general strategy for the solution of PDE's named Method of Lines (MOL)[1] which structure can accommodate different strategies of mesh discretization. Generally, the numerical solution of PDE's imply the approximation of the original differential problem defined over a continuous domain, to a system of algebraic equations defined on a discretized domain. This transformation may be done simultaneously on every independent variable. Alternatively, one may apply a sequenced strategy: discretization of the original problem in all directions except one (usually time for Initial-Boundary Value Problems) and integration in remaining direction using an integrator package. The PDE original problem is approximated to a system of ordinary differential equations (ODE's), which is solved by a standard ODE integrator. So, one can use a variety of different basis functions: FD approximations, different order polynomials, wavelets[2,3], radial basis functions[4], etc, to execute the discretization.

T. Sobh, K. Elleithy (eds.), *Innovations in Computing Sciences and Software Engineering*,
DOI 10.1007/978-90-481-9112-3_85,

B. Adaptation Concept

The classical approach to these kind of procedures is generally rigid and not adaptable to its evolution. One way to turn around the problems that may arise from the lack of flexibility of that approach is the introduction of the adaptation concept. Adaptivity implies the adjustment of algorithm parameters to the particular circumstances of the solution evolution. In the field of numerical solution of PDE´s it can assume the following purposes:

- h-refinement – grid refinement and relaxation.
- p-refinement – adjustment of approximating orders.
- r-refinement – introduction of nodal velocities.

These strategies are not mutually exclusive and may be combined in mixed adaptive methods. The application of adaptivity in the PDE solving field has already several decades, and the number and variety of methods proposed is rather extensive [5,6]. However, the primordial objectives of the adaptive procedure are generally the same: the construction of grids that concentrate nodes in the domain regions where the solution is more active (i.e. shows steeper gradients) and disperse them in the remaining regions, and follow efficiently the problematic features of the solution. The application of adaptivity into the MOL strategy concept is straightforward [7].

C. Dyadic Grids

We chose to construct grids at each time step of the integration, based in a series of embedded one-dimensional dyadic grids of decreasing level. A *k*-level one-dimensional dyadic grid is defined by a nodal mesh with 2^k intervals. Obviously, in a correspondent uniform grid, the size of a *k*-level grid is constant through the total domain. A higher level grid is constructed by adding nodes to the immediately previous one, at every interval middle position (Fig. 1).

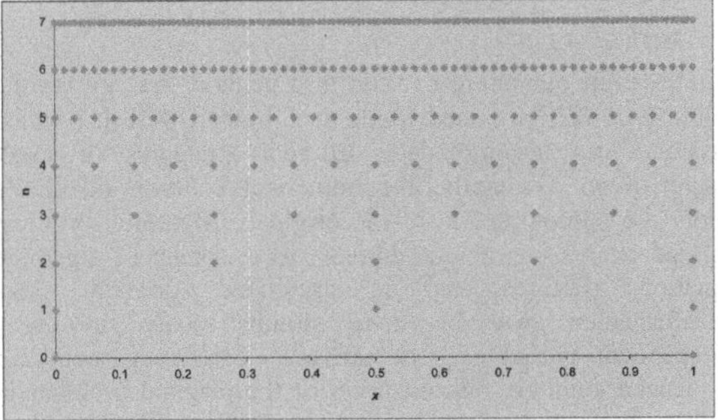

Fig. 1. Uniform dyadic grids of increasing level n.

It is important to note that a grid of level *k* is always included in all grids of higher level. So, the purpose is to generate grids that combine nodes of different levels according to the function activity at the various regions of the domain. It is obvious that the presented strategy can be easily extended to multidimensional domains.

For that purpose, we define a collocation strategy that uses function dependent features, to allow the activation (or deactivation) of nodes belonging to dyadic grids ranging from the lower resolution level (*M*) – the basis level; to a maximum allowed resolution level (*N*).

D. Numerical Algorithm

Applying the dyadic grid concept with finite differences approximations, we devise a collocation algorithm for grid generation which can be applied in MOL algorithm for the solution of PDE's. Considering a region of space domain defined by two consecutive dyadic grids (Fig. 2), a collocation algorithm is developed for activating the required nodes by the procedure described below.

Collocation Algorithm

- $k = M$
- **for** $i = 1, \ldots, 2^k - 1$
- estimate U_i^n (order n derivative at node *i*) by finite differences
- **if** collocation criterion is met: select intermediate nodes of level *k*+1: $x_{2i-1}^{k+1}; x_{2i}^{k+1}; x_{2i+1}^{k+1}$
- $k = k + 1$ (repeat **for** $k = M, \ldots, N - 1$)

$k+1$: x^{k+1}_{2i-1} x^{k+1}_{2i} x^{k+1}_{2i+1}

k: …… x^{k}_{i-1} x^{k}_{i} x^{k}_{i+1} ……

Fig. 2. Representation of the connection between nodes of consecutive levels.

The collocation criterion obeys to two different strategies. First, the grid size is calculated by,

$$\Delta x = \frac{x_{i+1}^k - x_{i-1}^k}{2}, \qquad (1)$$

Then, we define a criterion that captures oscillations on the finite difference estimate profile:

Criterion I

- calculate $\delta_1 = U_i^n \times U_{i-1}^n$ and $\delta_2 = U_{i+1}^n \times U_i^n$
- criterion verified if:
- $\left|U_i^n \times \Delta x\right| > \varepsilon_1$ or $\begin{cases} \delta_1 \le 0 \\ \delta_2 \le 0 \end{cases}$ and $\dfrac{\left|U_{i-1}^n\right| + \left|U_i^n\right| + \left|U_{i+1}^n\right|}{3} > \varepsilon_2$

Additionally, a second criterion that tracks high variations on the finite difference estimate profile is defined:

Criterion II

- calculate $\delta_1 = U_i^n - U_{i-1}^n$ and $\delta_2 = U_{i+1}^n - U_i^n$
- criterion verified if:
  - $|U_i^n \times \Delta x| > \varepsilon_1$ or $\delta_1 \times \delta_2 \le 0$ and $\dfrac{|\delta_1| + |\delta_2|}{2} > \varepsilon_2$

ε_1 and ε_2 represent the criteria tolerances. Both criteria tend to take advantage of the approximating nature of the space derivatives estimating scheme. The errors associated with the finite difference procedure induce artificial oscillations in the estimated derivative profiles mainly near the steep fronts regions, which can be identified. Therefore, we increase the grid resolution on these regions by activation of higher level nodes that do not verify the more demanding collocation criteria. The gathering of all active nodes in every dyadic grid, generate the overall grid. One advantage of this procedure is the possibility of applying the collocation algorithm sequentially, analyzing several derivative orders by stages, e.g. generating a grid that verify the first derivative condition and subsequently running the obtained grid through a second derivative analysis.

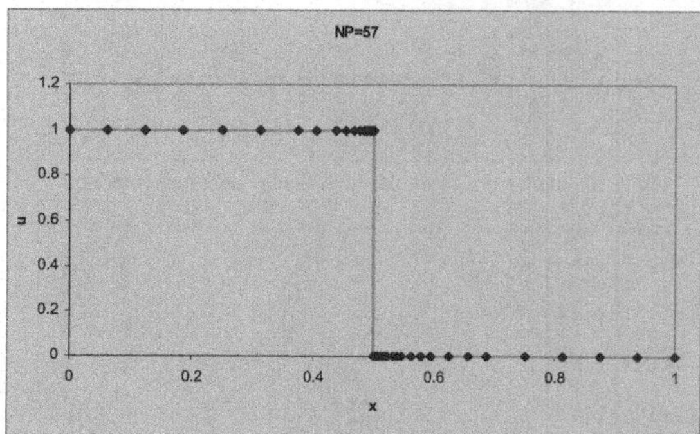

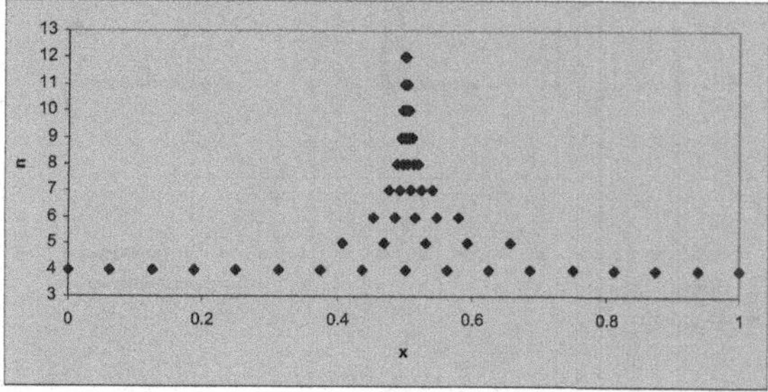

Fig. 3. Grid generated for the Step Function.

III. Grid Generation

First, we tested the performance of the collocation algorithm for the generation of grids that conform to the properties of selected one-dimensional functions.

A. *Example 1 – Step Function*

A simple function that represents a one-dimensional negative space step, i.e. a discontinuity located at the middle position of the domain [0,1],

$$\begin{cases} u(x) = 1 \ , & 0 \le x < 0.5 \\ u(x) = 0 \ , & 0.5 \le x \le 1 \end{cases}, \tag{2}$$

is tested using the collocation criterion I. We analyse the finite difference approximation (5 nodes centred) of the first derivative, with $\varepsilon_1 = \varepsilon_2 = 0.1$. The basis grid of lowest level is a uniform grid with 2^4 intervals and the highest dyadic grid level is N=12. The grid generated is presented in Fig. 3. We observe that the algorithm is able to detect the discontinuity quite satisfactorily and the constructed grid is adequate to represents the function main features with a reasonable total number of nodes (NP=57).

B. *Example 2 – TGH Function*

Now, we try to represent in a discrete fashion a function characterised by a very steep front located at the middle of the domain, surrounded by two flat plateaus at each side. The function is defined by the following hyperbolic tangent:

$$u(x) = \tanh(60x - 0.01). \tag{3}$$

Again, it is applied the collocation criterion I, by the analysis of the finite difference approximation (5 nodes centred) of the first derivative, with $\varepsilon_1 = \varepsilon_2 = 0.1$, M=4 and N=12. The results are resumed in Fig. 4. We conclude that the front is easily tracked and the generated grid allows the representation of the by a reasonable total number of nodes (NP=58).

The algorithm proves to be able to generate grids that efficiently detect and represent steep features in the studied functions.

IV. Simulation Experiments

The node collocation procedure is incorporated in an algorithm for the resolution of one-dimensional time-dependent PDE´s. This strategy is based on the conjugation of a MOL algorithm where the space derivatives are approximated by finite differences formulas, with grid generation procedure at specified times that reformulate the space grid according to the solution evolution. At these intermediate times the solution profiles are reconstructed through an interpolation scheme. The time integration is performed by the ODE integrator DASSL. Therefore the presented algorithm can be included in the class of h-refinement PDE solution adaptive procedures.

A. *Model 1 – Advection Equation*

We test the integration algorithm using a very simple equation known as the advection equation,

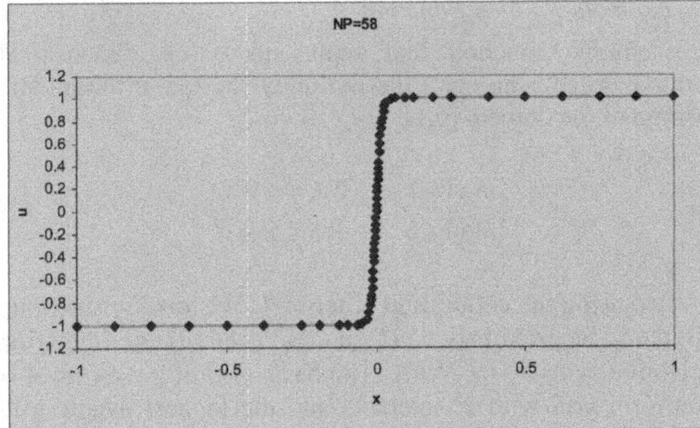

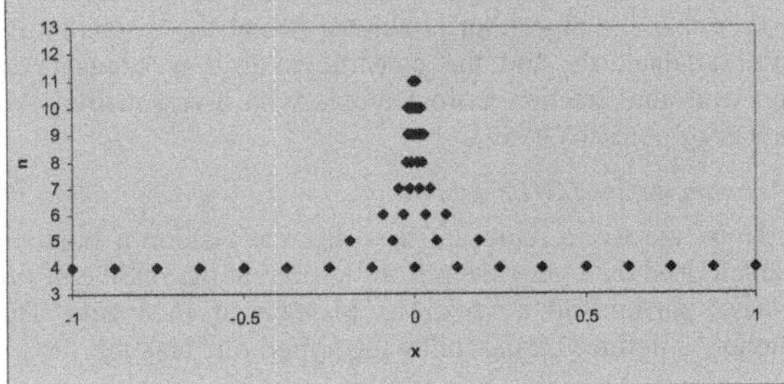

Fig. 4. Grid generated for the TGH Function.

$$\frac{\partial u}{\partial t} = -v\frac{\partial u}{\partial x}, \tag{4}$$

defined over the domain $x \in [0,1]$, with the boundary condition,

$$u(0,t) = 0. \tag{5}$$

In spite of its apparent simplicity, the solution of this equation can be rather problematic, depending on the initial conditions chosen. The solution space wave is propagated through time without distortion, with velocity v in the positive direction of the x referential. If the initial profile exhibits a steep front, the adequate numerical translation of the continuous problem by a uniform fixed grid, may prove to be difficult. So, we use the function,

$$u(x,0) = \exp\left(-\frac{(x-x_0)^2}{\varepsilon}\right), \tag{6}$$

TABLE I. SIMULATION PARAMETERS FOR MODEL 1

Collocation criterion	I or II
Derivative order for collocation	n=1 and 2; or n=1
Time step	10^{-3}
Finite Difference approximation	5 nodes centred - uniform grid
Interpolation strategy	Cubic splines with 9 nodes
Time integrator tolerances	10^{-6}
Dyadic grids levels	M=4; N=10
$\varepsilon_1 = \varepsilon_2 = 10^{-2}$	

with $x_0 = 0.5$ and $\varepsilon = 1\times10^{-4}$, which represents a steep wave to test the algorithm performance in the conditions described in Table I.

The results obtained are resumed in Fig. 5 and 6, using criterion I and II, respectively. It is observed that the algorithm provides rather good results, providing a close track of the wave propagation until it collides to the right boundary. The results obtained with the two criteria appear to be very similar.

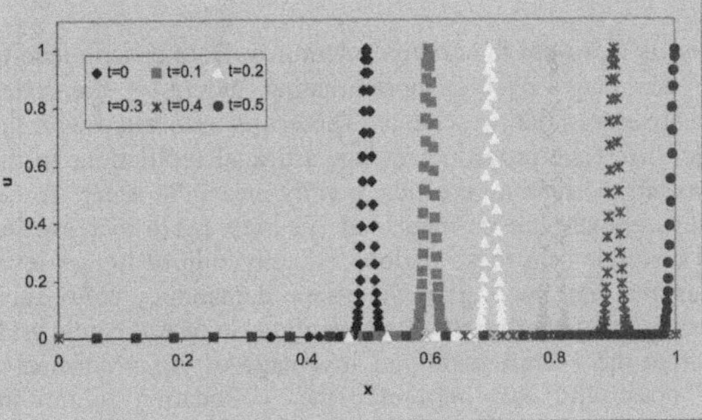

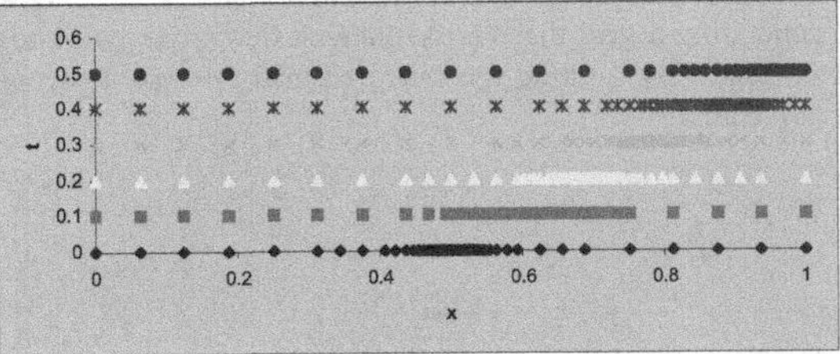

Fig. 5. Simulation results for the advection model using criterion I.

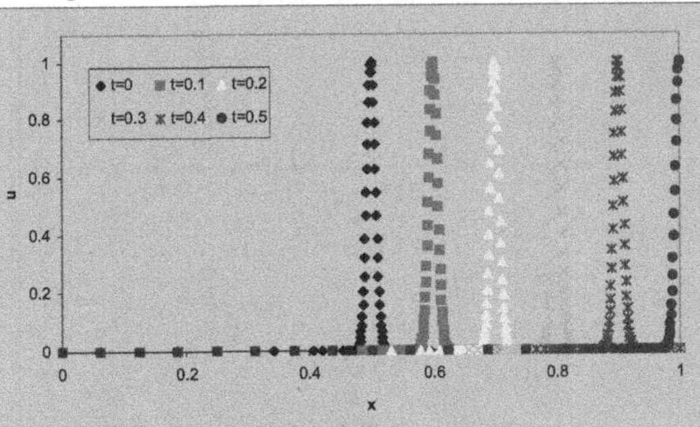

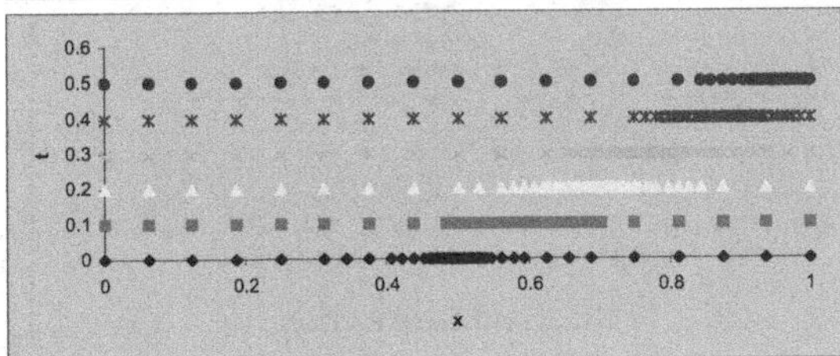

Fig. 6. Simulation results for the advection model using criterion II.

B. *Model 2 – 1-D Burgers' Equation*

The second test model is the widely studied 1-D inviscid Burgers' Equation[4],

$$\frac{\partial u}{\partial t} = -u\frac{\partial u}{\partial x} + \nu\frac{\partial^2 u}{\partial x^2}, \tag{7}$$

defined over the domain x∈ [0,1], with the boundary conditions:

$$u(0,t) = u(1,t) = 0. \tag{8}$$

This PDE represent an advection-diffusion problem, which, depending of the initial condition applied, may present some interesting challenges. Therefore, for the initial condition,

$$u(x,0) = \sin(2\pi x) + \frac{1}{2}\sin(\pi x), \tag{9}$$

as the advection velocities are the solution itself, the problem evolves from a rather smooth profile to a steep front forming at $x \approx 0,60$ by $t \approx 0,20$. From this instant on, the front moves on the positive direction of x until it eventually crashes onto the right boundary and slowly fades away. The size of the moving front thickness depends on the importance of the diffusion term, i.e. it is proportional with the scale of the diffusion coefficient (ν). In Table II, we resume the algorithm run conditions for $\nu = 10^{-3}$, using both collocation criteria. The simulation results for the criterion I are condensed in Fig. 7. We conclude that the algorithm successfully follows the formation and movement of the steep, with hardly any difficulty. The results obtained using the two collocation criteria seem to be very similar.

Now, the Burgers' equation is solved in more demanding conditions, decreasing the influence of diffusivity by fixing the parameter $\nu = 10^{-4}$. In these conditions, we apply the usual sequential first and second derivative analysis, associated with criterion I.

However, the maximum level grid is increased to N=12, to account to the reducing thickness of the moving steep front. The general conditions are resumed in Table III.

TABLE II. SIMULATION PARAMETERS FOR MODEL 2 ($\nu = 10^{-3}$)

Collocation criterion	I or II
Derivative order for collocation	n=1 and 2; or n=1
Time step	10^{-2}
Finite Difference approximation	5 nodes centred - uniform grid
Interpolation strategy	Cubic splines with 7 nodes
Time integrator tolerances	10^{-6}
Dyadic grids levels	M=4; N=10
Criterion I: $\varepsilon_1 = \varepsilon_2 = 10^0$;	Criterion II: $\varepsilon_1 = \varepsilon_2 = 10^{-1}$

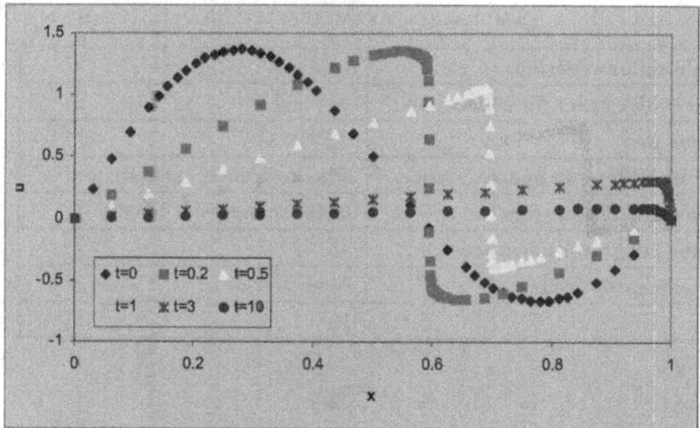

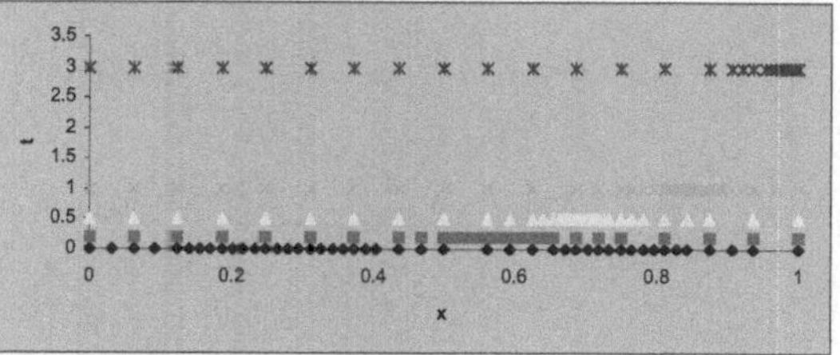

Fig. 7. Simulation results for the Burgers' model using criterion I ($\nu = 10^{-3}$).

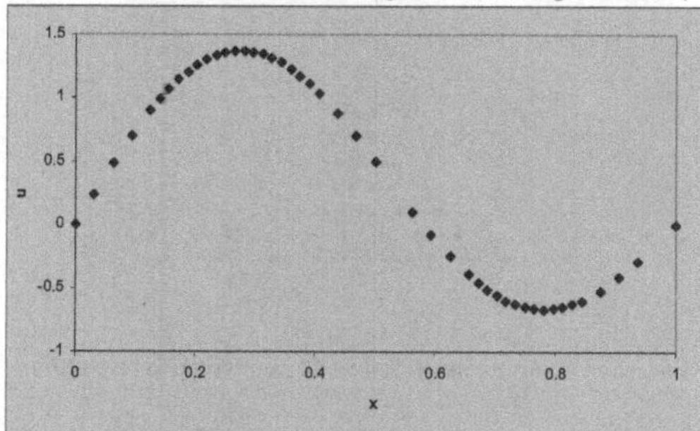

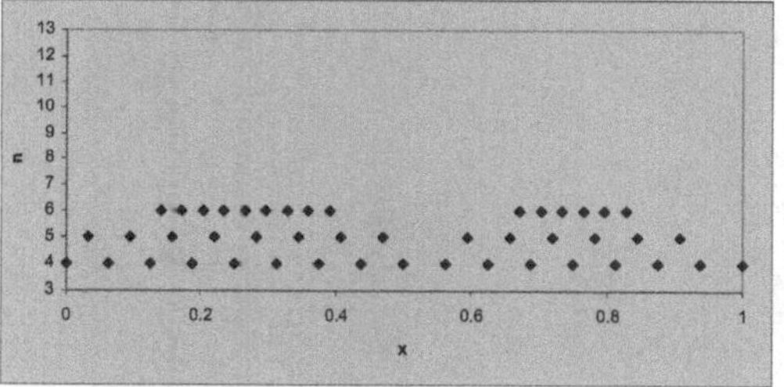

Fig. 8. Simulation results for model 2 at t=0, using criterion I ($\nu = 10^{-4}$).

In Fig. 8, we present the grid generation results concerning the initial condition profile. It is obvious that due to the smooth characteristics of this profile, the grid is relatively coarse and the maximum level attained is only a modest 6.

However, the situation changes radically for t=0.20 (Fig. 9). At this instant, the front is fully developed, and the procedure has to take advantage of the maximum level nodes to adequately conform to the front and its edges.

TABLE III. SIMULATION PARAMETERS FOR MODEL 2 ($\nu = 10^{-4}$)

Collocation criterion	I
Derivative order for collocation	n=1 and 2
Time step	2.5×10^{-3}
Finite Difference approximation	5 nodes centred - uniform grid
Interpolation strategy	Cubic splines with 7 nodes
Time integrator tolerances	10^{-6}
Dyadic grids levels	M=4; N=12
$\varepsilon_1 = \varepsilon_2 = 10^0$	

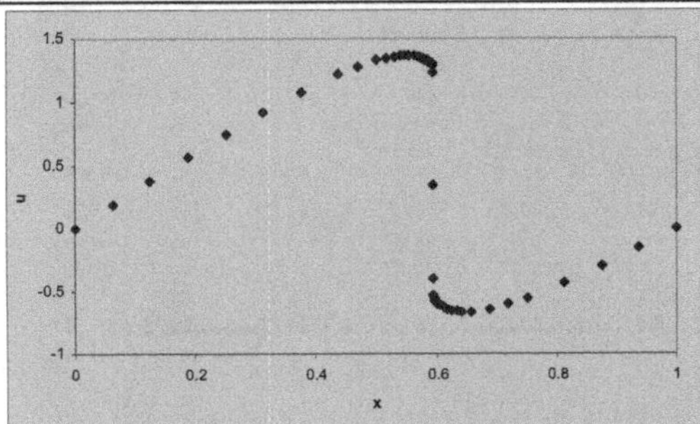

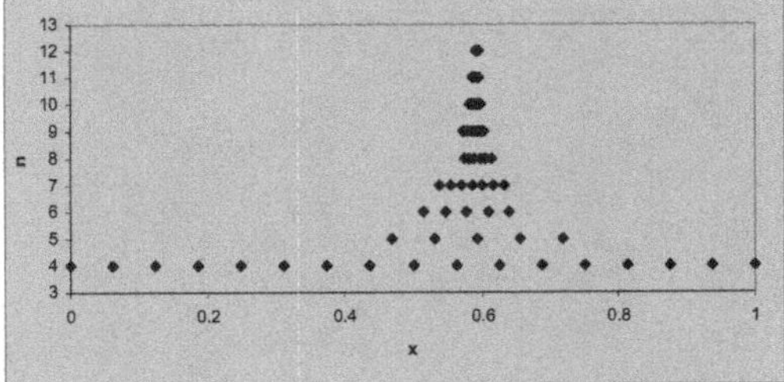

Fig. 9. Simulation results for model 2 at t=0.2, using criterion I ($\nu = 10^{-4}$).

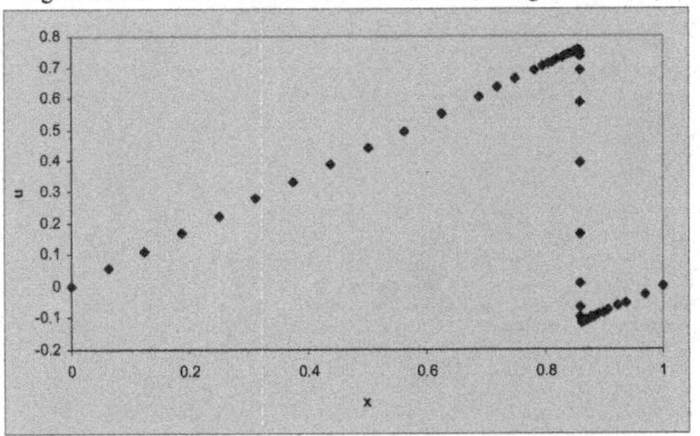

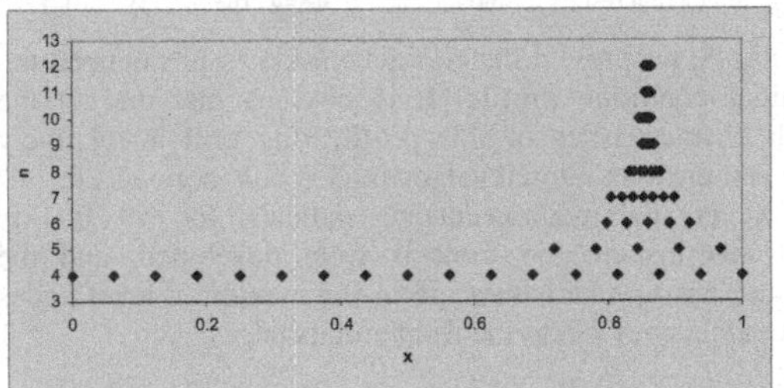

Fig. 10. Simulation results for model 2 at t=1.0, using criterion I ($\nu = 10^{-4}$).

After the formation of the steep front, the algorithm shows its ability to follow the movement of the front without introducing numerical distortions on the edges (Fig. 10).

The algorithm also proves its suitability by providing a adequately simulation of the front crash at the right boundary (Fig. 11). In general, the simulation is successfully carried out.

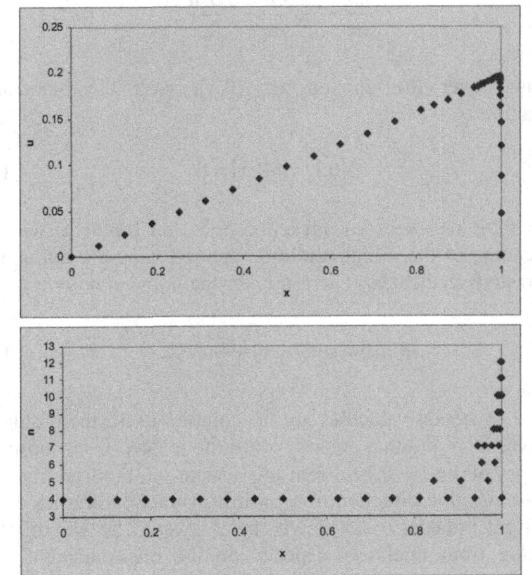

Fig. 11. Simulation results for model 2 at t=1.0, using criterion I ($\nu = 10^{-4}$).

V. CONCLUSIONS

We conclude that the integration algorithm that conjugates a MOL strategy with finite differences space discretizations, with a collocation strategy based on increasing level dyadic grids, revealed potential either as a grid generation procedure and a PDE integration scheme. It coped satisfactorily with a example characterized by a steep travelling wave and a example that presented a forming steep shock, which proves its versatility in dealing with different types of problems.

REFERENCES

[1] W. E. Schiesser, *The Numerical Method of Lines: Integration of Partial Differential Equations*, Academic Press, San Diego, 1991.

[2] J.C. Santos, P. Cruz, F.D. Magalhães and A. Mendes, "2-D Wavelet-based adaptive-grid method for the resolution of PDEs," *AIChe J.*, vol. 49, pp. 706-717, March 2003.

[3] P. Cruz, M.A. Alves, F.D. Magalhães and A. Mendes, "Solution of hyperbolic PDEs using a stable adaptive multiresolution method," *Chem. Eng. Sci.*, vol. 58, pp. 1777-1792, May 2003.

[4] T.A. Driscoll and A.R.H. Heryudono, "Adaptive residual subsampling methods for radial basis function interpolation and collocation problems," *Comput Math. Appl.*, vol. 53, pp. 927-939, March 2007.

[5] D.F. Hawken, J.J. Gottlieb and J.S. Hansen, "Review of some adaptive node-movement techniques in finite-element and finite-difference solutions of partial differential equations," *J. Comput. Phys.*, Vol. 95, pp. 254-302, August 1991.

[6] P. Brito, *Aplicação de Métodos Numéricos Adaptativos na Integração de Sistemas Algébrico-diferenciais Caracterizados por Frentes Abruptas*, MSc. Thesis, DEQ-FCTUC, Coimbra, Portugal, 1998.

[7] A. Vande Wouwer, Ph. Saucez, and W. E. Schiesser (eds.), *Adaptive Method of Lines*, Chapman & Hall/CRC Press, Boca Raton, 2001.

Educational Virtual Reality through a Multiview Autostereoscopic 3D Display

Emiliyan G. Petkov
St. Cyril and St. Methodius University,
Veliko Turnovo 5000, Bulgaria

***Abstract:* Nowadays the virtual reality technology is a topic of present and is an interest for research and development. There are different devices with which the user may enter, observe and interact with the computer-simulated three-dimensional world. For this reason applications of virtual reality can be in different areas. But the topical task nowadays is applying this modern technology in education. This report presents the results from the investigations into Philips multiview autostereocopic 3D displays and with the purpose of creating virtual reality applications for education objectives. An approach for creation of 3D video applications for the displays discussed in this paper is also presented.**

I. INTRODUCTION

Virtual reality (VR) created for educational objectives is a computer simulation of the three-dimensional environment, where the learner may interact with the contents of the modeled scene. The basic idea is the learner to be an integral part of the environment and to influence it in the same way as in the real world [2, 6]. So, VR for education can be described as a high-end technology that allows learners to go into a three-dimensional, computer-simulated world to learn.

There is a broad spectrum of technologies for VR. The interest in the usage of autostereoscopic 3D display systems is increasing rapidly [4, 9, 15]. This has been caused by the fact that in observing the 3D image the usage of some additional devices such as a headset, gloves, glasses and etc. is not necessary.

Fig. 1. Autostereoscopic 3D display.

Currently a number of different 3D displays are available on the market [11]. These displays together with the methods for creation of three-dimensional scenes allow the reproduction of a virtual world under the observer's eyes (fig. 1). This vastly enriches the experience and contributes to the best perception of the presented reality.

The technologies for VR are comparatively new instruments for perception of the surrounding environment. They may help us to obtain new knowledge. The integration of these 3D technologies in education is an innovative approach in the field of modern methods for education [1, 5, 7, 10]. It is known that 3D displays can be used in applications for games, 3D television, military and industrial manufacture [15]. However, the way learners can avail themselves of obtaining knowledge by means of autostereoscopic 3D displays in education has not been widely studied.

The set task in this research is a part of a bigger project of the University of Veliko Turnovo, titled «Virtual Reality in Education». The project aims to investigate the application of VR technologies in the process of teaching students at university and to equip a laboratory for 3D technologies. The project is in an advanced stage of development. Philips 42-inch multiview autostereoscopic 3D display has been chosen for the equipment of an auditorium. But the problem we encounter when creating Philips 3D technology applications is the lack of full set of software tools. The development of 3D contents for those kinds of displays requires appropriate software decisions. Philips gives documentation, drivers and a viewer, but there is no available software for 3D video production. In [12] the reader can be acquainted with all that Philips grants as information for the 3D displays and software tools for developing 3D applications for them.

The aims of this research are: to develop an approach for creating 3D applications which represent three-dimensional virtual computer models of real objects and spaces for Philips autostereoscopic 3D displays, to create an educational VR application for those 3D displays and to explore the benefits of that kind of educational applications.

The present investigation has been separated in three stages. The first stage includes the introduction into the 3D interface specifications of the displays – something very important before starting searching for a decision to the given problem. In the second stage an approach for creating 3D applications for the 3D displays has been developed and also an educational VR application has been created. The benefits of that kind of applications have been explored in the third stage. The most important findings from these three stages are presented in the next three sections of the report.

II. PHILIPS 3D DISPLAY SPECIFICATIONS

The goal of 3D displays is to get a distinct image into each eye of the viewer. From that point, the viewer's brain is processing each image in the same, natural way in which it

T. Sobh, K. Elleithy (eds.), *Innovations in Computing Sciences and Software Engineering*,
DOI 10.1007/978-90-481-9112-3_86, © Springer Science+Business Media B.V. 2010

processes the images it receives from the three-dimensional world. A characteristic common to all 3D displays is the creation and display of more than one view of a scene. Formerly, viewers had to wear special glasses to discern the views. In the last few years, a number of companies, among which Philips 3D Solutions [13, 14], have introduced *autostereoscopic* 3D displays - displays that do not require users to wear special 3D glasses. Multiview slanted lenticular lens technology leads to full brightness, full contrast, and true color representation. It allows multiple users to experience 3D at the same time.

The connection between the computer system and the 3D display makes use of a Digital Video Interface (DVI). For example some of the technical specifications for the 42-inch displays are: resolution – 1920 x 1080, refresh rate – 60 fps, display colors – 8-bits RGB, effective viewing area – 93.024 cm x 52.326 cm.

Philips has developed a set of technologies under the name of WOWvx [11]. WOWvx-based products make contents richer, more informative and more entertaining for the viewer so that it almost becomes 'alive'. A part of the WOWvx technology is the 2D-plus-Depth format [12]. A 3D image for the displays is described in that format. It contains two sub-images: 2D sub-image and Depth sub-image (fig. 4). A 2D sub-image has a resolution of half the native panel resolution in both horizontal and vertical direction. It is an R, G and B image with 8 bits per sub-pixel. A Depth sub-image has a resolution of half the native panel resolution in both horizontal and vertical direction. It contains disparity values with a range of 0 to 255, where a value of 0 corresponds with objects located with a maximum disparity behind the screen and 255 corresponds with objects located closest to the observer. In [13] the reader can be acquainted with the video data interface and WOWvx Declipse format.

III. One Approach to the Problem

A. A Choice of 3D Graphic System

The creation of 3D display contents, with regard to the set goal of this research, requires making virtual 3D computer models of real objects. Because of that, a 3D graphic system for modeling and creating photo-realistic images has to be chosen. This is a very important condition for the VR applications. The main requirement of the 3D models is to look like real. In this way a true VR is attained. Moreover, the 3D graphic system must have a module for computing of the depth along the z-axis (Z-depth) and tools for image composition in an animation. So, an investigation has been made into the capabilities of the 3D graphic systems [3] and Autodesk 3ds Max has been chosen [8].

B. A Model of the environment of observation

Philips multiview autostereoscopic 3D displays have determinate points of view in the space in front of the screen. For example 42-inch 3D display has nine positions where an observer could watch a good 3D image from. As a part of this research models of the environments for observation of the displays have been made in conformity with the technical specifications of the devices. These models also include the optimal virtual 3D space, where the objects of the animation should be placed in. Figure 2 shows the model of the environment of observation for Philips 42-inch 3D display.

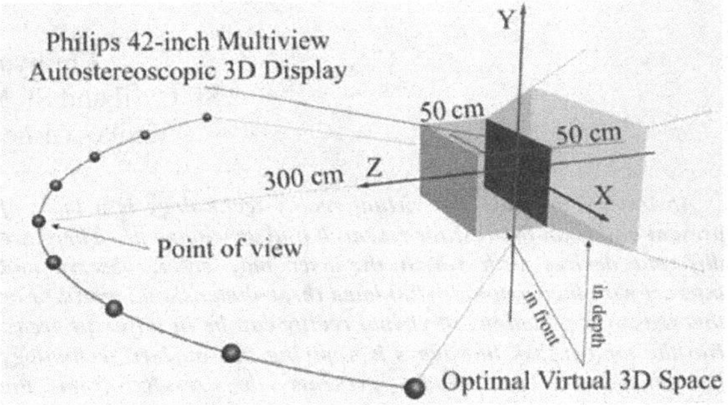

Fig. 2. A model of the environment of observation and optimal virtual 3D space for Philips 42-inch 3D display.

The effective viewing area of the 42-inch display is 93.024 cm x 52.326 cm and the optimal distance between the observer and the display is 300 cm [14]. The display can simulate 50 cm going out in front of the screen and 50 cm moving away behind the screen for every pixel. If the closest distance from the observer to the display is 100 cm and longest distance is unlimited, the optimal virtual 3D space for placing 3D objects in the coordinate space of the graphic system in front of the camera is formed. See figure 3 which shows the optimal distance of the camera in the scene from the middle (display) plane in the virtual 3D space.

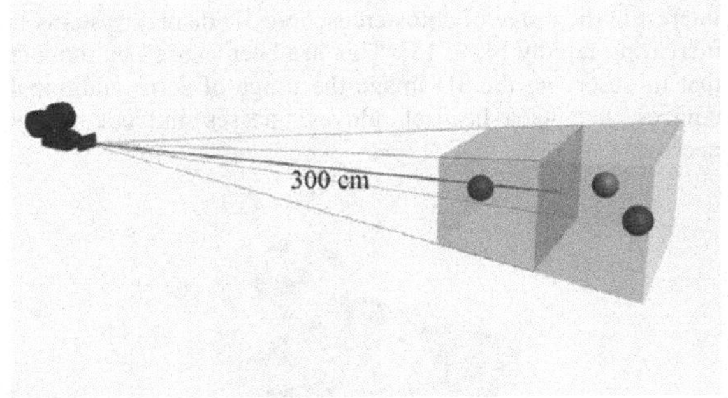

Fig. 3. Optimal distance of the camera in the scene from the middle (display) plane in the virtual 3D space.

C. Composition of the images

This sub-section presents the approach that has been developed as a part of this research in order to give a possibility for creating 3D video contents for the autostereoscopic 3D displays from Philips.

The 3D models and animation of real objects and environments are created in 3ds Max. A sequence of images which represent the frames of the animation is obtained after rendering. The Depth sub-images must be obtained as well. This graphic system includes a Z-Depth module. By means of using the Z-Depth module the depth of the every pixel from the 2D sub-images can be evaluated. The depth is the distance from the projection plane (the camera) to the surface of the object along the direction of the observation.

The Z-Depth module creates 2D images in Grayscale. To work correctly the Z-Depth module must have values for the minimum and maximum distance from the camera. It contains disparity values with a range of 0 to 255, where a value of 0 corresponds with objects located with a maximum distance and 255 corresponds with objects located closest to the camera. For example, having the model from the figure 3, the following values should be chosen: minimum distance – 250 cm and maximum distance – 350 cm.

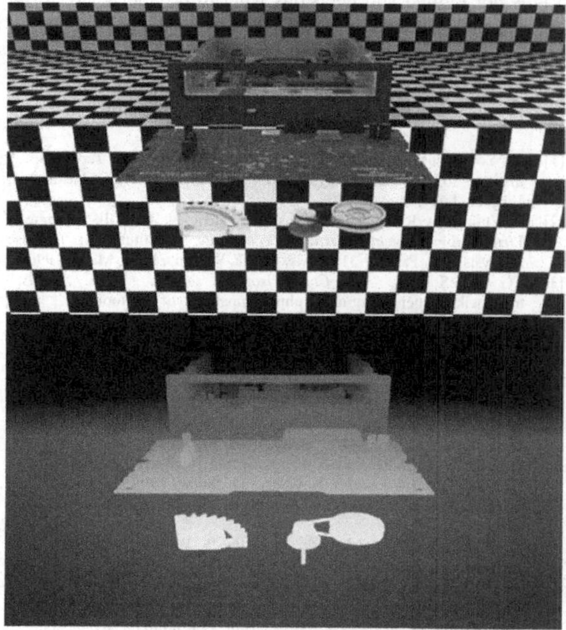

Fig. 4. A 2D sub-image and its Depth sub-image.

Thus a sequence of the 2D sub-images and a sequence of the Depth sub-images are obtained. After that, using a Video Post module of the graphic system, every 2D sub-image of the sequence together with its Depth sub-image are composed in one image with resolution of 1920 x 540 pixels in the 2D-plus-Depth format (.b3d files).

The sequence of the images in the 2D-plus-Depth format is composed in one video file and is stored in an appropriate format (.s3d file). That file can be played on a 3D display by the Philips 3DS Media Player.

D. 3D display application

An educational 3D video for Philips 42-inch multiview autostereoscopic 3D displays has been created to demonstrate the applicability of the approach presented here. It is titled "The elements of a DVD device". One image from the 3D video could be seen on figure 5. The objective of the project is to show all parts of a DVD device and the way it works. Thus the students will be able to see in front of themselves (in virtual environment) the structure of the DVD and the way it works without the necessity to disassemble such a device.

Fig. 5. The created image (fig. 4) in 2D-plus-depth format sent to the display.

The approach presented in this paper is taught in the subject "3D graphic systems" as a part of the master's programs at our university. In this way students can learn how to create applications for 3D displays by themselves.

IV. The Application in Education

Having the multiview autostereoscopic 3D displays and the 3D applications that are well prepared for them, the students get absorbed in a real atmosphere that they would not be able to witness in a natural way. For the first time they are able to see and fully perceive objects, spaces, phenomena, processes, etc. that appear and function just like the real ones. These objects can also be extinct things like animals, birds and microorganisms, or things extremely dangerous for humans, or objects much distant from the earth to be observed in any other way, but for all of them there is enough information to create their virtual model. The objects in this model can be observed from different viewpoints. Thus the learner gets unlimited possibility to move throughout this virtual world. Therefore, we can conclude that teachers should use virtual reality technologies to create a virtual world for exploration and experience.

Development of VR technologies shifts students' education to a higher level. After text-based teaching has been developed to multimedia, multimedia education now extends to learning in VR environments.

It is known that students (and people in general) quickly perceive by sight. So the natural striving is to develop materials which carry greater amount of information about the objects that are studied. Human brain is designed to perceive three-dimensional images. So the reproduction of three-dimensional space with three-dimensional objects in front of the eyes of the observer makes him or her fully apprehend the information – i.e. the way that human optical apparatus is designed – it perceives depth in direction of viewing.

Fig. 6. An anaglyph image showing the 3D effect achieved by the display.

In two-dimensional images depth is missing and as a result the observer is deprived of the full information about that part of the space the image is derived from. This refers even to three-dimensional modeled scenes, from which, however, a two-dimensional image is derived (via the rendering process). This is because the image carries no information about the depth of space that the image represents. In this case it carries the same information that a photographic image does.

But when the image also provides information about depth, then it is possible to recreate a part of the three-dimensional space in front of the eyes of the observer.

Figure 6 shows an anaglyph image aiming to give those who do not have the opportunity to observe VR on a multiview autostereoscopic 3D display but have red-cyan glasses, at least the vague idea of what it is like to observe a 3D image on such a display.

Conclusion

Integrating the real world with the virtual one offers the best solutions for qualitative perception of new knowledge. In the near future a large part of conventional training systems will be replaced with VR equipment. Using these innovative technologies in teaching will lead to a shift to a qualitatively new stage of education.

This approach of creating video applications in the format of 2D-plus-depth for Philips multiview autostereoscopic 3D displays has been developed in order to enrich the possibilities of creating applications for such displays. This approach can be used when developing 3D video contents for both educational and other objectives. However, "Virtual Reality in Education" project aims at exploring the issue of applying technologies for VR in education and creating applications for educational purposes. The results from this research give students the opportunity both to make use of VR products and to create such products by themselves.

The development of an approach for creating 3D video contents for 3D displays in the Declipse format can be a natural continuation of this research. This kind of video gives more 3D information than the 2D-plus-Depth format discussed here. The video in this format has a greater impact on the observer.

A matter of interest is also exploring the possibility for developing interactive applications for 3D displays. These applications give users the opportunity to interact with objects in virtual world in real time. Thus the time for remaining in VR is not limited and decisions what to do and where to go are made by participants in VR. This kind of applications will offer a new opportunity for creation of VR through the multiview autostereoscopic 3D displays.

References

[1] C. Youngblut, „*Educational Uses of Virtual Reality Technology,*" Institute for Defense Analysis, IDA Document D-2128, Alexandria, Virginia, USA, January 1998.

[2] C. Youngblut, R. Johnson, S. Nash, R. Wienclaw, C. Will, „*Review of Virtual Environment Interface Technology,*" Institute for Defense Analysis, IDA Paper P-3186, Alexandria, Virginia, USA, March 1996.

[3] CG Society, „*Comparison of 3d tools,*" http://wiki.cgsociety.org/index.php/Comparison_of_3d_tools.

[4] D. Ezra, G. Woodgate, B. Omar, N. Holliman, J. Harrold, L. Shapiro, „New autostereoscopic display system," *Proceedings of IS&T/SPIE Symposium on Electronic Imaging Science and Technology*, San Jose, California, 7 Feb. 1995.

[5] D. Vinciguerra, „Blink 3D: A Rapid Application Development Tool for Creating 3D Environments," *Virtual Reality in the Schools*, Volume 6, number 2, East Carolina University, USA, 1997.

[6] F. P. Brooks, „What's Real About Virtual Reality?," *IEEE Computer Graphics and Applications*, November/December 1999, pp. 16-27.

[7] G. Javidi, „*Virtual Reality and Education,*" University of South Florida, 1999.

[8] K. L. Murdock, „*3ds Max 9 Bible,*" Willey Publishing Inc., Indianapolis, Indiana, 2006.

[9] K. Langhans, D. Bezecny, D. Homann, D. Bahr, C. Vogt, Ch. Blohm, Karl-Heinz Scharschmidt, „New portable FELIX 3D display," *Proceedings of SPIE, Vol. 3296, 10th International Symposium at Photonics West '98 "Electronic Imaging: Science and Technology"*, San Jose, California, USA, 24-30 January 1998.

[10] M. Kuusisto, R. Launonen, „Virtual Reality in Education," *ERCIM News No.28*, January 1997.

[11] P. May, „*A Survey of 3D Display Technologies,*" The Society of Information Display (SID), USA, March/April 2005, pp28-33.

[12] Philips 3D Solutions, http://www.business-sites.philips.com/3dsolutions/home/index.page.

[13] Philips Electronics, „*3D Interface Specifications,*" White Paper, Philips 3D Solutions, 15 February 2008.

[14] Philips Electronics, „*42-inch 3D-Intelligent Display,*" 42-3D6C01/00, User Manual, Philips 3D Solutions, 23 September 2008.

[15] Z. Xia Jin, Y. Jun Zhang, X. Wang, T. Plocher, „Evaluating the Usability of an Auto-stereoscopic Display," *Human-Computer Interaction: 12th international conference, Part II, HCII 2007, LNCS 4551*, Springer-Verlag Berlin Heidelberg, pp. 605-614, 2007.

An Approach for Developing Natural Language Interface to Databases Using Data Synonyms Tree and Syntax State Table

Safwan shatnawi[*], Rajeh Khamis[**]
University of Bahrain, Applied Studies College
{sshatnawi[*], rkhamees[**]}@asc.uob.bh

Abstract: **The basic idea addressed in this research is developing a generic, dynamic, and domain independent natural language interface to databases. The approach consists of two phases; configuration phase and operation phase. The former builds data synonyms tree based on the database being implemented. The idea behind this tree is matching the natural language words with database elements. The tree hierarchy contains the database tables, attributes, attribute descriptions, and all possible synonyms for each description. The latter phase contains a technique that implements syntax state table to extract the SQL components from the natural language user request. As a result the corresponding SQL statement is generated without interference of human experts.**

Index-terms: *Natural language processing, Natural language interface, Database interface, Synonyms tree, Syntax table.*

1. INTRODUCTION

Natural language Interface (NLI) to database system is a work field that combines artificial intelligent (AI) and database management systems since database system was introduced till now [1]. Getting information stored in database system was computer specialists task [2]. By time, number of nontechnical users who deal with wide range of database has dramatically increased; therefore, adequate users training is needed on the underlying database applications. Such training is not always available and sometimes the database applications are very sophisticated and not designed to be used by such users. In general user training can be conducted by either teaching users formal query language (SQL for example), or giving the required training on graphical or form-based interface provided by the database applications. However the two proposals face some difficulties.

It is obvious that nontechnical users are unable to smoothly learn formal query languages. On the other hand, graphical interface and form-based interfaces are easier to use but still need different levels of training which consumes respected and valuable time and efforts.

For naïve users, an ideal communication between them and computer is natural languages since the users focus on what they want rather than how to do it. Evidently the user masters his native language much better than any artificial language, no matter which programming or visual interaction language would be used [3]. In addition, some requests are difficult to express using graphical or form-based interface, while can be easily expressed in natural language.

To solve this communication problem, many researchers investigated designing Natural Language (NL) interface to databases. Natural language interface to databases is a system that allows the user to access information stored in a database by typing requests in natural language [1]. The system then maps each natural language question to appropriate SQL statement(s) for answering questions (retrieving data) or even modifying the database structure [4]. At least six different architectures and approaches were found for database query [2, 5, and 6] and database design [4].

1.1 Natural Language Interface to Databases Challenges

Developing reliable natural language interface to database is complex task, since two categories of difficulties are usually faced; first, limitation of understanding natural language and second, interfacing to database problems. The following paragraph describes briefly these problems.

Once a natural language is processed many unexpected linguistic problems arise. Reference [2] gave many examples on these problems and some suggested solutions such as:

I. Modifier attachment: identifying the constituent to which each modifier has to be attached.
II. Quantifier scoping: which quantifier should be given a wider scope?
III. Conjunction and disjunction: the ambiguity of AND meaning.
IV. The nominal compound problem: the meaning of nouns when combined with preceding nouns.

In addition to the above general natural language problems, some specific problems may also arise when linking natural language with database systems.

One of the most critical limitations is the need for domain expert to configure Natural language Interface to database systems. Whenever they are being reconfigured for a new domain, someone has to teach the system the words and concepts used in the new domain, and how these concepts relate to the information stored in the database [2]. These Interfaces are domain dependent and need knowledge and database experts to successfully implement the system. As a result, budget and time limitations may make such approaches not widely used.

T. Sobh, K. Elleithy (eds.), *Innovations in Computing Sciences and Software Engineering*,
DOI 10.1007/978-90-481-9112-3_87,

This research aims to develop a database interface that could be built and configured dynamically without manual interference from domain experts or database engineers.

1.2 Organization

The paper is organized as follows. In section 2 we introduce the basic theory used to build the system. This includes the idea of Data Synonyms Tree and its four layers (section 2.1). Section 3.1 gives a brief description about the system components including the Meta data tables. Section 3.2 explains the technique used to understand the NL requests and how to link them with the actual attributes. The SQL generating method is discussed in section 3.2.5. Then a complete step-by-step example is discussed to clearly introduce the approach followed. After that we present some results that show the effectives of the proposed system. Finally we end with a brief conclusion and future work.

2. NL INTERFACE APPROACH

The proposed approach consists of two phases. In the first phase the system is configured via building Data Synonyms Tree (DST) while the second phase runs techniques that processes the user request to obtain the correct SQL statement resulting in displaying the required information.

2.1 Data Synonyms Tree (DST)

Based on the database addressed and an English dictionary [6] we have created a tree of data synonyms (DST). The aim of the tree is to map the NL request words –those which may be used in the natural language user request- to database elements (table and attributes). This tree consists of four main layers as illustrated in Figure 1. The first layer represents the database tables; the second one represents the attributes for each table. A description of each attribute is split into individual words in the third layer and each word has a set of synonyms placed in the fourth layer.

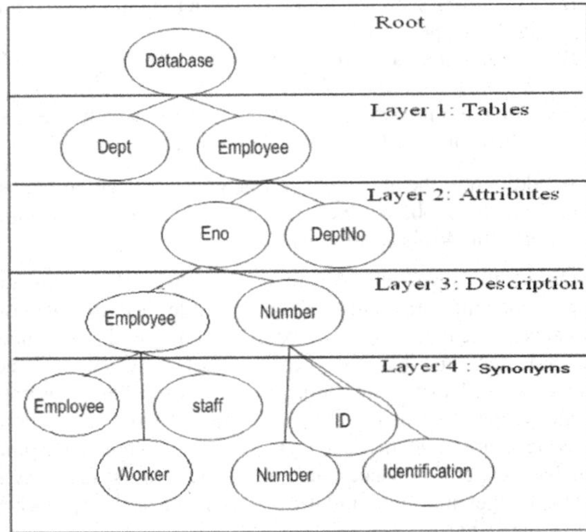

Figure [1] :Data Synonyms Tree DST

2.2 Extracting SQL from NL Request

After building the database's DST, a search procedure runs to extract the following components which are needed to generate the SQL statement that meet the user request:

A. Table name(s).
B. Attribute(s) required (column(s) in the database)
C. The condition which contains
   I. Attribute name (column in the Database)
   II. Comparison operator
   III. Specific value (if there is any)

The system processes the user request by removing all syntactic markers and articles such as (a, the, is, are ...), then splits the remaining into individual words (tokens). After that it performs direct search in the DST's layer four (synonyms) for the synonyms which match the request words and return its corresponding description just found in layer 3. Then a technique runs to classify the request words and their descriptions into three categories:

I. SQL command nature (retrieve, update ...etc)
II. Required field(s) and table(s)
III. Condition

Word descriptions (layer 3 entries) are then linked with the actual database attributes (layer 2). Finally, the approach finalizes the SQL statement by adding any join conditions for attributes come from multiple tables, executes it and retrieves the results.

3. THE PROPOSED SYSTEM

As mentioned in the previous section, the first phase was building DST to limit and match all NL request words. The proposed tree shown in Figure 1 has been represented in two linked tables added to the original database. Table 1 (Attribute Descriptions Table) is domain dependent as it has precise short description for each database attribute; however most of it could be automatically derived from database dictionary. On the other hand, the second table (Synonyms table) shown in table 2 is common and valid for almost all databases since it contains set of synonyms for each description [7].

Table 3 (Operator Semantic Table) has been built based on attributes data type to include operators used in database SQL statements.

3.1.1 Attribute Descriptions Table

Precise description for each database attribute is stored in this table along with information about the attribute's data type, name, and the host table. The description is short, precise and fully describes the database attribute. A sample entry is shown in table 1. Although it is clear that this table is domain dependent, it could be easily fetched from data dictionary.

TABLE[1]
ATTRIBUTE DESCRIPTIONS TABLE

Id	Attribute	Description	Table	Type
2	Dnumber	Department Number	Department	Number
3	Dname	Department Name	Department	Text

TABLE[2]
SYNONYMS TABLE

Word	Synonym	Id	Attribute	Table
Department	Subdivision	2	Dnumber	Department
Department	Branch	2	Dnumber	Department
Department	Unit	2	Dnumber	Department
Department	Responsibility	2	Dnumber	Department
Department	Section	2	Dnumber	Department
Department	Area	2	Dnumber	Department
Department	Field	2	Dnumber	Department

TABLE[3]
SEMANTIC OPERATOR TABLE

Data Type	Operator	Syntax
Number	>	Greater Than, Above, Higher Than,
Text	=	Equals, Begins With, Starts By, Contains,

3.1.2 Synonyms Table

This table contains all possible synonyms for the domain database. The system builds up the complete data by breaking down the attribute's description in Attribute Descriptions table -table 1- into individual words. Then an external synonym lexicon [7] has been used to generate a set of all synonyms for each word in the attribute description as shown in table 2.

3.1.3 Operator Semantic Table

In addition to the above two tables, we built domain independent table (Operator Semantic Table) to keep all possible data type operators like (>, <, etc...), and their equivalent syntax like (greater than, bigger than, less than, etc...) as illustrated in table 3.

3.2 System Description

After building the DST, the system follows syntactic and semantic techniques to generate SQL statements. The following paragraph describes the system.

The system makes use of data files that contain useful information such as semantic rules and actions to be taken. A brief description about the architecture components is given in the following section. The proposed system architecture is illustrated as level zero DFD shown in Figure 2. It involves five integrated components to convert the NL request into the corresponding SQL statement.

3.2.1 Tokenizer

In this section, the system takes the user NL query and split it into individual words. Each word is placed in one token, but all non useful word (such as articles, syntactic markers ...etc) are removed. The remaining tokens are sent to the Synonyms Matcher for further processing.

3.2.2. Synonyms Matcher

The synonyms matcher searches the Synonyms Table to identify whether the token is database field, value or others. The token represents a database field (attribute) if an entry in the Synonyms table matches the token. The token contains a value if it is not found in Synonyms table and its type is similar to database field type otherwise the token is classified as (others). This process is repeated for each token. All tokens are now ready to be processed by Sections Semantic Parser.

3.2.3. Sections Semantic Parser

Based on some semantic rules, the identified tokens are divided into three types; SQL type, required attributes, and condition attributes. This process uses two text files that contain some rules and predefined data to parse the identified tokens into their corresponding sections.

The first file contains list of all words that point to the type of SQL commands needed (query, update, delete, or insert). For example words such as find, display, list, and get, point to data query request while remove, delete, take out mean that the user wants to delete data. The second file contains list of English verbs and words that used to distinguish required fields and the condition like (who, works, where, etc…). Figure 3 shows the Deterministic Finite Automated (DFA) [8] state rules. Figure 4 shows sample of detailed NL syntax in BNF notation [9]. The corresponding states for this grammar are stored in external text file.

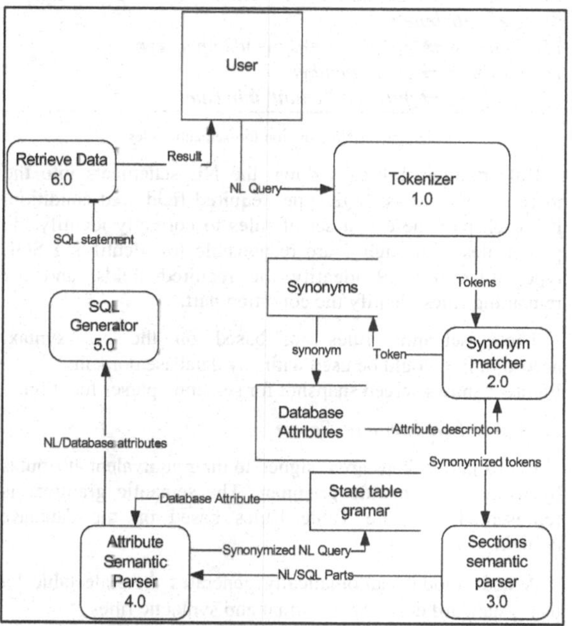

Figure [2]: The system architecture represented as level 0 DFD

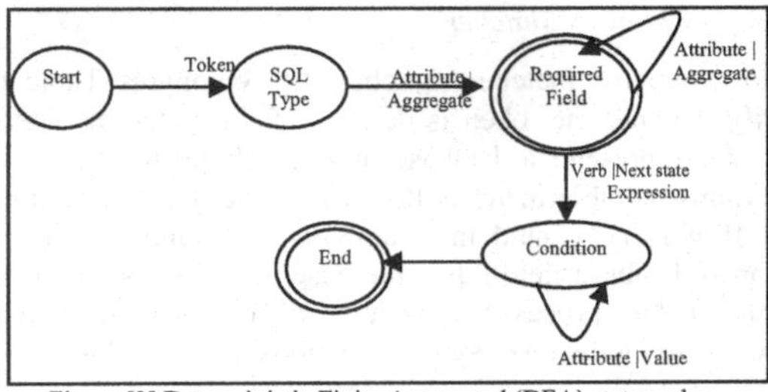

Figure [3] Deterministic Finite Automated (DFA) states rules

1. NL statement → <SQL Type> <Required fields> <Condition>
2. <SQL type> →<select> | <update> |<insert> | <delete>
3. <Select> →<WH> | <Verb>
4. <WH> →wh questions
5. <Verb> →imperative verbs.

6. <Required Fields> →<Attribute> | <Aggregate >
7. <Aggregate> →<Agg > Attribute>
8. <Attribute> →database fields.
9. <Agg> →max| avg| count| min |sum.

10.<Condition>→ <Text Condition>|<Num_date Condition>
11. <Text Condition> →<Attribute> <Op> <Value>
12. <Attribute> →database fields.
13. <Op> → = | like .
14. <Num_date Condition> →<Attribute> <Op> <Value>| <Agg><Attribute>
15. <Op> →>|<|<=|>=|<>|=|like|between
16. <value> →date | number
17. <Agg> →max| avg| count| min |sum.

Figure[4] :BNF Notation for semantic rules.

Rule number 1 breaks down the NL statements into the three main sections; SQL type, required field, and condition. For each part there is a set of rules to correctly identify the part. Rules 2 through 5 are responsible for identifying SQL type, rules 6 to 9 identify the required fields, and the remaining rules identify the condition part.

These semantic rules are based on the NL syntax, accordingly it could be used with any database domain.
Figure 5 shows screen snapshot for semantic parser function.

3.2.4 *Attribute Semantic Parser*

In this part, tokens are assigned to their equivalent attributes by using NL semantic grammar. The semantic grammar is represented as State Table Rules based on the database domain.

A code module automatically generates the state table by using standard description format and syntactic rules.

To explain the work done here, we will discuss the General NL Syntax State Table shown in table 4 before discussing a sample table.

The (NL word) represents all words that can be found in the attributes description we got from the previous section. The value (-1) means that the attribute is unidentified or irrelative, while the value (-99) represents final state (or simply identified attribute). Any other numbers mean that the attribute has been identified, but further information is expected.

Determining the attributes is not the only task done by this part, further more it identifies also the required database attribute (SELECT what), the source table (FROM) and the condition (WHERE)

The following paragraph shows with example how this part works. Consider the State Table shown in table 5. The table represents part of one of our testing database domain state table that used to identify the domain attributes from NL request. Assume that the following phrase has been found in NL request "*Employee First Name*"

First, the parser starts with initial state 0. The first NL word found is (*Employee*), so the entry for state 0 and word (*Employee*) is 1 which means that the state became now 1 therefore the parser moves to the second record where state is 1. The second NL word is (*First*); here the entry for state 1 and word (*first*) is 3 which makes the state equal to 3. The parser now goes to the forth record where the state is 3. The last word is (*Name*) which will send the machine to fifth record where state is 4. Here, the parser finds that all entries are -99 which means that the machine reached to the final state. Each state is linked with an actual database attribute and its table. For example state 4 is linked with (*Fname*) attribute and (*Employee*) table, the same scenario will be applied if the NL phrase was "*First Name*" as state 4 is the final state as well.

3.2.5. *SQL Generator*

After identifying the main SQL statement components, the remaining unidentified tokens are examined to be identified as value, operator, or aggregate function. The semantic rules mentioned in Figure 4 are applied here. The system will add join condition if the attribute comes from two or more tables, making use of Meta database information.

Finally the system combines, generates, and execute the SQL statement and retrieve the result. Figure 6 illustrates the Pseudo Code for the system. A complete example is shown in Figure 7.

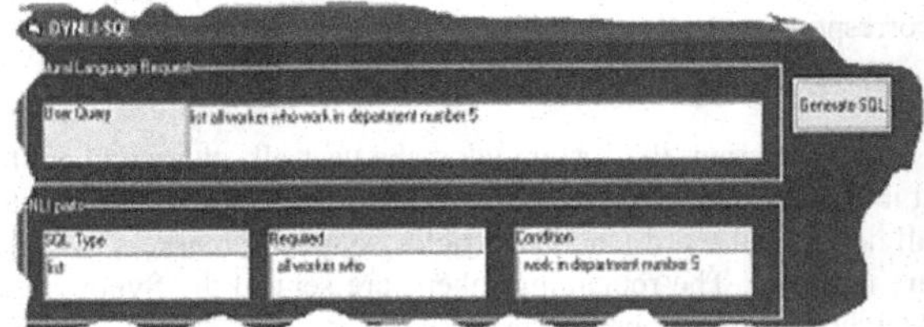

Figure [5] : screen snapshot of semantic parser

Pseudo code

1. *Let S be any English NL statement, W be set of words in database attributes' description, L be set of attributes' synonyms.*
2. *For each word s ; s ∈ S do*
   Search for w ∈ W; s =w or s ∈ L, where L* is set of all w synonyms.*
3. *Split S into its parts.*
4. *Identify the database attributes, aggregate functions, value, or operator.*
5. *Finalize SQL statement.*
6. *Retrieve data for S.*

Figure [6] Pseudo Code For The System

TABLE [4]
GENERAL NL SYNTAX STATE TABLE

State	Nl Word	Nl Word	Nl Word	Nl Word	Nl Word	Nl Word	Nl Word	Nl Word	Nl Word	Nl Word	Nl Word	Field	Table
0	1	2	3	5	7	9	10	11	12	13	30		
1	-1	2	3	5	7	9	10	-1	12	13	-1	Field1	Table 1
2	-99	-99	-99	-99	-99	-99	-99	-99	-99	-99	-99	Field1	Table 2

TABLE[5]
PART OF SYNTACTIC RULES STATE TABLE

State	Employee	Name	First	Initial	Last	Salary	Birth	Date	Manager	Sex	Field	Table
0	1	2	3	5	7	9	10	11	12	13		
1	-1	2	3	5	7	9	10	-1	12	13	Ssn Fname Minit Lname Address Salary Sex	Employee
2	-99	-99	-99	-99	-99	-99	-99	-99	-99	-99	Name	Employee
3	-1	4	-1	-1	-1	-1	-1	-1	-1	-1		
4	-99	-99	-99	-99	-99	-99	-99	-99	-99	-99	Fname	Employee

**Next state = (current_state, word)*

Tokenizer
input NL query : list staff first name who has the highest salary.
output : <list> <staff> <first> <name> <who> <has> <the> <highest> <salary>.
synonym matcher
input: <list> <staff> <first> <name> <who> <has> <the> <highest> <salary>.
output: <list> <employee> <first> <name> <who> <has> <the> <highest> <salary>.
section semantic parser
input: <list> <employee> <first> <name> <who> <has> <the> <highest> <salary>.
output: (<list>),(<employee> <first> <name>),(<who> <has> <the> <highest> <salary>).
attribute semantic parser:
input: (<employee> <first> <name>) , (<who> <has> <the> <highest> <salary>).
output: (Fname, table employee) , (<who> <has> <the> <highest>(<salary, table employee))
SQL Generator:
pass1 : input (Fname, table employee) , (<who> <has> <the> <highest>(<salary, table employee))
output: (Fname, table employee) , (<who> <has> <the> <max>(<salary, table employee))
pass 3:Input : (Fname, table employee) , (<who> <has> <the> <max>(<salary, table employee))
Output: select fname from employee where salary =(select max(salary) from employee);
Retrieve data
input : *select fname from employee where salary =(select max(salary) from employee);*
output : SQL result.

Figure [7] : NL request processing example (from NL to SQL)

4. Experimental Work And Analysis

In order to examine the system performance and efficiency, we prepared set of different levels of user requests written in natural language. These requests were written by both naïve users and database experts as well. The queries varied from simple queries that retrieve data from one table in a straight forward way, to sophisticated queries that retrieve information located in multiple tables.

It was found that almost all direct and simple questions - which have been prepared by naïve users- were successfully understood and the system retrieved the correct results. However the rate of successful response for expert questions was around 65%. When we analyzed the expert queries, it was found that database experts have good experience in generating complex requests that may need data from more than two tables. Part of unsuccessfully answered queries was domain dependent and requires more analysis to set semantic rules that complies with most of the database domain.

Another interesting point found is the nature of the SQL statement. The experiment statistics tells that data retrieving requests are much easier to be translated and understood than data updating requests. Although the proposed approach deals with all types of SQL commands, the aim of the research is to help naïve users who are most likely interested in retrieving data.

In general system did not provide good results when tested with poorly structured databases, because the DST was incomplete and the stored data was redundant.

The system showed an accepted efficiency in converting the NL queries although there are some rooms for enhancement.

4.1 System Performance

The system performance depends on the user request complexity, the machine specification, and network bandwidth

In this research we focused on the user requests only for developing and testing the introduced technique. However the system performance is clearly affected by NL requests' level of complexity because it broadens the search scope and increases the response time needed.

4.2 Intelligent Queries

In general, intelligent queries are database domain dependent therefore more analysis is needed to define relationships among the database entities. Ontology is the most suitable methodology to be used, however ontology is more complicated data integration approach.

4.3 Request Format

User NL requests do not follow any predefined format but it is clear that user requests to structured database imply sort of format that can be recognized, and formalized.

5. Conclusion

When proper Natural language interfaces to database is implemented, naïve users do not have to learn and master formal language in order to get access to information stored in databases. As most of naïve users' database requests are simple, their requests may be asked in natural language and automatically translated by NL interface to databases system.

By automatically building DST based on general purpose dictionary and database meta data, it was possible to develop NL interface to database without assistance from domain experts.

We also conclude that it is very important to have well normalized and well structured database system in order to be able to develop NL interface, otherwise the NL system is unable to successfully retrieve correct results.

Finally, it is strongly recommended to build general semantic information after studying many different databases and analysis NL requests from various users

6. Future Work

Our future work is adding adaptation capabilities so domain experts may help the system matching the NL requests to the database elements. It is also planned to build intelligent semantic rules to retrieve information beyond the stored data. In addition, further investigation is needed to analyze and implement data updating processes.

The system could be equipped with a suitable interface to be used as educational system in which students write their questions in natural language, then the system produces the correct SQL statement and vice versa. The level of NL request complexity controls the system performance so it is worth to investigate optimization issue to decrease the search time and hence improve the system.

Acknowledgment

Thanks go to deanship of College of Applied Studies at University of Bahrain for their support to this work.

References

[1]. Lappoon R. Tang, "Using Machine Learning Approach for Building Natural Language Interface for Databases," journal of Computer Science, Information & Electrical Engineering, volume 2, Issue 1, 2008.

[2] I. Androutsopoulos, G.D. Ritchie, and P.Thanisch, "Natural Language Interfaces to Databases – An Introduction", *Journal of Natural Language Engineering*, v. 1(1), Cambridge University Press, pp. 29-81, 1995.

[3] M. Samsonova, A. Pisarev, and m. Blagov, " Processing of natural language queries to relational database," *BIOINFORMATICS*, Oxford University press, Vol. 1, Suppl. 1, pp i241-i249, 2003.

[4] N. Omar, "Heuristics-based Entity-Relationship modeling through Natural Language Processing," PhD Thesis, University of Ulster, 2004.

[5] A. Mitrovic, "A Knowledge-Based Teaching System for SQL," *International Journal of Artificial Intelligence in Education,* IOS Press,*171-195, 13 (2003).*

[6] A. Yates, O. Etzioni, D. Weld, "A Reliable Natural Language Interface to Household Appliances," *Proceedings of the 8th international conference on intelligent user interfaces*, IUI'03, Miami, Florida, USA , ACM, 2003, January 12-15,2003.

[7]http://rovshan876.narod.ru/synonyms.html

[8] Introduction to Languages and the Theory of Computation, John Martin , McGraw-Hill ,2002.

[9] E. Terenzi, and B. Di Eugenio "Building lexical semantic representation for Natural Language instructions," North American Chapter of the Association for Computational Linguistics on Human Language Technology: companion volume of the Proceedings of HLT-NAACL 2003--short papers - Volume 2, Edmonton, Canada ,Pages: 100 - 102 , 2003

Analysis of Strategic Maps for a Company in the Software Development Sector

Marisa de Camargo Silveira – marisa@infostoreinf.com.br – Infostore - Project Manager - Brazil
Brandon Link – brandon.link@gmail.com - Graduate of The University of Kansas – United States
Silvio Johann - silviojohann@terra.com.br - Fundação Getúlio Vargas - Professor – Brazil
Adolfo Alberto Vanti – avanti@unisinos.br - UNISINOS University – Full Professor – Brazil
Rafael Espin Andrade – espin@ind.cujae.edu.cu - CUJAE – Full Professor - Cuba

Abstract- The present work develops the analysis of two strategic maps. One is based on the principles of Compensatory Fuzzy Logic (CFL) and the other studies Organizational Culture. The research is applied with a quali-quantitative approach and it studies the case of a software development company with the use of a technical procedure and a documentary base with the application of interviews and questionnaires. It concludes that the strategic maps based on and Organizational Culture are robust methodologies that identify and prioritize strategic variables. There is also an interrelationship amongst them in their consideration of important behavioral aspects. With this it was possible to analyze strategic aspects of the companies in a more complex and realistic way.

Key Words: Strategic Maps. Compensatory Fuzzy Logic, Organizational Culture

I. INTRODUCTION

The present study contemplates strategic maps using methodologies of control and prioritization of strategies for a company in the software development sector. This is accomplished through the following two strategic maps based on Compensatory Fuzzy Logic (CFL) and Organizational Culture. Analyzes of the strategic maps is based on environmental and organizational criteria.

In the world today change is continuous. Markets are constantly digitizing and significant difficulties are presented in the attempt to tailor classical administration theories to these intense new times of information technology. Significant investments in technology however do not always bring the necessary return if these investments are not parameterized in a way designed to reduce the separation between information systems, business strategy and organizational culture, thus allowing the manager an understanding of what operationally will adequately use their management information systems.

To direct the problem-question this work defines it as: How to analyze strategic maps based on environmental and organizational criteria?

II. STRATEGIC MAP BASED ON COMPENSATORY FUZZY LOGIC (CFL)

Due to the enormous difficulty in measuring qualitative aspects of decision making, we chose to use fuzzy logic to help improve the explanations of these data. Fuzzy logic can transform abstract information into more concrete data, easing the judgment and evaluation of them. These kind of logic is considered as set of concepts, principals and methods to handle vagueness and imprecision in a rational way. It allows dealing with values of intermediate membership or values of truth and to process them. There are several fields where the application of the fuzzy set was successful, such as analyzed in [1] and [2].

According to [3] and [4], the classical models of rationality in decision making are the bases of decision support systems (DSS) [5] and methodologies resulting from all decision making processes or Business Intelligence [6]. However the majority of these methods limit the viable form of human subjectivity and many times expensive projects are silently abandoned by companies considered benchmarking in the international market. So an appropriate methodology for this situation is CFL which can transform itself and adapt to new approaches for diverse administrative problems.

Definition of the problem is supported in the "Truth Tables" that are established by the value of truth of $p \wedge q$, $p \vee q$ and $\neg p$ to divide the corresponding values to p and q are, therefore functions whose domain is $\{0; 1\}x\{0; 1\}$ ($\{0; 1\}$ for $\neg p$) and its image $\{0; 1\}$. To introduce the "Principal of gradualness" it defines new logics where a predicate is a function of the universal X in the interval [0;1], and the operations $\wedge$, $\vee$, and $\neg$ are defined to restrict to the set $\{0; 1\}x\{0; 1\}$ ($\{0; 1\}$ for $\neg$) to obtain the operations of Boolean Logic and satisfy part of the axiom of Boolean Algebra without including the axiom of the third exclusion. In the case of business decisions of interaction with specialists shows the tendency to generate complex formula that also require complex predicates.

The truth values obtained to calculate these predicates should possess sensitivities to the changes of the truth values of the basic predicates, or to the "verbal

T. Sobh, K. Elleithy (eds.), *Innovations in Computing Sciences and Software Engineering*, DOI 10.1007/978-90-481-9112-3_88, © Springer Science+Business Media B.V. 2010

significance" of the calculated truth values. It renounces the accomplishments of the classic properties of conjunction and disjunction, opposing the idea that the increase or decrease of one of its components can be "compensated" with a corresponding decrease or increase of the other. In compensatory logic the operations $\wedge$ and $\vee$ are defined in the following way.

$$v(p_1 \wedge p_2 \wedge ... \wedge p_n) = (v(p_1).v(p_2)...v(p_n))^{1/n}$$

$$v(p_1 \vee p_2 \vee ... \vee p_n) = 1-((1-v(p_1)).(1-v(p_2))...(1-v(p_n)))^{1/n}$$

The data is structured as a continuity, the definitions of which are as follows: 0 = False; 0.1 = Almost false; 0.2 = Practically false; 0.3 = Somewhat false; 0.4 = More false than true; 0.5 = As much true as false; 0.6 = More true than false; 0.7 = Somewhat true: 0.8 = Practically true; 0.9 = Almost true; and 1 = True.

III. STRATEGIC MAP BASED ON ORGANIZATIONAL CULTURE

With the continued process of change, institutions see that observing Organizational Culture, when well managed, is able to provide a harmonic work environment, profitability and positive recognition of the institute's image in the marketplace. The map is referenced from [7] in order to gain information about the characteristic features of Organizational Culture and to verify that the mechanisms adopted to manage this culture are essential factors for the proper management of it. In accordance with [8] there are several factors that can determine the outside view of organizational culture. These include the study of the physical environment including location, observing that the organization's character emerges from its culture and how it is viewed by its public, especially from its receptiveness to visitors close to the organization, the course of its contributors in the company, and the comparison of what they carry out with what is proposed.

Culture can be understood as the way a social group responds to external pressure, following or conducting processes of adaptation through an outline of norms, perspectives and forms of internal thinking like a pattern of collective behavior [9].

High performance corporate culture could be defined as dense and flexible. Dense signifies when culture is shared with all and flexible signifies that the culture is able to continually absorb new cultural values. To measure the degree of cultural force, the study utilizes a five point scale in which number one corresponds to a dense culture directed towards high performance. Companies with strong cultural identification are believed to have excellent performance due to the reasons related below, [7]: share the same values and methods of doing business; subject people of different hierarchical levels to the same patterns; align goals in pluralist environments; create uncommon levels of motivation and loyalty; provide structure and control without the need of increasing bureaucracy; and permit transitions of power without major surprises.

One should pay attention to the dysfunctional elements that can attack strong cultures. One of these elements is gray areas. These areas are capable of generating dislike, not giving relevance to new strategies which can fractionalize and enhance their own corporate culture. A culture of success is one whose managers do not develop authoritarianism and leadership. Visionary companies, i.e., the best of the best, have many common qualities. They promote actions that enable the preservation of the core, they agree with a culture of devotion, they have great places to work and continued training with internal managers, and they worship the tireless stimulus to progress, each time setting goals more challenging and audacious. Institutions that have a strong cultural identification, or are characterized as dense, have a high degree of values and form shared beliefs. These institutions also believe that it is not successful to make decisions that do not meet their assumptions independently of the business strategy. When opinions are divided into segments or units, those units can be considered subcultures, and, if they significantly disagree with the core of the company, it is defined as an organizational counterculture.

In accordance with [7], "counterculture unites groups or subgroups that reject what the organization represents or what it tries to achieve in disguised opposition to the dominate values and/or power structure of the company. Arising from times of tension or in the course of big transformations [...], counterculture movements try to demean the dominate culture – or the new culture that the company intends to establish -, in an attempt to regain control over events."

What makes the battle against counterculture even more difficult is the way that it presents itself, because generally it doesn't submit to open confrontations instead acting behind the scenes using irony and subtlety. For [8] "these forms of resistance and conflicts express breeches in the system of formal power, [...] that include: the negation or hiding information; resistance to or boycott of innovations; failure of cooperation amongst workgroups," these attitudes come accompanying cynicism and sarcasm, corroborating with the ideas [7]. Organizational culture didactically decomposed into several layers that, as a whole, act in a quasi-chaotic disorderly fashion. I.E, in the same time that the whole company is driven in the same direction (driving force), they are constantly making references to a set of rules (central ideology), in parallel to elements that are unconscious (self) and even, undesirable (gray areas). Another important point in Organizational Culture is when resistance to the new values is responsible for its revaluation. Self is situated as the central point in the core of Organizational Culture. It represents the integration between conscience and unconscious systems that are by its time, joined to attitudes repeated over time, establishing this form, which become the guidelines adopted by the company. To identify the unconscious systems of an organization is in truth to recognize the gray areas, which can be identified as taboos and prejudices that somehow obscure the central ideal of the organization. Like the representation of the organizational images of [10] which highlights mechanisms, psychic prisons, political systems, instruments of domination, organic, cybernetic, flow and transformation, characterized in the following.

Mechanisms: Fits into this view of organizations that impose rigid routines and patterns, hierarchically distributed. Dealings are impersonal and control of the organization is bureaucratic. Because it is very predictable, it is no longer regarded as ideal, even in stable and authoritarian institutions. This also presents difficulties in innovation.

Psycic Prisons: Inflexibility is a characteristic of this image, becoming a prisoner of past events, allied to fundamental attitudes by their idealizers. Some of their traps are false assumptions, rules without questioning and fanaticism around the charisma of the leader that is beyond accommodation.

Political Systems: This view is often not in the interest of the group and often favors authoritarian executives. This includes companies with participatory management that is encompassed in political systems because although there is a certain distribution of power, the central objective will be executed by both subordinates and the owners of the capital.

Instruments of Domination: In organizations viewed as instruments of domination the employees and managers need to completely dedicate themselves to the company. They feel insecure about their employment and experience a lot stress on the job.

Organic: The fundamental principal of organic is that it is based on the employees' intellectual capital. Motivation is a substantial factor. Because of constant innovation and deadlines, the employees tend to obey a biological clock.

Cybernetic: Intellectual capital is highly valued and is constantly being stimulated to improve. Decision-making needs to be done "through formal or temporary processes, producing policies and plans that offer a point of reference or a structure for information processing" [7]. The definition of cybernetic is due to the fact that information technology is permanently present, which ensures better conditions in the review of political norms and procedures, beyond learning how to absorb changes in the environment.

Flow and Transformation: Organizations that better mirror flow and transformation are those that modify and evolve themselves to conform to change and evolution in the environment. Their survival depends on their internal and external environments.

I. RESEARCH METHOD

The research was applied with a quali-quantitative approach, a technical procedure and a documentary base with the application of interviews and questionnaires.

In approaching the problem the present work first identified the research as both quantitative and qualitative, with a qualitative emphasis that also quantifies part of that same data. This present work includes the development of strategic maps in a software company that serves companies in the industrial, commercial and service sectors, more specifically accounting offices within these sectors.

INSTRUMENTS OF DATA COLLECTION FOR THE STRATEGIC MAP BASED ON FUZZY LOGIC

The collection of data for this map was done through interviews based on the aforementioned truth tables. The questions were as follows:

1) Organizational Matrix Characteristics (strengths and weaknesses) x Environmental Characteristics (opportunities and threats):
How certain it is that each organizational characteristic (strengths and weaknesses) together with each Environmental Characteristic (opportunities and threats) should be considered in order to achieve the company's vision?

2) Column and Line Presence:
How each organizational characteristic (strengths and weaknesses) and Environmental (opportunities and threats) are presents (Field PRESENCE signaled)?

3) Organizational Matrix Characteristics (strengths and weaknesses) x Objectives:
How certain is it that each organizational characteristic (strengths and weaknesses) is related to the implementation of each objective?

4) Environmental Characteristics (opportunities and threats) x Objectives:
How certain is it that each environmental characteristic (opportunities and threats) is related to the implementation of each objective?

5) Objectives x Objectives:
How certain is it that each of the Objectives is related to the other Objectives?

6) Actions x Objectives:
How certain is it that each Action contributes to the achievement of each objective?

INSTRUMENTS OF DATA COLLECTION FOR THE STRATEGIC MAP BASED ON ORGANIZATIONAL CULTURE

The diverse views of the organization, previously presented, integrate the dynamic of organizations which can be understood, in its essence and constitution like an active phenomenon, alive, through which people create and recreate the worlds in which they live. In brief, any and all images can be considered as different ways of thinking about the organization and as the expression of Organizational Culture of the respective company. The administrators can use the approach of Organizational Culture to deal with the complexity.

Following is the structure of the strategic map based on Organizational Culture [11]. With this it is possible to define strategic priorities, to analyze the company and also to identify what type of information systems are implemented with the most ease or difficulty in the companies. The respondents answered the questionnaire using the criteria established below by identifying the option that best fits the situation in their company:

4 = Strong presence in my organization.
3 = Reasonable occurrence in my organization.
2 = Low incidence in my organization.
1 = Practically nonexistent in my organization.

1) Procedures, operations and processes are standardized.
2) Changes in the organization are normally a reaction to changes that already occurred in the macro business environment.
3) Administrators frequently talk about authority, power and superior-subordinate relationships.
4) Flexible and creative action.
5) Working in inadequate circumstances and conditions is considered a proof of loyalty to the organization.
6) The organization sees itself as a part of a larger system where there is an interdependence that involves the community, suppliers and the competition.
7) People and groups tend to display infantile behavior.
8) Past achievements are constantly cited as references and as examples for how to deal with present situations and how to face future adversities.
9) The organization evolves in harmony and balance with its macro environment.
10) People act under constant stress and pressure.
11) There is constant questioning and redirection of actions.
12) Power serves to provide discipline and achieve order in conflicts of interest.
13) The organization considers the motivations and needs of people.
14) There are rigid patterns and uniformity in people's behavior.
15) The company has and utilizes a great number of rules, norms and regulations about operational aspects of the business.
17) The delegation of power to operational levels tends to be very restricted.
18) Negative feedback is encouraged to correct organizational direction.
19) The organization expects complete devotion and dedication from its employees.
20) The company benefits more from external events (environmental, etc.) than from strict planning.
21) There are many taboos and prejudices in the organization.
22) The relationships between superiors and subordinates tend to contain elements of love and hate.
23) Long term achievement will be achieved in partnership with the forces acting with the macro-environment and not against it.
24) To dismiss people and streamline activities *is part of the game.*
25) Most people think about and influence the destiny of the company.
26) Interpersonal gossip consumes energy and diverts attention from productivity.
27) Organizational objectives and people's needs can be met simultaneously.
28) The organization is a realm of bureaucracy.
29) The organization is expected to operate in a routine, efficient, reliable and predictable manner.
30) Employees are seen as valuable resources who can offer rich and varied contributions to the organizations activities, provided that the organization attends to their needs and motivations.
31) Rumors and gossip are frequent.
32) The organization tends to offer quick answers to changes in their macro-environment.
33) The organization values executives who appear framed and faithful to the *mode of being* of the company
34) In strategic decision making the company normally abandons the simple view and prefers to take into account the complexity of the situation.
35) People are dedicated to the organization because they feel a *belonging to something greater*, which transcends their existence and individual limitations.

Table 1
Test Tabulation
Source: Johann (2008)

M	O	PS	C	ID	FT	PP
01:	02:	03:	04:	05:	06:	07:
14:	13:	12:	11:	10:	09:	08:
15:	16:	17:	18:	19:	20:	21:
28:	27:	26:	25:	24:	23:	22:
29:	30:	31:	32:	33:	34:	35:

For clarity the constant symbols are identified in the tabulation of the test:

M = Mechanism, O = Organic
PS = Political Systems C = Cybernetics
NS = Instruments of Domination
FT = Flow and Transformation PP = Psycic Prisons

TREATMENT AND ANALYSIS OF DATA AND STRATEGIC MAPS IN THE STUDIED CASE

The Infostore Company is focused on meeting the needs of its customers by suggesting operational and managerial systems to their target audience. It [12] is located in a strategically chosen point the city of Novo Hamburgo, in south of Brazil. It is a relatively new company that has only been in the market for three years and it has professional expertise and certifications in the areas of development and consulting.

The company also has commercial management, ensures their training, and expands their business that is spread across seven states in Brazil. Their products and services are recognized in diverse segments because their systems serve small, medium and large businesses. They develop flexible and totally integrated systems that integrate with other systems already used by their clients. The vanguard in services is noted as a fundamental feature of the organization. The construction and analysis of the proposed strategic maps will lead the company to the actual actions to be prioritized in order to realize this management.

The definitions of the strategies of the organization are based on the analysis of the factors that impact their results. This analysis is constructed with a base in the scenarios in which the organization is situated. The external factors correlated to the environmental factors of the company should be considered as well as macroeconomic and internal factors related to the functions existent within the organization. The analysis of the external factors permits the identification of the threats and opportunities of the environment in which the organization is positioned and helps to define the strategy to neutralize the threats and maximize the opportunities. Internal factors are analyzed as strong and weak points related to the existent functions in the organization. They are those controlled by the organization. Management starts with the translation of mission results, beliefs that are its core values, vision, desired future positioning and strategies.

Infostore [12] is focused on attending to the needs of information systems and services of the potential public consumer and on providing quality superior to the market average. They plan on doing this at a cost that will allow them to grow and penetrate the market while making the return on investment and remuneration that Infostore's members and staff. In this topic it's important that the organization conceptualizes what in fact is believed, which will be important to adapt to reality and to the businesses of it clients. They give them added value through the production and implementation of corporate programs and the addition of services and consultancies with a high standard of quality. The vision serves as a paradigm of what the institution really wants to be. In regard to this aspect, the actions of company concentrate on the development and implementation of corporate programs, especially on the service of clients of this segment, with an emphasis on the first group, developed from a technical and administrative body with elevated and growing professionalism and competency.

STRATEGIC MAP BASED ON COMPENSATORY FUZZY LOGIC

To elaborate on the strategic map based on CFL, it is necessary to cross various sets of data in order to form the guiding actions of the organization. These sets of data include such items as strengths, weaknesses, opportunities, threats [13] and [14], objectives and actions [15] and [16]. Following are the principal points within the items mentioned above.

Primary Strengths within the company:
a) Client Retention
b) Partner Network
c) Quick Solutions
d) Quality

Primary weaknesses within the company:
a) Low liquidity
b) Concentration on resale to major clients

Opportunities for the company:
a) Expansion of the internal market
b) Their computational system "Gesthor VI"

Threats to the company:
a) Increase in existing competition
b) Cancellation of contracts

Objectives listed:
a) Increased client satisfaction
b) Increased market share
c) Motivated employees

Actions the organization will adopt:
a) Management of the client relationship
b) Management of service with a goal of improvement
c) Management of productivity with a goal of improvement

Following are the results extracted from the CFL.

Characteristics of the Organization:
Strengths and weaknesses are described and confronted with the opportunities and threats. In the same form objectives, strategies and actions are confronted.

Strengths:
The principle strength of quality resulted in an index of 0.73. The post-sale satisfaction resulted in an index of 0.68. Partner network resulted in an index of 0.64. Quick Solutions resulted in an index of 0.60. Client Retention is noted as more false that true with an index of 0.37

Weaknesses:
Low liquidity resulted in an index of 0.64. Concentration of principal clients under resale responsibilities resulted in an index of 0.45.

Table 2
Results from the Strategic Themes Based on Fuzzy Logic

	OPPORTUNITIES			THREATS				OBJECTIVES		
	OP1	OP2	OP3	TR1	TR2	TR3	PRESENCE	OB1	OB2	OB3
STRENGTHS										
ST1	0.8	0.3	0.5	0	0	1	**0.7**	0	0.7	0.7
ST2	0.9	0.5	0.8	0.9	0.9	0.6	**0.8**	0.6	0.1	0.1
ST3	0.8	0.5	0.7	0	0.9	0.1	**0.7**	0	0	0
WEAKNESSES										
WE1	0	0	0.1	0	0.7	0.6	**0.4**	0	0	0
WE2	0	0	0.1	0	0.6	0.8	**0.2**	0.7	0	0
WE3	0.8	0	0.7	0	0.9	0.9	**0.1**	1	1	0.8
PRESENCE	**0.7**	**0.6**	**0.7**	**0.1**	**0.3**	**0.6**	**XX**			
OBJECTIVES										
OBJ1	0	0	0	0	0.6	0.6		1	0.4	0.6
OBJ2	0	0	0	0	0	0		0.4	1	0.7
OBJ3	0.8	0	0.8	0	0.7	0.6		0.6	0.7	1
ACTIONS										
AC1	x	x	x	X	X	x		0.80	0.8	0.7
AC2	x	x	X	X	X	x		0.95	0.78	0.8
AC3	x	x	x	X	X	x		0.78	0.92	0.85

Characteristics of the External Environment:
Here information like opportunities and threats were diagnosed after crossing of the variables.

Opportunities:
Expansion of the market is noted with the significant relevance of 0.81.

Threats:
Increased existing competition resulted in an index of 0.59. Cancellation of contracts was classified as a significant threat with an index of 1.0.

Strategic Objectives:
The increase in client satisfaction and how to increase market extraction resulted in an index of 0.73. Motivated employees was classified as an objective that needs further exploration as it resulted in an index of 0.68.

Actions:
Management of productivity with a goal of improvement resulted in an index of 0.75.

STRATEGIC MAP BASED ON ORGANIZATIONAL CULTURE

From the interview done with the board it was possible to identify the organizational *self* of the company, as the results in Table 3 show. It is followed by the tabulation of the received results. The organizational objectives can, in principle, admit as needs and as motivations of individuals, the organizational *self* which is the central point of the core and is directly linked to the process as a whole. The corresponding tabulation is presented in table 3:

Table 3
Organizational Self Test

M	O	SP	C	ID	FT	PP
01: 2	02: 2	03: 1	04: 3	05: 1	06: 3	07: 2
14: 1	13: 2	12: 1	11: 3	10: 3	09: 2	08: 4
15: 3	16: 3	17: 1	18: 2	19: 4	20: 4	21: 2
28: 2	27: 4	26: 3	25: 3	24: 1	23: 4	22: 1
29: 4	30: 4	31: 2	32: 2	33: 3	34: 3	35: 3
SUM 12	15	8	13	12	16	12

The results of Table 3 found 16 points for flow and transformation. The second most communicative result found 15 points for the organic self, which has great importance to the environment of the company. The third most communicative result found 3 points for the cybernetic aspect.

CONCLUSION

With the consolidation of the strategic maps it became possible to position and evaluate whether or not the organization had its objectives and initiatives channeled towards the purpose that they had proposed. These objectives that are to be exploited by different approaches were able to offer proposals that were not previously evident. They were also able to clarify that the placement of a major emphasis is not as important as respect for the company. The example mentioned above itself uses Fuzzy Logic that can clearly diagnose items that the company considers relevant and when confronted with the fuzzy analysis were demystified as irrelevant factors for the company, much like other points that were attributed and identified as real opportunities, objectives and actions. The study of Organizational Culture observes that the company represents flow and transformation consistent with the real reformulation of the organization to monitor the probable changes in the external environment

The goals, actions and Swot were analyzed by the CFL methodology and thus some of them had higher prioritization. The organizational culture of the studied company was also numerically measured. So this study aligned business efficiency using CFL and Organizational Culture. The scenario identified a map of Strategic

Objectives, an organizational culture represented by "Flow and Transformation" and the implementation of the CFL providing meaning in the range (range) [0,1] to each of the defined goals.

REFERENCES

[1] C. Ciupak, A. Vanti, A. Balloni, R. Espin and J. Marx-Gómez, Jorge. *Informational analysis involving application of complex information system* in Advanced Techniques in Computing Sciences and Software Engineering Elleithy, Khaled (Ed.) 2010, ISBN: 978-90-481-3659-9. *Published in International Joint Conferences on Computer, Information, and Systems Sciences, and Engineering. CISSE,* 2008.

[2] A.A. Vanti, R. Espin, A. Schripsema and D. Goyer, "The Importance of Objectives and Strategic Lagging and Leading Indicators in the Chain Import and Export Process using the Fuzzy Logic System". *Proceddings in ACM (SIGMIS)-CPR*, Claremont, USA, 2006, pp. 190-197.

[3] R. Espin, E. Fernández , G. Mazcorro, J. Marx-Gómez and M. Lecich 'Compensatory Logic: A fuzzy normative model for decision making'. *Investigación Operativa. Universidad de la Habana.*Vol 27, 2, (2006). pp. 188-197.

[4] R. Espin and A. A. Vanti. "Administração Lógica: um estudo de caso em empresa de comercio exterior". *Base Revista de Administração de Contabilidade da Unisinos*, São Leopoldo, p. 4-22, ago, 2005.

[5] R. Sprague and H. WATSON. *Decision Support Systems. Putting Theory in Practice.* Prentice-Hall 1993.

[6] E. Turban, R. Sharda, J. Aronson and D. King. *Business Intelligence. A managerial approach.* New Jersey: Pearson Education, 2008.

[7] S. Johann. *Gestão da cultura corporativa: como as organizações de alto desempenho gerenciam sua cultura organizacional.* Porto Alegre: Saraiva, 2004.

[8] M. E. Freitas *Cultura organizacional: formação, tipologias e impactos.* São Paulo: Makron, McGraw-Hill, 1991.

[9] R. Dagnino, E. Gomes, G. Costa, G. Stefanuto, S. Meneghel and T. Scalcu. *Gestão estratégica da inovação: metodologias para análise e implementação.* São Paulo: Cabral Editora e Livraria Universitária, 2002.

[10] G. Morgan. *Images of organization.* London: SAGE Publications, 1996.

[11] S. Johann. *Gestão da cultura organizacional. Apostila FGV Management - SIGA - Sistema de Informação e Gestão Acadêmica, da Fundação Getúlio Vargas,* RJ, FGV, 2008.

[12] Infostore Consultoria Ltda. *Disponível em http://www.infostoreinf.com.br*> Acesso em 10 mar. 2009.

[13] K. Andrews. *The Concept of Corporate Strategy.* Dow Jones Irwin. 1974.

[14] P. Wright, M. Kroll and J. Parnell. *Strategic Management: concepts.* USA: Prentice Hall, Inc., 1998

[15] R. Kaplan and D. Norton. *The Balanced Scorecard: Translating Strategy into Action.* Mass, 1996.

[16] R. KAPLAN and D. NORTON, *Strategy Maps.* HBS Press, 2004.

The RDF Generator (RDFG) - First Unit in the Semantic Web Framework (SWF)

Ahmed Nada
anada@itce.alquds.edu

Badie Sartawi
sartawi@alquds.edu

Department of Computer Science and Information Technology, Al-Quds University, Palestine

Abstract — **the Resources Description Framework RDF Generator (RDFG) is a platform generates the RDF documents from any web page using predefined models for each internet domain, using special web pages classification system. The RDFG is one of the SWF units aimed to standardize the researchers efforts in Semantic Web, by classifying the internet sites to domains, and preparing special RDF model for each domain. RDFG used web intelligent methods for preparing RDF documents such as ontology based semantics matching system to detect the type of web page and knowledgebase machine learning system to create the RDF documents accurately and according to the standard models. RDFG reduce the complexity of the RDF modeling and realize the web entities creating, sharing and reusing.**

Keywords — Semantic Web, RDF, Web Ontology, Semantics Matching, and Web Classification.

I. Introduction

The web is a large and growing source of information. This information is not organized, which make it difficult to reuse. The Semantic Web efforts enabled us to reuse this amount of unorganized text and make it into a database, but the researchers face some difficulty and problems to realize the Semantic Web Vision.

The Semantic Web provides a common framework that allows data to be shared and reused across application, enterprise, and community boundaries. It is a collaborative effort led by W3C, with participation from a large number of researchers and industrial partners [5]. The Semantic Web built on data is represented in the Resource Description Framework (RDF). The RDF is a framework for representing the information on the Web. RDF has a simple data model that is easy for applications to process and manipulate [5]. Fig. 1 shows that the Web RDF is organized and linked content.

So, we need tools and technologies to generate the RDF and for search in the RDF files. The researchers and programmers introduce projects and researches to build RDF out of Source-texts and make queries to retrieve useful information from it. Such as the Simple Protocol and RDF Query Language (SPARQL), this is a Query language for Semantic Web. But some of the introduced projects and efforts have weaknesses, such as each Semantic Web projects or researches prepared to solve a problem in specific domain or purpose. So by now, the researchers are working to make it not in closed domains; in addition to reduce the complexity of the RDF modeling and realize the web entities creating, sharing and reusing. This research is to make it possible by introducing RDF generator with knowledgebase machine learning system to be more intelligent and useful.

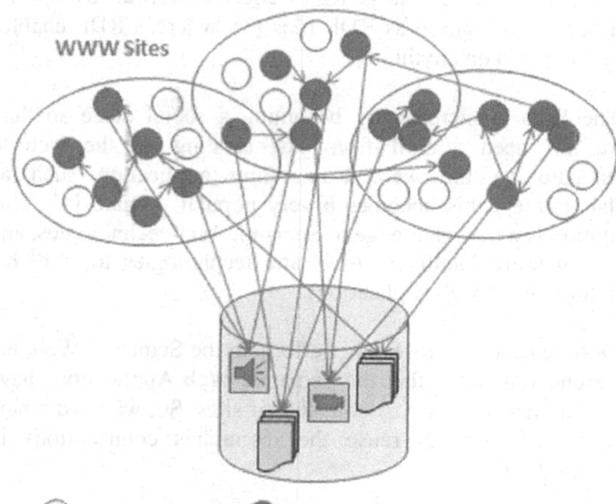

Fig. 1. The Semantic Web: RDF linked to each other and to the content available on the Web

The paper is organized as follows. Section2 talks about Semantic Web and RDF in general and introduce the problems in this field. Section3 introduces an abstract about our work in the Semantic Web Research Group at Al-Quds University, The Semantic Web Framework (SWF). Section 4 presents RDFG platform content and architecture. The last section summarizes this work.

T. Sobh, K. Elleithy (eds.), *Innovations in Computing Sciences and Software Engineering*, DOI 10.1007/978-90-481-9112-3_89,

II. Background

"The Semantic Web is an extension of the current web in which information is given well-defined meaning, better enabling computers and people to work in cooperation. " – Tim Berners-Lee, James Hendler and Ora Lassila [7]

The Semantic Web vision has inspired a large community of researchers and practitioners, who have achieved several early successes in the past six years [1]. Through these years the researches have introduced and developed tools and technologies to make the Semantic Web applicable. The main objective of this research is develops a platform for RDF generating by gathering the researchers efforts in this field.

The traditional Web technologies, which are based on a large amount of information, don't provide the semantic search and navigation in unorganized information. So the researchers are trying to find new technologies to navigate and search in the Web using semantic words to make these processes more intelligent. These efforts and technologies were named The Semantic Web.

Since the publication of the original Semantic Web Vision of Berners-Lee, Hendler and Lassile [2], the researcher develops and builds tools to realize this vision. Basically, the goal of Semantic web is to enable the machine understanding of the web resources. The Semantic Web vision involves the production and use of large amounts of RDF data; we can see the Semantic Web as a large Knowledgebase formed by sources that serve information as RDF files [3], whereas RDF enables the description on anything.

The Web is increasingly becoming a social place so that, there has been a shift from just existing on the web to participate on the web. Community application such as collaborative wikis becomes a very popular domain [4]. This evolution is a new challenge to Semantic Web technologies, and we need more intelligent tools and technologies to face this evolution in the web applications.

Despite of all the researcher efforts in the Semantic Web, the researchers assumed that the Semantic Web Applications have closed domains of manageable size of sites. So, we need a new way to arrange and reuse the researches contributions in different domains.

Recently the Database companies have introduced many of the new data management tools, such as the Oracle Database 11g introduce scalable, secure and reliable data management software for RDF applications [6]. But these technologies use the already created RDF documents in loading and querying, so we need another tool to generate RDF documents.

Our research solves these problems and realizes the visions in Semantic Web area. In this research we want to develop RDF generator platform contains all semantic web efforts, projects and researches.

III. The Semantic web framwork(SWF)

The Semantic Web Framework (SWF) is a new generation in the Semantic Web area being developed by Semantic Web Research Group at Al-Quds University. The SWF has an RDF generator that generates RDF documents from any web page using predefined model for each web domain, query processor to retrieve the requested data from RDF document. The framework also has page ranking system to provide it to the search engines. Fig. 2, Describe the status of the web after using the proposed framework.

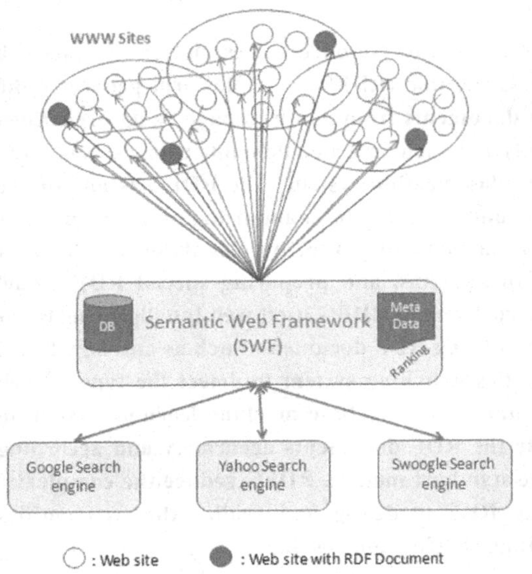

Fig. 2. The status of the Web after using the Semantic Web Framework.

This research is the first step in building the SWF. The RDFG is the basic unit in the SWF to generate the RDF document.

IV. The RDF Generator (RDFG)

RDFG is a platform to generate a standard description (RDF) for internet web sites using predefined model for each web site type. RDFG classify the web sites to help us while detecting the type of web site and extract the description from the pages.

1. Websites Classification

The web is continues to grow hugely, and the search process in the web become more complex also the direct access to what I need become impossible, so we need methods to arrange the web and help us while using it. The search engine can help us to search in the web but we face another problem is the need to search in the search engines results. SWF propose a new classification of websites to categories, to help us while detecting the type of page, and to help the search engines while preparing the search results and categories it.

Our proposed web classification based on previous classification with some adjustments to fit with our goal in RDFG, and create standard RDF model for each category. RDFG use our proposed web classification while detecting the type of web page and select the suitable RDF model to extract the pages description.

2. Websites Types Detection, and Suitable RDF Model Selection

Based on our classification, RDFG uses intelligent methods to determine the type of webpage. Semantics Matching System is the basic intelligent method we proposed, to determine the type of webpage then to extract the needed information to generate the RDF. This system depends on knowledgebase semantics for each web classification; this knowledgebase has machine learning system to be more intelligent and dynamic.

RDF models represent certain types of web categories models. After determine the type of web page, RDFG select the suitable RDF model to generate the description for the web page using the Semantics Matching System.

3. Machine Learning System

The RDFG contains an intelligent system used to learn the knowledgebase, so we can feed the RDFG while and after generate the RDF to change or modify the knowledgebase semantics to be more dynamic and intelligent. Also we can modify our classification, by feeding the knowledgebase automatically or manually by users. The machine work details are published in SWF Machine Learning paper.

4. RDFG Architecture

Basically we have represents the research idea using web service application to make testing and evaluation the idea. Fig 3 describes the RDFG platform contents. In the next section we talk about the RDFG web service.

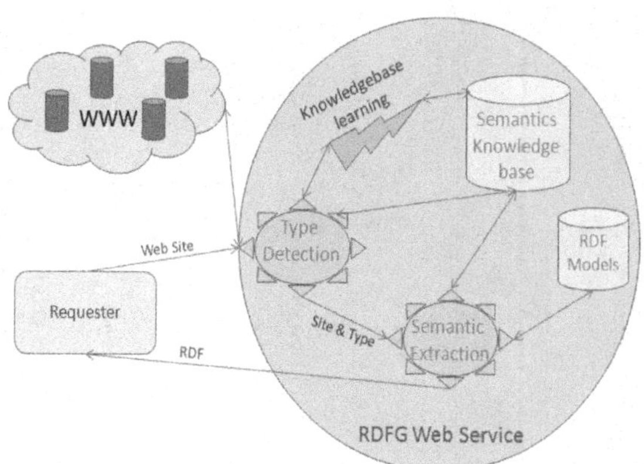

Fig. 3. The RDFG Architecture

5. RDFG Web Service

To build and test the RDFG we prepare a web service application using Microsoft C# .NET. This web service contains two ways to use it in the users and developers semantic web applications. The first one is a web page; the user enter the web page link to prepare the RDF for it, the RDFG prepare the RDF and export it to the user, and there is machine learning system to ask the user while generate the RDF if there are any suggestion for semantic extraction or type detection. Another one is a web service for web developers using XML request and response; the developer send the webpage using XML special syntax and the RDFG prepare the RDF.

V. Conclusion

We have proposed a new platform in Semantic Web area that can be used to generate the RDF documents from any web page using predefined models for each internet domain. The Resources Description Framework Generator (RDFG) is the first step in building the Semantic Web Framework (SWF). The RDFG aimed to standardize the RDF creation, by divided the internet sites to domains, and prepare special RDF model for each domain. We used intelligent methods for preparing RDF documents using RDFG such as ontology based semantics matching system and knowledgebase machine learning system, to create the RDF documents accurately and according to the standard models.

References

[1] A. ankolekar, M. Krotzsch, D.T. Tran, D. Varandecic, The Two Cultures: Mashing up web 2.0 and the semantic web, Journal of Web Semantics 6, 70-75, 2008.

[2] A. Aurona, A. Merwe, A. Barnard, A functional Semantic Web Architecture, 5th European Semantic Web Conference (ESWC2008), 2008.

[3] U. Bojars, J.G. Breslin, A. Finn, S. Decher, Using the Semantic Web for Linking and reusing data across Web 2.0 communities, Journal of Web Semantics 6, 21-28, 2008.

[4] R. Delbru, M Catasta, R Cyganiak, A Document-oriented Lookup Index for Open Linked Data, 5th European Semantic Web Conference (ESWC2008), 2008.

[5] W3C Web Site, URL: http://www.w3.org/.

[6] X. Lopez, S. Das, Semantic Data Integration for the Enterprise. Oracle Corporation, 2007.

[7] T. Berners-Lee, J. Hendler, and O. Lassila. The Semantic Web. Scientific American, 284(5):35–43, 2001.

Information Technology to Help Drive Business Innovation and Growth

Igor Aguilar Alonso, José Carrillo Verdún, Edmundo Tovar Caro
School of Computer Science,
Technical University of Madrid,
Campus de Montegancedo, C.P. 28660.
Madrid - Spain
iaguilar@zipi.fi.upm.es, jcarrillo@fi.upm.es, etovar@fi.upm.es

Abstract. This paper outlines how information technology (IT) can help to drive business innovation and growth. Today innovation is a key to properly managing business growth from all angles. IT governance is responsible for managing and aligning IT with the business objectives; managing strategic demand through the projects portfolio or managing operational demand through the services portfolio. IT portfolios offer the possibility of finding new opportunities to make changes and improve through innovation, enabling savings in capital expenditure and the company's IT operations staff time.

In the last century, IT was considered as a new source of infinite possibilities and business success through innovation.

Key Words: Innovation and Growth, Innovation Life Cycle, Innovation Business Models, Innovation Networks, Portfolio Management.

I. INTRODUCTION

Innovation develops at difficult times. It forces people to think of doing the things they need to do to improve operating procedures. Innovation is all about finding new ways to make people more productive. We have seen many advances in technology, ranging from improved predictive analysis embedded in a simple exposure to the analysis of trends and observational data from a lot of technological equipment. Organizations need to look for and identify the things people really need. This is where to start to think and change things and make improvements.

Business innovation can be supported by information technology governance (ITG). IT governance consists of the leadership and organizational structures and processes that ensure that the organization's IT sustains and extends the organization's strategies and objectives. [1]

Demand management, is a central element of IT governance, known as the management of all requests made to IT, and is really a great point at which to start to implement innovation through a governance strategy.

Business innovation should be implemented through portfolios other central element of IT governance, these portfolios manage different demand types, including strategic demand, operational demand and tactical demand.

The Chief Information Office (CIO) is responsible for managing demand and starting to implement business innovation. The CIO is characterized as a leading driver of change and business innovation, as well the Chief Executive Office (CEO).

To generate innovation in an enterprise, CIOs and other senior executives with similar potential need to be taken on to resolve the shortage of talent in IT. Additionally, they must be properly trained to develop this potential. As the global economy is characterized by the innovative application of technology, the evolution of business will be linked through the CIO to the senior executives who have the innovation to work within the enterprise and make the necessary changes according to business needs.

This paper discusses how information can help drive business innovation and growth. The paper is structured as follows. Section 1 introduces innovation. Section 2 defines innovation in demand and IT portfolio management. Section 3 defines the areas and components of innovation. Section 4 defines the innovation life cycle. Section 5 lists some conclusions.

II. INNOVATION IN DEMAND AND IT PORTFOLIO MANAGEMENT

As Figure 1 shows, IT demand management covers the needs of several business processes that are its customers. It can also be viewed as a mega project, which determines which IT projects should be classified and qualified to then be implemented by the IT department. [2].

The demand for IT resources comes from a variety of places and in different scales. Some requests are routine requirements such as recruitment help desk, new employee provisioning, whereas other demands are strategic and complex, such as new applications to support new business opportunities. With IT demand management, it is all channeled through a single point, where it can be consolidated, prioritized and executed. Demand management

T. Sobh, K. Elleithy (eds.), *Innovations in Computing Sciences and Software Engineering*,
DOI 10.1007/978-90-481-9112-3_90,

works closely with IT portfolio management to manage current and future IT investments [3].

Each demand type is managed by the respective portfolio, and all the portfolios together make up the IT Portfolio Management Office (PMO). It is in the PMO, and precisely the portfolios managing strategic operational demand, where innovation should start, using different types of technology. Portfolio management is a set of not necessarily related projects and/or programs that are combined in order to monitor, coordinate and optimize the entire portfolio.

A. IT Demand Types

IT demand types are segmented into three major categories: (1) strategic demand, (2) operational demand and (3) tactical demand [4]. As show in Figure 1, demand management deals with the influx of requests for IT services, maintenance, and operational support, each varying in its level of importance to the organization. Demand types are grouped by portfolios and by business needs for appropriate processing.

Reference [5], discusses demand management and IT types, which are the heart of IT governance. However, strategic demand and operational demand management haves a more detailed focuses, as they are managed by their respective portfolios. It is here that we find the ideas, proposals, projects and assets, and we can more consistently apply innovation.

Today, companies need to strategically change the way in which they think about how they do business. This calls for innovation within the company. Innovation should take on new ideas within the projects or services portfolio and from key stakeholders to drive change through innovation. This is the job of the CIO and senior IT management and involves strategic decision making, which is key to facilitating innovation through IT.

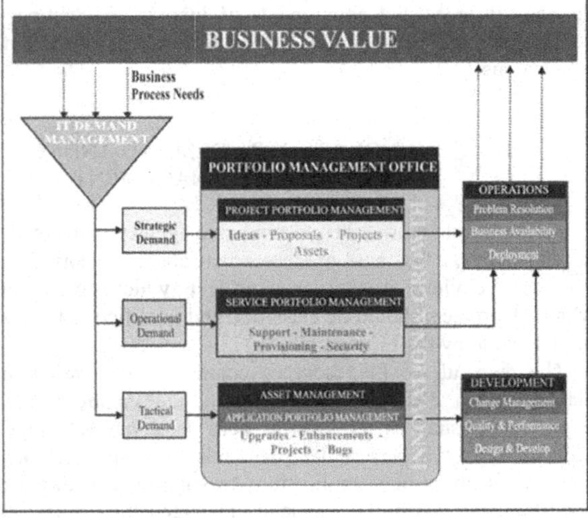

Figure 1. Types of IT Demand and Portfolios.

III. THE INNOVATION

Innovation takes place through the appropriate use of technology as a key element for achieving a competitive advantage over other companies. Many leading firms are successful in business and progressing at an impressive rate.

Companies that have a "strategic CIO" [6], use more technology to make innovations in products and services as well share technology more effectively in all areas of the company. CIOs are heavily involved in strategic decision-making have higher levels of: (1) Innovation in the business model through IT, (2) Innovation in products and services through IT, (3) Infrastructure and centralized shared services.

CIO and senior executives should play a central role in identifying projects and leadership for innovation and change.

At present, even though innovation attracts most CIOs, many govern their innovation efforts too rigidly [7]. These CIOs confine their mission to finding, funding, and rewarding innovation because they (1) miss lower impact opportunities by looking only for earth-shattering change; (2) fail to see ideas that are there for the picking while looking to a few smart people to innovate; and (3) obstruct innovation by managing it just like any other investment request.

According to Forrester Research [8], the question is, where do ongoing investments end and innovations begin? there is a gap between ongoing projects and new ideas, as shown in Figure 2. Precisely it is here where close cooperation and new ideas need to be exploited to address and fill this gap. Looking at ongoing investments, they have standardized operating procedures, are very low risk, developed incrementally, and demand is one way or operational.

By contrast, research teams managing a portfolio of ideas have to work very correctly because ideas are not standardized, are possibly high risk, unanticipated and are strategic in scope.

Many established enterprises have their own well-implemented research and development centers. They work within the demand management process and are able to liaise with IT portfolio management to manage current and future IT investments.

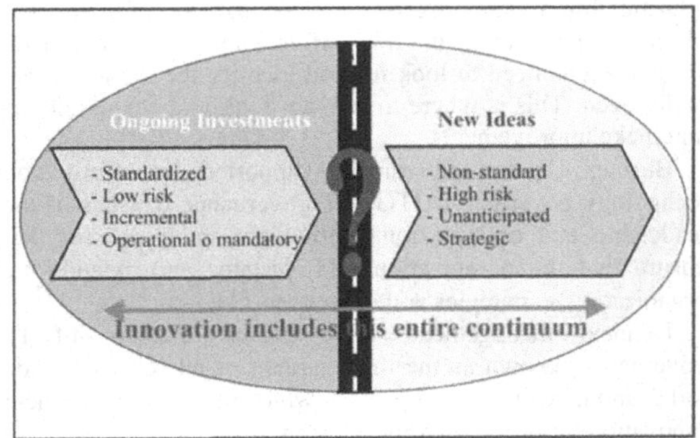

Figure 2. Innovation is a continuous process.

A. *Scope of business innovation areas*

Business innovation does not have to be stunning, but it must transform tasks across different areas, as well shows Figure 3; some of which are performed to create worth. Remember that innovation may not necessarily affect the IT organization, but innovation is closely related to technology.

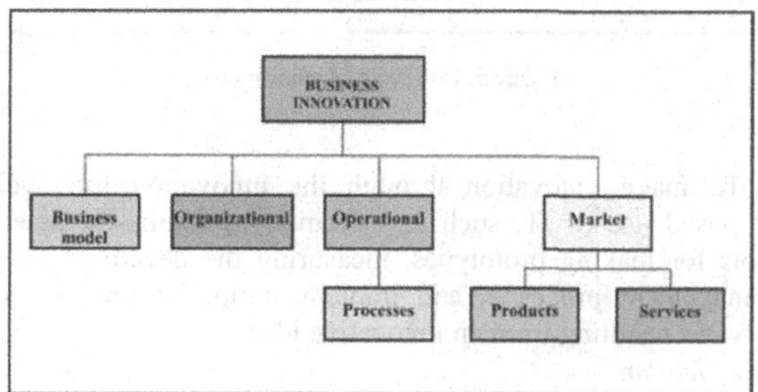

Figure 3. Scope of business innovation areas.

Companies are unable to design or introduce a new product or service or at least make changes to their business models without using technology. But in the era of emerging technology businesses, an IT organization may not be involved.

CEOs and CIOs are looking to transform their products, services, processes, and even business models in order to drive global competitive advantage. Recognizing this strategic imperative, CIOS are bent on helping their organizations innovate in different areas. [9]. Let us describe the most important innovation areas.

1. IT-based business model innovation

Companies set out to find a new way to interact with customers and partners without having to recreate a new physical infrastructure. New business models are often an enabling technology, and business model innovation can be the fastest way of increasing a company's margin growth. For leaders of business units, the challenge will be to create new, less expensive business models and to make new trade-offs between capital and labor. [10].

2. IT-based organizational innovation

A decision making committee on innovation, composed of staff from different business units, needs to be set up within the company. Committee members do not necessarily have to be business executives, although members should be creative and have innovative ideas on a range of issues, such as infrastructure or operational procedures to improve the business units across the company's entire organizational structure, starting with their own business units and passing on their proposals to their managers.

3. Operational innovation across business processes

Company innovation is reflected in operating procedures, low costs, speed cycle times, or better customer satisfaction.

At this stage, where processes are automated, today can see how many other companies are improving many manual processes. Innovation to automate manual processes will prevent a lot of mistakes.

4. Innovation for market penetration

Market innovation refers to the strategies adopted by companies seeking to penetrate new and existing markets by offering new products or services.

B. *The components of innovation*

Today an enterprise with successful and sustainable business innovation based on a solid foundation, including an understanding of the enterprise's core capabilities, assets, partners, customers, suppliers, funding, processes, measurable processes, where all of these key elements are interrelated, will drive change through business innovation [11]. Figure 4 shows the components involved in business innovation.

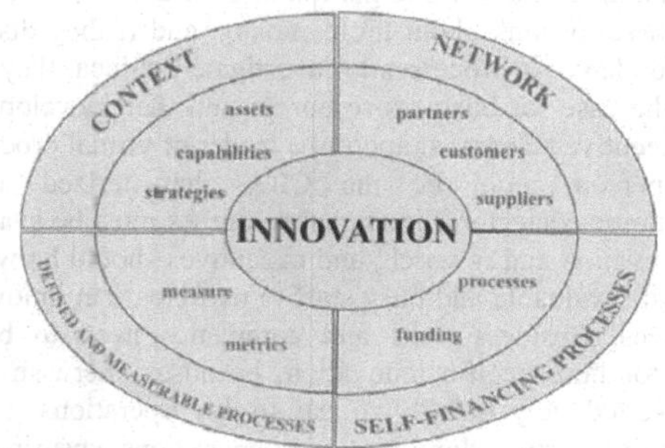

Figure 4. Innovation components.

Today companies look to innovate business models and operations across processes, as well as products and services in order to enter markets. Let us describe the most important innovation areas.

1. Innovation context

Within the context of innovation, committed strategically minded senior executives of the company with the will to succeed welcome new ideas, company executives work with other executives across the company to assess the enterprise's assets and capabilities portfolio, and business models must capitalize on the capabilities available to the company to enact its processes, thereby contributing to sustainable innovation. Understanding these capabilities involves a process of introspection. Within the context of innovation, strategies for achieving growth and excellence must be developed and articulated, and companies must decide whether to use the assets and capabilities with which to achieve operational excellence as a mark of distinction enabling them to position themselves in new markets or gain new market shares.

2. Innovation network

The innovation network engages the company's network of partners, customers, and suppliers, which is an extended group of people with similar interests or related in how they interact and keep in informal contact for mutual assistance or support. Senior executives must look inside and outside the enterprise for CEOs and senior executives to exploit the innovative potential that there is within the company, should regulate brainstorming meetings with IT, marketing and sales executives to solve problems and focus on the gaps in the current portfolio. CIOs must also look outwards, towards and inside the company. They must be constantly on the look out for ideas and opportunities for the company instead of regarding their vendors and consultants as mere suppliers. They should engage in brainstorming sessions and leadership exchange to build on open sharing of assets and gaps in company portfolios.

3. Self-financing processes

Companies should not expect to discover or invent great ideas and then find ways to get funding for their development. They have to think about the company, and if they discover that they have no processes to investigate the idea, they must build the case for business resources and their development. The executive team must appoint a leader of virtual processes. This person could be the CIO, characterized as an opportunities detector. Functional resources must be available for innovation and research, and executives should be willing to transfer valuable and busy staff to participate in innovation initiatives. Business units and companies need to budget funds for non-specific innovation, because otherwise funds are diverted very quickly to day-to-day operations. In this case, third parties should oversee operations ensuring that executives have the budget to finance possible innovations that conform to enterprise strategy and the executives' will to improve current capability or change the business model.

4. Defined and measurable processes

At this stage it is necessary to consider the objective of the process and relationships to other processes. A process is a series of activities that are executed to convert the input into an output and, finally, a result. The input is related to the resources that are used in the process. The output describes the results of the process. The result indicates the long-term process.

Control activities involve the input and output of each process, which are subject to policies and standards to provide information about the results that the process should produce. To analyze the results of the processes, metrics are required to take the appropriate measure in order to draw conclusions from the results.

IV. INNOVATION LIFE CYCLE

Today innovation is induced by several factors in the huge majority of businesses, including especially cultural and financial issues, and economic and technological changes in the world. Executives are very concerned about innovation through the use of IT helping their business to succeed. Executives from many companies have created their own structured process models that are scalable and replicable over time.

We propose a cyclical model to manage the innovation process, including the following steps as shown in Figure 5.

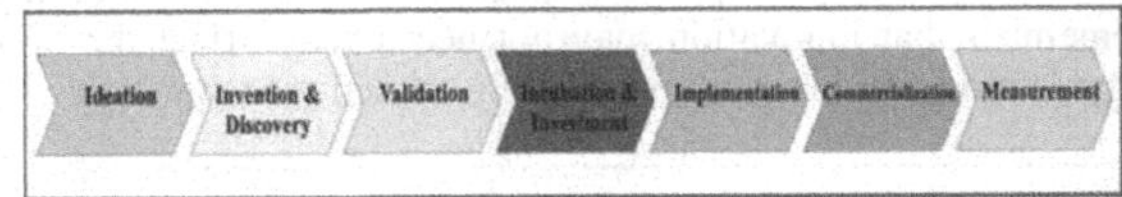

Figure 5. Life cycle of innovation.

To make innovation through the innovation life cycle proposed use of IT, such as information, databases, assets, tools for making prototypes, measuring the development of management processes and implementation of products or services resulting from an innovative idea.

A. Ideation

Ideation is the initial phase of the innovation process. This phase reflects all ideas from many different sources. The most common are suggested by employees, partners, customers and suppliers and vendors.

The first step is to create an inventory of all the potential ideas. This would be a good starting point for finding new ideas for entry in the innovation portfolio within the IT department.

After inventory, ideas must be streamlined. This should eliminate duplicate ideas, combine smaller ideas to make for a more sensible idea or split the big ideas into separate ideas.

The result of this process is an inventory of all potential ideas, with a short description of each one. The ideas should receive due attention in the subsequent steps to ensure they are properly documented before starting to be commissioned. Companies should:

1. Define the idea.

The next step is to clearly define the objectives of the idea at a level that enables the IT innovation committee to OK the idea for prioritization. This includes a brief outline of the objectives and preliminary workload, timeline, and cost and benefit estimates for the idea. These pieces of information quickly identify and help to provide a rough estimate of the relative cost of ideas.

Typically, the committee will design an innovation form, which should set out the critical information needed to understand and evaluate the ideas.

B. Invention and discovery

The purpose of the invention and discovery stage is simply to get ideas that can be evaluated. As part of setting up a culture that values and cultivates innovation, innovations must be the result of a funneled or well-managed approach. Innovations must be opportunists, enabled by the appropriate repeated context and the culture that conforms to the normal course of doing business or undertaking projects. To create an asset portfolio of ideas that work, companies must somehow create the environment for:

1. *Developing contextual issues at the executive level.*

CEOs should set up a framework for promoting ideas and foster a brainstorming culture. They should provide a context for examining innovation and design strategies for business growth and innovation.

2. *Creating innovation networks.*

Innovation networks involve partners, customers and suppliers who collaborate with each other. Companies clearly recognize that relations with partners are the source of innovation today, but are unable to put into place an explicit set of roles, expectations, and regular contact. Instead, companies need to divide roles and levels of partner commitment and then manage and monitor progress, and weigh up methods to speed up the pace of innovation. [12]

3. *Encouraging corporate employees to visit the work site daily.*

Businesses have the opportunity to innovate by getting their head office-based staff from IT or R&D departments to go out into field with customers or visit employees on site, or through sudden inspiration with developers and product partners within the innovation network.

4. *Incorporating new ideas with employees through internships, exchange, and outsourcing rotation.*

In business there are people that are set in their ways and routine. When CIOs seek to introduce new social networking tools in the enterprise, they typically meet with strong resistance from their own long-standing IT managers. Companies must refresh ideas by recruiting new employees, conducting regular exchanges between business units, intentionally rotating the roles of senior directives, and training staff to assume new responsibilities.

Global organizations can gather multiple ideas from a hierarchical perception channeled through a process of systematic and structured review. Global companies that depend on a steady flow of ideas must provide a work environment, in the shape of an online portal, with well-documented instructions for employees or people outside the company to submit their ideas or patents.

C. *Validation of the feasibility of an idea*

This stage aims simply to see if an idea is appropriate for innovation before taking research any further. The ideas that are feasible must be managed across the portfolio of ideas. This is the challenge at present, because innovative ideas are fragile, and underfunding, under response, the distractions of everyday processes and other mechanisms can lead to an error-prone business process. Companies should:

1. *Cultivate the proposed ideas.*

There should be an idea management system or online portal to gather the potentially innovative business ideas. These ideas should be tested with clients, researchers, financiers to be improved, and then go to inventory of ideas to further test the viability of proposed technologies with a defined set of contributors and testers.

2. *Use mentors.*

Companies with process patents must ensure that new sponsors are assigned to a high-level individual. This person will help with the process and criteria giving a clear understanding of the format for submitting ideas of any kind. The proponents of an idea must have some sort of guide, FAQ, and mechanisms to get the answers to the questions.

3. *Investigate inventions.*

Invention in the field of innovation is the result of the selection of a proper idea from a conglomerate of ideas or a project proposal. The idea must be aligned with the overall company strategy, related to the portfolio of capabilities identified at the higher level. For this phase of the innovation process there must be a virtual leader to ensure that the innovations proposed are suitable and adequate for cataloguing in the portfolio of ideas.

4. *Establish links.*

Companies must be careful not to lose track of unsuccessful ideas or ideas that are not well defined. They should be stored, returned to and rethought later. While one organization may not be able to use an idea today, technology or the concept of the idea may be feasible for use tomorrow or in another part of the company.

D. *Idea incubation and investment decision making*

At this stage where the best ideas are seen as potentially valuable for business innovation, it is up to the company to transform the concept of an idea into reality. The company should provide the foundation for the growth of and demonstrate the worth of the proposal. Companies should:

1. *Be clear about the decision making process.*

Companies need to establish a set of expectations for possible innovations. Within a project, the partners should have the autonomy to be creative, and decision-making must be based on established criteria for selecting the best idea through to its transformation into a product.

2. *Communicate the selection criteria.*

For innovation processes based on a wealth of ideas that are captured through online portals, the benefit and design of the selection criterion must be clearly identified, as with patent processes, where a company seeks to protect intellectual property. Apart from being posted on the portal, the criteria should be well communicated through the use of internal publications and by the executive management.

3. *Provide virtual and real resources.*

To transform an invention/idea into a product innovation, the idea should be developed in collaboration with a range of additional technologic resources or other type to achieve the goal, from inside or outside the company.

This should result in to the formation of cross-functional teams. Teams should bring onboard partners and suppliers to produce prototypes.

Prototypes are directly associated with a company supplier. This supplier is responsible for the preliminary design of a prototype technology.

E. Implementation

This phase implements the product produced and then marketed as a result of the innovative idea.

Remember that misinformation leads employees to think that ideas get to the market based on politics and whims. Although an organization's "standard project approaches" might work for these innovations, there will still be some obstacles, as innovations are likely to be higher risk. To surmount these risk-related hurdles, it is necessary to:

1. Promote rapid prototyping.

Organizations with the best track record of innovation are open to new ideas and to the possibility that they may not work. To promote these ideas, these organizations create prototypes, including Web-based content, to demonstrate feasibility. Within businesses, they may start to build prototypes based on their observation of the problems at the workplace and then present the prototype to the business executives as part of the recommendations for process improvement.

F. Commercialization

At the marketing stage the product is put on the market. Before this, though, the prototypes have to be tested. So, companies should:

1. Test with real customers.

Before transforming an innovative idea, the idea must be tested at the target destination and for the purpose or goal of the setting. The tests can be performed with the buyers in a virtual shopping environment, helping the teams to understand the validity of the innovation.

2. Reassess assets portfolio.

A well-proven concept of innovation is an opportunity to review overall company competitiveness, as well as exploring other product areas or new channels, where there are other customer segments or adjacent markets that could benefit from the new capabilities.

G. Measurement

Throughout the entire process of successful innovation, there is an ongoing current of cultural openness, reinforced by the deliberate effort of senior executives to:

1. Provide metrics and a premium based on the measurable business value.

As part of the sustainability of innovation, companies should offer incentives and cash bonuses based on patents, application success, or process improvement project success. They should motivate employees to seek and seize opportunities for professional development to enable them to leave their day-to-day business and work on new initiatives. They should use newsletters and company meetings to discuss the importance of innovation, encouraging the creation of new values, identifying what is patentable, and determining the number of patents that were submitted during the past year.

2. Provide and seek awards that recognize achievements.

Smart companies use a wide variety of mechanisms of formal and informal recognition, including the means for employees to take up more executive roles. To strengthen the market and future innovations, employees should submit a report on their work for publication in the awards program.

Managing the innovation process lifecycle calls for the support of senior company executives and especially the CIO as a leader of change and improvement through innovation within the company.

V. CONCLUSIONS

The conclusions can be drawn are as follows:

- Today business visions are changing due to the big impact of IT. IT facilitates business growth, reduces costs and increases return on investments.
- The use of IT has enabled growth and business innovation, and the CIO, together with partners and through networks of innovation, is the leading driver of change and innovation.
- Currently, large companies have established research teams and are continuously innovating their business models to the greater benefit of their companies.
- There are now many companies that are not applying innovation because the innovation budget is too small and they cannot grow their business.
- All companies have to form an innovation working group, and senior executives must allocate the necessary budget to that the group innovation achieves yours goals in the enterprise.

REFERENCES

[1]. IT Governance Institute (ITGI), Board Briefing on IT Governance (2nd Ed) Retrieved April 29 2003.

[2]. John Baschab, Jon Piot, Nicholas G. Carr. The Executive's Guide to Information Technology, Second Edition. Publisher: John Wiley & Sons Pub Date: March 23, 2007.

[3]. Cray Symons. IT Governance Framework. Best Practices. March 29, 2005.

[4]. Cray Symons. How IT Must Shape And Manage Demand. Best Practices. June 15, 2006.

[5]. Igor Aguilar, José Carrillo, Edmundo Tovar. "Importance of Process Management IT Demand", Magazine AEMES, (2), 235-238. 2008

[6]. Center for CIO Leadership. "La Profesión del CIO: Estimular la Innovación y Crear Ventaja Competitiva". 2007, IBM, New York, October 2007

[7]. "Make IT Matter for Business Innovation" report, November 3, 2005

[8]. Bobby Cameron, Alex Cullen and Brandy Worthington "CIOs: Don't Constrain Innovation". For CIOs. April 25, 2008/ Updated: July 15, 2008

[9]. Navi Radjou, Indian CIOs Excel As Chief Innovation Officers Western CIOs: Emulate Business-Focused, Well-Networked Indian CIOs. August 12, 2008.

[10]. William I. Huyett and S. Patrick Viguerie "Extreme competition" The McKinsey Quarterly, Nº 1, 2005.

[11]. Bobby Cameron, "IT Can Help Accelerate Business Innovation". Practices. February 21, 2008.

[12]. Navi Radjou, Bradford J. Holmes, Christine Ferrusi Ross, Heidi Lo. "Demystifying IT Service Innovation". July 3, 2007.

A Framework for Enterprise Operating Systems Based on Zachman Framework

S. Shervin Ostadzadeh
Computer Engineering Department,
Faculty of Engineering,
Science & Research Branch,
Islamic Azad University, Tehran, Iran
ostadzadeh@srbiau.ac.ir

Amir Masoud Rahmani
Computer Engineering Department,
Faculty of Engineering,
Science & Research Branch,
Islamic Azad University, Tehran, Iran
rahmani@srbiau.ac.ir

Abstract - **Nowadays, the Operating System (OS) isn't only the software that runs your computer. In the typical information-driven organization, the operating system is part of a much larger platform for applications and data that extends across the LAN, WAN and Internet. An OS cannot be an island unto itself; it must work with the rest of the enterprise. Enterprise wide applications require an Enterprise Operating System (EOS). Enterprise operating systems used in an enterprise have brought about an inevitable tendency to lunge towards organizing their information activities in a comprehensive way. In this respect, Enterprise Architecture (EA) has proven to be the leading option for development and maintenance of enterprise operating systems. EA clearly provides a thorough outline of the whole information system comprising an enterprise. To establish such an outline, a logical framework needs to be laid upon the entire information system. Zachman Framework (ZF) has been widely accepted as a standard scheme for identifying and organizing descriptive representations that have prominent roles in enterprise-wide system development. In this paper, we propose a framework based on ZF for enterprise operating systems. The presented framework helps developers to design and justify completely integrated business, IT systems, and operating systems which results in improved project success rate.**

Keywords: Enterprise Operating System, Zachman Framework, Enterprise Architecture, Enterprise Architecture Framework.

I. INTRODUCTION

Enterprises face a lot of challenges nowadays, however, fully utilizing and integrating rapid improvements of information technology remains one important challenge. This is due to the fact that proper development of information systems would have substantial impact on tuning activities in enterprises. An OS is an interface between hardware and user which simplifies development of applications.

The dynamic nature of activities in an enterprise brings up changes in relevant information systems. Managements are hesitant to adopt the regular changes due to the huge costs of information systems development and maintenance; as a result, outdated systems form a barrier toward the enterprise evolvement. Enterprise Architecture (EA) is introduced to specifically address this problem by organizing business processes and information technology infrastructure reflecting the integration and standardization requirements of an enterprise operating model [1].

An enterprise operating system is the center of IT activities in an enterprise. It manages all resources; connects all devices; and provides a virtual platform for enterprise services. To have an overall understanding of an enterprise, one should perceive different views of components contained in that enterprise, including EOS. It should be noted that handling this large amount of information is quite challenging and needs a well-developed framework. To address this problem, various enterprise architecture frameworks have emerged, such as, FEAF [2], TEAF [3], and C4ISR [4]. Zachman framework [5] originally proposed by John Zachman, is often referenced as a standard approach for expressing the basic elements of enterprise architecture.

In this paper we propose a framework for an enterprise operating system inspired by ZF. This is the first time that a framework is proposed for an enterprise considering operating system in it. However, using a framework in an enterprise is not a new term and has a long acquaintance. This resulted in a comprehensive structure for all aspects of EOS. ZF is widely accepted as the main framework in EA. Compared to other proposed frameworks, it has evident advantages to list [6]: (1) using well-defined perspectives, (2) using comprehensive abstracts, (3) normality, and (4) extensive usage in practice. They were the motivations for ZF adoption in our work.

The rest of this paper is organized as follows. In Section 2, we introduce some basic concepts and principles. We present the proposed framework in section 3. Finally, we make conclusions and suggest some comments for future works.

II. BASIC CONCEPTS

In this section we briefly introduce some basic concepts and principles. We believe these remarks can help readers to clearly understand what we mean by the concepts that are used throughout the paper.

A. Enterprise

An enterprise consists of people, information, and technologies; performs business functions; has a defined organizational structure that is commonly distributed in multiple locations; responds to internal and external events; has a purpose for its activities; provides specific services and products to its customers [7]. An IT-related enterprise is an enterprise in which IT plays an important role in its activities.

T. Sobh, K. Elleithy (eds.), *Innovations in Computing Sciences and Software Engineering*,
DOI 10.1007/978-90-481-9112-3_91,

In this paper, we refer to an IT-related enterprise as an enterprise.

B. Enterprise Architecture (EA)

Enterprise architecture is the science of designing an enterprise in order to rationalize its activities and organization. EA shows the primary components of an enterprise and depicts how these components interact with or relate to each other. EA typically encompasses an overview of the entire information system in an enterprise; including the software [8], hardware, and information architectures. In this sense, the EA is a meta-architecture. In summary, EA contains views of an enterprise, including work, function, process, and information, it is at the highest level in the architecture pyramid. For details refer to [9].

C. Enterprise Operating System Architecture

Enterprise Operating System Architecture is a view of the operating system used by an enterprise to accomplish its duty. It contains descriptions of various operating system layers integrated with other enterprise architecture views.

D. Zachman Framework (ZF)

The Zachman framework is a framework for enterprise architecture, which provides a formal and highly structured way of defining an enterprise. In 1987, the initial framework, titled "*A Framework for Information Systems Architecture*", was proposed by John A. Zachman [10]. An update of the 1987 original work was extended and renamed to the Zachman framework in the 1990s. In essence, the framework is a two dimensional matrix consisting of 6 rows and 6 columns.

Each row represents a total view of the enterprise from a particular perspective. These rows starting from the top include: Planner's View (Scope), Owner's View (Enterprise or Business Model), Designer's View (Information Systems Model), Builder's View (Technology Model), Subcontractor's View (Detail Representation), and Actual System View (The Functioning Enterprise).

The columns describe various abstractions that define each perspective. These abstractions are based on six questions that one usually asks when s/he wants to understand an entity. The columns include: The Data Description (What?), The Function Description (How?), The Network Description (Where?), The People Description (Who?), The Time Description (When?), The Motivation Description (Why?). Further information and cell definitions of ZF can be found in [11].

III. A Framework For EOS

As mentioned earlier, currently there are some frameworks for EA. However, none of them considers OS. In this section, we introduce our framework proposal based on ZF intended to support all aspects of enterprise operating system as a whole.

Figure 1 depicts the proposed framework schema. Similar to ZF, it is a two dimensions matrix. The columns are the same as ZF. They are based on six basic interrogatives that are asked to understand an entity. The columns include:

- ***Data (What is it made of?):*** This focuses on the material composition of the information. In the case of EOS, it focuses on data that can be used for operating system.
- ***Function (How does it work?):*** This focuses on the functions or transformations of the information used for operating system.
- ***Network (Where are the elements?):*** This focuses on the geometry or connectivity of the data used for operating system.
- ***People (Who does what work?):*** This focuses on the actors and the manuals and the operating instructions or models one uses to perform their services.
- ***Time (When do things happen?):*** This focuses on the life cycles, timings and schedules used for operating system.
- ***Motivation (Why do things happen?):*** This focuses on goals, plans and rules that prescribe policies and ends that guide an organization for operating system.

The rows represent various perspectives of the OS framework. These perspectives, starting from the top, are:

- ***Scope:*** This is the highest level of abstraction in the framework. It refers to the boundaries of the enterprise from the operating systems view. This row is the perspective of chief enterprise's managers.
- ***Services:*** This row stands beneath the Scope layer. In this row, the services that the operating system should provide in the enterprise will be addressed. This is the perspective of an enterprise's expertise.
- **Kernel:** This row stands below the services, and focuses on operating system behaviors to support operating system services. This is the perspective of the operating system development team.
- ***Core:*** This is the lowest level of abstraction in the framework. It focuses on basic management that an operating system should provide to support kernel layer. This row is the perspective of system programmers.

The framework contains 24 cells. Each cell describes a model that an organization might document to describe the enterprise operating system. Each of the cells in the framework is primitive and thus, each can be described or modeled independently. All of the cells on a given row make up a given perspective. All of the cells in a column are related to each other since they focus on the same type of elements.

Organizations may not keep all of the models described by the EOS framework. Some organizations do not formally define some of the cells; however, since all of the cells are logically necessary for a complete description of an organization, if they aren't formally described, they are implicit in assumptions made by people in the organization. Following sections present the framework's cells definitions.

EOS Framework	*Data*	*Function*	*Network*	*People*	*Time*	*Motivation*
Scope						
Services						
Kernel						
Core						

Figure 1. A framework for EOS based on Zachman Framework

A. Data Column

Scope-Data cell is simply a list of important operating system entities (or objects, or assets) that the enterprise is interested in. It is probably adequate that this list is at a fairly high level of aggregation. It defines the scope, or boundaries, of the rows 2- 4 models of entities that are significant to the enterprise.

Service-Data cell is a model of the actual operating system entities (objects, assets) that are significant to the enterprise. It typically would be at a level of definition that it would express concepts (terms and facts) used in the significant business objectives/strategies that would later be implemented.

Kernel-Data cell is a model of the kernel operating system entities (objects, assets) that are significant to the data of OS services.

Core-Data cell would be the definition of all the data specified by the Physical Data Model and would include all the data definition language required for OS implementation in the supervisor mode.

B. Function Column

Scope-Function cell is simply a list of important operating system processes (or functions) that the enterprise performs. It is probably adequate that this list is at a fairly high level of aggregation. It defines the scope, or boundaries, of the rows 2- 4 models of processes that the enterprise performs.

Service-Function cell is a model of the actual operating system processes (or functions) that the enterprise performs. It can be represented as a model expressing the business transformations (processes) and their inputs and outputs.

Kernel-Function cell is a model of the kernel operating system processes (or functions) that are significant to support the function of OS services.

Core-Function cell would be the algorithms specifications for the OS implementation in the supervisor mode.

C. Network Column

Scope-Network cell is simply a list of locations in which the enterprise operates. It is probably adequate that this list is at a fairly high level of aggregation. It defines the scope, or boundaries, of the models of locations that are connected by the enterprise and are found in rows 2- 4.

Service-Network cell is a model of the actual operating system locations (or nodes) and their connections that are significant to the enterprise. It would include identification of the types of facilities at the nodes and connections.

Kernel-Network cell is a model of the kernel operating system locations (or nodes) and connections that are significant to the locations of OS services.

Core-Network cell is the specific definition of the node addresses and the lines required for OS implementation in the supervisor mode.

D. People Column

Scope-People cell is simply a list of important operating system organizations to which the enterprise assigns responsibility for work. It is probably adequate that this list is at a fairly high level of aggregation. It defines the scope, or boundaries, of the models of organization that are responsible to the enterprise and depicted on rows 2- 4.

Service-People cell is a model of the actual operating system allocation of responsibilities and specification of work products.

Kernel-People cell is a model of the kernel operating system responsibilities that are significant to the work of OS services.

Core-People cell is the physical expression of work flow of the OS including the specific individual and their requirements and the presentation format of the work product required for OS implementation in the supervisor mode.

E. Time Column

Scope-Time cell is simply a list of important operating system events to which the enterprise responds. It is probably adequate that this list is at a fairly high level of aggregation. It defines the scope, or boundaries of the models of time that are significant to the enterprise and found in Rows 2- 4.

Service-Time cell is a model of the actual operating system business cycles that is comprised of an initiating event and an elapsed time (or cycle). It typically would be at a level of definition that it would express sequence, or relative time.

Kernel-Time cell is a model of the kernel operating system time (events, cycles) that are significant to the time of OS services. This model describes the system events that trigger the state to transition from one valid state (point in time) to another and the dynamics of that transition cycle.

Core-Time cell is the definition of interrupts and machine cycles required for OS implementation in the supervisor mode.

F. Motivation Column

Scope-Motivation cell is simply a list of major operating system goals (or objectives, or strategies, or critical success factors) that are significant to the enterprise and defines the relative to motivation. It is probably adequate that this list is at a fairly high level of aggregation. It defines the scope, or boundaries, of the models of goals (etc.) that are embraced by the enterprise and found in the constructs of Rows 2- 4.

Service-Motivation cell is a model of the business objectives and strategies (the "ends" and "means") of the enterprise that constitute the motivation behind Enterprise Operating System.

Kernel-Motivation cell is a model of the operating system rules of the enterprise in terms of their intent ("ends") and the constraints ("means").

Core-Motivation cell would be the specification of the operating system rules required for OS implementation in the supervisor mode.

IV. CONCLUSIONS

Business and IT integration is a critical challenge faced by IT industry. An EOS can be considered as the center of IT in an enterprise provided a virtual platform for enterprise services. In this paper, a framework for EOS based on ZF is proposed. Compared to other frameworks, ZF has some evident advantages. These advantages have caused its extensive usage as the basic framework of enterprise architecture. This research can be an initial step to demonstrate how the models in an EOS can be made coherent in order to avoid inconsistencies within the framework. In general, our proposed method is expected to increase the success rate of the projects in enterprises.

In order to develop an EOS, defining a methodology based on the proposed framework will unleash the full support of the presented framework, which should be considered in future work.

REFERENCES

[1] Peter Weill, "Innovating with Information Systems: What do the most agile firms in the world do?," Presented at the 6th e-Business Conference, Barcelona, Spain, March 2007. http://www.iese.edu/en/files/6_29338.pdf

[2] Chief Information Officers (CIO) Council, *Federal Enterprise Architecture Framework*, Version 1.1, September 1999.

[3] Department of the Treasury, *Treasury Enterprise Architecture Framework*, Version 1, July 2000.

[4] C4ISR Architecture Working Group (AWG), *C4ISR Architecture Framework*, Version 2.0, U.S.A. Department of Defense (DoD), December 1997.

[5] J. A. Zachman, *The Zachman Framework: A Primer for Enterprise Engineering and Manufacturing*, 2003.

[6] S. S. Ostadzadeh, F. Shams, S. A. Ostadzadeh, "A Method for Consistent Modeling of Zachman Framework," Advances and Innovations in Systems, Computing Sciences and Software Engineering, Springer, pp. 375-380, August 2007. (ISBN 978-1-4020-6263-6)

[7] M.A. Rood, "Enterprise Architecture: Definition, Content, and Utility," IEEE Trans., 1994.

[8] L. Bass, P. Clements, and R. Kazman, Software Architecture in Practice, 2nd Edition, Addison-Wesley, 2004.

[9] C.M. Pereira, and P. Sousa, "Enterprise Architectures: Business and IT Alignment," Proceedings of the 2005 ACM symposium on Applied computing, Santa fe, New Mexico, 2005.

[10] J. A. Zachman, "A Framework for Information Systems Architecture," IBM Systems Journal, Vol. 26, No. 3, 1987.

[11] J. A. Zachman, "The Framework for Enterprise Architecture – Cell Definitions," ZIFA, 2003.

A Model for Determining the Number of Negative Examples Used in Training a MLP

Cosmin Cernazanu-Glavan and Stefan Holban
University "Politehnica" of Timisoara, Romania
cosmin.cernazanu@ac.upt.ro, stefan.holban@ac.upt.ro

***Abstract*-In general, a MLP training uses a training set containing only positive examples, which may change the neural network into an over confident network for solving the problem. A simple solution for this problem is the introduction of negative examples in the training set. Through this procedure, the network will be prepared for the cases it has not been trained for. Unfortunately, up to the present, the number of negative examples that must be used in the training process was not mentioned in the literature. Consequently, the present article aims at finding a general mathematical pattern for training a MLP with negative examples. With that end in view, we have used a regressive analytic technique in order to analyze the data resulted from training three neural networks for a number of three datasets: a dataset for letter recognition, one for the data supplied by a sonar and a last one for the data resulted from the medical tests for determining diabetes. The pattern testing was performed on a new database for confirming its truthfulness.**

I. Neural Networks

The structure of the human brain consists of approximately 10^{11} neurons (nerve cells) interconnected through 10^{14} synapses [1]. For this reason, it is difficult to imagine an artificial device able to imitate completely this natural complexity.

Although the working speed of a biological neuron is highly reduced as compared to that of a computer, on account of the large number of neurons and connexions, the human brain is highly superior to any super computer used nowadays.

Starting from the biological neural networks, people tried to use and imitate its features and structure in order to create a similar artificial model.

This attempt resulted in developing the Artificial neural networks, special devices projected to adapt the activity of the biological neural networks to a certain detail level in order to reach (several) human brain characteristics.[2][3]

However, the main difference between the biological neural networks and computers consists in their structure. On the one hand, computers are made up of a high-speed main processor that performs the calculations, each component of the computer having a precise function. On the other hand, the human brain is made up of over 100 different types of special cells (neurons), their estimated number being between 50 billions and 100 billions (10^{11})[4].

An artificial neural network is a model that emulates a biological neural network. The nods from a neural network are based on a simplistic mathematic representation resembling to the real neurons.

The simulation of the cerebral action is eloquent for its two main actions:

- Knowledge is stored through a learning process
- Knowledge storage is performed by using the inter-neural connexions value, named synapse weights.

II. Training Neural Network

The neural networks essential utility consists in solving some difficult problems such as: estimation, identification and prediction or complex optimization. Their feasibility plan is very wide. They accompany us day-by-day either inbuilt in household appliances (cell phones, washing machines, TV sets, microwave ovens, etc.) or by interacting with them in our daily life (form recognition, speech recognition, automatic diagnosis, etc.).[5]

A network can be implemented by following several stages. In the first stage, we will select a certain type of neural network (feed forward, recursive, Kohonen,etc.) and we will define its configuration (number of layers, number of neurons, activating function, etc.). In the second stage, after selecting the network for a certain application, we will start the neural network training process. In the third stage, the neural network will be tested on a broad dataset and, depending on the result obtained, the process will be either restarted from stage 1, or the network will be successfully used in the future.

The neural network *classic* training implies the use of a number of examples in the training set and their random introduction at the network input until the error will decrease under a certain threshold. (Fig. 1)

After the training stage, an example that has not been previously used in the training will be introduced at the network input. If this example is similar to those previously used, it will successfully be recognized by the network. If an example totally different from those present in the training set is introduced at the network input, then the network will classify it as belonging to one of the categories of examples it has been trained with. In this case, we can define it as an over confident network. This type of errors is frequent in the classification problems that have an insufficient training set. [6]

For simply solving this type of problems, it is necessary to introduce some negative examples in the training set –

T. Sobh, K. Elleithy (eds.), *Innovations in Computing Sciences and Software Engineering*,
DOI 10.1007/978-90-481-9112-3_92, © Springer Science+Business Media B.V. 2010

examples that should not be recognized by the network as belonging to some of the already known categories. For

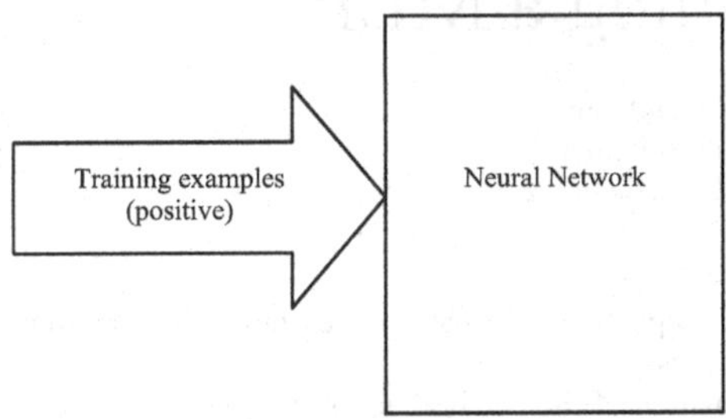

Fig. 1. Classic training

example, if a network is trained to recognize figures, it is recommendable that examples of other characters to be introduced in the training set (letters, punctuation marks, other signs). (Fig. 2)

In this case, the network is trained to recognize both examples from certain categories and examples that do not belong to the desired categories.

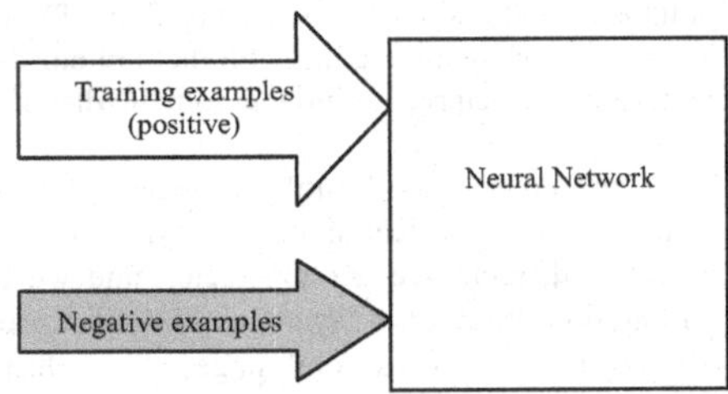

Fig. 2. Training a neural network with positive and negative examples

There have been cases when the use of negative examples visibly overran the number of positive examples. Therefore, the importance of the negative examples compared to the positive ones was decreased by a certain value. [7] In this way, a penalty of negative example has been introduced, by which, each negative example is able to influence the result only through a fraction depending on the total number of negative examples.

Unfortunately, there are no clear specifications about the percentage of negative examples (out of the total number of examples) that must be used in training a neural network. (Fig. 3) All the studies performed until the present moment are specific for a certain type of problem and the percentage of negative examples used in different applications vary between 5% and 80%. [7][8][9]

The value of the percentage is very important since its variation can significantly modify the recognition percentage of the neural network. For a training set with many negative examples, we will obtain low recognition rates for the desired patterns and high recognition rates for the undesired patterns.

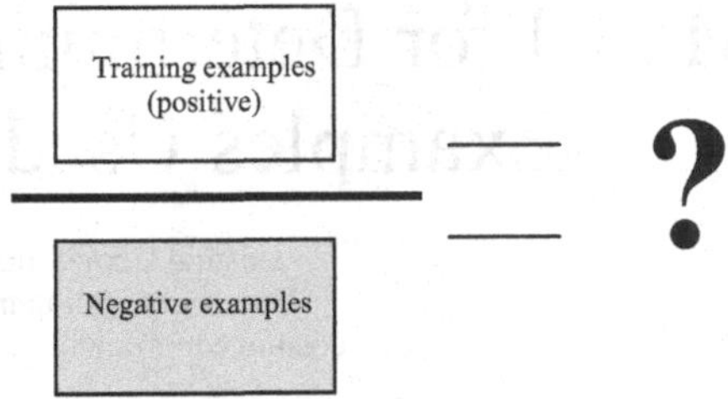

Fig. 3. Which is the optimum percentage of negative examples that must be used for best training a neural network?

A low number of negative examples in the training set cannot modify the network weights so that it could successfully recognize the undesired patterns. [13]

In order to solve the problem, we will start by detailing the problem of learning through examples which represents the basis of the artificial neural network supervised training.

The process of learning from examples applied to a neural network can be viewed as a problem of finding a function f modeled with a hypothetical class H and a training set of the type $D=\{ (x_i,y_i) \ , \ i = 1,..m\}$ where $x_i \in R^n$ is the *n*-dimensional example used for training, and y_i is the network output value.

The error resulted from this pattern-making process will have the following form:

$$J = Er_{aprox.}(n) + Er_{est.}\left(\frac{VC(H_n)}{m}\right) \tag{1}$$

where $VC(H)_n$ represent a measure of complexity for the hypothetical class. For minimizing this function, we must minimize the 2 components: the approximated error ($Er_{aprox.}$) and the estimated error ($Er_{est.}$).

The problem that arises is that the approximation error decreases proportionally to the increase of the pattern complexity, and the estimation error decreases proportionally to the reduction of the pattern complexity.

For this reason, a compromise of complexity must be found for these types of problems in order to obtain a minimum value of the error.

For the problem of learning from examples, the pattern of the hypothetical class will have the following form: [10]

$$H[f] = \sum_{i=1}^{m}(f(x_i) - y_i)^2 + \lambda\|Pf\|^2 \tag{2}$$

where λ is a positive regularization parameter, P is the differential operator and ||Pf||2 is a cost function that rapidly reduces the interval of possible solutions for any type of priority information.

According to the regularization theorem, the solution for this problem will have the following form:

$$f(x) = \sum_{i=1}^{m} a_i K(x, x_i) + b \tag{3}$$

where a_i represent the kernel function coefficients and b represents the bias function values.

When creating a number of negative examples of the type $D'=\{(x_i', y_i'), i = 1,..m\}$, the (2) will have the form [11]:

$$H[f] = \sum_{i=1}^{m} (f(x_i) - y_i)^2 - \sum_{i=1}^{m} \left(f(x_i') - y_i'^0\right)^2 + \lambda \|Pf\|^2 \tag{4}$$

where the second term corresponds to the negative examples and the final solution will have the form:

$$f(x) = \sum_{i=1}^{m} a_i K(x, x_i) + \sum_{i=1}^{m} a_i' K(x, x_i') + b \tag{5}$$

where a_i' represents the values of the negative functions.

The solution of the problem consists in finding all the values of the (5). In this way, the function by which the neural network is approximated will be clearly defined.

Starting from these theoretical grounds, we will experimentally try to find a calculus formula for the number of negative examples that will form the training set.

For each problem, we need a different number of negative examples. We will try to group these numbers and to find a formula able to interpolate these values.

The use of the negative examples in training the neural networks improves their recognition rate. Moreover, the negative examples are easier to built (virtually speaking all the other examples that are not positive will be negative) and there can be found in great number.

III. Mathematical Model For Determining The Number of Negative Examples Used For Training a MLP

For this purpose, we will use a regression analytic technique, by the aid of which, we will analyze the data resulted from training three neural networks for a number of three datasets, namely: a dataset for letter recognition, one for the recognition of data supplied by a sonar and one for the recognition of data resulted from the medical tests for determining diabetes. Further on, these three types of data will be generically referred to as: letter, sonar and diabetes. Stages:

- Determining a co-relation model for each of the three types of datasets
- Demonstrating that they all belong to the same pattern category
- Defining a new general model for the recognition with negative examples
- Testing the model on a new database for verifying its truthfulness.

For the whole process we use DataFit and Origin 6.0 tools.

A. *Letter, sonar and diabetes data analysis*

The data used [12] in the present analysis are all resulted from a recognition process. The data refer both to the percentage of negative examples used in the training process and to a normalized value provided by the proportion between the recognition percent obtained with negative examples and the recognition percent obtained with positive examples. Standardization is necessary because the recognition percentages vary according to the nature of application and to the patterns used for training the network.

The results obtained for the three types of data are presented in the table below (Table I)

TABLE I
THE NORMALIZED VALUES FOR THE THREE KNOWLEDGE DATABASE (DIABETES, SONAR AND LETTERS)

Neg. eg. %	Diabetes	Sonar	Letter
0	1	1	1
5	1.108482	1.114285714	1.039523689
10	1.221101	1.250892857	1.050924753
15	1.307723	1.296428571	1.055611857
16	1.279962	1.313749999	1.054725108
17	1.278027	1.307142856	1.054091715
18	1.297856	1.307142856	1.053204966
19	1.32343	1.339285714	1.056371928
20	1.307462	1.349999999	1.047377755
25	1.307775	1.214285714	1.048391183
30	1.290598	1.239285714	1.045604256
35	1.283814	1.226428571	1.049024576
40	1.267533	1.244285714	1.048771219
45	1.285275	1.246428571	1.042310616
50	1.226556	1.241071428	1.045097542
55	1.258814	1.228571428	1.041677223
60	1.235901	1.196428571	1.041297188
65	1.237989	1.210714285	1.038130225
70	1.22186	1.227678571	1.039016975
75	1.204118	1.197321428	1.041803902
80	1.212989	1.209821428	1.043577401
85	1.206205	1.166071428	1.032809729
90	1.223947	1.148214285	1.032936407
95	1.208292	1.149107142	1.033696478
100	1.193776	1.096428571	1.038510261

Our main aim is to find a function of the type:

Normalized recognition = f(Percentage of negative examples)

After the interpolation, the following three forms have been obtained for each of the three functions: (Figure 4, Figure 5, and Figure 6).

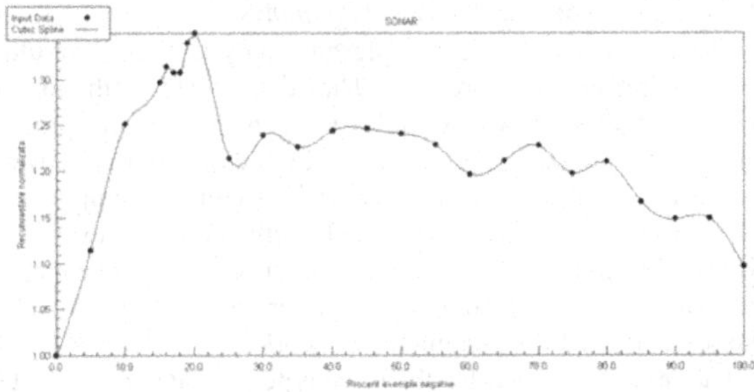

Fig. 4. The interpolation of normalized recognition percentages for SONAR

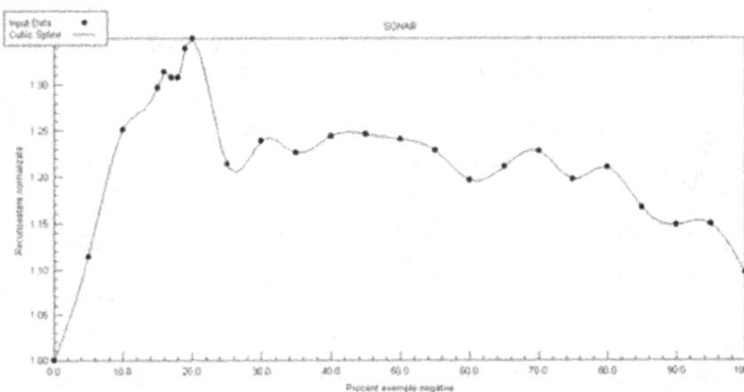

Fig. 5. The interpolation of normalized recognition percentages for DIABETES

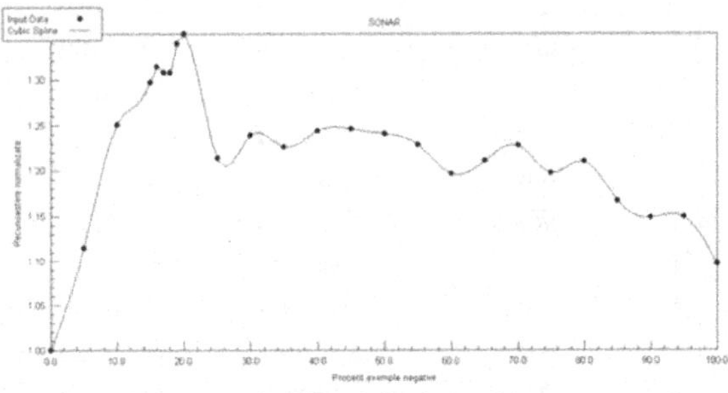

Fig. 6. The interpolation of normalized recognition percentages for LETTERS

Analyzing the three interpolation functions, we can notice that they have approximately the same form. Moreover, they present an increase of the maximum recognition rate for an interval of negative examples between 10% and 20% of the number of positive examples used for training.

As a first conclusion, we can mention that the process of training with negative examples induces a similar behavior in the recognition process. During this process, we can observe the presence of a maximum of instances recognized for each of the 3 examples.

The main interval for a number of negative examples where maximum is placed, is of [10, 20] % of the number of positive examples from the training set. The next stage consists in verifying to what extent this similar behavior can be defined through a model and if it can be defined, to what extent this pattern is correct from a statistic point of view.

B. *Determining the model of the training process with negative examples*

For determining a pattern for the training with negative examples, we suggested the use of a co-relational technique for defining the connections between the data in the same set. Each connection is analyzed for obtaining a truthful mathematic model.

In what follows, we will detail the analyze process performed for each dataset.

The mathematic pattern of the training process for SONAR, after performing a co-relational analysis, will have the following form:

TABLE II
THE MODEL OBTAINED ON SONAR DATABASE

Model definition	Y = a*x^4+b*x^3+c*x^2+d*x+e
Number of observations	25
Number of missing observations	0
Solver type	Nonlinear
Nunlinear iteration limit	250
Standard Error of the Estimate	3.53E-02
Coefficient of Multiple Determination (R^2)	0.8367
Proportion of Variance Explained	83.67%

The resulting model presents a credibility of 0.836 for a confidence of 95%. It has the following form:

$$f(x) = -6.91 * 10^{-8} * x^4 + 1.52 * 10^{-5} * x^3 - 1.14 * 10^{-3} * x^2 + 3.179 * 10^{-2} * x + 1.0126 \quad (6)$$

The data obtained for this model show its high quality, exhibiting a behavior pattern of 0.836 for a confidence of 95%.

For Diabetes and Letter database we have (7) and (8).

$$f(x) = -4.76 * 10^{-8} * x^4 + 1.15 * 10^{-5} * x^3 - 9.65 * 10^{-4} * x^2 + 0.0302 * x + 0.9997 \quad (7)$$

$$f(x) = -8.72 * 10^{-9} * x^4 + 2.03 * 10^{-6} * x^3 - 1.602 * 10^{-4} * x^2 + 4.638 * 10^{-3} * x + 1.0109 \quad (8)$$

The data obtained for these models shows their high qualities.

C. *Determining a general model of the training process with negative examples*

At this point, we will verify if the models determined in the previous stage are representative for the training with negative examples. If the result of the checking is affirmative, we will try to discover a general model by means of which we could determine the number of negative examples for a particular case.

First, we will verify if the three patterns belong to the same class. For this, we will use a test *t*, and the checking will be performed on the set of parameters (a, b, c, d, and e) which are characteristic for the patterns. The *t* test is performed for verifying if two patterns can significantly differ.

The checking will be performed with the help of the Origin 6.0 software tool, and parameters from two successive patterns will be used. The data verified in the analyze process are presented in the table below:

The conclusion of the present study is that all the three models describe the same phenomenon (they are characteristic for the same process of training with negative examples) and that they can represent the starting point for determining a global model for this type of training a neural network.

For building the model, we start from the average values of the parameters that define the three patterns previously mentioned, values that have been presented in a previous table (Table III).

The general pattern will have the following form:

$$f(x) = -4.18067 * 10^{-8} * x^4 + 9.57666 * 10^{-6} * x^3 - 7.5507 * 10^{-4} * x^2 + 2.2209 * 10^{-2} * x + 1.000773333 \quad (9)$$

D. Testing the general model on a new database

Using this general pattern, we have chosen a new database for testing its truthfulness. As we have made a great number of experiments with the network that is trained to determine the possible formation of some dangerous waves (WAVES), we have chosen these data for testing the general pattern.

The results obtained on this new database are presented in Figure 7. We can notice that the network is able to perform a precise localization of the optimum percentage of negative examples.

Moreover, all the recognition values of the network representing a percentage of negative examples situated in the interval [0% - 100%] are successfully interpolated by the general model.

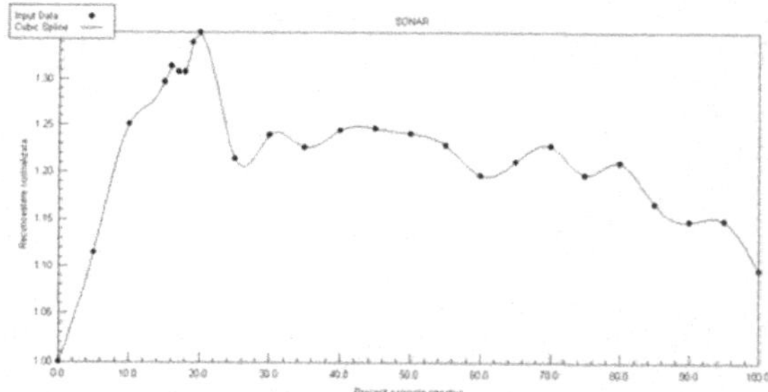

Fig. 7. The general pattern for training with negative examples used for WAVES

IV. CONCLUSION

The present article dealt exclusively with the problems of training neural networks with negative examples.

Such neural network may change into an overconfident network which could lead to high recognition rate of any example present at the input (even if the example is wrong).

The solution for this problem was the use of negative examples in the training process. The procedure is not new. However, it has not been sufficiently exploited until now, being both minimized and not currently used.

Unfortunately, up to the present, the number of negative examples that must be used in the training process was not mentioned in the literature. Consequently, the present article aims at finding a general mathematical pattern for training a MLP with negative examples.

For this purpose, we have used a regressive analytic technique in order to analyze the data resulted from training three neural networks. A pattern was created for each of the 3 trainings. All the three patterns analyzed (LETTER, DIABETES and SONAR) describe the same phenomenon (are characteristic for the same training process with negative examples) and represent the starting point for determining a global pattern for this type of training a neural network. The general pattern obtained has the form presented in the formula 5.5, and it has been tested on a new database (WAVES), a precise localization of the optimum percentage of negative examples being achieved.

REFERENCES

[1] Haykin, S., "Neural Networks. A comprehensive Foundation", *Macmillan College Publishing*, New York, 1994

[2] Rosenblatt, N., "Principles of Neurodynamics", *Spartan Books*, Washington, D.C., 1962

[3] Rumelhart, D.E., McClelland and J.L. & PDP Research Group, "Parallel Distributed Processing: Explorations in the Microstructure of Cognition", *The MIT Press*, Volume 1: Foundations, Cambridge, Massachusetts, 1986.

[4] Schwartz, J.T., "The New Connectionism: Developing Relationships Between Neuroscience and Artificial Intelligence", *Proceedings of the American Academy of Arts and Science*, Vol. 117, No. 1, p. 123 – 141, Daedalus, 1988

[5] Rabunal, J. R., "Artificial Neural Networks in Real-life Applications", *Idea Group Pub*, 2005

[6] Raudys, S, Somorjai, R and Baumgartner, R., "Reducing the overconfidence of base classifiers when combining their decisions", *4th International Workshop on Multiple Clasifier Systems* (MCS 2003), vol. 2709, pag. 65-73, 2003

[7] Hosom, J.P., Villiers, J. et al. "Training Hidden Markov Model/Artificial Neural Network (HMM/ANN) Hybrids for Automatic Speech Recognition (ASR)", *Center for Spoken Language Understanding (CSLU)*, 2006

[8] Qun, Z., Principe and J. C., "Improve ATR performance by incorporating virtual negative examples", *Proceedings of the International Joint Conference on Neural Networks*, pag. 3198-3203, 1999

[9] Debevec, P., "A Neural Network for Facial Feature Location", *CS283 Course Project*, UC Berkeley, 2001

[10] Tikhonov, A. and Arsenin, V., "Solutions of ill-posed problems", *W.H. Winston*, 1977

[11] Girosi, F., Poggio, B., T. and Caprile, "Extensions of a theory of networks for approximation and learning:outliers and negative examples.", *Advances in Neural Information Processing Systems 3*, R.P. Lippmann, J.E.Moody and D. S. Touretzky, pag. 750-756, San Mateo, CA, 1991

[12] Cernazanu, C., Holban, S., „Determining the optimal percent of negative examples used in training the multilayer perceptron neural networks", *International Conference on Neural Networks*, pag. 114-119, Prague, 2009

[13] Cernazanu, C., Holban, S., „Improving neural network performances – training with negative examples", *International Conference on Telecommunications and Networking/International Conference on Industrial Electronics, Technology and Automation, University of Bridgeport*, Novel Algorithms and Techniques in Telecommunications, Automation and Industrial Electronics, pag. 49-53, 2008

GPU Benchmarks Based On Strange Attractors

Tomáš Podoba
Department of Applied Informatics
Tomas Bata University
Zlín, Czech Republic

Jiří Giesl
Department of Applied Informatics
Tomas Bata University
Zlín, Czech Republic

prof. Karel Vlček
Department of Applied Informatics
Tomas Bata University
Zlín, Czech Republic

***Abstract*-The main purpose of presented GPU benchmark is to generate complex polygonal mesh structures based on strange attractors with fractal structure. Attractors have to be created as 4D objects using quaternion algebra. Polygonal mesh can have different numbers of polygons because of iterative application of this system. The major complexity of every mesh would provide efficient results using multiple methods such as ray-tracing, anti aliasing and anisotropic filtering to evaluate GPU performance. Our main goal is to develop new faster algorithm to generate 3D structures and apply its complexity for GPU benchmarking.**

Keywords-Benchmark, fractal, strange attractor, quaternion, marching cube algorithm

I. INTRODUCTION

Current computational power of personal computer is generally focused on CPU benchmark results which are actually going to be less powerful then GPU according to the amount of IPS. Recent years have been designed several changeless and linear benchmark applications that are basically after some period useless, moreover are not giving proper results corresponding to the 3Dmark. Our goal is to design and create a complex powerful computer benchmark application based on real-time rendering of a closed 3D mesh generated from attractors.

Different numbers of iterations and various attractor models may provide effective computational power results including special effects such us bump mapping, displacement, anti-aliasing, anisotropic filtering and ray-tracing. The main problem is to evolve specific algorithm that generates object based on strange attractors and modifies it as a closed 3D mesh.

II. STRANGE ATTRACTORS

Strange attractors are complicated sets with fractal structure which chaotic dynamical systems evolve to after a long enough time. These attractors can be generated in several ways – the most commonly used are quadratic map (1) and trigonometric map (2) where parameters *a, b, c, d, e, f, g, h, i, j, k, l* define each strange attractor.

$$\begin{aligned} x_{n+1} &= a + b\cdot x_n + c\cdot x_n^2 + d\cdot x_n y_n + e\cdot y_n + f\cdot y_n^2 \\ y_{n+1} &= g + h\cdot x_n + i\cdot x_n^2 + j\cdot x_n y_n + k\cdot y_n + l\cdot y_n^2 \end{aligned} \quad (1)$$

$$\begin{aligned} x_{n+1} &= a\cdot\sin(b\cdot y_n) + c\cdot\cos(d\cdot x_n) \\ y_{n+1} &= e\cdot\sin(f\cdot y_n) + g\cdot\cos(h\cdot x_n) \end{aligned} \quad (2)$$

The strange attractor can be revealed after several iterations of a map (1) or (2). When the strange attractor is represented geometrically, it is obvious that fixed points are locally unstable, but the system is globally stable.

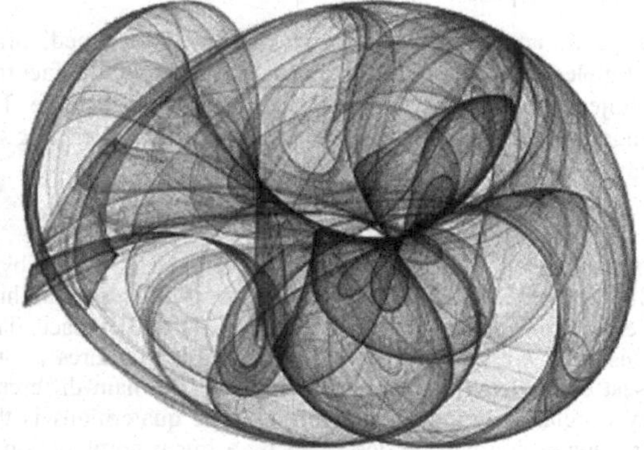

Figure 1. Example of Clifford attractor.

The attractor is chaotic when Lyapunov exponent for that map is positive. Two dimensional chaotic maps have not only a single Lyapunov exponent, but they have a positive one, corresponding to the direction of expansion, and a negative one corresponding to the direction of contraction. The signature of chaos is that at least one of these exponents is positive and the magnitude of the negative exponent has to be greater than the positive one [1].

T. Sobh, K. Elleithy (eds.), *Innovations in Computing Sciences and Software Engineering*,
DOI 10.1007/978-90-481-9112-3_93,

For a map $x_{n+1} = f(x)$ a small deviation δx_0 of coordinate x_0 leads to a small change in x_1.

$$\delta x_1 = \delta x_0 \cdot f'(x_0) \tag{3}$$

For n iterations

$$\delta x_n = \delta x_0 \cdot \prod_{i=0}^{n-1} f'(x_i) \tag{4}$$

Then the Lyapunov exponent is determined as

$$\Lambda = \lim_{n \Rightarrow \infty} \left(\frac{1}{n} \cdot \log \left| \frac{\delta x_n}{\delta x_0} \right| \right) = \lim_{n \Rightarrow \infty} \left(\frac{1}{n} \cdot \sum_{i=0}^{n-1} \ln |f'(x_i)| \right) \tag{5}$$

Deviation $|\delta x_n|$ grows with increasing n for a chaotic orbit and this leads to a positive Lyapunov exponent $\Lambda > 0$.

Strange (chaotic) attractors are associated with motion which is unpredictable. If we attempt to predict motion of a chaotic system then even the small deviation in the initial conditions will be amplified exponentially over the time and will rapidly destroy the accuracy of our prediction. Eventually, all we will be able to say is that the motion lies somewhere on the chaotic attractor in phase-space, but exactly where it lies the attractor at given time will be unknown to us. These properties of chaotic system, extreme sensitivity to initial conditions and unpredictability, can be very helpful for the encryption purposes.

Strange attractors themselves are markedly patterned, often having elegant, fixed geometric structures, despite the fact that the trajectories moving within them appear unpredictable. The strange attractor's geometric shape is the order underlying the apparent chaos. [2]

III. QUATERNIONS

Quanternion algebra has been developed in 1843 by a mathematician William Rowan Hamilton who was searching for extension of complex numbers from 2D to 3D space. This extension is not possible to create. Only 4D structures are the closest equivalents of complex numbers. The main difference between classic complex numbers and the quaternions is that every quaternion can be described by a linear combination of four orthogonal units: 1, *i*, *j* and *k*. Unit 1 is called scalar unit, units *i*, *j* and *k* are vector units. Quaternion is defined according to (6).

$$q = x + yi + zj + wk \tag{6}$$

Relations for mutual multiplications of the quaternion units are applied according to Tab. 1.

TABLE I.
MULTIPLICATIONS OF QUATERNION UNITS

Multiplicative operation	Result	Multiplicative operation	Result
1×1	1	j×1	j
1×i	i	k×1	k
1×j	j	i×j	k
1×k	k	j×i	-k
i×1	i	j×k	i
Multiplicative operation	**Result**		
k×j	-i		
k×i	j		
i×k	-j		
i×i=j×j=k×k	k		
i×j×k	-1		

Tab.1 shows that units of quaternion are not following a commutative law. Thus, quaternions do not create algebraic structure. If we want to multiply two quaternions.

$$q_1 = x_1 + y_1 i + z_1 j + w_1 k \tag{7}$$

$$q_2 = x_2 + y_2 i + z_2 j + w_2 k \tag{8}$$

we have to use the following scheme

$$\begin{aligned} q_1 q_2 = & 1(x_1x_2 - y_1y_2 - z_1z_2 - w_1w_2) + \\ & i(y_1x_2 + x_1y_2 + w_1z_2 - z_1w_2) + \\ & j(z_1x_2 - w_1y_2 + x_1z_2 + y_1w_2) + \\ & k(w_1x_2 + z_1y_2 - y_1z_2 + x_1w_2) \end{aligned} \tag{9}$$

Quaternions are very often used in computer graphics for the representations of objects, their rotations and orientations because of efficient computation in complex algorithms.

IV. MARCHING CUBE ALGORITHM

Marching cube algorithm is an algorithm for creating a polygonal surface representation of a 3D scalar field. This algorithm describes voxel-object by surface of connected polygons. This method is most often used for the representation of medical data, because of simple differentiation of its parts due to thresholding.

Let's have a set of voxels. This set is browsed and processed. Values of vertices of each cube (these means intensity of 8 voxels which the cube is created from) are compared with a threshold. If the value of vertex is lower than threshold, vertex is evaluated as "internal", otherwise as "external". Evaluation is expressed as an 8-bit value which is then used for the representation of corresponding configuration of the polygon of the resultant surface. Fig. 2 shows basic configurations of the cube, the rest of configurations are done by rotating of the basic configurations. The 8-bit value can be used as an index of 2D array with 256 rows where each row contains a proper sequence of vertices. Vertices in that table must be correctly organized in order to prevent light-collisions when drawing our object. [3]

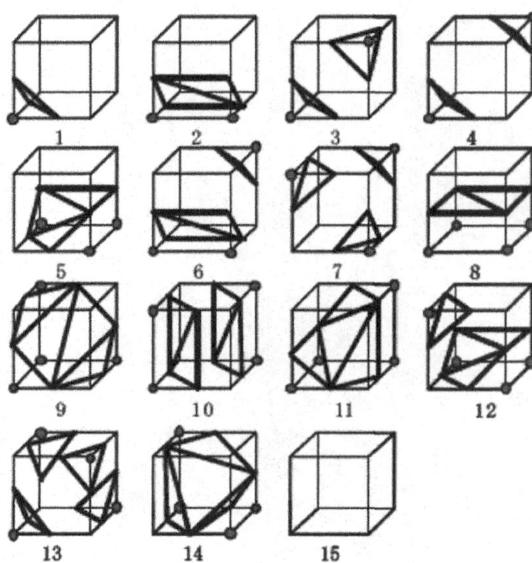

Figure 2. Basic cube configurations. Image taken from [4].

Shortly, the pattern of each cube is compared with 256 patterns which were previously generated by existence of measuring points and polygon is then rendered corresponding to the pattern. This procedure must be done for every cube and the 3D model is obtained this way.

V. Our Algorithm

Since Marching cube algorithm is quite time expensive and fast computing unit is needed. Ray tracing is a very realistic method of rendering geometric shapes. Graphical effects like shadows, reflection and refraction can easily be implemented. However the technique is very slow and near impossible to perform in realtime with today's computers, at least with a desired degree of quality.

Our algorithm, which is in development, would provide same result but in shorter time. Mesh generating method is based on Genetic Algorithm, Evolution or SOMA. The main purpose is to find out the net connections between highest peaks in points (voxel) environment. In the Fig 3., there is a basic example how method works. At the beginning the nearest points (reds) are selected and then connected into triangles. Blue dots represent back side of generated mesh from the point of view also connected and finally grey dots are points inside the mesh that are not visible and not connected together.

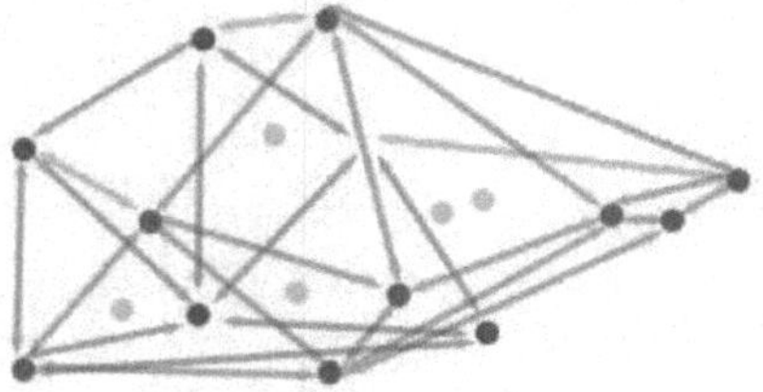

Figure 3. Connecting points.

Nevertheless, invisible points are ignored and visible points-red and blue represent a render able polygonal mesh of generated object in real time.

VI. Conclusion

In this preliminarily research paper, possible methods how to solve the main and very difficult problem of generating a closed 3D mesh based on strange attractors using quaternions or marching cube algorithm were briefly described. An increasing amount of parameters such us number of iterations, generating attractor values or usage of special effects, will exponentially grow the complexity of created 3D object.

A closed 3D mesh localized in virtual space and its real-time rendering process may be efficient to evaluate mainly the GPU and also the CPU performance also in the next decade. In our future work, we want to establish a proper method to create these objects and make an application that weigh evidence of computational power. Note that our algorithm is in development and final visible results will be published in future.

References

[1] Sprott, J.C. Strange attractors: *Creating Patterns in Chaos*. M&T Books, 1993.

[2] Giesl, J., Vlcek, K., *Image Encryption Based on Strange Attractor*, ICGST-GVIP Journal. 2009, vol. 9, is. 2, pp. 19-26. ISSN 1687-398.

[3] Bourke, P., Polygonising A Scalar Field, May 1994, Available at WWW: http://local.wasp.uwa.edu.au/~pbourke/geometry/polygonise/.

[4] Yokoyama, H., Chikatsu, H., *3D Representation of Historical Structure for Digital Archives by Laser Scanner*, The International Archives of the Photogrammetry, Remote Sensing and Spatial Information Sciences, Vol. XXXIV, Part 5/W12, pp. 347-350.

[5] Alan Norton, *Generation and Display of Geometric Fractals in 3-D*, Computers & Graphics, Vol. 16(nr 3), pp. 61–67, 1982.

[6] Yagel R., Cohen, D., Kaufman, A., *Discrete ray tracing*, Computer Graphics and Applications, IEEE , Volume: 12 Issue: 5, pp. 19–28, 1992.

Effect of Gender and Sound Spatialization on Speech Intelligibility in Multiple Speaker Environment

M. Joshi[1], M. Iyer[1], N. Gupta[1] and A. Barreto[2]
[1] University of Bridgeport, Bridgeport, U.S.A
[2] Florida International University, Miami, U.S.A

Abstract—**In multiple speaker environments such as teleconferences we observe a loss of intelligibility, particularly if the sound is monaural in nature. In this study, we exploit the "Cocktail Party Effect", where a person can isolate one sound above all others using sound localization and gender cues. To improve clarity of speech, each speaker is assigned a direction using Head Related Transfer Functions (HRTFs) which creates an auditory map of multiple conversations. A mixture of male and female voices is used to improve comprehension.**

We see 6% improvement in cognition while using a male voice in a female dominated environment and 16% improvement in the reverse case. An improvement of 41% is observed while using sound localization with varying elevations. Finally, the improvement in cognition jumps to 71% when both elevations and azimuths are varied. Compared to our previous study, where only azimuths were used, we observe that combining both the azimuths and elevations gives us better results (57% vs. 71%).

I. Introduction

A. HRTF (Head Related Transfer Functions)

Head-Related Impulse Responses (HRIRs) are used in signal processing to model the synthesis of spatialized audio which is used in a variety of applications, from virtual computer games to aids for the visually impaired [2]. HRTFs represent the transformation undergone by the sound signals, as they travel from their source to both of the listener's eardrums. This transformation is due to the interaction of sound waves with the torso, shoulder, head and outer ear of a listener [3]. Therefore, the two components of these HRTF pairs (left and right) are typically different from each other, and pairs corresponding to sound sources at different locations around the listener are different. Moreover, since the physical elements that determine the transformation of the sounds reaching the listener's eardrums (i.e., the listener's head, torso and pinnae), are somewhat different for different listeners, so should be their HRTF sets [4].

B. Measurement

The Ausim3D's HeadZap HRTF Measurement System was used for measurement in FIU lab [5]. This system measures a 256-point impulse response for both the left and the right ear using a sampling frequency of 96 KHz. Golay codes are used to generate a broad-spectrum stimulus signal delivered through a Bose Acoustimass speaker. The response is measured using miniature blocked meatus microphones placed at the entrance to the ear canal on each side of the head. Under control of the system, the excitation sound is issued and both responses (left and right ear) are captured (Fig. 1).

Since the Golay code sequences played are meant to represent a broad-band excitation equivalent to an impulse, the sequences captured in each ear are the impulse responses corresponding to the HRTFs. The system provides these measured HRIRs as a pair of 256-point minimum-phase vectors, and an additional delay value that represents the Interaural Time Difference (ITD), i.e., the additional delay observed before the onset of the response collected from the ear that is farthest from the speaker position. In addition to the longer onset delay of the response from the "far" or "contralateral ear" (with respect to the sound source), this response will typically be smaller in amplitude than the response collected in the "near" or "ipsilateral ear". The difference in amplitude between HRIRs in a pair is referred to as the Interaural Intensity Difference (IID).

Fig. 1. Measurement of HRTFs using Ausim3D's HeadZap System.

T. Sobh, K. Elleithy (eds.), *Innovations in Computing Sciences and Software Engineering*, DOI 10.1007/978-90-481-9112-3_94,

Our protocol records HRIR pairs from source locations at the 72 possible combinations of $\phi = \{-36^\circ, -18^\circ, 0^\circ, 18^\circ, 36^\circ, 54^\circ\}$ and $\theta = \{0^\circ, 30^\circ, 60^\circ, 90^\circ, 120^\circ, 150^\circ, 180^\circ, -150^\circ, -120^\circ, -90^\circ, -60^\circ, -30^\circ\}$. The left (L) and right (R) HRIRs collected for a source location at azimuth θ and elevation ϕ are symbolized by $h_{L,\theta,\phi}$ and $h_{R,\theta,\phi}$, respectively. The corresponding HRTFs are $H_{L,\theta,\phi}$ and $H_{R,\theta,\phi}$. The creation of a spatialized binaural sound (left and right channels) involves convolving the single-channel digital sound to be spatialized, s(n), with the HRIR pair corresponding to the azimuth and elevation of the intended virtual source location [6].

C. *Cocktail Party Effect*

The "cocktail party effect"' is the ability to focus one's listening attention on a single speaker among a discord of conversations and background noise. This specialized listening ability could be because of characteristics of the human speech production system, the auditory system, or high-level perceptual and language processing [7].

Listeners in a crowd can focus on a particular speaker easily if the sounds are coming from different directions rather than from the same direction. They can also segregate one sound above others if the speaker has a higher or lower pitch, a different accent and a different gender than the rest [8].

Teleconferences involve multiple participants communicating simultaneously. This can result in loss of intelligibility, particularly if the sound is monaural in nature. In this study, we exploit the "cocktail party effect", where a person can isolate one sound above all others using sound localization cues. HRTFs are used to create an auditory map of multiple conversations, where each participant (speaker) is assigned a separate direction.

II. PROCEDURE

A. *Recording*

In this study, an environment identical to a teleconference is created by recording and playing multiple sounds from multiple speakers. The sounds (voices) were recorded using Samson C01U USB Studio Condenser Microphone [9]. The first part of the experiment has two cases. Case I uses two male and one female voices and case II uses two female and one male voice. HRTFs from Florida International University (FIU) database were used [10]. HRTFs were used to create an auditory map of multiple conversations, where each voice was assigned a separate direction. The test sounds (voices) were convolved with HRTFs from different elevations and one azimuth (30°), i.e. vertical plane (Fig. 2) and repeated by varying the azimuths and elevations. Using convolution the three voices were given different directions and listening tests were performed. MATLAB (Version 9) was used to perform this convolution operation.

The speakers were all non native speakers of English. We used various test sentences. For case I with two males and one female, we used (a) "There are a lot of significant changes going on in this school" (Male voice - I); (b) "We just missed the bus, we will wait for the next one" (Male voice - II); and

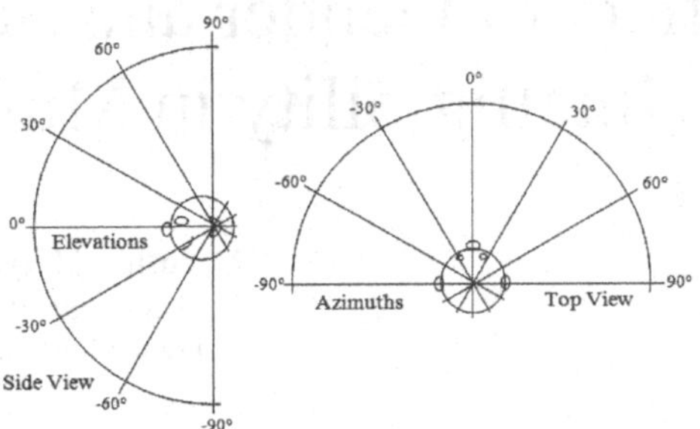

Fig. 2. Diagram of spherical coordinate system.

(c) "Since this is not working at all, we should drop the plan" (Female voice). For case II with two females and one male, we used (a) "There are a lot of significant changes going on in this school" (Male voice); (b) "Since this is not working at all, we should drop the plan" (Female voice - I); and (c)"We missed the bus, we will wait for the next one" (Female voice - II). The spoken lengths of these sentences were approximately of the same time duration.

Even though the recorded voices were of different intensity, they were eventually attenuated or amplified, so that the average intensities for all were almost the same. Fig. 3 shows the plot for recorded voices.

We introduced directions to these sounds using HRTFs. Current sound spatialization systems use HRTFs, represented by their corresponding impulse response sequences, the Head-Related Impulse Responses (HRIRs) to process, by convolution, a single-channel digital audio signal, giving rise to the two components (left and right) of a binaural localized sound. When these two channels are delivered to the listener through headphones, the sound will seem to originate from the source location corresponding to the HRIR pair used for the spatialization process.

B. *Listening Tests*

Listening tests were conducted on several subjects to find out the improvement in cognition because of the cocktail party effect. Each listening test lasted about 15-30 minutes. Analysis of results indicated a significant improvement in cognition when sounds came from different directions rather than the same direction.

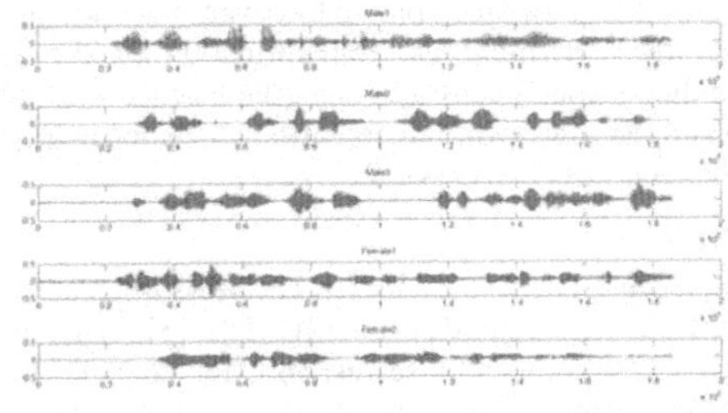

Fig. 3. Plots for recorded voices.

Fig. 4. Subject appearing for the listening test.

This method was tested over 15 human subjects. They were a combination of male and female within an age group of 20 to 35 years. Both the speakers and listeners involved in this test were from South Asia. Research subjects were asked to listen to three sounds (sentences) coming from a single direction via headphones and then they were asked to identify the sentence (in a female voice) and write it down. After this, they were asked to isolate one of the two male voiced sentences and write it down.

For each of the two steps, the listeners were given three trials to get used to the proceedings. This was followed by two trials each for identifying the male or the female voice. The accuracy of each reading was measured which was defined as the ratio of number of words identified correctly to the total number of words in that sentence. The same procedure was repeated with two female and one male voices. In this case the subject was asked to identify what the male voice was saying and also write down one of the female voices.

To examine the improvement due to cocktail party effect, we introduced a separate direction to each one of the three sounds. This was done using convolution and MATLAB was used. The same process as described above was used for sounds coming from (a) various elevations and (b) a combination of elevations and azimuths.

III. RESULTS

Fig. 5 shows the accuracy plot for all subjects in a male dominated environment. No spatialization was used. The fifteenth subject was an outlier; hence, it was not included in the results. It is quite obvious from Fig. 5 and Fig. 6 that a female voice is easier to understand in a male dominated environment and vice versa. Overall, we see 6% improvement in cognition while using a male voice in a female dominated environment and 16% improvement in the reverse case.

Fig. 7-9 show the improvement in accuracy when spatialization was introduced. An 'auditory map' was created with sounds coming from various elevations and azimuths. Significant improvement was observed in cognition (71%) when both elevation and azimuth were used.

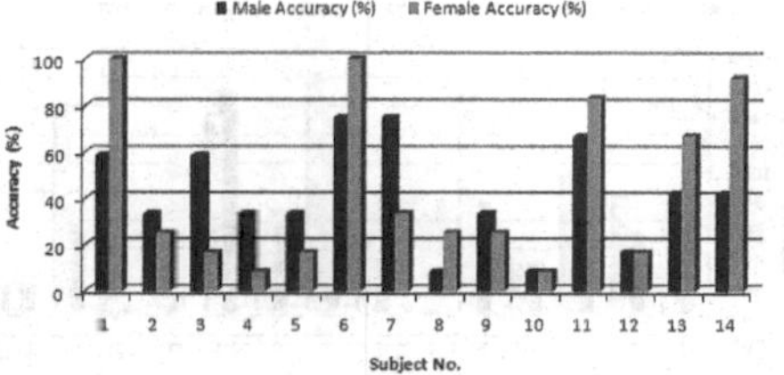

Fig. 5. Comparison of male and female accuracies in male dominated environment. Black bars represent accuracy for male voice and grey bars show accuracy for female voice.

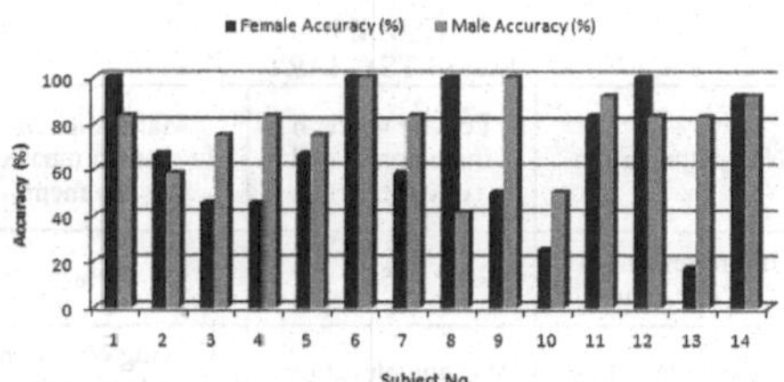

Fig. 6. Comparison of male and female accuracies in female dominated environment. Black bars represent accuracy for female voice and grey bars show accuracy for male voice.

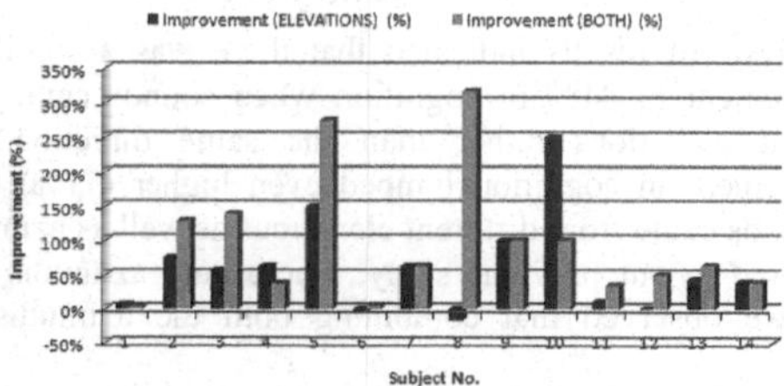

Fig. 7. Comparison of average improvement in cognition for a male dominated environment due to sound spatialization. Black bars represent accuracy for sounds with varying elevations and grey bars show accuracy for sounds with varying both elevations and azimuths.

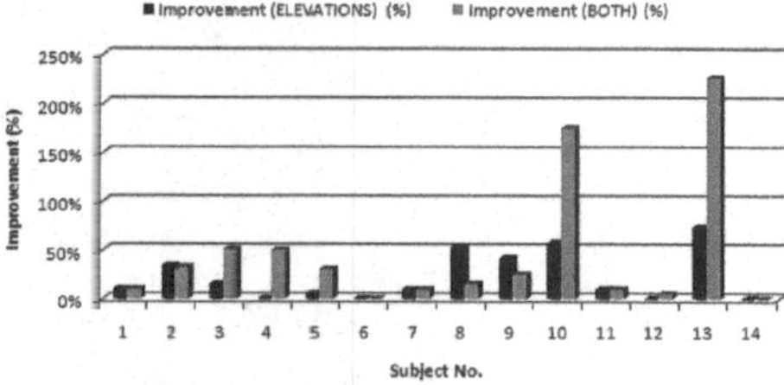

Fig. 8. Comparison of average improvement in cognition for a female dominated environment due to sound spatialization. Black bars represent accuracy for sounds with varying elevations and grey bars show accuracy for sounds with varying both elevations and azimuths.

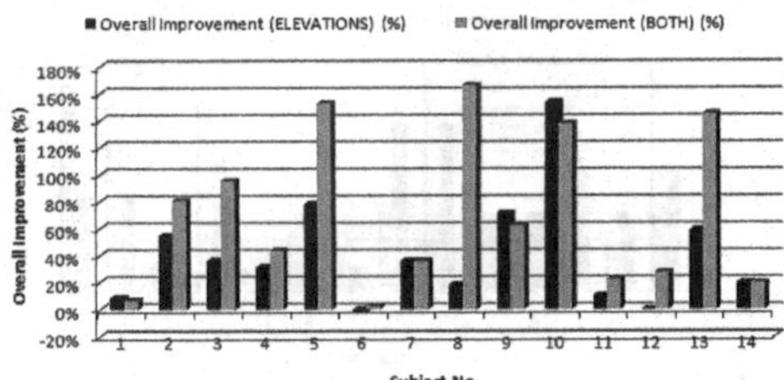

Fig. 9. Comparison of overall improvement in cognition due to sound spatialization. Black bars represent accuracy for sounds with varying elevations and grey bars show accuracy for sounds with varying both elevations and azimuths.

TABLE I
RESULTS CHART

No spatialization	Female voice in male dominated environment	Male voice in female doimnated environment
Improvement in Cognition	6 %	16%
With spatialization	Varying elevations	Varying elevations and azimuths
Overall Improvement in Cognition	41%	71%

IV. CONCLUSION

Analysis of results indicated that there was a significant improvement of 41% in cognition when sounds came from different elevations rather than the same direction. The improvement in cognition jumped even higher (71%) when the sounds came from different elevations as well as azimuths. Compared to our previous study, where only azimuths were used, we observed that combining both the azimuths and elevations gave us better results (57% vs. 71%) [1]. Furthermore, the female voice had a better accuracy compared to the male voice in a male dominated environment with a 6% improvement in cognition and a male voice had a better accuracy in a female dominated environment with a 16% improvement in cognition.

Sound spatialization finds widespread use in applications such as entertainment and navigation. Video games rely on immersive environments and auditory maps. Pilots in a cockpit can also use spatialization to understand multiple voices delivered over headphones. The results of this paper can help improve the intelligibility of such multiple speaker environments.

REFERENCES

[1] M. Joshi, K. Kotakonda, N. Gupta, and A. Barreto, "Improving Intelligibilty of Teleconferences Using Binaural Sounds", REV 2009.

[2] K. J. Faller II, A. Barreto, N. Gupta and N. Rishe, "Performance Comparison of Two Identification Methods for Analysis of Head Related Impulse Responses", CISSE 2005.

[3] Wenzel,E.M.,Arruda,M.,Kistler,D.J.and Wightman, F.L., "Localization Using Non-individualized Head-Related Transfer Functions," J.Acoust.Soc.Amer.,Vol.94,111-123, 1993.

[4] Begault, D. R., "A head-up auditory display for TCAS advisories." Human Factors, 35, 707-717, 1993.

[5] AuSIM, Inc., "HeadZap: AuSIM3D HRTF Measurement System Manual". AuSIM, Inc., 4962 El Camino Real, Suite 101, Los Altos, CA 94022, 2000.

[6] N. Gupta, A. Barreto and C. Ordonez, *"Spectral Modification of Head-Related Transfer Functions for Improved Virtual Sound Spatialization"*, Proceedings of the 2002 IEEE International Conference on Acoustics, Speech and Signal Processing (ICASSP 2002), May 13-17, 2002.

[7] http://xenia.media.mit.edu/~barons/html/cocktail.html

[8] Cherry, E. C., "Some experiments on the recognition of speech, with one and with two ears." Journal of Acoustical Society of America 25(5), 975—979, 1953.

[9] http://www.samsontech.com/products/productpage.cfm?prodID=1810

[10] http://dsp.eng.fiu.edu/HRTFDB/

Modeling Tourism Sustainable Development

O. A. Shcherbina[1], E. A. Shembeleva[1]
Nordbergstr., 15, University of Vienna,
Vienna 1090, Austria

***Abstract* - The basic approaches to decision making and modeling tourism sustainable development are reviewed. Dynamics of a sustainable development is considered in the Forrester's system dynamics. Multidimensionality of tourism sustainable development and multicriteria issues of sustainable development are analyzed. Decision Support Systems (DSS) and Spatial Decision Support Systems (SDSS) as an effective technique in examining and visualizing impacts of policies, sustainable tourism development strategies within an integrated and dynamic framework are discussed. Main modules that may be utilized for integrated modeling sustainable tourism development are proposed.**

Keywords-decision making; modeling; sustainable tourism; decision support systems; multicriteria analysis

I. Science as a Foundation For Tourism Sustainable Development

According to the World Travel and Tourism Council [1], world tourism receipts will reach approximately $727.9 billion by the end of 2004, with tourism generating more than 214 million jobs and contributing about $5.5 trillion of gross domestic product (GDP), 10.4% of the world's total. However, tourism's unplanned growth has significantly contributed to environmental degradation, negative social and cultural impacts. The realization of the damaging effects of tourism led to the paradigm of sustainable tourism. "Sustainable Development" is currently a topic of great social relevance and one that requires the integration of a challenging array of themes from a variety of disciplines spanning the physical and natural sciences, economics and other social sciences, and the humanities. The classic definition of **sustainable development** proposed in the World Commission on Environment and Development (WCED, 1987) report (so called the Bruntland report) "Our Common Future" [2] is: "Sustainable development is development that meets the needs of the present without compromising the ability of future generations to meet their own needs. It contains within it two key concepts:

• the concept of 'needs', in particular the essential needs of the world's poor, to which overriding priority should be given; and

• the idea of limitations imposed by the state of technology and social organization on the environment's ability to meet present and future needs."

This definition embraces three components: environmental responsibility, economic return and social development and requires that we see the world as a system - a system that connects space; and a system that connects time, i.e., a **spatio-temporal system**. "A great part of the challenge of modeling interactions between natural and social processes has to do with the fact that processes in these systems result in complex temporal-spatial behavior" [3].

Sustainable development is a wide concept and has over the years been introduced through many different definitions. These definitions have at least three common denominators; they all include a temporal perspective which entails a cross-generational responsibility and they all include a spatial perspective which entails a cross-system application. The temporal perspective indicates that the process is a long-term consideration with a focus on present behavioral modification for future preservation, while the spatial perspective is represented by a systems-approach advocating the dynamic interaction between natural and social systems.

In a report by the Global Environmental Change Programmes (a summary of the conclusions from the workshop "*Sustainable Development - The Role of International Science*", 4-6 February 2002, Paris) is written:

- "Research must move beyond a disciplinary focus to address sustainability issues in the framework of complex dynamical systems".
- "Building and delivering of predictive tools for enhanced understanding and decision-making, such as **system models** at local, regional and global scales".

In publications [4], [5] the issue of **regional sustainable development** has been considered under the three broad headings of **economic, social** and **ecological** concerns in a region.

The economic aspects are related to income, production, investments, market developments, price formation etc. The social concerns refer to distributional and equity considerations, such as income distribution, access to markets, wealth and power positions of certain groups or regions etc. And the ecological dimensions are concerned with quality of life, resource scarcity, pollution and related variables. This paradigm advocates a comprehensive decision-making that anticipates and manages scarce resource use, including environment and finance, while developing the regional system.

T. Sobh, K. Elleithy (eds.), *Innovations in Computing Sciences and Software Engineering*,
DOI 10.1007/978-90-481-9112-3_95, © Springer Science+Business Media B.V. 2010

Tourism has to contribute to sustainable development and tourism development should be based on criteria of sustainability.

Information plays a critical role in sustainable tourism development. Tourism and recreation are an information based business. Tourism and recreation information and destination management systems can be considered as one line of business with increasing acceptance and success in the e-commerce area of the Internet.

The importance of information, efficient information management, and decision support in recreation and tourism is steadily increasing due to the evolution of new technologies and high-capacity storage media.

The ability to identify, implement, and evaluate sustainable development strategies at all levels is inextricably linked to the effective identification, collection, use, and dissemination of information. The principles of sustainable development call for an integration of information about economic, environmental, and social factors in decision making. This information is required to support the identification of objectives, the development of policies or decision rules, and the evaluation of courses of action. While much of the reference to the role of information in sustainable development is directly linked to evaluation and decision making, access to information is also discussed in direct relationship to issues of equity and participation in decision making.

II. System Dynamics as a Modeling Tool for Sustainable Development

Tourism planning and management problems lie at the cross-roads of multiple disciplines, and for this reason may be described by a set of interacting models.

The **system dynamics** approach applies to dynamic problems (those that involve quantities that change over time) in feedback systems where feedback is defined as the transmission and return of information. System dynamics is an approach to understanding the behavior of complex systems over time. System dynamics is an aspect of systems theory as a method for understanding the dynamic behavior of complex systems. The basis of the method is the recognition that the structure of any system - the many circular, interlocking, sometimes time-delayed relationships among its components - is often just as important in determining its behavior as the individual components themselves.

An early attempt to model sustainable development was undertaken in "Limits to Growth" - models [6]. These models attempted to examine the impact of population growth, and pollution and resource use on planet. Despite numerous criticisms the system dynamics methodology can be used to build models of sustainable development. The systems dynamic approach to modeling sustainable development is based on the same methodology of difference equations represented as a set of interacting feedback loops.

A system dynamics based decision support system (DSS) to study the natural resources based tourism system has been developed in [7]. In [8] the suburb tourism trend based on system dynamics method is analyzed. A system dynamic approach was used in [9] to model the impacts of different tourism development strategies, accounting for interactions between ecology, economy and society.

Sustainability of development can be modeled with simulation supported by statistical and uncertainty analyses. These models are used to simulate possible scenarios for assessing novel and innovative technologies.

III. Multidimensionality of Tourism Sustainable Development

Sustainable tourism development is multidimensional in nature. Sustainability of tourism development is a broader concept that involves multiple criteria. It involves a pattern of economic development that would be compatible with a safe environment, biodiversity, and ecological balance, intergenerational and international equity.

Sustainable tourism development is a multidimensional paradigm, including socio-economic, ecological, technical and ethical perspectives. In making sustainability policies operational, basic questions to be answered are sustainability of what and whom? As a consequence, sustainability issues are characterized by a high degree of conflict. The design and development of sustainable development approaches is dependent upon the identification and development of an appropriate information infrastructure to support decision making. This information infrastructure must support the identification of objectives, the development and selection of appropriate actions toward those objectives, and the evaluation of progress toward those objectives.

The characterization of development sustainability in terms of a set of indicators makes very good sense. In fact, development sustainability is an abstract concept that is difficult to conceptualize and measure. These difficulties are due chiefly to the multidimensionality underlying the sustainability. Thus, development sustainability involves economic, ecological and sociological characteristics that are measured in very different units. What we should do in practice within such a complex scenario is to define and measure the different characteristics involved in the sustainability of a particular system in terms of suitable indicators. In general, it seems feasible to operationalize tourism sustainability by specifying a set of minimum (or critical) conditions to be fulfilled in any development initiative for a region. These conditions may relate to economic, social and environmental objectives. Such critical conditions are usually not specified via one single indicator, but require multiple criteria. As a consequence, multiple-criteria decision analysis (MCDA) paradigm may be seen as a helpful operational instrument for tourism sustainable development policy (Munda, 2005) [10], [11].

Consequently, it seems a practical approach (Nijkamp & Ouwersloot, 1997) [12] to describe environmental considerations and concerns mainly in terms of **reference values or threshold conditions** (limits, standards, norms) on resource use and environmental degradation (or pollution). This is in agreement with popular notions like carrying capacity, maximum yield, critical loads, environmental utilization space, maximum environmental capacity use and so forth. Usually optimization-based techniques are designed to create only single best solutions to problems. However, due to the presence of considerable system uncertainty and to the possibility that opposition from a dominant stakeholder can actually eliminate any single (even an optimal) solution from further consideration, environmental policy-makers faced with difficult and potentially controversial choices prefer to have the capability of selecting from a set of alternatives. MCDA has emerged as a powerful tool to assist in the process of searching for decisions which best satisfy a multitude of conflicting objectives, and there are a number of distinct methodologies for multicriteria decision-making problems that exist. Bousson (2001) [13] applies a multi-criteria methodology (ELECTRE) to the choice of the most preferred management alternative according to several criteria.

Belton and Stewart (2002) [14] define MCDA as "an umbrella term to describe a collection of formal approaches which seek to take explicit account of multiple criteria in helping individuals or groups explore decisions that matter". This general definition outlines three dimensions of MCDA, namely: (1) the formal approach, (2) the presence of multiple criteria, and (3) that decisions are made either by individuals or groups of individuals. MCDA approaches have been classified in a number of ways (Mendoza & Martins, 2006) [15]. One of the first categorizations makes a distinction between multi-objective decision making (MODM) and multi-attribute decision making (MADM). The main distinction between the two groups of methods is based on the number of alternatives under evaluation. MADM methods are designed for selecting discrete alternatives while MODM are more adequate to deal with multi-objective planning problems, when a theoretically infinite number of continuous alternatives are defined by a set of constraints on a vector of decision variables

The general classification of MCDA methods is suggested by Belton and Stewart [14] and classified MCDA methods into three broad categories:

(1) **Value measurement models**: "numerical scores are constructed in order to represent the degree to which one decision option may be preferred to another. Such scores are developed initially for each individual criterion, and are then synthesized in order to effect aggregation into higher level preference models";

(2) **Goal, aspiration or reference level models**: "desirable or satisfactory levels of achievement are established for each criterion. The process then seeks to discover options which are closest to achieving these desirable goals or aspirations";

(3) **Outranking models**: "alternative courses of action are compared pairwise, initially in terms of each criterion in order to identify the extent to which a preference for one over the other can be asserted. In aggregating such preference information across all relevant criteria, the model seeks to establish the strength of evidence favoring selection of one alternative over another".

Land-use planning has also been analyzed including the integration of MCDA methods with Geographic Information Systems (GIS) (Malczewski, 1999) [16].

In many cases, the concept and measurement of the sustainability of a tourism development is based upon an aggregation process of several indicators of different type and, consequently, expressed in very different units. Within this generally accepted scenario, this aggregation procedure can be done with a method based upon goal programming (GP) [17] with zero-one decision variables that turns out to be a powerful tool for determining the sustainability of tourism development. The proposed procedure flexibly determines the "most sustainable" system from a set of feasible tourism development plans in terms of several indicators of sustainability, as well as ordering or ranking the systems considered. GP technique has been used in the ecotourism [18] and for allocating resources in municipal recreation department [19].

Some of limitations of the traditional MCDA methods when dealing with the complexity of natural resources management were summarized by (Rosenhead, 1989)as follows: (1) "comprehensive rationality", which unrealistically presumes or aspires to substitute analytical results and computations for judgement; (2) the creative generation of alternatives is deemphasized in favor of presumably objective feasible and optimal alternatives; (3) misunderstanding and misrepresenting the reasons and motivations for public involvement; (4) a lack of value framework beyond the typical "utilitarian precepts".

In view of the above limitations, a more flexible, robust, and broad approach to MCDA application to tourism resources management is needed, one that is able to deal with ill-defined problems, with objectives that might be neither clearly stated or accepted by all constituents, with unknown problem components, and with unpredictable cause-and-effect relationships. A transparent and participatory definition of the planning and decision problems would also be desirable.

A number of authors (e.g. (Rosenhead, 1989) and (Checkland, 1981) [21]) proposed an alternative paradigm, known as "soft systems" methods to address what these authors described as wicked, messy, ill-structured or difficult to define problems. According to (Rosenhead, 1989) , these alternative paradigms are characterized by attributes such as: (1) search for alternative solutions, not necessarily optimal, but which are acceptable on separate dimensions without requiring explicit trade-offs; (2) reduced data demands through greater integration of hard and soft data including social judgments; (3) simplicity and transparency; (4) treatment of people as active subjects; (5)

facilitation of bottom-up planning; (6) acceptance of uncertainty guided by attempts to keep options open as various subtleties of the problem are gradually revealed. An excellent review of these "soft methods", or sometimes referred to as soft-operations research methods, can be found in (.

In general, soft systems approaches give less emphasis on generating solutions; instead, they give primacy to defining the most relevant factors, perspectives and issues that have to be taken into account, and in designing strategies upon which the problem can be better understood and the decision process better guided. They are also more adequate for addressing complex problems dominated by issues relevant to, and influenced by, human concerns and their purposeful schemes. By doing so, they recognize the intrinsically complex nature of social systems and consequently attempt to avoid prematurely imposing notions of objectivity, rationality, mechanistic and predictable causality among relevant components of the problem.

Two characteristic features that are central to the soft systems approach are facilitation and structuring. Facilitation aims to provide an environment where participants or stakeholders are properly guided and discussions or debate are appropriately channeled. Structuring, on the other hand pertains to the process with which the management problem is organized in a manner that stakeholders or participants can understand, and hence, ultimately participate in the planning and decision-making processes.

This need led to the development of approaches that formally analyze qualitative decision problems such as: artificial neural networks (, knowledge bases ((Reynolds et al., 1996) [23] and (Reynolds et al., 2000) [24]), and expert systems (Store & Kangas, 2001) [25]. Two applications in particular of these new approaches, developed as decision support systems, are the Ecosystem Management Decision Support System (EMDS) developed by Reynolds (1999) [26] and CORMAS (Common-pool Resources and Multi-Agent Systems) developed by Bousquet et al. (1998) [27].

IV. DECISION SUPPORT SYSTEMS (DSS)

DSS can be used by decision makers as an effective technique in examining and visualizing impacts of policies, sustainable tourism development strategies within an integrated and dynamic framework. In [28] the DSS for coastal-zone management is used to study the long-term impacts of different management measures, such as the construction of a storage lake or investments in tourism, on the coastal zone system. Different scenarios for the demographic, economic, and hydrological conditions can be introduced.

In [29] the current status and future directions of model-based systems in decision support and their application to sustainable development planning is comprehensively examined.

A **spatial decision support system** (SDSS) is an interactive, computer-based system designed to support a user or a group of users in achieving a higher effectiveness of decision making while solving a semi-structured spatial decision problem (Malczewski, 1999) [16]. The concept of SDSS has evolved in parallel with DSSs (Marakas, 1998) [30]. The first MC-SDSS have been developed during the late 1980s and early 1990s (Malczewski, 1999) [16]. Early research on MC-SDSS is especially devoted to the physical integration of the GIS and MCDA. According to (Densham, 1991) [31], a SDSS should (i) provide mechanisms for the input of spatial data, (ii) allow representation of spatial relations and structures, (iii) include the analytical techniques of spatial analysis, and (iv) provide output in a variety of spatial forms, including maps. A typical SDSS contains three generic components (Malczewski, 1999) [16]: a database management system and geographical information systems (GIS), a model-based management system and model base, and a dialogue generation system. Today's spatial decision support systems rely on a GIS component. Cowen (1988) [32] defined GIS "as a decision support system involving the integration of spatially referenced data in a problem solving environment". A GIS system is composed of a geographical database, an input/output process, a data analysis method, and a user interface. Such modern GIS techniques have been instrumental in developing interactive modes between quantitative modeling and spatial mapping (Giaoutzi & Nijkamp, 1993) [4]. Especially when tourism development plans have a bearing on land use, GIS may offer a powerful analytical tool for spatial sustainable development [33].

Multicriteria spatial decision support systems (MC-SDSS) can be viewed as part of the broader fields of SDSS. The specificity of MC-SDSS is that it supports *spatial multicriteria decision making*. Spatial multicriteria decision making refers to the use of MCDA. Web-based MC-SDSS is an active research topic which will be the subject of considerable additional interest in the future (Carver, 1999) [34].

A number of frameworks for designing MC-SDSS have been proposed including Diamond & Wright (1988) [35], Carver (1991) [36], Eastman et al. (1995) [37], and Jankowski et al. (1999) [38]. Despite differences in GIS capabilities and MCDA techniques, the generic framework contains three major components: a user interface, MCDA models (includes tools for generating value structure, preference modeling, and multiattribute decision rules), and spatial data analysis and management capabilities.

MC-SDSS have been developed for a variety of problems, including land use planning (Diamond and Wright, 1988) [35], (Thill & Xiaobai, 1999) [39], (MacDonald & Faber, 1999) [40], habitat site development (Jankowski et al., 1999) [38], health care resource allocation (Jankowski and Ewart, 1996) [41], land suitability analysis (Eastman et al., 1995) [37].

V. SPATIO-TEMPORAL INFORMATION SYSTEMS

Recently, the interest has been focused on dynamic applications with geographic reference. These applications are commonly called as spatio-temporal applications and examine phenomena, which occur in specific regions and change over time (Stefanakis & Sellis, 2000) [42], (Egenhofer & Golledge, 1998) [43], (Frank, 1992) [44]. Current GIS technologies have limited capabilities in modeling and handling complex spatio-temporal phenomena. A framework with enhanced capabilities in both representation and reasoning of geographic data is proposed in (Ratsiatou & Stefanakis, 2001) [45]. A unified model for spatial and temporal information is proposed in (Worboys, 1994) [46]. The semantic data model proposed in (Yazici et al., 2001) [47] utilizes unified modeling language UML for handling spatiotemporal information, uncertainty, and fuzziness especially at the conceptual level of database design. Bibliography on spatio-temporal databases is in (Al-Taha et al., 1993) [48]. In (Parent et al., 1999) [49] spatio-temporal conceptual models are discussed. Examples of spatial, temporal, and spatiotemporal applications include land management, weather monitoring, natural resources management, environmental, ecological, and biodiversity studies, tracking of mobile devices, and navigation systems. Paper (López et al., 2005) [50] contains many recent references on spatio-temporal databases. A comparative review (Pelekis et al., 2004) [51] is followed by a comprehensive description of the new lines of research that emanate from the latest efforts inside the spatio-temporal research community. Spatial information systems can be categorized into four main groups (Abraham & Roddick, 1999) [52]: Geographical Information Systems (GIS), which result from the automation of cartography and deal with digitized maps displaying geographic or thematic information, Automated Mapping/Facilities Management (AM/FM) systems which automate the management and maintenance of networks such as telephone lines or power grids, Land Information Systems (LIS), also known as cadastral systems) which manage information such as the details of land parcel ownership, and Image Processing systems which process remote sensing images acquired by aircraft and satellites.

The following main modules may be utilized for integrated modeling sustainable tourism development:

1. a base of mathematical models and/or meta-models for simulating land use changes as affected by alternative policy/management scenarios ;
2. a base of mathematical models and/or meta-models for the simulation of environmental impacts associated to tourism development scnarios producing quantitative indicators to be used by the multi-criteria analysis. Optimization and simulation modelling techniques have been widely used in the field of tourism and recreation planning and management (Shcherbina & Shembeleva) [53]. Examples of related publications include works by (Gearing, Swart, & Var, 1976) [54], (Lemeshev & Shcherbina, 1986) [55], (Penz, 1975) [56], (Shcherbina, 1980) [57];
3. MCDA models (includes tools for generating value structure, preference modeling, and multiattribute or multiobjective decision rules); and
4. GIS/spatio-temporal information system for the management and description of spatio-temporal variability.

ACKNOWLEDGMENT

Research partly supported by FWF (Austrian Science Funds) under the project P20900-N13.

REFERENCES

[1] World travel & tourism: A world of opportunity, The 2004 travel & tourism economic research. London: World Travel & Tourism Council, 2004.

[2] *Our Common Future*, Report of the World Commission on Environment and Development, World Commission on Environment and Development, 1987. Published as Annex to General Assembly document A/42/427, Development and International Co-operation: Environment August 2, 1987.

[3] R.M. Itami, "Simulating spatial dynamics: Cellular automata theory," *Landscape and Urban Planning*, vol. 30, pp. 27-47, 1994.

[4] M. Giaoutzi and P. Nijkamp, *Decision Support Models for Regional Sustainable Development*, Aldershot: Avebury, 1993.

[5] J.C.J.M. van den Bergh, *Ecological Economics and Sustainable Development*. London: Edward Elgar, 1996.

[6] D. H. Meadows, D.L. Meadows, J. Randers, and W.W. Behrens, *The Limits to Growth*. New York: Universe Books, 1972.

[7] K.C.Chen, "Decision support system for tourism development: system dynamics approach," *J. of Computer Information Systems*, vol. 45, pp. 104-112, 2004.

[8] Xia Jin, "An Analysis of Suburb Tourism Trend Based on System Dynamics Method," *International Conference on Computer Engineering and Technology*, vol. 2, pp.210-213, 2009.

[9] T. Patterson, T. Gulden, K. Cousins, and E. Kraev, "Integrating environmental, social and economic systems: a dynamic model of tourism in Dominica," *Ecological Modelling*, vol. 175, pp. 121–136, 2004.

[10] G. Munda, "Multiple criteria decision analysis and sustainable development," in *Multiple Criteria Decision Analysis: State of the Art Surveys*. New York: Springer, 2005, pp. 953-986.

[11] A. De Montis, G. Deplano, and P. Nijkamp, "Multicriteria evaluation and local environmental planning for sustainable tourism," in *Advances in Modern Tourism Research*, pp. 207-232, Physica-Verlag HD, 2007.

[12] P. Nijkamp and H. Ouwersloot, "A decision support system for regional sustainable development: the Flag model," in *Economic Modelling of Sustainable Development*, M. Hofkes and J. van den Bergh, Eds. Cheltenham: Edward Elgar, 1997.

[13] E. Bousson, "Development of a multicriteria decision support system adapted to multiple-use forest management: application to forest management at the management unit level in Southern Belgium," in *Criteria and Indicators for Sustainable Forest Management at the Forest Management Unit Level, EFI Proceedings*, vol. 38, A. Franc, O. Laroussinie, and T. Karjalainen, Eds, 2001, pp. 151–164.

[14] S. Belton and T.S. Stewart, *Multiple Criteria Decision* Analysis. *An Integrated Approach*. Kluwer Academic Publishers, Massachusetts, 2002.

[15] G.A. Mendoza and H. Martins, "Multi-criteria decision analysis in natural resource management: A critical review of methods and new modelling paradigms," *Forest Ecology and Management*, vol. 230, pp. 1-22, July 2006.

[16] J. Malczewski, *GIS and Multi-Criteria Decision Analysis*. New York: John Wiley & Sons, Inc., 1999.

[17] J.P. Ignizio, *Goal Programming and Extensions*. Massachussets: Lexington Books, 1976.

[18] Ch. Zografos; D. Oglethorpe, "Multi-criteria analysis in ecotourism: using goal programming to explore sustainable solutions," *Current Issues in Tourism*, vol. 7, pp. 20–43, 2004.

[19] F.P. Buffa, W.T. Shearon, "Goal programming for allocating resources in a municipal recreation department," *Journal of Leisure Research*, vol. 12, pp. 128-137, 1980.

[21] P.B. Checkland, *Systems Thinking, Systems Practice*, Chichester: John Wiley and Sons, 1981.

[23] K. Reynolds et al., "A knowledge-based information management system for watershed analysis in the Pacific Northwest U.S.," *AI Appl.*, vol. 10, pp. 9–22, 1996.

[24] K.M. Reynolds, M. Jensen, J. Andreasen, and I. Goodman, "Knowledge-based assessment of watershed condition," *Comput. Electron. Agric.*, vol. 27, pp. 315–333, 2000.

[25] R. Store and J. Kangas, "Integrating spatial multi-criteria evaluation and expert knowledge for GIS based habitat suitability modelling," *Landscape Urban Plan.*, vol. 55, pp. 79–93, 2001.

[26] K.M. Reynolds, *NetWeaver for EMDS Version 1.0 User Guide: a Knowledge Base Development System*. Gen. Tech. Rep. PNW-GTR-471. US Department of Agriculture, Forest Service, Pacific Northwest Research Station, Portland, 1999.

[27] F. Bousquet, I. Bakam, H. Proton, and C. Le Page, "CORMAS: common-pool resources and multi-agent systems", *Lecture Note in Artificial Intelligence, 1416*, Springer-Verlag, Berlin, pp. 826–838, 1998.

[28] J.-L. de Kok, G. Engelen, R. White, and H. G. Wind, "Modeling land-use change in a decision-support system for coastal-zone management," *Environmental Modeling and Assessment,* vol. 6, pp. 123–132, 2001.

[29] M.A. Quaddus and M.A.B. Siddique, Eds., *A Handbook of Sustainable Development Planning: Studies in Modelling and Decision Support.* Cheltenham: Edward Elgar Publishing, 2005.

[30] G.M. Marakas, *Decision Support Systems in the 21st Century.* Prentice-Hall, 1998.

[31] P.J. Densham, "Spatial decision support systems," in *Geographical information systems: Principles and applications*, vol. 1, D.J. Maguitre, M.F. Goodchild, and D. Rhind, Eds. London: Longman, 1991, pp. 403-412.

[32] D. Cowen, "GIS versus CAD versus DBMS: what are the differences?" *Photogrammetric Engineering and Remote Sensing*, vol. 54, pp. 1551-1555, 1988.

[33] R. D. Feick, G. B. Hall, "The application of a spatial decision support system to tourism-based land management in small island states," *Journal of Travel Research*, Vol. 39, No. 2, 163-171 (2000)

[34] S.J. Carver, "Developing web-based GIS/MCE: improving access to data and spatial decision support tools," in *Multicriteria decision-making and analysis: A geographic information sciences approach*, J.-C. Thill, Ed. Ashgate, 1999, pp. 49-75.

[35] J.T. Diamond and J.R. Wright, "Design of an integrated spatial information system for multiobjective land-use planning," *Environment and Planning Bulletin*, vol. 15, pp. 205-214, 1988.

[36] S. Carver, "Integrating multicriteria evaluation with GIS," *International J. of Geogr. Information Sys.*, vol. 5, pp. 321-339, 1991.

[37] J.R. Eastman, W. Jin, P.A.K. Kyem, and J. Toledano, "Raster procedures for multicriteria/ multiobjective decisions," *Photogram. Eng. Remote Sens.*, vol. 61, pp. 539-547, 1995.

[38] P. Jankowski, A. V. Lotov, and D. Gusev, "Application of a multiple criteria trade-off approach to spatial decision making," in *Spatial Multicriteria Decision Making and Analysis*, J. C .Thill, Ed. Hants: Ashgate Publishing Company, 1999, pp. 127-147.

[39] J.-C. Thill and Y. Xiaobai, "Urban Land Management in Transitional Economics: A Decision Support Prototype for Shangai," in *Spatial Multicriteria Decision Making and Analysis*, J. C .Thill, Ed. Hants: Ashgate Publishing Company, 1999, pp. 175-198.

[40] M.L. MacDonald and B.G. Faber, "Exploring the potential of multicriteria spatial decision support systems: a system for sustainable land-use planning and design," in *Spatial Multicriteria Decision Making and Analysis*, J. C .Thill, Ed. Hants: Ashgate Publishing Company, 1999, pp. 353-360.

[41] P. Jankowski and G. Ewart, "Spatial decision support system for health practitioners: Selecting a location for rural health practice," *Int. J. Geo.Inform. Sys.*, vol. 3, pp. 279-299, 1996.

[42] E. Stefanakis and T. Sellis, "Towards the design of a DBMS repository for temporal GIS,"in ESF- GISDATA Series Book: *Life & Motion of Socio-economic Units* (eds. Frank, A.U., Raper, J., & Cheylan, J.-P.) Taylor & Francis, 2000.

[43] M.J. Egenhofer and R.J. Golledge, *Spatial and Temporal reasoning in geographic information systems*, Oxford University Press, 1998.

[44] A. Frank, Ed., *Theories and methods of spatio-temporal reasoning in geographic space*, Lecture Notes in Computer Science 639, Springer-Verlag, 1992.

[45] I. Ratsiatou and E. Stefanakis, "Spatio-temporal multicriteria decision making under uncertainty," in *Proc. of the 1st Int. Symposium on Robust Statistics and Fuzzy Techniques in Geodesy and GIS*, Zurich, 2001, pp. 169-174.

[46] M.F. Worboys, "A unified model for spatial and temporal information," *Comput. J.*, vol. 37, pp. 26-34, 1994.

[47] A. Yazici, Q. Zhu, and N. Sun, "Semantic data modeling of spatiotemporal database applications," *International Journal of Intelligent Systems*, vol. 16, pp. 881-904, 2001.

[48] K.K. Al-Taha, R.T. Snodgrass, and M.D. Soo, "Bibliography on spatio-temporal databases", *SIGMOD Record*, vol. 22, pp. 56–67, 1993.

[49] C. Parent, S. Spaccapietra, and E. Zimanyi, "Spatio-temporal conceptual models: data structures + space + time," *Proc. ACM Int'l Symp. Advances in Geographic Information Systems (ACM-GIS),* pp. 26-33, Nov. 1999.

[50] I. F. V. López, R. T. Snodgrass, and B Moon, "Spatiotemporal aggregate computation: A survey," *IEEE Transactions on Knowledge and Data Engineering*, vol. 17, pp. 271-286, 2005.

[51] N. Pelekis, B. Theodoulidis, I. Kopanakis, and Y. Theodoridis "Literature review of spatio-temporal database models," *The Knowledge Engineering Review*, vol. 19, pp. 235-274, 2004.

[52] T. Abraham and J.F. Roddick, "Survey of spatio-temporal databases", *Geoinformatica*, , vol. 3, pp. 61–99, 1999.

[53] O. Shcherbina and E. Shembeleva, "Computer-based system of tourism and recreational systems study and optimization," *Tourism Analysis*, , vol.13, pp. 93-98, 2008.

[54] C.E. Gearing, W.W. Swart, and T. Var, *Planning for Tourism Development. Quantitative Approaches.* N.Y., Praeger Publishers, 1976.

[55] M.Ya. Lemeshev and O.A. Shcherbina, *Optimization of Recreational Activities,* Moscow, Economics, 1986.

[56] A.J. Penz, "Outdoor recreation area: capacity and formulation of use policy," *Management Science*, 22 (2), pp. 139-147, 1975.

[57] O.A. Shcherbina, "Mathematical methods for investigation recreational systems design abroad (Survey)," *Economics and mathematical methods*, N 6, 1980.

PI-ping - Benchmark Tool for Testing Latencies and Throughput in Operating Systems

J. Abaffy
Faculty of Informatics and Information Technologies
Slovak University of Technology
Bratislava, 842 16, Slovakia

T. Krajčovič
Faculty of Informatics and Information Technologies
Slovak University of Technology
Bratislava, 842 16, Slovakia

***Abstract* – In this paper we present a benchmark tool called PI-ping that can be used to compare real-time performance of operating systems. It uses two types of processes that are common in operating systems – interactive tasks demanding low latencies and also processes demanding high CPU utilization. Most operating systems have to perform well in both conditions and the goal is to achieve the highest throughput when keeping the latencies within a reasonable interval. PI-ping measures the latencies of an interactive process when the system is under heavy computational load. Using PI-ping benchmark tool we are able to compare different operating systems and we attest the functionality of it using two very common operating systems - Linux and FreeBSD.**

***Keywords* – Benchmark, Latency, Throughput, Linux, FreeBSD, Scheduling**

I. INTRODUCTION

Benchmarking of operating systems is very popular area and always when a new version of some OS comes to the scene, its authors and fans flood their websites with benchmarks showing the improvements made in the recent version compared to the older one and also compared to the other operating systems.

Most of the benchmarks are designed either for latency measurements or for performance comparison, but not both of them and when the performer of the test wants to highlight the improvement in the throughput; he uses benchmarks that can approve it. But increasing the throughput can lead into higher latencies [8].

Using PI-ping benchmark tool we are able to compare not only the latencies in OS but also the throughput. We attest the functionality of created benchmark using two very common operating systems - Linux and FreeBSD. Both of them were developed as general purpose operating systems without any consideration for real-time applications and are widely used as server operating systems. In recent years they have become attractive also as desktop operating systems, and nowadays they also find their way to the real time community due to their low cost and open standards.

Linux and FreeBSD have a huge community of contributors, fans and supporters and comparison of these kernels is popular in these communities [16]. These kernels are compared with one another and also in different versions of it to show the impact of changing the default schedulers in the recent years.

II. PI-PING BENCHMARK

PI-ping is based on two different types of process that occur in operating systems. In the first group there are processes that demand a lot of CPU. Other processes are interactive – they request good latencies. In this benchmark we use for the first group a computation of the number Л, and as interactive process we use network ping to localhost every 100 ms. This time was already a long time ago empirically determined as the maximum latency when the user considers the system as interactive [14]. Therefore it is widely used in different operating systems as a default amount of time assigned by the scheduler to the process between two task switches [13].

Computation of the number Л is used to prevent any optimization by the compiler because the ciphers are not predictable. This process demands as much CPU as it can gets compared to ping, which is demanding quick responses from the kernel.

With this tool we are able to compare how well the kernel and the scheduler is desirable for CPU consuming processes, and we can also see how many interactive process can under heavy load meet their deadlines. The main advantage of PI-ping is that it does not require exact time measuring. Lot of benchmarks desired for testing latencies in operating systems try to measure the time between the demand and the response. Latencies in operating systems are around microseconds and it is problematic to ensure desired precision using software tools [8].

To avoid the exact time measurement we run ping every 100 ms and measure only the time of the whole benchmark rounded up to 100 ms. After dividing this time by 100 we obtain the number of expected successful pings. The ratio of measured successful pings compared to the number of expected says how many deadlines were met. Parallel with the interactive ping process is running variable amount of CPU demanding

T. Sobh, K. Elleithy (eds.), *Innovations in Computing Sciences and Software Engineering*,
DOI 10.1007/978-90-481-9112-3_96,

calculations of the number Л, so we are able to see how the CPU consuming processes are impacting the latencies.

III. Testing Environment

We perform the PI-ping benchmark on five different kernels of operating systems. Two of them are Linux kernels and three are FreeBSD kernels. Linux is tested once in version 2.6.22 with O(1) scheduler and once in the version 2.6.28 with the to date newest CFS scheduler. FreeBSD also offers two different schedulers – 4BSD and ULE. There was made a lot of improvement in FreeBSD ULE scheduler [7], so we test it in version 7.1. and also in older implementation used in FreeBSD 6.3.

A. *Linux 2.6.22 with O(1) scheduler*

This kernel is the latest Linux kernel that uses O(1) scheduler. The name of the scheduler is based on the popular big O notation that is used to determine the complexity of algorithms. It doesn't mean that this scheduler is the fastest, but it means that it can schedule processes within a constant amount of time independent on the number of tasks running in the system. Therefore, this scheduler is suitable for real-time application because it guarantees the highest scheduling time.

B. *Linux 2.6.28 with CFS scheduler*

Since the version 2.6.23 Linux kernel comes with Completely Fair Scheduler (CFS) that is the first implementation of a fair queuing process scheduler in widely used general-purpose operating systems. Schedulers in other operating systems (and also O(1) scheduler) are based on run queues, but this scheduler arranges processes in a red-black tree. The complexity of this scheduler is O(log n).

The main advantage of a red-black tree is that the longest path in this tree is at most twice as long as the shortest path. This scheduler was written to accept different requirements in desktops and in servers.

C. *FreeBSD 7.1 with 4BSD scheduler*

4BSD is the default scheduler in all FreeBSD versions prior to 7.1, although there is a new scheduler called ULE since FreeBSD 5.0. It is the traditional Unix scheduler inherited from 4.3BSD, but in FreeBSD there were added scheduling classes. It is also based on run queues as the Linux O(1) scheduler.

D. *FreeBSD 7.1 with ULE scheduler*

The name of this latest scheduler in FreeBSD comes from the filename where is it located in source code of the kernel /sys/kern/sched_ule.c. In comparison to O(1) and 4BSD there are not two run queues, but in this case three: idle, current and next. Processes are scheduled from the queue current, and after expiration of their time slice they are moved to the queue next. Rescheduling is made by switching these two queues. In the queue idle there are idle processes.

The main advantage of this scheduler is that it can have run queues per processor, what enables better performance results on multiprocessors [9].

E. *FreeBSD 6.3 with ULE scheduler*

In this paper we perform benchmarks also on older ULE scheduler from FreeBSD 6.3 to see if there were made significant improvements as presented in [7].

F. *Hardware*

For testing and benchmarking was used a common laptop with 1 GB RAM and Celeron M processor at 1.6 GHz. Important is that the used processor is single-core. Using multi-core processor with enabled symmetric multiprocessing would affect the results in significant way [9].

IV. PI-ping Results

In the following graph (Fig.1.) there is shown how many deadlines were met by an interactive process ping.

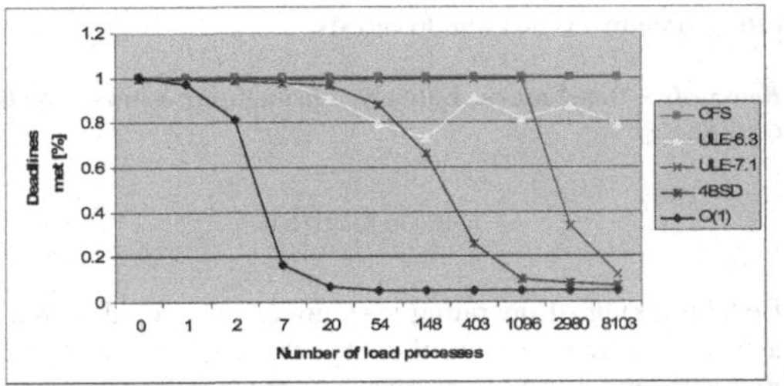

Fig. 1. Percentage of met deadlines in dependence of the number of load processes (higher is better)

In this benchmark CFS succeeded already under the load of more than 8000 processes, and always 100% of the interactive processes met their deadlines.

O(1), 4BSD and ULE-7.1 have similar characteristics, but be aware of the logarithmic axis used in this graph. The latest ULE scheduler in FreeBSD 7.1 can also be considered as a low latency scheduler since it also covers 100% deadlines when the number of load processes is in acceptable limits. Already servers are often limited by administrators to maximal 1024 processes, and now we are focusing on latencies in smaller systems.

Surprising was the decrease of O(1) scheduler, by only 2 load processes running in background the ping responsiveness was only around 80%.

PI-ping shows also problems with ULE scheduler in FreeBSD 6.3. Results in the graph (Fig.1.) are the average values measured in 3 benchmarks. Other schedulers have balanced characteristic, and the results were almost same in each experiment. In following graph there are the results of three measurements of ULE-6.3 scheduler.

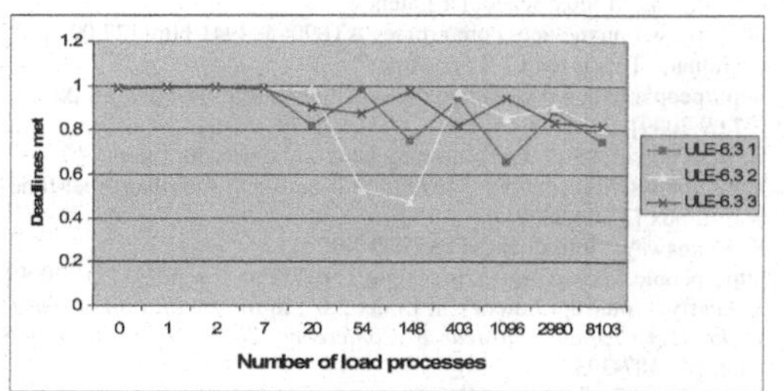

Fig. 2. Results of ULE-6.3 in 3 measurements

As you can see, by raising the number of processes the results of ULE scheduler become in FreeBSD 6.3 instable.

We also wanted to perform benchmark not only for interactive tasks, but also for CPU demanding processes like computation of the number Л. In the following graph CFS is used as reference scheduler and the speed of other schedulers is calculated as the time of CFS divided by the time of the other scheduler.

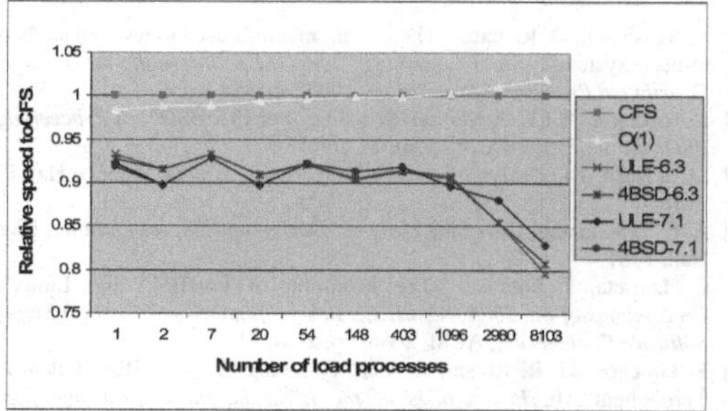

Fig. 3. Relative speed of Л computation compared to CFS (higher is better)

In this test FreeBSD is approximately 10% slower than Linux. It can be caused by optimization because Linux was compiled for i686 and FreeBSD for i386, by the different implementation of task switching routine, by the concept of forking processes, or by any other kernel options than scheduler. Important is that for the computation of Л the scheduler doesn't have high impact. These processes do not use any shared memory, pipes, mutexes, lot of IO operations et cetera and always use the whole time slice assigned by the scheduler which is 100 ms by default in the both operating systems. If we run for example 10 processes, each running for 10 seconds, the computation should take 100 seconds in ideal case. But in the real case it is higher because of the overhead caused by operating system, rescheduling, and other running processes in the system.

When comparing FreeBSD with ULE scheduler and with 4BSD, the results are almost the same. Small differences are only between different versions (7.1 versus 6.3), but the curves look similar. ULE and 4BSD are based on run queues with the complexity O(1), so for these non-interactive tasks they perform equal. But in case of Linux, we can see the confrontation of the CFS scheduler with O(log n) complexity with the older O(1) scheduler. For smaller numbers of processes CFS performs better, but if there are a lot of processes, O(1) takes advantage of its better complexity. In this case the intersection of O(1) and O(log n) was experimentally set at the point, where 500 processes are in the system.

V. HACKBENCH RESULTS

In PI-ping benchmark we have inspected instable results of ULE scheduler in FreeBSD-6.3 and demonstrated that CFS performs better for interactive processes and has also better results for non-interactive processes when there is not too much of them.

To approve the results of PI-ping benchmark we used another test called Hackbench. This benchmark launches a selected number of processes that either listen on a socket or on a pipe and complimentary the same number of processes that send 100 messages to the listening processes.

The results of the benchmark are in the graph (Fig.4.), but now we use not average values, but from only one benchmark, to depict the differences in stability of ULE-6.3 and ULE-7.1. In this benchmark ULE-6.3 performs better for smaller number of processes, but then becomes the instability predicted by PI-ping visible. CFS, O(1) and ULE-7.1 have linear characteristic.

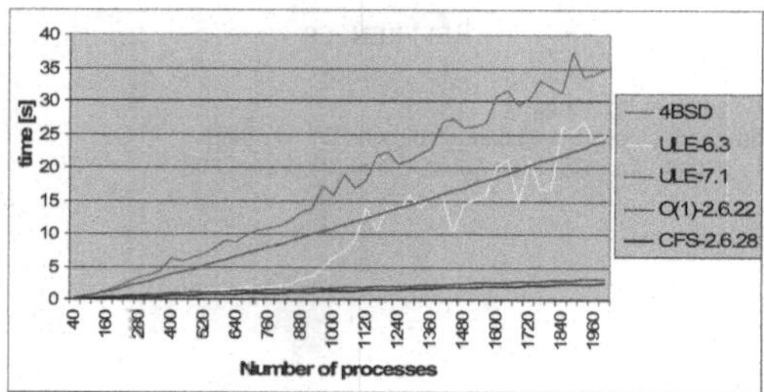

Fig. 4. Results of Hackbench benchmark (lower is better)

The curves of CFS and O(1) are very near to each other. To make it more visible, we show the results as the relative latency per process to CFS (Fig.5.). We can see, that O(1) nearest very slowly to CFS. In case of Pi-ping, the Л processes were CPU demanding, Hackbench processes are pure interactive. That is the reason why in PI-ping by already 500 processes O(1) performed better then CFS. CFS is designed to favoritism small and fast processes.

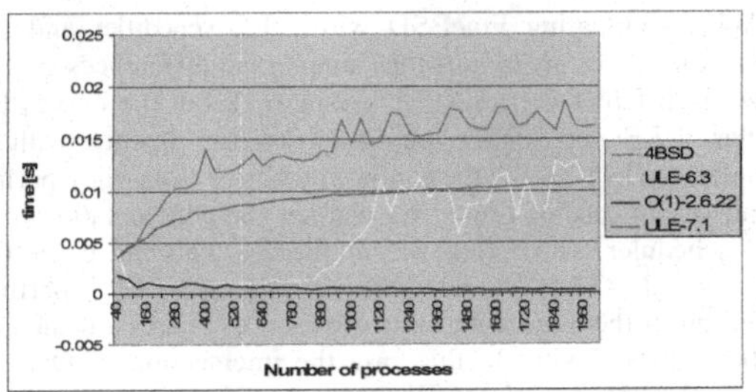

Fig. 5. Relative latency per process compared with CFS (lower is better)

VI. Conclusion

Using the PI-ping benchmark we were able to compare Linux and FreeBSD in both of problematic areas: latencies and throughput. The results were approved with the other benchmark called Hackbench.

We have also shown show that the complexity O(log n) of the CFS scheduler in Linux is not a handicap for real applications, and we can recommended also for embedded systems demanding real-time performance. Also the improvements of ULE scheduler made in the newer version of FreeBSD were approved. ULE in FreeBSD 7.1 performs better than long acting 4BSD and does not suffer the problems inspected by using this scheduler in FreeBSD 6.3.

Acknowledgment

This work was supported by the Grant No.1/0649/09 of the Slovak VEGA Grant Agency.

References

[1] Benchmark Programs. http://elinux.org/Benchmark_Programs [27.09.2009]

[2] L. Jelinek, *Jadro systemu Linux*, Computer press, 2008

[3] Sanjoy Baruah and Joel Goossens, "Scheduling Real-Time Tasks: Algorithms and Complexity", in *Handbook of Scheduling: Algorithms, Models and Performance Analysis*, Chapman & Hall/CRC, 2004

[4] C. Williams, "Linux Scheduler Latency" http://www.linuxdevices.com/articles/AT8906594941.html [27.09.2009]

[5] I. Molnar, "This is the CFS Scheduler" http://people.redhat.com/mingo/cfs-scheduler/sched-design-CFS.txt [27.09.2009]

[6] G. Ben-Yossef, "Soft, hard and ruby hard real time with Linux http://www.scribd.com/doc/3469938/Soft-hard-and-ruby-hard-real-time-with-Linux [27.09.2009]

[7] K. Kennaway, "Introducing FreeBSD 7.0" http://people.freebsd.org/~kris/scaling/7.0%20Preview.pdf [27.01.2009]

[8] J. Abaffy, "Interrupt Latency in Linux 2.6", in *Informatics and Information Technologies Student Research Conference 2008*, Vydavatelstvo STU, 2008, pp. 387-393

[9] J. Abaffy, "Performance Comparison of OS Schedulers on Symmetric Multiprocessors", in *Informatics and Information Technologies Student Research Conference 2009*, Vydavatelstvo STU, 2009, pp. 277-283

[10] J. Abaffy, T. Krajčovič, "Latencies in Linux and FreeBSD kernels with different schedulers - O(1), CFS, 4BSD, ULE.", in *Proceedings of the 2nd International Multi-Conference on Engineering and Technological Innovation*, IIIS, 2009, pp. 110-115

[11] Y. Etsion, D. Tsafrir, D. G. Feitelson, "Desktop scheduling: how can we know what the user wants?", in *Proceedings of the 14th international Workshop on Network and Operating Systems Support For Digital Audio and Video* (Cork, Ireland, June 16 - 18, 2004). NOSSDAV '04. ACM, New York, NY, pp. 110-115

[12] L. Nussbaum, O. Richard, "Lightweight emulation to study peer-to-peer systems," In *Parallel and Distributed Processing Symposium*, , 2006, pp. 454

[13] L. Nussbaum, O. Richard, "The current methods used to test and study peer-to-peer systems". in *Proceedings 20th IEEE International Parallel & Distributed Processing Symposium*, 2006, pp. 454

[14] J. Roberson, "ULE: A Modern Scheduler For FreeBSD", in *Proceedings of BSDCon '03*, USENIX Association, 2009

[15] M. J. Bach, *The Design of the UNIX Operating System*, Prentice Hall PTR., 1986

[16] A. S. Tanenbaum, Operating *Systems: Design and Implementation*, Prentice Hall, 1987

[17] C. Izurieta, J. Bieman, "The evolution of FreeBSD and Linux". In *Proceedings of the 2006 ACM/IEEE international Symposium on Empirical Software Engineering*, ACM, 2006, pp. 204-211

[18] E. Grochowski, R. Ronen, J. Shen, H. Wang "Best of Both Latency and Throughput", In *Proceedings of the IEEE international Conference on Computer Design,* IEEE Computer Society, 2004, pp. 236-243.

Towards Archetypes-Based Software Development

Gunnar Piho[a,b], Mart Roost[a], David Perkins[b], Jaak Tepandi[a]
[a] Department of Informatics, Tallinn University of Technology, Raja St. 15, Tallinn 12617, Estonia
[b] Clinical and Biomedical Proteomics Group, CRUK, LIMM, St James's Univ. Hospital, Beckett St, Leeds LS9 7TF, UK

Abstract. **We present a framework for the archetypes based engineering of domains, requirements and software (Archetypes-Based Software Development, ABD). An archetype is defined as a primordial object that occurs consistently and universally in business domains and in business software systems. An archetype pattern is a collaboration of archetypes. Archetypes and archetype patterns are used to capture conceptual information into domain specific models that are utilized by ABD. The focus of ABD is on software factories - family-based development artefacts (domain specific languages, patterns, frameworks, tools, micro processes, and others) that can be used to build the family members. We demonstrate the usage of ABD for developing laboratory information management system (LIMS) software for the Clinical and Biomedical Proteomics Group, at the Leeds Institute of Molecular Medicine, University of Leeds.**

I. Introduction

Software factory [1] is a domain specific RAD (Rapid Application Development) which applies traditional manufacturing techniques and principles to software development and captures a configuration of languages, patterns, frameworks, and tools. A crucial innovation of the software factory is a software product line [2] which captures knowledge about domains.

In the research work on archetypes based development, we investigate the research topics posed by Björner, [3] by combining the software engineering triptych [4; 5; 6] methodology with archetypes and the archetype patterns (A&AP) initiative by Arlow and Neustadt [7]. According to the software engineering triptych, in order to develop software we must first informally or formally describe the domain ($\mathfrak{D}$); then we must somehow derive the requirements ($\mathfrak{R}$) from these domain descriptions; and finally from these requirements we must determine software design specifications and implement the software ($\mathfrak{S}$), so that $\mathfrak{D}, \mathfrak{S} \models \mathfrak{R}$ (meaning the software is correct) holds [3]. According to Arlow & Neustadt [7], a business archetype pattern is a collaboration of business archetypes, where a business archetype is a "*primordial thing that occurs consistently and universally in business domains and in business software systems*". The archetype patterns, proposed by Arlow & Neustadt [7], are party, party relationship, product, order, inventory, quantity, money and rule. The main hypothesis of our studies in question are that archetypes and archetype patterns based software development: (a) increases dependability [8] of developed software; (b) reduces semantic heterogeneity [9] of models and data types; (c) improves the maturity [10] of the software development process; (d) is suitable for small and medium sized software houses; and (e) leads development of one-off software towards software factory [1].

In section II we give an overview of the ABD (archetypes based development) process we use for developing LIMS (laboratory information management system) software for the Clinical and Biomedical Proteomics Group, at the Leeds Institute of Molecular Medicine, University of Leeds. In section III (case study) we describe our current results in using the ABD method when developing the LIMS for the proteomics laboratory mentioned above. The ABD method and contribution is evaluated in the conclusions and discussions section.

II. Archetypes Based Development

The main target of ABD is RAD of product families. While general-purpose RAD uses logical information about the software captured by general-purpose development artefacts, the ABD uses conceptual information captured by domain specific models. ABD focuses on software factories i.e. on family-based development artefacts (domain specific languages, patterns, frameworks, tools, micro processes, and others) that can be used to build the family members.

A. Example of ABD

The following is an informal interpretation of ABD. We exemplify the ABD by using a domain of quantity. A quantity (for example "10 kilometres") is a measure. We can: (a) compare two quantities; (b) perform arithmetic operations with quantities; (c) round a quantity; and (d) convert a quantity from one unit to another. The simple narratives (structured and valid statements in natural language) [4] about the quantity can be as follows:

N.1. There are sorts, i.e., a types of *Quantity*, *Measure*, *Unit* and *Real*;

N.2. With *quantity* we can associate, i.e., we can observe:

N.2.1. The *unit* (*centimetre* for example) in which the quantity is measured;

N.2.2. The *amount* (1.86 for example), which is the numerical value of measurement;

N.3. With *unit* we can associate, i.e., we can observe:

N.3.1. The *measure* (distance for example) – means physical measure which has been measured;

N.3.2. The *factor* (for example 0.01 if talking about *centimetre* and if we take *metre* as a base unit for the distance measure) – the number which shows how many base units the particular unit is equal to;

N.4. We can define *arithmetic*, *comparing*, *rounding* and *converting* operations with quantity

T. Sobh, K. Elleithy (eds.), *Innovations in Computing Sciences and Software Engineering*,
DOI 10.1007/978-90-481-9112-3_97,

The domain model of quantity we designed (Fig.1.) is slightly different from the domain model of quantity described by Arlow and Neustadt [7]. There are no concrete measures, units and unit converting factors (or converting algorithms, for example in the case of converting Julian date to seconds) in our domain model ($\mathfrak{D}$) of quantity.

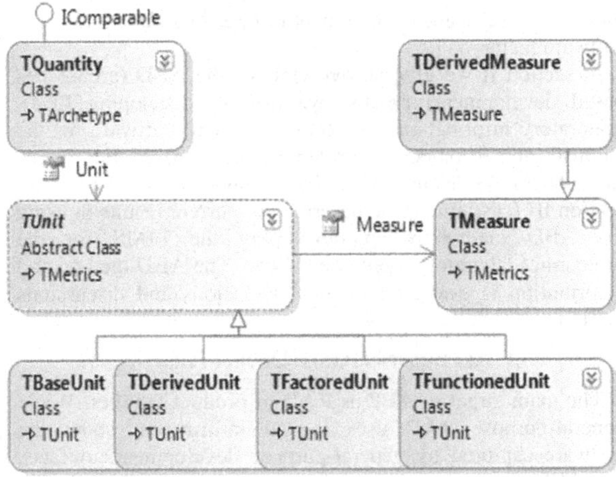

Fig. 1. Domain model of quantity

These concrete measures, units and factors are derived from particular software requirements ($\mathfrak{R}$). For instance, if area, volume and speed are needed as measures, we can formalize these requirements (in C# like pseudo-code) as follows:

Initially, by *RegisterMeasure* function, we are registering two base measures (*Distance* and *Time*) by defining their names and symbols accordingly.

```
//Measures - units must be defined
TMeasure Distance = RegisterMeasure("Distance", "s");
TMeasure Time = RegisterMeasure ("Time", "t");
```

Next, we are registering three derived measures (*Speed*, *Acceleration* and *Area*) by defining their names, symbols and formulas.

```
//Derived measures - units must not be defined
TMeasure Speed = RegisterMeasure( "Speed", "v", Distance, 1, Time, -1);
TMeasure Acceleration = RegisterMeasure("Acceleration", "a", Speed, 1, Time, -1);
TMeasure Area = RegisterMeasure("Area", "A", Distance, 2);
```

Finally, by the *RegisterUnit* function, we have to register all necessary units for all the base measures by defining their names, symbols and factors.

```
// Distance units
TUnit Meters = RegisterUnit( Distance, "Meters", "m", 1,0);
TUnit Microns = RegisterUnit( Distance, "Microns", "", 1E-6);
TUnit Millimeters = RegisterUnit( Distance, "Millimeters", "mm", 0.001);
...
// Time units
TUnit Seconds = RegisterUnit( Time, "Seconds", "sec", 1.0);
TUnit MilliSeconds = RegisterUnit( Time, "MilliSeconds","ms", 0.001);
```

The above mentioned is all that is required in order to have software ($\mathfrak{S}$), which is able to convert all the area, volume and speed (also distance and time) units from one particular unit to another. It also performs all arithmetic operations with physical measures. For instance, divides meters with seconds and gives the answer in kilometres per hour.

The correctness of software ($\mathfrak{D}, \mathfrak{S} \models \mathfrak{R}$) according to some particular requirement (for example converting "kilometres per hour" to "meters per second") we can validate by simple unit tests [11].

B. ABD Process Model

The ABD process model we use is based on the software engineering triptych [4; 5; 6] model and roughly consists of the following:

- We analyze the domain by Björners domain analysis methodology [6] and use A&AP [7] as the meta-model when developing the domain models. All models we developed are software artefacts (not only documentation artefacts) and are realized as .NET class libraries by using TDD [11] methodology;
- We investigate possibilities to use these domain models as the "ubiquitous language" [12] for prescribing (formalizing) requirements from customers. The aim, is to validate customer requirements according to the domain models;
- We investigate possibilities to generate the software by using domain models and formalized (according to this domain model) requirements. Our aim is to verify the generated software according to the requirements and to the domain model.

The Björner's domain analysis method [6] is based on domain stakeholders and on pragmatically chosen domain facets. Domain facets we use in domain analysis are intrinsic, business processes, supporting technologies, management and organization, rules and regulations, scripts and human behaviour.

C. Archetype Patterns

The following is a short description of archetype patterns described by Arlow and Neustad [7].

The *party archetype pattern* abstracts an identifiable and addressable unit that may have a legal status and that has some autonomous control over its actions. The *party relationship archetype pattern*, capturing a fact about semantic relationship between two parties in which each party plays a specific role, abstracts the relationships between parties. The *CRM* (customer relationship management) *archetype pattern* concretizes the party relationship archetype and abstracts features needed for customer management. The *product archetype pattern* abstracts product features and product related activities. The *inventory archetype pattern* abstracts a collection of inventory entities held in the stock by a business. The *order archetype pattern* abstracts selling as well as buying orders; the *rule archetype pattern* abstracts constraints on the operations of the business; and the *quantity* as well as the *money archetype patterns* abstract representatively physical measures and money.

D. Archetype Patterns as the Meta-model

We use A&AP described by Artlow and Neustadt as the meta-model for domain models. The reason we use these, and not similar initiatives from Fowler [13], Hay [14], or Silverston [15], is that we found the A&AP is harmonious with the triadic model of activity [16] (Fig.2).

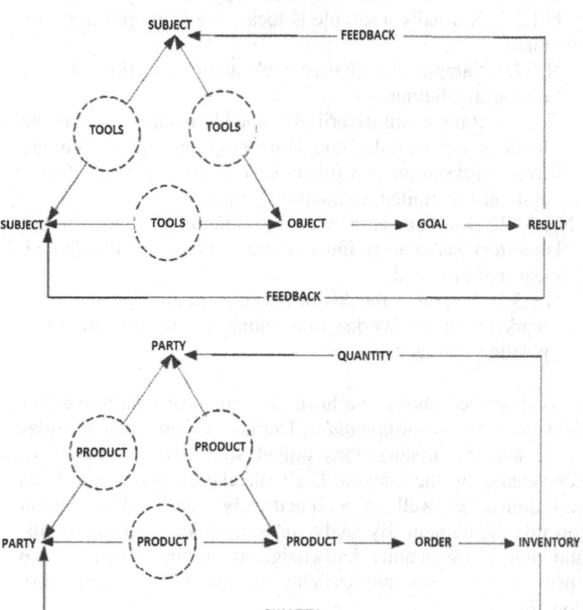

Fig. 2. Triadic model and its A&AP analogue

The triadic model of activity is used as a theoretical base in industrial-organizational psychology to describe human work, mind, culture, and activity. With the triadic model, all activities will be performed either by one or more subjects. So, the party archetype pattern is required. The product archetype pattern is also needed since when performing activities, the subjects can use tools (some product or service) and the outcome of activity is some object (also product or service). Each activity is triggered by a goal which in a business domain is some kind of order from a client - so the order archetype pattern is also essential. Each activity has a result, which in businesses will be a record in the inventory list - hence, the inventory archetype pattern is needed. From the inventory list the subject (manager, etc) gets feedback about the business activities. In businesses the feedback will be measured mainly by money or by some other physical measure - therefore, the quantity archetype pattern is also required. Finally, the arrows in Fig.2 are rules describing different conditions which must be followed. So, the rule archetype pattern is necessary

Fig.3 illustrates how we use A&AP in domain analysis and in domain engineering.

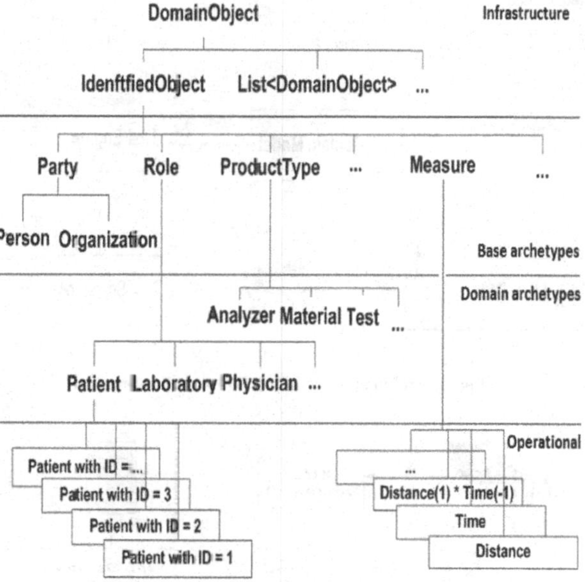

Fig. 3. A&AP as the meta-model

We have infrastructure, archetypes and operational layers. The operational layer represents customer requirements or customer data. An example of customer data are patient objects; examples of customer requirements are measures (objects). The knowledge about the customer data and requirements resides in archetypes (classes). Some archetypes (base) are universal and common for all businesses (party, measure, etc), but some archetypes are domain specific. Patient, analyzer, and test are laboratory (healthcare) specific archetypes. Different software, hardware, platform and related knowledge are encapsulated into infrastructure classes.

III. LIMS Software and LIMS Software Factory

The LIMS (laboratory information management system) software factory is the case study for the research, where the A&AP based techniques for the modelling, specifying and validating of domains, requirements and software will be evaluated and tested. The principal schema of components of the planned software factory for clinical laboratory software is illustrated in Fig. 4. The principal LIMS software architecture (borrowed from Helander [17 pp. 467-477]), which we generate by using the LIMS software factory, is shown in Fig.5. The working prototype of the domain model of the

LIMS factory (Fig.4) is almost complete and we are currently testing this domain model in a real laboratory environment (Clinical and Biomedical Proteomics Group, Leeds Institute of Molecular Medicine, University of Leeds) with real requirements.

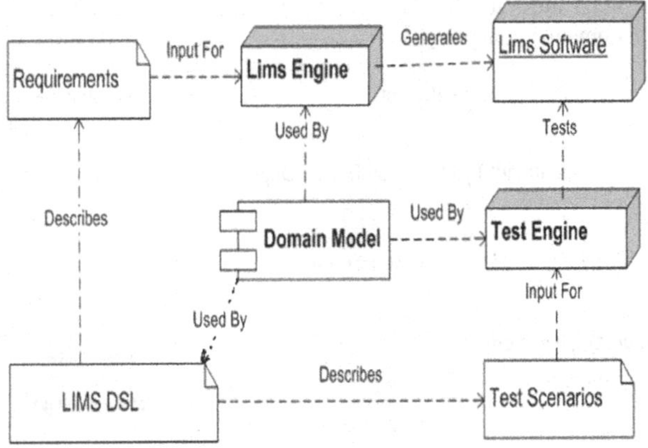

Fig. 4. Architecture of LIMS Software Factory

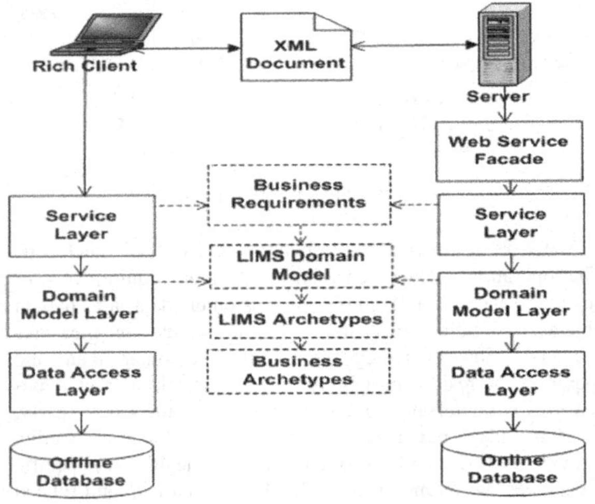

Fig. 5. Architecture of LIMS Software

In the current stage of the project, we have focused on the domain model layer (domain of clinical laboratory) and on the service layer (requirements of individual laboratories). We used the domain development methodology introduced by Dines Björner [4; 5; 6] when we implemented the domain model of laboratory. The terminology and the laboratory workflow description have been taken from the LIMS standard guide [17].

For example, we decided to take a sample, workstation and rack as an intrinsic (phenomena and concepts of a domain, which are basic to any other domain facet) of a clinical laboratory, and we described a clinical laboratory domain as a domain of sample management. The following narratives summarize clinical laboratory intrinsic:

N.1. Laboratory consists of one or more workstations; zero or more samples; and zero or more racks.
- N.1.1. Sample is an uniquely identified small piece of material (serum, urine, etc) in a tube;
  - N.1.1.1. Sample event describes a notable occurrence (logging - collecting can precede or follow, storing, distributing - can include taking aliquots, measuring, breaking - accident, disposing, waste removing) in the lifecycle of sample and must be trailed for auditing purposes.
- N.1.2. Rack is an uniquely identified container for samples;
  - N.1.2.1. Rack has a fixed number of positions for samples;
  - N.1.2.2. Normally a sample is located in some position of a rack;
  - N.1.2.3. Sample can change rack and/or position of rack during its lifetime;
  - N.1.2.4. Rack event describes a notable occurrence (sample loading, sample unloading, conversion of samples, moving from workstation to workstation) in the lifecycle of rack and must be trailed for auditing purposes.
- N.1.3. Workstation is a uniquely identified place in the laboratory (laboratory unit) where samples are distributed, measured or stored;
  - N.1.3.1. A sample resides in a workstation or moves from workstation to workstation alone or resides in some position of a rack.

As described above, we have also composed narratives for laboratory domain ***stakeholder***. Domain stakeholders are roles of persons or organizations united somehow in interest or dependency on the domain. Each stakeholder has some rights and duties, as well as a specifically identified viewpoint towards the domain. By analyzing stakeholders' views, rights, and duties, we acquire knowledge about the domain. Fig.6 abstracts the roles parties play in the clinical laboratory domain.

Other clinical laboratory domain facets we have analyzed are:

- **Business process** is a procedurally describable aspect of how a laboratory operates when manipulating the entities of the laboratory domain. The main business process in laboratory is sample management.
- Examples of **rules and regulations** in a laboratory are ambient temperature, sample temperature, sample age, sample volume and so on. Some rules and regulations, which have some legally binding power and may be contested in a court of law, are **scripts**. Examples of important scripts in clinical laboratory are RiliBÄK and Westgard QC, which can be used (depending on country) to regulate quality control procedures in a laboratory.
- **Support technology** is a way and means of implementing certain observed phenomena in a laboratory. Much work in a laboratory is done by machines called analyzers. Analyzers as

well as workstations are operated by MTSs (medical technical assistants) and are maintained (repairing and supplying requisites are included) by suppliers.

• **Management and organization** is the organization layout and the way a person is allowed to manipulate laboratory entities. When laboratory management mostly includes the process of determining and formulating rules and regulations, the laboratory organization is the structuring of staff, chains of command, and chains of reporting, liabilities as well as responsibilities. Laboratory organization also includes the working conditions (work shift, reporting periods, reporting terms, working hours…) of an organization.

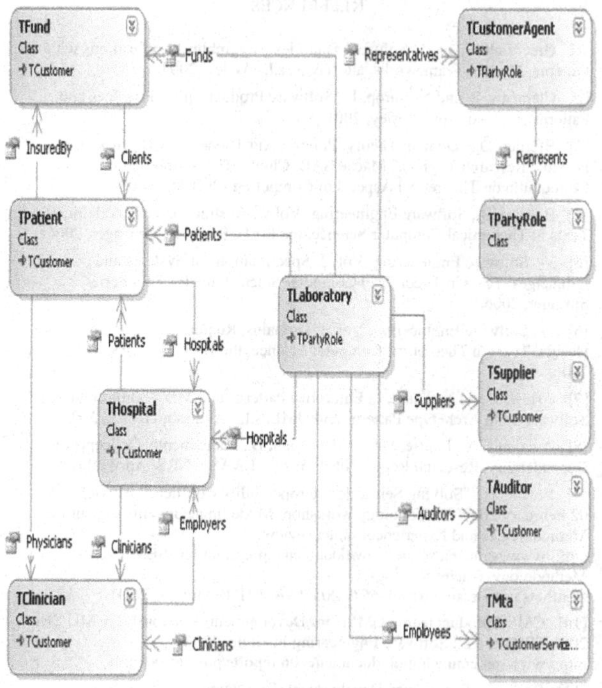

Fig. 6. Clinical Laboratory Stakeholders Abstraction

• **Human behaviour** is a quality spectrum (careful, diligent, accurate, sloppy, delinquent, criminal, etc) of carrying out assigned work by employees.

For each of these domain facets the narratives have been formulated. Based on these laboratory narratives we have modelled laboratory A&AP and have formalized them as .NET APIs in C#. Fig.7 illustrates the party archetype pattern of clinical laboratory. These APIs reside in the domain model (Fig. 4) of laboratory software factory and are used by LIMS DSL to prescribe LIMS requirements from some particular laboratory, similar to section "Example of ABD".

The following is the main list of tasks (for most tasks we have some preliminary working prototype) in our LIMS Software Factory project.

- Implementation of A&AP: critical analysis of A&AP; realization of A&AP API by using TDD (test driven development);
- Implementation of the domain model of a clinical laboratory: identification and acquisition of clinical laboratory domain knowledge; abstraction of clinical laboratory domain knowledge in terms of A&AP; realization of clinical laboratory domain model as an API by using of A&AP and TDD;
- Implementation of LIMS software factory (models, frameworks, tools, and languages): based on A&AP API and on clinical laboratory domain model API; implementation of the LIMS software factory framework (Fig 5.); implementation of DSL (Domain Specific Language) to identify custom requirements; verify; and to validate these custom requirements according to the laboratory domain model and A&AP API; implementation of tools to generate the UI as well as database schemas;
- Formalizing the custom requirements and partly generating LIMS software according to custom requirements by using the LIMS software factory.

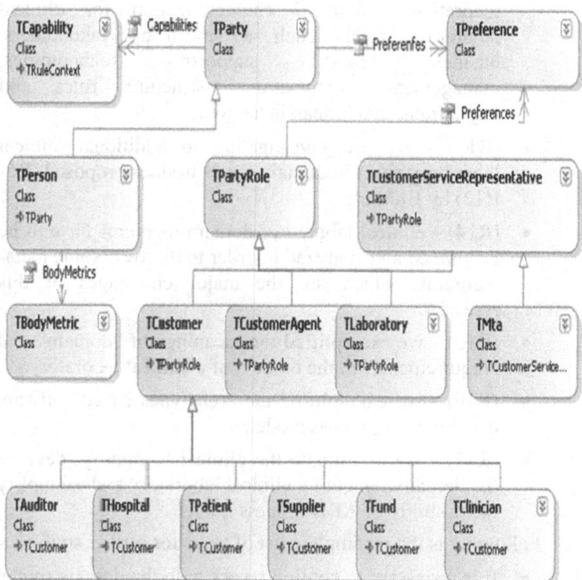

Fig. 7. Clinical laboratory Party archetype pattern

IV. Conclusion and Discussions

We described our ongoing research in analyzing the domain of a clinical laboratory and implementing the clinical LIMS software factory. The current hypothesis is that A&AP can be used as a base when modelling the business domains. We speculate, that the archetypes based approach: (a) is usable in small and medium sized software houses; (b) improves the maturity of software development in terms of CMMI [10]; (c) reduces semantic heterogeneity [9] of models and data types; (d) increases the dependability [8] of developed software; as well as (e) leads developed software towards the software factory [1]. We investigate domain and software engineering research topics described by Björner [3] in 2007 as below:

- (R1) - we exemplified the $\mathfrak{D}, \mathfrak{S} \Vdash \mathfrak{R}$ relation (from the domain model via requirement to software) in a real project: we implemented the domain model of the laboratory as an API by using domain modelling and TDD methods; used this API as the language for formulating requirements; and we work towards to generating the LIMS software according to these requirements;
- (R2) - we exemplified the lifting of domains by using business A&AP when implementing laboratory specific A&AP and by using laboratory A&AP when implementing clinical laboratory A&AP;
- (R3, R4) - we have preliminary results by generating the UI and database schemas not from client requirements, but from infrastructure and base archetypes;
- (R5 – R12) - our investigation leans towards the theoretically founded characterization for clinical laboratory facets such as intrinsic, stakeholders, business process, supporting technologies, management, organizational structure, rules and regulations, and human behaviour;
- (R13) - we are investigating to additional clinical laboratory specific domain facets besides proposed (R5-R12) by Björner;
- (R14) - clinical laboratory domain theorems have to be developed and analyzed in order to discover some meta-theorems, which are the major challenges of this research;
- (R15) - we exemplified the meanings of "domain" and "requirements" in the context of a clinical laboratory;
- (R16) - we exemplified the archetypes based software development process model;
- (R17) - we investigate the clinical laboratory, develop the domain model of a clinical laboratory and exemplify the usability of ABD process model.

Following is the incomplete list of tasks for further study:

- It is necessary to continue work with the domain model of a clinical laboratory (complete, analyze, formalize and verify the validity and especially the usability);
- Investigation of the influence and the place of communication protocols describing data transfer between: (a) LIMS and laboratory equipment [20; 21]; (b) health care systems (for example between LIMS and hospital information system [22]) is also essential;
- Future developments of domain specific language based on the domain model of a clinical laboratory for describing requirements and test scenarios (Fig. 4) are needed;
- Furthermore, future developments of LIMS Engine and Test Engine (Fig. 4) are also required;
- Influence of open EHR [17] (EHR - Electronic Health Records) community as well as HL7 [18] community works has to be studied and compared.

ACKNOWLEDGMENT

This work is supported by Estonian Science Foundation (grant 6839).

REFERENCES

[1] Greenfield, J., et al., Software Factories: Assembling Applications with Patterns, Models, Frameworks, and Tools. s.l. : Wiley, 2004.

[2] Clements, P. and Northrop, L., Software Product Lines: Practices and Patterns. s.l. : Addison-Wesley, 2001.

[3] Björner, D., "Domain Theory: Practice and Theories (A Discussion of Possible Research Topics)." Macau SAR, China : The 4thInternational Colloquium on Theoretical Aspects of Computing - ICTAC, 2007.

[4] Björner, D., Software Engineering, Vol. 1: Abstraction and Modelling. Texts in Theoretical Computer Science, the EATCS Series. : Springer, 2006.

[5] —. Software Engineering, Vol. 2: Specifications of Systems and Languages. Texts in Theoretical Computer Science, the EATCS Series. : Springer, 2006.

[6] —. Software Engineering, Vol. 3: Domains, Requirements, and Software Design. Texts in Theoretical Computer Science, the EATCS Series. : Springer, 2006.

[7] Arlow, J. and Neustadt, I., Enterprise Patterns and MDA: Building Better Software With Archetype Patterns and UML. s.l. : Addisson-Wesly, 2003.

[8] Avizienis, A., Laprie, J.-C. and Randell, B., Fundamental Concepts of Dependability. Research Report N01145. s.l. : LAAS-CNRS, April 2001.

[9] Wache, H., "Solving Semantic Interoperability Conflicts." Brussel : s.n., 02 February 2009. Methodology workshop: Modelling eGovernment entities Methodologies and Experiences under review. http://www.semic.eu/semic/view/documents/presentations/SEMIC-EU-Methodology-Wache-Solving-Conflicts.pdf;jsessionid=A065C6F205788A2F1E4E3366E9F24D10.

[10] CMMI product team., CMMI for Development, Version 1.2, CMU/SEI-2006-TR-008. s.l. : Software Engineering Institute, 2007. http://www.sei.cmu.edu/pub/documents/06.reports/pdf/06tr008.pdf.

[11] Beck, K., Test-Driven Development: By Example. Boston, MA : Addison-Wesley, 2003.

[12] Evans, E., Domain-Driven Design: Talking Complexity in the Heart of Software. Boston, MA : Addison-Wesley, 2004.

[13] Fowler, M., Analysis Patterns: Reusable Object Models. s.l. : Addison-Wesley, 2005.

[14] Hay, D. C., Data Model Patterns: Conventions of Thought. s.l. : Dorset House Publishing, 1996.

[15] Silverston, L., The Data Model Resource Book 1. A Library of Universal Data Models for All Enterprises. s.l. : Wiley, 2001. Vol. 1.

[16] Bendy, G.Z. and Harris, S.R., "The Systematic-Structural Theory of Activity: Applications to the Study of Human Work." Mind, Culture, and Activity. 2005, Vol. 12, 2, pp. 128-147.

[17] ASTM., E1578-06 Standard Guide for Laboratory Information Management Systems (LIMS). s.l. : ASTM International, 2006.

[18] openEHR., openEHR website. [Online] http://www.openehr.org/home.html.

[19] HL7., Health Level 7 (HL7) . [Online] http://www.hl7.org .

Dependability Aspects Regarding the Cache Level of a Memory Hierarchy Using Hamming Codes

*O. Novac, *St. Vari-Kakas, *Mihaela Novac, *Ecaterina Vladu and **Liliana Indrie

*University of Oradea, Faculty of Electrical Engineering and Information Technology,
** University of Oradea, Faculty of Textiles and Leatherworks,
1, Universităţii Str., Oradea, Romania, email: ovnovac@uoradea.ro

***Abstract*-In this paper we will apply a SEC-DED code to the cache level of a memory hierarchy. From the category of SEC-DED (Single Error Correction Double Error Detection) codes we select the Hamming code. For correction of single-bit error we use a syndrome decoder, a syndrome generator and the check bits generator circuit.**

I. Introduction

Cache memory is a fundamental component of all modern microprocessors. Caches provide for efficient read/write access to memory, and their reliability is essential to assure dependable computing. Among the primary threats to cache reliability are soft (transient) errors. When incident in a cache, these errors can corrupt data values or result in invalid state, and can easily propagate throughout the system to cause data integrity issues. In most modern processors, a significant portion of the chip area is dedicated to the L2 cache. In this paper, we examine the vulnerability (on a per bit basis) of different components of on-chip L2 caches, including data and tag bits.

There are many possible fault types in cache memories (that reduce the reliability): Permanent faults (Stuck-at, Short, Open-line, Bridging, Stuck-open, Indetermination), Transient faults, and Intermittent faults, [1]. Anothert metod to solve the problem of faults is the method of testing/correcting errors inside the chip, [2]. If we will use a error correcting code inside the chip, we will obtain memory chips with high reliability, low cost and greater memory capacity, [3]. We must give a special attention, if we use this technique, at the size of the memory chip when we test and correct the memory cells, and we must take count of additional cells for testing bits, [4], [5]. Correction of single error in the cache level of a memory hierarchy, is a correction of single error at parallel transfer and data memorizing, this correction can be done using the scheme presented in figure 3.

In figure 1, we present a typical memory hierarchy. Proceeding down the memory hierarchy, its reliability improves owing to the storage technology in different levels. There is of course a tradeoff between high reliability and performance, which is influenced beside the construction, by the transfer policy used among levels. A straightforward possibility is to *write through* to the most reliable, lowest level every time a data is transmitted from the CPU. This policy offers good reliability, but bad performance (high overhead for transferring data). On the other extreme, there is possible to *write back* data to lower level only when needed (for instance based on the amount of data in a level). This method yields a more reduced reliability (as data stays longer in a less reliable level), but better performance (less overhead for transferring data). At last, the third possibility is the *delayed write*, when data is written from level L to level L+1 after a time denoted $delay_L$. This is an acceptable compromise between the previous two methods and we will consider only this policy from this point forward.

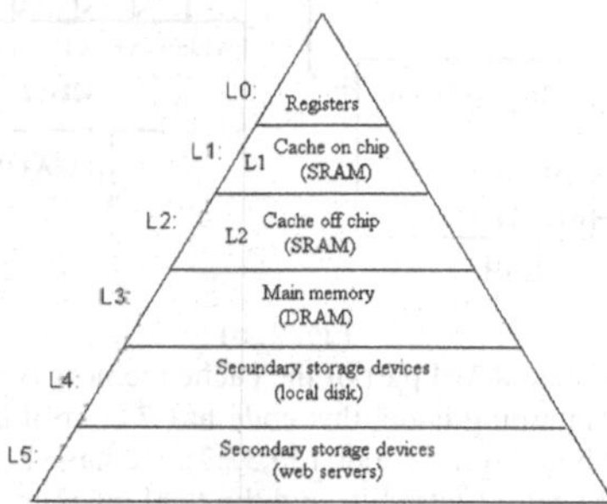

Fig. 1 Memory hierarchy

In modern computer systems, at the cache level of the memory hierarchy, we can succesfuly apply multiple error correction codes. This codes for detection and correction of errors are added to memories to obtain a better dependability. In high speed memories the most used codes are Single bit Error Correcting and Double bit Error Detection codes (SEC-DED), [6]. This codes can be implemented in parallel as linear codes for this type of memories. We have choose this Hamming code, because his properties. An important application of this code is in recovery from multiple errors. This is done with an automatic reconfiguration technique that uses the concept of address skewing to disperse such multiple errors into correctable errors. This Hamming code, makes the hardware and the speed of the encoding/decoding circuit optimal. Matrix H is presented above in figure 3.

T. Sobh, K. Elleithy (eds.), *Innovations in Computing Sciences and Software Engineering*,
DOI 10.1007/978-90-481-9112-3_98, © Springer Science+Business Media B.V. 2010

II. Block Diagramn Of A Cache Memory

În figure 2.a) is presented the block diagram of cache memory. This block diagram is presented because we want to present how is splited the cache memory in two parts. First part presented in figure 2.a) is the cache Tag memory (also named Tag RAM), and the second

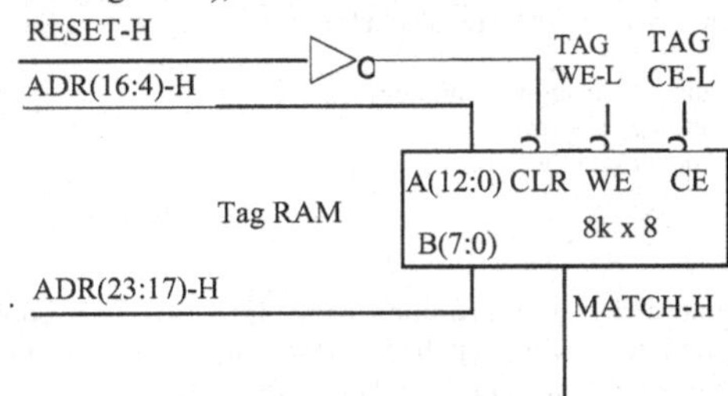

Fig. 2.a)

part, presented in figure 2. b) is the cache RAM memory.

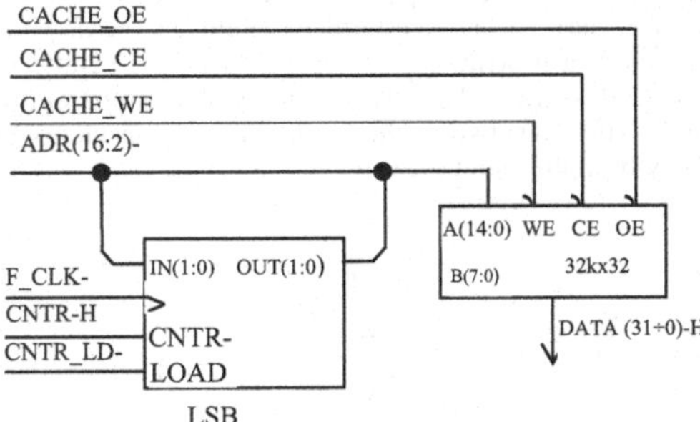

Fig. 2. b)

For the Cache RAM part of the cache memory we will use a (39,32,7), Hamming code, this code has 7 control bits and 32 data useful bits. For this code (39,32,7), we have k = 7 control bits, u = 32 useful (data) bits and the total number of code is t = 39. In this case for correcting single bit error, between this two values, u and k, we have satisfied the condition, $2^k > u+k+1$. Usualy it is enough a number of k= 6 control bits, but we will use k = 7 control bits, the last bit is used for double bit error detection.

The Hsiao code used for the part of cache RAM, is defined by matrix H, given by (1):

(1)

Fig. 3. Hamming Matrix

A typical codeword, of this matrix has the folowing form: $u=(c_0c_1c_2c_3c_4c_5c_6u_0u_1u_2u_3u_4u_5u_6u_7u_8u_9u_{10}u_{11}u_{12}u_{13}u_{14}u_{15}u_{16}u_{17}u_{18}u_{19}u_{20}u_{21}u_{22}u_{23}u_{24}u_{25}u_{26}u_{27}u_{28}u_{29}u_{30}u_{31})$ and has parities in position 1,2,3,4,5,6 and 7 and data bits elsewhere (from position 8 to 39). We have select for matrix H, this placement for 1's and 0's to obtain well-balanced equations for control bits. H matrix has on first six rows and six columns a unit matrix, and in continuare this matrix is constructed fromn columns with odd number of 1's and is equal to 3 or 5.

Control bits are calculated by the parity equations:

$$
\begin{aligned}
c_0&=u_0\oplus u_2\oplus u_6\oplus u_7\oplus u_8\oplus u_{13}\oplus u_{14}\oplus u_{15}\oplus u_{18}\oplus u_{21}\oplus u_{25}\oplus u_{27}\oplus u_{28}\oplus u_{29}\oplus u_{31}\\
c_1&=u_0\oplus u_1\oplus u_3\oplus u_7\oplus u_8\oplus u_9\oplus u_{15}\oplus u_{16}\oplus u_{19}\oplus u_{21}\oplus u_{22}\oplus u_{26}\oplus u_{28}\oplus u_{29}\oplus u_{31}\\
c_2&=u_1\oplus u_2\oplus u_4\oplus u_8\oplus u_9\oplus u_{10}\oplus u_{16}\oplus u_{17}\oplus u_{20}\oplus u_{22}\oplus u_{23}\oplus u_{27}\oplus u_{28}\oplus u_{29}\oplus u_{30}\oplus u_{31}\\
c_3&=u_2\oplus u_3\oplus u_5\oplus u_9\oplus u_{10}\oplus u_{11}\oplus u_{14}\oplus u_{17}\oplus u_{18}\oplus u_{21}\oplus u_{23}\oplus u_{24}\oplus u_{28}\oplus u_{30}\oplus u_{31} \quad (2)\\
c_4&=u_3\oplus u_4\oplus u_6\oplus u_{10}\oplus u_{11}\oplus u_{12}\oplus u_{15}\oplus u_{18}\oplus u_{19}\oplus u_{22}\oplus u_{24}\oplus u_{25}\oplus u_{28}\oplus u_{30}\oplus u_{31}\\
c_5&=u_0\oplus u_4\oplus u_5\oplus u_{11}\oplus u_{12}\oplus u_{13}\oplus u_{15}\oplus u_{19}\oplus u_{20}\oplus u_{23}\oplus u_{25}\oplus u_{26}\oplus u_{29}\oplus u_{30}\oplus u_{31}\\
c_6&=u_1\oplus u_5\oplus u_6\oplus u_7\oplus u_{12}\oplus u_{13}\oplus u_{14}\oplus u_{17}\oplus u_{20}\oplus u_{24}\oplus u_{26}\oplus u_{27}\oplus u_{29}\oplus u_{30}\oplus u_{31}
\end{aligned}
$$

The decoding of a received vector uses the syndrome equations, which are based on (2), and are given as follows (3):

$$
\begin{aligned}
s_0&=c_0\oplus u_0\oplus u_2\oplus u_6\oplus u_7\oplus u_8\oplus u_{13}\oplus u_{14}\oplus u_{15}\oplus u_{18}\oplus u_{21}\oplus u_{25}\oplus u_{27}\oplus u_{28}\oplus u_{29}\oplus u_{31}\\
s_1&=c_1\oplus u_0\oplus u_1\oplus u_3\oplus u_7\oplus u_8\oplus u_9\oplus u_{15}\oplus u_{16}\oplus u_{19}\oplus u_{21}\oplus u_{22}\oplus u_{26}\oplus u_{28}\oplus u_{29}\oplus u_{31}\\
s_2&=c_2\oplus u_1\oplus u_2\oplus u_4\oplus u_8\oplus u_9\oplus u_{10}\oplus u_{16}\oplus u_{17}\oplus u_{20}\oplus u_{22}\oplus u_{23}\oplus u_{27}\oplus u_{28}\oplus u_{29}\oplus u_{30}\oplus u_{31}\\
s_3&=c_3\oplus u_2\oplus u_3\oplus u_5\oplus u_9\oplus u_{10}\oplus u_{11}\oplus u_{14}\oplus u_{17}\oplus u_{18}\oplus u_{21}\oplus u_{23}\oplus u_{24}\oplus u_{28}\oplus u_{30}\oplus u_{31} \quad (3)\\
s_4&=c_4\oplus u_3\oplus u_4\oplus u_6\oplus u_{10}\oplus u_{11}\oplus u_{12}\oplus u_{15}\oplus u_{18}\oplus u_{19}\oplus u_{22}\oplus u_{24}\oplus u_{25}\oplus u_{28}\oplus u_{30}\oplus u_{31}\\
s_5&=c_5\oplus u_0\oplus u_4\oplus u_5\oplus u_{11}\oplus u_{12}\oplus u_{13}\oplus u_{15}\oplus u_{19}\oplus u_{20}\oplus u_{23}\oplus u_{25}\oplus u_{26}\oplus u_{29}\oplus u_{30}\oplus u_{31}\\
s_6&=c_6\oplus u_1\oplus u_5\oplus u_6\oplus u_7\oplus u_{12}\oplus u_{13}\oplus u_{14}\oplus u_{17}\oplus u_{20}\oplus u_{24}\oplus u_{26}\oplus u_{27}\oplus u_{29}\oplus u_{30}\oplus u_{31}
\end{aligned}
$$

We will apply this SEC-DED code to cache RAM memory of the system with the capacity of 128K x 8 bits. When we will read the information from the cache RAM, we will read the useful data bits ($u_0\ u_1\ u_2\ u_3\ u_4\ u_5\ u_6\ u_7\ u_8\ u_9\ u_{10}\ u_{11}\ u_{12}\ u_{13}\ u_{14}\ u_{15}\ u_{16}\ u_{17}\ u_{18}\ u_{19}\ u_{420}\ u_{21}\ u_{22}\ u_{23}\ u_{24}\ u_{25}\ u_{26}\ u_{27}\ u_{28}\ u_{29}\ u_{30}\ u_{31}$) and also the control bits ($c_0\ c_1\ c_2\ c_3\ c_4\ c_5$). We will implement with XOR gates, the equations (2). We will generate the control bits c_0' c_1' c_2' c_3' c_4' c_5' and c_6', from data bits that we have read from the cache Tag. For example, to generate the control bit c_2', we will use the equation:

$$c_2=u_1\oplus u_2\oplus u_4\oplus u_8\oplus u_9\oplus u_{10}\oplus u_{16}\oplus u_{17}\oplus u_{20}\oplus u_{22}\oplus u_{23}\oplus u_{27}\oplus u_{28}\oplus u_{29}\oplus u_{30}\oplus u_{31}$$

and to implement this equation we will use 15 XOR gates with 2 inputs, situated on four levels, aspect presented in figure 4. We will do in the same mode to generate all control bits, $c_0', c_1', c_3', c_4', c_5', c_6'$. The generated control bits ($c_0' c_1' c_2' c_3' c_4' c_5' c_6'$) are compared with control bits that we have read from the cache RAM ($c_0 c_1 c_2 c_3 c_4 c_5 c_6$), also with 2 input XOR gates, and we get as result syndrome equations: $s_0 = c_0 \oplus c_0'$, $s_1 = c_1 \oplus c_1'$, $s_2 = c_2 \oplus c_2'$, $s_3 = c_3 \oplus c_3'$, $s_4 = c_4 \oplus c_4'$, $s_5 = c_5 \oplus c_5'$, $s_6 = c_6 \oplus c_6'$. We will connect 7 NOT gates, on each syndrome line, and we will construct with 32 AND gates with 7 inputs, the syndrome decoder. The equations to built the syndrome decoder are:

$$
\begin{aligned}
u'_0 &= s_0 \cdot s_1 \cdot \overline{s_2} \cdot \overline{s_3} \cdot \overline{s_4} \cdot s_5 \cdot \overline{s_6} \\
u'_1 &= \overline{s_0} \cdot s_1 \cdot s_2 \cdot \overline{s_3} \cdot \overline{s_4} \cdot \overline{s_5} \cdot s_6 \\
u'_2 &= s_0 \cdot \overline{s_1} \cdot s_2 \cdot s_3 \cdot \overline{s_4} \cdot \overline{s_5} \cdot \overline{s_6} \\
u'_3 &= \overline{s_0} \cdot s_1 \cdot \overline{s_2} \cdot s_3 \cdot s_4 \cdot \overline{s_5} \cdot \overline{s_6} \\
u'_4 &= \overline{s_0} \cdot \overline{s_1} \cdot s_2 \cdot \overline{s_3} \cdot s_4 \cdot s_5 \cdot \overline{s_6} \\
u'_5 &= \overline{s_0} \cdot \overline{s_1} \cdot \overline{s_2} \cdot s_3 \cdot \overline{s_4} \cdot s_5 \cdot s_6 \\
u'_6 &= s_0 \cdot \overline{s_1} \cdot \overline{s_2} \cdot \overline{s_3} \cdot s_4 \cdot \overline{s_5} \cdot s_6 \\
u'_7 &= s_0 \cdot s_1 \cdot \overline{s_2} \cdot \overline{s_3} \cdot \overline{s_4} \cdot \overline{s_5} \cdot s_6 \\
u'_8 &= s_0 \cdot s_1 \cdot s_2 \cdot \overline{s_3} \cdot \overline{s_4} \cdot \overline{s_5} \cdot \overline{s_6} \\
u'_9 &= \overline{s_0} \cdot s_1 \cdot s_2 \cdot s_3 \cdot \overline{s_4} \cdot \overline{s_5} \cdot \overline{s_6} \\
u'_{10} &= \overline{s_0} \cdot \overline{s_1} \cdot s_2 \cdot s_3 \cdot s_4 \cdot \overline{s_5} \cdot \overline{s_6} \\
u'_{11} &= \overline{s_0} \cdot \overline{s_1} \cdot \overline{s_2} \cdot s_3 \cdot s_4 \cdot s_5 \cdot \overline{s_6} \\
u'_{12} &= \overline{s_0} \cdot \overline{s_1} \cdot \overline{s_2} \cdot \overline{s_3} \cdot s_4 \cdot s_5 \cdot s_6 \\
u'_{13} &= s_0 \cdot \overline{s_1} \cdot \overline{s_2} \cdot \overline{s_3} \cdot \overline{s_4} \cdot s_5 \cdot s_6 \\
u'_{14} &= s_0 \cdot \overline{s_1} \cdot \overline{s_2} \cdot s_3 \cdot \overline{s_4} \cdot \overline{s_5} \cdot s_6 \\
u'_{15} &= s_0 \cdot s_1 \cdot \overline{s_2} \cdot \overline{s_3} \cdot s_4 \cdot \overline{s_5} \cdot \overline{s_6} \\
u'_{16} &= \overline{s_0} \cdot s_1 \cdot s_2 \cdot \overline{s_3} \cdot \overline{s_4} \cdot s_5 \cdot \overline{s_6} \qquad (4) \\
u_{17} &= \overline{s_0} \cdot \overline{s_1} \cdot s_2 \cdot s_3 \cdot \overline{s_4} \cdot \overline{s_5} \cdot s_6 \\
u_{18} &= s_0 \cdot \overline{s_1} \cdot \overline{s_2} \cdot s_3 \cdot s_4 \cdot \overline{s_5} \cdot \overline{s_6} \\
u'_{19} &= \overline{s_0} \cdot s_1 \cdot \overline{s_2} \cdot \overline{s_3} \cdot s_4 \cdot s_5 \cdot \overline{s_6} \\
u'_{20} &= \overline{s_0} \cdot \overline{s_1} \cdot s_2 \cdot \overline{s_3} \cdot \overline{s_4} \cdot s_5 \cdot s_6 \\
u'_{21} &= s_0 \cdot s_1 \cdot \overline{s_2} \cdot s_3 \cdot \overline{s_4} \cdot \overline{s_5} \cdot \overline{s_6} \\
u'_{22} &= \overline{s_0} \cdot s_1 \cdot s_2 \cdot \overline{s_3} \cdot s_4 \cdot \overline{s_5} \cdot \overline{s_6} \\
u'_{23} &= \overline{s_0} \cdot \overline{s_1} \cdot s_2 \cdot s_3 \cdot \overline{s_4} \cdot s_5 \cdot \overline{s_6} \\
u'_{24} &= \overline{s_0} \cdot \overline{s_1} \cdot \overline{s_2} \cdot s_3 \cdot s_4 \cdot \overline{s_5} \cdot s_6 \\
u'_{25} &= s_0 \cdot \overline{s_1} \cdot \overline{s_2} \cdot \overline{s_3} \cdot s_4 \cdot s_5 \cdot \overline{s_6} \\
u'_{26} &= \overline{s_0} \cdot s_1 \cdot \overline{s_2} \cdot \overline{s_3} \cdot \overline{s_4} \cdot s_5 \cdot s_6 \\
u'_{27} &= s_0 \cdot \overline{s_1} \cdot s_2 \cdot \overline{s_3} \cdot \overline{s_4} \cdot \overline{s_5} \cdot s_6 \\
u'_{28} &= s_0 \cdot s_1 \cdot s_2 \cdot s_3 \cdot s_4 \cdot \overline{s_5} \cdot \overline{s_6} \\
u'_{29} &= s_0 \cdot s_1 \cdot s_2 \cdot \overline{s_3} \cdot \overline{s_4} \cdot s_5 \cdot s_6 \\
u'_{30} &= \overline{s_0} \cdot \overline{s_1} \cdot s_2 \cdot s_3 \cdot s_4 \cdot s_5 \cdot s_6 \\
u'_{31} &= s_0 \cdot s_1 \cdot s_2 \cdot s_3 \cdot s_4 \cdot s_5 \cdot s_6
\end{aligned}
$$

We will connect the output of AND gates to an input of an XOR gate, the second input of the gate has the data bit read from the cache Tag. To correct the data bits we will use 32 XOR gates with 2 inputs, this correction is realised with the following equations:

$$
\begin{aligned}
u_{0cor} &= u_0 \oplus u_0', \\
u_{1cor} &= u_1 \oplus u_1', \\
u_{2cor} &= u_2 \oplus u_2', \\
u_{3cor} &= u_3 \oplus u_3', \\
u_{4cor} &= u_4 \oplus u_4', \\
u_{5cor} &= u_5 \oplus u_5', \\
u_{6cor} &= u_6 \oplus u_6', \\
u_{7cor} &= u_7 \oplus u_7' \\
u_{8cor} &= u_8 \oplus u_8', \\
u_{9cor} &= u_9 \oplus u_9', \\
u_{10cor} &= u_{10} \oplus u_{10}', \\
u_{11cor} &= u_{11} \oplus u_{11}', \\
u_{12cor} &= u_{12} \oplus u_{12}', \\
u_{13cor} &= u_{13} \oplus u_{13}', \\
u_{14cor} &= u_{14} \oplus u_{14}' \\
u_{15cor} &= u_{15} \oplus u_{15}' \qquad (5) \\
u_{16cor} &= u_{16} \oplus u_{16}', \\
u_{17cor} &= u_{17} \oplus u_{17}', \\
u_{18cor} &= u_{18} \oplus u_{18}', \\
u_{19cor} &= u_{19} \oplus u_{19}', \\
u_{20cor} &= u_{20} \oplus u_{20}', \\
u_{21cor} &= u_{21} \oplus u_{21}', \\
u_{22cor} &= u_{22} \oplus u_{22}' \\
u_{23cor} &= u_{23} \oplus u_{23}', \\
u_{24cor} &= u_{24} \oplus u_{24}', \\
u_{25cor} &= u_{25} \oplus u_{25}', \\
u_{26cor} &= u_{26} \oplus u_{26}', \\
u_{27cor} &= u_{27} \oplus u_{27}', \\
u_{28cor} &= u_{28} \oplus u_{28}', \\
u_{29cor} &= u_{29} \oplus u_{29}' \\
u_{30cor} &= u_{30} \oplus u_{30}' \\
u_{31cor} &= u_{31} \oplus u_{31}'
\end{aligned}
$$

We generate the Hamming matrix, so that the column vectors corresponding to useful information bits to be different one from other. In figure 4 we will use three shift registers and one exclusive-or gate to implement the Hamming matrix. We present in figure 4 a scheme used for single error correction.

If we write in cache RAM memory the control bits are generated from useful data bits, and they are obtained from data bus using (2), in cache RAM memory we will write codewords with followimg :

$u=(c_0c_1c_2c_3c_4c_5c_6u_0u_1u_2u_3u_4u_5u_6u_7u_8u_9u_{10}u_{11}u_{12}u_{13}u_{14}u_{15}u_{16}u_{17}u_{18}u_{19}$
$u_{20}u_{21}u_{22}u_{23}u_{24}u_{25}u_{26}u_{27}u_{28}u_{29}u_{30}u_{31})$.

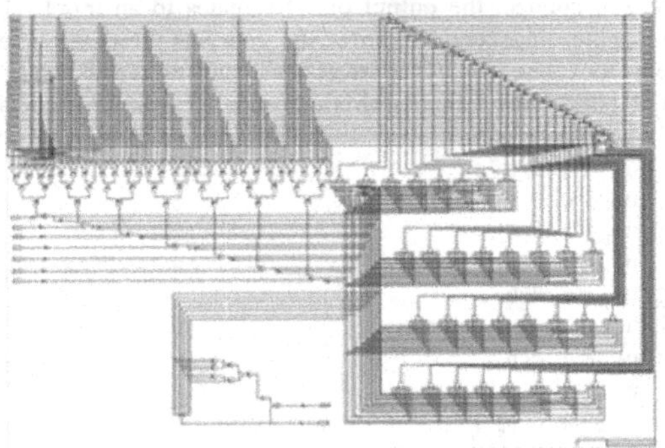

Fig. 4. Single error correction scheme

We have implemented Hamming code to the cache RAM memory also, and our results are presented in the foloowing table:

TABLE I
OVERHEAD OF HAMMING CODE AND PARITY CODE

Cache RAM Memory	Number of data bits u	Number of control bits c	Overhead O_1=c/u [%]	Overhead O_2=[%]
Without	8	0	-	-
Parity code	16	0	-	-
	32	0	-	-
With parity code on c bits	8	1	12,50	11,11
	16	2	12,50	11,11
	32	4	12,50	11,11
With Hamming code	8	5	62,50	38,46
	16	6	37,50	27,27
	32	9	28,12	21,95

Table 1 describes the introduction of Hamming code to the Cache RAM memory of 128 K x 32 bits. As we can observe in the table, if we increase the number of data bits of Hamming code, the overhead is decreasing.

CONCLUSIONS

In modern computer systems, at the cache level of the memory hierarchy, we can succesfuly apply multiple error correction codes. In the first implemetation of cache RAM memory with capacity 8K x 8 bits, without Hamming code, we have 2 groups of 2 memory circuits and each circuit store 4 bits, so we will store 8 bits.

In second implementation of cache RAM with Hamming code, we have 2 circuits that store 5 bits and 2 circuits that stores 6 bits , so we will store 22 bits. In this case we have an overhead of 29,32 % [7]. Overhead induced by the supplementary circuits for the error correction (AND gates, NOT gates, XOR gates, OR gates, is 6,19 %). This codes for detection and correction of errors are added to memories to obtain a better dependability. In high speed memories the most used codes are Single bit Error Correcting and Double bit Error Detection codes (SEC-DED). An important conclusion is the fact that, if we increase the number of data bits of Hamming code, the overhead is decreasing, so we must use SEC-DED codes with great number of data bits.

ACKNOWLEDGMENT

*"University of Oradea", Department of Computers, Faculty of Electrical Engineering and Information Technology, Oradea, Romania,

**"University of Oradea", Department of Electrotechnics, Measurements and using of Electrical Energy, Faculty of Electrical Engineering and Information Technology, Oradea, Romania.

REFERENCES

[1] David A. Paterson, John L. Henessy – "Computer architecture. a quantitative approach", *Morgan Kaufmann Publishers*, Inc. 1990-1996.

[2] Ovidiu Novac, Gordan M, Novac M., Data loss rate versus mean time to failure in memory hierarchies. Advances in Systems, Computing Sciences and Software Engineering, *Proceedings of the CISSE'05*, Springer, pp. 305-307, University of Bridgeport, USA, 2005.

[3] Ovidiu Novac, Vladutiu M, St. Vari Kakas, Novac M., Gordan M., A Comparative Study Regarding a Memory Hierarchy with the CDLR SPEC 2000 Simulator, Innovations and Information Sciences and Engineering, *Proceedings of the CISSE'06*, University of Bridgeport, Springer, pp. 369-372, USA, 2006.

[4] Ooi, Y., M. Kashimura, H. Takeuchi, and E. Kawamura, Fault-tolerant architecture in a cache memory control LSI, *IEEE J. of Solid-State Circuits*, Vol. 27, No. 4, pp. 507-514, April 1992.

[5] Philip P. Shirvani and Edward J. McCluskey, "PADded cache: a new fault-tolerance technique for cache memories", *Computer Systems Laboratory, Technical Report* No. 00-802, Stanford University, Stanford, California, December 2000.

[6] T.R.N. Rao, E. Fujiwara,"Error-Control Coding for Computer Systems ", Prentice Hall International Inc., Englewood Cliffs, New Jersey, USA, 1989

[7] Ovidiu Novac, Şt. Vari-Kakas, O. Poszet „Aspects Regarding the use of Error Detecting and Error Corecting Codes in Cache Memories", EMES'07, University of Oradea, 2007

Performance Evaluation of an Intelligent Agents Based Model within Irregular WSN Topologies

Alberto Piedrahita Ospina
GIDIA: Research and Development Group in Artificial Intelligence
Department of Computer Sciences
National University of Colombia at Medellin
Medellin, Colombia
aapiedra@unal.edu.co

Alcides Montoya Cañola
GICEI: Scientific and Industrial Instrumentation Group
Department of Physics
National University of Colombia at Medellin
Medellin, Colombia
amontoya@unal.edu.co

Demetrio Ovalle Carranza
GIDIA: Research and Development Group in Artificial Intelligence
Department of Computer Sciences
National University of Colombia at Medellin
Medellin, Colombia
dovalle@unal.edu.co

***Abstract*— There are many approaches proposed by the scientific community for the implementation and development of Wireless Sensor Networks (WSN). These approaches correspond to different areas of science, such as Electronics, Communications, Computing, Ubiquity, and Quality of Service among others. However, all are subject to the same constraints, because of the nature of WSN devices. The most common constraints of a WSN are the energy consumption, the network nodes organization, the sensor network's task reprogramming, the reliability in the data transmission, the resource optimization (memory and processing), etc. In the Artificial Intelligence Area is has proposed an Distributed System Approach with Mobile Intelligent Agents. An Integration Model of Mobile Intelligent Agents within Wireless Sensor Network solves some of the constraints presented above on WSN's topologies. However, the model only was tested on the square topologies. In this way, the aim of this paper is to evaluate the performance of this model in irregular topologies.**

Keywords- WSN (Wireless Sensor Networks); Multi-agent Systems; Mobile Agents;

I. Introduction

The observation and monitoring of physical environments are very important for some fields, such as Environment, Domotics, Enterprise Security, Ubiquitous Computing, among others. In Industrial production, for example, it is required the constant monitoring to ensure higher yields, optimum quality, and more efficient systems that contribute for improving utilities and quality of the products in the industry.

Wireless Sensor Networks or WSN are a distributed network nodes group, which act together in order to monitoring and controlling diverse kind of physical environments. The WSN nodes are small electronic devices that have wireless communication capabilities, storing, and processing. These can be programmed to interact within physical spaces. Through sensors and actuators, the nodes can perceive physical variables such as temperature, light, humidity, vibration, sound, etc. in order to act over a specific environment according to the application domain.

However, since a WSN is previously programmed, the system is therefore designed according to a priori events, which do not allow resolving future contingencies. So, What happens when the sensor network finds constraints and conditions for which it was not designed? How to achieve flexibility in the WSN? How can unexpected problems be solved?

To answer the above questions have been proposed in others papers to use an approach of Artificial Intelligence (AI), a branch of computer sciences that through learning techniques promotes the ability on hardware or software to solve unexpected problems. This, coupled with the complex behavior of a WSN, constitutes an excellent combination. Specifically the Distributed Artificial Intelligence (DAI) offers Multi-Agent Systems (MAS), a distributed system consisting of autonomous software modules so-called agents. This approach is appropriate for a WSN [1], since it provides mobility, autonomy, and intelligence to network nodes through software agents using perceptors and actuators for world's interaction purposes.

Therefore, the purpose of this paper is to evaluate an integration model for mobile intelligent agents within WSN into irregular topologies in order to solve the constraints normally found in WSN topologies, such as energy consumption, the organization of the nodes in the network, reprogramming of the sensor network, the reliability in the transmission of data, optimization of resources (memory and processing, etc.).

The rest of the paper is organized as follows: The first section presents the theoretical framework associated with WSN and Multi-Agent Systems followed by a review of the state of the art. Afterwards in it is presented the integration model proposed. Subsequently it is performed the model validation. Finally, it will present the conclusions and future work.

II. The Theoretical Framework

The definition of a WSN is initially given, followed by a short explanation of mobile agents. Finally, this section describes Agilla Framework, a middleware for programming mobile agents in a WSN that is the main tool used to develop the prototype associated to this research work.

A. *Wireless Networks Sensor*

The requirement for measuring, controlling, and computing, different physical variables in diverse environments that could be hostile, inaccessible or wide have originated the Wireless Sensor Network (WSN) has been emerged [2]. A WSN is

T. Sobh, K. Elleithy (eds.), *Innovations in Computing Sciences and Software Engineering*,
DOI 10.1007/978-90-481-9112-3_99, © Springer Science+Business Media B.V. 2010

defined as a distributed system of ubiquitous computing, which is composed of associated network nodes. Each node is a small electronic device strategically embedded in a real environment, which has the ability of processing, storing, and wireless data communicating. Network nodes have additionally input and output ports in order to interact with their close environment. Input ports are sensors to perceive or monitor changes in the environment, through physical environmental variables. On the other hand, output ports are analog-digital converters with the purpose of controlling peripherals and thus to manipulate the environment nearby.

Each node of a WSN, well known as "mote", is deployed in a geographical field, such as an invisible speck of dust that has the abilities to collect and process data and routing them to the "sink" node, which acts as a network gateway node for data gathering. It is important to notice that the WSN operates through an ad-hoc architecture of multiple hops (see figure 1).

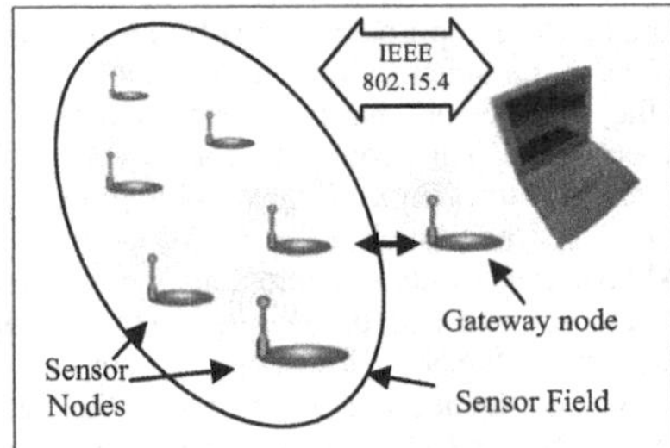

Figure 1. Wireless Sensor Networks basic topology

The design of a WSN depends on several factors such as fault tolerance, scalability, hardware constraints, topology, environment, transmission media, and energy consumption [3]. These factors strongly affect the implementation of the WSN, making more complex its programming and maintenance.

B. *Ubiquitous Computing and Ambient Intelligence*

Ubiquitous Computing is a new concept that is beginning to emerge, and was advertised and called by Mark Weiser [4] as the "Era Ubi" in 1988. Weiser predicted that computers could be found in TVs, toasters, ovens, Cars, Wallets, even in the Field. Inevitably the computers will penetrate even more into the lives of people; they will talk amongst themselves, and will form a computing invisible infrastructure in our lives. They are in common use and reduced costs, and improve quality of life of people.

The Weiser's view proposed two decades ago now is captured in a topic known as Ambient Intelligence [5], which is also the view of the European Community through ISTAG (Information Society Technologies Advisory Group), which proposes that the traditional desktop computer to become multiple devices in the environment with which they are interact naturally.

C. *Mobile Agents*

The mobile agents are computational processes that can travel through the network. Each agent has the ability to migrate or clone its code and state from one machine to another, as well as the self-destroy capability. These agents can interact with strange devices, gathering information in order to return to their home with the data obtained. The mobile agents have been widely accepted, because of their mobility. It is more efficient than an agent migrates to a remote location for performing a search in order to bring all the information to be processed and filtered.

III. The State of the Art

Giraldo and Montoya present in [6] a monitoring system for a greenhouse, which takes samples values of physical variables, such as temperature and humidity in order to send them through the Web. However, this system has a constraint, which the network topology is a star topology, so the nodes are always arranged around a central station in wired form. Therefore the system leads to a centralized control and it does not use a distributed approach computational model.

An application for seismic monitoring of the Tungurahua volcano in Ecuador is presented in [7], in which its basic programming was composed of NesC [8] code of TinyOS inserted within the device directly acting on native components of the sensor node. One advantage in this programming is that offers robustness, as well as optimization on the use of the hardware components. Disadvantages in this system are mainly the limited flexibility offered by the WSN, since it can only execute one application at a time. Other limitation is the impossibility to remotely reprogram the network.

An optimization to reduce the irrigation water used and improve the quality of Cabernet Sauvignon grapes is presented in Camelie Net [9]. Here sensors are deployed to measure soil moisture at several locations and depths of the vineyard, moreover, the pressure in the irrigation system is monitored in order to check its operation. Thus, an irrigation control is implemented to keep the moisture at optimal level. Camalie Net was used in 2005 and its implementation has improved yields and quality in the grapes. Despite the advantages of this system, it does not have an advanced program that allows each node in the network to make decisions independently, adapting itself to unexpected changes in environmental conditions.

G. Hackmann et al. developed in [10] the AgiTrack system, which aims at tracking freight containers using mobile agents in WSN. This system was implemented with Agilla framework [11]. In each container a sensor node is inserted, which serves for two purposes: first, to detect intrusions by motion and light sensors, and second, to store the manifest for the cargo container. The WSN also has two base stations, one located at the ship and the other is at the harbor, to manage and monitor the network. In AgiTrack the user deploys an agent Watchdog, whose role is to collect data from sensors, so, in case of any weaken event to alert the base station and to store in the device the information of the fault. In the AgiTrack system the user can inspect the manifests of each container. Although this system uses mobile agents, the purpose of the application is limited to the tracking of cargo. It is not possible to broaden the spectrum of applications to the measurement of environmental variables with the same agents, e.g. to monitor the quality of the cargo transported in containers.

IV. The Model

This paper evaluates the performance of a model that integrates intelligent mobile agents within WSN [12]. This model is based on a Multi-Agent System that provides distributed and ubiquitous computing to the sensor network. Each mobile agent model has the ability to move through the network with roles and rules of behavior that can give it a degree of deliberation in the decisions it makes, which will provide intelligence to the WSN.

The model allows to gathering of physical variables in a given environment. The physical variables could be, temperature, humidity, sound, etc., these will depend of the sensors or perceptors that have nodes in the network. In this way, the model could be used in different application domains, where it is required to monitor or control environments, like industrial production, environment, hydrology, food manufacturing, etc.

A. Agents in the Model

In the model there are 4 types of mobile intelligent agent, each of which play a certain role, and has defined rules of behavior.

1) Farmer agent: The role of this agent in the system is gather measurements of physical variables in network nodes, with a specific sampling frequency. To achieve this, the agent is propagated throughout the network, by means of clone agents during the diffusion process. In this way the agent acquires an ubiquitous feature in the WSN topology. It should be noted that to decrease energy consumption at each node, the farmer agent remains a large part of its time in sleeping state in order to increase its lifetime. The data obtained by this agent will be stored in each node, until they will be extracted from the base station by another kind of agent. The normal work cycle of the farmer agent is "sampling & sleeping". However, it is necessary to have a version of this agent (mutated) always ready to answer cloning requests, in order to repair those nodes lacking of farmer agents (see maintenance agent description).

2) Explorer Agent: The task of this agent is to identify anytime the status of the network nodes. The explorer agent will detect which network nodes are active or inactive. It is important to underline that inactive nodes are in that state possibly due to the lack of energy or affected by some damages produced by the environment. Once the agent is hosted on the device, it makes two queries to the local node related to the node id and the current location. This information is sent to the base station of the WSN using agent communication messages and then shown to the user. After explorer agent role has been completed the suicide mechanism is activated to release useful resources to the WSN.

3) Messenger Agent: this is a light agent whose mission is to migrate to a remote node by hops over the network, in order to gather the data collected there and send them to the base station. After the Messenger agent has sent the data to the base station, it opts for activating the suicide mechanism to release resources to the network. The deployment of a messenger agent occurs at the base station by the user who decides which node will be selected to extract the data.

4) Maintenance Agent: The goal of this agent is to guarantee that the network remains homogeneous in terms of programming of devices. To achieve this, an agent of this kind is deployed within the network looking for nodes in the WSN without farmer agent. When it matches a node with this feature makes a cloning request to the farmer mutated agent to obtain a clone of the farmer agent and thus the system can continue with the sampling of variables in the device. The maintenance agent guarantees that the node is repaired, awaiting the arrival of the clone and making several retries in case of no response from the base station. Once the clone farmer has reached the node and started its operation, the maintenance agent frees its resources through the mechanism of suicide.

TABLE I. AGENT'S PROPERTIES IN THE INTEGRATION MODEL PROPOSED

Agent	Size (bytes)	Number of Messages	Diffusion
Farmer Agent	154	7	Yes
Explorer Agent	88	4	Not
Messenger Agent	110	5	Not
Maintenance Agent	132	6	Yes

Table 1 shows the size employed by each of the agents that compound the Multi-Agent System implemented and the number of messages needed to clone an agent from one node to another. Additionally, the table shows if the diffusion process was needed for agents in the system.

B. Model's Considerations

In a WSN are many aspects to consider for any application or model which is intended to tackle this area. However, there are 4 considerations were taken into account when implementing the model. These were scalability, power consumption, topology and reprogramming.

1) Scalability, Size and Scope: The scope as well as the size refers to the ability of a WSN to cover large distances in outdoor. In the future will be feasible have a WSN with hundreds or thousands of nodes scattered in a geographical area. However, it is not enough to have large WSN is also expected to be able to add new nodes to the network, without affecting the operation of the network.

The model resolves that consideration through an ability of agents called "Diffusion by flooding". This skill enables an agent to know the entire network by making clones of itself, which migrate to neighboring nodes, these clones are also will clone into their neighboring nodes. This will be an iterative process and it is repeated to cover the entire network. When an agent decides to spread on the network, it acts like a virus "infecting" each of the nodes in the network with its code and state.

2) *Low power consumption:* Another consideration taken into account in the model is the energy consumption of the nodes in the network. Each of the agents must optimize their activities in the nodes, to achieve a state of sleep implemented in order to save energy and prolong the life of the host node. However, in this state the agent becomes reactive, waiting for external events to wake himself from sleep and execute its activities.

3) *Topology or Nodes Distribution:* The topology or nodes distridution in the field is refer to how the nodes are arranged in a geographical area. The topology will depend on certain factors such as, size and geography of the field, the obstacles, the need for concentrated measurements in some areas, and so on. Such factors can create WSN, larger or small, regular or irregular shapes, or with variable node densities along its structure.

The relationships nodes in the WSN depend on the organization of the nodes. A node can communicate with another if the latter is within its wireless communication range, and the reached node is denoted neighbor. The set of neighbors to which node can communicate denoted neighborhood. In the same topology of WSN, there could be diferents neighborhood, such as nodes that have a neighborhood of twenty neighboring nodes, as well as neighborhood with one neighbor.

In a WSN, the topologies that could be taken are infinite. However, it was necessary for the proposed model to reach all nodes in the WSN. Through the "Diffusion by flooding" the agents can reach all nodes in a WSN, regardless of topology. Thanks to flooding agent covers all possible paths in a WSN.

4) *Fault Tolerance and Repprograming:* In small devices such as nodes in a WSN, failures occur due to poor communication of data, lack of batteries, or simply environmental conditions. Faults that could affect the programming of the devices, because of is required the capability of reprogramming of the WSN.

To solve it the model introduce into Multi-Agent System a maintenance agent, this agent will be able to search the WSN nodes which have failures in their programming, in order to restart its operation and to send a new Agent Farmer.

V. Capabilities Proposals in the Model

This section describes two important properties of a mobile agent that were involved in the proposed model. These properties are composed of basic properties and have been developed by this work.

A. *Mutation*

This corresponds to a change in the agent programming with the purpose of playing other roles. Sometimes it is not appropriate to use another agent to perform other functions, just doing small changes in the normal structure of an agent to achieve different behaviors.

B. *Diffusion by flooding*

In this process an agent is propagated to every network node. The spread is based on a recursive process of flooding, where multiple clone agents are dispatched to neighboring nodes; these clones in the same way are cloned to their neighbors. Thus the cloning cycle is performed until to reach the entire network. This process may be interpreted similar to an epidemic, where the agent is reproduced in virus form, very quickly infecting the entire network (see figure 2).

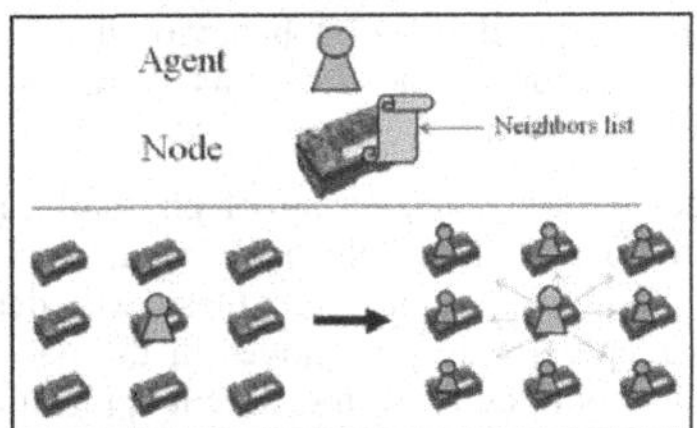

Figure 2. Diffusion by flooding process in a Wireless Sensor Network

VI. Interaction Among Agents

Interaction among agents in the system are established through the exchange of information among them, as shown in the sequence diagrams of figures 4, 5, and 6.

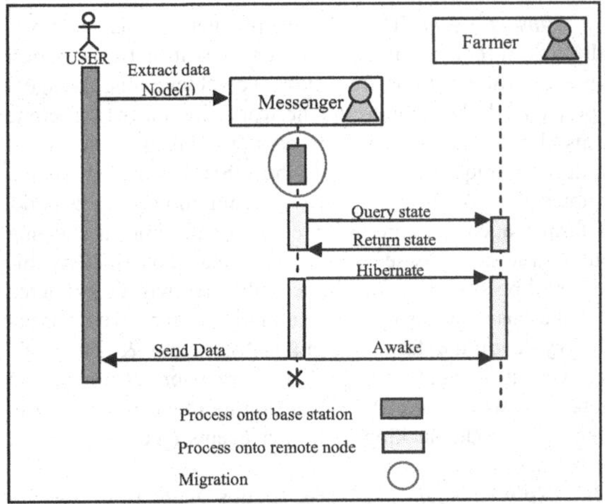

Figure 3. Sequence diagram among the user, the farmer and Messenger Agents

Figure 4 presents the interaction between the farmer and messenger agents. This is initiated by a user that makes a query aiming to extract data collected in the device. The interaction starts when a messenger agent is created in the base station. It begins a process of migration to the remote node where the query is performed. Once the Messenger has arrived to the remote node, it orders to the farmer agent (host) to hibernate, while the information is extracted. Finally, the agent wakes up the farmer, and next, dies thus releasing resources. In figure 5 the explorer agent's life cycle is shown. Its function begins with one explorer and ends with multiple copies or clones in each of the nodes in the WSN (diffusion). Then each explorer agent takes data available in the node to send them to the base station and dies.

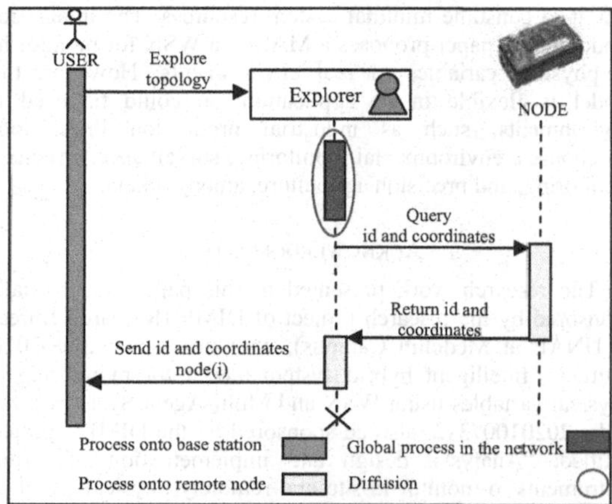

Figure 4. Sequence diagram among the user, the explorer agent, and the device

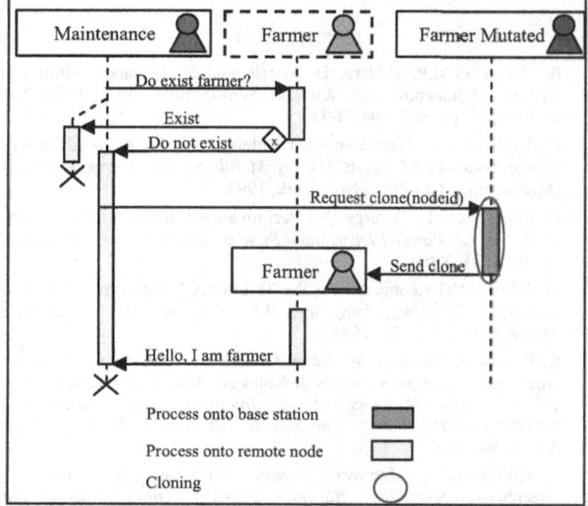

Figure 5. Sequence diagram between the maintenance, farmer and farmer mutated agents

Finally, figure 6 describes the relationship established between the maintenance agent and farmer agent. In this sequence diagram the process of cloning is highlight. When the maintenance command is executed, it originates a maintenance agent in the base station that spreads across the network looking for failures in the programming. In case of it finds a fail, the Agent is communicate with the farmer mutated agent at the base station, requests a clone on the remote node. After making the request, the maintenance agent wait that a clone arrives to the node in order to die and so release its resources.

VII. Model Validation

In this paper we validate the model in WSNs with different topologies in shape and size, i.e. irregular topologies. Then these are compared with model results in square topologies. The proposed model considers large WSN, with hundreds of nodes. However, to make a real validation of the model would need a WSN of such magnitude, which is not feasible due to WSN nodes price. For this reason, a theoretical analysis is performed to evaluate the model, and to offer results in terms of the efficiency which was raised by the model.

Figure 6 shows some possible topologies in sensor network for two and three-dimensional environments. Such as in the industry and civilian buildings, on maritime and air transport, so on.

Figure 6. Bi-dimensional and Three-dimensional Topologies

The topology of a WSN depends on the application domain. A key parameter in a topology of WSN is the density of nodes, which is defined as the number of WSN nodes per unit area or volume for two-dimensional or three-dimensional topologies respectively. In the equations 1 and 2 are showed the surface density of nodes and volumetric density of nodes.

$$\sigma = \frac{NodesNumber}{Area} \tag{1}$$

$$\rho = \frac{NodesNumber}{Volume} \tag{2}$$

Where:

- σ in (1) is the surface density of nodes.
- ρ in (2) is the volumetric density of nodes.

However, it is expected that the density of nodes in a WSN is variable, because there will be nodes with more neighbors than others into WSN. The equations 3 and 4, allow us to know all the relationships that exist among nodes in the network. The equations integrate the density function of topology throughout the geographical area of the WSN. Thus we can obtain an estimate of all interactions that occur within the WSN. Note that the equation 3 considers flat topologies and the equation 4 introduces the geographical height for the topologies with volume, which is denoted z.

$$TotalInteractions = range \bullet \iint \sigma(x, y)dxdy \tag{3}$$

$$TotalInteractions = range \bullet \iiint \rho(x, y, z)dxdydz \tag{4}$$

Where:

- x in (3) and (4) is the x coordinate in the space

- y in (3) and (4) is the y coordinate in the space
- z in (4) is the x coordinate in the space

Having defined all the interactions inside a WSN, it is possible to evaluate a WSN according to the density used, in order to analyze the performance of the model in different irregular topologies.

A. Performance in the Diffusion by Flooding Process

In the integration model proposed, is presented the diffusion by flooding process (DFP) described. This process is an important mechanism to disseminate agents within a WSN.

1) Efficiency: this component evaluates the process performance, comparing the utility with the waste of the clones throughout the topology. The DFP carried a series of steps, involving processes such as cloning and suicides in order to propagate agents on WSN. However, the suicides have a high associated cost, due to loss of code that is involved. Following equations indicate the efficiency as a function of topology order:

$$e = \frac{n-1}{TotalInteractions} \quad (5)$$

Where:

- e in (5) is the DFP's efficiency.
- n in (5) is the total nodes number in the topology

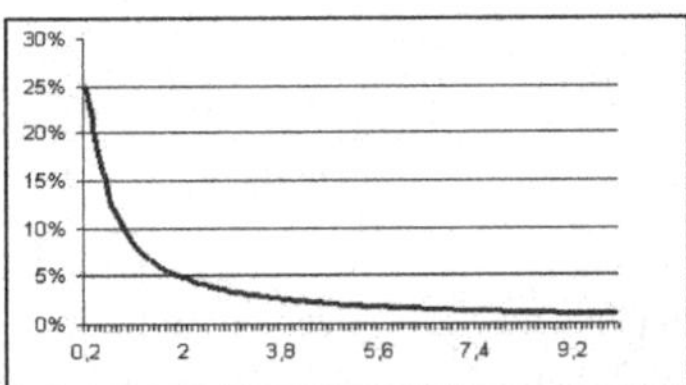

Figure 7. The Model's efficiency as a function of density topology

The figure 8 shows the efficiency in terms of the density topology. In the figure we can see that in topologies with more density the DFP is much less efficient, since the interaction between nodes is higher, which results in increased wastage of clones and therefore energy and code losses.

CONCLUSIONS AND FUTURE WORK

The techniques for mobile agents proposed and implemented in this paper, such as migration, cloning, diffusion, mutation and suicide, were very useful in the design model, due to the WSN structure. Some of the techniques of mobile agents presented may be trivial in platforms with better resources in processing, storing, and energy consumption. However, a WSN has devices with constrained resources; therefore to implement the same technique is a challenge.

As a continuation to the work presented is considerate to increase the efficiency in the DFP, or the design of new techniques for the deployment of agents in the WSN. Always aim at to consume minimal system resources. The integration model in this paper proposes a MAS in a WSN for monitoring of physical variables in real environments. However, this model is flexible in its application, so could be used in environments, such as industrial production lines, food warehouses, environmental monitoring, surveillance, structural monitoring, and precision agriculture, among others.

ACKNOWLEDGMENTS

The research work presented in this paper was partially sponsored by the research project of DIME (Research Bureau of UNAL at Medellin Campus), with time span 2008-2010, entitled: "Intelligent hybrid system model for monitoring of physical variables using WSN and Multi-Agent Systems" with code: 20201007312, also co-sponsored by the DIME's project entitled: "Analysis, design and implementation of virtual instruments to monitor in-situ and remotely physical variables in controlled environments using WSN" with code: 20101006725, both from the National University of Colombia at Medellin Campus.

REFERENCES

[1] R. Tynan, G.M.P. O'Hare, D. Marsh, and D. O'Kane. "Multi-agent System Architectures for Wireless Sensor Networks". ICCS 2005, LNCS 3516, pp. 687–694, 2005.

[2] D. Estrin et al., "Next Century Challenges: Scalable Coordination in Sensor Networks," *Proc. ACM Conf. Mobile and Computing Networking* (MobiCom), ACM Press, New York, 1999.

[3] L. Doherty et al., "Energy and Performance Considerations for Smart Dust," *Int'l J. Parallel Distributed Systems and Networks*, vol. 4, no. 3, pp. 121–133. 2001.

[4] M. Weiser, "The computer for the 21 century." *Reprinted in the IEEE Pervasive Computing Magazine, IEEE Computer Society, January-March 2002, pp. 18-25.* 1991

[5] R. Hervás, J. Bravo, S. W. Nava, G. Chavira, "Interacción Natural en Ambientes Inteligentes a través de Roles en Mosaicos de Visualización." *VII Congreso Internacional de Interacción Persona-Ordenador (INTERACCIÓN'2006). Puertollano (Ciudad Real), España, Noviembre.*2006

[6] L. Giraldo & N. Montoya. "Remote Monitoring and Controling of Greenhouses Variables". *Bachelor Thesis for physical Engineering degree.* National University of Colombia at Medellin. August, 2005.

[7] G. Werner-Allen, J. Johnson, M. Ruiz, J. Lees, and M. Welsh. "Monitoring Volcanic Eruptions with a Wireless Sensor Network". *EWSN '05*, 2005.

[8] D. Gay, P. Levis, R. V. Behren, M. Welsh, E. Brewer and D. Culler. "The nesC Languaje: A Holistic Approach to Networked Embedded Systems". In *Proceedings of the ACM SIGPLAN 2003 Conference on Programming Language Design and Implementation (PLDI).* 2003.

[9] M. Holler. "High Density, Multiple Depth, Wireless Soil Moisture Tension Measurements for Irrigation Management". *59th Annual Meeting ASEV (American Society for Enology and Viticulture's), Portland, Oregon.* Junio. 2008.

[10] G. Hackmann et al. "Agile Cargo Tracking Using Mobile Agents". In Proceedings of the Third Annual Conference on Embedded Networked Sensor Systems (SenSys 2005). November 2-4, Page 303, 2005.

[11] Ch-L. Fok, G-C. Roman and Ch. Lu. "Rapid Development and Flexible Deployment of Adaptive Wireless Sensor Network Applications". *Proceedings of the 25th IEEE International Conference on Distributed Computing Systems.* 2005.

[12] A. A. Piedrahita, A. Montoya and D. Ovalle. "Integration model of mobile intelligent agents within Wireless Sensor Networks." Communications, 2009. LATINCOM '09. IEEE Latin-American Conference on, vol., no., pp.1-6, 10-11 Sept. 2009.

Double Stage Heat Transformer Controlled by Flow Ratio

S. Silva-Sotelo[a], R. J. Romero [b,*], A. Rodríguez – Martínez [b]

[a] Posgrado en Ingeniería y Ciencias Aplicadas, Centro de Investigación en Ingeniería y Ciencias Aplicadas Tel.Fax +52(777)3297084.

[b] Centro de Investigación en Ingeniería y Ciencias Aplicadas, Universidad Autónoma del Estado de Morelos, Av. Universidad 1001, Col. Chamilpa, Cuernavaca, C.P. 62209, Morelos, México.

Corresponding author: rosenberg@uaem.mx

***Abstract*—this paper shows the values of Flow ratio (FR) for control of an absorption double stage heat transformer. The main parameters for the heat pump system are defined as COP, FR and GTL. The control of the entire system is based in a new definition of FR. The heat balance of the Double Stage Heat Transformer (DSHT) is used for the control. The mass flow is calculated for a HPVEE program and a second program control the mass flow. The mass flow is controlled by gear pumps connected to LabView program. The results show an increment in the fraction of the recovery energy. An example of oil distillation is used for the calculation. The waste heat energy is added at the system at 70 °C. Water ™ - Carrol mixture is used in the DSHT. The recover energy is obtained in a second absorber at 128 °C with two scenarios.**

Keywords: vapor absorption system, heat transformer, control strategies, double stage heat transformer, waste heat recovery

I. INTRODUCTION

An absorption double stage heat transformer (DSHT) is an advanced thermal machine. The DSHT is a system of 16 devices used in a thermodynamic cycle. The absorption heat transformer (AHT) is a Type of heat pump. The DSHT is a device of two AHP that has the capability of transform waste thermal energy into useful energy. The main advantage of the DSHT is that it uses only 0.2 kW of electric energy for revalorize each thermal kW of waste heat.

II. SINGLE STAGE AND DOUBLE STAGE HEAT TRANSFORMER

An AHT consists of an evaporator, a condenser, a generator, an economizer and an absorber. Fig. 1 shows a schematic diagram of an AHT. A working solution (water – lithium bromide + ethylene glycol) flows between absorber and generator. This solution is called water – Carrol™, it was created by Carrier Co. for air conditioner systems.

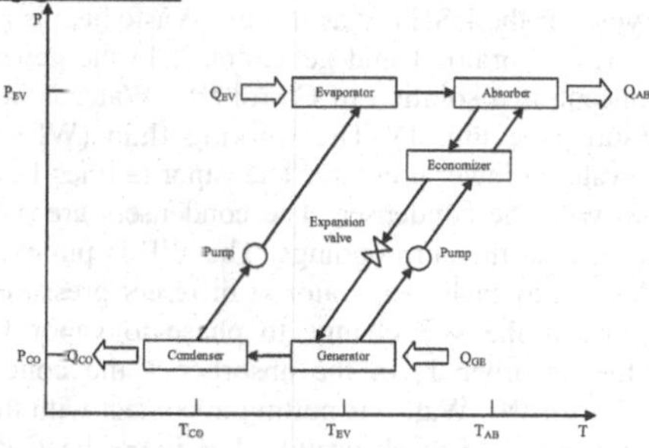

Fig. 1. Schematic diagram of an AHT.

A DSHT is a cascade set of two AHT. The connection between the two AHT has tree different modes:

a) The useful heat of the first absorber is added to the evaporator of the second stage.

b) The useful heat of the first stage is conducted to the generator of the second stage.

c) The total useful heat of the absorber of the first stage is splitting for second evaporator and second generator.

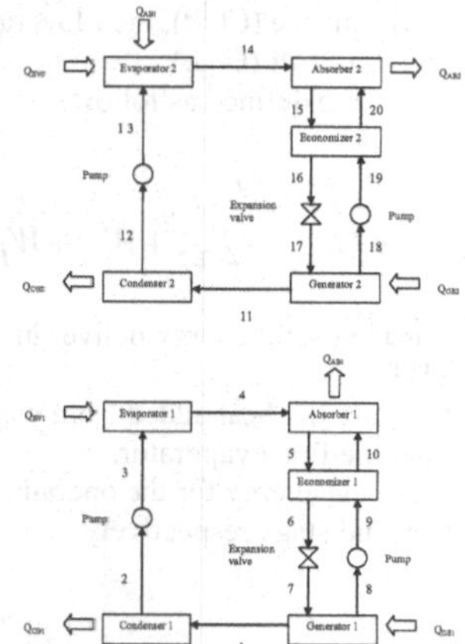

Fig. 2. Schematic diagram of the DSHT.

T. Sobh, K. Elleithy (eds.), *Innovations in Computing Sciences and Software Engineering*, DOI 10.1007/978-90-481-9112-3_100, © Springer Science+Business Media B.V. 2010

III. EXPERIMENTAL SET – UP

The DSHT was installed with ten plate heat exchanger made of stainless steel 316, of seven plates, thermal capacity by design of 1000W. Gear pumps are connecting the pressures zones between generators and condensers in the lines 2 to3 and 12 to 13, while the other gear pumps are connected the lines 8 to 9 and 18 to 19. Expansion valves control the diluted solution from the absorbers to the generators (see lines 6 to 7 and 16 to 17 in Fig.2).

The mode that DSHT is operating is the cited first in the past section. The useful heat of the first absorber is added to the evaporator of the second stage.

The Cycle for the DSHT is as follow: Waste heat is added to generator 1, evaporator 1 and generator 2. In the generators 1 and 2, concentrated solution of Carrol ™ - Water is boiling at low pressure (see Fig. 1). The working fluid (WF) for this DSHT is water at lower pressure. The vapor in lines 1 and 11 is condensed with the condenser. The condensers are delivering no useful heat to the surroundings. The WF is pumping from the condensers to each evaporator at different pressure. In the first evaporator the WF change to phase to vapor for goes through the absorber 1. In the absorber 1 the concentrated solution (Carrol ™ - Water) is putting in contact with the vapor from evaporator 1. The absorption 1 delivers heat at higher temperature than waste heat added to the first stage.

The heat from absorber 1 is added to the evaporator 2. The vapor from evaporator 2 is putting in contact with the second concentrated solution (Carrol ™ - Water) from generator 2. This absorption takes account into the absorber 2. The absorption in the absorber 2 delivers useful heat at the highest temperature at all system [1].

IV. MAIN PARAMETERS

The main parameters in the heat pump studies are the Coefficient of performance (COP), the Flow ratio (FR) and the Gross Temperature Lift (GTL).

These parameters are defined as follow:

$$COP = \frac{Q_{AB2}}{Q_{GE1} + Q_{EV1} + Q_{GE2} + W_{P1} + W_{P2}} \qquad (1)$$

Where: Q_{AB2} is the useful energy deliver in the second stage of the DSHT.

Q_{GE1}, Q_{EV1}, Q_{GE2} are the heat added from waste heat into the generators and the first evaporator.

W_{P1} and W_{P2} are the energy for the operating of the pumps in the first and second stage respectively.

$$FR = \frac{X_8}{X_8 - X_7} \qquad (2)$$

$$FR = \frac{X_{18}}{X_{18} - X_{17}} \qquad (3)$$

where X_i is the mass concentration of Carrol ™ in the line i.

$$GTL = T_{AB} - T_{EV} \qquad (4)$$

$$GTL_{DSHT} = T_{AB2} - T_{EV1} \qquad (5)$$

Where T_{AB2} is the highest temperature in the system and T_{EV1} is the operating temperature in the first evaporator after the heat transfer from waste heat.

Type T thermocouples were used, in each heat exchange are placed 8 thermocouples. The thermocouples are connected to a data logger for monitoring the temperature every five seconds. The temperature measures are sending in line to an Excel® file.

The total heat transferred from the DSHT is calculated by:

$$Q_{AB2} = m_{out}\, Cp\, (\Delta T) \qquad (6)$$

Where m_{out} is the flow that recover the useful energy from second absorber and Cp is the heat capacity of the fluid that is recovering the energy. ΔT is the difference of temperature from the application and the DSHT.

V. CONTROL BY FLOW RATIO

The control of the useful heat is based in mass the flow. The Q_{AB2} depends of the system as follow:

$$Q_{AB2} = Q_{GE1} + Q_{EV1} + Q_{GE2} - Q_{CO1} - Q_{CO2} \qquad (7)$$

Where each Q_i is calculated by previous thermodynamic model [2].

The Flow Ratio can be defined by a new and different way:

$$FR = \frac{m_5}{m_4} \qquad (8)$$

And

$$FR = \frac{m_{15}}{m_{14}} \qquad (9)$$

Where m_i is the flow in the "i" line.

From this new definition at T_4 and T_{15} defined by the GTL exist a constant ratio for calculate the mass flows into the DSHT. When the flows mass are calculated, the model for an AHT converges. And the DSHT's model is based by the AHT, so it is imperative to know the mass flow for the control of the system.

All the Qi are calculated with the actual Temperature, concentration and pressure for each component.

$$Q_{AB1} = Q_{EV2} \tag{10}$$

$$Q_{GE2} = M_{GE2,V} H_{GE2,V} + M_{GE2,S} H_{GE2,S} - M_{AB2,S} H_{VA2,S} \tag{11}$$

$$T_{EV1} = T_{GE1} = T_{GE2} \tag{12}$$

$$Q_{CO2} = M_{CO2}(H_{CO2,S} - H_{GE2,V}) \tag{13}$$

$$Q_{AB2} = M_{CO2} H_{EV2,V} + M_{GE2,S} H_{HX2,S} - M_{AB2,S} H_{AB2,S} \tag{14}$$

Whit the pressure in each component defined by:

$$P_{CO2} = P_{GE2} = P(T_{CO2}) \tag{15}$$

$$P_{EV2} = P_{AB2} = P(T_{EV2}) \tag{16}$$

VI. RESULTS AND DISCUSSION

The control was implemented as follow:

A gear pump was conditioned for each step corresponding to constant flow of 0.12 ml.

The density of the working fluid is constant and it is know by the LabView program. The program is shown in Figure 3. The DSHT is controlled by the calculation in a HPVEE program. This other program is shown in Figure 4.

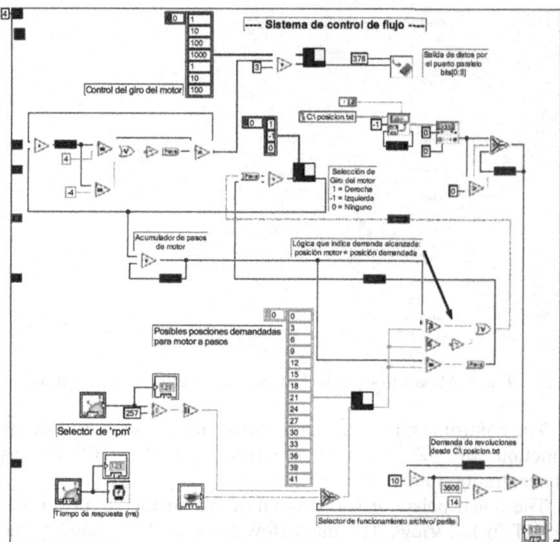

Figure 3. LabView program for flow control in a DSHT.

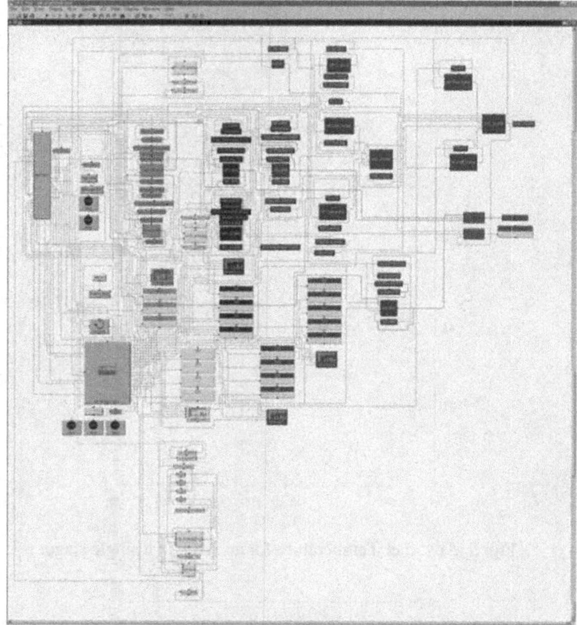

Figure 4. HPVEE program for DSHT control.

The experimental data were obtained, for steady state and that was validated with a Heat pump simulator designed by Romero [2].

The operating conditions show several operating conditions for the DSHT. The experimental data confirm that COP is bigger than an AHT.

The temperature of waste heat was simulated in laboratory conditions for oil refinery process. That energy is simulated b by each kW in the boiler – condenser equipment into a oil distillation process.

The energy simulated has a temperature of 70 °C for the adding into the generators and first evaporator. The surroundings have the capability to sink energy at 20 °C for the non useful energy at condensers.

The firs stage operates as literature [3], and the energy from first absorber is deliver for the second evaporator process at several conditions as show the figure 5.

In the figure 5, it is shown that a maximum COP_{AHT} exists. The maximum COP for the AHT is in the 100 °C for the firs absorber. The T_{AB1} at 128 °C has a COP of 0.239. This value means that only 23% of the waste energy is revalorized with an AHT.

While the energy from first absorber is added to the second evaporator, then the COP_{DSHT} is higher than COP_{AHT}. The energy at 100 °C is added to the second evaporator. The Flow ratio defines with the equation 7 the mass flow and the L293B integrate circuit send a signal to the pumps for control the thermodynamic cycle. With this action, the DSHT is controlled to get the highest temperature of the system.

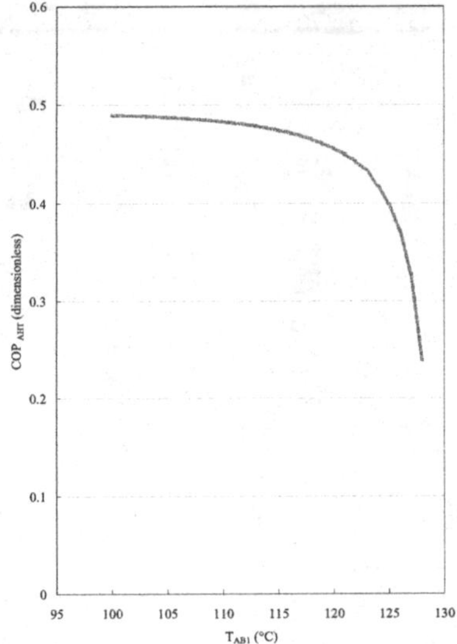

Fig. 5. Absorber Temperature for an AHT in a single stage.

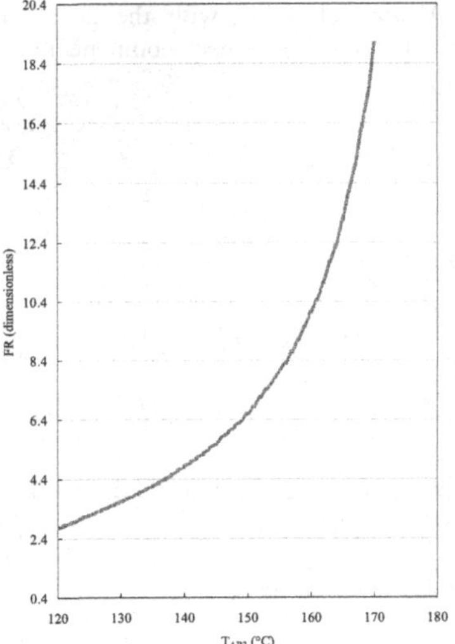

Fig. 7. Flow ratio as function of absorber temperature.

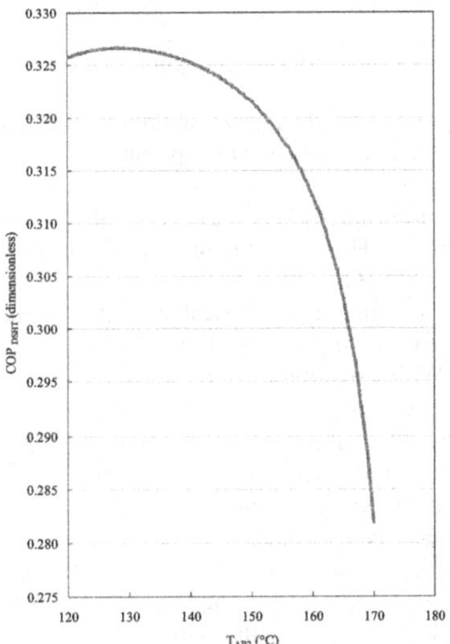

Fig. 6. DSHT energy recovering with FR control.

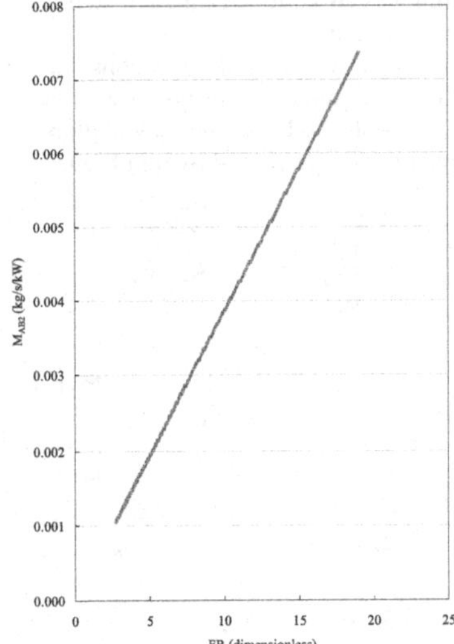

Fig. 8. Mass Flow per kW of load as function of flow ratio.

The maximum energy now, 28.1 % revalorized is at 170 °C instead 128 °C. Or in the other scenario for the oil distillation, the energy at 128 °C is revalorized until 32.6 %.

Both scenarios are more thermal efficient than the single stage, and the control implemented by Flow ratio is calculated for each single operating conditions. The function calculated in HPVEE and programmed in LabView for the mass flow control is show in the figure 7.

The control is based in a linear behavior of the mass flow as function of the calculation defined in the HPVEE as concentration functions.

The linear behavior was programming for the control of the DSHT in LabView. The mass flow for each kW added to the evaporator is show in the figure 7.

VII. CONCLUSIONS

The experimental set – up allows the measure of temperatures and the HPVEE program has the capability for the calculation of concentration of Carrol ™ - water for an absorption heat transformer (AHT) and for a double stage heat transformer (DSHT). A second program, in LabView programming, was implemented for control the mass flow. The flow ratio parameter was defined for the Control of the entire system. There is a linear behavior of the mass flow as function of the Flow ratio. The control of the mass flow by the flow ratio was observed for the DSHT. The main advantage of the control in the DSHT is the revalorized effect of the waste energy, in this case, of simulated oil distillation, waste heat. The maximum temperature for an AHT was reported at 128 °C with a Coefficient of performance of 0.239, instead the control in the DSHT leads to a higher temperature. The simulated and calculated maximum temperature for DSHT was 128 °C with a COP of 0.326. This means a increase of 36.4 % of increase in the recover and revaluation of waste heat.

VIII. REFERENCES

[1] R. J. Romero, Sotsil Silva – Sotelo, Comparison of instrumental methods for in-line determination of LiBr concentration in solar absorption thermal systems, Solar Energy Materials And Solar Cells, Vol. 90 ,Issue 15, 2006, pp. 2549 – 2555.

[2] Romero R. J.; Rivera W; Best R. Comparison of the theoretical performance of a solar air conditioning system operating with water / lithium bromide and an aqueous ternary hydroxide; Solar Energy Materials & solar Cells, Vol. 63, pp 387 – 399, 2000

[3] Romero R. J.; Rivera W.; Pilatowsky I.; Best R.; Comparison of the modeling of a solar absorption system for simultaneous cooling and heating operating with an aqueous ternary hydroxide and with water / lithium bromide; Solar Energy Materials & solar Cells, Vol. 70, pp 301 – 308, 2001

IX ACKNOWLEDGEMENTS

The authors thank to the project: "Desarrollo y aplicación de un sistema de refrigeración termo solar autosuficiente y sustentable para conservación de productos perecederos en comunidades costeras alejas de la red" for partial support.

Enforcement of Privacy Policies over Multiple Online Social Networks for Collaborative Activities

Zhengping Wu
Department of Computer Science and Engineering
University of Bridgeport
221 University Avenue Bridgeport, CT 06604
zhengpiw@bridgeport.edu

Lifeng Wang
Department of Computer Science and Engineering
University of Bridgeport
221 University Avenue Bridgeport, CT 06604
zhengpiw@bridgeport.edu

Abstract — **Our goal is to tend to develop an enforcement architecture of privacy policies over multiple online social networks. It is used to solve the problem of privacy protection when several social networks build permanent or temporary collaboration. Theoretically, this idea is practical, especially due to more and more social network tend to support open source framework "OpenSocial". But as we known different social network websites may have the same privacy policy settings based on different enforcement mechanisms, this would cause problems. In this case, we have to manually write code for both sides to make the privacy policy settings enforceable. We can imagine that, this is a huge workload based on the huge number of current social networks. So we focus on proposing a middleware which is used to automatically generate privacy protection component for permanent integration or temporary interaction of social networks. This middleware provide functions, such as collecting of privacy policy of each participant in the new collaboration, generating a standard policy model for each participant and mapping all those standard policy to different enforcement mechanisms of those participants.**

Keywords - social network, enforcement mechanisms, privacy, policy management, XACML, ontology

I. INTRODUCTION

Since social networking has been a buzzword, people began to register members of different social network websites one by one, to communicate with different friends on different social network websites or attempt new feature of new social network websites. Why we do not use only one ID to visit all the friends on different social network websites. So that we need only update information of this ID when there is something new or something change, then, all the updates are available for every friend on different social network websites. This should solve one problem summarized in [1] which is boring users of existing social networks. Theoretically, this idea is practical, because there are more and more social network websites try to support open source framework "OpenSocial". But to implement this idea, there are still lots of problems. One of the most sensitive problems is security protection. Of course, we can invoke privacy policy for both side of a connection by manually write source code. But we can see there is a way to map those policies to others automatically. We propose policy-based management to achieve requirements of security, and also propose an enforcement architecture to make this way more flexible and dynamic, because users can use any kinds of high level policy languages they want; system administrators can easily introduce a new privacy policy when a new cooperation is created; and semantic policy translation is flexible. Obviously, how to make it secure is the key point, and we also care about usability of users. So that users can make an interconnection for temporary cooperation or other purposes easily and secure between different social networks. In this paper, the second section describes some related works. The third section introduces policy language example XACML and discuss privacy policy settings of current social network websites. The fourth section offers the enforcement hierarchy. The fifth section describes details of enforcement architecture. The sixth section is case study. Then the conclusions are in the last section.

II. RELATED WORK

A social network is a social structure which, in general, facilitates communication between a group of individuals or organizations, which are related by one or more specific types of interdependency. People have used the social network metaphor for over a century to connote complex sets of relationships between members of social systems at all scales, from interpersonal to international. Today, we begin to simulate social networks online for interconnection with others, such as friends, schoolmates and colleagues. There are lots of social network applications for personal use, enterprise use or other purposes, such as Myspace, Facebook, IBM Lotus notes, BEA AquaLogic. All applications are developing rapidly but with many problems. One of those problems is that the usage scope of social networks is too limited, for purpose to visit your professional friends, you may have a Linkedin or Twitter account; for visiting your college friends, you may use a Facebook account; for entertainment, you may have a Bebo account. Unfortunately, there are some high school classmates are using Myspace, so you probably have to register an account of Myspace. Once you have some information needed to be updated, you have to login all of them and update them one by one. In order to extend those social networks, the best solution is to interconnect different social networks. Our paper intend to provide privacy protection mapping when interconnect decision made.

T. Sobh, K. Elleithy (eds.), *Innovations in Computing Sciences and Software Engineering*,
DOI 10.1007/978-90-481-9112-3_101,

Policy-based management is an administrative approach that is used to simplify the management of a given endeavor by establishing policies to deal with situations that are likely to occur. Policies are operating rules that can be referred to as a means of maintaining order, security, consistency, or other ways of successfully furthering a goal or mission. Different policies are used to play different roles or act at different stages in the management of federation activities. Some policies have already be defined by industrial standards. And there are also some policies without industrial standards, such as business rules, strategies, privacy policies [4] [5], provisional policies, and other potential policies. It is desirable to integrate all those policies into a coherent framework so that the expressiveness of original policies is not limited, the underlying infrastructure can be easily used to support interoperability and decision making, and the policies themselves can be transparently enforced, synchronized, and adapted. However, new issues arise when enforcing high-level policy languages with low-level mechanisms such as firewalls, web servers and databases and operating system security mechanisms, because they are faster and more difficult to avoid than rule interpreters. So a framework with flexible intermediate level process is needed. In this paper, a improved enforcement architecture is proposed to construct this framework with desired features.

III. POLICIES

Policies are operating rules that can be referred to as a meaning of maintaining order, security, consistency, or other ways of successfully furthering a goal or mission. In social networking sites, we use policies to define privacy protection rules. When people join social networking sites, they begin by creating a profile, then make connections to existing friends as well as those they meet through the site. A profile is a list of identifying information. It can include your real name, or a pseudonym. It possibly includes photographs, birthday, hometown, religion, ethnicity, and personal interest. Then, the users will update their own photos, videos, daily logs, etc. This information may content their hobbies and interests which are their privacies, such as current and previous schools, employers, drinking and drug habits and sexual preferences and orientation [12] [13]. As we know most of existing social networking sites have privacy configuration based on their own enforcement mechanism. All the access objects can be simply called "object" here, such as profile, photos, videos, daily logs. The group of people who desire to visit the "Resource" can be simply called "Subject". There are three privacy configurations of existing social networking sites; we will use those typical social networking sites as example.

For privacy protection, Facebook provide access control of Profile, Basic info, Personal info, Status and Links, Photos Tagged of You, Videos Tagged of You, Friends, Wall Posts, Education Info, Work Info. Those entire access objects can be seen as "Resource". The access groups include: Everyone, My Networks and Friends, Friends of Friends, Only Friends. All those access groups can be seen as "Subject". The screenshot of Facebook is shown by Figure 1.

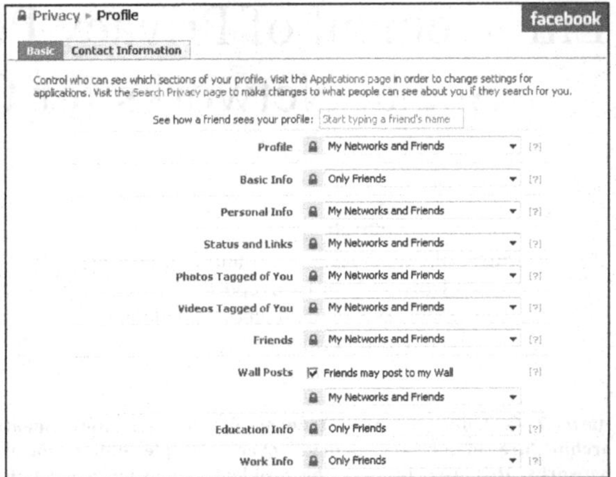

Figure 1. Screenshot of Facebook

Similar with Facebook, Myspace provide access control of Online Now, Birthday, Profile on Mobile, Comments, Friends, Photos, Status and Mood. Those entire access objects can be seen as "Resource". The access groups include: Anyone, Anyone 18 and over, Only my friends. All those access groups can be seen as "Subject". The screenshot of Myspace is shown by Figure 2.

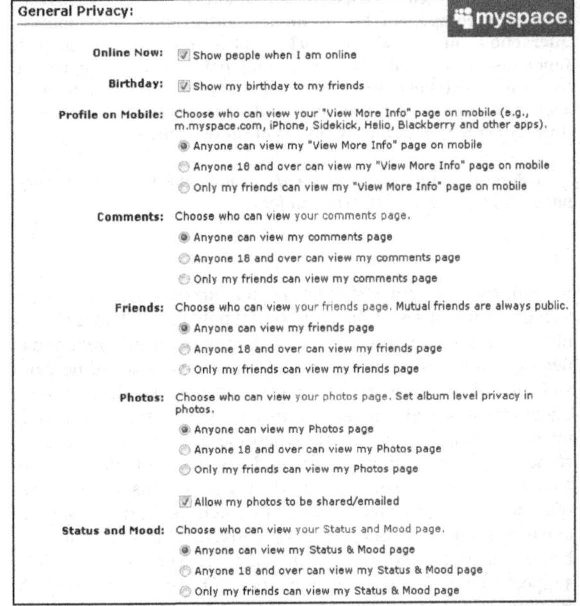

Figure 2. Screenshot of Myspace

We can use another example here, Linkedin provide access control of Research Surveys, Connections Browse, Profile Views, Viewing Profile Photos, Profile and Status Updates, Service Provider Directory, NYTimes.com Customization,

Partner Advertising, Authorized Applications. According to the usage of scope we concluded that here are some differences comparing with Facebook and Myspace, due to the usage of scope. Linkedin face to business and professional people. Most of their users are small and medium enterprises employees, consultants and sales personnel. So, there are lots of special privacy settings such as research surveys and partner advertising. All those special privacy settings can be seen as "special Resource"; the others are almost as same as Facebook and Myspace. The screenshot of Myspace is shown by Figure 3.

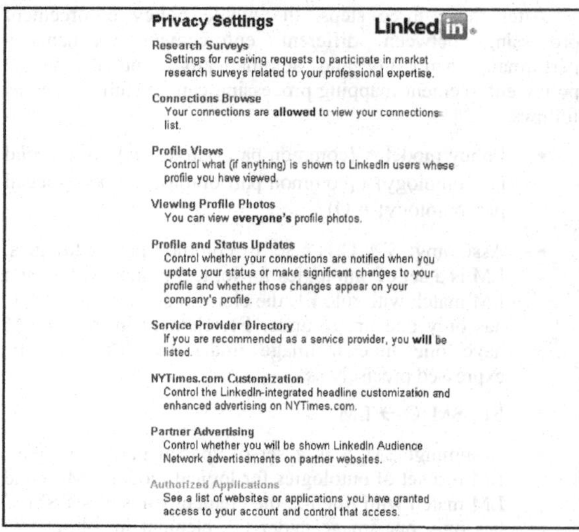

Figure 3. Screenshot of Linkedin

Based on all above examples of existing social network sites, we can see that, most of the privacy settings are similar, due to the similar features provided by different social network sites. Such as online status, profile, friends, photos, etc. but, some of the social network sites have characteristic features. Such as research surveys of Linkedin. All those similar part of settings may summarize as common part privacy settings, the others may summarize as special part privacy settings. Both of those two parts will be discussed later.

IV. ENFORCEMENT HIERARCHY

High-level policy languages are used to define enforcement rules, it's easy for users to use or understand, However it tends to be more and more complex with the development of mathematical languages and logic-based languages, such as Role-Based Access Control, Keynote, and General Access Control Language [6]. Actually, interconnections between social network websites are based on their agreements of privacy policies. Those agreements can be derived to standard policies by high-level policy languages, such as XACML we just mentioned in last section. Sometimes, these policies cannot be a one-on-one correspondence to low level enforcement mechanisms of social networks. So we resolve the discrepancy between high level languages and low level mechanisms with intermediate level. The hierarchy of enforcement as following:

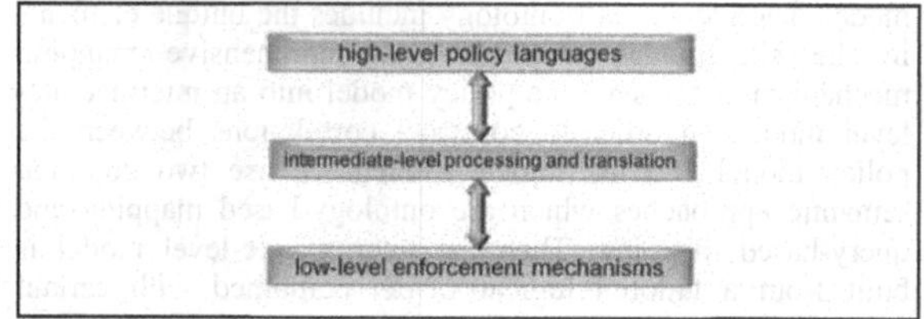

Figure 4. Policy enforcement hierarchy

The intermediate level translation mechanisms and corresponding intermediate level models must be flexible enough to bridge the semantic gap between high level policies and low level mechanisms in order to accommodate different models of high level policies. According to available low level enforcement mechanisms, ontology or a vocabulary specification is formed. Then domain experts translate high level policies to a specification using the ontology or vocabulary. This task has become a part of the responsibilities for IT department in every organization. Mapping mechanisms have been proposed to translate high level policies to low level mechanisms, such as top-down mappings and bottom-up mappings. Top-down mappings try to search corresponding features in low level mechanisms for high level policies. Bottom-up mappings present all the available mechanisms to the policy definer, and allow only enforceable features to be included in the policy. Bottom-up mappings usually need a good visualization to help a policy definer understand those low level features and mechanisms. We integrate the advantages of both top-down and bottom-up styles to build an intermediate level, and construct a comprehensive model translation in the intermediate level to bridge the gap.

V. ENFORCEMENT ARCHITECTURE

To reach the requirements and features we mentioned before, an intermediate-level middleware based on model translation is proposed to bridge the gap. Figure 5 and Figure 6 illustrates the enforcement architecture by using UML. (Figure 5 is the information flow, and Figure 6 is the control flow.)

The first step is to define the suitable privacy policy model to match the privacy protection settings of policy model by using an existing high-level language. The usability of the whole enforcement architecture will be affect by this privacy policy model due to it directly defines what feature are available and how can they be used.

The second step is to derive an intermediate-level model from a logical model. For example, the EM-enforceable policy model can be chosen as the logical mode. Each execution leads to a state in its finite state automate form, where enforcement mechanisms can be applied to check the validity and safety of that state. Then, together with the context information, enforcement mechanisms can determine whether the next execution is safe by checking the state it leads to. Then, there are two sets of ontology [3] to represent the policy model and the logical model respectively. The ontology for the policy model also includes two parts – a common part ontology and a special part ontology. The common part ontology includes the elements having direct corresponding elements in the logical model. The special part ontology includes the unique elements in the site model. We use a comprehensive mapping mechanism to translate the policy model into an intermediate-level model. In order to construct correlations between the policy model and the logical model, we use two common semantic approaches which are ontology-based mapping and query-based mapping. Then the intermediate-level model is built from a tailored logical model combined with certain extensions.

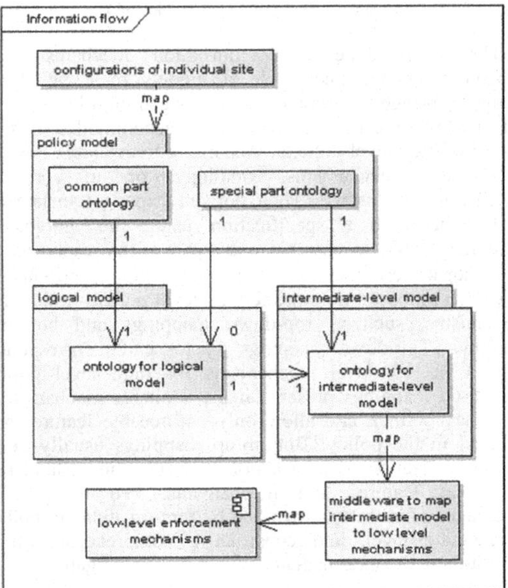

Figure 5. Information flow of the The enforcement architecture

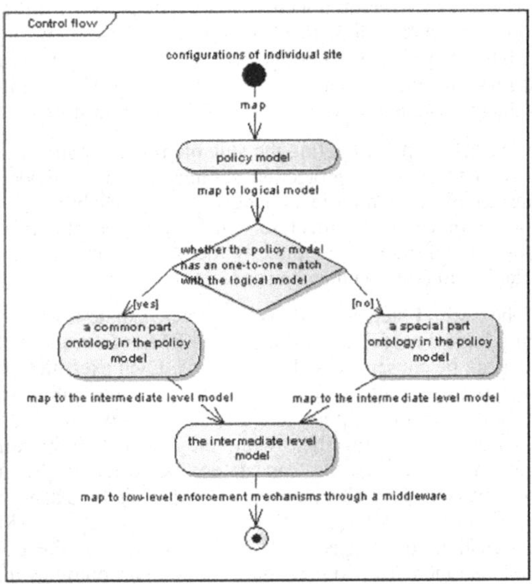

Figure 6. Control flow of the The enforcement architecture

The third step is using query-based construction to map the translated intermediate-level model to available low-level enforcement mechanisms. There are two merits of this architecture: the first is that users can choose their high–level policy languages to match the usability they want; the second, the domain administrator can introduce a new core logical model when it is more appropriate for the enforcement task. In this step, the requirement to achieve flexibility is the low-level enforcement mechanisms provide a clear set of APIs for query-based construction of mapping between the intermediate-level model and low-level mechanisms.

After those three steps, the whole policy enforcement processing between different enforcement mechanisms performance smoothly and automatically. And the whole policy enforcement mapping processing can be summarized as follows:

- Policy model = {common part ontologies} ∪ {special part ontology} ({common part ontologies} ∩ {special part ontology} = Ø)
- Assuming: SM_C is a set of common part ontologies. LM is a set of ontologies for logical model. SM_C and LM match with rule F1, the element sm_c of set SM_C has only one image under F1, element lm of set LM have one inverse image under F1. This can be expressed precisely as:

  $F1 : SM\_C \rightarrow LM$
- Assuming: SM_S is a set of special part ontologies. LM is a set of ontologies for logical model. SM_S and LM match with rule F2, the element sm_s of set SM_S has only one image under F2, element lm of set LM have none inverse image under F2. This can be expressed precisely as:

  $F2 : SM\_S \rightarrow LM$
- Assuming: SM_S is a set of special part ontologies. IL is a set of ontologies for intermediate-level model. SM_S and IL match with rule F3, the element sm_s of set SM_S has only one image under F3, element il of set IL has one inverse image under F3. This can be expressed precisely as:

  $F3 : SM\_S \rightarrow IL$
- Assuming: LM is a set of ontologies for logical model. IL is a set of ontologies for intermediate-level model. LM and IL match with rule F4, the element lm of set LM has only one image under F4, element il of set IL has one inverse image under F4. This can be expressed precisely as:

  $F4 : LM \rightarrow IL$
- Assuming: IL is a set of ontologies for intermediate-level model. LL is a set of ontologies for low-level enforcement mechanisms. IL and LL match with rule F5, the element il of set IL has only one image under F5, element ll of set LL have one inverse image under F5. This can be expressed precisely as:

F5 : IL → LL

VI. CASE STUDY

Currently, there are so many different social network websites run on the public internet, which are used by countless numbers of people. Those various social network websites don't usually work together. You thus have to reenter your profile and redefine your connections from scratch when you register for each new site. By using our enforcement architecture, the privacy protection can provide to the sites which look forward to interconnection with others.

A. Usecase

As we known, there are lots of famous social networking websites, such as Friendster, Facebook, Orkut, LinkedIn, Bebo, and MySpace, etc, they are all offer a lot of social networking functionalities. Usually, they offer the same basic functionalities: network of friends listings, person surfing, private messaging, discussion forums or communities, events management, blogging, commenting, and media uploading. So, all those social network sites should have almost the same privacy settings. For example, profile, personal info, status and links, photos, friends, education info, work info and so on. All those same privacy settings probably use different enforcement mechanisms of different social networks. Then, by using our enforcement mechanism, mapping all those similar policies as common part ontology. About the policy which is special for the others can be map as special part ontology. Then we got all the requirement of using our policy enforcement architecture. So, a desirous structure of social networks can be implemented by using our policy enforcement architecture as shown in Figure 4.

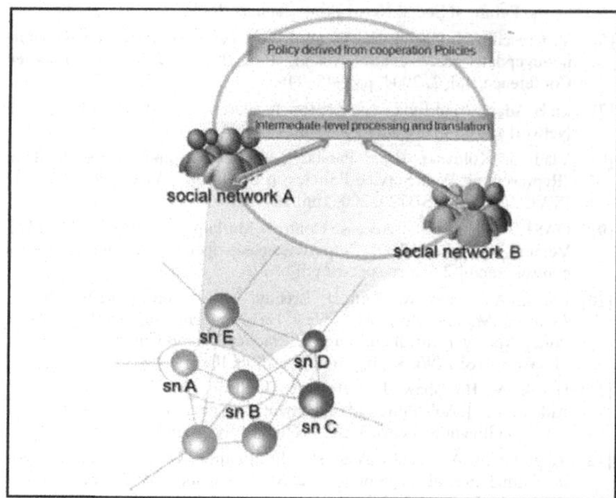

Figure 7. Desirous structure of social networks

As illustrated in Figure 4, the whole implement possessing follows the methods provided by our policy enforcement architecture exactly. As we mentioned in section three, assume Myspace is social network A, Facebook is social network B, so the common part ontology may represent things such as online status, profile, friends, photos, etc. The different privacy settings should be represented by special part of ontology. After we got the common part ontology and special part of ontology, both parts of ontologies can be mapped to intermediate-level processing and translation. Finally, map the intermediate-level processing and translation to low-level enforcement to both sides. Then, all the enforceable policies can be applied to other's enforcement mechanism. All the unenforceable policies will be given response back to notice user.

B. Privacy Policy Generating

In the section three, we have already mentioned the privacy policy management in some existing social network websites. All the cases describe to define access rules for similar operation: "Subject" access "Resource". Obviously, this is a question for defining access control decision. To illustrate the policy, we use OASIS standard XACML Policy [9]. Both the "Resource" and "Subject" can be mapped to XACML easily. As we known, XACML is used to describe both a policy language and an access control decision request/response language. The policy language is used to describe general access control requirements, and has standard extension points for defining new functions, data types, combining logic, etc. The request/response language lets you form a query to ask whether or not a given action should be allowed, and interpret the result. The response always includes an answer about whether the request should be allowed using one of four values: Permit, Deny, Indeterminate or Not Applicable. Some the features of XACML Policy are shown here:

- Resource = {Data, service, system component}
- Subject = {actors}
- Action = {operations}
- Environment = {attributes}
- Target = {resource, subject, action, Environment}
- Condition = {True, False, Indeterminate}
- Effect = {Permit, Deny}
- Rule = {target, effect, condition}
- Policy = {rules, Targets, policy-combining algorithm, obligations}
- Policy set = {policies, other policy sets, a policy-combining algorithm, obligations}

C. Implementation

The idea of implementation method is already mentioned in section five. The details of implementation will be described again with the combination of our use case. There are still three steps:

Firstly, we use XACML to translate the privacy policy configuration. So that we can get a policy file which match with the privacy protection settings of privacy model. Then, this policy file should be transformed to ontology format which is seemed as policy model.

Secondly, we map the policy model to logic model. All the one to one match part of ontology can be generated as common part ontology, the others can be seen as special part ontology. Both the common part ontology and special part ontology can be mapped to intermediate level model. In our use case, the common part should be online status, profile, friends, photos, etc. the others should be the special part.

Finally, there will be a query-based construction to map the intermediate-level model to available low-level enforcement mechanisms. Further, all the unavailable low-level enforcement mechanisms will be return to users. Such as there are not suitable enforcement mechanisms for "Education Info" and "Work Info", so both of them will be return to Facebook.

D. *Analysis of Implementation*

1) *Policy Dependencies*

The effectiveness of policy enforcement is predicated on the correct construction of policy assertions. Through the correct construction of policy assertions, we can use Web Ontology Language (OWL) to represent correct construction of ontologies which is one of core parts of our enforcement architecture. We don't care what kind of policy needed to be represented. Such as security policy, trust policy, authorization policy or privacy rules and so on. Then, all those correct policies can be represented to ontologies by using a similar way as [8]. We will also providing user interface to improve the usability as [10] [11]. Then, our enforcement architecture could performance well based on those correct ontologies.

2) *Performance*

As we mentioned there are three steps of mapping, the first step is to define the suitable privacy policy model to match the privacy protection settings of social network sites by using an existing high-level language. This is the only part required a human-machine interaction. Then all the steps are performed automatically, such as mapping new policies or modified policies to intermediate level, mapping intermediate level to low level enforcement mechanism, enforce enforceable policies and response all the unenforceable policies back to users.

Compare with traditional model, after programmers understand all the requirement of policy modifications, they will spend lots of time to modify source code and test the modified code. So the advantage of our enforcement architecture is obvious. In our workflow, even there are no programmers required. Almost all the works are automatically performed.

VII. CONCLUSIONS

Online social networking has become an indispensable activity for most people, our research base on the goal of improving existing social networking. We focus on solving the privacy protection issue when two or more social networking require interactions. Due to all the existing social networking is independent, when some permanent integration or temporary interaction of social networks is required, we must be puzzled by the trouble: different social networking used different policy enforcement mechanisms. In this paper, a policy enforcement architecture is provided, which can solve this trouble successfully. The merits of this enforcement architecture can be summarized as follows: users can use any kinds of high level policy languages they want; system administrators can easily introduce a new privacy policy or modify existing policies when a new cooperation is created; and the semantic policy translation is flexible.

We also think that much more research is necessary on the social networking. Especially we need to take more care about privacy protection, when some described social networking [7] need to interconnect with others. Such as enterprise social networking, there are more sensitive information. The policy is more complex. We will improve our enforcement architecture to meet the more complex requirements. And a friendlier interface will be provided also.

REFERENCES

[1] Breslin, J., and Decker, S., "The Future of Social Networks on the Internet: The Need for Semantics", Internet Computing, IEEE, Vol. 11, Issue 6, pp.86 – 90, Nov.-Dec. 2007.

[2] M. Blaze, J. Feigenbaum, and Jack Lacy, "Decentralized Trust Management," Proc.1996 IEEE Symposium on Security and Privacy, 1996, pp. 164 -173.

[3] Peter Mika, "Flink: Semantic Web Technology for the Extraction and Analysis of Social Networks", Web Semantics: Science, Services and Agents on the World Wide Web, Vol. 3(2-3), October 2005, pp. 211-223.

[4] Sören Preibusch, Bettina Hoser, etc., "Ubiquitous social networks – opportunities and challenges for privacy-aware user modeling", Proceedings of the Workshop on Data Mining for User Modelling at UM, 2007.

[5] Sören Preibusch and Alastair R. Beresford, "Privacy-Preserving Friendship Relations for Mobile Social Networking", W3C Workshop on the Future of Social Networking, January 2009.

[6] V. Crescini, Y. Zhang, W. Wang, "Web server authorization with the policyupdater access control system," Proc. 2004 IADIS WWW/Internet Conference, vol. 2, 2004, pp. 945–948.

[7] Lada Adamic and Eytan Adar, "How to search a social network", Social Networks, Vol. 27(3), July 2005, pp. 187-203.

[8] Vladimir Kolovski, Bijan Parsia, Yarden Katz, and James Hendler, "Representing Web Service Policies in OWL-DL", Y. Gil et al. (Eds.): ISWC 2005, LNCS 3729, 2005, pp. 461–475.

[9] OASIS, "eXtensible Access Control Markup Language (XACML) Version 2.0," Feb. 2005. http://docs.oasis-open.org/xacml/2.0/access_control -xacml-2.0-core-spec-os.pdf

[10] Uszok, A., Bradshaw, Lott, J. Breedy, M., Bunch, L.,Feltovich, P., Johnson, M. and Jung, H., "New Developments in Ontology-Based Policy Management: Increasing the Practicality and Comprehensiveness of KAoS". IEEE Workshop on Policy 2008, IEEE Press.

[11] Uszok, A., Bradshaw, J., Jeffers, R., Johnson, M., Tate A., Dalton, J., Aitken, S., "KAoS Policy Management for Semantic Web Services". In IEEE Intelligent Systems, Vol. 19, No. 4, July/August, p. 32-41.

[12] Ralph Gross, Alessandro Acquisti, "Information Revelation and Privacy in Online Social Networks", ACM Workshop on Privacy in the Electronic Society (WPES), 2005.

[13] Catherine Dwyer, Starr Roxanne Hiltz, "Trust and privacy concern within social networking sites:A comparison of Facebook and MySpace", Proceedings of the Thirteenth Americas Conference on Information Systems, Keystone, Colorado August 09 - 12 2007.

An Estimation of Distribution Algorithms Applied to Sequence Pattern Mining

Paulo Igor A. Godinho[1], Aruanda S. Gonçalves Meiguins[1,2], Roberto C. Limão de Oliveira[1], Bianchi S. Meiguins[1]

[1] Universidade Federal do Pará – UFPA, Belém, PA 66075-110 Brazil
[2] Centro Universitário do Pará – CESUPA, Belém, PA 66035-170 Brazil
piagodinho@gmail.com, aruanda@redeinformatica.com.br, limao@ufpa.br, bianchi.serique@terra.com.br

Abstract- **This paper presents a proposal of distribution's estimated algorithm to the extraction of sequential patterns in a database which use a probabilistic model based on graphs which represent the relations among items that form a sequence. The model maps a probability among the items allowing them to adjust the model during the execution of the algorithm using the evolution process of EDA, optimizing the candidate's generation of solution and extracting a group of sequential patterns optimized.**

I. INTRODUCTION

The necessity of extracting interesting information of complex database and with a great volume of data to obtain a competitive differential has become more often day bay day [7]. In almost every human knowledge area there are efforts from the scientific community do develop techniques and tools which can give a support and automate the process of information extraction with the objective of generating knowledge and help the process of taking decisions.

The mining of data is the process of discovering new meaningful correlations, patterns and tendencies in a great quantity of electronic storage data using patterns of recognition technology as well as math and statistics techniques [9].

There are many tasks and techniques of mining, the main ones are: Analysis of Association's Rules, Analysis of Sequential Patterns, Classification and Prediction, Cluster Analysis, Analysis of *Outliers* [5]. For each task there are many algorithms that can be used. Generally these algorithms are specific for one kind of database, or for one group of characteristic group of number data, categorized, continuous or discrete and it possesses application in a variety of areas, such as, engineering, biology, medicine, retailing and marketing [7].

Particularly the tasks of analyzing the sequenced patterns is the one that identifies frequent occurrences of a joint of elements sorted by event or pattern subsequences of data in a database. A sequence consists of element subsequences, or events, sorting, put in storage with, or without a concrete notion of time [5].

Among new evolution computer approaches which can help the analysis task of sequential pattern the highlighted ones are the Estimation of Distribution Algorithms (EDA), which possess a different evolution approach without the use of the crossover operators and candidates to the solution, trying to optimize them during the interactions of the algorithm to reach the desired results. On section 3 of EDA they are presented more detailed.

This, this work uses the EDA to extract sequential patterns optimizing the extraction of sequences and searching for interesting patterns. The algorithm uses a model based on graphs that represents the relations among the items that form a sequence. The model maps the probability among the items allowing adjusting the model during the algorithms execution using the evolution process of EDA, optimizing the generation of the candidates solutions and extracting a group of optimized sequential patterns.

This paper is organized in 6 sections. On section 2 it is presented the mining of sequential patterns and its main concepts. After, on section 3, the estimation sequential of algorithms and on section 4 it will be discussed related works, so it's presented, on section 5, the work developed performing a description of the proposed algorithm. In the sequence, on section 6, it will be presented the final considerations and future works.

II. MINING SEQUENTIAL PATTERNS

The mining sequential pattern consists of a discovery of frequent sequential patterns, in a sequence base. This is an important issue of mining data with a vast applicability [12], examples like, bioinformatics in the identification of patterns in DNA sequences, the assistance to the symptoms identification helping the medical diagnosis, besides the bases of commercial domain where the extraction of sequential patterns is a great utility of market campaigns, strategies to have the client's fidelity, organization of store shelves to sell products, promotional campaigns and a varied of other domains [5].

A sequence pattern is an expression in the format <I1, ..., In>, where each Ii is a group of items. The order in what they are aligned correspond to the chronological order the events occurred, for example the sequence <{TV},{DVD player, home theater}> represents the pattern "Clients who buy TV, after a period of time they buy a DVD player and a home theater".

The algorithms of sequential patterns use a parameter to indicate whether a found sequence can be considered a sequential pattern or not. This parameter named minimum support is specified by the user.

The minimum support is a parameter that identifies when a group of items is frequent in a database; its operation is given as following. If a group of items, or sequence, x1 repeats in 30% of the database and the other sequence x2, repeats 25%, considering the minimum support of 30%, only the first sequence (x1) will be considered a frequent sequence, or sequential pattern.

T. Sobh, K. Elleithy (eds.), *Innovations in Computing Sciences and Software Engineering*,
DOI 10.1007/978-90-481-9112-3_102, © Springer Science+Business Media B.V. 2010

For example, if a base with thousands of transactions and a joint of items <{TV},{DVD player, home theater}> occur in more than 30% of base transactions (supposing that 30% is the minimum support established), this joint possesses a frequency above the minimum support determined, so the sequence is considered frequent.

The development of algorithms and solutions that find sequential patterns interested in large databases are relevant due to their great extension and applicability, researches to optimize the space of searching and quality of the sequential patterns found, are inherent challenges of the sequential pattern mine [12].

The evolution approach of EDA is a recent topic of studies and researches in computer sciences and it is used in this work to develop an algorithm of sequential pattern extraction which is a new and different approach to the problem, generating new contributions to the area of data mining.

III. Estimation of Distribution Algorithms

The estimation of distribution algorithms are one more paradigm of evolutionary computer science. The EDA do not use the mutation and crossover operation, traditional in classical algorithms of evolutionary computer science like the Genetic Algorithms [6] and the Genetic Programming [8]. These operators are substituted by learning and sampling of the probability distribution of the best individuals from a population to each algorithm. Therefore, the EDA use a selection to a choice of individual subgroups from a population to the construction and optimization of probabilistic models which are used to generate candidates towards a solution to each generation [10].

The EDA were introduced in the field of Evolution Computer Science in the work of Muhlenbein and Paa (1996) [11]. Similar studies can be found on Zhigljavsky's book (1991) [19]. The estimation of distribution algorithms can be still found with other names and the most known ones are: Probabilistic Model Building Genetic Algorithms (PMBGA), Distribution Estimation Algorithms (DEA) e Iterated Density Estimation Algorithms (IDEA).

The execution of an EDA is formed by four main steps [10]:

1. Initially, a population of N individuals is produced, generally assuming a uniform distribution of variables.
2. An m < N individual number is then selected from the population to any of the selection methods used in evolution algorithms like, tournament, roulette or raking.
3. From the evaluation of selected individuals, it is created a better probabilistic model to the variables.
4. Based on the obtained distribution in the previous step, it is produced a new population of N individuals.

The algorithm repeats these steps until a stop criteria previously established can be attended like, for example, a maximum number of generations.

IV. Related Works

There are various algorithms to the sequential pattern mining based on the Apriori property proposed to the association of rules mining by Agrawal and Srinkant (1994) [2], the priority says that any subsequence of a frequent pattern will also be frequent. Algorithms like AprioriAll, AprioriSome, DynamicSome [1], GSP [16] and SPADE [17], use the same property to realize the sequential pattern mine.

Srikant e Agrawal (1996) [16] have developed the GSP algorithms, trying to attend some observed limitation of mining algorithms of sequential patterns, the lack of a time limit between the transactions of a sequence and the absence of taxonomy in the sequential patterns found in some of data groups were some of the highlighted limitations.

Through the GSP algorithm it is possible to find data sequence, with a taxonomy, defining parameters like: minimum and maximum lapse between each transaction, finding all the sequences with a better support than the minimum, also established by the user [16].

The AprioriAll also used in the Apriori property realizes to procedures to realize the search for the sequential patterns in the base. Firstly they generate the candidate sequences, they are named this way because they are only frequent sequences if they possess a better support than the minimum established, after the generation phase it comes the pruning phase, where it is applied the Apriori property to exclude sequences which will never be frequent sequences [1].

Algorithms based on Apriori need a great number of interactions about the whole database, realizing the same process many times until all the sequences can be found, turning the process extremely slow needing a high processing power. [18]

Another approach uses in the mining algorithms of sequential patterns, they are algorithms based on the database projection, they are algorithms much more efficient than the Apriori approach and they are able to deal with large databases [18].

Algorithms such as the PrefixSpan [12] use this approach to optimize the search process on database. To each interaction the algorithm projects one base part changing the smaller base, this projection process improves the algorithms performance in each projection.

The PrefixSpan algorithm does not need the candidates generation, only the database's recursive projection according to its prefixes. For example, in the first interaction the algorithm will get an *itemset* sizing 1 (*1-itemset*), example {DVD}, it will be the prefix, so it will be projected a base with all the *postfix* of the prefix {DVD}, which means that all the possible items that occur after the {DVD} prefix, this process will be realized recursively to each interaction.

Despite the algorithm PrefixSpan does not need to generate candidate sequences and realize the counting of support to the generated sequences, the algorithm still realizes a search for the entire base. The main cost of PrefixSpan is the process of generation of the projected base, sorting, to improve the performance on the next interaction [12].

The algorithm presented in this work shows a solution that, through the evolution approach, using the EDA, tries to optimize the results on the search for patterns in a large database, proceeding a probability graph of relations among items that compose the sequences, generating candidate solutions that are optimized during the algorithm interactions focusing the search of more optimized patterns to reach a group of interesting sequential patterns to the user.

V. ALGORITHM EDASP

The algorithm EDASP (Estimation of Distribution Algorithm for Sequence Pattern) is an Estimation of Distribution Algorithm to progress the sequential patterns through a probabilistic model based on a probability graph. The algorithm develops the graph that contains a linked item joint indicating the probability of each one occurs after another root item.

The probability graph is updated on each generation according to a sample of selected individuals. After upgrading the probability graph new individuals, or sequences, are created based on the distribution of probability of the graph. The interesting measure [13] of the generated sequences is evaluated and those with better interesting measure are kept to be presented in the algorithm final result.

The individual in the algorithm is represented by a sequence of items that represents a sequential pattern possible. Being t = {i1, i2, i3,..., in} a database group of items, a subgroup of items from group t would be considered an valid candidate individual in the algorithm (Ex.: <i1, i3, i5>).

The algorithm parameters specify the minimum and maximum sequence size and the minimum interesting measure value.

These parameters are crucial to determine the kind of sequence that the user wants to find on the database. The EDASP is part of algorithms that search for specified patterns, different of the algorithms which search for all the existent sequential patterns, such as the algorithm Apriori [1]. The size parameters help to direct the algorithm in the searching space improving the performance of the search.

The algorithm EDASP comprehend the steps of an EDA with the inclusion of one step to the partial extraction of the sequential patterns found on generation, as it can be observed on fig. 1 below:

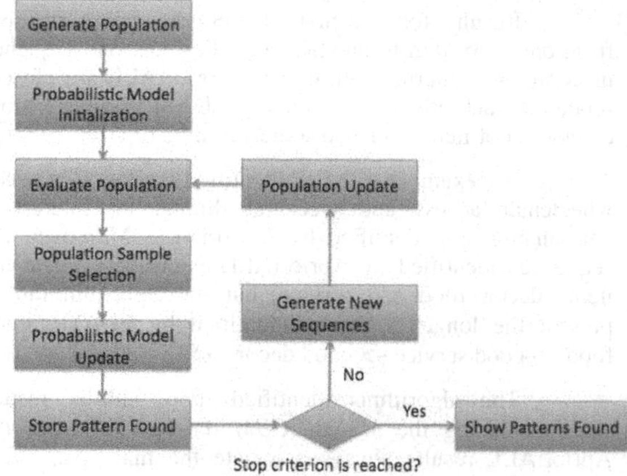

Fig. 1. EDASP Algorithm's Fluxogram.

The EDASP starts the population with database sequences, from these sequences it is initialized the probabilistic model, setting up the graph with all the existed values of first generation. On the following stages the algorithm repeats the evaluation stages of the population, sample selection, probabilistic model upgrade, extraction of the patterns found in generation, generation of new individuals from the present probabilistic model and population updated. The algorithm stages will be detailed and discussed in the following sections.

A. The Probabilistic Model

The estimation of distribution algorithm uses a probabilistic model able to express the problem's distributions probabilities [14]. In EDASP the model was represented through a noncyclical containing the relation and the distribution of probability among items existent on database. The items possess different probabilities depending on the position of the graph and the relation with its antecessors. The graph is initialized with the relation probabilities among all items contained in the initial population. The graph possess a root knot where they are linked with all the items and their items and their occurrence probabilities referred to the sample with initially is the proper group of initial sequences, after calculating and creating the knots linked to the root knot it is calculated the related probabilities, where one item will have one probability of occurring after a previous one. (Fig. 2). Thus, the graph is growing and being upgraded during the population formation on the extent that the algorithm finds new relations among the base items which were still not inserted in the graph. The graph is used in the generation process of sequences of the next generations.

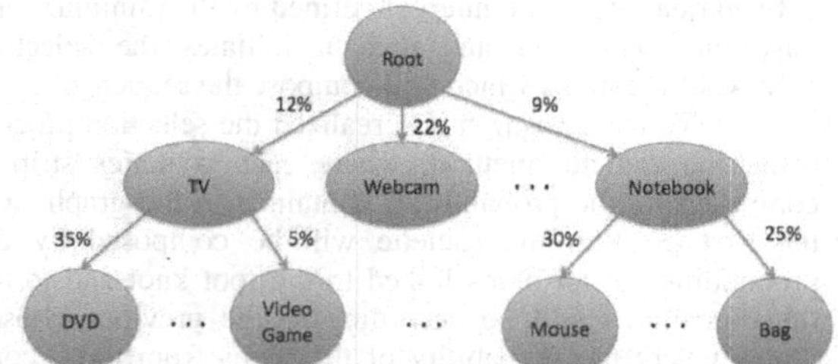

Fig. 2. Probabilistic model example based in a noncyclical graph.

B. Evaluation and Selection

After the probabilistic model is upgraded it starts the evaluation process of the population. The interesting measure (1) [13] of each sequence is calculated. Afterwards, a sample is selected by roulette [4] from the dataset to upgrade the probabilistic model. The method allows a chance for all the sequences to be selected, but the ones with better interesting measure values are proportionally more likely to be chosen.

$$inst(s) = \min_{s_p \subseteq s} \{ (\frac{1}{f_s(s_p)})^{\alpha} \} \times \frac{(f_s(s))^{(1+\alpha)}}{N} \quad (1)$$

C. New Sequences Generation

The selection determines the sample of the present main population that are used to upgrade the probabilistic model, but before actualizing the probability on the graph the calculated values are adjusted using the PBIL method [3], equation (2). The new item probability is adjusted considering the probability of the previous generation (pi(x)') and the probability calculated on the current generation (pi(x)"), the value of α vary between 0 and 1 and it indicates how much the new generation will be influenced by the previous and to the probabilities upgrade.

$$p_i(x) = (1-\alpha)p_i(x)' + \alpha * p_i(x)'' \quad (2)$$

The fig. 3 shows the process of the graphs probability upgrade and how the method PBIL is applied for the probabilities adjust.

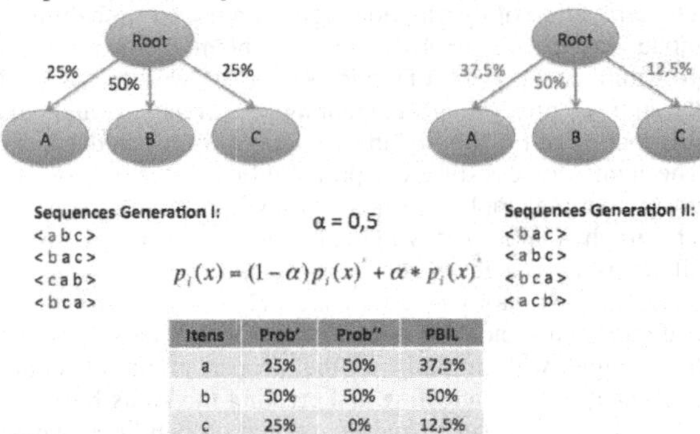

Fig. 3. Upgrade of graph possibilities usin the PBIL method.

The upgraded graph is used again to the generation of other individuals that are added on the population's upgrade. The new sequences are generated considering the parameters of a minimum and maximum size to one sequence, the algorithm generates the vector with a random defined quantity in the interval defined by the minimum and maximum parameter and then it initiates the selection process of the items which will compose the sequence.

To each position it is realized the selection process using the roulette method, where each roulettes strip is composed by the probabilities contained in the graph. On the first position the roulette will be composed by the probabilities of all items linked to the root knot and to the other positions will be according to the previous chosen items, where the probability of the items from the second position are dependents on the antecessor's items defined in the graph. The fig. 4 shows an example to a sequence of size 2.

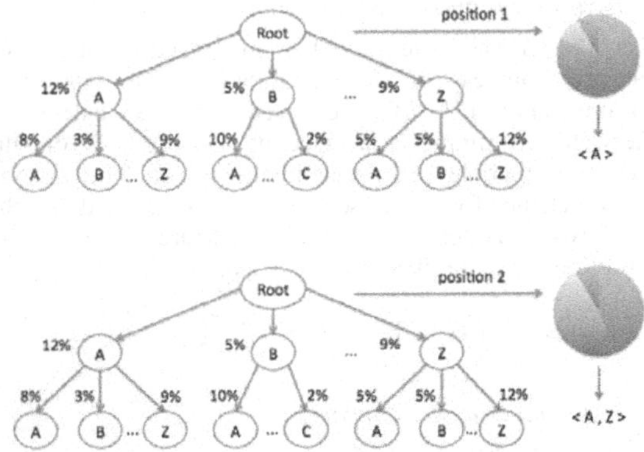

Fig. 4. Generation of an individual of size 2 using the roulette as a selection method of the sequence's items.

D. *The Upgrade of the Population*

To upgrade the population it will realized three stages, (1) it will be inserted the new individuals generated in the generation process from the graph, (2) it will be inserted new sequences from database on the population, to enable the algorithm realize searches in spaces that are still non-explored in the search space and (3) and finally the insertion of the best sequences of the previous population.

The quantity of inserted sequences in each one of the stages are parameters from algorithm and the new base sequences, selected to the population, are never repeated and the procedure occur until all the base sequences have been chosen by at least once to the population.

The insertion stage of new database helps to enrich the graph with new relation possibilities among the items not yet found on previous generations.

E. *Experiments*

Evaluation experiments of EDASP presented interesting results. Two datasets were used on the experiments, both from the *UCI Learning Machine Repository* [20]: *Entree Chicago Recommendation Data* and *MSNBC.com Anonymous Web Data*. The results of EDASP were compared to the results of the algorithm AprioriALL. Table 1 shows the five best patterns identified by each algorithm.

The *Chicago Recommendation* dataset contains information on user recommendation for restaurants, including criteria such as food, price and location. The *MSNBC.COM* dataset contains information on user interactions with the sections of a web site, such as sports, news, and business.

TABLE I
EXPERIMENTS RESULT

Base	EDASP Sequences	AprioriAll Sequences
Chicago Recomendation	Private parties; Private parties available	Excelent food; Excelent service
	Wheelchair access; Weekend dining	Excelent decor; Excelent service
	Good service; Good decor	Private parties; Private parties available
	Good food; Good service; Good decor; ($15-$30)	Excelent decor; Excelent food
	Good food; Good decor	Good decor; Excelent food
MSNBC.com	Main page; News	Main page; News
	On-air; Misc	Main page; Sports
	Main page; Bussiness	Main page; On-air
	Main page; Local	Main page; Local
	Main page; MSN sports	Main page; MSN sports

Results for the first dataset were very different from one algorithm to another, including just one sequence in common. Patterns identified by AprioriALL are closely related to each other. The results of EDASP include a more diverse set of items and also some variation of size.

For example, EDASP identified a relation between wheelchair access and weekend dining, an interesting combination not identified by AprioriALL. Moreover, the sequences identified by AprioriALL extensively relate the items decor, food and service, but the algorithm fail to present the longer sequence identified by EDASP: good food –> good service –> good decor -> $15-$30.

The algorithms identified more similar results when analyzing the *MSNBC.COM* dataset. However, the AprioriALL results always associate the main page to a second section of the web site, which is a rather common navigation. Using the interesting measure, the EDASP algorithm was able to identify a sequence that is not initiated by the main page: On-Air -> Misc.

These preliminary results indicate the potential of the new algorithm to identify semantically interesting results among the sequences with high support levels.

VI. FINAL CONSIDERATIONS AND FUTURE WORKS

The algorithm EDASP shows a different approach to the mining of sequential patterns with looks for improving the quality of the found patterns using an heuristic progress to optimize the search for patterns. The algorithm still possesses parameters to help the optimization of the search and to direct the results to attend better the user's expectations.

The probabilistic model created to attend the necessities of the problem serves as a contribution to the development of new models to the process improvement of generating new sequences, trying to optimize more the sequences generated. The model based on a graph possesses a great potential to represent visual information, this potential of representation also permits to realize studies to the construction of an informational visualization tool which makes possible to visualize and interact visually with data, with the objective of extracting new relations, patterns and different information that help in the process of new and interesting information extraction [15].

Other tests will be performed to validate the algorithm, analyze its performance, and compare the results with other algorithms and tools.

REFERENCES

1. Agrawal, R. e Srikant, R. "Mining Sequential Patterns". In Proc. of 1995 International Conference Data Engineering, Taipei, Taiwan, March, (1995).
2. Agrawal, R. e Srikant, R. Fast. "Algorithms for Mining Association Rules", In: Proc. 20th International Conference Very Large Data Bases, VLDB, (1994).
3. Baluja, S. e Caruana, R. "Removing the Genetics from Standard Genetic Algorithm". In Proceedings of the International Conference on Machine Learning. Morgan Kaufmann. p. 38-46, (1995).
4. Fogel, D. "Evolutionary Computation: Toward a new Philosophy of Machine Intelligence". 2ª Ed., IEEE Press, 312p, (2000).
5. Han, J.; Kamber, M. "Mining Sequence Patterns in Trasactional Databases. In: Data Mining: Concepts and Techniques". 2. ed. San Francisco: Elsevier. p. 23-498, (2006).
6. Holland, J. "Adaptation in Natural and Artificial Systems. University of Michigan Press", Ann Arbor, (1975).
7. Kantardzic, M. "Data Mining Concepts. In: Data Mining: Concepts, Models, Methods and Algorithms". New York: IEEE Press, (2003).
8. Koza, J. R. "Genetic Programming: On the Programming of Computers by Natural Selection". MIT Press, Cambridge, (1992).
9. Larose, D. L. "Introduction to Data Mining. In: Discovering Knowledge in Data". New Jersey: Wiley, (2005).
10. Larrañaga, P. e Lozano, J. "Estimation of Distribution Algorithms: A new tool for Evolutionary Computation", Kluwer Academic Publishers. 382p, (2002).
11. Muhlenbein, H. e PaaB, G. From recombination of genes to the estimation of distributions I . Binary parameters, Lecture Notes in Computer Science 1141: Parallel Problem Solving from Nature - PPSN IV, pp.178-187, Springer, (1996).
12. Pei, J., Han, J., Pinto, H., Chen, Q. e Dayal, U. "PrefixSpan: Mining Sequential Patterns Efficiently by Prefix-Projected Pattern Growth". Int. Conf. on Data Engineering, (2001).
13. Sakura, S.; Kitahara, Y.; Orihara, R. "A Sequential Pattern Mining Method based on Sequential Interestingness". International Journal Of Computational Intelligence, Paris, p. 252-260. (2008).
14. Santana, R., Larrañaga, P. e Lozano, J. "Interactions and Dependencies in Estimation of Distribution Algorithms". IEEE Press, 1418-1425, (2005).
15. Spence, Robert. Information Visualization. Barcelona: Acm Press, 459 p., (2001).
16. Srikant, R. e Agrawal, R. (1996) "Mining Sequential Patterns: Generalizations and Performance Improvements". Proc. 5th EDBT, 3-17.
17. Zaki, M., J. "Spade: An Efficient Algorithm for Mining Frequent Sequences". Machine Learning 42, ½, 31-60, (2001).
18. Zhao, Q. e Bhowmick, S. "Sequential Pattern Mining: A Survey". Technical Report, CAIS, Nanyang Technological University, Singapore, No. 2003118, (2003).
19. Zhigljavsky, A. Theory of Global Random Search. Kluwer Academic Publishers, (1991).
20. http://www.ics.uci.edu/~mlearn/. Acessado em: 24/10/2009.

TLATOA COMMUNICATOR
A Framework to Create Task-Independent Conversational Systems

D. Pérez, I. Kirschning

Department of Computing, Electronics and Mechatronics,
Universidad de las Américas, Puebla, Mexico

Abstract- **This paper presents an approach to simplify the creation of spoken dialogue systems for information retrieval, by separating all the task dependent information, such as vocabulary, relationships, restrictions, dialogue structure, the minimal set of elements to construct a query, and all the information required by the Dialogue Manager (DM), Automatic Speech Recognition (ASR), Natural Language Processing (NLP), Natural Language Generation (NLG) and the application. The task related information is kept in XML files, which can be read by the different modules, depending on the kind of data each one requires to function, providing task independence and making the design of spoken dialogue systems much easier.**

Index Terms: spoken dialogue systems, task independence, XML.

I. Introduction

Currently, in most of the conversational systems, the context, which is a crucial part of the system, is embedded in many parts of the source code, in such a way that when a new application is developed based on a different context, much effort and programming skill is required. This is because many parts of different files of the source code need to be modified and recompiled. However, we believe that it is possible to create a framework for the creation of conversational systems, where the application designer can specify all the elements of the interaction, in a simple straightforward way.

Spoken dialogue or conversational systems are a collection of several interacting modules: Automatic Speech Recognition (ASR), Natural Language Processing (NLP), Natural Language Generation (NLG), Dialogue Manager (DM), TTS, apart from the application itself. At the TLATOA Speech Processing Laboratory at our university we have developed mainly resources and tools for applications in Mexican Spanish. Thus there is a strong interest in creating Spanish conversational systems.

The present paper describes the result of a PhD research project focused on designing a framework for the development of conversational systems, based on the Galaxy architecture [1] and the CU Communicator. This framework has been called the TLATOA Communicator.

II. TLATOA Communicator

During the past few years others have also worked on how to make the development of a conversational system easier, underlining thus the need and tendency for more research and work in this area. Some examples of these efforts are MIT Speechbuilder [2], Microsoft Speech Server & Microsoft Speech Application SDK [3; 4], or the IBM Websphere Voice Toolkit [5]. Some of these are commercial products, where not many details are shown on the how and where task information is managed. Others have not given recent signs of new developments.

A. Dialogue structure

To determine the elements and structure required for the information to be stored outside the source code, we first collected a set of common, natural language dialogues for information retrieval. These dialogues were designed to contain all the elements of the user-computer interaction, including interaction to specify the query terms, clarification of miss-recognized elements, various ways to ask about the same type of information, etc.

Analyzing 38 different dialogues we identified the following elements during the flow of a conversation to request information (we denote as "facilitator" the system, which will provide the user with the desired information through a dialogue):

The facilitator begins with a welcome message to the user and usually provides some help about the context.

The user begins to interact in order to obtain certain information. At this point the user might have a clear idea of what he/she is looking for or not.

a) If the user does not know how to ask or what to say, then the facilitator repeats the help indicating the

T. Sobh, K. Elleithy (eds.), *Innovations in Computing Sciences and Software Engineering*,
DOI 10.1007/978-90-481-9112-3_103,

ways the user can interact with it. If the user should not collaborate, then the facilitator can finish the interaction;

b) If the user does know how to use the application then the facilitator will assist to generate a valid query.

This step is iterative until the user is satisfied and the facilitator has the minimum of required elements to launch the query, or until the user decides to cancel the search and break off the conversation.

When the user decides to stop the search for information, the facilitator gives a closing message and terminates de interaction.

B. Representing the context

In the TLATOA Communicator, each of the four elements shown above is defined in one text file using XML tags. Each module of the dialogue system interacts with these files to extract the information each of them requires to perform their function (see Fig. 1).

These four XML files are:

The database-file containing the information related to the database (.dbs.xml).

The task-file containing all the information related to the specific task (.tsk.xml).

The output-file with the system's messages and output structure (.out.xml).

The grammar-file with the grammar and the input (.gra.xml).

Since this work has focused on conversational systems for the retrieval of information, the file and database structure are defined with this purpose in mind. Any information for any domain can be stored in a database, for example, flight information, product catalogues, movie time tables, etc. Although a relational database can contain more than one table and the relations between these tables, in our current work we decided to map the context into only one table.

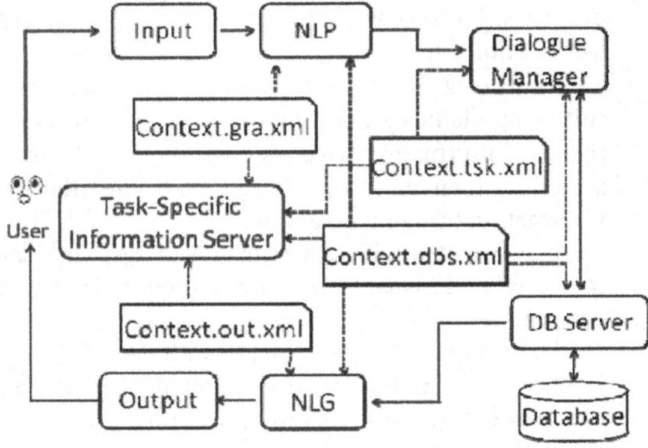

Fig. 1: Communication between servers and access to the context-files in the TLATOA Communicator.

This might not be the ideal way to store such information; however it is possible and simplifies the process significantly. Once the database has been created we can begin to define the four XML files. The following sections will describe the structure of each of these files.

B.1 Database file

The database file contains all the information elements that define de context of the application. Here, in an XML format we define the database's structure, the table from which the information will be retrieved, as well as the name and type of each field in the table.

The **root element** is **<database>**, and contains the items **<dbname>** and **<table>**.

<db_name> contains the name of the database;

<table> contains

<tname> or table name, and

<nfields> the number of fields in the table.

The item **<nfields>** contains one **<field>** for each field in the database's table, where each **<field>** contains **<name>** (of the field) and **<type>** (data type of the field). For practical reasons, the data types considered in this case are: integer, float, boolean, date, time and varchar or string. For the case where a field is declared as varchar, an element of **<size>** has to be added, defining the maximum length of the string.

B.2 Grammar File

To establish the kind of questions the user can ask, it is necessary to know the phrases that can be used, as well as the different forms a user can refer to the elements stored in the database, the way the restrictions are specified and the grammar of the valid utterances. This information is declared in the file with the extension .gra.xml

The root element is <**grammar**>. The grammar follows the W3C Speech Recognition Grammar Specification Version 1.0. This section shows the common elements for different tasks as tags, but in the grammar file these are stored as rules according to the SRGS v1.0.[6; 7]. These elements are:

<info_request> which identifies the beginnings of a request, such as "please tell me", "give me", "i'd like to know", etc.;

<repeat_request> tag for the phrases used to request that the last prompt be repeated. To achieve this all the prompts generated by the NLG are stored, generating also a log of the interaction, allowing for the resolution of context related requests, like "the first one", "the latter" and so on;

<polite_complement> is used to tag all the polite phrases a user might utter, which are ignored by the parser. (e.g. "please", "I'd like to know", etc.);

<affirmative> used for affirmative answers;

<negative> opposite of the <affirmative> tag;

<sort> denotes the different ways a user might ask for the results to be read in a certain order: "order by", "sort by",etc.;

<start_over> tags valid utterances to restart the conversation;

<exit> is a tag for utterances to end the conversation.

The grammar file also includes all the possible values for each field of the table, synonyms used for certain values, and references to other grammars for date, time, numbers, etc.

Additionally this file contains the restrictions that can be placed on certain fields, mapping them to their semantic interpretation. For example an utterance like "from the nineties on" is mapped to: year ≥1990.

B.3 Output File

This file contains the prompts and phrases used by the facilitator to give a welcome-message, provide some type of initial instructions to the first-time user, tips on how to make the information requests and navigate through the conversation, indicate keywords to repeat a prompt, restart, quit, etc. The extension of this file is .out.xml.

The **root element** is **<system_prompts>** which can contain the following items:

<welcome> first prompt when the application starts;

<short_instructions> initial instructions to the novice user;

<result_inform> tag that contains the phrase to begin the reading of the values obtained for <results_at_time> specified in the task-file;

<max_result_exceeded> Phrase used to inform the user when the query generated too many hits, more than the value indicated by **<max_db_results>** in the task-file;

<no_parse> tag for the feedback-prompt when the parser was unable to analyze the last utterance;

<no_parse_repeat> to add a specific message when the parser fails again;

<order_question> prompt used when the information returned by the query can be sorted in several ways, stating the criteria by which the results can be presented;

<ask_for_missing_info> prompts used to ask the user to complete the fields required for the minimal query. Each prompt will depend on the information specified by **<query_types>** in the task-file. For example:

```
  <ask_for_missing_info>
<field id=1>You need to specify a value for
      <field_name id="3">
    </field>
</ask_for_missing_info >
```

It is also possible to request values for more than one field, using the tag **<mixed>**:

```
<mixed>
    <req>
            <field_name id="1"/>
            <field_name id="2"/>
    </req>
  <out>Please specify a <field id="1"/> and a <field id="2"/>
    </out>
</mixed>
```

<req> indicates the fields for which a value is required to fill the item, and **<out>** denotes the corresponding prompt;

<query_responses> establishes how the results of the database query are to be read, since the number of expected fields depend on the type of query. This item has to correspond to the part of **<query_types>** in the task-file.

B.4 Task File

The contents of this fourth file with the extension .tsk.xml are related to the types of questions the user can make to obtain the adequate response, the restrictions used for sanity-checks and the form and amount of results to a query that can be presented to the user.

The **root element** of this file is <**task**> and it contains:

<max_instructions> integer representing the maximum number of times the system will repeat instructions before giving up;

<max_db_results> maximum number of results to be read to the user; when the number of results exceeds this value, the user is asked to confirm if all results are to be read of if he/she wishes to refine the query;

<results_at_time> number of results per group;

<query_types> Defines all the valid queries and contains several instances of:

<option> which contains
<input> and **<output>** which in turn contain a series of <field> items.

Here is where the developer determines what fields will be included in a response to the different queries. It is not always desirable or feasible to read out all the information stored in each record. To make the output easier to understand the developer has to decide which information to give to the user, depending on how or what was asked.

<task_restrictions> specifies the restrictions for the query and contains:

<restriction> which contains
<field> and one or more **<relation>** items.

<field> denotes the field upon which a restriction is put,

<relation> specifies the restriction, and Table 1 summarizes the values for the type attribute in <relation>.

The following example says that field 3 must be greater or equal 1900 and at the same time it must be less or equal 2009:

```
<restriction>
    <field> 3 </field>
    <relation type ="GOE"> 1900 </relation>
    <relation type ="LOE"> 2009 </relation>
</restriction>
```

And finally the **<sanity>** tag specifies the required sanity checks on the queries. For example, to indicate that when a value is specified for field 5 then the value of field 7 needs to be greater or equal than the one in field 5.

```
<restrict>
    <field id="7"/>
            <relation type ="GOE"/>
            <field id="5"/>
</restrict>
```

C. *Guarding consistency among records*

Each of the four configuration- or context files contain elements that have a strong correlation. This it is important to be careful and keep all the elements consistent with the ones in the other parts of the same file, and even in with the other files.

One method to guard their consistency and to check that all the elements are used correctly and well formed is the associated DTD. Among the consistency rules we can mention:

In the file containing the data base information (.dbs.xml) there is a section that defines the number of fields of the table, and those fields are enumerated.

In the file containing the task definition or task-file the types of valid database queries are specified, where each query has a set of input fields and a set of output fields, these values must be the ones defined in the database-file.

TABLE I
VALUES FOR THE TYPE ATTRIBUTE IN <RELATION>.

Value	Meaning
GOE	greater or equal
LOE	less or equal
LT	less than
GT	greater than
MAX	maximum
MIN	minimum
EQ	equals
DIF	different
LK	like

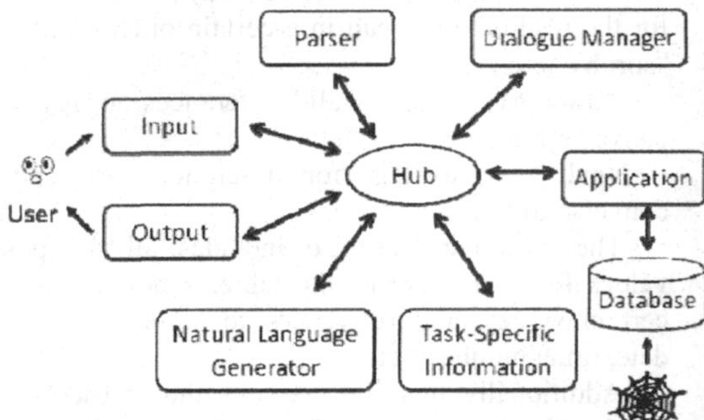

Fig. 2. Architecture of the TLATOA Communicator.

In the task-related restrictions, as well as sanity checks within the task-file, there are references to fields, which have to be valid fields according to the definition in the data base file. The grammar file must comply with W3C definitions.

In the output file, the parts referring to how the system asks for missing information, or how the user can ask to sort the results and the responses based on the results from the database queries, they all make reference to fields of the database, which necessarily need to correspond to the ones defined in the database-file.

D. *Task-Specific Information Server*

The proposed architecture for the TLATOA Communicator is similar to the modular GALAXY architecture for conversational Systems (see Figure 2). One module, the Hub, is responsible to route the messages between all the servers. All the messages between the modules must have the following structure:

[sender : addressee : message]

Where **sender** and **addressee** are integer values representing the port numbers where the sending and addressed servers are "listening"; and **message** is a string containing the message.

Since the task related information has been taken out of each of the modules, a new server is added: the Task-Specific Information Server (see Figure 1), which has the following responsibilities:

- To check consistency of the context-files at startup.
- Then send a message to the hub notifying that the files are valid and every server can use the files that it needs.

Table II summarizes which modules access each of the context-files.

TABLE II
THE FOUR CONTEXT-FILES AND MODULES THAT ACCESS THEM

Filename	Used by:
Context.dbs.xml	Dialogue Manager, Database server, Parser, NLG
Context.tsk.xml	Dialogue Manager
Context.out.xml	NLG
Context.gra.xml	Parser

III. CREATING THE DIALOGUE STRUCTURE

To create the four files that represent the dialogue's context and task information, a developer could work directly on the XML files and the database. However, to make sure that the consistency is kept, we recommend the use of a GUI.

Since the creation of these files follow a logical order, the GUI guides the developer safely through each step, adapting each screen to the information introduced by the designer. It is also possible to move back in the sequence of steps to add or remove fields, restrictions, etc. and the system will adapt to the changes, not allowing inconsistencies nor forcing the developer to remember which of the related files need to be modified. Thus allowing dialogue designers without special programming skills to adapt or create new contexts for conversational systems.

TABLE III
COMPARING EXISTING CONVERSATIONAL FRAMEWORKS (PART 1)

System	Objective	Domain information	Implementation Documentation
CSLU toolkit	Fast development of voice applications	Specified by the user using the Rapid Application Developer	There are no details on how it was implemented
CU Communicator	Dialog system in the flight- and hotel reservation and car rental domain	Defined in external text files, but also a lot is found embedded in the source code	There are some papers that describe the main ideas of the implementation [8]
SLS-Lite	Allow non expert users create conversational systems	Defined in external XML format files	Documented in a MIT master degree thesis[11]
SpeechBuilder	Allow non expert users create conversational systems	Defined in external XML format files	Documented in a MIT master degree thesis [10]
MS SASDK / SpeechServer	Allow non expert users to create conversational systems	Defined in external XML format files	It is a commercial product, thus we couldn't find details on how it was implemented
IBM Websphere	Allow non expert users to create conversational systems	Defined in external XML format files	It is a commercial product, thus we couldn't find details on how it was implemented
TLATOA Communicator	Allow non expert users to create conversational systems	Defined in external XML format files	Detailed document [12]

IV. COMPARISON WITH OTHER SIMILAR SYSTEMS

In this section we present two tables comparing our system to other similar systems. Table III compares the objective of each of the systems, location of the domain specific information and the type of the available documentation. In the second table (see TABLE IV) we compare the information available from the developer to learn to use the corresponding system, as well as the availability of the system itself, that is, how easy is to acquire the system and also their ease of use.

TABLE IV
COMPARING EXISTING CONVERSATIONAL FRAMEWORKS (PART 2)

System	Developer information	Availability	Ease of use
CSLU toolkit	There are enough information on how to use the toolkit to create a rapid application[9]	It's available online for non-commercial purposes [9]	The documentation is enough to learn to develop fast applications in a relatively short time
CU Communicator	There are tutorials that explains the parts where the domain is, but there are parts of the source code with the domain embedded [8]	Not anymore.	It was necessary to invest some time to learn how to install the system,
SLS-Lite	MIT master degree thesis [11]	No records found.	Easy, according to documented reports.[11]
SpeechBuilder	MIT master degree thesis [10]	It´s supposed to be available but when we tried to test it there was no support from the developers. [10]	Easy according to documented reports.[10]
MS SASDK / SpeechServer	Detailed Online Tutorials describing how to create new applications[3]	Commercial product. A license is needed to use it.[3]	Easy, according to the documentation. [3]
IBM Websphere	Detailed Online Tutorials describing how to create new applications [5]	Commercial product. A license is needed to use it. [5]	Easy, according to the documentation. [5]
TLATOA Communicator	Detailed document [12]	Once this work is finished it will be available online to get feedback and improve it	Easy, following step – by-step GUI.

V. CONCLUSIONS

In conversational systems, the design of the dialogue is a critical factor. It not only allows a user to retrieve successfully the desired information, but it is also crucial for a positive user experience. However, not every developer is an expert in dialogue design neither in human communication, nor has the required programming skills to create or adapt the software to accommodate all the elements, vocabulary end restrictions required in any context or language.

To simplify the task, this context or task-specific information can be created and managed in separate XML files, which then every module in the dialogue system can access and retrieve whatever they require.

For this to work properly each of the ASR, NLP, NLG and TTS engines or modules have to communicate properly with the task-information server. Each of them also needs to be programmed in a way that they don't rely on hard-coded restrictions and sanity-checks, but on the language models, vocabulary and their corresponding context specific restrictions and relations.

The application's information can be stored in a relational database, which can then be retrieved through the conversational interface. The interface will enable the user to construct the query for the desired information, as detailed as the application's developer decides.

By separating the task information into four different XML files, it is possible to separate all the context dependent data from the source code of a conversational system.

REFERENCES

[1] Seneff, S., Hurley, E., Lau, R., Pao, C., Schmidt, P., and Zue, V., "GALAXY-II: A Reference Architecture for Conversational System Development," in ICSLP 98, Sydney, Australia, November 1998.

[2] Glass, J., Seneff, S., Zue, V., "Building Japanese Conversational Systems based on the Galaxy Architecture", NTT Tech Rev, September, 2006.

[3] Microsoft. "MS-SDK". [Online]. http://msdn.microsoft.com/venus/library/ms986917.aspx, [Accessed: May 7, 2008]

[4] Microsoft, "MS-SDK", [Online] http://www.microsoft.com/downloads/details.aspx?FamilyId=1194ED95-7A23-46A0-BBBC06EF009C053A&displa%20 Microsoft,%20Speech%20Application%20SDK%201.0ylang=en &displaylang=en/ [Accessed: May 7, 2008].

[5] IBM. "WebSphere Voice Toolkit". [Online] http://www-01.ibm.com/software/pervasive/voice_toolkit/, [Accessed: May 9, 2008]

[6] W3C, "XML" [Online] http://www.w3.org/XML/ [Accessed: Feb 19, 2009]

[7] "Speech Recognition Grammar Specification Version 1.0" [Online] http://www.w3.org/TR/speech-grammar/ [Accessed: June 10, 2008]

[8] Wayne, W. and Pellom, B.. "The CU Communicator System". CSLR University of Colorado at Boulder, 1999

[9] "CSLU Toolkit Documentation", [Online]. http://cslu.cse.ogi.edu/toolkit/ [Accessed: Sep. 12, 2003]

[10] Eugene Weinstein "SpeechBuilder: Facilitating Spoken Dialogue System Development". MIT M. Eng. Thesis. 2001.

[11] Jeff Pearlman, "SLS-Lite: Enabling Spoken Language Systems Design for Non-Experts," M.S. thesis, Massachusetts Institute of Technology, Boston, MA, USA, 2000

[12] Daniel Pérez "TLATOA COMMUNICATOR: A Framework to Create Task-Independent Conversational Systems," Ph.D. Thesis, Universidad de las Américas, Puebla, Mexico, 2009.

Using Multiple Datasets in Information Visualization Tool

Rodrigo Augusto de Moraes Lourenço[2,3], Rafael Veras Guimarães[1], Nikolas Jorge S. Carneiro[1], Aruanda Simões Gonçalves Meiguins[3], Bianchi Serique Meiguins[1,2]

[1]Faculdade de Computação – Universidade Federal do Pará – UFPA, Belém, PA 66075-110 Brazil
[2]Programa de Pós-Graduação em Ciência da Computação – Universidade Federal do Pará Pará – UFPA, Belém, PA 66075-110 Brazil
[3]Área de Ciências e Tecnologias – Centro Universitário do Pará – CESUPA, Belém, PA 66035-170 Brazil
{rodrigo@redeinformatica.com.br, rafaelveras@ufpa.br, nikolas.carneiro@gmail.com, aruanda@redeinformatica.com.br, bianchi.serique@terra.com.br}

Abstract- The goal of this paper is to present an information visualization application capable of opening and synchronizing information between two or more datasets. We have chosen this approach to address some of the limitations of various applications. Also, the application uses multiple coordinated views and multiple simultaneous datasets. We highlight the application layout configuration by the user, including the flexibility to specify the number of data views and to associate different datasets for each visualization techniques.

I. Introduction

Business Intelligence (BI) is an area that has been increasing in recent years attracting the interest of many companies in many areas of business and any size all around the world. This interest comes from the companies' needs of gain knowledge about their own business to make decisions that can increase profits, improve competitiveness, achieve goals, among others.

This area triumphs today, where the technological arsenal is growing rapidly in terms of electronics, machines with high processing power and storage, information systems that collect and store data generated every second in every kind of transaction, such as shopping credit cards or bank transfers. Thus, the amount of data that can and are stored in repositories today is huge, and in most cases they are just stored, becoming just digital trash.

Thus, make a right business decision, with the range of data to analyze into reduced time becomes an extremely difficult task to do without the aid of a tool. In many cases, data were analyzed using a spreadsheet or tabular form with simple charts. In some situations, these sheets are very detailed (with multiple columns and large volume of pages), making the person who is looking unable to visualize all data at once and losing the information contained there. In the other hand, in case the spreadsheet is very synthesized (with a few columns and pages), preventing the analyst to perceive details that could be relevant to decision taking.

In this context, the area of Information Visualization (IV) has increased in recent decades [Spence 07], with the development of computational tools that assist decision-taking. The IV is intended to assist the analysis and understanding of the data [Kerren 07] for quick, intuitive and interactive, utilizing the human cognitive capability to extract information from data using visual representations of the data [Spence 07]. The human sense of sight, when correctly operated becomes a very effective resource for this task, since this effect has great ease and speed of detection of changes in the environment.

Beyond these needs, often come up the need to establish a relation between two or more data sources. To face it the usual way is join those datasets into one, but it could demand a rough effort and much time to be done, before submit this new dataset to a IV tool.

Given this scenario above, this paper presents a information visualization prototype which allow multiple dataset analysis and coordination using visualization techniques (as scatterplot [Spence 07], parallel coordinates [Inselberg 90], treemap [Shneiderman 92] and charts) and features like data overview, selection, brushing, filtering and on-demand details (IV "mantra" [Shneiderman 96]).

II. Information Visualization

The main purpose of using an information visualization tool is to interact with a dataset, generating organized images (data graphical representation) by user previously defined criteria. These images enable the user to contextualize the data and its relationships and extract information that will effectively assist him/her to better perform a task. This process should be fast, easy and intuitive, using the appropriate techniques, codifications and representations for data and user tasks [Kerren 07, Spence 07, Shneiderman 99].

The characteristics of a good visualization tool are: data overview, zooming, filtering and on-demand details [Shneiderman 96]. An IV tool may support a variety of tasks like identification, multi-derivative correlation, search, exploration and communication [Spence 07].

In an effort to improve user perception, IV tools have frequently applied multiple views from data [Kerren 07]. The user may simultaneously build several different graphical representations for the same dataset in order to better analyze the data [Baldonado 00, North 00]. This feature is called multiple coordinated views. The coordination ensures that all views keep consistent even after many user interactions with the visualized dataset and the graphical representations. The main coordination aspects are the visual attributes (color, shape and size),

T. Sobh, K. Elleithy (eds.), *Innovations in Computing Sciences and Software Engineering*,
DOI 10.1007/978-90-481-9112-3_104, © Springer Science+Business Media B.V. 2010

brushing, navigation and filters, used to reduce the analyzed dataset [Pillat 06].

III. Related Works

A. Snap-Together Visualization

Snap-Together [North 00] is a information visualization tool that allow visualizations and coordination in a fast and dynamic way with no need of programming skills. The tool is flexible in data (i.e. the user are allowed to load multiple datasets), visualizations and coordination. Furthermore, it is based on the relational data model.

To explore a dataset, the user should first load relations in visualizations. Next, build the coordinations specifying actions to tightly couple the visualizations. The possible coordination actions are selection, navigation, highlight and load, these are available according to the kind of visualization choose.

B. Improvise

Improvise [Weaver 04] is an environment that allows to the user build and explore visualizations from relational data through multiple visions, providing functionalities as load different kinds of data, create multiple visualizations over them and specify coordination using an abstractive visual language.

IV. Architecture and Technologies

The software visualization architecture was conceived to present a well-defined distribution of responsibilities, mainly inspired by the MVC model. The architecture is divided in three major modules (Fig. 1): VisualizationModule, SystemCore and Presentation. Each one of these modules is sub-divided into specialized modules. VisualizationModule and SystemCore internal modules contain structural models and controllers of their specific functionalities, on the other hand, Presentation internal modules are mainly views for these models.

Fig. 2, 3 and 4 details the internals of each one of the major modules, displaying the most important classes, interfaces and their relationship for a better understanding of the system.

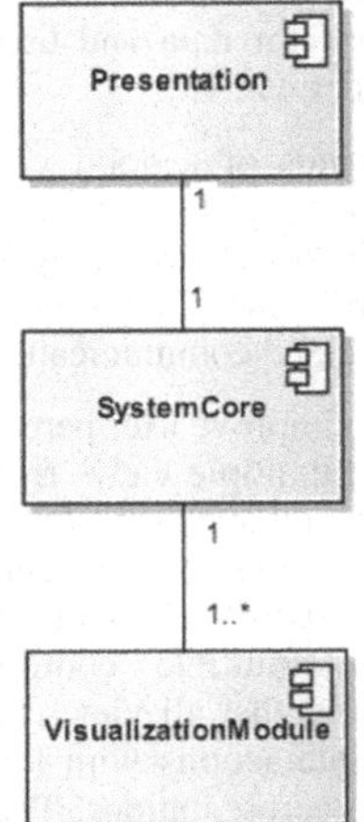

Fig. 1. Major application modules

Fig. 2 presents the internals of the VisualizationModule, it is composed of one dataset (XML, File or Database) for data input, one or more visualization techniques to generate the graphical views, one color manager, one filters manager and one on-demand details manager. It's main purpose is keep configuration information and generate the visualization's images based upon these configurations.

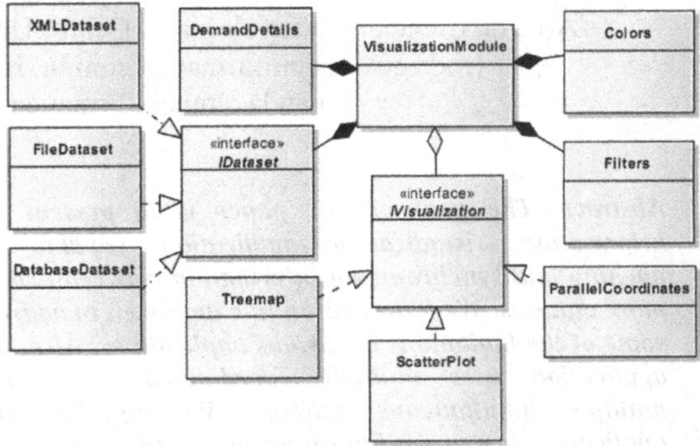

Fig. 2. VisualizationModule detailed

SystemCore is the main module, it is responsible for the creation of new VisualizationModules, for the coordination between VisualizationModules, for some of the actions from the Presentation's input and for binding Presentation's views to the VisualizationModules models.

SyncControl keeps a list of couples of coordinated columns between the datasets. It captures the model events from the VisualizationModule, and whenever a filter or color configuration is made on a model that references one of the listed columns the modification is propagated to the related column.

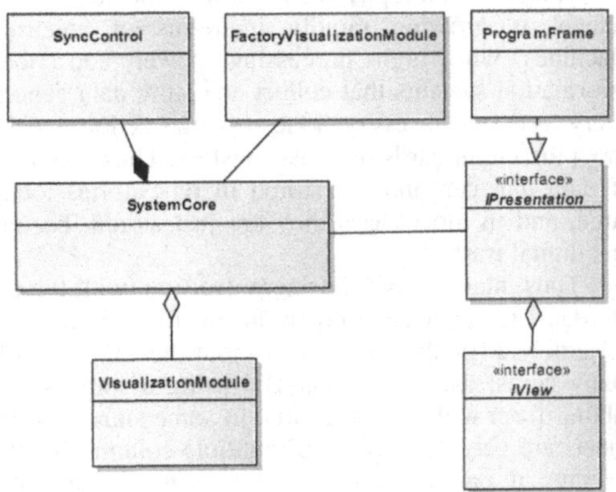

Fig. 3. SystemCore detailed

Presentation creates and manages a group of Graphic User Interface (GUI) components. These components are created according to the user's needs, adding a new dataset to the application will require new configuration panels for example. Presentation has a tight relation with the SystemCore, whenever it creates a new view (be it a configuration panel or a visualization panel) it makes a request to the SystemCore to bind the newly created view to the respective module.

This approach was chosen looking into web-based future works where the Presentation module might be a group of Servlets providing information and a communication path for a thin-client browser application.

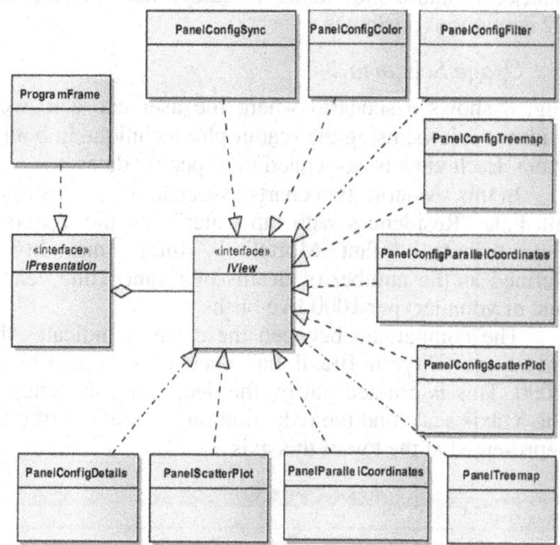

Fig. 4. Presentation detailed

V. PROTOTYPE

The prototype is a general-purpose information visualization tool with the following main characteristics:

- Customizable workspace
- Configurable coordination among views
- Simultaneous use of multiple datasets
- Support to different information visualization techniques
- Automatic generation of the client interface according to dataset information;

A. Customizable Workspace

The following figures present the graphic user interface (GUI) components used in the process of customizing the workspace with new datasets and visualization techniques. This allows the user to manage the visualization tool for his/her own needs. It is possible to select a set of datasets to be used, to specify visualization techniques and coordination options for each view.

Fig. 5A presents the first configuration step, when the user should decide from where to load a set of data, XML File, CSV File or from a Database. The next step (Fig. 5B, 5C) is to add the desired visualization techniques.

The user may interact with as many as simultaneous views as desired, these views are placed side by side inside a scrollable panel. During the writing of this paper the implemented techniques were: Scatter Plot, Treemaps, Parallel Coordinates and Pie Chart.

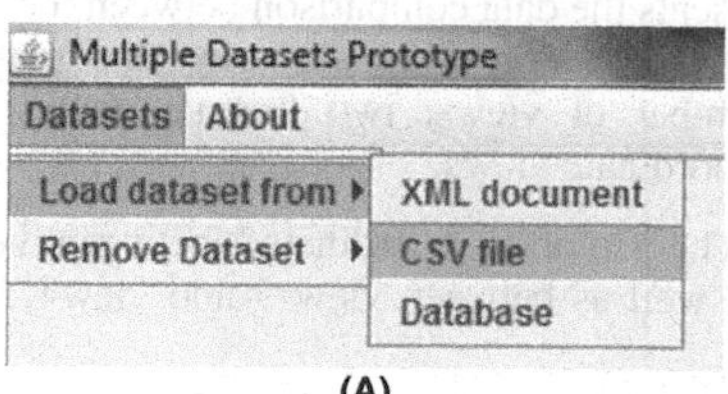

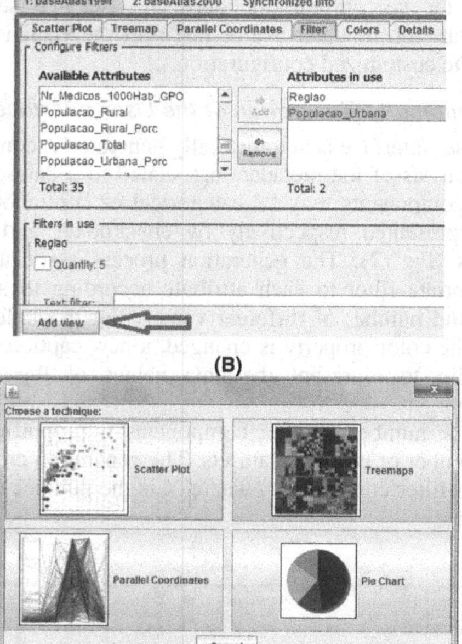

Fig. 5. First Steps: (A) Load dataset; (B) Add view button; (C) Choosing the desired technique

It's important to notice the strong colored borders, they link configurations and views, so that the configuration in the green border will affect the views in green border.

Fig. 6 presents the screen where the user is able to match columns from the different datasets. Matching two columns from different datasets means that these columns represent the same information, this implies that filters and colors are going to be coordinated between these datasets. In other words, if I match two columns that represent 'region' then whenever I filter or change color using the ' region ' attribute in any of the two datasets that same change will be reflected to the other dataset.

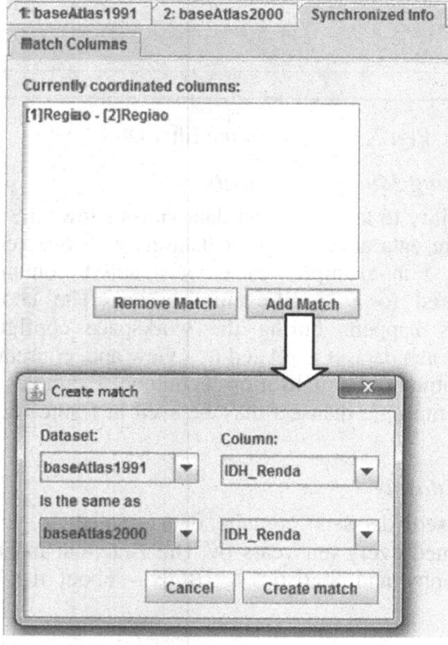

Fig. 6. Matching columns

After the configuration steps, the user may save the configuration for later use or just start the visualizations with the customized configuration.

B. *Automatic Generation of the User Interface*

The user interface is automatically generated according to the analysis of the metadata associated to a dataset. The filter components may be categorical or continuous and are represented respectively by checkboxes and range sliders (Fig. 7). The generation process associates the appropriate filter to each attribute according to its data type and number of different values. For example, each time the color property is changed, a new caption should be built to represent the data values of the chosen attribute.

The number of filter components is proportional to the number of selected datasets. The generation creates X sets of filter components, where X is the number of used datasets.

Fig. 7. Example of the filter tab.

C. *Using Multiple Datasets*

The ability to load different data views allows the user to compare data among similar datasets with different data values. For example, each view could contain data associated to a specific time period. The choice of datasets happens during the workspace configuration stage. Each dataset is related to a view and, consequently, an information visualization technique. Examples of the use of multiple datasets may be seen in figures 8, 9 and 10.

D. *Datasets*

The used datasets contain data related to a study performed every ten years by The Brazilian Institute of Geography and Statistics – IBGE – about the human development index (HDI) and other social and economic official indicators. The first dataset (baseAtlas1991) matches the 1991 study, while the second matches the study published in 2000 (baseAtlas2000). Dataset 1 and dataset 2 contain 5507 items, 12 categorical attributes and 22 continuous attributes.

E. *Usage Scenario 1*

Fig. 8 shows a scenario where the user chose to work with two views, using the scatter plot technique in both of them. Each view is associated to a specific dataset.

In this scenario, two charts associate the X axis to the attribute "Residences with tap water" and the Y axis to the attribute "Infant Mortality". Infant mortality is defined as the number of deaths of infants (one year of age or younger) per 1000 live births.

The comparison between these views indicates that infant mortality in Brazil has decreased from 1991 to 2000. This is pointed out by the decreasing tendency on the Y axis scale and the reduction on the number of cities represented at the top of this axis.

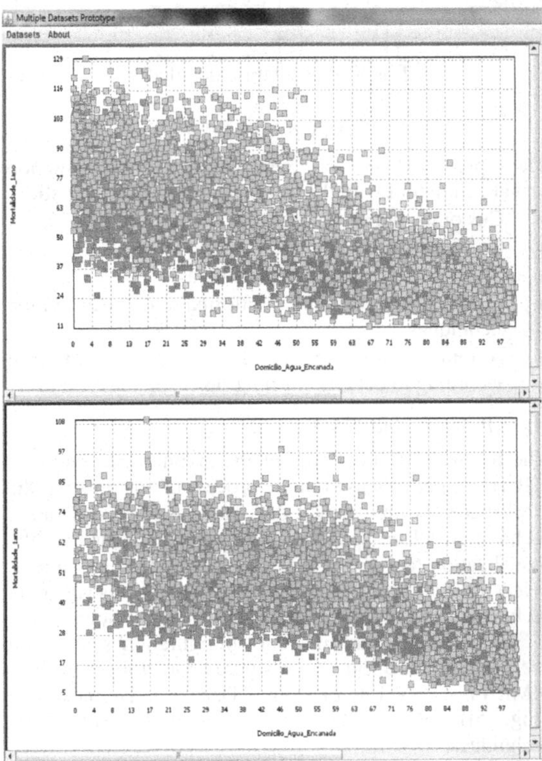

Fig. 8. Same information visualization technique for two different datasets

F. *Usage Scenario 2*

Fig. 9 presents the data comparison between the same two datasets from the previous scenario, this time with a larger number of views: two treemap views and two parallel coordinate views.

The Color is coordinated between view1 and view2, as well as between view 3 and view4. There are two distinct sets of colors representing the same attribute in all views: Income HDI. The Educational HDI attribute was categorized into the values low, medium-low, medium-high and high and used in the treemap hierarchy.

Views 1 and 3 (treemaps) present the changes in the Brazilian educational HDI. Many cities changed from medium to high. Highlighting only cities with high educational HDI in the treemap technique, the brushing feature indicates its correlations with other attributes in the parallel coordinate technique.

Despite the considerable increase in the educational HDI from 1991 to 2000, the Income HDI was not raised in the same pace.

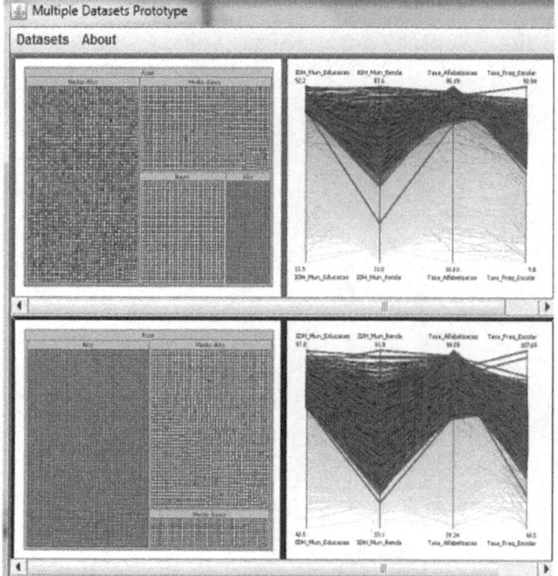

Fig. 9. two views for each one of the two datasets for determinate the educational HDI changes and point it non-directly relation to Income HDI

G. Usage Scenario 3

Two datasets were used in this scenario: baseAtlas2000 and baseAtlas2000(2). The latter is a replica of the first, which allows a direct comparison of those datasets. However, each one has its own independent filters and different configurations.

Three views and two techniques were used: treemap and pie chart. In view 3, treemap was grouped by region and had its color mapped by the IDH_Municipal_GPO attribute.

The Northeast region is the one that proportionally has the lowest number of cities with high HDI (represented in blue) and the largest number of cities with low HDI (represented in yellow).

In views 1 and 2, it is possible to analyze the Northeast region. In View 1 (treemap), items are grouped by "Number of doctors per 1000 inhabitants" and the properties size and color are both associated to the Literacy-Rate attribute.

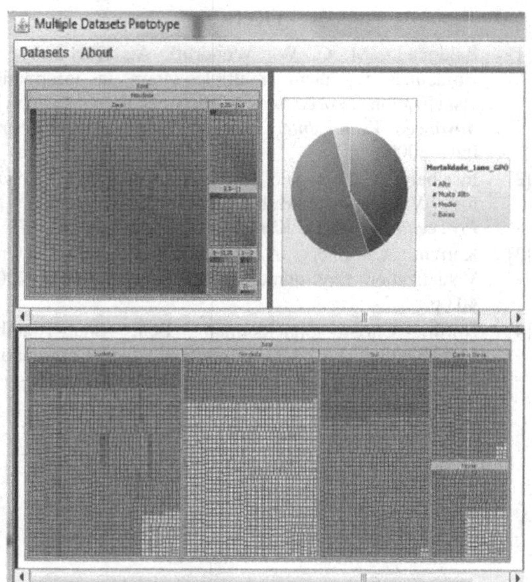

Fig. 10: Scenario 3, part/whole analysis of Northeast region.

VI. Final Remarks

The motivation for the development of this application was to contribute to the scenario of information visualization tools using a new approach.

The UI and functionalities were based on some of the most popular information visualization tools. Supported features include multiple views and coordination. The application still demands interface inspections by specialists and usability tests.

The example scenarios were used to present the potential power of these features on the process of extracting information of a dataset.

The main challenges were the management and coordination of multiple datasets and the automatic generation of the UI based upon the dataset.

VII. Future Works

We highlight the following potential future developments:

- Application of usability essays;
- Addition of other auxiliary charts, such as gauges, spider, etc;
- Deep zoom support on scatter plot, treemap and parallel coordinate techniques;
- Research and implementation of additional visualization techniques;
- Create a new web-based Presentation module;
- Expand the architecture to be able to handle multiple users at the same time;
- Scalability evaluation including network transfer performance tests;
- Study new usage scenarios about more distinct datasets.

REFERENCES

[1] Baldonado, M. Q. W.; Woodruff, A.; Kuchinsky, A. Guidelines for using multiple views in information visualization. *Proceedings of the working conference on Advanced Visual Interfaces*, pp. 110 – 119. Palermo. Italy. 2000.

[2] Inselberg, A.; Dimsdale, B. Parallel Coordinates: A Tool for Visualizing Multidimensional Geometry, In *Proceedings of IEEE Visualization'90* (1990), 361-375.

[3] Kerren, A.; Ebert, A.; Meyer, J. Human-Centered Visualization Environments. Germany: Springer, 2007. 403 p.

[4] North, Chris; Shneiderman, Ben. Snap-Together Visualization: A User Interface for Coordinating Visualizations via Relational Schemata. *Proceedings of the working conference on Advanced visual interfaces*, pp 128-135. Palermo, Italy. 2000.

[5] Shneiderman, B. Tree visualization with tree-maps: 2-d space-filling approach. *ACM Transactions on Graphics*, 1992.

[6] Shneiderman, B. The eyes have it: a task by data type taxonomy for information visualizations. *Procedings of IEEE Visual Language*, 336-343. 1996.

[7] Shneiderman, B.; Card, S. K.; Mackinglay, J. Readings in Information Visualization: Using Vision to Think. 1 ed. Morgan Kaufmann, 1999.

[8] Spence, R. Information Visualization: Design for Interaction. Barcelona: Acm Press. Second Edition, 2007.

[9] Pillat, R. M.; Freitas, C. D. S. Coordinating Views in the InfoVis Toolkit. Proceedings of Advanced Visual Interface. pp. 496-499. Venezia, Italy, 2006.

[10] Weaver, C. Building Highly-Coordinated Visualizations In Improvise. Proceedings of the IEEE Symposium on Information Visualization. Austin, TX, 2004.

Improved Crack Type Classification Neural Network based on Square Sub-images of Pavement Surface

Byoung Jik Lee
Department of Computer Science
Western Illinois University
Macomb, IL 61455
bj-lee@wiu.edu

Hosin "David" Lee
Department of Civil and Environmental Engineering
University of Iowa
Iowa City, IA 52242
hlee@engineering.uiowa.edu

Abstract— The previous neural network based on the proximity values was developed using rectangular pavement images. However, the proximity value derived from the rectangular image was biased towards transverse cracking. By sectioning the rectangular image into a set of square sub-images, the neural network based on the proximity value became more robust and consistent in determining a crack type. This paper presents an improved neural network to determine a crack type from a pavement surface image based on square sub-images over the neural network trained using rectangular pavement images. The advantage of using square sub-image is demonstrated by using sample images of transverse cracking, longitudinal cracking and alligator cracking.

Keywords-component; digital pavement image; crack type classification; neural networks; square sub-image decomposition;

I. INTRODUCTION

A cracking type is one of the most important factors in determining the most appropriate maintenance strategy for pavements [1][2]. Cracking is typically classified as longitudinal, transverse, block or alligator crack [4]. Previously, the proximity-based neural network was developed for automatically determining a proper crack type [7]. However, the digital images that were used for training the proximity-based neural network were rectangular rather than square, which has caused the neural network to make an error in classifying certain types of cracking. To overcome this limitation, the accuracy of the proximity-based neural network was improved by using a set of square sub-images rather than one rectangular image. This paper presents the analysis result of a new proximity-based neural network trained using square sub-images instead of using a rectangular pavement image. This paper proposes a square-split adaptation to remedy these problems so that the proposed system guarantees more accurate crack type classification.

A. Proximity-based Neural Network

The proximity-based Neural Network was previously developed based on typical rectangular images. The pavement image taken from the vehicle on the roads are converted into a set of two-dimensional binary images with crack tiles and no-crack tiles [5].

As shown in Equation (1), the proximity value is then computed by accumulating the differences between the numbers of cracked groups for adjacent image columns.

$$proximity[i] = \sum_{j=1}^{squaresize} \left| histogram[i][j+1], - histogram[i][j] \right|$$

$$, where\ i = 1\ for\ horizontal, 2\ for\ vertical \quad (1)$$

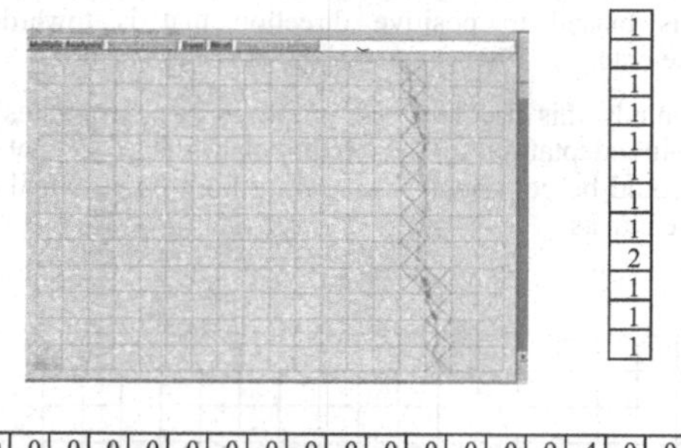

1
1
1
1
1
1
1
1
2
1
1
1

0	0	0	0	0	0	0	0	0	0	0	0	0	0	9	4	0	0

Figure 1. A longitudianl crack. Horizontal histogram and vertical histogram.

An image taken from a vehicle has 504 pixels x 756 pixels. This image is filtered and divided into 12 x 18 tiles. Each tile has 1600 pixels (40 rows and 40 columns). Each pixel in each group is converted into a binary value after applying threshold value. If a grayscale value of a pixel is higher than the threshold value, then the pixel retains a value of 1, otherwise, the pixel has a value 0. A pixel value 1 represents a crack [5]. Fig.1 shows an example of longitudinal crack image. After threshold process, if the tile exceeds the threshold, it is treated as a cracked tile and is marked red X as shown in Fig. 1 [6]. From this result, the matrix of horizontal histogram is [1,1,1,1,1,1,1,1,2,1,1,1] and the vertical histogram is [0,0,0,0,0,0,0,0,0,0,0,0,0,0,9,4,0,0]. Based on the equation (1), the given example has vertical proximity value as 18 and

T. Sobh, K. Elleithy (eds.), *Innovations in Computing Sciences and Software Engineering*,
DOI 10.1007/978-90-481-9112-3_105,

horizontal proximity value as 2. It has 13 cracked tiles. This result shows that a longitudinal crack has non-uniformity in the horizontal direction, but it has uniformity in the vertical direction. As a result, the horizontal proximity value is less than the vertical proximity value. A transverse crack would generate an opposite pattern to a longitudinal crack such that a transverse crack has non-uniformity in the vertical direction, but it has uniformity in the horizontal direction. An alligator crack and a block crack do not create uniformity either horizontally or vertically. The number of cracked tiles distinguishes a block crack from an alligator crack that has a larger number of cracked tiles [8].

However, because the original image is a rectangular image, the system is biased towards the transverse crack. The example is shown in Fig. 2 and Fig. 3. The matrix of horizontal histogram and vertical histogram of Fig. 2 are [0,0,0,18,0,0,0,0,0,0,0,0] and [1,1,1,1,1,1,1,1,1,1,1,1,1,1,1,1,1,1], respectively. The image has 18 cracked tiles and, based on the equation (1), the vertical proximity value is 0 and horizontal proximity value is 36. The matrix of horizontal histogram and vertical histogram of Fig. 3 are [1,1,1,1,1,1,1,1,1,1,1,1] and [0,0,0,0,12,0,0,0,0,0,0,0,0,0,0,0,0,0], respectively. The image has 12 cracked tiles, based on the equation (1), the vertical proximity value is 24 and horizontal proximity value is 0. The maximum horizontal proximity value of transverse crack is 36 and the maximum vertical proximity value of longitudinal crack is 24. When we treat the horizontal proximity as positive and the vertical proximity as negative, we can find that the system is biased to positive direction that is towards a transverse crack.

To remedy this problem, the proposed system applies the square-split adaptation to the rectangular image so that the system would be consistent in detecting both longitudinal and transverse cracks.

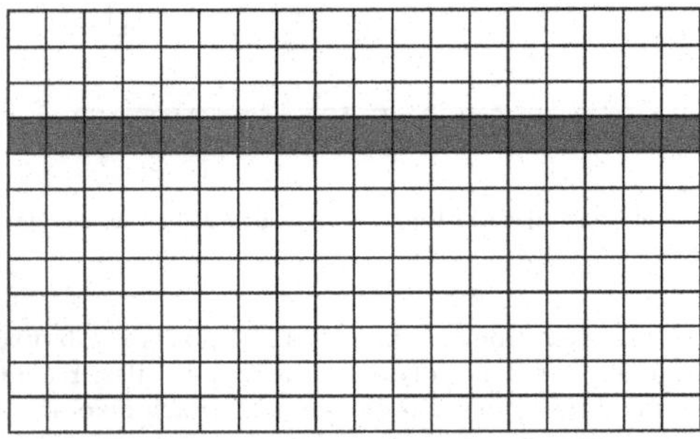

Figure 2. Transverse crack

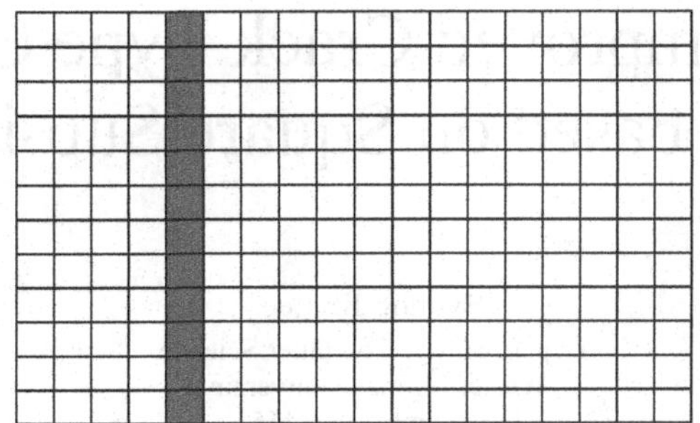

Figure 3. Longitudinal crack

II. Square-Split Adaptation with a New Proximity Method

A. System Architecture Based on Square Sub-images

As shown in Fig. 4, the system architecture has three modules; (1) square sub-image sectioning module, (2) neural network classification module and (3) crack type classification module. The first sub-image sectioning module is to apply the square sub-image sectioning algorithm to the original rectangular pavement image. The neural network module is to classify the crack type of the square sub-image using the proximity-based neural network. The third crack type classification module is to determine the crack type based on the analysis of a set of square sub-images.

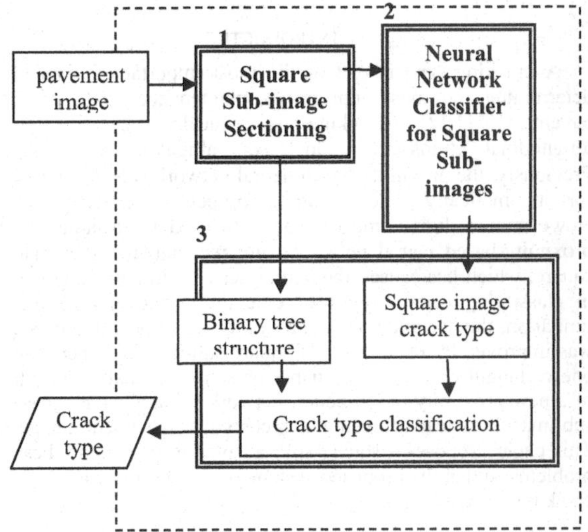

Figure 4. System architecture based on square sub-images

B. *Sectioning into Square Sub-images*

The square sub-image sectioning algorithm is programmed to automatically divide a rectangular image to square sub-images. The square sub-mage section algorithm is shown in Fig. 5.

```
While (an image is not a square image) {
Decompose it into a square image and a remainder image.
If an image is clean (does not have a crack), then discard it.
For the square image,
        apply the neural network classification system.
For the remainder image,
        continue the above procedure
}
```

Figure 5. Square Sub-image sectioning procedure

As shown in Fig. 6, the original rectangular pavement image is partitioned into a square image (A) and the rectangular image (B). If there is no crack, the image is discarded from a further analysis. Since the image A has a crack, the neural network classification module is applied. The rectangular image B is then partitioned into two square images, B1 and B2. Because B1 does not contain a crack, it is discarded. This square sub-image sectioning algorithm continues until the image cannot be further partitioned. Since the square image of B2 has a crack, the neural network classification module will be applied.

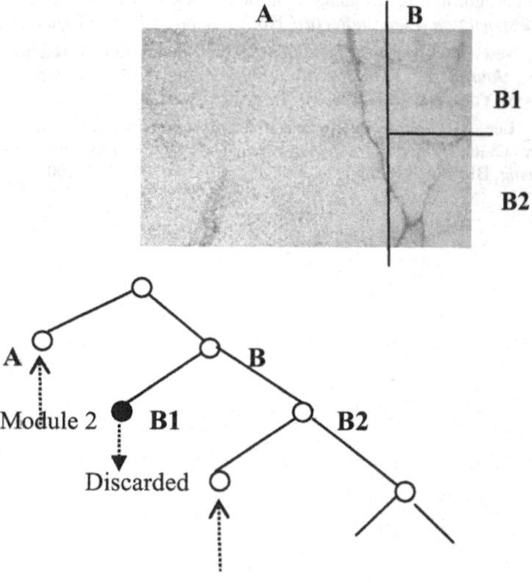

Figure 6. Square-split images and adaptation

The original rectangular image had 504 pixels x 756 pixels, which were grouped into 12 x 18 tiles. One rectangular image was then divided into one square image of 12x12 tiles and two square images of 6x6 tiles.

C. *Final Crack Type Classification*

This is the final neural network classification procedure based on the result of square sub-images from Module (1) and Module (2). As the result of sectioning, the given rectangular image is converted into three square images. Since each image has four types of cracking, the necessary number of training pattern is increased to 4^3.

III. ANALYSIS ON PROBLEM SOLUTION

The proposed proximity-based neural network with a square sub-image sectioning algorithm has distinct advantages over the one without it. First, with a square sub-image sectioning algorithm, the neural network system can save a significant amount of memory space since it does not store sections of the image where no crack is found. Second, the proposed the proposed neural network is more accurate than the system based on the entire original rectangular image. Some cases where the proposed algorithm is more robust than the original proximity-based neural network are demonstrated.

A. *Transverse Crack*

As shown in Fig. 2 earlier, the old horizontal proximity was 36, which would be biased to a transverse crack. However, by sectioning the rectangular image into a set of square sub-images, the horizontal proximity value of a large square image would be 24 and vertical proximity value of a large square image would be 0, which would still indicate it as a transverse crack. Since the lower-right sub-image has no crack, it will be discarded for a further analysis. The horizontal proximity value of the upper-right sub-image will be 12 and vertical proximity value would be 0, which also can be classified as a transverse crack.

Since two square images are classified as having transverse cracking, a whole image will be having a transverse crack. Based on these inputs (transverse crack for the first square image, no crack for the second square image, and a transverse crack for the third square image), the proposed proximity-based neural network based on the square sub-image sectioning algorithm will improve the accuracy of the neural network based on the original rectangular image.

B. *Longitudinal Crack*

As shown in Fig. 3, the old horizontal proximity was 0 and vertical proximity was 24. By sectioning the rectangular image into a set of square sub-images, the horizontal proximity value of a large square image would be 0 and vertical proximity value of a large square image would be 24, which would still indicate it as a longitudinal crack. Since the lower-right sub-image and upper-right sub-image do not have cracks, they will be discarded from a further analysis.

Since a square image is classified as having longitudinal cracking, a whole image will be considered having a longitudinal crack. Based on these inputs (longitudinal crack for the first square image, no crack for the second square image and the third square image), the proposed proximity-based neural network based on the square sub-image sectioning algorithm will also recognizes the given image as a longitudinal crack

C. *Alligator Crack/Block Crack*

As shown in Fig. 7, when a set of alligator cracking appear at the top and bottom half of the image, the horizontal and vertical proximity value are 90 and 68, respectively, which would recognize it as transverse cracking because it is biased towards to a transverse crack. By sectioning the rectangular image into a set of square sub-images, the horizontal proximity value of a large square image would be 30, vertical proximity value of a large square image would be 44, and the number of cracked tiles is 84, which would recognize it as an alligator crack. The horizontal proximity value of the upper-right sub-image will be 12, vertical proximity value would be 10, and the number of cracked tiles is 19, which can be classified as a block crack. The horizontal proximity value of the lower-right sub-image will be 15, vertical proximity value would be 10, and the number of cracked tiles is 48, which can be classified as an alligator crack.

Since two square images are classified as having alligator cracking, a whole image will be an alligator crack. Based on these inputs (alligator crack for the first square image, block crack for the second square image, and an alligator crack for the third square image), the proposed proximity-based neural network based on the square sub-image sectioning algorithm will improve the accuracy of the system based on the original rectangular image.

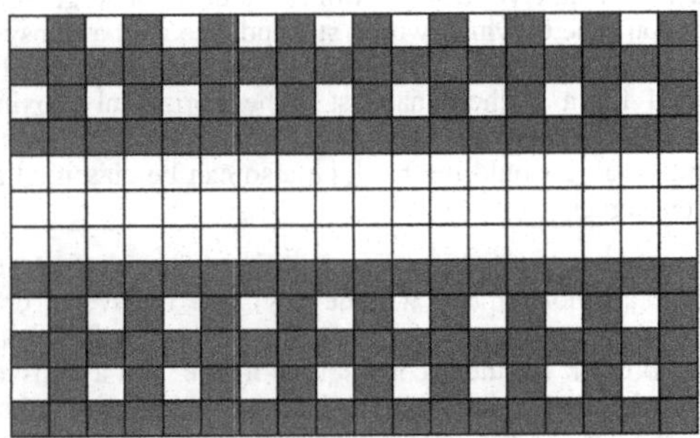

Figure 7. Distributed alligator cracks

IV. CONCLUSIONS

The original proximity values based on the histograms are biased towards a transverse crack because it was trained using a rectangular pavement image of 504 pixels x 756 pixels. The proposed square-split adaptation method is demonstrated as a consistent method to overcome such a limitation. By sectioning the rectangular image into a set of square sub-images, the proximity value based neural network is not biased towards transverse cracking. Further, because the proposed neural network is more dependent on the crack types of square images than the proximity values of entire image, the proposed neural network based on square sub-images would more accurately recognize a crack type. Another advantage of using square sub-image is to save a significant memory by discarding the sub-images which do not have cracks in them. In the future, the square-split partitioning should be applied to images with various dimensions.

REFERENCES

[1] Hudson, S. W., Hudson, W. R., Carmichael, R. F., Minimum Requirements for Standard Pavement Management Systems, *Pavement Management Implementation*, STP 1121, ASTM, Philadelphia, 1992, pp. 19-31

[2] Luhr, D. R.,: A Proposed Methodology To Qualify and Verify Automated Crack Survey Measurements, Transportation Research Record, 1999

[3] G. Eason, B. Noble, and I. N. Sneddon, "On certain integrals of Guralnick, S. A., Sun, E. S., Smith, C.,: Automating Inspection of Highway Pavement Surface, Journal of Transportation Engineering, Vol. 119, No. 1, 1993

[4] SHRP-P-338: Distress Identification manual for the Long-Term Pavement Performance Project, Strategic Highway Research Program, National Research Council, Washington D.C.

[5] Jitprasithsiri, S., Lee, H., Sorcic, R. G.,: Development of Digital Image Processing Algorithm to Compute a Unified Crack Index for Salt lake City, *Transportation research Record*, No. 1526, pp 142-148, (1996)

[6] Lee, H.,: New Crack-Imaging Procedure Using Spatial Autocorrelation Function., *Journal of Transportation Engineering*, Vol 120, No. 2, ASCE, New York, NY, 206-228, 1994

[7] Lee, B., Lee, H. : Position Invariant Neural Network for Digital Pavement Crack Analysis., *Computer-Aided Civil and Infrastructure Engineering*, Blackwell Publishers, Vol. 19, No. 2, pp 103-118, 2004

Building Information Modeling as a Tool for the Design of Airports

Júlio Tollendal Gomes Ribeiro
Faculdade de Arquitetura e Urbanismo, Universidade de Brasília, Brazil
juliotolendal@hotmail.com, http://lecomp.fau.unb.br
Neander Furtado Silva
Faculdade de Arquitetura e Urbanismo, Universidade de Brasília, Brazil
neander@unb.br, http://lecomp.fau.unb.br
Ecilamar Maciel Lima
Faculdade de Arquitetura e Urbanismo, Universidade de Brasília, Brazil
ecilamar@unb.br, http://lecomp.fau.unb.br

Abstract - **Building Information Modeling (BIM) may have obvious implications in the process of architectural design and construction at the present stage of technological development. However, BIM has rarely been really assessed and its benefits are often described in generic terms. In this paper we describe an experiment in which some benefits are identified from a comparison between two design processes of the same airport building, one run in an older CAD system and the other in a BIM based approach. The practical advantages of BIM to airport design are considerable.**

I. Introduction

The older bidimensional CAD systems used for conceptual design and analysis of airports project frequently results in inefficient processes. These systems are characterized by large amount of re-work, difficult information flow between the team members of design and construction, unnecessary expenditures and bigger environmental impact.

II. Research Problem

The problem treated in this paper results from the fragmented floor plans, sections and elevations of design projects and engineering works of INFRAERO, governmental institution responsible for management of the major Brazilian airports. This approach produces a long and serial process, besides documentation susceptible to various interpretations, dependent on paper communication that offering few subsides for decision making.

III. Hypothesis

Our hypothesis is that the systems of information of buildings design, BIM, can highly contribute for the reduction of time and steps of design processes of airports. For this article purpose we adopted the following concept:

> "BIM... (is) a modeling technology and associated set of processes to produce, communicate, and analyze building models" that "...are characterized by: building components that are represented with intelligent digital representations (objects) that "know" what they are, and can be associated with computable graphic and data attributes and parametric rules... components that include data that describe how they behave... consistent and non-redundant data such that changes to component data are represented in all views of the component...", and by last and not least, by the representation of "all views of a model" ... "in a coordinated way" (Eastman et al, 2008, p.13).

The present study is based in the above concept of a design process characterized as an object-based parametric modeling, including integration and coordination among all its elements through a tridimensional representation.
Other authors affirm that

> "the concept of BIM used for many software developers is based on the general idea of a tridimensional and parametric model as a central tool for the generation of everything since bidimensional drawings, material lists, other reporters and various kinds of analysis (for example, costs and structural design) and in addition serving as a primary base for interaction and interchange of information among all participants of the project and the construction process" [1]

As presented in the citation above the concept of BIM systems go beyond a three-dimensional modeling. "It is ... a model that takes into account performance characteristics, cost and other issues related to the construction and operation of a building, as well as its design" [2]. BIM systems include the development of the master model with its automatic and frequent up to date to all members of design teams allowing better coordination and integration among design elements, automatic production of documentation, etc. The use of BIM systems contributes to avoid inconsistencies, allows better analysis, saves time and costs through rapid simulation of design proposals, anticipated decision making and parallel activities among design, engineering and construction [3].

The contribution of BIM systems to the design process and construction can look obvious in general terms, but it has rarely been assessed and compared to the older CAD systems in a systematic and detailed form in a "posteriori" as we propose to do in this paper. There are important case studies about the use of BIM techniques and tools in design and construction such as the expansion of the factory Flint Global V6 of General

T. Sobh, K. Elleithy (eds.), *Innovations in Computing Sciences and Software Engineering*,
DOI 10.1007/978-90-481-9112-3_106, © Springer Science+Business Media B.V. 2010

Motors, Beijing National Aquatics Center, San Francisco Federal Building, etc. [4].

These case studies present the benefits of using BIM in the general way. For example, taking advantage of BIM systems the construction of the new factory of General Motors Glint Global V6 was concluded in 35 weeks instead of 60 or more in the traditional design build project, or 80 in the design-bid-build contract approach. The explanation for such reduction in time was that instead of working with the older bidimensional systems based on paper workflow and serial activities it was decided to run design, engineering and construction in parallel through frequent exchanges of the building model in order to up to date all participant teams [5].

IV. Research Method

In this paper we compare the design process of one airport terminal made in a traditional bidimensional system with another conceived and developed in the BIM system. Through this comparison it was possible do identify in the objective and systematic way some of the advantages of the use of BIM in the design process of airports.

For the purpose of investigation of this research it was used the design project for renovation and expansion of the airport terminal of the International Airport of Brasília (TPS-BSB). In order to verify some of the benefits of the BIM system, it was repeated the process of design previously done by INFRAERO in these two referred CAD system and after that compared the results.

One exclusive feature of BIM systems is the possibility of automatically extracting and printing the quantity bills of materials needed for the construction. These are essential to inform the budget and to plan the acquisition and delivery of materials in the construction site. However this is not automatic task in a "no BIM" system. The literature does not show analysis of this contrast in a systematic way. Filling this gap we decided to direct our investigation to the procedures needed to extract bills of quantity in the design process of the boarding room of the remote airport terminal (TPS-BSB). The tasks performed were the extraction of bills of quantity from slabs, columns, beams, walls and doors of the boarding room of TPS-BSB. We began our study modeling the TPS-BSB in the BIM system (ArchiCAD www.graphisoft.com, that was previously designed in the traditionally bidimensional representation. After that we represented this project using the traditional approach of representation according to the procedures adopted by INFRAERO.

This task involved the use of bidimensional resources of the CAD software currently used by INFRAERO (AutoCAD, www.autodesk.com) and the execution of manual calculation as in practice in this institution.

After that we compared the results gathered in each of the cited approaches, considering particularly the information related to time spent and number of steps in each task of the design. It was considered a step the execution of each command for the accomplishment of each task. The beginning of a command was considered a step, the entry of data in the same command was another step, while its conclusion was the final step of the task under analysis.

V. Analysis Of The Results

In the Table 1 below it is presented a comparison with only the common tasks developed by two softwares classified as traditional, AutoCAD, and as BIM approach, ArchiCAD. Both softwares were used in the same design process and for the same tasks of the TPS-BSB. However it is important to notice that any of these tasks when performed in the BIM system they involve much more information than in the bidimensional software such as the type of materials and their properties, the relation between de components, etc. The objective of the table below was to provide a simple comparison between these two systems considering only time and steps needed to perform the same tasks of the referred design process.

The numbers of the Table 1 show large differences of time spent and steps needed between the two systems. These figures show that the BIM system, ArchiCAD, allowed completing the design tasks in 35% of the time spent by AutoCAD. These advantages of this BIM system are due to the fact that in the BIM system the constructive components are represented as objects instead of generic geometric entities. In some tasks the time and the number of steps needed by ArchiCAD are longer than in AutoCAD due to the need of configuring and defining the parameters incorporated to objects.

In relation to the reasoning involved in the design process, the ArchiCAD contributes to focus in the conceptive and analytic activities. On the other hand, AutoCAD requires labor intensive drawing activities that distances architects from the design process, such as formal, functional, constructive, comfort and environmental aspects.

TABLE 1
COMPARATIVE COUNTING OF TIME AND STEPS USING TRADITIONAL DESIGN PROCESS AND BIM

Software used	AutoCAD	ArchiCAD
1- Time spent (in minutes)		
1- Open originals files of Terminal Satélite Norte (TPS-BSB) design.	1,5	1
2- Salve as new file: rename the file and save it.	1,25	2,58
3- Freeze layers.	4,66	0,26
4- Delete elements to be demolished.	11,5	2,35
5- Create new layers and configure existents ones.	20,41	11,25
6- Modeling of floor slabs of TPS.	6,33	4,88
7- Modeling of columns of TPS.	4,16	12,42
8- Modeling beams of TPS.	12,91	2,44
9- Modeling of walls of TPS.	1,84	2,22
10- Modeling of cladding components.	24,66	4,08
11- Modeling of accessory elements of the building.	13,6	2,51
12- Modeling the roof of TPS.	1,08	2,44
13- Generate floor plans, sections and elevations of the model.	130	35.6
Total	233,9	84,03
Softwares used	AutoCAD	ArchiCAD
1- Counting the steps (by tasks)		
1- Open originals files of TPS design.	15	3
2- Salve as new file: rename the file and save it.	15	3
3- Freeze layers.	21	3
4- Delete elements to be demolished .	99	96
5- Create new layers and configure existents ones.	21	45
6- Modeling of floor slabs of TPS.	27	66
7- Modeling of columns of TPS.	15	96
8- Modeling of beams of TPS.	39	36
9- Modeling of walls of TPS.	96	18
10- Modeling of cladding components.	42	36
11- Modeling of accessory elements of the building.	27	90
12- Modeling of the roof of TPS.	3	33
13- Generate floor plans, sections and elevations of the model.	1410	325
Total	2.043	850

Table 2 below shows the time and steps needed to extract or calculate bills of quantities. The figures corroborate to those shown in the previous table. This table shows time and number of steps needed to produce bills of quantities of the main elements of the TPS-BSB design. It does not provide a comparison between systems only, but between two design processes developed using different computer approaches. Therefore it includes not only what each system can do but also manual and automatic procedures required to complete the design tasks.

TABLE 2
COMPARATIVE STUDY BETWEEN TRADITIONAL DESIGN PROCESS AND BIM

Construction Components	Design Approach						Percentage of difference (BIM/ Traditional)	
	Traditional				BIM			
	Time of automatic calculation (sec.)	Time of manual calculation (sec.)	Total Time (sec.)	Steps	Time (sec.)	Steps	Time (sec.)	Steps
Slabs	189	73	262	45	135	9	51,53	20,00
Columns	352	24	376	96	135	9	35,90	9,38
Beams	384	50	434	99	135	9	31,10	9,09
Walls	174	43	217	75	135	9	62,21	12,00
Doors	352	46	398	96	135	9	33,92	9,38
Totals	1451	236	1687	411	675	45	40,01	10,95

The table above shows that the traditional design approach does not have tools to extract automatically those bills of quantities necessary for the TPS-BSB. In that approach several calculations needed to be done manually in addition to those automated for all elements. Although the sum of the time spent in manual calculations in the traditional approach of those elements represents only 16% in relation to the automatic ones, there is another important issue to be emphasized. It is related to the probability of errors from the manual calculations because the data basis of each element is separated without any connection as can be found in a master model of BIM systems.

The time needed to produce bills of quantities in the BIM system represents in average only 40% of the traditional. Such percentage of time spent decreases even more in relation to beams.

On the other hand, the difference is even larger in relation to the number of steps. Those calculations made through the BIM system require only 10,95% of the total of steps needed for the same tasks done in the traditional approach.

VI. CONCLUSION

The results obtained in this research are promising because they show a considerable reduction in time and steps needed in the BIM system. The traditional approach, according to the data in Table 2, requires 90% more steps and 60% more time to accomplish those tasks done in the BIM system. These numbers show that BIM systems can contribute with considerable savings of time and costs to the design process.

The data obtained in this research indicates important reasons in favor of a rapid adoption of BIM systems in the airport design and construction. They show the possibility of considerable savings in time and steps besides allowing better coordination. These advantages show the need for the major Brazilian authority that contracts airport design and construction to make mandatory the use of BIM systems by the design and construction companies.

REFERENCES

[1] Schodek, D., Bechthold, M., Griggs, K., Kao, K. M., Steinberg, M., "Digital Design and Manufacturing – CAD/CAM Applications in Architecture and Design", John Wiley & Sons, New Jersey, 2005, p. 123.

[2] Pittman, Jon., "Building Information Modeling: Current Challenges and Future Directions" in Architecture in the Digital Age – Design and Manufacturing, Kolarevic (editor), Taylor & Francis, New York and London, 2005, p. 256.

[3] Eastman, C. What is BIM. http://bim.arch.gatech.edu/? Accessed in 20/05/2009.

[4] Eastman, C., Teicholz, P., Sacks, R., Liston, K., "BIM Handbook – A Guide to Building Information Modeling", John Wiley & Sons, New Jersey, 2008, pp. 319-450.

[5] Eastman, C., Teicholz, P., Sacks, R., Liston, K., "BIM Handbook – A Guide to Building Information Modeling", John Wiley & Sons, New Jersey, 2008, pp. 326-327.

A Petri-Nets Based Unified Modeling Approach for Zachman Framework Cells

S. Shervin Ostadzadeh
Computer Engineering Department,
Faculty of Engineering,
Science & Research Branch,
Islamic Azad University, Tehran, Iran
ostadzadeh@srbiau.ac.ir

Mohammad Ali Nekoui
Intelligent Systems Laboratory,
Electrical Engineering Department,
K.N. Toosi University of Technology,
Tehran, Iran
manekoui@eetd.kntu.ac.ir

Abstract - **With a trend toward becoming more and more information based, enterprises constantly attempt to surpass the accomplishments of each other by improving their information activities. In this respect, Enterprise Architecture (EA) has proven to serve as a fundamental concept to accomplish this goal. Enterprise architecture clearly provides a thorough outline of the whole enterprise applications and systems with their relationships to enterprise business goals. To establish such an outline, a logical framework needs to be laid upon the entire information system called Enterprise Architecture Framework (EAF). Among various proposed EAF, Zachman Framework (ZF) has been widely accepted as a standard scheme for identifying and organizing descriptive representations that have critical roles in enterprise management and development. One of the problems faced in using ZF is the lack of formal and verifiable models for its cells. In this paper, we proposed a formal language based on Petri nets in order to obtain verifiable models for all cells in ZF. The presented method helps developers to validate and verify completely integrated business and IT systems which results in improve the effectiveness or efficiency of the enterprise itself.**

Keywords: Zachman Framework, Enterprise Architecture Framework, Petri Nets, Formal Modeling.

I. Introduction

An enterprise consists of people, information, and technologies; performs business functions; has a defined organizational structure that is commonly distributed in multiple locations; responds to internal and external events; has a purpose for its activities; provides specific services and products to its customers [1]. An IT enterprise is an enterprise in which IT plays an important role in its activities.

An IT enterprise can better respond to a business's demands if the applications in its portfolio

- are easy to integrate,
- implement similar processes in the same way, and
- have compatible perspectives on the enterprise's shared data.

Additionally, the organization's ability to support its application portfolio depends on the mix of technologies deployed and on the applications' durability and performance characteristics, both individually and collectively. Enterprise architecture organizations help development organizations address these issues [2].

The Enterprise Architecture Research Forum [3] defines EA as "... the continuous practice of describing the essential elements of a socio-technical organization, their relationships to each other and to the environment, in order to understand complexity and manage change". Another comprehensive definition of enterprise architecture is provided by the IFEAD (Institute for Enterprise Architecture Developments) as: "Enterprise architecture is a complete expression of the enterprise; a master plan which acts as a collaboration force between aspects of business planning such as goals, visions, strategies and governance principles; aspects of business operations such as business terms, organization structures, processes and data; aspects of automation such as information systems and databases; and the enabling technological infrastructure of the business such as computers, operating systems and networks [4]". Organizing such great amounts of information requires a framework. Various enterprise architecture frameworks have been proposed; among them are Zachman framework [5], FEAF [6], TEAF [7], and C4ISR [8].

ZF is widely accepted as the main framework in EA. Compared to other proposed frameworks, it has evident advantages to list: (1) using well-defined perspectives, (2) using comprehensive abstracts, (3) normality, and (4) extensive usage in practice [9]. They were the motivations for ZF adoption in our work, nevertheless; there are challenges to overcome, among them is the absence of an integrated formal language to model cells in the framework. In order to elegantly define and implement the concepts of EA, ZF needs a formal and verifiable modeling approach to describe its cells. Validity, sufficiency, necessity, integrity, authenticity, fitness and suitability of models are achieved through such a modeling method [9]. We aim to resolve the problem by proposing an approach based on Petri nets in order to model all cells in ZF.

The challenge we referred to is also addressed in other researches. A complete overview is given in [9,10]. Applying UML [10] and MDA [9] to ZF seems to be the best solution proposed up to now. Unfortunately, UML is not mature enough to support all aspects of an EA [11]; as a result, a lot of cells in ZF remain unmapped. MDA is a comprehensive

T. Sobh, K. Elleithy (eds.), *Innovations in Computing Sciences and Software Engineering*,
DOI 10.1007/978-90-481-9112-3_107, © Springer Science+Business Media B.V. 2010

method, but not a formal for verifiable. Some other solutions practice the use of nonstandard symbols which leave the initial problem intact.

The rest of this paper is organized as follows. In Section 2, we plot a Petri nets overview. We discuss our proposed approach in section 3, and finally, we make conclusions and suggest some comments for future works.

II. PETRI NETS

Petri Nets (PNs) [12] were invented by Carl Adam Petri for the purpose of describing chemical processes [13]. A Petri net (also known as a place/transition net or P/T net) is one of several mathematical modeling languages for the description of discrete distributed systems. A Petri net is a directed bipartite graph, in which the nodes represent transitions (i.e. discrete events that may occur), places (i.e. conditions), and directed arcs (that describe which places are pre- and/or post-conditions for which transitions).

Like industry standards such as UML, BPMN and MDA, Petri nets offer a graphical notation for stepwise processes that include choice, iteration, and concurrent execution. Unlike these standards, Petri nets have an exact mathematical definition of their execution semantics, with a well-developed mathematical theory for process analysis.

A Petri net consists of places, transitions, and directed arcs. Arcs run between places and transitions, never between places or between transitions. The places from which an arc runs to a transition are called the input places of the transition; the places to which arcs run from a transition are called the output places of the transition. Places may contain any non-negative number of tokens. A distribution of tokens over the places of a net is called a marking. A transition of a Petri net may fire whenever there is a token at the end of all input arcs; when it fires, it consumes these tokens, and places tokens at the end of all output arcs. A firing is atomic, i.e., a single non-interruptible step. A Petri net is a 5-tuple (P, T, I, O, M_0), where:

- P is a finite set of places
- T is a finite set of transitions
- P and T are disjoint, i.e. no object can be both a place and a transition
- I is a finite set of input arcs.
- O is a finite set of output arcs.
- $I \cup O$ is a multiset of arcs, i.e. it defines arcs and assigns to each a positive integer arc multiplicity; note that no arc may connect two places or two transitions.
- M_0 is the initial marking, a marking of the Petri net graph. A marking of a Petri net (graph) is a multiset of its places, i.e., a mapping. We say the marking assigns to each place a number of tokens.

One thing that makes PNs interesting is that they provide an interesting balance between modeling power and analyzability: many things one would like to know about concurrent systems can be automatically determined for Petri nets, although some of those things are very expensive to determine in the general case. Several subclasses of Petri nets have been studied that can still model interesting classes of concurrent systems, while these problems become easier.

III. FORMAL MODELS FOR ZF

As mentioned earlier, one of the difficulties we are facing to use ZF is the problem of formal and verifiable models. There is not a set of formal models across the entire cells. In this section, we investigate the use of Petri nets in Zachman framework in order to suggest a formal practical model for each cell. This can improve the verifiability of ZF for the developers who intend to put it in practice.

ZF contains six rows, each representing one stakeholder perspective. The question is: shall we propose a method for the entire rows? The first row of ZF specifies the architecture boundary. J.A. Zachman indicates that this row is a list of important things to the enterprise [14], and not a model. It seems that using natural language is the best way to describe this row. So, the first row does not exist in our problem space. Second till fifth rows model businesses, systems, technologies, and detailed-representations, respectively, and they exist in our problem space. The sixth row is not a model at all. It represents the actual deployed or running elements, data, and people of the organization. It is not a perspective, as such, but the "real world" in all its complexity. This row is usually omitted from ZF, and does not exist in our problem scope (see Fig. 1).

In the next, we plot our method to model ZF cells based on Petri nets. First, we use Zachman definition [14] for each cell. As follow, we investigate how to model them with places and transitions.

Data column focuses on data entities. Each data entity can be modeled by a place and the relations between entities can be modeled by transitions. Owner/Data cell is a model of the actual enterprise things (objects, assets) that are significant to the enterprise. In this cell, each actual thing is modeled by place. Designer/Data cell is a model of the logical (implementation - technology neutral) representation of the things of the enterprise about which it records information (in either automated or non-automated form). We use places to model logical things. Builder/Data cell is a technology constrained, or physical representation of the things of the enterprise. This is the same as previous cell, except that places are used for physical things. Contractor/Data cell would be the

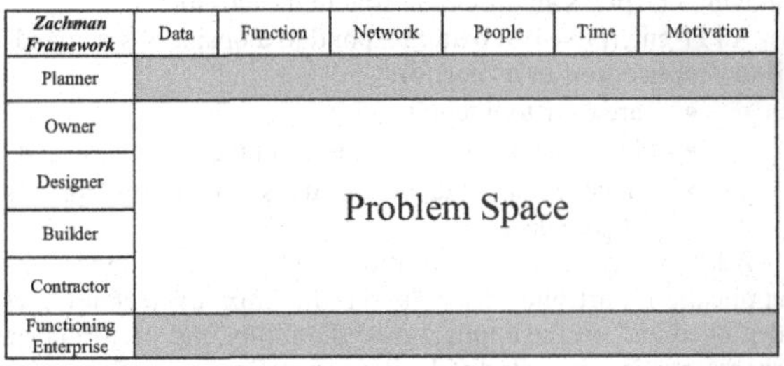

Zachman Framework	Data	Function	Network	People	Time	Motivation
Planner						
Owner	Problem Space					
Designer						
Builder						
Contractor						
Functioning Enterprise						

Fig 1. The Problem Space

Zachman Framework	Data	Function	Network	People	Time	Motivation
Planner	Out of problem space					
Owner	P=Things T=Relations	P=Process T=Workflows	P=Locations T=Connections	P=Agents T=Responsibilities	P=Cycles T=Events	P=Ends T=Means
Designer	P=Logic Obj. T= Relations	P=Systems T=Workflows	P=Logical Loc. T=Connections	P=Systems T=Roles	P=Cycles T=Events	P=Ends T=Means
Builder	P=Physical Obj. T= Relations	P=Applications T=Workflows	P=Physical Loc. T=Connections	P=Individuals T=Requirements	P=Cycles T=Events	P=Rules T=Constrains
Contractor	P=Data Obj. T= Relations	P=Programs T=Workflows	P=Nodes T=Lines	P=Individuals T=Jobs	P=Cycle T=Interrupt	P=Rules T=Constrains

Fig 2. Petri nets models for Zachman framework cells

definition of all the data objects specified by the Physical Data Model. In this cell, each data object is represented by a place.

Function column focuses on business processes. Processes are mapped to places, and workflows between processes are mapped to transitions. Owner/Function cell is a model of the actual Business Processes that the enterprise performs, quite independent of any "system" or implementation considerations and any organizational constraints. To model this cell, we plot each business process with place. Designer/Function cell is a model of the logical (implementation - technology neutral) "systems" implementation (manual and/or automated) supporting the Business processes and would express the "human/machine" boundaries. Each logical system is represented by a place, and the relations between systems are modeled by transitions. Builder/Function cell is system design. In this cell, applications will be shown by places. Contractor/Function cell is programs model. Similar to previous cell, each program will be modeled by a place, and the relations between programs will be depicted by transitions.

Network column focuses on locations. Owner/Network cell is a model of the locations of the enterprise and their connections. Places will be used to model locations, and transitions will be used to represent connections between locations. Designer/Network cell is a logical model of the Business Logistics System depicting the types of systems facilities and controlling software at the nodes and lines. Each logical location can be mapped to places. Builder/Network cell is the physical depiction of the technology environment for the Enterprise showing the actual hardware and systems software. This cell will be modeled in a similar way to previous cell. Places will show physical locations. Contractor/Network cell is the specific definition of the nodes and the lines. Each node will be modeled by a place, and each line will be depicted by a transition.

People column focuses on agents and responsibilities. Owner/People cell is the model of the actual Enterprise allocation of responsibilities and specification of work products. Each agent will be mapped to a place. Transitions will also use for responsibilities. Designer/People cell is the logical "systems" expression of work flow which would include the specification of the "roles" of the responsible parties. Each system is modeled by a place, and each role is modeled by transition. Builder/People cell is the physical expression of work flow of the enterprise including the specific individual and their ergonomic requirements and the presentation format of the work product. Places can be used for individuals, and transitions can be used for requirements. Contractor/People cell would be the identification of the individual accessing the system and the specification of the work or job they were authorized to initiate. Individuals are mapped to places, and their jobs are mapped to transitions.

Time Column focuses on scheduling and timing. Owner/Time cell is a model of the business cycles that is comprised of an initiating event and an elapsed time ("cycle"). Designer/Time cell is the logical (implementation - technology neutral) systems specification of points in time (systems events) and lengths of time (processing cycles). In both cells, business cycles are modeled by a place, and transitions will be used for events. Builder/Time cell is the physical expression of system events and physical processing cycles, expressed as control structure, passing "control" from one to another processing module. Physical cycles are depicted by places. Contractor/Time cell is the definition of interrupts and machine cycles. Machine cycles and interrupts can be modeled by places and transitions, respectively.

Motivation column focuses on goals and strategies. Owner/Motivation cell is a model of the business objectives and strategies (the "ends" and "means") of the enterprise that constitute the motivation behind enterprise operations and decisions. Designer/Motivation cell is a logical model of the business rules of the enterprise in terms of their intent ("ends") and the constraints ("means"). In both cells, "Ends" will be mapped to places, and "means" will be mapped to transitions. Builder/Motivation cell is a physical specification of the business rules, which can be modeled by places. Contractor/Motivation cell will be the "out-of-context" specification of the business rules, which can be depicted by places in a same way as previous cell.

Fig. 2 summarizes our proposed method. Each cell uses Places/Transitions as suggested by Petri nets.

IV. Conclusions

Business and IT integration has proven successful in delivering applications with improved value to the enterprise. We can achieve this integration by involving enterprise architecture framework. Compared to other frameworks, Zachman framework has some evident advantages. These advantages have caused its extensive usage as the basic framework of enterprise architecture in the present time. However, an architect should face the lack of formal and verifiable models for its cells. In this paper, we proposed a novel method based on Petri nets for modeling the ZF cells. This research demonstrated how the models in ZF cells can be made formal in order to verify within the framework. In general, our method can increase the success rate of information system projects within enterprises.

In future works, one is expected to suggest a methodology based on Petri nets for ZF. This methodology can be integrated with our proposed solution, achieving full support of the Zachman framework.

References

[1] M.A. Rood, "Enterprise Architecture: Definition, Content, and Utility," IEEE Trans., 1994.

[2] R.J. Parsons, "Enterprise Architects Join the Team," IEEE Software, Vol. 22, No. 5, September/October 2005.

[3] Enterprise Architecture Research Forum (EARF), http://hufee.meraka.org.za/Hufeesite/collaborations/earf

[4] IFEAD's Enterprise Architecture Standards Overview, http://www.enterprise-architecture.info/EA_Standards.htm

[5] J.A. Zachman, "A Framework for Information Systems Architecture," IBM Systems Journal, Vol. 26, No. 3, 1987.

[6] Chief Information Officers (CIO) Council, *Federal Enterprise Architecture Framework*, Version 1.1, September 1999.

[7] Department of the Treasury, *Treasury Enterprise Architecture Framework*, Version 1, July 2000.

[8] C4ISR Architecture Working Group (AWG), *C4ISR Architecture Framework*, Version 2.0, U.S.A. Department of Defense (DoD), December 1997.

[9] S. S. Ostadzadeh, F. Shams, S. A. Ostadzadeh, "A Method for Consistent Modeling of Zachman Framework," Advances and Innovations in Systems, Computing Sciences and Software Engineering, Springer, pp. 375-380, August 2007. (ISBN 978-1-4020-6263-6)

[10] A. Fatholahi, An Investigation into Applying UML to Zachman Framework, MSc thesis, Shahid Beheshti University, Tehran, 2004.

[11] D.S. Frankel, Model Driven Architecture: Applying MDA to Enterprise Computing, OMG Press, Wiley Publishing, 2003.

[12] C.A. Petri, "Petri net", Scholarpedia 3(4):6477. Retrieved on 2008-07-13.

[13] C.A. Petri, *Kommunikation mit Automaten*, Ph. D. Thesis, University of Bonn, 1962.

[14] J.A. Zachman, "The Framework for Enterprise Architecture – Cell Definitions," ZIFA, 2003.

From *Perspectiva Artificialis* to Cyberspace: Game-Engine and the Interactive Visualization of Natural Light in the Interior of the Building

Evangelos Dimitrios Christakou
Faculdade de Arquitetura e Urbanismo – Universidade de Brasília
vangelis@unb.br, http://lecomp.fau.unb.br
Neander Furtado Silva
Faculdade de Arquitetura e Urbanismo – Universidade de Brasília
neander@unb.br, http://lecomp.fau.unb.br
Ecilamar Maciel Lima
Faculdade de Arquitetura e Urbanismo – Universidade de Brasília
ecilamar@unb.br, http://lecomp.fau.unb.br

Abstract – **In order to support the early stages of conceptual design, the architect used throughout the years, mockups – scaled physical models - or perspective drawings that intended to predict architectural ambience before its effective construction. This paper studies the real time interactive visualization, focused on one of the most important aspects inside building space: the natural light. However, the majority of physically-based algorithms currently existing was designed for the synthesis of static images which may not take into account how to rebuild the scene - in real time - when the user is doing experiments to change certain properties of design. In this paper we show a possible solution for this problem.**

I. Computacional Visualization And Its Application In The Design Process

The beginning of the process of creation of architectural spaces and its developments is largely known among the Brazilian architects as design concept. In order to support the concept of design architects have used scale models – physical models of reduced dimensions – or perspectives drawings to represent designed space before its construction. These representation techniques have had important role, particularly by anticipating possible conflicts among the various architectural elements such as structural components, openings, plumbing, etc. These elements should be coordinated and consistent among themselves, allowing better choice of alternatives for the design process. Visualizing the building at the design stage, even before its construction, it has always been a big desire and need of the architect.

"During almost five centuries, the visual needs of the western civilization were met by a system of representation of the space known as "artificialis" perspective that is a visual representation that aims to achieve the sensation of depth based on objective laws of space created by Euclidian Geometry and its theory by Leo Batista Alberti" [1].

Centuries after the mathematical formula elaborated by Alberti, another important tool of representation was developed, based on the digital technology of computers allied to complex and sophisticated algorithms of simulation of the virtual space. "The image is the result of stimulus of luminance produced by one bidimensional support" [2]. The process that allow the conversion of data in image is known as computational visualization, translated in image of the synthesis generated by a computer from abstract data, independent of context of the real world.

The computational technology of visualization has contributed for the establishment of new user interfaces of computer, new paradigms to deal with complex data, even capable to represent new virtual worlds never seen before. These processes are present in the recent industry of virtual games and consoles, with exceptional power of processing computer graphics, promoted mainly by the use of techniques of rendering developed for processing directly in the Graphic Processing Unities (GPU) programmable (NVIDIA Tesla C1060 *Computing Processor* allied to CUDA system of paralleling graph processing). The Unities of Central Processing (UCP) in this case should be in charge of generic computational processing only.

The computational visualization had its beginning with the doctoral thesis entitled "*Sketchpad, a man-machine graphical communication system*" of Sutherland [3]. This thesis fundamentally contributes until nowadays to the developments of the relation between man and computer through graphic interface that permeate the interaction with the objects that are presented in the computer screen. The computational visualization of a building can be interactive and dynamic when generated in virtual environments. In these environments the architect eyes navigate through the computer screen that is transformed in a window of the virtual architectonic space, using Sutherland metaphor [4] (non-immersive process, known as Fishtank).

II. The Virtual Interactive Environments In Real Time And The Global Illumination

The interactive windows in real time, that means, those that do not require waiting time in its interactions with the user, in this research are entitled Real Time Virtual Interactive

T. Sobh, K. Elleithy (eds.), *Innovations in Computing Sciences and Software Engineering*,
DOI 10.1007/978-90-481-9112-3_108, © Springer Science+Business Media B.V. 2010

Environments (RTVIE), figure 1. It should be noticed that we do not use the expression "virtual reality" very common in Graphic Computation (CG) in order to avoid comparison among softwares that do not have the aim to use physical parameters as the basis for the generation of virtual images.

Our proposal in this paper is that the generation and manipulation of RTVIE should be based on the technology of computer games (CGm). Besides the entertainment experience, the games allow various multidisciplinary applications initially explored in the Massachusetts Institute of Technology (MIT), USA. Fundamental aspects such as immersion, the interactivity and the navigational spatiality allow promissory applications in the visualization of the architectonic space.

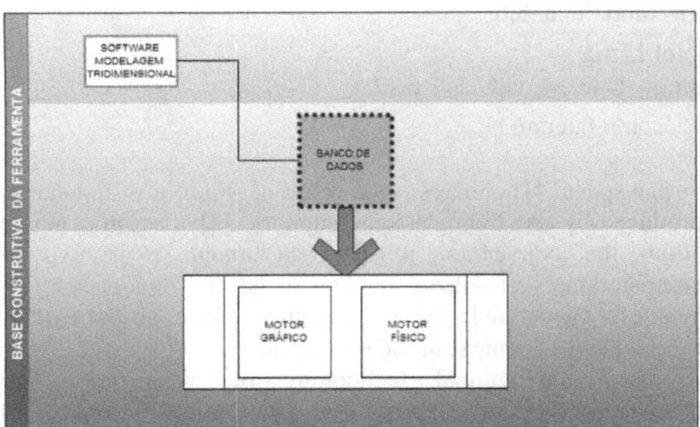

Figure 1 – Proposed tool, modeling software suported by data basis.

In order to allow that the RTVIE to be really useful it is not enough to be interactive. For the architect, besides to be physically correct, the forecast assessment should be in real time, allowing the dynamic assessment of the proposed changes in the future building. This is an useful resource, mainly in the initial stages of the design process, where there is high degree of undefined aspects to be decided. [5]. Each simulation of the architectural scene involves some thousands of facet and millions of polygons. In order to face such complexity for some time it was considered that the frequency of images needed to generate interactivity was incompatible with a synthesis to satisfy the principles of Global Illumination (GI).

According to Erlich the GI are physically correct because have their calculation based on physical and behavioral properties of the light, in its macro and micro scale. The first scale means light propagation directly from the source to the observer and the second is related to interactions of the light with the proprieties of surface [6].

One of the major obstacles for the effective use of GI in interactive environments in real time (RT) is that the majority of algorithms of GI was conceived for the synthesis of statics images that cannot solve the need to reconstruct one scene in RT when the user change one of its proprieties. When changes are made, even the most insignificant of them, all the calculation should be re-done since its beginning. This requires a high level of processing that is incompatible with the interactivity in RT [7].

The algorithms of GI take from some minutes up to hours to generate only one image. In the RT techniques it is not admissible that um tenth of one thousand of a second to be spent in such task. One revision about this subject in available in [8].

III. Literature Review

In interactivity, immersion and navigability of computer games (CG) is generated through game engines that refer to one collection of modules of codes of simulation that do not determine previously the logic of the game [9]. One introduction of programming techniques for game engine and one short history of the development of games can be found in [10].

The rendering techniques in RT have been developed and applied in virtual games, particularly in relation to the transfer of processing UPC to programmable UPG known as Vertex Shaders and Pixel Shaders that were discussed by [11].

Revision of techniques used by game engines and related softwares was presented by [12]. They demonstrated how game engines can be adopted to develop visualizations of architectural design. The architectonic environment is modeled through definitions of Constructive Solid Geometry (CSG) combining simple forms such as cubs, pyramids and spheres. Texture maps can be applied over these simplified tridimensional models. They can be synthetics or obtained from a data basis of photographs.

In relation to interactivity in RT, the most efficient strategies recently are among those that use hardware acceleration in the image processing by Pixel Shade and have the potential to render satisfactorily complex environments in frame rate per second (FRS). The minimum is 10 FRS for the interactive use, applying pre-computed textures, maps of environments and sophisticated shades cache of pixel and vertex [13].

Other authors such as [14] proposed an application of one algorithm of progressive GI processed in parallel in UGP. They presented experiments made in scenes of complex geometry where the objects and sources of light are moving. There were promising results in order to obtain high rates of FPS using *vertex* and *fragment shaders,* applied in hardware ATI Radeon 9800 [15].

IV. Application Of Virtual Computacional Games

The capability to visualize a virtual world with global illumination based on physical phenomenon's and dynamically, change the view point, the geometry and illumination is a great challenge for the research community in computer graphics.

Some computational limitations still need to be solved in the context of CGm. One of those limitations is that the camera should answer to unscripted events, that means, not foreseeable, that is the major difficulty to project systems in real time. The increasing use of animations in virtual environments marked by the inclusion of the physical modeling and complex systems of collision detection, means that the systems of camera should be still more efficient [16].

High-dynamic-range images obtained through specific photographic machines illuminate one scene using techniques or rendering based in images. Some aspects about the climatic specificity of the site of the future building need more attention in this research.

One new interface based on the paradigm of CGm amplifies the horizons of interactive simulation in real time. In this context the architect can experiment, examine and choose the best alternatives of project (figure 2). For this reason it is necessary to apply the graphic engine of CGm into the algorithms of GI and adopt efficient strategies of rendering in real time.

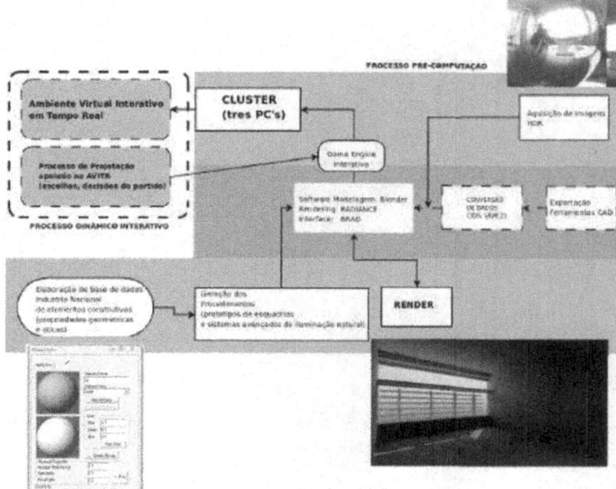

Figure 2: Virtual interactive environments in real time.

V. Discussion, Conclusions And Future research

The RTVIE as computational support to the design process potentially can allow simulations of the building under direct influence of the actions of the observer of the "Interactive Window". In this way a simultaneous experimentation of new data from the scenery, the volumetric parameters and those from the materials surfaces such as textures, colors and control of the natural light that illuminates the interior of the building are reflected automatically in the computer screen according to the architect's interventions.

In general this research aims to investigate the possibility to transfer an experience with RTVIE to the design process in architecture in its conceptual stage. More specifically, this research aims to study the control of natural light (NL) in the interior of the building. It aims forecasting the parameters of density of intensity of light that describes the amount of light that goes through or comes out of a specific surface, and the amount of light inside one environment and their special distribution.

Using RTVIE the architect can forecast and assess qualitative and quantitatively one natural light for taking decisions in the conceptual design with confidence in the sense that the image in the computer screen with which in interacting is a reliable. One future application of this research is the creation of integrative computational tool that incorporate graphic engine of Blender (software of tridimensional modeling) and the possibilities of simulation of natural light largely validated by Radiance [17]. Transporting interactivity and immersion from "Virtual Window" to the context of image synthesis based on the physical parameters of GI and at the same time in which includes the needs of experimentations of the initial stages of design process of architecture.

References

[1] MACHADO, A.: *A Ilusão Especular: introdução à fotografia*. Ed. Brasiliense, São Paulo, 1984, p. 63.

[2] GOMES, J. e VELHO, L.: *Computação gráfica: Imagem*. Rio de Janeiro: Editora IMPA/SBM, 1994, p. 131.

[3] SUTHERLAND, I.: *Sketchpad a man-machine graphical communication system*. Massachusets: Doctoral Thesis in Computer Science, MA, 1963.

[4] SUTHERLAND, I. : The Ultimate display in *Proceedings of the Int. Fed. of Information Processing Congress*, vol 2, 1965, p. 506–508.

[5] CHRISTAKOU, E. D.: *A simulação da luz natural aplicada ao projeto de arquitetura* . Brasília: Dissertação de Mestrado em Arquitetura e Urbanismo - Programa de Pesquisa e Pós-graduação, Universidade de Brasília, DF, 2004.

[6] ERLICH, C. K.: *Computer Aided Perception: A method to Evaluate the Representation of Glare in Computer Graphics Imagery*. Dissertação de mestrado em Ciência da Computação, Universidade de Berkeley, California, 2002.

[7] DAMEZ, C.; DIMITRIEV, K.; MYSZKOWSKI, K. : *State of art in global illumination for interactive applications and high-quality animations. Computer graphics forum*. 2003, p. 55-77.

[8] AKENINE-MOLLER, T. e HAINES, E. : *Real-Time Rendering*. Second ed. A K Peters Ltd, Massachusetts, 2002.

[9] LEWIS, M. e JACOBSON, J.: Game engines in scientific research, Communications of the ACM, 2002.

[10] GREBLER, E.: *Game programming for teens*. Boston: Thomas Course Technology,2006.

[11] WATT, A. e POLICARPO, F. : *3D games-animation and advanced real-time rendering*. Edinburgh: Pearson Education Limited-Addison Wesley, 2003, p. 189.

[12] KADA, M. e FRITSCH, D.: *Visualization using games engines*, em *XXth ISPRS Congress*. Istambul, 2004.

[13] TOLE, P.; PELLACINI, F.; WALTER, B.; GREENBERG, D. P.: *Interactive Global Illumination in Dynamic Scenes* in *Proceedings of the 29th annual conference on Computer graphics and interactive techniques*. San Antonio, Texas: ACM New York, NY, 2002, p. 537 – 546.

[14] NIJASURE, M, S PATTANAIK, and V GOEL. : "Real-Time Global Illumination on GPUs." *Journal of graphics tools*, 2005, p. 55-71.

[15] NVIDIA: 2009, Manual técnico em http://www.nvidia.com/object/product_tesla_c1060_us.html, accessed in January, 2009.

[16] HAIGH-HUTCHINSON, M.: Real-Time cameras: a guide for Game designers and developers, Morgan Kaufmann, 2009.

[17] WARD. hhtp://radsite.lbl.gov/radiance. Acessed in June, 2002.

Computational Shape Grammars and Non-Standardization: a Case Study on the City of Music of Rio de Janeiro

Félix A. Silva Júnior
Architect, Master Student, Universidade de Brasília
felixalsilva@hotmail.com

Neander Furtado Silva
Associate Professor, Faculdade de Arquitetura e Urbanismo, Universidade de Brasília
http://lecomp.fau.unb.br, neander@unb.br, neander.furtado@gmail.com

Abstract - **This paper shows how shape grammars can be applied in the analyze of new types of architecture through the case study of the project of the City of Music of Rio de Janeiro by Christian Portzamparc. It aims to indicate how shape grammars can still be constructed from designs which were created with the purpose of avoiding standardization.**

I. Introduction

The architecture of Christian Portzamparc is based on the concept of "open block" which is a set of principles developed by the architect himself during the 1980's [1]. Some of these principles consist in "no… façade conformity" and in an "overall avoidance of standardization" [1]. This consists in a clear departure from the principle of mass standardization provided by the industrial revolution which also drove the modern movement in architecture during most of the 20th century.

Novelty is often thought as being opposed to computation. Computation is often seen by the uninformed as a synonym for repetition and conformity. In this paper we will demonstrate through a simple example that modern computation can actually contribute for the designer's creativity.

We will show in this paper that it is possible to identify elements and computable procedures that may allow the construction of shape grammars based on the rules set in Christian de Portzamparc design methodology.

The analysis of the City of Music Project in Rio de Janeiro, shown in Figure 1, and the architect's design process makes it possible to formulate a shape grammar for this building and to verify the application of the architect's design methodology.

Figure 1. City of Music of Rio de Janeiro, by Christian de Portzamparc. (Source: Wikipedia, The Free Encyclopedia, 2009, http://en.wikipedia.org/wiki/Christian_de_Portzamparc)

Christian de Portzamparc, as a renowned French architect, has developed through his office several institutional projects (museums, concert halls, government buildings, cultural facilities, etc.) in many countries. Besides his vast design experience, Portzamparc has become an important reference regarding the development of form theories and critical analyses on the contemporary architecture as it can be seen in [1].

The invitation to Portzamparc for developing the project of the City of Music in Rio de Janeiro has been motivated by his great experience working with this kind of project [2].

II. Shape Grammars

The advent of the shape grammars theory occurred in the context of a growing preoccupation in searching for principles of design [3]. Its foundations are credited to the work of Stiny and Gips [4]. According to Smith and Edmonds [5] it followed a long established analogy between language and architecture:

> "Whereas semiotics deals with meaning, generative grammars are concerned with mechanisms for the construction of sentences, shape grammars follow this model and are applied to the generation of shapes. A shape grammar is a set of precise generating rules, which in turn, can be used to produce a language of shapes" [5].

Therefore, while in language letters are grouped to form words and words are grouped according to certain rules to form meaningful sentences, paragraphs and texts, in architectural design graphic symbols and geometric primitives are grouped according to a set of rules, a shape grammar, in order to produce shapes and shape languages.

The initial application of shape grammars was in analysis and criticism much like as linguistics is concerned with analyzing rather than with creating new languages. Much work has been developed in shape grammars regarding the analysis of precedents such as with the Palladian Villas [6] or Frank Lloyd Wright's prairie houses [7], just to name a few.

However, once the shape grammar is set, the same rules can be used to create new shapes in the language of the original. Smith and Edmonds [5] go on to explaining that:

> "Just as linguistic grammars provide a finite set of rules capable of generating an infinite set of linguistic

T. Sobh, K. Elleithy (eds.), *Innovations in Computing Sciences and Software Engineering*, DOI 10.1007/978-90-481-9112-3_109,

> constructions, so shape grammars consist of sets of rules that can be used to generate infinitely many instances of shape arrangements that conform to the specified rules." [5]

Therefore, shape grammars can be of two types: analytical and generative. The analytical shape grammars are created from the analysis of existing designs and result in sequences of rules that are made successive reductions resulting in a Boolean language type which allows to evaluate if the original sequence belongs or not to the sequence described by the shape grammar [8] The generative shape grammars correspond to that in which from a set and rules one can generate the entire sequence through substitution of an initial symbol.

The technique developed by Stiny and Gip had initially the purpose of establishing rules that could be applied to sculpture and painting in order to generate new forms from a predetermined set of symbols that would be grouped under a series of parameters. According to this model the artist wouldn't design what he was going to paint, but rather the set of rules would define the paint [4]

III. The City Of Music Of Rio De Janeiro

The project of the City of Music of Rio de janeiro, shown in Figure 2, has the primary object of hosting the Sinfonic Orchestra of Brazil.

Figure 2. City of Music of Rio de Janeiro, by Christian de Portzamparc. (Source: Wikipedia, The Free Encyclopedia, 2009, http://en.wikipedia.org/wiki/Christian_de_Portzamparc)

The design project was developed in 2002 and the construction started in setember 2003. The chosen site is located at the Tijuca district in the crossroads between the Ayrton Senna avenue and the avenue of Americas.

The brief of the project was divided in 4 parts distribuited in the 2 horizontals plans that make up the building. The finished buildign is comprised of: Great Concert Hall with 1.800 seats available; secundary hall with 800 seats; room for chamber music with 500 seats; 13 rooms for rehearsal; 13 classrooms; 3 movie theathers; 3 shops; media library; restaurant; coffee shop; music foyer and 738 parking spaces. The total built area is 87403 m² which makes the construction the largest cultural facility in Rio de Janeiro.

IV. The Open Block

Throughout his career Christian de Portzamparc developed a design process he called "open block" (Figure 3). This system is based on two basic entities: mass or volume and space. These entities directly influence the external form of his design projects.

Figure 3. "The Open Block", by Christian de Portzamparc. (Source: http://www.chdeportzamparc.com/content.asp?LANGUEID=2)

Christian's methodology proposes regarding volume that there must be autonomous structures defining free forms that receive light and provide views in all possible directions. He proposes also that the heights may be different, that the forms may be diverse and integrated, that the façades may not be semi-detached. It is also stressed that standardization should be avoided, mixing standard and custom elements. It should also be avoided the use of rigid planning rules enabling the street to evolve freely. Regarding the spatial entity, the open block, the architect says the study of the relationship of voids among the blocks should make up the volumetric set [1].

Another aspect of this method of work is the study of the internal spaces. Here Portzamparc recommends the creation of zones naturally ventilated and lighted to establish relationship with the street through of open plans avoiding corridors. He also proposes maintaining the use of partial alignment of the façade to cause visual impact of the buildings in the background.

V. Evaluation

The analysis of the building was carried out through the study of images of the work and the virtual models. Here we will attempt to identify the set of characters that may compose a shape grammar for this building.

In order to be able to identify the formal elements that constitute the formal grammar of the project the City of Music in Rio de Janeiro, we decided to take the principles and rules of the "open block" that directly affect the final volume of this building. In this case the entity mass establishes volumetric parameters (at different heights, autonomous structures, diverse and free forms) for the development of the architectural design.

Once our starting point was a existing project (the City of Music) and a set of established rules (the open block of Christian de Portzamparc), the type of the shape grammar used here is the analytical shape grammar.

Looking at the front (Figure - 4) and lateral (Figure - 5) views of the building we can see the application of the "open block". The building is composed by grouping the independent free-forms which are bounded by the horizontal planes of the roof slab and the elevated floor slab and by the voids between these blocks.

Figure 4. The City of Music of RJ, by Christian de Portzamparc. (Source: http://www.chdeportzamparc.com/content.asp?LANGUEID=2)

Figure 5. The City of Music of RJ, by Christian de Portzamparc. (Source: http://www.chdeportzamparc.com/content.asp?LANGUEID=2)

In Figure 6 and Figure 7 we highlighted the elements that are more often repeated in the building and the forms that obey the rules established by the methodology of Christian Portzamparc. In these figures we can see the elements that are repeated more frequently at this building and those that follow the formal parameters defined by the language of Portzamparc.

Figure 6. The City of Music of RJ, by Christian de Portzamparc. (Source: http://www.chdeportzamparc.com/content.asp?LANGUEID=2, adapted by the authors of this paper)

Figure 7. The City of Music of RJ, by Christian de Portzamparc. (Source: http://www.chdeportzamparc.com/content.asp?LANGUEID=2, adapted by the authors of this paper)

The most recurrent shape elements in this building, shown in Figure - 8 are the alphabet (or database of symbols) and the principles of the "open block" are the rules of the shape grammar from this building. They could be formalized as "if – then" statements in order to construct a rigorous shape grammars, not just for the analysis of this building, but also for creating new buildings which are faithful to the language of the original one.

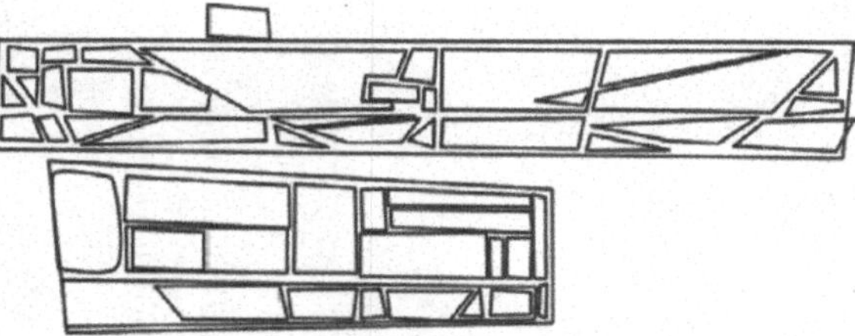

Figure 8. The City of Music of RJ, by Christian de Portzamparc. (Source: the authors of this paper)

The use of shape grammars, in this case study, made it possible to identify how the theoretical references of the architect are present in the building studied (City of Music of Rio de Janeiro). Another contribution of the shape grammar of this project is that it can serve as a first step for further study of the methodology and the architectural language of the architect Christian de Portzamparc.

REFERENCES

[1] Portzamparc, Christian de, "Open Block", available at: http://www.chdeportzamparc.com/content.asp?LANGUEID=2> accessed in August 16, 2009.

[2] Leonídio, O.: 2009, Cidade da Música do Rio de Janeiro: a invasora,Arquitextos 111.01. São Paulo, Vitruvius, set 2009. <http://www.vitruvius.com.br/arquitextos/arq111/arq111_01.asp>

[3] J. Wojtowicz, W. Fawcett, Architecture: Formal Approach, Academy Editions/St. Martin's Press, New York, 1986.

[4] Stiny, G.,Gips, J. :1972, Shape Grammars and the Generative Specification of Painting and Sculpture In: IFIP CONGRESS, 7.,Amsterdam.Proceedings of...:C.V. Freimanp. 1460-1465. Disponível em http://shapegrammar.org/ifip/ifip1.html

[5] Smith, M., Edmonds, E. Supporting design through the strategic use of shape grammars, Knowledge-Based Systems 13, 2000, pp.385-393.

[6] G. Stiny, W.J. Mitchell, The Palladian Grammar, Environment and Planning B 5, 1978, pp. 5-18.

[7] H. Koning, J. Eizenberg, The language of the prairie: Frank Lloyd Wright's Prairie Houses, Environment and Planning B 8, 1981, pp. 295-323.

[8] Celani G., Cypriano D., Godoi G., Vaz C.:2006, A gramática da forma como metodología de análise e síntese em arquitetura, Conexão,v.5, Caxias do Sul, PP 180-195.

Architecture Models and Data Flows in Local and Group Datawarehouses

R.M. Bogza[1], Dorin Zaharie[1], Silvia Avasilcai[2], Laura Bacali[3]

[1]Academy of Economic Studies of Bucharest, Romania, [2] Technical University "Gheorghe Asachi' – Iasi, Romania, [3] Technical University from Cluj – Napoca, Romania

romari_61@yahoo.com , zaharied@ase.ro, avasilcai@yahoo.com , laurabacali@gmail.com

ABSTRACT : **Architecture models and possible data flows for local and group datawarehouses are presented, together with some data processing models. The architecture models consists of several layers and the data flow between them. The choosen architecture of a datawarehouse depends on the data type and volumes from the source data, and inflences the analysis, data mining and reports done upon the data from DWH.**

Key words : local datawarehouse, group datawarehouse, data mart, layers, business intelligence

1. INTRODUCTION

The generally accepted definition for a datawarehouse is, as W.H. Inmon says : „A data warehouse is a subject-oriented, integrated, non-volatile and time-variant collection of data in support of management's decision." The main characteristics of an entreprisewide data warehouse are :

- Large scale implementation
- Scopes the entire business
- Data from all subject areas
- Developed incrementally
- Single source of entreprise data
- Synchronized enterprise data
- Single distribution point to dependent datamarts.

The typical data warehouse components are :

- The source systems : legacy, external, operational
- The staging area - where the data cleansing and preparation take place before the data is loaded to the data warehouse; it is both a storage area and a set of processes known as extraction, transformation and loading (ETL)
- The presentation area : data warehouse and datamarts
- Access tools allow simple to complex business modeling, trend analysis, complex drill-down activities, what-if analysis, forecasting and data mining.
- The metadata repository, that contains data about the data and supports the datawarehouse's technical, administrative and business user groups.

The main datawarehouse components are :

- Methodology
- Architecture
- Extraction, transformation and loading (ETL)
- Implementation
- Operation and support

The architecture provides the planning, structure and standardization needed to ensure integration of multiple components, projects and processes across time, and establishes the framework and the procedures for the DWH at the entreprise level. Some of the components of a datawarehousing architecture are :

- Data sources
- Data acquisition
- Data management
- Data distribution
- Information directory
- Data access tools

2. ARCHITECTURE MODEL FOR A GROUP DATAWAREHOUSE

The paper presents models for a group datawarehouse, that could be a multinational company. Each subsidiary, located within a country or region has its own local data warehouse, and one or more interface layers, through which the data are transferred to the group datawarehouse. Each local data warehouse has an OUT layer that will do all processing necessary to translate data from the local DWH to the DWH group.

Each local DWH, depending on the volume of managed data may have several layers. Local DWH is updated daily.

The group datawarehouse is updated daily or monthly (some dimensions may be daily, monthly etc.).

Local DWH is used for statutory local reporting and for internal company management.

Group DWH is used for reporting at the group.

For large enterprises with different types of activities, the following format can be used: if activities are big and bulky, and if their specifics vary greatly from one another, then we can create for each type of activity one DWH. But costs can be quite large in this case. Therefore, it is useful keep all data in one data warehouse.

DWH architecture and data models and flows are very important to quickly access data required for various reports. Therefore, it is preferably to organize data in DWH in various datamarts, each datamart being designed for a specific task. A specific datamart may be designed, built and should be used for assisting managers in that field, but there can be datamarts for managing the entire company. The datamarts can be used for profitability analysis of each type of activity, over a short, medium or long term.

T. Sobh, K. Elleithy (eds.), *Innovations in Computing Sciences and Software Engineering*, DOI 10.1007/978-90-481-9112-3_110, © Springer Science+Business Media B.V. 2010

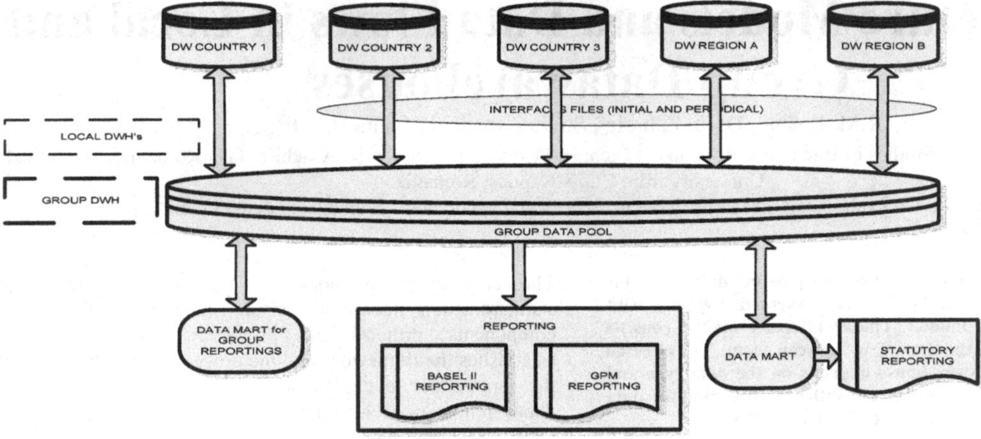

Fig. 1. DWH Model for a group / multinational company

The data for the group DWH are retrieved from the local DWH through a specific data-mart. The local DWH supports the reporting activity for the subsidiary in each country / region. Dynamic reports are obtained from data-mart. The business has no direct access to data from the data store, only the data from data-mart's, or through dynamic reports, or through user interfaces.

A group DWH is loaded with data from the local data warehouses through interfaces, having several layers, where the data is transformed and processed according to the format, granularity and rules asked by the group. This interface can be done through an extra level of staging - whose role is to prepare data in a format and structure required by the DWH group.

The group DWH supplies the data-marts at group level. These can be accessed by the user or through a graphical interface or on the basis of their reports are obtained.

In a financial institution, the group data pool (GDP) can offer some risk functions, beside the group data management, including also the group reporting. The data mart for group reporting can provide data for BASEL II reporting and treasury, exposure calculation, collateral allocation, risk weighted assets calculation, etc.

3. PROCESSES AND LAYERS IN THE GROUP DWH

The modules and processes in the group DWH are presented in “Fig. 2”.

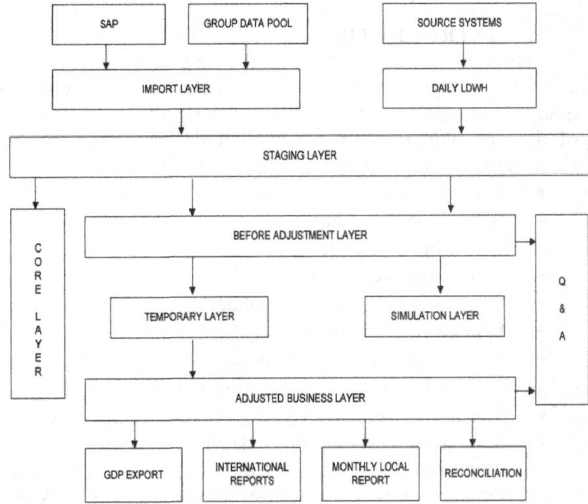

Fig.2. Processes and modules in a group DWH (for a multinational company)

3.1. THE LAYERS in THE GROUP DWH

<u>The CORE layer contains data from</u>:

• SAP Tables

• Transfer data from DWH + local transformations

<u>The staging layer</u>

- Has the same structure as import layer, only a few technical columns in addition for audit
- Inspection: Master - Detail and Detail – Master
- Rules for treatment of user errors
- Rules for treatment of data according to the regulations of group

<u>Before adjustment layer</u>

- The data is prepared in the required formats
- Certain rules are defined for loading data

The temporary layer

- Is the layer between DATA BEFORE AND AFTER ADJUSTMENT DATA
- Is used to run standard checks and rules (fixed rules) before checking non-standard rules (user rules)
- User Rules
- Fixed rules
- Group Rules
- Verifying Master-Detail
- Inspection Detail-Master
- Rules for treating errors

Simulation layer

- Is used to simulate user rules
- Data is in the same format as in adjusted for business

Adjusted for business layer

- Group rules
- User rules for the correction of data

After adjustment layer

After adjusting the data, a back-up is done on the data and final reporting is done for:
• International Bodies
• Internal Group Management
• regulatory bodies in the country where the group is located

3.2 THE ORDER FOR PROCESSING DATA FOR THE GROUP DWH

The following model presumes the data is exported from the out layer of the local datawarehouse into the group DWH monthly, after the end of a month. The proposed steps are :

- The list of values – LOV – are provided by the group to the subsidiary
- The domains and domain values are provided by the group, in specific locations, from where they are loaded through the import layer, to the staging layer
- The dimensions data are delivered from the group and loaded in the staging layer
- The SAP data are imported
- from the local datawarehouse, the data are delivered to the staging layer : exchange rates are the first, then the lines of basic data
- The initializing step prepares the monthly layer for processing data within a month, through : open processing, check processing and init to the tables in the staging layer
- After all data arrived in the staging layer , they are transformed and loaded to the core layer, and into the "before adjustment layer"
- The data are loaded in the temporary and simulation layer, where it is checked if some rules are applied; the rules are some constraints, that refer business and / or technical aspects; the technical constraints can be checked by using some sql scripts; the business constraints are implemented by the user via business GUI

4. INTEGRATION OF A LOCAL DATAWAREHOUSE IN A GROUP DATAWAREHOUSE

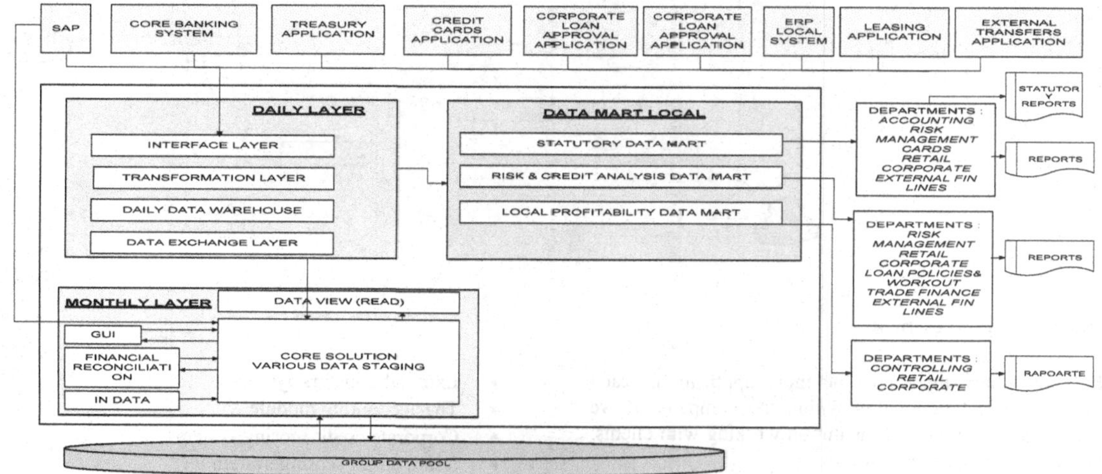

Fig. 3. Integration of a LDWH into a Group DWH (for a multinational company)

5. MODEL FOR A LOCAL DWH

5.1. Block shema for a local DWH

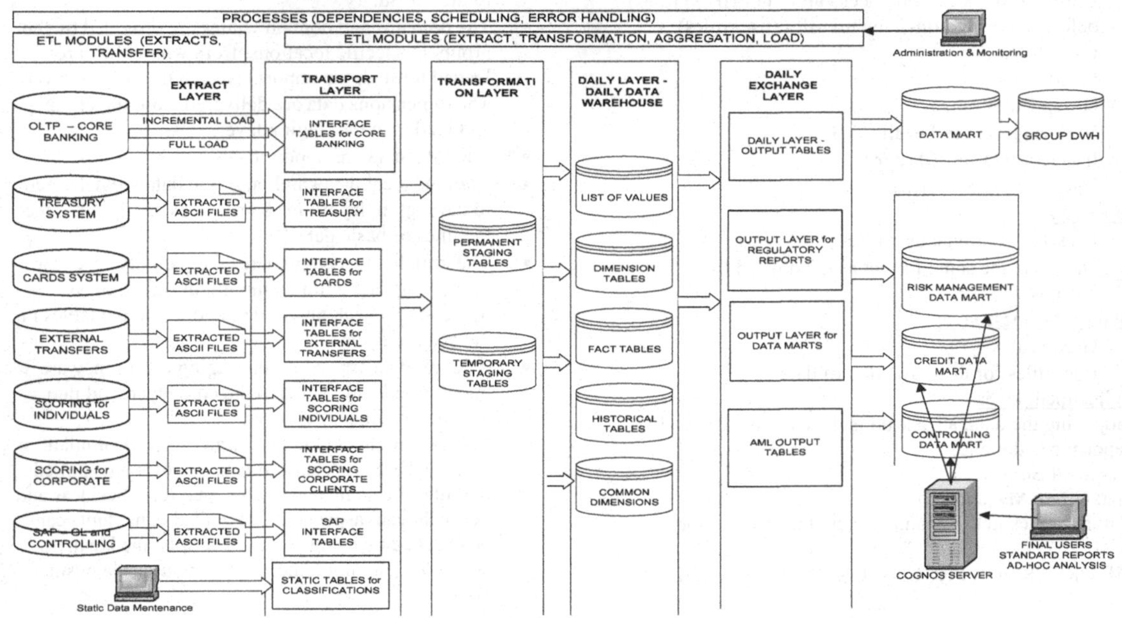

Fig.4. Block diagram – a model for a local DWH

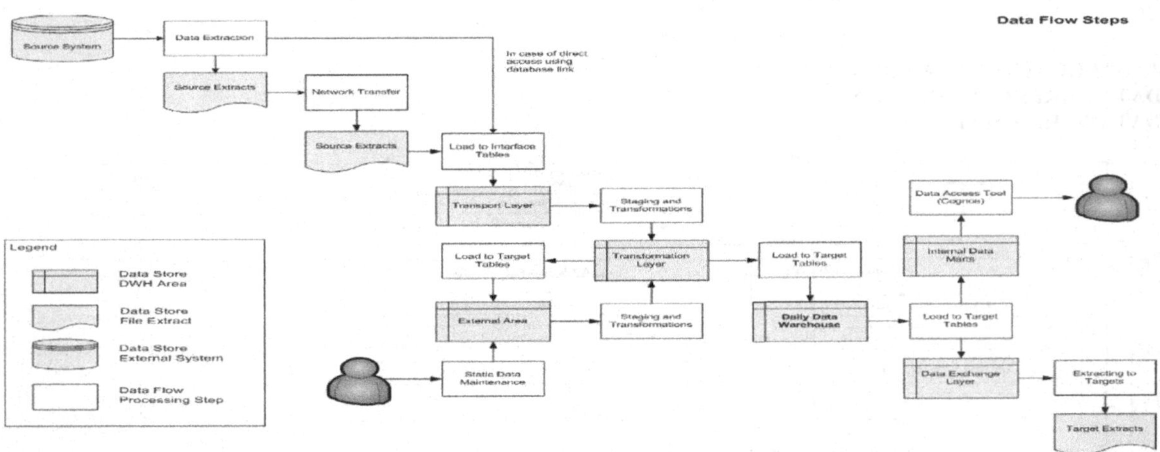

Fig. 5. Data Flow Steps in local DWH

In a subsidiary there may be more applications, each serving a specific functionality within the company. If we take for example, a financial institution working with clients, such information subsystems are:

- Transactional System (core banking)
- The cards system
- Treasury system
- External transfers system
- The accounting module
- Corporate credit scoring system
- Retail credit scoring system
- Leasing IT system
- Catalogs, classifications

Data is extracted from each source system, and follow an ETL process.

5.2. Extract process – transport layer

Data files are generated in the source systems and transferred in a buffer zone, specifically designated for that. ETL processes responsible for extracting data, load data from the buffer zone in the transport entities, providing log files that are accessible through the environment management and monitoring processes. Through log files, the end users can verify the accuracy of load data. After extracting the correct data from the source system, the files are archived.

Data can be loaded from the buffer zone in the transport layer by two ways:
• Incremental Load – the data from input source systems are loaded into the transport layer of data warehouse only if it differs from similar data record of the last extract. It is used for large tables, with more then one million records or for those who rarely change; Examples: balances, deposits, accounts, loans, clients, etc.
• Full Load - the selected data from input sources, are fully extracted from the input sources (all the records and all the attributes), daily or with another chosen frequency; it is used for classifications, catalogs, which are smaller, for entities that are changing frequently, such as: transactions, commissions, interest rates, or for the initial load.
Results of the extractions from source entities are found in tables of layer transport interface. In this phase, the data are not changed, but some auditing columns are added.

5.3. Transformation process

From the transport layer, the data are cleansed and processed by the transformation process to be ready for loading in the datawarehouse. We call this level : the staging layer, where data are subject of the data cleansing process and, structures are mapped on the structures from the next layer, being prepared for loading into the datawarehouse.
On this level:
• Data is transformed according to the model implemented in the datawarehouse
• Various filters and transformations are applied on data
• The surrogate (technical) keys are generated
• The data from various source systems are integrated.

5.4. The load process – the daily layer

Data are loaded into the datawarehouse, where you can find various types of entities:
• reference tables: lists of possible values for certain attributes / catalogs / classifications
• Dimension tables
• History tables
• Common Facts / Facts tables

5.5. The daily exchange layer

From the daily layer, the data is retrieved in the required format for the next level, DWH OUT, through the process of acquisition and data processing in order to get prepared for:

- interface with group datawarehouse
- Data-mart for special processing, ie preventing and combating money laundering
- Data-mart for statutory reports
- Data-mart for reporting financial performance / economic indicators
- Controlling Data-mart
- Risk management data-mart
- Credit data-mart
- Data-mart for treasury

The data are supplied from the DWH Out in the format agreed with the other target systems.

5.6. The out layer

The out layer is an interface layer between the daily exchange layer and the group DWH, in which, the data is transformed in order to be prepared for a direct load into the group DWH.

5.7. Reporting process – reporting server

The prepared data from data-marts are accessed by the user directly, or by a GUI , or through dynamic reports, which are implemented on a server that allows the OLAP techniques and the data mining techniques. It can be a COGNOS server.

5.8. Administration and monitoring layer

A GUI based tool can be used to schedule, execute and monitor all the ETL processes and loading of data extracts in the datawarehouse. Performing all the processes that allow the data extraction from the source systems, their cleansing and transformation, preparing them for loading in the datawarehouse, further processing for interfacing with the group DWH and for populating the data-marts, can be managed through this front-end tool, that allows:
• Process management: plan process, schedule and run process, monitor process execution, suspend process or restart canceled process.

- File management: load files, monitor / restart file loading.
- Notifications : send / resolve notifications
- Batch management: define batch of processes and / or file loads, run / schedule batch, monitor batch execution.
- Parameters configuration

Performing all the processes that allow the data extraction from the source systems, their cleansing and transformation , preparing them for loading in the datawarehouse, further processing for interfacing with the group DWH and for populating the data-marts , can be managed through a specific management and monitoring processes. It allows:

• Planning Processes
• running automatic processes
• re-running processes that didn't finish because of errors
• conditional running of processes

5.9. Data Flow in ETL processes

The data flow in the extract – transforming – loading processes is presented in fig. 6:

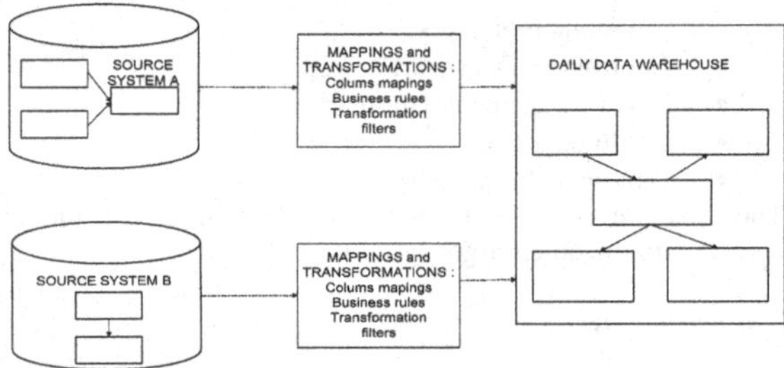

Fig.6. ETL processes in DWH

The data flow in the datawarehouse is determined by :

- the data stored in DWH
- the volume of data stored in DWH
- the architecture of DWH
- the data model in DWH
- the mappings and transformations applied to the data imported from the source systems

5.10. ETL versus ELT

All the processes through which the data are transported from the source systems , transformed and loaded in the datawarehouse is called ETL – Extract, Transform and Load. All these processes take place in the staging area. The extract, transform and load layers can be physically implemented on different machines, or on the same machine. The layers can be implemented on different databases or schemas, and so, physically delimited. But they also can be implemented in the same database, and only, functionally and logically delimited. There can be also other combinations, for example, the transport and transform layers in the same database, or the transform and the loading layers in the same database.
Another possibility for loading the data in the datawarehouse are the processes ELT – extract, load and transformation. In such case, the data extracted from the source systems are transported to the datawarehouse, and here, it is transformed in order to organize the data in dimension and fact tables. The advantages of such an approach are:

- the processing time could be shorter
- the datawarehouse keeps the history of the input data near the history of the datawarehouse data , so the reconciliation between data could be easier to be done.

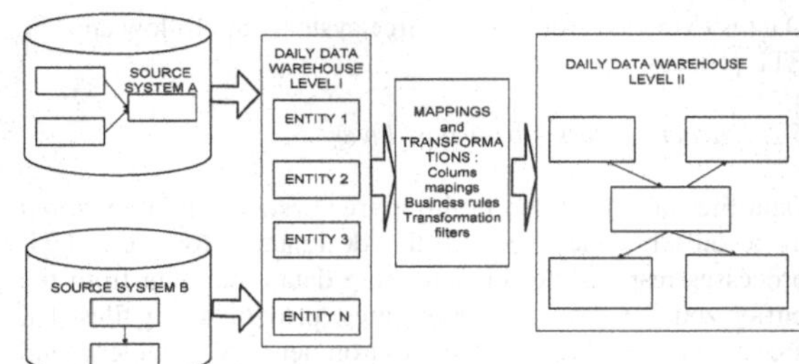

Fig.7. ELT Processes in DWH

6. CONCLUSIONS

The model and the architecture presented above offers the possibility to manage a large amount of data in order to obtain results at various levels of an organization or of a group. Of course, there are also other models and architectures that are much simpler and not so many layers. The layers of extract, transport and transformation/ staging can be performed with a special ETL-software application.

The advantages of such architecture are that it really offers the possibility to extract data from various systems and to assemble them, with an adequate model of data, in the desired format. It can be especially used in multinational groups, as they need to have a better control of the business, considering that the national regulations can be different from the international regulations or the regulations of the country where the headquarter of the multinational group is located. The model offers the possibility of having the same kind and format of financial and economic data from various subsidiaries, located in several countries or regions, or , in extension, even from several economical or financial activities and services.

The architecture of the datawarehouse and the implemented data model, impact directly the efficiency of the queries, analysis, data marts and the reports obtained from the datawarehouse. The impact consists in the quality of the analysis and of the reports, in the possibility of drilling top or down, and in the time response, aspects that are of high importance for the managers.

REFERENCES

[1] Peter Baker, Marco Canessa – Warehouse Design: A Structured Approach – European Journal of Operational Research 193 (2009) 425-436

[2] Rodica Maria Bogza – Strategic Intelligence with BI Competency Center - II International science conference "Knowledge Society", Nessebar, Bulgaria, ISSN 1313-4787

[3] Dorin Zaharie, Felicia Albescu, Veronica Ivancenco, Irina Bojan, Corina Vasilescu – Sisteme informatice pentru asistarea deciziei, Editura Dual Tech 2001, ISBN 973-85525-1-6

[4] Robert Reix – Systèmes d'information et management des organisations, Vuibert, Edition : 5e edition (2004), ISBN-10 : 2711775682, ISBN-13: 978-271177568

Index

T. Sobh, K. Elleithy (eds.), *Innovations in Computing Sciences and Software Engineering*, DOI 10.1007/978-90-481-9112-3, © Springer Science+Business Media B.V. 2010

E

F

G

H